REVOLUTIONARY RADICALISM

ITS HISTORY, PURPOSE AND TACTICS

WITH AN EXPOSITION AND DISCUSSION OF THE STEPS BEING TAKEN AND REQUIRED TO CURB IT

BEING THE

REPORT OF THE JOINT LEGISLATIVE COMMITTEE INVESTIGATING SEDITIOUS ACTIVITIES, FILED APRIL 24, 1920, IN THE SENATE OF THE STATE OF NEW YORK

PART I

REVOLUTIONARY AND SUBVERSIVE MOVEMENTS ABROAD AND AT HOME

VOLUME I

EVERY STRIKE IS A SMALL REVOLUTION AND A DRESS REHEARSAL FOR THE BIG ONE

—*The Labor Defender*, (*I. W. W.*) *Dec. 15, 1918*

ALBANY
J. B. LYON COMPANY, PRINTERS
1920

THE COMMITTEE

Clayton R. Lusk, *Chairman*

Louis M. Martin, *Vice-Chairman*

John J. Boylan, Frederick S. Burr,

Daniel J. Carroll, Edmund B. Jenks,

John B. Mullan, Peter P. McElligott,

William W. Pellet.

J. Henry Walters, *Ex-officio*

Thaddeus C. Sweet, *Ex-officio*

COUNSEL

Charles D. Newton, *Attorney-General.*

Archibald E. Stevenson, *Associated Counsel.*

Samuel A. Berger, *Deputy Attorney-General.*

Frederick R. Rich, *Special Deputy Atty.-Gen.*

STAFF

This Report was written and compiled, under the supervision of the Committee, by Archibald E. Stevenson in collaboration with Arthur L. Frothingham, Samuel A. Berger and Eleanor A. Barnes.

The maps of New York City showing Racial Colonies, accompanying Part II of this Report, were prepared for the Committee under the supervision of Special Deputy Attorney-General John B. Trevor.

The Committee's investigators were in charge of R. W. Finch, formerly of the Bureau of Investigation, United States Department of Justice.

The translations for the Report were made by Meta Rumel, George J. Starr and Charles M. Robinton.

TABLE OF CONTENTS

VOLUME I

SUBSECTION IV

Spread of Socialism in Educated Circles Through Pacifist, Religious, Collegiate Societies, Etc.

VOLUME II

PART I — Continued

SECTION II — Continued

SUBSECTION V

Propaganda

ADDENDUM

PART I

Subversive Movements Abroad and at Home

VOLUME III

PART II

Constructive Movements and Measures in America

SECTION I

Protective Governmental Measures

SECTION II

Organized Labor and Capital and Industrial Problems

CHAPTER III

CHAPTER IV

VOLUME IV

PART II — *Continued*

SECTION III — *Continued*

SUB-SECTION III — *Continued*

CHAPTER XII

CHAPTER XII

CHAPTER XIII

CHAPTER XIV

SUB-SECTION IV

Citizenship Training in all States Other than New York

CHAPTER I. ALABAMA

CHAPTER XIV. KANSAS

CHAPTER XV. KENTUCKY

CHAPTER XVI. LOUISIANA

CHAPTER XVII. MAINE

CHAPTER XVIII. MARYLAND

CHAPTER XIX. MASSACHUSETTS

ADDENDUM

PART II

Constructive Measures

SECTION I

Protective Governmental Measures

NOTE ON CHAPTER I

SECTION II

Organized Labor and Capital and Industrial Relations

NOTE ON CHAPTER V

NOTE ON CHAPTER XIII

SECTION III

Educational Training for Citizenship

NOTE ON SUB-SECTION II

NOTES ON SUB-SECTION III

Citizenship Training in the State of New York

NOTES ON SUB-SECTION IV

Citizenship Training in All States Other Than New York

LIST OF ILLUSTRATIONS

VOLUME I

VOLUME II

VOLUME III

VOLUME IV

CONCURRENT RESOLUTION AUTHORIZING THE INVESTIGATION OF SEDITIOUS ACTIVITIES

Whereas, It is a matter of public knowledge that there is a large number of persons within the State of New York engaged in circulating propaganda calculated to set in motion forces to overthrow the Government of this State and the United States, and

Whereas, Sufficient facts were adduced by the sub-committee of the Senate of the United States investigating this subject during the last session of Congress to indicate the necessity of further inquiry and action, and

Whereas, It is the duty of the Legislature of the State of New York to learn the whole truth regarding these seditious activities and to pass when such truth is ascertained such legislation as may be necessary to protect the government of the State and to insure the maintenance of the rights of its citizens,

Now, Therefore, Be It Resolved, That a joint committee of the Senate and Assembly be, and hereby is, created to consist of four members of the Senate to be appointed by the Temporary President of the Senate, and five members of the Assembly, to be appointed by the Speaker of the Assembly, of which joint committee the Temporary President of the Senate and the Speaker of the Assembly shall be members ex-officio, to investigate the scope, tendencies, and ramifications of such seditious activities and to report the result of its investigation to the Legislature; and be it

Further Resolved, That the said special committee shall have power to select its chairman and other officers to compel the attendance of witnesses and the production of books and papers; to employ counsel, stenographers and necessary clerical assistance; and shall have power to sit anywhere within the State, and shall otherwise have all the power of a legislative committee as provided by the Legislative Law, including the adoption of rules for the conduct of its proceedings, and be it

Further Resolved, That the sum of thirty thousand dollars ($30,000), or so much thereof as may be necessary, be and hereby is appropriated from the funds set aside for the contingent expenses of the Legislature, to be paid by the Treasurer on warrants of the Comptroller upon the certificates of the Chairman of the Committee and the approval of the Temporary President of the Senate or the Speaker of the Assembly.

Further Resolved, That the sum of thirty thousand dollars ($30,000), or so much thereof as may be necessary, be and hereby is, appropriated from the funds set aside for the contingent expenses of the Legislature, to be paid by the Treasurer on warrants of the Comptroller upon the certificates of the Chairman of the Committee and the approval of the Temporary President of the Senate or the Speaker of the Assembly.

STATEMENT OF CHAIRMAN

The present report has been compiled after a careful study of the evidence taken before the Committee, covering several thousand pages of testimony and a vast number of documents secured by the Committee in the course of its investigations.

The revolutionary movement, being of an international character, involved and necessitated a study of conditions existing not only in the State of New York but throughout the United States as well as in Europe and elsewhere: it is for that reason that this report necessarily is taken up, to a substantial extent, with a consideration of the conditions existing outside the State of New York.

The preparation of the report was begun shortly before the investigation by the Assembly of the State of New York into the qualifications of the five Socialist Assemblymen-elect to take their seats in that body. The records of this Committee were subpœnaed by the Judiciary Committee of the Assembly and used in that investigation. Counsel for the Committee were retained by the Assembly Committee to assist in its investigation, which was not concluded until the first of April. All this involved an interruption in the work of preparation which made it difficult to complete it before the closing of the legislative session on April 24th. This made it impossible to give as much time as the Committee desired to a careful consideration of the literary form and order of arrangement.

The report is very largely made up of documents the originals of which are in the possession of the Committee. It has been the desire of the Committee to eliminate personalities and put in only such evidence and documents as seemed absolutely necessary in order that a clear understanding might be had of the subjects under investigation.

The Committee has received much assistance in its work from various public officials. Early in the summer District Attorney Swann of New York county assigned Assistant District Attorney Alexander I. Rorke to this Committee. He has not only cooperated with the Committee in its work, but has so ably handled the criminal anarchy cases arising out of the investigations of this Committee in New York county that he has secured a conviction in every case of criminal anarchy which has been presented in court up to this time. The Committee has also received much assistance from the district attorneys of Bronx, Kings, Erie, Monroe, Oneida, Cortland and other counties in the State. The Committee also wishes to express its gratitude to Major George R. Chandler and Captain John A. Warner, of the State police, the police of the City of New York, especially Commissioner Richard E. Enright, Inspector Faurot (now Deputy Commissioner), and Sergeant James Gegan, head of the bomb squad, and to the police of Utica, Rochester, and Buffalo, for the able assistance furnished by these officials.

The Committee is under great obligation to Charles D. Newton, Attorney-General of the State of New York, Deputy Attorneys-General Samuel A. Berger and Frederick R. Rich, Archibald E. Stevenson, Esq., Prof. Arthur L. Frothingham of Princeton, N. J., and Miss Eleanor A. Barnes.

Much gratification has been afforded the chairman of the Committee by the fact that the work of the Committee has been entirely free from political or personal dissensions of any kind. Every member of the Committee has diligently and patriotically worked for an honest and fair investigation and presentation of the movement now on foot to undermine and destroy the government and institutions of the State and Nation.

CLAYTON R. LUSK,
Chairman.

PART I

REVOLUTIONARY AND SUBVERSIVE MOVEMENTS ABROAD AND AT HOME

GENERAL INTRODUCTION

In the report here presented the Committee seeks to give a clear, unbiased statement and history of the purposes and objects, tactics and methods, of the various forces now at work in the United States, and particularly within the State of New York, which are seeking to undermine and destroy, not only the government under which we live, but also the very structure of American society; it also seeks to analyze the various constructive forces which are at work throughout the country counteracting these evil influences and to present the many industrial and social problems that these constructive forces must meet and are meeting.

The Great War has shaken the foundation of European civilization. The same forces which promote civil strife in many of the countries of Europe are at work on this side of the ocean seeking to create a division in our population, stimulating class hatred and a contempt for government, which, if continued, must necessarily result in serious consequences to the peace and prosperity of this country. In doing this they are taking advantage of the real grievances and natural demands of the working classes for a larger share in the management and use of the common wealth.

The problems which were submitted by the Legislature to this Committee for investigation, are vital to the country's life. Upon the steps taken toward their solution, the Committee feels depends the perpetuation of our institutions. We therefore urge members of the Legislature and those into whose hands this report may come, to consider thoughtfully the facts here presented, in order to become acquainted with the subversive forces at work within our boundaries, and to give them careful and devoted study, so as to determine what steps shall and must be taken towards the solution of the problems they create.

In the section of this report dealing with American conditions, the Committee has attempted to describe in detail the various organizations masquerading as political parties, giving the principles and objects for which they stand, as well as the methods and tactics they employ or advocate in order to bring about the social revolution.

In every instance the Committee has relied upon the so-called party or organization's own statements with respect to these matters. They are permitted to speak for themselves. These organizations fall into two principal classes. The first group composes the Socialist movement; the second consists of the American adherents of the Anarchist philosophy.

Those representing the Socialist point of view are, the Socialist Party of America, the Communist Party of America, the Communist Labor Party, and the Socialist Labor Party. Each of these groups claims to be the most modern and aggressive body representing the Marxian doctrines.

A study of their platforms and official pronouncements shows that they do not differ fundamentally in their objectives. These objectives are: the establishment of the co-operative commonwealth in place of the present form of government in the United States; the overthrow of what they are pleased to call the capitalist system, namely, the present system under which we live, and the substitution in its place of collective ownership, and the management of means of production and distribution by the working class.

These organizations differ but slightly in the means advocated to bring about the social revolution. All are agreed that success can be obtained only through the destruction of the present trade union organizations of the working class, and by creating in their stead revolutionary industrial unions having the power (through industrial action involving the general strike and sabotage) to so cripple the government as to render it powerless to prevent the establishment of the co-operative commonwealth and the working-class rule.

A study of the chapters dealing with these organizations reveals the fact that they differ slightly in the matter of emphasis. The Socialist Party, the Socialist Labor Party and the American Labor Party believe that parliamentary action, participation in elections, offering candidates for public office, and taking part in legislative activities, afford an added weapon for the carrying on of revolutionary propaganda. On the other hand, the Communist Party and the Communist Labor Party feel that the time is ripe for immediate action, and in large measure deny the value of parliamentary action, laying the entire stress upon industrial organization, and the mass action of revolutionary organizations. The anarchist movement repudiates parliamentary or political action altogether. It seeks the overthrow of present organized society and the substitution for it of an ill-defined co-operative commonwealth. It is at one with the Socialist group, however, in advocating revolutionary industrial unionism as the means for accomplishing the destruction of the present form of government and the present system of society.

General strikes and sabotage are the direct means advocated. Anyone who studies the propaganda of the various groups which we have named, will learn that the arguments employed are the same; that the methods and tactics advocated cannot be distinguished from one another, and that articles or speeches made on the question of tactics or methods by anarchists could, with propriety, be published in Socialist or Communist newspapers without offending the membership of these organizations. The result of the propaganda of the quasi-political organizations which has been spread throughout the country broadcast to the working class organizations, and particularly among the foreign groups, has been to undermine the confidence of these workers in the conservative trade union organizations and lead to the formation of a large number of powerful and independent revolutionary industrial unions.

These organizations are treated in this report in the sub-section dealing with revolutionary Industrial Unionism.

The most successful of these organizations is the Industrial Workers of the World. Its propaganda is world-wide. Its members have invaded the membership of conservative organizations of labor, with the view of agitating within trade unions so as to weaken control of conservative labor leaders over a considerable number of their workmen. This method of "boring from within" has been extremely effective and has in large measure permeated the Central Federated Union of New York City as well as many union groups in other parts of the State, engendering radical and revolutionary spirit in their rank and file. It is this phase of the movement which presents the most serious aspect. These tactics are the ones which offer at least a promise of success in their undermining of society and of our present form of government.

The effect of this propaganda is particularly pernicious because it undermines and destroys the moral responsibility of the workers.

The motto " a fair day's pay for a fair day's work " is described as " impossible."

Men are taught that they must strike for higher and higher wages, shorter and shorter hours and slow up at the same time the working pace, ignoring the quality of work they turn out and in every way possible lowering production.

The avowed purpose is to drive business into bankruptcy, when it would be taken over by the workers. Strikes are called not with the idea of obtaining what is demanded but for the express purpose of failure — a failure that will leave the workman poorer and more embittered, will increase class hatred and make the workmen feel that only by violent revolution can they gain their demands.

It should not be necessary to point out the logical consequences of such propaganda. The per capita production of the men in industry is necessarily lowered and the cost of the product many times increased. This in the opinion of the Committee is one of the largest factors responsible for the high cost of living which is now a matter of grave concern to all classes of society in this country. While the Committee has been unable in the course of its investigation to make a study of the effects of profiteering and improper and useless handling of manufactured products and raw materials in the course of their distribution, it is certain that these elements also contribute toward the prevailing high prices. It is a matter of regret to the Committee that there has been no thorough investigation into the various elements which go to make up the costs of necessaries of life. It feels that no complete solution of the existing social and economic problems can be offered or suggested until all the facts bearing on this important question have been thoroughly studied and analyzed.

While the nature of this investigation has led the Committee to lay its emphasis upon the activities of subversive organizations, it feels that this report would not be complete if it did not state emphatically that it believes that those persons in business and commercial enterprise and certain owners of property who seek to take advantage of the situation to reap inordinate gain from the public, contribute in no small part to the social unrest which affords the radical a field of operation which otherwise would be closed to him.

As soon as the investigation was broadened so as to pass from the United States to a consideration of the European conditions during the last generation, it became perfectly clear that it would be impossible not only to understand what has led to this present condition in America but also impossible to understand the rapid changes and fluctuations in the American situation, unless we keep in touch with the past and present of the European movement in every country and unless we reach the fundamental principles and springs of action which have governed the councils of the leaders of radical thought in Europe ever since the time of the Revolution of 1848.

The very first general fact that must be driven home to Americans is that the pacifist movement in this country, the growth and connections of which are an important part of this report, is an absolutely integral and fundamental part of International Socialism. It is not an accretion. It is not a side issue. European Socialism concentrated its efforts in three directions:

The first was to organize labor as a step-daughter, an acolyte, a coadjutor of the great Socialist policy, in order to obtain a great mass of supporters for the revolution.

The second was the use of political action as a means and not an end; as a means for obtaining gradual control, or for obtaining paramount influence until the complete triumph of Socialism would make parliamentary government a thing of the past.

The third purpose was the creation of an International sentiment to supersede national patriotism and effort, and this internationalism was based upon pacifism, in the sense that it opposed all wars between nations and developed at the same time the class consciousness that was to culminate in relentless class warfare. In other words, it was not really peace that was the goal, but the abolition of the patriotic, warlike spirit of nationalities.

The entire program, in all its three sections, was based upon the ideas of one man and largely on the ideas expressed in one of his writings. The founder of Socialism and its present dominating force is Karl Marx. Its Ten Commandments are the Communist Manifesto of Marx, issued in 1848. This is true of the American, as it is true of the European movement. To understand every present campaign, every present alliance, we must read the Communist Manifesto.

The present program of the Third Communist International, founded at Moscow, is avowedly only the carrying out of the ideas of seventy-two years ago, as expressed in the Manifesto. If we want to know what the revolutionists expect to gain by the general strike, all we have to do is to read in the Manifesto that the general strike is to be the means of bringing about the revolution. When we read in the newspapers of general strikes, either threatened or carried out, in Great Britain, in Denmark, in Sweden, France, Italy, Germany, we must not for a minute look upon these movements as special nationalist movements, brought about by local causes and engineered by local groups. No! They are part of this big destructive program which the Socialists have been evolving during these years, bringing nearer and nearer the day when the general strike, instead of being either a threat or a passing phase, will bring about not concessions but the total destruction of present organized society.

In order to follow the evolution of this plan, in order to see how the popular support which was absolutely necessary was gradually developed in the different countries of Europe, the Committee has given in the report a general survey which starts with the origins of the Socialist and labor movements in the different countries of Europe. In this review it is impossible, as we see, to separate the nationalist from the international part of the program. The two wars, the Franco-German War of 1870 and the General War of 1914, were the two big interruptions in the rise of the waves of successful Socialist propaganda, because under the pressure of the nationalist feeling of defense of one's country, the theories of Socialist Internationalism receded into the background in the minds and hearts of a large part of the masses. But the difference in the attitude of the leaders between 1870 and 1914 is an index of the advance of internationalism.

We find that throughout Europe the labor unions, whether they were of the trades union type or of the Syndicalist type, were always closely linked with the Socialist movement, and were in many cases either founded by it or annexed by it in such a way as to take away from labor organizations any independence of policy or action. The Socialist gospel of the general strike and class hatred, of abolition of private property and the nationalization of all resources and industries were a program common to both branches. Of course, this meant the acceptance of political action and this theory was adopted by all but the most revolutionary, the Left Wing, of the Socialists and Syndicalists, who elected to stand aside from any co-operation with their national governments, waiting until the moment should arrive for direct action.

In analyzing the international situation and comparing the evolution in Europe with that in the United States, one thing emerges with great distinctness, and that is the different attitude toward Socialism assumed by organized labor in the United States from that which it assumed in Europe. From the beginning of the labor union movement in the United States the attempt was made by Socialist elements to get possession of the new organizations. These attempts, often repeated, were as often thwarted. Union labor in the United States was, therefore, considered by European labor as extremely conservative, even reactionary. A result of this difference of attitude, of the fact that union labor was very little contaminated with Socialism, was that American organized labor, as typified particularly by the American Federation of Labor, outlined for itself a policy of political non-intervention. It declined to form a separate party. It declined to take part in any political campaign directed by socialist forces. It refused the various suggestions made by European associations for a change of this policy. This policy, initiated in 1881, has continued consistently to the present time. It has been one reason for continual attempts on the part of the revolutionary element in labor to obtain influence in the direction of the Federation. The lack of success in this direction has led to various attempts to organize Socialist labor parties of quasi-political character.

These attempts have never enlisted any considerable element of organized labor. They have been overwhelmingly non-labor in their management. One of the results has been that European Socialism has shown favor to the movements in American labor that were distinctly different from or opposed to the Federation. This is particularly true of the I. W. W. movement; and the conflict between the I. W. W. representative and the representative of the Federation at the International Congress at Budapest in 1911, when each fought for recognition as representing the labor of the United States, is typical of the entire situation. At that time the I. W. W., although supported by France, lost the fight.

Another result of this difference of policy and purpose has been to intensify the opposition of the Federation of Labor to every form of revolutionary activity and to show this opposition in connection with the various international congresses that have taken place both before, during and after the war.

It is especially important to compare the different attitudes of American union labor and of British union labor at the present time, as these two branches of Anglo-Saxon labor have naturally very much in common and interact upon each other more than is the case with any other two groups.

A study of the situation in Great Britain will show us better than any other study of circumstances outside the United States how imminent is the danger in this country and what the situation might be with us if our organized labor took the same view of its relation to Socialism and to the government as British labor is doing.

Seeing the situation as we do, as something transcending not only the State but the nation, and as reaching down to the fundamentals of man's nature and of the organization of society, the Committee feels that it must appeal in the strongest way to every member of the Legislature, to every man who holds any position of authority or of influence, to take every possible step, not only to understand the cardinal facts of the situation but to devote his thoughts and his acts to a crusade in support of every agency, every policy, that will counteract and defeat this movement. Only complete knowledge will give us the leadership that is absolutely necessary, a leadership that will be based on clear conviction and a feeling for the necessity of action: a leadership that will understand that there must be a revival of religious and moral standards as the basis of any political and economic program. The community must be appealed to, must be given the facts, must be made to see the causes and the remedies, must be made to band itself together as a civic force in every center of the State in action that shall not be the action of individuals, the sporadic, ineffectual duplicating action that will lead us nowhere. If American ideals of individual freedom and initiative are to be maintained, every citizen must be militant in their defense.

But the very fact of organizing for social defense and for social offense against those who are attacking our life is in itself dangerous, because unless we are keen of insight, these very organizations are going to be, as they have been in the past, taken possession of by astute, hardworking, clearheaded revolutionists, and turned from the purposes of reconstruction to purposes of contamination.

As much energy and organized thought and action must be put by our leading men into the solution of economic and sociological problems as they have given to the solution of their own business problems. They must show as much altruistic energy in the defense as the radical leaders have been showing in the attack. The disjointed, unprincipled, unpractical or sentimental altruism which is doing so much harm as practiced in university, in church, in philanthropic and in social circles must be shown up or made to understand the realities and dangers of its efforts, and be led, by this new insight, to shift to the camp of constructive action.

The re-education of the educators and of the educated class must go hand in hand with the reorganization and extension of our educational system. We cannot give the right point of view to our foreign population and to our children unless it is clearly and firmly ingrained in all of us. Knowledge and convictions based on knowledge must be gained by the whole nation. This report aims to give this knowledge as far as it was humanly possible to do in the spheres it undertook to investigate. This Committee feels that it has only begun the work that the country as a whole must take up and carry on, heart and soul, beginning with the renovation and elevation of our school system, based on a generous and wise understanding of its financial needs. It therefore backed with all its influence the legislation granting increased salaries to public school teachers. Party differences, local claims, appropriations not fundamentally necessary, should be set aside until more than living wage is secured for those on whose teaching the spiritual and material prosperity of this country so largely depends.

RECOMMENDATIONS FOR EDUCATIONAL LEGISLATION

At the close of the Committee's investigation into various organizations engaged in seditious activities and those calculated to encourage such a movement, and after making just as careful a study of all the activities of constructive agencies seeking to counteract these influences, the Committee was confronted with the problem of making recommendations for legislative action. This was extremely difficult. The scope of the investigation is so broad, the problems presented of such great magnitude and importance, that the Committee has hesitated to make many or extensive recommendations.

I

After a thorough review of the educational facilities offered not only by the State and municipalities and school districts, but also by religious and philanthropic institutions, the Committee felt impelled to make certain very definite suggestions. It must be observed that no matter how imposing are the school buildings, how elaborate the curricula, how sound the text books, the success of the school system depends in the last analysis upon the character and viewpoint of the teachers and instructors who carry out the program, and who influence the pupils with whom they come in contact. It is apparent that these teachers must be acquainted with the forces at play upon public opinion. They must recognize the influences which seek to undermine the confidence and respect which their pupils or students should have for the government and laws of this commonwealth. They should be trained and eager to combat those influences, and, in order that they may do this, it is essential that they themselves shall be in full accord and sympathy with our form of government and the system of society under which we live. There is a further element which has been overlooked in the selection of teachers, and that is character. In the main, the teachers in our public schools and private and philanthropic institutions have been chosen because of their academic and pedagogical attainments. In other fields it has been found necessary to scrutinize the character of persons seeking to enter them, before they are granted special privileges. For instance, admission to the bar is not alone granted for legal knowledge, but the applicant must submit to a rigid and thorough investigation as to his character. If there exists a fiduciary relationship between the attorney and his client, there is even a greater reposing of trust on the part of the public in the teacher.

Having these considerations in mind, the Committee has recommended that a law be placed upon the statute books of this State which shall require the teachers in public schools to secure, before the first of January, 1921, a special certificate certifying that they are persons of good character and that they are loyal to the institutions of the State and Nation.

II

In another portion of this report descriptions are given of various so-called schools of social reform, masquerading under different names and being carried on by various subversive organinations. An examination of their curricula shows that the fundamental purpose of these schools is to destroy the respect of the students for the institutions of the United States. Many of them advocate the overthrow of the governments of this State and of the United States by force, violence or unlawful means. In many schools and courses of lectures and classes, class hatred and contempt for government are being preached, and all those fundamentals which make for good citizenship are either ignored or ridiculed. It is the fundamental purpose of these institutions to develop agitators to enter the labor fields, to preach the doctrine of revolt, and to divide the people of the United States into contending classes so that they may be instrumental in hastening the social revolution.

At the present time there are no methods by which the public authorities can protect the people of the State from the injurious effects of such institutions. Fundamentally, it is the duty of the State in the interests of its self-protection, to see that its citizens are trained to respect its laws, to revere its institutions and to accept the duties and responsibilities as well as the privileges of citizenship. It is also the duty of the State, in the opinion of this Committee, to protect its citizens from subversive teaching. Institutions holding themselves out to the public as institutions of learning, which have the ulterior purpose of undermining our social order, entice into their classrooms large numbers of students who are unfamiliar with the purposes of those institutions, unfamiliar with the principles and character of our form of government, who would be unwilling at the beginning to participate in the movement for which such schools are created, but who, after attending the courses of lectures and imbibing the false doctrines which are there enunciated, are made a part of and become active in movements which are detrimental to the interests of the State and of its people.

Years ago the State recognized its duty to protect its citizens from unqualified lawyers and from unskilled practitioners in medicine and dentistry, but it has neglected what this Committee considers the most fundamental of all questions, and that is the protection of its citizens from false and subversive teaching.

To meet this situation the Committee recommends to the Legislature the passage of a law requiring all schools, courses and classes that are not now under the supervision or control of the Department of Education, or are not created and maintained by well-recognized religious denominations or sects, to procure a license from the Board of Regents of this State. This bill was recommended in the preliminary report of this Committee, and it has been particularly interesting to note the way it has been received by the public of this State. A very considerable opposition has been aroused, not only among the subversive institutions against which it was directed, but also in the more conservative elements of our population. The latter have joined in a protest against this measure, largely because of a lack of understanding of the bill itself, the purposes for which it is prepared and the necessity for its enactment.

The opposition shown in the public prints against this measure is a clear demonstration of the methods by which public opinion is controlled by the subversive elements in this community. If any member of the Legislature or person into whose hands this report may come will follow the issues of the New York "Call" from the date of the submission of the preliminary report of this Committee, he will there see the methods adopted by Socialists and other radical groups to influence public opinion against this measure. The opposition began in a committee of the Rand School of Social Science. It was augmented by delegates from the various radical revolutionary organizations conducting subversive educational campaigns among their membership. It was joined by delegates from the Neighborhood Houses of New York City and if reference is made to the section of this report dealing with the pacifist movement as a means for the spread of Socialism, the reason for the participation of these particular individuals in these conferences at the Rand School will be understood. Through the agency of these committees, circularizing newspapers, and preparing and circulating petitions, they have secured the support of a large number of substantial and loyal citizens of this State in opposing this measure.

The measure itself is designed to give the same supervision over unincorporated schools, courses and classes which the Regents at present have over all incorporated educational bodies. It is claimed that such supervision would result in the suppression of free education, that it would be a bar to educational progress, that it would be a reversion to medieval methods. Precisely the same arguments were used at the time the control of the medical profession was placed in the State's hands. At that time the argument was used that State control would be a bar to the progress of medical science and knowledge. The opposition was as strong as that to this measure.

An examination of the schools and colleges of this State under the supervision of the Regents does not disclose any atrophying effect upon education: this supervision is recognized as essential in raising the standards of education in this State. It is these considerations that led the Committee to recommend this measure and to express the earnest hope that it will be placed upon the statute books of this State.

III

In the first chapter of the Educational section, in Part II of this Report, the problems created by the necessity to assimilate large bodies of alien peoples have been presented. The solutions of these problems rest primarily upon the teachers in our public and private institutions. They require extraordinary talent and special training. Heretofore it has been customary to employ teachers ordinarily qualified as public school teachers to deal with the problems of adult and immigrant education. Short courses of intensive training have been provided.

This Committee, however, feels that the problems are so vast that especial training of a substantial and thorough character is necessary in order to make effective the courses conducted in our public and private institutions in the fields of immigrant education and citizenship training.

The Committee, therefore, has proposed in its preliminary report legislation directing the Department of Education of this State to open and conduct special training courses for teachers in these fields, to have a duration of not less than one academic year.

IV

In the course of its investigation the Committee has been impressed by the need of a wide extension of the facilities offered to illiterate adults and minors over sixteen years of age. In another chapter the questions are fully presented. The factory extension education classes afford, in the opinion of the Committee, one of the most effective means of dealing with these problems. The Committee has, therefore, offered in its preliminary report a bill calculated to enable the Commissioner of Education to open more and more schools in factories and outside of school buildings, in such places as may be appropriate, so that it will become increasingly easy for the immigrant adult or minor over sixteen years of age to find a place in which he can become acquainted not only with the institutions and laws of this State and of the United States, but also with his duties and privileges as a citizen and resident thereof.

The texts of these four bills will be found at the close of this introduction.

SEARCH WARRANTS AND PROSECUTIONS

Soon after this Committee was organized it became apparent that the Criminal Anarchy statute of this State was being constantly and flagrantly violated. The reasons for this have already been pointed out in the preliminary report of this Committee.

In order to assist the prosecuting officers in the preparation and the presentation of cases involving a violation of this law, this Committee procured a number of search warrants against various organizations that were found to be the centers and sources of radical revolutionary propaganda.

The first search warrant was obtained on June 12, 1919, from Hon. Alexander Brough, city magistrate, and was directed against the office of the Russian Soviet Bureau at 110 West Fortieth street, New York city. The activities of this bureau have been described in another part of this report. This search warrant was executed on the day it was issued by special agents of the Committee assisted by the members of the State Constabulary, and large quantities of printed and written matter referred to in the search warrant were removed from 110 West Fortieth street to the headquarters of this Committee.

Counsel for the Soviet Bureau and for Ludwig C. A. K. Martens, the alleged representative of the Soviet government, endeavored to vacate the search warrant, but, after exhaustive argument, in which Attorney-General Charles D. Newton personally represented the Committee, the application for the vacating of the search warrant was denied, and the Committee permitted to retain possession of the papers and documents seized under and by virtue of the search warrant. Certain papers that were not deemed relevant or pertinent were voluntarily returned to the Soviet Bureau by representatives of the Committee.

On June 21, 1919, Hon. William McAdoo, Chief City Magistrate, issued three search warrants which were directed respectively against the Rand School of Social Science, situated at

7 East 15th street, in the borough of Manhattan, city of New York; the headquarters of the Left Wing Section of the Socialist Party, situated at 43 West 29th street, in the borough of Manhattan, city of New York; and the New York city headquarters of the I. W. W., situated at 27 East 4th street, in the borough of Manhattan, city of New York.

The three search warrants were executed simultaneously at 3 o'clock in the afternoon of June 21, 1919, by representatives of the Committee, members of the New York city police, members of the State constabulary, and volunteers from the American Protective League.

Large quantities of revolutionary, incendiary and seditious written and printed matter were seized in each of these three places under and by virtue of the search warrants that had been issued against them. Court proceedings were instituted in behalf of the Left Wing Section of the Socialist Party to vacate the search warrant that had been issued against it, but the application was denied by the court, and the validity of the search warrant sustained.

An application was made by counsel for the Rand School of Social Science for the vacating of the search warrant that had been issued against it but the attorney for the Rand School abandoned these proceedings. No application was made on behalf of the I. W. W. headquarters for a vacating of the search warrant directed against it.

In all of these places large quantities of written and printed matter of the character aforementioned were obtained, and in addition thereto much valuable information was had concerning the identity of the leaders of the radical revolutionary movement in America as well as the names and addresses of thousands of members of these various organizations, with a result that numerous indictments have been found in various counties of this State as a direct result of the information thus obtained. No arrests were made at the time of the execution of the search warrants against the Rand School, the I. W. W. headquarters, and the headquarters of the Left Wing Section of the Socialist Party, the purpose being not to make arrests, but to obtain evidence which was turned over to the prosecuting officers, as provided for by law.

On August 14, 1919, a search warrant was obtained by representatives of the Committee from Magistrate William Sweetser, directed against the headquarters of the Union of Russian Workers, situated at 133 East 15th street, in the borough of Manhattan, city of New York. These premises consist of an old private house in process of rather rapid decay. On the entrance or parlor floor was found a large room used as a schoolroom, containing a blackboard and crude desks and benches. Inquiry among the persons found therein disclosed the fact that many of them were led to gather in the premises on the supposition that they would there be taught both English and the reading and writing of their native tongue, Russian. As a matter of fact, this was but a blind, the real purpose being to gain recruits to the cause of revolution and anarchy. In the rear room, at the top floor of this building, were found the directors of this institution, and the editors of an anarchistic sheet called "Khlieb y Volya," the guiding spirits of which were one Peter Bianki, Naum Stepanuk and Peter Krawchuk. Large quantities of anarchistic literature were found secreted in various portions of the premises and were seized under the search warrant.

The three men above named were indicted by the extraordinary grand jury of New York county charged with criminal anarchy. They have since been deported to Russia on the "Soviet Ark" Buford.

This search warrant was executed by representatives of the Committee, together with Inspector (Now Deputy Commissioner) Joseph Faurot of the New York police department, who is best known as the Bertillon expert of the New York police department; Sergeant James Gegan, head of the bomb squad of the New York police department, and Officers Cornelius Brown, Charles J. Newman and other members of the bomb squad.

Shortly before this, representatives of the Committee had caused the arrest of two Finnish anarchist leaders named Carl Paivio and Gust Alonen, who were the editors and publishers of a rabid anarchist sheet called "Luokkataistelu." These two men, Paivio and Alonen, on complaint of the Committee, were indicted in New York county on the charge of criminal anarchy. They were tried and convicted before Mr. Justice Bartow S. Weeks in the Extraordinary Criminal Trial Term of the Supreme Court, and were sentenced to Sing Sing prison at hard labor, for a period of not less than four years and not more than eight years; and they are now in that prison serving their sentences.

On November 8, 1919, search warrants were issued by Chief

Magistrate William McAdoo at the request of the Committee, and directed against the seventy-one headquarters of the Communist Party of America in the various boroughs of the city. At 9 o'clock in the evening of that day all of these headquarters were simultaneously entered by representatives of the Committee, by members of the State constabulary, and by upward of 700 members of the New York police force under the leadership of Inspector Faurot, Detective Sergeant Gegan and other members of the bomb squad.

Many tons of seditious and anarchistic literature were seized in the execution of these search warrants and a large number of prisoners taken. Those concerning whom there was not absolutely positive proof of membership in the Communist Party of America were released, and those concerning whom indubitable proof was possessed were held for the action of the grand jury, and later indicted. Among those arrested on that date were Benjamin Gitlow, a former Socialist Assemblyman of the State of New York, and one of the editors of the "Revolutionary Age," and James J. Larkin, also one of the editors of the "Revolutionary Age."

Gitlow was recently tried on the charge of criminal anarchy before Mr. Justice Bartow S. Weeks, sitting in the Extraordinary Criminal Trial Term of the Supreme Court. He was convicted and sentenced to hard labor in Sing Sing Prison for a term of not less than five years, nor more than ten years.

Shortly afterward Harry M. Winitsky, Secretary of the Communist Party of America, Local Greater New York, was arrested and indicted on the charge of criminal anarchy. He also was recently tried before Mr. Justice Bartow S. Weeks, and convicted. He was sentenced to Sing Sing Prison at hard labor for a term of not less than five years nor more than ten years.

At the time of the preparation of this report James J. Larkin is being tried on the charge of criminal anarchy.

In the meantime, eighteen persons charged with criminal anarchy were arrested in Cortland county on complaint of the Committee, and the local headquarters of that organization entered and large quantities of seditious literature removed.

On December 28, 1919, search warrants were obtained by the Committee in the cities of Utica, Rochester and Buffalo. and simultaneously, at nine o'clock in the evening of that day the headquarters of the Communist Party of America, of the Union of Russian Workers, and of other revolutionary organizations were entered by representatives of the Committee, together with representatives of the local police force in each of these three cities, and of representatives of the district attorneys of these cities. Again, large quantities of seditious and revolutionary literature was seized under these search warrants, and formed the basis of numerous indictments found against the ringleaders of the revolutionary organizations in the cities mentioned.

In the city of Rochester the headquarters of the Communist party were in a building commonly known as "Dynamite Hall." Here was found a large circulating library containing books on anarchistic subjects, and a mass of literature urging the overthrow of organized government by unlawful means. There were also found in these premises a number of immoral books, and judging from the well-thumbed appearance of books of this character, and of anarchistic character, it seemed that this type of literature particularly appealed to the patrons of this library. In this "Dynamite Hall" was also found evidence of the fact that meetings had been held in public schools of the city of Rochester at which documents were circulated advising the propriety and the necessity of overthrowing organized government by force and violence, and in one instance a resolution had been passed in one of the public schools in the city of Rochester, at a meeting held by the Socialist local of that city, proposing that 10,000 copies of Nicolai Lenine's revolutionary appeal to the working men of America be printed and circulated.

We give below a table showing the number of indictments procured, the number of trials had, and convictions resulting therefrom.

TABLE OF CASES SHOWING PROSECUTIONS ON THE CHARGE OF CRIMINAL ANARCHY INSTITUTED THROUGH THE CO-OPERATION OF THIS COMMITTEE WITH THE DISTRICT ATTORNEYS OF THE COUNTIES NAMED

Name of defendant	County	Present status	Sentence upon conviction
James J. Larkin*	New York	On trial.	
Benjamin Gitlow	New York	Convicted	State prison, 5 to 10 yrs.
Isaac E. Ferguson*	New York	Awaiting trial.	
Charles E. Ruthenberg*	New York	Awaiting trial.	
Gust Alonen	New York	Convicted	State prison, 4 to 8 yrs.
Carl Paivio	New York	Convicted	State prison, 4 to 8 yrs.

*Since the submission of this report James J. Larkin, I. E. Ferguson and C. E. Ruthenberg have been convicted and are now serving sentences of 5 to 10 years in state prison.

Name of defendant	County	Present Status	Sentence upon conviction
Peter Bianki	New York	Deported on U. S. S. Buford to Russia.	
Naum Stepanuk	New York	Deported on U. S. S. Buford to Russia.	
Michael Krawchuk	New York	Deported on U. S. S. Buford to Russia.	
Harry Israel	New York	Awaiting trial.	
Isidore Cohen	New York	Awaiting trial.	
Nicholas Turkevitch	New York	Awaiting trial.	
Abe Schaiffer	New York	Awaiting trial.	
Joseph Sezwecuk	New York	Awaiting trial.	
Jay Lovestone	New York	Awaiting trial.	
Elias Marks	New York	Awaiting trial.	
John Holland	New York	Awaiting trial.	
Nathan Schechter	New York	Awaiting trial.	
Moses Zimmerman	New York	Awaiting trial.	
Hyman Bleiweiss	New York	Awaiting trial.	
Mike Stechner	New York	Awaiting trial.	
Hyman Feffer	New York	Awaiting trial.	
Benjamin J. Toback	New York	Awaiting trial.	
John Solsky	New York	Awaiting trial.	
Abraham Weinberg	New York	Awaiting trial.	
Louis Shapiro	New York	Awaiting trial.	
Harry M. Winitsky	New York	Convicted	State prison, 5 to 10 yrs.
Irving Potash	Kings	Pleaded guilty to unlawful assembly and awaiting sentence.	
Michael Zwarich	Kings	Pleaded guilty to unlawful assembly and awaiting sentence.	
Robert E. Fried	Kings	Pleaded guilty to unlawful assembly and awaiting sentence.	
John Janschuky	Kings	Pleaded guilty to unlawful assembly and awaiting sentence.	
Taft Novick	Kings	Pleaded guilty to unlawful assembly and awaiting sentence.	
Meyer Graubarid	Kings	Awaiting trial.	
Hyman Bleiwess	Bronx	Awaiting trial.	
Jay Lovestone	Bronx	Await ng trial.	
Charles M. O'Brien	Monroe (Rochester)	Awaiting trial.	
Ignatz Mizher	Cortland	Awaiting trial.*	
John Urchenko	Cortland	Awaiting trial.	
Corney Britt	Cortland	Awaiting trial.	
Nikita Zamry	Cortland	Awaiting trial.	
Louis Litonovitch	Cortland	Awaiting trial.	
Efim Capasin	Cortland	Awaiting trial.	
Acksenty Makovetsky	Cortland	Awaiting trial.	
Pimon Polonsky	Cortland	Awaiting trial.	
Steve Kostenko	Cortland	Awaiting trial.	
Jacob Hrikorash	Cortland	Awaiting trial.	
Sam Karpenko	Cortland	Awaiting trial.	

* Has since been tried, convicted, and sentenced to five to ten years in State's prison.

Name of defendant	County	Present status	Sentence upon conviction
Valerian Makovetsky	Cortland	Awaiting trial.	
Efim Pavlenko	Cortland	Awaiting trial.	
Ivan Kebanuk	Cortland	Awaiting trial.	
Dymtro Pastuck	Oneida (Utica)	Awaiting trial.	
Joseph Grigas	Oneida (Utica)	Awaiting trial.	
Michael Zlepko	Oneida (Utica)	Awaiting trial.	
Peter Kraus	Oneida (Utica)	Awaiting trial.	
Sewaren Skulski	Oneida (Utica)	Awaiting trial.	
John Korolenok	Oneida (Utica)	Awaiting trial.	
Alex Krucka	Oneida (Utica)	Awaiting trial.	
Fred Woznay	Oneida (Utica)	Awaiting trial.	
Dymtro Choptiany	Oneida (Utica)	Awaiting trial.	
Zygmund Ziminski	Erie	Awaiting trial.	
William J. Schwannekamp	Erie	Awaiting trial.	
Benjamin Keleman	Erie	Awaiting trial.	
Darcy Millikan	Erie	Awaiting trial.	
Anna M. Reinstein	Erie	Awaiting trial.	
Harry J. O'Neil	Erie	Awaiting trial.	
Crist Keegan	Erie	Awaiting trial.	
George A. Till	Erie	Awaiting trial.	
Oscar A. Peterson	Erie	Awaiting trial.	
W lliam Bradley	Erie	Awaiting trial.	
Anthony Gruensweig	Erie	Awaiting trial.	
Franklin P. Brill	Erie	Awaiting trial.	
Abraham Robiroff	Erie	Awaiting trial.	
Frank Rosenblatt	Erie	Awaiting trial.	
Paul Streamer	Erie	Awaiting tiral.	
Kyzma Olrinko	Erie	Awaiting trial.	
George H. Rosenberg	Erie	Awaiting trial.	

One defendant indicted but not yet arrested. Therefore his name is not here given.

In addition to the defendants above named six persons were indicted in New York county charged with criminal anarchy but have not been arrested, having fled the jurisdiction, and for obvious reasons their names are not given in this report.

The Committee desires to express its appreciation of the public service rendered by the district attorneys who procured the above indictments, who are: Hon. Edward Swann, of New York county; Hon. Harry E. Lewis, of Kings county; Hon. Francis M. Martin, of Bronx county; Hon. William F. Love, of Monroe county; Hon. W. R. Lee, of Oneida county, Hon. James Tobin, of Cortland county; and Hon. Guy Moore, of Erie county.

There have thus far been four trials under indictments charging Criminal Anarchy, and all four trials have resulted in convictions. The prosecution of these four cases was conducted by

Assistant District Attorney Alexander I. Rorke, who worked with the Committee for many months, and whose fidelity and ability merit the highest commendation from this Committee.

In the course of the public hearings held by the Committee, Ludwig C. A. K. Martens was summoned as a witness to attend before the Committee. He failed to obey the subpœna which had been duly served upon him, and an attachment was issued against him by Mr. Justice Leonard A. Giegerich of the Supreme Court. Martens was brought before the Committee at the City Hall, New York, on November 14, 1919, by Deputy Sheriff Murray, and upon his appearance was released under bond in the sum of $1,000. He appeared afterward before the Committee and was subjected to a careful examination. In the course of this inquiry Martens testified that he had received from Soviet Russia some $90,000 in money for the purposes of carrying on the work of his Bureau. Pressed as to the identity of the persons who brought to him this money, he declined to answer, and the Chairman of the Committee declared him in contempt.

Just before this he had made application through his attorney, Dudley Field Malone, for the vacating of the subpœna that had theretofore been duly served upon him. This application was heard by Mr. Justice Samuel Greenbaum of the Supreme Court. Mr. Malone advanced the argument that his client was clothed with diplomatic privileges and immunities. In his decision denying the application for the vacating of this subpœna, Judge Greenbaum brushed aside this alleged claim of diplomatic immunity, and decided there was no legal provision for the granting of such a motion, and Martens was compelled to answer the questions that were put to him. He declined, however, to divulge the identity of the couriers who had brought this money to him, and declined also to answer various other pertinent questions. He was declared in contempt of the Committee by the Chairman, and an application was made by the Attorney-General for an order requiring Martens to show cause why he should not be committed to the County Jail of New York County until he should answer the questions that had been propounded to him by the Committee.

The order to show cause was issued by Mr. Justice Greenbaum of the Supreme Court, but before it could be served upon him, Martens left the jurisdiction, and it was later learned he had gone to Washington, D. C., where he has since been.

Another contumacious witness who appeared before the Committee was Santeri Nuorteva, Martens' secretary, who also declined to answer pertinent and relevant questions, and was duly declared in contempt by the Committee. An order was issued by Mr. Justice Greenbaum directed to Santeri Nuorteva, requiring him to show cause why he should not be committed to the County Jail until he answer the said questions. Before this order could be served upon him he left the jurisdiction, went to Washington, D. C., with his chief, Martens, and is there at the time of the writing of this report.

Michael Mislig, a confrere of Martens and Nuorteva and the treasurer of the Russian Socialist Federation, who, as we have reason to believe, is a member of the Communist Party of America, followed the example of Martens and declined to answer material and relevant questions propounded to him by the Committee. He too was declared in contempt. A Supreme Court order was obtained by the Attorney-General requiring Mislig to show cause why he should not be committed to the County Jail until he answered the questions that had been thus properly propounded to him. Argument on this application for Mislig, which was vigorously contested by counsel, was had before Mr. Justice Vernon M. Davis of the Supreme Court. A final order was granted adjudging Mislig in contempt, and directing that he be confined in the County Jail until he should answer the questions that had thus been propounded to him by the Committee. Before this final order could be served upon him, Mislig too fled the jurisdiction, and though many months have elapsed, he is still out of the jurisdiction of the Supreme Court of the State of New York.

This Committee and its counsel have co-operated with the prosecuting authorities of various states in the investigation of seditious activities and with criminal prosecutions arising therefrom, as well as with the Department of Justice of the United States, and with the immigration authorities. Much valuable information has been placed at the disposal of these various prosecuting and investigating bodies by this Committee, resulting in prosecutions and deportations in large numbers.

STATE OF NEW YORK.

No. 1275. Int. 1121.

IN SENATE.

March 17, 1920.

Introduced by Mr. LUSK — read twice and ordered printed, and when printed to be committed to the Committee on Finance.

AN ACT

To amend the education law, in relation to the qualifications of teachers, and making an appropriation for expenses.

The People of the State of New York, represented in Senate and Assembly, do enact as follows:

Section 1. Chapter twenty-one of the laws of nineteen hundred and nine, entitled "An act relating to education, constituting chapter sixteen of the consolidated laws," as amended by chapter one hundred and forty of the laws of nineteen hundred and ten, is hereby amended by inserting therein a new section to read as follows:

§ 555-a. **Additional qualifications of teachers.** 1. In addition to the requirements for teachers and certification prescribed as provided in this article, each teacher employed in the public schools of each city, union free and common school district in the State shall obtain a certificate of qualifications as herein provided. Such certificates shall state that the teacher holding the same is a person of good moral character and that he has shown satisfactorily that he is obedient to and will support the constitutions and laws of this State and of the United States, and that he is desirous of the welfare of the country and in hearty accord and sympathy with the government and institutions of the State of New York and of the United States.

2. Such certificates of qualification shall be issued by, or under the direction of, the commissioner of education in conformity with rules to be adopted by the regents of the university of the State of New York.

3. No certificate shall be issued by the commissioner of education or by school authorities under any other provision of this article until the applicant therefor shall have been examined and a certificate of qualifications issued as provided in this section.

4. No teacher shall be employed in the public schools of the city, union free and common school districts of this State on and after January first, nineteen hundred and twenty-one, without having obtained a certificate of qualifications as provided in this section.

5. The certificate authorizing a person to teach may be revoked by the Commissioner of Education on the ground that such person is not of good moral character, or for any act or utterance showing that he is not obedient to the Constitution and laws of this State or of the United States, or that he is not desirous of the welfare of the country or that he is not in hearty accord and sympathy with the government and institutions of this State or of the United States.

§ 2. The sum of fifteen thousand dollars ($15,000), or such part thereof as shall be necessary, is hereby appropriated, out of money in the State Treasury not otherwise appropriated, for the purpose of carrying into effect the provisions of this act.

§ 3. This act shall take effect immediately.

STATE OF NEW YORK.

3d Rdg. 753. Nos. 1274, 1767. Int. 1120.

IN SENATE.

March 17, 1920.

Introduced by Mr. LUSK — read twice and ordered printed and when printed to be committed to the Committee on Finance — amended in said committee, ordered to a third reading and to be reprinted as amended.

AN ACT

To amend the education law, in relation to licensing and supervision of schools and school courses, and making an appropriation therefor.

The People of the State of New York, represented in Senate and Assembly, do enact as follows:

Section 1. Chapter twenty-one of the laws of nineteen hundred and nine, entitled "An act relating to education, constituting chapter sixteen of the consolidated laws,"as amended by chapter one hundred and forty of the laws of nineteen hundred and ten, is hereby amended by inserting therein, at the end of article three, a new section, to be section seventy-nine, to read as follows:

§ 79. **Licenses of schools; supervision.** 1. No person, firm, corporation, association or society shall conduct, maintain or operate any school, institute, class or course of instruction in any subjects whatever without making application for and being granted a license from the university of the state of New York to so conduct, maintain or operate such institute, school or class. Such application shall be made in the form and under the rules prescribed by the regents of the university of the state. The application for such license shall be accompanied with a verified statement showing the purposes for which the school, institute or class is to be maintained and conducted, and the nature and extent and purpose of the instruction to be given. No license shall be granted for the conduct of any such school, institute or class unless the regents of the university of the state are satisfied that the instruction proposed to be given will not be deterimental to public interest. Licenses shall not be required for the public schools of the city, union free and common school districts of the state nor for educational institutions which are now or may hereafter be incorporated by the university of the state or which are now or may hereafter be admitted to membership in the university of the state; nor shall such license be required of schools now or hereafter established and maintained by a religious denomination or sect well recognized as such at the time this section takes effect. A school, institute or class licensed as provided in this section shall be subject to visitation by officers and employees of the university of the state of New York.

2. A license granted to a school, institute or class as provided herein shall be subject to revocation by the regents of the university upon due notice after an opportunity to be heard before the board of regents or a committee thereof or an officer of the education department in each case designated by the board of regents. Such license shall be revoked when it shall appear to the satisfaction of the regents that the school, institute or class is being conducted in such manner as to be detrimental to public interests or is being conducted in a fraudulent or improper manner.

3. Any person, firm, corporation, association or society, or any representative or employee thereof, maintaining or conducting a school, institute, course or class without a license granted as herein provided shall be guilty of a misdemeanor and upon conviction therefor shall be punished by a fine not exceeding one hundred dollars, or by imprisonment not exceeding sixty days. Whenever it shall appear that any person, firm, corporation, association or society is maintaining or conducting a school, institute, course or class without such license an appropriate action and injunction proceedings may be brought on behalf of the state by the attorney-general to restrain such person, firm, corporation, association or society, or any employee or representative thereof, from continuing the maintenance or conduct of such school, institute, course or class without such license.

§ 2. The sum of ten thousand dollars ($10,000), or so much thereof as may be necessary, is hereby appropriated for the purpose of carrying into effect the provisions of section seventy-nine of the education law as added by this act.

§ 3. This act shall take effect immediately.

STATE OF NEW YORK.

3d Rdg. 740. Nos. 1276, 2047. Int. 1122.

IN SENATE.

March 17, 1920.

Introduced by Mr. LUSK — read twice and ordered printed, and when printed to be committed to the Committee on Finance — reported favorably from said committee, ordered to a third reading, amended and ordered reprinted, retaining its place in the order of third reading.

AN ACT

To amend the education law, in relation to teachers of foreign born and native adults and minors over sixteen years of age, and making an appropriation for expenses.

The People of the State of New York, represented in Senate and Assembly, do enact as follows:

Section 1. Subdivision eleven-a of section ninety-four of chapter twenty-one of the laws of nineteen hundred and nine, entitled "An act relating to education, constituting chapter sixteen of the consolidated laws," as amended by chapter one hundred and forty of the laws of nineteen hundred and ten, as added by chapter four hundred and twelve of the laws of nineteen hundred and eighteen, is hereby amended to read as follows:

11-a. [The commissioner of education is also authorized and empowered to organize, maintain and operate training institutes and regular courses of study in connection with the state normal institutions, and in the cities of the state for the purpose of training regular public school teachers and others in the best methods to be pursued in giving instruction to illiterates over sixteen years of age.] The commissioner of education is authorized and directed to establish and provide for the maintenance and conduct of courses of study or training in state normal institutions and in colleges and universities and other educational institutions and in connection with other educational agencies for the purpose of training teachers in principles and methods of instruction, and to give them knowledge to fit them to instruct foreign born and native adults and minors over sixteen years of age in evening, extension, factory, home and community classes. Such courses of study shall be prescribed by the Commissioner of Education and shall continue for a period of not less than one year. No teacher employed to instruct foreign born and native adults and minors over sixteen years of age shall be employed by the state or compensated in whole or in part by the state, unless he shall have completed such course of study or training or shall have an equivalent thereof to be determined under the rules and regulations of the Commissioner of Education. A special certificate shall be issued to teachers who have completed such course of study or a course of instruction which is equivalent thereto, provided, however, that temporary permits may be issued by the Commissioner of Education to teachers who are qualified to give such instruction pending the completion of such a course of study or training.

§ 2. The sum of forty thousand dollars ($40,000), or so much thereof as may be necessary, is hereby appropriated, out of moneys in the state treasury not otherwise appropriated, for the purpose of carrying into effect the provisions of this act.

§ 3. This act shall take effect immediately.

STATE OF NEW YORK.

3d Rdg. 1100. Nos. 1273, 2091. Int. 1119.

IN SENATE.

March 17, 1920.

Introduced by Mr. LUSK — read twice and ordered printed, and when printed to be committed to the Committee on Finance — reported favorably from said committee with amendments, by unanimous consent the rules were suspended and said bill ordered to a third reading and to be reprinted as amended.

AN ACT

To amend the education law, in relation to providing for educational extension facilities for foreign-born and native adults and minors over the age of sixteen years, relating to the employment of teachers, the payment of their compensation, and making an appropriation for expenses.

The People of the State of New York, represented in Senate and Assembly, do enact as follows:

Section 1. Section ninety-four of chapter twenty-one of the laws of nineteen hundred and nine, entitled "An act relating to education, constituting chapter sixteen of the consolidated laws," as amended by chapter one hundred and forty of the laws of nineteen hundred and ten, is hereby amended by adding at the end thereof a new subdivision, to read as follows:

11-d. The Commissioner of Education may provide for the establishment of courses of instruction of study and schools in connection with factories, places of employment, or in such other places as he may deem advisable, for the purpose of giving instruction to foreign-born and native adults and minors over the age of sixteen years. Such course of instruction of study shall include instruction in English, history, civics and other subjects tending to promote good citizenship and to increase vocational efficiency. Such course of instruction and study shall be prescribed by the regents of the university of the state of New York, and shall be in conformity with rules to be adopted by them.

The Commissioner of Education is authorized and directed to employ teachers and to fix the compensation of teachers especially trained and having certificates as provided in subdivision eleven-a of this section, and to assign such teachers to service in extension courses in factories and other places of employment, or in such other places as he may deem advisable throughout the state, established as provided by law.

§ 2. The sum of one hundred thousand dollars ($100,000), or so much thereof as may be necessary, is hereby appropriated, out of money in the state treasury not otherwise appropriated, for the purpose of carrying into effect the provisions of this act.

§ 3. This act shall take effect immediately.

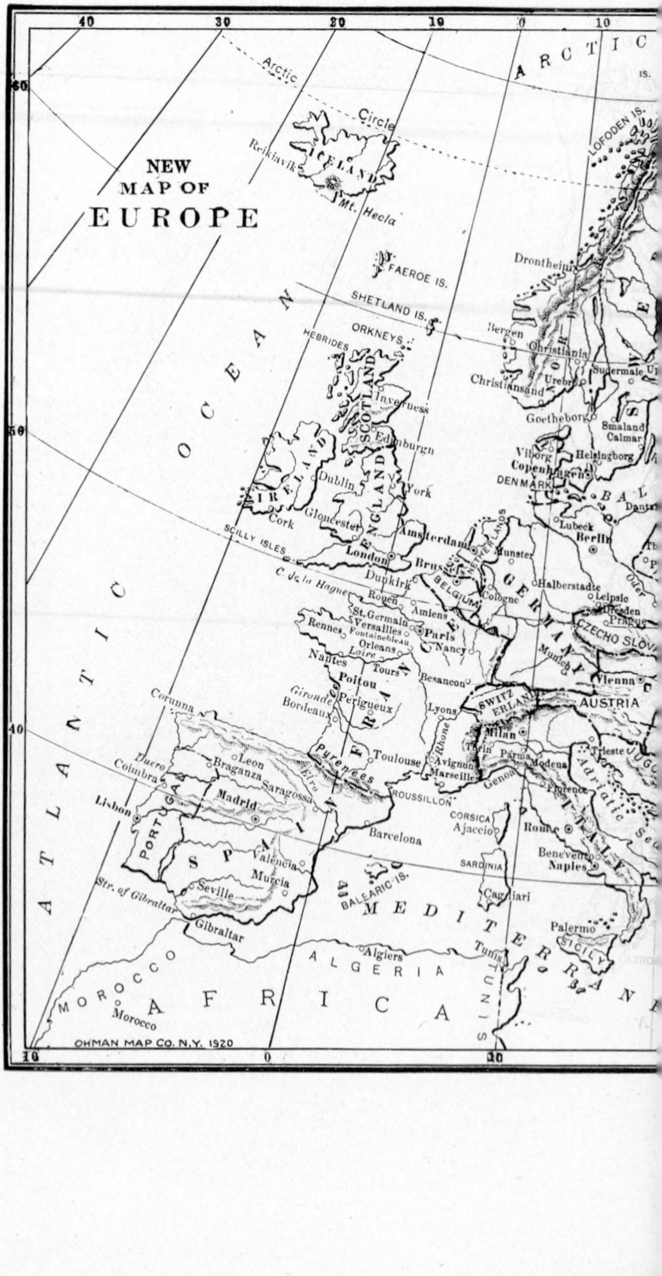
NEW
MAP OF
EUROPE
ARCTIC
Arctic Circle
ICELAND
Reikiavik
Mt. Hecla
FAEROE IS.
SHETLAND IS.
ORKNEYS
HEBRIDES
LOFODEN IS.
ATLANTIC OCEAN
SCOTLAND
Inverness
Edinburgh
IRELAND
Dublin
Cork
ENGLAND
York
Gloucester
London
SCILLY ISLES
Drontheim
Bergen
Christiania
Christiansand
NORWAY
Urebro
Sudermale
Goetheborg
Smaland
Calmar
Helsingborg
Viborg
Copenhagen
DENMARK
Lubeck
Berlin
Amsterdam
Brussels
NETHERLANDS
BELGIUM
Munster
Cologne
Halberstadt
Leipsic
Dresden
Prague
GERMANY
CZECHO SLOV
Munich
Vienna
AUSTRIA
Dunkirk
C. de la Hague
Rouen
Amiens
St. Germain
Versailles
Fontainebleau
Paris
Rennes
Orleans
Loire
Nancy
Nantes
Tours
Besancon
Poitou
Perigueux
Gironde
Bordeaux
FRANCE
Lyons
Rhone
Avignon
Marseille
Toulouse
ROUSSILLON
Pyrenees
SWITZERLAND
Milan
Turin
Parma
Modena
Genoa
Florence
Trieste
Adriatic Sea
ITALY
Rome
Benevento
Naples
CORSICA
Ajaccio
SARDINIA
Cagliari
Palermo
SICILY
Corunna
Leon
Braganza
Duero
Coimbra
Ebro
Saragossa
Madrid
Lisbon
PORTUGAL
SPAIN
Valencia
Barcelona
Murcia
Seville
BALEARIC IS.
Str. of Gibraltar
Gibraltar
MEDITERRANEAN
Algiers
ALGERIA
Tunis
TUNIS
MOROCCO
Morocco
AFRICA
OHMAN MAP CO. N.Y. 1920

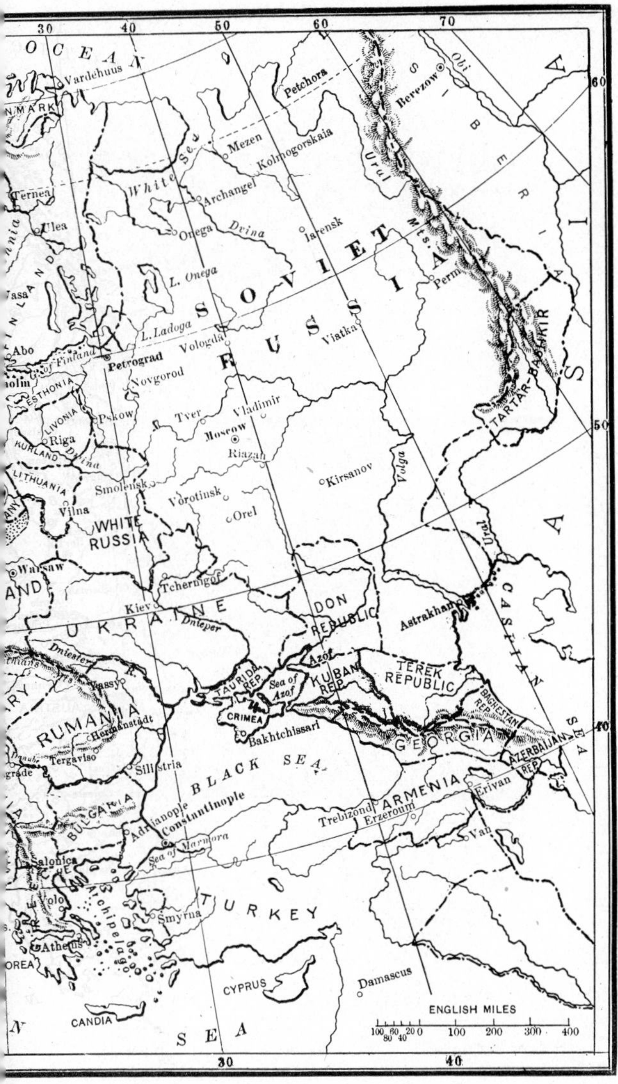

30
40
50
60
70
OCEAN
Vardehuus
Petchora
Berezow
Obi
SIBERIA
Mezen
Kolmogorskaia
White Sea
Archangel
Ural Mts.
Ternea
Ulea
Onega
Drina
Iarensk
SOVIET RUSSIA
Perm
L. Onega
Vasa
L. Ladoga
Viatka
Abo
G. of Finland
Petrograd
Vologda
Novgorod
ESTHONIA
LIVONIA
Pskow
Tver
Vladimir
Riga
Moscow
KURLAND
Riazan
TARTAR-BASHKIR
Volga
Kirsanov
LITHUANIA
Smolensk
Vorotinsk
Orel
Vilna
WHITE RUSSIA
Ural
ASIA
Warsaw
Tchernigof
Kiev
UKRAINE
Dnieper
DON REPUBLIC
Astrakhan
CASPIAN SEA
Dniester
Jassy
TAURIDA REP.
Sea of Azof
Azof
KUBAN REP.
TEREK REPUBLIC
DAGHESTAN REP.
CRIMEA
RUMANIA
Hermanstadt
Bakhtchissari
GEORGIA
AZERBAIJAN REP.
Danube
Tergaviso
Sillistria
BLACK SEA
ARMENIA
Erivan
BULGARIA
Adrianople
Constantinople
Trebizond
Erzeroum
Van
Sea of Marmora
Salonica
Volo
Archipelago
Smyrna
TURKEY
Athens
CYPRUS
Damascus
CANDIA
SEA
ENGLISH MILES
100 80 60 40 20 0 100 200 300 400

SECTION I

EUROPEAN CONDITIONS AND HISTORICAL REVIEW

CHAPTER I

Origin and Development of Socialist and Labor Movements in Europe

The most important questions of the day are Socialism and Labor. The men who are leading in both these fields of thought and action are quite aware of their international character. The American public is not. It must be educated to see that every big movement on the other side has its parallel in the United States, and that they are so closely interlocked and so governed by the same group of men that we cannot ignore the European situation. Otherwise our people cannot understand the centralized strategy behind the action. It cannot realize the tremendous forces at work nor the crises present and impending. It cannot measure the significance, for example, of the presence and free action in this country of Martens and Nuorteva, nor the meaning of simultaneous strikes here and in several European countries of the men who control the loading and unloading of ships and general trade and commerce, nor the meaning for America of the establishment in Holland of a base for International Communist propaganda by the Soviet government of Russia on behalf of the Third International, with sub-bureaus in the United States.

For this reason the present report aims to give a brief review of the rise of Socialism, of its spread in various countries, of its fundamental principles and accomplishments; to give also a sketch of the Labor movement and its connection both with Socialism and with more constructive ideas of industrial reform. It will describe the International side of these movements, which took shape in the First International; succeeded, after a short interval of preparation, by the Second International which is still in existence, now fighting for its life against the more destructive recent Soviet creation, the Third (Moscow) International.

The situation in each country, leading up to present conditions, will then be separately reviewed, in the fields of both Socialism and Labor. Only then will the connection between the European situation and our own be studied and the intensive propaganda of revolutionary forces in our country be outlined.

Several things must be borne in mind if we would understand Socialism and Labor in Europe as distinguished from America.

In the first place there is a small matter of terminology. When we read of the Social-Democratic Party in Germany, or in the Scandinavian or Balkan countries, it must be understood that this is the name adopted by the Socialist party whenever a political branch was established. All Social-Democratic or Social-Democratic Labor parties are Socialist parties. Only very recently, since the rise of the Bolsheviki, have groups of extreme Socialists, in breaking away from the regular party, called themselves Communists. Also practically all the Social-Democrats of Europe are followers of Karl Marx. There is no other system of philosophic and practical Socialism now being followed and applied.

The next and far more important point is that in considering the European situation we cannot pigeon-hole Labor by itself and Socialism by itself, as we can in the United States, in the case of organized labor of the American Federation of Labor type; nor as we also can in the case of Australia, where Labor has always been comparatively free from Marxism or any other form of doctrinaire socialism.

Throughout Europe, and to a large extent in Great Britain, Socialism and Labor must be bracketed. It is easy to study, in the Scandinavian countries, for instance, how the Socialist-Democratic Party fostered the establishment and extension of the trade unions, or vice-versa; and how the responsibility for the movements in the interest of the working classes was harmoniously divided between the two elements. The Social-Democratic Party took charge of the political and the trade unions took charge of the economic side of the struggle, and the campaigns were planned together by the leaders of the two groups.

In other countries like mercurial and individualistic France, there is an ebb and flow of collaboration, according to whether moderates or extremists are in power. The *Confédération Genérale du Travail,* even though it is Syndicalist, was more in sympathy with the moderate Socialism of Albert Thomas and Renaudel than it now is with the present dominant Bolshevik Party of Loriot, or even with the more moderate Longuet.

In Spain the Syndicalists and Socialists are at odds, but largely because the Spanish people are not yet sufficiently educated to really master the ideas of Socialism. In Italy, on the contrary, the people have had a long education in all these ideas and long practice in handling them, and notwithstanding the outspoken Bolshevism of the official Socialist Party, it has the almost solid backing of the big labor organizations and trade unions of the country which are largely Syndicalist. They work hand in hand and wait for the time when the economic and political revolutions will be brought about by their common action.

In Germany the interlocking of Labor and Socialism is even more complete and logical because founded on a long history and a thorough education in the theories underlying the alliance. The only obstacle to the dominance of Socialist theories of the revolutionary type over the German laboring man in his inborn thrift and his disinclination to endanger by uncertain experiments the basis of his material well-being.

Historical Evolution of Socialism

The evolution of Socialism has depended on the coming of economic crises. Engels, Marx's partner, believed that such crises came " about once every ten years," when over-production threw business out-of-joint. As that great early French Socialist, Fourier, described them, they were crises of plethora; as the present crisis, on the contrary, is a crisis of under-production, of depletion. Far more explanatory than Engels' theory is that which makes our present social upheaval depend on the tremendous concentration of capital and centralization of output through the modern combined development of machinery and invention; a concentration that also brought together great masses of the workers and gave them the idea of united effort and close organization in opposition to the capitalist concentration.

That such conditions led at first to a movement among thinkers and dreamers rather than workers was natural. Professor R. T. Ely says with regard to this early group in his "Socialism and Social Reform" (1894, p. 56): There existed early in the (nineteenth) century a Socialism of a Utopian type in France, England and Germany. France, in particular, had a number of thinkers who gained a great reputation at home and abroad and found followers in many lands. Cabet, Saint-Simon, and Fourier are names which, in this connection, occur to everyone who it at all familiar with the history of Socialism. They had schemes more or less fantastic. England had its Robert Owen, a wealthy manufacturer, who used up a fortune in endeavors to establish communistic villages in England and America. The United States had its wave of Fourieristic Socialism, and its Brook Farm and other settlements. Albert Brisbane, Horace Greeley, and George William Curtis . . . took part in the movement. About 1860 this early Socialism had well-nigh disappeared, or been absorbed by other Socialist movements." It had no roots among the workers, no reality, no practicability. It was very largely a literary Socialism. When the Paris Commune came, in 1871, it may be said that there did not exist any concrete, clearly-conceived Socialist or Labor movement in Europe. But during these years the foundations for one were being laid, by the combined energies of Ferdinand Lassalle and Karl Marx, both of them German Jews. Lassalle was instrumental in interesting the working class in Socialism with his brilliant progaganda and Marx assisted by Engels supplied the steady driving power, system and theory.

The revolution of 1848 coincided with the publication of the famous Communist Manifesto by Marx and Engels, one of the chief original documents in the history of modern Socialism. It is based upon his materialistic conception of history as a fatalistic natural evolution determined by economic conditions. If Marx's later and ponderous masterpiece "Das Kapital" is the Bible of present-day Socialism the "Manifesto" is its Ten Commandments, the basis for its bid for world-domination.

The Manifesto did not produce any apparent effect at first. Marx was exiled from Germany and went to live in London, to work and prepare. He saw the conservative reaction after the failure of the Republican wave of 1848. He saw the futility of the Utopians. He did not realize how much in the way of suggestion and originality he himself owed to the earlier French thinkers. He was building up the details of his system in "Das Kapital."

And now we come to the first step toward organizing a Socialist movement in the First International.

THE FIRST INTERNATIONAL.

What is meant by the First, Second and Third International of the Socialist Party?

It was in 1864 at St. James' Hall, London, on September 28th, that the First International was founded, largely through the efforts of Karl Marx, as the culmination of the fifteen years of educational work conducted by him and his friends and followers, such as Engels and Lasalle, ever since the Communist Manifesto of 1848. The organization was called "The International Working Men's Association." Its purpose was to unite all the different organizations of revolutionary tendencies in Europe. Hunter says in "Socialists at work" (p. 302): "It included working-class leaders, from the extreme anarchist to the moderate republican of the Mazzini type. In England the members were mostly trade unionists; in Germany, Socialists; in France and the Latin countries, anarchists. A few working men's organizations in America allied themselves, and in other countries there were many affiliated groups. Nearly all the leaders, however, were of the middle class, and many able thinkers sympathized with and supported the movement. It started with every promise of success; but it was loosely organized, and it mirrored the chaotic condition of the working class itself . . . bitter feuds broke out among the leaders, which added to the general confusion, and divided the workers even more grievously than before. . . . The Blanquists were conspirators, hoping to capture by stealth the French government. The Proudhonians were opposed to all parliamentary action . . . the International became the storm center of division . . . until finally Marx became a dictator."

Marx was a bitter polemist. He condemned the brilliant French Socialists as Utopians; he condemned State Socialists; his own disciple the brilliant Lasalle; Bakunin, the great Russian anarchist leader. The Franco-Prussian War of 1870 was a very serious blow to him. Finally in 1872 Marx wrecked the International in order to destroy the power of the anarchist wing. The Anarchists were growing very powerful. They had practical control of the revolutionary movement in Russia, and were influential in Italy, France and elsewhere. To Marx they were anathema, because they spelled the death of any system; and Marx wished to displace one system completely by another. Therefore, he pulled down the house he himself had built.

A brief survey of the main purposes of Socialism is in order, and an analysis of Karl Marx's Manifesto, the text of which will also be given in full.

Many persons, especially among the intellectuals and philanthropists, call themselves Socialists because they believe that for the selfishness of individual aims there should be substituted the altruism that subordinates the good of the individual to the good of society as a whole. This type of Socialist is as varied in opinion as Joseph's robe of many colors. Such general welfare theory has no connection with Socialism in its scientific and systematic sense. A Socialist in this sense is mainly an opponent of individualism: a constructive believer in this philosophy purposes to sacrifice no class but to improve and elevate all classes.

Socialism in its exact and scientific sense is based on certain definite principles, and not on various states of mind. It has a theory of both industrial and political society that involves a radical reconstruction of the present world, making its political organization subordinate to its economic or industrial organization. It is based on three main propositions.

The first principle is the common ownership of the material elements of production. It is collective industrialization. It has two forms:

(1) A constructive form, which allows certain kinds of wealth, not designed for further production, to remain private property; and

(2) A radical form, which abolishes all kinds of private property.

The second principle is the common management of production, which it is claimed would insure to the whole community the benefits of the things produced, and insure to all the opportunity and obligation for work under the best conditions.

The third principle relates to the distribution to the entire community of the wealth produced by the collective labor and management, a plan which is supposed to insure the satisfactory utilization of the surplus so produced, and its just distribution among the various classes of producers.

According to this the two principal sources of production, land and capital, must cease to be private property and become the collective property of society as a whole.

In the political sphere socialism aims to:

(1) Denationalize peoples,

(2) Denationalize governments, and

(3) Increase municipal and all local control,

(4) Transfer to economic authorities most powers now assigned to political authorities.

The political state by these means is so reduced in power and scope that it is practically wiped out.

It is a peculiar fact that there exists not a single system of Anglo-Saxon socialism, nor a single system of Latin race socialism. In fact, the only scientific, concrete and perfectly systematic scheme is of German-Jewish origin — the scheme of Karl Marx. This is the basis for the materialism inherent in present-day socialism, for its antagonism to religion, to ethics, and to all idealism based on principles, on sentiments and intellectual concepts that do not relate to purely material life and wealth interests.

Analysis of Marx's Communist Manifesto

The following outline of the Karl Marx Manifesto comprises its main points and will help in understanding the present Socialist and Communist attitude.

Modern society has evolved into only two classes: (1) the bourgeoisie, representing capital, and (2) the proletariat, representing wage-labor as a commodity.

This condition has been reached through the tremendous development of industry on a large scale, with gigantic means of production and exchange, through the subjection of Nature's forces.

The result is, with the help of machinery and the subdivision of labor, to divest labor of all delight and individualism, and to reduce it to slavery.

This despotic and egotistical despotism of capital has led to crises through over-production. The proletariat alone has withstood the conflict. All other classes have disappeared or are decaying.

The first stage of the class struggle must be national. In order to keep from sinking deeper into pauperism the laborer must develop civil war for the violent overthrow of the bourgeoisie.

Under the direction of the Communist leaders, who in all national struggles bring to the front the common interests of the entire proletariat, the working class passes to the phase of internationalism, of unification of purpose, organization and struggle.

Its theory may be summed up in the single sentence: "Abolition of private property," because present-day wage labor creates only one kind of private property — bourgeois property.

This means the doing away of buying and selling and of all the present bourgeois methods of production and distribution. Capital will be abolished with all its results in investments.

It means also the abolition of the family — the present bourgeois family will vanish. The Communists desire to introduce an openly legalized community of women. This involves also the children.

"The working-men have no country."

It is urged against communism that it "abolishes eternal

truths, it abolishes all religion and all morality, instead of constituting them on a new basis, its development involves the most radical rupture with traditional ideas."

The measures recommended to bring about the social transformation are mainly (1) abolition of property in land and application of all rents of land to public purposes; (2) heavy income tax; (3) abolition of all right of inheritance; (4) monopoly of credit by a single national bank; (5) means of transportation nationalized; (6) nationalization of means of production; (7) obligation of all to labor and establishment of industrial armies; (8) combination of agricultural and industrial interests; (9) free education of all children.

There will result the abolition of any political power or organization. Eventually class antagonism will cease because only one class will exist — the proletariat.

Reactionary and feudal socialism are ludicrous or deceptive. So-called "Christian Socialism is but the Holy water with which the priest consecrates the heartburnings of the aristocrat."

Then came petty bourgeois socialism, which, while recognizing clearly present industrial evils was, in its proposed remedies, "both reactionary and Utopian."

Based on Utopias, came a silly school-boy mountebank German school of so-called intellectuals, which became the bombastic representative of the petty bourgeois Philistine, which proclaimed the German nation to be the model nation. Far more serious was the conservative bourgeois socialism, worked out by economists and philanthropists in more or less complete systems of improvement; the critical-utopian and the communist-utopian schemes.

The attitude of the Communist Party itself is to everywhere support every revolutionary movement against the existing social and political order of things, always bringing to the front the property question and working for unity in all countries.

> "The Communists disdain to conceal their views and aims. They openly declare that their ends can be attained only by the forcible overthrow of all existing social conditions. Let the ruling classes tremble at a Communist revolution. The proletarians have nothing to lose but their chains. They have a world to win.
>
> "Working men of all countries, unite!"

An interesting summary of the situation is given by Marx's

partner Engels in a preface to the English translation of the Communist Manifesto written in 1888, the year before the founding of the Second International. It is here given almost entire. It includes a clear comparison of Communism with the early Utopian Socialism.

"The 'Manifesto' was published as the platform of the Communist League, a workingmen's association, first exclusively German, later on international, and, under the political conditions of the Continent before 1848, unavoidably a secret society. At a Congress of the League, held in London in November, 1847, Marx and Engels were commissioned to prepare for publication a complete theoretical and practical party programme. Drawn up in German, in January, 1848, the manuscript was sent to the printer in London a few weeks before the French revolution of February 24th. A French translation was brought out in Paris shortly before the insurrection of June, 1848. The first English translation, by Miss Helen Macfarlane, appeared in George Julian Harney's 'Red Republican,' London, 1850. A Danish and a Polish edition had also been published.

"The defeat of the Parisian insurrection of June, 1848 — the first great battle between proletariat and bourgeoisie — drove again into the background, for the time, the social and political aspirations of the European working class. Thenceforth the struggle for supremacy was again, as it had been before the revolution of February, solely between different sections of the propertied class; the working class was reduced to a fight for political elbow-room, and to the position of extreme wing of the middle-class Radicals. Wherever independent proletarian movements continued to show signs of life they were ruthlessly hunted down. As to the 'Manifesto,' it seemed to be thenceforth doomed to oblivion.

"When the European working class had recovered sufficient strength for another attack on the ruling classes, the International Workingmen's Association sprang up. But this association, formed with the express aim of welding into one body the whole militant proletariat of Europe and America, could not at once proclaim the principles laid down in the 'Manifesto.' The International was bound to have a programme broad enough to be acceptable to the English Trades' Union, to the followers of Proudhon in France,

Belgium, Italy and Spain, and to the Lassalleans in Germany. Marx, who drew up this programme to the satisfaction of all parties, trusted entirely to the intellectual development of the working-class, which was sure to result from combined action and mutual discussion. The very events and vicissitudes of the struggle against capital, the defeats even more than victories, could not help bringing home to men's minds the insufficiency of their various favorite nostrums, and preparing the way for a more complete insight into the true conditions of working-class emancipation. And Marx was right. The International on its breaking up in 1874 left the workers quite different men from what it had found them in 1864. Proudhonism in France, Lassalleanism in Germany, were dying out, and even the conservative English Trades' Unions, though most of them had long since severed their connection with the International, were gradually advancing towards that point at which in the year 1887 at Swansea, their President could say in their name, 'Continental Socialism has lost its terrors for us.' In fact, the principles of the 'Manifesto' had made considerable headway among the workingmen of all countries.

"The 'Manifesto' itself thus came to the front again. The German text has been, since 1850, reprinted several times in Switzerland, England and America. In 1872 it was translated into English in New York, where the translation was published in 'Woodhull and Claflin's Weekly.' From this English version a French one was made in 'Le Socialiste' of New York. Since then at least two more English translations, more or less mutilated, have been brought out in America, and one of them has been reprinted in England. The first Russian translation, made by Bakunin, was published at Hertzen's 'Kolokol' office in Geneva, about 1863; a second one, by the heroic Vera Zasulitch, also in Geneva, 1882. A new Danish edition is to be found in 'Socialdemokratisk Bibliothek,' Copenhagen, 1855; a fresh French translation in 'Le Socialiste,' Paris, 1886. From this latter a Spanish version was prepared and published in Madrid, 1886. The German reprints are not to be counted; there have been twelve altogether, at the least . . . Thus the history of the 'Manifesto' reflects, to a great extent, the history of the modern working-class movement; at present it is undoubtedly the most widespread, the most international production of all Socialist literature, the common platform, acknowledged by millions of working men from Siberia to California.

"Yet, when it was written we could not have called it a Socialist Manifesto. By Socialists, in 1847, were understood, on the one hand, the adherents of the various Utopian systems (Owenites in England, Fourierists in France, both of them already reduced to the position of mere sects, and gradually dying out); on the other hand, the most multifarious social quacks, who, by all manners of tinkering, professed to redress, without any danger to capital and profit, all sorts of social grievances; in both cases men outside the working class movement, and looking rather to the 'educated' classes for support. Whatever portion of the working class had become convinced of the insufficiency of mere political revolutions, and had proclaimed the necessity of a total social change, that portion, then called itself Communist. It was a crude, rough-hewn purely instinctive sort of Communism; still, it touched the cardinal point and was powerful enough among the working class to produce the Utopian Communism, in France, of Cabet, and in Germany, of Weitling. Thus, Socialism was, in 1847, a middle-class movement, Communism a working-class movement. Socialism was, on the Continent at least, 'respectable'; Communism was the very opposite. And as our notion, from the very beginning, was that 'the emancipation of the working class must be the act of the working class itself,' there could be no doubt as to which of the two names we must take. Moreover, we have ever since been far from repudiating it.

"The 'Manifesto' being our joint production, I consider myself bound to state that the fundamental proposition which forms its nucleus belongs to Marx. That proposition is: that in every historical epoch the prevailing mode of economic production and exchange, and the social organization necessarily following it, form the basis upon which is built up and from which alone can be explained, the political and intellectual history of that epoch; that consequently the whole history of mankind (since the dissolution of primitive tribal society, holding land in common ownership) has been a history of class struggles, contests between exploiting and exploited, ruling and oppressed classes; that the history of these class struggles forms a series of evolutions in which, now-a-days, a stage has been reached where the exploited and oppressed class (the proletariat) cannot attain its emancipation from the sway of the exploiting and ruling class (the bourgeoisie) without, at the same time, and once and for all, emancipating society at large from all exploitation, oppression, class-distinction and class-struggles.

"This proposition which, in my opinion, is destined to do for history what Darwin's theory has done for biology we, both of us, had been gradually approaching for some years before 1845. . . . From our joint preface to the German edition of 1872, I quote the following:

> "However much the state of things may have altered during the last 25 years, the general principles laid down in this 'Manifesto' are, on the whole, as correct to-day as ever. . . . In view of the gigantic strides of Modern Industry since 1848, and the accompanying improved and extended organization of the working class, in view of the practical experience gained, first in the February revolution, 1848, and then, still more, in the Paris Commune, where the proletariat for the first time held political power for two whole months, this programme has in some details become antiquated. . . . But then, the Manifesto has become a historical document which we have no longer any right to alter."

FRIEDERICK ENGELS.

LONDON, *30th January,* 1888.

SECOND INTERNATIONAL

After the dissolution of the First International in which Marx had not dared, as yet, to embody the radical ideas of his Manifesto, came a decade of intense and unifying education of workers for the cause of Communism, a marshalling of phalanxes of trained and educated leaders to direct the revolutionary movement of the working class and to eliminate the confusion of doctrines, the vagueness of unpractical doctrinaires, the irresponsible violence of anarchists, the sentimentalities of upper class socialists who knew nothing of the conditions and problems of the working classes.

Powerful leaders like Bebel and Liebknecht in Germany, Jaurès and Guesde in France, established that vital connection with the workers that was absolutely essential to success.

Although the Second International did not come to life until 1889, six years after Marx's death in 1883, it was even more thoroughly his work than the first had been, because through his educational efforts Socialist organizations had been everywhere founded in connection with labor and were based on Marxian theories in practically every case. Chaos was replaced by unity.

How had results been reached before 1889? The strength of the new doctrine of Marxism is its all-inclusiveness and its appeal to self-interest. It proposes a completely new society. It covers distribution as well as production and promises a millennium to the proletariat. If we accept the interpretation of Marxism given by its moderate followers it allows evolution as well as revolution as a method of transforming society. And this moderate or evolutionary and democratic theory is the one followed by the Second International; while the violent, revolutionary undemocratic theory of the dictatorship by a minority of the proletariat is the interpretation of his system supported, with logical force, by Lenin and the Third International.

During the ten or fifteen years before 1889, the situation was being transformed throughout Europe by the formation of national branches of a new party in politics, the Social Democratic Party, based on Marxism, and through the organization of workingmen's unions, imbued with the same ideas. They first took shape in Germany. It was in 1867 that the Social Democratic Party of Germany first went to the polls. The two great leaders of Socialism were Bebel and Wilhelm Liebknecht, who had studied with Marx in London. Bebel was a workingman, a powerful and rugged speaker, and under his influence the trade unions grew in power and became imbued with Socialism. This was between 1862 and 1867. But it was only in 1875 that a United Socialist Party, with the extensive support of a united workingmen's party entered German politics on a large scale, gaining steadily in 1877. Bismarck tried in vain to repress them. The Social Democratic Party secured power and influence over legislation, and gave a model in its organization and methods that was followed in other European countries. Extraordinary attention was paid by the party to educational matters and the rank and file of the workingmen were given an unequalled training that made them able to discuss economic questions with intelligence and to create a distinct class consciousness and unity of purpose and action.

Of France, Hunter, himself a brilliant Socialist, truly said in 1908: "France is the birthplace of nearly all the idealism that gave rise to the modern movement. Ever since the great revolution, the philosophy of Socialism has fascinated some of the most brilliant minds in France; but the fulness of their inspiration and the variation in their tendencies have prevented them from establishing one school." (*Op. cit.*, p. 57.) Before 1871 all groups worked against the government of Napoleon III, under the Old International — the Proudhon anarchists, the Blanqui conspirators, the Marxist working-class political agitators. All fell apart in 1871.

It was Jules Guesde, who, returning to France in 1877, full of the doctrines of Marx, started to capture for Socialism the working-class movement and to organize a political party that should abandon anarchism and conspiracy and have coherent political action. In October 1879 he organized a congress of workingmen at Marseilles, with the motto: "The land for the peasant; the tool for the laborer; and work for all." Out of the confusion of this "Socialist Labor Congress" arose a program written by Guesde and Paul Lafargue, Karl Marx's son-in-law, and so the French movement was captured by the Marxians, who alone had a clear program. But soon other French Socialist leaders, especially Brousse, revolted against Marxian dictatorship and gained control everywhere but in the north of France where Guesde remained supreme. Still Guesde was unable to capture the trade-union movement and turn it in favor of political action. When the Confédération Générale du Travail was founded in 1895, as the successor to the old Federation of Trade Councils of 1884, it decided against parliamentarism and in favor of the general strike as the only weapon. The Frenchmen glory in individual differences of opinion and despise the sheep-like following of cut-and-dried programs by the Germans. A new group of independents was formed led by men who were to loom so largely in French life — Millerand (the present premier), Jaurès (murdered in 1914), Viviani (also premier). This was the position in 1889.

In Italy the Socialist Party from the beginning has enlisted among its practical leaders men of the middle class, especially intellectual leaders — more than any other country. Also it is remarkable for its support on a large scale among the peasant class, who have organized even more thoroughly than the workmen in their trade unions. Before 1882, however, the anarchist ideas of the Russian Bakunin were more prevalent than the ideas of political Socialism, though both in 1882 and 1885 attempts were made with some slight success to organize workmen into a political party. But practically no progress had been made before 1889.

In England, during the eighties, the Fabian Society was formed, which still remains an influential group of intellectual Socialists, but without much direct influence on the workingmen or on parliament. At about the same time the Democratic Federation was formed under Socialist influence with a practical political program that was to be guided by such well-known labor leaders as John Burns and Tom Mann.

In 1886 the Socialist agitation gained tremendous headway, and Hyndman came into great prominence as leader. In November 1887 came the November uprising called "Bloody Sunday" in London.

As Hunter says: "A general awakening of the working class seemed to be taking place as a result of Socialist activity and 1889 (the year of the founding of the Second International) marks the beginning of a new epoch in English trade unionism — marked by two important successful strikes."

The Belgian movement was very early, but seemed so hopeless for many years that it veered, like the Russian working class, toward anarchism. In 1885 a small beginning of a Belgian Labor Party was made at Brussels. It was a practical movment, weary of the old literary, scholastic organization, objecting at first even to the word "Socialist" though it soon adopted the Socialist program. Vandervelde has well said: "Belgian Socialism, at the conflux of the great European civilizations, partakes of the character of each of them." From the English it adopted self-help and free association; from the Germans political tactics and fundamental doctrines, which were for the first time expounded in the Communist Manifesto, and from the French it took its idealist tendencies, its integral conception of Socialism, considered as the confirmation of the revolutionary philosophy (Hunter, p. 135).

The Belgian Labor Party was many sided, with trade unions,

co-operatives with houses of the people, stores and meeting halls; insurance societies; everything in one harmonious organization with its political policy, its press and its propaganda. It was prepared, when 1889 came, to take a leading part in the Second International.

Practically very little progress before 1889 had been made in Scandinavia, in Russia, in Spain, in Austria-Hungary or even in Holland toward the formation of Socialist or labor organizations. There was, to be sure, in Denmark, a Social Democratic organization on a small scale, founded in 1878, and another in Sweden. In Spain a small Socialist Party was formed in 1888 and 1889 under Pablo Iglesias.

The situation, then, when the organization of the Second International was attempted, was brilliant only in spots, except that there were trained leaders in Marxism almost everywhere ready to organize the workers.

The Second International Congress of 1889 took place in Paris, with nearly 400 delegates representing twenty countries. After that, meetings followed thick and fast, promoting more and more the international character of the Socialist movement: at Brussels in 1891, at Zürich in 1893, at London in 1896, important for its discussion of anarchism; at Paris in 1900, and especially at Amsterdam in 1904, when an important resolution on a policy of International Socialist tactics was adopted. At the latter meeting the Internationalism was stressed when the representatives of Japan and of Russia, whose countries were then at war, clasped hands amid the thunderous applause of 450 delegates. The next meeting of the Second International was in 1907 at Stuttgart, the first meeting in Germany. There were about 1,000 delegates representing thirty nations. Then in 1910 a meeting at Copenhagen and one at Basel in 1912.

During these eight years between 1889 and 1907 tremendous progress had been made in the forming of political Socialist parties throughout Europe. Almost everywhere there were splits.

The permanent International Socialist Bureau, which had been established at Brussels, with the Belgian leader Emile Vandervelde as chairman, was transferred later to the Hague, where the Belgium Socialists were put in charge under Camille Huysmans. In Italy the splits were typified more clearly than elsewhere; the Right Wing Reformists led by Turati, the Left Wing Syndicalists led by Labriola, the Integralists of the center, led by Ferri. While in Italy the labor unions still remained weak — weaker even than in France, they increased rapidly in strength throughout northern Europe, bringing the workingman more and more into the Socialist fold and giving him aggressive class consciousness. The details will be given later. Through pressure of both kinds — by strikes and by parliamentary methods — concessions were continually being secured. Solidarity of interest and action continued to spread the feeling of Internationalism.

Then came the Great War. What was its effect on Socialism? How did the doctrine of anti-militarism stand the inherent urge of national patriotism?

With few exceptions — the most notable, beside that of the American Socialist Party, being that of the Socialist Party of Italy — the Socialists put patriotism first.

This led to the temporary disruption of the Second International. It led, also, to the rise of a second, minor current of intransigeant Socialism which began an agitation against the regular Socialist International organization.

Before describing this movement and before giving the attitude of the Socialists in the various countries toward the war, it is necessary to give a picture of the condition of Socialism in each country, and its connection with the growing labor movement during the twenty-five years between the founding of the Second International in 1889 and the outbreak of the Great War in 1914.

The basis of the entire movement being the Communist Manifesto of Marx and Engels, of which a summary has just been given, its complete text is here inserted as an appendix to the chapter.

MANIFESTO OF THE COMMUNIST PARTY

By KARL MARX and FREDERICK ENGELS

A SPECTRE is haunting Europe — the spectre of Communism. All the powers of old Europe have entered into a holy alliance to exorcise this spectre; Pope and Czar, Metternich and Guizot, French Radicals and German police-spies.

Where is the party in opposition that has not been decried as communistic by its opponents in power? Where the Opposition that has not hurled back the branding reproach of Communism, against the more advanced opposition parties, as well as against its reactionary adversaries?

Two things result from this fact.

I. Communism is already acknowledged by all European Powers to be itself a Power.

II. It is high time that Communists should openly, in the face of the whole world, publish their views, their aims, their tendencies, and meet this nursery tale of the Spectre of Communism with a Manifesto of the party itself.

To this end, Communists of various nationalities have assembled in London, and sketched the following manifesto, to be published in the English, French, German, Italian, Flemish and Danish languages.

I.

BOURGEOIS AND PROLETARIANS

The history of all hitherto existing society is the history of class struggles.

Freeman and slave, patrician and plebeian, lord and serf, guild-master and journeyman, in a word, oppressor and oppressed, stood in constant opposition to one another, carried on an uninterrupted, now hidden, now open fight, a fight that each time ended, either in a revolutionary reconstitution of society at large, or in the common ruin of the contending classes.

In the early epochs of history, we find almost everywhere a complicated arrangement of society into various orders, a manifold graduation of social rank. In ancient Rome we have patricians, knights, plebeians, slaves; in the middle ages, feudal lords, vassals, guild-masters, journeymen, apprentices, serfs; in almost all of these classes, again, subordinate gradations.

The modern bourgeois society that has sprouted from the ruins of feudal society, has not done away with class antagonisms. It has but established new classes, new conditions of oppression, new forms of struggle in place of the old ones.

Our epoch, the epoch of the bourgeoisie, possesses, however, this distinctive feature; it has simplified the class antagonisms. Society as a whole is more and more splitting up into two great hostile camps, into two great classes directly facing each other: Bourgeoisie and Proletariat.

From the serfs of the middle ages sprang the chartered burghers of the earliest towns. From these burgesses the first elements of the bourgeoisie were developed.

The discovery of America, the rounding of the Cape, opened up fresh ground for the rising bourgeoisie. The East-Indian and Chinese markets, the colonization of America, trade with the colonies, the increase in the means of exchange and in commodities generally, gave to commerce, to navigation, to industry, an impulse never before known, and thereby, to the revolutionary element in the tottering feudal society, a rapid development.

The feudal system of industry, under which industrial production was monopolized by close guilds, now no longer sufficed for the growing wants of the new markets. The manufacturing system took its place. The guild-masters were pushed on one side by the manufacturing middle class; division of labor between the different corporate guilds vanished in the face of division of labor in each single workshop.

Meantime the markets kept ever growing, the demand ever rising. Even manufacture no longer sufficed. Thereupon, steam and machinery revolutionized industrial production. The place of manufacture was taken by the giant, Modern Industry, the place of the industrial middle-class, by industrial millionaires, the leaders of whole industrial armies, the modern bourgeois.

Modern industry has established the world-market, for which the discovery of America paved the way. This market has given an immense development to commerce, to navigation, to communication by land. This development has, in its turn, reacted on the extension of industry; and in proportion as industry, commerce, navigation, railways extended, in the same proportion the bourgeoisie developed, increased its capital, and pushed into the background every class handed down from the Middle Ages.

We see, therefore, how the modern bourgeoisie is itself the

product of a long course of development, of a series of revolutions in the modes of production and of exchange.

Each step in the development of the bourgeoisie was accompanied by a corresponding political advance of that class. An oppressed class under the sway of the feudal nobility, an armed and self-governing association in the mediaeval commune, here independent urban republic (as in Italy and Germany), there taxable "third estate" of the monarchy (as in France), afterwards, in the period of manufacture proper, serving either the semi-feudal or the absolute monarchy as a counterpoise against the nobility, and, in fact, cornerstone of the great monarchies in general, the bourgeoisie has at last, since the establishment of modern industry and of the world-market, conquered for itself, in the modern representative State, exclusive political sway. The executive of the modern state is but a committee for managing the common affairs of the whole bourgeoisie.

The bourgeoisie, historically, has played a most revolutionary part.

The bourgeoisie, wherever it has got the upper hand, has put an end to all feudal, patriarchal, idyllic relations. It has pitilessly torn asunder the motley feudal ties that bound man to his "natural superiors," and has left remaining no other nexus between man and man than naked self-interest, than callous "cash payment." It has drowned the most heavenly ecstacies of religious fervor, of chivalrous enthusiasm, of philistine sentimentalism, in the icy waters of egotistical calculation. It has resolved personal worth into exchange value, and in place of the numberless indefeasible chartered freedoms, has set up that single, unconscionable freedom — Free Trade. In one word, for exploitation, veiled by religious and political illusions, it has substituted naked, shameless, direct, brutal exploitation.

The bourgeoisie has stripped of its halo every occupation hitherto honored and looked up to with reverent awe. It has converted the physician, the lawyer, the priest, the poet, the man of science, into its paid wage-laborers.

The bourgeoisie has torn away from the family its sentimental veil, and has reduced the family relation to a mere money relation.

The bourgeoisie has disclosed how it came to pass that the brutal display of vigor in the Middle Ages, which Reactionists so much admire, found its fitting complement in the most slothful indolence. It has been the first to show what man's activity can bring about. It has accomplished wonders far surpassing Egyptian pyramids, Roman aqueducts, and Gothic cathedrals; it has conducted expeditions that put in the shade all former Exoduses of nations and crusades.

The bourgeoisie cannot exist without constantly revolutionizing the instruments of production, and thereby the relations of production and with them the whole relations of society. Conservation of the old modes of production in unaltered form was, on the contrary, the first condition of existence for all earlier industrial classes. Constant revolutionizing of production, uninterrupted disturbance of all social conditions, everlasting uncertainty and agitation distinguish the bourgeois epoch from all earlier ones. All fixed, fast-frozen relations, with their train of ancient and venerable prejudices and opinions, are swept away, all new-formed ones become antiquated before they can ossify. All that is solid melts into air, all that is holy is profaned, and man is at last compelled to face, with sober senses, his real conditions of life, and his relations with his kind.

The need of a constantly expanding market for its products chases the bourgeoisie over the whole surface of the globe. It must nestle everywhere, settle everywhere, establish connections everywhere.

The bourgeoisie has through its exploitation of the world-market given a cosmopolitan character to production and consumption in every country. To the great chagrin of Reactionists, it has drawn from under the feet of industry the national ground on which it stood. All old-established national industries have been destroyed or are daily being destroyed. They are dislodged by new industries, whose introduction becomes a life and death question for all civilized nations, by industries that no longer work up indigenous raw material, but raw material drawn from the remotest zones; industries whose products are consumed, not only at home, but in every quarter of the globe. In place of the old wants, satisfied by the productions of the country, we find new wants, requiring for their satisfaction the products of distant lands and climes. In place of the old local and national seclusion and self-sufficiency, we have intercourse in every direction, universal inter-dependence of nations. And as in material, so also in intellectual production. The intellectual creations of individual nations become common property. National one-sidedness and narrow-mindedness become more and more impossible, and from the numerous national and local literatures there arises a world-literature.

The bourgeoisie, by the rapid improvement of all instruments of production, by the immensely facilitated means of communication, draws all, even the most barbarian, nations into civilization. The cheap prices of its commodities are the heavy artillery with which it batters down all Chinese walls, with which it forces the barbarians' intensely obstinate hatred of foreigners to capitulate. It compels all nations, on pain of extinction, to adopt the bourgeois mode of production; it compels them to introduce what it calls civilization into their midst, *i. e.*, to become bourgeois themselves. In a word, it creates a world after its own image.

The bourgeoisie has subjected the country to the rule of the towns. It has created enormous cities, has greatly increased the urban population as compared with the rural, and has thus rescued a considerable part of the population from the idiocy of rural life. Just as it has made the country dependent on the towns, so it has made barbarian and semi-barbarian countries dependent on the civilized ones, nations of peasants on nations of bourgeois, the East on the West.

The bourgeoisie keeps more and more doing away with the scattered state of the population, of the means of production, and of property. It has agglomerated population, centralized means of production, and has concentrated property in a few hands. The necessary consequence of this was political centralization. Independent, or but loosely connected provinces, with separate interests, laws, governments and systems of taxation, became lumped together in one nation, with one government, one code of laws, one national class interest, one frontier and one customs-tariff.

The bourgeoisie, during its rule of scarce 100 years, has created more massive and more colossal productive forces than have all preceding generations together. Subjection of Nature's forces to man, machinery, application of chemistry to industry and agriculture, steam-navigation, railways, electric telegraphs, clearing of whole continents for cultivation, canalization of rivers, whole populations conjured out of the ground — what earlier century had even a presentment that such productive forces slumbered in the lap of social labor?

We see then: the means of production and of exchange on

whose foundation the bourgeoisie built itself up, were generated in feudal society. At a certain stage in the development of these means of production and of exchange, the conditions under which feudal society produced and exchanged, the feudal organization of agriculture and manufacturing industry, in one word, the feudal relations of property, became no longer compatible with the already developed productive forces; they became so many fetters. They had to burst asunder; they were burst asunder.

Into their places stepped free competition, accompanied by a social and political constitution adapted to it, and by the economical and political sway of the bourgeois class.

A similar movement is going on before our own eyes. Modern bourgeois society with its relations of production, of exchange and of property, a society that has conjured up such gigantic means of production and of exchange, is like the sorcerer, who is no longer able to control the powers of the nether world whom he has called up by his spells. For many a decade past the history of industry and commerce is but the history of the revolt of modern productive forces against conditions of production, against the property relations that are the conditions for the existence of the bourgeoisie and of its rule. It is enough to mention the commercial crises that by their periodical return put on its trial, each time more threateningly, the existence of the entire bourgeois society. In these crises a great part not only of the existing products, but also of the previously created productive forces, are periodically destroyed. In these crises there breaks out an epidemic that, in all earlier epochs, would have seemed an absurdity — the epidemic of over-production. Society suddenly finds itself put back into a state of momentary barbarism; it appears as if a famine, a universal war of devastation had cut off the supply of every means of subsistence; industry and commerce seem to be destroyed; and why? Because there is too much civilization, too much means of subsistence, too much industry, too much commerce. The productive forces at the disposal of society no longer tend to further the development of the conditions of bourgeois property; on the contrary, they have become too powerful for these conditions, by which they are fettered, and so soon as they overcome these fetters, they bring disorder into the whole of bourgeois society, endanger the existence of bourgeois property. The conditions of bourgeois society are too narrow to comprise the wealth created by them. And how does the bourgeoisie get over these crises? On the one hand by enforced destruction of a mass of productive forces; on the other, by the conquest of new markets, and by the more thorough exploitation of the old ones. That is to say, by paving the way for more extensive and more destructive crises, and by diminishing the means whereby crises are prevented.

The weapons with which the bourgeoisie felled feudalism to the ground are now turned against the bourgeoisie itself.

But not only has the bourgeoisie forged the weapons that bring death to itself; it has also called into existence the men who are to wield those weapons — the modern working-class, the proletarians.

In proportion as the bourgeoisie, *i. e.*, capital, is developed, in the same proportion is the proletariat, the modern working-class, developed: a class of laborers, who live only so long as they find work, and who find work only so long as their labor increases capital. These laborers, who must sell themselves piece-meal, are a commodity, like every other article of commerce, and are consequently exposed to all the vicissitudes of competition, to all the fluctuations of the market.

Owing to the extensive use of machinery and to division of labor, the work of the proletarians has lost all individual character, and, consequently, all charm for the workman. He becomes an appendage of the machine, and it is only the most simple, most monotonous, and most easily acquired knack that is required of him. Hence, the cost of production of a workman is restricted, almost entirely, to the means of subsistence that he requires for his maintenance, and for the propagation of his race. But the price of a commodity, and also of labor, is equal to its cost of production. In proportion, therefore, as the repulsiveness of the work increases, the wage decreases. Nay more, in proportion as the use of machinery and division of labor increases, in the same proportion the burden of toil also increases, whether by prolongation of the working hours, by increase of the work enacted in a given time, or by increased speed of the machinery, etc.

Modern industry has converted the little workshop of the patriarchal master into the great factory of the industrial capitalist. Masses of laborers, crowded into the factory, are organized like soldiers. As privates of the industrial army they are placed under the command of a perfect hierarchy of officers and sergeants. Not only are they the slaves of the bourgeois class, and of the bourgeois state, they are daily and hourly enslaved by the machine, by the over-looker, and, above all, by the individual bourgeois manufacturer himself. The more openly this depotism proclaims gain to be its end and aim, the more petty, the more hateful and the more embittering it is.

The less the skill and exertion or strength implied in manual labor, in other words, the more modern industry becomes developed, the more is the labor of men superseded by that of women. Differences of age and sex have no longer any distinctive social validity for the working class. All are instruments of labor, more or less expensive to use, according to their age and sex.

No sooner is the exploitation of the laborer by the manufacturer so far at an end, that he receives his wages in cash, than he is set upon by the other portions of the bourgeoisie, the landlord, the shopkeeper, the pawnbroker, etc.

The lower strata of the middle class — the small tradespeople, shopkeepers, and retired tradesmen generally, the handicraftsmen and peasants — all these sink gradually into the proletariat, partly because their diminutive capital does not suffice for the scale on which Modern Industry is carried on, and is swamped in the competition with the large capitalists, partly because their specialized skill is rendered worthless by new methods of production. Thus the proletariat is recruited from all classes of the population.

The proletariat goes through various stages of development. With its birth begins its struggle with the bourgeoisie. At first the contest is carried on by individual laborers, then by the work people of a factory, then by the operatives of one trade, in one locality, against the individual bourgeois who directly exploits them. They direct their attacks not against the bourgeois conditions of production, but against the instruments of production themselves; they destroy imported wares that compete with their labor, they smash to pieces machinery, they set factories ablaze, they seek to restore by force the vanished status of the workman of the Middle Ages.

At this stage the laborers still form an incoherent mass scattered over the whole country, and broken up by their mutual competition. If anywhere they unite to form more compact bodies, this is not yet the consequence of their own active union, but of the union of the bourgeoisie, which class, in order to attain its own political ends, is compelled to set the whole proletariat in motion, and is moreover yet, for a time, able to do so. At this stage, therefore, the proletarians do not fight their enemies, but the enemies of their enemies, the remnants of absolute monarchy, the landowners, the non-industrial bourgeois, the petty bourgeoisie. Thus the whole historical movement is concentrated in the hands of the bourgeoisie; every victory so obtained is a victory for the bourgeoisie.

But with the development of industry the proletariat not only increases in number, it becomes concentrated in greater masses, its strength grows, and it feels that strength more. The various interests and conditions of life within the ranks of the proletariat are more and more equalized, in proportion as machinery obliterates all distinctions of labor, and nearly everywhere reduces wages to the same low level. The growing competition among the bourgeois, and the resulting commercial crises, make the wages of the workers ever more fluctuating. The unceasing improvement of machinery, ever more rapidly developing, makes their livelihood more and more precarious; the collisions between individual workmen and individual bourgeois take more and more the character of collisions between two classes. Thereupon the workers begin to form combinations (Trades' Unions) against the bourgeois; they club together in order to keep up the rate of wages; they found permanent associations in order to make provision beforehand for these occasional revolts. Here and there the contest breaks out into riots.

Now and then the workers are victorious, but only for a time. The real fruit of their battles lies, not in the immediate result, but in the ever expanding union of the workers. This union is helped on by the improved means of communication that are created by modern industry, and that place the workers of different localities in contact with one another. It was just this contact that was needed to centralize the numerous local struggles, all of the same character, into one national struggle between classes. But every class struggle is a political struggle. And that union, to attain which the burghers of the Middle Ages, with their miserable highways, required centuries, the modern proletarians, thanks to railways, achieve in a few years.

This organization of the proletarians into a class, and consequently into a political party, is continually being upset again by the competition between the workers themselves. But it ever rises up again, stronger, firmer, mightier. It compels legislative

KARL MARX
Founder of "Scientific" Socialism.

JEAN LONGUET

Son-in-law of Karl Marx — Leader of "Centre" of French Socialist Party — Opposed to affiliation with Third International

recognition of particular interests of the workers, by taking advantage of the divisions among the bourgeoisie itself. Thus the ten-hour bill in England was carried.

Altogether collisions between the classes of the old society further, in many ways, the course of development of the proletariat. The bourgeoisie finds itself involved in a constant battle. At first with the aristocracy; later on, with those portions of the bourgeoisie itself, whose interest have become antagonistic to the progress of industry; at all times, with the bourgeoisie of foreign countries. In all these battles it sees itself compelled to appeal to the proletariat, to ask for its help, and thus, to drag it into the political arena. The bourgeoisie itself, therefore, supplies the proletariat with its own elements of political and general education, in other words, it furnishes the proletariat with weapons for fighting the bourgeoisie.

Further, as we have already seen, entire sections of the ruling classes are, by the advance of industry, precipitated into the proletariat, or are at least threatened in their conditions of existence. These also supply the proletariat with fresh elements of enlightenment and progress.

Finally, in times when the class-struggle nears the decisive hour, the process of dissolution going on within the ruling class, in fact, within the whole range of old society, assumes such violent, glaring character, that a small section of the ruling class cuts itself adrift, and joins the revolutionary class, the class that holds the future in its hands. Just as, therefore, at an earlier period, a section of the nobility went over to the bourgeoisie, so now a portion of the bourgeoisie goes over to the proletariat, and in particular, a portion of the bourgeois ideologists, who have raised themselves to the level of comprehending theoretically the historical movements as a whole.

Of all the classes that stand face to face with the bourgeoisie today, the proletariat alone is a really revolutionary class. The other classes decay and finally disappear in the face of modern industry; the proletariat is its special and essential product.

The lower middle-class, the small manufacturer, the shopkeeper, the artisan, the peasant, all these fight against the bourgeoisie, to save from extinction their existence as fractions of the middle class. They are, therefore, not revolutionary, but conservative. Nay more, they are reactionary, for they try to roll back the wheel of history. If by chance they are revolutionary, they are so only in view of their impending transfer into the proletariat: they thus defend not their present, but their future interests, they desert their own standpoint to place themselves at that of the proletariat.

The "dangerous class," the social scum, that passively rotting mass thrown off by the lowest layers of old society, may, here and there, be swept into the movement by a proletarian revolution; its conditions of life, however, prepare it far more for the part of a bribed tool of reactionary intrigue.

In the conditions of the proletariat, those of old society at large are already virtually swamped. The proletarian is without property; his relation to his wife and children has no longer anything in common with the bourgeois family-relations; modern industrial labor, modern subjection to capital, the same in England as in France, in America as in Germany, has stripped him of every trace of national character. Law, morality, religion, are to him so many bourgeois prejudices, behind which lurk in ambush just as many bourgeois interests.

All the preceding classes that got the upper hand, sought to fortify their already acquired status by subjecting society at large to their conditions of appropriation. The proletarians cannot become masters of the productive forces of society, except by abolishing their own previous mode of appropriation, and thereby also every other previous mode of appropriation. They have nothing of their own to secure and to fortify; their mission is to destroy all previous securities for, and insurances of, individual property.

All previous historical movements were movements of minorities, or in the interest of minorities. The proletarian movement is the self-conscious, independent movement of the immense majority, in the interest of the immense majority. The proletariat, the lowest stratum of our present society, cannot stir, cannot raise itself up, without the whole superincumbent strata of official society being sprung into the air.

Though not in substance, yet in form, the struggle of the proletariat with the bourgeoisie is at first a national struggle. The proletariat of each country must, of course, first of all settle matters with its own bourgeoisie.

In depicting the most general phases of the development of the proletariat, we traced the more or less veiled civil war, raging within existing society, up to the point where that war breaks out into open revolution, and where the violent overthrow of the bourgeoisie, lays the foundation for the sway of the proletariat.

Hitherto, every form of society has been based, as we have already seen, on the antagonism of oppressing and oppressed classes. But in order to oppress a class, certain conditions must be assured to it under which it can, at least, continue its slavish existence. The serf, in the period of serfdom, raised himself to membership in the commune, just as the petty bourgeois, under the yoke of feudal absolutism, managed to develop into a bourgeois. The modern laborer, on the contrary, instead of rising with the progress of industry, sinks deeper and deeper below the conditions of existence of his own class. He becomes a pauper, and pauperism develops more rapidly than population and wealth. And here it becomes evident, that the bourgeoisie is unfit any longer to be the ruling class in society, and to impose its conditions of existence upon society as an over-riding law. It is unfit to rule, because it is incompetent to assure an existence to its slave within his slavery, because it cannot help letting him sink into such a state that it has to feed him, instead of being fed by him. Society can no longer live under this bourgeoisie, in other words, its existence is no longer compatible with society.

The essential condition for the existence, and for the sway of the bourgeois class, is the formation and augmentation of capital; the condition for capital is wage-labor. Wage-labor rests exclusively on competition between the laborers. The advance of industry, whose involuntary promoter is the bourgeoisie, replaces the isolation of the laborers, due to competition, by their involuntary combination, due to association. The development of Modern Industry, therefore, cuts from under its feet the very foundation on which the bourgeoisie produces and appropriates products. What the bourgeoisie therefore produces, above all, are its own grave-diggers. Its fall and the victory of the proletariat are equally inevitable.

II

PROLETARIANS AND COMMUNISTS

In what relation do the Communists stand to the proletarians as a whole?

The Communists do not form a separate party opposed to other working-class parties.

They have no interests separate and apart from those of the proletariat as a whole.

They do not set up any sectarian principles of their own, by which to shape and mould the proletarian movement.

The Communists are distinguished from the other working class parties by this only: 1. In the national struggles of the proletarians of the different countries, they point out and bring to the front the common interests of the entire proletariat independently of all nationality. 2. In the various stages of development which the struggle of the working class against the bourgeoisie has to pass through, they always and everywhere represent the interests of the movement as a whole.

The Communists, therefore, are on the one hand, practically, the most advanced and resolute section of the working class parties of every country, that section which pushes forward all others; on the other hand, theoretically, they have over the great mass of the proletariat the advantage of clearly understanding the line of march, the conditions, and the ultimate general results of the proletarian movement.

The immediate aim of the Communists is the same as that of all the other proletarian parties; formation of the proletariat into a class, overthrow of the bourgeois supremacy, conquest of political power by the proletariat.

The theoretical conclusions of the Communists are in no way based on ideas or principles that have been invented, or discovered, by this or that would-be universal reformer.

They merely express, in general terms, actual relations springing from an existing class struggle, from a historical movement going on under our very eyes. The abolition of existing property relations is not at all a distinctive feature of Communism.

All property relations in the past have continually been subject to historical change consequent upon the change in historical conditions.

The French Revolution, for example, abolished feudal property in favor of bourgeois property.

The distinguishing feature of Communism is not the abolition of property generally, but the abolition of bourgeois property. But modern bourgeois private property is the final and most complete expression of the system of producing and appropriating products, that is based on class antagonism, on the exploitation of the many by the few.

In this sense, the theory of the Communists may be summed up in the single sentence: Abolition of private property.

We Communists have been reproached with the desire of abolishing the right of personally acquiring property as the fruit of a man's own labor, which property is alleged to be the ground work of all personal freedom, activity and independence.

Hard-won, self-acquired, self-earned property! Do you mean the property of the petty artisan and of the small peasant, a form of property that preceded the bourgeois form? There is no need to abolish that; the development of industry has to a great extent already destroyed it, and is still destroying it daily.

Or do you mean modern bourgeois private property?

But does wage-labor create any property for the laborer? Not a bit. It creates capital, *i. e.*, that kind of property which exploits wage-labor, and which cannot increase except upon condition of getting a new supply of wage-labor for fresh exploitation. Property, in its present form, is based on the antagonism of capital and wage-labor. Let us examine both sides of this antagonism.

To be a capitalist, is to have not only a purely personal, but a social status in production. Capital is a collective product, and only by the united action of many members, nay, in the last resort, only by the united action of all members of society, can it be set in motion.

Capital is therefore not a personal, it is a social power.

When, therefore, capital is converted into common property, into the property of all members of society, personal property is not thereby transformed into social property. It is only the social character of the property that is changed. It loses its class-character.

Let us now take wage-labor.

The average price of wage-labor is the minimum wage, *i. e.*, that quantum of the means of subsistence, which is absolutely requisite to keep the laborer in bare existence as a laborer. What, therefore, the wage-laborers appropriates by means of his labor, merely suffices to prolong and reproduce a bare existence. We by no means intend to abolish this personal appropriation of the products of labor, and appropriation that is made for the maintenance and reproduction of human life, and that leaves no surplus wherewith to command the labor of others. All that we want to do away with is the miserable character of this appropriation, under which the laborer lives merely to increase capital, and is allowed to live only in so far as the interest of the ruling class requires it.

In bourgeois society, living labor is but a means to increase accumulated labor. In Communist society, accumulated labor is but a means to widen, to enrich, to promote the existence of the laborer.

In bourgeois society, therefore, the past dominates the present; in communist society the present dominates the past. In bourgeois society capital is independent and has individuality, while the living person is dependent and has no individuality.

And the abolition of this state of things is called by the bourgeois abolition of individuality and freedom! And rightly so. The abolition of bourgeois individuality, bourgeois independence, and bourgeois freedom is undoubtedly aimed at.

By freedom is meant, under the present bourgeois conditions of production, free trade, free selling and buying.

But if selling and buying disappears, free selling and buying disappears also. This talk about free selling and buying, and all the other "brave words" of our bourgeoisie about freedom in general, have a meaning, if any, only in contrast with restricted selling and buying, with the fettered traders of the Middle Ages, but have no meaning when opposed to the Communistic abolition of buying and selling, of the bourgeois conditions of production, and of the bourgeoisie itself.

You are horrified at our intending to do away with private property. But in your existing society private property is already done away with for nine-tenths of the population; its existence for the few is solely due to its non-existence in the hands of those nine-tenths. You reproach us, therefore, with intending to do away with a form of property, the necessary condition for whose existence is the non-existence of any property for the immense majority of society.

In one word, you reproach us with intending to do away with your property. Precisely so; that is just what we intend.

From the moment when labor can no longer be converted into capital, money, or rent, into a social power capable of being monopolized, *i. e.*, from the moment when individual property can no longer be transformed into bourgeois property, into capital, from that moment, you say, individuality vanishes.

You must, therefore, confess that by "individual" you mean no other person that the bourgeois, than the middle-class owner of property. This person, must, indeed, be swept out of the way, and made impossible.

Communism deprives no man of the power to appropriate the products of society: all that it does it to deprive him of the power to subjugate the labor of others by means of such appropriation.

It has been objected that upon the abolition of private property all work will cease, and universal laziness will overtake us.

According to this, bourgeois society ought long ago to have gone to the dogs through sheer idleness; for those of its members who work, acquire nothing, and those who acquire anything, do not work. The whole of this objection is but another expression of the tautology: that there can no longer be any wage-labor when there is no longer any capital.

All objections urged against the Communistic mode of producing and appropriating material products, have, in the same way, been urged against the Communistic modes of producing and appropriating intellectual products. Just as, to the bourgeois, the disappearance of class property is the disappearance of production itself, so the disappearance of class culture is to him identical with the disappearance of all culture.

That culture, the loss of which he laments, is, for the enormous majority, a mere training to act as a machine.

But don't wrangle with us so long as you apply, to our intended abolition of bourgeois property, the standard of your bourgeois notions of freedom, culture, law, etc. Your very ideas are but the outgrowth of the conditions of your bourgeois production and bourgeois property, just as your jurisprudence is but the will of your class made into a law for all, a will, whose essential character and direction are determined by the economic conditions of existence of your class.

The selfish misconception that induces you to transform into eternal laws of nature and of reason, the social forms springing from your present mode of production and form of property — historical relations that rise and disappear in the progress of production — this misconception you share with every ruling class that has preceded you. What you see clearly in the case of ancient property, what you admit in the case of feudal property, you are, of course, forbidden to admit in the case of your own bourgeois form of property.

Abolition of the family! Even the most radical flare up at this infamous proposal of the Communists.

On what foundation is the present family, the bourgeois family, based? On capital, on private gain. In its completely developed form this family exists only among the bourgeoisie. But this state of things finds its complement in the practical absence of the family among the proletarians, and in public prostitution.

The bourgeois family will vanish as a matter of course when its complement vanishes, and both will vanish with the vanishing of capital.

Do you charge us with wanting to stop the exploitation of children by their parents? To this crime we plead guilty.

But you will say, we destroy the most hallowed of relations when we replace home education by social.

And your education! Is not that also social, and determined by the social conditions under which you educate, by the intervention, direct or indirect, of society by means of schools, etc.? The Communists have not invented the intervention of society in education; they do but seek to alter the character of that intervention, and to rescue education from the influence of the ruling class.

The bourgeois clap-trap about the family and education, about the hallowed co-relation of parent and child, becomes all the more disgusting, the more, by the action of Modern Industry, all family ties among the proletarians are torn asunder, and their children transformed into simple articles of commerce and instruments of labor.

But you Communists would introduce community of women, screams the whole bourgeoisie in chorus.

The bourgeois sees in his wife a mere instrument of production. He hears that the instruments of production are to be exploited in common, and, naturally, can come to no other conclusion than that the lot of being common to all will likewise fall to the women.

He has not even a suspicion that the real point aimed at is to do away with the status of women as mere instruments of production.

For the rest, nothing is more ridiculous than the virtuous indignation of our bourgeois at the community of women which, they pretend, is to be openly and officially established by the Communists. The Communists have no need to introduce community of women; it has existed almost from time immemorial.

Our bourgeois, not content with having the wives and daughters of their proletarians at their disposal, not to speak of common prostitutes, take the greatest pleasure in seducing each others' wives.

Bourgeois marriage is in reality a system of wives in common and thus, at the most, what the Communists might possibly be reproached with is that they desire to introduce, in substitution for a hypocritically concealed, an openly legalized community of women. For the rest, it is self-evident that the abolition of the present system of production must bring with it the abolition of the community of women springing from that system, *i. e.*, of prostitution, both public and private.

The Communists are further reproached with desiring to abolish countries and nationalities.

The workingmen have no country. We cannot take from them what they have not got. Since the proletariat must first of all acquire political supremacy, must rise to be the leading class of the nation, must constitute itself the nation, it is, so far, itself national, though not in the bourgeois sense of the word.

National differences and antagonisms between peoples are daily more and more vanishing, owing to the development of the bourgeoisie, to freedom of commerce, to the world-market, to uniformity in the mode of production and in the conditions of life corresponding thereto.

The supremacy of the proletariat will cause them to vanish still faster. United action, of the leading civilized countries at least, is one of the first conditions for the emancipation of the proletariat.

In proportion as the exploitation of one individual by another is put an end to, the exploitation of one nation by another will also be put an end to. In proportion as the antagonism between classes within the nation vanishes, the hostility of one nation to another will come to an end.

The charges against Communism made from a religious, a philosophical, and generally, from an ideological standpoint, are not deserving of serious examination.

Does it require deep intuition to comprehend that man's ideas, views, and conceptions, in one word, man's consciousness, changes with every change in the conditions of his material existence, in his social relations and in his social life?

What else does the history of ideas prove than that intellectual production changes in character in proportion as material production is changed? The ruling ideas of each age have ever been the ideas of its ruling class.

When people speak of ideas that revolutionize society, they do but express the fact that within the old society, the elements of a new one have been created, and that the dissolution of the old idea keeps even pace with the dissolution of the old conditions of existence.

When the ancient world was in its last throes, the ancient religions were overcome by Christianity. When Christian ideas succumbed in the eighteenth century to rationalist ideas, feudal society fought its death-battle with the then revolutionary bourgeoisie. The ideas of religious liberty and freedom of conscience, merely gave expression to the sway of free competition within the domain of knowledge.

"Undoubtedly," it will be said, "religious, moral, philosophical and juridical ideas have been modified in the course of historical development. But religion, morality, philosophy, political science, and law, constantly survived this change."

"There are, besides, eternal truths, such as Freedom, Justice, etc., that are common to all states of society. But Communism abolishes eternal truths, it abolishes all religion, and all morality, instead of constituting them on a new basis; it therefore acts in contradiction to all past historical experience."

What does this accusation reduce itself to? The history of all past society has consisted in the development of class antagonisms, antagonisms that assumed different forms at different epochs.

But whatever form they may have taken, one fact is common to all past ages, viz., the exploitation of one part of society by the other. No wonder, then, that the social consciousness of past ages, despite all the multiplicity and variety it displays, moves within certain common forms, or general ideas, which cannot completely vanish except with the total disappearance of class antagonisms.

The Communist revolution is the most radical rupture with traditional property-relations; no wonder that its development involves the most radical rupture with traditional ideas.

But let us have done with the bourgeois objections to Communism.

We have seen above, that the first step in the revolution by the working class, is to raise the proletariat to the position of ruling class, to win the battle of democracy.

The proletariat will use its political supremacy, to wrest, by degrees, all capital from the bourgeoisie, to centralize all instruments of production in the hands of the State, i. e., of the proletariat organized as the ruling class; and to increase the total of productive forces as rapidly as possible.

Of course, in the beginning, this cannot be effected except by means of despotic inroads on the rights of property, and on the conditions of bourgeois production; by means of measures, therefore, which appear economically insufficient and untenable, but which, in the course of the movement, outstrip themselves, necessitate further inroads upon the old social order, and are unavoidable as a means of entirely revolutionizing the mode of production.

These measures will of course be different in different countries.

Nevertheless in the most advanced countries the following will be pretty generally applicable:

1. Abolition of property in land and application of all rents of land to public purposes.
2. A heavy progressive or graduated income tax.
3. Abolition of all right of inheritance.
4. Confiscation of the property of all emigrants and rebels.
5. Centralization of credit in the hands of the State, by means of a national bank with State capital and an exclusive monopoly.
6. Centralization of the means of communication and transport in the hands of the State.
7. Extension of factories and instruments of production owned by the State; the bringing into cultivation of waste lands, and the improvement of the soil generally in accordance with a common plan.
8. Equal liability of all to labor. Establishment of industrial armies, especially for agriculture.
9. Combination of agriculture with manufacturing industries; gradual abolition of the distinction between town and country, by a more equable distribution of population over the country.
10. Free education for all children in public schools. Abolition of children's factory labor in its present form. Combination of education with industrial production, etc., etc.

When, in the course of development, class distinctions have disappeared, and all production has been concentrated in the hands of a vast association of the whole nation, the public power will lose its political character. Political power, properly so called, is merely the organized power of one class for oppressing another. If the proletariat during its contest with the bourgeoisie is compelled, by the force of circumstances, to organize itself as a class, if, by means of a revolution, it makes itself the ruling class, and, as such, sweeps away by force the old conditions of production, then it will, along with these conditions, have swept away the conditions for the existence of class antagonisms, and of classes generally, and will thereby have abolished its own supremacy as a class.

In place of the old bourgeois society, with its classes and class antagonisms, we shall have an association, in which the free development of each is the condition for the free development of all.

III

SOCIALIST AND COMMUNIST LITERATURE

1. *Reactionary Socialism*

a. FEUDAL SOCIALISM

Owing to their historical position, it became the vocation of the aristocracies of France and England to write pamphlets against modern bourgeois society. In the French revolution of July, 1830, and in the English reform agitation, these aristocracies again succumbed to the hateful upstart. Thenceforth, a serious political contest was altogether out of the question. A literary battle alone remained possible. But even in the domain of literature the old cries of the restoration period had become impossible.

In order to arouse sympathy, the aristocracy were obliged to lose sight, apparently, of their own interests, and to formulate their indictment against the bourgeoisie in the interest of the exploited working class alone. Thus the aristocracy took their revenge by singing lampoons on their new master, and whispering in his ears sinister prophecies of coming catastrophe.

In this way arose feudal socialism; half lamentation, half lampoon; half echo of the past, half menace of the future; at times, by its bitter, witty and incisive criticism, striking the bourgeoisie to the very hearts' core, but always ludicrous in its effect, through total incapacity to comprehend the march of modern history.

The aristocracy, in order to rally the people to them, waved the proletarian alms-bag in front for a banner. But the people, so often as it joined them, saw on their hindquarters the old feudal coats of arms, and deserted with loud and irreverent laughter.

One section of the French Legitimists, and "Young England," exhibited this spectacle.

In pointing out that their mode of exploitation was different to that of the bourgeoisie, the feudalists forget that they exploited under circumstances and conditions that were quite different, and that are now antiquated. In showing that, under their rule, the modern proletariat never existed, they forget that the modern bourgeoisie is the necessary offspring of their own form of society.

For the rest, so little do they conceal the reactionary character of their criticism, that their chief accusation against the bourgeoisie amounts to this, that under the bourgeoisie regime a class is being developed, which is destined to cut up root and branch the old order of society.

What they upbraid the bourgeoisie with is not so much that it creates a proletariat, as that it creates a revolutionary proletariat.

In political practice, therefore, they join in all coercive measures against the working class; and in ordinary life, despite their high falutin phrases, they stoop to pick up the golden apples dropped from the tree of industry, and to barter truth, love, and honor for traffic in wool, beet-root sugar and potato spirit.

As the parson has ever gone hand in hand with the landlord, so has Clerical Socialism with Feudal Socialism.

Nothing is easier than to give Christian asceticism a Socialist tinge. Has not Christianity declaimed against private property, against marriage, against the State? Has it not preached in the place of these, charity and poverty, celibacy, and mortification of the flesh, monastic life and Mother Church? Christian Socialism is but the Holy Water with which the priest consecrates the heart-burnings of the aristocrat.

b. PETTY BOURGEOIS SOCIALISM

The feudal aristocracy was not the only class that was ruined by the bourgeoisie, not the only class whose conditions of existence pined and perished in the atmosphere of modern bourgeois society. The medieval burgesses and the small peasant bourgeoisie were the precursors of the modern bourgeoisie. In those countries which are but little developed, industrially and commercially, these two classes still vegetate side by side with the rising bourgeoisie.

In countries where modern civilization has become fully developed, a new class of petty bourgeois has been formed, fluctuating between proletariat and bourgeoisie, and ever renewing itself as a supplementary part of bourgeois society. The individual members of this class, however, are being constantly hurled down into the proletariat by the action of competition, and, as modern industry develops, they even see the moment approaching when they will completely disappear as an independent section of modern society, to be replaced, in manufactures, agriculture and commerce, by overlookers, bailiffs and shopmen.

In countries like France, where the peasants constitute far more than half of the population, it was natural that writers who sided with the proletariat against the bourgeoisie, should use, in their criticism of the bourgeoisie regime, the standard of the peasant and petty bourgeois, and from the standpoint of these intermediate classes should take up the cudgels for the working class. Thus arose petty bourgeoise Socialism. Sismondi was the head of this school, not only in France, but also in England.

This school of Socialism dissected with great acuteness the contradictions in the conditions of modern production. It laid bare the hypocritical apologies of economists. It proved, incontrovertibly, the disastrous effects of machinery and division of labor; the concentration of capital and land in a few hands; overproduction and crises; it pointed out the inevitable ruin of the petty bourgeois and peasant, the misery of the proletariat, the anarchy in production, the crying inequalities in the distribution of wealth, the industrial war of extermination between nations, the dissolution of old moral bonds, of the old family relations, of the old nationalities.

In its positive aims, however, this form of Socialism aspires either to restoring the old means of production and of exchange, and with them the old property relations, and the old society, or to cramping the modern means of production and of exchange, within the frame work of the old property relations that have been, and were bound to be, exploded by those means. In either case, it is both reactionary and Utopian.

Its last words are: corporate guilds for manufacture; patriarchal relations in agriculture.

Ultimately, when stubborn historical facts had dispersed all intoxicating effects of self-deception, this form of Socialism ended in a miserable fit of the blues.

c. German or True Socialism

The Socialist and Communist literature of France, a literature that originated under the pressure of a bourgeoisie in power, and that was the expression of the struggle against this power, was introduced into Germany at a time when the bourgeoisie, in that country, had just begun its contest with feudal absolutism.

German philosophers, would-be philosophers, and beaux esprits, eagerly seized on this literature, only forgetting, that when these writings immigrated from France into Germany, French social conditions had not immigrated along with them. In contact with German social conditions, this French literature lost all its immediate practical significance, and assumed a purely literary aspect. Thus, to the German philosophers of the eighteenth century, the demands of the first French revolution were nothing more than the demands of "Practical Reason" in general, and the utterance of the will of the revolutionary French bourgeoisie signified in their eyes the laws of pure Will, of Will as it was bound to be, of true human Will generally.

The work of the German literati consisted solely in bringing the new French ideas into harmony with their ancient philosophical conscience or, rather, in annexing the French ideas without deserting their own philosophic point of view.

This annexation took place in the same way in which a foreign language is appropriated, namely, by translation.

It is well known how the monks wrote silly lives of Catholic Saints over the manuscripts on which the classical works of ancient heathendom had been written. The German literati reversed this process with the profane French literature. They wrote their philosophical nonsense beneath the French original. For instance, beneath the French criticism of the economic functions of money, they wrote "Alienation of Humanity," and beneath the French criticism of the bourgeois State they wrote, "Dethronement of the Category of the General," and so forth.

The introduction of these philosophical phrases at the back of the French historical criticisms they dubbed "Philosophy of Action," "True Socialism," "German Science of Socialism," "Philosophical Foundation of Socialism," and so on.

The French Socialist and Communist literature was thus completely emasculated. And, since it ceased in the hands of the German to express the struggle of one class with the other, he felt conscious of having overcome "French one-sidedness" and of representing, not true requirements, but the requirements of Truth, not the interests of the proletariat, but the interests of Human Nature, of Man in general, who belongs to no class, has no reality, who exists only in the misty realm of philosophical phantasy.

This German Socialism, which took its school boy task so seriously and solemnly, and extolled its poor stock-in-trade in such mountebank fashion, meanwhile gradually lost its pedantic innocence.

The fight of the German, and especially of the Prussian, bourgeoisie, against feudal aristocracy and absolute monarchy, in other words, the liberal movement, became more earnest.

By this the long-wished-for opportunity was offered to "True Socialism" of confronting the political movement with the Socialist demands, of hurling the traditional anathemas against liberalism, against the representative government, against bourgeois competition, bourgeois freedom of the press, bourgeois legislation, bourgeois liberty and equality, and of preaching to the masses that they had nothing to gain, and everything to lose, by this bourgeois movement. German Socialism forgot, in the nick of time, that the French criticism, whose silly echo it was, presupposed the existence of modern bourgeois society, with its corresponding economic conditions of existence, and the political constitution adapted thereto, the very things whose attainment was the object of the pending struggle in Germany.

To the absolute governments, with their following of parsons, professors, country squires and officials, it served as a welcome scarecrow against the threatening bourgeoisie.

It was a sweet finish after the bitter pills of floggings and bullets, with which these same governments, just at that time, dosed the German working-class risings.

While this "True Socialism" thus served the government as a weapon for fighting the German bourgeoisie, it, at the same time, directly represented a reactionary interest, the interest of the German Philistines. In Germany the petty bourgeois class, a relic of the sixteenth century, and since then constantly cropping up again under various forms, is the real social basis of the existing state of things.

To preserve this class, is to preserve the existing state of things in Germany. The industrial and political supremacy of the bourgeoisie threatens it with certain destruction; on the one hand, from the concentration of capital; on the other, from the rise of a revolutionary proletariat. "True Socialism" appeared to kill these two birds with one stone. It spread like an epidemic.

The robe of speculative cobwebs, embroidered with flowers of rhetoric, steeped in the dew of sickly sentiment, this transcendental robe in which the German Socialists wrapped their sorry "eternal truths," all skin and bone, served wonderfully to increase the sale of their goods amongst such a public.

And on its part, German Socialism recognized, more and more, its own calling as the bombastic representative of the petty bourgeois Philistine.

It proclaimed the German nation to be the model nation, and the German petty Philistine to be the typical man. To every villainous meanness of this model man it gave a hidden, higher, socialistic interpretation, the exact contrary of its true character. It went to the extreme length of directly opposing the "brutally destructive" tendency of Communism, and of proclaiming its supreme and impartial contempt of all class struggles. With very few exceptions, all the so-called Socialist and Communist publications that now (1847) circulate in Germany belong to the domain of this foul and enervating literature.

2. *Conservative or Bourgeois Socialism*

A part of the bourgeoisie is desirous of redressing social grievances, in order to secure the continued existence of bourgeois society.

To this section belong economists, philanthropists, humanitarians, improvers of the condition of the working class, organizers of charity, members of societies for the prevention of cruelty to animals, temperance fanatics, hole and corner reformers of every imaginable kind. This form of Socialism has, moreover, been worked out into complete systems.

We may cite Proudhon's "Philosophie de la Misère" as an example of this form.

The socialistic bourgeois want all the advantages of modern social conditions without the struggles and dangers necessarily resulting therefrom. They desire the existing state of society minus its revolutionary and disintegrating elements. They wish for a bourgeoisie without a proletariat. The bourgeoisie naturally conceives the world in which it is supreme to be the best; and bourgeois Socialism develops this comfortable conception into various more or less complete systems. In requiring the proletariat to carry out such a system, and thereby to march straightway into the social New Jerusalem, it but requires in reality, that the proletariat should remain within the bounds of existing society, but should cast away all its hateful ideas concerning the bourgeoisie.

A second and more practical, but less systematic, form of this Socialism sought to depreciate every revolutionary movement in the eyes of the working class, by showing that no mere political reform, but only a change in the material conditions of existence, in economical relations, could be of any advantage to them. By changes in the material conditions of existence, this form of Socialism, however, by no means understands abolition of the bourgeois relations of production, an abolition that can be effected only by a revolution, but administrative reforms, based on the continued existence of these relations; reforms, therefore, that in no respect affect the relations between capital and labor, but, at the best, lessen the cost, and simplify the administrative work, of bourgeois government.

Bourgeois Socialism attains adequate expression, when, and only when, it becomes a mere figure of speech.

Free trade: for the benefit of the working class. Protective duties: for the benefit of the working class. Prison reform: for the benefit of the working class. This is the last word and the only seriously meant word of bourgeois Socialism.

It is summed up in the phrase: the bourgeois is a bourgeois—for the benefit of the working class.

3. *Critical-Utopian Socialism and Communism*

We do not here refer to that literature which, in every great modern revolution, has always given voice to the demands of the proletariat: such as the writings of Babeuf and others.

The first direct attempts of the proletariat to attain its own ends were made in times of universal excitement, when feudal society was being overthrown. These attempts necessarily failed, owing to the then undeveloped state of the proletariat, as well as to the absence of the economic conditions for its emancipation, conditions that had yet to be produced, and could be produced by the impending bourgeois epoch alone. The revolutionary literature that accompanied these first movements of the proletariat had necessarily a reactionary character. It inculcated universal asceticism and social leveling in its crudest form.

The Socialist and Communist systems properly so-called, those of Saint Simon, Fourier, Owen and others, sprang into existence in the early undeveloped period described above, of the struggle between proletariat and bourgeoisie. (See Section I. Bourgeoisie and Proletariat.)

The founders of these systems see, indeed, the class antagonisms, as well as the action of the decomposing elements in the prevailing form of society. But the proletariat, as yet in its infancy, offers to them the spectacle of a class without any historical initiative or any independent political movement.

Since the development of class antagonism keeps even pace with the development of industry, the economic situation, as they find it, does not as yet offer to them the material conditions for the emancipation of the proletariat. They therefore search after a new social science, after new social laws, that are to create these conditions.

Historical action is to yield to their personal inventive action, historically created conditions of emancipation to fantastic ones, and the gradual, spontaneous class organization of the proletariat to an organization of society specially contrived by these inventors. Future history resolves itself, in their eyes, into the propaganda and the practical carrying out of their social plans.

In the formation of their plans they are conscious of caring chiefly for the interests of the working class, as being the most suffering class. Only from the point of view of being the most suffering class does the proletariat exist for them.

The undeveloped state of the class struggle, as well as their own surroundings, cause Socialists of this kind to consider themselves far superior to all class antagonisms. They want to improve the condition of every member of society, even that of the most favored. Hence, they habitually appeal to society at large, without distinction of class; nay, by preference, to the ruling class. For how can people, when once they understand their system, fail to see in it the best possible plan of the best possible state of society?

Hence, they reject all political, and especially all revolutionary, action; they wish to attain their ends by peaceful means, and endeavor, by small experiments, necessarily doomed to failure, and by the force of example, to pave the way for the new social Gospel.

Such fantastic pictures of future society, painted at a time when the proletariat is still in a very undeveloped state, and has but a fantastic conception of its own position, correspond with the first instinctive yearnings of that class for a general reconstruction of society.

But these Socialist and Communist publications contain also a critical element. They attack every principle of existing society. Hence they are full of the most valuable materials for the enlightenment of the working class. The practical measures proposed in them, such as the abolition of the distinction between town and country, of the family, of the carrying on of industries for the account of private individuals, and of the wage system, the proclamation of social harmony, the conversion of the functions of the State into a mere superintendence of production, all these proposals point solely to the disappearance of class antagonisms which were, at that time, only just cropping up, and which, in these publications, are recognized under their earliest, indistinct and undefined forms only. These proposals, therefore, are of a purely Utopian character.

The significance of Critical-Utopian Socialism and Communism bears an inverse relation to historical development. In proportion as the modern class struggle develops and takes definite shape, this fantastic standing apart from the contest, these fantastic attacks on it lose all practical value and all theoretical justification. Therefore, although the originators of these systems were, in many respects, revolutionary, their disciples have, in every case, formed mere reactionary sects. They hold fast by the original views of their masters, in opposition to the progressive historical development of the proletariat. They, therefore, endeavor and that consistently, to deaden the class struggle and to reconcile the class antagonisms. They still dream of experimental realization of their social Utopias, of founding isolated "phalansteres," of establishing "Home Colonies," of setting up a "Little Icaria" — duodecimo editions of the New Jerusalem, and to realize all these castles in the air, they are compelled to appeal to the feelings and purses of the bourgeois. By degrees they sink into the category of the reactionary conservative Socialists depicted above, differing from these only by more systematic pedantry, and by their fanatical and superstitious belief in the miraculous effects of their social science.

They, therefore, violently oppose all political action on the part of the working class; such action, according to them, can only result from blind unbelief in the new Gospel.

The Owenites in England, and the Fourierists in France, respectively, oppose the Chartists and the "Reformistes."

IV

POSITION OF THE COMMUNISTS IN RELATION TO THE VARIOUS EXISTING OPPOSITION PARTIES

Section 2 has made clear the relations of the Communists to the existing working class parties, such as the Chartists in England and the Agrarian Reformers in America.

The Communists fight for the attainment of the immediate aims, for the enforcement of the momentary interests of the working class; but in the movement of the present, they also represent and take care of the future of that movement. In France the Communists ally themselves with the Social-Democrats, against the conservative and radical bourgeoisie, reserving, however, the right to take up a critical position in regard to phrases and illusions traditionally handed down from the great revolution.

In Switzerland they support the Radicals, without losing sight of the fact that this party consists of antagonistic elements, partly of Democratic Socialists, in the French sense, partly of radical bourgeois.

In Poland they support the party that insists on an agrarian revolution, as the prime condition for national emancipation, that party which fomented the insurrection of Cracow in 1846.

In Germany they fight with the bourgeoisie whenever it acts in a revolutionary way, against the absolute monarchy, the feudal squirearchy, and the petty bourgeoisie.

But they never cease, for a single instant, to instill into the working class the clearest possible recognition of the hostile antagonism between bourgeoisie and proletariat, in order that the German workers may straightway use, as so many weapons against the bourgeoisie, the social and political conditions that the bourgeoisie must necessarily introduce along with its supremacy, and in order that, after the fall of the reactionary classes in Germany, the fight against the bourgeoisie itself may immediately begin.

The Communists turn their attention chiefly to Germany, because that country is on the eve of a bourgeois revolution, that is bound to be carried out under more advanced conditions of

European civilization, and with a more developed proletariat, than that of England was in the seventeenth, and of France in the eighteenth century, and because the bourgeois revolution in Germany will be but the prelude to an immediately following proletarian revolution.

In short, the Communists everywhere support every revolutionary movement against the existing social and political order of things.

In all these movements they bring to the front, as the leading question in each, the property question, no matter what its degree of development at the time.

Finally, they labor everywhere for the union and agreement of the democratic parties of all countries.

The Communists disdain to conceal their views and aims. They openly declare that their ends can be attained only by the forcible overthrow of all existing social conditions. Let the ruling classes tremble at a communistic revolution. The proletarians have nothing to lose but their chains. They have a world to win.

Workingmen of all countries, unite!

CHAPTER II

Socialism and Labor in Germany *

In reviewing the European situation of Socialism and Labor for twenty-five years before the War, it is natural to begin with Germany, because the establishment of the Social Democratic Party in Germany was earlier than in any other country, and the movement was also stronger and better organized. Its relation to labor and to the co-operative movement was from the beginning harmonious and close. Educational commissions were appointed by the social democracy in conjunction with the labor unions, and a labor system of educational facilities for the labor classes, including education in economic and sociological questions, was established and developed in a way unequalled in any other country. A Socialist press of unrivalled importance was established.

The principles of the Karl Marx Communist Manifesto were adopted as early as 1869 as the basis of the first Social Democratic Labor Party, and, quoting from page 168 of Hunter, "Socialists at Work," we find that "In 1875, in order to achieve unity between the Lasallians and the Marxists, the program was altered, and many ideas of Lasalle were accepted in the face of the very vigorous opposition of Marx. Finally, however, in 1891, the German Congress revised its program and adopted a thorough and comprehensive Marxian position.

"This is expressed in the so-called Erfurt program of October, 1891, which remained the basis of the German party from that time forward."

Long before this, as far back as 1875, there had been a United Workingmen's Party which, at the elections of 1877, polled nearly half a million votes, electing twelve representatives to the Reichstag. Bismark attempted to block the increasing influence of Social Democracy, but was powerless to prevent its steady increase in voting power and in its representation in the Reichstag. The party secured one after the other a large measure of economic reform and labor legislation. This included a well-developed insurance system, according to which every employee receiving less than $500 a year in wages must be insured against accident, sickness, invalidism and old age.

The effect was especially evident in the German cities which

* See Addendum, Part I.

developed municipal ownership to a considerable extent under Socialist influence. The most brilliant philosophical and literary exponent of Marxism in Germany before the war was Karl Kautsky, who occupied an intermediary position between the Left Wing, headed by Liebknecht, and the Right Wing headed by Scheidemann. Because Kautsky led the moderately radical section in deprecating the more violent theories of immediate action of the Left Wing, he was stigmatized as not a true interpreter of Marx by all those who afterwards followed the lead of Lenin. It is interesting that during the period before the war the German Socialist leaders of the Center and Right Wings would not agree to the theory of peace at any price in case of war, but were in favor, under certain restrictions, of defending the Fatherland.

The analysis of the voting situation at the two elections of 1903 and 1907 will show how successful the Social Democratic Party had become. The party had over 3,000,000 votes in 1903, by far the largest number of votes cast for any party, the nearest approach being the 1,875,000 votes of the Catholic Party. It was almost the same in 1907. The Socialists polled over 3,250,000 votes and the Catholics 2,183,000 but, owing to the peculiarly unjust methods of counting votes in the cities, the Socialists never obtained the proportion of representatives in Parliament to which they were entitled. The especial value set upon the close alliance between the Social Democracy and labor unions is shown by that portion of the program of the Socialist Congress at Stuttgart in 1907, which followed largely the dictation of German leaders.

The following quotation does not touch upon other important declarations of the conference, its opposition to the war, and its review of the ways in which Socialism had prevented recent wars; nor does it touch on the discussion in regard to the general strike as a preventive of war, which was favored by the French under Jaurès, and opposed by the Germans under Bebel. We give here that part which relates to the trade unions and to industrial policy:

> "To emancipate the proletariat completely from the bonds of intellectual, political, and economic serfdom, the political and economic struggle are alike necessary. If the activity of the Socialist Party is exercised more particularly in the domain of the political struggle of the proletariat, that of the unions displays itself in the domain of the economic

struggle of the workers. The unions and the party have, therefore, an equally important task to perform in the struggle for proletarian emancipation. Each of the two organizations has its distinct domain, defined by its nature, and within whose borders it should enjoy independent control of its lines of action, but there is an ever-widening domain in the proletarian struggle of the classes in which they can reap advantages only by concerted action and by co-operation between the party and the trade unions.

"As a consequence, the proletarian struggle would be carried on more successfully and with more important results if the relations between unions and the party are strengthened without infringing the necessary unity of the trade unions.

"The Congress declares that it is to the interest of the working class in every country that close and permanent relations should be established between the unions and the party.

"It is the duty of the party and of the trade unions to render moral support the one to the other and to make use only of those means which may help forward the emancipation of the proletariat. When divergent opinions arise between the two organizations as to the effectiveness of certain tactics they should arrive by discussion at an agreement.

"The unions will not fully perform their duty in the struggle for the emancipation of the workers unless a thoroughly Socialist spirit inspires their policy. It is the duty of the party to help the unions in their work of raising the workers and of ameliorating their social conditions. In its parliamentary action, the party must vigorously support the demands of the unions.

"The Congress declares that the development of the capitalist system of production, the increased concentration of the means of production, the growing alliance of the employers, the increasing dependence of particular trades upon the totality of bourgeois society, would reduce trade unions to impotency if, concerning themselves about nothing more than trade interests, they took their stand on corporate selfishness and admitted the theory of harmony of interests between capital and labor.

"The Congress is of the opinion that the unions will be able more successfully to carry on their struggle against exploitation and oppression, in proportion as their organizations are more unified, as their benefit system is improved, as the funds necessary for their struggle are better supplied, and as their members gain a clearer conception of economic relations and conditions, and are inspired by the Socialist ideal with greater enthusiasm and devotion."

The attitude of the Socialists during and after the War will be treated in a later chapter in connection with the Spartacide movement.

CHAPTER III

Socialism and Labor in Italy *

The Socialist Party was rather late in taking form in Italy as compared with Germany, Belgium and Denmark, but it was very quickly organized and became extremely powerful, owing to the fact that it not only joined forces with and helped to organize the industrial worker, but also helped to form unions among the peasants in a way that was unknown either in Germany or in France. This led to a very early development of co-operative societies in which the peasant unions played a very important part. These peasant organizations were not only economic and political but had strong leanings from the beginning toward Republicanism, which was engineered very quickly into Socialism. The leader in this peasant movement was Enrico Ferri.

These unions were among the first to establish special banks, which facilitated agricultural operations on a large scale. The industrial workers developed very much in the French manner, meeting in labor chambers or local centers which were called "Camere di Lavoro." These workmen's organizations were often under the protection of local municipal officials, and this added to the ease with which they were organized and developed.

The Socialist Party, almost from the beginning, directed the political action of both the industrial and peasant branches. The Socialist vote is reckoned as having grown from about 26,000 in 1902 to 320,000 in 1904 in the parliamentary elections. In the city elections the domination of the Socialists has been remarkable even in the largest cities. Socialist propaganda in Italy is not so much carried on in literary and journalistic forms in the north, as it is through the efforts of brilliant orators.

Between 1880 and 1900 the Socialists became divided into three sections or parties; the first, under the direction of Ferri, which was opportunist in character; the second, under the direction of Turati, whose program was distinctly Marxian, and who exercised the strongest influence among the intellectual classes, and especially in the north of Italy; the third party, led by Labriola, which was far more violent and revolutionary in its program and did not take much account of parliamentary methods, and which was supported by the Syndicalists.

---

* See Addendum, Part I.

The Italian parties are naturally rather extreme in their expressions of opinion and the differences among the three factions for a long time prevented unity of program, but more and more influence was gained by the radical section until it became evident, long before the war, that the Italian Socialist Party as a party would be defeatist.

The trade union membership in Italy in 1912 was already close to 1,000,000, larger in proportion to the population than that of France. The struggles between the groups were shown at the various congresses. In 1906 the Syndicalists and the Socialists had a bitter fight, the Moderates winning by about five to one. Shortly afterward Labriola resigned and formed a separate group. At the Congress of Rome in 1910 the Reformist Party, led by Turati, obtained a large majority against both the Radical Revolutionists, headed by Lazzari, and the Integralists, headed by Ferri. At the time of the war in Tripoli (1912) the party took a decided stand against the war, expelling one of its important leaders, Bissolati, and forecasting its action in 1914.

During the year before the war, in 1913, after the extension of the franchise, the Socialist Party obtained 960,000 votes, while the new moderate wing recently formed by Bissolati and his friends, called the Socialist Reformist Party, had 200,000 votes. The proportion of the total votes cast for the Socialists represented about one-quarter, as compared with more recent votes after the war, which total about one-third of the whole electorate. Notwithstanding the increased radicalism of the party as a whole, the labor elements in Italy remained in alliance with it.

The activities of the Socialist Party in Italy, its attitude toward the war, and toward the Bolsheviki, have many points of contact with past and possible conditions in the United States.

Was the Italian Socialist Party loyal to its government during the war, when Italian independence was in danger of being destroyed by the invasion of the Central Powers?

The answer is that it was not. It betrayed its country in every way possible.

The Socialist Party issued an official manifesto at the opening of the war in which it opposed the war and urged the soldiers to throw down their arms and go home. This was in 1915. The Socialists organized an elaborate defeatest campaign in the army, by leaflets and pamphlets and personal propaganda. As a result of this came the so-called Caporetto disaster, which nearly resulted in Italy's conquest. The Austrian and German armies penetrated through gaps left open for them by Socialized Italian regiments. Even after the popular national revolution and stiffening of patriotic resolve, the Socialist Party again issued another defeatist manifesto against the war.

The official statements of the Italian government, in and out of parliamentary debate, admit that this Socialist treachery almost brought about Italy's downfall. The theoretical Socialist opposition to war was, therefore, in Italy's case, inexorably carried out in practice.

The attitude of the Italian Socialists toward Lenin and Trotzky has been one of consistent approval and co-operation. The propaganda in the army was modelled on that of the Bolsheviki to disrupt the Russian army's morale, discipline and patriotism. Their efforts since the war have turned in the direction of gaining control of labor and of bringing on mass strikes. They planned a universal strike throughout Italy on July 20–21, 1919, to protest against interfering with the Bolsheviki in Russia and Hungary. They celebrated, on November 7, 1919, the anniversary of the Bolshevist revolution in Russia, by demonstrations in the principal cities of Italy. The extraordinary success of the Socialist candidates at the polls, due largely to the discontent with the high cost of living, has made the party a formidable element in the Italian Chamber.

It is generally considered that as a party the Italian Socialists approach more closely to the Bolshevik type than any other European section of the party. There must be a certain reaction of this attitude in that of the Italians in this country who have Socialist sympathies.

"The Italian Socialist Party was the first Socialist Party of power and influence to ally itself with the Third (Moscow) International, and which openly endorsed the program and manifesto of the Moscow Conference. This important step was taken by the National Executive Committee of the party which met in March, 1919, at Milan, by a vote of ten to three, and which was later endorsed by an overwhelming vote at the National Convention of the party. At the previous convention, the party decided to withdraw from the International Socialist Bureau and declined to send delegates to the Berne International Conference. The National Executive Committee later decided, however, to send two of its members to Berne to observe the activities of the

Conference. At the same convention, the party reiterated its anti-war position, called the Socialist deputies to task for failing to take a more aggressive stand in the Chamber of Deputies, and gave the Executive Committee power to expel recalcitrant deputies. It also refused to send delegates to the Inter-Allied Socialist and Labor Conference in London on the ground that it admitted the American Federation of Labor, while delegates from the Socialist Party of America and the Russian Communist Party were not present. The party also repudiated both the mission from the American Federation of Labor and the Social-Democratic League of America, which visited Italy.

"The National Executive Committee submitted a proposition in December, 1918, to the party subdivision favoring the elimination of all minimum demands from the party program which is used in electoral campaigns. The proposition met with almost unanimous approval of the different sections of the party. It also issued a declaration in which it sponsored the establishment of a Socialist Republic and the dictatorship of the proletariat, with the following scope: (1) The socialization of the means of production and transportation, land, mines, railroads, steamships operated and managed directly by the peasants, sailors, miners and workers; (2) distribution of commodities through co-operatives or municipal agencies exclusively; (3) abolition of military conscription and universal disarmament following the union of all Socialist proletarian international republics of the world.

"The declaration also vigorously advocated the withdrawal of troops from Russia, and announced that the Socialist Party "would not join in the homage to the representative of the United States," so that when President Wilson addressed the Chamber of Deputies, he found nearly forty seats, usually occupied by the Socialists, empty. The party convention also went on record against readmission of all those former members of the party who supported the government in the prosecution of the war and instructed its subdivisions to strictly observe this mandate.

"The Socialist Union, which was organized by pro-war Socialists, did not succeed in attracting to itself many of the members of the party. It formed an alliance with the so-called "Reformist Socialists," who had split away from the party, following the war with Tripoli.

"During 1919 the party continued its agitation for amensty

for political prisoners, and secured the release of several of its leaders, among whom were Constantino Lazzari, veteran secretary of the party, his assistant, Nicola Bombacci, and the editor of the party organ "Avanti," Giacinto Serrati.

"In June, 1919, the International Socialist Bureau sent a committee consisting of Ramsay Macdonald and Jean Longuet to discuss with the Italian Party the reconsideration of the withdrawal from the Second International. The negotiations proved of no avail. The Italian Party, however, joined the international demonstration decided upon by the International Socialist Bureau on July 21st with the result that Italian Socialists alone among the "Allied" Socialists, conducted a general strike in protest against the Russian blockade. Entire provinces were prostrated by the industrial standstill. All traffic and communication ceased and in more than 240 municipalities, among them, Genoa and Florence, Soviets were established.

"The Socialist Party has denounced the Paris Peace and the proposed League of Nations, seeing in this attempt the "recreating of the Holy Alliance among the conquerors, to oppress not only politically, but also economically, the conquered populations, dumb victims of the mistakes and rapacity of the bourgeoisie, captained by imperialistic capitalism and against the international proletariat."

"Preparatory to the next congress of the Socialist Party, the National Executive Committee issued a draft of a program, in which the party is called upon to prepare for the coming revolution by the formation of agencies which would be in a position to direct the course of the revolution, with the aim of establishing a Soviet form of government. The program even goes as far as to promulgate certain fundamental principles underlying the dictatorship of the proletariat, such as the disenfranchising of persons who do not do any socially useful work.

"In the Parliamentary elections of November 1919, the Socialist Party scored a tremendous victory, receiving about 3,000,000 votes as against 883,409 in 1913, or more than a third of the votes cast, and increasing its representation in the Chamber from 44 to 159. The campaign was waged on an anti-war and revolutionary program, which included unqualified support to the Russian Soviet Government.

"The industrial labor movement is divided into two distinct groups, one co-operating closely with the Socialist Party, and the other consisting of the syndicalist organizations, which are not interested in political action. The General Confederation of Labor, which is the strongest labor federation, has endorsed the war position of the party and was instrumental in forcing the Italian Government to discontinue its participation in the anti-Russian campaign. The government was also forced to publicly announce that no more troops would be sent to Russia, that no munitions would be dispatched, and that no Italian steamers would be allowed to transport munitions or materials to the Russian counter-revolutionary elements. At a national conference in April, the Italian labor unions demanded the convocation of a constituent assembly for a revision of the form of government favoring the transformation of the national parliament as constituted at present into a national soviet.

"The membership of the Italian labor unions is estimated at present to be about 1,000,000, which is an increase of almost 300,000 since 1917, and an organization campaign is at present on throughout the country to enroll more workers into the unions."

(These statements are taken from the able summary published in the American Labor Year Book, 1919–1920, pp. 372–4.)

The National Executive Committee of the Socialist Party arranged for a Congress in October, 1919, at Bologna. There were four groups within the Socialist Party which prepared four distinct programs that were considered throughout Italy by the members several weeks before the meeting.

These four programs were as follows:

The first was that of the Reformists led by Turati, who was the founder of the party in Italy and had been its leader until 1918. Turati had been consistently opposed to the war but was opposed also to revolutionary direct action, and was not among those who favored the Soviet program. He wanted the party to keep co-operating with the present government in Italy with a program of conquering public power through the ballot and meanwhile securing reform measures. He was of the same type of Marxian Socialist as the German Socialists led by Kautsky.

Opposed to Turati were the Maximilists led by Serrati. This section of the party had gained control at the Congress in Rome in 1918 and had pledged themselves to absolute sympathy and co-operation with the Soviet government in Russia. Serrati himself had come from the United States where he had directed a

Socialist newspaper and the organization of an Italian Socialist Party. He was the coming man in the Italian group.

The only difference between the program of Serrati and that of Lenin was that Serrati believed the party should take part in the present government; should send as many deputies to Parliament as possible; should use the parliamentary platform for spreading Socialist ideas and keeping out pseudo Socialists. Meantime, the program of the party was to be a Soviet program, including arming of the proletariat, disarming of the bourgeoisie, and establishing the dictatorship of the proletariat. This was to be done while ostensibly supporting the parliamentary regime through the progressive establishment of Soviet workers' organizations throughout the country, and educating the proletariat for its coming supremacy.

A third party of Centrists was headed by Lazzari. It was a rather colorless timid party, which coalesced with the Reformists when the Congress opened, reducing the groups from four to three before it came to the voting.

The last of the parties was that of the Abstentionists, headed by the young leader named Bordiga, who was even more extreme than Serrati and the Maximilists, preaching of course abstention from parliamentary action and immediate direct action to bring about the revolution.

The voting on the three programs was:

For the Maximilists of Serrati, 48,411; for the Unitarians of Lazzari and Turati, 14,886; and for the Abstentionists of Bordiga, 3,417.

This meant an even greater triumph for the Soviet section of the Socialist Party than in the Congress of 1918.

The party had then to decide on its policy in the approaching elections; and it nominated its candidates from all three of the above groups in proportion to their voting strength, on condition that all elected candidates should follow the policy, not of their group, but of the whole party. A very characteristic and important condition was that no one could be a candidate of the party who had in any way favored or aided the late war.

It must be remembered that Serrati had taken part in the Turin uprising during the war, which was considered by the government an act of treason of the Socialist Party behind the lines, and had led to his imprisonment for eight months.

This incident also had led Premier Orlando in Parliament to

state that after the Caporetto diaster, Italy had been in worse danger from traitors behind the lines than from enemies in front, and to agree with a speech of one of the former Socialist leaders that he would be ready to shoot down any traitorous Socialist.

The pronounced Soviet character of the Congress, it was thought, might bring about disagreement with the great Italian labor organization which was largely Syndicalist. But this break did not occur and the elections were very successful from a Socialist point of view. They secured almost one-third of the membership of the Chamber of Deputies, electing 156 candidates.

On the day of the opening of the Italian Parliament, they asserted their lack of loyalty to the Royal government by remaining seated while the King ascended the throne, and by rising from their seats and shouting, "Long live Socialism," and leaving the chamber as soon as the Royal address was delivered.

This action led to disturbances and strikes throughout a large part of Italy. The Italian Socialists are as a body very level-headed and do not expect to bring about an immediate revolution until two things have occurred:

In the first place, a very much wider education of the people and its organization in Soviet form; and in the second place, a wider international diffusion of adherence to the Soviet idea; because they feel that only as an international movement can Communism succeed.

The program of the Italian Socialist Party as declared in 1892 is retained practically intact by the present party, except for the details of Soviet organization and the preparations for direct action.

The latest development of the Socialist Soviet campaign will be given in the later chapter on the Third International.

CHAPTER IV

Socialism and Labor in France *

We have already spoken of the brilliant French Utopian Socialists whose ideas were so influential with Karl Marx, though he did not acknowledge their influence upon him. The influence of Guesde at the time of the founding of the Second International has already been referred to. There were at that early time two parties in the Socialist movement, who were called the Possibilists and the Impossibilists, according as they accepted or did not accept any modifications in the present organization of society. In 1893 as many as forty Socialists were elected to the Chamber of Deputies. Even Socialists who approved of taking part in parliamentary life were for the most part opposed to having Socialist leaders accept office in the government ministries. In fact, some of the ablest Socialist leaders were read out of the party on account of accepting portfolios in the ministry. This was the case with Millerand in 1904, and with Viviani and Briand in 1906. In the first decade of the century the parliamentary Socialists advocated the dis-establishment of the Church, the secularization of education, labor legislation and the diminution of the army. The increased voting power of the party is shown by comparison of the 20,000 votes in 1885 with the 1,400,000 votes in 1914 when the Socialists had about one-sixth of the total votes.

It was in 1877 that the Socialist organization began and that their organ, "L'Egalité," was started to promote Marxian ideas. Socialism was indorsed by the labor union congress at Marseilles in 1879 and soon after a Socialist Labor Party was founded, which took part without any success in the elections of 1881. Its first real political victory was in 1893, when they polled 487,000 votes and elected forty representatives. As in Italy, the Socialists gained great influence in the municipal elections, especially in those of the large cities.

In 1912, 282 cities and towns came under the control of the Socialists. In great contrast to the condition in Germany is the relation of labor to the Socialist Party in France. For a long time there was very little contact between the two radical groups. The French labor movement, being Syndicalist and not trade union in character, and relying on the general strike as a weapon,

* See Addendum, Part I.

was out of sympathy with the political action of the Socialist Party. It was only the approach of the war that led to closer contact between the "Confédération Générale du Travail" and the Socialist Party, as we shall see. Consequently, in the matter of law-making in the interest of labor, in the matter of parliamentary influence, the labor Confederation was quite negligible before the war.

France has no large trade union organization, comparable with those of America and Great Britain. Business and labor are not organized in the same way, nor are the problems of labor considered as in these two countries largely on the basis of evolutionary processes. The struggle between employers and employees is not being abridged. The possibility of immediate and violent revolutionary action is continually in mind. The "hot-air" revolutionists are not held in check by a mass of practical wage-earners. The various Syndicates composing the "Confédération Générale du Travail" are practically at one in their policies with the Socialist Party, if one can speak of a Socialist policy in view of the many sections of the party each with different policies. At the same time the practical French character leads the Confederation to draw back at the last moment from extreme measures. The Syndicalist theory includes the class struggle and the abolition of the State as its ultimate aim and direct action through the general strike and sabotage as the means for realizing the change by which all industry shall be in the hands of the producers.

The Confédération Générale du Travail is composed of two kinds of federations: one is the national federations of crafts and the other the departmental federations of joint local organizations. The departmental federation has for its main object propaganda, among other aims for "the general social transformation." Communications from the C. G. T. with affiliated bodies are addressed to both the national and departmental federations, most of the latter having their headquarters in local Bourse halls. These organizations have not all the character of trade unions.

The similarity between the aims of the Syndicalist leaders and those of the Socialists makes it possible for a Socialist organ to represent them both. The paper "L'Humanité," the Socialist daily, has recently been supplemented by another Socialist organ "Le Proletaire."

The fact that Syndicalism is opposed to taking part in parliamentary life is one of its points of difference with the conservative wing of the Socialists. The greater community of views with the more revolutionary Socialists, includes opposition to community ownership and control of industry.

The attitude of the Confederation is expressed in the following statement issued in April, 1919:

"The Confédération Générale du Travail to Public Opinion. To the Workers.

"From August, 1914, to November, 1918, we were told repeatedly that we were fighting the war of right. This assurance implied that peace would confer upon the nations the liberty of self-determination and that it would be based on general disarmament, the only possible method of liquidating the debts of war.

"To-day these solemn promises are being broken. Our diplomats offer us a plan of a League of Nations which is not the society of nations described in the Fourteen Points of President Wilson. The peoples of the whole world in their thirst for justice have acclaimed these fourteen propositions. We have made them ours.

"The French working class, faithful to its conception of "war against war," rises against the sabotage of peace.

"On coming out of torment, the nations cannot be condemned to have no other object than the payment of taxes destined to support the burden of armament.

"The Confédération Générale du Travail condemns any foreign policy of blockade, of force, of diplomatic or armed intervention.

"It recalls the formula of the French Revolution: 'Each nation by itself has the right to make its laws, the inalienable right to change them; to wish to despoil a foreign people of that right is to become the enemy of the human race.'

"The C. G. T. vigorously protests the expedition against Russia, a friendly country against which no declaration of war has ever been made.

"The continuation of this policy of intervention makes France a power guarding the privileges and the reactionary institutions of all countries.

"The working class, the French people, can never subscribe to this humiliating and dishonorable attitude.

"Since liberty of thought and opinion was the very foundation of the declaration of the rights of man, the C. G. T. appeals to public opinion, to the conscience of the trade union organizations, to agitate against this state of things.

"The C. G. T. condemns any continuation of the war, and urgently demands the conclusion of a real peace to which all peoples can subscribe."

In its Congress held at Lyons during July, 1919, the Confédération Générale du Travail by a vote of 1,393 against 586 repudiated Bolshevism and upheld Jouhoux, its patriotic leader and secretary who opposed the proposed general strike of July 21st, which had been called as a protest against the blockade of Russia and as a mark of sympathy with Bolshevism. Consequently, on July 19th, the strike was officially countermanded by the Confederation, and Italy was left practically alone to carry it out on a large scale.

In a notable speech of Merrheim, also, like Jouhoux, a Syndicalist leader and therefore supposed to be an advocate of Bolshevism, he described his meeting with Lenin at the famous Zimmerwald Conference in 1915. At that time the Germans were only forty kilometres from Paris and France was in danger of perishing. Lenin worked hard to persuade Merrheim to return to France and declare a general strike as a war against war. This would have put France at Germany's mercy. From that moment Merrheim says that he became the enemy of Lenin and Trotzky.

At the same time the Confederation's Congress passed a resolution ordering the Syndicalist transportation organizations to refuse to handle any shipments of farms and ammunition and other stores that were intended for the use of the anti-Bolshevik armies of Kolchak and Denikin in Russia. This order was obeyed and was paralleled by action of the port workers and seamen in Italy.

The Confederation also put forth a manifesto based on a theory of Revolutionary Syndicalism, which differed from the Bolshevist plan in its method, because it forbids the use of conspiracy, of minority terrorism and the bringing on of a state of anarchy. Since then the Confederation has taken another step forward. (American Labor World, Feb. '20.)

FRENCH LABOR'S RECONSTRUCTION PLAN

In the "American Labor World" for February, 1920, Wm. English Walling outlines the plan of the C. G. T. for the reconstruction of France. Mr. Walling says: "The French project is perhaps the first reconstruction plan the world has seen which rests upon economic and not upon political democracy. It aims frankly to bring about by gradual and by peaceful means the substitution of industrial democracy in place of the present political state and the control of that state by private or capitalistic interests."

The new project consists not in a program of reforms but in a new method of evolving such a program. Let the C. G. T. speak for itself:

> "The C. G. T., representing organized labor, examined the general problems that confronted the country immediately after the armistice and pointed out in a general way the solution of these problems through a National Economic Council.
>
> "To its proposition to create this National Economic Council with the duty of confronting these difficult and essential problems the government replied only by offering to enact a grotesque caricature of the project. The General Confederation of Labor then decided itself to constitute an Economic Council of Labor.
>
> "The C. G. T. intends to have recourse to the new form of organization and to introduce, by new methods, a changed direction into the entire economic activity of the country.
>
> "In order to assure to the organism which it has created the necessary maximum of competency and authority, the C. G. T. has appealed to the following organizations of consumers and technicians, all of which have agreed to give it their undivided support:
>
> "National Federation of Co-operatives;
>
> "National Federation of Government Employees and Functionaries.
>
> "Union of Technicians of Industry, Commerce and Agriculture.
>
> "The Economic Council of Labor thus constituted is placed under the protection of the C. G. T. The end pursued is to contribute to economic reconstruction by means of practical principles aimed solely at the common good and giving to labor a just share in the management and control of production and distribution.

"Such work cannot be the result of fragmentary studies and discontinuous efforts."

Hence the establishment of this permanent council.

Most remarkable in this new plan is the appeal to "the common good" and not to the "class struggle." French labor here repudiated not only the Bolshevism which now completely dominates the French Socialist Party but also the whole Marxist "class struggle" dogma which underlies the entire political Socialist movement of Continental Europe and America. Undoubtedly the C. G. T. would still claim that it adheres to the "class struggle" but its new interpretation converts that doctrine into industrial democracy.

The C. T. G. then proceeds to throw over a second reactionary dogma of orthodox Marxism — the proposition that the problem of production is now solved and that only the problem of a more equal distribution remains.

On the contrary, the French labor unions base their new project primarily on the proposition that the problem of production is not solved and that the present government and capitalistic methods cannot solve it. Therefore the new project.

Let us again give the floor to the C. G. T.:

> "The salvation of industry demands organization for increased production. This organization for increased production can only be realized by appealing for the help of (1) those who are participating in production itself, workingmen and the technical and managerial staff; (2) those who have, or rather should have, as their professional task the co-ordination of various activities — the government functionaries and employees, and (3) finally, those who represent the interests of the consumers — the co-operators.
>
> "Increased production is possible only under two conditions:
>
> > "First, it must be organized in such a way that the natural resources, the capacities of the people, the mechanical equipment of industry and the instrumentalities of exchange shall be exploited to the full, and that everybody shall participate in the labor which produces the objects necessary to the life of the individual and of society.
> >
> > "Second, it is necessary that the producers, whose interests have been hitherto denied or not fully recog-

nized, should have the certainty that their labor is for the benefit of all society and not for the benefit of private interests.

"In adopting the principle of industrialized nationalization the Economic Council of Labor does not by any means intend to perpetuate or to strengthen the present tendency toward governmentalism which has done practically nothing to justify the hopes that have been placed upon it.

"The nationalization which the labor movement demands consists in putting into the hands of the combined producers and consumers the means of production and exchange of which they have been dispossessed to the profit of a few."

What are prospects that the plan of French Labor will receive a fair hearing and perhaps a fair trial?

These prospects are excellent because of the fact that France is in a more difficult economic position than any other country of western Europe — and also because of the fact that the government has offered no plan whatever for dealing effectively with the situation.

The C. G. T. believes that France is headed towards bankruptcy and that the government has devised no method to save the country.

"A year after the end of hostilities there has been no improvement in the economic situation of the country. The continued rise in the cost of living is in itself a sufficient barometer of the disorder throughout the industry of any country. No measure has been proposed which might even be conceived as promising to put an end to this disorder; and to face the terrible financial burdens of France, the only plan devised by the government is the endless issue of banknotes. No general plan for industrial reconstruction has been devised and there has been no serious effort to put an end to speculation and to tax the scandalous profiteering that continues in France (as in other countries)."

French Labor is aware that its project, though constructive and democratic, is also revolutionary.

"The organizations of producers and consumers which compose the new council, have weighed the immensity of the task to be accomplished. The new order must arise out of the disorder of the regime that is passing away. . . .

> To disarm the State while making it evolve towards the time when it will no longer be anything more than the representative of the collective organizations of production and distribution — to take away from the hands of capital the direction of industry — such is the work to be accomplished."

The ultimate aim of the C. G. T. plan for social reconstruction may be revolutionary. The method proposed is evolutionary. The government is not to be overthrown; on the contrary, it is to be made to evolve towards that time when it will meet the requirements of industrial democracy.

The new project of the C. G. T. is to be compared with the constructive plans of British labor unions.

A slight amendment to Mr. Walling's comparison between the plans of French and British would be that the French plan is far more like that of the National guilds of Great Britain than that of the trade unions.

The official point of view of the American Socialist party as to the attitude of French Socialists is expressed in the following statement in the American Labor Year Book for 1919–20.

French Socialism During the War

"In France as in other European countries Socialism passed through a profound crisis during the war. But in France the crisis was more serious than elsewhere, because from the morrow of the declaration of war the abdication of the French Socialist Party was complete, and it was only after long tenacious efforts on the part of obscure party members that French Socialism returned to the principles and tactics of opposition to the war, class struggle, internationalism and revolution.

"A few months before the outbreak of the war, in May, 1914, the party won a great victory at the legislative elections, receiving some 1,400,000 votes and electing 100 deputies. The party had at that time 72,000 dues-paying members, and its daily paper, "L'Humanité," printed 150,000 copies daily.

"The assassination of Juarès and the declaration of war were two mortal blows for the party. The deputies and leaders of the party could not or dared not resist the wave of chauvinism. The parliamentary group voted the military credits without discussion, accorded unlimited confidence to the bourgeois government, and joined the "Union Sacrée" (political truce), thus disavowing its political past and renouncing Socialism. Two Socialist deputies, Jules and Marcel Sembat, entered on August 28, 1914, the bourgeois ministry.

"To justify their attitude the Socialist leaders invoked the "national defense theory." They declared that France had been attacked by Germany and that Socialists should participate in a war of defense, help defeat imperialist Germany, abolish Prussian militarism and establish a just and democratic peace.

"This treason of the Socialist leaders led to the collapse of the entire party. Those who remained clear-visioned and faithful to Socialism could not make their voices heard; all civil liberties were suppressed, meetings were forbidden, the censor blanked in the newspapers every expression of a point of view different from the official and governmental view of the war.

"The party, most of whose members were mobilized, had lost its best forces. The locals and federations no longer met. Political life was suspended. For a year it was a veritable eclipse of Socialism.

"Toward the middle of 1915, when the majority of the party was increasing its responsibilities by approving the entry of Albert Thomas into the ministry (May 22, 1915) and subscribing to the policy of the capitalist rulers, Socialist and trade union men began to raise their voices in protest.

"The locals began to meet again, letters from the front told of the sufferings of the combatants and revealed the horror of the massacres, the mistakes of the generals, the horrible waste of every kind. Discontent increased, the spirit of criticism reawoke. The flag of opposition was raised in the party by the Federation of the Haute-Vienne which in June sent to the other federations of the party a circular letter calling attention to the attitude of Liebknecht and his friends in Germany, recalling the decisions of the international congresses, and proposing to take advantage of any opportunity for peace.

"The spirit of opposition grew in the ranks of the party. A group of Russian Socialists, among them Leon Trotzky, sustained the international elements and helped their propaganda. Bourderon, Loriot, Rappoport, Louis Saumonneau, were the spokesmen of the Extreme Left. Longuet, Pressemane, Mistral, Mayeras, Verfeuil, Delepine, Frossard, Maurin, and others were the spokesmen of the more moderate Left which was forming.

"The Zimmerwald Conference with German and other Socialists, met on September 5, 1915. Bourderon, of the Socialist Party, and Merrheim, secretary of the Metal Workers' union, represented the French working class.

"Wide approval of Bourderon's and Merrheim's attitude was expressed. The Committee for the Resumption of International Relations was founded, and undertook propaganda for peace and for the reconstitution of the International. There were disputes in all the federations; the party shook itself out of its torpor. The Permanent Administrative Committee of the party (C. A. P.) became disturbed, and on November 6 passed a resolution repudiating the action of the Zimmerwald Conference.

"The National Congress of the party met on December 25, 1915 (the National Councils of the French Socialist Party are gatherings of the officials of the various departmental federations; the Congresses are gatherings of representatives elected by the party members); the Left and Extreme Left both made their protests heard, but once more the Left capitulated, and voted with the majority whose resolution passed by 1,736 votes against the 76 Zimmerwaldians, with 102 abstentions.

"For the first time the Left came out firmly at the National Council on April 9, 1916, but the majority resolution was passed by 1,996 votes to 960.

"The Kienthal Conference met April 24, 1916. Three French Socialist deputies, Brizon, Raffin-Dugens, and Blanc, were present. On June 24th the three voted against the military credits for the first time, and their act created a stir in the country.

"The minority had founded a weekly, "Le Populaire," on May 1, 1916, and it became the organ of the Internationalists.

"A New National Council met August 7, 1916. The majority had 1,837 votes, the minority 1,081. To intensify the minority propaganda, the Committee for the Defense on International Socialism was founded.

"It was impossible to express the minority point of view openly in the press, for the censor suppressed " subversive " articles, so, in November, the minority published secretly a pamphlet expressing its thesis (partial responsibility of all nations in the war; opposition to the hate campaigns and to participation in bourgeois ministries; immediate resumption of international relations with Socialists even of enemy countries; immediate peace on basis of no annexation as the only means of saving France from destruction; international tribunal to settle questions of indemnities and of Alsace-Lorraine). This was signed by thirty-one deputies and by eight members of the C. P. A.

"At the National Congress in December, 1916, the vote stood 1,537 to 1,407. The forces of the minority were steadily increasing. In reality the minority was already the majority, but the party leaders voted as majority votes the votes of the federations of the invaded provinces, which could not be consulted. At the meeting of the National Council on March 3d, the vote was 1,556 to 1,337.

"Then the Russian Revolution broke out in mid-March, giving the internationalist elements an irresistible impulse. A telegram from Camille Huysmans announcing the convocation of the International Conference at Stockholm May 15th was answered on April 27th by the majority of the C. A. P. by a refusal to participate. The National Conference of the Minoritaires met at Paris May 6th to protest, and three weeks later, May 29th, the National Council voted unanimously to join the Conference at Stockholm. The internationalists had won their victory.

"Following this victory the Right Wing Majoritaires shifted position and disavowed the decision. The government refused passports, and the old struggle was resumed. At the National Council in October, 1917, the two factions preserved their respective force, the Zimmerwaldians obtaining 118 votes for a separate motion. Another National Council in February showed no change.

"Le Populaire" became a daily evening paper in April, 1918, under the direction of Jean Longuet; and the July, 1918, National Council at last gave a clear majority to the internationalists, as follows:

Longuet resolution (Moderate Left)	1,544
Renaudel resolution (Conservative Right)	1,172
Loriot resolution (Extreme Left)	152

"Two months later, the National Congress confirmed this result. Marcel Cachin supplanted Renaudel as editor of the official party daily "L'Humanité." The internationalists gained the majority of the C. A. P. and took the leadership of the paty.

"The party and its journals made rapid progress under the new leadership as the following figures show:

Dues-Paying Members of the Party

July, 1914	92,000
December, 1915	17,000
December, 1916	18,000
December, 1917	24,000
December, 1918	36,000
August 1919	102,000

"L'Humanite," which had fallen to less than 50,000 copies per day, reached 300,000 during the June, 1919, strikes, and maintains an average of 200,000. "Le Populaire" reached 100,000 during the strikes, and maintains a circulation of 60,000. "Le Journal du Peuple," which unites Socialist and Syndicalist elements of the extreme left, prints 50,000 copies daily." (Boris Souvarine.)

Addendum

"At the Congress held in April, 1919, the Socialist Party voted to remain in the Second International with the proviso "that those Socialists who are Socialists only in name" be expelled from it. The motion of Loriot to join the Third (Moscow) International immediately was defeated with 894 votes against 270. The Congress also adopted an electoral program of immediate demands which included among others the demands for the convocation of a constituent assembly, the granting of universal suffrage, the initiative and proportional representation, a single legislative chamber, decentralization of administration, representation of workers in the management of industrial affairs, nationalization of essential industries and advanced labor legislation. It also went on record against the ratification of the Versailles Peace and the proposed League of Nations by a vote of 1,420 to 114.

"Paul Faure, editor of "Le Populaire," drew up a declaration which outlined the party policy on several important matters. This declaration, which was adopted by the Congress in the form of a resolution, declared against the punitive peace against Germany and greeted the German republic, declaring "that it (the party) is entirely with the true German Socialists who courageously endeavor to give the real labor and Socialist complexion to their revolution," and continues, "it bows before their heroes and will not cease to honor the memory of Karl Liebknecht, Rosa Luxemburg and Kurt Eisner, who have crowned with the martyr's laurels three lives wholly devoted to the struggle against empire and to the liberation of the universal proletariat." After extending fraternal greeting to the Russian Soviet government, the resolution explained the party's position on the policy of the Russian Soviets. "The Socialist Party," it explains, "recalls in the same way that its thinkers from Karl Marx to Jaurès have always recognized the necessity of the dictatorship of the proletariat on the morrow of the triumphant revolution. This latter had naturally the need of force not only to establish itself and accomplish its work, but to shatter the inevitable attempts of the counter-revolution." The declaration later declares for unmitigated opposition to bourgeois control, the systematic and symbolical refusal of the military and civil credits and the whole of the budget and the absolute autonomy of the Socialist Party as the political party of the working class, excluding naturally all possibility of alliance or electoral coalition in the case of a first or only ballot. It concluded with the following significant words: "It is with the pre-occupation of re-establishing the real unity of doctrine and action of the proletariat that the party declares to those who do not recognize these ideals, and particularly to the members of Parliament who may continue to vote for the credits of bourgeois governments, that they will thus be putting themselves outside their party."

"Two Communist groups were formed as a result of this Congress. Both are so far committees to organize "Parties in agreement with the Third International," and are led in the main by Syndicalists. Loriot and his adherents of the extreme left propose to remain in the Socialist Party, believing that they will soon control the policies of the party. At a recent meeting of the National Council, it was decided that only such candidates should be placed on the party ticket in the forthcoming general parliamentary elections as are opposed to the ratification of the Versailles Treaty and are in favor of the recognition of the Russian Soviet government.

"The parliamentary elections of November, 1919, resulted in a victory, but a disappointment for the French Socialists. While their total vote mounted to 1,750,000, a gain of about 40 per cent. over that in 1914, their representation in Parliament, because of a complicated system of disproportionate representation and gerrymandering, was lowered from 105 to 55. If their representation in the Chamber had been proportionate to their total vote, they would have elected 160 deputies. The Haute Vienne, where the internationalist revival began, was the only department in which the Socialists elected their entire ticket, bettering even their record of 1914. In addition, a number of anti-war and Extreme Left Socialists were elected from other departments.

"In the municipal elections held two weeks later the Socialists made greater gains still, electing mayors in the great industrial cities Lille, Roubaix and Tourcoing in the devastated district, in Strassburg, and in several jumped in two weeks from 28 to 35 per cent. of the total.

"The French Syndicalists in the main favored the war, recognized it as a war of national defense and entered a "civil truce" with the government. The Syndicalist daily, "La Bataille Syndicaliste," was frequently so chauvinist that it was severely criticized by the Socialist organs.

"The Internationalist and anti-war minority in the Labor Confederation as in the Socialist Party was growing in influence under the leadership of Merrheim of the metal-workers. At the first Congress of the Confederation in July, 1918, the internationalist faction was so strong that the majority leaders were obliged to accept a compromise resolution embodying the demands which the minority made on the leadership of the Confederation throughout the war, especially dealing with the question of the participation of the Confederation in the International. The next Congress, held in September, 1919, showed the same tendency to return to the traditional revolutionary policy of French Syndicalism. The Confederation numbered 600,000 members before the war. It claims now 1,500,000 members.

"The Confederation has on many occasions joined the Socialist Party in important proclamations and manifestoes, demanding the restoration of civil liberties, hailing the German Revolution, opposing intervention in Russia, etc. The Confederation also decided to participate on July 21st in the twenty-four-hour demonstration general strike against the invasion of Russia and for the democratization of the political and economic institutions of France. On the eve of the strike, the Executive Committee of the Confederation declared the strike off, presumably because the government promised to withdraw troops from Russia and decrease the cost of living."

The French Socialist Congress in Strassburg

The National Congress of the French Socialist Party was called for January 25–29 in Strassburg to consider the following questions:

First. The political situation; (a) the general election; (b) the parliamentary policy of the party; (c) organization of propaganda throughout the country.

Second. The international situation; (a) resolutions of the last International Conference, and (b) the Geneva Congress.

Before the Congress met it seemed as if it would be dominated by the extreme revolutionary groups. But the proposition to affiliate with the Third Moscow International, advanced by this group, was defeated. So was a similar proposition of the Right Wing to maintain affiliation with the Second International. The policy of the party was expressed in a resolution by which the executive committee was instructed to enter into negotiations with the Socialist parties already affiliated with the Third International, for the purpose of convening, in collaboration with the Independent Socialist Party of Germany, and with the Swiss and Italian Socialist parties, an International Socialist Conference for the purpose of forming a Third International composed of those parties in every country that based their action upon the traditional principles of Socialism. The executive committee at once sent out delegates of the party to Great Britain, Germany, Russia, Italy, Spain and Switzerland to report the action of the Strassburg Congress and to obtain their views on the reconstruction of the International. The sentiment of the Strassburg meeting was to reaffirm certain general policies. That the Socialist Party is a class party; that it condemns Socialist participation in capitalized industries; that it undertakes to organize the proletariat for the complete conquest of the public powers by every means, not excluding mass action; that it entirely approves of the Soviet government of Russia. What the party is at present aiming at is to reorganize the battle-front of International Socialism broken by the war. It declined to accept the leadership of Russia in this task, though it is willing to accept Russia's co-operation. The ambassadors that have been sent out to advise on their return under what conditions the conference that is desired by the Independent Socialists of Germany as well as by the French Socialists shall be convened, and to do so as quickly as possible.

CHAPTER V

Socialism and Labor in Belgium

The main outlines of the movement in Belgium have already been sketched and it is seen to have been very much closer in its organization to the German than to the French plan. After the organization of the Labor Party in 1885 it gave itself up for several years to the fight for universal suffrage. In 1893, after years of unsuccessful propaganda, a general strike, which brought out 200,000 workmen, was staged as a demonstration in favor of suffrage, and resulted in the granting of a limited form of franchise which resulted in a Socialist vote of 345,000 and the election of twenty-nine parliamentary representatives. In 1913 a general strike was called in order to obtain better electoral laws.

The wonderfully strong organization of the Belgian Party led to its being considered the strongest element in the international, and the making of Brussels the center of the International Secretariat. The most active Socialist leader at that time, as well as the most radical, was Edouard Anseele, a born militant, as well as an able business man. On the other hand, the most scholarly and able parliamentary leader was Vandervelde, who shared with Huysmans the leadership of the International Socialist Bureau. It must not be understood that at that time the trade unions or syndicates, which are more important in the commercial life of Belgium than in any other country, were all affiliated with the Socialist Party. This was far from being the case. A large section was affiliated with the clerical party; another with the liberal party, while a third remained independent. Of the total membership before the war, however, about three-fourths were affiliated with the Socialists.

In the development of the co-operative movement in Europe it is probable that the example of its wonderful success in Belgium has been the strongest single reason for its wide spread, first in England and finally in Russia. In the matter of Socialist programs, the very breadth of the movement has made the political program of the Belgian Labor Party about the broadest and the most valuable to study of all the National Labor Party programs. It is interesting to compare this program, which is published by Hunter ("Socialists at Work," pp. 172–177), with the famous Erfurt Social Democratic program of the German Party, issued in October, 1891, and which has served as a basis for German Socialist work ever since, and as an excellent short embodiment of a moderate interpretation of Karl Marx (p.169).

CHAPTER VI

Socialism and Labor in Holland

The recent closing of its frontier on the German side by the Dutch government, in order to prevent the inroad of Bolshevist propagandists, has called attention to an extraordinary situation in Holland; unexpected on account of the thrifty and cautious individualism of the Dutch character. During the war German propaganda was intense in Holland and gained control of banks, of big business and of political and intellectual leaders. The German policy of using Bolshevist agencies to disintegrate national sentiments and integrity found able exponents. Leading Dutchmen were tied to German apron-strings. Holland's international position makes the results important for us to understand, and to watch the Dutch government's struggle to prevent the possibility of a similar *coup d'etat* as that which Germany engineered in Russia through Lenine and Trotzky.

The Dutch leader of political Bolshevism is David Wijnkoop, who, we are informed, is a Jew. He and two other Communists, were elected in 1918 to represent Amsterdam in the Parliament, and he has been able to lead into the advocacy of revolutionary demands a considerable group of Socialists, Social Democrats and Laborites who do not belong to the Communist group. The effects on Labor programs in Holland is evident. The Social Democrat, Troelstra, is the leader in this radical swing.

The intellectual field is even more frankly invaded by Communism than it is in the United States. The presence of university leaders such as Mannoury, the mathematical professor, and Pannekoeke, the astronomer, on the executive board of the Communist Party, is a powerful aid to the spread of Bolshevik doctrines among the student body of every class. In the case of these men, the right to absolute freedom of speech and teaching has been raised by the government's refusal to appoint Dr. Pannekoeke to the professorship of astronomy at the University of Leiden.

As two further sources of danger among the Dutch themselves there are: The religious zealots, led by that fiery Communist preacher of the Dutch Reformed Church, Dr. Schermerhorn; and the sentimental idealists led by the greatest of living Dutch poets, Mme. Roland Holst, who urges the people " to rise and sacrifice themselves for the common good because it is the holocaust on the barricades that must bring peace on earth and good will among men."

The present Spartacan revolutionary movement in Germany is increasing the danger in Holland and intensifying the call for immediate action. Thus far there have been no overt acts except the strike engineered by the Communists that will now be described.

The central figure, however, in Dutch Socialism is still the same as it has been for over twenty years — Troelstra and his career must be sketched to explain the present situation. It was in 1894 that he and eleven others — known as the Twelve Apostles — founded the Social Democratic Labor Party of Holland, and entered politics, electing four members of Parliament in 1897, seven in 1901, nineteen in 1913, and twenty-two in the present Assembly. From the beginning it was troubled with both anarchist and Syndicalist elements, but they never gained control. In 1913 the question of allowing Socialists to take part in the ministry was decided in the negative at a party convention which definitely stated that "a party like the Socialist Labor Party, which in its origin, its nature and its aims, is diametrically opposed to the political domination of the capitalist class, is under no obligation to join a capitalist ministry." A small radical group broke away in 1909, calling itself the Social Democratic Party, claiming to be purely Marxian. It sent representatives to the Zimmerwald and Kienthal Conferences which the main body of Dutch Socialists had declined to recognize and it has now joined the Third (Moscow) International, changing its name to the Communist Party, and taking the usual anti-patriotic, anti-war, anti-parliamentary and ultra-international attitude. Meanwhile Troelstra continues to advocate for the main body of the S. D. L. P. participation in parliamentary life, even though it is unrepresented in the ministry. In this it is supported by the Federation of Trade Unions which backs up its political work. At present the Communists have three representatives in the Second Chamber (Wijnkoop, Van Ravesteyn) and the Social Democratic Labor Party has twenty-two members, under Troelstra and Schaper.

The present crisis has been brought on by the strike at Amsterdam and Rotterdam, which began on February 14th, by the Netherland Federation of Transport Workers. It had been threatening for some time and had received the support of the Social-Democratic Labor Party. But the official organ of this Socialist Party, the "Volk," which had previously approved the strike movement, withdrew its support on February 14th, after it had been shown by the Algemeen Handelsblad that Messrs. E. Bouwman and H. Sneevliet, chairman and treasurer respectively of the Federation, had been the guests of the Secret Communist Congress held at Amsterdam on February 3d, and following days, when they accepted the direction of the Communist Party for the Labor movement and pledged themselves to organize strikes in Holland as part and parcel of the Bolshevist movement in Western Europe and to give such strikes as far as possible a revolutionary character. "By associating the strike of the transport workers with the Bolshevist movement," says the "Volk" (14), "they have sold and betrayed the interests of the workers in question entrusted to their care, they have deceived the leaders of the League, and played such a double game that there can no longer be any agreement between them and us (meaning the Socialists of the S. D. L. Party) with regard to this conflict. While on the one hand, Sneevliet and Bouwman were exploiting the strike in the interest of the Communist movement, Bouwman, on the other, was issuing a strike manifesto in which he declared the whole dispute to be purely a question of wages and labor conditions which would be ended and done with the moment the employers agreed to concede their demands."

The S. D. L. Party does not propose to have Holland come under the heel of the Bolshevist dictatorship. (Dutch Socialist Press in the "Political Review," February 27th.)
and the character of her business the transport workers are the

The food supplies for Germany, relief for Austria and Hungary, were all held up by the strike. Owing to Holland's position key-note and determining factor of her commerce. It is freely stated that the strike may end in revolution. The head emissary from Russia, in charge of the International propaganda and relations, appears to be Rutgers, who represented the Dutch revolutionary Socialists at the organizing of the Third International in Moscow.

CHAPTER VII

Socialism and Labor in Scandinavia and Finland *

The three Scandinavian countries — Norway, Sweden, Denmark — and Finland must be considered together because of the close interaction of their various labor and Socialist organizations. It is true that of the four Norway seems the more revolutionary and Denmark the more conservative, while Socialism of the less revolutionary type is more dominant in Sweden than in any of the rest of the group. In fact in Sweden the question of the day was whether the Socialist Party should not take upon itself the formation of a complete government instead of merely forming part of a coalition government. The leader of the Majority Socialists in Sweden, Branting, has long been known as one of the ablest leaders in Europe.

A movement is on foot to add to the above four nations of the league not only Iceland but the new Baltic states of Esthonia, Latvia and Lithuania, in a scheme for uniform Northern legislation and policy. It was announced in the "Reval Social-Demokrat" of January 27th that at the end of February a conference of the Socialists of Finland, Poland, Esthonia would be held for the purpose of discussing questions of general policy. This was to follow closely on the meeting of the Scandinavian Socialist Congress of December and the Scandinavian Labor Congress of January which are here reported.

Scandinavian Socialist Congress

A Congress of Scandinavian Socialists of the Left — the revolutionary branch of the party — met in Stockholm, December 8 and 10, 1919. It was attended by 143 delegates from Sweden, 107 from Norway and 18 from Denmark. The Norwegians, with Tranmael at their head, played a very prominent part. They advocated revolutionary methods in nearly all their speeches, Olaussen, the principal leader after Tranmael, especially stating that the final struggle must be fought out with arms.

The Congress split up into Communists and Syndicalists. The revolutionary methods proposed by the Norwegians were not well received by the Swedes, one of whom, Severin, asked Tranmael: "Why, if the Norwegian Labor Party is so unanimous in this

---

* See Addendum, Part I.

view, does it not raise a revolution in Norway, instead of coming to Sweden to talk about it?" The Swedish radical paper "Social-Demokraten" showed that the Bolsheviks and the Syndicalists, who formed the two big groups of the Congress, were hopelessly divided and could not come to any agreement. It appeared as if the Syndicalists were in the majority.

The final resolution showed that the Congress did not regard Moscow as "the new Mecca," as it postponed the question of adherence to the Third International for further deliberation. Owing to the same reason — the disagreement with the radical attitude of the Norwegian delegates — the negotiations for Scandinavian co-operation was also postponed.

There was a discussion of the relations between Scandinavian working-class organizations and world revolution, and of the duties, methods and forms of the trade union movement. Here, again, the Syndicalists carried the day against the Bolshevists, who lacked solidarity. Syndicalism showed signs of joining forces with the political Socialists of the Left.

Shortly before this the Communal elections in Norway had shown a decided veering of public sentiment away from revolutionary radicalism, resulting in a Socialist defeat as well as the defeat of the party of the Left. (Quotations from Swedish and Norwegian Press in the "Political Review," January 9, 1920.)

SCANDINAVIAN LABOR CONGRESS

More than a month after the Revolutionary Socialists of Scandinavia met at Stockholm, there was opened, on January 21st, at Copenhagen, the Ninth Scandinavian Labor Congress. Four hundred delegates were present, representing a million organized workers. Sweden sent 109 and Norway 76 delegates, and 3 came from Finland. The rest of the 400 represented Denmark. The foreign delegates were welcomed by the Danish Social Democratic Party.

The last previous Congress had been in Stockholm in 1912.

The matters dealt with by the Congress cover socialization, industrial democracy, the position as regards the International, future Scandinavian co-operation, mutual aid in trade disputes, social legislation, the high cost of living and co-operation. ("Social-Demokraten," 20, 22.)

Among the resolutions passed was one upholding the continuance of both political and trade union co-operation throughout

Scandinavia. Another expressed continued adherence to the Second International. Both these resolutions had large majorities.

The long resolution on socialization (only six votes, all Norwegian, against it) states that the aim of Social Democracy is to conquer economic and political power with the object of transferring the ownership of the means of production to the people and of socializing production. In order to attain this end the workers must organize themselves industrially as producers, co-operatively as consumers, and politically as citizens. The increased share of workers in the control of industry will be a useful preparation for the future, when Capitalism is replaced by Socialism, and it will also counteract the tendency toward bureaucracy now in evidence in large undertakings, whether public or private. Industrial democracy is, therefore, to be regarded as a step in the process of socialization.

Another resolution favored working for uniform social legislation in the four countries. (Scandinavian Press in the "Political Review," London, February 13, 1920.)

SOCIALISTS' CONGRESS IN FINLAND

A Congress of the Finnish Social-Democratic Party opened on December 10, 1919, in Helsingfors. The election of the committee resulted in fifty-eight for the Left Socialist list and ninety for the Socialists of the Right, showing that the Communists formed about one-third of the party. It was decided to support the present government in order to avoid bringing in a conservative government with a bourgeois coalition. The Congress also decided to continue to support the Second International. The Communist leaders threaten to split and form a separate party of action. The local Helsingfors Social-Democratic organization has already voted to leave the Second International without as yet joining the Third (Moscow) International.

The government has not agreed to the demand of the Socialists for a complete amnesty but has released 3,000 more prisoners and restored citizenship rights to 40,000 previously released. It is to be remembered that these prisoners were supposed to be supporters of the "Red Terror" which was suppressed by the "White Terror" when Finland expelled the Bolsheviks and established independence. The fear of subjugation by Lenine and Trotzky appears to be what is keeping the naturally revolutionary Finnish Socialists from becoming more generally Bolshevik. (Finnish Press in the "Political Review" of January 16, 1920.)

SWEDISH SOCIALIST CONGRESS

The Congress of the Social-Democratic Party of Sweden opened February 8, 1920, in Stockholm. In the opening speech Branting declared that now that power is in the hands of democracy, the Social Democrats must concentrate on the new problems of economic changes. If civilization is to be maintained immense changes will be necessary; building up as well as pulling down, and lessons may be learned from countries that have tried a dictatorship of the proletariat. Progress toward Socialism must not be through minority dictatorship, but must be based on democracy. The Congress refused to go on record as supporting in its political programme "a single-chamber system," such as at present forms the representative government of the country. For this expression it substituted "a democratic system of representation." In the discussion Branting maintained that it was by no means certain that the single-chamber system would prevail in the Socialist state. He thought that the much discussed and misunderstood Soviet system should be examined from the Social-Democratic point of view. There was perhaps something of value in the idea that groups of producers should as producers send representatives to an assembly other than one resulting from a general election. Such an assembly might be conceived as existing side by side with the popularly-elected chamber. (Nya Dagliga Allehanda, II.)

The Congress passed a resolution calling for an immediate discussion of the introduction of a system of industrial democracy. (Swedish Press in the "Political Review," March 5, 1920.)

COMPARATIVE CONDITIONS IN SCANDINAVIA

The Scandinavian Socialists acknowledge quite generally the weakness of the International — by which they mean the Second International — due to its "straddling" policy and to the weakness, they believe, of Social Democracy in England and France. The Third International is in danger of causing a schism in Scandinavia as everywhere else. Even Branting, the Swedish leader, while adhering to the Second International and protesting against the Soviet principle of dictatorship by a minority, has suggested a careful study of the Soviet system with the view of adopting some of its features.

Throughout Scandinavia there has been the same epidemic of strikes as elsewhere, with this difference, that lockouts by the employers have been quite frequent. There have also been organized conferences for attempted adjustments between aggregations of employers and workers. In no case, however, has there been any violence, though in many cases agreement has not been found possible.

In Denmark the workers are not by any means represented by one political and economic party. The Social Democrats (Socialist Party) represent the interests of the workers in the towns, the Radicals represent largely the agricultural workers, the Party of the Left the farmers, while the Conservatives represent the upper and middle classes of town and country. (Hovedstaden, 19, of Copenhagen, in "Political Review," February 13, 1920.) Thus far there is no very clear political economic outlook.

In Norway the extreme revolutionary tendency, noted in the case of the Norwegian delegates to both the Socialist and Labor Congress, just reported, was accentuated at a recent meeting of the Norwegian Labor Party in connection with a dispute between the Socialist leader, Buen, and the Extremist leader Tranmael.

Buen asked whether it was not the case that indifference, and not actual hostility, had lately been exhibited, by those in power in the Labor Party, towards the question of universal suffrage and parliamentary routine. Tranmael replied that the Social Democrats continued to take an interest in universal suffrage and would participate in the elections. At the same time they had no confidence in the efficacy of the Storting (the Parliament of Norway) as an instrument of Socialism, and would be glad to see it abolished. As long as the present system continued the Social Democrats would insist upon proportional representation and equal suffrage. Their aim, however, was a complete reconstruction of political life, "beginning in the workshops." The workers must appropriate the economic power.

Zinoviev, head of the Third (Moscow) International, in his manifesto, reproduced elsewhere names the most violent Bolshevist in Norway, the deputy, Hoglund, whom he compares to Liebknecht in Germany, as rendering incomparable service in Sweden to the Soviet cause.

With the great increase of power throughout Scandinavia of the Labor and Socialist elements in their more advanced form, it is a debatable question whether their Congresses will adhere to the old International that is to meet in Geneva on July 1st, or will pass over to the Soviet Third International of Moscow. Whatever they do there is hardly any question that parliamentary government in Scandinavia will be radically modified or superseded before very long.

The two most recent events in Scandinavia are the assumption of power by the Socialist Party in Sweden and the threat of the general strike in Denmark to coerce the King into changing his policy toward Socialism and labor.

On March 7th the Liberal Socialist Eden Cabinet resigned, as the Socialist members could no longer agree in policy with the liberal element. The Socialist Party had a considerable majority in Parliament. What had been anticipated for some time happened. The Socialist Party of the Right Wing decided to assume power. It made up a ministry composed entirely of Socialists, which was accepted by the King. H. Branting, lifelong leader of the Right Wing Socialists, became President of the Council. The opposition is made up at present mainly of the Left Wing Socialists, who are part of the Third (Moscow) International, and who call themselves Communists. There is no apparent intention on the part of the Socialists of overturning the present form of government. Insofar as any policy is concerned, the speeches and program previously outlined by Branting himself give the main outlines.

In Denmark, the King demanded, on March 29th, the resignation of the Zahle Cabinet. The situation was made tense by the fact that the Parliament was not in session. It was almost a *coup d'etat.* The King called upon the liberal leader, Neergaard, to form a cabinet. The Socialist and labor leaders at once decided to proclaim a general strike. For some time revolution was talked of and the proclaiming of a republic. The Socialist and radical elements forming the majority of Parliament were absolutely opposed to the proposed new ministry. The King decided to form a new cabinet under Liebe, who was acceptable to the Socialist and radical elements. The general strike was called off. It had succeeded in changing the political situation of the country. In other words, it is one of the first times that the general strike has passed out of the economic into the political field.

To explain the present situation in Norway as a result of a conservative reaction against the Communist movement, it is necessary to refer to the program of the Socialist Party in 1918, when it went over, by a considerable majority, to the Syndicalists led by Martin Tranmael, and declared in favor of the "red" communist Kienthal program. At that time he outlined a program of Soviet Communist Revolution, to which the Socialist Party then committed itself. It involved the destruction of parliamentary government by direct class action; if necessary by a minority.

"Hitherto," he says, "strikes have concerned themselves chiefly with the special demands of certain unions; but they will develop into revolutionary and political measures. By means of the general strike every man and woman will be forced to take sides for or against labor's ideal of organized society. When not only the industrial workers and artisans, but the transportation workers, the crofters, the farm laborers and small farmers, and the fishermen, have been organized for class war, the position of labor will be very strong. If then the upper classes are deprived of the support they have had in the military, the chances for a successful revolution ought to be very good indeed."

He advocates Soviet councils in place of a constitutional assembly. He favors workmen's and soldiers' councils, based on labor unions and social organizations. He would have soldiers' councils at first merely for the sake of getting the protection of the bayonets for the revolution, but after the fight is won, he would have only workmen's councils and the bourgeois would be completely dissolved and disfranchised.

The first step in organization by the Socialist Party looking toward the carrying out of their revolutionary program was in fact this organization of soldiers' Soviets for the contamination of the army.

Some time after this, in September, 1919, the Commission appointed by the Norwegian National Organization of Labor Unions, and the Socialist Party, to investigate the participation of workmen in industrial management, reported recommending the establishment of industrial councils. This report was given in the "Morgenbladet" of Christiania, of September 6th.

It recommends the establishment of industrial councils in all concerns employing as many as ten persons, to consist of three persons where there are not over fifty employees, five persons for between fifty and 100, up to nine members for concerns employing more than 200 persons. The council shall represent as far as possible the different branches in each concern, including not only manual but professional and clerical workers, who shall also take part in the voting by secret ballot. The council is to be elected for a year. It shall look out for the interests of the employees and work towards socialization of industry. It shall demand for the workingmen the right to elect their foreman, and for the council itself the right to influence the opinion of officials in the company, and to influence the management and distribution of the work, the purchase and utilization of machinery.

The council shall look after the housing and maintenance of workers; shall inform itself with regard to the business and technical management, with access to the books of the company, shall exercise the right of mediation in cases of dispute between employees and managers; and shall insist on having its decisions respected by the employers, if necessary through support of the labor unions.

DOCUMENTS

A SWEDISH PARTY CORRESPONDENCE

We print below all the documents in the negotiations that were conducted by the executive representation of the Social Democratic Party of the Left (P. L.) with the management of the Right Socialist Party, with regard to the requirements for carrying out the great democratic and socialistic demands of the working class. It is clear from these documents where the blame for the failure of these negotiations must be laid, namely, with the management of the Right Socialists, who, in order to continue their shameful alliance with the enemies of the working class, are inventing all sorts of imaginary obstructions of a "democratic" character, in the way of a co-operation with their class comrades of the Left.

I. The Offer of the Social Democratic Party of the Left (P. L.)

In this revolutionary era, which is now raising one nation after the other into a full political and social democracy, the working class of Sweden also demands that our country shall take its place among the democratic nations of the world. If this is to be realized, the working class must, as far as is feasible, advance on a common front against all the reactionary enemies of society. The necessity of removing all obstructions in the path of this realization impels the Swedish S. D. P. L. to do all in its power to arrange a common action by a united working class. With this object, the S. D. P. L. asks the S. D. L. whether it will recognize a socialistic plan of action, for the impending struggles, of the following general content:

1. General political and communal suffrage, without restriction, for all men and women over twenty years old.

2. Abolition of the Upper House of the Riksdag.
3. A Republican Constitution.
4. A maximum of eight hours' work a day.
5. Complete liquidation of the military system.
6. Socialization of banks and the most important branches of industry, as well as workers' control of industry.
7. Substantial reductions in the land holdings of corporations and estates, and transfer of the land, with assured title, to the propertyless workers of the soil.
8. Complete right of public assembly and demonstration.

In order to secure the realization of these aims the S. D. P. L. is ready and willing to support a Socialist government that will accept this plan of action. Should the program not be realizable without the use of force, the S. D. P. L. invites the co-operation of the S. D. Workers' Party in a mass action to be inaugurated in the form of a general strike.

As the representatives of the S. D. P. L. are at present gathered in Stockholm, an answer is requested in the course of the day.

II. The Old Party is Afraid of "Bolshevism"

To the S. D. P. L.:

In answer to your communication the S. D. P. executive states the following:

That the party executive is always ready to offer its co-operation to secure the national or international solidarity of the working class in accordance with the general fundamental principles of Democratic Socialism; but that, since the party executive has had more and more occasion to observe the contradiction existing between a democratic solution of the problems of society, and a Bolshevist minority dictatorship, it would appear to behoove the S. D. P. L. to create the prerequisites for a practical political co-operation, by making a definite statement of its position with regard to the principles of democracy.

The party executive, in order to secure the introduction of democracy into the Swedish body politic, would greet with satisfaction a complete union of all the elements in our social system that are in principle and without reserve based on the foundations of democracy.

Yet the P. L.'s program of action contains points which in our opinion are manifestly of such nature as to require a reference of these questions, either in an election or a referendum, to the people. For this reason alone the party executive cannot recognize it as a basis for a common action to realize the reforms that should be immediately introduced.

Should the S. D. P. L. feel able to accept without reserve the already indicated democratic principles, and to adopt the minimum program set up by the S. D. Party executive as a basis for co-operation, the party executive would have not the slightest objection to working together with the S. D. P. L.

The S. D. Party Executive,

HJ. BRANTING.
GUSTAF MOELLER.

III. The Left Answers: Not Minority Dictatorship, But Complete Democracy

To the S. D. Party Executive:

In connection with your answer to our request of yesterday, touching the possibility of a common action by a united working class in the present situation, we have the honor to state the following:

Let us first emphasize that our party has never come out in favor of a minority dictatorship. The question of a dictatorship of the proletariat, already indicated in Karl Marx "Communist Manifesto," the basic document of modern Socialism, is for the present not a burning one in our country, at least not to the extent of allowing a difference of opinion on this question to preventing a co-operation when on all other matters there would be a possibility of such co-operation. We have clearly and distinctly, through our demand for a National Constituent Assembly, placed ourselves on the broadest democratic basis. We have surely in this way answered your objection with regard to what you call a "first requirement for a practical political co-operation."

Touching the minimum program you propose, we must make the general observation that it concerns itself almost exclusively with purely political reforms, neglecting the great social and economic demands which cannot or ought not to be postponed to an indefinite future in the present situation. Such proposals as were made by us in our minimum program — the socialization of the money system and of big industry, workers' control of industry, and the provisional solution of the land question — have not been considered at all in your program.

But even in connection with your political demands we must deplore that they provide no guarantees whatever for a speedy and thorough solution. We find, among other things, that such old democratic demands as a republic and a single legislative chamber, which have long since been accepted by the bourgeois circles of the country, have not seemed to you to be capable of immediate realization.

Instead, you point out that "binding assurances" should be given in advance by the state powers, regarding the removal of all disabilities in voting (but you seem to have forgotten the age restriction), while the question of a one-chamber system or of a republic should be decided either by a Riksdag constituted under the new election laws, or by a new popular election in accordance with those laws.

We believe, however, that Sweden's workers have learnt through long and bitter experience how much "assurances" and "promises" from the ruling classes are worth, and they would, in our opinion, be guilty of a serious mistake politically, if not of a crime against themselves and their future, if they should permit an opportunity for action to slip by, that might solve these questions at a single stroke.

As far as the only social demand in your program is concerned — that of the eight-hour day — we note that even its realization has been postponed without so much as a suggestion of a provisional solution. Particularly this omission must cause great discouragement among the entire Swedish working class.

To accept the minimum program you set up, as suggested by you in your communication, as a basis for our co-operation, would be impossible for use, for the reasons above-named. The program, which limits itself entirely to a bourgeois-democratic action, seems to be adapted rather for a continued co-operation with the liberal party than for a common basis for the entire Swedish working class, which would have been more natural.

Nevertheless, we hope, in spite of the form of your communication, that you may again consider whether there is no possibility for a common action between us, along lines that may lead more clearly and speedily to the democratic and social transformation that is desired by both the S. D. parties.

Should you find that a continued discussion is advisable, we suggest that it is desirable for both parties to appoint special representatives for the continuance of the negotiations.

The question as to the resources of power which the working

class must, in those demands which it advances, mobilize in their support — even if they should be of the limited nature proposed by you — would in such meetings require detailed examination.

We suggest the desirability of an early answer to this communication.

Stockholm, Nov. 16, 1918.

For the S. D. P. L.,
EXECUTIVE COMMITTEE.

IV. The Old Party Answers One Question When You Ask Them Another

To the S. D. P. L.:

In answer to your last communication we beg leave to say: To our plain question whether "you can without reserve accept the principles of democracy" you have replied that "our party has never been for a minority dictatorship," and that the question of a dictatorship of the proletariat "is not a burning one in our country at present." These are subterfuges that would be more in place in the notes of the old diplomacy than in a declaration of a party which, in accordance with its loudly proclaimed principles, should place a certain value upon straightforwardness. We must, therefore, again emphasize that the necessary prerequisite for a co-operation on our part is the unconditional renunciation of Bolshevism by your party. The Social Democratic Party's executive feels that it has the support of an overwhelming opinion among the Swedish working class, in declaring that it will not enter into any co-operation with Bolsheviks.

You have answered our question with regard to your attitude on our program of action, by saying that it is impossible for you "to accept it as a basis for co-operation as it stands." We herewith point out that this minimum program was adopted after a careful scrutiny by the political and craft leaders, with the specific purpose of bringing about the strongest possible rally of all the democratic forces in our country around it. Your Sunday resolution is a blow in the face to this unity thought and asks, on the contrary, a split in the front of democracy.

We, therefore, point out that in both the points we have drawn up the answers made by your executive have been either evasive or negative.

Stockholm, Nov. 18, 1918.

For the Executive Committee of the S. D. P.,
HJ. BRANTING.
GUST. MOLLER.

V. Final Reply From the Left: You Prefer Unity With the Liberal Party to Unity Within the Working Class

To the S. D. P. Executive:

At a meeting held yesterday, of the S. D. P. L. Committee and the Y. P. S. L. Committee, as well as the Riksdag members and the representatives in Stockholm, as well as other representatives, it was unanimously decided to send the following communication to the S. D. P. executive concerning the question of unity in the workers' movement:

As a prerequisite for your co-operation you demand in your last communication of November 18th that the S. D. P. L. "should unreservedly renounce Bolshevism." The answer of the S. D. P. L. is a categorical negative, if by this means you seek to secure the party's moral or practical support for the policy of intervention and isolation inaugurated by Entente capitalism against Soviet Russia. The latter is a brutal denial both of the right of national self-determination as well as of the solidarity of the international proletariat, and, if it should prove successful, would be equivalent to a triumph for Russian and European reaction. Our party, furthermore, declines to set itself up in judgment over the fighting methods used by the November Revolution in Russia, which are the result partly of the counter-revolution and its methods, and partly of the general conditions of the country.

As regards our goal and tactics in the people's struggle that has begun in Sweden, the S. D. P. L. refers you to its former declaration, that the party has never declared itself in favor of a minority dictatorship, and that it takes its stand on the broadest democratic foundation. Any other interpretation of our answer we must definitely reject.

Our party offered its co-operation on the basis of a pure socialistic-democratic program, calculated to gather the entire working class in a common front. The S. D. Workers' Party passed a program of action that was chiefly bourgeois-democratic in character, which, on the one hand, postponed to an indefinite future certain important democratic constitutional demands, and, on the other hand, overlooked entirely the weighty economic and social demands of the working class. As you refuse any radicalizing of your program of action in the direction of the program of action of the S. D. P. L., it must be admitted that the executive of your party prefers a unity with the liberal party to a unity within the working class. Under these circumstances, the S. D. P. L. is obliged to note with regret that its attempt to create a united S. D. front on a socialistic platform has for the time met with failure. But the party simultaneously expresses its confident hope and certainty that the workers of Sweden, under the pressure of the world's revolutionary events, will succeed in forcing a socialistic unity of action, which is necessary if the present situation is to be the introduction to a completely democratic and socialistic Sweden.

CHAPTER VIII

Socialism and Labor in Switzerland

The Bolshevik Revolution in Russia was really started in Switzerland, whence the two famous trainloads headed by Lenin started for Petrograd, passing across Germany with the consent, if not at the instigation, of the German government. Late in 1916 Lenin acknowledged the importance of Switzerland as his center of action up to the present, when he outlined the policy he expected to follow, first in Russia and then in the whole world. He says:

> "Before our departure we wish . . . to state our views on the task of the Russian Revolution. We feel all the more bound to do this since it is through the medium of the Swiss workers . . . also thanks to their countries' varieties of languages, that we have been enabled to address ourselves to the German, French and Italian workers . . . We are not pacifists. We are the opponents of imperialistic wars which are conducted by capitalists, on account of their share in the imperialistic booty. We declare it absurd to suppose that the revolutionary proletariat will renounce revolutionary wars, which appear to be necessary in the interest of Socialism. The Russian Proletariat is not in a position alone to accomplish the social revolution, but it can give the present Russian Revolution an impetus which would bring about the best conditions for such a revolution, and, in a sense, be its beginning. It can make easier the conditions under which its principal and most faithful ally, the European and American proletariat, would enter upon the decisive struggle.
>
> "The future of German Socialism is represented not by the traitors, Scheidemann, Legien, David and Company, nor by the vacillating, characterless figures of Haase, Kautsky and Company, held fast in the routine of the times of peace. The future of German Socialism belongs to that tendency which produced Karl Liebknecht, formed the Spartacus group, and found its expression in the Bremen 'workers' policy.'"

At the beginning of 1916 he expressed his plan as follows, in a pamphlet on conditions in France, in which he said:

> "What is necessary now is effort: systematic, slow, serious, obstinate, creative effort, with illegal organization and literature — for preparing a revolutionary movement of the masses against their governments. It is not true that the French working class is incapable of carrying on systematic illegal action. It is false! The French have quickly accustomed themselves to the trenches; they will soon adapt themselves to the new conditions of illegal action and of preparation for a revolutionary movement of the masses."

The principal associate of Lenin in Switzerland during this period of incubation and propaganda was a naturalized German-Swiss, Fritz Platten, who is said to be a Saxon Jew. He was secretary of the Swiss Social Democratic Party and had charge of the issuing of Bolshevik propagandist books and pamphlets in Switzerland and foreign countries. He and Lenin issued in Geneva a paper in Russian called the "Social-Demokrat." In the October, 1914, number (33) of this paper Lenin makes perfectly clear the attitude on the war which he would take. He was willing to turn his own country, Russia, over to German control for the sake of securing the defeat of the Czar. He says:

> "In the present state of affairs it is impossible, from the point of view of the International proletariat, to say what would be the least evil to Socialism — the defeat of the Germans and Austrians, or the defeat of the Franco-Russian-English alliance. For us Russian Social Democrats there is no doubt that, from the point of view of the working classes and the oppressed masses of all the Russian peoples, the least evil would be the defeat of the Czarist monarchy."

Except in industrial centers, like Basel and Zürich, the extreme Socialist Party has a relatively small following in Switzerland. It has practically no adherents in the mountainous districts. During the recent elections the Socialists gained a number of seats through a change in the electoral laws. For a long time it was thought that the extreme Socialist section would obtain control of the party and follow the dictates of the Executive Committee which pledged the party to join the Third (Moscow) International. The party was canvassed in detail on this question for about two months and then a referendum vote was taken, and to the general surprise there was a large majority against joining the Third International. There had been some scandal in connection with the alleged bribing of the Swiss Socialist Grimm by Germany through Hoffman, and this probably had some influence.

During 1919 Switzerland was obliged to take a firm stand in the matter of being used as a center for Bolshevik propaganda in its world-wide campaign. In May there had arrived in Berne from Russia about a dozen emissaries to establish a regular legation under the direction of a Lettish Bolshevik, Jean Berzine. He established a bureau for propaganda which was taken charge of and developed the next month in Berne by a new Bolshevik agent named Lipnitski. A number of Swiss papers, specially German-Swiss, were flooded with propaganda news, telegrams, advertisements, all calculated both to forward the cause of the Soviet government and to undermine all other existing governments. The work included the establishment of a printing and publishing house for the circulating and exploiting of propaganda literature, especially under the direction of Platten. This developed, with the assistance of Herzog and other followers of Lenin among Swiss Socialists, to turn all economic discontent into revolutionary aspirations.

The Swiss government found that it was harboring a regular conspiracy against itself as well as against neighboring governments. It felt obliged, therefore, to expel the entire Bolshevik delegates from the country early in November, 1918, just before the Armistice.

CHAPTER IX

Socialism and Labor in Spain

The Federation of Employers in Catalonia started a lockout on November 3, 1919, on account of the exorbitant demands of labor, and in order to prevent a general strike. This lockout continued for nearly three months, ending in January. It showed that though the Socialists in Spain had gained, they were neither as practical nor as well organized as the Syndicalists, and also showed that the two groups were not in harmonious relations. The Syndicalists' Congress, in December, passed a resolution against the amalgamation of the Syndicalist organization, "Confederacion Natcional del travajo," with the Socialist organization "Union General De Trabajadores," but in favor of the absorption of the latter by the former.

The resolution also decreed that a manifesto be addressed to all the workmen in Spain, giving them three months in which to join the Syndicalist Confederacion, and should they fail to do so, they would be classed as blacklegs. (See the "Epoca" of Madrid, in "Political Review" of January 9, 1920.)

The main Barcelona strike was complicated by contemporaneous strikes through a great part of Spain, in a great variety of fields. Terrorism and bomb explosions ruled Barcelona for a time, but public service was not seriously interrupted. Strikes occurred in Madrid, Valencia, Vigo, in the mines of Almaden, and so forth.

As indications of Bolshevist propaganda in Spain, the "Figaro" of Madrid publishes a letter from the Bolshevist Committee at Basle, dated October 4, 1919, making arrangements for supplying funds for Bolshevist work in western Europe. It further states that two German Bolshevist agents, Brockmann and Albrecht, well provided with funds, reached Portugal, and commenced operations in the Balkans, but were detected by the police, and passed into Spain. They approached the People's Institute (Socialist headquarters) in Madrid, but were repulsed. However, they found supporters amongst certain Spaniards, who acted as German agents during the war. ("Epoca," 18, of Madrid, in "Political Review," February 13, 1920.) The elections that have just taken place show that the Spaniards are gravitating to the two extremes. The revolutionary camp of the Syndicalists on the one hand, who practically kept out of the voting, and the anti-revolutionary camp of reactionaries. The government openly characterized the Syndicalists as a criminal association. They seemed to have obtained the upper hand in Catalonia and northern Spain.

The Syndicalists issued a manifesto declaring that although the ultimate object of the organization was the complete overthrow of the State, as at present constituted, the abolition of the army and of frontiers, its immediate action demands the application of these principles, and although communism was its goal, it would reach out slowly and quietly. ("Sol." of Madrid, No. 31, in "Political Review," January 16, 1920.)

The Employers' Federation refused to recognize the union of workmen, and issued a manifesto outlining the terms on which they would put back the men whom they had dismissed in the lockout.

The government, however, put an end to the lockout by ordering a resumption of work, and putting both parties in the wrong. It was a form of compulsory arbitration. Barcelona gradually resumed its normal life during February. The fight between the Syndicalists and the Socialists, however, continued. The Socialist deputies, Saborit and Menendez, proclaimed themselves Syndicalists at a meeting in the People's Institute in Madrid. The bulk of the workmen in the industrial regions of the north are clearly Syndicalists, considering the Socialists as largely a party of theorists.

Until recently the Socialist Party had remained under their old leader, Pablo Iglesias, a lifelong Marxian, who was their sole representative in Parliament; but since the war, the body has changed hands. A Socialist Conference was held in the spring of 1919, in Madrid. It voted to remain attached to the Second International, and not to join the Third (Moscow) International, but it declared against any interference with Soviet Russia. It sent representatives to the Berne and Luzerne Conferences of the Second International. The "Red" section, under Bonefacio Martinez, has been constantly gaining strength, and it favors violent revolutionary tactics for the party. Such organizations as the Juventud Socialista of Madrid, and such publications as the "Red Wave" have adhered to the Left Wing.

It was the strikes of 1917 which gave Socialism its first popularity in Spain, and brought it into rather painful prominence. The General Workers' Union, and the General Confederation of

Labor in March, 1917, issued a manifesto declaring that unless the economic situation was relieved by legislation, a general strike was inevitable. Strikes were called during the summer, culminating in a railroad strike followed by a general strike. The government claimed that the object of this strike was the revolutionary overthrow of the State, and the army was used in industrial centers to break it up. In the course of the disorders several hundred workers were shot, and many of the leaders and the rank and file were arrested. Among these were Caballero, Anguiano, and Saborit, as well as the university professor, Bestiaro. These four men were nominated as candidates in December, 1917, in the municipal elections of Madrid. Although elected, their election was declared invalid by the government. They were re-elected in 1918, on the Socialist ticket, and the Cortez was forced to grant them complete amnesty. This triumph is considered to have inaugurated the real practical Socialist movement.

CHAPTER X

Socialism and Labor in Austria and Czechoslovakia *

The situation in the whole Austro-Hungarian Empire was complex and unfavorable to unified action either in fields of Socialism or labor. This was due largely to two reasons. The first was the multiplicity of languages and races in the Empire which split up the Austrian Social Democratic Party into a number of national groups, such as Germans, Czechs, Poles, Italians, Slavs, Ruthenians, respectively grouped in different sections of the empire. It was not until nearly 1890 that any organization began which drove the trade unions into affiliation with the Socialist Party in order to secure political influence. The tyrannical exercise of autocratic power by the government was more drastic than in northern Germany, largely because the labor element in Austro-Hungary was not sufficiently large to insure respect on the part of the government.

However, in 1901, the Socialists elected ten members to the Reichrath, and succeeded in their extensive campaign to secure universal manhood suffrage. This campaign was not successful until the enormous increase of the influence of Socialism in 1905 and 1906 combined with the threat of a general strike, to force the government to carry out to a certain extent the Socialist demands for universal suffrage in December, 1906. This led to a tremendous increase in the Socialist vote throughout the empire, which amounted to over a million, or nearly a third of the total vote. It secured an increase of Socialist members of Parliament from eleven to eighty-seven and it coincided with the increase in two years of the number of trade unionists from 180,000 to over 500,000. This applies to the Austrian half of the empire, and does not include the development of Socialism and trade unionism in Hungary, where a larger proportion of the population is of agricultural instead of industrial character. The agitation for universal suffrage carried on in Hungary at the same time as in Austria was even more violently opposed by the government which dissolved 354 trade unions in 1906 in its attempt to suppress the whole trade union movement.

This led to giving to the Socialist Party of Hungary a more extreme and radical view than to the Socialist Party in Austria.

The organization of the Social Democratic Labor Party in Austria was in two branches. The Austrian party proper, centered in Vienna, and the Czecho slovak party, centered in Prague,

---

* See Addendum, Part I.

The break between these two elements came in connection with the election of 1911, when, after years of harmonious work, the Czech or Bohemian separate labor unions were created, introducing a nationalist fight in the labor movement. This break in the party entered also into the parliamentary membership, resulting in the cleavage between the two parliamentary groups. Although the International Congress at Copenhagen blamed the Bohemian Separatists, no attention was paid to the attitude of the Congress. The principal leader of the Austrian Party before the war, and practically its founder, was Victor Adler, father of the more recent leader, Friederich Adler.

The Socialist Labor Union press before the war consisted of fifty German, forty-four Czech, eight Polish, one Slovak, one Ruthenian and three Italian organs.

While the Union Labor movement in Austria-Hungary was so strongly thwarted in its development by government opposition, the other phase of labor development, the co-operative movement, was remarkably successful. It increased from 483 branches, with 206,620 members in 1908 to 560 branches with 590,000 members in 1914. Co-operative labor organizations were established in practically every city with an industrial population.

The attitude of the Social Democratic and Labor groups during the war will be studied later.

The Socialist Party of Austro-Hungary, on account of the great variety of languages and nationalities already noticed, and the Separatist tendencies within its ranks, has been termed quite rightly "The Little International," because it represents on a small scale practically all the important characteristics which have to be considered in connection with the big international meetings. This accounts for the lack of influence which the party has exercised in the general international conference.

> "There are two Socialist parties in Czecho slovakia: the Social Democratic, which is undoubtedly much stronger, and the former National Socialist Party, now the Socialist Party. Marxism has played a very small part in the Czech Socialist movement. The great majority of the Czech workers regard Socialism primarily as an idealistic conception of a better human society . . . Revolutionary Marxism, or Bolshevism, is foreign to the Czech mind and has therefore no future in Bohemia . . . and on January 16 (1919) the Socialist Party executive published an explicit repudiation of Bolshevik propaganda."

This statement by Alexander Broz in the "New Europe" (No. 124) will explain why the Bohemians in the United States are an element that can be counted upon for law and order. As a prominent Czech Socialist deputy wrote, "Bolshevism seduces the suffering working classes into a policy that drives the whole nation to still greater misery and involves all classes in political extinction."

The Czecho slovak government by the stand it took against Bela Kun's invasion of Slovakia in July, 1919, by guarding against a general strike, by arresting the Bolshevik agitator Muna and Mme. Janishek, helped to bring about the failure, on June 15, of the Bolshevik rising in Vienna. This was an attempt to turn Austria into a Soviet state as had already been done in Hungary. It was all a part of Bela Kun's plan, and to be done with his money. The conspirators in Vienna were mostly Hungarian propagandists. Fortunately the troops of the garrison refused to be stampeded into joining the Bolsheviks. The Hungarian Bolshevik funds were siezed, including immense quantities of jewelry, and Bela Kun's agents were arrested. The fate of Central Europe had hung by a thread. Bolshevism might have spread to Italy and France if Bohemia had gone to pieces.

SOCIALISM IN AUSTRIA SINCE THE WAR

During the war, Austrian Socialism had even less opportunity to show any independence than German Socialism, being kept so absolutely under oppression. This oppression resulted in the extraordinary assassination of the Austrian Prime Minister, Count Stuergkh, by Friederich Adler, the leader of the militant branch of the Socialist Party. The majority Socialists, as in Germany, supported the government. Only the Left Wing, under young Adler, attempted to remain true to international pacifist Socialism.

The insistent call for peace by the Socialists may have hastened the disintegration of Austria at the close of the war. There is no question but that the misery and hunger in Vinena and throughout Austria after the war, which was more extreme perhaps than in any other part of Europe, was responsible for the rise of Socialist conditions in Vienna which have led during the last year to the practical dictation by extra-governmental Socialist organizations. A condition of partial Communism exists in Vienna, including expropriation of houses for the poor, the dictating of measures by meetings of the workingmen's associations, the cowing of the middle and upper classes by the Socialists. The attempt to establish a Bolshevik Communist rule in Austria by means of funds sent both directly from Russia by proxy — funds that were refused by Adler in the name of his party— and through funds and jewelry showered by Bela Kun, the Communist ruler of Hungary, in his attempt to repeat in Austria the successful uprising in Hungary, resulted in failure, through the vigilance of the authorities.

The situation in Austria is extremely serious and it is impossible to say how far the despotism of the Socialist Labor Party may go.

CHAPTER XI

Socialism and Labor in the Balkans *

There has been considerable Socialist activity throughout the Balkans, notwithstanding the abnormal destruction due to the war. The three principal national groups are the Serbian and Bulgarian and Roumanian, as Greek Socialism is negligible. In all three of these countries, the character of the Socialist movement is decidedly radical, much more so than in the neighboring Czecho-Slovak region of Bohemia, and Slovakia. This is shown by the adhesion of all three groups to the Zimmerwald and Kienthal programs, by their refusal to join the Second International Conferences, and by their adhesion to the Third (Moscow) International. The Roumanian Socialists, reorganized after the war, almost provoked a revolution at the time of the invasion of Hungary. In the political field, it is in Bulgaria that the Socialists, or, as they call themselves, the Social Democrats, have obtained the greatest power, electing a large number of deputies to the recent Parliament, notwithstanding the repressive measures of the government. The Socialist Party in Serbia is, since the war, rather disorganized. In Bulgaria, there are two sections to the party; one called the broad-minded, which supported the war and governmental positions, the latter called the narrow-minded, which endorsed the Zimmerwald Conference, and more than 1,000 of whose members were imprisoned. It was in May, 1919, that the radical section of the party broke away and called itself the Communist Party, adopting a program thoroughly in harmony with the Communist International.

During the last year the Serbian Socialist Party has been reorganized and has decided to join the Third (Moscow) International. It sent a delegate to attend the organization meeting in Moscow in December, 1919. In certain sections of the new Jugo-Slav State, especially Croatia, the Communist section of the Social Democrats have made great gains.

Bulgaria was also represented at that time by a delegate who gave to the Congress in his speech a verbatim reproduction of the Manifesto recently issued by the Bulgarian Socialists.

The Communist Party has gained steadily in Bulgaria since the close of the war. In the 1919 elections, notwithstanding the

---

* See Addendum, Part I.

very drastic opposition of the government, it gained a number of seats in Parliament. In fact, the Communist Socialists won forty-eight seats, the Moderate Socialists twenty-five seats, against the government block of 113. The Bolshevist propaganda in Bulgaria is extremely active.

CHAPTER XII

Labor and Socialism in Great Britain *

The movement of the Socialist and Labor groups in Great Britain is extremely complicated and not easily to be traced in a few words. Its beginnings have already been referred to, down to the time when, almost contemporaneously with the formation of the Second International, a series of strikes in England gave a tremendous impetus to the movement. However, at that time British Socialism lacked unity and lacked able leaders. The gulf between the Socialists and the workmen was not yet bridged. Even as late as 1899, there was very little practical Socialism in charge of the labor movement. The Independent Labor Party was unimportant, at that time, notwithstanding the wonderful personality of its founder, Keir Hardie. The failure of the so-called Social Democratic Federation in the various elections emphasized the lack of political power of the Socialists. But a complete transformation took place during the succeeding years, so that when a labor party congress met at Belfast in 1907 almost all the delegates were workingmen.

In 1908 the old confederation changed its name to that of the Social Democratic Party. In 1911 the party coalesced with other organizations under the new name of the British Socialist Party. This party adopted the Marxian point of view but remained of very little influence in politics.

In 1903, a new party called the British Labor Party was formed, growing out of the action of the Trades Union Congress of 1899 and of the combined activity of Ramsay MacDonald and Arthur Henderson. This party quickly acquired great political influence, electing in 1910 as many as forty labor members to the Parliament.

In 1907 the Congress of the British Labor Party declared in favor of "the socialization of the means of production, distribution and exchange, to be controlled in a democratic state in the interest of the entire community, and the complete emancipation of labor from domination of capitalism and landlordism, with the establishment of social and economic equality between the sexes."

We have already called attention to the Fabian Society as an interesting group of intellectual Socialists who engaged in a very brilliant campaign of propaganda.

---

* See **Addendum, Part I.**

Another association which began as an intellectual and theoretical group, but which expanded very soon into an extremely important association, is the so-called National Guild League, founded by G. D. H. Cole, in 1905. This group and its theory will be very carefully studied in another chapter.

Even here we wish to call attention to the wonderfully important document, which will be later published, called "Labor and the New Social Order," which, though not written until 1918, expresses the ideas and the plans that were already current in the British Party before the war.

The British labor movement is political as well as economic and is composed of four large organizations besides a number of minor ones. These are described as follows in the Report of the National Civic Federation ("The Labor Situation in Great Britain and France," p. 112):

"(1) The Trade Union Congress, meeting annually to decide principally upon the several measures to be asked of Parliament and to elect its "Parliamentary Committee," whose mandate is "to watch all legislation affecting labor." In 1918 the membership fees were $4,532,085; the number of delegates 881, representing 262 societies.

(2) The General Federation of Trade Unions described by its secretary as "the largest purely trade union organization outside of the United States," and as having March 31 (1919), 1,215,107 of a gross membership, with 140 affiliated societies.

(3) The Co-operative Union, its fraternal delegate to the Congress reporting a membership of 3,500,000, the great bulk trade unionists; associated since 1917 in the Labor Party.

(4) The British Labor Party, its membership composed of wage-workers and other citizens, mixed, polling a vote equal to somewhat more than half the total membership claimed for the trade unions in the Congress and represented in Parliament by fifty-nine out of 707 members."

There is no national organization of trade unionists in Great Britain in the way they are organized in the United States. Of dock and riverside unions there are fifteen; none national; of seamen and boatmen, nineteen, only three in the Congress. Bricklayers, masons and plasterers have seventeen societies, only two national, etc. There is little unity either or policy or organization. In the National Federation of General Workers there are nine organizations (four of them having "national" in their titles), all separately represented in the Congress, each with its own headquarters and independent administrative machinery, and mostly with special fields of operation, local or regional, the total membership claimed being 961,466. Arthur Henderson, the foremost labor leader in Great Britain, says: "The pressing need of organized labor is fewer trade unions and more trade unionists," and J. H. Thomas, secretary of the National Union of Railwaymen, says: "The greatest difference now is not between the government and the railwaymen, but between the unions themselves."

No reference to British working class effort in the pursuit of its own welfare would be complete without mention of the co-operative movement. It has now more than 1,300 distributive societies, with 3,500,000 members, and more than 100 productive and three wholesale societies. Its employees number at least 125,000, and the sum total of all the sales annually runs up to $1,000,000,000, from which its members are reimbursed nearly $100,000,000. The movement promotes voluntary co-operation and resists any legislative or administrative inequality which would hamper its progress. Its biggest aim is "that eventually the processes of production, distribution and exchange" (including the land) "shall be organized on co-operative lines in the interest of the whole community." The co-operative movement is now associated with the political labor movement and has a "platform" of eleven planks, the objects stated in the final paragraph being the "breaking down of the caste and class system," and "the democratizing of State services — civil, commercial and diplomatic."

The Independent Labor Party of Great Britain

The most radical labor leader in Great Britain among those who do not adhere to the Third International and believe in democratic parliamentary methods is J. Ramsay MacDonald, who yet is a sympathizer with the Soviet idea among English labor men. He made one of the most important addresses at the International Labor and Socialist Conference at Berne, in 1919. He gave an authoritative statement of the Independent Labor Party's character and aims in the "N. Y. Nation" of June 14, 1919, under the above title, and from it the following important passages are quoted. As he is its foremost exponent it is authoritative.

"The Independent Labor Party is for the moment the red rag to the bull of ordinary British opinions. For years it has been the subject of almost daily attack in the newspapers. . . . It is a Socialist Party, and must not be confused with the Labor Party, with which, however, it is affiliated, and with which it acts for electoral purposes. Its parliamentary candidates, for instance, are run in the general list of candidates for which the Labor Party is responsible. Its Socialism is not of the dogmatic type. It believes in the collective control of land and capital, but it interprets itself as a continuation of British liberal tradition, and connects its economic and industrial theories with the British trade union movement. Evolution is the breath of its life. When it was started, a quarter of a century ago, chiefly by the efforts of the late Mr. Keir Hardie, it had a clear conception of a goal — Socialism; and an equally clear conception of a method — the welding of the working class, especially the trade unionists, into a political party separate from the other parties.

"After strenuous work — generally in the nature of attack upon old leaders like Mr. Ben Pickard, Mr. C. Fenwick and Mr. H. Broadhurst — it swung the British trade unions around into politics and formed the Labor Party. When the war broke out it took up an attitude which exposed it to the wildest ravings of misrepresentation and calumny; its total destruction under the wrath of popular passion and the repressive action of the government was confidently expected; at the recent election it lost its parliamentary leaders; it is regarded by some sections of the Labor Party as something of an ugly duckling of imperturable persistence but of unpopular activity. Yet the party leaders have never forfeited their personal power within the councils of the working classes. . . .

"Meanwhile the party itself, after the first rending turmoil of the outbreak of the war, began to right itself. Its public meetings were always crowded . . . and the propaganda of the party was continued through every channel that could be kept open. Twelve times was its printing business raided . . . but arrests were confined to the less known men. . . . The membership of the party steadily increased, its recruits coming mainly from the

"WRITE IT OVER AGAIN, GEORGE, AS FOLLOWS ---"

This cartoon vividly portrays British Labor's attitude toward its government.

(*The Liberator*, Oct. 1920.)

young educated democracy. . . . There are now 783 branches of the party. . . .

"The party's position on the war has always been misrepresented. It was 'pro-German'; it consisted of the 'agents of the Kaiser'; and what not. The truth was that it was simply democratic and international. Despite what is said to the contrary, it took with it the overwhelming majority of British Socialists. . . .

"When the Russian Revolution came, the Independent Labor Party, in Parliament and out, begged the government to regard it as an opportunity by which to get at the German democracy rather than as one to reconstitute a Russian offensive. . . .

"The industrial strike for political purpose is a very old idea. It was revived by the modern movement of syndicalism in France; it was encouraged by the failure of the Labor Party after 1906 to effect dramatic changes in politics; since the war, the strike and the threat to strike have won enormous advantages for labor, even when the trade union officials were opposed to any action being taken. Industrial or 'direct' action has therefore come to the center of the stage of British labor politics.

"Moreover, two movements have given it a new authority. The National Trade Guilds have been battering at Parliament as the representatives of industrial democracy and at the State as absolute authority in a nation. They argued that the workers as workers had to create something like an industrial legislature with authority over industrial affairs, because geographical areas called constituencies, full of a medley of electors removed in mind and in interests from the problems of the workshop, could never create a body of representatives whose industrial mind would be sufficiently definite to make it a satisfactory authority to deal with the real life of the people.

"Then came the Russian Soviets and the rule of the workers secured by the disfranchisement of all those who did not work. To industrial democrats here, this method of government causes less shock than might be imagined. For up to the present time our House of Commons has been elected by a franchise which deprived millions of workmen of the right to vote, and our House of Lords is the purest example of a Soviet which the world has ever seen — a Soviet, however, not of the workers, but of the aristocracy.

"The Independent Labor Party is, therefore, peculiarly exposed to the movements for the political strike and for the reconstruction of our Constitution on Soviet models. These movements, however, do not really go deep — its leaders — all . . . believe in parliamentary democracy.

"Still the party will undoubtedly respond to industrial movements . . . its allegiance to parliamentary methods will be tested under a terrible strain. . . . In any event, the party is steadily returning to its old commanding place in the labor movement."

A British Industrial Council

A plan was proposed in 1919, which was somewhat in advance of the Whitley type of National Councils in the field of labor. The National Industrial Conference called by the British government early in 1919, to meet the threat of the general strike, which involved the Triple Alliance — railway men, miners and transport workers — accepted the report of its Joint Committee of Employers and Workers' Representatives, to recommend the establishment of a permanent representative National Industrial Council of 400 members, under the direction of the Minister of Labor.

The representatives of capital and labor were to be evenly divided. The Council was to form a permanent standing committee of fifty members, equally divided between the two parties. The objects of the proposed Council were:

"(a) The consideration of general questions affecting industrial relations.

"(b) The consideration of measures for a joint or several action to anticipate and avoid threatened disputes.

"(c) The consideration of actual disputes involving general questions.

"(d) The consideration of legislative proposals affecting industrial relations.

"(e) To advise the government on industrial questions, and on the general industrial situation.

"(f) To issue statements for the guidance of public opinion on industrial issues."

How the Railroad Strike of 1919 was Broken in Great Britain

There is a great difference between the outlaw railroad strike in this country in April, 1920, and the railroad strike in Great Britain in September-October, 1919. The British strike involved half a million workers and immediately paralyzed the railroads of the whole country. It was a walkout of an official character, arranged by the railroad workers themselves, the most powerful of the members of the Triple Alliance.

That strike lasted nine days. There was no resort to injunction proceedings. The British public immediately rose as one man and proceeded to run the railroads, and public opinion practically expressed broke the strike.

The similarities between the two strikes were that in both cases the workers were irritated by the government's delay in settling their claims for wage increases. In both cases the leaders knew that the men were getting out of hand. In both cases the railroad workers were jealous of wage increases granted to higher-priced workers and other groups. Another point of similarity is the suddenness of the strike, which broke out without previous warning. In both cases the impression was given that the strike was not for wages or for better conditions, but for revolutionary purposes, as a feeler toward a general revolutionary strike.

The "Round Table" for December, 1919, gives an excellent summary of the strike in Great Britain. It shows that through the suddenness of the strike passengers were stranded on the line, and trainloads of milk, fish and other perishable goods were left to decay where they stood. For all practical purposes the stoppage of the railways was complete for the first two or three days of the strike. Of course, this fact places the British strike in an entirely different category from the American.

The British government took the position that the strike must be fought with all the resources of the country; fortunately, a plan of campaign had already been prepared for the maintenance of the essential public services, and particularly the distribution of food supplies. Taking advantage of the powers which the government still wielded under "The Defense of the Realm Act," the Food Controller immediately armed himself with authority to requisition all horses and road vehicles suitable for the transport of goods. Strict rationing of meat, bacon and margerine was reimposed, hoarding prohibited, and public meals restricted. Milk was taken by the farmers to prearranged spots, where it was collected by motor lorries. Hyde Park was converted into a calling station. Wholesalers drew their supplies there and passed them on to retailers. These plans worked so smoothly that the effect of the strike on the food supplies of the big towns was almost unnoticeable.

The Ministry of Transports set up an organization of volunteers to replace the strikers in running the railways, some of whom needed a short course of training. Owing to some disorder an appeal was issued to all loyal citizens to enroll themselves in citizen guards for the protection of life and property. It is a recognized fact that it was the public, by its willingness and efficiency in its co-operation with the government, and the energy and promptness of the government itself, which showed the strikers that they could not control the country and coerce the government.

Revolutionary Industrial Unionism and the Triple Alliance

We read in the "National Labor Digest," as far back as September, 1919, page 13, a warning against the plans of the famous Triple Alliance:

> "For months England has been on the verge of the greatest strike in her history of industrial troubles. Three of the largest British labor unions, the Miners' Federation, consisting of over 800,000 members; the National Union of Railwaymen, comprised of over 450,000 members, and the Transport Workers' Union, made up of over 500,000 members, form the Triple Alliance. This association presented a program of demands on the British government unequalled in the history of that nation. A general strike was threatened if these demands were refused. The program of the Triple Alliance was far-reaching, dealing, not merely with matters of higher wages, shorter hours, and improved working conditions, but demanding also the immediate nationalization of all the coal mines, iron mines, railways, and canals of Great Britain. . . .
>
> "A special commission set up by Parliament to investigate points at issue have been trying to find some way out of the dilemma. . . . The situation is so critical that England is applying itself assiduously to the task of staying the tide of Bolshevism and preventing, so far as possible, further inroads upon the commerce and industry of the nation. . . .
>
> "All parties now realize that the situation has become a

menace to the established government. The 'Morning Post' (London) announced, 'The real cause of the strike by the Triple Alliance of miners, railwaymen and transport workers is a long and carefully concocted plan to overthrow the existing order of things and place the whole nation at the mercy of one section — the Bolsheviki.' The 'Daily Express' (London) declared, 'Extremist leaders of the striking miners in the Yorkshire fields are in constant communication with the Bolsheviki of Russia, the Spartacans of Germany, and the Industrial Workers of the World in America.'"

A letter printed in the London "Times," written by one British Soviet worker to another, shows that the famous Clyde strike was connected fundamentally with the Soviet movement. This letter says:

"Dear Comrade: Enclosed is a copy of a program arranged by our comrades of the Clyde workers' Soviet committee and drafted from the articles arranged by the German Spartacists' Union. The original draft of the above was translated direct from the German. Our own ideas are not in agreement with the Clyde and no responsibility is accepted by the sub-committee."

The program enclosed with the foregoing letter, as published by the London "Times," follows:

"1. Disarming of all non-proletarian soldiers.

"2. Seizure of arms and ammunition by the workers and soldiers' councils.

"3. Arming of the entire labor population as a Red army.

"4. Voluntary discipline of all soldiers in place of the present brutal and degrading slavery, all superiors to be nominated by the rank and file, with abolition of courts-martial.

"5. Nomination of authorized representatives of the soldiers' and workers' councils for all political organs.

"6. Creation of a revolution tribunal, chiefly responsible for the harsh treatment accorded our comrades now in prison and of political prisoners.

"7. Immediate seizure of all means of subsistence to secure success to the revolution.

"8. Removal of parliament and municipal councils to be taken over by the revolutionary council.

"9. Abolition of all class distinctions, titles and orders; social equality of the sexes.

"10. Reduction of working hours to avoid unemployment and to conform to the limitation of the working day to six hours and a minimum wage of $35, seven pounds, per week.

"11. Confiscation of all Crown estates and revenues, which will become common property.

"12. Annulment of State debts and other debts.

"13. Appropriation of all lands and properties, funds, and other securities now in the possession of the ruling and non-proletariat classes.

"14. Expropriation of all banks, mines, industrial and commercial establishments by the revolutionary committee.

"15. A Republican Committee to take over all means of communication, and means of transport."

Of course, the above program is not one that is accepted by the entire rank and file, but the actual official program of the triple union is sufficiently revolutionary to have led to the speech by Lloyd George, sounding the alarm, a part of which is published elsewhere.

The Triple Alliance is merely one of the combinations which is forming the rank and file of labor into a unified combination under the banner of industrial unionism, as Kellogg and Gleason, the authors of "British Labor and the War," say, p. 176:

> "The labor movement is not weakening toward a split. It is amalgamating. In twenty-two organizations are found three-quarters of all trade union membership. The cohesive force of the trade union movement is clearly revealed in these terms, and there are eight effective industrial combinations, each with at least 100,000 members, and a total membership of 2,500,000. The eight combinations are: The miners (800,000), the railway men (400,000), the Amalgamated Society of Engineers (270,000), Workers' Union (350,000), National Union of General Workers (250,000), Amalgamated Weavers' Association (200,000), Amalgamated Society of Carpenters, Cabinet Makers and Joiners (110,000), and the National Amalgamated Union of Labor (117,000).
>
> "This is the striking blow behind the bargaining power of the industrial movement. And not only that, but when coal, cotton, transport and metal workers decide on a program of action, Great Britain will listen, and, more simple

yet, if the Triple Alliance wills it, the industrial life in Great Britain will stop short."

THE NATIONALIZATION OF RAILROADS IN GREAT BRITAIN

Under the stress of railway strikes, the House of Commons passed a bill on July 11, 1919, by which the British government created a system of unified control and operation in England, involving railways, roads, canals, docks and coastwise traffic, under Sir Eric Geddes, now popularly known as the government's right hand man. ("National Labor Digest," August, 1919, p. 29.)

It is considered by many as the first step toward the nationalization of the entire transportation system of Great Britain. The advantages of the bill, as outlined by Sir Eric Geddes, before the Commons, were as follows:

Elimination of wasteful competitive services, common use by all roads of passenger and freight cars; elimination of privately owned cars, increased capacity of railroads and decreased cost of traction by extension of electrification; increased carrying capacity by increased size of cars; reduction of idle time of cars; standardization of materials.

Another object is the more efficient use of canals and docks and the reviving of the coastwise trade which has suffered thus far from what has amounted to government subsidizing of railroads. Another new feature is the development of road transport by motor trucks. It will be remembered that the wholesale use of motor trucks at the time of the railroad strike was one of the principal means for breaking the strike. The new scheme is supposed to be temporary, to tide over a period of crisis and prepare for a fundamental plan.

The Britism Labor Party in January, 1918, at its annual conference, had submitted to it, by its executive committee a report on reconstruction entitled "Labor and the New Social Order." This program was submitted for consideration with a view to its being adopted somewhat later at the summer conference in June. The draft submitted in January was actually the basis for "Resolutions on Reconstruction," adopted by the British Labor Party in June, but the text of these resolutions naturally eliminated a great deal of the reasoning and basic general considerations of the original draft. Therefore, it is the original draft which we will here reproduce, because it is an eloquent and fundamental document which was of great value as a piece of propaganda, and, which being widely circulated, not only in Great Britain, but all over the world, created a tremendous sensation, and was the basis for a great deal of reconstructive program-making, during 1918 and 1919. It is therefore here given in full. Both this document and the final resolutions have been published by the Labor Party with an introductory article by the Party leader, Arthur Henderson.

To our own country the effect of this pronouncement of the British Labour Party is evident in some of the documents studied in this Report, especially the "Social Reconstruction" pamphlet issued by the National Catholic War Council, and the Triennial Report of the Social Service Commission of the Episcopal Church presented to the Detroit Convention in October, 1919. It affected not merely the Socialistically inclined members of the clergy of the various Christian denominations, but also to a great extent the intellectuals of various radical and sentimental groups. It helped to popularize in the best circles the name and theory of the New Social Order and to minimize the dangers of revolutionary change.

What are the cardinal points of this document:

(1) It pledges the Labor Party not to help to reconstruct our present shaken civilization but to help to complete its destruction.

(2) After this destruction of the Capitalist System and all its works the new order must secure for all people the proper 'minimum conditions of healthy existence,' through 'the elimination from the control of industry of the private capitalist,' through the common ownership of the means of production, and 'the equitable sharing of the proceeds.' This involves common ownership of land, nationalization of basic industries, of means of transportation, and of raw material, both national and imported. This means a revolution in national finance, based on a very heavy direct taxing of incomes above the necessary cost of family maintenance, on the limiting of inheritances and on the heavy assessment of capital. All the national surplus is to be applied to the common good.

It might be objected that the document appears to be based on the assumption of the co-existence of two irreconcilable systems — the old Capitalist and the new Communistic Society. The system of national finance presupposes the large fortunes of capitalism, while the National Minimum of comfortable living is based on the elimination of private ownership and control, which would quite preclude the creation of any such fortunes as would make the above financial scheme practicable.

"LABOUR AND THE NEW SOCIAL ORDER

"Submitted by the Executive Committee of the British Labour Party at the 17th Annual Conference, Nottingham, January 23–25, 1918

"A Draft Report on Reconstruction

"It behoves the Labour Party, in formulating its own programme for Reconstruction after the war, and in criticising the various preparations and plans that are being made by the present Government, to look at the problem as a whole. We have to make it clear what it is that we wish to construct. It is important to emphasize the fact that, whatever may be the case with regard to other political parties, our detailed practical proposals proceed from definitely held principles.

"The End of a Civilization

"We need to beware of patchwork. The view of the Labour Party is that what has to be reconstructed after the war is not this or that Government Department, or this or that piece of social machinery; but, so far as Britain is concerned, society itself. The individual worker, or for that matter the individual statesman, immersed in daily routine — like the individual soldier in a battle — easily fails to understand the magnitude and far-reaching importance of what is taking place around him. How does it fit together as a whole? How does it look from a distance? Count Okuma, one of the oldest, most experienced and ablest of the statesmen of Japan, watching the present conflict from the other side of the globe, declares it to be nothing less than the death of European civilization. Just as in the past the civilizations of Babylon, Egypt, Greece, Carthage, and the great Roman Empire have been successively destroyed, so, in the judgment of this detached observer, the civilization of all Europe is even now receiving its death-blow. We of the Labour Party can so far agree in this estimate as to recognize, in the present world catastrophe, if not the death, in Europe, of civilization itself, at any rate the culmination and collapse of a distinctive industrial civilization, which the workers will not seek to reconstruct. At such times of crisis it is easier to slip into ruin than to progress into higher forms of organization. That is the problem as it presents itself to the Labour Party today.

"What this war is consuming is not merely the security, the homes, the livelihood and the lives of millions of innocent families, and an enormous proportion of all the accumulated wealth of the world, but also the very basis of the peculiar social order in which it has arisen. The individualist system of capitalist production, based on the private ownership and competitive administration of land and capital, with its reckless 'profiteering' and wage-slavery; with its glorification of the unhampered struggle for the means of life and its hypocritical pretence of the 'survival of the fittest'; with the monstrous inequality of circumstances which it produces and the degradation and brutalisation, both moral and spiritual, resulting therefrom, may, we hope, indeed have received a death-blow. With it must go the political system and ideas in which it naturally found expression. We of the Labour Party, whether in opposition or in due time called upon to form an Administration, will certainly lend no hand to its revival. On the contrary, we shall do our utmost to see that it is buried with the millions whom it has done to death. If we in Britain are to escape from the decay of civilisation itself, which the Japanese statesman foresees, we must ensure that what is presently to be built up is a new social order, based not on fighting, but on fraternity — not on the competitive struggle for the means of bare life, but on a deliberately planned co-operation in production and distribution for the benefit of all who participate by hand or by brain — not on the utmost possible inequality of riches, but on a systematic approach towards a healthy equality of material circumstances for every person born into the world — not on an enforced dominion over subject nations, subject races, subject Colonies, subject classes or a subject sex, but, in industry as well as in government, on that equal freedom, that general consciousness of consent, and that widest possible participation in power, both economic and political, which is characteristic of Democracy. We do not, of course pretend that it is possible, even after the drastic clearing away that is now going on, to build society anew in a year or two of feverish 'Reconstruction.' What the Labour Party intends to satisfy itself about is that each brick that it helps to lay shall go to erect the structure that it intends, and no other.

"The Pillars of the House

"We need not here recapitulate, one by one, the different items in the Labour Party's programme, which successive Party Conferences have adopted. These proposals, some of them in various publications worked out in practical detail, are often carelessly derided as impracticable, even by the politicions who steal them piecemeal from us! The members of the Labour Party, themselves actually working by hand or by brain, in close contact with the facts, have perhaps at all times a more accurate appreciation of what is practicable, in industry as in politics, than those who depend solely on academic instruction or are biased by great possessions. But today no man dares to say that anything is impracticable. The war, which has scared the old Political Parties right out of their dogmas, has taught every statesman and every Government official, to his enduring surprise, how very much more can be done along the lines that we have laid down than he had ever before thought possible. What we now promulgate as our policy, whether for opposition or for office, is not merely this or that specific reform, but a deliberately thought out, systematic, and comprehensive plan for that immediate social rebuilding which any ministry, whether or not it desires to grapple with the problem, will be driven to undertake. The Four Pillars of the House that we propose to erect, resting upon the common foundation of the Democratic control of society in all its activities, may be termed, respectively:

"(a) The Universal Enforcement of the National Minimum;

"(b) The Democratic Control of Industry;

"(c) The Revolution in National Finance; and

"(d) The Surplus Wealth for the Common Good.

"The various detailed proposals of the Labour Party, herein briefly summarised, rest on these four pillars, and can best be appreciated in connection with them.

"The Universal Enforcement of a National Minimum

"The first principle of the Labour Party — in significant contrast with those of the Capitalist System, whether expressed by the Liberal or by the Conservative Party — is the securing to every member of the community, in good times and bad alike (and not only to the strong and able, the well-born or the fortunate), of all the requisites of healthy life and worthy citizenship. This is in no sense a 'class' proposal. Such an amount of social protection of the individual, however poor and lowly, from birth to death is, as the economist now knows, as indispensable to fruitful co-operation as it is to successful combination; and it affords the only complete safeguard against that insidious Degradation of the Standard of Life, which is the worst economic and social calamity to which any community can be subjected. We are members one of another. No man liveth to himself alone. If any, even the humblest is made to suffer, the whole community and every one of us, whether or not we recognise the fact, is thereby injured. Generation after generation this has been the cornerstone of the faith of Labour. It will be the guiding principle of any Labour Government.

"THE LEGISLATIVE REGULATION OF EMPLOYMENT

"Thus it is that the Labour Party today stands for the universal application of the policy of the National Minimum, to which (as embodied in the successive elaborations of the Factory, Mines, Railways, Shops, Merchant Shipping, and Truck Acts, the Public Health, Housing, and Education Acts and the Minimum Wage Act — all of them aiming at the enforcement of at least the prescribed minimum of Leisure, Health, Education, and Subsistence) the spokesmen of Labour have already gained the support of the enlightened statesmen and economists of the world. All these laws purporting to protect against extreme degradation of the standard of life need considerable improvement and extension, whilst their administration leaves much to be desired. For instance, the Workmen's Compensation Act fails, shamefully, not merely to secure proper provision for all the victims of accident and industrial disease, but what is much more important, does not succeed in preventing their continual increase. The amendment and consolidation of the Factories and Workshop Acts, with their extension to all employed persons, is long overdue, and it will be the policy of Labour greatly to strengthen the staff of inspectors, especially by the addition of more men and women of actual experience of the workshop and the mine. The Coal Mines (Minimum Wage) Act must certainly be maintained in force, and suitably amended, so as both to ensure greater uniformity of conditions among the several districts, and to make the District Minimum in all cases an effective reality. The same policy will, in the interests of the agricultural labourers, dictate the perpetuation of the Legal Wage clauses of the new Corn Law just passed for a term of five years, and the prompt amendment of any defects that may be revealed in their working. And, in view of the fact that many millions of wage-earners, notably women and the less-skilled workmen in various occupations, are unable by combination to obtain wages adequate for decent maintenance in health, the Labour Party intends to see that the Trade Boards Act is suitably amended and made to apply to all industrial employments in which any considerable number of those employed obtain less than 30s. per week. This minimum of not less than 30s. per week (which will need revision according to the level of prices) ought to be the very lowest statutory base line for the least skilled adult workers, men or women, in any occupation, in all parts of the United Kingdom.

"THE ORGANISATION OF DEMOBILISATION

"But the coming industrial dislocation, which will inevitably follow the discharge from war service of half of all the working population, imposes new obligations upon the community. The demobilisation and discharge of the eight million wage-earners now being paid from public funds, either for service with the colours or in munition work and other war trades, will bring to the whole wage-earning class grave peril of unemployment, reduction of wages, and a lasting degredation of the standard of life, which can be prevented only by deliberate National Organisation. The Labour Party has repeatedly called upon the present Government to formulate its plan, and to make in advance all arrangements necessary for coping with so unparalleled a dislocation. The policy to which the Labour Party commits itself is unhesitating and uncompromising. It is plain that regard should be had, in stopping Government orders, reducing the staff of the national factories and demobilising the army, to the actual state of employment in particular industries and in different districts, so as both to release first the kinds of labour most urgently required for the revival of peace production, and to prevent any congestion of the market. It is no less imperative that suitable provision against being turned suddenly adrift without resources should be made, not only for the soldiers, but also for the three millions operatives in munition work and other war trades, who will be discharged long before most of the Army can be disbanded. On this important point, which is the most urgent of all, the present Government has, we believe, down to the present hour, formulated no plan, and come to no decision, and neither the Liberal nor the Conservative Party has apparently deemed the matter worthy of agitation. Any Government which should allow the discharged soldier or munition worker to fall into the clutches of charity or the Poor Law would have to be instantly driven from office by an outburst of popular indignation. What every one of them who is not wholly disabled will look for is a situation in accordance with his capacity.

"SECURING EMPLOYMENT FOR ALL

"The Labour Party insists — as no other political party has thought fit to do — that the obligation to find suitable employment in productive work for all these men and women rests upon the Government for the time being. The work of resettling the disbanded soldiers and discharged munition workers into new situations is a national obligation; and the Labour party emphatically protests against it being regarded as a matter for private charity. It strongly objects to this public duty being handed over either to committees of philanthropists or benevolent societies, or to any of the military or recruiting authorities. The policy of the Labour Party in this matter is to make the utmost use of the Trade Unions, and equally for the brain workers of the various professional associations. In view of the fact that, in any trade, the best organization for placing men in situations is a national Trade Union having local branches throughout the kingdom, every soldier should be allowed, if he chooses, to have a duplicate of his industrial discharge notice sent out, one month before the date fixed for his discharge, to the Secretary of the Trade Union to which he belongs or wishes to belong. Apart from this use of the Trade Union (and a corresponding use of the professional association) the Government must, of course, avail itself of some such public machinery as that of the Employment Exchanges; but before the existing Exchanges (which will need to be greatly extended) can receive the cooperation and support of the organized Labour Movement, without which their operations can never be fully successful, it is imperative that they should be drastically reformed, on the lines laid down in the Demobilization Report of the 'Labour after the War' Joint Committee; and, in particular, that each Exchange should be placed effectively under the supervision and control of a Joint Committee of Employers and Trade Unionists in equal numbers.

"The responsibility of the Government, for the time being, in the grave industrial crisis that demobilization will produce, goes, however, far beyond the eight million men and women whom the various departments will suddenly discharge from their own service. The effect of this peremptory discharge on all the other workers has also to be taken into account. To the Labour Party it will seem the supreme concern of the Government of the day to see to it that there shall be, as a result of the gigantic 'General Post' which it will itself have deliberately set going, nowhere any degradation of the standard of life. The Government has pledged itself to restore the Trade Union conditions and 'pre-war practices' of the workshop, which the Trade Unions patriotically gave up at the direct request of the Government itself; and this solemn pledge must be fulfilled, of course, in the spirit as well as in the letter. The Labour Party, moreover, holds it to be the duty of the Government of the day to take all necessary steps to prevent the standard rates of wages, in any trade or occupation whatsoever, from suffering any reduction, relatively to the contemporary cost of living. Unfortunately, the present Government, like the Liberal and Conservative Parties, so far refuses to speak on this important matter with any clear voice. We claim that it should be a cardinal point of Government policy to make it plain to every capitalist employer that any attempt to reduce the customary rate of wages when peace comes, or to take advantage of the dislocation of demobilisation to worsen the conditions of employment in any grade whatsoever, will certainly lead to embittered industrial strife, which will be in the highest degree detrimental to the national interests; and that the Government of the day will not hesitate to take all necessary steps to avert such a calamity. In the great impending crisis the Government of the day should not only, as the greatest employer of both brainworkers and manual workers, set a good example in this respect but should also actively seek to influence private employers by proclaiming in advance that it will not itself attempt to lower the standard rates of conditions in public employment; by announcing that it will insist on the most rigorous observance of the Fair Wages Clause in all public contracts, and by explicity recommending every local authority to adopt the same policy.

"But nothing is more dangerous to the standard of life, or so destructive of those minimum conditions of healthy existence, which must in the interests of the community be assured to every worker, than any widespread or continued unemployment. It has always been a fundamental principle of the Labour Party (a point on which significantly enough it has not been followed by either of the other political parties) that in a modern industrial community, it is one of the foremost obligations of the Government to find, for every willing worker, whether by hand or by brain, productive work at standard rates.

"It is accordingly the duty of the Government to adopt a policy of deliberately and systematically preventing the occurrence of unemployment, instead of (as heretofore) letting unemployment occur, and then seeking, vainly and expensively, to relieve the unemployment. It is now known that the Government can, if it chooses, arrange the public works and the orders of national departments and local authorities in such a way as to maintain the aggregate demand for labour in the whole kingdom (including that of capitalist employers) approximately at a uniform level from year to year; and it is therefore a primary obligation of the Government to prevent any considerable or widespread fluctuations in the total numbers employed in times of good or bad trade. But this is not all. In order to prepare for the possibility of there being any unemployment, either in the course of demobilization or in the first years of peace, it is essential that the Government should make all necessary preparations for putting instantly in hand, directly or through the local authorities, such urgently needed public works as (a) the rehousing of the population alike in rural districts, mining villages, and town slums, to the extent, possibly, of a million new cottages and an outlay of 300 millions sterling; (b) the immediate making good of the shortage of schools, training colleges, technical colleges, etc., and the engagement of the necessary additional teaching, clerical and administrative staffs; (c) new roads; (d) light railways; (e) the unification and reorganisation of the railway and canal system; (f) afforestation; (g) the reclamation of land; (h) the development and better equipment of our ports and harbours; (i) the opening up of access to land by co-operative small holdings and in other practicable ways. Moreover, in order to relieve any pressure of an overstocked labour market, the opportunity should be taken, if unemployment should threaten to become widespread, (a) immediately to raise the school-leaving age to sixteen; (b) greatly to increase the number of scholarships and bursaries for secondary and higher education; and (c) substantially to shorten the hours of labour of all young persons, even to a greater extent than the eight hours per week contemplated in the new Education Bill, in order to enable them to attend technical and other classes in the daytime. Finally, wherever practicable, the hours of adult labour should be reduced to not more than forty-eight per week, without reduction of the standard rates of wages. There can be no economic or other justification for keeping any man or woman to work for long hours, or at overtime, whilst others are unemployed.

"SOCIAL INSURANCE AGAINST UNEMPLOYMENT

"In so far as the Government fails to prevent unemployment—wherever it finds it impossible to discover for any willing worker, man or woman, a suitable situation at the standard rate—the Labour Party holds that the Government must, in the interest of the community as a whole, provide him or her with adequate maintenance, either with such arrangements for honorable employment or with such useful training as may be found practicable, according to age, health and previous occupation. In many ways the best form of provision for those who must be unemployed, because the industrial organisation of the community so far breaks down as to be temporarily unable to set them to work, is the Out of Work Benefit afforded by a well administered Trade Union. This is a special tax on the trade unionists themselves which they have voluntarily undertaken, but towards which they have a right to claim a public subvention—a subvention which was actually granted by Parliament (though only to the extent of a couple of shillings or so per week) under Part II of the Insurance Act. The arbitrary withdrawal by the Government in 1915 of this statutory right of the Trade Unions was one of the least excusable of the war economies; and the Labour Party must insist on the resumption of this subvention immediately the war ceases, and on its increase to at least half the amount spent in Out of Work Benefit. The extension of state unemployment insurance to other occupations may afford a convenient method of providing for such of the unemployed, especially in the case of badly paid women workers and the less skilled men, whom it is difficult to organise in Trade Unions. But the weekly rate of the state unemployment benefits needs, in these days of high prices, to be considerably raised; whilst no industry ought to be compulsorily brought within its scope against the declared will of the workers concerned, and especially of their Trade Unions. In one way or another remunerative employment or honorable maintenance must be found for every willing worker, by hand or by brain, in bad times as well as in good. It is clear that, in the twentieth century, there must be no question of driving the unemployed to anything so obsolete and discredited as either private charity, with its haphazard and ill-considered doles, or the Poor Law, with the futilities and barbarities of its 'Stone Yard,' or its 'Able-bodied Test Workhouse.' Only on the basis of a universal application of the policy of the National Minimum, affording complete security against destitution, in sickness and health, in good times and bad alike, to every member of the community of whatever age or sex, can any worthy social order be built up.

"THE DEMOCRATIC CONTROL OF INDUSTRY

"The universal application of the policy of the National Minimum is, of course, only the first of the Pillars of the House that the Labour Party intends to see built. What marks off this party most distinctively from any of the other political parties is its demand for the full and genuine adoption of the principle of democracy. The first condition of democracy is effective personal freedom. This has suffered so many encroachments during the war that it is necessary to state with clearness that the complete removal of all the wartime restrictions on freedom of speech, freedom of publication, freedom of the press, freedom of travel and freedom of choice of place of residence and kind of employment must take place the day after Peace is declared. The Labour Party declared emphatically against any continuance of the Military Service Acts a moment longer than the imperative requirements of the war excuse. But individual freedom is of little use without complete political rights. The Labour Party sees its repeated demands largely conceded in the present Representation of the People Act, but not yet wholly satisfied. The party stands, as heretofore, for complete adult suffrage, with not more than a three months' residential qualification, for effective provision for absent electors to vote, for absolutely equal rights for both sexes, for the same freedom to exercise civic rights for the 'common soldier' as for the officer, for shorter parliaments, for the complete abolition of the House of Lords, and for a most strenuous opposition to any new Second Chamber, whether elected or not, having in it any element of heredity or privilege, or of the control of the House of Commons by any party or class. But unlike the Conservative and Liberal Parties, the Labour Party insists on Democracy in industry as well as in government. It demands the progressive elimination from the control of industry of the private capitalist, individual or joint-stock; and the setting free of all who work, whether by hand or by brain, for the service of the community, and of the community only. And the Labour Party refuses absolutely to believe that the British people will permanently tolerate any reconstruction or perpetuation of the disorganisation, waste and inefficiency involved in the abandonment of British industry to a jostling crowd of separate private employers, with their minds bent, not on the service of the community, but — by the very law of their being — only on the utmost possible profiteering. What the nation needs is undoubtedly a great bound onward in its aggregate productivity. But this cannot be secured merely by pressing the manual workers to more strenuous toil, or even by encouraging the 'Captains of Industry' to a less wasteful organisation of their several enterprises on a profit-making basis. What the Labour Party looks to is a genuinely scientific reorganisation of the nation's industry, no longer deflected by individual profiteering, on the basis of the common ownership of the means of production; the equitable sharing of the proceeds among all who participate in any capacity and only among these, and the adoption, in particular services and occupation, of those systems and methods of administration and control that may be found, in practice, best to promote, not profiteering, but the public interest.

"IMMEDIATE NATIONALISATION

"The Labour Party stands not merely for the principle of the common ownership of the nation's land, to be applied as suitable opportunities occur, but also, specifically, for the immediate nationalisation of railways, mines, and the production of electrical power. We hold that the very foundation of any successful reorganisation of British industry must necessarily be found in the provision of the utmost facilities for transport and communication, the production of power at the cheapest possible rate, and the most economical supply of both electrical energy and coal to every corner of the kingdom. Hence the Labour Party stands, unhesitatingly, for the national ownership and administration of the railways and canals, and their union, along with harbours and roads and the posts and telegraphs — not to say also the great lines of steamers which could at once be owned, if not immediately directly managed in detail, by the Government — in a united national service of communication and transport; to be worked, unhampered by capitalist, private or purely local interests (and with a steadily increasing participation of the organised workers in the management, both central and local), exclusively for the common good. If any Government should be so misguided as to propose, when peace comes, to hand the railways back to the shareholders; or should show itself so spendthrift of the nation's property as to give these shareholders any enlarged franchise by presenting them with the economics of unification or the profits of increased railway rates; or so extravagant as to bestow public funds on the re-equipment of privately owned lines — all of which things are now being privately intrigued for by the railway interests — the Labour Party will offer any such project the most strenuous opposition. The railways and canals, like the roads, must henceforth belong to the public, and to the public alone.

"In the production of electricity, for cheap power, light and heating, this country has so far failed, because of hampering private interests, to take advantage of science. Even in the largest cities we still 'peddle' our electricity on a contemptibly small scale. What is called for, immediately after the war, is the erection of a score of gigantic 'super-power stations,' which could generate, at incredibly cheap rates, enough electricity for the use of every industrial establishment and every private household in Great Britain; the present municipal and joint-stock electrical plants being universally linked up and used for local distribution. This is inevitably the future of electricity. It is plain that so great and so powerful an enterprise, affecting every industrial enterprise and, eventually every household, must not be allowed to pass into the hands of private capitalists. They are already pressing the Government for the concession, and neither the Liberal nor the Conservative Party has yet made up its mind to a refusal of such a new endowment of profiteering in what will presently be the life-blood of modern productive industry.

The Labour Party demands that the production of electricity on the necessary gigantic scale shall be made, from the start (with suitable arrangements for municipal co-operation in local distribution), a national enterprise, to be worked exclusively with the object of supplying the whole kingdom with the cheapest possible power, light, and heat.

"But with the railways and the generation of electricity in the hands of the public, it would be criminal folly to leave to the present 1,500 colliery companies the power of 'holding up' the coal supply. These are now all working under public control, on terms that virtually afford to their shareholders a statutory guarantee of their swollen incomes. The Labour Party demands the immediate nationalisation of mines, the extraction of coal and iron being worked as a public service (with a steadily increasing participation in the management, both central and local, of the various grades of persons employed); and the whole business of the retail distribution of household coal being undertaken, as a local public service, by the elected Municipal or County Councils. And there is no reason why coal should fluctuate in price any more than railway fares, or why the consumer should be made to pay more in winter than in summer, or in one town than another. What the Labour Party would aim at is, for household coal of standard quality, a fixed and uniform price for the whole kingdom, payable by rich and poor alike, as unalterable as the penny postage stamp.

"But the sphere of immediate nationalisation is not restricted to these great industries. We shall never succeed in putting the gigantic system of health insurance on a proper footing, or secure a clear field for the beneficent work of the Friendly Societies, or gain a free hand for the necessary development of the urgently called for Ministry of Health and the Local Public Health Service, until the nation expropriates the profit-making industrial insurance companies, which now so tyrannously exploit the people with their wasteful house-to-house industrial life assurance. Only by such an expropriation of life assurance companies can we secure the universal provision, free from the burdensome toll of weekly pence, of the indispensable funeral benefit. Nor is it in any sense a 'class' measure. Only by the assumption by a state department of the whole business of life assurance can the millions of policy holders of all classes be completely protected against the possibly calamitous results of the depreciation of securities and suspension of bonuses which the war is causing. Only by this means can the great staff of insurance agents find their proper places as civil servants, with equitable conditions of employment, compensation for any disturbance and security of tenure, in a nationally organised public service for the discharge of the steadily increasing functions of the Government in vital statistics and social insurance.

"In quite another sphere the Labour Party sees the key to temperance reform in taking the entire manufacture and retailing of alcoholic drink out of the hands of those who find profit in promoting the utmost possible consumption. This is essentially a case in which the people, as a whole, must assert its right to full and unfettered power for dealing with the licensing question in accordance with local opinion. For this purpose, localities should have conferred upon them facilities:

"(a) To prohibit the sale of liquor within their boundaries;

"(b) To reduce the number of licences and regulate the conditions under which they may be held; and

"(c) If a locality decides that licences are to be granted, to determine whether such licences shall be under private or any form of public control.

"Municipalisation

"Other main industries, especially those now becoming monopolised, should be nationalised as opportunity offers. Moreover, the Labour party holds that the municipalities should not confine their activities to the necessarily costly services of education, sanitation and police; nor yet rest content with acquiring control of the local water, gas, electricity, and tramways; but that every facility should be afforded to them to acquire (easily, quickly and cheaply) all the land they require, and to extend their enterprises in housing and town planning, parks, and public libraries, the provisions of music and the organisation of recreation; and also to undertake, besides the retailing of coal, other services of common utility, particularly the local supply of milk, wherever this is not already fully and satisfactorily organised by a Co-operative Society.

"Control of Capitalist Industry

"Meanwhile, however, we ought not to throw away the valuable experience now gained by the Government in its assumption of the importation of wheat, wool, metals, and other commodities, and in its control of the shipping, woollen, leather, clothing, boot and shoe, milling, baking, butchering, and other industries. The Labour Party holds that, whatever may have been the shortcomings of this Government importation and control, it has demonstrably prevented a lot of 'profiteering.' Nor can it end immediately on the declaration of peace. The people will be extremely foolish if they ever allow their indispensable industries to slip back into the unfettered control of private capitalists, who are, actually at the instance of the Government itself, now rapidly combining, trade by trade, into monopolist trusts, which may presently become as ruthless in their extortion as the worst American examples. Standing as it does for democratic control of industry, the Labour Party would think twice before it sanctioned any abandonment of the present profitable centralization of purchase of raw materials; of the present carefully organized 'rationing,' by joint committees of the trades concerned, of the several establishments with the materials they require; of the present elaborate system of 'costing' and public audit of manufacturers' accounts, so as to stop the waste heretofore caused by the mechanical inefficiency of the more backward firms; of the present salutary publicity of manufacturing processes and expenses thereby ensured; and, on the information thus obtained (in order never again to revert to the old-time profiteering) of the present rigid fixing, for standardized products, of maximum prices at the factory, at the warehouse of the wholesale trader and in the retail shop. This question of the retail prices of household commodities is emphatically the most practical of all political issues to the woman elector. The male politicians have too long neglected the grievances of the small household, which is the prey of every profiteering combination; and neither the Liberal nor the Conservative party promises, in this respect, any amendment. This, too, is in no sense a 'class' measure. It is, so the Labour Party holds, just as much the function of Government, and just as necessary a part of the democratic regulation of industry, to safe-guard the interests of the community as a whole, and those of all grades and sections of private consumers, in the matter of prices, as it is, by the Factory and Trade Boards Acts, to protect the rights of the wage-earning producers in the matter of wages, hours of labour, and sanitation.

"A Revolution in National Finance

"In taxation, also, the interests of the professional and housekeeping classes are at one with those of the manual workers. Too long has our national finance been regulated, contrary to the teaching of political economy, according to the wishes of the possessing classes and the profits of the financiers. The colossal expenditure involved in the present war (of which, against the protest of the Labour Party, only a quarter has been raised by taxation, whilst three-quarters have been borrowed at onerous rates of interest, to be a burden on the nation's future) brings things to a crisis. When peace comes, capital will be needed for all sorts of social enterprises, and the resources of Government will necessarily have to be vastly greater than they were before the war. Meanwhile innumerable new private fortunes are being heaped up by those who take advantage of the nation's need; and the one-tenth of the population which owns nine-tenths of the riches of the United Kingdom, far from being made poorer, will find itself, in the aggregate, as a result of the war, drawing in rent and interest and dividends a larger nominal income than ever before. Such a position demands a revolution in national finance. How are we to discharge a public debt that may well reach the almost incredible figure of 7,000 million pounds sterling, and at the same time raise an annual revenue which, for local as well as central government, must probably reach 1,000 million a year? It is over this burden of taxation that the various political parties will be found to be most sharply divided.

"The Labour Party stands for such a system of taxation as will yield all the necessary revenue to the Government without encroaching on the prescribed national minimum standard of life of any family whatsoever; without hampering production or discouraging any useful personal effort, and with the nearest possible approximation of equality of sacrifice. We definitely repudiate all proposals for a protective tariff, in whatever specious guise they may be cloaked, as a device for burdening the consumer with unnecessarily enhanced prices, to the profit of the capitalist employer or landed proprietor, who avowedly expects his profits or rent to be increased thereby. We shall strenuously oppose any taxation, of whatever kind, which would increase the price of food or of any other necessary of life. We hold that indirect taxation on commodities, whether by customs or excise, should be strictly limited to luxuries; and concentrated principally on those of which it is socially desirable that the consumption should be actually discouraged. We are at one with the manufacturer, the farmer and the trader in objecting to taxes interfering with production or commerce, or hampering transport and communications. In all these matters — once more in contrast with the other political parties, and by no means in the interests of the wage-earners alone — the Labour Party demands that the very definite teachings of economic science should no longer be disregarded.

"For the raising of the greater part of the revenue now required the Labour Party looks to the direct taxation of the incomes above the necessary cost of family maintenance; and for the requisite effort to pay off the national debt, to the direct taxation of private fortunes both during life and at death. The income tax and super-tax ought at once to be thoroughly reformed in assessment and collection, in abatements and allowances, and in graduation and differentiation, so as to levy the required total sum in such a way as to make the real sacrifice of all the taxpayers as nearly as possible equal. This would involve assessment by families instead of by individual persons, so that the burden is alleviated in proportion to the number of persons to be maintained. It would involve the raising of the present unduly low minimum income assessable to the tax, and the lightening of the present unfair burden on the great mass of professional and small trading classes by a new scale of graduation, rising from a penny in the pound on the smallest assessable income up to sixteen or even nineteen shillings in the pound on the highest income of the millionaires. It would involve bringing into assessment the numerous windfalls of profit that now escape, and a further differentiation between essentially different kinds of income. The excess profits tax might well be retained in an appropriate form; while so long as mining royalties exist the mineral rights duty ought to be increased. The steadily rising unearned increment of urban and mineral land ought, by an appropriate direct taxation of land values, to be wholly brought into the public exchequer. At the same time, for the service and redemption of the national debt, the death duties ought to be regraduated, much more strictly collected, and greatly increased. In this matter we need, in fact, completely to reverse our point of view, and to rearrange the whole taxation of inheritance from the standpoint of asking what is the maximum amount that any rich man should be permitted at death to divert, by his will, from the national exchequer, which should normally be the heir to all private riches in excess of a quite moderate amount by way of family provision. But all this will not suffice. It will be imperative at the earliest possible moment to free the nation from at any rate the greatest part of its new load of interest-bearing debts for loans which ought to have been levied as taxation; and the Labour Party stands for a special capital levy to pay off, if not the whole, a very substantial part of the entire national debt — a capital levy chargeable like the death duties on all property, but (in order to secure approximate equality of sacrifice) with exemption of the smallest savings, and for the rest at rates very steeply graduated, so as to take only a small contribution from the little people and a very much larger percentage from the millionaires.

"Over this issue of how the financial burden of the war is to be borne, and how the necessary revenue is to be raised, the greatest political battles will be fought. In this matter the Labour Party claims the support of four-fifths of the whole nation, for the interests of the clerk, the teacher, the doctor, the minister of religion, the average retail shopkeeper and trader, and all the mass of those living on small incomes are identical with those of the artisan. The landlords, the financial magnates, the possessors of great fortunes will not, as a class, willingly forego the relative immunity that they have hitherto enjoyed. The present unfair subjection of the Co-operative Society to an Excess Profits Tax on the 'profits' which it has never made — specially dangerous as 'the thin end of the wedge' of penal taxation of this laudable form of democratic enterprise — will not be abandoned without a struggle. Every possible effort will be made to juggle with the taxes, so as to place upon the shoulders of the mass of labouring folk and upon the struggling households of the professional men and small traders (as was done after every previous war) — whether by customs or excise duties, by industrial monopolies, by unnecessarily high rates of postage and railway fares, or by a thousand and one other ingenious devices — an unfair share of the national burden. Again at these efforts the Labour Party will take the firmest stand.

"THE SURPLUS FOR THE COMMON GOOD

"In the disposal of the surplus above the standard of life society has hitherto gone as far wrong as in its neglect to secure the necessary basis of any genuine industrial efficiency or decent social order. We have allowed the riches of our mines, the rental value of the lands superior to the margin of cultivation, the extra profits of the fortunate capitalists, even the material outcome of scientific discoveries — which ought by now to have made this Britain of ours immune from class poverty or from any widespread destitution — to be absorbed by individual proprietors; and then devoted very largely to the senseless luxury of an idle rich class. Against this misappropriation of the wealth of the community, the Labour Party — speaking in the interests not of the wage-earners alone, but of every grade and section of producers by hand or by brain, not to mention also those of the generations that are to succeed us, and of the permanent welfare of the community — emphatically protests. One main pillar of the house that the Labour Party intends to build is the future appropriation of the surplus, not to the enlargement of any individual fortune, but to the common good. It is from this constantly arising surplus (to be secured, on the one hand, by nationalisation and municipalisation and, on the other, by the steeply graduated taxation of private income and riches) that will have to be found the new capital which the community day by day needs for the perpetual improvement and increase of its various enterprises, for which we shall decline to be dependent on the usury-exacting financiers. It is from the same source that has to be defrayed the public provision for the sick and infirm of all kinds (including that for maternity and infancy) which is still so scandalously insufficient; for the aged and those prematurely incapacitated by accident or disease, now in many ways so imperfectly cared for; for the education alike of children, of adolescents and of adults, in which the Labour Party demands a genuine equality of opportunity, overcoming all differences of material circumstances; and for the organisation of public improvements of all kinds, including the brightening of the lives of those now condemned to almost ceaseless toil, and a great development of the means of recreation. From the same source must come the greatly increased public provision that the Labour Party will insist on being made for scientific investigation and original research, in every branch of knowledge, not to say also for the promotion of music, literature and fine art, which have been under Capitalism so greatly neglected, and upon which, so the Labour party holds, any real development of civilisation fundamentally depends. Society, like the individual, does not live by bread alone — does not exist only for perpetual wealth production. It is in the proposal for this appropriation of every surplus for the common good — in the vision of its resolute use for the building up of the community as a whole instead of for the magnification of individual fortunes — that the Labour Party, as the party of the producers by hand or by brain, most distinctively marks itself off from the older political parties, standing, as these do essentially for the maintenance, unimpaired, of the perpetual private mortgage upon the annual product of the nation that is involved in the individual ownership of land and capital.

"THE STREET OF TO-MORROW

" The House which the Labour Party intends to build, the four Pillars of which have now been described, does not stand alone in the world. Where will it be in the Street of To-Morrow? If we repudiate, on the one hand, the imperialism that seeks to dominate other races, or to impose our own will on other parts of the British Empire, so we disclaim equally any conception of a selfish and insular 'non-interventionism' unregarding of our special obligations to our fellow-citizens overseas; of the corporate duties of one nation to another; of the moral claims upon us of the non-adult races, and of our own indebtedness to the world of which we are part. We look for an ever-increasing intercourse, a constantly developing exchange of commodities, a steadily growing mutual understanding, and a continually expanding friendly co-operation among all the peoples of the world. With regard to that great Commonwealth of all races, all colours, all religions and all degrees of civilisation, that we call the British Empire, the Labour Party stands for its maintenance and its progressive development on the lines of local autonomy and 'Home Rule All Round'; the fullest respect for the rights of each people, whatever its colour, to all the democratic self-government of which it is capable, and to the proceeds of its own toil upon the resources of its own territorial home; and the closest possible co-operation among all the various members of what has become essentially not an empire in the old sense, but a Britannic alliance. We desire to maintain the most intimate relations with the Labour parties overseas. Like them, we have no sympathy with the projects of 'Imperial Federation,' in so far as these imply the subjection to a common imperial legislature wielding coercive power (including dangerous facilities for coercive imperial taxation and for enforced military service), either of the existing self-governing dominions, whose autonomy would be thereby invaded; or of the United Kingdom, whose freedom of democratic self-development would be thereby hampered; or of India and the colonial dependencies, which would thereby run the risk of being further exploited for the benefit of a 'White Empire.' We do not intend, by any such 'Imperial Senate,' either to bring the plutocracy of Canada and South Africa to the aid of the British aristocracy or to enable the landlords and financiers of the mother country to unite in controlling the growing popular democracies overseas. The absolute autonomy of each self-governing part of the empire must be maintained intact. What we look for, besides a constant progress in democratic self-government of every part of the Britannic alliance, and especially in India, is a continuous participation of the ministers of the Dominions, of India, and eventually of other dependencies (perhaps by means of their own ministers specially resident in London for this purpose) in the most confidential deliberations of the Cabinet, so far as foreign policy and imperial affairs are concerned; and the annual assembly of an Imperial Council, representing all constituents of the Britannic alliance and all parties in their local legislatures, which should discuss all matters of common interest, but only in order to make recommendations for the simultaneous consideration of the various autonomous local legislatures of what should increasingly take the constitutional form of an Alliance of Free Nations. And we carry the idea further. As regards our relations to foreign countries, we disavow and disclaim any desire or intention to dispossess or to impoverish any other State or nation. We seek no increase of territory. We disclaim all idea of 'economic war.' We ourselves object to all protective customs tariffs; but we hold that each nation must be left free to do what it thinks best for its own economic development, without thought of injuring others. We believe that nations are in no way damaged by each other's economic prosperity or commercial progress; but, on the contrary, that they are actually themselves mutually enriched thereby. We would therefore put an end to the old entanglements and mystifications of secret diplomacy and the formation of leagues against leagues. We stand for immediate establishment, actually as a part of the treaty of peace with which the present war will end, of a universal league or society of nations, a supernational authority, with an international high court to try all justifiable issues between nations; an international legislature to enact such common laws as can be mutually agreed upon, and an international council of mediation to endeavor to settle without ultimate conflict even those disputes which are not justiciable. We would have all the nations of the world most solemnly undertake and promise to make a common cause against any one of them that broke away from this fundamental agreement. The world has suffered too much from war for the Labour Party to have any other policy than that of lasting peace.

"MORE LIGHT — BUT ALSO MORE WARMTH!

"The Labour Party is far from assuming that it possesses a key to open all locks; or that any policy which it can formulate will solve all the problems that beset us. But we deem it important to ourselves as well as to those who may, on the one hand, wish to join the party, or, on the other, to take up arms against it, to make quite clear and definite our aim and purpose. The Labour Party wants that aim and purpose, as set forth in the preceding pages, with all its might. It calls for more warmth in politics, for much less apathetic acquiescence in the miseries that exist, for none of the cynicism that saps the life of leisure. On the other hand, the Labour Party has no belief in any of the problems of the world being solved by good will alone. Good will without knowledge is warmth without light. Especially in all the complexities of politics, in the still undeveloped science of society, the Labour Party stands for increased study, for the scientific investigation of each succeeding problem, for the deliberate organization of research, and for a much more rapid dissemination among the whole people of all the science that exists. And it is perhaps specially the Labour Party that has the duty of placing this advancement of science in the forefront of its political programme. What the Labour Party stands for in all fields of life is, essentially, democratic co-operation; and co-operation involves a common purpose which can be agreed to; a common plan which can be explained and discussed, and such a measure of success in the adaptation of means to ends as will ensure a common satisfaction. An autocratic Sultan may govern without science if his whim is law. A plutocratic party may choose to ignore science, if it is heedless whether its pretended solutions of social problems that may win political triumphs ultimately succeed or fail. But no Labour Party can hope to maintain its position unless its proposals are, in fact, the outcome of the best political science of its time; or to fulfill its purpose unless that science is continually wresting new fields from human ignorance. Hence, although the purpose of the Labour Party must, by the law of its being, remain for all time unchanged, its policy and its programme will, we hope, undergo a perpetual development, as knowledge grows, and as new phases of the social problem present themselves, in a continually finer adjustment of our measures to our ends. If law is the mother of freedom, science, to the Labour Party, must be the parent of law.

THE BRITISH GOVERNMENT AND LABOR

During 1919 and the early part of 1920 Premier Lloyd George became convinced that the ultimate aim of the various labor and socialist organizations of Great Britain was to secure the triumph of the new social order by any and every means; that at the proper moment parliamentary action would be deserted for economic pressure and violent action if necessary. He believed that the conservative old-time Labor leaders who would try to hold the rank and file in leash would be swept aside and the younger and more radical leaders placed in command. The premier felt so strongly the imminence of the attempt either to establish a super-government of Labor in virtual command, or an entirely new state, that he proposed a coalition of the various Conservative and Liberal groups, uniting against the tyranny of Labor. This he was unable to accomplish.

More and more the leadership of British labor had been assumed by the head of the Miners and of the Triple Alliance, Robert Smillie. He is quoted as saying, immediately after the Armistice, on November 19, 1918, that the workers must "utterly refuse to recognize a Coalition Government and at once form the Soviet Workers' Government, as the time has now arrived for the workers to control their destiny."

Even more radical was John MacLean of Glasgow, who was also the leader in the Clyde revolutionary movement. He came out in January, 1919, with an approval and intensifying of Smillie's appeal. He proposed sabotage in the mining and other industries, and added: "With a determined revolutionary minority we shall be able to take control of the country and the means of production at once, and hold them tight through disciplined production under the Workshop Committees and the District and National Councils. Through the co-operative movement we shall be able to control the full distribution of the necessaries of life and so win the masses to Socialism."

Such statements as these, which could easily be multiplied, give ground for Lloyd George's premonitions.

LATEST ATTITUDE OF BRITISH LABOR

Over against the pessimism of Lloyd George there is the opinion epitomized by Arthur Gleason in a recent number of the "World" that even the great radical labor leader of Britain, Robert Smillie, head of the miners and of the Triple Alliance, does not believe in gaining Labor's votes by coercion. He says:

> "Smillie's social revolution is a capture of Parliament by votes, and the creation of legislation by a duly elected majority. 'Five, ten, fifteen years,' he says — whatever time is necessary to do the job peaceably by persuasion."

The latest strike threat in Britain, that of the miners, has just been compromised by giving the miners two-thirds of the increase in wages which they demanded. The acceptance of this solution by the miners, temporarily, was probably due to the decision of the British Trades Union Congress, representing practically all the elements of labor in Great Britain, which decided against a general strike, proposed by the miners. The "National Labor Digest" of April, 1920, gives a summary of the situation to date:

> "The question came up in connection with the nationalization of the coal mines. John R. Clynes, president of the National Union of General Workers, and former food controller, arguing against 'Direct Action,' said:
>
> > "Force, as it has been proposed to employ it, is not a British, but a Prussian characteristic.
>
> "J. H. Thomas, leader of the railwaymen, voicing opposition to the miners' plan to force nationalization through a general strike, asked:
>
> > "What right have we to call upon men and women to force the hands of the government by action which cannot fail to inflict on the nation an upheaval that will inevitably entail bloodshed while not necessarily achieving our object?
>
> "In their attempt to force nationalization of the coal industry 524,000 miners had voted in favor of a general

> strike, while 346,000 had opposed it. The miners, however, decided to abide by the decision of the Trades Union Congress, which voted against a general strike by a majority of 2,820,000 in a total vote of 4,920,000, the radicals losing by nearly four to one."

This conservative decision of the Trades Union Congress has, for the moment, put off the labor crisis in Great Britain.

AUSTRALIA AND NEW ZEALAND

Australia and New Zealand occupy an absolutely unique position in history, in that they were the first countries in which labor has taken possession of the government. The experiment of New Zealand in socialism, and the later experiment in Australia, after the Labor Party gained a majority in the Federal Senate and House, was not in the least on the basis of scientific Socialism or Marxian theory. It was simply a plain practical out-and-out labor government. The crisis that brought about the growth of the Labor Party as an organization, was the result of the great strike in 1890, which brought the country, on the side both of capital and labor, to the bring of ruin. In 1891, twenty-four representatives of the Labor Party were elected to the New South Wales Legislature, and from that time the movement grew with great rapidity.

From 1901 to 1909, the liberal protectionists carried on the government for the support of the Labor Party against the conservative free traders. A further step in advance was made during the election of 1911, when the Labor Party secured a majority, both in the Federal Senate and House of Representatives, and remained in power for three years up to the election of 1913.

Then, as before, it was opposed by a fusion party. It increased its majority in the Senate, and lost the House by only one vote. When the war broke out in 1914, labor had reached its high-water mark. Every state, except Victoria, had a labor government, and labor was in charge of the Federal Government. Between then and 1917, through the change in sentiment caused by the war, the Labor Party lost ground, and in 1917, the only state where the Labor Party remained in power was Queensland. The most important split in the party occurred in 1916, when Prime Minister Hughes visited England. His extreme imperialism divided the party, which also differed on the issue of conscription. In the elections of May 5, 1917, the Labor Party polled 47 per cent. of the votes, and the fusion ticket 53 per cent. Meanwhile, Hughes had been expelled from the party and had joined the Liberals.

In 1918–1919, a new movement started in the labor field in Australia, through the I. W. W. propaganda, and the idea of the one big union was endorsed by many unions. The W. I. U. of Australia was formed, "to bind together in one organization all wage workers in every industry, to achieve the purposes set forth in the preamble." This preamble was practically identical with the union preamble of the American I. W. W's, and declared for the abolition of capitalistic class-ownership and the establishment of social ownership by the whole community. For this reason, it was opposed by the bulk of Australian labor, and in the summer of 1919, the Australian labor conference put itself on record as strongly opposed to the one big union. This movement to differentiate between industrial unionism and craft unionism has led to great recent increase in the membership of the trade unions, which has risen from about 55,000 in 1894, to 590,000 in 1918.

A special Socialist Party in Australia was very late in developing, and was divided, as most Socialist parties, into several factions of either revolutionary or non-revolutionary character. All these branches, however, were against the war, and in this policy they had the co-operation of the militant wing of the Labor Party. It is said, however, that the theory of Socialism in its usual scientific Marxian expression, is of very little influence in Australia. The work of the Labor Party during the course of its administration in different states and in the Federal Government has been extremely constructive, and practically none of its legislation has been seriously criticized by the fusion parties of opposition.

There is an interesting statement in the "Christian Science Monitor" of October 29, 1919, of the present labor and Socialist situation in Australia. It says:

> "Today, the Australian labor movement, industrially and politically, is in a flux, and the position is unprecedented. The seamen have concluded to strike, which they claim means a victory for direct action. The one big union have reorganized their campaign, and the labor party in New South Wales has been split by the secession from the official ranks of the movement of some prominent leaders who have formed a Socialist Party of their own.
>
> "The seamen's strike, however, is the most important factor in the recent developments, for the strike had much more behind it than the demand of the seamen for increased wages and altered working conditions. It was essentially an attack upon the Arbitration Court, and the leaders of the seamen openly proclaimed that they would determine that the court would no longer be recognized by the seamen. In fact, it

was the first attempt by a great industrial organization to establish the plan of direct action as against arbitration, and the rest of the industrial movement awaited the result with keen interest, because officials realized that upon the issue depended vital decisions of policy by other organizations.

"Broadly put, the result has been a victory for the seamen, inasmuch as they have been granted a round table conference to deal with their claims by the government, which, at the outset, took up the position that the men must go to the Arbitration Court for the rectification of their grievances.

"The seamen after 101 days' strike, have been able to compel the government to grant a round table conference to consider their claims, the proviso being that the decisions of the conference shall be ratified by the Court. . . .

"The advocates of direct action have been quick to seize the opportunity, and they have succeeded in getting the Melbourne Trades Hall Council to authorize a ballot among the unions on the question of whether they favor 'direct action' or arbitration. This ballot is now in progress, meanwhile the Council is debating a motion in favor of the one big union form of organization."

In New South Wales, a new party was formed at this juncture by the advocates of the one big union, after they failed to capture the State Labor Conference. This new party is known as the Australian Industrial Socialist Party. It is really a political wing of the one big union, and its strength at the polls will be tested at the next New South Wales election.

The Broken Hill miners, who are a revolutionary group, struck for a six-hour day, and they declared that they are the pioneers of the coming industrial struggle in Australia. Their propaganda is in harmony with the direct action policy of the seamen.

Since then, in December, the official Manifesto of the Federal Labor Party, has been issued by its leader, Frank Tudor. It includes the repeal of the compulsory clauses of the Australian Defense Act, with the promise of more liberal and efficient clauses. Measures would be introduced to give the workers in industry a better standing and representation in the control of industry, and to provide for a minimum wage, which would automatically vary with the cost of living. National insurance against unemployment was promised. The laws relating to seafaring labor would be made to conform with modern conditions. An effective tariff would be introduced. Workers in all industries would get their full share of the benefits of protection. The use of Australian products by government contractors and departments would be made compulsory. Primary production was to be stipulated, and the wheat-growers guaranteed five shillings a bushel. A labor system of rural credits was to be arranged. On the question of the amendment of the constitution, the Manifesto says:

> "When returned to power, we intend to submit to the people for approval, proposals for the amendment of the constitution, providing for complete Australian self-government, as a British community, and for unlimited legislative powers in Australian affairs to be vested in a Commonwealth Parliament, with devolution of adequate local powers upon subordinate legislatures and municipalities."

One of the prominent politicians of Australia, after visiting America, on his departure in April, left as a message to us that he considered our method of settling industrial disputes by voluntary arbitration preferable and more successful than the Australian method of compulsory arbitration. This feeling seems to be quite universal in Australia, both among employers and in labor circles. The feeling is summarized in the "National Labor Digest" for April, page 29. According to the labor leader of Toronto, in a dispatch from Melbourne, Australian employers now admit that "it is obvious, after an experience of twenty years, that our industrial laws have lamentably failed to secure industrial peace." These words are taken from a report by a committee of the Central Council of Australia, appointed to study industrial unrest and to establish improved relations between employers and workers.

This report states that:

> "During the six years from 1913 to 1918, inclusive, there were 2,153 Australian strikes, involving 603,716 people, with a direct wage loss of $25,000,000. The workers won 837 of these disputes, while the employers won 706. There were 521 compromises and 89 not definitely settled."

In this report it is evident that the employers are not anxious to have the compulsory provisions of the Industrial Relations

Law continued in force. A similar feeling has grown among the workmen themselves, as we have already noticed.

SOCIALISM AND LABOR IN CANADA

Before the war, Socialism was practically non-existent in Canada. The little that there was of it was an importation from the United States — a branch of the American Socialist Party. The war stimulated the growth of a more independent Socialist group, especially in western Canada, with its center at Winnipeg.

The result of this movement was to cause the trade unions of this part of Canada to declare their separation from the American Federation of Labor, and to declare themselves in sympathy with the one big union, or the I. W. W. On March 16, 1919, the Western-Canadian Labor Conference declared in favor of the one big union. As a consequence, it declared in favor of immediate action of Soviet control, and of the overturning of the government. Its declarations were partly as follows:

> "Industrial Soviet control by selection of representatives from industries is more efficient and of more value to producers than the present form of Canadian political government, and we accept without alteration the principle of proletarian dictatorship, as a means of transforming society from a capitalistic to a communal basis."

Among the demands made by this Conference was "Six-hour day and five days' work a week."

NOTE.— See Addenda, Part I, for further information on Canadian problems.

CHAPTER XIII

European Socialism and the War

The crucial question before the Socialist parties even for several years before the war broke out was the attitude of the party toward militarism and war, and it was on the rock of nationalism at the time of the outbreak of the war that the ship of international socialism temporarily split. This fact and the attitude and acts of the Socialists of different countries have already been discussed in this report, but this should be supplemented by a notice of the official pronouncements of International Socialism. At the very beginning of the Second International in 1889 the demand was made at the opening Congress that standing armies should be abolished, that international arbitration tribunals should be formed, and that the people should have a voice in the question of peace and war. These general demands were stated at each successive congress. They are best typified by a resolution offered by the French Socialist leader, Jaurès, at the Paris Congress of 1900:

"1. That it is necessary for the Labor Party in each country to oppose militarism and colonial expansion with redoubled effort and increasing energy.

"2. That it is absolutely necessary to reply to the alliance of the bourgeois classes and the governments for the perpetuation of war by an alliance of the proletarians of all lands for the perpetuation of peace — that is to say, to give up more or less platonic demonstrations of international solidarity and adopt energetic international action in the common struggle against militarism.

"The Congress suggests three practical courses for carrying this out —

"1. The Socialist Parties everywhere shall educate the rising generations to oppose militarism tooth and nail.

"2. Socialist members of Parliament shall always vote against any expenditure for the army, the navy, or colonial expeditions.

"3. The standing International Socialist Committee shall be instructed to organize uniform movements of protest against militarism in all countries at one and the same time, whenever there shall be occasion to do so."

It will be remembered that it was the Franco-Prussian war of 1870 with the participation of the masses of both peoples in the war that was one of the causes for the breaking up of the First International. But since then the tremendous increase of all national armies was making any future war the war of whole nations in arms instead of a comparatively small-armed minority. This was what led to an ever greater detemination of the Socialist parties to vote against increasing armaments and to take every occasion to weaken nationalist sentiment. The most dramatic scene at the Amsterdam Conference in 1904 was the hand clasp of the representatives of Russia and Japan, then at war. The use of the general strike as a means to prevent wars was discussed at the Stuttgart Congress of 1907.

The efforts of the Socialist parties during the period before 1914 to prevent declarations of war, for instance; at the time of the Fashoda incident between England and France, at the time of the Morocco crisis between France and Germany, at the time of the separation of Sweden and Norway, to prevent a Scandinavian war. All these occasions were utilized by the Socialists to diminish the frictions that might lead to hostilities. The Stuttgart Congress, besides emphasizing the use of the strike to prevent wars, emphasized the probability that future wars would be due to economic ambitions and causes. Its resolution is more radical by far than that of Jaurès at the Paris Congress of 1900:

"The Congress reasserts the resolutions adopted by former International Congresses against militarism and imperialism and declares afresh that the war against militarism must proceed hand in hand with the general class war. Wars between nations are as a rule the consequences of their competition in the world market, for each state seeks not only to secure its existing markets, but also to conquer new ones. This means the subjugation of nations and lands, and, therefore, spells war. But wars result furthermore from the continual attempts of all lands to outstrip their neighbors in military armaments — one of the chief supports of the capitalist class supremacy, and therefore of the economic and political oppression of the proletariat. . . .

> They will cease only when the capitalist system declines or when the sacrifices of men and money have become so great . . . that the people will rise in revolt against them and sweep capitalism out of existence."

There was great opposition, especially from the German Socialists during many years to the general strike as obligatory on Socialist parties to prevent wars. Bebel, the great German leader, was against the obligation to use the general strike and against the obligation to refuse to defend the Fatherland in case of war. It was the Frenchman, Jaurès, who was most eloquent in opposition to Bebel. The Congress adopted a middle attitude, recommending the use of the general strike as a possible but not a required weapon against war. This Congress, as well as the geenral Congress at Copenhagen in 1910, demanded that Socialist representatives should vote against military grants. It is an interesting fact that the Socialists and the working class generally were more conscious in 1913 than in 1914 of the danger of a general war. They fought unsuccessfully both in Germany and in France against the tremendous increases in military budgets and in the size of the national armies. This consciousness of the approach of war was shown at the national French Socialist Congress held July 15-17, 1914, only two weeks before the declaration of war. This Congress passed a resolution that:

> "The French Party considers the spontaneous general strike of the workers of all countries, combined with anti-war propaganda among the masses, as the most workable of all means in the hands of the workers to prevent war and to force international arbitration of the dispute."

The question of the general strike and its use was to have been brought for decision before the International Congress that was to meet but never did, on August 23, 1914, in Vienna.

During the famous thirteen days which elapsed between the Austrian ultimatum to Serbia and the outbreak of the general war, the Socialists of different countries held hurried and agitated meetings against the war and attempted to bring about the adoption of some common policy, but in vain. The agitation was so great that it resulted in France in the assassination of Jaurès by a Nationalist fanatic who considered that his anti-war attitude was dangerous to the country.

SOCIALIST ATTITUDE AFTER DECLARATION OF WAR

Immediately on the declaration of war the attitude of the Socialist leaders as well as the rank and file shifted with marvellous rapidity. It was natural that Belgium should react in the most patriotic way against its brutal invaders. The leader of the Belgian Socialists, as well as chairman of the International Bureau, Emile Vandervelde, entered the Belgian Cabinet, and there were no opponents among Belgian Socialists to his action and to the patriotic loyalty of the party. In France the Socialist deputies voted in favor of war credits, the two principal leaders of the party, Sembat and Guesde, at once became members of the Cabinet, and soon after Albert Thomas, the leader of the conservative section of the party became Minister of Munitions.

In Germany the bulk of the party followed the same policy of upholding the government, whether they were or were not aware of the aggressive nature of their government's action in bringing on the war and of the fact that they were not under the same moral obligation to support their government as was the case with the Belgian, French, British and Russian Socialists. There were, however, two groups of German Socialists who differed. One of these groups was formed of "trimmers," led by Haase and Kautsky, who, while they condemned the war, were willing to abide by a caucus decision of the party to support the government. They afterwards broke away, however, and formed what they called the Independent Socialist Party. There was a second group of more logical, uncompromising Socialists, led by Karl Liebknecht and Rosa Luxembourg, who refused to abide by the decision of the majority.

Karl Liebknecht, as a member of the Reichstag, voted against the war budget and carried on a violent propaganda against the war. So much so that he was first imprisoned by the government and then sent to the front, notwithstanding his immunity as a deputy.

In Russia a small group of members of the Duma, especially the members of the Social Revolutionist Party, frankly condemned the war.

In Great Britain, the opposition to the war of the Labor and Socialist parties was at first extremely aggressive, but gradually patriotism got the better of internationalism in all but a minority.

The British Socialist Party acknowledged the right of nations to defend themselves by arms. In the same month the Parliamentary Committee of the Trades Union Congress declared itself in favor of whole-hearted support of the war.

In October, the representatives of the Labor Party in Parliament defended their position in favor of war, which had been decided on as early as August 5th and 6th, a policy which caused a split between the majority branch led by Henderson and the minority led by Ramsay MacDonald, who led the Independent Labor Party in its anti-war policy, a policy in which it was supported only by the Left Wings of the other Labor and Socialist organizations. In fact, the anti-war influence of Socialism in Great Britain was negligible.

The Socialist Party in Italy was the only national group among the belligerents which adhered consistently throughout the war and after to its pre-war policy of uncompromising opposition to war and opposition to national interests as superior to international class interests and sympathy.

Berne Socialist Conference

Early in February (2/2/19) an International Socialist Conference met at Berne, Switzerland, called by the International Socialist Bureau, as part of the Second International. Twenty-five countries were represented by ninety delegates. Its program did not satisfy either the conservative or the revolutionary extremes. The American Federation of Labor and the Social Democratic League of America refused to attend because of its anticipated revolutionary and pacifist tendencies. At the other end the Communists kept from it because they considered it unfriendly to Bolshevism, to direct action, and to extreme internationalism. Therefore, the Socialist parties of Italy, Norway, Switzerland and the United States, as well as other Communist groups, such as the Balkan groups, refused to send delegates.

Among the more prominent delegates who did attend were: Kunfi for Hungary; Troelstra, for Holland; Longuet, Renaudel, Cachin, Loriot and Thomas, for France; Adler for Hungary; MacDonald, J. H. Thomas and Henderson for Great Britain; Kautsky, Haase, and Eisner, for Germany; Huysmans, for Belgium.

The pervading spirit of the Conference was the spirit of nationalism. Some anxiety was in the air concerning the meeting and relations between the German and French delegates. The question of the responsibility for the war had to be discussed and was the question most likely to cause angry disputes. The

German delegates were willing to acknowledge, to a certain extent, the responsibility of their government, and the Congress refrained from any extreme imputation of guilt in Germany. The acknowledgment of Germany's guilt by Eisner, the Bavarian Premier, provoked a storm of protest from other German delegates and was, undoubtedly, the reason for his assassination on his return to Munich. The text of the resolution that was passed is as follows:

> "The Conference at Berne acknowledges that the question of the immediate responsibility of the war has been made clear, through the discussion and through the declaration of the German majority, stating the revolutionary spirit of new Germany and its entire separation from the old system, which was responsible for the war. In welcoming the German revolution and the development of democratic and Socialist institutions which it involves, the conference sees the way clear for the common work of the International."

The other principal topics for the Conference were the League of Nations, territorial readjustments, the Labor Charter and the Russian situation. The Labor Charter is given fully elsewhere and was, apparently, the model that was followed later by the American Federation of Labor at the Washington Conference. It is also closely connected with the section on labor passed by the Peace Conference in Paris, to which the Berne Conference appealed. In regard to territorial adjustments the resolution passed favored the self-determination of peoples, elections or plebiscites, in disputed territories, the protection of nationalities forming a minority or a majority in a country, the protection of vital economic interests by the League, the increasing of the rights of subject populations in the colonies in the matter of free self-determination through the founding of schools, the granting of local autonomy, freedom of speech and press, etc.

The Conference expressed its decided adherence to a democratic League of Nations of a popular character which should abolish standing armies and establish a free trade with international control of commercial thoroughfares.

It was reckoned that the delegates present at this Conference from Great Britain, France, Holland, Germany, Austria, the Baltic Provinces, the Ukraine, and other parts of old Russia, represented at least 50,000,000 people. The Belgian Socialists sent no delegates because they refused to meet the Socialists of the Central Powers until the latter had confessed their guilt.

The resolution on Russia led to an acrimonious discussion, because, while hailing the political revolutions in Russia and elsewhere, it criticized the idea of dictatorship of the proletariat and the oppression of free speech and free press, because creating "conditions which might accurately be described as a transition from one form of tyranny to another. Liberty, democracy, and freedom must be their steady and unchangeable goal. The revolution that did not establish liberty was not a revolution towards Socialism, and was not a revolution which Socialists ought to make themselves responsible for, nor should it allow the outside bourgeois reaction to impose upon them responsibility."

The minority that fought against this resolution was headed by Longuet and Adler.

7

APPENDIX

Chapter XIII

Reports and Documents

1. The Berne Conference.
2. Charter of Labor of the Berne Conference.
3. The Lucerne Conference.
4. Clauses for insertion in the treaty of peace.

Document No. 1

The following ample summary of both the Berne and the Lucerne conferences of the Second International are quoted from *The American Labor Year Book* for 1919–1920, pp. 308–311.

"The Berne Conference

"The International Socialist Conference held at Berne February 2–9, 1919, was called together at the initiative of the International Socialist Bureau. Hjalmar Branting, of Sweden, presided at the Conference. Among those who actively participated in the discussions were Kautsky, Haase, Eisner, Muller, Janson and Wells, Germany; Adler, Austria; MacDonald, Bunning, Ethel Snowden, J. H. Thomas, MacGuirk, Shirkie, and Henderson, Great Britain; Longuet, Renaudel, Milhaud, Cachin, Thomas, Mistral, Loriot, Verfeuil, France; Huysmans, Belgium; Troelstra, Holland; O'Brien, Ireland; Kunfi, Hungary; Justo and de Tomasso, Argentina; Locker, Palestine. In addition there were present delegates from Alsace-Lorraine, Czecho-slovakia, Denmark, Sweden, Finland, Lettland, Georgia, Esthonia, Russia, Poland, Greece, Bulgaria, Armenia, Spain and Canada, making altogether twenty-five countries represented with ninety delegates in attendance.

"Norway, Switzerland, Italy, Roumania, Serbia, and the Communist groups of other countries refused to send delegates to the Conference. Delegates from the American Socialist Party could not come in time for the Conference, while those of Australia and Ukrania arrived too late to attend the meetings.

"The resolutions which were taken up at the Conference dealt with the following matters:

> "(a) *Responsibility for the War.*—After an extended discussion on the subject, it was decided to leave the question for decision at the next international congress when there should be a larger representation and when more material would be available on this issue.

"(b) *League of Nations.*— Favoring that the League aims to prevent future wars; to abolish all standing armies and bring about disarmament; that it should create an international court of mediation and arbitration; that it should use economic weapons to enforce its decisions; that it should protect the small nationalities; that it should provide for free trade among nations and that it should secure the enforcement of the International Labor Charter adopted by this Conference.

" (c) *Territorial Question.*—Advocating self-determination of nationalities and against annexations and economic and political spheres of influence.

" (d) *Democracy and Dictatorship.*—A spirited discussion ensued on this momentous question brought about by experiences of the Russian revolution. The majority of the committee proposed a resolution in which it was claimed that democracy with various constitutional guarantees provides opportunities for Socialist work. Longuet and Adler, who were members of the committee, brought in a minority report in which they charged those favoring the resolution with working against unity in the International. They claimed that the forces who were responsible for the disruption in the International and who have supported their respective governments during the war, are anxious to attack the revolutionary Socialist elements in various countries, particularly in Russia, which attacks may be utilized against them by the bourgeoisie. The Conference adopted a resolution which also provided for the sending of a mission to Russia and placing the subject of Bolshevism on the agenda of the next international congress. The resolution, which expressed the sentiment of the majority of the conference, contained the following:

> "As a result of recent events, the Conference desires to make the constructive character of the Socialist program absolutely clear to all. Socialization consists in the methodical development of different branches of economic activity under the control of democracy. The arbitrary taking over of a few undertakings by small groups of men is not Socialism, it is nothing less than capitalism with a large number of shareholders.
>
> " Since in the opinion of the Conference the effective development of Socialism is only possible under demo-

cratic law, it follows that it is essential to eliminate from the outset all methods of socialization which would have no chance of gaining the adhesion of the majority of the people.

"Such dictatorship would be all the more dangerous if it rested upon the support of only one section of the proletariat. The inevitable consequence of such a regime could only be to paralyze the forces of the proletariat by fratricidal war. The result would be the dictatorship of reaction.

"(e) *The Labor Charter.*—Provisions of the Labor Charter are given in full in another part of this book.

"(f) *Resolution Dealing with the Return of Prisoners of War.*

"(g) *Resolution Dealing with the Continuation of the Work of the Conference.*—A commission was elected consisting of two delegates from each party represented, with Henderson, Branting and Huysmans as an Executive Committee. This commission was instructed to put before the Paris Peace Conference the decisions of the Conference and to carry on the work of unification among the Socialist forces.

"It was also empowered to convoke the next international congress, prepare an agenda, and take the necessary steps for an early reorganization of the International.

No. 2

"THE INTERNATIONAL CHARTER OF LABOR OF THE BERNE CONFERENCE (See also p. 128)

"Under the wage system, the capitalists seek to increase their profit in exploiting the workers by methods which, unless the exploitation is limited by international action of the workers, would lead to the physical, moral and intellectual decay of the workers.

"The emancipation of labor can be entirely realized only by the abolition of the capitalist system itself. Meanwhile, the resistance of the organized workers can lessen the evil; thus the worker's health, his family life and the possibility of bettering education, can be protected in such fashion that he may fulfill his duties as a citizen in the modern democracy. The capitalist form of production produces a competition in the various countries which puts the backward countries in a state of inferiority to the more advanced.

"The need of a normal basis for international labor legislation has become doubly urgent as a result of the terrific upset and enormous ravages which the popular forces have suffered because of the war. We regard the present remedy of this situation to be the constitution of a league of nations applying an international labor legislation.

"The International Trade Union Conference met at Berne and asks the league of nations to institute and apply an international system fixing the conditions of labor.

"The present conference supports the decisions of the Trades Union Conference of Leeds (1917) and Berne (1918), and asks that their essential provisions, already applied in several countries, be applied internationally and be inscribed in the treaty of peace as an international charter of labor, as follows:

"(1) The conference considers primary instruction obligatory in all countries; pre-apprenticeship everywhere. Higher schooling should be free and accessible to all, special aptitudes and aspirations not being blocked by the material conditions of life in which the children may be placed.

"Children below fifteen shall not be employed in industry.

"(2) Children from fifteen to eighteen shall not be employed more than six hours per day, with one and one-half hours rest after four hours of work. For two hours per day both sexes shall take technical continuation courses to be established for them between six in the morning and eight at night.

'The employment of children shall be prohibited (a) between eight at night and six in the morning; (b) Sundays and holidays; (c) in unhealthy industries; (d) in underground mines.

"(3) Women workers shall have a Saturday half-holiday and shall work only four hours that day; exceptions which are necessary in certain industries being compensated by a half-holiday some other day in the week.

"Women workers shall not work at night. Employers shall be forbidden to furnish home work after the regular hours of labor. Women shall not be employed in dangerous industries where it is impossible to create sufficiently healthy conditions, as, for instance, in mines where the handling of harmful matters is injurious to the health of weak constitutions.

"The employment of women for four weeks before and six weeks after maternity shall be forbidden.

"A system of maternity insurance shall be established in all countries and benefits paid in case of illness. Women's work shall be free and based on the principle of equal pay for equal work.

"(4) The hours of labor shall not exceed eight per day and forty-four per week. Night work, after eight at night and before six in the morning, shall be forbidden except where the technical nature of the work makes it inevitable.

"Where night work is necessary, the pay shall be higher.

"(5) The Saturday half-holiday shall be introduced in all countries. The weekly repose shall be of at least thirty-six hours. When the nature of the work requires Sunday work, the weekly repose shall be arranged during the week. In industries of continuous fire, the work shall be arranged so as to give the workers holidays on alternative Sundays.

"(6) To protect health, and as a guarantee against accidents, the hours of labor shall be reduced at least eight hours in very dangerous industries. The use of harmful matters is forbidden wherever they can be replaced. A list of prohibited industrial poisons shall be made; the use of white phosphorus and white lead in decoration shall be forbidden. A system of automatic coupling shall be applied internationally on the railroads.

"All laws and regulations concerning industrial labor shall in principle be applied to home work; the same is true for social insurance.

"(7) Work which may poison or injure health shall be excluded from homes.

"(8) Food industries, including the manufacture of boxes and sacks to contain food, shall be excluded from homes.

"(9) Infectious diseases must be reported in home industries and work forbidden in houses where these diseases are found. Medical inspection shall be established.

"Lists of workers employed in home industries shall be drawn up and they shall have salary-books. Committees of representatives of employers and workers shall be formed wherever home industries prevail, and they shall have legal power to fix wages. Such wage-scales shall be posted in the work-places.

"Workers shall have the right to organize in all countries. Laws and decrees submitting certain classes of workers to special conditions or depriving them of the right of organization shall be abrogated. Emigrant workers shall have the same rights as native workers, including the right to join unions and to strike. Punishment shall be provided for those who oppose the rights of organization and association.

"Foreign workers have the right to the wages and conditions of labor which have been agreed upon between the unions and employers in all branches of industry. Lacking such agreements, they shall have the right to the wages current in the region.

"(10) Emigration shall in general be free. Exceptions shall be made in the following cases:

"(a) A state may temporarily limit immigration during a period of economic depression in order to protect the native as well as the foreign workers.

"(b) Any state may control immigration in the interests of public hygiene and may temporarily forbid it.

"(c) States may demand of immigrants that they be able to read and write in their own tongue—this in order to maintain a minimum of popular education and to render possible the application of labor laws in industries employing immigrants.

"The contracting states agree to introduce without delay laws forbidding engaging workers by contract to work in other countries, thus putting an end to the abuse of private employment agencies. Such contracts shall be forbidden.

"The contracting states agree to prepare statistics of the labor market based upon local reports, mutually exchanging information as often as possible through a central international office. These statistics shall be communicated to the trade unions of each country. No worker shall be expelled from any country for trade union activity; he shall have the right of appealing to the courts against expulsion.

"If wages be insufficient to assure a normal life, and if it be impossible for employers and workers to agree, the government shall institute mixed commissions to establish minimum wages.

"(11) In order to combat unemployment, the trade union centers of the various countries maintain relations and exchange information relative to the demand and supply of labor. A system of insurance against unemployment shall be established in all countries.

"(12) All workers shall be insured by the state against industrial accidents. The benefits paid the injured or their dependents shall be fixed according to the laws of the worker's country of origin. Old age and invalidity insurance, and insurance for widows and orphans, shall be established with equal benefits for natives and foreigners.

"A foreign worker may, on departure, if he has been victim of an industrial accident, receive a lump sum—if such an agreement has been concluded between the country where he has been working and his country of origin.

"(13) A special international code shall be created for the protection of seamen, to be applied in collaboration with the seamen's unions.

"(14) The application of these measures shall in each country be confided to labor inspectors. These inspectors shall be chosen among technical, sanitary and economic experts and aided by the workers of both sexes.

"The trade unions shall watch over the application of the labor laws. Employers employing more than four workers speaking foreign tongues shall post the labor regulations and other important notices in the respective languages and shall at their own expense teach the language of the country to their employees.

"(15) To apply the international labor legislation the contracting states shall create a permanent commission constituted half of delegates of the states which are members of the league of nations and half of delegates of the international federation of labor unions.

"This permanent commission shall convoke annually the delegations of the contracting states to perfect the international labor legislation. This conference should be one-half composed of representatives of the organized workers of each country; it shall have power to make resolutions having the force of international law.

"The Permanent Commission shall collaborate with the International Labor Office at Bale and with the International Union of Trade Unions.

No. 3

"THE LUCERNE CONFERENCE

"The Committee for the Reconstitution of the International convened an international conference at Lucerne, August 2–9, 1919, to receive reports of the activities of the various committees elected at the Berne Conference. The various discussions at this Conference followed the tenor of the discussions at Berne. With a few exceptions, the decisions and resolutions of the Lucerne Conference represent the points of view expressed by the delegates at Berne, primarily because almost the same groups and individuals were represented at both conferences. Wells of the German Majority Socialists was concerned about Germany's admission into the League of Nations; Vandervelde argued that there can be no unity between the Second and Third International; Bernstein, Tsereteli and De Brouckere attacked the Russian Bolsheviks, while Hilferding, Adler, Longuet and Troelstra criticized the majority of the Conference for their failure to recognize the changes which had taken place in the revolutionary struggles of the workers.

"The Conference adopted a series of resolutions protesting against the reactionary *coup d'etat* in Hungary, allied military intervention in Russia, the continuance of the blockade against Soviet Russia and the economic support of Russian counter-revolutionary governments. The Conference again reiterated the desire to send a commission of inquiry to Soviet Russia to find out about the work of the Bolshevik government and hear testimony of the various Russian Socialist groups opposed to the Bolsheviks.

"The Conference accepted the recommendation of the Committee for the Reconstitution of the International that a plenary meeting of an International Labor and Socialist Congress should be convoked in Geneva on February 2, 1920, to which all international sections of the labor and Socialist movements accepting the principles of international Socialism should be invited. It was agreed that the agenda for this congress should include the following subjects: 1. The adoption of the draft statutes of the International. 2. Questions of responsibilities. 3. General policy of International including Peace, Democracy, Dictatorship, Socialization and Labor Legislation. 4. Organization of the press. The Permanent Committee of Action was instructed to circulate reports of the following subjects, not later than one month before the Geneva Congress: 1. Forms of democracy and its representative institutions. 2. Place of revolution in the transformation of society. 3. Relations between industry and political organization. 4. Plans for the socialization of industry in view of the present struggle between the proletariat and capitalist power. Altogether 408 votes were allotted to all the delegates from the various countries with France, Germany, Great Britain, Russia and the United States receiving thirty votes each.

"It was also decided that a concurrent meeting of parliamentary representatives of Labor and Socialist parties be held with a view to the creation of a permanent commission of Labor and Socialist parliamentary groups and to consider how joint action between parliamentary groups in different countries may be promoted, through the exchange of information and the study of questions of common interest, and to decide upon the steps which may be necessary for securing the universal adoption of decisions which have as their object the establishment of international labor standards.

"The secretary of the International Socialist Bureau is Camille Huysmans, Maison du Peuple, Brussels, Belgium."

At a meeting in London in December of the Arrangements Committee of the Second Socialist International under the Presidency of Arthur Henderson, it was decided to postpone until July 1, 1920, a meeting of the International Socialist Congress at Geneva, which had previously been arranged for February 2d. This change of date was proposed by the Swiss, Austrian and Danish parties, which are strongly tinged with Bolshevism. The schism between the various sections of the European Socialists have been growing more and more acute. The old or Second International had organized headquarters at Brussels. The new, extreme or Third International, organized at Moscow, had been joined by the branches of the Socialist Party of the Balkans, as well as by the Spartacides, by the whole Italian Socialist Party, and by the Norwegian Socialists. It was thought possible that before July there would be further changes of the allegiance between the Second and Third Internationals. The meeting of the French Socialists at the close of January in Strassburg was expected to lead to developments in the direction of a Third International distinct from that established at Moscow. which had been foreshadowed by a meeting of the Independent Socialists of Germany.

No. 4

"CLAUSES PROPOSED FOR INSERTION IN THE TREATY OF PEACE.

"The High Contracting Parties declare their acceptance of the following principles, and engage to take all necessary steps to secure their realization in accordance with the recommendation to be made by the International Labor Conference as to their practical application:

"1. In right and in fact the labor of a human being should not be treated as merchandise or an article of commerce.

"2. Employees and workers should be allowed the right of association for all lawful purposes.

"3. No child should be permitted to be employed in industry or commerce before the age of fourteen years, in order that every child may be ensured reasonable opportunities for mental and physical education.

"Between the years of fourteen and eighteen, young persons of either sex may only be employed on work which is not harmful to their physical development and on condition that the continuation of their technical or general education is ensured.

"4. Every worker has a right to a wage adequate to maintain a reasonable standard of life, having regard to the civilization of his time and country.

"5. Equal pay should be given to women and to men for work of equal value in quantity and quality.

"6. A weekly rest, including Sunday or its equivalent, for all workers.

"7. Limitation of the hours of work in industry on the basis of eight hours a day of forty-eight hours a week, subject to an exception for countries in which climatic conditions, the imperfect development of industrial organization or other special circumstances render the industrial efficiency of the workers substantially different. The International Labor Conference will recommend a basis approximately equivalent to the above for adoption in such countries.

"8. In all matters concerning their status as workers and social insurance foreign workmen lawfully admitted to any country and their families should be ensured the same treatment as the nationals of that country.

"9. All States should institute a system of inspection in which women should take part, in order to ensure the enforcement of the laws and regulations for the protection of the workers" (American Labor Year Book, 1919–1920, p. 128).

CHAPTER XIV.

The Russian Soviet Regime *

The extraordinary impetus given to the radical movement in the past two years, both in Europe and in the United States, is due in large measure to the success of the Russian Communist Party in overturning the Kerensky regime in Russia and in setting up a Soviet government founded upon the principles of that party.

The vital concern of the people of the United States in the Soviet regime results from the international character of its principles. Its leaders consider themselves to be the highest exponents of the doctrines of Marxian Socialism. Their ambition is the establishment of a world Soviet regime. Their hope is to instigate the social revolution in all countries.

It is this attitude towards foreign countries which makes it necessary for all students of the revolutionary movement to acquaint themselves as fully as possible with the history of the conditions in Russia which gave rise to this movement, and to study the character of the government established by Lenin and Trotzky. If it were not for this international aspect, the experiments in government being made in Russia would have little more than an academic interest for the American people.

Historical Sketch of the Socialist Movement in Russia

The fact that the so-called proletarian dictatorship was achieved in Russia with such apparent ease has been considered by radical workingmen in other European countries, as well as in the United States, as an indication that the time is ripe everywhere for the adoption of an active revolutionary program seeking a speedy and violent overthrow of the existing political and social order, the seizure of the machinery of government by the working class, and the introduction of a Communist regime.

In many countries the basic principles of modern society, namely, the rights of private property, individual freedom, the equality of every citizen before the law, and the equality of economic opportunity, have been put in jeopardy through the activities of revolutionary agents seeking to emulate the Russian Communist Party.

The moral and religious standards that have safe-guarded society have been sedulously and successfully undermined; class

* See Addendum, Part I.

hatred and disregard for public safety and comfort continuously preached and applied. This has been done on the basis of the Marxian system of the materialistic interpretation of history which aims to destroy the religious and ethical side of human nature.

Acting upon the Marxian doctrine that the workers of the world should unite in order to seize control of governmental machinery as well as the instruments of production and distribution, the Russian Communist Party or Bolsheviki soon after the November revolution of 1917, by means of the Central Soviet of People's Commissaries, issued a decree appropriating 2,000,000 rubles for international revolutionary propaganda.

This decree, which is signed by Lenin and Trotzky, is as follows:

"FINANCING THE INTERNATIONAL MOVEMENT

"Inasmuch as the Soviet power firmly adheres to the principles of international solidarity of the proletariat and of fraternity of the toilers of all lands; and

"Inasmuch as the struggle against war and imperialism can be brought to victory only on an international scale:

"Therefore, the Soviet of People's Commissaries deems it necessary to bring all possible means, including money, to the aid of the Left International Wing of the workers' movement of all lands, quite regardless of whether these countries are at war or in alliance with Russia; or whether they are neutral.

"To that end the Soviet of People's Commissaries, orders to appropriate for the needs of the revolutionary international movement 2,000,000 rubles, to be taken charge of by the foreign representative of the Commissariat of Foreign Affairs.

"(Signed)

President, Soviet People's Commissaries,

VL. ULIANOFF (LENIN),

"(Signed)

People's Commissary of Foreign Affairs,

L. TROTZKY."

(Published in "Izvestia," No. 250, Dec. 13, 1917, p. 9.)

Apparently as a result of this decree revolutionary emissaries were dispatched by the Soviet regime of Russia to various European countries and to the United States, sufficiently supplied with funds, well organized and acting under definite instructions from Soviet Russia. These emissaries succeeded in promoting a strong revolutionary propaganda among the working classes throughout the world. By taking advantage of the general social unrest which came as a result of the World War, these agents were instrumental in fomenting and spreading dissatisfaction among the various classes of modern society.

The strike epidemic prevailing at present on both sides of the Atlantic has received powerful support from the followers of the Soviet regime who recognize in industrial action the only weapon which gives promise of success to the revolutionary movement, as will be pointed in the following sections of this report. In fact, the various interlocking international strikes are apparently due to a distinct program worked out by the Soviet government.

All the international revolutionary Socialist elements recognize the necessity of stimulating and encouraging a wide strike movement in different countries, because it accentuates the class difference, stimulates class hatred, increases the sodidarity of the workers in different industries and offers the greatest opportunity for spreading the doctrine of open revolt of the laboring class against the existing order, thus bringing about "liberation" of the toiling masses who, according to Marx, "have nothing to lose but their chains, and the world to gain."

It is therefore considered necessary to give in this report a brief historical sketch of the development of the radical Socialist movement in Russia, because of the leadership which this movement has taken as a world movement. Such historical data may help to disclose the nature of the destructive movement referred to, as well as its correlation with the revolutionary aims proclaimed by the various Socialist-Communist factions throughout the world.

The first evidence of a revolutionary movement in Russia in recent times took place in 1825. It was not a popular movement, and was never supported by the mass of the Russian people. It was the work of three secret societies, the first aiming at a constitutional monarchy, the second at a republic and the third at a federation. The December revolt of 1825 was instigated largely by a group of Russian noblemen belonging to the Imperial Court circles. Many were officers of the Imperial

Russian Guard who sought to force the Czar, Nicholas I, to grant a series of liberal reforms, including the liberation of the Russian peasants. These were mostly officers who had returned from France after the downfall of Napoleon and who sought to implant in Russia western liberal ideas. The revolt proved a failure, being easily suppressed by the loyal regiments, and its leaders were either executed or imprisoned.

The second phase of the Russian revolutionary movement which took form in the '60s divided the two camps. The first was begun and guided by liberal idealists of aristocratic origin. Prince Peter Kuropatkin and Michael Bakunin were the founders of theoretical anarchism, while Alexander Hertzen and N. G. Chernyshevsky became the recognized leaders of the radical movement generally.

The latter soon headed a new movement among the Intelligentsia, who formed a Central Revolutionary Committee in 1862, which fomented disorders in the schools.

An imperial manifesto of February 19, 1861, granted freedom to more than 20,000,000 Russian peasants. Under the provisions of this manifesto the peasants were made owners of a considerable area of land.

In 1863 Czar Alexander II granted to the Russian people an elaborate system of local (provincial and municipal) self-government which is known under the title of the "Zemstvo" institution.

On the 20th of November, 1864, Jury Courts were established throughout Russia, and a more liberal judiciary system was instituted.

The liberal tendencies of the imperial government at that time undoubtedly encouraged the radical movement among the so-called Intelligentsia or educated classes of the Russian people.

The concessions of the imperial government, instead of tending to quiet revolutionary activities, increased the opportunity for more extended agitation against the reactionary regime of the Czar. Abstract theories of anarchism were spread among students in the universities and colleges throughout the Empire, especially through the efforts of Bakunin, Tchaykowsky and Hertzen; and for the first time in Russian history the demand was made by the Russian radical groups to confiscate all lands owned by the nobility and the Crown, and to distribute the same among the peasant population. In fact, at about this time the leaders gave up the hope of winning the ruling classes of Russia and devoted themselves to stirring up the masses.

In 1874 a secret society was established by the revolutionaries in St. Petersburg under the name of "Land and Freedom." The aims of the society were as follows:

(a) Organization of riots and uprising throughout the country.

(b) Propagation of revolutionary ideas among the toilers and peasants.

(c) Organization of fighting detachments and supplying them with arms.

(d) Establishment of systematic communications with dissenters from the Greek Orthodox Church.

Agitation carried on by this society among the peasants of Russia resulted in an attempt on the part of many peasants to seize the estates of the land owners, particularly in the district of Kiev. Disorders, however, were readily suppressed by the government.

In 1876 the members of the "Land and Freedom" group held their first demonstration in front of the Kazan Cathedral in St. Petersburg. This public protest, however, proved to be a complete failure. In general the revolutionary propaganda was unsuccessful among the peasants. The doctrines of abstract Socialism were too involved to appeal to the minds of the rural population. Very often agitators received rough treatment at the hands of the peasants themselves.

The leaders of the "Land and Freedom" group soon recognized the necessity of changing their tactics, and in 1879 a special executive committee was formed to carry out systematic terrorist tactics against government officials. This committee formed the nucleus of a revolutionary party subsequently known as "Will of the People." The extreme Wing of this revolutionary organization decided upon the assassination of Czar Alexander II in the hope that such an act would kindle flames of revolution throughout Russia.

The first attempt on the life of Alexander II, who had been the most liberal of Russia's czars, was made on February 4, 1880. The attempt was a failure, but on March 1, 1881, a group of terrorists headed by A. I. Zheliabov succeeded. A second bomb was thrown at the Emperor when on his way to the Winter Palace in St. Petersburg, severely wounded the Czar who died a few hours later.

The Terrorists issued a manifesto, signed by N. Morozov, which defined their program:

> "We must bring knives, dynamite, bombs and poison into play. By such action the authorities will be kept in fear, the general public will be continually excited, the people will be demoralized, the party will assert its vitality and the prestige of the present authority will be shattered." (Antonelli, "Bolshevik Russia," p. 13.)

Contrary to the expectations of the Terrorists the murder of the Czar did not result in a revolution throughout the country. The overwhelming majority of the Russian people still remained loyal to the Empire, the only result of the act being to cause the adoption of severe repressive measures under the reign of Czar Alexander III.

Agitation, however, was continuously carried on. The study of Marxian theories continued to attract the students of the universities and the Intelligentsia. Some workingmen's organizations had sprung up throughout Russia, among them the "Union of Struggle for the Liberation of the Working Class," founded in 1895. Among its leaders was Nicolai Lenin. It was as a result of demonstrations carried on by this organization in 1896 that Ludwig C. A. K. Martens, then a student in the technological institute of St. Petersburg, now unrecognized representative of the Soviet regime in the United States, was arrested, and after three years imprisonment deported from Russia into Germany. (See pp. 1050–52, stenographer's minutes, Committee hearings.)

In the same year (1895) the Russian Social-Democratic Labor Party was founded to co-operate with the political branch of the Socialist Party just mentioned. At the same time the party "The Will of the People" gradually developed into a Socialist revolutionary organization. While the Social Democrats conducted their propaganda among the industrial workmen in the cities, who were assuming increasing importance, the Social Revolutionists devoted their attention to the revolutionary education of the peasant masses. Destructive ideas denouncing the fundamental principles of law and order were systematically promulgated among the Russian people, and, at the same time, a number of government officials were murdered by members of the Social Revolutionary Party. The Marxian doctrines gained increasing foothold, especially through the efforts of Plechanov and his followers, including Lenin.

In 1902 the Minister of the Interior, Sypiagin, was shot by a revolutionist.

In 1903 a second Minister of the Interior, Mr. von Plehve, was murdered by a bomb thrown by another member of the Social Revolutionary Party. At the same time a number of other government officials were shot in various cities of Russia. Finally, Grand Duke Sergius was murdered in February, 1905.

At the second convention of the Russian Social-Democratic Party, which took place in London in the year 1903, a strong divergence of opinion manifested itself which led to a definite split among the members of that party. The majority insisted upon an immediate revolt against the imperial government, while the minority faction argued that Russia was not ready for a revolution, and that the changes in her political and social structure must come gradually as a result of the development of the capitalist system of production and of the education of the masses. It also was against representative electoral assemblies, stood out for centralized government, while the minority upheld a constituent national assembly and a decentralized federalist government.

The majority "Bolshinstvo" faction, which was headed by Nicolai Lenin, whose real name is Vladimir Vlianov, founded a separate group, the members of which were called the Bolsheviki. The minority of the convention, headed by Plechanov, assumed the name of Mensheviki, meaning the supporters of the minority. Thenceforth the Bolsheviki and Mensheviki constituted contending factions, and the Russian Social Democratic Party thus became divided into two hostile camps. Nevertheless, on various occasions the Mensheviki co-operated with the Bolsheviki. Each section retained the name it was given in 1903, though the Mensheviki soon became the majority instead of the minority of the Social-Democratic Party.

The third party, far more numerous and more distinctly different in program, was the party of the peasants of Russia, the Social Revolutionaries.

In 1904 the war between Russia and Japan broke out. The revolutionaries belonging to the different factions and creeds determined to take advantage of war conditions to overthrow the imperial government at a moment of national weakness.

In January, 1905, a general strike was ordered in St. Petersburg, and the revolutionary leaders succeeded in organizing a powerful demonstration of workmen, which proceeded to the Winter Palace, headed by Father Gapon.

It was to present a petition to the Czar asking for universal suffrage, a constituent assembly, free speech, press and assembly, general compulsory education, ministers responsible to the representatives of the people, separation of Church and State, tax reform, protection of labor by law and adequate wage rates. A demand was made by the mob that the Emperor should come out and speak to the workmen. This demand was flatly rejected by the military authorities who were defending the imperial headquarters. Thereupon the mob became threatening, and as a result, a massacre took place during which hundreds of workmen and other civilians were killed. This was called "Bloody Sunday."

The January riots in St. Petersburg were only a signal for the nation-wide strike movement accompanied by uprising, terroristic acts and increased revolutionary activities throughout the country.

In various parts of Russia the peasants, led by the Social Revolutionaries, succeeded in seizing the estates of land-owners. Private property was subjected to wholesale destruction. Agricultural implements were burned and destroyed, cattle killed, and for a time a wave of extreme disorder swept over Russia.

The government experienced great difficulty in coping with the situation, since the war against Japan required all of its energies in order to supply the Manchurian armies. These demonstrations constituted the first Russian revolution, and it is important to emphasize the fact that they were marked by strong Socialistic tendencies. The various political demands made by the revolutionaries played but an insignificant part in the general movement. The peasants, under the guidance of the social revolutionary and anarchist leaders, adopted the slogan "All Land for the Peasants."

The industrial workmen, or proletariat of the city, led by Social Democrats, insisted not only upon the overthrow of the imperial government, but also upon an economic revolution.

At the same time the property class was divided in its attitude toward the revolution. The majority of the so-called bourgeoisie, however, protested against the revolution on account of its distinctly unpatriotic character. It was felt that it was disloyal to the nation to fight against the government while engaged in defending the country against the danger of the Japanese invasion.

Moreover, it was pointed out that the revolutionary movement had lost its *raison d'etre* since August 6th, when the government had granted substantial concessions to the liberal parties, and authorized the creation of the Duma.

The radical factions of the bourgeois, however, insisted upon a republican form of government, and the convocation of a constituent assembly. In fact, the imperial ukase of October 17, 1905, calling for the establishment of the Imperial Duma, satisfied neither the conservative elements nor the radical faction of the property classes. The former blamed the government for having made unnecessary concessions to the revolutionists, while the radicals insisted upon the immediate establishment of a republic.

The Socialist factions, however, were neither satisfied with the existing order, nor did they support the radical factions of the bourgeois.

On October 13, 1905, the first Soviet of Workers' Deputies was founded in St. Petersburg. The society was absolutely independent of the Socialist parties. The majority of its members were self-appointed leaders of the labor movement. At some factories, however, the workmen selected their own deputies to the Soviet, but the bulk of the working population in St. Petersburg refrained from taking part in such elections. Owing to the revolutionary propaganda of the Bolsheviki, Mensheviki and Social Revolutionaries, the political situation grew more acute.

In October, 1905, a general railroad strike was called, and soon after the traffic throughout Russia became paralyzed. In many instances the revolutionary railway committees seized the telegraph stations, and by use of physical violence, compelled satisfied workmen to join the strike. In the meantime, the activities of the Soviet of St. Petersburg were growing bolder. Count Witte, Premier of the Russian cabinet, continued a hesitating and wavering policy, and for a time it looked as though the imperial government would recognize, to a certain extent at least, the authority of the Soviet.

The December revolt at Moscow, however, put an end to the policy of leniency. The imperial government decided to exercise its full power in order to suppress the revolutionary movement throughout the Empire. Regiments of the Russian Guard were dispatched to Moscow, and after five days of hard fighting the revolt was suppressed both in Moscow itself and in the vicinity.

An interesting illustration of the international character of the Socialist movement is found in the exchange of correspondence between the Japanese Socialists and the Russian Revolutionists at this period. On the 20th of March, 1904, a letter was addressed by the Japanese Socialists to their Russian comrades, which was as follows:

> "Dear Comrades:
>
> "Our governments have plunged us into a war to satisfy their imperialistic desires. But to the Socialist there exists no barriers of race, territory or nationality. We are comrades, brothers and sisters, and have no cause to battle against one another. Your enemy is not the Japanese people, but your own militarism, the so-called patriotism of your country. Our enemy is not the Russian people, but the militarism and patriotism of our ruling class. Patriotism and militarism are our common enemies, are the enemies of Socialists all over the world. It is the highest duty of Socialists everywhere to fight bravely and unafraid against them. . . . when you are suffering under the cruel persecution of your government and its spies, remember that there are thousands of comrades in a distant land who are praying for your well being and your success in their inmost hearts."
>
> "The Russian Social Democrats know only too well the difficulties that confront us in time of war when the entire machinery of government is working to the utmost to create a blind patriotic fervor . . . How much more difficult and embarrassing is the position of our Japanese comrades, who, at a moment when nationistic feeling was at its highest pitch, openly extended to us the hand of brotherhood."

(Note: "One Year of Russian Revolution," published by the Socialist Publication Society, page 17. These documents are in an article by Sen Katayama, a Japanese Socialist who has been active in the radical revolutionary movement in this country in recent years.)

In another part of this report attention is called to a dramatic climax in the International Socialist Convention at Amsterdam in 1904, during the war, when the audience was roused to a pitch of enthusiasm by the hand-clasp of international solidarity of the representatives of the Russian and Japanese parties.

Upon the restoration of peace between Russia and Japan,

owing in large part to the mediation of Theodore Roosevelt, the imperial government was enabled to devote more attention to the internal situation.

The cabinet of Stolypin adopted a number of important agrarian reforms which restored order in the rural districts. In many provinces the farmers became owners of the land which they had cultivated for decades.

In the first Duma there were 166 deputies representing the peasants; and this representation was increased in the second Duma. But the government aimed to make of the Duma merely a debating society. The Soviets were suppressed, prominent agitators arrested and exiled, the atrocities of the Black Hundreds were renewed; and by 1907 reaction was again in the saddle and all hopes of a pacific application of liberal reforms by the government coming to an end. By the law of June, 1907, the majority of the peasants and industrial workers were deprived of the suffrage, and landed proprietors given ten votes to one of the peasants.

That revolutionary activities were carried on through underground channels is illustrated by the testimony of Ludwig C. A. K. Martens before this Committee.

Mr. Martens testified that while he resided at Berlin he was engaged in Russian revolutionary activities in connection with Russian revolutionary organizations in Berlin. He stated that he was in constant communication with revolutionaries in Russia, and engaged in smuggling into Russia propaganda which had been prepared largely in Switzerland and in France. The quiet and underground activities of these revolutionaries were laying the foundations for the development of those organizations which were to play so decisive a part in the revolution of November 7, 1917.

In August, 1914, the first shots were exchanged between Russia and Germany in the Great War. A wave of genuine patriotic fervor swept over the Russian Empire. With the first day of mobilization the workmen who had been on strike in Petrograd and Moscow resumed their work. The national crisis apparently united the entire Russian people. This might have been the case had the war been swift and decisive in Russia's favor; but soon after the beginning of hostilities it became apparent that Russia was not prepared to conduct military operations on so gigantic a scale against Germany, Austria and Turkey.

Reports coming out of Russia revealed that there was a sad lack of ammunition, and that the equipment of the Russian armies was in every way inadequate. The government itself admitted that the estimates of the Empire were entirely erroneous. Rumors circulated that the minister of war General Soukhomlinoff was a paid German agent, and had used his position to betray Russia. Public opinion insisted upon his immediate trial.

In August, 1915, after the historic retreat of the Russian armies, the Czar, Nicholas II, ordered an investigation of General Soukhomlinoff's activities which revealed that the Minister had in fact, together with his associates, consciously kept Russia unprepared for a war with the Central Powers. By order of the Czar he was imprisoned, while several officers of the general staff were condemned by courts as traitors to their country, and were thereupon executed. Although during the spring of 1916 the military situation on the Russian front considerably improved, and notwithstanding the fact that the Russian offensive in Galicia resulted in the capture of an enormous number of prisoners, in Russia itself there was a feeling of general discontent, mainly because the food situation in the large cities had become extremely acute.

In addition dark rumors were circulated in Petrograd and in Moscow to the effect that the Czarina was conducting secret negotiations with the Imperial German government for a separate peace. Although tales of this kind had never been corroborated, yet they furnished ground for a solid opposition on the part of the liberal elements of the country which sought to take advantage of the existing conditions to force from the government a grant of further concessions to the liberal movement in general.

The appointment of Stuermer, an avowed pro-German, as premier, and the consequent ghastly betrayal of Roumania to Germany, increased the feeling of desperation.

The revolutionary parties also revived their activities beginning with the summer of 1916. Revolutionary propaganda was started among the soldiers behind the fighting lines, and among the workmen in industrial districts. Labor was urged to stop work at munition plants, and thus force the Russian government to give up the "Capitalistic and bloody enterprise" in which it was engaged. The Social Democrats distributed hundreds of thousands of leaflets among Russian soldiers in which it was argued that the Russian laboring population had no quarrel with the German people, and that the soldiers should disobey their officers. Immediate "democratic" peace with Germany was urged by the extremists, and the slogan was proclaimed that Russia objected to indemnities and annexations. This was the same kind of revolutionary and pacifist propaganda which was later circulated by Boloists in France, by socialists and Industrial Workers of the World in the United States, as well as by German sympathizers and paid agents.

The tactless policy of the Russian government at that time, its hostile attitude toward the legitimate aims of the Imperial Duma, the sinister influence of Rasputin at the Russian court, the instability of the Imperial cabinet, and the general uncertainty of political and military conditions accelerated the first outbreak of the revolutionary movement in Russia.

The March or So-Called Bourgeois Revolution

In dealing with the history of Russian revolutions in March, 1917, and November 7th of that year, this Committee will have recourse for its information, aside from unquestionable historic data, solely to the revolutionary press, to such copies of the official Bolsheviki newspapers as have come into its hands, and to the statements made by sympathizers with the Russian Soviet regime.

While this policy of the Committee may result in describing the Russian revolution and the subsequent conduct of the Soviet regime in their most favorable light, the Committee feels that by depicting the Russian Soviet regime in the words of its advocates, it can show more clearly and more effectively how completely subversive of democratic institutions and destructive of civil liberty are the principles and programs of that regime.

The Committee is thus able to show that the advocates of these revolutionary principles in this country know and understand the precise meaning of their own propaganda. In other words, it is of little consequence to the people of the United States what precise conditions exist in Russia, but it is of great consequence to determine what the revolutionary elements of this country believe them to be.

It will be recalled that the first revolutionary outbreak occurred in Petrograd on March 11, 1917, after a general strike had been ordered on the previous day. At the beginning the movement was confined to mere food riots, but when the government foolishly decreed the dissolution of the Duma all parties united against it and the reserve garrisons joined the mob. After a four days' struggle the loyal military units, as well as the police, were overthrown, and the provisional government consisting mainly of members of the Imperial Duma was established on March 13th.

On March 15th the Emperor, Czar Nicholas II, issued a manifesto by which he abdicated the throne for himself and his son in favor of Grand Duke Michael, who in turn refused to accept the crown without the approval of the Constituent Assembly.

Although the unstable political conditions of Russia were well known to the allied governments, the swiftness and success of the revolution came as a great surprise to the people of other countries at large, and the revolution was generally hailed as the beginning of a new era for the Russian people, and was looked upon as a victory of the democratic principles for which the war was being fought against Germany.

The swift success of the bourgeois revolution of 1917 is attributed in large measure by Lenin to the struggles of 1905 to 1907, and also to a fortuitous co-operation between contending groups and factions. He is quoted as saying:

> "The rapid success of the revolution, and, at first glance, its 'radical' success, was produced by the unusual historical conjuncture, in a strikingly 'favorable' manner, of *absolutely* opposed movements, *absolutely different* class interests, and *absolutely hostile* political and social tendencies. The Anglo-French imperialists were behind Milyukov, Guchkov & Co., in their seizure of power *in the interests of prolonging an imperialistic war,* with the objects of waging the war more savagely and obstinately, accompanied by the slaughter of new millions of Russian workers and peasants, that the class of Guchkov might have Constantinople, the French might have Syria, the English Mesopotamia, etc. That was one element in the situation, which united with another and opposite element,—the profound proletarian and popular mass movement, consisting of all the poorest classes of the cities and the provinces, revolutionary in character and demanding *bread, peace, and real freedom.*" (Words attributed to Nicolai Lenin in a book entitled "The Proletarian Revolution in Russia," edited by Louis C. Fraina, p. 22.)

With full liberty of the press and peaceable assembly proclaimed by the provisional government, the pacifist, socialist and anarchist propaganda assumed an extremely aggressive character.

Soldiers both in the rear and at the front were urged by the provisional agitators and German agents to lay down their arms and fraternize with their "German comrades."

At the same time alongside of the provisional government, headed first by Prince Lvoff (whose importance was later dwarfed by Milyukov), the Socialist and anarchist elements of Petrograd's population established a Soviet of Soldiers', Workmen's and Sailors' Deputies, which body was gradually turned into the center of all disloyal activities. Through continuous agitation the power of this body increased rapidly. Its president was at first Tcheidze and its vice-president Kerensky, neither of them Bolsheviki, the former being a leader of the Mensheviki.

In May, 1917, the Soviet forced the resignation of the first cabinet of the provisional government, which was accused of imperialistic aims and of secret diplomacy, as well as of representing not the people but the bourgeoisie.

The program of the provisional government was merely liberal, not revolutionary, and reflected the timid ideas of the Duma. This condition was what Trotzky calls "the farce of dual authority," and better yet, "the epoch of dual impotence, the government not able and the Soviet not daring."

The Soviet denounced all secret treaties concluded by the allied governments in connection with the prosecution of the World War, and insisted upon an immediate conclusion of peace with Germany on the basis of "No indemnities and no annexations."

Kerensky who succeeded Prince Lvoff, the first premier of the provisional government, proved to be a weak and vacillating character. The Constitutional Democratic Party, of which Milyukov was the most prominent representative, was discredited. Nicolai Lenin who, during his exile in Switzerland, had continued his connection with the revolutionaries in Russia, and was one of the leading spirits of the Bolsheviki element of the Social Democratic Party, as well as the leading figure in the International revolutionary Conferences at Zimmerwald and Kienthal, was permitted by the Imperial German government to pass through Germany from Switzerland to Russia. This man and Leon Trotzky, who had proceeded to Russia from New York City in March, 1917, became the recognized leaders of the Soviet elements of Petrograd and Kronstadt. In other words, the Soviet had become the organized expression of International Revolutionary Socialism.

An open struggle for control immediately developed between the Soviets and the provisional government.

Lenin says:

> "The Soviet of Workers' and Soldiers' Delegates constitute the form of a government by the workers, and represents the interest of all the poorest of our people, of nine-tenths of the population, aiming to secure peace, bread and liberty. . . . The only *guarantee* of liberty and of a complete abolition of czarism is the arming of the proletariat, the strengthening, broadening, and development of the role and empire of the Soviets of workers and soldiers. Accomplish this, and the liberty of Russia will be invincible, the monarchy incapable of restoration, the republic assured. . . . 'Our revolution is a bourgeois revolution,' say we Marxists, 'therefore, the Socialist workers should open the eyes of the people to the deceptive practices of the bourgeois politician, should teach the people not to believe in words, but to depend wholly on their own strength, and on their own organization, on their own unity, and on their own military equipment.'" (Words attributed to Nicolai Lenin in a book entitled "The Proletarian Revolution in Russia," edited by Louis C. Fraina, pp. 24–25.)

The provisional government was thus attacked as bourgeois. Patriotism was decried and Marxian principles of proletariat dictatorship were everywhere heralded as the only hope of the revolution.

The liberal decrees of the provisional government on the other hand had destroyed the discipline of the army, and the disintegration of the once powerful Russian military machine became almost complete.

In July, 1917, the Russian lines of defense in Galicia were broken by the German troops, and the retreat of the Russian units was soon converted into a rout. This was the first tangible result of the weak policy of the provisional government under Kerensky, and of the Bolshevist propaganda.

In the Soviet, the May 14th vote of forty-one to nineteen in favor of joining in a coalition ministry, indicates less than one-third in favor of Bolshevik theories at that time. This Bolshevik section was reduced in a later vote to seven. This was on May 18th. On the previous day, May 17th, was the first meeting of over 1,000 peasants who formed the first All-Russian Congress of Peasants, the delegates being from all parts of Russia. Hardly any of these held Bolshevik views, a large majority being Socialist Revolutionists.

There is evidence that the Bolsheviki agitators continued to become more and more aggressive. In June they had bitterly condemned the military offensive. A plot of theirs to seize power on June 24th was thwarted, but on July 17, 1917, the first Bolshevist uprising took place in Petrograd. Although after two days of street fighting the Cossacks succeeded in quelling the revolt, nevertheless, owing to the weakness of the provisional government, the leaders of the revolt, namely, Lenin, Trotzky and Apfelbaum, alias Zinoviev, succeeded in making their escape to Finland.

The provisional government was obviously losing its power. The Russian armies themselves were melting away, leaving the front defenseless — leaving the vast territory of Russia exposed to German intrigue and aggression. The strong measures necessary to curb disloyal propaganda and to restore military discipline were not attempted by Kerensky.

On various occasions conservative Russian leaders warned the provisional government of the imminent danger. At the national convention held in Moscow on the 27th of August, 1917, General Kornilov, commander-in-chief of all Russian armies, is quoted as having said that an immediate restoration of discipline was absolutely necessary.

In much the same way General Kaledine, the elected representative of the Cossacks of twelve regions, warned the provisional government that "in the bitter struggle for existence which Russia is now waging, it should utilize all the Russian people, all the vital forces of all classes in Russia."

The provisional government, however, remained deaf to all appeals. It feared to be accused of being reactionary. It apparently believed that the only method to deal with the socialist elements which were undermining its power must be to grant them greater liberties and freedom to carry on their program of national destruction.

Two months later the provisional government was overthrown, an event which was the direct result of the vacillating, timorous and conciliatory policy which it had always maintained toward domestic enemies.

Before its downfall it had issued a call for the election of a general Constituent Assembly, to meet in December and decide on the form of government for Russia.

The Bolsheviki were among the loudest in clamoring for the election of the Assembly and in blaming the delay in the election.

THE BOLSHEVIST REVOLUTION OF NOVEMBER 7TH

From the time Nicolai Lenin arrived in Petrograd on the night of April 16, 1917, his entire energies were aimed at guiding and directing revolutionary propaganda with the object of making possible the proletarian revolution. He thought he saw in the revolution of March the first stage of the Socialist revolution which deprived the autocracy of power and put the control of government into the hands of the bourgeoisie.

He felt it to be his mission to hasten the second stage of the revolution which was to "give the power to the proletariat and the poorest peasantry."

He speaks of the fact that Russia under the bourgeois government had become the freest of all belligerent nations of the world, and comments upon the absence of violence, and particularly on the trustful and unconscious attitude of the masses towards the government of the capitalists which he characterizes as the worst enemy of peace and Socialism.

In commenting upon this situation he says:

> "This peculiarity demands of us the ability to adapt ourselves to certain conditions of partisan work among broad masses of the proletariat, who have only now awakened to political life. No support for the Provisional Government; explanation of the emptiness of its promises, especially concerning the repudiation of annexations. The revelation of the real character of this government, instead of the illusory 'demand' that *this* government, a government of capitalists, should *cease* to be imperialistic."

In order to carry on the work of the revolution Lenin says there must be "recognition of the fact that in the majority of Soviets of Workmen's Delegates our party is in the minority, and thus far in a small minority, against the block of all the petty bourgeoisie opportunistic elements, who have come under the influence of the bourgeoisie and who carry this influence into the ranks of the proletariat."

He further says, "As long as we are in the minority we are

carrying on the work of criticism and explanation of errors; preaching, in the meantime, the necessity of a transference of the old government power to the Soviets in order that the masses should rid themselves of their errors by experience. Not a parliament republic — a return to it from Soviets of Workmen's Delegates would be a step backwards — but a republic of the Soviets of Workmen's and Peasants' Delegates, throughout the whole country." (Page 54, "Proletarian Revolution in Russia," by N. Lenin and Leon Trotzky, edited by Louis C. Fraina.)

At this time he also advocated the necessity of changing the name of the party to the Communist Party, which was later effected.

The constant struggle which had been going on between these conflicting agencies of government culminated on November 7, 1917, when the provisional government was overthrown, Kerensky driven into exile, and the city of Petrograd was captured by the Red Guard, almost without a struggle, because of lack of leadership and policy on the part of the large anti-Bolshevik majority. The overthrow was also due to the fact that a new All-Russian Congress of Soviets had been packed so as to have a Bolshevik majority, and that a successful propaganda had been carried on among the soldiers.

The official announcement of the Bolshevist revolution reads as follows:

"FROM MILITARY REVOLUTIONARY COMMITTEE OF PETROGRAD, SOVIET OF WORKERS' AND SOLDIERS' DEPUTIES

"*To the citizens of the Russian Republic:*

"The provisional government has been overthrown. The sovereign authority has passed to the Petrograd Soviet of Workers' and Soldiers' Deputies of the Petrograd Proletariat and the Garrisons. The cause for which the people have been fighting, immediate proposals of a democratic peace, repeal of freehold land properties, and workers' control over production, the establishment of the Soviet government — is guaranteed.

"Long live the revolution of the workers, soldiers and peasants!

"(Signed) MILITARY REVOLUTION COMMITTEE OF PETROGRAD'S SOVIET OF WORKERS' AND SOLDIERS' DEPUTIES."

At the same time the Duma of Petrograd, which was about to meet, was forcibly dissolved by the Bolsheviki on the ground that the majority of its members were opposed to Bolshevism.

The mere capture of governmental power by the Soviets of Petrograd and other districts was but the initial step in the consolidation of the proletarian dictatorship.

This dictatorship was later described by Lenin as that of a very small minority.

"Just as 150,000 lordly landowners under Czarism dominated the 130,000,000 of Russian peasants, so 200,000 members of the Bolshevik Party are imposing their proletarian will on the mass, but this time in the interest of the latter." (Text of Lenin in the "New International," April, 1918.)

In commenting upon this situation Lenin says in a pamphlet entitled "The Soviets at Work" (published by the Rand School of Social Science, Page 10):

> "We have defeated the bourgeoisie, but it is not yet destroyed and not even completely conquered. We must therefore resort to a new and higher form of the struggle with the bourgeoisie; we must turn from the very simple problem of continuing the expropriation of the capitalists to the more complex and difficult problem — the problem of creating conditions under which the bourgeoisie could neither exist nor come anew into existence. It is clear that this problem is infinitely more complicated and that we can have no Socialism until it is solved."

The precise meaning of this transition from capitalism to Socialism is described by Lenin in the same pamphlet, at page 30, as follows:

> "In the first place, it is impossible to conquer and destroy capitalism without the merciless suppression of the existence of the exploiters, who cannot be at once deprived of their wealth, of their advantages in organization and knowledge, and who will, therefore, during quite a long period inevitably attempt to overthrow the hateful (to them) authority of the poor. Secondly, every great revolution, and especially a Socialist revolution, even if there were no external war, is inconceivable without an internal war, with thousands and millions of cases of wavering and of desertion from one side to the other, and with a state of the greatest uncertainty, instability and chaos."

Despite the pleasing pictures which have been drawn of Russian conditions subsequent to the November revolution by sympathizers of the Soviet regime returning to this country from Russia, it is evident from an examination of documents published in the various official journals of the Soviet regime that the description of the conditions necessarily attending upon the Socialist revolution given by Lenin which we have just quoted was fully realized throughout the territory over which the Soviets exerted their power.

While the Russian Communist Party under the leadership of Lenin and Trotzky had succeeded in gaining control of the machinery of the Soviets, it was quite evident that it had not succeeded in gaining the support of the majority of the population. This was shown at the first meeting of the Constituent Assembly, elected three weeks after the Bolshevik Revolution, the election of which had been authorized by the Kerensky government.

This Assembly met in Petrograd in January to take charge of the government. But it was at once dissolved by force by Lenin and Trotzky because it was found to have a large anti-Bolshevik majority.

For the purposes of this report the description of conditions bearing on this subject may best be taken from admissions of Ludwig C. A. K. Martens, Soviet representative in the United States, at the public hearing of this Committee on December 11, 1919, when he was asked the following questions:

"Q. After the November revolution of 1917, when the Russian Communist Party assumed control of the government, did they not allow the greatest freedom of speech, of the press and of assembly in Russia? A. Yes, they did.

"Q. And subsequent to that time were there elections held for a Constituent Assembly? A. Yes.

"Q. And were those elections held throughout the entire territory under the control of the Soviets? A. Yes.

"Q. About how long a period was occupied in the campaigns for these elections? A. I think a couple of months.

"Q. And were delegates chosen during those campaigns for members of the Constituent Assembly? A. Yes, they were.

"Q. And what were the various parties that ran candidates for that Assembly? A. The three main parties: One, the

NIKOLAI LENIN

LEON TROTZKY

THE BEGINNING OF THE BOLSHEVIST JULY UPRISING IN PETROGRAD
This Photograph Was Taken From an Official Album of the Russian Revolution, Issued by the Russian Soviet Bureau.

A DETACHMENT OF RED GUARD SAILORS WHO DISSOLVED CONSTITUENT ASSEMBLY

This Photograph Was Taken From an Official Album of the Russian Revolution, Issued by the Russian Soviet Bureau

so-called Bolsheviks; the other the Social Revolutionaries; the other the Mensheviks and Constitutional Democrats—four parties.

"Q. And what was the result of that election; what were the various proportions of delegates returned to that Assembly? A. I do not remember exactly the figures. It was about approximately 40 per cent. Bolsheviks, and about as many Social Revolutionists, and the rest for the other parties.

"Q. So that the majority of that Assembly constituted other than Bolshevik representatives? A. Nobody constituted a majority.

"Q. I mean a majority of the delegates were not Bolshevik representatives? A. Yes.

"Q. Did that Assembly ever meet? A. Yes.

"Q. When did it meet? A. In December, 1917, I think.

"Q. And where did it meet? A. Petrograd.

"Q. And was that Assembly permitted to sit? A. Until a certain time, yes.

"Q. And then what was done to it? A. Well, then the Soviets demanded a revolutionary assembly and it was dissolved.

"Q. It was dissolved? A. Yes."

As a matter of fact the following things occurred: The Bolshevik seizure of power happened November 7. The elections took place November 25. The Bolshevik government represented by the Petrograd Soviet issued a manifesto to the workers and soldiers, which appeared in the "Izvestia" of November 11, as follows:

"The bourgeoisie land magnates, Kerensky's government, have done everything possible during eight months in order to put off elections to the Constituent Assembly. Persistently and stubbornly did they endeavor to break it up, for they knew that in the matter of land and peace the Constituent Assembly cannot help but come out against the land magnates and capitalists. The only guarantee of really convening the Assembly has been the overthrow of Kerensky's government, the victory of the workers, soldiers and peasants over the bourgeoisie.

"The elections to the Constituent Assembly are now assured and must be held on time.

"The Petrograd Soviet calls upon all workers, soldiers, sailors, administrative staffs, upon all citizens to go to the balloting places on the 12th and 13th of November without fail. Failure to vote is playing into the hands of the bourgeoisie who may be depended on to mobilize their entire strength for the elections. The ballot must aid the gun.

"Workers and soldiers, go to the ballot box and vote for those who helped with their blood to attain the soldier-worker victory. Vote for the Bolsheviks for List 4."

The above appeal was issued after Lenin had issued an official decree on the same day, announcing the election for the 25th.

The first informal meeting of the Constituent Assembly was December 12th and for two successive days, under great difficulty, and the third day the deputies were driven out by a body of sailors. It was a military *coup d' etat*. Of the 730 members of the Assembly, only 165 were Bolsheviki. The official meeting was fixed for January 5th, notwithstanding Bolshevik opposition and intimidation. Two prominent anti-Bolshevik deputies, Kokoshkin and Shingarie, were murdered cold-bloodedly in bed by Bolsheviki ruffians. When the session was opened Bucharin, on behalf of the Bolsheviki, announced that the Assembly must bow to the decisions of the Soviet before it could be recognized. A few hours later a decree was issued by Lenin dissolving it as a counter-revolutionary body. On January 6th Trotzky, in speaking of it before the Third Congress of Soviets, acknowledged: "In dissolving the Constituent Assembly we violated the formal principles of Democracy."

In other words, as late as December of 1917, the majority of the representatives chosen by suffrage of the entire people of Russia were not supporters of the Russian Communist Party, known as "Bolsheviki."

It is evident that the powerful parties whose participation in government had been denied them were openly resentive of the action of the Soviets, and must have constituted a serious menace to the control of the governmental power, because we find the Soviets setting up revolutionary tribunals for the purpose of prosecuting so-called counter-revolutionists; and also revolutionary tribunals of the press for the purpose of silencing all criticisms of the conduct of the Soviet authorities.

The Bolsheviki acknowledged that their worst enemies, those against whom they used the severest form of "Red Terror," including wholesale executions, were not members of the bourgeoisie, but members of the other two Socialist parties, the Mensheviki and Social Revolutionaries, against whom they raised the absurd accusation of being "counter revolutionists."

Mr. Martens, in his testimony before the Committee, says, in answer to the question:

> "Q. And the purpose of these tribunals was to prosecute counter-revolutionary activities? A. Exactly.
>
> "Q. And then parties agitating against the Soviets were constituted counter-revolutionaries, were they? A. Yes, several parties. One of them was the anarchists, constituted to overthrow the government, and the Constitutional Democrats.
>
> "Q. Were they the Cadets? A. Yes.
>
> "Q. So they were the principal parties that had been active in the campaign for the Constituent Assembly, were they not? A. Oh, no.
>
> "Q. Well, the Cadets you mentioned? A. Yes, the Cadets and Social Revolutionaries.
>
> "Q. Those two parties were treated as counter-revolutionists, were they not? A. Yes, and the anarchists, too."

It is particularly interesting to note that the Social Revolutionaries which represented the rural or peasant population in the struggle against the Czarist regime was among the first of the parties to be treated as counter-revolutionary. Perhaps for this reason the constitution of the Soviet Republic makes a distinction between the city and rural voters, and gives to the rural inhabitants only one-fifth the representation in the Soviet councils given to the city proletariat.

During the summer of 1918, as a part of the campaign of "merciless suppression of the bourgeoisie" and effectually to silence all persons or parties who sought to resist the usurpation of power by the Soviets, the Red Terror was allowed free reign.

In the official publication of the Petrograd council of Workmen's, Peasants' and Red Guard Deputies, the "Red Gazette," an editorial was published on the 31st of August, 1918, referring to the Red Terror as follows:

> "Only those men among the representatives of the bourgeoisie class, who, during the period of nine months succeeded in proving their loyalty to the Soviet rule should be

spared. All the others are our hostages, and we should treat them accordingly. Enough of mildness. *The interest of the revolution necessitated physical annihilation of the bourgeoisie class. It is time for us to start.*"

Another official Communist publication, namely, the "Izvestia," published on the 29th of September, 1918, in the fourth issue, an article under the title "The Voice of Tombs," the closing lines of which read as follows:

"Nay, we have already left the path of all errors. We have found the right track of struggle with our hated enemies, and this track is the Red Terror."

A Bolshevist proclamation issued in the City of Kotelnich in 1918, in North Russia, reads in part as follows:

"We take oath not to leave a stone unturned in these nests where the terrible parasites and their partisans are living. When compelled to evacuate the cities, we will turn them into deserts, and every step of ours will be abundantly soaked with blood. In this struggle between the world's capital and those oppressed, let the world tremble before the horror of the mode in which we shall demolish and annihilate everything which oppresses us. . . . You, rich peasants, who have drunk the blood of the poor for centuries long, you should remember that the above also applies to you."

Thus the bourgeoisie as a whole, as well as the prosperous peasants, were declared enemies of the Russian Soviet Republic.

Although the revolutionary Socialists have for many years been loudest in protesting against any infringement of the right of free speech or free press on the part of any government, one of the first steps taken by the Soviets after they gained control in the November revolution was to set up the revolutionary tribunal of the press. In a decree signed by I. Z. Steinberg, People's Commissar of Justice, the organization of this tribunal, its jurisdiction and powers were set forth as follows:

"THE REVOLUTIONARY TRIBUNAL OF THE PRESS

"1. Under the Revolutionary Tribunal is created a Revolutionary Tribunal of the Press. This Tribunal will have jurisdiction of crimes and offenses against the people committed by means of the press.

"2. Crimes and offenses by means of the press are the publication and circulation of any false or perverted reports and information about events of public life, in so far as they constitute an attempt upon the rights and interests of the revolutionary people.

"3. The Revolutionary Tribunal of the Press consists of three members, elected for a period not longer than three months by the Soviet of Workers, Soldiers, and Peasants' Deputies. These members are charged with the conduct of the preliminary investigation as well as the trial of the case.

"4. The following serve as grounds for instituting proceedings: Reports of legal or administrative institutions, public organizations or private persons.

"5. The prosecuting and defense are conducted on the principles laid down in the instructions to the General Revolutionary Tribunal.

"6. The sessions of the Revolutionary Tribunal of the Press are public.

"7. The decisions of the Revolutionary Tribunal of the Press are final and are not subject to appeal.

"8. The Revolutionary Tribunal imposes the following penalties: (1) Fine; (2) expression of public censure, which the convicted organ of the press brings to the general knowledge in a way indicated by the tribunal; (3) the publication in a prominent place or in a special edition of a denial of the false report; (4) temporary or permanent suppression of the publication or its exclusion from circulation; (5) confiscation to national ownership of the printing shop or property of the organ of the press if it belongs to the convicted parties.

"9. The trial of an organ of the press by the Revolutionary Tribunal of the Press does not absolve the guilty persons from general criminal responsibility."

It will be noted that the crimes and offenses by means of the press are publication and circulation of any false or perverted reports, and information about the events of public life in so far as they constitute an attempt upon the rights and interest of the revolutionary people.

It is difficult in passing not to comment upon the cries of anguish and reproach which would arise in the columns of the New York "Call" and other radical newspapers published in the United States should the government of the State of New York attempt to put into force a statute to control the press in precisely the same terms as that adopted by the much praised Soviet Republic. Through the operations of this tribunal all protests against the actions taken by the Soviet government, by means of newspaper publicity, were effectually silenced.

It should be pointed out that the very acts of government which for years had been decried by revolutionary Socialists in all countries as oppressive and destructive of all human liberty were immediately adopted and put into effect by the Soviet regime. In all countries military training has been seriously opposed by revolutionary Socialists, and yet in a speech made by Leon Trotzky at the city conference of the Russian Communist Party of Moscow on March 28, 1918, we find him saying:

> "Thus far, comrades, many decrees, many provisions have existed only on paper. The task of first importance for the party should be to see to it that the decrees concerning compulsory military training in the industrial plants, factories, workshops, schools, etc., which we shall publish in the course of the next few days, are actually carried out in practice. Only the extensive military training of the masses of workers and peasants wherever it can be immediately put into practice will make it possible to convert the voluntary cadres into that skeleton which at the instant of danger can be surrounded with flesh and blood, that is, with really extensive armed masses." (Page 379 of "Class Struggle," issue of November, 1919.)

At the beginning of the revolution the general elective system for the selection of officers was put into effect in the hastily organized groups of Red Guards. It soon became apparent to the less violent extremists in the revolutionary movement that this method of selection of armed men must of necessity reduce the military machine to a chaotic and ineffective weapon.

Trotzky in the same speech approaches the question of doing away with the elective system in the following words:

> "The second question concerns the so-called principle of election of the army. The whole purpose of this principle lies in its use to fight the old make-up of the officers' machine, to control the commanding personnel. As long as the power was vested in the class that is our enemy and the commanding personnel appeared a tool in the hands of this power, it was our duty to strive, through the election principle, to break the class opposition of the commanding personnel.

> But at the present time the political power lies in the hands of the same working class from whose ranks the army is recruited. Under the present regime in the army — I tell you this with absolute frankness — the election principle appears politically unnecessary and from the technical point of view impracticable, and in the decree it is to all intents abolished." (Page 381, "Class Struggle," issue of November, 1919.)

With the adoption of this decree the last vestige of democratic control in the army disappeared. Further the same principles of military discipline, and the choice of military commanders from the central government which had been in vogue in all European armies was adopted.

Even the much hated principle of military conscription was put into effect.

In an article appearing in "Soviet Russia," of November 1, 1919, we find the following:

> "The strong conscientious discipline introduced by Trotzky which was enforced even by capital punishment,— since the method of administration has been rendered efficient by the communistic principles which exist in the Red Army, — is fully recognized by these officers as a very important element of morale of any military organization, though lacking in the army of the fallen empire." (Page 7.)

At this time similar disciplinary measures were being introduced in the industrial field. In the pamphlet entitled "Soviets at Work," by Nicolai Lenin, the author constantly recurs to the necessity of increasing production in all lines through well-organized and disciplined workers. He acknowledges that industry had been completely disrupted; that inefficiency, laziness and ignorance were universal; that there was chaos; that no work was being done. He says, at page 38, "Our gains, our decrees, our laws, our plans must be secured by the solid forms of *every-day labor discipline*. This is the most difficult, but also the most promising problem, for only its solution will give us Socialism. We must learn to combine the stormy, energetic breaking of all restraint on the part of the toiling masses, with *iron discipline during work, with absolute submission* to the will of one person, the Soviet director, *during work*." It was military dictatorship in industry. This speech of Lenin was made at the meeting of the All-Russian Soviet Congress in March, 1918.

The promoters and leaders of the Proletarian Revolution had fired the toiling masses and poor peasantry of Russia with the hope of unlimited freedom; had laid before them the plans for an elective system in industry which would constantly put into the hands of the workers, in factory or field, the selection of their immediate superiors and give them the opportunity to recall such superiors at any time.

These principles were extremely inviting, and caught the ear of no small number of the masses. It was such promises and such prospects that made possible the organization of the workers into revolutionary units which effected the November revolution. As with the armies, so with the industrial organizations. The principles which had been enunciated in so authoritative a manner were found to be impracticable. It was early discovered that the ignorant masses were not acquainted with the methods or the technique of production and distribution. It became necessary to compromise with the technical experts and the especially trained elements of the bourgeoisie, in order to prevent the whole economic machinery from falling into chaos.

Not only was it necessary to effect such compromise, but it became imperative that the system of the universal election in industry should be abolished.

In dealing with this question Leon Trotzky says:

> "Let me ask you: is the election principle applied throughout in your industrial unions and co-operatives? No. Do you elect the officials, bookkeepers, clerks, cashiers, the employees of definite professions? No. You elect from among the workers of the union in whom you have most confidence your supervisory council and leave to this body the appointment of all necessary employees and experts."

The code of labor laws which has been adopted, and which is published in the official organ of the Russian Soviet Bureau, "Soviet Russia," February 21, 1920, as the last phase of Soviet government policy, indicates that the principle of conscription has also been applied, in large measure, in the industrial field. This is made possible by the universal military conscription that has been enforced, and by keeping this big army undisbanded, and turning it into a militarist economic labor machine. Lenin and Trotzky found that the workmen's Soviets in the various industrial plants, which were the basis of the famous Soviet rule, interfered with the absolute rule of the government commissioners and managers. Therefore all such Soviets have now been abolished throughout Russia.

The first article of this code deals with compulsory labor. Section 1 says:

> "All citizens of the Russian Socialist Federated Soviet Republic, with the exceptions stated in sections 2 and 3, shall be subject to compulsory labor."

These exceptions are:

(a) Persons under sixteen years of age;

(b) All persons over fifty years;

(c) Persons who have become incapacitated by injury or illness.

Temporary exemptions are granted as follows:

(a) Persons who are temporarily incapacitated owing to illness or injury, for a period necessary for their recovery;

(b) Women, for a period of eight weeks before and eight weeks after confinement.

Section 4 of this article says that all students shall be subject to compulsory labor at the schools.

Article 5 deals with the transfer and discharge of wage earners. This gives authority to the governing boards of industry to transfer the workers from one industry to another; and even from one place to another.

The full significance of the labor code, as well as the entire instrument, will be discussed and reproduced in that portion of this report which deals with labor problems.

It is cited here for the purpose of showing that the liberty of the individual in various walks of life has been subordinated completely to the necessities of the State as a whole, and that to all intents and purposes the individual, unless he be elected to high political office, exists under a tyranny more oppressive and more exacting than any that has yet been devised.

Long before all these changes had taken place in the life of Russia those really guiding the destinies of the political machinery were engaged in the preparation of a constitution which would vest them permanently with power and give them complete control over the destinies of the people.

This instrument was finally adopted by resolution of the Fifth All-Russian Congress of Soviets at Moscow on July 10, 1918, and is appended in full elsewhere.

It puts in practice the extreme form of Marxian Socialism and includes the following main features:

(1) A federation of Soviet National Republics.

(2) Abolition of private ownership of land, which becomes national property.

(3) Forests, mines, waters, equipments become national property.

(4) Banks become property of the government.

(5) Everybody must work.

(6) Workers to be armed, bourgeoisie disarmed.

(7) Establishment of dictatorship of urban and rural proletariat and poorest peasantry.

(8) Establishment of local, provincial and regional Soviets headed by the All-Russian Congress of Soviets with continuous power vested in the All-Russian Central Executive Committee.

(9) Separation of Church and State.

(10) Abolishing of all press, except that representing the Soviet government.

(11) Free education.

(12) Universal military conscription except non-workers.

(13) Equal rights to all foreigners.

(14) All inimical individuals or groups are deprived of their rights.

(15) All decrees and orders are issued by the Council of People's Commissars, but can be revoked or suspended by the Central Executive Committee.

(16) There are seventeen People's Commissars (heads of Government Departments).

(17) In elections a city representative represents 5,000 votes, and a rural 25,000 votes, etc., in such proportions that it takes five rural voters to equal one urban voter.

(18) Persons over eighteen years of age of both sexes can vote with the following exceptions: (a) persons who have an income; (b) persons who employ any labor; (c) clergy; (d) defectives and criminals; (e) persons suspected of enmity to the government.

(19) The Soviets levy taxes only for local needs. State needs are covered by the State treasury.

In the elaborate Land Law the rules are given that govern the apportioning and working of the land by the local inhabitants, the standards of production and consumption per acreage; the shifting of workers to sections requiring more labor, the use of implements and live-stock, etc.

International Policies of the Russian Soviet Regime

From the very beginning of the Russian revolution it was recognized that its success and the permanent establishment in power of a proletariat depended in large measure upon the coming of the social revolution in all of the western countries.

As early as April, 1917, the Council of Workers and Soviets of Petrograd, through Tcheidze, president of the Executive Committee, issued a manifesto to the workers and Socialists of all countries in the following terms:

> "We, Russian workers and soldiers, united in the Petrograd Council of Workers' and Soldiers' Delegates, send you our warmest greetings and the news of great events. The democracy of Russia has overthrown the century-old despotism of the Czars and enters your ranks as a legitimate member and a powerful force in the battle for our common liberation. Our victory is a great victory of the freedom and democracy of the world. The principal supporter of reaction in the world, the 'gendarme of Europe,' no longer exists. May the earth over his grave become a heavy stone. Long live liberty, long live the international solidarity of the proletariat and its battle for the final victory!
>
> "Our cause is not yet entirely won. Not all the shadows of the old regime have been scattered, and not a few enemies are gathering their forces together against the Russian Revolution. Nevertheless, our conquests are great. The people of Russia will express their will in the Constituent Assembly which is to be called within a short time on the basis of universal, equal, direct and secret suffrage. And now it may already be said with certainty in advance that the democratic republic will triumph in Russia. The Russian people is in possession of complete political liberty. Now it can say an authoritative word about the internal self-government of the country, and about its foreign policy. And in addressing ourselves to all the peoples who are being destroyed and ruined in this terrible war, we declare that the time has come in which the decisive struggle against the attempts at conquest by the governments of all nations must begin. The time has come in which the peoples must take into their own hands the questions of war and peace.
>
> "Conscious of its own revolutionary strength, the democracy of Russia declares that it will fight with all means

against the policy of conquest of its ruling classes and it summons the peoples of Europe to united, decisive action for peace.

"We appeal to our brothers, to the proletarians of the German-Austrian coalition, and above all to the German proletariat. The first day of the war you were made to believe that in raising your weapons against absolutist Russia you were defending European civilization against Asiatic despotism. In this many of you found the justification of the support that was accorded to the war. Now also this justification has vanished. Democratic Russia cannot menace freedom and civilization.

"We shall firmly defend our own liberty against all reactionary threats, whether they come from without or within. The Russian Revolution will not retreat before the bayonets of conquerors and it will not allow itself to be trampled to pieces by outside military force. We call upon you to throw off the yoke of your absolutist regime, as the Russian people have shaken off the autocracy of the Czar. Refuse to serve as the tools of conquest and power in the hands of the kings, junkers and bankers, and we shall, with common efforts, put an end to the fearful butchery that dishonors humanity and darkens the great days of the birth of Russian liberty.

"Workingmen of all countries! In fraternally stretching out our hands to you across the mountains of our brothers' bodies, across the sea of innocent blood and tears, across the smoking ruins of cities and villages, across the destroyed gifts of civilization, we summon you to the work of renewing and solidifying international unity. In that lies the guaranty of our future triumph and of the complete liberation of humanity.

"Workers of all countries, unite!" (Pages 56–7, "Proletarian Revolution," by Lenin and Trotzky, edited by Louis C. Fraina.)

From the beginning Lenin and his followers recognized the necessity of organizing and stimulating the activities of revolutionary groups in other countries. Soon after the November revolution the Soviets set up a bureau of international revolutionary propaganda in which were prepared, for distribution in other countries, incendiary documents calculated to encourage the masses of the western democracies to emulate the Russian revolution.

Lenin is quoted as saying:

> "Only after we have completely forced down and expropriated the bourgeoisie of the whole world and not of one country alone, will wars become impossible." (Page 137, "The Proletarian Revolution in Russia," by Lenin and Trotzky, edited by Louis C. Fraina.)

Mr. Ludwig C. A. K. Martens, the so-called representative of the Russian Socialist Federation of the Soviet Republic in the United States, was asked:

"Q. Mr. Martens, you are a member of the Russian Communist Party, are you not? A. Yes, sir.

"Q. And that party is the party which is now in control of the government of Soviet Russia, is it not? A. Yes, sir.

"Q. Mr. Martens, as a matter of fact, the Russian Soviet Republic is based upon the principles of the Communist Party of Russia, is it not? A. Yes, sir.

"Q. Isn't it one of the principles of the Communist Party that the workers of the world should unite? A. Yes, sir.

"Q. And that they should unite to overthrow the capitalist system the world over? A. Yes, sir.

"Q. Isn't it a fact that in overthrowing the capitalist system (referring to the Soviet government) they wish and state they wish the overthrow of capitalist governments? Answer my question, please. A. Do they wish the overthrow of capitalist government, or do they not wish it, is that the question?

"Q. Yes, sir. A. That is their wish. Their wish is to change from the capitalist system to the Socialist system —

"Q. I ask this question again. Isn't it a fact that the Soviet government issues propaganda advising the propriety of overthrowing the capitalist governments in other countries? A. They are issuing propaganda as a defense.

"Q. I am asking you this question; isn't it a fact that the Soviet government issues propaganda advising the propriety of overthrowing the capitalist governments in other countries? A. No, it is not a fact; I deny it.

"Q. In answer to that question before you said it does? A. It does in a specific way as a means of defense against attacking.

"Q. But it does, does it not? A. Yes, as a means of defense." (See p. 1076, stenographer's minutes Committee hearings.)

As to whether the United States was included among the capitalist governments which the Soviet government sought to overthrow, Mr. Martens was asked:

"Q. Under the definition which you have given yourself of capitalistic government do you call the government of the United States a capitalistic government? A. Yes." (See p. 1123, stenographer's minutes Committee hearings.)

The character of the government which had been set up by Lenin and Trotzky, and the nature of the propaganda which was issued by its government bureau made it impossible for the Entente Powers to recognize the Russian Soviet regime. Diplomatic representatives were withdrawn and a blockade of Russian ports instituted.

Counter-revolutions were early started against the Soviet regime in Siberia, southern Russia, and in the Murmansk district. Admiral Kolchak leading the revolt in Siberia in co-operation with the Czecho-slovak units, and General Denikin in the south, and the counter-revolutionists of the Archangel district were assisted by allied troops among which were American units. The blockade thus instituted, together with the revolutionary groups on other fronts, rendered it difficult, if not impossible, for the Soviet regime to import necessary raw materials and manufactured products from western countries as well as from other parts of the world.

The foreign policy of the Soviet government had always been frank. It declared itself the enemy of every existing government and took every means of upsetting them. It fomented the revolutionary movement of the Spartacides in Germany through its agents Radek and Joffe; in Bavaria through Axelrod; in Hungary through Bela Kun; less successfully in Austria and in other countries. As Lenin held the theory that on account of economic conditions survival was possible only through world-wide triumph, no other policy was possible. He was frankly more inimical to the governments of the Entente Powers than to

Germany. The disgraceful Brest-Litovsk treaty with Germany which not only left Germany free on the East but gave her advantages in Russia; the control of the Soviet policy by the German ambassador, Mirbach, until he was assassinated; the selling of Russian business to Germans, were all part of a settled policy.

The revolutionary Socialist propaganda that was being carried on with increasing success in almost every country by Russian agents was not proceeding fast enough. Economic conditions in Russia were becoming daily more desperate.

It became apparent, therefore, that the Soviet government as a government must seem to change its attitude with respect to the stimulation of the International revolution, and to make promises of good behavior in exchange for recognition by the western powers. In order that such a position might be taken without the sacrifice of the principle that the International Socialist revolution must be stimulated, the leaders of the party in power, according to the testimony of Mr. Martens and to numerous pronouncements and documents which have come out of Russia, set up in Moscow a new instrument for the propagation of International revolutionary propaganda. This was the bureau of the Third Communistic International Committee.

It is given here as the culminating appeal of International Communism. We are giving elsewhere the stages in the evolution of Socialism that have led up to it and its connection with the Socialist movement in general.

This Congress adopted as a statement of principles the following manifesto which has been published in this country in the "Revolutionary Age" of Boston in the May 12, 1919, issue; and also printed in pamphlet form by the literature department of the Socialist Party of America, and distributed by the party throughout the country. Another version appeared in the "Nation" which was reprinted in the American Labor Year Book 1919–1920.

In December the meeting which took place in Petrograd, at which it was decided to convoke the Third International in March, brought together many of the leading propagandists for Bolshevism in the various countries of the East and West. At this meeting the speeches disclosed a remarkably widespread activity. The Conference also issued a remarkable program for the International which will be published in full together with the manifesto of the International itself, in a following chapter.

The basis of the program is the carrying out of the Communist Manifesto of Karl Marx. The capitalist cliques of democratic countries are attacked as bitterly as the dethroned dynasties. The complete deterioration of paper money is hailed as a proof of the deadly crisis in capitalist finance. The present dilemma is put before the world either of bowing to the International bourgeois finance enslavement of the Entente Powers, or of letting the working classes take into its own hands the entire economic life. The national state must be replaced by the universal proletarian dictatorship, which will among other things liberate the colonial slaves of Africa and Asia. This spells the downfall of political democracy, together with that of the bourgeois state, and that of nationalist sentiment. This can be carried out only by civil war and the "Red Terror" in case of resistance. This civil war will be made as short as possible. This is the historic result of the evolution of the last half-century since the establishment of the First International. The work at first had to be based on national spirit and organization. The opportunism of the reformist elements in the party caused the disruption of the Second International and the war made traitors of the so-called Social patriots of the Socialist groups. "Against these hypocrites we Communists are founding in the Third International the International of deeds; to join which we call on the proletarians of all lands, to rise in a war of revolutionary struggle for power."

THE NEW RUSSIAN LABOR LAW

The latest stage in the internal policy of the Soviet regime is expressed in the new code of labor laws promulgated and applied in 1919, the text of which is given in the documents at the end of this chapter. It is both a most extraordinary and important official Soviet document. This is because it has to be actually applied in every particular, contrary to the majority of the Soviet laws, including the constitution, which remains for the most part paper laws that are a dead letter. Where the Labor Law has *not* been followed it has been because of more severe and tyrannical rulings by the Soviet government; such as capital punishment for failure to work and substitution of a longer day for the eight-hour day.

Speeches by Leon Trotzky cabled over during the last few months explain the new labor laws as the only means of forcing the people to work, to insure adequate production, transportation and distribution of production. The Soviet leaders and newspapers freely acknowledge the paralysis of Russian production and transportation, the failure of the Soviet form of management by workmen, and the necessity for autocratic government of labor.

Lenin's appeals to the people to work during 1918 and 1919 were found to be useless. There were more non-working, non-productive government officials, from clerks to inspectors and commissioners, than there were workers. Consequently, after the necessity of fighting armies of Denikine, Kolchak and Yudenitch passed, universal conscription law put into operation for the army was maintained and applied to labor, the army not being disbanded but held together under military rule. Labor service was put under military law. Every man between the ages of eighteen and fifty, liable for military service, was made liable for working service under government rule, as a service to the State. Labor was not merely compulsory. It was so directed as to take away absolutely any liberty from the workmen.

The limitation to an eight-hour day, according to cabled information, is not carried into effect in certain industries where ten- and twelve-hour days are enforced.

A brief summary of the outstanding features of the new law shows that:

(1) Nobody is free to choose his kind of work. The Bureau of Labor assigns individuals or groups to any trade that is short of workers. (II, 10, 28, 29.)

(2) Nobody is free to choose his place of work. The Bureau sends individuals or groups to any locality or establishment that is found to need more workers. (II, 27.)

(3) Anybody who is not working must register at once, and cannot remain idle unless sick and provided with doctor's certificate, or belonging to a category exempt through disability or otherwise. (II, 21–26, and appendix.)

(4) Violation of the rules of labor distribution is punished by fine or imprisonment.

(5) There are elaborate arrangements for the transfer and discharge of workers, and for re-employment.

(6) Wages are fixed by tariff (VI, 55), which shall cover minimum living expenses as fixed by the Labor Commissariat.

(7) There is a classification of wages by groups and categories. (The old idea of the single wage was long ago abandoned and

Soviet wages were differentiated into nearly thirty categories from the low grade to the highest expert grade.)

(8) Every worker must have a labor booklet in which everything is entered relating to his work and payments. (Sec. 80 and appendix.)

(9) In case more than eight hours are required in any work there must be shifts. For children the hours must not exceed six. Overtime work is permitted under certain restrictions.

(10) To insure efficiency and standard of amount and quality of work is obligatory, and must be followed under penalty of discharge.

(11) There is an elaborate system of inspectors for enforcement of these laws, for medical inspection, for the granting of subsidies, etc.

BOLSHEVIK PROPAGANDA AMONG THE SOLDIERS OF THE ENTENTE AND AMERICAN ARMIES

Among the documents given at the close of this chapter are a number of the proclamations issued by the Soviet government and scattered broadcast among the soldiers of the American and Entente armies, combined against the Bolshevik fronts in Russia, especially the northern Archangel front. Considerable prominence has been given to these propaganda sheets in the Bolsheviki press of the United States, especially "The Liberator" and "The Class Struggle." The result was not, by any means, a failure. Among the speakers at the meeting held in Petrograd in December, 1919, to organize the Third International, there were a number of American, English and French army men, with one exception, prisoners taken on the front by the Bolsheviki and so well treated and so propaganized as to become converts. These isolated instances, brought forward very prominently at this International meeting and stressed by the Bolsheviki for obvious purposes, were merely examples of quite a widespread condition.

This skillful system of propaganda was successfully extended from the soldiery to the ranks of all the other workers of Entente and American nationality in Russia. It was successful in a large number of cases of both representatives of the Y. M. C. A. and Red Cross.

It was apparently the hope of the propagandists that converts in these extra-military agencies would prove of value in undermining the morale of American troops in Russia and in America.

One of the results of the skillful and psychological work of this sort done by Soviet agents has been that after their return to this country a number of Americans of this type have devoted themselves largely to spreading pro-Bolshevik propaganda in this country in every form.

PROPAGANDA OF THE SOVIET GOVERNMENT IN THE EAST

The general public is hardly aware that the Soviet government of Russia is conducting fully as active a propaganda throughout the entire East, as it is in Europe and America. It is a propaganda, the results of which might be almost too terrible to contemplate, because it involves letting loose so many hundreds of millions of people in a low stage of civilization. There is in Moscow a university or college for the teaching of propagandists, in which men from every part of the world, belonging to every conceivable nationality, are educated in the essentials of Bolshevik propaganda. It is reported that as many as sixty Hindu dialects and forty Chinese dialects are in use in this college.

At the meeting held in December, 1918, for the purpose of issuing the call for the Third International, there were in attendance native representatives of the following Eastern nationalities or groups —Turkestan, Persia, Afghanistan, India, Korea, China, Japan. These men all made speeches, in which they pledged the adhesion of large groups of their countrymen to the Soviet program.

At about the same time Vosniesansky, who is the Soviet Commisar for Asiatic affairs, returned to Moscow from a mission to Kabul, Tashkend and Samarkand, together with Bravine, Soviet Commisar in Persia. He had established connections between Teheran and Kabul, as well as between Kabul, Herat, Samarkand and Tashkend. All disagreements between the Soviet of Tashkend and Afghanistan had been arranged, and a close organization effected. Vosniesanky brought back with him a number of Afghans and delegates from Tashkend, whose purpose was to arrange at Moscow for a Bolshevik Afghan Convention.

The Chinese situation is even more dangerous, on account of the close connection between a large number of Chinese in Russia and China itself. It is a fact of common knowledge, that about 60,000 Chinese laborers, who were in Russia at the time of the advent of the Bolsheviki to power, were drafted into the Bolshevik army, and were turned into the professional executioners of the Red Terror. They have been used as the nucleus for very extensive propaganda in China.

In January, 1919, Lenin issued a decree placing the Chinese under the particular protection of the Soviet Republic, and organizing a special department for Bolshevik propaganda in China, under a Chinaman named Chun Yun Sun. A regular line of communication was established with China through Turkestan and Thibet.

The Bolshevik propaganda in India is very well known, and is linked up, as is so generally the case, with previous pro-German propaganda. The United States had quite a share in unwittingly helping along this propaganda, by affording refuge to the conspirators.

One of the Bolshevist leaders, specially connected with propaganda in Afghanistan and India, is a Commisar by the name of Kumaroff, who was connected with the well-known uprising in Afghanistan in 1918.

In November, 1919, an Afghan Ambassador to Soviet Russia was received with great pomp by Lenin in Moscow. The Ambassador expressed the hope that the Soviet would help to emancipate the peoples of the East. Lenin replied that that was exactly what the Soviet wished to do, but that it would be necessary for the Mohammedans in the East to help Soviet Russia first in its great war of emancipation.

It is hardly necessary to say that the arguments used by Soviet propaganda in the Orient have no connection whatsoever with the arguments used in the propaganda among advanced and educated peoples.

The contact which has been established through the recent Bolshevist victories, with Turkestan and Persia, as well as with the Turks, has brought about closer contact between the Russian agents and their Oriental propagandists, and has brought them within striking distance of Afghanistan. The leaders of the Pan-Turkish movement have been reported as favoring the Bolshevists.

APPENDIX

CHAPTER XIV

Documents of the Russian Soviet Regime

APPENDIX

CHAPTER XIV

Official and Other Documents of the Russian Soviet Regime

Document No. 1

CONSTITUTION OF THE RUSSIAN SOCIALIST FEDERATED SOVIET REPUBLIC

" Resolution of the Fifth All-Russian Congress of Soviets, adopted on July 10, 1918.

" The declaration of rights of the laboring and exploited people (approved by the Third All-Russian Congress of Soviets in January, 1918), together with the Constitution of the Soviet Republic, approved by the Fifth Congress, constitutes a single fundamental law of the Russian Socialist Federated Soviet Republic.

" This fundamental law becomes effective upon the publication of the same in its entirety in the 'Izvestia of the All-Russian General Executive Committee.' It must be published by all organs of the Soviet Government and must be posted in a prominent place in every Soviet institution.

" The Fifth Congress instructs the People's Commissariat of Education to introduce in all schools and educational institutions of the Russian Republic the study and explanation of the basic principles of this Constitution.

A. "Article One

"Declaration of Rights of the Laboring and Exploited People

" CHAPTER ONE

" 1. Russia is declared to be a Republic of the Soviets of Workers', Soldiers', and Peasants' Deputies. All the central and local power belongs to these Soviets.

" 2. The Russian Soviet Republic is organized on the basis of a free union of free nations, as a federation of Soviet national republics.

" CHAPTER TWO

" 3. Bearing in mind as its fundamental problem the abolition of the exploitation of men by men, the entire abolition of the division of the people into classes, the suppression of exploiters, the establishment of a Socialist society, and the victory of Socialism in all lands, the Third All-Russian Congress of Soviets of Workers', Soldiers', and Peasants' Deputies further resolves:

"(a) For the purpose of attaining the socialization of land, all private property in land is abolished, and the entire land is declared to be national property and is to be apportioned among agriculturists without any compensation to the former owners, in the measure of each one's ability to till it.

"(b) All forests, treasures of the earth, and waters of general public utility, all equipment whether animate or inanimate, model farms and agricultural enterprises, are declared to be national property.

"(c) As a first step toward complete transfer of ownership to the Soviet Republic of all factories, mills, mines, railways, and other means of production and transportation, the Soviet law for the control by workmen and the establishment of the Supreme Soviet of National Economy is hereby confirmed, so as to insure the power of the workers over the exploiters.

"(d) With reference to international banking and finance, the Third Congress of Soviets is discussing the Soviet decree regarding the annulment of loans made by the Government of the Czar, by landowners and the bourgeoisie, and it trusts that the Soviet Government will firmly follow this course until the final victory of the international workers' revolt against the oppression of capital.

"(e) The transfer of all banks to the ownership of the Workers' and Peasants' Government, as one of the conditions of the liberation of the toiling masses from the yoke of capital, is confirmed.

"(f) Universal obligation to work is introduced for the purpose of eliminating the parasitic strata of society and organizing the economic life of the country.

"(g) For the purpose of securing the working class in the possession of complete power, and in order to eliminate all possibility of restoring the power of the exploiters, it is decreed that all workers be armed, and that a Socialist Red Army be organized and the propertied class disarmed.

"CHAPTER THREE

"4. Expressing its fixed resolve to liberate mankind from the grip of capital and imperialism, which flooded the earth with blood in its present most criminal of all wars, the third Congress of Soviets fully agrees with the Soviet Government in its policy of abrogating secret treaties, of organizing on a wide scale the fraternization of the workers and peasants of the belligerent armies, and of making all efforts to conclude a general democratic peace without annexations or indemnities, upon the basis of the free determination of peoples.

"5. It is also to this end that the third Congress of Soviets insists upon putting an end to the barbarous policy of the bourgeois civilization which enables the exploiters of a few chosen nations to enslave hundreds of millions of the working population of Asia, of the colonies, and of small countries generally.

"6. The third Congress of Soviets hails the policy of the Council of People's Commissars in proclaiming the full independence of Finland, in withdrawing troops from Persia, and in proclaiming the right of Armenia to self-determination.

"CHAPTER FOUR

"7. The third All-Russian Congress of Soviets of Workers', Soldiers', and Peasants' Deputies believes that now, during the progress of the decisive battle between the proletariat and its exploiters, the exploiters should not hold a position in any branch of the Soviet Government. The power must belong entirely to the toiling masses and to their plenipotentiary representatives — the Soviets of Workers', Soldiers', and Peasants' Deputies.

"8. In its effort to create a league — free and voluntary and for that reason all the more complete and secure — of the working classes of all the peoples of Russia, the third Congress of Soviets merely establishes the fundamental principles of the Federation of Russian Soviet Republics, leaving to the workers and peasants of every people to decide the following question at their plenary sessions of their Soviets, namely, whether or not they desire to participate, and on what basis, in the Federal Government and other Federal Soviet institutions.

B. "Article Two

"General Provisions of the Constitution of the Russian Socialist Federated Soviet Republic

"Chapter Five

"9. The fundamental problem of the constitution of the Russian Socialist Federated Soviet Republic involves, in view of the present transition period, the establishing of a dictatorship of the urban and rural proletariat and the poorest peasantry in the form of a powerful All-Russian Soviet authority, for the purpose of abolishing the exploitation of men by men and of introducing Socialism, in which there will be neither a division into classes nor a state of autocracy.

"10. The Russian Republic is a free Socialist society of all the working people of Russia. The entire power, within the boundaries of the Russian Socialist Federated Soviet Republic, belongs to all the working people of Russia, united in urban and rural Soviets.

"11. The Soviets of those regions which differentiate themselves by a special form of existence and national character may unite in autonomous regional unions, ruled by the local Congress of the Soviets and their executive organs.

"These autonomous regional unions participate in the Russian Socialist Federated Soviet Republic upon a federal basis.

"12. The supreme power of the Russian Socialist Federated Soviet Republic belongs to the All-Russian Congress of Soviets, and, in periods between the convocation of the Congress, to the All-Russian Central Executive Committee.

"13. For the purpose of securing to the workers real freedom of conscience, the church is to be separated from the state and the school from the church, and the right of religious and anti-religious propaganda is accorded to every citizen.

"14. For the purpose of securing freedom of expression to the toiling masses, the Russian Socialist Federated Soviet Republic abolishes all dependence of the press upon capital, and turns over to the working people and the poorest peasantry all technical and material means for the publication of newspapers, pamphlets, books, etc., and guarantees their free circulation throughout the country.

"15. For the purpose of enabling the workers to hold free meetings, the Russian Socialist Federated Soviet Republic offers to the working class and to the poorest peasantry furnished halls, and takes care of their heating and lighting appliances.

"16. The Russian Socialist Federated Soviet Republic, having crushed the economic and political power of the propertied classes, and having thus abolished all obstacles which interfered with the freedom of organization and action of the workers and peasants, offers assistance, material and other, to the workers and the poorest peasantry in their effort to unite and organize.

"17. For the purpose of guaranteeing to the workers real access to knowledge, the Russian Socialist Federated Soviet Republic sets itself the task of furnishing full and general free education to the workers and the poorest peasantry.

"18. The Russian Socialist Federated Soviet Republic considers work the duty of every citizen of the Republic, and proclaims as its motto: 'He shall not eat who does not work.'

"19. For the purpose of defending the victory of the great peasants' and workers' revolution, the Russian Socialist Federated Soviet Republic recognizes the duty of all citizens of the Republic to come to the defense of their Socialist Fatherland, and it therefore introduces universal military training. The honor of defending the revolution with arms is accorded only to the workers, and the non-working elements are charged with the performance of other military duties.

"20. In consequence of the solidarity of the workers of all nations, the Russian Socialist Federated Soviet Republic grants all political rights of Russian citizens to foreigners who live in the territory of the Russian Republic and are engaged in work and who belong to the working class. The Russian Socialist Federated Soviet Republic also recognizes the right of local Soviets to grant citizenship to such foreigners without complicated formality.

"21. The Russian Socialist Federated Soviet Republic offers shelter to all foreigners who seek refuge from political or religious persecution.

"22. The Russian Socialist Federated Soviet Republic, recognizing the equal rights of all citizens, irrespective of their racial or national connections, proclaims all privileges on this ground, as well as oppression of national minorities, to be contrary to the fundamental laws of the Republic.

"23. Being guided by the interests of the working class as a whole, the Russian Socialist Federated Soviet Republic deprives all individuals and groups of rights which could be utilized by them to the detriment of the Socialist Revolution.

C. "ARTICLE THREE

"ORGANIZATION OF THE SOVIET POWER

"I. Organization of the Central Power

"CHAPTER SIX

"The All-Russian Congress of Soviets of Workers', Peasants', Cossacks' and Red Army Deputies

"24. The All-Russian Congress of Soviets is the supreme power of the Russian Socialist Federated Soviet Republic.

"25. The All-Russian Congress of Soviets is composed of representatives of urban Soviets (one delegate for 25,000 voters) and of representatives of the provincial (Gubernia) congresses of Soviets (one delegate for 125,000 inhabitants).

"Note 1.—In case the Provincial Congress is not called before the All-Russian Congress is convoked, delegates for the latter are sent directly from the County (Ouezd) Congress.

"Note 2.—In case the Regional (Oblast) Congress is convoked indirectly, previous to the convocation of the All-Russian Congress, delegates for the latter may be sent by the Regional Congress.

"26. The All-Russian Congress is convoked by the All-Russian Central Executive Committee at least twice a year.

"27. A special All-Russian Congress is convoked by the All-Russian Central Executive Committee upon its own initiative, or upon the request of local Soviets having not less than one-third of the Russian Socialist Federated Soviet Republic.

"28. The All-Russian Congress elects an All-Russian Central Executive Committee of not more than 200 members.

"29. The All-Russian Central Executive Committee is entirely responsible to the All-Russian Congress of Soviets.

"30. In the periods between the convocation of the Congresses, the All-Russian Central Executive Committee is the supreme power of the Republic.

"CHAPTER SEVEN

"*The All-Russian Central Executive Committee*

"31. The All-Russian Central Executive Committee is the supreme legislative, executive, and controlling organ of the Russian Socialist Federated Soviet Republic.

"32. The All-Russian Central Executive Committee directs in a general way the activity of the Workers' and Peasants' Government and of all organs of the Soviet authority in the country, and it co-ordinates and regulates the operation of the Soviet Constitution and of the resolutions of the All-Russian Congresses and of the central organs of the Soviet power.

"33. The All-Russian Central Executive Committee considers and enacts all measures and proposals introduced by the Soviet of People's Commissars or by the various departments, and it also issues its own decrees and regulations.

"34. The All-Russian Central Executive Committee convokes the All-Russian Congress of Soviets, at which time the Executive Committee reports on its activity and on general questions.

"35. The All-Russian Central Executive Committee forms a Council of People's Commissars for the purpose of general management of the affairs of the Russian Socialist Federated Soviet Republic, and it also forms departments (People's Commissariats) for the purpose of conducting various branches.

"36. The members of the All-Russian Central Executive Committee work in the various departments (People's Commissariats) or execute special orders of the All-Russian Central Executive Committee.

"CHAPTER EIGHT

"37. The Council of People's Commissars is entrusted with the general management of the affairs of the Russian Socialist Federated Soviet Republic.

"38. For the accomplishment of this task the Council of People's Commissars issues decrees, resolutions, orders, and, in general, takes all steps necessary for the proper and rapid conduct of government affairs.

"39. The Council of People's Commissars notifies immediately the All-Russian Central Executive Committee of all its orders and resolutions.

"40. The All-Russian Central Executive Committee has the right to revoke or suspend all orders and resolutions of the Council of People's Commissars.

"41. All orders and resolutions of the Council of People's Commissars of great political significance are referred for consideration and final approval to the All-Russian Central Executive Committee.

"Note.—Measures requiring immediate execution may be enacted directly by the Council of People's Commissars.

"42. The members of the Council of People's Commissars stand at the head of the various People's Commissariats.

"43. There are seventeen People's Commissars: (a) Foreign Affairs; (b) Army, (c) Navy, (d) Interior, (e) Justice, (f) Labor, (g) Social Welfare, (h) Education, (i) Post and Telegraph, (j) National Affairs, (k) Finances, (l) Ways of Communications, (m) Agriculture, (n) Commerce and Industry, (o) National Supplies, (p) State Control, (q) Supreme Soviet of National Economy, (r) Public Health.

"44. Every Commissar has a Collegium (committee) of which he is the president, and the members of which are appointed by the Council of People's Commissars.

"45. A People's Commissar has the individual right to decide on all questions under the jurisdiction of his Commissariat, and he is to report on his decision to the Collegium. If the Collegium does not agree with the Commissar on some decisions, the former may, without stopping the execution of the decision, complain of it to the executive members of the Council of People's Commissars or to the All-Russian Central Executive Committee.

"Individual members of the Collegium have this right also.

"46. The Council of People's Commissars is entirely responsible to the All-Russian Congress of Soviets and the All-Russian Central Executive Committee.

"47. The People's Commissars and the Collegia of the People's Commissariats are entirely responsible to the Council of People's Commissars and the All-Russian Central Executive Committee.

"48. The title of People's Commissar belongs only to the members of the Council of People's Commissars, which is in charge of general affairs of the Russian Socialist Federated Soviet Republic, and it cannot be used by any other representative of the Soviet power, either central or local.

"CHAPTER NINE

"Affairs in the Jurisdiction of the All-Russian Congress and the All-Russian Central Executive Committee

"49. The All-Russian Congress and the All-Russian Central Executive Committee deal with questions of state, such as:

"(a) Ratification and amendment of the Constitution of the Russian Socialist Federated Soviet Republic.

"(b) General direction of the entire interior and foreign policy of the Russian Socialist Federated Soviet Republic.

"(c) Establishing and changing boundaries, also ceding territory belonging to the Russian Socialist Federated Soviet Republic.

"(d) Establishing boundaries for regional Soviet unions belonging to the Russian Socialist Federated Soviet Republic, also settling disputes among them.

"(e) Admission of new members to the Russian Socialist Federal Soviet Republic, and recognition of the secession of any parts of it.

"(f) The general administrative division of the territory of the Russian Socialist Federated Soviet Republic, and the approval of regional unions.

"(g) Establishing and changing weights, measures, and money denominations in the Russian Socialist Federated Soviet Republic.

"(h) Foreign relations, declaration of war, and ratification of peace treaties.

"(i) Making loans, signing commercial treaties and financial agreements.

"(j) Working out a basis and a general plan for the national economy and for its various branches in the Russian Socialist Federated Soviet Republic.

"(k) Approval of the budget of the Russian Socialist Federated Soviet Republic.

"(l) Levying taxes and establishing the duties of citizens to the State.

"(m) Establishing the bases for the organization of armed forces.

"(n) State legislation, judicial organization and procedure, civil and criminal legislation, etc.

"(o) Appointment and dismissal of the individual People's Commissars or the entire Council, also approval of the president of the Council of People's Commissars.

"(p) Granting and cancelling Russian citizenship and fixing rights of foreigners.

"(q) The right to declare individual and general amnesty.

"50. Besides the above-mentioned questions, the All-Russian Congress and the All-Russian Central Executive Committee have charge of all other affairs which, according to their decision, require their attention.

"51. The following questions are solely under the jurisdiction of the All-Russian Congress:

"(a) Ratification and amendment of the fundamental principles of the Soviet Constitution.

"(b) Ratification of peace treaties.

"52. The decision of questions indicated in paragraphs (c) and (h) of section 49 may be made by the All-Russian Central Executive Committee only in case it is impossible to convoke the Congress.

"II. Organization of Local Soviets

"CHAPTER TEN

"*The Congresses of the Soviets*

53. Congresses of Soviets are composed as follows:

"(a) Regional: of representatives of the urban and county Soviets, one representative for 25,000 inhabitants of the county, and one representative for 5,000 voters of the cities — but not more than 500 representatives for the entire region — or of representatives of the provincial congresses, chosen on the same basis, if such a congress meets before the regional Congress.

"(b) Provincial (Gubernia): of representatives of urban and rural (Volost) Soviets, one representative for 10,000 inhabitants, from the rural districts, and one representative for 2,000 voters in the city; altogether not more than 300 representatives for the entire province. In case the county congress meets before the provincial, election takes place on the same basis, but by the county congress instead of the rural.

"(c) County: of representatives of rural Soviets, one delegate for each 1,000 inhabitants, but not more than 300 delegates for the entire county.

"(d) Rural (Volost): of representatives of all village Soviets in the Volost, one delegate for ten members of the Soviet.

"Note 1.—Representatives of urban Soviets which have a population of not more than 10,000 persons participate in the county congress; village Soviets of districts of less than 1,000 inhabitants unite for the purpose of electing delegates to the county congress.

"Note 2.—Rural Soviets of less than ten members send one delegate to the rural (Volost) congress.

"54. Congresses of the Soviets are convoked by the respective executive committees upon their own initiative, or upon request of local Soviets, comprising not less than one-third of the entire population of the given district. In any case they are convoked at least twice a year for regions, every three months for provinces and counties, and once a month for rural districts.

"55. Every Congress of Soviets (regional, provincial, county or rural) elects its executive organ — an executive committee the membership of which shall not exceed: (a) for regions and provinces, twenty-five; (b) for a county, twenty; (c) for a rural district, ten. The executive committee is responsible to the congress which elected it.

"56. In the boundaries of the respective territories the congress is the supreme power; during intervals between the convocations of the congress, the executive committee is the supreme power.

"CHAPTER ELEVEN

"*The Soviet of Deputies*

"57. Soviets of Deputies are formed:

"(a) In cities, one deputy for each 1,000 inhabitants; the total to be not less than fifty and not more than 1,000 members.

"(b) All other settlements (towns, villages, hamlets, etc.) of less than 10,000 inhabitants, one deputy for each 100 inhabitants; the total to be not less than three and not more than 50 deputies for each settlement.

"Term of the deputy, three months.

"Note.—In small rural sections, whenever possible, all questions shall be decided at general meetings of voters.

"58. The Soviet of Deputies elects an Executive Committee to deal with current affairs; not more than five members for rural districts, one for every 50 members of the Soviets of cities, but not more than 15 and not less than three in the aggregate (Petrograd and Moscow not more than 40). The Executive Committee is entirely responsible to the Soviet which elected it.

"59. The Soviet of Deputies is convoked by the Executive Committee upon its own initiative, or upon the request of not less than one-half of the membership of the Soviet; in any case at least once a week in cities, and twice a week in rural sections.

"60. Within its jurisdiction the Soviet, and in cases mentioned in section 57, note, the meeting of the voters is the supreme power in the given district.

"CHAPTER TWELVE

"*Jurisdiction of the Local Organs of the Soviets*

"61. Regional, provincial, county, and rural organs of the Soviet power and also the Soviets of Deputies have to perform the following duties:

"(a) Carry out all orders of the respective higher organs of the Soviet power.

"(b) Take all steps for raising the cultural and economic standard of the given territory.

"(c) Decide all questions of local importance within their respective territories.

"(d) Co-ordinate all Soviet activity in their respective territories.

"62. The Congresses of Soviets and their Executive Committees have the right to control the activity of the local Soviets (i. e., the regional Congress controls all Soviets of the respective region; the provincial, of the respective province, with the exception of the urban Soviets, etc.); and the regional and provincial Congresses and their Executive Committees have in addition the right to overrule the decisions of the Soviets of their districts, giving notice in important cases to the central Soviet authority.

"63. For the purpose of performing their duties, the local Soviets, rural and urban, and the Executive Committees form sections respectively.

D. "ARTICLE FOUR

"THE RIGHT TO VOTE

"CHAPTER THIRTEEN

"64. The right to vote and to be elected to the Soviets is enjoyed by the following citizens of both sexes, irrespective of religion, nationality, domicile, etc., of the Russian Socialist Federated Soviet Republic, who shall have completed their eighteenth year by the day of election:

"(a) All who have acquired the means of livelihood through labor that is productive and useful to society, and also persons engaged in housekeeping which enables the former to do productive work, i. e., laborers and employees of all classes who are employed in industry, trade, agriculture, etc., and peasants and Cossack agricultural laborers who employ no help for the purpose of making profits.

"(b) Soldiers of the army and navy of the Soviets.

"(c) Citizens of the two preceding categories who have in any degree lost their capacity to work.

"Note 1.—Local Soviets may, upon approval of the central power, lower the age standard mentioned herein.

"Note 2.—Non-citizens mentioned in section 20 (article 2, chapter 5) have the right to vote.

"65. The following persons enjoy neither the right to vote nor the right to be voted for, even though they belong to one of the categories enumerated above, namely:

"(a) Persons who employ hired labor in order to obtain from it an increase in profit.

"(b) Persons who have an income without doing any work, such as interest from capital, receipts from property, etc.

"(c) Private merchants, trade and commercial brokers.

"(d) Monks and clergy of all denominations.

"(e) Employees and agents of the former police, the gendarme corps, and the Okhrana (Czar's secret service), also members of the former reigning dynasty.

"(f) Persons who have in legal form been declared demented or mentally deficient, and also persons under guardianship.

" (g) Persons who have been deprived by a Soviet, cf their rights of citizenship because of selfish or dishonorable offenses, for the period fixed by the sentence.

" CHAPTER FOURTEEN

" *Elections*

" 66. Elections are conducted according to custom on days fixed by the local Soviets.

" 67. Election takes place in the presence of an election committee and a representative of the local Soviet.

" 68. In case the representative of the Soviet cannot for valid causes be present, the chairman of the election committee takes his place, and in case the latter is absent, the chairman of the election meeting replaces him.

" 69. Minutes of the proceedings and results of elections are to be compiled and signed by the members of the election committee and the representative of the local Soviet.

" 70. Detailed instructions regarding the election proceedings and the participation in them of professional and other workers' organizations are to be issued by the local Soviets, according to the instructions of the All-Russian Executive Committee.

" CHAPTER FIFTEEN

" *The Checking and Cancellation of Elections and Recall of the Deputies*

" 71. The respective Soviets receive all the records of the proceedings of the election.

" 72. The Soviet appoints a commission to verify the election.

" 73. This commission reports the results to the Soviet.

" 74. The Soviet decides the question when there is doubt as to which candidate is elected.

"75. The Soviet announces a new election if the election of one candidate or another cannot be determined.

" 76. If an election was irregularly carried on in its entirety, it may be declared void by a higher Soviet authority.

" 77. The highest authority in relation to questions of elections is the All-Russian Central Executive Committee.

" 78. Voters who have sent a deputy to the Soviet have the right to recall him, and to have a new election, according to general provisions.

E. "ARTICLE FIVE

"THE BUDGET

"CHAPTER SIXTEEN

"79. The financial policy of the Russian Socialist Federated Soviet Republic in the present transition period of dictatorship of the proletariat facilitates the fundamental purpose of expropriation of the bourgeoisie and the preparation of conditions necessary for the equality of all citizens of Russia in the production and distribution of wealth. To this end it sets forth as its task the supplying of the organs of the Soviet power with all necessary funds for local and state needs of the Soviet Republic, without regard to private property rights.

"80. The state expenditure and income of the Russian Socialist Federated Soviet Republic are combined in the State budget.

"81. The All-Russian Congress of Soviets or the All-Russian Central Executive Committee determine what matters of income and taxations shall go to the state budget and what shall go to the local Soviets; they also set the limits of taxes.

"82. The Soviets levy taxes only for the local needs. The state needs are covered by the funds of the state treasury.

"83. No expenditure out of the state treasury not set forth in the budget of income and expense shall be made without a special order of the central power.

"84. The local Soviets shall receive credits from the proper People's Commissars out of the state treasury, for the purpose of making expenditures for general state needs.

"85. All credits allotted to the Soviets from the state treasury, and also credits approved for local needs, must be expended according to the estimates, and cannot be used for any other purposes without a special order of the All-Russian Central Executive Committee and the Soviet of People's Commissars.

"86. Local Soviets draw up semi-annual and annual estimate of income and expenditure for local needs. The estimates of urban and rural Soviets participating in county congresses, and also the estimates of the county organs of the Soviet power, are to be approved by provincial and regional congresses or by their executive committees; the estimates of the urban, provincial, and regional organs of the Soviets are to be approved by the All-Russian Central Executive Committee and the Council of People's Commissars.

"87. The Soviets may ask for additional credits from the respective People's Commissariats for expenditures not set forth in the estimates, or where the allotted sum is insufficient.

"88. In case of an insufficiency of local funds for local needs, the necessary subsidy may be obtained from the state treasury by applying to the All-Russian Central Executive Committee or the Council of People's Commissars.

F. "ARTICLE SIX

"THE COAT OF ARMS AND FLAG OF THE RUSSIAN SOCIALIST FEDERATED SOVIET REPUBLIC

"CHAPTER SEVENTEEN

"89. The coat of arms of the Russian Socialist Federated Soviet Republic consists of a red background on which a golden scythe and a hammer are placed (cross-wise, handles downward) in sun-rays and surrounded by a wreath, inscribed:

Russian Socialist Federated Soviet Republic
Workers of the World, Unite!

"90. The commercial, naval, and army flag of the Russian Socialist Federated Soviet Republic consists of a red cloth, in the left corner of which (on top, near the pole) are in golden characters the letters R. S. F. S. R., or the inscription: Russian Socialist Federated Soviet Republic.

"*Chairman of the fifth All-Russian Congress of Soviets and of the All-Russian Central Executive Committee* — J. SVERDLOV.

"*Executive Officers — All-Russian Central Executive Committee:*

T. I. TEODOROVITCH, F. A. ROSIN, A. P. ROSENHOLZ, A. C. MITROFANOV, K. G. MAXIMOV.

"*Secretary of the All-Russian Central Executive Committee* —

V. A. AVANESOV."

LAWS AND DECREES

The following documents are taken in part from a collection in the Library of Congress at Washington and in part from a volume of laws, regulations, and decrees published by the Executive Committee of the Workers' and Soldiers' Deputies of the province of Tomsk, Russia. The documents selected have appeared in various issues of the International Relations section of the "Nation."

LAND LAW

The "Fundamental Law of Socialization of the Land" went into effect in September, 1918, replacing the earlier and briefer Land Decree of November 7, 1917.

Document No. 2

DECREES AND CONSTITUTION OF SOVIET RUSSIA

---

a. LAND LAW

"DIVISION I

"General Provisions

"Article 1. All property rights in the land, treasures of the earth, waters, forests and fundamental natural resources within the boundaries of the Russian Federated Soviet Republic are abolished.

"Article 2. The land passes over to the use of the entire laboring population without any compensation, open or secret, to the former owners.

"Article 3. The right to use the land belongs to those who till it by their own labor, with the exception of special cases covered by this decree.

"Article 4. The right to use the land cannot be limited by sex, religion, nationality, or foreign citizenship.

"Article 5. The sub-surface deposits, the forests, waters and fundamental natural resources are at the disposition (according to their character) of the county, provincial, regional and Federal Soviet powers and are under the control of the latter. The method of disposition and utilization of the sub-surface deposits, waters and fundamental natural resources will be dealt with by a special decree.

"Article 6. All private live stock and inventoried property of non-laboring homesteads pass over without indemnification to the disposition (in accordance with their character) of the land departments of county, provincial, regional and Federal Soviets.

"Article 7. All homestead structures mentioned in Article 6, as well as all agricultural appurtenances, pass over to the disposition (in accordance with their character) of the county, provincial, regional, and Federal Soviets without indemnification.

"Article 8. All persons who are unable to work and who will be deprived of all means of subsistence by force of the decree socializing all lands, forests, inventoried property, etc., may receive a pension (for lifetime or until the person becomes of age) upon the certification of the local courts and the land departments of the Soviet power, such as a soldier receives, until such time as the decree for the insurance of the incapacitated is issued.

"Article 9. The apportionment of lands of agricultural value among the laboring people is under the jurisdiction of the Volostnoi (several villages), county, provincial, regional and Federal land departments of the Soviets in accordance with their character.

"Article 10. The surplus lands are under the supervision, in every republic, of the land departments of the regional and Federal Soviets.

"Article 11. The land departments of the local and central Soviets are thus entrusted with the equitable apportionment of the land among the working agricultural population, and with the productive utilization of the natural resources. They also have the following duties:

"(a) Creating favorable conditions for the development of the productive forces of the country by increasing the fertility of the land, improving agricultural technique, and, finally, raising the standard of agricultural knowledge among the laboring population.

"(b) Creating a surplus fund of lands of agricultural value.

"(c) Developing various branches of agricultural industry, such as gardening, cattle-breeding, dairying, etc.

" (d) Accelerating the transition from the old unproductive system of field cultivation to the new productive one (under various climates), by a proper distribution of the laboring population in various parts of the country.

"(e) Developing collective homesteads in agricultural (in preference to individual homesteads) as the most profitable system of saving labor and material, with a view to passing on to Socialism.

"Article 12. The apportionment of land among the laboring population is to be carried out on the basis of each one's ability to till it and in accordance with local conditions, so that the production and consumption standard may not compel some peasants to work beyond their strength; and at the same time it should give them sufficient means of subsistence.

"Article 13. Personal labor is the general and fundamental source of the right to use the land for agricultural purposes. In addition, the organs of the Soviet power, with a view to raising the agricultural standard (by organizing model farms or experimental fields), are permitted to borrow from the surplus land fund (formerly belonging to the Crown, monasteries, clergy, or landowners) certain plots and to work them by labor paid by the state. Such labor is subject to the general rules of workmen's control.

"Article 14. All citizens engaged in agricultural work are to be insured at the expense of the state against old age, sickness, or injuries which incapacitate them.

"Article 15. All incapacitated agriculturists and the members of their families who are unable to work are to be cared for by the organs of the Soviet power.

"Article 16. Every agricultural homestead is to be insured against fire, epidemics among cattle, poor crops, dry weather, hail, etc., by means of mutual Soviet insurance.

"Article 17. Surplus profits, obtained on account of the natural fertility of the land or on account of its location near markets, are to be turned over for the benefit of social needs to the organs of the Soviet power.

"Article 18. The trade in agricultural machinery and in seeds is monopolized by the organs of the Soviet power.

"Article 19. The grain trade, internal as well as export, is to be a state monopoly.

"DIVISION II

Who Has the Right to Use the Land

"Article 20. Plots of land may be used in the Russian Federated Soviet Republic for the following social and private needs:

"A. Cultural and educational:

"1. The state, in the form of the organs of the Soviet power (Federal, regional, provincial, county, and rural).

"2. Social organizations (under the control and by permission of the local Soviets).

"B. For agricultural purposes:

"3. Agricultural communities.

"4. Agricultural associations.

"5. Village organizations.

"6. Individuals and families.

"C. For construction purposes:

"7. By the organs of the Soviet power.

"8. By social organizations, individuals, and families (if the construction is not a means of obtaining profits).

"9. By industrial, commercial, and transportation enterprises (by special permission and under the control of the Soviet power).

"D. For constructing ways of communication:

"10. By organs of the Soviet power (Federal, regional, provincial, county, and rural, according to the importance of the ways of communication).

"DIVISION III

"The Order in Which Land is Apportioned

"Article 21. Land is given to those who wish to work it themselves for the benefit of the community, and not for personal advantage.

"Article 22. The following is the order in which land is given for personal agricultural needs:

" 1. To local agriculturists who have no land or a small amount of land and to local agricultural workers (formerly hired), on an equal basis.

" 2. Agricultural emigrants who have come to a given locality after the issuance of the decree of socialization of the land.

" 3. Non-agricultural emigrants in the order of their registration at the land departments of the local Soviets.

" Note.— When arranging the order of the apportionment of land, preference is given to laboring agricultural associations over individual homesteads.

"Article 23. For the purpose of gardening, fishing, cattle breeding, or forestry, land is given on the following basis:

" (1) Land which cannot be tilled; (2) land which can be tilled, but which on account of its location is preferably to be used for other agricultural purposes.

"Article 24. In rural districts, land is used for construction purposes in accordance with the decision of the local Soviets and the population.

" In cities, land may be obtained in the order in which applications are filed with the respective local Soviets, if the construction planned does not threaten to harm the neighboring buildings and if it answers all other requirements of the building regulations.

" Note.— For the purpose of erecting social buildings, land is given regardless of the order in which applications are filed.

" DIVISION IV

" *The Standard of Agricultural Production and Consumption*

"Article 25. The amount of land given to individual homesteads for agricultural purposes, with a view to obtaining means of subsistence, must not exceed the standard of agricultural production and consumption as determined on the basis indicated in the instruction following:

" INSTRUCTION FOR DETERMINING THE PRODUCTION AND CONSUMPTION STANDARD FOR THE USE OF LAND OF AGRICULTURAL VALUE.

" 1. The whole of agricultural Russia is divided into as many climatic sections as there are field cultivation systems historically in existence at the given agricultural period.

"2. For every agricultural section a special production and consumption standard is set. Within the section the standard may be changed in accordance with the climate and the natural fertility of the land, also, in accordance with its location (near a market or railway) and other conditions which are of great local importance.

"3. For an exact determination of the standard of each section, it is necessary to take an All-Russian agricultural census in the near future.

"Note.—After the socialization of the land has been accomplished, it is necessary to survey it immediately and to determine its topography.

"4. The apportionment of land on the production and consumption basis among the agricultural population is to be carried on gradually in various agricultural sections, according to regulations stated herein.

"Note.—Until the socialization of land is entirely accomplished, the relations of agriculturists will be regulated by the land departments of the Soviets in accordance with a special instruction.

"5. For the determination of the production and consumption standard of a given climatic section, it is necessary to take the standard (an average agricultural homestead) of one of the counties of that section (or another agricultural standard of equal size) with a small population, and with such a proportion of various agricultural advantages as, in the opinion of the local inhabitants (regional or provincial congress of the land departments of the Soviets), will be recognized as the most normal, i. e., the most favorable for the type of field cultivation which predominates in that climatic section.

"6. For the determination of what an average agricultural homestead is, it is necessary to take into consideration only those lands which were actually in the possession of working peasants down to 1917, i. e., lands bought by peasant organizations, associations, individuals, and entailed and rented lands.

"7. Forests, sub-surface deposits, and waters are not to be considered in this determination.

"8. Private lands which were never used for agricultural purposes, and which were actually in the possession of the state, private banks, monasteries, or land owners, will not be taken into consideration in this determination, as they will constitute the surplus land fund which will serve to supply the landless peasants and those who have less land than the peasant's production and consumption standard calls for.

"9. For determining the entire amount of land which was in actual possession of the working peasants down to the revolution ..of 1917, it is necessary to determine its quantity according to its special character (field, pasture, meadow, drainage, gardens, orchards, estates).

"10. This determination must be made in exact figures, as well as in the proportion of the entire quantity to each individual homestead, settlement, village, county, province, or region, or the entire climatic section of the given system of field cultivation.

"11. When thus determining the entire quantity of land, it is necessary to determine the quality of each acre of a typical field of meadow by ascertaining the amount (in poods) of grain or hay yielded by an acre of land of the given section for the past ten years.

"12. When determining the quantity and quality of land, it is necessary to determine at the same time the entire population of the given climatic section engaged in agriculture, and also that part of the population which subsists at the expense of agriculture.

"13. The census of the inhabitants engaged in agricultural work is to be taken by sex, age, and family for each homestead separately, and later the information obtained is to be classified by villages, counties and provinces of the given section.

"14. When taking the census of the population it is necessary to determine the number of workingmen and members dependent upon them and for that purpose the entire population is divided into the following classes according to ages:

"Those Unable to Work

"Girls, to 12 years of age.

"Boys, to 12 years of age.

"Men, from 60 years of age.

"Women, from 50 years of age.

"Those incapacitated by physical or mental illness are recorded separately.

"Those Able to Work

"Men from 18 to 60 — 1.0 unit of working strength.

"Women from 18 to 50 — 0.8 unit of working strength.

"Boys from 12 to 16 — 0.5 unit of working strength.

"Girls from 12 to 16 — 0.5 unit of working strength.
"Boys from 16 to 18 — 0.75 unit of working strength.
"Girls from 16 to 18 — 0.6 unit of working strength.

"Note.— These figures may be changed in accordance with climatic and customary conditions by decision of the appropriate organs of the Soviet power.

"15. By dividing the number of acres by the number of working units, the number of acres to each unit may be obtained.

"16. The number of incapacitated members to each working unit may be obtained by dividing the entire incapacitated element by the total of working units.

"17. It is also necessary to describe and figure out the number of work animals and cattle that can be fed on one acre of land and with one working unit.

"18. For determining what an average landowning peasant is in a county, it is necessary to ascertain the average acre in quality and fertility. This average is the sum of crops from various soils divided by the number of the soil categories. (Paragraph 9.)

"19. The average obtained as above is to serve as a basis for determining the production and consumption standard by which all the homesteads will be equalized from the surplus land fund.

"Note.— In case the average, as indicated above, obtained after preliminary calculations, proves insufficient for existence (see Division I, Article 12), it may be increased from the surplus land fund.

"20. For determining the amount of land needed for additional distribution among peasants, it is necessary to multiply the number of acres of land to each working unit in a county by the sum of agricultural working units of the given climatic section, and to subtract from the product the amount of land which the working population have on hand.

"21. Further, upon ascertaining the number of acres of land (in figures and percentage according to character) which the surplus land fund has, and comparing this figure with the quantity of land necessary for additional distribution among peasants who have not sufficient land, the following is to be determined: is it possible to confine the emigration within the boundaries of the given climatic sections? If so, it is necessary to determine the size of the surplus land fund and its capacity.

If it is not possible to confine it within the given climatic section, ascertain how many families will have to emigrate to another section.

"Note.— The main land departments of the Soviet power must be informed of the quantity of surplus land, as well as of a lack of the same; and the location, amount and kind of unoccupied lands must be indicated.

"22. When additional distribution takes place, it is necessary to know the exact amount and quality of land which the peasants have, the number of cattle on hand, the number of members of the families, etc.

"23. When additional distribution takes place in accordance with the production and consumption standard, this standard must be raised in the following cases:

"(1) When the working strength of a family is overtaxed by the number of incapacitated members; (2) when the land which the family has on hand is not sufficiently fertile; (3) in accordance with the quality of such land of the surplus fund as is given to the peasant (the same applies to meadows).

"25. When an additional apportionment of land takes place and the given district lacks certain advantages, the peasant gets a certain amount of land possessing other advantages.

"DIVISION V

"*Standard for the Utilization of Land for Construction, Agricultural, and Educational Purposes, Etc.*

"Article 26. When land is apportioned for educational and industrial purposes and also for the erection of dwellings, for cattle breeding and other agricultural needs (with the exception of field cultivation), the quantity of land to be apportioned shall be determined by the local Soviets in accordance with the needs of the individuals or organizations which ask permission to use the land.

"DIVISION VI

"*Emigration*

"Article 27. In case the surplus land fund in the given section proves to be insufficient for additional distribution among peasants, the surplus of the population may be transferred to another section where there is sufficient surplus land.

"Article 28. Transfer from one section to another is to take place only after the peasants of the latter section are all distributed.

"Article 29. The emigration from one section to another, as well as the distribution of the inhabitants within the section, must be carried on as follows: At first those who are furthest away from the surplus fund are to emigrate, so that

" (a) The land of the surplus fund is used first of all by the peasants of that village or hamlet in the vicinity of which the surplus land fund lies.

"Note.— If there are several such villages, preference is given to those that tilled the land before.

" (b) The second place is given to the peasants of the volost within the boundaries of which the surplus land lies.

" (c) The third place is given to the peasants of the county within the boundaries of which the surplus land lies.

" (d) Finally, if the given system of field cultivation covers several provinces, the peasants of the province within the boundaries of which the surplus land lies receive additional land.

"Article 30. The emigration accordingly runs in the following order: (a) Volunteers are the first to emigrate; (b) those organizations which suffer most from lack of land; (c) agricultural associations, communities, large families, and small families which have small amounts of land.

"Article 31. The apportionment of land among agriculturists who have to emigrate is to be carried on as follows: In the first place, small families suffering from lack of land; second, large families suffering from lack of land; third, other families suffering from lack of land; fourth, agricultural associations; and, finally, communities.

"Article 32. The transfer of peasants from one section to another is to be done with consideration, so that the new place shall give the peasant a chance to cultivate land successfully and the climatic conditions shall be analogous to those of his previous domicile. In that case it is necessary to take into consideration the customs and nationality of the emigrants.

"Article 33. The cost of transferring peasants to new places is to be provided by the state.

"Article 34. In connection with the transfer, the state is to help the peasants in the building of homes, roads, drains, and wells, in obtaining agricultural machinery and artificial fertilizers, by creating artificial water systems (when necessary), and by erecting educational centers.

"Note.—For the purpose of expediting the establishment of agricultural work on a socialistic basis, the state offers to extend to the emigrants every aid necessary for a systematic and scientific management of collective homesteads.

"DIVISION VII

"Form of Utilization of Land

"Article 35. The Russian Federated Soviet Republic, for the purpose of attaining socialism, offers to extend aid (cultural and material) to the general tilling of land, giving preference to the communistic and co-operative homesteads over individual ones.

"Article 36. Lands of co-operative and individual homesteads must, if possible, be in the same location.

"DIVISION VIII

"Obtaining Rights to the Use of Land

"Article 37. Land may be obtained:

"(a) For educational purposes:
"1. Social usefulness.

"(b) For agricultural purposes:
"1. Personal labor.

"(c) For building purposes:
"1. Social buildings.
"2. Dwellings.
"3. The necessity of conducting a working homestead.

"(d) For the purpose of constructing ways of communication:
"1. Public necessity.

"DIVISION IX

The Order in Which the Right to Use the Land May Be Obtained

"Article 38. An application must be filed with the land department of the Soviet power in whose jurisdiction the desired land lies.

"Article 39. The application shows the order in which the permission to use the land is granted. The permission is granted on the basis of the general provisions of this decree.

"Note.— The application should contain the following information, in addition to the full name and address of the person who desires to use the land: former occupation, the purpose for which land is desired, the inventory on hand, the location of the desired plot and its size.

"Note.— If the land department of the Volostnoi Soviet refuses to grant the permission to use the land, the question may be brought (within one week) to the notice of the land department of the county Soviet; if the county Soviet refuses, it may be presented to the land department of the provincial Soviet within two weeks.

"Note.— The right to use land (sub-surface deposits, waters, forests, and fundamental natural resources) cannot be obtained under any circumstances through purchase, rental, inheritance, or any other private transaction.

"DIVISION X

"Article 40. The right to use the land becomes effective in the following order.

"Article 41. The right to use land for construction purposes becomes effective upon actual occupation of the plot or upon preparations for its occupation, but not later than three months after the receipt of permission from the local Soviet.

"Note.— By actual preparations is meant the delivery of building materials to the place of destination or the closing of a contract with workers.

"Article 42. The right to use land for agricultural purposes (on the basis of personal labor) becomes effective upon beginning the work at the opening of the next agricultural season.

"Article 43. The right to use the land for field cultivation becomes effective upon the actual beginning of field work (without hired help) at the opening of the agricultural season next after the receipt of a permit from the local Soviet.

"Note.— Buildings may be erected on plots of land that may be tilled only by special permission of the land department of the Soviet government.

"Article 44. In case of actual inability to use the plot in the period of time allowed by the land department, the latter may extend this period if there is valid cause, i. e., the illness of the working hands, trouble brought about by epidemics, etc.

"DIVISION XI

"Transfer of Right to Use Given Plots of Land

"Article 45. The right to use the land is not transferable.

"Article 46. The right to use land may be obtained by anyone on the basis of this decree, and it cannot be transferred from one person to another.

"DIVISION XII

"Temporary Cancellation of the Right to Use the Land

"Article 47. Any land-borrower's right to use the plot of land may be suspended for a certain length of time, without cancelling it entirely.

"Article 48. Any land-borrower may cease utilizing the land at a certain time and still have the right to it (a) if natural calamities (floods, etc.) deprive him of the possibility; (b) if the agriculturist is temporarily ill; (c) if the agriculturist is called to do some government duty; or for other cause valid from the social point of view. He may hold it until such time as conditions are favorable for the utilization of his plot.

"Note.— The period of such temporary cessation is to be determined in each case by the land department of the local Soviet.

"Article 49. Upon every temporary cessation of the use of the land (as indicated in Article 48), the local Soviet either organizes community help to the agriculturist or calls upon the workers, paid by the state and subject to the general regulations of workers' control, to do the work of the afflicted agriculturist (temporary incapacity, death, etc.), so as to save his property and proceed with production.

"DIVISION XIII

"Cessation of the Right to Use the Land

"Article 50. The right to use the land may cease for an entire agricultural unit, or for individual members of the same.

"Article 51. The right of the given individual to use the land may cease for the whole plot or for a part of it.

"Article 52. The right is cancelled (a) if the organization, or the purpose for which it had taken land, is declared void; (b) if units, associations, communities, etc., disintegrate; (c) if the individual finds it impossible to cultivate the field or do other agricultural work, and if at the same time the individual has other means of subsistence (for instance, a pension paid to the incapacitated); (d) upon the death of the individual, or when his civil rights are cancelled by the court.

"Article 53. The right to use a plot of land ceases (a) in case of a formal refusal to use the plot; (b) in case of obvious unwillingness to use the plot, although no formal refusal has been filed; (c) in case the land is used for illegal purposes (e. g., throwing garbage); (d) in case the land is exploited by illegal means (e. g., hiring land secretly); (e) in case the use of the land by a given individual brings injury to his neighbor (e. g., manufacture of chemicals).

"Note.— The land borrower, upon cessation of his right to the use of the land, has the right to demand from the respective land departments of the Soviets a fee for the unused improvements and labor invested in the land, if the given plot did not bring him sufficient profit.

"*Chairman of the All-Russian Central Executive Committee:*
SVERDLOV.
"*Members of the Executive Body:*
SPIRIDONOVA, MOURANOV, ZINOVIEV, OUSTINOV, KAMKOV, LANDER, SKOULOV, VOLODARSKY, PETERSON, NATANSON-BOBROV.
"*Secretaries of the Central Executive Committee:*
AVANESOV, SMOLIANSKY.
"*Chairman of the Soviet of People's Commissaries:*
V. OULIANOV (LENIN).
"*People's Commissar of Agriculture:*
A. KOLEGUEV."

It is not necessary in this report to give a detailed history of the changes which have taken place in the Soviet government. Those who may be interested in acquiring such knowledge will find at the close of this section a bibliography to which they can refer.

The purpose here is simply to indicate in a general way the nature of that system so that there can be a general understanding of what is advocated by the revolutionary Socialists and the sympathizers with the Soviet regime when they urge the American workers to emulate their Russian comrades.

The principal interest of this Committee in Soviet Russia is the attitude which it takes toward the government of other countries.

---

b. CHURCH AND STATE

"1. The church is separated from the state.

"2. Within the limits of the Republic, it is prohibited to pass any local laws or regulations which would restrict or limit the freedom of conscience or establish any kind of privileges or advantages on the ground of the religious affiliations of citizens.

"3. Every citizen may profess any religion or none at all. Any legal disabilities connected with the profession of any religion or none are abolished.

"Note.— From all official acts any indication of the religious affiliation or non-affiliation of citizens is to be omitted.

"4. The proceedings of state and other public legal institutions are not to be accompanied by any religious customs or ceremonies.

"5. The free observance of religious customs is guaranteed in so far as the same do not disturb the public order and are not accompanied by attempts upon the rights of the citizens of the Soviet Republic. The local authorities have the right to take all necessary measures for the preservation, in such cases, of public order and security.

"6. No one may decline to perform his civil duties, giving as a reason his religious views. Exemptions from this law, conditioned upon the substitution of one civil duty for another, are permitted by decision of the people's court in each individual case.

"7. Religious or judicial oaths are abolished. In necessary cases a solemn promise only is given.

"8. Acts of a civil nature are performed exclusively by civil authorities, such as the departments of registration of marriages and births.

"9. The school is separated from the church. The teaching of religious doctrines in all state and public, as well as in private, educational institutions in which general subjects are taught, is forbidden. Citizens may teach and study religion privately.

"10. All church and religious societies are subject to the general regulations governing private associations and unions, and do not enjoy any privileges or subsidies either from the state or from its local autonomous and self-governing institutions.

"11. Compulsory collection of payments and assessments for the benefit of church or religious societies, or as a means of compulsion or punishment of their co-members on the part of these societies, is not allowed.

"12. No church or religious society has the right to own property. They have no rights of a juridical person.

"13. All the properties of the existing church and religious societies in Russia are declared national property. Buildings and articles specially designated for religious services are, by special decisions of the local or central state authorities, given for the free use of corresponding religious societies.

"*President of the Council of the People's Commissars:*

"OULIANOV (LENIN).

"*Commissars:*

"PODVOISKY, ALGASSOV, TRUTOVSKY, SHLIKHTER, PROSHIAN, MENZHINSKY, SHLIAPNIKOV, PETROVSKY.

"*Director of the Affairs of the Government:*

"BONCH-BRUYEVITCH.

"*Secretary to the Council of the People's Commissars:*

"GORBOUNOV."

---

c. NATIONALIZATION OF BANKS

"In the interest of the regular organization of the national economy, of the thorough eradication of bank speculation, and the complete emancipation of the workmen, peasants, and the whole laboring population from the exploitation of banking capital, and with a view to the establishment of a single national bank of the Russian Republic which shall serve the real interests of the people and the poorer classes, the Central Executive Committee resolves:

"1. The banking business is declared a state monopoly.

"2. All existing private joint-stock banks and banking offices are merged in the state bank.

"3. The assets and liabilities of the liquidated establishments are taken over by the state bank.

"4. The order of the merger of private banks in the state bank is to be determined by a special decree.

"5. The temporary administration of the affairs of the private banks is entrusted to the board of the state bank.

"6. The interests of the small depositors will be safeguarded.

"December 14, 1917."

d. THE PEOPLE'S COURT

The Council of People's Commissaries resolves:

"1. To abolish all existing general legal institutions, such as district courts, courts of appeal, and the governing Senate with all its departments, military and naval courts of all grades, as well as commercial courts, and to replace all these institutions with courts established on the basis of democratic elections.

"Regarding further procedure and the continuation of unfinished cases a special decree will be issued.

"Beginning October 25 of this year, the passage of time limits is stopped until the issuance of a special decree.

"2. To abolish the existing institution of justices of the peace, and to replace the justices of the peace heretofore elected by indirect vote, by local courts consisting of a permanent local judge and two jurors, the latter of whom are summoned in pairs to each session from special lists of jurors. Local judges are henceforth to be elected on the basis of direct democratic vote, and, until the time of such elections, are to be chosen by regional and township Soviets, or, where there are none such, by district, city, and provincial Soviets of Workmen's, Soldiers' and Peasants' Deputies.

"These same Soviets make up the lists of alternating jurors and determine the time of their presence at the session.

"The former justices of the peace are not deprived of the right to be elected as local judges, either temporarily by the Soviets or finally by a democratic election, if they express their consent thereto.

"Local judges adjudicate all civil cases to an amount not exceeding 3,000 rubles, and criminal cases if the accused is liable to a penalty of not more than two years' deprivation of freedom. The verdicts and rulings of the local courts are final and no appeal can be taken from them. In cases in which the recovery of over 100 rubles in money or deprivation of freedom for more than seven days is adjudged, a request for review is allowed.

" The court of cassation is the district session, and in the capitals the metropolitan session, of local judges.

" For the trial of criminal cases at the fronts, local judges are elected by regimental Soviets in the same order, and, where there are none, by the regimental committees.

" Regarding procedure in other legal cases, a special decree will be issued.

" 3. To abolish all existing institutions of investigating magistrates and the procurator's office, as well as the grades of counsellors-at-law and private attorneys.

" Until the reformation of the entire system of legal procedure, the preliminary investigation in criminal cases is made by the local judges singly, but their orders of personal detention and indictment must be confirmed by the decision of the entire local court.

"As to the functions of prosecutors and counsel for defence, who are allowed even in the stage of preliminary investigation, and in civil cases the functions of solicitors, all citizens of moral integrity, of either sex, who enjoy civil rights, are allowed to perform them.

" 4. For the transfer and further direction of cases and suits, proceedings of the legal bodies as well as of officials engaged in preliminary investigation and the procurator's office, and also of the associations of counsellors-at-law, the respective local Soviets elect special commissaries, who take charge of the archives and the properties of those bodies.

"All the lower and clerical personnel of the abolished institutions are ordered to continue in their positions and to perform, under the general direction of the commissaries, all duties necessary in order to dispose of unfinished cases, and also to give information on appointed days to interested persons about the state of their cases.

" 5. Local judges try cases in the name of the Russian Republic, and are guided in their rulings and verdicts by the laws of the governments which have been overthrown only in so far as those laws are not annulled by the revolution, and do not contradict the revolutionary conscience and revolutionary conception of right.

" Note.— All those laws are considered annulled which contradict the decrees of the Central Executive Committee of the Soviets of Workmen's, Soldiers', and Peasants' Deputies and the Workmen's and Peasants' Government, also the minimum programmes of the Russian Social-Democratic Labor Party and the party of Socialist Revolutionaries.

"6. In all civil as well as criminal cases the parties may resort to the arbitration court. The organization of the arbitration court will be determined by a special decree.

"7. The right of pardon and restoration of rights of persons convicted in criminal cases belongs henceforth to the legal authorities.

"8. For the struggle against the counter-revolutionary forces by means of measures for the defence of the revolution and its accomplishments, and also for the trial of proceedings against profiteering, speculation, sabotage, and other misdeeds of merchants, manufacturers, officials, and other persons, workmen's and peasants' revolutionary tribunals are established, consisting of a chairman and six jurors, serving in turn, elected by provincial or city Soviets of Workmen's, Soldiers', and Peasants' Deputies.

"For the conduct of the preliminary investigation in such cases, special investigating commissions are formed under the above Soviets.

"All existing investigating commissions are abolished, and their cases and proceedings are transferred to the newly-formed investigating commissions.

"*President of the Council of People's Commissars:*
V. OULIANOV (LENIN)
"*Commissars:*
A. SHLIKHTER, L. TROTZKY, A. SHLIAPNIKOV, I. DJUGASHVILI (STALIN), N. AVILOV (N. GLYEBOV), P. STUCHKA.

"November 24, 1917."

e. INSTRUCTIONS TO THE REVOLUTIONARY TRIBUNAL

The Revolutionary Tribunal is guided by the following instructions:

"1. The Revolutionary Tribunal has jurisdiction in cases of persons (a) who organize uprisings against the authority of the Workmen's and Peasants' Government, actively oppose the latter or do not obey it, or call upon other persons to oppose or disobey it; (b) who utilize their positions in the state or public service to disturb or hamper the regular progress of work in the institution or enterprise in which they are or have been serving (sabotage, concealing or destroying documents or property, etc.); (c) who stop or reduce production of articles of general use without actual necessity for so doing; (d) who violate the decrees, orders, binding ordinances and other published acts of the organs of the Workmen's and Peasants' Government, if such acts stipulate a trial by the Revolutionary Tribunal for their violation; (e) who, taking advantage of their social or administrative position, misuse the authority given them by the revolutionary people. Crimes against the people committed by means of the press are under the jurisdiction of a specially instituted Revolutionary Tribunal.

"2. The Revolutionary Tribunal for offences indicated in Article 1 imposes upon the guilty the following penalties; (1) fine, (2) deprivation of freedom, (3) exile from the capitals, from particular localities, or from the territory of the Russian Republic, (4) public censure, (5) declaring the offender a public enemy, (6) deprivation of all or some political rights, (7) sequestration or confiscation, partial or general, of property, (8) sentence of compulsory public work.

"The Revolutionary Tribunal fixes the penalty, being guided by the circumstances of the case and the dictates of the revolutionary conscience.

"3. (a) The Revolutionary Tribunal is elected by the Soviets of Workmen's, Soldiers', and Peasants' Deputies and consists of one permanent chairman, two permanent substitutes, one permanent secretary and two substitutes, and forty jurors. All persons, except the jurors, are elected for three months and may be recalled by the Soviets before the expiration of the term.

"(b) The jurors are selected for one month from a general list of jurors by the Executive Committees of the Soviets of Workmen's, Soldiers', and Peasants' Deputies by drawing lots, and lists of jurors numbering six, and one or two in addition, are made up for each session.

"(c) The session of each successive jury of the Revolutionary Tribunal lasts not longer than one week.

"(d) A stenographic record is kept of the entire proceedings of the Revolutionary Tribunal.

"(e) The grounds for instituting proceedings are: reports of legal and administrative institutions and officials, public, trade, and party organizations, and private persons.

"(f) For the conduct of the preliminary investigation in such cases an investigating commission is created under the Revolutionary Tribunal, consisting of six members elected by the Soviets of Workmen's, Soldiers', and Peasants' Deputies.

"(g) Upon receiving information or complaint, the investigating commission examines it and within forty-eight hours either orders the dismissal of the case, if it does not find that a crime has been committed, or transfers it to the proper jurisdiction, or brings it up for trial at the session of the Revolutionary Tribunal.

"(h) The orders of the investigating commission about arrests, searches, abstracts of papers, and releases of detained persons are valid if issued jointly by three members. In cases which do not permit of delay such orders may be issued by any member of the investigating commission singly, on the condition that within twelve hours the measure shall be approved by the investigating commission.

"(i) The order of the investigating commission is carried out by the Red Guard, the militia, the troops, and the executive organs of the Republic.

"(j) Complaints against the decisions of the investigating commission are submitted to the Revolutionary Tribunal through its president and are considered at executive sessions of the Revolutionary Tribunal.

"(k) The investigating commission has the right (1) to demand of all departments and officials, as well as of all local self-governing bodies, legal institutions and authorities, public notaries, social and trade organizations, commercial and industrial enterprises, and governmental, public, and private credit institutions, the delivery of necessary documents and information, and of unfinished cases; (2) to examine, through its members or special representatives, the transactions of all above-enumerated institutions and officials in order to secure necessary information.

"4. The sessions of the Revolutionary Tribunal are public.

"5. The verdicts of the Revolutionary Tribunal are rendered by a majority of votes of the members of the Tribunal.

"6. The legal investigation is made with the participation of the prosecution and defence.

"7. (a) Citizens of either sex who enjoy political rights are admitted at the will of the parties as prosecutors and counsel for the defence, with the right to participate in the case.

"(b) Under the Revolutionary Tribunals a collegium of persons is created who devote themselves to the service of the law, in the form of public prosecution as well as of public defence.

"(c) The above-mentioned collegium is formed by the free registration of all persons who desire to render aid to revolutionary justice, and who present recommendations from the Soviets of Workmen's, Soldiers', and Peasants' Deputies.

"8. The Revolutionary Tribunal may invite for each case a public prosecutor from the membership of the above-named collegium.

"9. If the accused does not for some reason use his right to invite counsel for defence, the Revolutionary Tribunal, at his request, appoints a member of the collegium for his defence.

"10. Besides the above-mentioned prosecutors and defence, one prosecutor and one counsel for defence, drawn from the public present at the session, may take part in the court's proceedings.

"11. The verdicts of the Revolutionary Tribunal are final. In case of violation of the form of procedure established by these instructions, or the discovery of indications of obvious injustice in the verdict, the People's Commissar of Justice has the right to address to the Central Executive Committee of the Soviets of Workers', Soldiers', and Peasants' Deputies a request to order a second and last trial of the case.

"12. The maintenance of the Revolutionary Tribunal is charged to the account of the state. The amount of compensation and the daily fees are fixed by the Soviets of Workers', Soldiers', and Peasants' Deputies. The jurors receive the difference between the daily fees and their daily earnings, if the latter are less than the daily fees; at the same time the jurors may not be deprived of their positions during the session.

"*People's Commissar of Justice:*

"I. Z. STEINBERG.

"December 19, 1917."

---

f. THE REVOLUTIONARY TRIBUNAL OF THE PRESS

"1. Under the Revolutionary Tribunal is created a Revolutionary Tribunal of the Press. This Tribunal will have jurisdiction of crimes and offences against the people committed by means of the press.

"2. Crimes and offences by means of the press are the publication and circulation of any false or perverted reports and information about events of public life, in so far as they constitute an attempt upon the rights and interests of the revolutionary people.

"3. The Revolutionary Tribunal of the Press consists of three members, elected for a period not longer than three months by the Soviet of Workmen's, Soldiers', and Peasants' Deputies. These members are charged with the conduct of the preliminary investigation as well as the trial of the case.

"4. The following serve as grounds for instituting proceedings: reports of legal or administrative institutions, public organizations, or private persons.

"5. The prosecution and defence are conducted on the principles laid down in the instructions to the general Revolutionary Tribunal.

"6. The sessions of the Revolutionary Tribunal of the Press are public.

"7. The decisions of the Revolutionary Tribunal of the Press are final and are not subject to appeal.

"8. The Revolutionary Tribunal imposes the following penalties: (1) fine, (2) expression of public censure, which the convicted organ of the press brings to the general knowledge in a way indicated by the Tribunal, (3) the publication in a prominent place or in a special edition of a denial of the false report, (4) temporary or permanent suppression of the publication or its exclusion from circulation, (5) confiscation to national ownership of the printing-shop or property of the organ of the press if it belongs to the convicted parties.

"9. The trial of an organ of the press by the Revolutionary Tribunal of the Press does not absolve the guilty persons from general criminal responsibility.

"*People's Commissar of Justice:*

"I. Z. STEINBERG.

"December 18, 1917."

---

g. TO THE SOVIET OF WORKMEN'S, SOLDIERS', AND PEASANTS' DEPUTIES

A REQUEST FOR THE IMMEDIATE ELECTION OF COMMISSARIES OF JUSTICE, THEIR DUTIES AND RIGHTS

"By the decree of the Council of the People's Commissaries (November 24, 1917) the general legal institutions and justices' courts, the procurator's office, the institutions of investigating magistrates, counsellors-at-law, and private attorneys, are abolished. Until the creation of permanent legal institutions, elect immediately Commissaries of Justice.

"The duties of the elected Commissaries are the safe-keeping of archives and the property of the courts, the direction of unfinished cases, and the giving of information to interested persons. In view of the approach of the time for rendering semi-annual and annual financial reports for 1917, the elected Commissaries are requested to take measures for the immediate preparation and delivery of the above-mentioned reports in the established form and order. The publications of the official 'Gazette of the Provisional Workmen's and Peasants' Government' are to serve as a guide to the local authorities.

"Report the beginning of the activity of the new courts, their structure, the names of the Commissaries of Justices. Report the tentative budgets of the legal department for 1918.

"The credits of the legal department which were not used locally in 1917, you may use by order of the Soviets.

"Instructions for the Revolutionary Tribunal of the Press, and for general courts, criminal and civil, are being prepared.

"*People's Commissar of Justice:*
"I. Z. STEINBERG."

---

h. MARRIAGE, CHILDREN, AND REGISTRATION OF CIVIL STATUS

"The Russian Republic henceforth recognizes civil marriage only.

"*Civil marriage is performed on the basis of the following rules:*

"1. Persons who wish to contract marriage declare (their intention) orally or by a written statement to the department of registration of marriages and births at the city hall (regional, district, township, Zemstvo institutions), according to the place of their residence.

"Note.— Church marriage is a private affair of those contracting it, while civil marriage is obligatory.

"2. Declarations of intention to contract marriage are not accepted (a) from persons of the male sex younger than eighteen years, and of the female sex, sixteen years of age; in Transcaucasia the native inhabitants may enter into marriage upon attaining the age of sixteen for the groom and thirteen for the bride; (b) from relatives in the direct line, full and half-brothers and sisters; consanguinity is recognized also between a child born out of wedlock and his descendants on one side and relatives on the other; (c) from married persons, and (d) from insane.

"3. Those wishing to contract marriage appear at the department of registration of marriages and sign a statement concerning the absence of the obstacles to contracting marriage enumerated in Article 2 of this decree, and also a statement that they contract marriage voluntarily.

"Those guilty of deliberately making false statements about the absence of the obstacles enumerated in Article 2 are criminally prosecuted for false statements and the marriage is declared invalid.

"4. Upon the signing of the above-mentioned statement, the director of the department of registration of marriages records the act of marriage in the book of marriage registries and then declares the marriage to have become legally effective.

"When contracting marriage the parties are allowed to decide freely whether they will henceforth be called by the surname of the husband or wife or by a combined surname.

"As proof of the act of marriage, the contracting parties immediately receive a copy of the certificate of their marriage.

"5. Complaints against the refusal to perform marriage or incorrect registration are lodged, without limitation of time, with the local judge in the locality where the department of registration of marriage is; the ruling of the local judge on such complaint may be appealed in the usual way.

"6. In case the former books of registration of marriages have been destroyed, or lost in some other way, or if for some other cause married persons cannot obtain a certificate of their marriage, those persons are given a right to submit a declaration to the respective department of registration of marriages, according to the place of residence of both parties or one of them, to the effect that they have been in the state of wedlock since such and such time. Such declaration is attested, in addition to the statement stipulated by Article 3 by a further statement of the parties that the book of registration has really been lost or that for some other sufficient cause they cannot obtain a copy of the certificate.

"REGISTRATION OF BIRTHS

"7. The registration of the birth of a child is made by the same department of registration of marriages and births in the place of residence of the mother, and a special entry of each birth is made in the book of registration of births.

"8. The birth of a child must be reported to the department either by his parents or one of them; or by the persons in whose care, because of the death of his parents, the child remained, with an indication of the name and surname adopted for the child and the presentation of two witnesses to attest the fact of birth.

"9. The books of registration of marriages as well as the books of registration of births are kept in two copies, and one copy is sent at the end of the year to the proper court for preservation.

"10. Children born out of wedlock are on an equality with those born in wedlock with regard to the rights and duties of parents towards children, and likewise of children towards parents.

"The persons who make a declaration and give a signed statement to that effect are registered as the father and mother of the child.

"Those guilty of deliberately making false statements regarding the above are criminally prosecuted for false testimony and the registration is declared invalid.

"In case the father of a child born out of wedlock does not make such a declaration, the mother of the child or the guardian or the child itself has the right to prove fatherhood by legal means.

"REGISTRATION OF DEATHS

"11. The record of the death of a person is made in the place where the death occurred by the department which has charge of the registration of marriages and births, by entry in a special book for registration of deaths.

"12. The death of a person must be reported to the department by the legal or administrative authorities or persons in whose care the deceased was.

"13. Institutions in charge of cemeteries are henceforth forbidden to place obstacles in the way of the burial in cemetery grounds in accordance with the ritual of civil funerals.

"14. All religious and administrative institutions which hitherto have had charge of the registration of marriages, births, and deaths according to the customs of any religious sect, are ordered to transfer immediately all the registration books to the respective municipal district, rural, or Zemstvo administrations.

"*President of the Council of People's Commissars:*
"V. OULIANOV (LENIN).
"*President of the Central Executive Committee of the Soviets of Workmen's, Soldiers', and Peasants' Deputies:*
"YA. SVERDLOV.
"*Director of the Affairs of the Council of People's Commissars:*
"BONCH-BRUYEVITCH.
"*Secretary:*
"N. GORBOUNOV.

"December 18, 1917."

i. "DIVORCE

"1. Marriage is annulled by the petition of both parties or even of one of them.

"2. The above petition is submitted, according to the rules of local jurisdiction, to the local court.

"Note.— A declaration of annulment of marriage by mutual consent may be filed directly with the department of registration of marriages in which a record of that marriage is kept, which department makes an entry of the annulment of the marriage in the record and issues a certificate.

"3. On the day appointed for the examination of the petition for the annulment of marriage, the local judge summons both parties or their solicitors.

"4. If the residence of the party who is to be summoned is unknown, the petitioner is allowed to file the petition for annulment of marriage in the place of residence of the absent party last known to the petitioner, or in the place of residence of the petitioner, stating to the court, however, the last known place of residence of the defendant.

"5. If the place of residence of the party who is to be summoned is unknown, then the day for the trial of the case is set not earlier than the expiration of two months from the date of the publication of a notice of summons in the local government gazette, and the summons is sent to the address of the last known place of residence of the defendant given by the petitioner.

"6. Having convinced himself that the petition for the annulment of the marriage really comes from both parties or from one of them, the judge personally and singly renders the decision of the annulment of the marriage and issues a certificate thereof to the parties. At the same time, the judge transmits a copy of his decision to the department of registration of marriages where the annulled marriage was performed and where the book containing a record of the marriage is kept.

"7. When annulling a marriage by mutual consent, the parties are obliged to state in their petition what surnames the divorced parties and their children are to bear in the future. But when dissolving the marriage by the petition of one of the parties, and in the absence of an understanding about this matter between the parties, the divorced parties preserve their own surnames, and the surname of the children is determined by the judge, and in case of disagreement of the parties, by the local court.

"8. In case the parties are agreed on the matter, the judge, simultaneously with the decision of annulment of the marriage, determines with which of the parents the minor children begotten of the marriage shall live, and which of the parents must bear the expense of maintenance and education of the children, and to what extent and also whether and to what extent the husband is obliged to furnish food and maintenance to his divorced wife.

"9. But if no understanding shall be reached, then the participation of the husband in furnishing his divorced wife with food and maintenance when she has no means of her own or has insufficient means and is unable to work, as well as the question with whom the children are to live, is decided by a regular civil suit in the local court, irrespective of the amount of the suit. The judge, having rendered the decision annulling the marriage, determines temporarily, until the settlement of the dispute, the fate of the children, and also rules on the question of the temporary maintenance of the children and the wife, if she is in need of it.

"10. Suits for adjudging marriages illegal or invalid belong henceforth to the jurisdiction of the local court.

"11. The operation of this law extends to all citizens of the Russian Republic irrespective of their adherence to this or that religious sect.

"12. All suits for annulment of marriage which are now tried in ecclesiastical consistories of the Greek-Catholic and other denominations, in the governing synod and all other institutions of Christian and non-Christian religions, and by officials in charge of ecclesiastical affairs of all denominations, and in which no decisions have been rendered or the decisions already rendered have not become legally effective, are declared by reason of this law null and void, and are subject to immediate transfer to the local district courts for safe-keeping, with all archives in the possession of the above-mentioned institutions and persons having jurisdiction in divorce suits. The parties are given the right to file a new petition for the annulment of the marriage according to this decree, without awaiting the dismissal of the first suit, and a new summons of absent parties (paragraphs 4 and 5) is not obligatory if such a summons was published in the former order.

"*President of the Central Executive Committee of the Soviets of Workers', Soldiers', and Peasants' Deputies:*

"YA. SVERDLOV.

"*President of the Council of People's Commissars:*

"V. OULIANOV (LENIN).

"*Director of the Affairs of the Council of People's Commissars:*

"BONCH-BRUYEVITCH.

"*Secretary:*

"N. GORBOUNOV.

"December 18, 1917."

---

j. ORDERS OF THE PEOPLE'S COMMISSAR OF EDUCATION OF THE WESTERN PROVINCES AND FRONT

The following orders are selected from a group of six educational documents published at Petrograd, March 10, 1918. The omitted orders, Nos. 3–5, relate to the budget for 1919 and to routine matters.

No. 1

"*To all primary and secondary educational institutions of the western provinces:*

"I propose to the administration of all the above-mentioned educational institutions, from the date of the publication of this order, not to discharge students for non-payment of dues. As to those who have already been discharged before this order was published, they must immediately be reinstated.

"I propose to all departments of public education in local Soviets of Workmen's, Soldiers', and Peasants' Deputies, to attend strictly to the carrying out of my order. The question of the legal position of students who have not paid their school dues will be explained in the near future.

"No special notification will be given to each educational institution, and the present order becomes the law of the land from the date of its publication in the newspaper 'Sovietskaya Pravda' (Soviet Truth).

"No. 2

"Having in mind to afford to the large popular masses access to books, the Commissariat of Public Education will shortly proceed to regulate the library business and its reorganization on new principles. In view of this the Commissar directs that:

"I. All libraries found within the boundaries of the western provinces and front, and belonging to municipalities, public institutions, or organizations of various sorts, or to private persons, are taken over for the benefit of public educational institutions in local Soviets of Workmen's, Soldiers' and Peasants' Deputies, and, in the city of Smolensk, by the local section of public education of the provincial commissariat.

"II. All institutions, organizations, and private persons possessing libraries in the city of Smolensk must, within five days following the date of the publication of this order in the newspaper 'Sovietskaya Pravda,' present to the Commissariat of Public Education exact information concerning:

"(1) The location of the libraries belonging to them;

"(2) The number of volumes found in the libraries;

"(3) The contents of the libraries (complete catalogues of the books must be presented, and in case such do not exist, then general information concerning the character of the books collected);

"(4) The periodical publications subscribed to by the libraries;

"(5) The number of subscribers;

"(6) The rules adopted for the use of these books.

"Note.— This order does not affect persons who have libraries consisting of less than 500 volumes, if these libraries are not intended for public readers.

"III. In case reading-rooms are found at such libraries, it is necessary to indicate:

"(1) The list of periodical publications found in the reading-room;

"(2) Statistical data, if such are at hand, regarding the reading-room visitors.

"IV. Institutions, organizations, and private persons possessing libraries outside the boundaries of the city of Smolensk and of the Government of Smolensk must present the information indicated above, within a week from the date of the publication of this order, to the proper section of local Soviets of Workmen's, Soldiers', and Peasants' Deputies. The latter, upon receipt of the data, must furnish copies of the same to the Commissar of Public Education of the western provinces and front.

"V. Those who fail to comply with this order will be turned over to the Military Revolutionary Tribunal.

"No. 6

"It is the duty of all owners of moving-picture houses in the city of Smolensk, from the date of the publications of this order in the newspaper 'Sovietskaya Pravada' to present for approval to the provincial Commissariat of Public Education the programme and librettos of the pictures proposed to be exhibited by them.

"It is forbidden to show pictures not approved by the Commissariat.

"In those cases in which the Commissariat shall find it necessary the pictures, before being shown to the public, must be shown for examination to persons specially designated by the Commissariat.

"Moving-picture enterprises not complying with this order will be at once confiscated.

"*The Commissar of Public Education of the Western Provinces and Front:*

"PIKEL."

---

k. ABOLITION OF INHERITANCE

"I. Inheritance, whether by law or by will, is abolished. After the death of an owner, the property which belonged to him, whether movable or immovable, becomes the property of the government of the Russian Socialist Federated Soviet Republic.

"Note.— The discontinuance and transfer of rights of utilization of farm lands is determined by the rules provided in the fundamental law of the socialization of the land.

"II. Until the issuance of a decree dealing with general social arrangements, relatives who are in need (i. e., those who do not possess a minimum maintenance), and who are incapable of work — such relatives being in a directly ascending or descending line, full or half-brothers or sisters, or spouse, of the deceased — receive support from the property left by the deceased.

"Note 1.— No distinction is made between the relationship that arises within wedlock and that which arises outside of wedlock.

"Note 2.— Adopted relatives or children and their descendants are put upon the same footing as relatives by descent whether as to those who adopted them or as to those who have been adopted.

"III. If there is not enough of the property remaining to support a spouse and all surviving relatives, as enumerated above, then the most needy of them must be provided for first.

"IV. The amount of allowance to be given a spouse and surviving relatives from the property of the deceased is determined by the institution conducting the affairs of social security in the governments, and in Moscow and Petrograd by the municipal Soviets of Workmen's and Peasants' Deputies, in agreement with the persons who have the right to receive the allowance, and, in case of dispute between them, by the local court, according to the usual legal procedure. Cases of this sort are under the jurisdiction of the Soviets of Workmen's and Peasants' Deputies and the local courts of the last place of residence of the deceased.

"V. All property of the deceased, other than that enumerated in Article IX of this decree, comes under the jurisdiction of the local Soviet, which turns it over to the bureaus or institutions having control in those localities of similar property of the Russian Republic, according to the last place of residence of the deceased or according to the place where the property is situated.

"VI. The Local Soviet publishes, for the purpose of general notification, the death of the property owner, and calls upon the persons who have a right to receive support from the said property to appear within a year from the date of the publication.

"VII. Those who do not declare their claims before the expiration of the year following the publication, as provided in the above article, lose their right to receive support from the property of the deceased.

"VIII. From the property of the deceased are paid, first, the expenses of the administration of the property. The relatives and spouse of the deceased receive their allowances before the creditors are paid. The creditors of the deceased, if their claims are recognized as proper to be paid, are satisfied from the property after the deductions indicated above, on condition, in case the property is insufficient to cover all demands of the creditors, that the general principles of the meeting of creditors be applied.

"IX. If the property of the deceased does not exceed 10,000 rubles, or in particular consists of a farm house, domestic furniture, and means for economic production by work, in either city or village, it comes under the immediate control of the spouse and relatives enumerated in Article II of the present decree, who are present. The method of control and management of the property is arranged by agreement between the spouse and relatives, and, in case of their disagreement, by the local tribunal.

"X. The present decree is retroactive as regards all inheritances discovered before it was issued, if they have not yet been acquired by the heirs, or, if acquired, if they have not yet been taken possession of by the heirs.

"XI. All suits now pending respecting inheritances, the probate of wills, the confirmation of the rights of inheritance, etc., are deemed to be discontinued, and the respective hereditary property is to be at once turned over for administration to the local Soviets or institutions indicated in Article V of the present decree.

"Note.— Concerning hereditary properties discovered before the present decree is issued — properties enumerated in Article 9 of the present decree — a special regulation will be issued.

"XII. The People's Commissar of Justice is empowered, in agreement with the Commissariat of Social Security and Work, to issue a detailed instruction concerning the enforcement of the present decree.

"The present decree is of force from the date of its signature, and is to be put into operation by telegraph.

"*President of the Central Executive Committee:*

"SVERDLOV

"*Secretary of the Central Executive Committee:*

"AVANESOV

"April 27, 1918."

Document No. 3

CIRCULAR OF THE SOVIET COMMITTEE OF THE SOVIET GOVERNMENT OF RUSSIA

General Instructions (Issued Summer 1919)

The Revolutionary Work of the Communist Party

"The work of Bolshevist organizations in foreign countries is regulated as follows:

"1. In the Domain of International Relations:

"(a) Assist all chauvinistic measures and foster all international discords.

"(b) Stir up agitation that may serve to bring on industrial conflict.

"(c) Try to assassinate the representative of foreign countries.

"(Thanks to these methods interior discords and coups d'etat will occur, such agitation working to the advantage of the Social Democratic party.)

"2. In the domain of internal politics:

"(a) Compromise by every possible means the influential men of the country; attack people in office; stir up anti-governmental agitation.

"(b) Instigate general and particular strikes; injure machinery and boilers in factories, spread propaganda literature.

"(Thanks to these methods destruction of governments and the seizure of power will be facilitated.)

"3. In the economic sphere:

"(a) Induce and sustain railroad strikes; destroy bridges and tracks; do everything possible to disorganize transport.

"(b) Interfere with and prevent if possible the transport of food supplies into the cities; provoke financial troubles; flood the markets with counterfeit bank notes, appoint everywhere special committees for this work.

"(In this way economic disorganization will bring its inevitable catastrophe and the resulting revolution against the government will have the sympathy of the masses.)

"4. In the Military Sphere:

"(a) Carry on intensive propaganda among the troops. Cause misunderstandings between officers and soldiers. Unite the soldiers to assassination of the higher officers.

"(b) Blow up arsenals, bridges, tracks, powder magazines. Prevent the delivery of supplies of raw materials to factories and mills.

"(Thus the complete destruction of the army will be accomplished and the soldiers will adopt the program of the social democratic workers.)

Document No. 4

RUSSIAN SOVIET INDUSTRIAL PROGRAM

N. BOUKHARIN

PROGRAM OF THE COMMUNISTS

(BOLSHEVIKS)

1. Labor Discipline of the Working Class.
2. End of Money Power.
3. Nationalization of the Foreign Commerce.

(Fifth Issue Published by Russian Socialistic Federation, New York, 1919.)

a. LABOR DISCIPLINE OF THE WORKING CLASS AND PEASANT POVERTY.

To remedy production in such a manner that it should be possible to live without bosses, on a co-operative basis, is a pretty good idea. But it is one thing to say, another to perform. There are so many difficulties that they might be lessened; first, we now have the inheritance of the severe and unfortunate war which ultimately ruined our country; the working class must drink the stew brewed by Nikolas Romanoff and his servants — Sturmers, Sukhomlinoffs, Protopopoffs, and which was then stirred up more by Goutchkoff and Rodzianko, with their servants — Kerensky, Tzeretelli, Dan and the rest of the treacherous gang; second, the working class has to begin to organize production, repelling the blows of malicious enemies, who with grinding teeth of cannibals are attacking it externally, and of others who attempt to disrupt the laboring forces internally; under such conditions in order to conquer once and for all, the working class must swallow entirely its own portion (of this stew). In organizing an army of labor, there must also be organized a revolutionary labor discipline in this army. The reason is that there are such workers who do not seem to believe that they themselves are beginning to comprise the bosses of the land. As the treasury is now, the workers' peasants' treasury; factories are folk-factories; the soil is folk-soil; woods, machines, mines, implements, houses, all these are being transferred to the toiling people themselves. The management of all this, is the workers' management. At present the worker or peasant cannot look at this wealth with the same eyes, as formerly it belonged to the proprietors, now it is the people's. The proprietor squeezed from the workers all he could. The baron landowner tore the very skin from the poor peasant or laborer. And the peasant and laborer were, therefore, right when they didn't consider themselves obligated to work under the whip of their masters for the sake of strengthening the power and authority of their torturers. This is the reason why there could be no talk about any labor discipline at that time when the whip and club of the capitalist and landowner hissed upon the laborer and peasant. Now it is another thing. Whips are no more. The working people toil for themselves, they make no money for the capitalist, but they are engaged in a common labor, labor of the toiling masses which formerly was slavery.

And, nevertheless, we repeat that there still exist such unconscientious workers who seem not to see all this. Why? Because they were slaves too long. The thoughts of slaves and menials are cropping up in their minds all the time. In the depths of their souls they think that they can perhaps not go along without God and boss. And therefore they will try to profit by revolution as much as possible to fill their own pockets wherever there is a chance. And they never think of their obligation to the task. This negligence and fraud of their duty is now a crime against the working class itself. For at present not the boss is supported by labor; this labor supports the workers — the "poverty" which stands at the social rudder now. Not directors and bankers are they deceiving now, but the members of workers' offices, workers' unions and workers' peasants' government. If they handle the machines carelessly, if they break the tools, if they strive to do nothing in the appointed hours of labor in order to do their daily task during overtime hours and get double pay, they do not deceive the boss in this way, they do not harm the capitalist but the working class *in toto.* The same is with the soil; those who loot now the tools which are taken by the laborers and peasants under check, those rob society, and not the landowner who has long been deposed. Who cuts the woods in spite of the interdiction of the peasants' organization, he steals from " poverty." He, who instead of tilling the soil appropriated from the landowner, is occupied with bread speculation or in the secret manufacture of intoxicating drinks, he is a scoundrel and criminal against the workers and peasants.

At present, it is evident to all that in order to establish and organize production, the workers ought also to organize themselves, to establish their own laboring-order. In the factories and works the workers themselves ought to take care that every comrade should perform so much work as is required. Professional industrial unions and working councils are managing the sources of production. They can, if possible, shorten the working day; and we shall strive to such a good organization of production, that to the burden of every shift should fall not eight but six hours labor. But these same workers' organizations and, together with them, the workers' authority *in toto* can and must *demand* from their members the most careful devotion to the popular wealth and most conscientious care to their work. The workers' organizations — professional unions, in the first instance — are themselves arranging the standard form of production, i. e., that quantity of commodities which every one has to produce during the working day. Who doesn't accomplish this extent, he is a sabotager (of course, exceptions are allowed to weak and sick), he interrupts the work of the construction of a new free socialistic order, he impedes the working class from going its own way to complete communism.

Production — it is an immense machine, all parts of which must be adjusted to one another in order to make them work in harmony. A poor tool in the hands of a good worker is twaddle; a good tool in the hands of a poor worker is also twaddle. It is necessary that both the tool and worker be good.

Therefore, we ought to strive with all our power to organize the supply of fuel and raw materials, perfect the transportation facilities, distribute this fuel and raw stuff precisely, and on the other hand, take all measures of self-discipline, steadfastness, and conscientiousness necessary for the working masses.

To perform all this in Russia is much more difficult than in any other country. The working class (and, in still smaller degree, the peasant "poverty") haven't yet acquired that schooling in organization possessed by the South European and American workingmen. We have many workers, who have just recently become workers, who are just now becoming accustomed to social labor, who are breaking away from their accustomed thought that "I mind my own business." Such are always pulling in all different directions. The more we will have such types whose minds are occupied with the idea: to become petty bosses themselves, to save a little money and open a little shop, the more difficult it is to organize a real labor discipline. But the more intensive must be the efforts of the advance guard of the revolution, of the foremost workers, the workers of organization, to bring into existence, establish and reinforce such a discipline. If this will be successful, then we will succeed in organizing everything; and the working class will emerge victorious from its difficulties, created by the war devastation, sabotage, all barbarities and bestialities of the capitalistic order.

b. End of Money Power

(State "Finances" in the Soviet Republic and Monetary System)

At present, money is a mere medium for the procurement of goods. Therefore, he who possesses much money is able to buy many different things, he is a rich man. Irrespective of the low value of money, he who has the most of it, is better off. The rich classes who have plenty of this money are even now able to live perfectly well. In the city, the merchants, shop-keepers, capitalists, speculators; in the village, the tight-fisted peasant, who had during the war stuffed their pockets to the brim, accumulated hundreds of thousands of bills of varied colors and shades. This matter went so far that they had to bury their money in pitchers and jars deep in the soil, so much had they accumulated of this money medium.

And, on the other hand, the workers' peasants' government is in dire need of money. The further printing of paper money reduces its value; the more it appears, the cheaper it becomes. But the factories and works must be supported by money; the workers must be paid; the administration, the clerks, must be paid. Whence, then, is this money to be procured? For this purpose, it is in the first place necessary to impose taxes on the rich classes. Income and property taxes, i. e., taxes on large profits and big properties — such ought to be the fundamental tax, the tax on the rich, and those who get excessive incomes.

But now, when all are undergoing revolutionary fever, when it is difficult to organize at once the collection of taxes, all other means of procuring funds are permissible and expedient! For instance, such measure is expedient and wise, that the government declare that until a certain time all money be exchanged into new, the old money losing its value. It means that every one must empty his jars, drawers and chests, and bring their contents to the bank for exchange. And here can be inaugurated such a story. The savings of the petty people are not to be touched, a ruble is to be given for a ruble, old ruble for new, and from certain sums part is to be retained for the benefit of the government; and the more the sum accumulated, the more ferociously we would retain, say, in such a manner, up to five thousand, ruble for ruble exchanged; from the next five thousand, the tenth part would be taken; from the third five-thousand portion, the seventh part; from the fourth, the fourth; from the fifth, half; from the sixth, three-fourths; and from a certain sum — confiscate the whole.

Then the power of the rich would be adequately broken, it would be possible to obtain additional funds for the needs of the workers' government, everyone would be more or less equal in income.

In revolutionary time contribution from the bourgeoisie is also permissible, i. e., compulsory donations once and for all by decision of the Soviet organization. Of course, it is not at all satisfactory for one council to besiege the bourgeoisie according to one manner, for another by another, for the third by a third manner; it is just as bad as the various taxes which are placed on sites.

Therefore we must strive to unite the entire machinery of taxation in a decisive plan, which may be suitable for the Soviet republic *in toto*. But while such system does not exist — contribution is permissible. "When there is no fish craw-fish is also a fish," as the proverb says. It is always necessary to remember, that the problem of the party, the problem of the councils, the problem of the working class, and the peasant "poverty," lies precisely in uniting and centralizing the work of taxation; in ordering it so that the bourgeoisie could gradually be pushed from its entrenched economic position.

Nevertheless, it is necessary to remark that the further the work of organizing production advances according to the workers' new principles, the more the value of money in general depreciates. Formerly when private enterprises were dominant, these private enterprises sold their wares to each other; now-a-days as we go along, these sources of production are more united and are transformed in the various channels of social productivity. The product can be distributed among them, not through the means of a free market, but after a plan, indicated by the distribution of Workers' functions. Here happens something similar to the capitalistic and so-called complex enterprises.

Complex enterprises are those enterprises which combine various channels of production. In America, for instance, there are such enterprises which possess iron works, coal mines, iron mines, and steamship companies. One branch of the enterprise supplies the other with raw products, or provides finished products. But since all these different branches are only parts of one enterprise, it is understood that one section does not at all sell its products to the other section, on the contrary this product is distributed according to the orders of the central general bureau regulating the different sections of the complex enterprise. Let us take another example. In the factory a half-finished product is transferred from one section to another section, but at the same time, within the factory no buying — selling operations have been transacted. The same story will occur also in the course of entire production. When the main branches of production will be organized, which means that they will be transformed into one immense social enterprise under the workers' control, among all parts thereof will ensure a just distribution of the important means of production; fuel, raw materials, half-finished products, auxiliary materials; etc. And this means that money loses its value, and has its value only when production is not organized; the more it is organized, the smaller becomes the role of money, and, subsequently, the need of it diminishes.

And what about the Chamber of Workers, we might be asked?

Here, again, is the same story. The better organized production will be in the hands of the working class, the less social will workers be paid in money, and the more they will obtain natural remuneration, i. e., with products. We spoke already about co-operative communities and about workers' registration books. In such a manner, after registration, all the products wanted by the workers will be issued from the reserves without money, merely upon the certificate that such a man is working and earning his commodities. Of course this work cannot be arranged at once. Much time will pass until this will all be organized, arranged and ends made to meet. It is a new affair, existent, nowhere else in the world and therefore very difficult. But one thing is clear, the more the workers will come in possession of production and the distribution thereof, the less will be the need of money, and then it will little by little die away entirely.

Without money the realization begins of *"exchange" between town and village;* the urban industrial organizations give to the village, drygoods, iron works, and the like; in return, the rural organizations give to the town, bread. And here too, the less will be the value of money, the closer the rural and urban organizations, of the workers' and rural "poverty" will unite.

At present, at *the very minute,* the working government is in need of money, urgent need of it. Because the organization of production and distribution only *begins* to function, and money plays yet a very, very big role. Finances — pecuniary expenses and incomes of the government — are at present of enormous importance. Therefore the question of *taxes* is so acutely prominent, they are needed at any rate; confiscation of financial surpluses of the urban and the rural bourgeoisie is needed at any rate; from time to time contributions are also required. But eventually the tax system will also die. Already now, as far as the nationalization of production has gone on, so far has disappeared the incomes from the hands of the capitalists; the landowners are annihilated, with them, the taxes of the landowners' incomes, the so-called land rent. Houses are appropriated from the landlords, with them disappears the source of property taxes. Excessive riches are being confiscated, the rich lose their basis of support, and gradually everybody becomes a worker in the service of the proletariat government organization (afterwards, when full communism is established, when even the state dies, all, as we have seen, are transformed into equal comrades, and every remembrance of the former divisions of bourgeoisie and workers disappears).

And if so, it is evident that it is much simpler to pay less at the beginning, than to offer high salaries and then from these salaries to make deductions in the form of taxes. It is useless to waste breath and energy on a tale of the "House that Jack built."

On the other hand, we have seen that when the production and distribution are organized *to the end,* money doesn't play the least role. This means that money exactions will be required from no one. Money will cease to be necessary *altogether*. That is, it will cease to be necessary also for the government power. The monetary system *will die*.

We repeat, that this state is still far off. There can be no talk whatever about this in the nearest future. At present we ought to be anxious about how to *find* means. But now we are already taking steps which are leading us to the road of annihilating the financial system, in general. Society is being transformed into an immense association of workers which produces and distributes its products without any production of gold metal or paper money. The power of money comes to an end.

---

c. NO COMMERCIAL RELATION WITH IMPERIALISTIC FOREIGN COUNTRIES FOR RUSSIAN BOURGEOISIE!

(*Nationalization of Foreign Commerce*)

Every country in our time lives among other countries and greatly depends upon them. It would be very difficult to get along without trading with other countries; one country produces more products of one kind, the other, of another. The blockade of Germany brings home the difficulty of getting along without import from other countries. And if, for instance, England would have surrounded by such a closed circle as Germany was surrounded, she would have long already perished. Likewise Russian industry nationalized by the working class cannot go on without procuring certain wares from abroad. On the other hand, foreign countries, and particularly Germany are in dire need of raw materials. We ought not forget even for a minute that we are living among brigand capitalistic governments. And there is no wonder that these brigand governments will make every effort to obtain everything necessary for them on their robber highways. And on the other hand, the Russian bourgeoisie, which has now such a hard time in Russia, will be glad to come in contact with foreign imperialists. There is no doubt that the foreign bourgeoisie would be likely to pay the Russian speculators still more than our own, patriotic, real-Russian bourgeoisie. And the speculator supplies those who pay him most. Naturally, should we only allow our bourgeoisie to transport abroad all kinds of goods, and give permission to the foreign ravishers to establish here all kinds of commercial affairs which they like, then it would not greatly benefit the Soviet Socialistic Republic.

Formerly, when questions of foreign commerce were discussed, two things were considered: must high customs be charged for foreign wares or, on the contrary, ought the customs to be repealed altogether? During the last years of the reign of capital, merchants have adopted the policy of high tariff. Thanks to them the trusts have secured additional profits; in their own government they are monopolist possessors of the market, they have no competitors or rivals; and from the foreigners they were protected by the tariff wall. That is, through the help of high tariff, the trusts, *i. e.*, the biggest sharks of capital skinned their compatriots shamelessly. Matters grew to such extent that profiteering by this additional extortion of their compatriots, the trusts started to export wares abroad at very low rates, with the sole aim to drive their rivals' trusts from other countries. Naturally, these cheap prices existed only until a certain time. As soon as the rivals were pushed out, they immediately started to raise their prices in the newly-conquered markets also. In order to maintain such policy they were also in need of custom duties. The trusts, crying for *protection* of the industry, cried in fact for one of the means of *attack*, for one of the means of the economic conquest of the foreign market. And, as was usual in such cases, they, the professional swindlers of the populace hid their robbery under the pretended protection of popular interests.

Some of the socialists, seeing this, were ready to proclaim free trade among countries. This would mean that full freedom for economic struggle is granted to different bourgeoisie. But this proclamation remaining in the air, was simply good for nothing. Because, what trust would refuse to become an additional income?

And since this additional profit is obtained by the trust, thanks to the protection by high tariffs from foreign rivalry, how then can the trust refuse to receive custom duties? At first *must be overthrown the trust,* first must be established a socialistic revolution. This is the way, how real socialists answered this question, *i. e.,* Communist Bolsheviki. And socialist revolution — it means establishing social order, when everything is under the control of the *organized into a government working class.* We have seen what harm causes private trade within the country. No less harm is caused by such trading between countries. Consequently it is fully absurd to abolish free trade within the country and establish it beyond. The same absurd, according to the viewpoint of the working class, appears the system of imposition foreign capitalists. A *third* escape is necessary, and this escape consists of the *nationalization of foreign commerce by the proletarian government.*

What does it mean? This means that none who live on the Russian territory has the right to transact commercial affairs with foreign capitalists. He who will be caught in this affair must be fined or jailed. The whole foreign trade ought to be intersected by the workers'-peasants' government. The government has to arrange all business affairs, case by case. For instance, America offers us machines in exchange for a certain ware, or a certain amount of gold pieces. And Germany offers the same machine at a different price or under other conditions. The workers' organization (of the government, of Soviet,) realizes whether they have to make this sale and where there is an advantage. Where advantage is shown, there they buy. The purchased products are sold to the populace without profit. Because this business is transacted, not by capitalists who rob the workers, but by the workers themselves. In such a manner the domination of capital ought to be driven out of these trenches. And the workers must take (and they take, and they have taken) the affair of foreign trade in their own hands and to organize it in such a way that no swindler, no speculator, none of the marauders should succeed in escaping the workers' patrol.

It is understood that a relentless chastisement is required with regard to the capitalist-smugglers. They ought to be, once forever, disaccustomed from all kinds of tricks. The affair of economic life is now the affair of the toiling masses. Only through further continuation of *reinforcement* of such order, the working class will succeed in final liberation from every reminder of the damned capitalistic regime.

Document No. 5

THE RED TERROR

In the official publication of the Petrograd Council of the Workmen's, Peasants' and Red Guards' Deputies, the "Red Gazette," an editorial article was published on the 31st of August, 1918. This article referred to the Red Terror. The whole article is naturally an expression of the official point of view of the Soviet officials on the subject of class struggle. The following is stated in the above article:

> "Only those men among the representatives of the bourgeois class who, during a period of nine months, succeeded in proving their loyalty to the Soviet rule, should be spared. All the others are our hostages and we should treat them accordingly. Enough of mildness. *The interests of the revolution necessitate physical annihilation of the bourgeois class. It is time for us to start.*"

Another official Bolshevist publication, namely, "The Izvestia," of the Executive Committee of the Kotelinich Soviet of the Workmen's, Soldiers', and Peasant Beggars' Deputies, published on September 29, 1918, in the fourth issue, an article under the title "The Voice of Tombs," the closing lines of which read as follows:

> "Nay, we have already left the path of all errors and we have found the right track of struggle with our hated enemies and this track is—*Red Terror.*"

Another Bolshevist proclamation, issued by the Terrorists in the city of Kotelnich in 1918, North Russia, partly reads as follows:

> "We take oath not to leave a stone unturned in those nests where the terrible parasites and their partisans are living. When compelled to evacuate the cities, we will turn them into deserts and every step of ours will be abundantly soaked with blood. In this struggle between the world's capital and those oppressed let the world tremble before the horror of the mode in which we shall demolish and annihilate everything which oppresses us. . . . *You, rich peasants, who have drunk the blood of the poor for centuries long, you should remember that the above also applies to you.*"

Document No. 6

ON THE BREST-LITOVSK PEACE

In March, 1918, Lenin made an endeavor to invent some excuses with regard to the treacherous attitude of the Bolsheviki at the Brest-Litovsk Peace parleys. In a pamphlet under the title "To the History of the Question of the Unfortunate Peace," Lenin stated as follows:

"By concluding a separate peace, we free ourselves, to the highest degree possible under the present circumstances, from the two belligerent imperialistic groups (the Allied group and the Central Powers), moreover taking advantage of their war and their hostilities, which, in turn, hampers their deal against us. We also avail ourselves of a certain period of free-hands in order to continue and to strengthen the socialistic revolution. The reorganization of Russia on the basis of proletarian dictatorship as well as on the basis of nationalization of banks and of the big industry, accompanied by a natural exchange of goods between the cities and the rural consumers' societies of the small farmers, is quite possible, provided several months of peaceful work are assured. A reorganization of this kind will make socialism unconquerable, both in Russia and throughout the whole world, and at the same time it will establish a firm economic basis for a powerful workmen's and peasants' red army." (Page 8, translation from the "Russian Edition," March, 1918, published by the Kronstadt Commune of the Russian Communist Party.)

Document No. 7

DEFENSE OF BERKMAN

Matters which were confined to the internal situation in the various Allied countries, and which stood in no relation with the state of affairs in Russia herself were lively debated by the Soviet officials and by the various radical organizations in Russia. In corroboration of the above statement the following resolution of a group of anarchists on the yacht "Polar Star" might be of interest:

"*Resolution*

"Session of Helsingfors group of anarchists of December 23, 1917, on the yacht 'Polar Star.'

"*To the Ambassador of the United States of North America:*

"We, sailors, soldiers and workmen of the city of Helsingfors, having become fully acquainted with the fact of the persecution by the government of the United States of No. America, of our comrade Alexander Berkman, whose only guilt culminates in that he has given his whole life to the service of the toiling class and the disinherited, demand the immediate release of our Comrade Alexander Berkman. In the event of refusal we openly declare that we will hold personally responsible the representatives of the government of the United States for the life and liberty of the revolutionary fighter for the people's cause, Comrade Alexander Berkman."

"(Signed) *Chairman:*
"S. KRILOFF.
"*Secretary:*
"F. KUTZEY."

("Izvestia" of the Central Executive Committee of the Soviets of Peasants', Workmen's and Soldiers' Deputies and of the Petrograd Soviet of Workmen's and Soldiers' Deputies, No. 13, Jan. 18, 1918.)

Document No. 8

SUICIDE LETTER OF A BOLSHEVIK COMMISSAR

On April 24, 1919, N. Lopoushkin, chairman of the Kirsanov Soviet, issued a letter to the Central Soviet of Workmen's Deputies at Moscow, which probably throws more light on the present conditions in Soviet Russia than many exhaustive treaties. In part this letter reads as follows:

"My colleagues of the Kirsnov Soviet are writing to tell you that I am no longer fit to hold the position of President of the Soviet, that I am a counter-revolutionary, that I have lost my nerve, and am a traitor to our cause. Perhaps they are right—I only wish I knew. . . . Speaking frankly, we are, in my opinion, on the brink of a terrible disaster, which will leave its imprint, not only upon Socialism, but upon our nation for centuries, a disaster which will give our descendants the right to regard us Bolsheviks at the best as crazy fanatics, and at the worst, as foul impostors and ghastly muddlers, who murdered and tortured a nation for the sake of an unattainable Utopian theory, and who in our madness sold our birthright amongst the peoples for less than the proverbial mess of pottage.

"All around me, wherever I look, I see unmistakable signs of our approaching doom, and yet no one responds to my appeals for help; my voice is as the voice of one crying in a wilderness. In the towns I have just come from, chronic hunger, murder, and the license and libertinage of the criminal elements, who undoubtedly hold numerous executive positions under our Soviets, have reduced the population to the level of mere brute beasts, who drag out a dull semi-conscious existence, devoid of joy in to-day, and without hope for the morrow. Surely this should not be the result of the earthly Paradise which the Soviets were to introduce into our lives. Nor did I find the position any better on the railways. Everywhere a people living under the dread of famine, death, torture, and terror, everywhere groaning and utter misery. My countrymen, whom I love, and whom I had hoped to assist to render happy above all nations, look at me either with the mute uncomprehending eyes of brutes condemned to slaughter, or else with the red eyes of fury and vengeance. . . .

"Speculation is rife amongst even the most humble inhabitants in the country villages, who have forced a lump of sugar up to four rubles, and a pound of salt up to forty rubles. And the Bolshevik militia and the Soviets? When they are called upon to deal with various infringements of the Bolshevik Decrees, they either try to get out of taking action altogether, or else they pretend that there is insufficient evidence to commit for trial. . . .

"No member of the Red Guard dare risk his life by returning to his native village, where his father would be the first to kill him. I maintain that there must be something wrong with a regime which has aroused such universal hatred, in such a comparatively short time; and amongst whom? Amongst the very class it strove to uplift, to free, to benefit, and to render happy. . . .

"I feel tired and depressed. I know that the Red Terror was a mistake, and I have a terrible suspicion that our cause has been betrayed at the moment of its utmost realization.

"Yours in fraternal greeting,

"N. LOPOUSHKIN."

It will be of interest to know that immediately after having issued the above letter, Lopoushkin committed suicide. (Published in "the New Europe" and "Struggling Russia.")

Document No. 9

MANIFESTO ISSUED ON DECEMBER 19, 1917, BY THE SOVIET OF RAILWAY, PETROGRAD DISTRICT, TO THE RAILROAD EMPLOYEES OF ALL THE RUSSIAN RAILWAY SYSTEMS

COMRADES! — The general confusion into which the country was plunged by the government of the landholders and capitalists, which for eight months has been operating without the slightest accounting or control, has been particularly manifest in the railways, which constitute one of the most important functions of the national economic life.

Even without this, the transportation system, after being dislocated by the war, had fallen into complete disorganization because of the criminal carelessness, ignorance, and lack of preparation on the part of the higher officials of the railroads, of the guardians, who, although they were entrusted with the guidance of the hundreds of thousands of white slaves constituting the lower ranks of the service, were interested only in keeping their own jobs safe, completely forgetting the hopeless situation of the lower employees.

Thus the railroads of our country were gradually enveloped in an increasing state of disorder, the possibility of through traffic and transportation over the roads was reduced to a minimum, the rolling stock was in bad repair, the number of "sick" cars and locomotives was increasing day by day, the lack of traction material is becoming seriously felt; there is a constant increase in the difficulties experienced at traffic centers and transfer points; the normal flow of "empties" to the important points from which provisions are constantly moving to the capitals and to the army, was being constantly interrupted; the most important centers, Moscow and Petrograd, were congested; there, at other times, an insufficiency of rolling stock was felt when thousands of cars that were being held up at transfer points were preventing the proper operation of the roads.

It is not possible to give a detailed picture here of the whole mess, but it is necessary to point out that if, in this vast confusion, it is still possible for a citizen of Russia to move about somewhat in his own country, this possibility must be ascribed to the slavish devotion alone, the almost intolerable exertions of the lower ranks of railway employees — workmen, foremen, clerks, especially the men working out on the line.

The consciousness of our duty to the country and to the revolution impels us, the lower employees of the railroads, to stand by our posts under conditions that are intolerably severe, in spite of the fact that the coalition ministry of agreement (Kerensky Cabinet), in a number of proclamations, criminally betraying the interests of the toiling masses for the advantage of capital, completely forgot the railway slaves, fed them on promises and used only the most merciless measures in dealing with the disobedient.

Ministers changed, the wording of their promises changed, but the poverty of the poor railway employees increased.

The hopes of the railway men to have the aid of their own Trade Organization have not been realized.

This organization, the All-Russian Railway Organization, the so-called "Vikzhel" (Vserossiskyi Zhelyeznodorozhny Sayuz), from the very beginning of its existence, assumed the impress of the policy of coalition and compromise which was characteristic of the Kerensky government.

Being elected at a removal of two, three and even four degrees from the original voter, "Vikzhel," consisting of persons cut off from the great masses of the railway workers, has not reflected, and does not reflect the will and the hopes of these masses, and has never fought for their demands.

On the contrary, all this time, especially at the moment when there were bitter conflicts between the broad masses of the workers with the landholders and capitalists, this organization stood openly by the side of those who fought, with a policy of union with the landholders and capitalists, against the workers and the peasants.

This fight against the workers and peasants came out with particular clearness in November, at the time of the successful uprising of the workers and soldiers.

Comrades! There are still many struggles ahead, the workers and peasants will still have many conflicts with the landholders and capitalists, the Kaledins, Kornilovs, and Kerenskys; all workers, all toilers, should unite in one faithful family around their peasants' and workers' government, born in the Second All-Russian Congress of Soviets of Workers', Soldiers' and Peasants' Delegates.

Comrades! All for one and one for all! Only by our united strength and not by the wretched policy of agreement pursued by the "Vikzhel," can we improve our lot. Only by supporting the outspoken policy of the Council of People's Commissaires can we prevent the sabotage and the opposition now being practised by our superior officials, those managers and servants of the roads who were formerly the chinovniks and employees of the Czarist government, in their fight against the success of our workers' and peasants' government.

This criminal sabotage must be stopped!

Comrades, support the Council of People's Commissaires!

Document No. 10

FROM THE PEOPLE'S COMMISSARIAT OF LABOR TO ALL WORKERS

COMRADES: — Hard and difficult times are ahead of us for the industries of our country which were mobilized without any system during three and a half years of the war and were conducted for the sole purpose of war-profiteering, are now losing a considerable part of their contracts. The slowdown of war industries is taking place at the moment of the greatest struggle between two classes, two worlds — the world of capitalist exploitation and oppression, and the world of fraternal co-operation of all the oppressed. The political struggle between capital and labor throughout the whole country is being accompanied by a threatening economic disorganization. The organizers of the capitalist production — the owners of plants, factory owners, bankers with all their clique of lackey partisans (officials, engineers, and others) fed on the crumbs of the profiteers attempt to utilize the coming crisis so that the deadly grip of hunger and disorganization will tighten the noose on the necks of the working class and thus crush the revolution.

Every worker, soldier, peasant,— all the sons of the revolution must at this crucial hour unite and consciously use their capabilities, strong hands and mighty shoulders to preserve our economic system from that disorganization. Enterprises released from war orders and labor organizations must adapt themselves to the production of the vital necessaries for national consumption. Everyone must now remember that he works not for accumulating profits for capitalists but for the benefit of all the toilers; that the workers and peasants are becoming the real masters of our country and all must regard the factories, plants, other enterprises and forms of work with such unselfish considerations as befits the Socialist state of society.

The slowdown of war orders, the horrible disorganization which results in the cessation of work at the plants would bring grief to the worker's heart, and the spectre of hunger and the fear of oncoming unemployment hovers over the heads of the large toiling masses. This fear inherited from our enslaved fathers keeps our vigorous thoughts in capitalist captivity, dwarfs our great aspirations for the emancipation of the whole mankind from the yoke of exploitation, and overcomes them with fears for the morrow.

Only when the control shall rest in the hands of labor organizations, central as well as local, and energetically and actively applied, not hesitating even to use most drastic measures against capitalists, should the latter deliberately neglect the duties imposed on them;—only when the control shall be put in close and direct contact with the general regulation and organization of production, in individual enterprises, as well as in a whole branch of an industry—only then will it accomplish its aims and justify the expectations held out for it.

Control should be precisely understood as a transitory step toward an organization of the whole economic structure of the country on a social basis, as the immediate and necessary step in that direction, made by the masses themselves, and parallel with the work done in the central organs of the national economy.

Petrograd, July, 1918.

Document No. 11

SOVIET CIRCULARS

(Issued to Foreign Soldiers on Russian Soil)

RUSSIAN SOCIALIST FEDERAL SOVIET REPUBLIC

a. WHY HAVE YOU COME TO UKRAINE?

To British and American Soldiers:

FELLOW WORKINGMEN!—Why have you come to Ukraine? Do you not know that the war is over? An armistice is declared on the Western front, and preparations are being made for the peace conference. Yet instead of arrangements being made for you to return home, to those dear ones, who with keen longing will be expecting you, you have been brought here to start a new war in Russia.

What have you got to fight for now?

When the allied governments invaded Russia from the North, in Mourmansk, and Archangel, and the East from Vladivostok, they publicly made a solemn declaration that they had no hostile intentions against the Russian people. They said, they had come in fact to help us to get out of the clutches of German Imperialism. President Wilson gave as an additional reason that he desired to protect the Czecho-Slovaks, who he alleged were in danger of being betrayed to the Germans.

These were merely hypocritical pretexts. Russia was not in the grip of the Kaiser. Russia did not want this kind of assistance of the Allies. The Czecho-Slovaks were in no danger of betrayal. They were at perfect liberty to leave Russia unharmed, but they were bribed by the Allies to take up arms against the Russian Republic, and were until we had defeated them, a source of danger to us.

But what excuse is there now for this fresh landing in the Ukraine, openly directed against Russia? It may be that you have been kept in ignorance of the tremendous events that have taken place during the last month, although that is hardly possible. We tell you then, that there have been revolutions in Bulgaria, Austria-Hungary and Germany.

Prussianism has been overthrown by the German workers and soldiers. Kaiser Wilhelm has fled to Holland. The Crown Prince has been shot. There is a new government in Berlin controlled by a Workers' and Soldiers' Council.

On the west front fighting has ceased and the Germans, French, and British soldiers are fraternizing.

In Austria-Hungary too the old order has been overthrown by the workers. The Emperor Karl has abdicated. Hungary has broken away from Austria, and the Czecho-Slovaks, as well as the other nations hitherto under the dominion of the Hapsburgs have established their independence.

What pretext have the Allied governments now for invading Russia from the South? The menace of Prussian militarism no longer exists thanks to the German revolution. We have offered to the Czecho-Slovaks all facilities to return to their own country, to join their liberated countrymen. There is no excuse at all for your landing in the Ukraine. If there was ever the slightest doubt as to the intentions of the Allied governments, there can be none now. The purpose of the Allied invasion of Russia is to crush the Socialist Republic, and re-establish the reign of capitalism and landlordism. You surely cannot be unaware of the tremendous change that has taken place in Russia. We have abolished capitalism and landlordism. The land belongs to the whole people. So, too, do the factories, mines, railways and all the means of wealth production. All these things are under the direct control of workers, and peasants. We are constructing a new society in which the fruits of labour will go to those who work. But the financiers of Wall Street and the City have greedy eyes for our vast storehouse of wealth. They want to control the rich coal basin of the Don, the oil wells of Baku, the cotton fields of Turkestan and minerals of the Caucasus, the great timber forest of the North, and the vast corn lands of the South. They want to convert the million of workers and peasants of Russia into wage slaves to grind out profits for them.

Fellow workingmen, this is the purpose for which you have been brought here. You have not come to fight Prussian militarism, that is finished. You have not come to fight for liberty. You have come to overthrow the first real workers' republic. There is another important fact which you should know. In this attack on Soviet Russia from the South, your government will be co-operating with the present government of the Ukraine. Last year we had a Soviet Republic in the Ukraine. But the present head of the government, Skoropadski, with the assistance of the Kaiser, suppressed the Soviet Republic, and since then has maintained an iron rule over the Ukraine people with the aid of German bayonets.

The German soldiers have now refused any longer to be the policemen for the Ukrainian-German capitalists and landlords, and are going home to their now free country.

Skoropadski, has now turned to the Allied governments and they, not in the least troubled by the fact that he has been actually co-operating with the Kaiser, have come to an arrangement with him, to keep the Ukrainian people down, and to sacrifice you in the interests of International capitalism. If you were told that your landing will be welcomed by the people, do not believe it. During the whole period of the German occupation the Ukrainian people have been in a state of rebellion. The German Commanding General was assassinated. Numbers of other acts of violence, and strikes showed the hostility of the people to the present regime, not merely because it was German, but because it was capitalist. At any moment we expect our comrades in the Ukraine to overthrow Skoropadski and to re-establish the Soviet Republic.

Now you have come to the assistance of the South Russian landlords and capitalists. Comrades, are you going to do the dirty work that the German soldiers refused to do any longer?

The supreme motive which animates the capitalist governments of the Allies for invading Russia is to suppress this stronghold of the revolutionary Socialist movement. They fear above everything else that the working people in their own countries will overthrow them and take the power into their own hands. They hope, by crushing the Russian revolution, to take the heart out of the tremendous movement for working class emancipation that is spreading everywhere. And how rapidly it is spreading. The soldiers, who only yesterday were slaughtering each other on the Western front are now mingling as brothers. Will it be long before the voice of revolution is heard in France, England, America and Italy?

Comrades, if the workers of England or America made a revolution would you suppress it? You would not. You would side with your own class. We also are workers, we belong to the same class as you do. Will you then, fight against us?

Comrades, we are living today at the beginning of a new period in the history of mankind. This is the last struggle between capital and labor. If you continue your present job, you will be siding with the gang of imperialists, who during four years have sacrificed ten millions of the flower of manhood, have mutilated thirty millions more, have caused unutterable misery and devastation, and who, if allowed to remain in power, will reduce us workers to a worse slavery than has ever been known.

Comrades, don't do it. You have arms in your hands. Your officers are powerless against you. Raise the red flag of working-class freedom. Join with us, and with the revolutionary workers of Germany and Austria to make the world free for labor.

Down with capitalism! Long live the Social Revolution!

Signed: N. LENIN,

President of the Council of Peoples' Commissaries.

C. CHICHERIN,

Peoples' Commissary for Foreign Affairs.

QUIT FIGHTING, BRITISH SOLDIERS AND JOIN YOUR RUSSIAN COMRADES!

(b. English prisoner from Archangel front writes to his brother Scots)

Is it right for working people of one country to kill working people of another?

The Allied troops, invading Russia, have so often been told that if they are taken prisoner they will be tortured and killed by the Bolsheviks, that it is interesting to see what in fact happens when an English soldier falls into the hands of the Russian workmen's and peasants' army. Here is the letter of a private of the Royal Scots taken prisoner last month near Archangel:

CUTLAS, *Monday*, Oct. 14th, 1918.

"*To the men of the Royal Scots:*

"I wonder if you all know the kind of men you are fighting. I do. You are fighting an army of working-men and there are no officers amongst them. Everybody is the same. They ask, why do we fight them. Well, that is more than I can say; in fact, I don't know why we have come to fight them, and another thing that counts is, they don't want to fight us. They are not fighting their own class, the working class, but the capitalists of Russia and all countries. Since I have been a prisoner I have been treated as one of themselves, and given me plenty to eat and drink. I have also seen one of our men that lies in hospital wounded. He tells me he has been well treated and looked after and as a friend, a workingman, and not as a soldier.

"Now, I ask you this question; is it right, that the working class of one country should come and fight the working class of another country? We are not at war with Russia, and the Russians are not at war with us, but with the capitalist of all the countries, the people whom we work for and keep in plenty, while we, the working class, merely exist. If the working class knew why they are fighting and for who, they would refuse to fight any longer. Think things over and ask yourselves, is it worth while killing each other to please other people, who care not what happens, as long as their pockets are being filled at our expense. From what I have seen the Russians are a good people and they are fighting for a good cause, a cause that every country in the world should follow.

"Private LAPHAM, 10th Royal Scots."

Now, isn't it clear that English and American soldiers are being fooled when they believe that a mob of robbers and criminals have seized power in Russia and are murdering right and left. Here is an example of a Scotch soldier taken prisoner in square fight. He says himself he did not know what sort of people he was fighting, till he was in their hands. He had probably been told by his officers and by some rag like the "Daily Mail" that the most terrible things would happen to him if he fell in the hands of the bloodthirsty Bolshevike. Of course he was told that, because the rich people who rule England must hide from English workmen the truth about the Russian people and their revolution. But what happens in fact when an English soldier gets into the hands of the Red army? The Russian soldier, who is a working man or peasant, like the English soldier, looks upon him at once like a comrade and sees that his interests lie not in killing his prisoner but in treating him as a fellow worker, who has the same hard life of toil as he has. But the Russian workman and peasant is trying to improve his lot. He has turned out his criminal government and put an end to the rich parasites that have lived so long at his expense,— landlords, war profiteers, bankers, industrial bosses. He is making a new world here now, where only those people rule, who labor by muscle and brain. Therefore, every workingman and peasant from any country in the world, no matter what language he speaks, is welcome to him and will find a home in Russia. He wants to make Russia the refuge of all those who are oppressed under the cruel regime of capitalism and wage slavery. He has abolished that regime in his country and invites fellow workers of other lands to come and see what he has done and then go home and do the same.

For this reason a special order has been issued by the commander of the Red army on the Archangel and Murmansk fronts to all soldiers of the Red army to treat all prisoners with the utmost kindness and consideration, to provide for their material wants and to send them down to the bases, where they will be welcome as fellow workers. The commander of every battalion is now responsible for the safety of prisoners taken. If any prisoner is shot, then he answers for it with his life before the military revolutionary tribunal of the republic.

---

c.

To the British Soldiers:

COMRADES.— Great events are taking place. We have just been celebrating the anniversary of the great Russian proletarian revolution. This revolution has overthrown the government of the landlords and capitalists. It has brought to the working class of Russia not only political but also economic liberty. The big landlords have been driven off the land, the land has become the common property of the people and those who toil are utilizing it for the good of the people. The capitalists have been deprived of the factories, works and mines; these are now being controlled by the workers themselves.

By the February revolution the Russian people liberated themselves of the Czar's autocracy with its evils; a capitalist government was established. The Russian middle class tried to introduce a system of government similar to yours, a system the main object of which is the exploitation of the working class and its subjugation to a few trust magnates. The capitalist governments have not only unmercifully exploited the people but have been and are using them as gun-fodder for almost five years.

The Russian working class however did not fight through its revolution in order to continue the murderous fratricidal war, or to maintain such a system of slavery as you have in Great Britain. The Russian working class has overthrown the capitalist government and established an entirely new system of government by the working class. Soviets (Councils) of Workers', Soldiers' and Peasants' Deputies have been established which have complete political power and are managing the industries of the country for the welfare of the working people. In each village, town or district such Soviets are at work. These are united in one central body which is being elected every three months at the all-Russian Congress of the Soviets. The People's Commissaries such as the people's commissary for foreign affairs, for home affairs, for war and so forth, are appointed by this central body and are directly responsible to the working people—instead of lawyers and self-seeking professional politicians, the workers and peasants are themselves managing their affairs. We communists are acting in accordance with the principle: the emancipation of the working class is the task of the workers themselves.

The fact that the Russian working class is striving for its economic and political liberty induced the British capitalists to use all means in order to prevent us from establishing Socialism. The British, French and American capitalists know pretty well that as soon as the truth about the Russian worker's revolution becomes evident to the proletarians of their respective countries these will follow our example and liberate themselves of wage-slavery. Therefore they supported our counter-revolutionary capitalists, landlords and generals against the Soviets of the working people. Now, not being satisfied with the streams of blood that are flowing everywhere—in the West, in the East, in the South, they send you, British workers, to fight against us, the Russian workingmen. They wish to enslave us in order to keep you in slavery, yet you allow yourselves to be used as tools for this vile purpose.

Your capitalists and officers have been telling you that you are fighting against Prussian militarism. Prussian militarism has already been destroyed by the Prussian people themselves. Influenced by the Russian revolution, the German working class has risen and has overthrown the regime of the bloody kaiser. He is in prison, his government is dispersed, Soviets are being formed everywhere; the soldiers have joined hands with the working class; the German sailors at Kiel and elsewhere have shot their officers and taken possession of the navy. Berlin is in the hands of the revolutionary soldiers and workers. Severe fighting is taking place all over Germany; a great Socialist revolution has commenced. Similar events are taking place in Austria and Hungary. The Emperor Karl has escaped and Vienna and Budapest are in the hands of the Soviets of workers and soldiers. At the Western front the German soldiers have arrested the peace delegation of the old government and are negotiating directly with the French and British soldiers.

At this time you are called upon by your capitalist government to play the part of international gendarmes. You are called upon to assist the Russian and German capitalists and landlords to enslave those peoples. In the meantime the British, French and American capitalists are strengthening the shackles of slavery and are forging chains for yourselves. In Great Britain liberty of the press, the liberty of the subject, the rights of the trade unions have been completely abolished, the country is misgoverned by a gang of adventurers and profiteers who for the sake of a few millions of profit do not mind killing millions of British and other workingmen. The flower of the manhood of the nation is being crippled. Industries which produced necessities of life for the people have been destroyed, famine and misery are reigning everywhere. The armament ring which dictates it policy through the Northcliffe press is ruling supreme.

Hundreds of thousands of British workingmen are protesting against this unbearable state of affairs; they demand peace and liberty. Hundreds of the best men of the nation, such as John Maclean, are in prison.

At this time you serve as tools of your exploiters. British Soldiers! Is it not time for you to face the truth, and to decline to serve as the gendarmes of international capitalism?

Demand your immediate withdrawal from free soil of the Russian Federative Soviet Republic!

Return home and join those workers who are fighting for the liberation of the working class.

PETER PETROFF.

---

d. BOLSHEVIST PROPAGANDA

I. WHY DON'T THEY SEND YOU HOME?

To the American and British Soldiers:

Did you ever stop to think why they don't send you home?

The war is over. Armistice is concluded. Peace negotiations are already being conducted. Months have already elapsed since the great slaughter has stopped.

Millions of soldiers — French, British, American, are returning home from the battlefields. Millions of prisoners are returning home from prison. This is a time of joy and happiness for thousands of humble homes — the boys are coming back! Hundreds of ships are carrying American boys in khaki from the Western front back to the shores of Columbia.

Why, then, don't they let you go home?

"Sweet Home" is waiting for you. Those whom you love are waiting for you. Your wives and children, your sisters and sweethearts are waiting for you. Your gray, old dear mothers are waiting for you.

Are they waiting in vain?

Your mother is asking every newcomer from the front: "Where is my boy?" "Don't know! Somewhere in the steppes of Russia."

What are you doing here, "somewhere in Russia?" What do they want you here for?

The war is over because there is nothing left to fight for, and nothing to fight against.

They have been telling you that this was a war against German autocracy, against German imperialism, against kaiserism.

But now there is no more kaiserism, there is no more autocracy. The German workers have arisen in revolt — and they have themselves defeated kaiserism. Themselves! — without the help of British and American troops. There is no more imperialism in Germany. The kaiser and the cruel "war-lords" have fled. Germany, like Russia, is now the land of revolution. Germany, like Russia, will be governed not by a bunch of cruel masters, but by the people, by revolutionary workers.

Is it true that you have been fighting for freedom and democracy? If this was true you would have been sent home on the very day the German revolution broke out. But instead of home you are sent to the steppes of Russia. Why?

Because this is not a war for Freedom. This is not a war for Democracy, but against Democracy.

Do you know that Russia is the freest and most democratic country in the world? Do you know that all the wealth of Russia now belongs, not to a small group of greedy capitalists, but to the vast majority of the people, to the workers and the poor peasants? Do you know that the land, the mines, the shops, the factories of Russia are now owned and governed by the people and operated for the benefit of the people? Do you know that the present government of Russia — the government of the Soviets (councils of workmen's and peasants' deputies) is the only real democratic government in the world?

Of course you don't know all this. Because your masters are afraid to tell you the truth about revolutionary Russia. They are telling you lies about the atrocities of the Bolsheviks. Don't believe them! There is no disruption, no anarchy, no disorder in Russia. Revolutionary Russia is, indeed, as one of your American journalists has said, the paradise of the workers and the poor.

The capitalists and imperialists of France, Great Britain and the United States, the Rothschilds, the Rockefellers, the Morgans want to destroy this paradise of the workers and the poor. The bloodthirsty exploiters of the Entente want to defeat the revolution. Why? Because the revolution is making headway, because revolutionary ideas are being spread in all countries. Country after country is getting revolutionized; the German workers have followed the example of the Russians. The French and Italian and British are going to follow the example of the Germans. This is the time of Revolts! The workers of the whole world are going to throw off the capitalist yoke! The Russian and the German revolutions are just the first two acts of the Great World Revolution. The capitalists of the Entente are trembling. Don't they hear the sounds of revolt all around? Don't they realize, don't they know that "it" is coming? And this is why they want to defeat the revolution before the revolution defeats them. This is why they declared war on revolutionary Russia. And this is why they don't want to send you home.

You are here to fight against Democracy and Freedom. You are here to fight against the Russian workers and poor peasants.

Do you realize that in this great battle of labor against capital, of freedom against exploitation, of real democracy against the fake democracy of Rockefeller and Morgan — you are to fight on the side of your cruel masters against your brethren, against your fellow workers? Are you not workingmen yourselves?

You are going to shed your blood and our blood for the benefit of the Allied plutocrats, for the benefit of the Rockefeller-Morgan kaiserism.

We don't want war. We want peace with you American and British fellow-workers! Don't you want peace with us? Don't you want to go home?

The war is over, but a new war is starting. This new war is the class war. The oppressed of all countries are rising against the oppressors, because the war has brought so much distress and so much sufferings to the poor that they can suffer no longer. Do you realize that you are shedding your blood in the interests of the oppressors and not of the oppressed? Do you realize that you are to defend oppression and exploitation and that you are to give your very lives for the interests of those who are now, after the fall of the Kaiser, the only kaisers in the world?

Do you want to sacrifice your lives in order that the capitalists may obtain a greater hold on our class, the workers? Of course not!

Demand to go home. Hold meetings in your regiments, form Soldiers' Councils, and force your demands on your governments and your officers. If you are convinced in the justness of the cause of labor then come over to our side and we will give you a hearty welcome into the ranks of those who are fighting for the emancipation of labor.

THE GROUP OF ENGLISH SPEAKING COMMUNISTS.

II. WHY DON'T YOU RETURN HOME?

To the American and British Soldiers:

Comrades.—The war is over, why are you not returning home? The people in England and America went nearly mad with joy when the long hoped for peace at last arrived. But why is there no peace for you, and for us? President Wilson and his colleagues are in Europe, the other Allied governments have also appointed their delegates, and soon the Peace Conference will assemble. But in the meantime you are still condemned to fight and die, and war with all its horrors is raging in Russia.

For many long, weary agonizing months, perhaps years, your old folks, your wives, your little ones have been overwhelmed with anxiety about you. Now in their innocence their anxiety has been turned into joyful expectation of your return. Can you not picture them—every knock, every footstep they hear makes their hearts leap in the belief that it is someone bringing tidings of your homecoming. But your dear ones will wait in vain. Your masters continue to drive you through the valley of death, and you do not know, but that your bodies may rot in the mud and blood of the battlefield. Don't you want to mingle with your loved ones again?

The war is over. Why don't you go home?

For over four years your governments have kept you at war, and have condemned millions of your fellow citizens to death, and millions more to a fate worse than death. You made these fearful sacrifices for what you were led to believe to be the defense of Europe against the domination of the kaiser, and once and for all to relieve the world from the crushing burden of armaments; from the menace of Prussian militarism.

Well, this menace is removed. Prussian militarism is crushed. The kaiser is a fugutive. The German workers have risen in revolt and have delivered a death blow to the power of the reactionary Junker class.

Why, then, are you still fighting? Above all, why are you in Russia?

The help of the Allied governments against Germany was never desired by Russia. It is now quite unnecessary. It was never intended that the Allied troops in Russia were to fight Germans. This is perfectly obvious now since the war with

Germany is apparently over, and yet the war against the Russian people still continues. Why? The reason is not far to seek.

The workers and peasants in Russia have done what your rulers fear you will do; they have swept the whole — class of parasites, courtiers, landlords, and capitalists out of power, and have taken possession of the land and the means of production for the use of the whole people. The Russian people refuse to be the slaves of an idle class any longer. They are constructing a new order of society in which the products of the labor will go to those who work. The spirit which animates the Russian people has spread westward, and now the Austrian, Hungarian, and German people have overthrown their rulers, and are rapidly traveling along the same lines as the workers of Russia. It is the awakening of the real democracy that we are witnessing today. The common workers in field, factory, and mine are asserting their right and power to rule, and be masters of their own destiny.

Your masters see that the spirit of revolt is spreading to your countries. In both England and America the idea of Bolshevism is making rapid headway. Great labor demonstrations frequently take place at which the workers demand that the means of wealth production shall be taken over by the workers. At these meetings strong protests are expressed against the invasion of Russia. Your masters know that the source and center of the revolutionary world movement is Russia, and they are determined therefore to crush it out, and remove the menace to their power. That is why you are here. That is why your masters will not permit you to rejoin your loved ones who are eagerly looking forward to your return.

You see that the war has now been converted into a gigantic conflict between labor and capital. It is a conflict between progress and reaction. A conflict between those who are inaugerating a new area of social and economic liberty for the toiling masses, and those who desire to retain the present sordid commercial system, with its sweating, poverty and war. And you who obey the orders of your governments are fighting to maintain the old order, you are fighting on the side of reaction against the forces of labor and progress.

Is this worth dying for? Do you really desire to bleed and die in order that capitalism may continue? Say no!

Form Soldiers' Councils in each regiment, and demand of

your governments, demand of your officers to be sent home. Refuse to shoot your fellow workers in Russia—refuse to crush our workers' revolution.

The Group of English Speaking Communists.

III. PARLIAMENT OR SOVIET

To American and British Soldiers:

You are told that you are fighting for democracy. But what kind of democracy are you fighting for? On one side is the Russian Socialist Federated Soviet Republic, on the other side the capitalist "democracies" of England, France and the United States.

The fact is clear, and you have to choose between two existing systems of management of public life—by the workers for the workers; or by the workers and the capitalist for the capitalists. The political system under which you live appears to give the right to control public affairs to the people. But who actually controls affairs in your countries? Is it not the Morgans and Rockefellers, the Devenports, Rhondas or men like these; big business men, capitalists and financiers. At elections they make fine promises, but when they are returned do nothing, and when some petty reform is demanded they wonder where the money is to come from. If the workers get more insistent in their demands these so called representatives of the people will call out troops to shoot the people down, as they did at Ludlow, Colorado, Tonypandy, Wales, and Dublin.

In our democracy only the workers have a voice, only those that produce the useful things decide how to enjoy the results of their common efforts. We are a commonwealth of fellow-workers and we don't want parasites and their supporters to interfere with our affairs.

This kind of democracy is not to the liking of those who wish to live upon the labor of others. Being a minority they want a democracy that secures the rule of the few over the many and you are made to fight for this kind of "democracy."

You may argue since we have general suffrage it is our own stupidity if we elect the wrong representatives to Parliament and we are going to change this gradually.

But even if it was possible to secure a majority of the right people in Parliament, this would not help you out since Parliament is only one of the institutions of capitalist power and not the most important either. There is the government with its bureaucratic machinery, the police, the judges, the army. In the Parliaments the representatives were allowed to talk, but it is the executive power, the government that acts. And this government in all countries is becoming more and more powerful, whereas the influence of the Parliament is on the decline. It would be absurd to believe that it will be possible to vote the capitalists out of power, out of their privileges. Parliament is a capitalist institution to further capitalist interests and if it ceases to further those interests it will be simply reorganized or abolished altogether.

More than that, political control is useless if it does not carry with it control of the means of life; in your country Parliament has only a very limited control of industry. The means of production are owned and controlled almost exclusively by capitalists. Those who own the means of life, own every thing. In Russia the means of life are owned by the whole nation, and the control is vested in the local and National Soviets. The Soviets are elected from the workers in the factories, mines or railroads as the case may be. We have thus direct and exclusive labor representation. Ours is a real labor republic, and when you come against us to overthrow the Soviets and establish the kind of democracy that exists in your countries, you are attempting to overthrow the rule of the workers and re-establish the rule of kings and capitalists.

Fellow workingmen, refuse to be the suppressors of your own class. Strive rather to establish your rule in your countries. Form soldiers' councils in your regiments. Send your representative to your officers and demand to be sent home. And when you get home remove the sham capitalist democracy reigning there, and establish true republics of labor as we have done in Russia.

THE GROUP OF ENGLISH SPEAKING COMMUNISTS

BOLSHEVIST PROPAGANDA

(Distributed among British and American Soldiers in North Russia)

IV. THE SOVIET GOVERNMENT AND PEACE

To British and American Soldiers:

Comrades — Now that the war with Germany is over, you no doubt, in common with your fellow-countrymen in France and at home, are demanding to be discharged from further military service, and to be allowed to return to your dear ones. Do you know that your comrades in France and at home are practically "raising hell" because demobilization is not proceeding quickly enough? Why are you not being sent home?

You are probably being told that peace cannot be restored in Europe until peace is restored in Russia, and that you are still required for that purpose. But who stands in the way of peace in Russia? Not the Soviet government.

The Soviet government has made repeated offers to the Allied governments no discuss peace. In November last through the medium of neutral governments it informed the Allies of its readiness and willingness to open negotiations. On the occasion of the departure of the Swedish consul from Russia the Soviet government requested him to convey to the Allied governments its desire to discuss peace. At the last All-Russian Convention of Workers', Soldiers' and Peasants' Deputies, the supreme parliament of Russia, a resolution was carried instructing the Soviet government to offer to negotiate peace with the Allies. This resolution was telegraphed far and wide. Finally a letter was sent to President Wilson personally when he arrived in Europe, to the same effect. No reply was received to any of these offers. Towards the end of December Reuter's Agency sent out a message to the effect that the peace offers of the Soviet government had been received, but as the Allies did not recognize the Bolsheviks, no reply would be sent.

In the meantime, however, the workers and soldiers in your home countries had discovered the real reason for the Allied armed intervention in Russia. They saw through the lies and calumny spread by the capitalist press about the Bolsheviks. They know that intervention was undertaken for the purpose of overthrowing the working class government, and restoring the reign of monarchy and capitalism. There is now a tremendous agitation which is taking on a revolutionary character in your home countries against the war on Russia. Huge protest meetings of workers are held in the big cities under the motto "Hands off Russia!" Strikes have broken out in the mines and railroads, and in some places riots have taken place in which workers and police have been injured. The strongest agitation against the continuation of the war on Russia is carried on by the soldiers. Discipline in the army at home has completely gone. Soldiers are parading the streets demanding immediate demobilization. In

Aldershot, the largest military camp in England, there were huge demonstrations of soldiers shouting: "You want to send us to Russia, but we won't go!"

In order to allay the storm of popular indignation the Allied governments sent out a statement in which they expressed their deep concern and sympathy for the sad plight in which the Russian people found themselves. They expressed their keen desire to assist Russia to get out of its difficulties. They had no wish to interfere in the internal politics of Russia, they said, nor endeavor to impose any particular kind of government on the Russian people. They definitely declared that they recognized the Russian revolution, and would under no circumstances support any counter-revolutionary attempts. They invited all the political groups which had achieved or were striving to achieve governmental power in Russia to meet Allied representatives on the Prince Islands in the Sea of Marmora in order to submit their claims. They suggested in the meantime that any armistice should be arranged between the warring sections, and demanded that the Soviet government should withdraw its troops from those territories outside of European Russia.

If this were a sincere offer of peace it would have been communicated to the Soviet government through the usual diplomatic channels. But it was not even addressed to the Russian government, but sent out by wireless for anybody to read who cared to take notice of it. The Allies still refuse to recognize the Soviet government. The other political groups referred to are the counter-revolutionaries Tchaikovsky, Admiral Kolchak, and Generals Denikin and Krasnoff. In inviting them the Allies place them on the same level as the government of Russia. The Allies have been, and are still, helping the counter-revolution. That is what you American and British soldiers are here for. In demanding an armistice with these, and the withdrawal of the Soviet troops, the Allies demand that the Red Army give up the fight just when it is beating the Tsarist counted-revolutionaries hands down. It is not a peace offer, but a demand to the Bolsheviks to surrender. These conditions were attached to the invitation, as the London "Times" frankly stated, with the expectation that the Soviet government would refuse it. The Allied governments would then be able to say to their people: "You see, we have offered peace to the Bolsheviks, but they refuse. There is nothing else for us but to go on with the war."

But it does not say much for the cuteness of the Allied governments if it imagined that the Soviet government would walk into the trap so clumsily laid. As a matter of fact the tables have been turned. The Soviet government in the note published below accepts almost all the conditions attached to the Allies invitation and announces its readiness to meet the Allied representatives wherever and whenever they desire. It is now the turn of the Allied governments to show whether they desire to discuss peace with the Soviet government or not.

Document No. 12

SOVIET'S NOTE TO ALLIED GOVERNMENTS

To the Government of Great Britain, France, Italy, Japan, and the United States of North America:

The Russian Soviet government has learned from a press telegram of an alleged invitation from the Entente Powers to all the de facto governments in Russia, calling upon them to send delegates to a conference to the Prince Islands.

Having received no invitation and learning from press radios that the absence of a reply is being interpreted as a refusal to answer the invitation, the Russian Soviet government wishes to remove from its line of action every possibility of misrepresentation. Taking into consideration further that its acts are being systematically presented by the foreign press in a false light, the Russian Soviet government takes this opportunity to state its attitude quite clearly and openly.

Although the situation of Soviet Russia is becoming every day more and more favorable both from a military and interior point of view, the Russian Soviet government places such value on the conclusion of an agreement which will put an end to the hostilities that it is ready to enter immediately into negotiations to that end, and even, as it has so often before declared, to pay the price of serious sacrifices under the express condition that the future development of the Soviet Republic will not be endangered.

Considering that its enemies derive their force of resistance solely from the help given them by the Entente Powers, and that these are consequently the only real adversaries with whom it has to deal, the Russian Soviet government states herewith to the Entente Powers the points on which it would consider possible such sacrifices in order to put an end to every difference with these powers.

Seeing the special importance assigned in the press, and also in the repeated declarations made by the representatives of the Entente governments to the question of the Russian state loans, the Russian government declares itself in the first place ready to make a concession on this point to the demands of the Entente governments. It does not refuse to recognize its financial obligations towards its creditors belonging to the Entente Powers whereas the details of the realization of this point must become the object of special agreements as a result of the proposed negotiations.

Further, seeing the difficult financial situation of the Russian Soviet Republic and the unsatisfactory state of its credit abroad, the Russian Soviet government proposes to guarantee the interests with raw material which will be enumerated in the suggested agreements.

Thirdly, seeing the great interest which has always been shown by foreign capital for the exploitation of Russia's natural riches, the Russian Soviet government is disposed to grant concessions upon mines, forests, and so on, to citizens of the Entente Powers, under conditions which must be carefully determined so that the economic and social order of Soviet Russia should not suffer from the internal rule of these concessions.

The fourth point upon which the Russian Soviet government finds it possible to negotiate with the Entente Powers is the question of territorial concessions. Seeing that the Russian Soviet government is not determined to exclude at any price from these negotiations the discussion of eventual annexations of Russian territory by the Entente Powers, the Russian Soviet government adds further that in its opinion, by annexations is understood the maintenance in some regions formerly making part of the old Russian Empire with the exclusion of Poland and Finland, of armed forces of the Entente, or maintained at the expense of the Entente, or enjoying the military, technical, financial, or any other support of these same powers.

As regard the second, third, and fourth points, the extent of the concessions that can be expected from the Russian Soviet government will depend upon its military situation towards the Entente Powers which at the present period is ameliorating itself every day. On the Northern front the Soviet troops have just re-conquered Shenkursk, on the Eastern front having temporarily lost Perm they have re-captured Ufa, Starlitamak, Belebey, Orenburg, and Uralsk, the railway communications with Central Asia being now in their hands. On the Southern front they have recently taken the important railway stations of Povorino, Alexikovo, Uriopino, Talovaya, Kalach, Boguchar, the railways of the region thus passing into their power, whilst from the Southwest the Ukrainian Soviet troops moving from Lougansk are threatening Krasnoff's rear. In the Ukraine the Soviet troops of that republic have taken Kharkof, Ekaterinoslav, Poltava, Kremenschug, Chernigoff, Ovruch, as well as numerous other less important towns. White-Russia, Lithuania, Lettland have almost completely passed into the hands of the Soviet troops of these republics together with the large towns of Minsk, Vilna, Riga, Dvinsk, Mitau, Windau and others.

The remarkable consolidation of the internal situation of Soviet Russia is shown by the negotiations with the Russian Soviet government begun by members of the previous Constituent Assembly whose representatives Rakitnikoff, chairman of their Congress, Sviatitsky, secretary, Volsky, Khmelev, Burevoy, Tchernenkoff, Antonoff, all members of the Central Committee of the Social Revolutionary Party, arrived yesterday, February 3d, in Moscow, these well-known social revolutionaries having with great force pronounced themselves against Entente intervention in Russia. The amelioration of the relations between the Soviet government and those elements of Russian society hitherto hostile is being illustrated by the change of attitude of the Menesheviks whose conference has likewise protested against Entente intervention and whose paper "Vperiod" (Forward) appears now in Moscow. The growing internal order is seen by the suppression of the district extraordinary commissions.

As to the false news of the foreign press concerning alleged disorders in Petrograd and elsewhere these are, from beginning to end, only fiction. Emphasizing once more that the situation of Soviet Russia will necessarily influence the extent of the sacrifices to which it will consent, the Russian Soviet government nevertheless maintains its proposition to negotiate upon the points enumerated above.

As to the frequent complaints of the Entente press about the Russian revolutionary international propaganda, the Russian Soviet government, whilst pointing out the fact that it cannot restrain the liberty of the revolutionary press, declares its readiness in case of necessity to include in a general agreement with the Entente Powers the pledge to refrain from any interferenc in their internal affairs.

On the indicated basis the Russian Soviet government is disposed to begin negotiations immediately whether on Princes Island or elsewhere, with the Entente Powers collectively or else with some of them separately, or else with some Russian political groups, according to the desires of the Entente Powers. The Russian Soviet government asks to name without delay the place to which its representatives are to be sent, as well as the date of the meeting and the route to be followed.

People's Commissary for Foreign Affairs:

TCHITCHERIN.

Moscow, February 4, 1919.

The acceptance of the Allies' invitation has by no means been prompted by the mere desire to score a diplomatic success. Nor must it be taken as a sign of weakness. As the official note of Tchitcherin points out in detail, the military position of the Red Army is immensely favorable; and all the signs are that the counter-revolutionary forces are on the verge of utter defeat. The acceptance of the invitation is prompted by the earnest desire of the Soviet government to avoid further bloodshed, and to bring peace to Russia, so that she may have the opportunity of proceeding with the work of constructing the new Socialist order.

In accepting the invitation the Soviet government was under no delusions as to the nature of the people they will have to meet, or the business they will have to transact. It knows perfectly well that just as it is impossible for a tiger to master his instinct, so it is impossible for capitalist governments to be guided by any other motive than that of serving the interests of the exploiting class. It knows that the Allies' ardent avowals of friendship for the Russian people, and their profuse offers of assistance are only worthy screens behind which to conceal their eagerness to lay their hands upon the undeveloped resources of Russia.

With its rough revolutionary candor, therefore, the Soviet government completely disregards the silk and suavity, the posing and hypocrisy of traditional diplomacy, and frankly says to the Allies: "Never mind sympathy and good wishes, you may cut that out; we make you a purely business proposition, we want peace and are prepared to pay for it. You want us to repay the Tsar's loans, you want concessions on our forests, our mines, on railway construction — very well, we are prepared to consider it; *name your price.*" What can be more fair or outspoken than this?

It is for the Allies to accept or refuse. So far no reply has been received, and the war goes on.

British and American soldiers! You can see now who stands in the way of peace. It is the capitalist governments of your countries, who compel you to undergo the horrors of war, and who keep you away from your loved ones who are yearning for your return. It is they, and not the Bolsheviks, who are bringing ruin and anarchy into Russia. It is they who maintain the civil war in Russia, for without the support which they are giving through you, the counter-revolutionaries would long ago have been crushed, and normal life restored in Russia. Do not permit yourselves to be deceived by the lies of your officers. Your country-men at home, soldiers as well as civilians, are violently opposed to the attempt to crush the Russian workers' revolution. Their protests have so far been so strong as to compel your government to pretend to desire peace. You can help to make the desire real, by refusing any longer to do the dastardly work you have been brought here to do. Why, if you refuse to fight, then peace is made, and there is no more to it! That is sense, is it not?

Your fellow-workers at home have given up their blind obedience to the capitalist and military class; they are going to dictate the policy of the governments. Are you going to lag behind? You, too, wake up, be men, and we shall soon sweep away the reign of capitalist exploitation and plunder!

THE GROUP OF ENGLISH-SPEAKING COMMUNISTS.

Document No. 13

A UKRAINIAN SOVIET MESSAGE TO GREECE

("Soviet Russia," Nov. 1, 1919 issue, page 22)

To the Ministry Of Foreign Affairs, at Athens:

The units of the regular Greek army operating in conjunction with French subjects have continued to occupy the territory of the Black Sea coast of the Ukrainian Socialist Soviet Republic. Of late they occupied Aleckki and Bereslav. This intrusion on foreign territory without any legitimate reason and without a formal declaration of war is considered by all international law as an act of brigandage. If the Greek government supposes that its alliance with France makes it immune against the consequences of its policy of gross violence towards the workers and peasants of the Ukraine, and that it is immune against any punishment which it may thus incur, the Greek government is harboring illusions. Before long it will have to yield to the judgment of the Greek workers and peasants and render account for the violations committed not only against them, but also toward the workers and peasants of other countries, in which the Greek army, playing the part of mediæval mercenaries, is shedding its blood in defense of the interests of international capitalism. The Ukrainian Socialist Soviet government is aware of the methods of agitation to which the Greek government resorts in order to encourage the Greek soldiers who refuse to fight against the workers and peasants of the Ukraine. It is acquainted with the nationalistic and religious campaign which the Greek government is conducting in order to slander the Soviet power as persecuting religion and the Greek elements in Southern Ukraine. If they have in mind the Greek speculators and stock exchange brokers, whose system of exploitation includes the coast of the Black Sea belonging to the Ukraine and Russia — to fight against them as well as against all exploiters of the Ukraine without distinction of nationality is the principal aim of every Socialist government. So far as the poor Greek fishermen are concerned who constitute the population of the coastlines of the Ukraine and Crimea or the 150,000 poor Greek peasants who live in Transcaucasia, their sympathies are entirely on the side of the Soviet power, and all attempts of the Greek bourgeoisie to divert the attention of the Greek fishermen and landless peasants from the class struggle, by means of panhellenic propaganda, have thus far been and will remain futile. Nevertheless, the Greek government, not sufficiently cognizant of these circumstances, not only continues to interfere with the affairs of the Greek peasants and workers of the Black Sea coast, but it even has the audacity to fit out special missions which it intends to send to the Ukraine and Southern Russia for the purpose of stirring up nationalistic passions and civil strife. Thus for example, through their efforts the agencies throughout Europe have published the following telegram emanating from Constantinople:

> "With the sanction of the Holy Synod the Greek government decided to send to Russia, simultaneously with its troops, which are completely ready to embark, three bishops, four archimandrites, and forty priests, with a coterie of clergymen who are well versed in the Russian lauguage and who possess the gift of oratory. The aim of the expedition is to exercise a religious influence over the Russians."

It is by no means the intention of the Ukrainian Socialist Soviet government to take note of the blissful ignorance in which both the Greek government and the Holy Synod yet remain as regards the new intellectual level of the "Moujiks" of the Ukraine, who have been robbed and fooled for centuries by the Greek monks who used to come from Mount Athos or Constantinople and who fooled and robbed them in the name of Christ. But in order to avoid any misunderstanding, the provisional government of the Ukraine deems it its duty to warn the Greek government that it declares the eloquent bishops, archimandrites and priests, with all the clergymen who accompany them, to be agents provocateurs and spies who will be arrested and immediately arraigned before the revolutionary court-martial. The provisional government of the Ukraine at the same time calls the attention of the Greek government that its policy of military intervention in the affairs of the Ukraine must needs affect the destiny of the Greek bourgeoisie residing on Ukrainian territory.

President of the Ukrainian Provisional Workers' and Peasants' Government:

People's Commisary for Foreign Affairs,

RAKOVSKY.

Kharkov, February 26th.

Document No. 14

OFFICIAL CORRESPONDENCE BETWEEN SOVIET RUSSIA AND POLAND

("Soviet Russia," October 25, 1919 issue, page 11-12)

a. THE POLISH SOCIALIST PARTY TO THE COMMUNIST PARTY OF RUSSIA

"Izvestia," Moscow, *April* 15, 1919.

To the Central Committee of the Communist Labor Party of Russia:

"We deem it our duty, making use of this opportunity, to convey to the Central Committee of the Communist Labor Party of Russia a detailed formulation of the position taken by the Polish Socialist Party, which is the expression of the views and tendencies of the broad masses of the Polish proletariat.

1. We consider the full sovereignty and independence of Poland a necessary condition for the success of our class struggle for Socialism, an indispensible presupposition for the develop-

ment of Polish culture and, consequently, of the culture of the Polish proletariat as well. We shall consider any attempts on the part of the Soviet troops at an invasion of Polish territory as an encroachment upon the independence of the country and shall repel such attempts with firm determination.

2. The same refers to the attempts at interference on the part of the Soviet government in the internal affairs of Poland. Such attempt is, beyond contradiction, the fact of the formation of a Polish Soviet government in Vilna, as well as the assistance rendered by the Russian Soviet government to the Communist Labor Party of Poland. We categorically insist on the liquidation of the pseudo-Polish government now existing in Vilna, of which the Polish working class knows nothing, and which it had absolutely no share in producing.

3. The question of the boundaries of the Polish Republic we wish to solve by way of self-determination of the population living in the disputed territories and, in the first place, in Lithuania and White Russia. We insist upon the withdrawal from these territories of all foreign troops and the carrying out of the people's vote under the conditions of full political freedom. The will of the working class of Lithuania, alleged to be already expressed in favor of a union with Russia on the basis of federation, we consider as a fiction, because of the fact that no popular vote had been held in Lithuania and White Russia.

Being convinced of the fact that the Russian Workers' Party will not be indifferent to the opinion of the Polish proletariat, we are sending fraternal greetings to all workers and all Socialists.

The Central Workers' Committee of the Polish Socialist Party:

M. NIEDZIALKOWSKI.

B. THE RUSSIAN SOVIET GOVERNMENT TO THE POLISH REPRESENTATIVE

March 24, 1919.

To the Citizen Delegate Extraordinary of the Government of the Polish Republic:

DEAR SIR, ALEXANDER YANOVICH: The letter of the Central Workers' Committee of the Polish Socialist Party to the Central Committee of the Communist Labor Party of Russia, which was handed to me, and to which the latter has called my attention, touches upon some questions in regard to which I consider it necessary to express myself in the name of the government of the Russian Republic. I beg to request of you that my declarations be brought to the knowledge of the Polish Republic and of the Polish people.

With reference to point one of the letter of the Central Workers' Committee I must declare that no attempts at invasion of the Polish territory by the Soviet armies were or are being contemplated, and the protest of the Central Workers' Committee is a result of absolutely false information.

With reference to point two of the same letter I declare that, so far as my knowledge goes, no Polish government is in existence in Vilna, and that in this case again the Central Workers' Committee has undoubtedly been misinformed.

As regards point three, relating to the eastern boundaries of Poland, we find it fully expedient that in this matter a vote of the toiling people should be taken in the respective territories under the condition of the withdrawal of foreign troops, and we shall defend this standpoint before the Lithuanian-White-Russian Republic, while the details of this plan may be elaborated during further negotiations of the interested parties with our co-operation, and we think that no difficulties will be encountered on the part of the Lithuanian-White-Russian Republic.

I beg of you, dear sir, to accept the assurance of my highest esteem.

Chicherin,
People's Commissaire for Foreign Affairs.

Document No. 15

Decree Relating to Conscientious Objectors

(Soviet Russia, October 11, 1919 issue, page 16)

Decree of the Soviet of Commissaries of the People, Dated 4th of January, 1919

Freedom from Military Service on the Ground of Religious Convictions

(1) People who on account of their religious convictions are unable to undertake military service are obliged, in accordance with the decrees of the National Tribunal, to substitute for it an equal term of service to their fellow creatures by such service as work in hospitals for contagious diseases, or some other work of public utility to be chosen by the individual concerned.

(2) The National Tribunal in deciding questions as to the substitution of civil work for military service is to be assisted by "The Joint Council of Religious Groups and Communes of Moscow," for each individual case; the Joint Council to report as to whether the religious conviction concerned makes military service impossible, as well as on the sincerity and honesty of the applicant.

(3) In exceptional cases the Joint Council of Religious Groups and Communes may have recourse to the All-Russian Central Executive Committee, with a view to securing complete freedom from service, without the substitution of any other service, if it can be shown that such substitution is incompatible with religious convictions; the proof to be taken from writings on the question and also from the personal life of the individual concerned.

NOTE.— Steps to secure freedom from service may be initiated by the individual concerned or by the Joint Council, and the latter can require the case to be tried by the National Tribunal of Moscow.

(Signed) *President of the Soviet Commissaries:*
LENIN.
Commissary of Justice:
KURSKY.
Chancellor of State:
BONCH-BRUYEVITCH.
Secretary:
FOTNIEVA.

Dated from The Kremlin, Moscow, January 4, 1919.
(Translation of the Original on Opposite Page.)

Document No. 16

UKRAINIAN SOCIALIST SOVIET REPUBLIC

PROLETARIANS OF ALL COUNTRIES, UNITE! DOWN WITH THE POGROM-MAKERS!

COMRADES.— The czarist government, which protected the interests of the capitalists and landed proprietors, always resorted to Jew-baiting for the purpose of strengthening its power.

The czarist government organized hundreds of Jewish pogroms; it spent millions of the people's money for the purpose of arousing national animosity.

Through the oppression of nationalities it endeavored to divide the toiling masses of different nationalities, and hindered the workers of different nationalities from joining hands for a united struggle against their common enemy: the autocracy, the landed proprietors and the capitalists.

And now Grigoriev's rascals incite their robber bands against the defenseless Jews, vent on them all their anger, and torture women, old men and children.

Comrades! Those who direct and inspire these bands and gangs — Grigoriev and his like, are the same protectors of the interests of the capitalists and landed proprietors. *They have the same traitorous aim: To divide the working class and to break the united proletarian front.*

The black hundred and the Grigorievists, in union with the world bourgeoisie, are trying to drown the Communist revolution in the blood of innocent victims, in the blood of poverty-stricken Jews. Jewish pogroms are the straw at which the outworn world is clutching in order to save its capital.

Comrades, Red-Guardists, Workers and Peasants! Do not be misled by the scoundrels and provocature who sold themselves to the bourgeoisie and nobility and who urge you to make pogroms. Over the corpses of the Jewish poor the capitalists and landed proprietors are trying to find a way to the millions and the houses which they lost.

Together with the torrents of blood of the Jewish poor will swim away the *lands* from the peasants and *the factories and workshops* from the workers, will swim away the freedom and the power from the toilers, which have been won at such cost.

Comrades, Red Guardists, be firm, do not yield to provocation. Let your answer to the Black Hundred agitation be the brave and proud call:

Down with the pogrom-makers!

Hold firmly in your hands the red banner — the banner of struggle and freedom.

Long live the International Workers' and Peasants' Army.

Long live the Ukrainian Socialist Soviet Republic.

Long live the power of the workers of all countries and of all nations.

ODESSA COMMITTEE OF THE COMMUNIST (BOLSHEVIST)
PARTY OF UKRAINE.

(*Published by the Department of Soviet Propaganda attached to the Executive Committee of the Odessa Council of Workers' Deputies.*)

Document No. 17

POLITICAL PROPAGANDA AND EDUCATIONAL ACTIVITY IN THE VILLAGES

("Soviet Russia," July 12, 1919, pages 13–14)

A RESOLUTION OF THE 8TH CONVENTION OF THE RUSSIAN COMMUNIST LABOR PARTY

Bearing in mind the necessity of a firm and lasting alliance between the proletariat and the poorest peasants and peasants of medium means; also bearing in mind the political darkness, the general ignorance and the low standard of agricultural knowledge in the villages, which are serious obstacles and which condemn the poorest peasantry and the peasantry of medium means to poverty and stagnation -the Communist Party is compelled to pay the most serious attention to the matter of education in the villages in the broadest sense of the word.

For the purpose of educational activities in the villages the following elements must co-operate:

1. Communistic propaganda;
2. General education;
3. Agricultural education.

1. Political propaganda in the villages must be carried on among the literate peasants as well as among the illiterate.

The propaganda among the literate must consist first of all in the distribution of popular literature and newspapers of a communistic character, specially prepared for this purpose. Such literature must be sold at very low prices in schools, reading huts and in all Soviet stores.

It is necessary to strive for the organization of reading rooms in every school with a political department and that such reading rooms should be in every village a people's house; and, in places where there are not such people's houses, popular political books must be an essential part of every reading hut.

The courses for children, and especially those for adults — the academic as well as the special (agricultural for instance), must include: (1) popular history of culture from a scientific socialistic point of view and with a specially prepared part devoted to Russian history and to the history of the Great Russian revolution; (2) the interpretation of the Soviet constitution. For both of these courses proper text-books are to be prepared immediately.

The teachers are obliged to look upon themselves as upon agents not only of a general but also of a communistic education.

In this respect they must be subjected to the control of their immediate heads, as well as of the local party organizations.

Moving picture houses, theatres, concerts, exhibitions, etc., inasmuch as they will reach the villages (and all effort is to be exerted for this purpose), must be utilized for communistic propaganda directly, i. e., through the upkeep of these and also by way of combining these with lectures and meetings.

Departments of public education, provincial and county, with the assistance and under the control of the local party organizations, must organize collegiums of propagandists who are partly permanent, i. e., attached to their locality; and partly traveling, i. e., such as will cover a more or less wide section.

In the big city centers it is necessary that the party organizations should form collegiums of propagandists-instructors (in accordance with the local organs of the Commissariat of Education), who would carry on a traveling propaganda directly among the masses, and also instruct the less experienced comrades in the localities.

In this connection the convention calls special attention to the possibility of utilizing the work of the regiments of industrial workers, who are under the direction of the All-Russian Soviet of Professional Unions.

For the illiterate, periodical readings must be arranged in the schools, on the premises of the volost Soviet of Deputies, in the reading huts, etc., for which purpose the departments of public education, with the assistance of the local party organizations, create special circles of readers, including the local teaching staff, with obligatory readings by the literate elements. The subjects of the readings should be the decrees and administrative order of the Soviets, together with specially prepared popular interpretations sent out by the centers (party or Soviet centers), also stories from readers, which are being constantly revised. It would be advisable to accompany such reading with illustrations by way of motion pictures or stereopticon slides; also with a reading of fiction, as well as concerts for the purpose of attracting large audiences.

2. General education — within school and outside of school including artistic education: theatres, concerts, motion pictures, exhibitions, etc.), endeavoring not only to shed the light of a varied knowledge on the dark villages, but primarly to aid in the

creation of self-consciousness and of a clear conception of things, must be closely connected with the communistic propaganda. There are not any forms of science and art which are not connected with the great ideas of communism and with the various tasks of creating communistic economy.

As far as the schools are concerned, the question of revising them on principles of continuity and labor has been decided. It is necessary to pay special attention to all forms of out-of-school education for adults. The party must by all means assist the Soviet authorities and the local population in the organization of a large system of community centers (people's houses), for which purpose the Soviet estates are to be used first of all. The community centers must be peasants' clubs for resting, for sensible amusements and broad enlightenment, general as well as communistic.

The Communist Party, permitting and encouraging the utilization of the knowledge of the specialists and other educated persons for conducting courses and for aiding in conducting communistic centers, must take care at the same time that the elements hostile to the Soviet power should not make use of the apparatus of general education and should not introduce in the form of literature, science and art any counter-revolutionary, or anti-social tendencies, and should not thereby paralyze the efforts of communistic propaganda.

3. The peasants feel keenly the need of agricultural education.

The Soviet estates, as well as the farm schools, must become the lighthouses of agricultural education. Agricultural institutions, organized and maintained by the People's Commissariat of Education, must be in closest contact with the agricultural institutions of the People's Commissariat of Agriculture.

There must not be any schools, colleges or any other educational organizations in the villages, which would not endeavor (in accordance with the principle of combining studies with productive labor) to function at the same time as an organization of a model husbandry — complete or in part.

Agricultural education must be carried on in such a way as to combine this with communistic ideas and it should serve as a pillar to the general effort of the party to reconstruct private establishments into one organized socialistic institution.

Propaganda among peasants must not be apart from life problems of agriculturists, but must be closely connected with the questions of rural economy.

The state school must be freed from all religious instruction and every attempt at counter-revolutionary propaganda under the guise of religious sermons must be thwarted.

But the constitution of Soviet Russia recognizes full freedom of religious propaganda for all citizens and this convention calls special attention to the absolute impossibility of any such restrictions of this right and even of a shadow of violence in the questions of religion. Persons, who encroach upon religious liberties of citizens of any creed, must be subjected to strict judgment.

"Northern Commune," April 6, 1919.

Document No. 18

SOVIET RUSSIA'S CODE OF LABOR LAWS

I. The Code of Labor Laws shall take effect from the moment of its publication in the Compilation of Laws and Regulations of the Workmen's and Peasants' Government. This code must be extensively circulated among the working class of the country by all the local organs of the Soviet government and be posted in a conspicuous place in all Soviet institutions.

II. The regulations of the Code of Labor Laws shall apply to all persons receiving remuneration for their work and shall be obligatory for all enterprises, institutions and establishments (Soviet, public, private and domestic), as well as for all private employers exploiting labor.

III. All existing regulations and those to be issued on questions of labor, of a general character (orders of individual establishments, instructions, rules of internal management, etc.,) as well as individual contracts and agreements, shall be valid only in so far as they do not conflict with this code.

IV. All labor agreements previously entered into, as well as all those which will be entered into in the future, in so far as they contradict the regulations of this code, shall not be considered valid or obligatory, either for the employees or the employers.

V. In enterprises and establishments where the work is carried on in the form of organized co-operation (section 6, Labor Division A of the present code) the wage earners must be allowed the widest possible self-government under the supervision of the Central Soviet authorities. On this basis alone can the working masses be successfully educated in the spirit of socialist and communal government.

VI. The labor conditions in the communal enterprises organized as well as supported by the Soviet institutions (agricultural and other communes) are regulated by special rules of the All-Russian Central Executive Committee and of the Council of People's Commissars, and by instructions of the People's Commissariat of Agriculture and labor.

The labor conditions of farmers on land assigned them for cultivation are regulated by the Code of Rural Laws.

The labor conditions of independent artisants are regulated by special rules of the Commissariat of Labor.

a. ARTICLE I

On Compulsory Labor

1. All citizens of the Russian Socialist Federated Soviet Republic, with the exceptions stated in sections 2 and 3, shall be subject to compulsory labor.

2. The following persons shall be exempt from compulsory labor:

(a) Persons under sixteen years of age;

(b) All persons over fifty years;

(c) Persons who have become incapacitated by injury or illness.

3. Temporarily exempt from compulsory labor are:

(a) Persons who are temporarily incapacitated owing to illness or injury, for a period necessary for their recovery.

(b) Women, for a period of eight weeks before and eight weeks after confinement.

4. All students shall be subject to compulsory labor at the schools.

5. The fact of permanent or temporary disability shall be certified after a medical examination by the Bureau of Medical Survey in the city, district or province, by accident insurance offices or agencies representing the former, according to the place of residence of the person whose disability is to be certified.

Note 1.— The rules on the method of examination of disabled workmen are appended hereto.

Note 2.— Persons who are subject to compulsory labor and are not engaged in useful public work may be summoned by the local Soviets for the execution of public work, on conditions determined by the Department of Labor in agreement with the local Soviets of trade unions.

6. Labor may be performed in the form of:
(a) Organized co-operation;
(b) Individual personal services;
(c) Individual special jobs.

7. Labor conditions in government (Soviet) establishments shall be regulated by tariff rules approved by the Central Soviet authorities through the People's Commissariat of Labor.

8. Labor conditions in all establishments (Soviet, nationalized, public and private) shall be regulated by tariff rules drafted by the trade unions, in agreement with the directors or owners of establishments and enterprises, and approved by the People's Commissariat of Labor.

Note.— In cases where it is impossible to arrive at an understanding with the directors or owners of establishments or enterprises, the tariff rules shall be drawn up by the trade unions and submitted for approval to the People's Commissariat of Labor.

9. Labor in the form of individual personal service or in the form of individual special jobs shall be regulated by tariff rules drafted by the respective trade unions and approved by the People's Commissariat of Labor.

b. ARTICLE II

The Right to Work

10. All citizens able to work have the right to employment at their vocations and for remuneration fixed for such class of work.

Note.— The district exchange bureaus of the Department of Labor Distribution may, by agreement with the respective unions, assign individual wage earners or groups of them to work at other trades if there is no demand for labor at the vocations of the persons in question.

11. The right to work belongs first of all to those who are subject to compulsory labor.

12. Of the classes exempt from compulsory labor, only those mentioned in subdivision "b" of section 2 have a right to work.

13. Those mentioned in subdivisions "a" and "c" of section 2 are absolutely deprived of the right to work, and those mentioned in section 3 temporarily deprived of the right to work.

14. All persons of the female sex, and those of the male sex under 18 years of age, shall have no right to work during night time or in those branches of industry where the conditions of labor are especially hard or dangerous.

Note.— A list of especially hard and health-endangering occupations shall be prepared by the Department of Labor Protection of the People's Commissariat of Labor, and shall be published in the month of January of each year in the Compilation of Laws and Regulations of the Workmen's and Peasants' Government.

c. ARTICLE III

Methods of Labor Distribution

15. The enforcement of the right to work shall be secured through the Department of Labor Distribution, trade unions, and through all the institutions of the Russian Socialist Federated Soviet Republic.

16. The assignment of wage earners to work shall be carried out through the Department of Labor Distribution.

17. A wage earner may be summoned to work, save by the Department of Labor Distribution, only when chosen for a position by a Soviet institution or enterprise.

18. Vacancies may be filled by election when the work offered requires political reliability or unusual special knowledge, for which the person elected is noted.

19. Persons engaged for work by election must register in the Department of Labor Distribution before they are accepted, but they shall not be subject to the rules concerning probation set forth in Article IV of the present code.

20. Unemployed persons shall be assigned to work through the Department of Labor Distribution in the manner stated in sections 21-30.

21. A wage earner who is not engaged on work at his vocation shall register in the local Department of Labor Distribution as unemployed.

22. Establishments and individuals in need of workers should apply to the local Department of Labor Distribution or its division (Correspondence Bureau) stating the condition of the work offered as well as the requirements which the workmen must meet (trade, knowledge, experience).

23. The Department of Labor Distribution, on receipt of the application mentioned in section 22, shall assign the persons meeting the requirements thereof in the order determined by the same.

24. An unemployed person has no right to refuse an offer of work at his vocation, provided the working conditions conform with the standards fixed by the respective tariff regulations, or in the absence of the same by the trade unions.

25. A wage worker engaged for work for a period of not more

than two weeks, shall be considered unemployed, and shall not lose his place on the list of the Department of Labor Distribution.

26. Should the local Department of Labor Distribution have no workers on its lists meeting the stated requirements, the application must be immediately sent to the District Exchange Bureau, and the establishment or individual offering the employment shall be simultaneously notified to this effect.

27. Whenever workers are required for work outside of their district, a roll-call of the unemployed registered in the Department of Labor Distribution shall take place, to ascertain who are willing to go; if a sufficient number of such should not be found, the Department of Labor Distribution shall assign the lacking number from among the unemployed in the order of their registration, provided that those who have dependents must not be given preference, before single persons.

28. If in the Department of Labor Distribution, within the limits of the district, there be no workmen meeting the requirements, the District Exchange Bureau has the right, upon agreement with the respective trade union, to send unemployed of another class approaching as nearly as possible the trade required.

29. An unemployed person who is offered work outside his vocation shall be obliged to accept it, on the understanding, if he so wishes, that this be only temporary, until he receives work at his vocation.

30. A wage earner who is working outside his specialty, and who has stated his wish that this be only temporary, shall retain his place on the register on the Department of Labor Distribution until he gets work at his vocation.

31. Private individuals violating the rules of labor distribution set forth in this article shall be punished by the order of the local board of the Department of Labor Distribution by a fine of not less than 300 rubles or by arrest for not less than one week. Soviet establishments and officials violating these rules on labor distribution shall be liable to criminal prosecution.

d. ARTICLE IV

Probation Periods

32. Final acceptance of workers for permanent employment shall be preceded by a period of probation of not more than six days; in Soviet institutions the probation period shall be two weeks for unskilled and less responsible work and one month for skilled and responsible work.

33. According to the results of the probation the wage earner shall either be given a permanent appointment, or rejected with payment for the period of probation in accordance with the tariff rates.

34. The results of the probation (acceptance or rejection) shall be communicated to the Department of Labor Distribution.

35. Up to the expiration of the probation period, the wage earner shall be considered as unemployed, and shall retain his place on the eligible list of the Department of Labor Distribution.

36. A person who, after probation, has been rejected, may appeal against this decision to the union of which he is a member.

37. Should the trade union consider the appeal mentioned in the preceding section justified, it shall enter into negotiations with the establishment or person who has rejected the wage earner, with the request to accept the complainant.

38. In case of failure of negotiations mentioned in section 37, the matter shall be submitted to the local Department of Labor, whose decision shall be final and subject to no further appeal.

39. The Department of Labor may demand that the person or establishment who have without sufficient reason rejected a wage earner provide the latter with work. Furthermore, it may demand that the said person or establishment compensate the wage earner according to the tariff rates for the time lost between his rejection and his acceptance pursuant to the decision of the Department of Labor.

e. ARTICLE V

Transfer and Discharge of Wage Earners

40. The number of wage earners in all enterprises, establishments, or institutions employing paid labor can take place only if it is required in the interest of the business and by the decision of the proper organ of management.

Note.— This rule does not apply to work with private individuals employing paid labor, if the work is of the subdivisions mentioned in "b" and "c" of section 6.

41. The transfer of a wage earner to other work within the enterprise, establishment or institution where he is employed may be ordered by the managing organs of said enterprise, establishment or institution.

42. The transfer of a wage earner to another enterprise,

establishment or institution situated in the same or in a different locality, may be ordered by the corresponding organ of management with the consent of the Department of Labor Distribution.

43. The order of an organ of management to transfer a wage earner as mentioned in section 40 may be appealed from to the respective Department of Labor (local or district) by the interested individuals or organizations.

44. The decision of the Department of Labor in the matter of the transfer of a wage earner may be appealed from by the interested parties to the District Department of Labor or to the People's Commissariat of Labor, whose decision in the matter in dispute is final and not subject to further appeal.

45. In case of urgent public work the District Department of Labor may, in agreement with the respective professional unions and with the approval of the People's Commissariat of Labor, order the transfer of a whole group of wage earners from the organization where they are employed to another situated in the same or in a different locality, provided a sufficient number of volunteers for such work cannot be found.

46. The discharge of wage earners from an enterprise, establishment or institution where they have been employed is permissible in the following cases:

(a) In case of complete or partial liquidation of the enterprise, establishment or institution, or of cancellation of certain orders or work;

(b) In case of suspension of work for more than a month;

(c) In case of expiration of term of employment or of completion of the job, if the work was of a temporary character;

(d) In case of evidence of unfitness for work, by special decision of the organs of management and subject to agreement with the respective professional unions.

(e) By request of the wage earner.

47. The organ of management of the enterprise, establishment or institution where a wage earner is employed, or the person for whom a wage earner is working must give the wage earner two weeks' notice of the proposed discharge, for the reasons mentioned in a, b and d of section 46, notifying simultaneously the local Department of Labor Distribution.

48. A wage earner discharged for the reasons mentioned in subdivisions "a," "b" and "d" of section 46 shall be considered

unemployed and entered as such on the lists of the Department of Labor Distribution and shall continue to perform his work until the expiration of the term of two weeks mentioned in the preceding section.

49. The order to discharge an employee for the reasons mentioned in subdivisions "a," "b" and "d" of section 46 may be appealed from by the interested persons to the Local Department of Labor.

50. The decision of the Local Department of Labor on the question of discharge may be appealed from by either party to the District Department of Labor, whose decision on the question in dispute is final and not subject to further appeal.

51. Discharge by request of the wage earner from enterprise, establishment or institution must be preceded by an examination of the reasons for the resignation by the respective organ of workmen's self-government (works and other committees.)

Note.— This rule does not apply to the resignation of a wage earner employed by an individual, if the work is of the character mentioned in subdivisions "b" and "c" of section 6.

52. If the organ of workers' self-government (works or other committee) after investigating the reasons for the resignation finds the resignation unjustified the wage earner must remain at work, but may appeal from the decision of the committee to the respective professional union.

53. A wage earner who quits work contrary to the decision of the Committee, pursuant to section 52, shall forfeit for one week the right to register with the Department of Labor Distribution.

54. Institutions and person employing paid labor shall inform in each case when a wage earner quits work the Local Department of Labor Distribution and the professional union of which the wage earner is a member, stating the date and the reason thereof.

f. ARTICLE VI

Remuneration of Labor

55. The remuneration of wage earners for work in enterprises, establishments and institutions employing paid labor, and the detailed conditions and order of payment shall be fixed by tariffs worked out for each kind of labor in the manner described in sections 7–9 of the present code.

56. All institutions working out the tariff rates must comply with the provisions of this article of the Code of Labor Laws.

57. In working out the tariff rates and determining the standard remuneration rates, all the wage earners of a trade shall be divided into groups and categories and a definite standard of remuneration shall be fixed for each of them.

58. The standard of remuneration fixed by the tariff rates must be at least sufficient to cover the minimum living expenses as determined by the People's Commissariat of Labor for each district of the Russian Socialist Federated Soviet Republic and published in the Compilation of Laws and Regulations of the Workmen's and Peasants' Government.

59. In determining the standard of remuneration for each group and category attention shall be given to the kind of labor, the danger of the conditions under which the work is performed, the complexity and accuracy of the work, the degree of independence and responsibility, as well as the standard of education and experience required for the performance of the work.

60. The remuneration of each wage earner shall be determined by his classification in a definite group and category.

61. The classification of wage earners into groups and categories within each branch of labor shall be done by special valuation commissions, local and central, established by the respective professional organizations.

Note.—The procedure of the valuation commissions shall be determined by the People's Commissariat of Labor.

62. The tariff regulations shall fix the standard of remuneration for a normal working day or for piece work, and particularly the remuneration for overtime work.

63. Remuneration for piece work shall be computed by dividing the daily tariff rate by the number of pieces constituting the production standard.

64. The standard remuneration fixed for overtime work shall not exceed time and a half of the normal remuneration.

65. Excepting the remuneration paid for overtime work done in the same or in a different branch of labor, no additional remuneration in excess of the standard fixed for a given group and category shall be permitted, irrespective of the pretext and form under which it might be offered and whether it be paid in only one or in several places of employment.

66. Persons working in several places must state in which place of employment they wish to receive their pay.

67. Persons receiving excessive remuneration, in violation of

section 65, shall be liable to criminal prosecution for fraud, and the remuneration received in excess of the normal (standard) may be deducted from subsequent payments.

68. From the remuneration of the wage earner may be deducted the excess remuneration received in violation of section 65, and the remuneration earned by the wage earner during his vacation; deduction may also be made for cessation of work.

69. No other deductions, except those mentioned in section 68, shall be permitted, irrespective of the form or pretext under which they might be made.

70. Payment of remuneration must not be made in advance.

71. If the work is steady, payment for the same must be made periodically, at least once in every fortnight. Remuneration for temporary work and for special jobs, provided the same continues at least for two weeks, shall be paid immediately upon completion of work.

72. Payments shall be made in money or in kind (lodgings, food supplies, etc.).

73. To make payments in kind special permission must be obtained from the Local Department of Labor which shall determine the rates jointly with the respective trade unions.

Note.— The rates thus determined must be based on the standard prices fixed by the respective institutions of the Soviet authority (valuation commissions of the Commissariat of Victuals, Land and Housing Department, Price Committee, etc.)

74. Payments must take place during working hours.

75. Payments must be made at the place of work.

76. The wage earner shall be paid only for actual work done. If a cessation of work is caused during the working day by circumstances beyond the control of the wage earner (through accident or through the fault of the administration), he shall be paid for the time lost on the basis of the daily tariff rates, if he does time work, or on the basis of his average daily earning, if he does piece work.

77. A wage earner shall be paid his wage during leave of absence (sections 106–107).

78. During illness of a wage earner the remuneration due him shall be paid as a subsidy from the hospital funds.

Note.— The manner of payment of the subsidy is fixed by rules appended hereto.

79. Unemployed shall receive a subsidy out of the funds for unemployed.

Note.— Rules concerning unemployed and the payment of subsidies to them are appended hereto.

80. Every wage earner must have a labor booklet in which all matters pertaining to the work done by him as well as the payments and subsidies received by him are entered.

Note.— Rules regarding labor booklets for wage earners are appended hereto.

g. ARTICLE VII

Working Hours

81. Working hours are regulated by the tariff rules made for each kind of labor, in the manner described in sections 7–9 of the present code.

82. The rules for working hours must conform with the provisions of this article of the Code of Labor Laws.

83. A normal working day shall mean the time fixed by the tariff regulations for the production of a certain amount of work.

84. The duration of a normal working day must in no case exceed eight hours for day work and seven hours for night work.

85. The duration of a normal day must not exceed six hours: (a) for persons under 18 years of age, and (b) in especially hard or health-endangering branches of industry (note section 14 of the present code).

86. During the normal working day time must be allowed for meals and for rest.

87. During recess machines, beltings and lathes must be stopped, unless this be impossible owing to technical conditions or in cases where these machines, beltings, etc., serve for ventilation, drainage, lighting, etc.

88. The time of recess fixed by section 86 is not included in the working hours.

89. The recess must take place not later than four hours after the beginning of the working day, and must continue not less than a half hour and not more than two hours.

Note.— Additional intermissions every three hours, and for not less than a half hour, must be allowed for working women nursing children.

90. The wage earners may use their free time at their own discretion. They shall be allowed during recess to leave the place of work.

91. In case the nature of the work is such that it requires a working day in excess of the normal, two or more shifts shall be engaged.

92. Where there are several shifts, each shift shall work the normal working hours; the change of shifts must take place during the time fixed by the rules of the internal management without interfering with the normal course of work.

93. As a general rule, work in excess of the normal hours (overtime work) shall not be permitted.

94. Overtime work may be permitted in the following exceptional cases:

(a) Where the work is necessary for the prevention of a public calamity or in case the existence of the Soviet government of the R. S. F. S. R. or human life is endangered;

(b) An emergency, public work in relation to water supply, lighting, sewerage or transportation, in case of accident or extraordinary interruption of their regular operations;

(c) When it is necessary to complete work which owing to unforseen or accidental delay due to technical condition of production, could not be completed during the normal working hours. If leaving the work uncompleted would cause damage to materials or machinery;

(d) On repairs or renewal of machine parts or construction work, wherever necessary to prevent stoppage of work by a considerable number of wage earners.

95. In the case described in subdivision C of section 94, overtime work is permissible only with the consent of the respective trade union.

96. For overtime work described in subdivision D of section 94 permission must be obtained from the local labor inspection, in addition to the permit mentioned in the preceding section.

97. No females and no males under eighteen years of age may do any overtime work.

98. The time spent on overtime work in the course of two consecutive days must not exceed four hours.

99. No overtime work shall be permitted to make up for a wage earner's tardiness in reporting at his place of work.

100. All overtime work done by a wage earner, as well as the remuneration received by him for the same, must be recorded in his labor booklet.

101. The total number of days on which overtime may be permitted in any enterprise, establishment or institution must not exceed fifty days per annum, including such days, when even one wage earner worked overtime.

102. Every enterprise, establishment or institution must keep a special record book for overtime work.

103. All wage earners must be allowed a weekly uninterrupted rest of not less than forty-two hours.

104. No work shall be done on specially designated holidays.

Note.— Rules concerning holidays and days of weekly rest are appended hereto.

105. On the eve of rest days the normal working day shall be reduced by two hours.

Note.— This section shall not apply to institutions and enterprises where the working day does not exceed six hours.

106. Every wage earner who has worked without interruption not less than six months shall be entitled to leave of absence for two weeks, irrespective of whether he worked in only one or in several enterprises, establishments or institutions.

107. Every wage earner who has worked without interruption not less than a year shall be entitled to leave of absence for one month, irrespective of whether he worked in only one or in several enterpises, establishments or institutions.

Note.— Sections 106 and 107 shall take effect beginning January 1, 1919.

108. Leave of absence may be granted during the whole year, provided that the same does not interfere with the normal course of work in enterprise, establishment or institution.

109. The time and order in which leave of absence may be granted shall be determined by agreement between the management of enterprise, establishment or institution and proper self-government bodies of the wage earners (works and other committees).

110. A wage earner shall not be allowed to work for remuneration during his leave of absence.

111. The remuneration of a wage earner earned during his leave of absence shall be deducted from his regular wages.

112. The absence of a wage earner from work caused by special circumstances and permitted by the manager shall not be counted as leave of absence; the wage earner shall not be paid for the working hours lost in such cases.

h. ARTICLE VIII

Methods to Assure Efficiency of Labor

113. In order to assure efficiency of labor, every wage earner working in an enterprise, establishment or institution (governmental, public or private) employing labor in the form of organized collaboration, as well as the administration of the enterprise, establishment or institution, shall strictly observe the rules of this article of the code relative to standards of efficiency, output and rules of internal management.

114. Every wage earner must during a normal working day and under normal working conditions perform the standard amount of work fixed for the category and group in which he is enrolled.

Note.— Normal conditions referred to in this section, shall mean:

(a) Good condition of machines, lathes and accessories;

(b) Timely delivery of materials and tools necessary for the performance of the work;

(c) Good quality of materials and tools;

(d) Proper hygienic and sanitary equipment of the building where the work is performed (necessary lighting, heating, etc.)

115. The standard output for wage earners of each trade and of each group and category shall be fixed by valuation commissions of the respective trade unions (section 62).

116. In determining the standard output the valuation commission shall take into consideration the quantity of products usually turned out in the course of a normal working day and under normal technical conditions by the wage earners of the particular trade group and category.

117. The production standards of output adopted by the valuation commission must be approved by the proper Department of Labor jointly with the Council of National Economy.

118. A wage earner systematically producing less than the fixed standard may be transferred by decision of the proper valuation commission to other work in the same group and category, or to a lower group or category, with a corresponding reduction of wages.

Note.— The wage earner may appeal from the decision to transfer him to a lower group or category with a reduction of wages, to the local Department of Labor and from the decision of the latter to the District Department of Labor, whose decision shall be final and not subject to further appeal.

119. If a wage earner's failure to maintain the standard output be due to lack of good faith and to negligence on his part, he may be discharged in the manner set forth in subdivision "d" of section 46 without the two weeks' notice prescribed by section 47.

120. The supreme Council of National Economy jointly with the People's Commissariat of Labor may direct a general increase or decrease of the standards of efficiency and output for all wage earners and for all enterprises, establishments and institutions of a given district.

121. In addition to the regulations of the present article relative to standards of efficiency and output in enterprises, establishments and institutions, efficiency of labor shall be secured by rules of internal management.

122. The rules of internal management in Soviet institutions shall be made by the organs of Soviet authority with the approval of the People's Commissariat of Labor or its local departments.

123. The rules of internal management in industrial enterprises and establishments (Soviet, nationalized, private and public) shall be made by the trade unions and certified by the proper Departments of Labor.

124. The rules of internal management must include a clear, precise and, as far as possible, exhaustive directions in relation to —

(a) The general obligations of all wage earners (careful handling of all materials and tools, compliance with instructions of the managers regarding performance of work, observance of the fixed standard of working hours, etc.);

(b) The special duties of the wage earners of the particular branch of industry (careful handling of the fire in enterprises using inflammable materials, observance of special cleanliness in enterprises producing food products, etc.);

(c) The limits and manner of liability for breach of the above duties mentioned above in subdivisions "a" and "b."

125. The enforcement of the rules of internal management in Soviet institutions is entrusted to the responsible managers.

126. The enforcement of the rules of internal management in industrial enterprises and establishments (Soviet, nationalized, public or private) is entrusted to the self-government bodies of the wage earners (works or similar committees).

ARTICLE IX

Protection of Labor

127. The protection of life, health and labor of persons engaged in any economic activity is entrusted to the labor inspection — the technical inspectors and the representatives of sanitary inspection.

128. The labor inspection is under the jurisdiction of the People's Commissariat of Labor and its local branches (Departments of Labor) and is composed of elected labor inspectors.

129. Labor inspectors shall be elected by the Councils of Professional Unions.

Note 1.— The manner of election of labor inspectors shall be determined by the People's Commissariat of Labor.

Note 2.— In districts where there is no Council of Trade Unions, the Local Department of Labor shall summon a conference of representatives of the trade unions which shall elect the labor inspectors.

130. In performing the duties imposed upon them concerning the protection of the lives and health of wage earners the officers of labor inspection shall enforce the regulations of the present code, and decrees, instructions, orders and other acts of the Soviet power intended to safeguard the lives and health of the workers.

131. For the attainment of the purposes stated in section 130 the officers of labor inspection are authorized —

(a) To visit at any time of the day or night all the industrial enterprises of their districts and all places where work is carried on, as well as the buildings provided for the workmen by the enterprise (rooming houses, hospitals, asylums, baths, etc.);

(b) To demand of the managers of enterprises or establishments, as well as of the elective organs of the wage earners (works and similar committees) of those enterprises or establishments in the management of which they are participating, to produce all necessary books, records and information;

(c) To draw to the work of inspection representatives of the elective organizations of employees, as well as officials of the administration (managers, superintendents, foremen, etc.);

(d) To bring before the criminal court all violators of the regulations of the present code, or of the decrees, instructions, orders and other acts of the Soviet authority intended to safeguard the lives and health of the wage earners;

(e) To assist the trade unions and works committees in their efforts to ameliorate the labor condition in individual enterprises as well as in whole branches of industry.

132. The officers of labor inspection are authorized to adopt special measures, in addition to the measures mentioned in the preceding section for the removal of conditions endangering the lives and health of workmen, even if such measures have not been provided for by any particular law or regulation, instructions or order of the People's Commissariat of Labor or of the Local Department of Labor.

Note.— Upon taking special measures to safeguard the lives and health of wage earners, as authorized by the present section, the officers of inspection shall immediately report to the Local Department of Labor, which may either approve these measures or reject them.

133. The scope and the forms of activity of the organs of labor inspection shall be determined by instructions and orders issued by the People's Commissariat of Labor.

134. The enforcement of the instructions, rules and regulations relating to safety is entrusted to the technical inspectors.

135. The technical inspectors shall be appointed by the Local Departments of Labor from among engineering specialists; these inspectors shall perform within the territory under their jurisdiction the duties prescribed by section 31 of the present code.

136. The technical inspectors shall be guided in their activity, besides the general regulations, by the instructions and orders of the People's Commissariat of Labor and by the instruction issued by the technical division of the Local Department of Labor.

137. The activity of the sanitary inspection shall be determined by instructions issued by the People's Commissariat of Health Protection in conference with the People's Commissariat of Labor.

APPENDIX TO SECTION 79

j. *Rules Concerning Unemployed and Payment of Subsidies*

1. An "unemployed" shall mean every citizen of the Russian Socialist Federated Soviet Republic subject to labor duty who is registered with the local Department of Labor Distribution as

being out of work at his vocation or at the remuneration fixed by the proper tariff.

2. An " unemployed " shall likewise mean:

(a) Any person who has obtained employment for a term not exceeding two weeks (section 25 of the present code);

(b) Any person who is temporarily employed outside his vocation, until he shall obtain work at his vocation (sections 29 and 30 of the present code).

3. The rights of unemployed shall not be extended —

(a) To persons who in violation of sections 2, 24 and 29 of the present code, have evaded the labor duty, and refused work offered to them;

(b) To persons not registered as unemployed with the local Department of Labor Distribution (section 21 of the present code);

(c) To persons who have wilfully quit work, for the term specified in section 54 of the present code.

4. All persons described in section 1 and subdivision "b" of section 2 of these rules shall be entitled to permanent employment (for a term exceeding two weeks) at their vocations in the order of priority determined by the list of the Department of Labor Distribution for each vocation.

5. Persons described in section 1 and subdivision "b" of Article 2 of these rules shall be entitled to a subsidy from the local fund for unemployed.

6. The subsidy to unemployed provided in section 1 of the present rules shall be equal to the remuneration fixed by the tariff for the group and category on which the wage earner was assigned by the valuation commission (section 61).

Note.— In exceptional cases the People's Commissariat of Labor may reduce the unemployed subsidy to the minimum of living expenses as determined for the district in question.

7. A wage earner employed temporarily outside of his vocation (subdivision "b" of section 2) shall receive a subsidy equal to the differences between the remuneration fixed for the group and category in which he is enrolled and his actual remuneration, in case the latter be less than the former.

8. An unemployed who desires to avail himself of his right to a subsidy shall apply to the local funds for unemployed and shall present the following documents: (a) his registration card from the local Department of Labor Distribution; and (b) a certificate

of the valuation commission showing his assignment to a definite group and category of wage earners.

9. Before paying the subsidy the local funds for unemployed shall ascertain, through the Department of Labor Distribution and the respective trade union, the extent of applicant's unemployment and the causes thereof, as well as the group and category to which he belongs.

10. The local funds for unemployed may for good reasons deny the application for a subsidy.

11. If an application is denied, the local fund for unemployed shall, within three days from the filing of the application, inform the applicant thereof.

12. The decision of the local fund for unemployed may within two weeks, be appealed from by the interested parties to the local Department of Labor, and the decision of the latter may be appealed from to the District Department of Labor. The decision of the District Department of Labor is final and subject to no further appeal.

13. The payment of the subsidy to an unemployed shall commence only after he has actually been laid off and not later than after the fourth day.

14. The subsidies shall be paid from the fund of unemployed insurance.

15. The fund of unemployment insurance shall be made up:

(a) from obligatory payments by all enterprises, establishments and institutions employing paid labor;

(b) from fines imposed for default in such payments;

(c) from casual payments.

16. The amount and the manner of collection of the payments and fines mentioned in section 15 of these rules shall be determined every year by a special order of the People's Commissariat of Labor.

APPENDIX TO SECTION 80

K. Rules Concerning Labor Booklets

1. Every citizen of the Russian Socialist Federated Soviet Republic, upon assignment to a definite group and category (section 62 of the present code), shall receive, free of charge, a labor booklet.

Note.— **The form of the labor booklets shall be worked out by the People's Commissariat of Labor.**

2. Each wage earner, on entering the employment of an enterprise, establishment or institution employing paid labor, shall present his labor booklet to the management thereof, and on entering the employment of a private individual — to the latter.

Note.— A copy of the labor booklet shall be kept by the management of the enterprise, establishment, institution or private individual by whom the wage earner is employed.

3. All work performed by a wage earner during the normal working day as well as piece work or overtime work, and all payments received by him as a wage earner (remuneration in money or in kind, subsidies from the unemployment and hospital funds), must be entered in his labor booklet.

Note.— In the labor booklet must also be entered the leaves of absence and sick leave of the wage earner, as well as the fines imposed on him during and on account of his work.

4. Each entry in the labor booklet must be dated and signed by the person making the entry, and also by the wage earner (if the latter is literate), who thereby certifies the correctness of the entry.

5. The labor booklet shall contain:

(a) The name, surname and date of birth of the wage earner;

(b) The name and address of the trade union of which the wage earner is a member;

(c) The group and category to which the wage earner has been assigned by the valuation commission.

6. Upon the discharge of a wage earner, his labor booklet shall under no circumstances be withheld from him. Whenever an old booklet is replaced by a new one, the former shall be left in possession of the wage earner.

7. In case a wage earner loses his labor booklet, he shall be provided with a new one into which shall be copied all the entries of the lost booklet; in such a case a fee determined by the rules of internal management may be charged to the wage earner for the new booklet.

8. A wage earner must present his labor booklet upon the request:

(a) Of the managers of the enterprise, establishment or institution where he is employed;

(b) Of the Department of Labor Distribution;

(c) Of the trade union;

(d) Of the officials of workmen's control and of labor protection;

(e) Of the insurance offices or institutions acting as such.

APPENDIX TO SECTION 5

Rules for the Determination of Disability for Work

1. Disability for work shall be determined by an examination of the applicant by the Bureau of Medical Experts, in urban districts, or by the provincial insurance offices, accident insurance offices or institutions acting as such.

Note.— In case it be impossible to organize a Bureau of Medical Experts at any insurance office, such a Bureau may be organized at the Medical Sanitary Department of the local Soviet, provided, however, that the said Bureau shall be guided in its actions by the general rules and instructions for insurance offices.

2. The staff of the Bureau of Experts shall include:

(a) Not less than three specialists in surgery;

(b) Representatives of the Board of Directors of the office;

(c) Sanitary mechanical engineers appointed by the Board of Directors of the office;

(d) Representatives of the trade unions.

Note.— The specialists in surgery on the staff of the bureau shall be recommended by the medical sanitary department, with the consent of the Board of Directors, preferably from among the surgeons connected with the hospital funds, and shall be confirmed by a delegates' meeting of the office.

3. During the examination of a person at the Bureau of the Medical Commission, all persons who have applied for the examination may be present.

4. An application for the determination of the loss of working ability may be made by any person or institution.

5. Applications for examination shall be made to the insurance office nearest to the residence of the person in question.

6. Examinations shall take place in a special room of the insurance office.

Note.— If the person to be examined cannot be brought to the insurance office, owing to his condition, the examination may take place at his residence.

7. Every person who is to be examined at the Bureau of Medical Experts shall be informed by the respective insurance office of the day and hour set for the examination and of the location of

the section of the Bureau of Medical Experts where the same is to take place.

8. The Bureau of Medical Experts may use all methods approved by medical science for determining disability for work.

9. The Bureau of Medical Experts shall keep detailed minutes of the conference meetings, and the record embodying the results of the examinations shall be signed by all members of the Bureau.

10. A person who has undergone an examination and has been found unfit for work shall receive a certificate from the Bureau of Medical Experts.

Note.— A copy of the certificate shall be kept in the files of the Bureau.

11. The records as well as the certificates shall show whether the disability is of a permanent or temporary character. If the disability for work be temporary, the record and certificate shall show the date set for examination.

12. After the disability for work has been certified the proper insurance office shall inform thereof the Department of Social Security of the local Soviet, stating the name, surname and address of the person disabled, as well as the character of the disability (whether temporary or permanent).

13. The decision of the Bureau of Medical Experts certifying or denying the disability of the applicant may be appealed from by the interested parties to the People's Commissariat of Health Protection.

14. The People's Commissariat of Health Protection may either dismiss the appeal or issue an order for the re-examination of appellant by a new staff of the Bureau of Experts.

15. The decision of the new staff of the Bureau of Experts shall be final and subject to no further appeal.

16. Re-examinations to establish the recovery of working ability shall be conducted in the same manner as the first examination, with the observance of the regulations of the present article of the code.

17. The expenses incurred in connection with the examination of an insured person shall be charged to the respective insurance office. The expenses incurred in connection with the examination of a person not insured shall be charged to the respective enterprise, establishment or institution.

18. The People's Commissariat of Labor may, if necessary, modify or amend the present rules for the determination of disability for work.

M. Rules Concerning Payment of Sick Benefits (Subsidies) to Wage Earners

1. Every wage earner shall receive in case of sickness a subsidy and medical aid from the local hospital fund of which he is a member.

Note 1.— Each person may be a member of only one insurance fund at a time.

Note 2.— A person who has been ill outside the district of the local hospital fund of which he is a member shall receive the subsidy from the hospital fund of the district in which he has been taken ill. All expenses thus incurred shall be charged to the hospital fund of which the particular person is a member.

2. The sick benefits shall be paid to a member of a hospital fund from the first day of his sickness until the day of his recovery, with the exception of those days during which he has worked and accordingly received remuneration from the enterprise, establishment or institution where he is employed.

3. The sick benefit shall be equal to the remuneration fixed for a wage earner of the respective group and category.

Note 1.— The group and category in which the wage earner is enrolled shall be ascertained by the local hospital fund through the Department of Labor Distribution or through the trade unions.

Note 2.— The subsidy for pregnant women and those lying-in shall be fixed by special regulations of the People's Commissariat of Labor.

Note 3.— In exceptional cases the People's Commissariat of Labor may reduce the subsidy to the minimum of living expenses as determined for the respective district.

4. Besides the subsidies, the hospital funds shall also provide for their members free medical aid of every kind (first aid, ambulatory treatment, home treatment, treatment in sanatoria or resorts, etc.).

Note.— To secure medical aid any hospital fund may, independently or in conjunction with other local funds, organize and maintain its own ambulatories, hospitals, etc., as well as enter into agreements with individual physicians and establishments.

5. The resources of the local hospital funds shall be derived:

(a) From obligatory payments by enterprises, establishments and institutions (Soviet, public and private) employing paid labor;

(b) From fines for delay of payments;

(c) From profits on the investments of the funds;
(d) From casual payments.

Note.—The resources of the local hospital funds shall be consolidated into one common fund of insurance against sickness.

6. The amount of the payments to local hospital funds by enterprises, establishments and institutions employing paid labor shall be periodically fixed by the People's Commissariat of Labor.

Note 1.—In case these obligatory payments be not paid within the time fixed by the local hospital funds, they shall be collected by the local Department of Labor; moreover, in addition to the sum due, a fine of 10 per cent. thereof shall be imposed for the benefit of the hospital fund.

Note 2.—In case the delay be due to the fault of the responsible managers of the particular enterprise, establishment, or institution, the fine shall be collected from the personal means of the latter.

7. The decision of the hospital funds may be appealed from within two weeks to the Department of Labor. The decision of the Department of Labor shall be final and subject to no further appeal.

8. The People's Commissariat of Labor may, whenever necessary, change or amend the foregoing rules concerning sick benefits to wage earners.

CHAPTER XV

Revolutionary Socialist Activities in Europe Since 1917

(A) Prussian "Spartacide" Communists

Beginning even before the signing of the Armistice, the revolutionary Socialist element in Germany started a concerted movement to take possession of the State. A group, with touch of intellectual pride characteristically German, to show its knowledge of history and past revolutions, took the name of Spartacans, from that ancient Roman revolutionary proletarian, Spartacus, who started a bloody revolt against the Roman state. The Spartacans formed the extreme Left Wing of the Socialist aggregation. Lenin's accusation is that all German Socialists except the Spartacus group were guilty of the betrayal of Socialism and of the proletariat through their absolute or partial loyalty to the Fatherland during the Great War. This, together with the corresponding loyalty of French and the majority of British Socialist and labor leaders, had led to the collapse of the Second Socialist International, which had been based on the fundamental idea that loyalty to revolutionary Socialism must replace loyalty to one's country.

Between October, 1918, and January, 1919, the Spartacus movement developed rapidly in Northern Germany. On December 31st the Spartacus unions of all Germany had a meeting in Berlin at which Karl Liebknecht said:

> "The introduction of the class struggle into the country is a decisive matter for us. . . . We want to lift the mailed fist against every one who opposes the social revolution of the proletariat. The next thing we have to expect is the internationalization of civil war."

The party then issued a manifesto calling for revolution and the dictatorship of the proletariat, signed by four leaders: Clara Zetkin, Rosa Luxemburg, Karl Liebknecht and Franz Mehring. Armed bands of Spartacides were organized, and riots took place in many towns and cities. The Spartacides demanded that all power be given to the Councils of Workers' and Soldiers' Deputies; that the proletariat be armed and bourgeoisie disarmed; that the government proceed to the immediate socialization of industry and should itself be turned into a dictatorship

KARL LIEBKNECHT

One of the Principal Leaders of the Spartacides or Communist Party of Germany. Killed January 15, 1919.

of the proletariat. They opposed the calling of a Constituent Assembly, because they were in favor of minority dictatorship and never claimed to be backed by the majority of the people.

The Spartacans followed the scheme of working up passionate sentiment among the workmen of the cities by rushing motor trucks through the streets, which distributed thousands of circulars warning the people that the revolution was in danger and calling for protest meetings against the timid policy of all other parties. This propaganda plan was borrowed from the program which had been followed so successfully by Lenin and Trotzky before their *coup d'etat* in Russia in November, 1917. The deciding element in inducing the Spartacans to act when they did appears to have been: (1) That the new Congress of Councils of Workers' and Soldiers' Deputies, which met December 16, 1918, showed at once that it favored the moderate and not the revolutionary element among the Socialists, refusing to allow either Liebknecht or Rosa Luxembourg to address the delegates, and expressing its confidence in the Ebert government; (2) the decision to convoke the national assembly on January 19th, instead of in March, and the abolishment of the Berlin Soviet executive.

The following program was issued early in December by the Spartacans:

> "Disarmament of the police officers, non-proletarian soldiers and all members of the ruling classes; confiscation by the Soldiers' and Workers' Council of arms, munitions and armament works; arming of all adult male proletarians and the formation of a workers' militia; the formation of a proletarian red guard; abolition of the ranks of officers and non-commissioned officers; removal of all military officers from the Soldiers' and Workers' Councils; abolition of all parliaments and municipal and other councils, the election of a general council which will elect and control the Executive Council of the Soldiers and Workmen; repudiation of all state and other public debts, including war loans down to a certain fixed limit of subscriptions; expropriation of all landed estates, banks, coal mines and large industrial works; confiscation of all fortunes above a certain amount."

It was on December 23d that the first revolutionary outbreak occurred in Berlin, being occasioned by the refusal of 2,000 revolutionary sailors to disband, which led to fights between them and the republican guards and to the seizure of the office of the *Vorwaerts.* This developed into street fights, to the passing over of several regiments to the Spartacans, and to the bringing in from the front of troops by the government to put down the uprising. The bloody suppression of the revolt led to the resignation of three cabinet members of the Independent Socialist Party, which did not approve of the drastic policy of the majority Socialists. The Independents put this question to the government:

> "Is the Council of the same view with us that the Socialist Republic must not rest on the support of generals and the rest of the standing army, but on citizens' guards to be formed on democratic principles? Does the Council approve that the socializing of industries as far as practicable should begin at once?"

The Council referred to is the Council of Workmen's and Soldiers' Deputies.

These questions not having been answered satisfactorily, the three independent Socialists resigned on December 30th. However, the Independents led by Haase, Dittman and Barth were not willing to go the length of the Spartacans, and adopted by 485 votes to 195, at a conference of the party, a motion calling for the election of a National Assembly.

On December 30th, after their failure to stampede the Independents, the Spartacans decided to operate alone, forming a new party which called itself "The Revolutionary Communist Labor Party of the German Spartacus League."

The Spartacus group was in constant communication with the Soviet government whose propaganda was in charge of Joffe, the official Bolshevik Ambassador in Berlin, and of Radek, the most powerful and able of the Russian propagandist agents outside of Russia. The first Spartacan uprising was ostensibly in defense of Eichhorn, head of the Berlin police, accused of protecting Joffe in his propaganda work. This began January 5th, 1919; for two weeks the street of Berlin were the scene of open battle between the government forces and the Spartacan revolutionists, who seized newspaper offices, fortresses, railway stations, breweries, telegraph stations, gas plants, electric power houses and water works, and proclaimed a new government under the direction of a revolutionary committee. The Spartacans started similar riots and attempts in Bremen, Brunswick, Halle, Dusseldorf, Essen, Hamburg and other cities. The government proclaimed martial law on January 9th, and on January 10th a general strike was called by the Spartacans to save the collapse of their movement. The next four or five days saw the success of the government in suppressing the insurrection and on January 15th the death blow to the movement, not only for the time being but for the immediate future, was given through the killing of Karl Liebknecht and Rosa Luxembourg by an unauthorized group of soldiers and civilians.

Order having been restored, the elections for the National Assembly took place the following week, with the result that the majority Social Democrats obtained 164 seats and the Independent Socialists twenty-four seats, the Spartacans taking no share in the voting. When the Assembly met, Ebert was elected President on February 12th. After that time the Council of Workmen's and Soldiers' Deputies had but little influence on the government. In April, at its second Congress, it demanded representation in the government, but was refused except in an advisory capacity; and in July the workmens' councils, which had by that time come under the domination of the Independent Socialists, decided on a general strike. The opposition of the Independents increased and was expressed in a number of strikes and riots during the summer. The shooting of the ablest leader of the Independents, Haase, on October 8th, which resulted in his death, was the culmination of this agitation.

The Spartacan movement, while it apparently sank into the background during the rest of 1919, was in reality gaining renewed power, not only through acquisition to its own ranks but through a rapidly increasing rapprochement with the Independent Socialists, especially after Haase's death.

The Independent Socialist Party met in Congress at Leipsig in December, 1919, and decided to declare its affiliation with the Third (Moscow) International by a vote of 227 to 54. The resolution read:

> "Should the parties of the states outside Germany refuse to enter the Moscow International along with us, the German Independent Socialist Party must take the step by itself."

A motion made by the leader of the Extremists, Crestien, sent fraternal greetings to revolutionary Russia. Crestien, and the other Extremist, Daumig, were appointed chairmen. The whole trend of the Congress was toward union with the Communists or Spartacides, now that the restraining influence of Haase was removed.

Also during December there was formed at Dusseldorf a "Propaganda Bureau for the Councils' System," by the local committee for direct action organized in the Rhenish Westphalian industrial districts. Seventy delegates from forty towns attended, and the extension of the councils' system was to be pushed through the already existing Workers' Councils and Workmen's Committees. The purpose was to use direct action as both an economic and a political weapon and to turn the trades unions into fighting industrial organizations.

The results of this propaganda were shown in the revolutionary movement at the end of March, when the workmen of the region were seen to have an organized army, provided with artillery, and commanded by experienced officers.

The above two facts are indications of the penetration of the Communist idea into both the political and the economic and labor fields. They resulted in the Communist uprising throughout Germany after the militarist reactionary attempt under Kapp. The Ebert government used the revolutionary movement as a club to defeat the militarists through the use of the Communist and Syndicalist general strike.

While there is no question, therefore, that the Communist hold upon the German people has increased tremendously during 1919 and the early part of 1920, it remains to be seen whether the Independent Socialists, who have a larger following than the Spartacides, will take the lead in violent reactionary movements. The fact that they did support the Spartacides in the attack on the National Assembly in January, would indicate the probability of an eventual complete coalition.

Only the thrift and conservatism natural to the German workmen would seem to stand in the way of the establishment of Communism in Northern Germany.

(B) BAVARIAN COMMUNISTS

At the time of the armistice Bavaria was planning a revision of the election laws that would give a more popular result to the next election, but early in 1919, a liberal and intellectual element felt that it was necessary, in order to preserve Bavarian particularism, to proceed to stronger measures, in the form of a movement corresponding in a certain theoretical way with the Spartacan movement in northern Germany. But the agents of Lenin in Bavaria took possession of this revolutionary movement in Munich and turned it into an artificial, short-lived attempt at Soviet government similar to that in Hungary. However, its genuine character is more than doubtful. It lasted only three weeks during March, 1919, but was disastrous in handing over Bavaria to the tender mercies of Prussianism. The revolutionary movement was started by Landauer and Muehsam, both of them Bavarian patriots, and was based on the conservative Peasants' Councils, together with representatives of the organized professional corporations. It was a movement for the expression in political life of a traditional rather than a revolutionary Bavarian particularism and real democracy. In fact, it had a touch of feudalism. Bavaria had always hated Prussia and objected to being swamped in the centralized republican government. It had no large element of workmen engaged in industrial life. It was essentially an agricultural country.

The new government hoped for speedy recognition by the Entente Powers. But this never came. It was only when this movement for an autonomous rule in Bavaria, under these native liberal leaders, was in danger of being overwhelmed by military attack from the Prussian government, through an invasion of a northern army, that the Bolshevik agents were called in to help continue the movement. In fact, this action has been considered to have been brought about, not by Landauer and Muesham, but through a *coup d' etat* by the Bavarian Minister of War, Schneppenhorst, who instead of using his military power to back up the liberal leaders installed in their place the gang of Lenin's agents led by the two well-known propagandists, Axelrod and Levine. It is practically certain that this was a plot between Schneppenhorst and the German government to make the advent of these Russian Bolshevik agents the excuse for a triumphant entry of Prussian troops into Munich. It was another phase of the Prussian Bolshevik entente. It was a death blow to Bavarian particularism. The thought that Bavaria would ever be the focus of any revolutionary Communist movement or take part in any of its propaganda may be dismissed.

(c) HUNGARIAN COMMUNISTS

The population of Hungary, in its various classes and occupations, its social and economic structure, is fairly representative of normal conditions the world over. Its experiment in Bolshevism is, therefore, more instructive for Americans than is the Russian experiment where the class and educational situation is so abnormal, if we would judge of the results of an attempt at violent Communistic Socialist revolution in our own country.

The desperation and political confusion, the isolation and economic helplessness in Hungary, at the close of the war, made radical changes inevitable. Universal suffrage was granted, but elections were put off. The Communist group became more numerous between December, 1918, and March, 1919. The principal trouble-maker was a Jew named Bela Kun (whose real name is Cohen), who had been an intimate of Lenin in Russia where he was at first a liberated prisoner. Later he had been sent back to Budapest by Lenin with Russian money to start Bolshevik propaganda on a huge scale. Bela Kun's Bolshevik agents masqueraded, in some cases, as Red Cross officials. Keen advantage was taken of prevalent misery and unrest. During January and February, 1919, Bela Kun provoked outbreaks in Budapest, in the only coal mines — those of Salgotorjan — and was arrested, February 20th, in a raid where he got a broken head fighting the police.

The mistaken hostile policy of the Entente obliged Count Karolyi, who was then President of the Hungarian Republic, to resign in despair, March 20th, after the Entente had insisted on sending both Roumanian and Entente troops to occupy a large strip of Hungarian territory. On March 21st he turned over the reins of government to a group of moderate Communists headed by Bohm and Garbai. But soon the more radical Communists, Bogany and Kunfi, gave things a different tone, and Bela Kun, released from prison, took the absolute leadership proceeding at once to carry out Lenin's Russian program. He was in fact in constant communication with Lenin by courier and by wireless; and at one time it seemed as if a Russian Bolshevik army was attempting to come through to effect a junction with the Communist Hungarian Army in an attempt to overwhelm Roumania.

There was no organized opposition to Bela Kun. Like Lenin, he surrounded himself with commissars, having absolute authority. Of the thirty-two principal commissars, twenty-five were Jews, which was about the same proportion as in Russia. The most prominent of these formed a directorate of five: Bela Kun, Bela Varga, Joseph Bogany, Sigmund Kunfi and one other.

Other leaders were Alpari and Samuely, who had charge of the Red Terror and carried out the torturing and executing of the bourgeoisie, especially the groups held as hostages, the so-called counter-revolutionists and peasants.

Nominally, Alexander Garbai was President and Bela Kun Foreign Minister. The government's first decree was as follows:

> "The proletariat of Hungary from to-day has taken all power in its own hands. By the decision of the Paris Conference to occupy Hungary, the provisioning of revolutionary Hungary becomes utterly impossible. Under these circumstances the sole means open for the Hungarian government is a dictatorship of the proletariat.
>
> "Legislative, executive and judicial authority will be exercised by a dictatorship of the Workers', Peasants' and Soldiers' Councils. The Revolutionary Government Council will begin forthwith work for the realization of Communist Socialism.
>
> "The Council decrees the socialization of large estates, mines, big industries, banks and transport lines, declares complete solidarity with the Russian Soviet government, and offers to contract an army to march with the proletariat of Russia."

With this decree not only all industries carried on on a large scale were seized, but all retail stores employing more than ten workers. Small stores were put out of business. All houses used for residential purposes were made the property of the Soviet Republic. The basis of housing was that no family should be allowed more than three rooms and single adults one room each. No extra allowance was made for children. Agricultural guilds were formed on the old large estates. Each family received produce in proportion to its members, the remaining produce to be taken to the Central District Agricultural Association. Suffrage was based on the same principle as in Russia. No person except a productive worker was allowed to vote. The same plan of denying the vote to counter-revolutionists, that is, to the workers not in sympathy with Communism, that obtained in Russia was enforced, the electoral lists being prepared by the Communist Party caucus. No representative assembly of a democratic character was called. The Soviet constitution was based on that of Russia. It consisted of a national Congress of Soviets, a directing central committee, which elected the revolutionary Soviet government and its President. In mines and factories the workmen were represented by Soviets with a maximum of seven members. Theatres were socialized. The educational system was revolutionized and both amusement and education were placed at the service of Communist propaganda.

In the suppression of property which, of course, was one of the basic principles, house to house confiscation was carried on as had been the case in Russia. All jewelry, all objects of precious metal, were confiscated and apparently retained by the Commissars as a part of public funds. A considerable part of this loot was used in furthering Bolshevik propaganda, not only throughout Hungary, but outside, in Bohemia and Austria. For example, when Bela Kun was attempting to bring about a Communist revolution in Vienna, a search by the Austrian government of the rooms of Bela Kun's agent resulted in the seizing of several millions, worth of this jewelry.

Bela Kun attempted to obtain recognition from the Allied governments during the late spring and early summer, but the Allies declined to enter into negotiations with the Bela Kun government, though it offered to do so in case this government was replaced by a genuine social democratic government. Meanwhile war was being carried on between the Roumanian invaders, backed by the Entente Powers and the Hungarian army. The Communist army was at first unorganized, and while it seemed willing to attack the peasants who refused to allow the establishment of a Communist regime in their districts, it showed no discipline in front of the attacks of the regular troops, until Bela Kun followed the same plan adopted by Trotzky in Russia, bringing back the strictest discipline into the army, and placing at its head experienced officers. After this the Hungarian Red army obtained a number of victories over the Roumanians.

The management of the financial side of the Communist government was even more destructive than the Russian. The same scheme of destroying money as a medium was carried out. During the 132 days of its supremacy the government spent, with the exception of about $150,000,000 worth of notes, the entire note reserve of the Austro-Hungarian Bank in Budapest, amounting to nearly two milliard kronen, and issued so-called white money — paper money of a certain description — to the amount of between two and three milliards, besides so-called green money to the amount of three hundred millions and other smaller groups of financial output. The paralysis of industry by violent socialization, the confiscation of capital and the destruction of the bourgeois and upper classes, made the production of economic wealth practically impossible. It is not merely the extravagance of the Communist government, but the confusion which it introduced into national and individual finances that will make the revival of Hungarian finances a long and difficult problem. The overthrow of the Soviet government was hastened by the regrouping of political forces throughout the country in four different groups: (1) The Christian Socialist Party, especially in the west; (2) the Peasant Party, especially in the center and the west; (3) the Bourgeois Democratic Party, particularly in the towns; (4) the old Social Democratic Party, consisting of organized labor in the towns. The latter party was comparatively small; the Peasant Party was by far the most powerful.

The final blow was dealt by two agencies: first, the successful invasion of the Roumanian army at the end of August, and second, the defection of the trade unions during June from the support of the Communist Party.

As organized industrial labor had been the main support of the revolution, its defection combined with the invasion and the Allied blockade, made the abdication of Bela Kun on August 1st an absolute necessity. After a short interval of a phantom Social Democratic government, power came into the hands of the reactionary element, which almost immediately established a White Terror as bad as the Red Terror of Samuely and Bela Kun. This included wholesale imprisonment, executions of Communists and persecution of the Jewish element of the population, which was considered mainly responsible for the situation. The persecution of the Socialist and Democratic element in the country has extended to the exclusion from parliamentary life.

The Social Democratic Party in Hungary consequently issued, in early September, a protest which stated:

> "It was through an act of desperation on the part of Hungarian labor that Bolshevism came. It came only, and could only have come, after all hope in the west seemed vain. Bolshevism has now collapsed, and Hungarian labor emerging from this most frightful and critical illness of its sorely tried existence, is now turning itself towards social democracy, trusting to the political methods of the west.

> "We Social Democrats can only condemn the methods of the dictatorship and the Red Terror. Yet at the moment that we are in the mood to make up for past mistakes we find ourselves face to face with a cruel White Terror of a medieval and barbaric character. We have for Bolshevism only words of condemnation. Nevertheless, we are compelled to point out, and can establish it by documentary evidence, that the White Terror in the four weeks since the usurpation of the Archduke Joseph of Hapsburg and the government of his adventurer lackey Friederich, has spilt a hundredfold more blood than the dictatorial regime of the new overthrown Soviet Republic did in the whole four months of its existence."

It is this reactionary situation in Hungary that creates a dangerous center of possible Bolshevist trouble in the future.

At the same time, the experiment in Hungary, being better known in its details to Europe and the United States through authentic information, has through its failure, financial, economic and social, given more of a death blow to the success of Bolshevik propaganda in Europe than any other Bolshevik movement has done.

ROSA LUXEMBURG

One of the Principal Leaders of the Spartacides or Communist Party of Germany. Killed January 15, 1919.

Copyrigt by Underwood & Underwood

BELA KUN
Founder of Hungarian Soviet Regime

APPENDIX

CHAPTER XV

Official Documents

1. German Revolution and Russia.
2. Appeal of "Spartacus" Group to Berlin Workmen.
3. An Appeal of "Spartacus" Group to Workers of all Countries.
4. The Agrarian Program of Communist Party of Germany.
5. To Workers and Soldiers of the Entente.
6. Constitution of Hungarian Socialist Federated Soviet Republic.
7. The Last Appeal of the Hungarian Soviet Government to Working Class of Hungary.

Document No. 1

ORIGINAL DOCUMENTS

THE GERMAN REVOLUTION AND RUSSIA IN 1918

The Russian legation at Stockholm received (October 4th) the following dispatch from the Russian Ambassador at Berlin:

"I have been notified that the meeting, recently held by the Central Executive Committee, the Moscow Soviet and other organizations of Moscow, adopted the following resolution, which later was approved by the All-Russian Central Executive Committee.

"The All-Russian Central Executive Committee considers it necessary that the working classes of all nations should state their position on the latest events. The imperialists of the Central Powers are rapidly approaching a great catastrophe. Bulgaria and Turkey have bolted the alliance, and Austria will soon follow suit. The internal front of Germany is tottering. The policy of the ruling classes is wavering between military dictatorship and a parliamentarian cabinet composed of representatives of liberals, Catholics and Socialist traitors. The British-French, American and Japanese imperialistic exploiters now seem to be almighty, just as Germany half a year ago, during the Brest-Litovsk parleys, seemed to be almighty. Encouraged by their newest victories, the Allied exploiters appear as more dangerous and merciless enemies of the Soviet Republic than the Germans.

But just as we, during the period of the greatest triumph of the German military power, foresaw its inevitable catastrophe and the impossibility of its annexation plans, likewise we now express our unshakable conviction of the approaching downfall of the Entente Powers. The deep-going inner conflicts among the partners of the world's exploitation and the deep-felt bitterness among the deceived masses of the people, are driving the capitalistic world toward social revolution. Now, as in October last year, and as during the negotiations at Brest-Litovsk, the Soviet government bases its whole policy on the conviction of the oncoming social revolution in both imperialistic camps. The firmness of this conviction allowed us to accept the vile terms of the Brest-Litovsk peace, which terms we did not for a moment believe to be the last word of history.

"As we now again are joining the fate of Ukraine, Poland, Lithuania, Baltic Provinces and Finland to the fate of the Russian workers' revolution, we do not contemplate any kind of an alliance with the Allied imperialists for the purpose of obtaining modifications of the Brest-Litovsk treaty. Those chains wherewith the British-French and Japanese-American exploiters are burdening the peoples of the world are not in the least better than those of the German-Austrian exploiters. The German military dictatorship is no more able than a parliamentary coalition between bourgeois agents and socialistic compromisers to change the course of the events. These events are relentlessly leading the working classes of Germany to power.

"The war between the British-American and Austrian-German exploiters may at any moment develop into a war between imperialism and the German working class. The All-Russian Central Executive Committee declares before the whole world that in this struggle the whole of Soviet Russia with all its power and with all possible means will support the German workers. The All-Russian Central Executive Committee is convinced that the revolutionary working class of France, England, Italy, America and Japan will come to the same camp together with Russia and revolutionary Germany.

"Awaiting the coming revolutionary events, it is the duty of the All-Russian Central Executive Committee to fight with double strength against the brigands who are invading our territory, and at the same time to prepare effective aid for the working class of Germany and Austria, military aid as well as in respect to the food situation.

"The All-Russian Central Executive Committee, therefore, orders the revolutionary military council immediately to outline a broad program for the organization of the Red Army based on the conditions of the new International situation. The All-Russian Central Executive Committee orders the food commission immediately to outline a program for sending food reserves to the working masses in Germany and Austria, in order to strengthen their struggle against the internal as well as external brigands and violators of their rights. All Russian Soviet institutions, central as well as the local, all trade unions, factory committees, the committees of the poor peasants and the co-operative societies are ordered to partake in a most effective manner in the mobilization of a powerful Red Army and in the organization of the food reserves of the social revolution.

"JOFFE.

"Berlin, October 4, 2 A. M." [1918]

Document No. 2

THE APPEAL OF THE "SPARTACUS" GROUP TO THE BERLIN WORKMEN, 1918

(From the Moscow "Izvestia" of October 19th; appeared in the "Novy Mir," December 18th.)

WORKERS, Awake!—The dreams of the German imperialists of world domination, which they sought to rear on heaps of corpses, in a sea of blood, have gone up in smoke. Vain are their efforts! The sword cannot forever rule the world. In one night everything has tumbled down with a crash. The shameless commerce with peoples in the East over the corpse of the strangled revolution has brought its fruits; it forced the peoples of the West to unite for a desperate war of self-defense. Everything goes down. In the battlefields of Flanders, the Balkans and Palestine defeat after defeat. The alliance of the Central Powers, that was to serve as a foundation for world domination by Germany, has failed completely. Hardly had the robbers terminated their quarrels about the booty—Poland for Germany and Austria, Roumania for Bulgaria and Turkey, Dobrudja for Germany, Austria and Bulgaria — when Bulgaria left the coalition and concluded a separate peace with France and England. The German people do not any longer want a German protectorate and war, the people desire peace. And already the German soldiers are being driven from the West in order to force Bulgaria to continue the war. The German proletarian, who has nothing to eat — whose wife and children pine away from their husband and father — this proletarian must now take by the throat the Bulgarian proletarian and force him to go on fighting.

Thus the ruling clique in Germany tries to remain in power. It feels that the ground is slipping away beneath it. It is bankrupt — bankrupt in the battlefields, bankrupt in its internal and external policies. And now it stands aghast before the consequences of its criminal military adventure. It is appalled at the very thought of the awakening of the tortured, misled proletariat, at the thought of the coming judgment of the people.

And at this very moment the government Socialists, the Scheidemanns, offer their services in order to sustain the tottering power of the German bourgeoisie. At this hour of a possible world revolution they are busy with petty bargaining, attempting to get a few ministerial seats; and to get them they stand ready to save the situation for the imperialistic bourgeoisie, ready to force the people to a further waiting for the war's end, and to prolong the slaughter among the peoples. They want merely to put up a few patches and blur the class rule of the capitalists and Prussian reaction, so that their rule may be more acceptable to the people. What were the conditions for which they consented to do these lackey's services? The solemn promise of the German government to abandon the idea of annexations and indemnities in the sense of the famous July resolution of the Reichstag. Yes, right now, when the English and French field-guns are exerting their efforts not to give any indemnities and contributions. More; the franchise reform in Prussia. Yes, right now, after the universal franchise, thanks to the shameless and piteous role which the Reichstag has played during the war, has become an empty mockery. And these arm-bearers of the bourgeoisie dared not even demand an immediate revocation of the martial laws, did not demand even that the Reichstag should sit intermittently. Thus they declare their readiness, in return for a few contemptible ministerial seats, to play the comedy of "reformed" Germany, and thus defend the rule of the capitalist class against the outburst of the people's wrath. This is the meaning of all this talk about the "reforms." Our task consists precisely in that we must destroy this agreement at the expense of the proletariat and the future of Socialism. Now everything is at stake. Down with the whole refuge of Prussian reaction and the rule of the capitalists! The thing now is to obtain an immediate and a permanent peace! But to attain a stable peace these things are required: Destruction of militarism, rule of the people, and a republic. Thus, the German proletariat must become the master of the whole situation. Forward with the banner of Socialism! Long live the revolution of the international proletariat!

We must not look forward to a victory of Anglo-French imperialism. If arms dictate peace, then the cause of freedom and socialism will be lost. No matter which guns be victorious, whether German or English, the working class everywhere will have to pay the bill. The international reaction and militarism, in case they are victorious, will put on the working class chains ten times heavier than before.

The proletariat of all countries must stop the slaughter by rising. They are called to dictate peace in the interests of freedom and Socialism.

Now the hour has come to act. At this moment the English and French workmen may follow the signal given by the German workers. This signal must be given. Forward, German workers, soldiers, male and female! Forward to the battle for freedom, for an immediate peace and Socialism! Forward toward the brotherhood of all peoples under the banner of free labor! Down with the class rule of the bourgeoisie! All power to the proletariat! Long live the German republic! Long live the international revolution of the proletariat!

Document No. 3

AN APPEAL OF THE "SPARTACUS" GROUP TO THE WORKERS OF ALL COUNTRIES

CHRISTMAS, 1918.

PROLETARIANS! MEN AND WOMEN OF LABOR! COMRADES!— The revolution in Germany has come! The masses of the soldiers who for four years were driven to slaughter for the sake of capitalistic profits, the masses of workers, who for four years were exploited, crushed, and starved, have revolted. Prussian militarism, that fearful tool of oppression, that scourge of humanity, lies broken on the ground. Its most noticeable representatives, and therewith the most noticeable of those guilty of this war, the kaiser and the crown prince, have fled from the country. Workers' and soldiers' councils have been formed everywhere.

Workers of all countries, we do not say that in Germany all power actually lies in the hands of the working people, that the complete triumph of the proletarian revolution has already been attained. There still sit in the government all those Socialists who in August, 1914, abandoned our most precious possession, the International, who for four years betrayed the German working class and the International.

But, workers of all countries, now the German proletarian himself speaks to you. We believe we have the right to appear before your forum in his name. From the first day of this war we endeavored to do our international duty by fighting that criminal government with all our power and branding it as the one really guilty of the war.

Now at this moment we are justified before history, before the International and before the German proletariat. The masses agree with us enthusiastically, constantly widening circles of the proletariat share the conviction that the hour has struck for a settlement with capitalistic class rule.

But this great task cannot be accomplished by the German proletariat alone; it can only fight and triumph by appealing to the solidarity of the proletarians of the whole world.

Comrades of the belligerent countries, we are aware of your situation. We know full well that your governments, now that they have won the victory, are dazzling the eyes of many strata of the people with the external brilliancy of their triumph. We know that they thus succeed through the success of the murdering in making its causes and aims forgotten.

But we also know that in your countries the proletariat made the most fearful sacrifices of flesh and blood, that it is weary of the dreadful butchery, that the proletarian is now returning to his home, and is finding want and misery there, while fortunes amounting to billions are heaped up in the hands of a few capitalists. He has recognized, and will continue to recognize, that your governments, too, have carried on the war for the sake of the big money bags. And he will further perceive that your governments, when they spoke of "justice and civilization" and of the "protection of small nations," meant capitalist profits as surely as did ours when it talked about the "defence of home;" and that the peace of "justice" and of the "League of Nations" are but a part of the same base brigandage that produced the peace of Brest-Litovsk. Here as well as there the same shameless lust for booty, the same desire for oppression, the same determination to exploit to the limit the brutal preponderance of murderous steel.

The imperialism of all countries knows no "understanding," it knows only one right—capital's profits; it knows only one language—the sword; it knows only one method—violence. And if it is now talking in all countries, in yours as well as ours, about the "League of Nations," "disarmament," "rights of small nations," "self-determination of the peoples," it is merely using the customary lying phrases of the rulers for the purpose of lulling to sleep the watchfulness of the proletariat.

Proletarians of all countries! This must be the last war! We owe that to the twelve million murdered victims, we owe that to our children, we owe that to humanity.

Europe has been ruined by this damnable slaughter. Twelve million bodies cover the grewsome scenes of this imperialistic crime. The flower of youth and the best man power of the peoples have been mowed down. Uncounted productive forces have been annihilated. Humanity is almost ready to bleed to death from the unexampled blood-letting of history. Victors and vanquished stand at the edge of the abyss. Humanity is threatened with famine, a stoppage of the entire mechanism of production, plagues, and degeneration.

The great criminals of this fearful anarchy, of this unchained chaos—the ruling classes—are not able to control their own creation. The beast of capital that conjured up the hell of the world war is incapable of banishing it, of restoring real order, of insuring bread and work, peace and civilization, justice and liberty, to tortured humanity.

What is being prepared by the ruling classes as peace and justice is only a new work of brutal force from which the hydra of oppression, hatred, and fresh, bloody wars raises its thousand heads.

Socialism alone is in a position to complete the great work of permanent peace, to heal the thousand wounds from which humanity is bleeding, to transform the plains of Europe, trampled down by the passage of the apocryphal horseman of war, into blossoming gardens, to conjure up ten productive forces for every one destroyed, to awaken all the physical and moral energies of humanity, and to replace hatred and dissension with fraternal solidarity, harmony, and respect for every human being.

If representatives of the proletarians of all countries could but clasp hands under the banner of Socialism for the purpose of making peace, then peace would be concluded in a few hours. Then there will be no disputed questions about the left bank of the Rhine, Mesopotamia, Egypt or colonies. Then there will be only one people — the toiling human beings of all races and tongues. Then there will be only one right — the equality of all men. Then there will be only one aim — prosperity and progress for everybody.

Humanity is facing the alternative: Dissolution and downfall in capitalist anarchy, or regeneration through the social revolution. The hour of fate has struck. If you believe in Socialism, it is now time to show it by deeds. If you are Socialists, now is the time to act.

Proletarians of all countries, if we now summon you for a common struggle it is not done for the sake of the German capitalists who, under the label of "German nation," are trying to escape the consequences of their own crimes; it is being done for our sake as well as for yours. Remember that your victorious capitalists stand ready to suppress in blood our revolution, which they fear as they do their own. You yourselves have not become any freer through the "victory," you have only become still more enslaved. If your ruling classes succeed in throttling the proletarian revolution in Germany and in Russia, then they will turn against you with redoubled violence. Your capitalists hope that victory over us and over revolutionary Russia will give them the power to scourge you with a whip of scorpions and to erect the thousand-year empire of exploitation upon the grave of Socialism.

Therefore the proletariat of Germany looks toward you in this hour. Germany is pregnant with the social revolution, but Socialism can only be realized by the proletariat of the world.

And, therefore, we call to you: "Arise for the struggle! Arise for action! The time for empty manifestos, platonic resolutions, and high-sounding words is gone! The hour of action has struck for the International!" We ask you to elect workers' and soldiers' councils everywhere that will seize political power, and, together with us, will restore peace.

Not Lloyd George and Poincarré, not Sonnino, Wilson, and Erzberger or Scheidemann, must be allowed to make peace. Peace must be concluded under the waving banner of the Socialist world revolution.

Proletarians of all countries! We call upon you to complete the work of Socialist liberation, to give a human aspect to the disfigured world and to make true those words with which we often greeted each other in the old days and which we sang as we parted: "And the International shall be the human race!"

KLARA ZETKIN,
ROSA LUXEMBURG,
KARL LIEBKNECHT,
FRANZ MEHRING.

Document No. 4

THE AGRARIAN PROGRAM OF THE COMMUNIST PARTY OF GERMANY

At the moment of publishing this agrarian program Germany is for the first time experiencing far-reaching strikes of the agricultural workers in Bielefeld, in Pomerania, in East Prussia. Smaller, short-breathed strike activity had preceded these in Magdeburg, in West Prussia, in Lubeck. Here and there communities of small farmers had favored the apportionment of the large estates within their district—this happened back in the May days of the Ebert-Haase government—but the armed power of the Ebert Republic let them know at once that property is inviolable, and they sank back at once into their former lethargy.

The present strikes of the agricultural workers in Bielefeld, Pomerania, East Prussia, etc., once more open the dispute between the agricultural proletariat and the large land owning class. The former is for the time being fighting for individual economic demands, still unconscious of the revolutionary significance of its newly begun fight. The Junkers on the other hand, with the sure instinct of the ruling class, have immediately grasped the fact that the strikes of the farm workers are more than any individual move of the agrarian proletariat in "normal" times. In a number of Pomeranian districts a state of siege has been declared, government troops have been ordered to forcibly put down the rebellion of the rural proletariat. Thus Junkerdom answers the first independent move of the proletariat of the land with the last word of the bourgeois state—with musket and sword. This act expresses its knowledge that this is a fight for the whole, for its ruling position on the land. And the power of state of the Ebert Republic, in placing itself at the disposal of the Junkers at the first hint that the class struggle is smouldering in the lowlands, stands opposed to the rural proletariat from the beginning as the tool of Junkerdom. Thus they are seeing to it that the workers of the country may speedily become aware of the revolutionary significance of their movement.

The reasons that the rural proletariat is so late in taking up the quarrel with the large landowners are obvious. Its division into small communities and its isolation place much greater hindrances in the way of independent action than in the case of the urban proletariat. In the pre-revolutionary period the Junker power succeeded in hermetically shutting off the agricultural workers from every political movement. Only the revolution made political life accessible to the country folk. In the first months of the revolution they had to take up the studies that the urban working class had hammered into it during two generations. To them even the hackneyed demagogic phrases of the Scheidemanns, regarding bourgeois democracy, were a revelation. What wonder then, that in the elections to the National Assembly they streamed in large bodies into the camp of the Majority Socialists and that they, together with the petty bourgeoisie, stepped into the gaps which the desertion of the metropolitan workers had torn in the ranks of the Majority Socialist Party organization. Then there is another thing: The economic ruin did not show itself in so harsh a form to the rural proletariat as it confronted the proletarian masses of the cities — as naked hunger and wholesale unemployment. The country had become accustomed during the war, first of all to nourish itself duly — many small farmers who in normal times had sold the food they raised and underfed themselves with substitutes of various kinds, now for the first time eating the butter, cheese, eggs, poultry, meat, fruit, etc., themselves. Only the excess over their own needs was shipped to the cities. Thus hunger in its most glaring aspect was spared the country people during the war and during the Revolution itself.

Unemployment among the agricultural workers, particularly after the departure of the prisoners of war, was unheard of; on the contrary, there was a dearth of hands.

The end of the war, the return to the native village or estate, the destruction of the old militarism, bourgeois democracy, these things at first sufficed the rural proletariat. Those who did not take part in uniform in the military rebellion that was such a significant feature of the ninth of November, had followed the urban proletariat passively in the November revolution. This passivity of theirs had — aside from the unripeness of the city revolution itself — enabled the bourgeoisie to win its isolated counter-revolutionary victories in revolutionary centers — in Berlin, in Bremen, in the Ruhr region, in Central Germany, in Munich. Not only did the passivity of the country permit the bourgeoisie to throw itself undivided upon the revolutionary centers, but the military power of the counter-revolution, the volunteer troops, were recruited largely from the ranks of the land proletariat and the small farmers. In the re-establishment of militarism in the shape of the volunteer system, the political passivity and revolutionary immaturity of the rural workers were revealed.

As long as the rural working class itself sat quiet, as long as the country itself did not bring up the land question, the Scheidemann servants of the bourgeoisie and the Junkers had no cause for grasping this hot iron. Some of the medieval rubbish, such as the rules for servants, was abolished on paper; the estate districts were abolished, likewise on paper; and finally the settlement law was accepted — which also leads a quiet existence on paper, which never has harmed the hair of a Junker's head, and was never intended to. It was really no more than the inheritance of the Hindenburg-Ludendorff plans of colonization in the Baltic region that the Ebert-Scheidemann government was executing through this innocent legislation, which on its own account fitted perfectly into the Junker settlement policy. The purpose of the move in both cases was the settlement of the land with squatters, as a reservoir for the labor needs of the large landowners, with the only difference that to some extent the settlement plans of Hindenburg were meant seriously, being at the same time intended for "dependable" border protection, military and political, in the east, while the land settlement law of Ebert-Scheidemann was from the start nothing but a demagogic trick.

The former passivity of the country is revealed drastically in another phenomenon; in the peasants' councils. While the workers' and soldiers' councils were crystalized directly from the revolutionary movement of the workers and soldiers, and therefore from the first bore a decided class character in their composition, the peasants' councils were an artificial creation of the Ebert-Haase government, that is to say, a clumsy deception. Under the name of "peasants' councils," the Farmers' League presented the country with an organization which, a brazen caricature of the Soviets, coupled the Junker and large estate owner with the rural workers and small farmers and gave this organization a suffrage privilege that afforded an excellent substitute for the abandoned three-class voting system. It is characteristic that the erstwhile independent Food Minister Wurm gave official recognition to this brazen swindle and unblushingly defended it. It is clear that such a caricature of the Soviet organization in the country was possible only because the country was still asleep, and that at the first independent action on the part of the rural workers it must be cast aside.

The country population has thus far been the last great reservoir of the counter-revolution, both through its passivity and through its active participation in counter-revolutionary actions and organizations. The incursion of troops in East Prussian and Pommeranian land districts for the purpose of quelling the landworkers is beginning in earnest. But this means that the question of militarism and Junker rule is only at this moment being attacked at the root. For militarism can be torn out by the roots only where it has gone most deep, in the Prussian "heart provinces," and the political domination of the Junkers can be torn down for good and all, not in the streets of Berlin — to say nothing of a Weimar or Berlin National Assembly — but only in the 30,000 estate districts, only through the uprising of the rural workers. And only now is the land question moving out of the twilight of theory or of demagogic routine into the light of the practical revolutionary conflict.

There are two chief elements that are bringing the rural proletariat into the revolutionary arena. First, its own passivity has permitted the Junker counter-revolution to recover from its first stupefaction and not only to hold all its positions of power in rural government, but to strengthen them and to more and more boldly to take the offensive in re-establishing the pre-revolutionary despotism of the Junker domain. The land-proletariat, which saw the chains that had enclosed its limbs loosen without any effort on its own part, now struggles with all its might against a return to the conditions previous to November 9th. The second factor is the effect of the increasing economic and financial disorder upon the rural workers and the small farmers; the growing depreciation of money which forces the agricultural workers into mass strikes. The small farmers still try to make up for this condition by raising prices, but these attempts are becoming constantly less satisfactory, and the pressure of direct taxation imposed by native and foreign capital must stir them to action completely. The small peasants before the revolution followed the Junkers in politics because they were attached to them economically. The bankruptcy of capital and state financiers is breaking this economic union. Necessarily it must also sooner or later break the political bond.

Thus the agrarian program of the Communist Party of Germany comes at exactly the right moment. The program itself is the product of the first independent movements of the rural proletariat, leading to the founding of the Communist Agricultural Workers' and Small Peasants' League in Central Silesia. The agrarian program was worked out in common by the party headquarters and officers of the League, and in appearance coincides with the first great mass movement of the agricultural workers. Thus it will soon be more than a piece of paper. Soon it will be the battle-cry of millions of country proletarians when they attack the Junker strongholds.

For not until this standard is carried before the country folk, will the ranks of the revolution close, then only will the revolution be irresistible. Therefore, let the city proletarians with all their strength carry the revolutionary message to the farm lands. The rural and urban proletariat divided cannot gain the victory, only their union will be their triumph.

Here follows the text of the agrarian program (it should be remarked that it is yet to be presented for ratification at a party conference):

I

The immense economic work of destruction of the World War has undermined the foundations of capitalism in Germany. In this hell-fire the apparatus of production has melted. Labor power, machinery, raw material, auxiliary materials, currency, all have been decimated. And in the same degree that these values of use were destroyed the war debt rose, and with it rose the demands of the capitalist class upon the fruits of labor. In the same degree anarchy in production increased. Capital, whose historic role was the widest development of the forces of production, has itself developed into a pure parasite upon the body of society, into a force of destruction and confusion. Its historical hour has struck. The proletariat is called upon to execute the sentence of history under pain of the decay of production.

The military collapse of German imperialism on the fields of France gave the impetus to this conflict which has been lying ready in the womb of society. Its signal was the revolution of November 9th. But this revolution, although carried on by war-weary and disappointed soldiers and the workers, has left the foundations of the capitalistic system untouched. It attacked only the outer state form. It transformed the monarchistic military state into a bourgeois republic, with the traitors of Socialism as officers of the firm. The political form of the dominion of capital was reformed, given a new base.

But the political revolution was at the same time the point of departure of the conflict between capital and labor which swept over Germany in a series of violent strike waves and armed uprisings and the result of which can be only the overthrow of a capitalist rule. The industrial proletariat introduced the rebellion of wage labor against capital. In its steps followed the employes of commercial and financial capital.

It is obvious that the conflict between capital and labor cannot be restricted to the cities. More severely than upon the urban proletariat, the domination of capital weighs down the proletariat of the country. Its collapse threatens also the petite-bourgeoisie with destruction.

The rural proletariat and the small farmers are hindered in their fight against capital by territorial division and rural isolation. These obstacles can be overcome only by the closest co-operation with the proletariat of the cities.

II

In agriculture on a large scale socialistic production is prepared for by capital itself. All that is needed is to break the restrictions of private ownership, to appropriate the land and the means of labor for society, and to establish a close co-operation with socialized industry and commerce, so that here, too, the socialistic mode of labor may develop. The class of small farmers and the tenant farmers on the large estates suffer no less than the agricultural proletariat under the pressure of the capitalistic mode of labor. But its system of management is not yet developed to the point where it could pass over into a socialistic system. The latter cannot be put through by force. Bourgeois management has undermined bourgeois petty ownership by applying for centuries a violent process of economic uprooting and of fraud which simply hurls the small farmer down into the proletariat or causes him to lead a hybrid existence between the industrial proletarian and the agricultural proletarian, separating him from the soil and from his implements of labor, and placing him under the domination of the landlord or the industrial employer. Very frequently he has been converted into an agricultural day-laborer or an industrial wage. Else his farm has been so dwarfed or mortgaged as to become a drag upon him, forcing him down into the position of a bondsman of landlordism and industrial capital. On the other hand, the attitude of the working class in power toward the small farmer can be only that of assistance and education, so that he may find the way to Socialism. The idea is to lighten the economic burden of the small farmer in his position as a small farmer by means of every possible support from socialized industry and commerce. It is our purpose to free the small farmer from the bureaucratic clerical gang that has been running his affairs, and to open to him the way to the independent management of his own business; it is our purpose finally to extend the beginnings of his own business, its co-operatives, so that he may step by step attain to co-operative production on a large scale. In order to accomplish the end of freeing the small farmer from capitalistic exploitation and to establish the socialistic mode of production in agriculture, the Communistic Party sets up the following demands:

1. Large-scale agricultural enterprises are such as constantly employ outside labor for wages, for the purpose of obtaining capitalistic profits. Small-scale enterprises are farms which do not employ outside labor at all, or else under such conditions that these workers form an integral part of the farm-household, like the owner and his family.

Management of Large Estates

2. All large estates worked on a large scale, together with all livestock and equipment, as well as all the auxiliary industrial plants and their working capital, shall be confiscated without compensation by the Socialist state. They shall become the common property of socialistic society.

3. Landlord rights and titles (landlord hunting and fishing rights, tax exemptions, police rights, etc.), as well as all rights of entailed property, shall be cut off without compensation.

4. On every large estate the steadily employed farm hands, mechanics, employees, and domestics form an estate council.

5. The estate council shall take over the co-operative management of the state under the central administrative organization, which shall be uniform for all the large agricultural enterprises.

6. The estate council, within the bounds of the regulations of the central organization, shall take over:

1. Employment and discharge of workers.
2. Determination of working hours and wages.
3. Cultivation and use of the fields and the supervision of the industrial plants connected with the estate.
4. The distribution of the agricultural products in excess of the needs of the estate itself.
5. The determination of the needs of the estate in the way of agricultural accessories which it does not itself produce (seeds, cattle for slaughter, dairy cattle, breeding stock, agricultural machines and implements, fertilizers, feeds, chemicals, building materials, etc.).
6. The determination and distribution of the necessary industrial products, articles for individual use (food, furniture and domestic equipment, clothing) and of the products of literature and art.
7. The determination of the necessary working capital.

The amount of the agricultural and industrial products of the estate that are necessary for home use shall be determined by the central organization, the excess shall be delivered to local centers, likewise the needs of the estates in the way of agricultural, industrial, and commercial articles shall be referred to the local assembling and distributing centers.

7. The excess products of the estate shall be credited to the co-operatives of the estate as delivered.

The financing of the estate shall be vested in central banks.

8. The forests and hunting preserves shall be managed centrally through the co-operatively organized forest workers and officials who shall also form councils.

9. The right of exploitation of forests hitherto owned by peasant communities shall be retained by these communities within the limits of their local needs. They shall be centrally managed like all the other forests.

10. The water courses shall be uniformly managed according to river systems.

11. During the busy seasons, in agricultural work requiring completion within definite periods (sowing, harvesting), gangs of agricultural workers shall be formed, their local distribution to be determined by the central organization.

12. In order to make up the quota of agricultural workers in the busy seasons at all times, it is necessary also that the industrial workers shall be trained from their earliest youth in the elements of agriculture.

On the other hand it is necessary that the resident agricultural workers should be trained in the elements of agricultural and industrial mechanics, in the interest of the technical development of agriculture itself as well as to enable those who cannot be employed in agriculture to transfer to industry without friction.

13. Instruction, study materials, and means of subsistence at the general as well as technical and agricultural schools shall be free.

14. For agricultural reclamation work on a large scale (clearing of waste lands, irrigation, drainage, road building, animal and plant experimentation, etc.) the State shall place means and labor power at the disposal of the estate councils.

15. Estates not being worked on a large scale, but parcelled out in small rent farms shall be confiscated, like the large enterprises, without compensation. As much of this land as was formerly worked on a small scale shall be given over to the local agricultural workers' and small farmers' councils, which shall regulate their manner of exploitation and management with a view to the interests of the former managers, the small farmers.

16. Government lands, in so far as they have not been divided into small rent farms, shall be made into model and experimental farms under the immediate direction of the provincial or state central organizations. In connection with these lands, agricultural schools and colleges shall be established.

17. The State shall attempt to equalize the cultural differences between city and country by making all the elements of city culture available to the rural population, through the development of an extensive rapid transit system and other means of transportation; also, in the interests of production itself, by supplying the country adequately with electric power, gas, etc., and finally through the systematic unification of the agricultural with the industrial establishments.

Small Farm Management

18. The private property of the small farmer shall remain untouched. The land hitherto under his cultivation may be disposed of by him as he sees fit.

19. The small farmer shall manage his economic and administrative affairs himself in accordance with the Soviet Constitution. This self-management is to take the place of the system of bureaucratic tutelage under the capitalistic state.

20. The farm hands working on the small farms, as well as the female domestic workers, shall organize into local small farm councils.

The membership of the small farm councils shall include the resident village craftsmen and small merchants who do not employ outside labor.

The local small farm councils in turn join with the estate councils of the large estates within the township to form village councils together with any industrial workers that may be resident in the village.

The small farm councils shall manage the economic affairs of the group of small farmers in common. The village councils shall manage the economic affairs and the administration of the village in common.

21. The small farm councils shall care for the common purchasing of fertilizers, feed, seeds, breeding cattle, agricultural implements, machinery, and the various necessities of life.

In conjunction with the local estate councils and workers' councils, they shall manage the delivery of their excess agricultural products to the local assembling and distributing centers.

22. The socialistically organized industries shall supply the small farmers with industrial necessities of life. They shall encourage the formation of co-operatives out of small enterprises through the extension of a finely woven net of electrical power

systems, by supplying machinery and buildings to be used by co-operatives, by the extension of general and technical education, by supplying specialists gratis to manage technical undertakings, etc.

23. The transition to large scale co-operative agricultural production shall be the combination of the small farms of the township into a common enterprise, the district co-operative, to be worked in common by all the members of the township.

A township co-operative may be formed by the free decision of the small farm inhabitants of the township.

The beginnings of a township co-operative may be formed through the free organization of any number of small farmers who combine for co-operative work.

24. The socialized industries shall aid the township co-operatives by the construction of township barns, township stables, and other township buildings, by supplying geometricians, technicians, agricultural experts, and gangs of workers for sowing and harvesting time, as well as capital for stock and upkeep.

25. Education, including general and technical training, school supplies, and subsistence during the school year shall be free.

26. All schools in city and country shall be equipped by the State with appropriate means for the practical training of the pupils in the main branches of agricultural work.

27. Mortgages and real estate titles shall be taken over by the State. They may not be broken, even though the State shall have the right to declare them void.

Economic and Political Structure of the Estate, Small Farm, and Village Councils

28. The estate, small farm, and village councils shall be united according to economic districts and finally for the entire State.

Each of these council organizations shall elect from among its members an executive committee, which shall conduct ordinary business and have the right to enlist the services of experts. The supreme economic Soviet body for agriculture shall be the central congress of agricultural workers' and small farmers' councils. The congress shall elect from among its members as its executive organ the central agricultural council. This body shall belong to the central economic bureau and in common with the latter decides the general rules for the management of agriculture.

29. The village communities shall govern themselves through

the village councils. Current business shall be conducted by the executive committee of the village council.

The members of the executive committee, as also those of the village council may at any time be recalled by their constituents. The village councils shall send their delegates to the precinct workers' and peasants' councils, these to the district workers' and peasants' councils, etc., which together with the other councils shall wield the political power in their respective territories.

The former tutelage of the agricultural population by the bureaucrats shall be replaced by their self-government. (*The Class Struggle,* November, 1919.)

Document No. 5

To the Workers and Soldiers of the Entente!

Berlin, *October* 31, 1918.

Friends, Comrades, Brothers! — In the midst of the earthquake of the World War, of the chaotic collapse of the czaristic imperialist society, the Russian proletariat, in spite of misunderstanding, hatred and slander, has established its rule — the Socialist Republic of Workers, Soldiers and Peasants. It is the titanic beginning of the Socialist construction of the world, the work which constitutes now the historic task of the international proletariat. The Russian revolution has tremendously stimulated the revolutionizing process of the world's proletariat. Bulgaria and Austria-Hungary are already drawn into the struggle. The German revolution, too, is awakening. Still, tremendous difficulties are arising on the way to victory of the German proletariat. The bulk of the people of Germany are with us. The power of the most bitter enemies of the working class is breaking down. Still they are striving by means of lies and deception to chain the masses to their chariot and to put off the hour of the emancipation of the people of Germany.

And just as the imperialism of the Entente Powers was strengthened by the robberies and murders perpetrated by German imperialism in Russia, so have the German rulers made use of the assault of the Entente Powers upon Socialist Russia for the maintenance of their power in Germany.

Have you seen how a few weeks ago Kaiser Wilhelm II, who,

after the overthrow of Czarism as the representative of the most infamous reaction, made use of the intervention of the Entente Powers against proletarian Russia to arouse anew the war spirit of the masses of workers?

We cannot allow that such welcome opportunities for demagogy be placed into the hands of our contemptible enemies — the most abominable enemy of the world proletariat. It cannot be that the proletariat of the Entente Powers should allow such a thing to happen. Of course we know that you have already raised your voice against the machinations of your governments. But the danger is constantly growing. The united front of the world imperialism against the proletariat is becoming a reality in the case of the campaign against the Russian Soviet Republic.

It is to fight to prevent this that I am appealing to you!

The world proletariat cannot allow the hearth of the Socialist Revolution to be put out if it does not want to see its own hopes and power vanish. The downfall of the Russian Soviet Republic would mean the defeat of the world proletariat.

Friends, Comrades, Brothers! Raise your arms against your masters!

Long live Russia of the workers, peasants and soldiers!

Long live the revolution of the French, British, Italian and American proletariat!

Long live the emancipation of workingmen of all countries from the hell of war, exploitation and slavery!

KARL LIEBKNECHT.

Document No. 6

THE CONSTITUTION OF THE HUNGARIAN SOCIALIST FEDERATED SOVIET REPUBLIC

Fundamental Principles

Section 1. In establishing the Soviet Republic the proletariat has taken into its hands full liberty, full right and full power for the purpose of doing away with the capitalistic order and the rule of the bourgeoisie and putting in its place the socialistic system of production and society. The dictatorship of the proletariat is, however, only a means to the destruction of all exploitation and class rule of whatever kind, and the preparation for the social order which knows no classes and in which also the most important instrument of class rule, the power of the state, ceases to exist.

Section 2. The Hungarian Soviet Republic is the Republic of the Workers', Soldiers' and Peasants' Councils. The Soviet Republic will not grant to the exploiters a place in any council. In the Workers', Soldiers' and Peasants' Councils the working people shall create the laws, execute them, and pass judgment upon all who transgress against these laws. The proletariat exercises all central and local authority in the Councils.

Section 3. The Soviet Republic is a free league of free nations. In its foreign policy the Soviet Republic shall aim, with the aid of the world revolution, to bring about the peace of the workers' world. It desires peace without conquest and without indemnities, based upon the right of self-determination of the workers.

In place of imperialism, which caused the World War, the Soviet Republic desires the union, the federation of the proletarians of all lands, the international Soviet Republic of the workers. Hence it is opposed to war as a mode of exploitation, opposed to all forms of oppression and subjugation of the people. It condemns the means employed by class governments in their foreign relations, particularly secret diplomacy.

The Rights of the Workers in the Hungarian Federated Soviet Republic

Section 4. For the sake of checking exploitation and organizing and increasing production the Soviet Republic aims to transmit all the means of production into the profession of the society of the workers. To this end it shall take over as public property all industrial, mining and transportation establishments exceeding retail dimensions.

Section 5. The domination of financial capital shall be checked in the Hungarian Soviet Republic by turning all financial institutions and insurance companies into public property.

Section 6. In the Hungarian Soviet Republic only those who work shall have the right to live. The Soviet Republic prescribes compulsory labor and, on the other hand, insures the right to work. Those who are incapacitated for work, or to whom the state cannot offer employment, shall be supported by the state.

Section 7. In order to insure the power of the toiling masses and in order to thwart the re-establishment of the power of the exploiters, the Soviet Republic shall arm the workers and disarm the exploiters. The Red Army shall form the class-army of the proletariat.

Section 8. In the Soviet Republic the workers shall be able to express their opinion freely in speech and writing, for that power of capital which enabled it to degrade the press to an agency for disseminating the capitalistic ideologies and obscuring the self- consciousness of the proletarians, the dependency of the press upon capital, has ceased. The right to publish literature of every kind belongs to the workers, and the Soviet Republic shall see to it that the ideas of Socialism shall be propagated freely throughout the country.

Section 9. In the Soviet Republic freedom of assemblage of the workers shall be absolutely guaranteed. All proletarians shall have the right to meet freely or organize processions. With the overthrow of the rule of the bourgeoisie all obstacles to the free right of organization of the workers are removed, and the Soviet Republic shall not only bestow upon the workers and peasants the fullest freedom of union and organization, but shall also, in order to secure the development and permanency of their freedom of organization, extend to them every material and moral support.

Section 10. The Soviet Republic shall do away with the cultural privilege of the bourgeoisie and extend to the workers the opportunity for the positive appropriation of culture. It shall guarantee to the working class and the peasants free instruction, offering a high degree of education.

Section 11. The Soviet Republic shall preserve the true freedom of conscience of the workers by complete separation of church and state and of church and school. Everyone may exercise his own religion freely.

Section 12. The Soviet Republic proclaims the proposition of the unification of the proletarians of all lands, and, therefore, grants to every foreign proletarian the same rights that are due to the proletarians of Hungary.

Section 13. In the Hungarian Soviet Republic every foreign revolutionist shall possess the right of asylum.

Section 14. The Hungarian Soviet Republic recognizes no differences of race or nationality. It shall not permit any form of oppression of national minorities nor any abridgement of the use of their language. Everyone shall be permitted to use his mother tongue freely, and it shall be the duty of all officials to accept any document written in any language in use in Hungary, to hear everyone in his native tongue, and to deal with him in that tongue.

The Central Organization of the Soviet Government

Section 15. In the Soviet Republic the supreme authority shall be vested in the National Congress of the Federated Soviets.

Section 16. The jurisdiction of the National Congress of Soviets shall extend over all state affairs of high importance, in particular (1) the establishment and amendment of the Constitution of the Hungarian Socialist Federated Soviet Republic; (2) the establishment and modification of the boundaries of the country; (3) the declaring of war and the negotiating of peace; (4) the closing of international agreements; (5) the raising of state loans; (6) the supreme direction of external and internal policies; (7) the division of the country into districts; (8) the definition of the jurisdiction of the local councils; (9) the general direction of the economic life of the country, in its entirety as well as in its separate branches; (10) the establishment and modification of the monetary system and the system of weights and measures; (11) the drawing up of the budget of the Soviet Republic; (12) the determination of the public burden; (13) the determination of the system of defense; (14) the regulation of the right of state citizenship; (15) state, civil, and criminal legislation; (16) the determination of the structure of the judicial system; (17) general or partial amnesty; (18) the supreme direction of cultural affairs.

All questions relating to the affairs over which the National Congress of Federated Soviets has established its authority shall be brought up in the National Congress of Soviets. During the time that the National Congress of Federated Soviets is not in session its jurisdiction shall be exercised by the Directing Federal Central Committee.

The following, however, shall come unconditionally and solely under the jurisdiction of the National Congress of Federated Soviets:

(a) The establishment and amendment of the Constitution;
(b) The declaring of war and the negotiation of peace;
(c) The determination of the boundaries of the country.

Section 17. The National Congress of Soviets shall be convened by the Directing Federal Central Committee at least twice in each year.

Section 18. The National Congress of Soviets must be convened by the Federal Central Committee upon demand of the Councils of districts and cities whose population totals at least one-third of the population of the country.

Section 19. The Directing Federal Central Committee, which is to be elected by the National Congress of Federated Soviets, shall consist of not more than 150 members. All nationalities living in the country shall be represented in the Central Committee in proportion to their population.

Section 20. The Directing Central Committee shall, during the time that the National Congress of the Councils is not in session, assume the conduct of state affairs; it shall exercise supreme legislative and executive power. During the other time it shall always participate directly in the control of state affairs. From among its members shall be chosen, besides the People's Deputies, all committees assigned to the People's Commissariats and supplementing the work of the People's Deputies.

Section 21. The Directing Central Committee directs the activities of the Workers', Soldiers' and Peasants' Councils as well as of all representative publications of the Councils. It shall care for the practical working out of the Soviet Constitution and carry out the decisions of the National Congress of Soviets.

Section 22. The Directing Central Committee shall report to the National Congress of Soviets concerning its operations. It shall keep the Congress informed of the general political and economic situation, as also concerning definite questions of greater importance.

Section 23. The Directing Central Committee shall be responsible for its actions to the National Congress of Soviets.

Section 24. The Directing Central Committee shall elect the Revolutionary Soviet Government and its President.

Section 25. The members of the Revolutionary Soviet Government are the People's Deputies. The Revolutionary Soviet Government shall appoint the People's Deputies to the heads of the various People's Commissariats and of the main sections of the People's Council for Political Economy.

Section 26. It shall be the duty of the Revolutionary Soviet Government to transact the affairs of the Soviet Republic in accordance with the injunctions of the National Congress of Soviets, as well as of the Federal Central Committee.

Section 27. The Revolutionary Soviet Government shall have the power to issue decrees. In general it may order all that is necessary for the speedy transaction of state business.

Section 28. The Revolutionary Soviet Government shall inform the Directing Central Committee forthwith of its decrees, decisions, and any measures taken in important affairs.

Section 29. The Directing Central Committee shall examine the decrees, decisions, and measures of the Revolutionary Soviet Government, the People's Council for Political Economy, and all other People's Commissariats, and shall have power to amend them.

Section 30. The Soviet Government may take steps in state matters of decisive importance without previous dispensation of the Directing Central Committee only in case of extraordinary urgency.

Section 31. The members of the Revolutionary Soviet Government are responsible to the National Congress of Soviets and the Directing Federal Central Committee.

Section 32. The various People's Commissaires shall be as follows: (1) The people's Council for Political Economy; (2) the People's Commissariat for Foreign Affairs; (3) for Military Affairs; (4) for the Interior; (5) for Justice; (6) for Public Welfare and Health; (7) for Education; (8) the German; (9) the Russian People's Commissariat.

Section 33. The various People's Deputies may, within the jurisdiction of their respective People's Commissariats, and the People's Council for Political Economy in questions coming under its jurisdiction, issue decrees and injunctions. The Revolutionary Soviet Government shall have power to amend the decrees of the People's Council for Political Economy as well as those of the various People's Commissariats.

Section 34. The jurisdiction of the People's Council for Political Economy shall extend over the uniform control of production and the distribution of goods, the issuing and executing of decrees affecting the national economy, and the technical economic control of the agencies of production and distribution.

Section 35. The main divisions of the People's Council for Political Economy are as follows: (a) General administration of production, husbandry of raw materials, and foreign trade; (b) agriculture and cattle-raising; (c) technical direction of industrial production and channels of distribution; (d) finance;

(e) public relief; (f) traffic; (g) economic organization and control; (h) labor.

Organization of the Local Soviets

Sections 38 to 65 concern the structure of the local system of councils, the prescriptions for suffrage, the powers and the mutual relations of the councils, which hold all political power in their hands. On account of lack of space we can reproduce only a few of the most important dispositions.

The working rural population sends one member to the village council for each 100 inhabitants, the working urban population sends only one member for each 50 inhabitants to the city council. The village and city councils of a district elect the District Workers', Peasants' and Soldiers' Council, in which the delegates of the cities may not comprise more than one-half. For every 1,000 inhabitants there is one member. The district councils of each county (comitat) elect the county councils, one delegate being elected for each 5,000 inhabitants.

Section 48. The function of the village, city, district, and county councils shall be to promote in every way the economic and cultural welfare of the working people living within the borders of their respective territorial units. To this end they shall decide all matters of local significance and execute all decrees referred to them by their superior councils and People's Commissariats.

Section 49. The previously existing machinery of local administration herewith ceases to exist. The personnel taken over by the councils with the public offices and public works shall be at the disposal of the councils. The administration and other public buildings that have heretofore served the purposes of local government shall be transferred, together with their equipment, into the hands of the councils.

Section 52. The councils shall constantly observe whether the ordinances of their superior administrative bodies prove satisfactory. They shall direct the attention of the latter or of the appropriate People's Commissariat to any shortcomings and may present suggestions, if in their opinion any measure of the higher administration or of any other body seems necessary.

Section 53. The councils shall preserve all the public works and institutions serving the dietary, hygienic, economic, cultural and similar needs of the population and may create new ones and recommend the establishment of others to their superior councils.

Section 54. The villages, cities, districts and counties shall conduct their financial affairs independently, within the limits ordained by the People's Council for Political Economy.

Section 55. The councils shall have power to choose and discharge officials and other trained workers, including the transferred personnel of the former administration. Any trust conferred upon an officer of the Hungarian Republic may be revoked at any time.

Section 58. In counties, cities and districts special committees of experts (sub-committees) shall be regularly formed for the following affairs: (1) economic, financial and industrial; (2) roads and public traffic; (3) public welfare and health; (4) housing; (5) public relief; (6) cultural affairs.

Section 62. The councils shall see to it that disputing parties receive prompt and accurate advices in regard to their cases without any formalities and in their mother-tongue; that appropriate agencies exist for receiving oral complaints and requests; that, after the hearing of the interested parties and after a complete disposition of the cases — based, wherever possible, upon direct observation of the circumstances — the requests be discharged within the shortest time possible, without awaiting solicitation, and the parties be notified thereof in appropriate form.

Suffrage

Section 66. In the Hungarian Socialist Federated Soviet Republic only the working people shall have the right to vote. All those are voters and eligible for election to membership in the councils, regardless of sex, who have passed their eighteenth year and as workers or employees, etc., live by work that is useful to society, or occupy themselves with household labor which makes possible the labor of the above mentioned workers or employees, etc. Further, soldiers of the Red Army are voters and are eligible for election, as well as those workers and soldiers who have formerly lived by useful labor, but have entirely or partially lost their capacity for labor.

Section 67. Citizens of other states shall also be voters and eligible for election, provided, they fulfill the conditions contained in preceding sections.

Section 68. The following may not vote and are not eligible for election: (a) all those who employ wage-workers for the purpose of obtaining profit; (b) those who live off unearned income; (c) merchants; (d) clergymen and members of religious orders; (e) those mentally deranged and those living under guardianship; (f) those whose political rights have been suspended because of a crime committed from base motives, for the period of time stipulated in the conviction.

The Budget Privilege

Section 78. The Hungarian Soviet Government shall be guided in its financial policy exclusively from the point of view of the satisfaction of the needs of its workers. It shall show no consideration for unearned income.

Section 79. The branches of the Soviet Republic may collect receipts and defray expenditures only within the limits of an approved budget.

Section 80. The estimate of costs for the village, district, city and county shall be determined by the appropriate local council upon the suggestion of the directing committee, the estimate of costs for the Soviet Republic by the National Congress of Soviets upon the suggestion of the Revolutionary Soviet Government or of the Directing Central Committee.

The Rights of Nationalities in the Hungarian Socialist Federated Soviet Republic

Section 84. All nationalities living in the Hungarian Socialist Federated Soviet Republic may use their language freely and foster and promote their own culture. To this end any national group, even if it does not live in a continuous territory, may create a federal council for the promotion of its culture.

Section 85. As a result of the Soviet system the local administration will be conducted by the workers of those nationalities whose workers form the majority in their respective local unit. This sort of local administration will naturally find expression in the matter of the language. The national minorities may, nevertheless, use their own speech in dealing with the agents of the Soviets. This system cannot disturb the Soviet organization based upon territorial principles.

Section 86. Wherever the workers of any particular nationality in a continuous territory extending over several districts find themselves in the majority, independent counties shall be created.

Where any particular national group in a continuous territory extending over several counties finds itself in the majority, the districts may unite into one national county.

The counties united in this manner are, through the national county, parts of the Hungarian Socialist Federated Soviet Republic.

Section 87. The Hungarian continuous counties with German majority or Russian majority are herewith recognized under the Constitution of the Federated Soviet Republic as German and Russian national counties. In matters affecting the universal interests of the Soviet Republic the decisions of the Federated Soviet Republic extend to the national counties.

Section 88. The Hungarian Socialist Federated Soviet Republic shall interpose no obstacle if the national groups of the increasingly independent territories, empowered by their population and their economic strength, decide to form a separate Soviet Republic allied with the Hungarian Soviet Republic.

Section 89. The provisions of the Constitution relating to the rights of nationalities may be amended only with the consent of the Federal Council of the workers of the participating national groups.

Document No. 7

THE LAST APPEAL OF THE HUNGARIAN SOVIET GOVERNMENT TO THE WORKING CLASS OF HUNGARY

To the Working People of Hungary:

COMRADES! PROLETARIANS! — The international and the Hungarian counter-revolution are swooping down with grim fury upon the Hungarian Soviet Republic, the state of the poor and the workers, the destroyer of the dominion of capital, the constructor of Socialism.

The police force of the international counter-revolution of the capitalists, the Entente, has set its armed hordes upon us. The misled and terrorized mass of proletarians which has been welded to the slave-chains of the Roumanian boyars or forced to groan under the yoke of the Czecho-Slovakian capitalists is stirring against us in order to drive the proletariat of Hungary back into that pool of misery, of bondage, and exploitation which the Dictatorship of the Proletariat has dried up. On command of French, English, and American capitalists and Czech and Roumanian nationalists, Czecho-Slovakian, French, colored peasants and workers are attempting to force the liberated Hungarian proletariat once more under the yoke of the capitalists and oppressors. The attack which they are directing against the rule of the Hungarian proletariat *purposes to re-establish the private ownership of the means of production.*

They want to return the banks and hence the complete dominion over the economic life of the country to the money-kings.

They want to return to the stockholders their dividends and their unearned income and to turn the hard labor of the miner and the industry of the factory worker once more into a source of prosperity and ease for the idlers.

They want to give back all the means of production, the factory, the machine, the raw material, the transportation facilities, to the exploiters and once more set upon the workers' necks the boss, the director, the slave-driver.

They want to force the workers to pay the interest on the war loans and surrender a tithe out of the return from their labor to the drones, the various rent-profiteers.

They want to reinstate the landlords whom the country people have driven out and to thrust the poor peasants, the small landholder, the squatter, the agricultural workers back into the condition of serfdom.

They want to put the confiscated money and jewels back into the hands of the rich so that they may be able to continue their luxurious, indolent, frivolous life which is a bane to society.

The house-rent usurers and the usurious dealers who without any necessity or cause have raised the price of every commodity — these they want to let loose once more upon the proletarian consumer, so that the value of his money may decrease still more. They want to reduce wages and increase the hours of labor, in short, *whatever the revolution has built up in the way of Socialist institutions* they want to tear down and distort.

The international counter-revolution aims to force upon us once more with armed might the dominion of private property, the strength of the capitalists, and it aims to drown in the blood of the workers that mighty work of the Dictatorship of the Proletariat, a work which has carried us amid a thousand dangers and sufferings but with giant strides toward the world of Socialism.

Under the protection of the international capitalistic counter-revolution preparations are being made to organize *the Hungarian counter-revolution.*

Under the protection of the Roumanian and Czecho-Slovakian army of occupation the great Hungarian patriots have gathered to lay waste the Hungarian land with the force of arms. In Arad the landlords, the capitalists, and their beholden retinue of bourgeois politicians have established an opposing government. Like the Russian leaders of 1849, so to-day the representatives of the ruling classes are clearing the way for the present hostile invasion. They are trying to organize *a white guard for the white government.* The justices of the peace, the notaries, the little autocrats of the comitats, the former congressional representatives of privileges, the grafters, who have been deprived of their business, the bankrupt adventurers, all the derelicts of the worn-out and overthrown political parties, finding support in the Roumanian and French arms are preparing to revive the class government of tyranny and oppression, they are organizing to wrest the political power from the poor workers and peasants and to entrust it again to those mercenary oppressors and politicians, to those classes whom only the storm of two revolutions was able to shake out of their political seats of power.

The Dictatorship of the Proletariat as transition stage of the state to Socialism — that is the watchword of the Hungarian Soviet Republic.

The dictatorship of the oppressors and exploiters as a permanent form of government — that is the emblem of the counter-revolution.

In the factories, in the fields, in the offices, all power to belong to the workers, the producers — that is the significance of our red banner.

All authority vested in the landlord, the manufacturer, the banker, the bishop — that is the motto which sullies the white flag of our opponents.

The preparing and establishing of Socialism — that is the purpose and the reason for existence of the Soviet Republic.

The vain attempt to revive capitalism — that is the economic program of the counter-revolution.

Hence it is not a war, whose furies are now being loosed upon us, even though it is being conducted by the force of arms, but an *armed class struggle* which Hungarian and International capitalism is carrying on against the proletariat of Hungary, the advance guard of the world revolution. This conflict is the struggle for the existence and development of the working class, a life and death struggle which will mean the realization or the overthrow of Socialism, and every proletarian is a traitor to himself, a traitor to his class, a traitor to the sacred cause of the social world revolution, a traitor to the world-redeeming idea of Socialism, who does not now with all his readiness to sacrifice, with all his energy, with all his courage, his life and limb, his work, his manhood, stand by the endangered revolution, the besieged Dictatorship of the Proletariat, the hard-pressed cause of Socialism!

The organized workers of Budapest are at this moment at the front holding over the dominion of the proletariat a shield made of their own living bodies. The pick of the workers have taken up arms in order, even at the cost of their lives, to defend the great idea of the rule of the workers, to protect the *cause of the social world revolution* from any reverse.

"We believe that the great energies of Socialism poured forth in an inexhaustible stream will render this Red Army, which is fighting the class struggle of the workers against the hordes of the exploiters and oppressors, invincible. But this struggle necessitates the work, the sacrifices of the workers and poor peasantry of the whole country! We, therefore, call all proletarians, the workers of city and village, all the adherents of outraged Poverty demanding power, to arms. We call upon the proletariat of the occupied districts to prevent with all lawful and unlawful means, with all methods of open and underground warfare, the organization of the white counter-revolution and to fight with every weapon of individual and mass action against all counter-revolutionary classes, groups, and individuals! We call upon every proletarian of the occupied districts to *obstruct by means of sabotage the war which the international and Hungarian capitalists* are waging against the Hungarian Revolutionary Soviet Republic, against the rule of the toiling masses of the poor.

But let the capitalists and the counter-revolutionists heed the following:

The cause of the Proletariat, of the social revolution cannot fall, in fact it is obviously making strides the world over. And the forces of the proletariat will advance to the points where at this moment the counter-revolutionists are hiding under cover of the arms of the imperialistic conquerors, and then our settlement with those who introduced armed civil war against the rule of the proletariat will be merciless and unsparing! But until we are able to extend the power of the proletariat to those districts which have been wrested from us, we owe it to our proletarian brothers fighting at the front, to our own principles, and the obligation which we have assumed toward the world revolution, to work with all our might to destroy root and branch the economic system of capitalism and the state based upon oppression and force, and *out of the constructive forces of Socialism* to rebuild and perfect it as much as possible in the triumphant, indomitable spirit of the Dictatorship of the Proletariat!

Long live the International Socialist World Revolution!

Long live the Dictatorship of the Proletariat!

Long live the Hungarian Soviet Republic!

THE REVOLUTIONARY SOVIET GOVERNMENT.

THE HUNGARIAN SOCIALIST PARTY.

(*The Class Struggle,* August, 1919)

CHAPTER XVI

The Third Socialist International *

The culminating and fundamental event in international Socialism of the present time has been the founding of the Third International of Moscow and it is very important to trace the steps which led up to this climax.

The uncompromising Socialists who were in favor of peace at any price and who wished to destroy the division of peoples into nations with separate interests, found themselves in a minority at the opening of the war, as has already been noticed. There is no question that all Socialists, whether they were conservative and nationalists, or revolutionary and internationalists, were driven to almost despair by the divisions and divergences occasioned by the outbreak of the war. Many thought that this meant the downfall of Socialism as a power, because for years the Socialist parties had been advocating the abolition of armaments and the ending of war. And now the greatest war of all times had begun. The majority parties in the Socialist field, except in the case of Italy, having decided to side with their governments, it was only the neutrals and the minorities in Russia, Germany and France that could plan to carry on the anti-militarist campaign. This they attempted to do almost at once. These uncompromising anti-nationalists, peace-at-any-price Socialists, urged on by Swiss Socialists and by certain Russians then in Switzerland, but especially by the whole Italian Socialist Party and by Lenin himself, called a conference in September, 1915, at Zimmerwald, in Switzerland. This conference became the startingpoint of what has now culminated in the Third International, organized at Moscow in March, 1919. It has already been referred to in this Report.

Meanwhile there had been in January 1915 a futile Conference at Copenhagen, attended only by sixteen delegates, representing only the neutrals of Scandinavia and Holland, calling for peace. Whereas in February a Conference of Socialists of the Allied Countries had expressed itself in favor of victory.

The Zimmerwald Conference was attended by about forty Italian, Roumanian, Bulgarian, German, French, Swedish, Norwegian, Swiss, Polish, Dutch and Russian delegates. British

* See Addendum, Part I.

delegates were not allowed by the government to attend. It issued a manifesto addressed " To the Proletariat of all Nations," accusing the capitalists and jingoes of bringing on the war. It called on the workers of the world, no longer deceived by the fair promises of the selfish ruling classes, to condemn the war, as a crime, to call for the restoration of Belgian independence and to warn against annexation.

All wars were declared wars of aggression; and civil insurrection against war in all countries was urged: war against war. Another conference of the same group was held in April, 1916, at Kienthal, Switzerland. The principal leaders who signed the Zimmerwald manifesto were Ledebour and Hoffman for Germany, Bourderon and Merrheim for France, Modigliani and Lazzari for Italy, Lenin, Axelrod and Babroff for Russia and Kolarov for Bulgaria.

One of the French delegates, Merrheim, long after, told how for a whole day Lenin argued with him to induce him on his return to France from Zimmerwald to make open war on war, to induce French labor to go on a general strike and throw down its arms. Merrheim said that as at that moment the German armies were within thirty miles of Paris this proposal to betray his country made him from that time Lenin's enemy.

The Conference at Kienthal on April 24-30, 1916, was also attended by about forty delegates, but the majority were members of the official Italian Socialist Party, as well as some Swiss and Russians, two Germans and three Frenchmen (Brizon, Blanc and Raffin-Dugens). At neither of these conferences were there any representatives of the Major Socialist parties of France or Germany and none at all from England. The general Congress of French Socialists, held at Christmas, 1915, specifically repudiated the Zimmerwald program by 2,736 votes to 76. The National Council in April, 1916, did the same by 1,996 votes to 960, repudiating the peace-at-any-price program.

The French Socialist leaders without exception rallied to the government and several entered the ministry. There were however many of the minor leaders and of the rank and file who became defeatists and caused anxious moments.

The German Socialists did the same, with certain important qualified or unqualified exceptions. A large group formed the Independent Socialist Party because it did not approve of the purpose of the war. It was led by Haase. This group, however, did not refuse to vote for the war credits. A smaller group of the so-called "Spartacans" led by Karl Liebknecht openly opposed the war and refused to vote for the war credits.

In England the Independent Labor Party and the British Socialist Party opposed the war and suffered greatly from popular indignation in consequence. But their influence was negligible and was not aggressive except in theory.

It was in Italy that the disloyalty of the Socialist Party led to the verge of a national catastrophe, which will be later referred to.

Meanwhile various attempts were being made at International Socialist Peace Conferences. Early in 1917 the Socialist Party of the United States cabled a suggestion for a conference, which the Dutch-Scandinavian neutral committee acted upon, to bring together delegates from the warring as well as the neutral countries. This was opposed by the Allied governments and was abandoned.

But a peculiar situation arose when Henderson the English Labor Socialist leader, then a member of the British Cabinet, visited Russia in the Spring of 1917, and met there Albert Thomas, the French Socialist leader, then Minister of Munitions. This was after the fall of the Czar and before the advent of the Bolsheviki, when the Allies were arranging for the continuation of Russia in the war. The Russian Socialist leaders Skobilev, Tzeretelli and Tcheidze favored an International Socialist meeting and the All-Russian Council of Workers' and Soldier's Delegates issued a call for a conference to meet at Stockholm in August. It was an irregular call because not issued by the International Bureau of The Hague, but the invitation was accepted by nearly all the Socialist groups, by the French Socialist Party, the two German parties, the Austrian and Hungarian groups, the Belgian S. D. L. P., the United States Socialist Party and in England by the Independent Labor Party, British Socialist Party and Labor Party, and the Italian Socialist Party. The Congress never met because the Allied governments refused passports to the delegates.

On the other hand a conference of the adherents to the Zimmerwald program took place in September at Stockholm, which was made the seat of the bureau of its permanent committee, which had previously been at Berne. This so-called Zimmerwald Agitation Committee was reorganized with the exclusion of the Swiss delegate Grimm, owing to the scandalous intrigue called the

"Grimm affair," connected with German bribery of Socialist leaders.

Serious efforts to resuscitate the Second International were made after the close of the war in the two important conferences at Berne, February 2-9, 1919, and at Lucerne, August 2-9, 1919.

Kienthal Conference—April, 1916

The Manifesto issued by the Socialist Conference at Kienthal, reads as follows:

> "The Second International Socialist Conference offers warmest sympathy and greetings of solidarity to all the faithful, courageous, pioneers, who, in the midst of a bloody world catastrophe held high the flag of Socialism, and who, in spite of domestic truce and reconciliation theories, recognize no armistice in the battle against capitalism.
>
> "While the Conference extends greetings to all those brave fighters for freedom, right and peace, at the same time, it expresses its disgust and its vigorous protest against the reactionary measures, and unheard of persecutions, whose victims our comrades are, in Germany as in Russia, in England as in France, yes, even in neutral Sweden.
>
> "The Conference directs the attention of the workingmen of all countries on the one hand to the ruthless raging of the forces of reaction, which stands out in such sharp contrast with the legend of 'War for Freedom;' and on the other hand, directs attention to the imposing, enthusiastic, stirring rise of the revolutionary social democrats who are waging war, just as expressly against social patriotism, its confusing teachings, and its hypocritical spokesman, as against the policy of their own governments.
>
> "The Conference greets the newly-freed representatives of the Socialist women in Germany and in France, whose incarceration has only increased that influence upon the masses.
>
> "The Conference raises a decided protest against the persecution of the Jews by the Russian Government, and by their helpers, 'Liberal Bourgeoisie,' which, according to its accustomed system, endeavors to make the Jews pay for the dissatisfaction of the population as well as for military disasters.

"The Conference calls upon all parties, organizations and minorities, who took part in the Zimmerwald Conference, in imitation of their persecuted comrades, to stamp out the spirit of dissatisfaction and of protest in the masses, to educate them in the spirit of the International Socialist Democracy, in order that the individual sparks and coals of discontent may rise to a mighty flame of invective and widespread protest and in order that the International Proletariat may, in accordance with its historic mission, hasten the world liberating task — the fall of capitalism."

THE REVOLUTIONARY INTERNATIONAL SOCIALIST MEETING AT STOCKHOLM, IN 1917

The meeting planned for September, 1917, at Stockholm, for the Socialist parties belonging to the Second International, to go with representatives of the more radical parties, which was planned in connection with the Russian government preceding the Bolshevik, was prevented by the Entente governments, as we have seen. In its place, there met, in Stockholm, September 5-7, a conference of revolutionary Socialists, who issued a manifesto reaffirming the Zimmerwald Manifesto of 1915. This meeting may be considered as the third meeting of the revolutionary Socialists, the other two having been Zimmerwald and Kienthal. There attended representatives of the Independent Socialist Party of Germany, of the opposition group of Austria, and nearly all the Russian Socialist organizations, of the regular Socialist parties of Finland, Roumania, Poland and Switzerland, and of the radical wings of Sweden, Norway and Denmark. The United States were represented by members of the Socialist Propaganda League, and International Brotherhood. The delegates from England, France and Italy were prevented by their governments from attending. The long manifesto issued by this conference was practically a reiteration of the Zimmerwald and Kienthal documents, and called for a general international strike, to bring the war to an immediate close.

DOCUMENTS

I. CALL FOR A THIRD INTERNATIONAL AT MOSCOW

In January 1919, the Russian Soviet government sent out a call for the Congress of the Third International. It proposed the following platform:

1. The present period is the period of the dissolution and ruin of the whole capitalist system of the world and the disappearance of European culture.

2. The task of the proletariat consists today in taking possession at once of the governmental power — this power signifies the annihilation of the present apparatus of government — in order to replace it by the apparatus of proletarian power.

3. This new governmental apparatus should incorporate the dictatorship of the working class and, in some places, that also of the small peasants and agricultural laborers, and shall be the instrument of the systematic overthrow of the exploiting classes.

4. The dictatorship of the proletariat should aim at the immediate expropriation of capitalism and the suppression of private property and in its transfer to the proletarian state under Socialist administration of the working class.

5. In order to make the Socialist revolution secure, the disarming of the bourgeoisie and of its agents and the general arming of the proletariat are necessary.

6. The fundamental condition of the state is the mass action of the proletariat going as far as open conflict with arms in hand against the governmental power of capitalism.

7. The old International has split into three principal groups: the openly patriotic Socialists; the minority Socialists, composed of always hesitant elements, lastly the revolutionary Left Wing.

8. Against the Social patriots — only a combat without mercy is possible. As to the Centre, the tactics consist in separating out the revolutionary elements, in a pitiless criticism of its leaders, and in systematically dividing its adherents.

9. On the other side it is necessary to proceed to a *bloc* movement with those elements of the revolutionary workers who, although they have not formerly belonged to the party, now adopt as a whole the point of view of the dictatorship of the proletariat under the form of Soviet power, especially the Syndicalist elements of the labor movement.

10. Lastly it is necessary to rally the groups and the proletarian organizations which, while not having joined the revolutionary current of the left, have nevertheless shown the development of a tendency in that direction.

11. We propose that the representatives of the following parties, groups and tendencies take part in the Congress as plenipotentiary members of the Labor International: (1) The Spartacus League (Germany); (2) The Bolsheviks or Communist Party (Russia); the Communist parties of (3) German Austria; (4) Hungary; (5) Finland; (6) Poland; (7) Esthonia; (8) the Lettish provinces; (9) Lithuania; (10) White Russia; and (11) the Ukraine; (12) the revolutionary elements among the Czechs; (13) the Bulgarian Social Democratic Party, (14) the Roumanian Social Democratic Party; (15) The Left Wing of the Serbian Social Democratic Party; (16) the Left of the Swedish Social Democratic Party; (17) The Norwegian Social Democratic party; (18) in Denmark those groups standing for the class struggle; (19) the Dutch Communist Party; (20) the revolutionary elements of the Belgian Labor Party; (21) and (22) the groups and organizations within the Socialist and trade union (Syndicalist) movement in France, as a whole solidary with Loriot; (23) The Left of the Swiss Social Democratic Party; (24) the Italian Socialist Party; (25) the elements of the Left in the Spanish Socialist Party; (26) and in the Portuguese Socialist Party; (27) The British Socialist Party (the elements in it most nearly approaching us are those represented by MacLean); (28) I. S. L. P. (England); (29) I. W. W. K. (England); (30) I. W. W. (Great Britain); (31) the revolutionary elements in the labor organizations in Ireland; (32) and among the shop stewards (Great Britain); (33) S. L. P. Socialist Labor Party (America); (34) the elements of the Left of the American Socialist Party (tendencies represented by Debs and the Socialist Propaganda League). (Note: This was issued, it must be remembered, before the forming in Chicago of the two pro-Soviet parties, the Communist and Communist Labor parties, both of which have been welcomed into the International); (35) American I. W. W.; (36) I. W. W. (Australia); (37) American Workers International Industrial Union; (38) the Socialist groups of Tokio and Yokohama represented by Katayama; (39) the Young People's Socialist International.

MEETING FOR ISSUANCE OF THE CALL OF THE THIRD INTERNATIONAL

The Committee has come into possession of an extremely interesting document, the authenticity of which is duly established, and which is an historical document of such importance that we here publish it in full.

It does not give a full account of the meeting itself with the resolutions that were passed, but these resolutions are published from other authentic sources and are given elsewhere in this report.

The circumstances leading up to and attending the calling of this conference, and the resolutions there adopted, have been treated in this chapter. This particular document is a verbatim report of all the speeches that were made by the delegates to this conference: they are of especial interest because a number of them report on the character of the progress of Bolshevik International propaganda in the different countries of the world by men who came to Russia to report the status of that movement.

The importance of the revolutionary movement in the Balkans, and especially throughout the East, including the Eastern countries adjacent to and within the British Empire is emphasized.

This meeting to prepare for the Conference and to issue its program was held in Petrograd, while the Congress itself was to be held in Moscow. The avowed purpose of this movement was to place the Soviet Government of Russia at the head of the International Socialist movement.

II. SOVIET RUSSIA AND THE NATIONS OF THE WORLD

WITH A PREFACE BY MAXIM GORKY

Speeches made at the International Meeting in Petrograd; a publication of the Petrograd Soviet of the Deputies of Workingmen and Red Guardists.

PETROGRAD, 1919.

The International meeting on December 19th was a holiday of the Russian proletariat, and it is desirable that this great day of the Russian revolution would remain in the memory of the workingmen for a long time, forever.

The speeches are not so important, the words said to the Russian people by the representatives of diverse empires and nations of Europe and Asia are not so new and brilliant as the feeling of flaming trust towards laboring Russia; the deep understanding of her historic mission, expressed by twenty-three orators, is important and significant.

The Hindu and the Korean, the Englishman, the Persian, the Frenchman, the Chinaman, the Turk and all the rest talked, essentially, about one and the same topic — the topic of imperialism which has rushed in its greediness to mad and shameful massacre, choked in the blood of nations, intoxicated by it, and digged itself a grave, exposing in a most terrifying clearness before the whole working world its inhumanity and cynicism.

But, I say, not this known and already familiar to the ear of the toiling masses criticism of the crimes of the worn-out social structure, not the judgment of international justice on the band of international robbers, who fought among themselves about the dividing of the spoils,— not this was the fundamental significance of the meeting.

Its significance was in the unanimous feeling, which manifested itself as the funeral song to the past and in joyful good tidings, calling all nations to the assistance of revived revolutionary Russia, calling her to the assistance of the working people of all countries. In all speeches sounded the assurance that Russia, after having taken on herself through the will of history the mission of the foremost army of Socialism, will fulfill with honor and success this hard, great mission and will carry along with her all nations to the creation of new life.

These speeches in different languages sounded wonderful, filled with only one sentiment, and once more one thought with conviction that only the intelligently directed will of the people is able to create wonders.

Truly, is it not a wonder? From the end of the eighteenth century the people of monarchistic Russia infallibly accomplished the shameful and bloody task of an extinguisher of all revolutionary and liberating movements of the nations of the West and East; our soldiers fought blindly against the revolutionary army of the great French Revolution, they crushed several times cruelly the national revolutionary movements of Poland. In '48 they helped monarchistic Austria to annihilate the Hungarian revolution: in the years of '78–79 they killed the constitution of Turkey, violated Persia, drowned in blood the national movements of China — took the part of hangmen of freedom everywhere where they were sent by the selfish and cowardly hand of autocracy.

And now towards this people are attracted the hearts and eyes of all nations, of all the toilers in the world; all look at the Russian people with a strong hope, with the assurance that it will meritoriously and vigorously accomplish the part of power it has assumed, liberating them from the rusty chains of the past.

This assurance, these hopes, were expressed strongest by comrade Usupoff, the representative of Turkestan and Bokhara, in his speech; he expressed most convincingly and flamingly the sense of a universal world-wide significance of the Russian revolution.

"Don't complain about your hardships," he said, "you have undertaken a work which demands the greatest sacrifices from you, which demands self denial, unfaltering valor, disinterestedness and untiring work."

Such was the meaning of his speech, and it was said at a most opportune time. Actually, the Russian workingman socialist has attracted the attention of the whole world. It seems as if he were taking an examination of his political maturity before the face of humanity. He shows himself to all people of the world as the creator of new forms of life. For the first time the decisive experiment of the realization of the ideas of Socialism is produced on such an enormous scale,—the experiment of incarnation into life of the theory, which may be called the religion of the toilers.

The intense attention accorded to Russia by the whole of toiling humanity is fully understandable — we are doing a universal world-wide work.

And the intense interest of the working world for the Russian socialist obliges the latter to hold his banner tight and high. He through the will of history becomes the teacher and example to hundred thousands, millions, of people. Regardless of the whole difficulty of the conditions in which he is living at the present time, he is compelled to be manly, firm, intelligently magnanimous, unselfish and persevering in the work.

He must know that he himself is poisoned by the same poison with which the proprietors have infected the whole world, he must know that cruelty, bestial relations towards his fellow creatures and everything that the old world was resting on, has been inoculated also into his flesh and blood.

He, now free, still feels towards work like a slave, like the oxen towards the yoke, but only intense, obstinate, disinterested work can change from the roots up the whole ugliness of the old world.

I do not think that these anxious thoughts are out of place here before the lauding speeches to the Russian workingman at his first international holiday.

Comrades! The entire working world on earth is looking at us with a burning hope; it wants to see in you new, honest, disinterested people untiring in the working of building a new world.

Then show yourself to your whole world as new people, show the world all the best, all the most human in you,— your love, magnanimity, incorruptible honesty, your skill to work.

M. GORKY.

SOVIET RUSSIA AT AN INTERNATIONAL MEETING

PETROGRAD, *December* 19, 1918.

ZINOVIEV.— Comrades: In the name of the Petrograd Soviet, and I hope also in the name of all assembled, I greet the dear guests, sent to us by workingmen, soldiers and the poorest peasantry of different countries and who are today among us, (Applause.)

Comrades, I recall the first small international meeting, held in Zimmerwald after one year of war. Then the frame of mind was such that it seemed somehow criminal for a German to meet with a Frenchman, shake each other's hands, say a few words. The Bourgeoisie of all countries, especially the German and the French, had enflamed chauvinism, called forth such an abyss of human hatred, incited against each other the workingmen and soldiers to such a degree, that only the fact that a Frenchman sat with a German at the same table, was declared to be treachery and treason, just the same as the delegates of that time were declared traitors in Germany. Those few workingmen in France were persecuted who had the courage to appear at the meeting of the representatives of the international proletariat.

Since then about three years have gone by. The Third International has not yet been formally constituted. But — and this is much truer — it exists already in reality.

I look upon our meeting of today only as a small vestibule of the coming great assembly of the actual Third International, which, I am sure, will assemble also in Petrograd, in that city, which was the first to raise the banner of international revolution, the first to throw down the bourgeoisie.

At the present time the frame of mind of the wide masses of nations throughout the whole of Europe is such, that chauvinism is living its last days. And although the English, American and French bourgeoisie is intoxicated by the victory over Germany, and although it is making now a last effort to enflame once more the hatred of one nation towards another, yet they do not succeed any more and won't succeed. These are the last convulsions of the expiring bourgeois structure. The widest circles of the people, not only workingmen, but also the adjoining groups of the population, are now in a different frame of mind. Now at last, the people in all countries of the world present an account to the bourgeoisie of all countries.

Now, when the war is dying out before our eyes, the nations are putting forth the account of the broken dishes and presenting everywhere the indictment to the governing classes, in some places loudly with an angered protest, at other places simply with a mute reproach. They ask the governing class: In the name of what was this massacre brought on? In the name of what was Europe watered for four and a half years with blood? In the name of what did ten million people perish? In the name of what were all the European countries devastated so that now we have not even a plough in order to till the soil?" Nowhere there is bread, everywhere the very foundations for the existence of humanity have been destroyed, everywhere people have become savage, everywhere the death rate of children has risen to unheard of dimensions, everywhere the women of the working classes die and starve as never before.

I say that now the masses of the people live under a different frame of mind than they did when the first dare-devils of the new Third International were gripping each others' hands. Even those workingmen who do not stand consciously under the banner of communism, are awakening, nevertheless, to a new life. And they cannot help but ask themselves such a clear, natural elementary question: What was this war fought for?

If, during four and a half years the bourgeois succeeded in deceiving "their" soldiers, "their" workingmen. If the fairy tales were told everywhere that this war is "liberating," "national," "cultural," etc., then even now the very darkest backward laborer understands that this is a lowdown lie, imagination, fairy tale.

Now everyone sees the real cause of the outbreak of the war. It started in order that one group of the capitalists should have a possibility to rob a bigger amount of lands in Asia, America, Africa. It started in order that small bands of English-American capitalists should get a chance to strangle the revolution in Russia and Germany. That is why the eyes of hundreds of thousands of people, perhaps millions of people, are opening now. Everywhere the women of the working class, the working class itself, the soldiers, inevitably are asking themselves this question, and everywhere the answer will be the same: "This was an abominable, pillaging war!" Everywhere the people will say that the bourgeoisie is guilty of this war. Everywhere the people are resolving that by no possibility shall there be repetition of this horror! But when they ask the question what should be done in order that this horror should not reoccur, the answer is everywhere the same: down with the bourgeoisie, long live the Soviet power in the whole world! (Applause, the orchestra plays the "International.")

The comrades and workingmen of all countries are presenting an indictment not only to the bourgeoisie, not only to a bunch of millionaires, but tlso to those parties who called and continue to call themselves Socialists, but actually are the servants of the capitalists. The workingmen vent the whole force of their just wrath and burning disapproval against these parties who carry just as heavy a responsibility for this war, as the bourgeoisie themselves are carrying.

Even now in Germany, which attracts the attention of us all, we see how an entire party which calls itself socialist is actually a chained dog of the bourgeoisie. In Germany an attempt is being made to change the universal historical meaning of the revolution. There is taking place the swindling attempt of the bourgeoisie to take away from the workers their conquests. Only a few weeks from the beginning of the German revolution we see the attempt of Scheideman and Bros., for instance Wehls, the commandant of Berlin, who calls himself a socialist and even an independent one — an attempt which amounts to a repetition of the Korniloff affair, where people calling themselves socialists gathered the white guard troops and tried to shoot Liebknecht and his followers and to take away from the workers and the soldiers their power, which they had achieved with such pains.

Do you know that Germany is going the same road that our great revolution went? We are told many fairy tales; not long ago the Mensheviki said at the Moscow meeting that the German revolution is taking a special course, that it is a fine orderly, decent revolution, without bloodshed and civil war. That is a lie! The German revolution takes the same course as our revolution.

There is a little episode I read about three days ago in the German papers. In the town of Cassel (one of the small German towns) the workingmen and soldiers raised the red banner on the station. The general staff did not like it, they selected among themselves one of the most brilliant officers and sent him to take down the red banner and to replace it with the national one. That dare-devil ascended to the third floor in order to tear down the red banner and when the soldiers saw that, they, without long musings, took aim and shot him like a partridge. (Applause.)

I say, comrades, this little episode is enough to make us realize that Germany is taking the same course as we took. This bitter cup of civil war won't pass her by, because there also the laborers have no other choice except to leave everything to the bourgeoisie or to raise their banner over the entire country; either to give to the bourgeois the power over millions of people or to begin the most decisive fight with fire and sword against the class which led entire humanity to this terror which is now reigning, and so eliminate the possibility of the recurrence of wars, such as have been fought up to now.

Today there will be among you people who are not all Marxists and Communists. Not all agree with us on all points of our program; but we agree with all the numerous comrades who appear here on one point; in the similar hatred to the bourgeoisie, in the hatred to this class who annihilated millions of people in the interest of a small clique; we agree in the mutual hot brotherly love to the red banner, which the white guard officers, together with Scheideman and all his followers who are in power, want to take down in order to give their own banner a chance to soar; we agree in the mutual burning hope that Socialism is not a matter of the coming generation, that not tens and hundreds of years still remain to wait for it; we also agree on the fact that Socialism is dawning, that it is near and it is the duty of us all to fight like one man now, today, tomorrow and in the nearest future for the full victory of the socialistic revolution.

Greeting these comrades once more I say that now the time is not far when honest socialists, they who did not give the banner to the enemy but who remained the friends of the people at a time when the whole world was intoxicated with madness, with war, to which the bourgeoisie had led it, will give a brotherly hand to these socialists with the exclamation: "Long live the Third International, the imperishable, the eternal!" (Loud applause, the music plays the "International.")

THE REPRESENTATIVE OF THE AMERICAN SOCIALIST PARTY, COMRADE REINSTEIN

Comrades: At the present time, the attention of everybody in Russia and of all the toilers of the whole world is concentrated almost exclusively on the American Republic and what the head of this Republic of the United States of America proposes. All agree now as well in Russia as abroad — I speak of course about the millions of the working people — that President Wilson is at the present time trying to follow the footprints of Nicholas I, when he in the year of '48 crushed with the force of the Russian army the revolution in Hungary.

I, comrades, while greeting you, want to remind you that in respect to America it is necessary to say the same as it is in respect to Russia, France and other countries. There is a Russia and a Russia; a Russia of the white guards and a Russia of the proletariat. There is a France and a France; the bourgeoisie of France and her proletariat. There is an America of Wilson and the millionaire Morgan and other stranglers of the American working class; there is an America of the proletariat, the workers, striving toward liberty the same as you are striving here. And in the name of these millions of the American proletariat, not only socialistically revolutionarily inclined, but, I tell you, bolshevistically inclined, I appear here. (Applause.) I know, some doubting may ask: you talk about the millions of Bolshevik-minded American workingmen, but where are the barricades in Washington? No, one must not have such a view, one must understand that in any country it is necessary to have a certain time limit. Many nations recognized the hopelessness of their position and the necessity to grip the gun, to start an armed battle. I know the American people sufficiently to have the right to assure you it is not necessary for us to wait as many months for an armed uprising in America as it was necessary for the proletariat abroad to wait years for an armed fight of the Russian proletariat of the Russian people. I remember how in the emigrant years the comrades in Germany, Switzerland, France and America said: but when will this Russian people arise at last, when at last will it gather its strength and actually enter on a serious fight against the autocracy? They did not understand that there are time limits, that it is necessary to have a certain ripening of conditions in order that a successful fight can be fought. But the Russian revolution was not expected in vain. When the political economic conditions ripened, the comrades abroad were rewarded for their long patience; they did not only wait to see the February revolution of the last year but saw that the Russian proletariat had ripened even to something greater and after having destroyed the monarchy dared the bourgeoisie and the landowners in the month of October. They saw that the proletariat of Russia is now the vanguard of the Socialism of the world.

Comrades, in so far as America is concerned, the conditions are ripening. I have no time to draw a full picture of the conditions there, but I must say that when the American bourgeoisie, looking out for its own interests, led the American people to the massacre, from that moment the American proletariat made a tremendous advance. At the present time there are no official accounts because we are cut off; but when the comrades will come from America (some will succeed in doing so) they will tell you that the revolutionary battle there is ripening more and more. There are already not only tens and hundreds but thousands of American revolutionary proletariats, who are starting the fight against American imperialism with sufficient resolution to pay for it by languishing behind the bars of jails. But in America that kind of repression adds only oil to the fire. Now when the mask has fallen, or rather has been torn from the face of Wilson: when he can no more deceive the people, he cannot continue the game which he played together with the Amrican capitalists; now they have appeared before the world without a mask as the hangmen and gendarmes of the toiling population of Europe. Now the American proletarians are beginning to understand their part, and the revolutionary mood ripens, takes fire. The idea of a social revolution in a universal sense was looked upon skeptically. I'll admit to you that if five or six years before the war, which destroyed the foundation under the feet of the bourgeoisie of Europe and America — annihilating millions of lives, destroying the transportation, the production of articles of foremost necessity, etc.— if, I tell you, even a year before that I would have been asked: "Is it possible to think about a socialistic revolution in a universal sense as of something very imminent," I would have answered: "I never was a pessimist or skeptic, but still, No." At the present time, it is too early to talk about a socialist revolution, as of something very imminent. And suddenly we perceive that at the present time it is impossible to talk about a socialistic revolution in a universal sense as of something which is going to happen after fifteen or twenty years. The alarm is sounding. The time is up. The Russian proletariat, supported by the peasantry, have lifted the banner of battle against oppression and exploitation by the bourgeoisie and the landowners, this Russian proletariat faces during the last thirteen months not only the population of Russia, but faces all those oppressed by the iron fist of imperialism in England, France, Germany, Austria, America. It stands holding tightly in one hand the gun and with the other one writing into the dictionary of every nation two Russian words which were entirely unknown to these people before the revolution. These words have a magic significance, an enflaming, inspiring influence on the peoples of all countries. These two words are: Soviet and Bolshevism. The Soviet — as a concrete practical manifestation of the proletariats' dictatorship for the removal of the exploiters of all kinds. Bolshevism — as a way of looking at the world's destiny, as an answer to this question on the part of the masses to make them understand that a social revolution is not something unattainable, and that through the course of the so-called scientific process of evolution the bourgeoisie ought to have been prepared for this. Bolshevism is convinced that the proletariat understands already that the political economic conditions in all countries have ripened sufficiently so that the united proletariat of the world may take up "the last and decisive battle" with the exploiters and throw them down into an historical grave which the exploiters digged themselves with their cannons, bombs, explosives, etc. The commanding classes themselves prepared a grave for them just the same as the Russian autocracy. We saw how easy it was to push into the grave this autocracy. It was not even necessary for the entire working class to arise; only the vanguard of the proletariat arose decisively in order to give a push to the rotten tree of autocracy and it toppled down.

And at the present time not only we, comrades, here in Russia, but the proletariat of England, Germany, America, the numerous millions of the downtrodden masses of India and other enslaved peoples are confronted with the same problem. And actually history shows once more that no great pressure is needed to fell the tree of imperialism everywhere. You see how strongly Bolshevism differs from Menshevism, which talked about the general unification of the democratic front and also to give the bourgeoisie another twenty to twenty-five years to ride on the back of nations and to prepare the ground for the Socialists — and then, if you please — "with God's help, go into the fight against the bourgeoisie."

Actually the time has arrived for the workers of all countries to give each other the hand and to throw off with a mutual attack the yoke of the exploiters!

The words "Soviet" and "Bolshevism" are now accepted by all nations. "Soviet" and "Bolshevism are now the guiding stars for all the oppressed, no matter in what part of the world they may be. "Soviet" and "Bolshevism" grow like thunder clouds. As soon as the laboring masses succeed in arising and getting into motion, the first thing they organize is the Soviet. We notice that as well in Bulgaria as in Germany. Perhaps at first these Soviets are not quite given up to such aims as they should follow, but in general they are on the right track and are inevitably coming to the same thing as they have come to in Russia. And under the motto, "The Soviet power in a universal sense" we will overthrow the bourgeoisie of all countries and not after fifty or 100 years, but now, in the nearest future. For that purpose every one of us must be on the job. We must arrange our governmental apparatus, the elementary apparatus, production, and we not forget our fighting organ — the Red army. We must work, and not fold our hands, in order to stand before our examiner, before history, and to hear from her: "You proletarians wanted to be the leading class in the country and were really the leaders of the furthest progress of humanity. You solved the problem of the organization of the governmental apparatus, of production, and the problem of the organization of military forces." Yes, we work on that; it is possible that we have not fully solved these questions. Perhaps we are still clumsily governing the country, perhaps we are clumsily struggling in the water wherein we suddenly found ourselves. We must swim or go under. We will solve our problem: we will stand our test and will win. (Applause.)

Captain SADOUL (speaks in French).— Comrades: I have come to Russia convinced of the possibility to make peace among the socialists of different camps. I arrived here as the representative of the French mission and appearing at this meeting, I tell you I feel at this moment how solemn all this is which has been happening here during three days.

Just today is the anniversary of the day when I with comrade Trotsky went to the representative of the French government. Then I believed that the governments of the allied powers were actually fighting for the freedom and equality of humanity. Comrade Trotzky did not believe any more in it. And after the negotiations with the official representative of the French government, General Voulanso, he expressed to me his conviction that these negotiations will lead nowhere, and that the representatives of all governments fear Socialism much more than the so-called enemy. Then I could not become convinced how correct the viewpoint of Trotzky and the other Russian communists was. Now I am convinced that the French people, the organized workers, the Left side of the Socialists and the whole thinking part of the working peasant and socialistic population of France, have entirely the same standpoint as comrade Maxim Gorky, who said, recently, that at the present time the world will have to decide between the politics of Wilson and the politics of Lenin. The French people made their decision long ago. It has understood that by helping actively the Russian revolution it can pay off its debt concerning the Russian revolution, the ideal of freedom, equality and brotherhood. The events show how much the French nation has adopted this point of view. Even the most moderate Socialists who up to the most recent time fought Bolshevism had to announce unanimously they will fight with all their might against the invasion of Russia by the Allies and they cannot acknowledge that France has any right to attack the Russian socialistic republic. This understanding of the Russian proletariat revolution by the people of France and its deep solidarity toward it are great. That cannot be crushed with any obstacles and persecutions. And I, in the name of the French Socialists of the Left side and in my own name, assure the Russian proletariat that the day is not far when the French people will enter into active fight against imperialism and against the enemies of the Russian revolution. And when the French people unite with the Russian, German and Austrian people, then the great revolution of the proletariat will be unconquerable, then socialism will win! (Applause; the orchestra plays the "International.")

LAO (the representative of Northern China).— Comrades: When in the twelvth year the revolution broke out in China, which by many was called the great revolution; when the best of us Chinese set ourselves as a goal the overthrow of the rotten monarchistic structure, it seemed as if this revolution would actually bring China the desired freedom. But this revolution was only an exterior one. Only the dynasty perished. Only the throne of the potentate was destroyed. All the rest remained the same.

Meanwhile the European War broke out and showed once more that the revolution brought nothing new to China; she is as before in the power of not only her own capital but the capital of the world. Japan, taking advantage of this war, took in the Far East all economic life into her hands, and now especially presents continually new demands to China. The Chinese people, who have lived so long a peaceful life, benefiting from the blessing of an agricultural civilization, are now fully crushed under Japanese imperialism. The task of the Chinese people, therefore, is the fight against universal imperialism, and one of the chief representatives of it for China is the imperialism of Japan.

Rumors reach us (unfortunately we are scattered far away in a foreign land and do not have exact news) that a revolution has started in Southern China which is setting itself ideals like the Russian; it wants to declare a socialistic Soviet republic.

I am not sure whether that is actually so, but it is true that there are revolutionary fermentations. Russia is separated from Southern China by Great Siberia, with its many thousand versts, but if that were not so, if China could learn all the truth about Russia, she would send not only moral but also physical support and would call out to the world, "Long live the Great Russian revolution!" (Applause, "International.")

COMRADE FEINBURG, the representative of England speaks in English: As a representative of the Socialist Party, I thank the comrades for the occasion which gives me a chance to greet you in the name of the socialistic British proletariat. Although the present International situation is serious, although the danger which threatens us is really great, nevertheless, I do not doubt that the Russian proletariat, together with the proletariat of Austria, Germany and other countries, can repulse the robbers of the world. It has become entirely clear to the proletarians of the Allied countries that there is no difference between the imperialists of England, France, America and Italy of one side and their former enemies of the other side. Millions understand that this war was actually a war between two robbers. And, just as the Geman imperialists, at the time of Brest-Litovsk wanting to strangle the Russian revolution, extracted from Russia what they could, but in the end tore up the ground from under their own feet, and were crushed by Brest-Litovsk and perished, thus, I am convinced, the English, American, French, Italian and Japanese imperialism will also be crushed by Brest, which it arranges for Socialism but prepares for itself.

AHMED (the representative of India): I speak in the name of 330,000,000 of the Hindu people, who are oppressed by English imperialism and express a deep gratitude for the chance to be with you — to see the success of the Russian proletarian movement and for the possibility to talk to you about my country. I only regret that I have no time to initiate you into all the terrible details of the English oppression over the numerous millions of the Hindu people. But you must understand that if it was hard for you to get along with your autocracy, it is even more difficult for the much suffered Hindu people to fight the foreign imperialism! In India every year millions of Hindus die of hunger in the literal sense of the word in spite of the fact that this country is fruitful and is not in the same condition as Russia is now, when she is surrounded from all sides by enemies who are blockading her. The dying out of the Hindu people is explained exclusively only by the fact that the English imperialism presses all the juices out of us by exporting everything that is needed by the Hindu people to Europe. I have heard and know what a terrible fight is fought against the Russian liberating movement, but the words of the preceding orator, the English representative convinced me also that the Russian people have not only enemies but also allies,— and such an ally is also the nation in whose name I am now speaking. This harassed, much suffered, thirsting for liberation from an imperialistic oppression, people understand the hopes and sufferings of the Russian people, share its ideals and hopes that the time will come when it will be able to render actual assistance. I want to attract your attention to the following. Before me the representation of the English people, Comrade Feinberg, had the word . . . I do not see in him an enemy but, on the contrary my brother in the struggle because the enemy of the Hindu and the English toiling peoples are not Englishmen but the English imperialists. Once more I want to thank you for the hospitality, with the conviction that the united efforts of all oppressed nations will succeed to strengthen on earth the triumph of justice, freedom and socialism. (Applause. The International.)

Redcheb Bombi. (The representative of Persia). Greetings to you, comrades and brothers, from the laboring revolutionary people of Persia! A greeting to Soviet Russia, who has lifted the banner of the real liberation of the working people of the entire world and the toiling classes from the oppression and exploitation of the world's capital. Greetings to you comrades, greetings to Soviet Russia, from the revolutionary party of Persia.

Several years ago our famous poet expressed himself against the bourgeoisie in the following verses (speaks in Persian) which means translated: "Don't make agreements with a rich man, do not expect success from an agreement with him, it amounts to the same as to hold in the pocket a poisonous snake, which, some way or other, will sting you." Comrades, you are sons of the people. We fight for its rights. The bourgeoisie is our eternal enemy. We waive all agreements with this unexampled greedy and cruel oppressor of the working class of all nations. We accept the struggle, death or victory. There are no ways of retreat. We are sons of the people, we believe in it. We believe in our victory, we believe that the dawn which has lighted the world will embrace also revolutionary Persia.

Considering the fact that during recent events in Persia despotism ruled in Russia and that the Russian people is unacquainted with these events, I find it necessary to relate before you the treachery of the bourgeoisie and to tell you something about the history of Persia.

Comrades, Persia was robbed twice by organized capitalistic bands. One is the European organized band, the other is the Asiatic organized band. The European consisted of Russian and English capitalists, who came to Persia and leased there from the government or the landowners settlements, and organized there an armed force out of the runaway convicts, the arms for which were distributed by the embassy. During harvesting time they took everything from the poor peasants that they had, so that the peasants had nothing left of their labors for their living, and in order to support their families the peasants had to leave their native country and look for work, and in the meantime their families died of starvation and cold. The Asiatic organized band conducted themselves even worse. The officials of the Shah sold entire provinces for a certain sum to some grandees who went out there with their farmers and robbed the poor peasants and treated them as they pleased. For that reason the people revolted. And, at last, there was organized in Persia a group of republicans. This group considered it its first duty to put an end to its bitterest enemy, the Shah, who was killed. As a consequence of the repressions, which were effected after this murder, the movement quieted down in Persia, but the underground work continued all the time, and after ten years a new revolution broke out. As a consequence there came the conquest of a broad constitution, but it could not last long, because now the foreign imperialism would not stand for the growth of revolution in Persia. It was decidedly unprofitable to despotic England, because she could not get big concessions. The imperialists crushed with all their might the first Persian revolution, sometimes even by having recourse to the Russian army. The same condition prevailed also after the February revolution because Kerensky was an humble servant of English imperialism, and only the October revolution showed all the oriental people the sincerity of Russian Socialism in the form of the Bolsheviki.

The October revolution destroyed the treaty of 1907 between Russia and England; renounced all annihilation ideas; called back from Persia the army and laid a solid foundation to the social revolution of the world.

Comrades, after the October revolution, we appeal to you as to friends and brothers. We have succeeded in getting 13,800 Persians into the lines of the Red Army and we would be happy to organize a still closer union between Russia and revolutionary Persia.

Comrades, give us a chance to fight in line with you and we will put forth a Red Army of 100,000. (Applause. Shouts, Hurrah.)

We will start to fight in line with you and at the same time we will organize a group of propagandists whom we will send through Persia and India, and they uniting with the Indian revolutionaries will destroy English imperialism. (Applause.)

Comrades, we the representatives of the East, were brought here by the mutual enemy, and we are happy to say this to you and to entire Russia. (Applause.)

Halders (a young American workingman, the first American soldier taken as a prisoner from the camps of the reign of capitalism and brought into the camp of Socialism).— I left America thinking that we were taken to fight Germany. Our transport consisting of twelve vessels left New York on July 16th for Liverpool. In England we were told that from there we would be taken to London and further to the French front in order to escape navigation on the British water on account of mines. Our 85th Division was, however, sent on the 21st of August instead of to France to Archangelsk, where we were taken supposedly to guard the railroad. But actually after our arrival in Archangelsk on the 16th of September, we were sent to the Russian front to fight against the Russian people, being assured that the Russians stole provisions, ammunitions, metals and arms and in general everything that could be carried away and took it into Germany. "If you are taken prisoners by them," was said of the Russians, "then you are done for with absolute mercilessness, like an animal."

Surrounded by Russians, we were taken prisoners in November and awaited a quick end. Great was my surprise, when on the order of an officer I was turned over to the Russians and was treated better than I had been in my own division. Then only I understood why we were told legends about the Russians!

With great pleasure I was present in Vologda on the anniversary of the October revolution and must express my surprise about the work which the Russian people did in these months in spite of the fact that it had been kept for a long time during the former regime in ignorance and darkness, without any schools. And I have nothing more to say except to wish a further success to the Russian Soviet Federated and Socialistic Republic. After you and following your example the red flag will soon wave everywhere, in the whole world, to the blessing of the toiling people. In any case when I return to America, then on my side I shall do everything possible in order to help to hoist this banner also in America and to conquer also for the American workingmen a chance to enjoy true freedom and the fruits of their hands! (Applause "International.")

SUBHI (the Turkish Communist, speaks in the Turkish language).— What a happiness it is to speak here in Petrograd in the center of the great revolution, which must change the future of the whole world, to speak in the name of the oppressed Turkish proletariat and the Turkish peasants, in the name of that nation which has suffered so much from the oppression of rapacious imperialism, and is perishing in the tenacious clutches of the forcible civilization of the West! The Turkish people, crushed and oppressed, is called a barbaric nation. Unquestionably there are in Turkey as in every other country many barbarians and traitors committing murders and sucking the blood of the people: these are the Turkish pashas, drinking not only the Armenian blood, but also the blood of the Turkish proletariat. Not the masses of the oppressed people but the pashas and the Sultans are these barbarians. The comrades, the representatives of the working men and peasants, who were in Russia after the October revolution, decided to arise and fight capital and before all to destroy the rapacious barbarians who are called rulers.

Eight months ago when the Turkish generals intended to send a Turkish army to take the banks of the Caspian Sea, Persia and Turkestan, the Turkish revolutionaries raised bravely in Moscow the red banner and set forth against the adventurous strivings of the Turkish generals. The Turkish ambassador in Moscow, desiring to deafen our voice, bombarded the government of the Russian Republic with persistent notes wherein he demanded that we be deported immediately from Russia, at the same time conducting a propaganda against us in the centers of the Mussulman nations, in Tashkent, Orenburg, Kazan, and trying with all their might to destroy their work. In the articles of bourgeois papers directed against us questions of this kind appeared: Who are the people who play wth the faith and most sacred ideas of the Turco-Tartar nation at a time when the Mussulman world celebrates a victory of the Turkish army in the depths of Asia? To what religion do these people belong and what is their nationality? And when the embassy tried to fool with these Jesuistic questions the whole eastern Mussulman world, we the Turkish Internationalists, declared solemnly that the whole world is our home country and the whole humanity is our nation. And thus raising boldly the red banner of revolution, we decided to go against the current, against the people who have united around the Turkish imperialism. It is true for a time we remained alone on the road leading to the fulfillment of our ideas. But now the entire East goes with us. Comrades when the English-French robbers took Constantinople together with the Turkish imperialists, all lying voices who talked against us disappeared; it became clear that the oppressed poor class does not have a better friend than the great Russian revolution!

Already in 1908 a part of the Turkish youths understood that the people could find its salvation only in a social revolution. But every tie with Socialism was suppressed and the loud voice of the unforgettable Shores, raised in defense of the oppressed people, remained the clamouring voice in the desert. Only the friends of Shores did not give up the work started by him, and now here, in Russia, has been organized the revolutionary hearth. The conviction of the Russian comrades that through a universal social revolution may be accomplished the economic and social rebirth of the Orient strengthened even more in us after the great October events.

I will give an interesting example which shows that this conviction is not only shared among the Turkish proletariat but also among the Turkish intellectuals. After the October revolution when the question was decided at the Constantinople University who should receive the Noble Prize, the Turkish youths, regardless of the pressure of the Turkish professors, awarded it to Comrade Lenin (applause) and showed thereby once more that the ideas of a social revolution have rooted strongly in the Orient. The great teacher, Comrade Lenin, with his ideas, strivings and actions, represents in himself the revolutionary world, and the Turkish youths have shown by their selection how they are attached to this world. I do not find it necessary to talk any more about the sympathy of the Turkish people toward the Russian revolution. But let it be known by the fighters of the Russian social revolution that they are not alone on the field of battle, that is the Turkish proletariat, who together with its intellectuals live by their life, and their hearts are beating in accord with our hearts.

May these heroes be assured that under a southern sun ripens the deep revolt of the Turkish proletariat, who is also under pressure and therefore only awaits the battle cry from its Russian comrades who are older in the field of fighting activity.

Comrades, also in the Near East among the Turkish people live vehement revolutionaries, who feel with all their soul for the Russian revolution!

I shall touch in broad lines the question, what bearing the movement in the East has upon the universal revolution.

According to my deep conviction the revolution in the East has a direct bearing upon the revolution in the West. We, the Turkish revolutionaries, working in the lines of the Russian revolution, are fully convinced that the revolution in the East is necessary not only for the liberation of the East from European imperialism, but also from the support of the Russian revolution.

Comrades, the head of the French-English capitalism is in Europe but its stomach rests on the fertile fields of Asia and Africa. And the first and foremost task of us, the Turkish Socialists, is to hew under the capitalism in the East. Thus only will the French-English exploiting industries be deprived of the raw material. Closing the door to the French-English industry Turkey, Persia, India and China deprive it of the chance for sales on the European stock exchanges, and by that bringing about an inevitable crisis, and as a result the power passes into the hands of the proletariat, and socialistic order will be established. This can be achieved only by inciting a local revolutionary movement and the revolt of the oriental people against the English-French imperialism.

But how to revolutionize the East?

I have often been present at meetings where the oriental question was discussed, where the mystical life of the oriental nations was talked about and wish expressed to study these nations deeper. The study of the Orient was practiced already under the Czar regime with the aim to find the best ways and means of exploitation of oriental countries. But now this problem is being studied in order to liberate the oppressed East. Leaving the study of the East to experienced investigators we must hold the weapons firmly in our hands and not leave our goal out of sight — the organization of a revolutionary hearth in the East. The revolt of the peoples of the East against European capital is just as necessary for the Russian as it is for the young German revolution, the existence of which agitates at the present time the proletariat of all countries. And the German revolution is under the constant threat of the English-American violence and expects the help of the Orient.

In order to create a united revolutionary front the first task of the Soviet power ought to be the occupation of the territory cleared up by the German army. The support of the revolutionary movement in the East is not less important in order to abstract the western capital from the young German revolution.

The Turkish military revolutionary organizations exist already in Russia. Thousands of Turkish Red army men are serving in now the lines of the Red army on the different fronts of the Soviet Republic. Soon they will move together into Turkey.

When the universal revolution will be accomplished by a full victory of the proletariat, we picture Stamboul, the most fairy-tale-like city in the world, as the capital of the International. Aja-Sofia, which up to now was the cause of constant bloodsheds of the greedy imperialism — Aja-Sofia must become the temple of the Soviets of the Universal Socialistic Republic, and instead of a cross and a half-moon, for which a bloody battle has been fought for centuries, on the mosque of the Aja-Sofia will shine the Red Star of the International! (Applause. "International.")

Usupoff (the representative of Turkestan and Bokhara).— Comrades: Allow me to greet the huge auditorium, which has gathered to hear us, the representatives of the Eastern nations! Some time ago I did not have the right even to open my mouth, now I have a chance to exchange thoughts with you, like with older brothers who have raised the banner of the universal revolution.

Greetings from the Mussulman nations of twelve millions The population of Turkestan is cut off from one side by the army of Dutoff and from the other by the imperialistic English army; notwithstanding it is already a year that Turkestan is holding out stoutly, and she sends you her radio-telegram saying that she will hold out to the last. (Applause.) Comrades, your revolution happened in October but in Turkestan it happened already in September. Remember that the population of Turkestan has not yet had a chance to unite with you, but when she unites you will gain 12,000,000 Mussulmen (applause) who will fight with you hand in hand. Our Red army fights on the Ashabad front against the imperialistic English army, and our army is not mobilized in order to go and defend Turkestan. (Applause.) The greatest honor has come to you. The Russian workingmen were the first to raise the banner for the liberation of the whole world, among others the oppressed Orient. To tell the truth, I never thought that this great honor would be ours; I thought that the sacred banner of liberation would be raised by the West-European proletariat; but it turned out that you obtained the immortal name in history, you were the first to raise this banner and reached out your hand to the workers of the whole world. I remember, how learning about your happenings, we wavered: is this the real revolution, has the Russian people actually thrown off the heavy yoke of the oppressors? — and suddenly we received from the universal leader Lenin the proclamation to the "Eastern Nations," and especially, to Turkestan: "liberate and govern yourself." We plucked up courage, conquered the conciliating parties and stepped forth with a gun in our hands, and on the 13th of September it was proclaimed in Turkestan: "All power to the Soviets of the Soldiers' and Workers' Deputies!" (Applause.) As a proof that the Oriental people strive for liberation is the fact that in Bokhara where, up to this time ruled a Toy Chan, who oppressed his people, the revolution flamed up and in this little Chandom rules now the young Committee of Bouhara.

Several hundred versts in circumference of whole settlements were burnt down in order to wipe off the earth this young Bokhara Committee. But, very fortunately, the Russian workingman came to our assistance and saved the young Bokhara Committee with its leaders who, at the given moment, are working with you in Moscow. Now to describe all the horrors we went through during a whole year, cut off from the whole world! We died silently, without complaint in the name of the revolution for which we were fighting; not once did we complain that we are dying without bread. We did not cry: "Down with the power of Soviets." Comrades, if you are going to suffer still more, perhaps you will have to sit three days without bread, die silently and never cry out "down with the Soviets," because this power which you yourself created, which you brought forth according to your own choice, these same leaders are the best people; they are also fighting for you, they are also suffering for you. (Shouts. Hurrah. Applause.) We will suffer, be tortured, starve, we know that perhaps, we won't see heaven on earth, but your and our children will see it, grandchildren, great grandchildren, who will remain after us and who will benefit by these blessings. We must not live and toil for ourselves but for the coming generations who will bless you for a free life. That is how I understand your revolution and our revolution and hope that you will understand it the same way and as uncomplainingly as we in Turkestan die without a lament, fighting in the name of liberty for which you are fighting. From you and in the name of Turkestan I send a warm greeting to the fighters who have been fighting under Orenburg already several months against Dutoff, who is surrounding us for the third or fourth time, cutting us off from you. I greet this army because it is not like the one of Nikolarfsk; it does not come to conquer us but comes to our assistance, frees us from hunger; it brings along with it bread and products. Remember that we prepared for you innumerable quantities of flock and wool. These are the riches of Turkestan and as soon as the road opens we will send this wool to you. We have 12,000,000 pounds of wool in store. Be not afraid that the textile factories will stop, that you will remain without fabrics. No, there will be fabrics, Turkestan guarantees it! Will give it! (Applause.) Only it is necessary to be firm and not to waver as you are wavering, or perhaps you are assailed with doubt? Suddenly the Soviet power will not take root? But what are the international orators saying? They say that a universal fight is going on. Remember that when Turkestan is liberated you will be united with Persia, who will give you, as the orator has stated here, a Red army of 100,000. And Persia lives a common life with us. Back of Persia is much suffering — numerous millions of India. And thus revolutionary Turkestan, as we call it — the Red Turkestan — will be the first disciple who will bring the red banner to the Far East for the liberation of the Far Eastern people, who were most oppressed. Because it is on their account that the World War was fought, on their account the imperialists are fighting for four years, not being able to agree how to divide among them Turkey, India, Persia and Turkestan. They could not agree and raised the arms and stirred the nations of the whole world, pushed them into a bloody massacre in order to decide, with bayonets in their hands, who is stronger. England moved in order to crush the Russian revolution. But the deeper she is going to invade the more she will be involved in the massacre and the shorter will be the duration of her existence. Napoleon is an example — he plunged, and perished.

The English imperialism has a very short time left to exist, because it has gone too far, but it cannot go back, it cannot stop and cannot hold off the indigation of the people; it cannot lead any longer the people to a massacre by treachery; and the bayonets which are directed against you will be in a near future — perhaps within a month or two — directed against it. A little more patience and you live to see the longed-for moment, only trust, compactness and unity are necessary in order to wait for the brothers who are coming to help you. We waited long for you, you will not have to wait long for us.

A warm greeting to the comrades — Communists! (Applause.)

AN. (the representative of Korea).— Comrades: Rumors of Korea seldom reach you. But in the meantime there, in the Far East, a nation consisting of 20,000,000 Koreans are fighting against their enslavers the same as the people of India and Southern China. From the time the Japanese conquered our country, expelling from there the Chinese and the Russians, all our aims were directed toward a liberation from the usurpers. The same as we fought before the Chinese usurpers, as we fought later on the officials of the Czar, thus we are now fighting the Japanese. Korea was once upon a time the wealthiest country of Asia and attracted the greedy glances of the Asiatic imperialists. Our ancient culture exists already about five thousand years and was considered the highest culture of Eastern Asia. Now we are destroyed, robbed, changed into laborers for the Japanese. Our riches have been exported from Korea, our land is in the hands of the conquerors. The regime of the Japanese is so despotic that several years ago a whole department of the Japanese administration resigned as a protest against the violence and inhumanity of the Japanese general, Teranchi, the same who, together with the Englishmen and Americans, intended to crush also your Soviet Republic. The higher classes in Korea are bribed by the Japanese. The revolutionary organizations are suppressed. The government of the Czar and later on also the Kerensky government made an agreement with the Japanese to deliver our emigrants and revolutionaries who were hiding in Siberia to the Japanese hangmen. I myself saw in the archives of the oriental department of the people's commissariat for foreign affairs documents, which prove that the Kerensky government invited Japanese spies and provocaturs in order to cause terroristic deeds in Russia, supposedly committed by Koreans and thus justify the delivery of our comrades into the hands of the Japanese. Yes, comrades, you must know how you were dealt with, not only in Korea, but also in Russia. In your country the white guardists kill every workingman — one out of ten; in our country the Japanese hang generally everybody who is only suspected to love his own country. And these victims were augmented by those who were sold by Kerensky and Tereschenko to the Japanese. Yes, comrades, there is one road left open for us — the terror, and we will and shall adopt it. Thus my relative killed with his own hand the Japanese premier, the Prince Ito, when he returned from Russia after having discussed with the Tzar's government how it would be best to deal with us. You do not know that no week goes by that we do not kill either here or there one of the Japanese officials. When it became impossible to work in Siberia we transferred our activity to America. And tens of thousands of Korean workingmen organized there our revolutionary committee. We had our own papers and breathed freely. But Wilson led the American people into the universal massacre and when the American bankers, robbers, found it necessary to negotiate with the Japanese we were expelled from America. The only country where we can find refuge is the Soviet Republic. Russia has ceased to be a stepmother to us. She is now our beloved mother. Under her protection our revolution is being created, the new generation of Korea is brought up according to your socialistic teaching. Outside our union with you we have no freedom. Your happiness, your peril is our peril. Great dangers are nearing us from the North, the South, the East and the West. And in this threatening hour we, the Korean workingmen and peasants, have come to you, in order to either die with you or to conquer. This is the feeling shared by everyone of the 20,000 of our workingmen on the territory of the Soviet Republic and hundreds of thousands of our workers in Siberia. And I speak in the name of our revolutionary national Soviet; we must win, because in this victory lies the liberation and salvation of entire Asia. Long live the united laboring class of Russia and Asia. Long live the proletariat of the whole world!

Forward — either victory or death! (Applause. "International.")

TCHAN (the representative of Northern China).—Comrades: The poorest workingmen of Northern China are greeting you, the whole Soviet power, Comrade Lenin and his comrades. I say that we, the Chinese workers, strive together with you for a republic, for a universal revolution, for Soviet power against all exploiters. In the near future you will find out in practice, that the workingmen of Northern China work hand in hand with you! (Applause.)

GORI (the representative of the Austrian Soviet of the Workers' and Soldiers' Deputies).— Unfortunately, in place of the Hapsburg dynasty which for so long oppressed the people, a new oppression has appeared now, the bourgeois government, which evidently does not consider sufficient the four years during which the Austrian people did not cease to bleed, not sufficient these humiliations and injustices which it suffered during recent times. But the hopes and expectations of the bourgeoisie are in vain, it cannot hold off any longer the wrath of the people and the development of the communist movement in Austria, and this can be proven. Only recently I read that the Austrian government did not dare to take measures against the Communists because it knew how it would be endangered if measures would be taken against the conscious element of the Austrian proletariat. When the day arrives, and this is not far off, the Austrian proletariat will also succeed in having an October revolution, whether it is going to be called an October, March or April revolution, whether it is going to be in Vienna or Budapest, is immaterial, but at the time when the proletariat will get the power the conciliators Bauer and Pomer will come to grief, they who betrayed the Austrian proletariat during the January revolt, which was an expression of protest of the Austrian proletariat.

Every prisoner in war who had to live in Russia during the revolutionary period knows that when he returns to his home-country, which is still oppressed by capitalism, all conscious workers will turn to him with the question, what is going on in Russia and how was liberty conquered? And it will be the duty of everyone returned to tell what he succeeded to observe in

Russia. The Austrian proletariat, after having had the revolution, and the Russian proletariat will become the strongest and truest allies. I am speaking not only in the name of the war prisoners who are here, but I am convinced that I am expressing the wishes and hopes of the entire Austrian proletariat. Long live the communistic socialistic universal republic! Long live Lenin and Tinaviev! (Applause. "International.")

LENIVUDI (the representative of Scotland).— Comrades: I want to say to you a few words about the things which we have seen since our imprisonment in October.

To begin with our chiefs told us that we are going to Archangelsk front in order to do garrison duty and will return as soon as we have finished with the band of robbers who have destroyed the country, whom the local population is fighting; that these bands are supposedly led by Germans, that at the head of the Russian Red Army were German officers. We were told that our enemy is only a handful of Petrograd workingmen, without discipline and war training. But I can state that they fight like regular soldiers who have trained many months. All these stories about the German officers and about the fact that our prisoners are being shot by the Russians and therefore we must shoot them, turned out to be fairy tales. In the battle where I was taken prisoner and where we were convinced that a handful of Petrograd workingmen are stronger than we, there were many casualties just because we were afraid to be taken prisoners. But from the very first moment of our imprisonment we experienced that we were in the hands of our Russian comrades — workingmen, who are not fighting us, but the capitalists; and that, on the contrary, the capitalists are using us in order to crush the Russian workers in order to enrich themselves. Therefore, I hope that this is understood soon by us and that the matters will take the same course with us as they did with you. By the way, in one village a Russian Red guardist talked with me. The Russians do not want to fight with us but must defend themselves from an assault. I answered that we, the English soldiers, do not want to fight against the Russians and are beginning to see the truth only now. If we could have known it before, the present condition would very likely not continue long. We know that the Russians are defending the country which belongs to them because the land is the property of the Russian people. We were welcome in prison as we were not at home. In all the villages where we have been we saw a desire to do everything to help us. We were well fed. I did not see anywhere any signs of these bands of robbers and German officers we had been told about. And therefore I will end by thanking our Russian comrades for the warm relationship, and wish success to the Russian revolution, which, I hope, will enflame the revolutionary movement also in England.

The English War Prisoner.— Comrades: My speech will be short. I am not an orator and ask to be pardoned. However, I will try to tell what I and my comrades were told about the aim of the English expedition and what actually, as we have learned now, is the authentic aim of this expedition. My comrades and I were taken prisoners on Sunday, October 27th, on this best of days, on the anniversary of the best events. The Russian soldiers with whom we came in contact have asked us why we fight against them. They could not understand it because they themselves do not want to fight against us. The English public opinion is suggesting to us through the press that we are going to help Russia by destroying the German influence. But now we have been already four months in Russia and have not seen a sign of German influence. We were told that the Allied intervention bears a purely temporary character and that as soon as the German influence will be destroyed the Allied troops will be withdrawn from Russia. Then just imagine the frame of mind of myself and my comrades after the Armistice had been signed between Germany and the Allies. It became clear that the Allied troops had no more reason to stay in Russia and that a further stay could not be justified by anything. We are simply being deceived.

We were told that we were going to fight against a bloodthirsty gang of the rabble who kill all the prisoners and that if we are taken prisoners it is best to shoot oneself. It is hard to imagine how far that is from the truth! My comrades and myself, wounded and not wounded, were all met with the same warm welcome by those who made us prisoners and by those with whom we came in contact. We were treated more like guests than prisoners and we are only hoping very much that the Russian comrades, whom the misfortune befalls to be taken prisoners by the Allies, will be treated as well as we are.

We know now exactly why the Allies attacked Russia. We have already seen enough of Russian life in order to be enlightened that the Russian people are busy with the reconstruction of their economic and social life in order to guarantee to the workers the fruit of their toil. The Allied governments fear that if they permit such a state of affairs to develop other countries will follow the example of Russia. For that reason the Allies decided to crush Russia before the new order would have a chance to become stable. In other words, they want to strangle Socialism with the hands of their own workingmen.

We understand that the American soldiers on the Archangel front already comprehend this truth. They have bluntly refused to fight against the Russians and are returning home.

We hope that the Allied troops in this country will also soon learn the truth and leave. Then and only then the Russian people will be left alone in order to have a chance to arrange its own affairs, according to its own will.

SIROLA (the representative of Finland, one of the foremost leaders of the Finnish labor movement, a member of the red government of Finland, the present chairman of the Finnish Communist Party; his appearance is met with applause).— I appear in the name of the Finnish people who at the present time is enduring the hardest, most terrible, inexpressible results of the bourgeoise dictatorship, which does not shrink from any cruelty, from any bestiality, destroys everything living, profanates the dead, trying through starvation and shootings to extinguish the red Finnish people. In the name of this oppressed people I turn to the Scandinavian, the Germans and the whole West European proletariat and say: Comrades, once for all time do not believe in the phrases about democracy and liberty! The Finnish people have paid dearly for this belief. There was a time when the Finnish people, the Finnish proletariat, thought that by fighting on national ground it was possible to become free. The Finnish people lived in the conviction that being a small nation it cannot have any imperialistic problems and it is necessary to become free only nationally in order to continue on the general road of liberation. But the governing classes proved how much the Finnish people were mistaken. And the people had to pay dearly for this mistake! It paid with its own blood. The Finnish bourgeoisie who had talked much about national independence started by selling the freedom and independence of the people to Nicholas, "the Bloody," and then to Wilhelm. At the present moment this Finnish bourgeoisie crawls on its knees before the bloody Allied imperialism. I ask this solemn meeting of nations not to believe a word that the Finnish bourgeoisie press is saying and that the bourgeoisie press of the whole world is repeating: that the Finnish people has lost faith in the final victory of revolution. The Finnish proletariat (the conscious working class and peasantry) was annihilated by tens of thousands by shootings, was subjected to terrible, inexpressible tortures of hunger; the Finnish working class and the Finnish peasantry are dying out under the yoke of the bourgeois dictatorship, of hunger, of horror, of all kinds of sickness, which are the result of the chastising expeditions of the bourgeoisie.

But there is one thing, comrades, there is a feeling and consciousness which cannot be destroyed by starvation, by sickness nor by chastising expeditions: that is the knowledge of the Finnish proletariat, that the day will come when it will be able to become once more the vanguard of the universal revolution. And this day is dawning, is being prepared for. And I am not saying this only from a general knowledge of the matter; the bourgeois papers write again about it that in Finland the red ghost is beginning to threaten the bourgeois order and dictatorship. On the other hand, during the elections of the diet, in spite of the fact that the Finnish working class and the red Finnish proletariat are deprived of the right to vote, the small bourgeoisie and the red peasantry voted for the Socialists. And thus the bourgeoisie did not gain its gaol. It thought that by depriving the red Finnish working class of the ballot it would deprive it of socialistic representation; but it was wrong in its calculations. The peasantry proved that it also can arise to this understanding. I do not doubt that the time will arrive when the Finnish proletariat will anew raise its head and will not only defend itself but will know how to attack the bourgeoisie, the democracy of the bourgeoisie. I draw the attention of the masses of the West-European proletariat to one of this bloody experiences of the Finnish revolution.

This is the deduction, comrades: the peoples and workingmen and peasants pay dearly who even for one minute let themselves be tempted by some ideas and illusions that their exists some kind of a native country. No, down with the bourgeois native country! The proletariat has no native country but it has only one hope and one banner around which it must gather, the socialistic, the International banner. The day will come when the Finnish proletariat with the help of the Russian proletariat, the Russian Red army, supported by the revolution throughout Europe, will once more raise its mighty red banner. Down with capitalism, down with the native country of the bourgeoisie! Long live the only native country of the working class, long live the communistic revolution! (Applause.)

TINOVIEV.— Long live red Finland, Hurrah! (Applause, calls, hurrahs, the orchestra plays the "International.")

A VOICE.— Death to the Hangman Svinhuvfud!

PERTZ (a member of the Soviet of German soldier deputies, speaks in German).— Comrades: The German Petrograd Soviet of workingmen's deputies sends you its greeting and recalls how a month ago the rumor about the German revolution was spread, how the conscious Russian workingmen and soldiers were thrilled with joy, pride and hope because during four years German imperialism threatened Russian freedom most. The German bayonets threatened the Russian people most during the last year. All who were living in Russia during the war learned to understand and to love the Russian revolution. And although at the present time traitors are at the head of the German government who once more want to encroach upon the dignity and the life of the German people, although there again people are ruling who have been bought by the Allies, who are throwing to the worn out German people a crumb of bread, and for this crumb of bread demand from the German people a possibility to crush forever all liberty not only in Germany but in the whole world, anyway, comrades, in the name of the German working class I assure you that we won't allow to have a new yoke put upon us, a new slavery. And all who have been in Russia feel now what a danger threatens our people. But as long as the present generation is alive all those who together with you lived through the great revolutionary days will not lift their hands against German liberty. All who lived here, who burned with your fire, who were present while you were fighting capitalism; all these war prisoners, Socialist Communists, upon their return to Germany will not only tell about your successes and victories but will fight to the last drop of blood so that the great beginnings of the Russian revolution will be continued and carried out in Germany and in the whole world! (Applause. The "International.")

A VOICE.—Long live the leader of the German working class, comrade Liebnecht! Hurrah!

RUTGERS, the representative of Holland (speaks in Dutch).—The Labor and socialistic movement could not help being reflected in our country. Holland itself, a small country, was a toy in the imperialistic massacre and in the rivalry between Germany and England; it had to subjugate now to one and then to the other imperialism. And the labor movement there had a small bourgeois character with a strong social-patriotic tinge. Many years ago there was a split in Holland between the adherents of the former Second International and those who considered it indispensable to create a Third International on the foundation of a class international movement of the workers of the whole world. And from the year of 1905 the events in Russia were reflected in Holland in the most serious way.

The Marxists left the party of the opportunists and, after having formed the Social Democratic Party, have now changed into the Communist Party, which has about 2,000 members. The members of this party are the adherents of Bolshevik tactics. They were always posted concerning the events in Russia, and the names of the comrades Lenin, Tinoviev, Kameneo and others enjoy the greatest popularity among the conscious workers of Holland; just the same as I have had the opportunity to become assured that the names of comrade Roaland Holst and others are far from being unknown to the Russian proletariat. Recently, under the pressure of the imperialism of both countries, the movement in Holland has sharpened. It is clear that at the present time the victorious Allies desire to make use of the dependent position of Holland in order to make out of it a weapon in their own hands and in order to use it for more exploitation. However, in spite of all efforts the communist movement develops in Holland. And not long ago on account of the celebrations in honor of the great Russian revolution on the streets of Amsterdam and other centers of the industrial movement there were encounters with the police. And on account of the celebration of the German revolution there were in these towns encounters which resulted in the death of four comrades and the wounding of more than eight workers. This proves that the Dutch proletariat, in spite of its small number, does not cease to struggle under the banner of International Socialism. Will it be possible to keep the national independence of Holland unknown to the Dutch communists? It does not interest them, they are not striving to conquer national independence and self-determination; they want to become a member of the international, socialistic, federated republic. Other national independence they do not need. And they greet in the name of the Dutch communistic party the first alvevle, the link of the great socialistic fatherland in the shape of the Russian proletariat and the Russian revolution! (Applause.)

MARKOVICH (the representative of Serbia).— Comrades: Our great teacher Marx said that when consciousness belongs to one person, then this is like one consciousness, one idea, small and feeble, but when consciousness enters the hearts and minds of millions of proletarians, then this consciousness becomes a mighty elementary force which must throw over the entire rotten and corrupt bourgeois structure. I am not going to occupy your attention long but I will say this: that the only road, the only tactic and the only party, which will lead to the destruction of this accursed world is the party of the Communists. (Applause.) Whom does the proletariat of the Balkans follow and whom does it join? Those who first lifted the banner of revolt, who first started the internal war against the band of robbers. The proletariat of the Balkans goes with the party which exposed the bourgeoisie, destroyed the routine of the church, the lies of the schools and all this hypocrisy which was used by the bourgeoisie and the so-called intellectuals who were serving the bourgeoisie, in order to befool the people. (Applause.) We go with the party which creates a new world, a new life, a new science on socialistic foundations. The proletariat of the Balkans goes with the party which does not march under a conciliatory slogan with the bourgeoisie and which goes with a gun in its hands against the bourgeoisie, that is the party of the Communists; the people of the Balkans, who are now awakening from a lethargic sleep and cursing these hangmen leaders who for such a long time made people kill each other by inciting people against people, follow this party and its tactics. The people of the Balkans go now with the party which abolished all nationalities, recognizing only the proletariat of the whole world. Now there won't be any Musselmen nor Buddhists nor Christians, those will be only one proletariat. This party destroyed the lies of the church not only in Russia but also in the whole world and now there exists only one faith — that is Communism.

We, comrades, the same as you, follow the only slogans which have become the world force, talked about by Karl Marx. This force is the deliverance of the entire humanity from these terrible shackles, it is the fraternization of the poor of the whole world, it is the creation of the reign of Socialism where there will be no more terrible massacres. And we extend a hand to our comrades the Turks, the Germans, the Hungarians, and together we enter the battle against the bloodthirsty Serbian bourgeoisie, which is now trying to fight the Hungarian revolution on the Balkans. We consider all the agents of the bourgeoisie, all conciliators on the same level with the bourgeoisie itself. And our definite tactics are — death to it! (Applause.)

The conciliators of the Mensheviki you have already conquered, they are going now with you; in our country, however, they have not yet been conquered. But we will handle them! They are on the other side of the barricades, they oppose us by word and by deed. But there is a great, terrible weapon in this last battle. Long live, comrades, not only the physical force, not only the great Red army, but long live also the only powerful weapon, long live the word, the great word, which is above all other weapons! Comrades, long live also the Red army of the world, long live the great brotherhood of the proletariat! We will fight with the weapons in our hands. Wilson and other bourgeois bloodsuckers propose that we should lay down the weapons and create a brotherhood of nations. But we know what this brotherhood of nations means, what the slogan of the liberation of Belgium and Serbia means! The slogans are meant for hy* ! Now it is already late, now consciousness has become elementary. No bourgeoisie lies will counteract this elementary force. It will ruin the bourgeois system of the world. And we know, comrades, that the fire was started here. To us this city of Petrograd martyrs is sacred. And the voice from here will not remain the voice crying in the wilderness. Your love has taught us to love Socialism and to fight for it. We will go with you, with the proletariat of the world and will fight until the last drop of blood, until we have killed the last bloodsucker of the bourgeoisie. We are with you, only, with you, and following your tracks! (Applause. The "International.")

COMRADE ANTONOFF (the representative of Bulgaria).— Comrades: When the executors of the October overthrow unfurled the red banner of the revolution of the proletariat and started energetically to realize in actuality the principles of Socialism they declared that it would be childish artlessness to think that a

* So in original

tiny little socialistic island among the stormy ocean of coarse capitalism will stand the hits of the powerful waves of international imperialism.

They laid all their hopes on the support of the international proletariat. And actually, these hopes came true. The red banner of revolution is taken up by the proletariat of literally all countries. The revolution is victoriously advancing toward the existing heights: "Socialism," the liberation of the proletariat, "death to capital," etc.

The first task of the Russia of October was to discredit the abominable massacre of the world, to end it. This task has been accomplished brilliantly.

The first support came from there, whence, perhaps, no one expected it, from the Balkan Peninsula, in the shape of the Bulgarian revolutionary proletariat, which proved to be the first ally of Red Russia.

The Bulgarian workingman and peasant by his energetic refusal to shed his blood any longer for interests which are alien to him, forced the Bulgarian camarilla to discontinue the war. By opening a front which proved to be far from secondary, this workingman commanded the respect of the Bulgarian bourgeoisie for his vote.

Bulgarian withdrawal from the war, as the events have shown, the imperialistic war, received a death blow in a strategic sense. It was finished.

Comrades, now a new war is approaching, has already approached, the war of the English-American imperialism against Soviet Russia, rather, the war of capitalism against labor.

The international proletariat is deeply interested so as not to give the Anglo-American imperialism a chance to crush Soviet Russia. Here not only the fate of Russia is decided, but the fate of the international proletariat.

One aim, one task should at the given moment inspire absolutely all adherents of the liberation of labor from the yoke of capitalism: the victory over the Anglo-American imperialism. In the name of this victory everything must be undertaken.

The aggressive plan of the Anglo-American imperialism on Russia must be destroyed in the root. And, therefore, it is necessary to pay due attention again to the Balkan Peninsula where the imperialistic war was strategically discredited.

The strategic position of the Balkan Peninsula is such that the British will make and are already making it their main base for the operation against Soviet Russia. On the Balkan Peninsula and not in the Murmansk or on the Baltic Sea will be the outcome of the planned campaign against Red Russia.

However paradoxical it may seem, comrades, it is so! The Anglo-Americans cannot and will not undertake any operations in the Murmansk and on the Baltic Sea because behind them is the stormy Germany about whose conduct they cannot be calm. This is confirmed by the fact that they have not undertaken anything during forty days. The South is more favorable to them. They consider themselves the masters on the Balkans. The prospect to join Krasnoff and Denikin through Roumania and the Ukraine is more tempting to them. All their preparations are being conducted in the Bulgarian port Varna, from where they intend to send their punitive expedition to Odessa in order to join Krasnoff.

That is why I maintain that the plan of attack of the British must be destroyed, just there where it was conceived, the Balkan Peninsula. There also should be turned the attention to the strategic politics of Soviet Russia.

The next task of revolutionary Russia is to enflame the fire of revolution on the Balkans in order to deprive the enemy of his strategic point of support.

There is a soil favorable for this. No doubt about that. If for the time being there is no reason to declare Bulgaria the center of the Balkan revolution, I have the courage to maintain that the Bulgarian proletariat can be in a short time prepared for a revolt. There is only organized work needed, and only that. The psychology of Bulgaria's toiling masses is sufficiently revolutionary.

The first revolution in Bulgaria was, as you already know, crushed by the bayonets of the Anglo-French. Although the set aim — to end the war — was attained gloriously, but inasmuch as the revolution was checked there by the Anglo-French hangmen, the interruption assumes the character of a lost battle.

But to think that this ended the matter would be wrong. In Russia also October came after July.

In Bulgaria the throne of Boris, as saved by the Allied troops of occupation, itself creates conditions for the discontent of the masses. The masses of the people to whom the occupation is unbearable as an oppression are collecting their strength in order to throw off the yoke.

Comrades, keep in mind that Bulgaria is not Africa, as Comrade Lenin expressed it. It is a democratic country which during a half century has lived a free political life, and is penetrated with a deep hatred to all kinds of oppression. It is a country where the condition of life made it possible for four political parties to flourish, a country which sent to its small parliament eleven Socialist deputies, a country which has preceded by its professional movement even some of the Middle European countries, a country having 98 per cent literate, a country where there is not a single workingman who would not consider himself a Social Democrat; such a country cannot long tolerate the oppression of occupation.

A foreign yoke remains a yoke, no matter with what kind of sauce it is served.

After the first Bulgarian revolution was crushed, in August, through the realization of the German revolution and recrudescent agitation, comradely support against the nearing danger of the abominable imperialism intends to crush the free existence of the awakening international proletariat, with the accuracy of one to ten. It is possible to foresee that in this small — but great on account of its strategic position — country the second revolution will arrive inevitably. The sound political logic of things demands this. The preparations for this, the second revolution, are on the way.

You have sent already agitators to Bulgaria whose duty it is to inform the Bulgarian proletariat about the development of the Russian socialistic revolution and about the hopes which the international revolution sets on her in the sense of destroying the plan of aggression of the Anglo-Americans from the South on Soviet Russia.

To disclose to you everything intended in this connection I cannot, in such a public meeting, and you are not going to try to make me to, I hope.

Allow me only to read the manifesto which the executive committee of a group of Bulgarian Communists prepared to be sent to Bulgaria. Perhaps after the manifesto has been honored by the attention of the representatives of the proletariat of the Far and Middle East, it will have a stronger influence upon the proletariat, too, of the Near East.

MANIFESTO TO THE TOILING PEOPLE OF BULGARIA

Comrades, workingmen and peasants: Few months ago you accomplished a great deed. With your unexampled action of the Saloniki front you started the beginning of the end of the mad universal slaughtering. The breakdown of the powerful German imperialism started when you threw down your guns and refused to continue the senseless and criminal extermination of your brothers — workingmen and peasants. Your revolt broke a long and painful silence on the revolutionary front. During the distressed summer days, when many were beginning to lose their hope of a possibility of a European revolution, your action renewed the revolutionary fire and the revolution was carried over to Germany, enveloped Austria and Hungary and began to knock at the gates of France and Italy. This strengthened the position of Soviet Russia, encouraged the workingmen and peasants of all countries and for the first time the bourgeoisie for the whole world felt that a threatening sword is suspended over its head. That is where your services before the revolution are invaluable.

Comrades, workingmen and peasants, the growth of revolution has caused great fear among the lines of the bourgeoisie of all countries. The robbers of the world do not want to give up the inheritance of centuries — the exploitation of workingmen and peasants. That is why, not choosing the means, they exert their last strength and prepare for a last and decisive battle with the oppressed. They know that the base of the universal revolution is Soviet Russia and, therefore, are doing everything in order to destroy the Soviet power and thereby strangle the revolution and reinstate their firm rule.

Comrades, workingmen and peasants, there are many signs that the imperialism of the whole world prepares to attack Soviet Russia from the South through the Balkans Peninsula. Perhaps you have already witnessed the most shameful deed of the bankrupt bourgeois civilization; perhaps you see how the files of slaves of civilized Europe, black skinned, red skinned, yellow skinned and generally of every race on earth, are landed in your ports and they are sent to a new slaughter against Soviet Russia. Your duty, your obligation, comrades, workingmen and peasants, is to prevent this hellish plan of the insolent imperialists. You are called upon to accomplish the last fatal act for the revolution. Your action will start the beginning of the end of the other conceited imperialism — the Anglo-French-American. You must do this by word and deed. By word, you must explain to the imperialistic slaves the whole shame of a campaign against the Russian people. By deed, you must not allow the imperialists to make use of your roads, your ports and in general of all your means for sending troops against Soviet Russia. If during the summer on the Saloniki front, when you were entirely alone, you dared to take action, so much more it is now your duty to raise the flag of revolt because revolutionary Germany and Austria will not interfere with you any more, but Soviet Russia and Soviet Ukraine will help you with all means.

Comrades, workingmen and peasants, the moment is extremely serious! Time won't wait. Fate is doing everything in your favor. And if we do not make use of the favorable moment we will become the victims of international imperialists and will inflict upon ourselves a slavery more terrible, more severe than before.

The twelfth hour of revolution is sounding and calls all the oppressed; woe to them who do not answer the call of fate! Long live they who hold tightly the red flag of revolution!

Long live the creators of a new world!

Long live renewed Europe!

Long live the free and peaceful Balkans! (Applause; the "International.")

THE EXECUTIVE COMMITTEE OF THE PETROGRAD GROUP OF BULGARIAN COMMUNISTS.

THE SOVIETS IN ITALY

We are publishing the so-called Bombacci Plan, a working plan for the establishment of the Soviet system in Italy, which was drawn up for the purpose of serving as a subject of study and a model for use when the time came to put it into practice.

The "Workers' Dreadnought" of London for February 27th, quoted in "The Nation" of April 17, 1920, published an article from Italy on the situation as it has developed since the Congress of Bologna. In October the Italian Socialist Party agreed to take part in parliamentary elections only on condition that the party should at the same time organize a system of Soviets in order to prepare the people to carry out the revolution and replace the parliamentary by the Soviet system at the proper time.

The plan was carried into effect at a meeting of the National Council of Regional Delegates of the Socialist Party held in Florence in February. Between October and February immediate action was made necessary by the activity of the so-called Turin movement. This was led by Antonio Granacci, one of the younger leaders, who agitated for immediate action, accusing the Federation of Labor of hesitating to carry out the decision of the Congress. He was in control of the metal industry and, therefore, during November and December he organized Soviets in all the chief factories of the metal industry with the help of the labor union. This produced an embarrassing situation which had to be faced by the entire party at the Florence convention. It was then decided to put forth the so-called Bombacci Plan for Soviets, which was then drawn up in almost perfect duplication of the Russian Plan. The plan was to be circulated through all the locals of the association and to be discussed by them in special meetings.

After a two months' discussion the delegates are to meet again, bringing to the conference the decision of their locals for or against the plan. Already the various factions are criticizing the plan. The anti-parliamentary abstentionists under Bordiga insist that the project does not give sufficient power to the party. The Turin group, headed by Granacci, insists that the plan is not harsh enough in its ejection of the capitalist element from the factory through the industrial action that is to precede the political.

While this agitation is being carried on in all the branches of the Socialist Party and in the labor confederation or *Camere di Lavoro*, a corresponding agitation is effervescing in the spheres of the trade unions and the peasants. In the industrial field the councils of exploitation, as they are called, or factory councils, are being developed with great rapidity. It is a scheme which we have described in detail in connection with both the British and the American labor situation. That is, it is what is usually called the works' committee. This works' committee or factory council, which started in the region of Turin, is another form of preparation for the taking over of industry by the workmen. On the other hand, the peasants, especially in Tuscany, and in the Romagna region, have been agitating for reforms in their relations with the landowners. They have insisted on the suppression of forced labor; of the gifts in kind from tenants; of the right of arbitrary eviction of peasants. They have insisted on arbitration councils of equal numbers of landowners and tenants. The landowners, however, did not accede to the demands of the tenants to be allowed a share in the technical management.

The landowners are grouped together in associations which deal as bodies with the labor chambers of the Federation of Agricultural Laborers. The keynote to the agitation, so far as it concerns the demands of labor, is that the demands are made in such a way that labor knows they cannot be granted. In other words, labor wishes to create an impossible situation that will lead to expropriation or revolution. The labor representative said:

> "Our conditions are impossible. We know it. That is why we make them. The landowners, no longer masters on their own land, forced to employ three times as much labor as is necessary, prevented from bettering or extending the land under cultivation, will be forced to quit. If they stop producing, or produce less than they could under normal conditions, they become subject to expropriation. So we hasten the coming of the necessary reform."

All this seems to show that matters are working toward a catastrophe or a reaction in Italy. All this is the latest development of the Third International outside of Russia.

THE BOMBACCI PLAN

"The following provisional plan, drawn up by Signor N. Bombacci for the establishment of a Soviet system within the present industrial and political system in Italy, was printed in "Avanti" (Milan) for January 28th:

GENERAL PRINCIPLES

1. The Soviets (councils of workingmen, artisans and peasants) must form the basis of the Socialist state of workingmen, the sole organs of power and of supreme direction for the organization of production and of communist distribution as well as for the regulation of all economic, social and political relations, both internal and external.

2. The formation and arrangement of the Soviets must necessarily be made effective, during the revolutionary period (which is the present state of Italy) preceding the actual beginning of the social revolution, by transferring all power into the hands of the Soviets for the exercise of the dictatorship of the proletariat. It is not only to accomplish with greater success this particular historic duty that the institution of Soviets must first have complete organization and thorough preparation, but because only a national body broader than the local Soviets can have control during the period before the final revolutionary struggle against the bourgeois régime and its false democratic illusion — parliamentarism.

3. The conditions of the present period, characterized by a want of liberty of action, of speech, and even of thought for the workingman, as well as the constant pressure and defamation to which the laboring classes are subjected by the bourgeoisie, make it absolutely necessary for the highest interests of these classes to protect and guarantee, by means of a proletarian vanguard, the Soviets of the workingman against any pressure and against any insidious schemes, direct or indirect, of the bourgeoisie. These guarantees must express themselves in the control and close vigilance on the part of the proletarian vanguard (the Socialist Party, organizations of resistance and of Socialist co-operation) of the Soviet. From this the necessity arises on the one hand for the introduction of an adequate representation in the local and central Soviets and, on the other, for the formation of administrative regulations so that the bourgeoisie cannot undermine the free expression of the will of the laboring classes.

THE FORMATION OF THE SOVIET ORGANS

I. Provisional Central Executive Committee

Initiated by the Italian Socialist Party, there shall be formed, with its headquarters at Rome, a Provisional Central Executive Committee composed of ten members, four from the Italian Socialist Party, three from the General Confederation of Labor, two from the Socialist Union, and one from the Coöperative League.

The political secretary of this committee must be one of the representatives of the Italian Socialist Party.

II. Duties of the Central Executive Committee

The duty of the Provisional Central Executive Committee shall be to proceed to organize Soviets throughout the whole of Italy on the basis of the present plan, and its functions shall continue until the completion of the work and the convocation of the National Congress of Soviets of all Italy, which Congress shall be convoked by this same committee and shall maintain its relations with the committee during the entire period of organization.

The provisional Central Executive Committee shall have the complete control during this period and to it shall belong the right of direction and control of the management of all the Soviet organizations. Besides directing the work of organizing the Soviets during the initial period, it shall have the right to dissolve those formed irregularly or in contradiction to the accepted standards of the Soviets and to bring about new elections.

III. Provisional Executive Subcommittees

From the Provisional Central Executive Committee there shall be formed regional, provincial, district and local provisional executive committees whose duties shall be to form Soviets in each of the regions, provinces, districts, and localities under the direction of and on the basis of the instructions sent to them by the Central Executive Committee at Rome; which provisional committee shall continue to function until they are replaced by the deputies from the Central Committee for the locality (district), province, and region. The Provisional Executive Committees shall be composed in greater part of representatives of the Italian Socialist Party, of members of the Chamber of Confederated Labor, and of the organizations of resistance, as well as of Socialist co-operators.

IV. Territorial Subdivisions

For the formation of Soviets, Italy shall be divided into regions having a specific economic character, whether rural, commercial or industrial. In conformity with this specific character the subdivisions into provinces and districts shall be made, irrespective of whether those subdivisions conform to the present divisions of the bourgeois state. For the subdivisions of the province into districts, each city or industrial center with its surrounding rural communes which depend upon such centers or cities shall form the Soviet district. For the formation of the Soviets in the large public utilities (railroads and transport, post, telegraph, telephones, etc.) and for their representation in the General Soviet, their particular subdivision must conform to those indicated above.

V. General District Soviets

Soviets of workingmen shall be formed in every city, as well as in every industrial center of the region.

In every commune an elementary Soviet shall be formed whose councils of peasants, corresponding to the Soviet of workingmen for the cities or for the industry, form the center of the economic district.

The workingmen's Soviets of the principal place in a district, together with those of the peasants and of the employees in public works, shall form the General District Soviet. These shall form the basis of all Soviet organizations.

VI. Soviets of Workingmen

The Workingmen's Soviets shall be composed of delegates elected by the workingmen and employees of factories and works, as well as by all manual and brain workers. Any one over eighteen years of age who does not employ labor for his own profit may be a voter or a delegate. The peasants, however, must belong to the Socialist Soviet or to a revolutionary organization of resistance or a co-operative Socialist organization.

Elections will be held in factories employing over 200 persons, and at the rate of one delegate to 200 voters or a fraction of that number. Factories of minor importance will combine in conformity with instructions from the Executive Committee to conduct elections. On account of the difficulty of holding meetings in factories where large numbers are employed, the elections shall be held by groups of laborers who shall elect deputies. These in turn shall designate the delegates to the Soviet. When councils within the factory have already been formed, composed of deputies elected by a single body, the appointment of the representative to the Soviet may be made by the deputies themselves, who will inform the people of the delegates elected and will serve to keep them in touch with the working people. The same procedure holds for the people working in their own homes and not concentrated in one place. In the Soviet elected in this way the aggregate shall be composed of representatives of the Italian Socialist Party, of revolutionary organizations of defense and of co-operatives, and of experts on specified questions under dispute, not to exceed 20 per cent, representatives having been appointed by these same organizations in agreement with the provisional Central Executive Committee.

The Soviets of workers in public utilities (transport, post, and telegraph, teachers and public administrators) shall be formed in the same way as those of working men.

VII. Soviets of Peasants

The elementary Soviets of peasants shall be elected in every commune by farmers and small proprietors who do not employ labor for their own profit. The minimum age for voting and for eligibility is eighteen years. One delegate is to be chosen for each fifty voters or fraction of that number. Only one-fourth of the small Soviet of the commune shall be sent as delegates to the District Soviet, thus equalizing the representation of peasants with the other categories in the General District Soviet. Those elected must belong to a political or economic organization of their class. An adequate representation of revolutionary class organizations and also of experts on questions under discussion may be added by the provisional Central Executive Committee to the small Soviet of communes, as well as to the District Peasant Soviet in numbers not exceeding 20 per cent.

VIII. Sections of the Soviet

All the Soviets in this category shall form sections of the General District Soviet; sections to be kept if possible in the same proportion in the election of the executive committees as in that of the provincial, regional, and national Soviets.

IX. Meetings

The workingmen's Soviets in the cities shall meet not less than once a week, also in small peasant Soviets and those of the workingmen in public utilities. The General District Soviet shall meet not less than once a week. At least once a month it shall meet in the chief place of the province. The Conference of Soviets is composed of delegates from the Soviets.

Not less than once in three months the Regional Conference of Soviets shall meet in the chief places of the region and in another place designated by the executive committee. This Regional Conference is composed of delegates from the nearest Provincial Conference.

Not less than once in six months there shall meet at a place designated by the Central Executive Committee, the National Congress of Soviets, composed of delegates from District Soviets.

X. Executive Committees

The executive committee for the Provincial and Regional Conferences and for the National Congress shall be elected from the District Soviets. All the executive committees continue to function during the period included between the two national congresses. The number composing them and the functions of the executive committees shall be regulated by laws made by the provisional Central Executive Committee.

The provisional Central Executive Committee, the organ of general direction for the organization of the Soviet, as well as the regional, provincial and district executive committees, shall have the task of elaborating the labor programs of their respective assemblies, of providing in every way for the development and co-ordination of the individual sections of the Soviets, as well as developing any activities with which they may be charged by their respective assemblies.

XI. Convocation of Meetings

The Soviet, the Conferences, and the Congress shall be convoked by the same executive committees in general and in special sessions. Thus convocation must be made on the demand of one-fourth of those composing the assembly whose convocation is demanded by its respective executive committee with the approval of the Central Executive Committee.

XII. Election and Recall of Delegates

The elections in the Soviets of workingmen shall take place every six months. A delegate may at any time be deprived of his power by failing to obtain a majority vote in the assembly of his electors and of the deputies from the factory councils called together for the purpose and to which the delegate in question will be invited for explanation. Also, any member of an executive committee must resign in whom a want of confidence is expressed by his own elective assembly.

All elections, whether in the Soviets, in the Conferences, in the Congress, or in the Executive Committee shall be made in proportion to the different categories of labor (workingmen, peasants, employees, etc.).

A detailed and definite Constitution of the Soviet organizations shall be elaborated on a basis of the present plan of the provisional Central Executive Committee and presented to the Soviets to be approved by the National Congress after prior discussion.

FOUNDING OF THE THIRD INTERNATIONAL

THE MOSCOW INTERNATIONAL COMMUNIST CONFERENCE

Following a call for a constituent congress to organize the Third International, sponsored by the Russian Communist Party and supported by the Communist parties of Poland, Hungary, German-Austria, Lettland, Finland and the Balkan Revolutionary Socialist Federation, a conference was held March 2–6, 1919, at Moscow, consisting of thirty-two delegates, and representing communist and radical Socialist groups of twelve different countries. In addition to accredited delegates from Russia, Germany, Hungary, German-Austria, Sweden, Norway, Bulgaria, Roumania, Finland, Ukrainia, Esthonia and Armenia, there were admitted, with voice but no vote, persons connected with the Socialist movements of Switzerland, Holland, Bohemia, Jugo-Slavia, France, Great Britain, Turkey, Turkestan, Persia, Korea and the United States. The American representative was Boris Reinstein, a member of the Socialist Labor Party, who has resided in Russia for over a year and had no mandate from his party.

Among those who actively participated in the work of the Conference were Lenin, Trotzky, Bucharin, Kamenev, Tchitcherin, N. Steklov of the Russian Communist Party, Rakovsky of the Balkan Socialist Federation; Skripnik of Ukrainia; Stang, representing the Norwegian Left Socialists; Grimlund of the Swedish Socialist Party; Captain Sadoul and Guilbau of the French Socialist Party; Platten of the Swiss Socialist Party; Albrecht of the German Spartacus group, and Sirola of the Finnish Communists.

The agenda of the Conference consisted of the following questions:

1. Program of the Communist International. 2. Dictatorship of the Proletariat and Bourgeois Democracy. 3. Attitude toward other Socialist parties and the Berne International Conference. 4. The present international situation and the policy of the Allies. 5. The election as of a Bureau of the new International.

The Spartacan, Albrecht, was the only delegate who opposed the immediate formation of the Third International, claiming that not all Socialist parties had had the opportunity to send delegates to the Conference or to make known their attitude toward the Second International. The prevailing opinion was that the immediate formation of a new International would stimulate discussion and decision on the part of the Socialist parties with regard to their affiliation with the elements who were attempting to revive the Second International.

The Conference liquidated the Zimmerwald movement, perfected the organization of the new International and entrusted the direction of the work to an Executive Committee consisting of one representative from the Communist parties of the more important countries. The parties in Russia, Germany, German-Austria, Hungary, Switzerland, Sweden and the Balkan Federation were directed to send members to the Executive Committee. Parties which have declared their adherence to the new International will be given seats in the Executive Committee, pending the arrival of delegates from other countries. The members of the committee from the country in which the Executive Committee has its seat were empowered to plan the work of the new organization. The Executive Committee was authorized to elect a bureau consisting of five members to do the actual work of the committee. The various decisions of the Conference pertaining to national and international problems and the Socialist Party are summarized in the following manifesto drafted by a committee consisting of Nicolai Lenin, Leon Trotzky and L. Zinoviev (Russia), Charles Rakovsky (Roumania), Fritz Platten (Switzerland), and issued in behalf of the Moscow Conference.

APPEAL OF THE MOSCOW INTERNATIONAL OF SEPTEMBER 1, 1919

DEAR COMRADES.— The present phase of the revolutionary movement has, along with other questions, very sharply placed the question of parliamentarism upon the order of the day's discussion. In France, America, England, and Germany, simultaneously with the aggravation of the class struggle, all revolutionary elements are adhering to the Communist movement by uniting among themselves or by co-ordinating their actions under the slogan of Soviet power. The anarchistic-syndicalist groups and the groups that now and then call themselves simply anarchistic are thus also joining the general current. The Executive Committee of the Communist International welcomes this most heartily.

In France the syndicalist group of Comrade Pericat forms the heart of the Communist Party; in America and also to some extent in England, the fight for Soviets is led by such organizations as the I. W. W. (Industrial Workers of the World). These groups and tendencies have always actively opposed the parliamentary methods of fighting.

On the other hand, the elements of the Communist Party that are derived from the Socialist parties are, for the most part, inclined to recognize action in Parliament, too. (The Loriot group in France, the members of the A. S. P. in America, possibly meaning the American Socialist Party, the Independent Labor Party in England, etc.). All these tendencies, which ought to be united as soon as possible in the Communist Party at all cost, need uniform tactics. Consequently, the question must be decided on a broad scale and as a general measure, and the Executive Committee of the Communist International turns to all the affiliated parties with the present circular letter, which is especially dedicated to this question.

The universal unifying program is at the present moment the recognition of the struggle for the dictatorship of the proletariat in the form of the Soviet power. History has so placed the question that it is right on this question that the line is drawn between the revolutionary proletariat and the opportunists, between the Communists and the social traitors of every brand. The so-called Centre (Kautsky in Germany, Longuet in France, the I. L. P. and some elements of the B. S. P. in England. Hillquit in America), is, in spite of its protestations, an objectively anti-Socialist tendency, because it cannot, and does not wish to, lead the struggle for the Soviet power of the proletariat.

On the contrary, those groups and parties which formerly rejected any kind of political struggles (for example, some anarchist groups) have, by recognizing the Soviet power, the dictatorship of the proletariat, really abandoned their old standpoint as to political action, because they have recognized the idea of the seizure of power by the working class, the power that is necessary for the suppression of the opposing bourgeoisie. This, we repeat, a common program for the struggle of the Soviet dictatorship has been found.

The old divisions in the international labor movement have plainly outlived their time. The war has caused a regrouping. Many of the anarchists or syndicalists, who rejected parliamentarism, conducted themselves just as despicably and treasonably during the five years of the war as did the old leaders of the Social Democracy who always have the name of Marx on their lips. The unification of forces is being affected in a new manner: some are for the proletarian revolution, for the Soviets, for the dictatorship, for mass action, even up to armed uprisings — the others are against this plan. This is the principal question of today. This is the main criterion. The new combinations will be formed according to these labels, and are being so formed already.

In what relation does the recognition of the Soviet idea stand to parliamentarism? Right here a sharp dividing line must be drawn between two questions which logically have nothing to do with each other: The question of parliamentarism as a desired form of the organization of the State and the question of the exploitation of parliamentarism for the development of the revolution. The comrades often confuse these two questions something which has an extraordinary injurious effect upon the entire practical struggle. We wish to discuss each of these questions in its order and draw all the necessary deductions.

What is the form of the proletarian dictatorship? We reply: The Soviets. This has been demonstrated by an experience that has a world-wide significance. Can the Soviet power be combined with parliamentarism? No, and yet again, no. It is absolutely incompatible with the existing parliaments, because the parliamentary machine embodies the concentrated power of the bourgeoisie. The Deputies, the Chambers of Deputies, their newspapers, the system of bribery, the secret connections of the parliamentarians with the leaders of the banks, the connection with all the apparatuses of the bourgeois state — all these are fetters for the working class. They must be burst. The governmental machine of the bourgeoisie, consequently also the bourgeois parliaments, are to be broken, disrupted, destroyed, and upon their ruins is to be organized a new power, the power of the union of the working class, the workers' "Parliaments," i. e., the Soviets.

Only the betrayers of the workers can deceive the workers with the hope of a "peaceful" social revolution, along the lines of parliamentary reforms. Such persons are the worst enemies of the working class, and a most pitiless struggle must be waged against them; no compromise with them is permissible. Therefore, our slogan for any bourgeois country you may choose is: "Down with the Parliament! Long live the power of the Soviets!"

Nevertheless, a person may put the question this way: "Very well, you deny the power of the present bourgeois parliaments; then why don't you organize new, more democratic parliaments on the basis of a real universal suffrage?" During the Socialist revolution the struggle has become so acute that the working class must act quickly and resolutely, without allowing its class enemies to enter into its camp, into its organization of power. Such qualities are only found in the Soviets of workers, soldiers, sailors, and peasants, elected in the factories and shops, in the country and in the barracks. So the question of form of the proletarian power is put this way. Now the government is to be overthrown: Kings, Presidents, Parliaments, Chambers of Deputies, National Assemblies; all these institutions are our sworn enemies, they must be destroyed.

Now we take up the second basic question: Can the bourgeois parliaments be fully utilized for the purpose of developing the revolutionary class struggle? Logically, as we just remarked, this question is by no means related to the first question. In fact: A person surely can be trying to destroy any kind of an organization by joining it and by "utilizing" it. This is also perfectly understood by our class enemies when they exploit the official Social Democratic parties, the trade unions and the like for their purposes.

Let us take the extreme example: The Russian Communists, the Bolsheviki, voted in the election for the Constituent Assembly. They met in the hall. But they came there to break up this Constituent within twenty-four hours and fully to realize the Soviet power. The party of the Bolsheviki also had its deputies in the Czar's Imperial Duma. Did the party at that time recognize the Duma as an ideal, or at least, an endurable form of government? It would be lunacy to assume that. It sent its representatives there so as to proceed against the apparatus of the Czarist power from that side, too, and to contribute to the destruction of that same Duma. It was not for nothing that the Czarist government condemned the Bolsheviks' "parliamentarians" to prison for "high treason." The Bolshevist leaders were also carrying on all illegal work, and though they temporarily made use of their 'inviolability' in welding together the masses for the drive against Czarism.

But Russia was not the only place where that kind of "parliamentary" activity was carried on. Look at Germany and the activities of Liebknecht. The murdered comrade was the perfect type of a revolutionist, and so was there then something non-revolutionary in the fact that he, from the tribune of the cursed Prussian Landtag, called upon the soldiers to rise against the Landtag? On the contrary. Here, too, we see the complete admissibility and usefulness of his exploitation of the situation. If Liebknecht had not been a deputy he would never have been able to accomplish such an act; his speeches would have had no such an echo. The example of the Swedish Communists in Parliament also convince us of this. In Sweden Comrade Hoglund played, and plays, the same role as Liebknecht did in Germany. Making use of his position as a deputy, he assists in destroying the bourgeois parliamentary system; none else in Sweden has done as much for the cause of the revolution and the struggle against the war as our friend.

In Bulgaria we see the same thing. The Bulgarian Communists have successfully exploited the tribune of Parliament for revolutionary purposes. At the recent elections they won seats for forty-seven deputies. Comrades Blagoief, Kirkof, Kolarov, and other leaders of the Bulgarian Communist Party understand how to exploit the parliamentary tribune in the service of the proletarian revolution. Such "parliamentary work" demands peculiar daring and a special revolutionary spirit; the men there are occupying especially dangerous positions; they are laying mines under the enemy while in the enemy's camp. They enter Parliament for the purpose of getting this machine in their hands in order to assist the masses behind the walls of the Parliament in the work of blowing it up.

Are we for the maintenance of the bourgeois "democratic" parliaments as the form of the administration of the State?

No, not in any case. We are for the Soviets.

But are we for the full utilization of these parliaments for our Communist work — as long as we are not yet strong enough to overthrow the Parliament?

Yes, we are for this — in consideration of a whole list of conditions. We know very well that in France, America, and England no such parliamentarians have yet arisen from the masses of the workers. In those countries we have up to now observed a picture of parliamentary betrayal. But this is no proof of the incorrectness of the tactics that we regard as correct! It is only a matter of their being revolutionary parties there like the Bolsheviki or the German Spartacides. If there is such a party then everything can become quite different. It is particularly necessary: (1) That the deciding center of the struggle lies outside Parliament (strikes, uprisings and other kinds of mass action); (2) that the activities in Parliament be combined with this struggle: (3) that the deputies also perform illegal work: (4) that they act for the Central Committee and subject to its orders: (5) that they do not heed the parliamentary forms in their acts (have no fear of direct clashes with the bourgeois majority, "talk past it," etc.)

The matter of taking part in the election at a given time, during a given electoral campaign, depends upon a whole string of concrete circumstances which, in each country, must be particularly considered at each given time. The Russian Bolsheviki were for boycotting the elections for the first Imperial Duma in 1906. And these same persons were for taking part in the elections of the second Imperial Duma, when it had been shown that the bourgeois agrarian power would still rule in Russia for many a year. In the year 1918, before the election for the German National Assembly, one section of the Spartacides was for taking part in the elections, the other section was against it. But the party of the Spartacides remained a unified Communist Party.

In principle we cannot renounce the utilization of the parliamentarism. The party of the Russian Bolshevik declared, in the spring of 1918, at its seventh congress, when it was already in power, in a special resolution, that the Russian Communists, in case the bourgeois democracy in Russia, through a peculiar combination of circumstances, should once more get the upper hand, could be compelled to return to the utilization of bourgeois parliamentarism. Room for manœuvring is also to be allowed in this respect.

The comrades' principle efforts are to consist in the work of mobilizing the masses; establishing the party, organizing their own groups in the unions and capturing them; organizing Soviets in the course of the struggle; leading the mass struggle; agitation for the revolution among the masses — all this is of first line importance; parliamentary action and participation in electoral campaigns only as one of the helps in this work — no more.

Insists Upon Unity of Communists

If this is so — and it undoubtedly is so — then it is a matter of course that it doesn't pay to split into those factions that are of different opinions only about this, now secondary, question. The practice of parliamentary prostitution was so disgusting that even the best comrades have prejudices in this question. These ought to be overcome in the course of the revolutionary struggle. Therefore, we urgently appeal to all groups and organizations, which are carrying on a real struggle for the Soviets, and call upon them to unite firmly, even despite the lack of agreement on this question.

All those who are for the Soviets and the proletarian dictatorship wish to unite as soon as possible and form a unified Communist Party.

With Communist greetings
G. ZINOVIEV,
President of the Executive Committee of the Communist International

September 1, 1919.

Printed in German Communist papers, reprinted in the Socialist paper the "New Yorker Volkszeitung" of January 4th. See New York "Times" of January 25.

SECRET INTERNATIONAL COMMUNIST CONGRESS AT AMSTERDAM

In February it was disclosed in the paper "Algemeen Handelsbad" that there had recently been at Amsterdam a secret meeting of the International Communist Congress which is arranging for revolutionary Communist action all over the world. Holland was selected by Lenin for the gathering because in that country reaction was weak and communication with other countries easy. The expenses were to be met by contributions by each country, but the Soviet government at once placed at the disposal of the Congress diamonds, pearls and other precious stones to the value of 20,000,000 rubles.

A resolution was carried to the effect that revolutionary action was necessary to compel capital to make peace with Russia and so have the Soviet regime and hasten the world revolution. Communists should, therefore, take advantage of every strike movement and every mass demonstration to promote their objects.

An international strike should be organized in opposition to intervention in Russia; this demonstration to be supplemented by coercive strikes. It was expressly resolved that it was the duty of the Bureau to support every strike and revolutionary movement and that the 20,000,000 rubles be devoted to this object.

The Dutch chairman of the Netherlands Federation of Transport Workers, Bouwman, who, with Sneevliet, both of them Syndicalists, is leading the dock strike at Amsterdam and Rotterdam, declared that the independent trade unionists did not want intensive production, which would only help to maintain capitalism. It was resolved that the Bureau be instructed to see (1) to the dissemination of literature, (2) to propaganda, (3) to the financing of all movements and strikes of a revolutionary character, and that *branches be established* in *North America* and *Eastern* Asia, the latter to carry on operations in British India and in the Dutch East Indies. Miss Pankhurst and Mr. John Thomas Murphy were among those who represented England at the Congress, the latter insisted that trusted men should be sent among the trade unions in order to install revolutionary sentiments and detach the men from their leaders. (Reported in "Political Review," March 5, 1920.)

The secret meetings were mostly held in the house of the leader of the Dutch Communists, Wijnkcop. Beside the representatives of England there were delegates from America, Germany, Switzerland, Belgium, India, Russia and Hungary. A number of foreigners were arrested and expelled. The manifesto that was issued speaks of the spring offense of the Soviet government against Poland, with a view to breaking through to Germany and also forecasts the revolutionary outbreak in Germany itself, which had long been planned in co-operation with Russia. "The Red army," it says, "is coming to free the proletariat of Poland and as the army approaches Holland workmen must join in like brethren . . . further they must force capitalism to make peace with the Soviets and thus hasten the world revolution. . . If the revolution breaks out in Russia or elsewhere the international proletariat must be ready for a general strike, especially transport workers in America, England, France and Italy.

Every three months the countries where sub-bureaus are established, including Mexico and Spain, are to send a representative to Holland.

This attempt to establish a base for the Third International outside of Russia is said to be placed by Lenin, in charge of an agent named Rutgers, sent from Russia to Holland. An elaborate service is being established of spies, press agents, financial agents, courier service, reports, propagandisers among trade unions and in the army, a bureau for false passports, etc.

MANIFESTO OF THE THIRD (MOSCOW) COMMUNIST INTERNATIONAL

To the Proletariat of All Lands:

Seventy-two years have gone by since the Communist Party of the World proclaimed its program in form of the manifesto written by the greatest teachers of the proletarian revolution, Karl Marx and Frederick Engels. Even at that early time, when Communism had scarcely come into the arena of conflict, it was hounded by the lies, hatred and calumny of the possessing classes, who rightly suspected in it their mortal enemy. During these seven decades Communism has traveled a hard road; storms of ascent followed by periods of sharp decline; successes, but also severe defeats. In spite of all, the development at bottom went the way forecast by the Manifesto of the Communist Party. The epoch of the last decisive battle came later than the apostles of the social revolution expected and wished. But it has come.

We Communists, representatives of the revolutionary proletariat of the different countries of Europe, America and Asia, assembled in Soviet Moscow, feel and consider ourselves followers and fulfillers of the program proclaimed seventy-two years ago. It is our task now to sum up the practical revolutionary expense of the working class, to cleanse the movement of its admixtures of opportunism and social patriotism, and to gather together the forces of all the true revolutionary proletarian parties in order to further and hasten the complete victory of the communist revolution.

I

For a long span of years Socialism predicted the inevitableness of the imperialistic war; it perceived the essential cause of this war in the insatiable greed of the possessing classes in both camps of capitalist nations. Two years before the outbreak of the war, at the Congress of Basle, the responsible Socialist leaders of all countries branded Imperialism as the instigator of the coming war, and menaced the bourgeoisie with the threat of the Socialist revolution — the retaliation of the proletariat for the crimes of militarism. Now, after the experience of five years, after history has disclosed the predatory lust of Germany, and has unmasked the no less criminal deeds on the part of the Allies, the State Socialists of the Entente nations, together with their governments, again and again unmask the deposed German kaiser. And the German social patriots, who in August, 1914, proclaimed the diplomatic White Book of the Hohenzollern as the holiest gospel of the people, today, in vulgar sycophancy, join themselves with the Socialists of the Entente lands to accuse as arch-criminal the deposed German monarchy which they formerly served as slaves. In this way they hope to erase the memory of their own guilt and to gain the good will of the victors. But alongside the dethroned dynasties of the Romanoffs, Hohenzollerns, and Hapsburgs, and the capitalistic cliques of these lands, the rulers of France, England, Italy and the United States stand revealed in the light of unfolding events and diplomatic disclosures in their immeasurable vileness.

The contradictions of the capitalist system were converted by the war into beastly torments of hunger and cold, epidemics and moral savagery, for all mankind. Hereby. also the academic quarrel in Socialism over the theory of increasing misery, and also of the undermining of capitalism through Socialism, is now finally determined. Statisticians and teachers of the theory of reconciliation of these contradictions have endeavored for decades to gather together from all corners of the earth real and apparent facts which evidence the increasing well-being of the working class. To-day abyssmal misery is before our eyes, social as well as physiological, in all its shocking reality.

Finance-capital, which threw mankind into the abyss of war, has itself suffered catastrophic changes during the course of the war. The dependence of paper money upon the material basis of production was completely destroyed. More and more losing its significance as a medium and regulator of capitalistic commodity circulation, paper money becomes merely a means of exploitation, robbery, of military-economic oppression. The complete deterioration of paper money now reflects the general deadly crisis of capitalist commodity exchange.

As free competition was replaced as the regulator of production and distribution in the chief domains of economy, during the decades which preceded the war, by the system of trusts and monopolies, so the exigencies of the war took the monopolies and gave them directly to the military power. Distribution of raw materials, utilization of petroleum from Baku or Romenia, of coal from Donetz, of cereals from the Ukraine; the fate of German locomotives, railroad cars and automobiles, the provisioning of famine-stricken Europe with bread and meat — all these basic questions of the economic life of the world are no longer regulated by free competition, nor yet by combinations of national and internatianol trusts, but through direct application of military force.

Just as complete subordination of the power of the State to the purposes of finance-capital led mankind to the imperialistic shambles, so finance-capital has, through this mass slaughter, completely militarized not alone the State but also itself. It is no longer able to fulfill its essential economic functions otherwise than by means of blood and iron.

The opportunists who before the war exhorted the workers, in the name of the gradual transition into Socialism, to be temperate, who, during the war asked for submission in the name of Burgfrieden and defense of the Fatherland, now again demand of the workers self-abnegation to overcome the terrible consequences of the war. If this preaching were listened to by the workers, capitalism would build out of the bones of several generations a new and still more formidable structure, leading to a new and inevitable world war. Fortunately for humanity, this is no longer possible.

The absorption by the State of the economic life, so vigorously opposed by capitalist liberalism, has now become a fact. There can be no return either to free competition nor to the rule of the trusts, syndicates and other economic monsters. The only question is, who shall be the future mainstay of State production, the Imperialistic State or the State of the victorious proletariat. In other words, shall the entire working humanity become the feudal bond-servants of the victorious Entente bourgeoisie, which under the name of a League of Nations aided by an "international" army and an "international" navy here plunders and murders, there throws a club, but everywhere enchains the proletariat, with the single aim of maintaining its own rule? Or will the working class take into its own hands the disorganized and shattered economic life and make certain its reconstruction of a Socialist basis?

Only the proletarian dictatorship, which recognizes neither inherited privileges nor rights of property but which arises from the needs of the hungering masses, can shorten the period of the present crisis; and for this purpose it mobilizes all materials and forces, introduces the universal duty of labor, establishes the regime of industrial discipline, this way to heal in the course of a few years the open wounds caused by the war and also to raise humanity to a new undreamed-of height.

The national State, which was given a tremendous impulse by capitalistic evolution, has become too narrow for the development of the productive forces. And even more untenable has become the position of the small States, distributed among the great powers of Europe and in other parts of the world. These small States came into existence at different times as fragments split off the bigger States, as petty currency in payment for services rendered, to serve as strategic buffer States. They, too, have their dynasties, their ruling gangs, their imperialistic pretensions, their diplomatic machinations. Their illusory independence had until the war precisely the same support as the European balance of power, namely, the continuous opposition between the two imperialistic camps. The war has destroyed this balance. The tremendous preponderance of power which the war gave to Germany in the beginning compelled these smaller nations to seek their welfare and safety under the wings of German militarism. After Germany was beaten the bourgeoisie of the small nations, together with their patriotic "Socialists," turned to the victorious imperialism of the Allies and began to seek assurance for their further independent existence in the hypocritical points of the Wilson program. At the same time the number of little States has increased; out of the unity of the Austrian-Hungarian monarchy, out of the different parts of the Czarist Empire, new sovereignties have formed themselves. And these, as soon as borne, jump at each others throats on account of their frontier disputes. Meanwhile the Allied Imperialists brought about certain combinations of new and old small States through the cement of mutual hatreds and general weakness. Even while violating the small and weak peoples and delivering them to famine and degredation, the Entente Imperialists, exactly as the Imperialists of the Central Powers before them, did not cease to talk of the right of self-determination of all peoples, a right which is now entirely destroyed in Europe and in the rest of the world.

Only the proletarian revolution can secure the existence of the small nations, revolution which frees the productive forces of all countries from the restrictions of the national States, which unites all peoples in the closest economic co-operation on the basis of a universal economic plan, and gives even to the smallest and weakest peoples the possibility freely and independently to carry on their national culture without detriment to the united and centralized economy of Europe and the whole world.

The last war, after all, a war against the colonies, was at the same time a war with the aid of the colonies. To an unprecedented extent the population of the colonies was drawn into the European War. Indians, Arabs, Madagascans battled on the European continent—what for?—for their right to remain slaves of England or France. Never did capitalist rule show itself more shameless, never was the truth of colonial slavery brought into such sharp relief. As a consequence we witnessed a series of open rebellions and revolutionary ferment in all colonies. In Europe itself it was Ireland which reminded us in bloody street battles that it is still an enslaved country and feels itself as such. In Madagascar, in Annam, and in other countries, the troops of the bourgeois Republic have had more than one insurrection of the colonial slaves to suppress during the war. In India the revolutionary movement has not been at a standstill for one day, and lately we have witnessed the greatest labor strike in Asia, to which the government of Great Britain answered with armored cars.

In this manner the colonial question in its entirety became the order of the day, not alone on the green table of the diplomatic conferences at Paris, but also in the colonies themselves. The Wilson program, at the very best, calls only for a change in the firm name of colonial enslavement. Liberation of the colonies can only happen together with liberation of the working class of the capital cities. The workers and peasants not only of Annam, Algeria, Bengal, but also of Persia and Armenia, can gain independent existence only after the laborers of England and France have overthrown Lloyd George and Clemenceau and taken the power into their own hands. Even now in the more advanced colonies the battle goes on not only under the flag of national liberation, but it assumes also an open and outspoken social character. Capitalistic Europe has drawn the backward countries by force into the capitalistic whirlpool, and Socialistic Europe will come to the aid of the liberated colonies with its technique, its organization, its spiritual influence, in order to facilitate their transition into the orderly system of socialistic economy.

Colonial slaves of Africa and Asia! The hour of triumph of the proletarian dictatorship of Europe will also be the hour of your liberation!

II

The entire bourgeois world accuses the Communists of destroying liberties and political democracy. That is not true. Having come into power the proletariat only asserts the absolute impossibility of applying the methods of bourgeois democracy and creates the conditions and forms of a higher working-class democracy. The whole course of capitalistic development undermined political democracy, not only by dividing the nation into two irreconcilable classes, but also by condemning the numerous petty bourgeois and half-proletarian elements, as well as the slum proletariat, to permanent economic stagnation and political impotence.

In those countries in which the historical development has furnished the opportunity, the working class has utilized the regime of political democracy for its organization against capitalism. In all countries where the conditions for a worker's revolution are not yet ripe, the same process will go on. But the great middle layers on the farm lands, as well as in the cities, are hindered by capitalism in their historic development and remain stagnant for whole epochs. The peasant of Bavaria and Baden who does not look beyond his church spire, the small French winegrower who has been ruined by the adulterations practiced by the big capitalists, the small farmer of America plundered and betrayed by bankers and legislators — all these social ranks which have been shoved aside from the main road of development by capitalism, are called on paper by the regime of political democracy to the administration of the State. In reality, however, the finance-oligarchy decides all important questions which determine the destinies of nations behind the back of parliamentary democracy. Particularly was this true of the war question. The same applies to the question of peace.

If the finance-oligarchy considers it advantageous to veil its deeds of violence behind parliamentary vote, then the bourgeois State has at its command in order to gain its ends all the traditions and attainments of former centuries of upper-class rule multiplied by the wonders of capitalistic technique: lies, demagogism, persecution, slander, bribery, calumny and terror. To demand of the proletariat in the final life and death struggle with capitalism that it should follow lamblike the demands of bourgeois democracy would be the same as to ask a man who is defending his life against robbers to follow the artificial rules of a French duel that have been set by his enemy but not followed by him.

In an empire of destruction, where not only the means of production and transportation, but also the institutions of political democracy represent bloody ruins, the proletariat must create its own forms, to serve above all as a bond of unity for the working class and to enable it to accomplish a revolutionary intervention in the further development of mankind. Such apparatus is represented in the workmen's councils. The old parties, the old unions, have proved incapable, in the person of their leaders, to understand, much less to carry out, the tasks which the new epoch presents to them. The proletariat created a new institution which embraces the entire working class, without distinction of vocation or political maturity, an elastic form of organization capable of continually renewing itself, expanding, and of drawing into itself over new elements, ready to open its doors to the working groups of city and village which are near to the proletariat. The indispensable autonomous organization of the working class in the present struggle and in the future conquests of different lands, tests the proletariat and represents the greatest inspiration and the mightiest weapon of the proletariat of our time.

Whenever the masses are awakened to consciousness, workers', soldiers' and peasants' councils will be formed. To fortify these councils, to increase their authority, to oppose them to the State apparatus of the bourgeoisie, is now the chief task of the class-conscious and honest workers of all countries. By means of these councils the working class can counteract that disorganization which has been brought into it by the infernal anguish of the war, by hunger, by the violent deeds of the possessing classes, and by the betrayal of their former leaders. By means of these councils the working class will gain power in all countries most readily and most certainly when these councils gain the support of the majority of the laboring population. By means of these councils the working class, once attaining power, will control all the fields of economic and cultural life, as in the case of Russia at the present time.

The collapse of the imperialistic State, czaristic to most democratic, goes on simultaneously with the collapse of the imperialistic military system. The armies of millions, mobilized by imperialism, could remain steadfast only so long as the proletariat remained obedient under the yoke of the bourgeoisie. The complete breakdown of national unity signifies also an inevitable disintegration of the army. Thus it happened, first in Russia, then in Austria-Hungary, then in Germany. The same also is to be expected in other imperialistic states. Insurrection of the peasants against the landowner, of laborer against capitalist, of both against the monarchy or "democratic" bureaucracy, must lead inevitably to the insurrection of soldier against commander and, furthermore, to a sharp division between the proletarian and bourgeois elements within the army. The imperialistic war which pitted nation against nation has passed and is passing into the civil war which lines up class against class.

The outcry of the bourgeois world against the civil war and the red terror is the most colossal hypocrisy of which the history of political struggles can boast. There would be no civil war if the exploiters who have carried mankind to the very brink of ruin had not prevented every forward step of the laboring masses, if they had not instigated plots and murders and called to their aid armed help from outside to maintain or restore their predatory privileges. Civil war is forced upon the laboring classes by their arch-enemies. The working class must answer blow for blow, if it will not renounce its own object and its own future which is at the same time the future of all humanity.

The Communist parties, far from conjuring up civil war artificially, rather strive to shorten its duration as much as possible, in case it has become an iron necessity, to minimize the number of its victims, and above all to secure victory for the proletariat. This makes necessary the disarming of the bourgeoisie at the proper time, the arming of the laborers, and the formation of a Communist army as the protector of the rule of the proletariat and the inviolability of the social structure. Such is the Red army of Soviet Russia which arose to protect the achievements of the working class against every assault from within or without. The Soviet army is inseparable from the Soviet state.

Conscious of the world-historic character of their mission, the enlightened workers strove from the very beginning of the organized socialistic movement for an international union. The foundation-stone in this union was laid in the year 1864 in London, in the First International. The Franco-Prussian War, from which arose the Germany of the Hohenzollerns, undermined the First International, giving rise at the same time to the national labor parties. As early as 1889 these parties united at the Congress of Paris and organized the Second International. But during this period the center of gravity of the labor movement rested entirely on national ground, confining itself within the realm of national parliamentarism to the narrow compass of national states and national industries. Decades of organizing and labor reformism created a generation of leaders most of whom gave verbal recognition to the program of social revolution but denied it in substance. They were lost in the swamp of reformism and adaptation to the bourgeois state. The opportunistic character of the leading parties of the Second International was finally revealed, and led to the greatest collapse of the movement in all its history, when events required revolutionary methods of warfare from the labor parties. Just as the war of 1870 dealt a death blow to the First International by revealing that there was not in fact behind the social-revolutionary program any compact power of the masses, so the war of 1914 killed the Second International by showing that above the consolidated labor masses there stood labor parties which converted themselves into servile organs of the bourgeois state.

This includes not only the social patriots who today are openly in the camp of the bourgeoisie as preferred confidential advisers and reliable hangmen of the working class, but also the hazy, fickle and irresolute Socialist Center which is today trying to revive the Second International, i. e., the narrowness, opportunism and revolutionary impotence of their predecessors. The Independents of Germany, the present Majority of the Socialist Party in France, the Independent Labor Party in England, and similar groups, are actually trying to re-establish themselves in the position which the old official parties of the Second International held before the war. They appear as before with proposals of compromise and conciliation and hereby paralyze the energy of the proletariat, lengthening the period of crisis and consequently increasing the misery of Europe. War against the Socialist Center is a necessary condition of successful war against imperialism.

Spurning the half-heartedness, hypocrisy and corruption of the decadent official Socialist parties, we, the Communists assembled in the Third International, feel ourselves to be the direct successors of the heroic efforts and martyrdom of a long series of revolutionary generations from Baboeuf to Karl Liebknecht and Rosa Luxembourg. As the First International foresaw the future development and pointed the way, as the Second International gathered together and organized millions of the proletariats, so the Third International is the International of open mass-action of the revolutionary realization, the International of deeds. Socialist criticism has sufficiently stigmatized the bourgeois world order. The task of the International Communist Party is now to overthrow this order and to erect in its place the structure of the Socialist world order. We urge the working men and women of all countries to unite under the Communist banner, the emblem under which the first great victories have already been won.

Proletarians of all lands! In the war against imperialistic barbarity, against monarchy, against the privileged classes, against the bourgeois state and bourgeois property, against all forms and varieties of social and national oppression — UNITE!

Under the standard of the Workingmen's Councils, under the banner of the Third International, in the revolutionary struggle for power and the dictatorship of the proletariat, proletarians of all countries UNITE! (Translation by Ida Ferguson.)

GOVERNING RULES OF THE COMMUNISTIC INTERNATIONAL

The new era has begun! The era of the downfall of capitalism — its internal disintegration. The epoch of the proletarian communist revolution; in some countries, victorious proletarian revolution; increasing revolutionary ferment in other lands; uprisings in the colonies; utter incapacity of the ruling classes to control the fate of peoples any longer; that is the picture of present world conditions.

Humanity, with its entire culture now lying in ruins, faces danger of complete destruction. There is only one power which can save it — the power of the proletariat. The old capitalistic "order" can exist no longer. This ultimate result of the capitalistic mode of production is chaos — a chaos to be overcome only by the great producing class, the proletariat. It is the proletariat which must establish real order, the order of communism. It must end the domination of capital, make war impossible, wipe out state boundaries, transform the whole world into one co-operative commonwealth, and bring about real human brotherhood and freedom.

World capitalism prepares itself for the final battle. Under cover of the "League of Nations" and a deluge of pacifist phrase mongering, a desperate effort is being made to pull together the tumbling capitalist system and to direct its forces against the constantly growing proletarian revolt. This monstrous new conspiracy of the capitalist class must be met by the proletariat by seizure of the political power of the State, turning this power against its class enemies, and using it as a lever to set in motion the economic revolution. The final victory of the proletariat of the world means the beginning of the real history of free mankind.

THE CAPTURE OF POLITICAL POWER

Seizure of political power by the proletarian means destruction of the political power of the bourgeoisie. The organized power of the bourgeoisie is in the civil state, with its capitalistic army under control of bourgeois-junker officers, its police and gendarmes, jailers and judges, its priests, government officials, etc. Conquest of the political power means not merely a change in the personnel of ministries but annihilation of the enemy's apparatus of government; disarmament of the bourgeoisie, of the counter-revolutionary officers, of the White Guard; arming of the proletariat, the revolutionary soldiers, the Red Guard of Workingmen; displacement of all bourgeois judges and organization of proletarian courts; elimination of control by reactionary government officials and substitution of new organs of management of the proletariat. Victory of the proletariat consists in shattering the enemy's organization and organizing the proletarian power; in the destruction of the bourgeois and upbuilding of the proletarian state apparatus. Not until the proletariat has achieved this victory and broken the resistance of the bourgeoisie can the former enemies of the new order be made useful, by bringing them under control of the communistic structure and gradually bringing them into accord with its work.

Democracy and Dictatorship

The proletarian state, like every state, is an organ of suppression, but it arrays itself against the enemies of the working class. It aims to break the opposition of the despoilers of labor, who are using every means in a desperate effort to stiffle the revolution in blood, and to make impossible further opposition. The dictatorship of the proletariat, which gives it the favored position in the community, is only a provisional institution. As the opposition of the bourgeoisie is broken, as it is expropriated and gradually absorbed into the working groups, the proletarian dictatorship disappears, until finally the state dies and their is no more class distinction.

Democracy, so-called, that is, bourgeois democracy, is nothing more not less than veiled dictatorship by the bourgeoisie. The much vaunted "popular will" exists as little as the undivided people. In reality, there are the classes, with antagonistic, irreconciliable purposes. However, since the bourgeoisie is only a small minority, it needs this fiction of the "popular will" as a flourish of fine-sounding words to reinforce its rule over the working classes and to impose its own class will upon the people. The proletariat, on the contrary, as the overwhelming majority of the people, openly exercises its class power by means of its mass organizations and through its councils, in order to wipe out the privileges of the bourgeoisie and to secure the transition, rather the transformation, into a classless communistic commonwealth.

The main emphasis of bourgeois democracy is on formal declarations of rights and liberties which are actually unattainable by the proletariat, because of want of the materials means for their enjoyment; while the bourgeoisie uses its material advantages, through its press and organizations, to deceive and betray the people. On the other hand, the council type of government makes it possible for the proletariat to realize its rights and liberties. The council power gives to the people palaces, houses, printing offices, paper supply, etc., for their press, their societies and assemblies. And in this way alone is actual proletarian democracy made possible.

Bourgeois democracy, with its parliamentary system, uses words to induce belief in popular participation in government. Actually the masses and their organizations are held far out of reach of the real power and the real state administration. In the council system the mass organizations rule and through them the mass itself, inasmuch as the councils drew constantly increasing numbers of workers into the state administration; and only by this process will the entire working population gradually become part of the government. The council system also builds itself directly on the mass organizations of the proletariat, on the councils themselves, the revolutionary trade unions, the co-operatives, etc. Bourgeois democracy and its parliamentary system sharpen the separation of the masses from the state by division of the government into legislative and executive powers, and through parliamentary mandates beyond popular recall. The council system, by contrast, unites the masses with the organs of government by right of recall, amalgamation of legislative and executive powers, and by usue of working roads. Above all this union is fostered by the fact that in the council system elections are based not on arbitrary territorial districts, but on units of production.

In this way the council system brings about true proletarian democracy, democracy by and for the proletarians against the bourgeoisie. The industrial proletariat is favored in this system because it is the most aggressive, best organized and politically ripest class, under whose leadership the half-proletarians and small farmers will be gradually elevated. These temporary privileges of the industrial proletariat must be utilized to draw the small farmers away from the control of the big landowners and bourgeoisie and to organize and train them as helpers in the building of the communistic structure.

EXPROPRIATION OF THE BOURGEOISIE AND SOCIALIZATION OF PRODUCTION

The breakdown of the capitalistic order and the disruption of capitalistic industrial discipline makes impossible the reorganization of production on the capitalistic basis. Wage wars of the workingmen, even when successful, do not bring the anticipated betterment of conditions of living; the workers can only become emancipated when production is no longer controlled by the bourgeoisie but by the proletariat. In order to raise the standards of productivity, in order to crush the opposition on the part of the bourgeoisie (which only prolongs the death struggle of the old regime and thereby invites danger of total ruin), the proletarian dictatorship must carry out the exportation of the greater bourgeoisie and junkerdom and convert the means of production and distribution into the common property of the proletarian state.

Communism is now being born out of the ruins of capitalism — there is no other salvation for humanity. The opportunists who are making utopian demands for the reconstruction of the economic system of capitalism, so as to postpone socialization, only delay the process of disintegration and increase the danger of total demolition. The Communist revolution, on the other hand, is the best, the only means, by which the most important social power of production, the proletariat, can be saved, and with it society itself.

The dictatorship of the proletariat does not in any way call for partition of the means of production and exchange; rather, on the contrary, its aim is further to centralize the forces of production and to subject all of production to a symmetrical plan. As the first steps toward socialization of the entire economic system may be mentioned: the socializing of the great banks which now control production; the taking over by the state power of the proletariat of all government-controlled economic utilities; the transferring of all communal enterprises; the socializing of the syndicated and trustified units of production, as well as all other branches of production in which the degree of concentration and centralization of capital makes this technically practicable; the socializing of agricultural estates and their conversion into co-operative establishments.

As far as the smaller enterprises are concerned, the proletariat must gradually unite them, according to the degree of their importance. It must be particularly emphasized that small properties will in no way be expropriated and that property owners who are not exploiters of labor will not be forcibly dispossessed. This element will gradually be drawn into the socialistic organization through the force of example, through practical demonstration of the superiority of the new order of things, and the regulation by which the small farmers and the petty bourgeoisie of the cities will be freed from economic bondage to usurious capital and landlordism, and from tax burdens (especially by annulment of the national debts), etc.

The task of the proletarian dictatorship in the economic field can only be fulfilled to the extent that the proletariat is enabled to create centralized organs of management and to institute workers' control. To this end it must make use of its mass organizations which are in closest relation to the process of production. In the field of distribution the proletarian dictatorship must re-establish commerce by an accurate distribution of products, to which end the following methods are to be considered: the socialization of wholesale establishments; the taking over of all bourgeois state and municipal apparatus of distribution; control of the great co-operative societies, which organizations will still have an important role in the production epoch; the gradual centralization of all these organs and their conversion into a systematic unity for the rational distribution of products.

As in the field of production so also in the field of distribution all qualified technicians and specialists are to be made use of, provided their political resistance is broken and they are still capable of adapting themselves, not to the service of capital, but to the new system of production. Far from oppressing them the proletariat will make it possible for the first time for them to develop intensive creative work. The proletarian dictatorship, with their co-operation, will retrieve the separation of physical and mental work which capitalism has developed and thus will science and labor be unified. Besides expropriating the factories, mines, estates, etc., the proletariat must also abolish the exploitation of the people by capitalistic landlords, transfer the large mansions to the local workers' councils, and move the working people into the bourgeois dwellings.

During this great transition period the power of the councils must constantly build up the entire administrative organization into a more centralized structure, but on the other hand constantly draws ever increasing elements of the working people into the immediate control of government.

THE WAY TO VICTORY

The revolutionary era compels the proletariat to make use of the means of battle which will concentrate its entire energies, namely, mass action, with its logical resultant, direct conflict with the governmental machinery in open combat. All other methods, such as revolutionary use of bourgeois parliamentarism, will be of only secondary significance.

The indispensable condition for successful struggle is separation not only from the direct servitors of capitalism and enemies of the communist revolution, in which role the Social Democrats of the Right appear, but also from the Party of the Centre (Kautskians), who desert the proletariat at the critical moment in order to come to terms with its open antagonists. On the other hand, there are essential elements of the proletariat, heretofore not within the Socialist Party, who stand now completely and absolutely on the platform of the dictatorship of the proletariat in the form of council rule, for example, the corresponding elements among the Syndicalists.

The growth of the revolutionary movement in all lands, the dangers of suppression of this revolution through the coalition of capitalistic states, the attempts of the Socialist betrayers to unite with one another (the formation of the Yellow "International" at Berne), and to give their services to the Wilsonian League; finally, the absolute necessity for co-ordination of proletarian actions, all these demand the formation of a real revolutionary and real proletarian Communist International. This International, which subordinates the so-called national interests to the interests of the international revolution, will personify the mutual help of the proletariat of the different countries, for without economic and other mutual helpfulness the proletariat will not be able to organize the new society. On the other hand, in contrast with the Yellow International of the social-patriots, the proletarian Communist International will support the plundered colonial peoples in their fight against imperialism, in order to hasten the final collapse of the imperialistic world system.

The capitalistic criminals asserted at the beginning of the World War, that it was only in defense of the common Fatherland. But soon German imperialism revealed its real brigand character by its bloody deeds in Russia, in the Ukraine and in Finland. Now the Entente states unmask themselves as world despoilers and murderers in the proletariat. Together with the German bourgeoisie and social-patriots, with hypocritical phrases about peace on their lips, they are trying to throttle the revolution of the European proletariat by means of their war machinery and stupid barbaric colonial soldiery. Indescribable is the White Terror of the bourgeois cannibals. Incalculable are the sacrifices of the working class. Their best — Liebknecht, Rosa Luxembourg — they have lost. Against this the proletariat must defend itself, defend at any price. The Communist International calls the entire world proletariat to this final struggle.

Down with the imperial conspiracy of Capital!

Long live the International Republic of the Proletarian Councils!

Moscow, March 2-6, 1919.

THE THIRD INTERNATIONAL

The problem as phrased by the Third International manifesto is this: "Is the whole of laboring mankind to become serfs and day-laborers under a victorious international clique, which, in the name of the League of Nations, and assisted by an 'international' army and an 'international' fleet, alternately plunders or casts a morsel of bread to the needy, but everywhere keeps the proletariat in chains with the sole aim of retaining its own power; or shall the working classes in Europe and the most civilized countries in other parts of the world take into their own hands the shaken and ruined world economy and thus ensure its restoration on the basis of Socialism?"

To bring to an end the prevailing crisis will only be possible with the help of proletarian dictatorship, which will not look back to the past nor show consideration for inherited privileges or rights of property.

The national state, which gave such a mighty impulse to capitalist development, has become too restricted for the continued development of the productive forces. The collapse of the imperialist state, from the Czarist to the most democratic, as proceeding simultaneously with the collapse of the national unity, is synonymous with the inevitable collapse of the army, to the revolt of the soldier against his officer, and later to a sharp division between the proletarian and bourgeois elements in the army. Imperialist war, which opposes one nation against the other, is followed by civil war where class is opposed to class.

The outcry by the bourgeois world against civil war and the Red Terror is the most abominable hypocrisy ever noted in the history of political fighting. There would be no civil war if the profiteering cliques who have brought mankind to the verge of ruin did not oppose all progress on the part of the working masses.

Civil war is forced on the working classes by their mortal enemy. The working classes must return blow for blow. The Communist parties never try by artificial means to encourage civil war, but exert themselves, as far as possible, to shorten the duration of it, and if it does become an imperative necessity, they endeavor to keep down the number of victims, and above all to secure victory for the proletariat. From this will clearly be seen the necessity of disarming the bourgeoisie and arming the proletariat and thus raising an army for the protection of the power of the proletariat and the inviolability of the Socialist Social Community.

CHAPTER XVII

Socialism in Mexico, Central and South America *

It may seem unnatural, but it is quite logical, that the developments of the socialistic and labor situations in Mexico and South America, although on our own continent, should have less vital connection with our own situation than any of the European developments. In the first place, the soil was not propitious for the development either of organized labor or of political or economic Socialism. It is only during the years just before and after 1900 that any beginning was made either to organize labor or to the development of a socialist party.

It was natural that the first developments should take place in Argentina, because of the very large proportion among the workmen there of hundreds of thousands, not to say millions, of emigrants from Italy and Germany, who brought with them to the Argentine the socialistic and unionizing tendencies of their motherlands. The Socialist Party in the Argentine was founded in 1896 and it almost immediately established connections with the International Socialist Bureau, which it joined in 1904, taking part in their subsequent Congress. It took part also in parliamentary elections at home, electing two deputies in 1912 and four in 1913, and nine in 1914. There was no corresponding development of trade unionism or of co-operative organization.

In Chile, where the miners formed a very strong element among the workingmen, there was an early development of socialist and democratic tendencies among the workers without an exact definition of socialist principles or the organization of a definitely socialist party, until, in 1912, there was formed in the northern part of the country a socialist labor party which was strengthened by the already existing organization in the Argentine.

A difference between the Chilean and the Argentine situation is the far greater development of union labor in Chile. The only reason why the unions did not sooner obtain political power, is the lack of a close federation of unions. Brazil was even later in coming into line, no socialist party being formed until 1916, and there being no organization of workmen's unions of any importance.

In Peru there is a federation called the Centro-Latino Americano, composed of three sections or sub-federations of labor, made up of workmen of every sort, from hod carriers to street car men,

* See Addendum, Part I.

in the General Federation of Workers; of printers, carpenters, painters and others, in the Federation of Artisans; and of every class of workman in the Federation of Mutual Benefit Societies. The organizations have very little to do with politics or economics, and are simply a basis upon which socialism and labor unionism can build, especially as they form the main link with the corresponding classes, in Chile, with which country their own is politically at swords' points.

In Mexico, with one exception, the situation is even less propitious for organized labor, and theoretical Socialism in connection with labor, than in the Argentine. Yet, in one province of Mexico, in Yucatan, which is industrially speaking, very advanced, a socialistic government has actually been applied for several years with communistic elements in the administration. In the rest of Mexico a vague sort of Socialism, quite lacking in the scientific characteristics of real Socialism, has made progress since the beginning of the war.

During 1918 and 1919, partly owing to the influence of outside agitators, the scheme of the general strikes and of special strikes in public utilities was attempted to exercise pressure on the governments in a number of South American states. In the American Labor Year Book for 1919-1920, page 324, we read:

> "General unrest was manifested among the workers of South American countries during 1918-1919. Argentina, Uruguay, Chile and Peru have experienced a general strike movement, which, though industrial in origin, had assumed political importance, and brought the workers in direct conflict with their respective governments. In many instances, troops had to be used to quell the riots which were a result of the oppressive measures, practiced by the local police authorities.
>
> "The railway workers of Argentina declared a general strike in the winter of 1918, which paralyzed transportation throughout the country. The steel workers followed with a strike in the beginning of 1919, and a sympathetic general strike was proclaimed to aid the striking steel workers. Strikes of longshoremen, clerks, telephone operators and workers of many other callings took place during the spring and summer of 1919. The strike movement greatly aided the Socialists, who were among the leaders of the striking workers. In the municipal elections of Buenos Aires in October, 1918, which was soon after the railway strike, the

Socialists elected twelve members of the council. In the Federal elections in March, 1919, the Socialists polled 56,000 votes out of the 150,000 votes, cast for two deputies in Buenos Aires.

"Several strikes were inaugurated in Uruguay, in sympathy with the striking railway and transport workers of Argentina. As a result of the strike an eight-hour law was declared by the government. Two Socialists sit in the National Legislature of Uruguay.

"Several strikes took place in Chile where the Socialist movement is growing rapidly and is supported by the labor organization."

A split in the Socialist movement of Mexico occurred at the convention of the Socialist Party in the fall of 1919, when a seceding faction organized the Communist Party. The split is attributed to the undue influence exercised by the representatives of the A. F. L. in Mexico, who are also members of the Socialist Party.

Two Pan-American Congresses took place in 1918 and 1919. The first of these was a Pan-American Labor Conference at Laredo, Texas, in November, 1918. It was under the patronage of the American Federation of Labor and was attended by delegates of the labor unions of Mexico, Guatemala, Costa Rica, Salvador, and Colombia. The sequel to this was a Congress in New York in July, 1919. In both cases, the South American and the Central American delegates showed signs of radical tendencies and socialistic and, at times, communistic ideas, which led the American delegates of the Federation of Labor to show a lack of sympathy with a part of the proceedings, which did not please the Mexican delegate, J. deBorran, who complained of the reactionary character of the A. F. of L. in a communication to the New York "Call."

Of quite a different character was the first Pan-American Socialist and Labor Congress, which met at Buenos Aires, Argentina, between April 26th and May 1st, 1919. The representatives of the American Socialist Party could not be present, as they were denied passports. The countries represented were Chile, Argentina, Peru, Bolivia, Uruguay and Paraguay. The Socialist member of Parliament of Argentina, Dr. Bravo, was made President. The Congress showed its communistic tendencies by the messages it sent to the revolutionary proletariats of

Russia, Germany and Hungary. It passed resolutions elaborating a very detailed program of economic and social and even political character. It established a permanent labor and socialist secretary at Buenos Aires, charged with the interests of the Socialist and labor movement in America, and empowered to select the time and place of the next congress.

It must be noted that the Argentine Socialist Party was represented at the Berne conference by two delegates, Drs. Tomasso and Justo. To complete the picture of the circumstances and the results of the strikes during 1919, which were referred to above, we must add that the strikers in Lima and Callao, Peru, in January, 1919, demanding an eight-hour day and a 50 per cent. increase in wages, were successful in obtaining from the government an eight-hour day decree and the designation of the Supreme Court as arbitrator in labor disputes. But in the course of the strike there was great disorder. The strikers were shot and arrested and troops were used to quell the disturbance. In connection with the disturbances among the miners in Chile in December, 1918, the President, in discussing martial law, spoke of the disorders as provoked "by Bolsheviks who have managed to reach the country." This connection of I. W. W., Russian or other alien agitators, with the South American labor troubles, is generally considered to be more a fact in the case of the Argentine troubles, where the strikes, curiously enough, broke out at about the same time as the Peruvian strikes, both in and near Buenos Aires. The strike involved not only industrial workers, but almost every branch of municipal employees; martial law was declared and machine guns were used against the workers in street fights. The strike of the harbor workers was the most difficult to settle, and here again was seen the hand of the International agitators.

There is the beginning of an extensive Bolshevist agitation in Central America centered in Guatemala, looking toward a union of the five republics in a single communistic state.

SECTION II

AMERICAN CONDITIONS—AN HISTORICAL REVIEW

SECTION II

AMERICAN CONDITIONS — AN HISTORICAL SKETCH

INTRODUCTION

In the preceding section of this report an analysis has been given of the revolutionary movement in the various countries of Europe in order that a more complete and comprehensive understanding may be had of the revolutionary movement in the United States.

Conditions in Europe inevitably have a reflex action upon the people of the United States. So long as the Communist elements are in control of the masses of Russia and remain a force to be reckoned with in the other countries of Europe, so long will they continue a menace to the institutions of the United States.

As an illustration of the effect of European movements upon the United States, we may make reference to the influence which the Jacobin Clubs of the French Revolution had upon the malcontents in the United States in the latter part of the eighteenth century.

The Whiskey Rebellion of Western Pennsylvania was the outgrowth of agitation carried on by so-called democratic societies acting under the guise of protectors of civil liberties, which received their inspiration from the French revolutionary societies.

The power of these agitators continued to grow until Robespierre was brought to the guillotine, and the political power of the revolutionary clubs of France was destroyed.

In referring to this condition, John Marshall, in his "Life of Washington," published in Philadelphia in 1832, says on page 353: "Not more certain is it that the boldest streams must disappear, if the fountains which feed them be emptied than was the dissolution of the democratic societies of America, when the Jacobin Clubs were denounced by France."

In this section of this report the Committee will outline the history and development of the various quasi-political groups having revolutionary objectives which represent in this country various branches of the revolutionary movement in Europe.

The Socialist, Communist, and Anarchist movements in this country, as well as the industrial organizations which are the outgrowth of their propaganda, are not spontaneous expressions of unrest brought about by critical economic conditions in this country, but are the result of systematic and energetic propaganda, spread by representatives of European revolutionary bodies. The agitation was begun many years ago largely among the elements of foreign workmen who had come to this country, and was carried on almost exclusively by alien agitators. But with the increasing number of aliens and the renewed activity of agitators the propaganda has spread from alien groups, so that today it permeates all classes of society in this country.

It is the purpose of this section to describe the history of each of the quasi-political revolutionary parties, to show their relationship to the world movement, and the effect of the propaganda in its attempt to destroy the conservative organizations of labor, as well as its further attempt to substitute therefor industrial unions having the same revolutionary objective and seeking the same revolutionary goal.

SUB-SECTION I

SOCIALIST MOVEMENT IN AMERICA

SUB-SECTION I

SOCIALIST MOVEMENT IN AMERICA

CHAPTER I

Historical Sketch

In its widest aspect the Socialist movement in the United States today includes the activities of the Socialist Party, the newly created Communist Party of America, the Communist Labor Party, and the Socialist Labor Party.

The inspiration afforded by the success of the Russian Communist Party in setting up a Soviet regime in Russia, however, has in addition to giving impetus to the revolutionary movement throughout the world, modified the tactics of each of the organizations named, so as to make it difficult to distinguish one from the other in their economic ambitions and tactics.

The present Socialist movement in the United States must be distinguished from the early experiments in Utopian ideals, represented by the sectarian communities such as the Shakers, or the experiment in Communism made by the Owenites, or the Fourierists and the Icarian communities.

The modern movement of organized Socialism may be dated from the formation of the Social Party of New York and Vicinity which was organized in January, 1868, in the Germania Assembly rooms on the Bowery. The membership of this organization was recruited solely from the German labor circles, and its policies and platform were in accord with the principles then set down by the International Workingmen's Association.

In 1868 this party nominated an Independent ticket, but the number of votes which it secured was negligible. The organization did not survive this defeat, but in the same year some of the leading spirits of this organization organized what has been termed by Morris Hillquit "The first strictly Marxian organization of strength and influence on American soil," which was known as the Allgemeiner Deutscher Arbeiter Verein.

In 1869 this organization was admitted to the National Labor Union as Labor Union No. 5 of New York, and in the following year joined the International Workingmen's Association as Section 1, New York. It should be noted that the pioneer element of the radical and revolutionary movement in this country was German.

During the next succeeding years the number of sections of the International grew to thirty or more, being located in New York, Chicago, San Francisco, Newark, New Orleans, Springfield, Washington and Williamsburgh (Brooklyn, N. Y.).

The activities of these sections of the International attracted considerable attention during that period. The movement was generally stimulated by the action taken in transferring the seat of the General Council of the International from London to New York. The general secretary of the council at this time was S. A. Sorge, who was an intimate friend of both Carl Marx and Frederick Engels. He became the most active of the organizers in the new movement.

It was not, however, until the panic of 1873 that the International came prominently before the American people. The agitation among the laboring classes generally, which was occasioned by the unemployment resulting from economic disturbances, afforded the German Socialists an opportunity to spread their propaganda and gain recruits. The "Arbeiter Zeitung," says Morris Hillquit in his "History of Socialism in the United States," p. 182, "official organ of the International," published a plan for the relief of the unemployed, which consisted of the three following measures:

"First: Employment of the unemployed on public works.

"Second: Advances of money or food for at least one week to all who stand in need of it.

"Third: Suspension of all laws for the dispossession of delinquent tenants."

As a result of this agitation a demonstration of unemployed was held on the 13th day of January, which was broken up by the police. Similar demonstrations were held in Chicago and other cities.

In speaking of the Second National Convention of the American sections of the International held in Philadelphia on the 11th of April, 1874, Mr. Hillquit says, "It did not assemble in very auspicious circumstances. The events in the labor movement just described had given rise to sharp controversies as to the policy to be pursued in the future by the International."

These divergencies of opinion resulted in the formation of a competing Socialist Party known as the Labor Party of Illinois, and the New York sections left the International to form a new party known as the Social Democratic Workingmen's Party of North America.

In 1876 the First International ceased to exist. At the last convention of this organization held in Philadelphia on the 15th day of July, the following proclamation was adopted:

"FELLOW WORKINGMEN.—The International Convention at Philadelphia has abolished the General Council of the International Working-Men's Association, and the external bond of the organization exists no more.

"'The International is dead!' The bourgeoisie of all countries will again exclaim, and with ridicule and joy it will point to the proceedings of this convention as documentary proof of the defeat of the labor movement of the world. Let us not be influenced by the cry of our enemies! We have abandoned the organization of the International for reasons arising from the present political situation of Europe, but as a compensation for it we see the principles of the organization recognized and defended by the progressive workingmen of the entire civilized world. Let us give our fellow-workers in Europe a little time to serenghten their national affairs, and they will surely soon be in a position to remove the barriers between themselves and the working men of other parts of the world.

"Comrades! You have embraced the principles of the International with heart and love; you will find means to extend the circle of its adherents even without an organization. You will make new champions who will work for the realization of the aims of our association. The comrades in America promise you that they will faithfully guard and cherish the acquisitions of the International in this country until more favorable conditions will again bring together the working men of all countries to common struggle, and the cry will resound again louder than ever:

"'Proletarians of all countries, unite!'"

Afater the dissolution of the First International, the Socialist movement was carried on in America principally through the agency of the Social Democratic Workingmen's Party of North

America, which had been formed on the 4th of July, 1871. The platform of the party is given by Mr. Hillquit as follows:

"The Social Democratic Working-Men's Party seeks to establish a free state founded upon labor. Each member of the party promises to uphold, to the best of his ability, the following principles:

"1. Abolishment of the present unjust political and social conditions.

"2. Discontinuance of all class rule and class privileges.

"3. Abolition of the working men's dependence upon the capitalist by introduction of co-operative labor in place of the wage system, so that every laborer will get the full value of his work.

"4. Obtaining possession of the political power as a prerequisite for the solution of the labor question.

"5. United struggle, united organization of all working men, and strict subordination of the individual under the laws framed for the general welfare.

"6. Sympathy with the working men of all countries who strive to attain the same object."

It was the purpose of this organization to unite into one party the various groups of Socialists which were scattered throughout the United States. Conferences were held with representatives of numerous societies, but apparently without result. However, the convention of the National Labor Union, held at Pittsburgh, on April 17, 1876, was seized upon as an opportunity for strengthening the Socialist movement, and this convention was captured by the Socialists and was instrumental indirectly in uniting the various Socialist groups.

A convention was held in Philadelphia on July 19 to 22, 1876, which resulted in the consolidation of the North American Federation of the International Workingmen's Association, the Social Democratic Workingmen's Party of North America, the Labor Party of Illinois and the Socio-political Labor Union of Cincinnati into a new organization known as the Workingmen's Party of the United States. This was founded upon the Marxian principles, and the year following assumed the name of the Socialist Labor Party of North America.

For about twenty years the Socialist Labor Party was the dominant factor in the Socialist movement in this country. It was recruited largely from alien elements, and particularly under the influence of German leaders. It was wholly out of touch with American life and American principles. The despotic character and extremely narrow viewpoint of the party leadership finally resulted in alienating newly converted Socialists from the party, and a new party known as the Social Democratic Party of America came into being in 1899.

An attempt to harmonize the difference was made in the following year and a convention was held in Indianapolis on July 29, 1901, representing the various Socialist organizations with the exception of the New York faction of the Socialist Labor Party. The result of this convention was the formation of the Socialist Party of America which has led the Socialist movement in this country since that time. The part played by this new party in the revolutionary movement of today will be described in the succeeding chapter of this report.

CHAPTER II

Socialist Party of America*

"The social revolution, not political office, is the end and aim of the Socialist Party."

(Resolution, National Convention Socialist Party 1917.)

The expression "Socialist Party of America" is really a misnomer, for the group operating under this name is not in reality a party. As commonly understood and accepted in American political life, a political party is a group of citizen voters differing from other groups of voters, as to certain political principles or policies to be worked out under the Constitution of the United States or the Constitution of the particular state wherein the party may be operating, but at all times functioning under, through, and by our republican form of government, and having as its purpose the putting into effect of these principles and policies in our political system in a lawful way and by means of the ballot only.

The Socialist Party is in reality a membership organization, numbering among its members infants and aliens, as a part of an international group, and with a program that is not basically political.

A distinction must be drawn at this time between the members of the Socialist Party of America and the enrolled Socialists. Neither citizenship nor the voting age are essential prerequisites to membership in the Socialist Party of America, for its constitution provides as follows:

"ARTICLE II. MEMBERSHIP

"Sec. 1. Every person, resident of the United States of the age of eighteen years and upward, without discrimination as to sex, race, color or creed, who has severed his connection with all other political parties and political organizations, and subscribes to the principles of the Socialist Party, including political action and unrestricted political rights for both sexes, shall be eligible to membership in the party.

Note.— Political action within the meaning of this section is participation in elections for public offices and practical legislation and administration work along the line of the Socialist Party platform to gain control of the powers of government in order to abolish the present capitalist system and the substitution of the co-operative commonwealth.

---

* See Addendum, Part I.

"Sec. 2. No person holding an elective public office by gift of any party or organization other than the Socialist Party shall be eligible to membership in the Socialist Party without the consent of his state organization; nor shall any member of the party accept or hold any appointive public office, or honorary or remunerative (Civil Service positions excepted), without the consent of his state organization. No party member shall be a candidate for public office without the consent of the city, county or state organizations, according to the nature of the office.

"Sec. 3. A member who desires to transfer his membership from the party in one state to the party in another state may do so upon the presentation of his card showing him to be in good standing at the time of asking for such transfer and also a transfer card duly signed by the secretary of the local from which he transfers.

"Sec. 4. No member of the party, in any state or territory, shall under any pretext, interfere with the regular or organized movement in any other state."

It will thus be seen that minors and aliens, and even alien enemies, are eligible to membership in this organization.

A person enrolling under the Socialist Party emblem on registration day in this state does not thereby become a member of the Socialist Party of America. He has no right to participate in its management, or to dictate or take part in formulating its policies, its platform, its program or propaganda.

To become a member of the Socialist Party of America an application for membership must be made in the following form which is prescribed in the National Constitution of the organization:

"Sec. 5. All persons joining the Socialist Party shall sign the following pledge: . . .

"I, the undersigned, recognizing the class struggle between the capitalist class and the working class, and the necessity of the working class organizing itself into a political party for the purpose of obtaining collective ownership and democratic administration and operation of the collectively used and socially necessary means of production and distribution, hereby apply for membership in the Socialist Party.

"I have no relations (as member or supporter) with any other political party.

"I am opposed to all political organizations that support and perpetuate the present capitalist profit system, and I am opposed to any form of trading or fusing with any such organizations to prolong that system.

"In all my political actions while a member of the Socialist Party I agree to be guided by the constitution and platform of that party."

This pledges the applicant, if admitted to membership in this organization, to abide by the provisions in its National and State constitutions.

An examination of these constitutions reveals the fact that they provide for a strong party discipline which applies, not only to actions of the members within the party itself, but which exercises an effective control over such members of the party as may be elected to public office. This is clearly shown by the following provision of the New York State Constitution of the Socialist Party which, in Article VIII, section 4, provides as follows:

"Section 4. Elected Socialist Officials shall submit the names of the proposed or contemplated appointments for heads of departments, members of mayor's cabinets, commissioners, deputies and members of commissions or any other appointees to position of administrative or executive character for the approval of the local or county organizations. If said local or county organization shall disapprove of any proposed appointment, it may submit its choice of appointment to the said elected official. In case of further disagreement, the local or county organization and the elected officials have the right to appeal to the State Executive Committee."

Under the State constitution of the Socialist Party a member may be expelled:

"For failing or refusing, when elected to a public office or while acting as a delegate to an official party convention, to abide and carry out such instructions as he may have received from the dues-paying party organization or as prescribed by the State or National constitutions."

Under the regulations of the New York Local:

"The affairs of the local shall be conducted by a Central Committee."

The Socialist constitution of the State expressly indorses all of the provisions of the national platform.

The State Socialist Constitution expressly provides:

> "RESIGNATION OF CANDIDATES AND APPOINTEES.
>
> "Art. VIII, Sec. 1. All candidates for public office or appointees to public office selected by the dues-paying membership of the Socialist Party of the State of New York or any of its sub-divisions shall sign the following resignation blank before nomination is made official, or appointment is made final.
>
> "FORM OF RESIGNATION.
>
> "Section 2. Recognizing the Socialist Party as a purely democratic organization in which the source and seat of all powers lies in the dues-paying membership, as an elected (or appointed) official of the party it shall be my duty to ascertain and abide by the wish of the majority of the dues-paying members of my local or political sub-division.
>
> "To the end that my official acts may at all times be under the direction and control of the party membership I hereby sign and place in the hands of local . . . to which I may be elected (or appointed), such resignation to become effective whenever a majority of the local shall so vote.
>
> "I sign this resignation voluntarily as a condition of receiving said nomination (or appointment) and pledge my honor as a man, a Socialist, to abide by it."

A similar provision is contained in the county regulations.

The strict party discipline which is, as a matter of fact, enforced under the provisions of the State and National constitutions of the Socialist Party, and the by-laws of the New York County Local, indicates the complete subservience of the dues-paying member of the Socialist Party elected to public office as a candidate of that party to the will of its dues-paying membership. It further indicates that a person so elected does not acknowledge responsibility to the State, nor responsibility to his constituency, but solely to the dues-paying organization which, as heretofore pointed out, is entirely separate and distinct from the body of persons who may have enrolled under the Socialist emblem in conformity with the provisions of the Election Law of this State, and illustrates the distinction between the Socialist Party of America and the recognized political parties in this country.

It embodies an idea alien to our institutions and hostile to democratic ideas.

In order that a full appreciation of the structure of this organization may be had, there is appended at the close of this chapter the National Constitution of the Socialist Party as amended by the referendum of 1919, a copy of the State Constitution, and the by-laws of the New York County Local.

The strict discipline of these constitutions is enforced upon the members in order to enable the party to carry out more effectively the principles and objects for which it is created. It adheres to the theory that the proletariat of the United States, as well as the proletariat of all countries, are concerned with no other consideration than a continuing and bitter struggle between two imaginary classes of society, the one seeking to keep the other in perpetual bondage; that it is only in this struggle that those who adhere to the principles and policies of the Socialist Party of America can possibly be interested; that inasmuch as this is a capitalistic government, its aims and its purposes do not deserve, and will not receive, the encouragement, support and fidelity of those who constitute the membership of this party, and that it is necessary, therefore, in order to secure the triumph of the principles of that party, that the government of the United States should be overthrown and in its place should be substituted a so-called co-operative commonwealth. This would be operated as part of an international institution of the same character, devoted not to the interests of the entire people of the United States, but exclusively to the alleged interest and for the imaginary benefit of the propertyless elements throughout the entire world, called the proletariat of all countries, in whose hands, in the phrase of its present chief exponent, Nicolai Lenin, there shall be placed an immutable and perpetual dictatorship.

On April 2, 1917, President Wilson addressed the Congress of the United States and asked that there be declared a state of war existent between this country and the Imperial German Government. On April 6, 1917, the die was cast, and this country took its proper place with the Allies against the aggression and attacks which had been perpetrated upon our national honor by the Imperial German Government.

On April 7, 1917, the Socialist Party of America met in national convention at St. Louis, and continued in session until the 14th day of that month. It was after this country had entered the war that the Socialist Party adopted and issued its war proclamation and program.

In this instrument the party shaped its policy with respect to the war which had just been declared, as well as restated its position with relation to the international revolutionary groups in other countries.

The war program began with the following statement:

> "The Socialist Party of the United States in the present grave crisis, solemnly reaffirms its allegiance to the principle of internationalism and working class solidarity the world over, and proclaims its unalterable opposition to the war just declared by the Government of the United States."

With this country then at war the Socialist Party called upon the "workers of all countries to refuse support to their governments in their wars."

This, of course, included an appeal to the workers of the United States to refuse support to this country in its war. The program repudiated and discredited the idea of national patriotism, and denied the propriety of national allegiance in the following language:

> "As against the false doctrine of national patriotism we uphold the ideal of international working-class solidarity."

While the Socialist Party of America took a stand in opposition to the war, it must not be understood that the Socialists are pacifists. Mr. Hillquit, in his testimony before the Judiciary Committee of the Assembly of the New York Legislature, stated that the Socialists are not pacifists. This was made clear by the following statement in the war proclamation and program, which indicates that in the prosecution of the so-called class struggle, the Socialists were not averse to employing armed force in order to effect their purpose:

> "The only struggle which would justify the workers in taking up arms is the great struggle of the working class of the world to free itself from economic exploitation and political oppression."

The great struggle in which the United States was then about to engage meant nothing to the members of the Socialist Party of America. Indeed, they sought to take advantage of the crisis to stimulate the class struggle. This is shown by the following language in this instrument:

> "The Socialist Party emphatically rejects the proposal that in time of war the workers should suspend their struggle for better conditions. On the contrary, the acute situation created by war calls for an even more vigorous prosecution of the class struggle, and we recommend to the workers and pledge ourselves to the following course of action:
>
> "1. Continuous, active, and public opposition to the war, through demonstrations, mass petitions, and all other means within our power.
>
> "2. Unyielding opposition to all proposed legislation for military or industrial conscription.
>
> "Should such conscription be forced upon the people, we pledge ourselves to continuous efforts for the repeal of such laws and to the support of all mass movements in opposition to conscription. We pledge ourselves to oppose with all our strength any attempt to raise money for payment of war expenses by taxing the necessaries of life or issuing bonds which will put the burden upon future generations. We demand that the capitalist class, which is responsible for the war, pay its cost. Let those who kindled the fire, furnish the fuel."

The war proclamation and program will be found in full appended at the end of this chapter.

Under the heading of "Immediate Program," and among the measures which the Socialist Party in its war proclamation and program believed of immediate practical importance and for which it urged its members to wage an especially energetic campaign, we find the following:

> "VI . . Resistance to compulsary training and to the conscription of life and labor.
>
> "VII. . . The repudiation of war debts."

These demands and planks in its platform have never been repealed by the Socialist Party, and adopted, as they were, by the referendum of the party membership, they today stand as one of the principles under which this party is operating. As above pointed out, it was only the passage of the Espionage Act that prompted the deleting of this demand from the published copies of the party's platform, which were circulated throughout the country.

Seymour Stedman, at the investigation into the qualifications of the five Socialist Assemblymen before the Judiciary Committee of the Assembly, conceded that about 1,000,000 copies of the St. Louis platform were circulated throughout the length and breadth of the United States in the fall of 1917, and used as campaign documents.

Reference has heretofore been made to the First and Second Internationals. These international conventions or congresses maintained an International Socialist Bureau with an executive committee and a secretary acting in the interim between congresses. The conventions or congresses themselves were composed of the Socialist parties of the various countries as represented in these congresses and affiliated with these bureaus, this constituting the Socialist International. The Socialist Party of America recognized the fact that the Second International had ceased to exist, and has affiliated with the new international organization known as the Third International, for the purpose of co-ordinating and securing co-operation among the various radical revolutionary Socialist elements in all countries.

In the latter part of August and the early part of September, 1919, a National Emergency Convention was held by the Socialist Party in Chicago. This was the first convention held since the St. Louis Convention of 1917.

The reason given for the failure to hold regular annual conventions was the fear on the part of party leaders that a frank and full discussion of the party purposes would lead to their arrest and imprisonment.

Practically the first thing the party did at its convention was to declare its appreciation not only of the importance but of the absolute necessity for the immediate organization of a new International, and to declare its adherence to, and firm belief in, the idea that such new International should be based, in clear and unmistakable terms, upon the fundamental principle, "that the real struggle in the modern world is one between the workers of all countries as against the ruling classes of all countries."

It is significant to note, in this connection, that the Socialist Party of America immediately after the war repudiated and denominated as traitors to the Socialist cause those Socialists in other countries who had supported their countries during the war and who were engaged in an attempt to revive the Second International, which had ceased to function by reason of the same. At the same time the Socialist Party of America entered into affiliation and co-operation with the Third International, the international group or body set up in Moscow to carry out in all countries and wherever organized government was found, the principles, program, and methods which Lenin and Trotzky are carrying out in Soviet Russia at the present time.

The Socialist Party of America has consistently, since the outbreak of the European War, denominated as traitors to the Socialist cause, those Socialist groups in various countries that stood by their respective governments during the war, that participated in the war in support of their respective countries; and the party has acclaimed as true followers of Socialism only those groups that opposed their respective countries during the war. The Majority Socialists of Germany who set the Socialist creed aside and came to the support and assistance of their country at the outbreak of the war have again and again been repudiated and denounced by the Socialist Party, and as will hereafter be more fully demonstrated, it was the Independent group and the Spartacide group in Germany, headed by the late Karl Liebknecht and the late Rosa Luxemburg, which the Socialist Party of America idealized as true Socialists. The Socialist Party of America was submissive to the high moral authority of the International that existed until the outbreak of the war (we get the word "moral" in this connection from the lips of Algernon Lee, educational director of the Rand School). This old or Second International ceased to have authority because of the refusal of those groups of the Socialist movement to participate, who were criticized, condemned and repudiated as pro-war Socialists by the Socialist Party of America for having set their country above their allegiance to the creed of radical revolutionary Socialism. It adhered to the principles of radical revolutionary Socialism during the period of national stress and crisis, and a new International was sought to be formed on radical revolutionary lines. During the war the Socialist Party of America continued as a part of this international program by its adherence to the uncompromising group of international radical revolutionary Socialists, who under the leadership of Lenin met at Zimmerwald in September, 1915, at Kienthal in 1916 and on whose program the Third International has been erected. The word "uncompromising" in this connection has a distinct meaning. It is found in the Chicago manifesto adopted by the Socialist Party at its convention in the early part of September, 1919, and the Socialist Party of America referred to the anti-national, anti-patriotic, anti-coalition stand which the other radical revolutionary groups of Socialists in Europe took during the war. The main groups that adopted this uncompromising attitude, so highly lauded at all times by the Socialist Party of America, are the Bolsheviki of Russia, the Spartacides and independent groups in Germany (as against the majority Socialists at present represented by Ebert, President of Germany), and the Socialist Party of America. This word "uncompromising" is again and again referred to in the declarations, manifestos and official pronouncements of the Socialist Party of America since 1914.

As part of the program of the Chicago Convention of September, 1919, a referendum, known as "Referendum D," was submitted to the party membership. The question presented was to which of these groups the Socialist Party of America should ally itself in a new International.

This referendum providing for the participation in an International, only if Communist and Spartacide groups were included, was overwhelmingly adopted, and indicated the sentiment of the majority of that party to be distinctly revolutionary.

At the emergency Convention of 1919, when it became necessary for the Socialist Party to determine its foreign affiliations, two reports were made to the convention, known as the majority and minority reports, respectively. The two reports were in agreement that the Socialist Party should affiliate only with an International made up of the revolutionary elements of the Socialist movement in Europe, that is to say, those elements which had refused to support their respective governments in the late war. In addition to repudiating the attempt of the so-called social patriotic elements of the Socialist movement in Europe, which sought to revive the Second International at the Berne Conference, these reports differed, in that the so-called majority report wished to have the Socialist Party of America take the lead in the formation of the new International to which the Communist Party of Russia should be invited, while the minority report wished to bind the party in direct affiliation with the Moscow International, which has been shown in a previous chapter to be the creature of the Russian Communist Party or Bolsheviki.

These two reports were submitted by order of the Convention, to the party membership for a referendum vote, and as appears from an admission made by counsel for the five Socialist Assemblymen who have been excluded from the Assembly of the State of New York, the minority report was overwhelmingly adopted by the party vote.

These interesting and important documents are appended at the close of this chapter.

The adoption of the minority report unequivocally bound the membership of the Socialist Party of America to the principles and the doctrines and the dictates of the revolutionary Communist parties of the world, and has effectually taken away from the Socialist Party any possible claim to its being a political party seeking to effect political changes through parliamentary action only.

A letter from Alexander Trachtenberg, Director of the Department of Labor Research in the Rand School of Social Science in New York City, urging the adoption of this minority report, appeared in the "New York Call" of November 26, 1919. This letter may be taken as fairly representing the ideas and sentiments of the majority membership of the Socialist Party of America. The interesting historical review which it makes prompts the Committee to give it here in full:

"EDITOR OF THE 'CALL:' — The members of the Socialist Party now have before them two referenda — Referendum E, consisting of the various changes in the party constitution which were decided upon at the Chicago convention and Referendum F, on international Socialist relations.

"With regard to the changes in the Constitution, I believe that most of these changes will make for a greater efficiency in the administration of our party. I wish to suggest that the proposed new section dealing with membership (Article II, section 8) should be defeated, as it is entirely out of accord with Socialist policy. This section provides that every new member should within three months of his admission, wherever possible, make application for citizenship. Membership in the Socialist Party should not, in my opinion, be based upon the desire to become a citizen. There may be large numbers of persons who are sojourning in this country, but who expect to return to the countries of their origin, and while here wish to belong to the Socialist Party. They should not be excluded from the possibility of participating in the activities of the Socialist movement, if they are Socialists and wish to do Socialist work.

"The question of international affiliation is at this moment, probably the most important before the Socialist Party. The two reports which emanated from the convention, known as the majority and minority reports, will no doubt receive very careful consideration by the members. In the controversy which preceded the Chicago convention, the question of international affiliation was one of the most important before the party membership. In fact this matter is the most important in the life of the entire International Socialist movement.

"A close examination of the two reports reveals that the condition laid down for the International, with which the Socialist Party cares to affiliate itself, are the same. Both reports agree that:

"(a) The Second International is dead.

"(b) The Berne International Conference hopelessly failed in its endeavor to reconstitute the International.

"(c) The new International must consist only of those parties;

"1. Which have remained true to the revolutionary International Socialist movement during the war.

"2. Which refused to co-operate with bourgeois parties and are opposed to all forms of coalition.

"In short, both reports agree that the Socialist Party will go only into such an International the component parties of which conduct their struggle on revolutionary class lines. The difference between the two reports is, that while the majority report leaves the matter of the reconstruction of the International hang in the air, the minority report has something tangible to offer. It also more specifically outlines the Socialist policy on the question of international affiliation, and gives several reasons for joining the Third (Moscow) International.

"The criticism of the minority report that I heard at the convention and since then in talking with comrades is two-fold:

"1. That the Russian Socialists who sponsored the Third International and will undoubtedly play a leading role in its councils, insist that the component parties repudiate parliamentary activity.

"This belief is entirely unfounded, as we find that Lenin in his second letter to European and American workers says the following:

'Socialists who are fighting for the deliverance of the toilers from exploitation must use the bourgeois parliament as a tribunal, as long as our struggle confines itself within the boundaries of the bourgeois social order.'

"2. That the Moscow International, with which the minority report, if passed, would affiliate us, is not an International in the real sense, as only a few Russian groups participated in the conference.

"It is true that the Moscow Conference was not as representative as International Congresses formerly held. This is due to the fact that the various parties which accepted the invitation of the Russian Socialists could not send official delegates to the Conference.

"What is important is the fact that since that conference some of the most important parties have officially affiliated themselves with this International. These parties include the Socialist Party of Italy, which has just quadrupled its representation in Parliament; the Socialist parties of Norway, Serbia, Greece, Ireland, Roumania and the strong Left sections of the Socialist movements in Bulgaria and Sweden. The British Socialist Party of England and several sections of the Independent Socialists of Germany have voted to join the Moscow International.

"The Swiss Socialist Party, at two successive conventions, voted by large majorities to affiliate with the Third International, which decision was recently reversed in a referendum by the votes in the French Sections of Switzerland, where the movement is more moderate.

"In addition, the Communist Parties of Russia, Hungary, Letvia, Esthonia, Poland, Finland and Lithuania, as well as Germany and Austria, are members of the new International. The Socialist Party of Spain at the Congress which is about to meet, will undoubtedly go with the Third International, while a strong movement to have the Independent Labor Party of England and the French Socialist Party affiliate with the Third International is evidenced among those organizations.

"The Third International already comprises the greatest portion of the revolutionary Socialist elements in Europe. Any attempt to organize another International would naturally come in conflict with this already created and popularized International among the membership of the various parties.

"By its past record — the adoption of the Zimmerwald program in 1915, the support of the Kienthal Manifesto in 1916, the adoption of the St. Louis resolution in 1917, the general position of the party and the sentiment of the rank and file throughout the last five years — the Socialist Party could not do anything else but ally itself with those Socialist groups, who have, like itself, remained steadfast to the revolutionary and internationalist spirit of the Socialist movement.

"The various decisions of the Chicago convention, and especially the manifesto adopted at the convention, proved beyond a doubt the spiritual adherence of our party to the principles enunciated at the Moscow International Conference. Anyone who had read carefully both the Moscow and Chicago manifestoes, will note the similarity of ideas which underlie both of these documents. It is because of this that many of us who stood by the party during the recent controversy, had the right to brand the assault upon the party by some groups as criminal and as aiming to destroy an organization which remained true to the principles of the revolutionary class struggle.

"The minority report also urges our affiliation with the Third International, because of the moral support it would give to the Russian comrades who have initiated that International. Surely they, the Russian Socialists, who have for the past two years stood the brunt of the great struggle for Socialism, earned the right to sponsor the reconstitution of the Socialist International. Their auspices is a guarantee that the new International will not fail when the test will come.

"The Russian Socialists do not intend to dictate the policies of the new International, and the minority report is perfectly right when it claims that our party, if affiliated with it, will have an equal right to share in the formulation of the principles and policies upon which it will be based. Our affiliation at this time can only mean a moral affiliation. When the blockade is lifted and free intercourse with Russia is secured the new International will assemble all its adherent parties and groups, and will then proceed to mould Socialist policies and tactics in the light of the old principles and new facts.

"The Socialist Party of America cannot afford to remain amorphous at the present stage of the building of the new International. It has refused to go with those elements who have either betrayed or were unwilling to remain true to their professions. It belongs among those parties which have remained true to International Socialism and who alone have the right to build the edifice of the new International.

"By voting for the minority report the comrades will give expression to what they have professed and believed in during the past critical years in the life of the International Socialist movement.

"ALEXANDER TRACHTENBERG."

In a letter from Morris Hillquit, appearing in the "New York Call" of May 21, 1919, with regard to the "Socialist Task and Outlook," we find the following interesting statements:

"It is safe to assert that at no time since the formation of the First International has the Socialist movement of the world been in a state of such physical disunion, moral ferment and intellectual confusion as it is today. The World War, so sudden in its outbreak, so titanic in its dimensions and so disastrous in its effects, had placed the Socialist movement in Europe before a situation, which it had not foreseen as a concrete reality and, for which it was entirely unprepared, and it reacted to it in a most unexpected and disheartening manner. Far from proving the formidable bulwark against war which their friends and enemies alike had believed them to be, the powerful cohorts of European Socialism on the whole supported their capitalist governments in the capitalist war, almost as enthusiastically and unreservedly as the most loyal Junker classes, and when, with the collapse of the war, the Socialist revolutions broke out in several countries, their forms of struggle were equally startling."

This is a frank criticism of the Socialist elements of Europe who supported their governments, and emphasizes the disloyal character of the Socialist Party of America which did not support this country in the war.

The letter continues:

"The bourgeoisie, against whom the revolutions were directed, made little or no effective resistance, and the fight, repressive and sanguinary at times, was principally among those, who before the war called each other Comrades in the Socialist movement.

"There is something radically wrong in a movement that could mature such sad paradoxes and that wrong must be discovered and eliminated, *if the international Socialist movement is to survive as an effective instrument of the working-class revolution.* What was wrong with the Second Socialist International, and how are its mistakes to be avoided in the future? This is the main question which agitates and divides the Socialist movement today, and upon the solution of which the future of our movement depends.

"It may be somewhat premature to pass conclusive judgment upon the contending views and methods of contemporary Socialism or to attempt to formulate a complete revision of the Socialist program. Socialist history is still in the making, and history has recently shown an almost provoking disregard for preconceived theories and rigid formulae. But enough has happened since August 1, 1914, to justify several definite conclusions, both as to the wrongs and remedies of the situation.

"Why did the Second International fail? Some of our neo-revolutionary ideologists conveniently account for it upon the theological theory of lapse from grace. The Socialists of the pre-war period had become too materialistic and 'constructive,' they paid too much attention to political office and reforms, they were corrupted by bourgeois parliamentarism — 'they forgot the teachings of the founders of scientific Socialism' (how reminiscent of the familiar ecclesiastic complaint — 'they abandoned the faith of their fathers!').

"Marxian Socialists, accustomed to look to material causes for the explanation of political events and manifestations, can hardly accept this explanation, which after all only reiterates and describes, but does not explain, and furnishes no guide for correction. It asks sternly: What were the economic causes which deflected the Socialist movement of Europe from the path of revolutionary, proletarian internationalism? And the answer is as startling and paradoxical as the entire recent course of the Socialist movement. It was the economic organization of the European workers, and the pressure of their immediate economic interests (as understood by them) that broke the solidarity of the Socialist International.

"It was not parliamentarism which was primarily responsible for the mischief. Excessive parliamentarism in the Socialist movement of Europe had undoubtedly contributed substantially to the disaster, negatively as well as positively, but on the whole the Socialists in Parliament expressed the sentiments of their constituents pretty faithfully.

"The Social-Democratic Deputies of Italy, Russia, Serbia and Bulgaria knew how to use the Parliaments of their countries as revolutionary tribunals, and so did Liebknecht, Rueble and Ledebour in Germany.

"The Parliaments of Germany and France were the scenes of Socialist betrayal. Its mainsprings lay much deeper.

"The countries in which the Socialist movement failed most lamentably are precisely those in which the movement was most closely linked with organized labor, while the principles of international solidarity were upheld most rigorously in countries in which the economic labor movement was either very weak or quite detached from the Socialist movement. In the United States, where this detachment was more complete than in any other modern country, the American Federation of Labor, under the leadership of Samuel Gompers, outdid all jingoes in the orgy of profiteering, while the Socialist Party adopted the St. Louis platform. The bulk of the Social Democracy in Germany was made up of workers organized upon the same structure and looking to the same immediate ends as the American Federation of Labor. The German workers were more progressive than their American brethren. They acted politically within the Social Democratic Party. They had their own representatives in Parliament, and their social patriotic stand found parliamentary expression, just as the social patriotic spirit of the 'non-political' American Federation of Labor vented itself in extra-parliamentary action. What is true of Germany applies also, though perhaps in varying degree, to Austria, Belgium, France and Great Britain. Conversely, in Russia, Italy and the Balkan countries, in all of which the element of organized labor was a negligible factor in the Socialist movement, the Socialists have on the whole successfully withstood the wave of nationalistic reaction, and when the first break came, it was Carl Liebknecht, Rosa Luxemburg and Franz Mehring in Germany, Fritz Adler in Austria, Lenine and Trotsky in Russia, and Jean Longuet in France, all intellectuals, that led the Socialist revolts in their countries.

"What, then, is the inference to be drawn from these facts? Shall revolutionary Socialism hereafter disassociate itself from organized labor? By no means. A Socialist movement without the support of the workers is a sort of disembodied spirit; in fact, a spook. Socialism must remain the political and spiritual guide of the working class, but it must reorganize and re-educate the working class.

"The fundamental weakness of the organized labor movement has been that it was a movement of a class within a class, a movement for the benefit of the better-situated strata of labor — the skilled workers. As such semi-privileged class, the economic organizations of labor had attained large power in the leading countries of Europe and in the United States before the war. They enjoyed a sort of government recognition, and had accumulated considerable material wealth. They had certain 'vested interests' in the capitalist regimes of their respective countries. In addition to this basic shortcoming, and largely because of it, the workers were organized along the narrow lines of separate trades and crafts. This form of organization naturally limits the efforts and activities of the workers to the petty struggles and interests of their own special trades. It creates a psychology of craft solidarity, rather than class solidarity, and deflects the workers' attention from the ultimate goal to immediate benefits.

"In such conditions the parliamentary activities of labor's political representatives cannot but reflect the narrow economic policies of their constitutents. The petty political reform measures of the pre-war Socialists correspond to the craft organization in the economic field, and the striving of the organized workers to preserve their economic position within the industrial system of their country and to protect it against the menace of enemy capitalists is the basis of the war-patriotism of their parliamentary representatives.

"The first task of the post-war Socialist International must, therefore, be to organize and reorganize all grades and strata of labor on broad class lines, not only nationally, but internationally. Not as trade unions, nor even as mere industrial unions, but as one working-class union.

"This first lesson to be drawn from the recent experiences and failures of the old International applies, of course, mainly, if not exclusively, to the countries still remaining under capitalist-class control. In the countries that have passed, or are passing, to a regime of Communist or Socialist government, the problem presents itself in a different and more advanced form. Shall the socialization of industries and national life be attempted by one master-stroke, or shall it be carried out gradually and slowly? Shall the working-class immediately assume the sole direction of the government as a working-class government, or shall it share governmental power and responsibilities with the capitalist class, at least 'during the period of transition?'

"While the question involved is primarily one of power, to be determined in each country according to the conditions existing at the critical moment, there can be no doubt about the stand which the Socialist International must take on it. In all cases in which the proletariat of a country in revolution has assumed the reins of government as a pure working class government, determined upon the immediate socialization of the country, the true Socialists of all countries will support it. Whether we approve or disapprove of all the methods by which such proletarian government has gained or is exercising its power is beside the question. Each revolution develops its own methods, fashioning them from the elements of the inexorable necessities of the case.

"The Socialists of the foreign countries are faced by an accomplished fact and by the simple alternative of supporting the revolution or counter-revolution. It is thus quite evident that no Socialist or Socialist Party that makes common cause with the ultra-reactionary elements of bourgeois and Czarist Russia in supporting foreign military intervention against the Soviet government, or in any other way actively opposes that government in the face of its life-and-death struggle with international capitalism and imperialism, has a legitimate place in the international Socalist movement. The same may, of course, be said of the Socialist attitude toward Hungary.

"In countries like Germany, in which the struggle for mastery lies between two divisions of the Socialist movement, one class-conscious and the other opportunist, one radical and the other temporizing, the support of the Socialist International must, for the same reason, go to the former.

"Such, it seems to me, must be the main outline of the guiding policy of the new International. Upon such or similar general program must the Third International be built. . . .

"The attitude of the Socialist Party of the United States toward International problems is thus clearly outlined. From the temper of its membership and from the official utterances of its administrative bodies, fragmentary as they necessarily had to be under extraordinary restriction, there can be no doubt about the party's advanced and militant position. How is that position to be translated into a domestic program?

"The platform and the policies of the Socialist party must be revised in keeping, not only with the development of Socialism abroad, but also with regard to the changes wrought by the war in the United States.

"The United States emerges from the war the strongest capitalist country in the world, not only because of the superiority of its material and military resources, but also because the power of capitalism has been less shaken in the United States than in any of the advanced countries of Europe. Our 'liberal' administration has turned to the lowest depths of reaction and repression without effective resistance or opposition on the part of any considerable sec-

> tion of the population. The 'progressive' elements in politics and social reform have collapsed like a house of cards, and organized labor has so far remained inert and passive. The only voice of protest and the only vision of progress have come from the Socialist Party and a negligible group of industrial workers and radical individuals. But the Socialist Party is as yet an insignificant factor in the political and social life of America. The importance of American Socialism lies in the future, probably the immediate future. The futility of the war, the failure of 'peace,' the governmental persecution and repression, the stupid obscurantism of the press and the terrorism of countless private and public agencies are bound to cause a reaction of revolt, and a period of unemployment and intensified exploitation will arouse the American workers from the narcotics of their leaders' empty phrases."

The letter then reviews what it calls the so-called split between the Left Wing and the Right Wing of the Socialist Party; and referring to the disaffected elements, Morris Hillquit says:

> "Let them separate honestly, freely and without rancor. Let each side organize and work in its own way, and make such contribution to the Socialist movement in America as it can. Better a hundred times to have two numerically small Socialist organizations, each homogeneous and harmonious within itself, than to have one big party torn by dissensions and squabbles, an impotent colossus on feet of clay. The time for action is near. Let us clear the decks."

The official pronouncements of the Socialist Party can really only be properly understood when this steadfast adherence to the revolutionary and international spirit of the Socialist movement is properly appreciated. One of the leaders of the Socialist movement in the State of New York is James Oneal, who was sent to Europe by the Socialist Party of America and who returned to this country in the latter part of April, 1919. On May 7, 1919, he made a report which was submitted to the national secretary of this party. His visit to England was immediately after the holding of the Moscow Congress, at which the Third International was established, in March, 1919. It was shortly after the Berne Conference, whose program had been rejected by the

Socialist Party of America because it was too conciliatory and savored somewhat of nationalism, and because it was not sufficiently radical and revolutionary. This report was before the members of the Socialist Party of America at the time of the holding of the Emergency Convention in Chicago, in September, 1919. It contains an explanatory statement of the nature of the Third International. It was with this letter before it that the Socialist Party of America decided to affiliate with the Moscow, or Third International. We give below a copy of this letter:

"DEAR COMRADE GERMER.— I am enclosing the story of my experience on arrival in England, which appeared in the Call. Owing to the police espionage I had to be very careful and I decided to wait until I returned before I wrote you or made any reports.

"I did not go to any other country for a number of reasons. First, the situation is still so unsettled in the other countries that in my judgment it will probably be a year before we can make any definite alliance with comrades abroad. The Italian comrades have refused to attend the Berne Conference, and when I was in London, news came that the Italian Party had also definitely withdrawn from the International Bureau. The Swiss comrades also refused to attend and I learned that there is no likelihood of them affiliating with the Berne crowd.

"The British Socialist Party, which corresponds to the Socialist Party in this country, had intended to send delegates, though not satisfied with all the elements that would attend at Berne. In the meantime, the Labor Party claimed a monopoly of choosing all delegates representing Great Britain. The Independent Labor and the British Socialist Party protested, and the latter announced its intention of ignoring the decision of the Labor Party, but could not elect its delegates in time. But as soon as the decision of the Berne Conference became known, the British Socialist Party comrades, if the members of the executive are to be relied upon, and I think they speak for the membership — decided that they would not care to affiliate with the Berne organization.

"In France the situation has not changed and owing to this fact, I questioned the advisability of going to Paris. Some of the French delegates formed a healthy 'Left' in the Berne Conference, and the tendency is in that direction in the French movement. Now that the war hysteria is passing the chauvinists in the French movement are losing what standing they had and the whole movement will eventually plant itself on a sound international basis. May Day events will undoubtedly hasten this result.

"I could have stayed another week and attended a meeting of the commission of the Berne Conference which was called to meet in Holland on April 24th. I could have claimed a seat in the commission, but in doing so I would have been morally bound to pay $100 dues to the old International Bureau. I would not take that responsibility as it was in conflict with my judgment. The next best thing was to write a statement of what had occurred in the United States, the activity of the social patriots who had left the party, how the party had been persecuted, the complete collapse of the American Federation of Labor officialdom to imperialism and autocracy, and the position of the party regarding the League of Nations, war and internationalism. This I did and I gave copies to J. Ramsay MacDonald of the Independent Labor Party, and to Comrade Inkpin, Secretary of the British Socialist Party. MacDonald attended the meeting of the Commission, and no doubt brought this statement to the attention of the members, and they know what the attitude of the American Party is. Whether it will help in eliminating the chauvinist elements of the Berne organization I do not know, but it is certain they will gather no comfort from it. I regret that I did not make another copy of this statement to send on to you, but it will probably appear in the 'Call,' the organ of the B. S. P." (that is, the English "Call," it is not the New York "Call"), "as Inkpin promised it would, and if I can get a copy of it I will send it on to you.

"There is the further fact that the Scheidemann patriots were accepted at Berne, a fact, of course, which we knew before I left this country. They correspond to the Social patriots in the Allied countries and there is little difference between them except that they represent the bourgeoisie classes of their respective countries and are in conflict with each other.

"A large part of Central and Eastern Europe is still in a state of turmoil and it will be many months and possibly a year or two before any definitely established party group will be formed that will have time to consider the founding of a new International.

"While in London I secured some information regarding the Communist Congress held in Moscow. It had to be called in an atmosphere of secrecy if delegates in other countries were to attend and a number of delegates were arrested while on their way to the Congress. Despite opposition thirty-two delegates were present representing the following fourteen countries: Germany, Russia, Hungary, Sweden, Norway, Switzerland, America, Bulgaria, Roumania, Poland, Finland, Ukraine, Esthonia and Armenia. The Berne Conference had 100 delegates representing twenty-five countries, but the delegates did not have the same difficulties to face that the Moscow delegates did.

"Fifteen other organizations were represented at Moscow with a voice but no vote. These included representatives of Czech South Slav (Jugo-Slav), British and French Communist groups, Dutch Social Democratic Party, Socialist Propaganda League of the United States, Swiss Communist group and similar groups in Turkestan, Turkey, Georgia, Persia, China and Korea. These representatives were probably comrades who were marooned in Russia and were accepted as fraternal delegates but unable to speak authoritatively for their organization.

"An article in the central organ of the Soviets 'Izvestiya' refers coolly to the commission elected by the Berne Conference to go to Russia and investigate the Soviet regime. An extract from it undoubtedly reflects the view of the Moscow Congress. I quote:

> 'The establishment of the Communist International, which places itself in opposition to the International of opportunists and social traitors, has now confronted all the hesitating elements in the Socialist movement who have not yet sold their principles to the imperialist bourgeoisie with the option either of joining the advance guard of the proletariat in its fight for the social revolution, or of going over to the league of capitalists struggling for social reaction. There is no longer a third way. The social revolution is knocking at the door of the Old World. With the establishment of the Third

International the proletariat has reached the very gates of the Socialist era and will know how to open them, in spite of all the obstacles which have been accumulated in its way by the will of the ruling class and the treachery of its former leaders.'

"The Moscow Congress resolved to take over the work of the Zimmerwald and Kienthal groups after a report by Balabanoff, secretary of the Zimmerwald International Socialist Committee, in which he was joined by Lenin, Trotzky, Zinovieff, Rakowsky and Platten as members of the Zimmerwald Association.

"On the matter of organization I quote the following decision of the Moscow Congress:

'In order to expedite the commencement of activity of the new International the Congress at once elects the necessary organs with the provision that the final constitution of the Communist International will be submitted by the Bureau to the next Congress. The direction of the Communist International is entrusted to an Executive Committee consisting of one representative from the Communist parties of the more important countries. The parties in Russia, Germany, German-Austria, Hungary, the Balkan Federation, Switzerland and Sweden are to send their delegates to the first Executive Committee without delay. Parties from other countries, which will have declared their adhesion to the Communist International, before the second Congress, will also receive a seat on the Executive Committee. Pending the arrival of delegates from abroad, the comrades of the country in which the Executive Committee has its seat will undertake their work. The Executive Committee elects a bureau of five members.'

"So far as I know there was unity at the Moscow Congress, which was quite in contrast with the Berne Conference. There is little doubt that in selecting the name 'Communist' the Moscow Congress did so for the same reason that the Marxists did in 1847, that is, to distinguish themselves from the many sects and groups going under the name of Socialist. The world war has resulted in the same confusion regarding the use of the word that was apparent in the days when various Utopian sects of divergent views called themselves Socialist. The Moscow Congress certainly have in mind the ideals of Socialism, not the concept of communism of wealth which has characterized many religious sects. Its membership is made up of all the elements of the Socialist movement that oppose war and militarism, relies upon the class struggle to chart the course of the movement and keeps in mind the fact that the real struggle in the modern world is one between the workers of all countries as against the ruling classes of all countries.

"In conclusion will state that I could have gone to other countries and probably have acquired more information, but learning what I did in London, I felt I could not justify the expenditure of a few more hundred dollars for what additional information I might have secured. There was the additional consideration that if I stayed longer I had no assurance of getting passage back before June and perhaps later. I would have, therefore, piled up a large expense which would have hardly been compensated by any additional information I might have secured.

"My impression is that as the work of the Paris Peace Conference becomes better known, the dispelling of illusions that the diplomats might be persuaded to make a 'people's peace,' illusions, strange to say, many who called themeselves Socialists apparently believed, the drift away from the Berne Conference will become pronounced and this survival of the old International will disappear. There were some revolutionary elements at the Berne Conference who hoped that they could swing it to adopt declarations that would be a challenge to the Paris diplomats. A statement made at the Berne Conference by Loriot of France, for example, was read at the Moscow Congress and was heartily cheered. I was unable to get the text of this statement, but it is evident that there were delegates at Berne, though in the minority, who would be acceptable to Moscow. The Irish delegation was also of the same type.

"Then there are elements like the I. L. P. of Great Britain who from the beginning of the war maintained a critical attitude toward their own government and suffered persecution for it. Their offices were raided, their literature confiscated and many of their number served terms of imprisonment. They have occupied a center position, but they will inevitably be driven to a course that will bring them to hearty support of a genuine International pledged to international solidarity of the workers and against imperialist wars. Their fault has been hesitation to draw logical conclusions from facts which they repeatedly brought to the attention of their own membership and the workers in general. Events are dispelling their illusions as they admitted to me when I talked with them.

"The International was the work of years and it will require time to rebuild it on a sound foundation. The process of getting together is now under way and will proceed more rapidly as the wounds of the war are healed. Whether the party desires to take any immediate action regarding the International upon the basis of our knowledge is for the party itself to determine.

(Signed) "JAMES ONEAL."

As expressive of the immediate program and purposes of the party, and as a reflection of its international affiliation, we refer to a speech made by Scott Nearing, formerly of the University of Pennsylvania, and now of the Rand School of Social Science, which he delivered at a meeting on the night following the signing of the Armistice, which meeting was held at the Park View Palace, 110th Street and Fifth Avenue, New York City.

In the course of his remarks, Scott Nearing used the following language:

"So while we rejoice that the Russian revolutionists are breaking economic chains; while we send our good wishes and cheer to the German revolutionists as they throw off autocracy and set up a government of the people, let us not forget that expressions of good cheer and messages of encouragement are not the things that the Russian and German workers want from us. They want from us a Workers' and Soldiers' Council in New York City. (Applause.) They want from us a Workers' and Soldiers' Government in the United States. (Applause.) When we have established government, we will have made good our claim to brotherhood and comradeship with the workers of Russia and Germany."

Similar views were expressed upon the occasion of the celebration of the second anniversary of the Soviet Republic on November 2, 1919, by Alexander Trachtenberg, Director of the Department of Labor Research at the Rand School of Social Science; by the excluded Socialist Assemblymen Claessens and Waldman, and by other leaders of the Socialist movement in New York City and elsewhere.

In Chapter VII of Section I of this report there are discussed in detail the principles and objects of the Third or Moscow International, as well as an analysis of the principles and program set out in the Manifesto issued by that body.

The mere statement that the Socialist Party of America adopted the minority report at the Chicago convention, and thereby pledged its allegiance to the Moscow International means nothing without an appreciation of what is contained in this manifesto. The Committee deems it proper at this point to quote again a few passages from that manifesto. We find therein the following:

> "The collapse of the imperialistic State, czarist to most democratic, goes on simultaneously with the collapse of the imperialistic military system. The armies of millions, mobolized by imperialism, could remain steadfast only so long as the proletariat remained obedient under the yoke of the bourgeoisie. The complete breakdown of national unity signifies also an inevitable disintegration of the army. Thus it happened, first in Russia, then in Austria-Hungary, then in Germany. The same also is expected in other imperialistic States. Insurrection of the peasants against the landowner, of laborer against capitalist, of both against the monarchic or 'democratic' bureaucracy, must lead inevitably to the insurrection of soldier against commander and, furthermore, to a sharp division between the proletarian and bourgeois elements within the army.
>
> "The imperialistic war which pitted nation against nation, has passed and is passing into the civil war which lines up class against class.
>
> "The outcry of the bourgeois world against the civil war and the red terror is the most colossal hypocrisy of which the history of political struggles can boast. There would be no civil war if the exploiters who have carried mankind to the very brink of ruin had not prevented every

forward step of the laboring masses, if they had not instigated plots and murders and called to their aid armed help from outside to maintain or restore the predatory privileges. Civil war is forced upon the laboring classes by their arch-enemies. The working class must answer blow for blow, if it will not renounce its own object and its own future which is at the same time the future of all humanity.

"The Communist parties, far from conjuring up civil war artificially, rather strive to shorten its duration as much as possible — in case it has become an iron necessity — to minimize the number of its victims, and above all to secure victory for the proletariat. This makes necessary the disarming of the bourgeoisie at the proper time, the arming of the laborers, and the formation of a Communist army as the protector of the rule of the proletariat and the inviolability of the social structure. Such is the Red army of Soviet Russia which arose to protect the achievements of the working class against every assault from within or without. The Soviet army is inseparable from the Soviet state."

The International scope of this new movement with which the Socialist Party of America has allied itself is evident in the following differentiation between the Second and Third International:

"During this period"— the period of the Second International — "the center of gravity of the labor movement rested entirely on national ground, confining itself within the realm of national parliamentarism to the narrow compass of national states and national industries."

The purpose of the Third International as distinguished from the First and Second which preceded it, is thus declared:

"As the First International foresaw the future development and pointed the way; as the Second International gathered together and organized millions of the proletariat, so the Third International is the International of open mass action, of the revolutionary realization, the International of Deeds. Socialistic criticism has sufficiently stigmatized the bourgeois world order. The task of the International Communist Party is now to overthrow this structure and to erect in its place the structure of the Socialist world order. We urge the workingmen and women of all countries to unite under the Communist banner, the emblem under which the first great victories have already been won."

We have here indicated a definite purpose to overthrow organized government wherever found, including the Government of the United States, by force and violence, and it was the foregoing principles and program that the Socialist Party, by its action at the Emergency National Convention in September, 1919, adopted and with which the party expressed its full accord and sympathy. The manifesto concludes as follows:

"Proletarians of all lands! In the war against imperialistic barbarity, against the monarchy, against the privileged classes, against the bourgeois state and bourgeois property, against all forms and varieties of social and national oppression — Unite!

"Under the standard of the Workingmen's Councils, under the banner of the Third International, in the revolutionary struggle for power and the dictatorship of the proletariat, proletarians of all countries — Unite!"

That the Socialist Party of America has taken its stand with the uncompromising, revolutionary, radical forces of Russia, Hungary, and other countries is proven by the language contained in Referendum D, referred to above, to the effect that the Socialist Party of America would join the International provided only that the Communist parties of the world would be admitted to said International, as well as by the language of the report of the Chicago Convention of September, 1919 (to be found at the end of this chapter), which proves the radical revolutionary character of this organization.

The following article, appearing in the "New York Call" of October 28, 1919, entitled "Independents of Germany Back Stand of U. S. Socialists," proves very clearly that the purpose of the Socialist Party of America is anti-national and anti-patriotic, practically non-political and extra-parliamentary:

"Independents if Germany Back Stand of U. S. Socialists. Letter signed by Haase, Crispien and Stoerker indorses move for new International. Opposing majority. Ask whether American party will support efforts for convocation of Conference.

"In communications just received here the Independent Socialists of Germany express their satisfaction with the action taken by the recent Emergency Convention of the Socialist Party of America on the formation of a new International, and state that the Independents are making an earnest effort to bring about an understanding between all the radical Socialist organizations of Eastern, Southern and Northern Europe and the Russian comrades. Then also invite the American Socialists to send representatives to the Congress of the Independents at Leipsic next month. The letter, dated September 27th and signed by Haase, Crispien and Stoerker of the Central Committee of the Independent Social Democratic Party of Germany, was sent to Morris Hillquit, who was International Secretary for America of the International Socialist Bureau, for transmission to the National Executive Committee of the Socialist Party of America.

"In commenting upon the letter, Hillquit said last night:

"'The interesting thing about it is that the Independents take a position very much like that of the Socialist Party of the United States. With this letter they also sent a copy of the program adopted by them at their last convention. They placed themselves in this platform squarely with the radical revolutionary wing of the International Socialist movement and in very clear opposition to the Majority Socialists of Germany.

"'They advocate the establishment of Workers' Councils, or Soviets, as permanent institutions and as part of the governmental machinery of Germany. They advocate the immediate socialization of the most important industries and oppose co-operation with bourgeois elements in the government.

"'Their position on the Socialist International is very similar to that of the Socialist Party of America in that they, too, seek to exclude the so-called social-patriotic elements of the Socialist movement in all countries and to include the Bolshevik Socialists of Russia. The fact that the Independents decided upon such a reorganization of the International at about the same time as our party, and quite independent of it, indicates that the need of such a reorganization is beginning to be felt all through the movement.

"'I also have a cablegram from the Independent

Social Democratic Party of Germany, received yesterday,' said Hillquit, 'inviting the American Socialist Party to send representatives to the coming Congress of the Independent Socialists of Germany, to be held at Leipsic, November 16 to 22.'

"The letter from the Independents follows:

"'*To Morris Hillquit, for transmission to the National Executive Committee of the Socialist Party of America:*

"DEAR COMRADES: As much as we regretted that no representative of your party has been here since the end of the war, we now welcome most enthusiastically the step which you have undertaken for the re-establishment — and carrying the story from the first to the third page apparently a line was omitted, because the first line of the third page begins with 'tional,' apparently a part of the word 'International.'

"Unfortunately, your action has reached us only in the form of a brief press dispatch.

"We send you our revolutionary program and some material on our attitude toward the International. The latter will be formally defined at the convention of our party, which is to be held shortly.

"The governing body of our party at its last session has directed us to make an earnest effort to bring about the co-operation of all truly revolutionary Socialist parties, such as the radical Socialist organizations of Switzerland, Italy, Austria, France and England, and more particularly the Socialists of the Scandinavian countries and of the Balkans, in order to bring about a joint explanation with the Russian comrades. By these means it will undoubtedly be possible to remove many misunderstandings and difficulties which at present seem to be insurmountable.

"We shall welcome it most profoundly if your party will support this undertaking of ours and further it with all your might, for we must succeed in establishing a true revolutionary International of Socialism. We shall be very grateful to you if you will communicate to us your views on the subject at an early date, and particularly if you will inform us whether you will support efforts looking toward the convocation of a conference for the above-mentioned purposes.

"With fraternal greetings,

"*The Central Committee of the Independent Social Democratic Party of Germany.*

"HAASE,
"CRISPIEN,
"STOERKER."

A reading of the foregoing indicates very clearly that the Socialist Party of America, in the carrying out of its international program and its adherence to the principles enunciated in the Communist Manifesto, subordinates national allegiance at all times to the principles of internationalism; that it denied such allegiance at that time of the nation's stress and crisis; and that it purposes to establish in this country and to impose upon the people of this country the program enunciated in the Communist Manifesto.

The Socialist Party of America is attempting to bring about a revolution in this country (and the word "revolution" is here used in its commonly accepted meaning), as part of the International, social revolution; and in the words of James Oneal, it it is not to be "a pink tea affair." It is to be a revolution of the character of the French Revolution, and as James Oneal puts it, it is not to be accomplished "by going out into the street and slapping a Bolshevik on the wrist and saying 'Come, let us have a revolution.'"

In a publication issued by the Rand School of Social Science, and edited by Alexander Trachtenberg, entitled: "Americans, Socialists, and the War," there are set forth concisely and clearly the program and policy of the Socialist Party. This book was issued about June 26, 1917, subsequent to our entry in the war and was prefaced by an introduction by Morris Hillquit. It will be necessary at this point to discuss briefly some of the pronouncements, declarations, and acts of the Socialist Party, antedating our entry into the war, because of their very close relation to other acts and declarations of the party following our entry into the war, and because of the further fact that the unbroken chain of utterances and declarations of the party, beginning with the commencement of the World War, and still continuing, show the true purpose and aim of this organization, as well as the tactics by which it hopes to accomplish its purpose.

Immediately after the sinking of the Lusitania, the National Executive Committee of the Socialist Party, at a meeting held in May, 1915, prepared a new section of the party constitution, reading as follows:

> "Article II, Section 6. Any member of the Socialist Party, elected to an office, who shall in any way vote to appropriate moneys for military or naval purposes, or war, shall be expelled from the party."

This was submitted to a referendum of the party membership and was ratified by a vote of 11,041 for and 782 against. Standing alone and not followed by any other declaration, this might be regarded merely as a pacifist utterance, but note the following paragraph from a manifesto addressed by the Executive Committee of the Socialist Party to the American people, adopted at this same convention:

> "Let us proclaim in tones of unmistakable determination: 'Not a worker's arm shall be lifted for the slaying of a fellow worker of another country, nor a wheel turned for the production of man-killing implements or war supplies! Down with war! Forward to International peace and the world-wide solidarity of all workers.'"

In connection with this must be read the declaration contained in the St. Louis platform of 1917, after the entry of our country in the war, to the effect that the only war in which the workers would be justified in taking up arms is the war of the working class to free itself from economic exploitation, showing that the foregoing amendment to the Constitution and the manifesto following it were not purely pacifist utterances, but simply expressed the anti-American attitude of the party.

In September, 1915, when the Allies were suffering one defeat after another at the hands of the Central Powers, Lenin, Trotzky, Zinoviev, Rakowsky and Fritz Platten organized the Zimmerwald Conference. This was intended to become a new International to take charge of the critical conditions existing in the various countries at war and to bring about the International Social revolution. The program included the general strike, and the Socialist Party of America responded to this destructive suggestion. On

April 21, 1916, when the situation between the Imperial German Government and the United States was highly critical by reason of the use of submarines against American vessels, the national secretary of the Socialist Party of America met with the secretaries of the various foreign language federations of the party and drew up a proclamation. This was disseminated in all foreign languages to the party membership and closes with the following appeal to force and violence:

> "We suggest and appeal that the workers as a measure of self-defense and as an expression of their power exert every effort to keep America free from the stain of a causeless war, *even to the final and extreme step of a general strike and the consequent paralyzation of all industry.*"

In the same year the Zimmerwald Conference reconvened at Kienthal, Switzerland, and a manifesto, very similar to the Zimmerwald proclamation was issued. The Socialist Party of America was again responsive to the International program of Lenin, Trotzky and other Socialists. By the wanton depredations of the Imperial German Government upon our ships on the high seas, our country was being drawn closer and closer to participation in the World War. While the Imperial German Government was spending millions of dollars in propaganda in this country, while munition factories were being blown up by German agents, and while our national honor was being defiantly flaunted by Germany, the Socialist Party of America did everything possible to render this country impotent to protect its national honor, and impotent to maintain its rights against all the world. It adopted the following in its presidential platform of that year:

> "Therefore, the Socialist Party stands opposed to military preparedness, to any appropriations of men or money for war or militarism, while control of such forces through the political state rests in the hands of the capitalist class. *The Socialist Party stands committed to the class war, and urges upon the workers in the mines and forests, on the railways and ships, in factories and fields, to use of their economic and industrial power, by refusing to mine the coal, to transport soldiers, to furnish food or other supplies for military purposes, and thus keep out of the hands of the ruling*

EUGENE V. DEBS

Convicted for Violation of Espionage Act. Sentenced to 10 Years in the Federal Prison. Presidential Nominee of Socialist Party of America.

MORRIS HILLQUIT
The acknowledged leader of the Socialist Movement in America.

class the control of armed forces and economic power, necessary for aggression abroad and industrial despotism at home."

These pronouncements were followed, after the declaration of war upon Germany by the United States, by the war proclamation and program which we have previously discussed, and which carried out to the letter the same spirit and purpose which these previous utterances had expressed.

Had the call of the Socialist Party to the workers of America to refuse to support their government in the war been heeded no coal would have been mined, not a wheel in factory, shop or railroad would have turned, no troops would have been transported, no munitions would have been produced, no food would have been distributed, none of those articles needed in the prosecution of the war would have been produced. The nation would have been paralyzed in the throes of the general strike and would have fallen an easy prey and a ready victim to the force and power of its enemies.

Yet while the Socialist Party of America took this anti-patriotic, anti-national stand, the Majority Socialists of Germany casting away the Socialist creed in the hour of their nation's war, bled and died on the field of battle for their country and while the Majority Socialists of Germany were assisting their government in their endeavor to crush the United States, the Socialist Party of America refused its support to this country, decried the idea of national patriotism, and attempted to render this country weak and helpless. The plainly visible intent of the St. Louis platform of 1917 was indicated in the language of the platform, in part quoted above, and this at a time when all the loyal men and women of this country were enlisting in the only struggle before the people—the struggle for the maintenance of the national honor and integrity of the country. At such a time the Socialist Party of America was urging participation of the workers in the party's struggle, the class struggle, and the taking advantage of the acute situation created by the war.

At this same convention of April, 1917, occurred a very significant change in the party's constitution. The sinister purpose and intent of this change can be readily grasped from the following recitals:

The practice of sabotage had been forbidden up to this time by the party's constitution since 1912, the prohibition against sabotage having been embodied in Article II, section 6, of its national constitution; but with the declaring of a state of war existent between this country and the Imperial German Government in April, 1917, this provision of the Socialist Party constitution was repealed. No longer was there a check upon this iniquitous practice in the party's decrees.

Read in connection with the war program of the party, with its insistent urge to allow its members to use all means within their power to resist the prosecution of the war, with the declaration that the only struggle which would justify the workers in taking up arms was not the nation's struggle, but the class struggle, the removal of restraint on the use of sabotage becomes manifestly clear. Now might the workers throw a monkey wrench into the machinery of production, now might they slow up, now might they idle and loaf on the job, now were they notified that even the negative restraint contained in Article II, section 6, of the Socialist Party's National Constitution was removed. What but an invitation to the continued commission of sabotage was the repeal of this section? These proceedings of the National Convention of April, 1917, were circulated broadcast throughout the country, as was the war program adopted by the various Socialist Party locals throughout the United States. The platform was also distributed for the consideration and vote of the Socialist Party's locals, as was also the repeal of the anti-sabotage clause. They were all adopted by referendum vote.

And here came a break in the Socialist Party. Those members of the Socialist Party who had placed love of their country above their Socialist creed, deserted its ranks and stood by their country in the hour of its need. Among the men who left the party at this time were J. G. Phelps Stokes, Allen Benson, John Spargo, William English Walling, Henry Slobodin, and others.

Said Allen Benson, the Socialist Party's candidate for President in 1916:

> "The present foreign-born leaders of the American Socialist Party, if they had lived during the Civil War, would doubtless have censured Marx for congratulating Lincoln.
>
> "For these reasons I now take leave of the Socialist Party a year after I ceased to agree with it. It seemed to me that,

having been at the head of the National ticket, two years ago, it was particularly my duty to wait and see if the party would not right itself. It has not righted itself. I, therefore, resign as a protest against the foreign-born leadership that blindly believes a non-American policy can be made to appeal to many Americans."

And while the Socialist Party of America took the stand here outlined, the American Federation of Labor immediately preceding the entry of this country into the war issued the following declaration:

'In this solemn hour of our nation's life, it is our earnest hope that our Republic may be safeguarded in its unswerving desire for peace; that our people may be spared the horrors and the burdens of war; that they may have the opportunity to cultivate and develop the arts of peace, human brotherhood and a higher civilization.

But despite all our endeavors and hopes, should our country be drawn into the maelstrom of the European conflict, we, with these ideals of liberty and justice herein declare as the indispensable basis for national policies, offer our services to our country in every field of activity to defend, safeguard, and preserve the Republic of the United States of America against its enemies whomsoever they may be, and we call upon our fellow workers and our fellow citizens in the holy name of Labor, Justice, Freedom and Humanity to devotedly and patriotically give like service."

No convention of the Socialist Party of America was held between April, 1917, and September, 1919. This is explained by the statement of the National Executive Committee, published in the Official Bulletin, as follows:

"To have held the convention would have subjected many comrades to persecution and imprisonment."

But throughout the war the program of the party was carried into effect by the circulation of millions of pieces of propaganda. The foremost leaders of the party were indicted, tried, and convicted for the dissemination of the disloyal publications of the party, as well as for treasonable utterances, and among them was Eugene V. Debs, the Socialist Party's choice for President in the year 1920, who is now serving a ten-year sentence for violation of the Espionage Act. Other violators of the law, tried and convicted, are Adolph Germer, executive secretary; J. Louis Engdahl, editor of the "American Socialist," the party organ; William F. Kruse, secretary of the Young People's Socialist League, and the following members of the National Executive Committee: Shiplacoff, Clark, and Victor L. Berger. Herman Krafft and A. Wagenknecht, of the National Executive Committee, have served terms in prison. Victor L. Berger, upon whom a sentence of twenty years imprisonment has been imposed, on his conviction for violation of the Espionage Act, has four additional indictments pending against him and has been refused his seat in Congress. Irwin St. John Tucker, one of the leaders of the party, has been convicted and all the Socialist candidates for Congress in Wisconsin, as well as the state secretary, were under indictment in September, 1919.

The Socialist Party program contemplates the use of industrial mass action, involving the use of unlawful means in an endeavor to effect a change in our form of government. During the war the party took every means within its power to oppose and obstruct the government of the United States in all matters relating to the national defense. These measures involved the use of industrial action and, as will be hereafter pointed out, this connotes the use of unlawful means in an endeavor to bring about a political objective. It is really nothing new in the Socialist program, for the Brussels Congress of 1868 adopted resolutions in which may be found the following:

> "The Congress recommends above all to workers to cease work in case a war be declared in their country.
>
> "The Congress counts upon the spirit of solidarity which animates the workingmen of all countries and entertains a hope that means would not be wanting in such an emergency to support the people against their government."

And in the Stuttgart Conference of 1907, we find a resolution concluding with the following paragraph:

> "In case war should break out notwithstanding, they shall be bound to intervene for its being brought to a speedy end. and to employ all their forces for utilizing the economical

and political crisis created by war, in order to rouse the masses of the people and to hasten the downfall of the predominance of the capitalistic class."

In the Chicago Manifesto of September, 1919, we find the following:

"To insure the triumph of Socialism in the United States the bulk of the American workers must be strongly organized politically as Socialists in constant, clean-cut and aggressive opposition to all parties of the possessing class. They must be strongly organized in the economic field on broad industrial lines, as one powerful and harmonious class organization, co-operating with the Socialist Party, and ready in cases of emergency to reinforce the political demands of the working class by industrial action." (See Manifesto in full at end of this chapter.)

We desire to direct particular attention to the concluding phrase in this paragraph:

"To reinforce the political demands of the working class by industrial action."

Under the laws of this State this is unlawful. In making this statement we do not want to be misunderstood as desiring to infringe in the slightest degree upon the right of labor to strike. Labor has that right. Some of the most marked reforms and some of the greatest benefits that labor has received have been brought about through strikes, but it never has been recognized that the general strike, with the resultant paralysis of all industry, might lawfully be used to bring about a political change. This is where the sharp line of demarcation is drawn. We recognize in this country but one lawful manner and method of effectuating political changes or political reforms, and that is by the voice of the people as expressed at the polls.

When means other than the ballot are used we then find ourselves outside of the pale of the law. In the recently adopted preamble to the constitution of the Socialist Party its objective is stated in the following language:

"The workers must wrest the control of the Government from the hands of the master class and use its powers in the upbuilding of the new social order — the co-operative commonwealth."

And the methods to be employed are stated in the following paragraph of this preamble, which was adopted as part of the changes of the constitution in the year 1919:

> "The Socialist Party seeks to organize the working class for independent action on the political field, not merely for the betterment of their conditions, but also and above all with the revolutionary aim of putting an end to exploitation and class rule. Such political action is absolutely necessary to the emancipation of the working class, and the establishment of genuine liberty for all."

While political action is considered essential it is also held by the Socialist Party to be ineffectual, and this is made clear by this paragraph which immediately succeeds the one just quoted:

> "To accomplish this aim it is necessary that the working class be powerfully and solidly organized also on the economic field, to struggle for the same revolutionary goal; and the Socialist Party pledges its aid in the task of promoting such industrial organization and waging such industrial struggle for emancipation."

The leaders of the Socialist Party on all occasions strive to impress upon the rank and file of that organization that it is impossible to obtain their ultimate goal by political action only. Every platform, every manifesto, practically every utterance of the Socialist orators convey the idea that the workers of America should be organized industrially so as to be submissive to the command of the revolutionary leadership; and it is for this reason that the American Federation of Labor and its leaders are continually attacked and abused by the members of the Socialist Party. It is also for this reason that the latter declares the program of the American Federation of Labor, archaic, non-progressive and inimical to the cause of the working class.

Eugene V. Debs, originally an enthusiastic advocate of the trade union, repudiated his former trade union associates after joining the Socialist Party, and uttered the following sentiments:

> "The trade union is outgrown and its survival is an unmitigated evil to the working class. Craft unionism is not only impotent but a crime against the workers."

The Socialist Party has consistently assumed this attitude, for witness this declaration of this party at the time of our entry into the war:

> "The Socialist Party will ever be ready to co-operate with the labor union in the task of organizing the unorganized workers, and urges all labor organizations, which have not already done so, to throw their doors wide open to the workers of their respective trades and industries, abolishing all onerous conditions of membership and artificial restrictions, with the view that their organizations be eventually developed into industrial, as well as militant, class-conscious and revolutionary unions with the development of the industries.
>
> "In the face of the tremendous powers of the American capitalists and their close industrial and political union, the workers of this country can win their battles only through a strong class-consciousness and closely united organization on the economic field, a powerful and militant party on the political field and by joint attack of both on the common enemy."

In the course of his examination in the investigation of the five excluded Socialist Assemblymen elect at Albany, Mr. Algernon Lee testified that "Very frequently the general strike is used to back up political action, not always," and that, if the circumstances should exist which make it necessary, it is a part of the program of the Socialist Party in the United States to utilize the general strike for the purpose of affecting political action.

Mr. Claessens, one of the five excluded Socialist Assemblymen elect, an instructor in the Rand School of Social Science, in the course of a speech at the Park View Palace, on November 7, 1919, on the occasion of the celebration of the second anniversary of the founding of the Russian Federated Soviet Republic, had this to say:

> "*Now, thank goodness, Socialists are not only working along political lines. If we thought for a minute it was merely a dream on our part, a great political controversy, until we have a majority of men elected, and then by merely that majority, declare the revolution, if any of you smoke that pipe-dream, if that is the quality of opium you are puffing now, give it up, give it up.*"

The advocacy of a program of industrial action involving the use of the general strike for political purposes indicates very clearly that the Socialist Party of America is today a revolutionary, radical organization; and the proposition hardly admits of argument that if the Socialist Party were truly a political party, it would depend upon political means alone for the effectuation of political objectives.

The Socialist Party of America has as members various foreign language federations, namely:

The Scandinavian Socialist Labor Federation,
The South Slavonian Socialist Labor Federation,
The Hungarian Socialist Labor Federation,
The Lettish Socialist Labor Federation,
The Jewish Socialist Labor Federation.

These foreign language federations are an integral part of the Socialist Party of America and are under its jurisdiction. Within the year, certain of the foreign language federations have been expelled for the doing and saying of things that were displeasing to the Socialist Party itself or to the members of its Executive Committee. They exist for propaganda purposes to bring within the fold persons not conversant with the English language but who are likely to make good Socialists and who may add to the strength of industrial activity of the party.

Some of the boldest and frankest propaganda of the Socialist Party is to be found in the publications of these foreign language federations, presumably on the theory that being printed in a foreign tongue they are less apt to come to the attention of the authorities, whose duty it is to concern themselves with these matters.

The party has not refrained from direct advocacy of violence to bring about its much-heralded co-operative commonwealth; and we give below a few excerpts from statements made by leaders of the party on this point. In the National Convention of the Socialist Party in 1908, Victor L. Berger, recently excluded from Congress and now under sentence of twenty years for his conviction on the charge of violating the Espionage Act, said the following:

> "Comrade Chairman and Comrades: There is a growing tendency, not only in this country, but in other countries to deprecate political action. That tendency you can see in Italy and France, even in Germany to some extent, although less there than anywhere else, and in this country.

The Syndicalists in Italy fight political action. They call themselves Socialists and are members of the Socialist Party. There is a strong element or was at least in this country doing the same thing, and I have heard it pleaded many a time right in our own meetings by speakers that come to our meetings, that the only salvation for the proletariat of America is direct action; that the ballot box is simply a humbug. Now I don't doubt that in the last analysis we must shoot and when it comes to shooting Wisconsin will be there. We always make good."

The following year in the "Social Democratic Herald," of Milwaukee, under date of July 31, 1909, Victor L. Berger used the following language:

"No one will claim that I am given to the reciting of 'revolutionary' phrases. On the contrary, I am known to be a 'constructive' Socialist.

"However, in view of the plutocratic lawmaking of the present day, it is easy to predict that the safety and hope of this country will finally lie in one direction only — that of a violent and bloody revolution.

"Therefore, I say, each of the 500,000 Socialist voters and of the 2,000,000 workingmen who instinctively incline our way, should, besides doing much reading and still more thinking, also have a good rifle and the necessary rounds of ammunition in his home and be prepared to back up his ballot with his bullets if necessary."

On January 12, 1919, a meeting was held in the City of Milwaukee, arranged by the Socialists of Milwaukee, and at which the Socialist mayor of Milwaukee presided. William Bross Lloyd, who had recently been the Socialist Party candidate for United States Senator from the State of Illinois, and who, by the way, has since been indicted in Illinois for his connection with the Communist Party of America, used the following language:

"We know that the readier we are to fight, the bigger army we have got, the bigger navy, the more ammunition, the less chance there is for us to have to fight. So what we want is revolutionary preparedness. We want to organize, so if you want to put a piece of propaganda in the hands of everybody in Milwaukee, you can do it in three or four hours. If you want every Socialist in Milwaukee at a certain place, at a certain time, with a rifle in his hand, or a bad egg, he will be there. We want a mobilization plan and an organization for the revolution. We want to get rifles, machine guns, field artillery and the ammunition for it. You want to get dynamite. You want to tell off the men for the revolution, when it starts here. You want to tell off the men who are to take the dynamite to the armory doors and blow them in, and capture the guns and ammunition there so that the capitalists won't have any. You want to tell off the men to dynamite the doors of the banks to get the money to finance the revolution. You want to have all this ready, because the capitalist propaganda of unpreparedness teaches that if you have it ready, you won't need it, and you won't because if you have that sort of an organization when you get a political victory, and you can get it, the other side will lay down. If they don't you go take their laws, their police and their military and use it against them. Let's see how they will like that. It is bourgeoisie to conspire to commit treason or every crime under the sun. A Bolshevik is a man that don't care whether school keeps or not, so long as the revolution goes on."

In September of that same year, 1919, Louis Waldman, delegate to the Chicago Convention, one of the five Socialist Assemblymen, used this language:

"If I knew we could sway the boys when they get guns to use them against the capitalist class I would be for universal military training."

In a speech made at the Park View Palace on November 7, 1919, and which has heretofore been referred to, August Claessens, lecturer in the Rand School, declared that the great mass of the American people were brutal, bestial, and inferior to the Russian comrades of the Socialists, that his auditors had no chance in court with the representative of a crook sitting on the Bench, that the courts were elected by illegal practice and the judges held their seats by fraud. He said: "If they are not thieves, a great many of them are receivers of stolen goods, and you can imagine — you can imagine — how much justice you can get from this bunch." He said that there is no American Republic, that it is merely one huge institution, based upon fraud, and that the members of the Assembly fill their seats and sit in the Assembly with stolen property. He concluded this strain of invective with the following language: . . . "But another reason and argument that proves the necessity of not merely a political victory, but a social revolution."

The Socialist Party of America looks upon Eugene V. Debs, now in prison under a ten-year sentence on a conviction of violating the Espionage Act, as its chief guide and prophet. He is the party's candidate for President. The Chicago Convention of the Socialist Party in September, 1919, went on record as favoring his nomination for the presidency in 1920.

In the call for the Third International appear certain groups that are invited to participate in that Third International, since held at Moscow. In the 33rd group, referred to therein, after practically all the radical, revolutionary and communistic organizations throughout the world had been listed, we find the following:

> "The elements of the Left of the Socialist Party of America (especially that group which is represented by Debs and the Socialist Propaganda League.")

Here falls the claim that the Socialist Party of America is a "Right" organization. It is practically as much "Left" as the Communist Party of America.

On March 12, 1919, at a Socialist rally at Cleveland, Debs said: "With every drop of blood in my veins I despise their laws and I will defy them. . . . I am going to speak to you as a Socialist, as a Revolutionist, and as a Bolshevist, if you please."

Further proof of the fact that the Socialist Party of America advocates the use of unlawful means to effect political purposes is found in its acceptance of the program promulgated by Lenin and Trotzky, and very clearly set forth in the Manifesto of the Third International. The leaders of the Socialist Party in their public utterances and in their writings have approved of the program and the methods set out in this Manifesto.

James Oneal, heretofore referred to, used this language in a speech made by him at the Brownsville Labor Lyceum on November 7, 1919:

> "But, they say, that there has been violence in Russia. Some violence in a revolution! Just imagine! Do they

> think a revolution is a pink tea party, for men and women to gather around the table and say, 'Now, let us have a revolution. Have a drink with me. Let us have a drink. Let us drink to the success of the revolution'—and then you go out and slap a Bolshevik on the wrist, and say, 'Please depart; we want a little revolution!' (laughter.) Is that the way you have a revolution?
>
> "Every tremendous appeal in the world's history that has brought about new institutions, every great revolution, the French Revolution, the American Revolution, the Russian Revolution — all such revolutions have been accompanied with more or less violence, and it is impossible to dispense with it."

Lenin, in his "Soviets at Work," more fully referred to in the section of this report dealing with the Russian situation, declares:

> "Every great revolution and especially a Socialist revolution, even if there were no external war is inconceivable without an internal war, with thousands and millions of cases of wavering and of desertion from one side to the other and with a state of the greatest uncertainty, instability and chaos."

The Socialist's concept of revolution is very clearly expressed in the utterance of Oneal, above referred to, and we find a similar sentiment expressed in a publication issued by the Jewish Socialist Federation, entitled, "The Dictatorship of the Proletariat," from which we quote the following:

> "Revolution is war, civil war, one class wars on the other for power, and as surely as the war cannot be conducted on sound democratic maxims, neither can a revolution be conducted in a democratic manner. And the revolution in Russia has not ended yet.
>
> "The class struggle in time of revolution, says Lenin, has always assumed the inevitable form of a civil war, and a civil war is unthinkable without destruction, without terror and without the elimination of democracy. One would have to be a sickly sentimentalist not to understand or comprehend this."

We have referred to the fact that the Socialist Party of America today is "Left" and not "Right," and have stated that there is really no substantial difference between the Socialist Party of America and the Communist Party of America, other than their estimate of present American conditions. This seems to be borne out by an open letter written by Morris Hillquit, published in the "New York Call" of September 22, 1919, and which follows:

"The split in the ranks of American Socialism raises an interesting question of policy. What shall be the attitude of the Socialist Party toward the newly formed "Communist" organization?

"Any attempted solution of the problem must take into account the following fundamental facts:

"First: The division was not created arbitrarily and deliberately by the recent conventions in Chicago. It had become an accomplished and irrevocable fact many months ago, and the Chicago gatherings did nothing more than recognize the fact and give the divergent movements concrete form and expression.

"Second: The division was not brought about by differences on vital questions of principles. It arose over disputes on methods and policy, and even within that limited sphere it was largely one of emphasis rather than fundamentals. The division within the ranks of American Socialism is an echo, but by no means a reproduction of the Socialist movement in Europe.

"Third: The separation of the Socialist Party into three organizations need not necessarily mean a weakening of the Socialist movement as such. Our newly baptized 'Communists' have not ceased to be Socialists even though in a moment of destructive enthusiasm they have chosen to discard the name that stands for so much in the history of the modern world. They are wrong in their estimate of American conditons, their theoretical conclusions and practical methods, but they have not deserted to the enemy. The bulk of their following is still good Socialist material, and when the hour of the real Socialist fight strikes in this country, we may find them again in our ranks." . . .

According to the "New York Call" August Claessens, in a speech made at the Brownsville Labor Lyceum, made the following statements regarding the Socialist Party and the Communists:

"There is little real difference between the Socialist Party and the Communists. We want to get to the same place, but we are traveling different roads. The reason that they are being raided and we unmolested is not because we are considered more conservative, but because we are more powerful than those litile groups."

And further, to emphasize this oneness of purpose and harmony of design in the Communist Party and the Socialist Party, note the following letter from Walter M. Cook, Secretary of the State Executive Committee of the Socialist Party of America, addressed to all Socialist Party Locals, State of New York:

"NEW YORK STATE COMMITTEE, SOCIALIST PARTY

"Room 311, Dolan Building, 467 Broadway, Albany, N. Y.

"WALTER M. COOK, *Secretary,* Rochester Communist.

"*September* 27, 1919.

To all Socialist Party locals, State of New York:

"DEAR COMRADES.— It has come to the attention of the State Executive that a situation has developed in various sections of the State wherein members of the Communist or of the Communist Labor parties, have been nominated for public office on the Socialist Party ticket.

"It is imperative that the working class shall stand as a unit in its struggle against the capitalist class.

"You are urged to go forward with your campaign just as vigorously as ever regardless of the makeup of the ticket at the present moment. Whatever the personnel of the ticket may be, you will be voting for the working class and Socialism. Let us prove our devotion to the slogan, 'Workers of the World, Unite! You have nothing to lose but your chains. You have a world to gain!' Forget the personalities and wage the strongest campaign we have ever yet put up.

"Yours for Socialism,

"STATE EXECUTIVE COMMITTEE,
SOCIALIST PARTY,

WALTER M. COOK, *Secretary.*"

The unity of purpose between the Socialist Party of America and the revolutionary forces of Soviet Russia was clearly expressed by Alexander Trachtenberg, (who has several times been referred to,) at a public meeting arranged by the Socialist Local of New York to celebrate the Second Anniversary of the founding of the Russian Socialist Federated Soviet Republic at Park View Palace, 110th Street and Fifth Avenue on November 7, 1919, when he said:

"Now, comrades, we will have to celebrate this matter very swiftly. Comrades, we will have, I say, to celebrate the Anniversary of the Russian Revolution very swiftly tonight, because we have the several meetings to cover with the same number of speakers. By the way, there are tonight, perhaps, a dozen meetings being held throughout the city, celebrating the very same occasion, but here in this very hall we have a meeting here, a meeting downstairs, and I understand that people are going now to the cellar. We will have a meeting there and then one outside (laughter).

"This meeting has been arranged by the Socialist Party of New York County, to celebrate the Second Anniversary of the proletarian revolution which took place in Russia on November 7, 1917. Those of you who are members of the party, those of you who are Socialist sympathizers, those of you who read the "Call" or "Forwarts," or any other Socialist publication, are well acquainted with the history of the Russian revolution beginning March, 1917, up to the uprising in 1917, in November, and the establishment of a Soviet government. When we celebrate the Second Anniversary of the Russian revolution, as we celebrate the first anniversay and in fact as we celebrate the establishment of the Soviet government, we always try to draw a few lessons for us in America, for the organized Labor and Socialist movement in this country, because there is no use having revolutions somewhere else if the workers of the other countries cannot profit by it.

"The reason for such a thing as an isolated revolution in some corner of the earth, where the people of the other parts of the world will not profit by it — and therefore, on this Second Anniversary, we ought to think, and think very deeply as to what the meaning is of that revolution; what it means not only to the Russian worker; what it means to the workers of the world; what it means to the movement we have been working for and fighting for for so many years, and what it means for us in the future. It seems to me as it seems to the Socialists of America that this establishment of the workers' government in Russia proves one thing, that if the workers are organized, organized politically and economically, and organized in a way we have to understand not only their immediate conditions, not only their immediate requirements, but understand the great purpose of an organized labor movement, with them to understand the great mass of the working class and what they have to perform in this world — then we can have not only a Soviet Russia, but a Soviet government in England, Germany, and a Soviet America, just as well. (Applause.) We can, comrades, take great heart in what the Russian workers have accomplished; and at this very minute when we are celebrating the Second Anniversary, we are celebrating not only the establishing of some ethereal thing, not an idle thing, but some very concrete proposition. (Applause; here the flag of the Russian Soviet was exposed amidst loud applause.) And we are really celebrating the working out of the Socialist revolutionary program, which the Russian workers have been promulgating for the past twenty-five or thirty years.

"We are now celebrating the working out of the practical dream, not a purely idle dream, but a practical dream, of those of the Russian revolutionists who have organized the Russian Socialist movement away back there and have now borne fruit.

"We must now take this lesson, but if the American working class were organized on the same basis as the Russian workers were, fully understanding the mission of the working class, we probably today in America would perhaps be celebrating our own establishment of a working government, our own establishment of a Soviet government, instead of only celebrating what has happened there on the other side of the ocean.

"The Socialist Party is very anxious in organizing these meetings, in putting forth proclamations on this subject, to call attention to the workers of America, that the Russian Socialist revolution in November, 1917, teaches the workers of the world that great lesson, that solidarity, class consciousness, sacrificial idealism which the Russian workers have manifested in this great work, is not only purely a Russian method, but it is an international method; and if our hearts and our minds link together with those Russian comrades and we understand them, then we know what it is up to us to do in this country.

"I have no more to tell you. You reason it out for yourselves."

And August Claessens, referring to this speech of Trachtenberg, said as follows:

"Yes, as Comrade Trachtenberg said, when we read and when we hear of these things, we immediately begin to grasp the significance of what Socialists call 'the social revolution.'"

The membership of the Socialist Party is given in the American Labor Year Book of 1917-18 from 1903 to 1917. These are the latest figures available. The following table shows the average paid up membership for each year, beginning with 1903:

1903	15,975	1911	84,716
1904	20,763	1912	118,045
1905	23,327	1913	95,957
1906	26,784	1914	93,579
1907	29,270	1915	79,374
1908	41,751	1916	83,284
1909	41,470	1917 (10 mos.)	81,000
1910	58,011		

The membership given for the foreign language federations, from 1907 to 1911 inclusive, is as follows:

FOREIGN LANGUAGE FEDERATIONS OF THE SOCIALIST PARTY

Name	Year Organized	Members When Organized	Present Membership
Finnish	1907	2928	9396
German	1913	3620	5150
Jewish	1913	1631	3214
Lithuanian	1915	1554	2262
So. Slavic	1911	1133	2604
Lettish	1916	900	900
Hungarian	1912	770	1037
Bohemian	1912	674	1421
Slovak	1913	431	867
Italian	1911	411	800
Scandinavian	1911	400	1404
Total		14452	29055

Contrasted with this limited membership is the large Socialist vote cast at the polls. The rapid growth of the movement is illustrated by states in the following table, which appears in the American Labor Year Book for 1917-1918:

BIENNIAL VOTE OF SOCIALIST PARTY, 1900–1912

State	1900	1902	1904	1906	1908	1910	1912
Alabama	928	2,312	853	839	1,399	1,633	3,029
Arizona	......	510	1,304	1,995	1,912	......	3,163
Arkansas	27	......	1,816	2,164	5,842	9,106	8,153
California	7,572	9,592	29,533	17,515	28,659	47,819	79,201
Colorado	684	7,177	4,304	16,938	7,974	9,603	16,418
Connecticut	1,029	2,804	4,543	3,005	5,113	12,179	10,056
Delaware	57	......	146	149	240	556	556
Florida	603	......	2,337	2,530	3,747	10,204	4,806
Georgia	......	......	197	98	584	224	1,028
Idaho	......	1,567	4,954	5,011	6,400	5,791	11,960
Illinois	9,687	20,167	69,225	42,005	34,711	49,896	81,249
Indiana	2,374	7,111	12,013	7,824	13,476	19,632	36,931
Iowa	2,742	6,360	14,847	8,901	8,287	9,685	16,967
Kansas	1,605	4,078	15,494	8,796	12,420	16,994	26,779
Kentucky	770	1,683	3,602	1,819	4,185	5,239	11,647
Louisiana	......	......	995	603	2,538	706	5,249
Maine	878	1,973	2,106	1,553	1,758	1,641	2,541
Maryland	908	499	2,247	3,106	2,323	3,924	3,996
Massachusetts	9,716	33,629	13,604	20,699	10,781	14,444	12,662
Michigan	2,826	4,271	8,941	5,994	11,586	10,608	23,211
Minnesota	3,605	5,143	11,692	14,445	14,527	18,363	27,505
Mississippi	......	......	393	173	978	23	2,061
Missouri	6,128	5,335	13,000	11,528	15,431	19,957	28,466
Montana	708	3,131	5,676	4,638	5,855	5,412	10,885
Nebraska	823	3,157	7,412	3,763	3,524	6,721	10,185
Nevada	......	......	925	1,251	2,103	3,637	3,313
New Hampshire	790	1,057	1,090	1,011	1,299	1,072	1,980
New Jersey	4,609	4,541	9,587	7,766	10,253	10,134	15,928
New Mexico	......	......	162	211	1,056	......	2,859
New York	12,869	23,400	36,883	25,948	38,451	48,982	63,381
North Carolina	......	......	124	......	345	437	1,025
North Dakota	518	1,245	2,017	1,689	2,421	5,114	6,966
Ohio	4,847	14,270	36,260	18,432	33,795	62,356	89,930
Oklahoma	815	1,964	4,443	4,040	21,799	24,707	42,262
Oregon	1,495	3,771	7,651	17,033	7,339	19,475	13,343
Pennsylvania	4,831	21,910	21,863	18,736	33,913	59,639	83,614
Rhode Island	......	......	956	416	1,365	529	2,049
South Carolina	......	......	22	32	101	70	164
South Dakota	169	2,738	3,138	2,542	2,846	1,675	4,662
Tennessee	410	......	1,354	1,637	1,870	4,571	3,504
Texas	1,846	3,615	2,791	3,065	7,870	11,538	24,896
Utah	717	3,069	5,767	3,010	4,895	4,889	9,02?

State	1900	1902	1904	1906	1908	1910	1912
Vermont	371	......	844	512	547	1,067	928
Virginia	145	155	218	......	255	987	820
Washington ...	2,006	4,739	10,023	8,717	14,177	15,994	40,134
West Virginia.	268	......	1,572	2,611	3,679	8,152	15,336
Wisconsin	7,095	15,970	28,220	24,916	28,164	40,052	33,481
Wyoming	......	552	1,077	1,827	1,715	2,155	2,760
Total	96,931	223,494	408,230	331,043	424,488	607,674	901,062
Presidential Totals	96,116	......	402,321	......	420,973	......	901,062

The Vermont vote of 547, in 1908, was for the State ticket. No electoral ticket was in the field. The vote in New Mexico and Arizona, in 1910, has never been compiled by the State authorities.

APPENDIX

CHAPTER II

Official Documents

1. National Constitution — Socialist Party of America.
2. State Constitution of Socialist Party of State of New York.
3. By-Laws of Socialist Party, New York County.
4. War Proclamation and Program, Socialist Party adopted at St. Louis Convention, April, 1917.
5. Manifesto of Socialist Party — Chicago Convention, September, 1919.
6. Majority Report rejected by Membership of Party by Referendum after submission to the Emergency National Convention held at Chicago, September, 1919.
7. Minority Report adopted by overwhelming party vote on Referendum after submission to Emergency National Convention held at Chicago, September, 1919.

Document No. 1

NATIONAL CONSTITUTION OF THE SOCIALIST PARTY

"The Socialist Party of the United States is the political expression of the interests of the workers in this country, and is part of the international working-class movement.

The economic basis of present day society is the private ownership and control of the socially necessary means of production, and the exploitation of the workers who operate these means of production for the profit of those who own them.

The interests of these two classes are diametrically opposed. It is the interest of the capitalist class to maintain the present system and to obtain for themselves the largest possible share of the product of labor. It is the interest of the working class to improve their conditions of life and get the largest possible share of their own product so long as the present system prevails, and to end this system as quickly as they can.

In so far as the members of the opposing classes become conscious of these facts, each strives to advance its own interest as against the other. It is this active conflict of interests which we describe as the class struggle.

The capitalist class, by controlling the old political parties, controls the powers of the State and uses them to secure and entrench its position. Without such control of the State its position of economic power would be untenable. The workers must wrest the control of the government from the hands of the masters and use its powers in the upbuilding of the new social order — the co-operative commonwealth.

The Socialist Party seeks to organize the working class for independent action on the political field, not merely for the betterment of their conditions, but also and above all with the revolutionary aim of putting an end to exploitation and class rule. Such political action is absolutely necessary to the emancipation of the working class, and the establishment of genuine liberty for all.

To accomplish this aim, it is necessary that the working class be powerfully and solidly organized also on the economic field, to struggle for the same revolutionary goal; and the Socialist Party pledges its aid in the task of promoting such industrial organization and waging such industrial struggle for emancipation.

The fundamental aim of the Socialist Party is to bring about the social ownership and democratic control of all the necessary means of production — to eliminate profit, rent and interest, and make it impossible for any to share the product without sharing the burden of labor — to change our class society into a society of equals, in which the interest of one will be the interest of all.

As subordinate and accessory to this fundamental aim, it supports every measure which betters the conditions of the working class, and which increases the fighting power of that class within the present system.

CONSTITUTION

ARTICLE I

Section 1. The name of this organization shall be the Socialist Party, except in such States where a different name has or may become a legal requirement.

ARTICLE II

Membership

Section 1. Every person, resident of the United States, of the age of eighteen years and upward, without discrimination as to sex, race, color or creed, who has severed his connection with all other political parties and political organizations, and subscribes to the principles of the Socialist Party, including political action and unrestricted political rights for both sexes, shall be eligible to membership in the party.

Section 1. (a) Political action within the meaning of this section is participation in elections for public offices and practical legislation and administration work along the line of the Socialist Party platform to gain control of the powers of government in order to abolish the present capitalist system and the substitution of the co-operative commonwealth.

Section 2. No person holding an elective public office by gift of any party or organization other than the Socialist Party shall be eligible to membership in the Socialist Party without the consent of his state organization; nor shall any member of the party accept or hold any appointive public office, honorary or remunerative (civil service positions excepted), without the consent of his state organization. No party member shall be a candidate for public office without the consent of the city, county or state organizations, according to the nature of the office.

Section 3. A member who desires to transfer his membership from the party in one state to the party in another state may do so upon the presentation of his card showing him to be in good standing at the time of asking for such transfer and also a transfer card duly signed by the secretary of the local from which he transfers.

Section 4. No member of the party, in any state or territory, shall, under any pretext, interfere with the regular or organized movement in any other state.

Section 5. All persons joining the Socialist Party shall sign the following pledge:

APPLICATION FOR MEMBERSHIP IN THE SOCIALIST PARTY

"'I, the undersigned, recognizing the class struggle between the capitalist class and the working class, and the necessity of the working class organizing itself into a political party for the purpose of obtaining collective ownership and democratic administration and operation of the collectively used and socially necessary means of production and distribution, hereby apply for membership in the Socialist Party.

"'I have no relations (as a member or supporter) with any other political party.

"'I am opposed to all political organizations that support and perpetuate the present capitalist profit system, and I am opposed to any form of trading or fusing with any such organizations to prolong that system.

"'In all my political actions while a member of the Socialist Party I agree to be guided by the Constitution and platform of that party.

"'Upon the acceptance of my application for membership in the Socialist Party, I promise within three months, wherever possible, to make application for citizenship.'"

Section 6. Any member of the Socialist Party, elected to an office, who shall in any way vote to appropriate moneys for military or naval purposes, or war, shall be expelled from the party.

ARTICLE III

Section 1. (a) The affairs of the Socialist Party shall be administered by the National Executive Committee and national officials, the National Committee on Appeals, National Conventions and the general vote of the party.

(b) The National Executive Committee shall be composed of seven members, elected by the National Convention at its annual sessions; not more than two shall be from one state. The Committee shall take office immediately following its election and shall hold office until the next regular convention, and until their successors shall have been elected.

(c) The National Executive Committee shall be elected by secret ballot. The convention shall first elect seven members who shall constitute the National Executive Committtee.

(d) The Convention shall, by secret ballot, further elect seven additional members as alternates to the Executive Committee.

(e) A majority vote of all the votes cast at the convention shall be required to elect either the members of the Executive Committee or alternates to the Executive Committee.

(f) In case of a vacancy on the Executive Committee it shall be filled by one of the alternates in the order of the votes they received.

Section 2. (a) Members of the National Executive Committee may be recalled by a referendum of the members of the party.

(b) A motion for the recall of any or all members of the National Executive Committee may be initiated by any one local, and shall require the seconds of locals with a membership of at least 10 per cent. of the total membership of the party, located in at least five different states.

(c) A motion to recall any or all members of the National Executive Committee shall be open for seconds for not more than ninety days, and shall be published in the party Bulletin.

(d) If sufficient seconds are procured before the expiration of ninety days, the National Secretary shall send the referendum out immediately.

(e) Motions for the recall of a member or members of the National Executive Comittee failing to receive sufficient seconds during the time allowed for seconds, shall be dropped and cannot be renewed again during the period of the service of the member or the Committee.

(f) In submitting ballots to a vote on the recall of any or all members of the National Executive Committee, the local initiating the motion, and the member or members who are to be recalled, shall have the right to submit a statement giving the reasons for the recall or in the defense as the case may be, such statement not to exceed one thousand words. This statement to be submitted with the ballots for a vote.

(g) If more than one member of the National Executive Committee is to be recalled, each member shall have the right to submit a statement of not more than 300 words, such statement to be submitted with the ballots for referendum vote.

(h) The time for voting on referendum for the recall of members of the National Executive Committee shall be sixty days from the time the ballots were sent out from the National office, and all state, local or branch organizations must retain the individual ballots for at least six months, and must send them either to the state or National Office when demanded.

(i) Only members in good standing who have been in the party at least six months can vote on the recall of members of the National Executive Committee.

(j) Referendum for the recall of members of the National Executive Committee shall not be submitted if the National Convention is to meet prior to, or within sixty days of, the closing of the vote for the recall.

Section 3. (a) The call for the regular election of members of the National Executive Committee shall be issued on the first day of January, 1918, and on January 1st of each odd numbered year thereafter. Members elected in 1918 shall retire July 1, 1919.

(b) Forty days shall be allowed for nominations, twenty days for acceptances and declinations, and sixty days for the referendum. The candidates receiving the highest votes shall in each case be declared elected. The term of their office shall be for two years beginning on the first day of July.

Section 4. Three years consecutive membership in the party shall be necessary to qualify for membership on the National Executive Committee and executive officials.

ARTICLE IV

Section 1. The duties and powers of the Committee shall be:

(a) To represent the party in all national and international affairs.

(b) To call National Conventions decided upon by the referendum of the party.

(c) To make reports of the membership and condition of the party organization to National Conventions, with recommendations thereon.

(d) To perfect and strengthen the organization and promote propaganda.

(e) To formulate the rules and the order of business of the National Conventions of the party not otherwise provided for by this constitution, and subject to amendment and adoption by the conventions.

(f) To receive dues and reports from state organizations.

(g) To conduct the national referendums in the manner provided by this constitution.

(h) To supervise the work and transact all current business of the National office.

(i) To print the minutes of its meetings in the official organ.

(j) To print in the official organ a specific statement of all moneys expended for printing leaflets and books, with titles and authors of the same.

(k) To maintain in connection with the National office such bureaus and departments as may be necessary.

Section 2. Members of the National Executive Committee shall be eligible to serve as organizers. Any member may be appointed lecturer on courses arranged by the National office and may be given temporary assignment for special party work.

Section 3. The National Executive Committee, as required by the Federal Corrupt Practices Act, shall elect a permanent chairman who shall serve without salary.

Section 4. The Committee shall formulate its own rules of procedure, not inconsistent with the provisions of this constitution.

Section 5. Meetings of the National Executive Committee shall be held at least once every three months, except by unanimous consent.

Section 6. The National Executive Committee shall be the custodian of all party property.

Section 7. Members and officers of the National Executive Committee shall be subject to recall by the membership of the party through referendum.

Section 8. The location of the National headquarters shall be determined by the National Executive Committee.

Section 9. (a) No funds of the National organization shall be appropriated by the National Executive Committee for any purpose not directly connected with the propaganda of Socialism or the struggles of labor. No more than $100 shall be appropriated to any one organization other than a subdivision of the party; and no application for financial assistance coming from locals or other subdivisions of state organizations shall be entertained unless they have the endorsement of the state organization.

(b) The committee shall not have power to appropriate funds, except for the current expenses of the National office, unless the party has sufficient funds on hand to meet all outstanding obligations, or unless the regular income will in the natural course of events cover such appropriations before the end of the current year. The committee shall make no appropriations directly or indirectly for the support of any paper or periodical not owned by the National office.

Section 9. The National office mailing lists of locals and branches and of subscribers shall not be given out to anyone outside the membership, nor shall they be given to members for private purposes. Appropriate portions of them may be given to members and party officials at any time for purposes of organization, propaganda and renewals of subscriptions.

Section 10. The National Executive Committee may publish and mail to every party member a weekly organization paper devoted exclusively to party activities.

ARTICLE V

Executive Secretary

Section 1. The Executive Secretary shall be employed by the National Executive Committee. He may be removed at any time by the committee or by referendum vote of the membership. He shall give bonds in the amount fixed by the committee. His compensation shall be fixed by the National Executive Committee.

Section 2. The Executive Secretary shall have charge of all affairs of the National office, including the employment of necessary help subject to the directions of the National Executive Committee. He shall supervise the accounts of the National office and its departments.

Section 3. The Executive Secretary shall cause to be published in the official organ of the party all important official reports and announcements; a monthly report of the financial affairs of the party; a summary of the conditions and the membership of the several states and territorial organizations and language federations; the principal business transacted by the National officials and such other matters pertaining to the organization of the party as may be of general interest to the membership.

ARTICLE VI

National Committee on Appeals

Section 1. (a) The National Committee on Appeals shall consist of seven members elected by the National Convention in the same manner as provided for the election of the National Executive Committee, not more than two shall be from any one state and no member or alternate of the National Executive Committee shall be a member of the National Committee on Appeals.

(b) The committee shall meet immediately following the adjournment of the convention at which it is elected, and shall organize by electing a chairman and secretary, the names and addresses of which shall be kept standing in the official organ of the party.

Section 2. (a) It shall be the duty of the National Committee on Appeals to hear cases involving the revocation of charters, or suspension of organizations on appeal from the actions of the National Executive Committee and on no other matters.

(b) The committee shall formulate its own rules of procedure not inconsistent with this constitution, or with a fair and impartial hearing of the matter before it.

Section 3. (a) All acts of revocation of charters or suspension of organizations by the National Executive Committee shall have full force and effect on and after their adoption by the National Executive Committee, unless rescinded by the National Committee on Appeals.

(b) The National Executive Committee shall have the right to appeal from any decision from the National Committee on Appeals to the next succeeding National Convention, but the decision of the National Committee on Appeals shall be final, unless rescinded by the National Convention.

Section 4. When a charter of an organization affiliated with the party is by action of the National Executive Committee revoked, or when an organization affiliated with the party is suspended from membership, such organization shall have the right to appeal to the National Committee on Appeals within thirty days after the decision of the National Executive Committee. All appeals must be submitted to the committee in writing, addressed to the secretary of the National Committee on Appeals, and a copy of the appeal sent to the National Executive Committee secretary. On the receipt of an appeal for a rehearing, the secretary of the National Committee on Appeals shall immediately arrange for a meeting of the committee which shall be held within thirty days from the date the appeal was filed.

ARTICLE VII

Representatives in Congress

Section 1. Members of Congress elected on the ticket of the Socialist Party shall submit reports of their actions in Congress to the National Conventions.

Section 2. In the support of all measures proposed by the Socialist Party, they shall carry out instructions which may be given by the National Conventions, the National Executive Committee or by a general referendum of the party.

Section 3. In all legislative bodies, as Congress, State Legislatures, Boards of Supervisors or Town Council, Socialist Party members shall organize into a group separate and apart from all other parties. They shall elect a chairman and in the support of all measures definitely declared for in the platform of the party, they shall vote as a unit.

ARTICLE VIII

Conventions

Section 1. There shall be a National Convention of the Socialist Party each year.

Section 2. The date and place of the regular convention shall be fixed by the National Executive Committee.

Section 3. The representation at regular National Conventions shall be one delegate from each organized state having a membership of 1,000 or less, and one additional delegate for every additional thousand members, or a major fraction thereof based upon the sale of dues stamps during the year preceding the National Convention.

Section 4. In presidential years the National Convention shall be composed of 200 delegates to be apportioned among the states in the following manner:

One from each state or territory and the remainder in proportions to the average national dues paid by the organization of such states or territories during the preceding year.

Delegates to National Convention must be resident members of the state from which they present credentials, and must be members of the Socialist Party for at least three years.

Section 5. Railroad fare, including tourist sleeping car fare of delegates to and from the conventions, and a per diem of $5 to cover expense, shall be paid from the National Treasury from a Special Convention Fund to be created by the sale to the members of a special Convention stamp.

Section 6. These special Convention stamps shall be sold for fifty cents, and no member of the party shall be considered in good standing in the party on and after the Convention for which the stamp is issued, unless such stamp is attached to his or her membership book.

Section 7. (a) Delegates to the National Convention shall, be elected by referendum vote of the members.

(b) The election of delegates shall, wherever possible, be completed not later than sixty days preceding the Convention, and the respective state secretaries shall furnish the Executive Secretary with a list of accredited delegates immediately after said election.

(c) The Executive Secretary shall prepare a printed roster of the accredited delegates to be sent to each delegate and forwarded to the party press for publication. Such list shall contain the occupation of each delegate at the time of his nomination and his office or employment in the party. All official reports required to be presented to the National Convention shall be printed and sent to each delegate elected at least fifteen days before the date of the Convention and furnished to the party press for publication.

(d) At the time and place set for the opening of the National Convention, the Executive Secretary shall call the Convention to order, and shall call the roll to ascertain the number of uncontested delegates, and they shall permanently organize the Convention.

Section 8. The National Convention shall have the power to nominate candidates for President and Vice-President, to adopt a National platform, and to transact such other business as the Convention may see fit. Vacancies on the National tickets shall be filled by the National Executive Committee.

Section 9. All National platforms, amendments of platforms, and resolutions adopted by any National Convention shall be submitted seriatim to a referendum vote of the membership. One-fourth of the regularly elected delegates shall be entitled to have alternate paragraphs to be submitted at the same time. Such alternative paragraphs, signed by one-fourth of such delegates, shall be filed with the Executive Secretary not later than one day after the adjournment of the Convention.

ARTICLE IX

State Organizations

Section 1. The formation of all state or territorial organizations or the organization of state or territorial organizations which may have lapsed shall be under the direction of the Executive Committee.

Section 2. No state or territory may be organized unless it has at least ten locals or an aggregate membership of not less than 200, but this provision shall not affect the rights of states and territories organized prior to the adoption of this constitution. When the membership of any state averages less than 150 per month for any six consecutive months the National Committee may revoke the charter of that state.

Section 3. (a) The platform of the Socialist Party shall be the supreme declaration of the party, and all state and municipal platforms shall conform thereto. No state or local organization shall under any circumstances fuse, combine or compromise with any other political party or organization, or refrain from making nominations, in order to favor the candidate of such other organizations, nor shall any candidate of the Socialist Party accept any nomination or endorsement from any other party or political organization.

(b) No member of the Socialist Party shall, under any circumstances, vote in any political election for any candidate other than Socialist Party members nominated, endorsed or recommended as candidates by the Socialist Party, or advocate voting for them. To do so will constitute party treason and result in expulsion from the party.

Section 4. In states and territories in which there is one central organization affiliated with the party, the state or territorial organizations shall have the sole jurisdiction of the members residing within their respective territories, and the sole control of all matters pertaining to the propaganda, organization and financial affairs within such state or territory; provided, such propaganda is in harmony with the National platform and declared policy of the party. Their activities shall be confined to their respective organizations, and the National Committee, its subcommittees or officers shall have no right to interfere in such matters without the consent of the respective state or territorial organizations.

Section 5. (a) The state committees shall make monthly reports to the Executive Secretary concerning their membership, financial condition and general standing of the party.

(b) During the months of January and July of each year, or at any other time required by the Executive Committee or by this Commission, the state secretaries shall furnish the Executive Secretary a list of all locals affiliated with their respective state organizations, together with the number of members in good standing, and the name and address of the corresponding secretary of each local. Refusal, failure or neglect to comply with this section shall subject the state organization to suspension from the Socialist Party and deprive such state organization of participation in the affairs of the Socialist Party, and shall be a forfeiture of the right to representation in the National Executive Committee, the conventions and congresses of the party.

Section 6. (a) The dues of the members to be paid to the Socialist Party shall be not less than $1.50 a quarter, of which the National office shall receive from the state organization thirty cents. The state organizations shall retain forty-five cents, and thirty cents to go to the county or city organizations in organized counties or cities. The state organizations to sell quarterly dues stamps at the rate of $1.05 in unorganized counties.

(b) Only dues stamps issued by the National Executive Committee shall be affixed to members' dues cards as valid receipts for the payment of dues.

(Dues may be collected monthly where practical.)

Section 7. (a) The National office shall also issue to the state secretaries exempt stamps, both regular and special, free of charge, to be used by party members temporarily unable to pay dues on account of unemployment caused by sickness, strikes, lockouts or any other condition not within their control.

(b) Any member desiring to use such exempt stamps shall make application therefor to the financial secretary of his local organization, and such application shall be passed upon by such organization. Exempt stamps shall be issued only to members in good standing who have paid dues for at least three months and who are by the same action exempt from the payment of dues to the state and local organization. The number of exempt stamps shall not exceed 10 per cent. of the total number of stamps obtained by the respective state organizations. The acceptance of exempt stamps by any member shall in no way disqualify such member from any rights and privileges of party membership.

(c) The National office shall also issue a double perforated stamp to the state secretaries to be sold at the same rate as the regular dues stamps.

One-half of such stamp to be affixed to the membership card of the husband and the other half to that of the wife. Husband and wife desiring to use such stamps shall make application to the financial secretary of their local, and such application shall be passed upon by such organization.

Section 8. All state organizations shall provide in their constitutions for the initiative, referendum and imperative mandate.

Section 9. No person shall be nominated or endorsed by any subdivision of the party for candidate for public office unless he is a member of the party and has been such for at least two years, except with the consent of the state organization. But this provision shall not apply to organizations which have been in existence for less than two years.

Section 10. When a controversy exists in a state organization, the executive secretary shall continue to sell dues stamps to the secretary recognized by him before such controversy is officially brought before him, until a state referendum has decided otherwise. He shall take no action except on petition of 10 per cent. of the locals (but not less than three locals), which must be located in different localities, appearing on the last official list filed with him by the State Secretary at least three months prior to controversy, and then only if there is doubt as to who is State Secretary. In such case he shall hold a referendum of those locals reported on the last official list to determine who is State Secretary. The individual signed ballots in such referendum shall be sent to the Executive Secretary.

ARTICLE X

Delegates to the International Congress and the International Secretary shall be elected by the National Convention. There shall be one delegate for every 20,000 members, ascertained by computing the average membership for the preceding year.

Members to be eligible must have been members of the party for at least three years at the time of their election. The expense of the delegates and a per diem equal to the per diem fixed for delegates to the National Convention shall be paid from the National Treasury.

ARTICLE XI

Foreign-Speaking Federations

Section 1. Five branches of the Socialist Party working in any other language than English shall have the right to form a National Federation under the supervision of the Executive Secretary and the Executive Committee.

Section 2. Such National Language Federation shall have the right to elect an officer known as Translator-Secretary, who shall be conversant with his own language as well as the English language, and whose duty it shall be to serve as a medium of communication between his Federation and the National Organization of the Socialist Party.

Section 3. When such National Language Federation shall have at least 1,000 members, their Translator-Secretary shall be entitled to necessary office room in the National office, and to a salary from the National body not to exceed $28 per week, not to be less than $15, the exact sum to be fixed by the Executive Committee of the Socialist Party. Such Translator-Secretary must be at least three consecutive years a member of the party, except when his federation has not been affiliated with the party that length of time. When any language Federation is reduced to 1,000 members the rights of that Language Federation to office room and salaries shall be suspended at the discretion of the Executive Committee.

Section 4. Language Federations shall pay to the National office the same sum monthly per capita as paid by the state organizations, receiving in exchange therefor dues stamps. They shall also pay through the Translator-Secretary to the regular state and county or city organization 50 per cent. of the dues paid by the English speaking branches.

The Translator-Secretary shall pay monthly to the respective state secretaries the quota of all monthly dues paid by the branches of his Federation in the state. The State Secretary shall forward the county dues to the respective county secretaries, wherever there is an organized county.

Section 5. (a) Branches of Language Federations shall be an integral part of the county and state organizations, and must in all cases work in harmony with the constitution and platform of the state and county organizations of the Socialist Party.

Language branches, not affiliated with a Federation of their respective language, shall work in harmony with such Federation, restricting their work within the territorial jurisdiction of such branches. In no case, however, shall such branches indulge in or permit their members to carry on work against the interests of the Federation. The Federations shall not be permitted to organize additional branches within the territorial jurisdiction of branches not affiliated with them, except with the consent of the state organization. The charter of any language branch not affiliated with a Federation, that condones or conducts work aiming at the destruction of a Federation, shall be revoked by the state organization in accordance with the method of procedure provided by the constitution of the state organization. When the charter of such branch is revoked, such of its members who will agree to refrain from similar objectionable work in the future shall be organized in a new branch. But no member of a branch the charter of which has been revoked for the offense mentioned above, shall be denied admission to the new branch, if a statement is signed obligating himself to work in harmony with the provisions of this section.

(b) A language Federation may, if its constitution so provides, exclude for cause any of the branches or local affiliated with it. Such excluded locals and language branches shall lose only the rights and privileges dependent upon affiliation with the Federation. They shall continue to be an integral part of the county and state organizations until such time as the exclusion has been approved by the county and state organizations.

Members of a Federation cannot be suspended or expelled from the party by the Federation or by any of its subdivisions, the power to suspend or expel members from the party being vested exclusively in the county and state organizations. The accused members shall be accorded a fair trial in the manner provided by the county and state constitutions or local by-laws.

Members of a Federation can be suspended from membership in any of its subdivisions by the subdivision to which the member belongs, for work detrimental to the welfare of Federation involved. Such suspended members, unless the suspension has been approved by the county and state organizations, shall continue to be members of the party, and the county and state organizations shall either attach them to some other local or branch, or recognize them as members-at-large.

Section 6. All propaganda work of the Language Federations shall be carried out under the supervision of their executive officers according to the by-laws of the Federations. Such by-laws must be in conformity with the constitution of the Socialist Party.

Section 7. Each Translator-Secretary shall submit a monthly report of the dues stamps sold during that period to the National and State offices. He shall make every three months, also, a report of the general standing of his Federation to the National office.

Section 8. The National Party shall not recognize more than one Federation of the same language.

Section 9. Each National Federation shall be entitled to elect one fraternal delegate to the National Conventions of the party; provided, that such delegate shall have a voice but no vote. He shall receive railroad fare and per diem from the party the same as regular delegates.

ARTICLE XII

Section 1. Motions or resolutions to be voted upon by the entire membership of the party except proposed amendments to the National Constitution and the recall of the National Executive Committe shall be submitted by the Executive Secretary to the referendum vote of the party membership upon the request of the locals representing at least 5 per cent. of the entire membership on the basis of dues paid in the preceding year.

Section 2. Each motion and resolution shall be printed in the official bulletin and remain open ninety days from the date of first publication, and, if it has not been received, the requisite number of seconds shall be abandoned. The vote on each referendum shall close sixty days after its submissions.

Section 3. Referendums shall be submitted without preamble or comment. But comment not to exceed 200 words both for and against may accompany the motion when printed.

Section 4. Only members of the party in good standing and who have been members of the Socialist Party for at least six months can vote on National Referendums. (Ballots for National Referendums shall contain a line where members can state as to their length of membership in the Socialist Party.)

Section 5. Any officer who attempts to interfere with the processes of the membership shall be expelled from office.

Section 6. Whenever a motion, resolution or an amendment has been regularly initiated and passed upon by the party membership, another motion that conflicts with the same, shall not be considered for at least six months.

ARTICLE XIII

The National Executive Committee shall employ a director for propaganda and education among the young. The director of propaganda among the young shall organize and co-operate with the existing Young People's Socialist Organization for the extension of Socialist propaganda and education among the young people.

ARTICLE XIV

Amendments

Section 1. This constitution may be amended by a referendum of the party membership; amendments may be proposed by the National Convention, upon the request of locals representing at least 8 per cent. of the entire membership on the basis of dues paid in the preceding year. All such amendments to be submitted seriatim to a referendum vote of the party membership.

The term " local " as herein used shall be construed to mean a local or branch of a local, but not a body composed of delegates from branches or locals.

Section 2. All amendments shall take effect sixty days after being approved by the membership.

Document No. 2

STATE CONSTITUTION OF THE SOCIALIST PARTY OF THE STATE OF NEW YORK

ARTICLE I

Organization

NAME. Section 1. The Socialist Party of the State of New York is a part of the national organization of the Socialist Party of the United States, and shall be governed by the platform, constitution and resolutions of said party.

LOCALS. Sec. 2. The state organization shall consist of all present local organizations of the Socialist Party, within the State of New York, and of all such as may hereafter be organized within the State.

FORMATION OF LOCALS. Sec. 3. Five or more persons within a town, city or village, in which no local of the party is in existence, may form a local of the Socialist Party upon declaring their adherence to the national and state platforms of the party and their readiness to conform to the national and state constitutions of the party.

APPLICATIONS FOR CHARTERS. Sec. 4. Applications for the formation of such locals shall be made to the State Committee, and shall be accompanied by a list of the names, addresses and occupations of the proposed members and an initiation fee of ten cents for every member.

SEMI-ANNUAL REPORTS. Sec. 5. (a) Each local shall send every three months a statement showing its numerical strength and financial condition, also its progress and prospects, and shall report the names and addresses of members to the State Committee.

(b) Each local shall send every month to the State Committee a report containing the names and addresses of the members admitted during the month.

LOCAL BY-LAWS. Sec. 6. Locals or County and General Committees of said locals may adopt by-laws to govern their own proceedings, but such by-laws shall not be in conflict with the national or state constitution. A copy of the same shall be forwarded to the State Committee.

OFFICERS OF LOCALS. Sec. 7. Every local shall elect from its membership the following officers: An Organizer, a Recording Secretary, a Financial Secretary, a Treasurer, a Literature Agent and such other officers as it may find necessary. The Organizer shall act as Corresponding Secretary unless otherwise provided by the local.

MEMBERS IN LOCALS. Sec. 8. A qualified applicant residing within the territorial jurisdiction of a local may become a member by filing with the secretary of such local the application for membership, provided that the application shall be read at the next regular meeting of the local and accepted.

MEMBERS AT LARGE. Sec. 9. A qualified applicant residing outside of the jurisdiction of any local may become a member at large by filing with the State Secretary his application for membership, subject to the approval of the State Executive Committee, and the payment of an initiation fee of ten cents, and the payment of six months' dues in advance at fifteen cents per month.

OBJECTIONS TO ADMISSION OF MEMBERS. Sec. 10. Should objection be made to the admission of any applicant for membership, two-thirds of the membership of the local voting shall be necessary to admit.

MEMBERSHIP CARDS AND CONSTITUTIONS. Sec. 11. There shall be issued to each member on admission, a membership card in the form prescribed by the State Executive Committee. Such card to be signed by the Financial Secretary of the local of which the applicant becomes a member, or in case of a member at large, by the State Secretary. With the membership card each member shall receive a copy of the state and national constitutions.

TRANSFER OF MEMBERS. Sec. 12. (a) In case of removal of a member from the jurisdiction of one local to that of another, his membership card showing payment of dues to date shall be taken as prima facie evidence of his qualification to membership to the latter local, when submitted with transfer card duly issued by the Financial Secretary of the local or branch that he is leaving.

(b) The State Committee shall provide locals or branches with transfer cards. No others than those provided by the State Committee shall be recognized.

SUSPENSION AND EXPULSION. Sec. 13. (a) A member may be expelled from the party, or may be suspended for a period not exceeding one year for the following offenses:

(b) For supporting or aiding in the election of a candidate for any office, in either a primary or final election, of any other than the Socialist Party, or in opposition to the regularly selected candidates of the Socialist Party.

(c) For accepting the endorsement of a party other than the Socialist Party.

(d) For the larceny, embezzlement or corrupt misappropriation for his own use or benefit of party funds.

(e) For accepting or holding any appointed position, under a non-Socialist administration, except a civil service position, or a position to which the Socialist Party is entitled under the law.

(f) For failing or refusing, when elected to a public office or while acting as a delegate to an official party convention, to abide and carry out such instructions as he may have received from the dues paying party organization or as prescribed by the state or national constitutions.

(g) For the wilful violation of any provisions of this constitution.

APPEALS FROM DECISIONS. Sec. 14. (a) An expelled or suspended member shall have the right to appeal to the State Committee against such suspension or expulsion. When appeals are filed with the State Committee they are to be investigated by the State Executive Committee and the results of the investigation, together with the recommendations of the State Executive Committee, shall be submitted to a vote of the members of the State Committee for approval or rejection.

(b) The action of the State Committee shall be final unless an appeal is filed for a referendum vote of the membership of the entire state; notice of such appeal, however, shall be filed not later than fifteen days after the receipt of the verdict of the State Committee.

(c) An expelled or suspended local shall have the right to appeal to the entire membership of the state by the referendum vote. Such appeal must be made within fifteen days after the decision of the State Executive Committee has been declared final, or approval of by the State Committee.

REVOCATION OF CHARTERS. Sec. 15. The charter of any local may be revoked for the following reasons:

(a) For wilfully adopting and adhering to a constitution or platform in violation of the national and state constitutions of the Socialist Party.

(b) For aiding in the nomination to any political office of any person not a dues paying member of the party.

(c) For failing to support all regular nominees of the Socialist Party.

(d) For failing to prosecute, and if found guilty, to punish a member for a violation of the provisions of the state and national constitutions.

(e) For failing to remit for dues to the State Committee for three consecutive months, provided, however, that notice of the intention to revoke such charter shall be given the local at least thirty days in advance.

Charges — Appeals

PROCEEDINGS, HOW INSTITUTED AND PROSECUTED. Sec. 16. (a) Proceedings against a local for violation of any section of this or the national constitution shall be instituted upon a written complaint, signed by at least three (3) members of the party in good standing, or by the State Secretary. Said complaint shall state specifically and clearly the nature of the offense or offenses, with which the local is charged.

(b) The written charges shall be filed with the State Executive Committee, which is to appoint at its discretion a committee to investigate the said charges. The State Executive Committee shall report the findings of this committee with their recommendations to the State Committee. If no objections to the recommendations of the State Executive Committee from a member of the State Committee is filed with the State Secretary within fifteen days, such recommendation shall be the final decision of the State Committee.

(c) In case of an objection on the part of any one member of the State Committee (the members of the State Committee from the local under charges not included) it shall be submitted to a vote of the entire State Committee.

(d) Proceedings against a member for the commission of an offense shall be instituted only upon a written complaint signed by a member in good standing, said complaint shall state clearly the offense or offenses with which the member is charged.

(e) The written charges shall be filed with the Secretary of the local who must read the same at the next meeting. The charges may be tried either by the entire local, or by a committee elected for the purpose. The verdict or recommendation of such committee shall be submitted to the local for final ratification.

LOCAL MEETINGS. Sec. 17. Each local shall hold a regular business meeting at least once a month.

CENTRAL COMMITTEES. Sec. 18. In any local which is divided into two or more branches, all business of the local with the party's National and State Committees shall be carried on by a Central Committee.

CHARTERS. Sec. 19. (a) Not more than one charter shall be granted to any city, unless such city consists of more than one county, in which case one charter shall be granted to each county organization.

(b) More than one charter may be granted to such county with the consent of the existing organization.

COUNTY COMMITTEES. Sec. 20. All counties composed of two or more locals shall organize County Committees composed of three or more delegates from each local in the county; such County Committees to work toward unifying the agitation and organization in the county, and especially assist in organizing the unorganized territory of their respective counties.

MEMBERS IN ARREARS. Sec. 21. (a) Members who are in arrears in the payment of their dues for more than three months shall stand suspended from all membership rights until they have paid up such arrears.

(b) Members in arrears in the payment of their dues for more than one year may be dropped from the membership roll of the local.

EXEMPTION FROM DUES. Sec. 22. On application to their local, sick or unemployed members shall be excused from payment of dues.

NAMES AND ADDRESSES OF OFFICERS. Sec. 23. Upon the election of new officers, locals shall notify the State Committee within ten days after such election, giving the names and addresses of such officers.

CANDIDATES AND FUSION. Sec. 24. Under no circumstances shall the state or local organization co-operate with any other political party, or independent organization organized to advance the interests of a candidate for public office; and no local shall nominate any one as a candidate for public office who has not been a member of the party for at least two years, except locals which have been in existence less than two years.

ARTICLE II

Administration of State Organization

CONDUCT OF AFFAIRS. Sec. 1. The affairs of the organization shall be conducted by the State Committee, State Executive Committee and the general vote of the members.

STATE COMMITTEE. Sec. 2. The State Committee shall consist of one member from each organized county in the state, and one additional member for every five hundred members in good standing; same to be based on the due stamps bought by the local or locals in such counties during the year ending in the month of September.

ELECTION. Sec. 3. The members of the State Committee shall be elected and may be recalled and their successors chosen by referendum vote of the members of the local or locals in the county. In cases, however, when one local covers the whole county and conducts its business through a county committee, such county committee shall have the power to fill vacancies, and shall also have the power to suspend State Committeemen, but shall immediately submit such suspension to a referendum of the members in the county. The members of the State Committee must be members in good standing for at least two years, except in the counties not organized for that period of time.

TERM OF OFFICE. Sec. 4. The members of the State Committee shall be elected in the month of December for a term of one (1) year. The term of office to begin in the month of January.

DUTIES OF STATE COMMITTEE. Sec. 5. (a) The State Committee shall meet on the second Sunday in April, except in years when a State Convention is to be held, and it shall then meet at the same time and place with the convention. The expenses of State Committeemen in attending these meetings shall be paid out of the Treasury of the State Committee.

(b) The State Committee shall have the power to review and revise the actions of the State Executive Committee. The Platform Committee, Committee on Rules and all other important committees of the State Convention shall be elected by the State Committee at its meeting prior to the State Convenion, and all these committees to be so appointed shall render reports of their work through the party press not later than two months prior to the date set for the State Convention.

(c) At its annual meeting the State Committee shall elect a State Secretary.

(d) The State Committee shall call the State Conventions of the party.

(e) Any three members of the State Committee, other than members of the Executive Committee, may initiate a motion which shall be submitted to a vote of the State Committee.

(f) The State Committee at its annual meeting shall determine the location of the State headquarters.

COMPOSITION OF STATE EXECUTIVE COMMITTEE. Sec. 6. The State Executive Committee shall consist of nine members of the party, elected by the State Committee at its annual meeting. Nominations to be made by the State Committeemen at least one month prior to the annual meeting, and a list of those accepting the nominations shall be sent to the State Committeemen in advance of such meeting.

Vacancies shall be filled by the State Committeemen voting by correspondence. Members of the State Executive Committee must have the same qualifications as required of members of the State Committee.

DUTIES OF STATE EXECUTIVE COMMITTEE. Sec. 7. The State Executive Committee shall have immediate charge of the work of organization, agitation and campaign throughout the state; shall elect a treasurer and such other officers as may be deemed necessary for the proper transaction of its business; pass upon all applications for charters; furnish to locals the monthly due stamps bought of the National Committee, at the price of ten cents each; furnish the locals quarter-annual report blanks. It shall meet at least once a month, and carry on a general correspondence between the locals and the state organization; and at its meeting not later than thirty days before a State Convention shall appoint a Committee on Rules; prepare and present to the State Convention a draft of a platform for the action of the convention. To prepare the order of business for the State Convention and have same published in the party press at least two months prior to the date set for the holding of the same.

REPORT OF STATE EXECUTIVE COMMITTEE. Sec. 8. The State Executive Committee shall furnish reports of its meetings and actions taken thereon to the State Committee after each meeting. Upon the demand of two members of the State Committee, other than members of the State Executive Committee, made within fifteen days after submission of report, any act of the Executive Committee must be submitted to a vote of the State Committee. The minutes of the State Executive Committee shall be sent to all the members of the State Committee for their approval, and unless objections are raised within fifteen days after their submission, all actions contained therein shall stand approved.

QUORUM. Sec. 9. Five members of the State Executive Committee shall constitute a quorum for the transaction of business.

VACANCIES. Sec. 10. Any member of the State Executive Committee absent for three consecutive meetings of the committee shall have his seat declared vacant.

RULES OF PROCEDURE. Sec. 11. The State Committee and State Executive Committee shall adopt their own rules of procedure not inconsistent with this constitution or the national constitution of the party.

STATE SECRETARY — DUTIES. Sec. 12. The State Secretary shall be the executive officer of the State Organization. His duties shall include the following:

(a) Have charge of the State office and all records or documents.

(b) He shall be ex-officio member of the State Executive Committee and State Committee and shall have a voice but no vote at their meetings.

(c) He shall act as Financial Secretary of the State Committee and in this capacity shall receive and receipt for all moneys of the organization, and pay out the same in the discharge of current expenses and obligations duly authorized.

(d) He shall submit quarterly a written financial report to the members of the State Committee, and annual reports to all locals.

(e) He shall submit his books to the Auditing Committee every three months, or whenever called upon either by the Auditing Committee, State Committee, or State Executive Committee.

(f) Turn over to his successor in office all books, papers, money or any other property belonging to the State Committee, which may have been in his possession.

(g) He shall have charge of and supervise the work of the State organizers and speakers, subject to instruction from the State Executive Committee.

(h) He shall be authorized to employ the necessary clerical help, subject to the approval of the State Executive Committee.

(i) He shall perform such special duties as may be prescribed by the State Committee or State Executive Committee.

AUDITING COMMITTEE. Sec. 13. An Auditing Committee of three members shall be elected for a term of one year by the State Executive Committee, whose duties shall be to audit the accounts of the State Committee every three months or whenever called upon by the State Committee or State Executive Committee, a copy of such audited report to be sent to every member of the State Committee and to the locals.

ARTICLE III

State Conventions

REGULAR CONVENTIONS. Sec. 1. Regular State Conventions of the party shall be held in all years when a Governor of the State is to be elected.

SPECIAL CONVENTIONS. Sec. 2. Special conventions may be called whenever decided upon by a general vote. The question of calling a special convention may be submitted to a general vote of the membership by the State Committee on its own motion and shall be submitted upon the demand of any three locals located in three different counties.

REPRESENTATION. Sec. 3. At all State organization conventions the representation shall be by locals, each local being entitled to one delegate and one additional delegate for every 100 members in good standing to be determined by the number of due stamps purchased during the six months preceding the call for the election of such delegates.

Delegates to the State Convention must be members of the party for at least two years, except from locals which have not been organized for that period. They must also be members of the county which they are to represent.

POLITICAL CONVENTION. Sec. 4. All statutory political conventions where the work of the convention has been prescribed by referendum, convention or committees of the dues-paying organization, shall be held at the seat of the State organization, and the State Executive Committee may direct that the delegates near or at the seat of the State headquarters shall constitute a quorum at such conventions and shall assemble and hold such convention as the law provides.

DELEGATES EXPENSES. Sec. 5. The railroad fare of the delegates in going to or from the place of convention shall be paid from the treasury of the State organization. The fund for this purpose shall be raised by a per capita assessment on the membership, or in such other manner as the State Committee shall find expedient.

ARTICLE IV

National Committeemen

ELECTION. Sec. 1. The locals in the State of New York shall elect by referendum vote in the month of January each year, such number of representatives of the National Committee of the party as the state may be entitled to, provided, however, that not more than one member shall be from the same local.

To qualify as a candidate for National Committeeman, such candidate shall be nominated by not less than two locals in two different counties.

TERM OF OFFICE. Sec. 2. The election of National Committeemen shall be conducted by the State Committee, and the National Committeemen elected shall hold office for the term of one year and until their successors are elected.

VACANCIES. Sec. 3. Any vacancies occurring in the offices of National Committeemen shall be filled by a referendum vote without delay.

WRITTEN REPORTS. Sec. 4. The National Committeeman shall make a written report to the State Committee in the months of January, April, July and October of each year, and to the State Convention whenever it meets. The seat of any National Committeeman who shall fail to make reports for two consecutive quarters shall be declared vacant and a new election ordered.

INSTRUCTIONS. Sec. 5. The State Committee or State Executive Committee may call upon the National Committeemen at any time to appear before it to discuss such questions as the committee deems important, and the decisions arrived at by majority vote of the committee shall be binding upon the National Committeemen and they shall vote as instructed.

ARTICLE V

Amendments

METHOD OF AMENDING THIS CONSTITUTION.—Any amendment of this constitution shall be submitted to a general vote upon motion of the State Committee or upon demand of at least three locals in three different counties.

ARTICLE VI

Referendums

WHEN TAKEN. Sec. 1. The State Committee or three or more locals in three different counties with at least 500 members may demand a referendum vote on all questions.

DEMANDS ON REFERENDUM. Sec. 2. A demand for a referendum vote made by a local must stand open for six weeks for two locals to second it. If no endorsement is received from two locals within the specified time such motion shall be null and void.

Sec. 3. All referendum votes shall be open for six weeks for locals to vote, and no extension of time shall be made by the State Committee.

Sec. 4. It shall be the duty of the State Secretary to submit every proposed referendum to the locals within three weeks after it has been duly initiated.

ARTICLE VII

National Conventions

METHOD OF ELECTION AND APPORTIONMENT OF DELEGATES.—The election of delegates to national conventions of the party shall be through the county organizations. The number of delegates to be apportioned by the State Committee in proportion to the membership in the county organizations.

ARTICLE VIII

Miscellaneous Regulations

RESIGNATION OF CANDIDATES AND APPOINTEES. Section 1. All candidates for public office or appointees to public office selected by the dues-paying membership of the Socialist Party of the State of New York or any of its subdivisions shall sign the following resignation blank before nomination is made official, or appointment is made final.

FORM OF RESIGNATION. Sec. 2. Recognizing the Socialist Party as a purely democratic organization in which the source and seat of all powers lies in the dues-paying membership, as an elected (or appointed) official of the party it shall be my duty to ascertain and abide by the wish of the majority of the dues-paying members of my local or political subdivision.

To the end that my official acts may at all times be under the direction and control of the party membership I hereby sign and place in the hands of Local —, to which I may be elected (or appointed), such resignation to become effective whenever a majority of the local shall so vote.

I sign this resignation voluntarily as a condition on receiving said nomination (or appointment) and pledge my honor as a man, a Socialist, to abide by it.

FORMS OF RESIGNATION TO BE SUPPLIED BY STATE EXECUTIVE COMMITTEE. Sec. 3. The State Executive Committee shall supply each local with the necessary resignation forms.

APPOINTMENT FOR NON-COMPETITIVE OFFICES. Sec. 4. Elected Socialist officials shall submit the names of the proposed or contemplated appointments for heads of departments, members of mayor's cabinets, commissioners, deputies and members of commissions or any other appointees to position of administrative or executive character for the approval of the local or county organizations. If said local or county organization shall disapprove of any proposed appointment, it may submit its choice of appointment to the said elected official. In case of further disagreement, the local or county organization and the elected officials have the right to appeal to the State Executive Committee.

SELECTION OF CANDIDATES TO BE VOTED FOR AT THE FALL PRIMARIES. Sec. 5. (a) All candidates for public offices other than for county, township, municipal offices, or candidates lying wholly within one county, to be nominated at the primary elections, shall be selected by a referendum vote of the dues-paying membership in such districts, or by a convention of delegates from the locals of such districts.

(b) The selections made through such referendums or conventions shall be binding on the members composing the official committees authorized by law to make the designations for the primary elections.

ELIGIBILITY FOR PUBLIC OFFICE. Sec. 6. No person shall be eligible as a candidate of the Socialist Party for any political or public office (this not to include members of the political committee elected for the purpose of designating candidates) who is not a member in good standing at the time of his nomination, and has been such for a period of two years preceding the date of his nomination. Provided that this rule shall not apply where there has been no local organization in existence for the prescribed period.

No one but party members in good standing shall be nominated for member of political committees, authorized by law to designate candidates.

ARTICLE IX

National Constitution

TAKES PRECEDENCE.—In case of conflict between any provisions of this constitution and the national constitution, the latter shall take precedence.

Document No. 3

BY-LAWS OF SOCIALIST PARTY, NEW YORK COUNTY

(Adopted 1918.)

ARTICLE I

Name

The name of the organization shall be "Local New York Socialist Party."

ARTICLE II

Organization

Section 1. Local New York shall be composed of all organizations of the Socialist Party within the borough of Manhattan in the city and county of New York.

Article III

Management

Section 1. The affairs of the Local shall be conducted by a Central Committee, and by the officers and committees elected by the Central Committee.

Sec. 2. The officers of the Local shall be: An Executive Secretary, a Recording Secretary, a Treasurer. No member shall hold more than one of these offices.

Sec. 3. All acts of officers and committees shall be binding and inclusive unless rescinded by the Central Committee, and all acts of the Central Committee shall be binding and conclusive unless rescinded by a general party meeting or by a general vote of the members.

Article IV

Central Committee

Section 1. The Central Committee shall be composed of delegates from the various branches of Local New York, and of the officers and members of the standing committees of the Local.

Sec. 2. The basis of representation shall be as follows: One delegate for every twenty-five members in good standing in the branch. The number of delegates shall be determined by the number of dues stamps bought by a branch during the twelve months preceding the month of November before the election.

Sec. 3. Newly organized branches shall be entitled for the first year to not more than two delegates; the regular representation shall be given them only after an existence of at least one year.

Sec. 4. The delegates to the Central Committee shall be elected at the second regular meeting of the branches in the month of December, and their term shall be for twelve months, unless withdrawn as hereinafter provided.

Sec. 5. Delegates to the Central Committee must be in good standing and members of the Socialist Party for at least two years, excepting delegates of newly organized language branches.

Sec. 6. Delegates to the Central Committee who have absented themselves without excuse from three consecutive meetings shall thereby forfeit their seats in the Central Committee, and branches shall be requested to elect other delegates.

Sec. 7. The Central Committee shall elect an Executive Committee of nine, a Grievance Committee of five, an auditing Committee of three, a Recording Secretary, a Treasurer, and a

Sergeant-at-Arms, all of whom serve for one year and until their successors are elected.

Sec. 8. Nominations are to be made at the first meeting of the Central Committee in January, and elections at the first meeting thereafter. Additional nominations may be made on the date of election.

Sec. 9. The officers and members of committees of Local New York, if not delegates, shall have a voice, but no vote in the Central Committee.

Sec. 10. The Central Committee shall have the right to donate a sum not exceeding $50 by majority vote at a meeting when such donation is proposed; all donations of larger sums shall be referred to the next meeting, so that the delegates may consult their constituents.

ARTICLE V

Duties of the Central Committee

Section 1. The Central Committee shall meet at least once a month.

It shall:

(a) Elect the officers of the Local and Committees as hereinbefore mentioned.

(b) Receive reports from Officers and Committees and to act on such reports.

(c) Receive reports from branches of the Local through their respective delegates.

(d) Carry out the decisions of general party meetings and of referendums of the members of Local New York.

(e) Enforce the attendance of delegates.

(f) Order general meetings of all members to be called whenever it shall deem such meetings necessary.

(g) Perform such other functions, not inconsistent with these by-laws, as may be required in furtherance of Socialist propaganda.

ORDER OF BUSINESS. Sec. 2. The meetings of the Central Committee shall be opened by the Executive Secretary, or in his absence by the Recording Secretary or any other officer of the local. The business of the Central Committee shall be transacted in the following order:

Election of Chairman and Vice-Chairman.
Reading of minutes.
Communications.

Reports of special committees.
Report of Executive Committee.
Report of standing committees and officers.
Roll call and reports of branches.
Unfinished business.
New business.
Good and welfare.
Adjournment.

Robert's Rules of Order shall govern the proceedings of the Central Committee in so far as special rules are not provided.

ARTICLE VI

The Executive Committee

Section 1. The Executive Committee shall consist of nine (9) members elected by the Central Committee and the District Representatives, elected by all the party members in each Assembly district at a joint meeting of all the branches within the territory of the Assembly district branches. Vacancies are to be filled in the same manner.

Sec. 2. No member shall be eligible to the Executive Committee who has not been a member of the party in good standing continuously for at least three years, and who has not identified himself with the party by active participation in its work.

Sec. 3. The Executive Committee shall elect the following standing committees: On Organization, Education, Propaganda, Public Affairs, Finance, Naturalization, Propaganda among Women, and Young People's Socialist League. The Chairman of each committee shall be elected by the Executive Committee.

Sec. 4. The Executive Committee shall:

(a) Meet at least twice a month; act as Campaign Committee, carry out all instructions of the Central Committee and appoint such committees as may be necessary.

(b) Prescribe a uniform system of bookkeeping for all branches.

(c) Receive and pass upon applications for membership.

(d) Call conventions of the Socialist Party in the County of New York, whenever required, as hereinafter provided.

(e) Investigate disputes between branches of the Local.

(f) Pass upon the formation of new branches or changes in the present divisions of the Local.

(g) Pass on all candidates for political offices within the County of New York, and in case of objection to any candidate so nominated, refer such objection to the Central Committee.

(h) Submit to general vote all propositions referred to Local New York by the National or State Committees.

(i) Pass upon all credentials of delegates to the Central Committee as soon as they are presented, and report thereon to the Central Committee.

(j) Provide for the raising of funds.

(k) Call mass meetings and arrange demonstrations whenever it may consider such meetings and demonstrations necessary and proper.

(l) Supervise the work of all branches of Local New York, of all standing committees and of the Executive Secretary.

ARTICLE VII

Standing Committees

COMMITTEE ON ORGANIZATION. Sec. 1. The Committee on Organization shall consist of a Chairman elected by the Executive Committee and the organizers of all branches: It shall:

(a) Keep a correct record of the names, addresses, dates of admission, occupations, and other useful information regarding all members of the Local.

(b) Supervise the work of organization of the Local and the branches.

(c) Take steps to induce the unaffiliated Socialists in the County of New York to become members of the Socialist Party.

(d) See to it that all members of the party who allow their membership to lapse be induced to resume active work and membership within the party.

(e) Report to the Executive Committee on its work.

COMMITTEE ON EDUCATION. Sec. 2. Committee on Education shall consist of a Chairman elected by the Executive Committee and the chairman of the educational committees of the branches, language groups and a representative of the Y. P. S. L.; it shall:

(a) Supervise the educational work of the Local.

(b) Conduct one or more systematic lecture courses on Socialism or on topics of the day from a Socialist point of view.

(c) Organize classes for the study of Socialism among members of the party and classes for the training of Socialist speakers.

(d) Organize special study clubs among young people and children's Socialist schools.

(e) Co-operate with all agencies of Socialist instruction inside and outside of the Socialist Party.

(f) Report to the Executive Committee.

PROPAGANDA COMMITTEE. Sec. 3. The Propaganda Committee shall consist of a Chairman, elected by the Executive Committee and the chairman of the propaganda committees of all branches or subdivisions of the Local; it shall:

(a) Supervise the propaganda work of the Local.

(b) Supervise and print popular Socialist literature.

(c) Supervise the distribution of literature and open air meetings and act jointly with Committee on Education and Committee of Propaganda among Women where their work coincides.

(d) Report to the Executive Committee.

COMMITTEE ON PUBLIC AFFAIRS. Sec. 4. Committee on Public Affairs; it shall:

(a) Issue public statements, proclamations, or resolutions, on all matters and events of general public interest, setting forth the position of the Socialist Party toward such matters and events, whenever necessary and practical, under the supervision and with the approval of the Executive Committee.

(b) Report to the Executive Committee.

FINANCE COMMITTEE. Sec. 5. The Finance Committee shall consist of a Chairman elected by the Executive Committee and a representative from each branch; it shall:

(a) Supervise the financing of the party work and of all its branches.

(b) Provide for raising of funds.

(c) Report to the Executive Committee.

NATURALIZATION COMMITTEE. Sec. 6. The Naturalization Committee shall consist of a Chairman elected by the Executive Committee and such assistants as may be appointed by the Chairman with the approval of the Executive Committee; it shall:

(a) Maintain one or more naturalization bureaus in the county under supervision and with the approval of the Executive Committee.

(b) Procure and keep on hand copies of the latest rules, statutes, and decisions on naturalization.

(c) Distribute printed instructions for the guidance of applicants for naturalization and aid applicants for naturalization in every possible way, and maintain a bureau for that purpose.

(d) Make public propaganda for a more liberal naturalization law and a more liberal administration of existing statutes.

COMMITTEE ON PROPAGANDA AMONG WOMEN. Sec. 7. The Committee on Propaganda among Women shall consist of a Chairman elected by the Executive Committee and a delegate from each branch; it shall:

(a) Supervise propaganda among women and take measures to bring them into the party and co-operate with the Committees on Propaganda and Education for that purpose.

(b) Report to the Executive Committee.

LABOR UNION COMMITTEE. Sec. 8. The Labor Union Committee shall consist of a Chairman, elected by the Executive Committee and one delegate from each branch, who must be members of labor unions; it shall:

(a) Keep a correct record of the names, addresses, dates of admission, occupations, and other useful information regarding all members of the local.

(b) Keep a list of members who are also members of labor organizations.

(c) Organize work among the trade unions and other labor organizations.

(d) Report to the Executive Committee.

YOUNG PEOPLE'S COMMITTEE. Sec. 9. The Young People's Committee shall consist of three members elected by the Executive Committee and two elected by the Young People's Socialist League; it shall:

(a) Direct in conjunction with the supervisors the education and organization of the young people.

(b) Report to the Executive Committee.

ARTICLE VIII

Grievance Committee

The Committee on Grievances shall:

Section 1. Elect a Chairman and a Secretary and adopt a uniform method of procedure, and submit the same for approval to the Central Committee to be incorporated in its Rule Book.

Sec. 2. (a) Shall investigate such charges against members of the Local as are referred to it by the Central Committee, and report its recommendations on same to the Central Committee.

(b) It shall proceed to investigate each case without unnecessary delay, hearing the witnesses on both sides.

(c) The committee shall send a copy of the charges to the accused.

(d) Shall have authority to summon to its hearings the accusing and accused persons and such other persons whose testimony may be deemed material or necessary. Such summons to be mailed by registered letter to the last known address of persons whose attendance is required.

Sec. 3. A detailed report of the investigation and conclusion of the committee shall be drawn and laid before the Central Committee not later than the second regular meeting following the taking of testimony. The accused and accuser being notified by the Secretary of the Grievance Committee in due time to appear there.

ARTICLE IX

Auditing Committee

The Auditing Committee shall:

Section 1. Investigate once a month all the financial books, reports and accounts of the Local, of the Finance Committee and of any other committees handling party funds, and report on their condition to the Central Committee.

Sec. 2. See whether the balance shown by the books of the Local is deposited in the bank, or its equivalent can be shown in cash by the Executive Secretary.

Sec. 3. Keep the monthly financial reports represented by the Executive Secretary and submit them to the Executive Committee every three months or whenever the books are audited.

ARTICLE X

Executive Secretary

Section 1. The Executive Secretary shall be elected by a referendum vote of Local New York; he shall:

(a) Devote his entire time to the work of the Local.

(b) Act as Corresponding Secretary of the Local.

(c) Act as Campaign Secretary during all campaigns of the Local.

(d) Call special meetings of the Central and Executive Committees whenever he deems it proper and whenever requested by one-third of the delegates.

(e) Be a member ex-officio of all committees of the Local.

(f) In every way assist the divisions of the Local in the work of organization and propaganda.

(g) Keep a correct record of the names, addresses, dates of admission, occupations and other useful information regarding all members of the Local.

(h) Have charge of the seal, office, books, and other property belonging to the Local.

(i) Prepare and furnish to branches all supplies ordered by the Central Committee.

(j) Keep correct accounts of the income and expenditures of the Local.

(k) Attend to all bookkeeping and other matters of business and routine of the Local.

(l) Submit all bills against the Local to the Executive Committee.

(m) Render a report every month of the financial condition of the Local to the Executive Committee.

(n) Buy dues stamps from the State Committee for the Local and sell the same to the branches for cash only, at such rates as may be fixed by the Central Committee. He shall also have charge of and sell all assessment stamps, tickets and subscription lists.

(o) Supply the Executive Committee of the Local, every year, and whenever new delegates are elected, with a membership report and an account of the dues stamps bought by every branch during the preceding year.

(p) Receive applications for membership and collect the initiation fees.

(q) Prepare annual reports of the work of propaganda, education and organization, and of the financial affairs of the Local.

(r) Report to the Central Committee and carry out its instructions.

(s) Turn over at the end of his term of office, to his successor in office, all books, funds and other property of the Local in his possession.

Sec. 2. The Executive Secretary shall furnish a bond to be approved by the Executive Committee in a sum of not less than $1,000.

Sec. 3. All funds to be received by the Executive Secretary shall be deposited in a bank to be approved by the Executive Committee and all bills ordered to be paid by the Executive Committee wherever possible shall be paid by check to be signed by the Treasurer and counter-signed by the Executive Secretary.

Sec. 4. The term of office of the Executive Secretary shall begin with the first week in May, nominations to be made during the month of January and the election to take place ending with the last day in March.

Sec. 5. The Executive Secretary must be a member in good standing and a member of the Socialist Party for at least three consecutive years.

Article XI

Treasurer

Section 1. The treasurer shall be elected by the Central Committee for a term of one year; he shall:

(a) Have the custody of the funds and supervise all accounts of the income and expenditure of the Local and sign all checks or bills approved by the Executive Committee when counter-signed by the Executive Secretary.

(b) Prepare semi-annually a report of his receipts and disbursements.

(c) Turn over at the end of his term of office to his successor in office all funds and other property of the Local in his possession.

Sec. 2. The Treasurer shall furnish a bond in a sum of not less than $1,000 to be approved by the Executive Committee.

Sec. 3. The Treasurer shall be a member ex-officio of the Finance Committee.

Article XII

Recording Secretary

Section 1. The Recording Secretary shall:

(a) Keep a correct record of the proceedings of the Central Committee.

(b) Furnish accurate reports of the Central Committee meetings to all Socialist Party papers of New York City.

ARTICLE XIII

Sergeant-at-Arms

Section 1. The Sergeant-at-Arms shall:

(a) Provide seats for visiting members in the rear of the meeting hall, separate from those occupied by the delegates.

(b) Require of all delegates and visiting members their membership cards.

(c) Use his efforts in preserving decorum and good order in the meeting halls.

ARTICLE XIV

Branches or Subdivisions

Section 1. The branches or subdivisions of Local New York shall be organized on the basis of Assembly districts. The Central Committee may combine two or more Assembly districts into one branch.

Sec. 2. (a) Separate language branches or groups may be formed whenever necessary among those members desiring to transact their business in a language other than English.

(b) But no more than one branch in any one foreign language shall exist in one Assembly district.

(c) Language branches should be designated to a definite political subdivision and no language branch should cover a larger territory than the English branch, except where only one language branch is in the Local.

(d) Whenever there are more than one branch in any language, they shall form a committee for agitation purposes and transact business of common interest to all of such branches.

(e) Language branches shall in all party matters co-operate with the English speaking branches in their territory and shall in every respect be subject to the jurisdiction and decisions of the Local.

Sec. 3. It shall be the duty of every officer of the branch to transmit promptly to his branch all official communications sent to him by the Executive Secretary or any other officer of the party for that purpose.

Sec. 4. The presiding officer of the branch shall explain to every applicant, before he is admitted to membership, the significance of the class struggle and the uncompromising policy of the party, and the applicant shall pledge in writing to its recognition and support. A copy of the National Platform, National and

State Constitution and By-Laws of the Local shall be handed to every new member.

Sec. 5. A member in good standing of one branch shall have the right to attend and speak at any meeting of another branch, but shall not be allowed to vote.

Sec. 6. (a) The branches in each organized political subdivision shall meet jointly at least once a month to transact business of common interest and to organize and carry on the propaganda and agitation in the district.

(b) At the joint meeting in the month of January, they shall elect a district organizer and such other officers and committees as is necessary to carry on the work of the organization, each branch in the district shall have at least one member on each of the committees elected by the joint meetings.

Sec. 7. (a) The district organizer shall represent the district on the Executive Committee of the Local.

(b) He shall act as corresponding secretary for the district on all matters concerning the district as a whole.

(c) He shall look after the agitation and organization of the party in the district and for this purpose should visit all the branches in the district regularly, co-operate and assist them in their work and report to them on the work of the Local and the district.

(d) He shall be elected for a term of one year.

ARTICLE XV

Duties of Branches

Section 1. The branches shall meet at least once a month, and at least one-half of the number of meetings shall be devoted to education, such as lectures, discussions, etc.

Sec. 2. The regular order of business for the branch meetings shall be: Election of Chairman, reading of minutes, proposal of new members, admission of new members, communications and bills, report of Executive Committee, reports of delegates to the Central Committee, reports of committees and special delegates, unfinished business, roll call of members, new business, good and welfare.

Sec. 3. The branches may fix such special order of business as they may find necessary from time to time.

Sec. 4. The branches shall elect their officers, delegates and standing committees at their second regular meetings in December.

Sec. 5. Every branch shall elect from its members the following officers, delegates and such standing committees as the branches may desire to have:

(a) An Organizer; (b) a Financial Secretary; (c) a Recording Secretary; (d) a Treasurer; (e) Delegates to the Central Committee; (f) an Auditing Committee of three members, and at least the following committees: An Executive Committee, a Membership Committee, a Committee on Education, and a Propaganda Committee.

Sec. 6. No member can be an officer of a branch who has not been a member of the party for at least one year.

Sec. 7. The result of every election within a branch shall be sent immediately, and a list of all members in arrears, suspensions, and change of address, at least once a month, to the Executive Secretary of the Local.

Sec. 8. The branches shall submit to their membership for a vote all propositions referred by the Executive Committee for a general vote.

Sec. 9. The branches shall purchase their dues stamps from the Executive Secretary of the Local.

Sec. 10. Each branch shall, through its delegates, make monthly reports to the Central Committee about its organization, propaganda work, and such other matters as the Central Committee may require. It shall send in the months of July and January a report of its financial condition, such report to contain the names, addresses, standing and such other information as the printed forms furnished by the Executive Committee may require.

Sec. 11. No branch shall be dissolved without the consent of the Executive Committee.

Sec. 12. In case of dissolution of any branch, all the property belonging to the same shall be turned over to the Executive Committee of the Local.

EXECUTIVE COMMITTEE. Sec. 13. (a) The Executive Committee of a branch shall consist of three members elected by the branch and of the Chairman of all standing committees.

(b) The Executive Committee shall perform the routine work of the branch subject to the approval of the branch meetings.

MEMBERSHIP COMMITTEE. Sec. 14. (a) It shall be the duty of the Membership Committee to increase and consolidate the membership, by calling upon delinquent and indifferent members, by visiting enrolled voters and sympathizers, and by holding organization meetings at regular intervals.

(b) It shall elect a permanent chairman who shall supervise the activities of the committee and keep an accurate record of the work done.

(c) The Financial Secretary of the branch shall be a member ex-officio of this committee.

PROPAGANDA COMMITTEE. Sec. 15. (a) All election district captains within the territory of an Assembly district shall constitute the Propaganda Committee for that district.

(b) Each Assembly District Propaganda Committee shall meet once a month for the transaction of business.

(c) The district organizer shall act as chairman of this committee, shall supervise its activities, shall keep a record of the work done, and shall, subject to the approval of the committee, appoint captains for those election districts in which a regular agitation is carried on.

(d) It shall be the duty of every election district captain to supply the residents of his election district with literature as often as possible; he shall endeavor to obtain the assistance of as many members as are necessary to canvass the entire election district regularly; he shall assign a definite block or group of houses to each of his assistants for careful canvassing; and at regular intervals he shall furnish to the district organizer a correct list of the members and sympathizers residing within his election district.

ARTICLE XVI

Dues

Section 1. The dues per member to be paid by the branches to the Local shall be ten cents more than the Local pays to the State Committee, but the Central Committee shall have the power to fix the amount of dues as the circumstances may require. The various subdivisions may fix such additional dues as they may see fit, providing that such is adopted by two-thirds of the members voting. All members in good standing shall receive notification of such proposed changes.

Sec. 2. The dues shall be receipted by dues stamps purchased from the Financial Secretary.

Sec. 3. Members shall refuse to pay dues unless the Financial Secretary shall furnish the dues stamps. It is the duty of every member to immediately inform the Executive Secretary of the

Local whenever his Financial Secretary collects dues without giving the necessary dues stamps.

Sec. 4. To be in good standing a member's dues must not be more than three months in arrears.

Sec. 5. Sick or unemployed members will be excused from payment of dues, but the fact must be noted each month upon their cards.

Sec. 6. A member who has withheld payment of his dues for three months, unless known to be sick or unemployed, shall be immediately notified in writing by the Financial Secretary of the subdivision, and at the conclusion of a fourth month of delinquency shall stand suspended, and a suspension notice shall be sent to the member.

Sec. 7. A member suspended for the non-payment of dues, may be reinstated upon the payment of back dues, or in extraordinary cases may be reinstated without payment by the branch making such suspension.

Sec. 8. The Executive Committee shall supply the subdivisions with printed circulars for delinquent and suspended members.

Sec. 9. Members in arrears in the payment of their dues shall have no right to vote on any questions to be voted upon by the members of the party unless excused on account of sickness or unemployment.

Sec. 10. The Executive Secretary of the Local shall have a correct list of all members suspended or dropped from the rolls by the various branches.

ARTICLE XVII

Membership

Section 1. Any person eighteen years of age or over, who agrees to abide by the National Platform and Constitution and Resolutions of the Socialist Party, may become a member of the party.

Sec. 2. Candidates for membership in the party shall be proposed at a regular meeting of the subdivision; they must be present when proposed, except in cases of compulsory night work when the application may be accepted in the absence of the candidate.

Sec. 3. All applications must be signed by the Financial Secretary and the applicant and forwarded to the Executive Secretary with an admission fee of twenty-five cents.

Sec. 4. All objections filed with the Executive Secretary shall be reported by him to the Executive Committee; the latter shall cause an investigation to be made thereon and report its findings to the Central Committee.

Sec. 5. The candidates for membership against whom objections were made can be admitted by the Central Committee by a two-thirds affirmative vote of the delegates present.

Sec. 6. Every member must belong to the branch in whose territory he resides except by special permission of the Central Committee.

Sec. 7. The subdivision should transfer any member as soon as he moves out of its territory, and the fact so entered in the minutes of the district. A transfer card shall be given to the member acknowledging that he paid all his dues, and that the subdivision has no other claim against him; the Financial Secretaries of both branches, the one issuing and the one receiving the transfer, shall send stub of transfer to the Executive Secretary of the Local.

Sec. 8. Any member transferring to any of the subdivisions of Local New York from any other Local or State shall be accepted on the presentation of his membership card in good standing, but the fact must be at once communicated to the Executive Secretary, so that he may write for further information to the Secretary of the Local of which such comrade was formerly a member.

ARTICLE XVIII

Charges

Section 1. Charges against members of the Local must be made in writing and signed either by the individual member making the charges or by the Executive Secretary in behalf of the Central Committee.

Sec. 2. All such charges shall be referred immediately to the Grievance Committee.

Sec. 3. Charges shall not be debated until the Grievance Committee has thoroughly investigated the case and reported to the Central Committee.

Sec. 4. A two-thirds vote of the delegates to the Central Committee present and voting shall be required to expel a member of the Local. A majority shall be sufficient to suspend or censure.

Sec. 5. A member of the Local shall not be suspended for a longer period than one year.

Sec. 6. An expelled or suspended member may appeal from within two months to a general vote, or to the State Committee, but he shall not enjoy the privileges of membership pending the appeal.

ARTICLE XIX

Secret Ballot Election

Section 1. The Executive Secretary:

(a) Delegates to City, State and National Conventions shall be elected by secret ballot of the membership of the Local.

(b) Each subdivision is entitled to nominate as many candidates as there are offices to be filled.

(c) No one shall be placed on the list of candidates unless he or she receives the nomination of at least one subdivision of the Local.

(d) The names of all such candidates for the various offices shall be placed on the ballot in alphabetical order.

(e) After receiving notice of such secret ballot election, the Assembly district branch designates a meeting for the election within the four weeks that are allowed for it.

(f) The branch notifies the Executive Committee of the meeting so selected. The Executive Committee in turn delegates one of its members to supervise such election as its representative.

(g) The Executive Committee shall tabulate the vote, and the comrade or comrades receiving the highest number of votes shall be declared elected for the respective offices and committees.

Sec. 2. In case of referendums, the Executive Committee, with the approval of the Central Committee, may order the vote to be taken by secret ballot, in which case it shall be so directed in the letter to the subdivisions accompanying ballots for use on such referendums.

Sec. 3. The delegates to the Central Committees and officers of subdivisions, whenever there are more than the required number of candidates, shall be elected by a secret ballot.

ARTICLE XX

Secret Balloting

Section 1. Each subdivision of the Local shall elect by a majority vote a Board of Elections consisting of three members.

Sec. 2. Whenever an election is to take place the financial

secretaries of the various subdivisions shall be required to prepare from their books a list of members in good standing, such list to be verified by the Board of Elections of the respective subdivisions.

Sec. 3. In voting every member shall hand in the folded ballot to the Board of Elections, whereupon a check shall be marked on the list of good standing members supplied by the Financial Secretary. When the voting is over, the Board must count the number of ballots, the total to correspond with the number of checks on the list.

Sec. 4. After the ballots are counted they shall be canvassed by the Board of Elections. The representative of the Executive Committee of the Local acting as chairman.

Sec. 5. After the vote is canvassed for each candidate, three statements containing the report of the votes cast are to be signed by the three members of the Board of Elections and the representative of the Executive Committee of the Local. Each of these statements shall be put in a separate envelope and sealed. One of these envelopes to remain in the custody of the Recording Secretary of the branch until the total vote in the Local is canvassed and published. The second is addressed to the Executive Committee of the Local to be taken there by its representatives. The third is to be addressed to the Executive Secretary of Local New York and mailed.

Sec. 6. For secret balloting in subdivision elections, the same method shall prevail, except that the Board of Elections itself shall constitute the Canvassing Board.

ARTICLE XXI

General Meetings

Section 1. General meetings may be called by the Central Committee of the Executive Committee whenever it deems it necessary.

Sec. 2. Upon the request of two or more branches representing not less than 400 members in good standing, the Central Committee shall call a general meeting of the Local. In requesting a general meeting, the branches shall state the order of business for which such general meeting is to be called.

Sec. 3. The Executive Secretary of the Local shall notify all good standing members of the Local whenever a general meeting is to be held, stating time, place and order of the day for which such meeting is called. Such notice to be published in the party press and mailed to every member at least three days before the date of meeting.

Sec. 4. Only members in good standing shall be admitted to such meetings, and only members of Local New York shall be allowed to vote.

Sec. 5. General meetings shall act only on subjects that are mentioned in the call for such meetings.

Sec. 6. If a quorum is present, all actions of such general meetings shall be binding upon the Local and its officers and committees.

Sec. 7. The presence of one-seventh of the good-standing members of the Local is necessary to constitute a quorum.

Sec. 8. The membership of the Local shall be determined from the last annual membership report.

Sec. 9. If no quorum is present at a general meeting, the meeting may, nevertheless, proceed to discuss the order of business before it, but in that case its decision shall have no binding force, and shall be regarded merely in the nature of recommendations.

Sec. 10. The point of no quorum may be raised before taking any vote.

Sec. 11. Upon the demand of one-third of the members present and voting, any or all the decisions of the general meeting shall be referred to a referendum vote of the members of the Local.

Sec. 12. A general meeting shall not be continued in session and no vote shall be taken after midnight.

ARTICLE XXII

General Discussion Meetings

Section 1. General discussion meetings may be called by the Central Committee whenever deemed necessary, or by the Executive Secretary upon the request of three or more subdivisions.

ARTICLE XXIII

Referendums

Referendum votes shall be taken:

Section 1. On all matters submitted to a referendum vote by either the National or State Committee.

Sec. 2. On any decision of the Central Committee, when demanded by one-third of the delegates present and voting or when requested by subdivisions representing not less than 400 members in good standing.

Sec. 3. On amendments to the By-Laws when asked for by subdivisions representing not less than 400 members.

Sec. 4. All referendum votes shall be submitted without comment and ballots containing the subjects to be voted upon shall be sent to the financial secretaries of the subdivisions in proportion to their number of good standing members.

Sec. 5. In case of referendums, the Executive Committee, with the approval of the Central Committee, may order the vote to be taken by secret ballot, in which case it shall be so directed in the letter to the subdivisions accompanying ballots for use on such referendums.

Sec. 6. Only members in good standing shall be entitled to vote on any referendum.

Sec. 7. The individual ballot shall be signed by the members and shall be retained by the Secretary of the subdivision for two months, after which they may be destroyed. The Secretary shall send to the Executive Secretary a ballot containing the tabulated vote cast for and against every subject voted upon.

Sec. 8. The members may vote only at their meetings, and the referendum shall stand open for members to be voted upon until the last meeting of the subdivision prior to the date set by the Local for the closing of the vote.

Sec. 9. No ballots shall be sent by mail to any of its members by any of the subdivisions of the Local, exception being made with those known to be sick or working nights.

Article XXIV

Amendments

Section 1. The By-Laws of Local New York may be amended or altered in the following way:

The Central Committee may amend the by-laws, by a majority vote of the delegates present. Such amendment to be referred to the branches for discussion and shall come up at the next meeting of the Central Committee for final adoption when a two-thirds majority is necessary.

ARTICLE XXV

Quorums

Section 1. One-seventh of all the members of the Local in good standing shall constitute a quorum for the transaction of business at a general meeting of the Local.

Sec. 2. One-third of the total membership of the Central Committee shall constitute a quorum for the transaction of business.

Sec. 3. One-third of the total number of delegates shall constitute a quorum for the transaction of business at a Convention of Local New York.

ARTICLE XXVI

Conventions

Section 1. Upon the request of four or more branches it shall be the duty of the Central Committee to issue a call for a local convention.

Sec. 2. The Executive Committee shall prepare and publish in the Socialist press the order of business for the Convention at least one month before the date set for same.

Sec. 3. The basis of representation at such conventions shall be as follows: One delegate for each branch, one delegate for each language group, and one additional delegate for every twenty members of such branch or group in good standing.

Sec. 4. The convention shall meet at the call of the Executive Secretary, and may adjourn from time to time and continue its sessions until its business has been fully completed.

Sec. 5. The convention shall hear reports from all officers and standing committees of the Local; review the work of the organization and determine the general plan of work.

Sec. 6. The decisions of the convention shall be binding upon all members, officers and committees of the Local, unless reversed by a general vote.

ARTICLE XXVII.

Miscellaneous Regulations

Section 1. None but party members shall speak for or represent the party.

Sec. 2. A member ex-officio of a committee shall have a voice, but no vote, in the sessions of such committee.

Sec. 3. The officers of Local New York shall be elected for a period of one year.

Sec. 4. Any member of the Local in good standing is eligible to all offices and committees of the Local, whether he is a delegate to the Central Committee or not, provided the special requirements of these by-laws are complied with.

Sec. 5. Any member of a committee, officer or delegate, may at any time be withdrawn by the body that has elected him.

Sec. 6. Acquaintance with the current affairs of the party being essential for the intelligent discharge of the duties and responsibilities of party membership, each subdivision shall insist upon each member being a reader of a party paper.

Sec. 7. No subdivision shall enter into any compromise with any other political organization or party. No candidate of the party for any public office shall accept any nomination or indorsement from any other political organization or party, or permit such indorsement to stand without public protest, otherwise his nomination must be at once withdrawn.

Sec. 8. On accepting a nomination of the party for public office, the candidate shall at once give to the Executive Committee a signed resignation, dated —, of the office for which he is nominated and shall assent in writing to its being filed with the proper authorities if, in case of election, he proves disloyal to the party.

Sec. 9. In case of conflict between any clause of these by-laws and the National or State constitution, it shall be deemed void, and the National or State constitution shall take precedence.

ARTICLE XXVIII

Eligibility for Political Office

Sec. 1. No member shall be eligible to become a candidate for political office who has not been a member of the party in good standing continuously for at least three years.

Sec. 2. No member of the party who has previously been a candidate on old party tickets, shall be eligible for candidacy on the Socialist Party ticket except after five years continuous membership in the party.

Document No. 4

WAR PROCLAMATION AND PROGRAM ADOPTED AT NATIONAL CONVENTION, SOCIALIST PARTY, ST. LOUIS, MO., APRIL, 1917

The Socialist Party of the United States in the present grave crisis, solemnly reaffirm its allegiance to the principle of internationalism and working-class solidarity the world over, and proclaims its unalterable opposition to the war just declared by the Government of the United States.

Modern wars as a rule have been caused by the commercial and financial rivalry and intrigues of the capitalist interests in the different countries. Whether they have been frankly waged as wars of aggression or have been hypocritically represented as wars of "defense," they have always been made by the classes and fought by the masses. Wars bring wealth and power to the ruling classes, and suffering, death and demoralization to the workers.

They breed a sinister spirit of passion, unreason, race hatred and false patriotism. They obscure the struggles of the workers for life, liberty and social justice. They tend to sever the vital bonds of solidarity between them and their brothers in other countries, to destroy their organizations and to curtail their civic and political rights and liberties.

The Socialist Party of the United States is unalterably opposed to the system of exploitation and class rule which is upheld and strengthened by military power and sham national patriotism. We, therefore, call upon the workers of all countries to refuse support to their governments in their wars. The wars of the contending national groups of capitalists are not the concern of the workers. The only struggle which would justify the workers in taking up arms is the great struggle of the working class of the world to free itself from economic exploitation and political oppression, and we particularly warn the workers against the snare and delusion of so-called defensive warfare. As against the false doctrine of national patriotism we uphold the ideal of international working-class solidarity. In support of capitalism, we will not willingly give a single life or a single dollar; in support of the struggle of the workers for freedom we pledge our all.

The mad orgy of death and destruction which is now convulsing unfortunate Europe was caused by the conflict of capitalist interests in the European countries.

In each of these countries, the workers were oppressed and exploited. They produced enormous wealth but the bulk of it was withheld from them by the owners of the industries. The workers were thus deprived of the means to repurchase the wealth which they themselves had created.

The capitalist class of each country was forced to look for foreign markets to dispose of the accumulated "surplus" wealth. The huge profits made by the capitalists could no longer be profitably reinvested in their own countries, hence, they were driven to look for foreign fields of investment. The geographical boundaries of each modern capitalist country thus became too narrow for the industrial and commercial operations of its capitalist class.

The efforts of the capitalists of all leading nations were, therefore, centered upon the domination of the world markets. Imperialism became the dominant note in the politics of Europe. The acquisition of colonial possessions and the extension of spheres of commercial and political influence became the object of diplomatic intrigues and the cause of constant clashes between nations.

The acute competition between the capitalist powers of the earth, their jealousies and distrusts of one another and the fear of the rising power of the working class forced each of them to arm to the teeth. This led to the mad rivalry of armament, which, years before the outbreak of the present war, had turned the leading countries of Europe into armed camps with standing armies of many millions, drilled and equipped for war in times of "peace."

Capitalism, imperialism and militarism had thus laid the foundation of an inevitable general conflict in Europe. The ghastly war in Europe was not caused by an accidental event, nor by the policy or institutions of any single nation. It was the logical outcome of the competitive capitalist system.

The 6,000,000 men of all countries and races who have been ruthlessly slain in the first thirty months of this war, the millions of others who have been crippled and maimed, the vast treasures of wealth that have been destroyed, the untold misery and sufferings of Europe, have not been sacrifices exacted in a struggle for principles or ideals, but wanton offerings upon the altar of private profit.

The forces of capitalism which have led to the war in Europe are even more hideously transparent in the war recently provoked by the ruling class of this country.

When Belgium was invaded, the government enjoined upon the people of this country the duty of remaining neutral, thus clearly demonstrating that the "dictates of humanity," and the fate of small nations and of democratic institutions were matters that did not concern it. But when our enormous war traffic was seriously threatened, our government calls upon us to rally to the "defense of democracy and civilization."

Our entrance into the European War was instigated by the predatory capitalists in the United States who boast of the enormous profit of $7,000,000,000 from the manufacture and sale of munitions and war supplies and from the exportation of American food stuffs and other necessaries. They are also deeply interested in the continuance of war and the success of the Allied arms through their huge loans to the governments of the Allied powers and through other commercial ties. It is the same interests which strive for imperialistic domination of the Western Hemisphere.

The war of the United States against Germany cannot be justified even on the plea that it is a war in defense of American rights or American "honor." Ruthless as the unrestricted submarine war policy of the German government was and is, it is not an invasion of the rights of the American people, as such, but only an interference with the opportunity of certain groups of American capitalists to coin cold profits out of the blood and sufferings of our fellow men in the warring countries of Europe.

It is not a war against the militarist regime of the Central Powers. Militarism can never be abolished by militarism.

It is not a war to advance the cause of democracy in Europe. Democracy can never be imposed upon any country by a foreign power by force of arms.

It is cant and hypocrisy to say that the war is not directed against the German people, but against the Imperial Government of Germany. If we send an armed force to the battlefields of Europe, its cannon will mow down the masses of the German people and not the Imperial German Government.

Our entrance into the European conflict at this time will serve only to multiply the horrors of the war, to increase the toll of death and destruction and to prolong the fiendish slaughter. It will bring death, suffering and destitution to the people of the United States and particularly to the working class. It will give the powers of reaction in this country the pretext for an attempt to throttle our rights and to crush our democratic institutions, and to fasten upon this country a permanent militarism.

The working class of the United States has no quarrel with the working class of Germany or of any other country. The people of the United States have no quarrel with the people of Germany or any other country. The American people did not want and do not want this war. They have not been consulted about the war and have had no part in declaring war. They have been plunged into this war by the trickery and treachery of the ruling class of the country through its representatives in the National Administration and National Congress, its demagogic agitators, its subsidized press, and other servile instruments of public expression.

We brand the declaration of war by our government as a crime against the people of the United States and against the nations of the world.

In all modern history there has been no war more unjustifiable than the war in which we are about to engage.

No greater dishonor has ever been forced upon a people than that which the capitalist class is forcing upon this nation against its will.

In harmony with these principles, the Socialist Party emphatically rejects the proposal that in time of war the workers should suspend their struggle for better conditions. On the contrary, the acute situation created by war calls for an even more vigorous prosecution of the class struggle, and we recommend to the workers and pledge ourselves to the following course of action:

1. Continuous, active, and public opposition to the war through demonstrations, mass petitions, and all other means within our power.

2. Unyielding opposition to all proposed legislation for military or industrial conscription. Should such conscription be forced upon the people we pledge ourselves to continuous efforts for the repeal of such laws and to the support of all mass movements in opposition to conscription. We pledge ourselves to oppose with all our strength any attempt to raise money for payment of war expense by taxing the necessaries of life or issuing bonds which will put the burden upon future generations. We demand that the capitalist class, which is responsible for the war, pay its cost. Let those who kindled the fire, furnish the fuel.

3. Vigorous resistance to all reactionary measures, such as censorship of press and mails, restriction of the rights of free speech, assemblage, and organization, or compulsory arbitration and limitation of the right to strike.

4. Consistent propaganda against military training and militaristic teaching in the public schools.

5. Extension of the campaign of education among the workers to organize them into strong, class-conscious, and closely unified political and industrial organizations, to enable them by concerted

and harmonious mass action to shorten this war and to establish lasting peace.

6. Widespread educational propaganda to enlighten the masses as to the true relation between capitalism and war, and to rouse and organize them for action, not only against present war evils, but for the prevention of future wars and for the destruction of the causes of war.

7. To protect the masses of the American people from the pressing danger of starvation which the war in Europe has brought upon them, and which the entry of the United States has already accentuated, we demand —

(a) The restriction of food exports so long as the present shortage continues, the fixing of maximum prices and whatever measures may be necessary to prevent the food speculators from holding back the supplies now in their hands;

(b) The socialization and democratic management of the great industries concerned with the production, transportation, storage, and the marketing of food and other necessaries of life;

(c) The socialization and democratic management of all land and other natural resources now held out of use for monopolistic or speculative profit.

These measures are presented as means of protecting the workers against the evil results of the present war. The danger of recurrence of war will exist as long as the capitalist system of industry remains in existence. The end of wars will come with the establishment of socialized industry and industrial democracy the world over. The Socialist Party calls upon all the workers to join it in its struggle to reach this goal, and thus bring into the world a new society in which peace, fraternity, and human brotherhood will be the dominant ideals.

Document No. 5

MANIFESTO OF THE SOCIALIST PARTY ADOPTED AT THE NATIONAL EMERGENCY CONVENTION, CHICAGO, SEPTEMBER, 1919

The capitalist class is now making its last stand in its history. It was intrusted with the government of the world. It is responsible for the prevailing chaos. The events of recent years have conclusively demonstrated that capitalism is bankrupt, it has become a dangerous impedient to progress and human welfare. The working class alone has the power to redeem and to save the world.

In every modern country, whether monarchial or republican in form, the capitalist class was in control, monopolized the national wealth and directed the industrial processes.

Its rule has been one of oppression, disorder and civil and international strife.

The capitalist interests of every leading nation fully exploited the resources of their country and reduced their peoples to wretchedness and then set out to conquer the markets of the world for the sale of their surplus commodities, for the investment of their surplus capital and for the acquisition of additional sources of raw materials and national wealth.

Struggle for Market Grows Desperate

A new era dawned upon the world, the mad era of capitalist imperialism. The weak peoples of the globe were subjugated by the strong nations. Asia, Africa, Central and South America with their hundreds of millions of peaceful inhabitants were forcibly parcelled out into colonies, so-called — protectorates and spheres of influence for the capitalist conquerers.

The struggle for foreign markets became ever more desperate and acute. A violent clash among competing imperialistic nations became even more imminent and threatening.

The great rival powers of the world were uneasily and distrustfully watching each other and arming against each other. Millions of workers were taken from productive labor and trained in the savage art of killing their fellowmen. Civilizing and life-sustaining activities were subordinated to the mad race for military and naval supremacy. The nations of Europe groaned under the oppressive burdens of great armaments and became frantic with fear of mutual attacks. Capitalism in its full development caused human society to revert to the primitive conditions of savage tribal warfare.

Statesmen at Versailles Blinded by Greed

Then came the inevitable collapse. The world was precipitated into the most savage and inhuman slaughter in history.

Millions of young men were killed. Millions more were maimed and crippled. Countries were devastated and depopulated. Industries were disorganized. Famine, disease and misery ravaged the people of many lands.

Finally, the ghastly combat ended. The Central Powers, vanquished and exhausted, laid down their arms. Imperialistic statesmen of victorious Allies dictated a so-called peace. It is a peace of hatred and violence, a peace of vengeance and strangulation. The reactionary statesmen at the Versailles Peace Conference were blinded by greed, passion and fear. They refused to heed the terrible lesson of the Great War. They have left open the old international sores and have inflicted innumerable and grievous new wounds upon a distracted world.

To strengthen their precarious rule of violence and reaction, the triumphant representatives of Allied capitalism have created an executive committee of their governments, which they have the insolence to parade under the counterfeit label of a League of Nations.

WEAKER NATIONS WILL BE BULLIED

The true aim of this alliance of capitalist powers is to safeguard their plunder, to bully and dominate the weak nations, to crush proletarian governments and to thwart everywhere the movements of the working class.

It was the world-wide struggle between the working class and the capitalist class which dictated the decisions of the Versailles Conference. This is clearly shown on the one hand by the desperate attempts to crush Soviet Russia and by the destruction of Soviet Hungary, on the other hand, by its recognition of the unsocialistic coalition government of Germany.

The so-called League of Nations is the capitalist black international against the rise of the working class. It is the conscious alliance of the capitalists of all nations against the workers of all nations.

WORKERS MUST REBUILD SOCIAL ORDER

It now becomes more than ever the immediate task of international Socialism to accelerate and organize the inevitable transfer of political and industrial power from the capitalist class to the workers. The workers must reorganize the economic structure of human society by eliminating the institution of the private ownership of natural wealth and of the machinery of industry, the essence of the war breeding system of international commercial rivalry. The workers of the world must reorganize the economic structure of human society by making the natural wealth and the machinery of industry the collective property of all.

The workers of the world are already ushering in the new order of true civilization.

The workers of Germany and Austria are now the dominant political powers. While the leaders of the workers of these two countries have as yet proved too timid to use their political power for the abolition of economic exploitation, the masses are showing an ever-increasing determination to end the impossible government copartnership between capital and labor and to establish in its place a genuine Socialist industrial democracy.

The workers of Great Britain, France and Italy, the workers of the newly created nations, and the workers of the countries which remained neutral during the war, are all in a state of unprecedented unrest. In different ways, and by different methods, either blindly impelled by the inexorable conditions which confront them, or clearly recognizing their revolutionary aims, they are abandoning their temporizing programs of pre-war labor reform. They are determined to control the industries, which means control of the governments.

In the United States, capitalism has emerged from the war more reactionary and aggressive, more insolent and oppressive, than it has ever been.

Having entered the war "to make the world safe for democracy," our government has enthusiastically allied itself with the most reactionary imperialism of Europe and Asia. In the preparation of the infamous Peace Treaty, acts of violence and of plunder were sanctioned by our peace delegates. Acts of infamy were masked by our eloquent President in idealistic and sanctimonious phrases.

And, while thus serving as an accomplice of black reaction abroad, our Administration and the capitalist interests behind it were busily engaged in the ruthless work of suppressing civil rights and liberties at home.

PATRIOTISM SCREENS CAPITALISTS

Under the pretext of wartime necessity, Congress and State Legislatures enacted drastic laws, which effectively nullified the right of political criticism and opposition, freedom of speech, of the press and of assemblage. Although these laws were clearly unconstitutional, our courts skilfully avoided declaring them invalid. The Socialist Party, which during the war was the only party of peace and progress and the sole political defender of civil rights and labor's interests in the United States, was brutally outlawed. Its press was crippled, many of its meetings were dispersed, a great number of its defenders were persecuted and jailed.

Under the cloak of false patriotism and behind a barrage of terroristic jingo sentiment, deliberately incited by them, the capitalists of America launched an orgy of profiteering which all but ruined the nation. The administration permitted a relatively small number of men to make profits amounting to billions of dollars, while the price of the necessaries of life rose to overwhelming heights.

While the war created thousands of new millionaires, the short sighted workers of the United States were appeased by increases of their nominal wages, which left them behind their pre-war standards of life. While the vain, conservative labor leaders were bribed by meaningless posts of honor, the courageous spokesmen for the radical labor groups were put behind prison bars.

SPIRIT OF REVOLT GROWS STEADILY

It is not surprising, therefore, that the end of the war has found the organized workers of America far behind their brothers in Europe, who are everywhere strengthening their forces to throw off the chains of industrial and political subjugation.

But even in the United States the symptoms of a rebellious spirit in the ranks of the working masses are rapidly mutiplying. The widespread and extensive strikes for better labor conditions, the demand of the 2,000,000 railway workers to control their industry, the sporadic formation of labor parties apparently, though not fundamentally, in opposition to the political parties of the possessing class, are promising indications of a definite tendency on the part of American labor to break away from its reactionary and futile leadership and to join in the great emancipating movement of the more advanced revolutionary workers of the world.

PRO-WAR SOCIALISTS REPUDIATED

Recognizing this crucial situation at home and abroad, the Socialist Party of the United States at its first National Convention after the war, squarely takes its position with the uncompromising section of the International Socialist movement. We unreservedly reject the policy of those Socialists who supported their belligerent capitalist governments on the plea of "National Defense," and who entered into demoralizing compacts for so-called civil peace with the exploiters of labor during the war and continued a political alliance with them after the war.

We, the organized Socialists of America *declare our solidarity with the revolutionary workers of Russia —

In the support of the government of their Soviets, with the radical Socialists of Germany, Austria and Hungary in their efforts to establish working-class rule in their countries, and with those Socialist organizations in England, France, Italy and other countries, who during the war as after the war, have remained true to the principles of uncompromising international Socialism.

The people of Russia, like the American Colonists in 1776, were driven by their rulers to the use of violent methods to obtain and maintain their freedom. The Socialist Party calls upon the workers of the United States to do all in their power to restore and maintain our civil rights to the end that the transition from capitalism to Socialism may be effected without resort to the drastic measures made necessary by autocratic despotism.

RUSSIAN BLOCKADE MUST BE LIFTED

We are utterly opposed to the so-called League of Nations. Against this international alliance of capitalistic governments, we hold out to the world the ideal of a federation of free and equal Socialist nations.

A genuine and lasting peace can be built only upon the basis of reconciliation among the peoples of the warring nations and their mutual co-operation in the task of reconstructing the shattered world.

We emphatically protest against all military, material or moral support which our government is extending to Czarist counter-revolutionists in Russia, and reactionary powers in Hungary, and demand the immediate lifting of the indefensible and inhuman blockade of those countries.

We demand the unconditional and immediate liberation of all class war prisoners convicted under the infamous Espionage Law and other repressive legislation.

We demand the immediate and unconditional release of all conscientious objectors.

We demand the full restoration to the American people of their constitutional rights and liberties.

* Other texts read: "pledge our support to."

WORKERS MUST TAKE INDUSTRIES

The great purpose of the Socialist Party is to wrest the industries and the control of the Government of the United States from the capitalists and their retainers. It is our purpose to place industry and government in the control of the workers with hand and brain, to be administered for the benefit of the whole community.

To insure the triumph of Socialism in the United States the bulk of the American workers must be strongly organized politically as Socialists, in constant, clearcut and oppressive opposition to all parties of the possessing class. They must be strongly organized in the economic field on broad industrial lines, as one powerful and harmonious class organization, co-operating with the Socialist Party, and ready in cases of emergency to reinforce the political demands of the working class by industrial action.

To win the American workers from their ineffective and demoralizing leadership, to educate them to an enlightened understanding of their own class interests, and to train and assist them to organize politically and industrially on class lines, in order to effect their emancipation, that is the supreme task confronting the Socialist Party of America.

To this great task, without deviation or compromise, we pledge all our energies and resources. For its accomplishments we call for the support and co-operation of the workers of America and of all other persons desirous of ending the insane rule of capitalism before it has the opportunity to precipitate humanity into another cataclysm of blood and ruin.

Long live the International Socialist Revolution, the only hope of the suffering world!

Document No. 6

MAJORITY REPORT REJECTED BY THE MEMBERSHIP OF PARTY BY REFERENDUM AFTER SUBMISSION TO THE EMERGENCY NATIONAL CONVENTION HELD AT CHICAGO, IN SEPTEMBER, 1919

The Second International is no more. We repudiate the Berne Conference as retrograde and failing to act in the interests of the working class. It is the duty of the Socialist Party of the United States actively to participate in the speediest possible convocation of an International Socialist Congress and to make every effort to reconstitute the functioning of the International.

In the reconstituted Socialist International only those organizations and parties should be given representation which declare their strict adherence by word and deed to the principle of the class struggle.

To such an International must be invited the Communist parties of Russia and Germany, and those Socialist parties in all countries which subscribe to the principle of the class struggle. No party which participates in a government coalition with the parties of the bourgeoisie shall be invited.

In such Congress our party should urge the reconstruction of world-wide organization of the Socialist proletariat upon closer and firmer lines than have prevailed in the past, to the end that the revolutionary proletarian forces of the world may at every critical moment be effectively mobilized for simultaneous and harmonious action.

Document No. 7

MINORITY REPORT ADOPTED BY OVERWHELMING PARTY VOTE ON REFERENDUM AFTER SUBMISSION TO THE EMERGENCY NATIONAL CONVENTION HELD AT CHICAGO, SEPTEMBER, 1919

We consider that the Second International ceased to function as an International Socialist body upon the outbreak of the World War.

All efforts to bring together the elements that made up the former International have only added strength to this conviction. The Berne Conference was a notable example of this collapse, especially with reference to its failure to take a helpful attitude toward Russia, and its policy of hanging onto the tails of the Peace Conference in Paris and placid acceptance of rebuffs given it by members of that conference, the refusal of Russian passports, for instance.

Any International, to be effective in this crisis, must contain only those elements who take their stand unreservedly upon the basis of the class struggle, and their adherence to this principle is not mere lip loyalty.

When leading Socialists join their national governments upon a coalition basis they accept and sanction policies which hinder Socialists and the working class generally from taking full advantage of the opportunities for deep-seated change which the war creates. This makes the workers content with superficial reformist changes which are readily granted by the capitalist class as a means of self-protection from the rising tide of working class revolt.

And when Socialists use the military organization of the master class as a means of crushing the agitation of their more radical comrades, they flatly take their position with the counter-revoluaries whom they serve.

The Second International is dead. We consider that a new International which contains those groups which contributed to the downfall of our former organization must be so weak in its Socialist policy as to be useless.

The Socialist Party of the United States, in principle and in its past history, has always stood with those elements of other countries that remained true to their principles. The manifestoes, adopted in national convention at St. Louis (1917) and Chicago (1919), as well as Referendum "D" 1919, unequivocally affirm this stand. These parties, the majority parties of Russia, Italy, Switzerland, Norway, Bulgaria and Greece, and growing minorities in every land, are uniting on the basis of the preliminary convocation, at Moscow, of the Third International. As in the past, so in this extreme crisis, we must take our stand with them.

The Socialist Party of the United States, therefore, declares itself in support of the Third (Moscow) International, not so much because it supports the "Moscow" programs and methods, but because:

(a) "Moscow" is doing something which is really challenging world imperialism.

(b) "Moscow" is threatened by the combined capitalist forces of the world simply because it is proletarian.

(c) Under these circumstances, whatever we may have to say to Moscow afterwards, it is the duty of the Socialists to stand by it now because its fall will mean the fall of the Socialist republics in Europe, and also the disappearance of Socialist hopes for many years to come.

CHAPTER III

Activities of the Russian Soviet Regime and its Sympathizers in the United States*

In order to appreciate the significance of the activities of the Russian Soviet regime and its sympathizers in the United States, a careful study should be made of those chapters of this report which deal with the Russian revolution, and the formation of the Third International. It must also be remembered that the Russian Soviet regime is founded upon the principles of International revolutionary Socialism and is simply an achievement of part of the plan for world-wide social revolution. It is the international character of this great movement which renders the activities of the agents of Soviet Russia in this country, and those who aid and abet them, a real menace to the institutions of this country.

For a number of years prior to the Russian proletarian revolution in 1917 a large number of members of the Social revolutionary party in Russia and the Social Democrats emigrated to the United States, coming in particularly large numbers after the unsuccessful revolution of 1905. Revolutionary organizations were formed in the Russian colony for the purpose of assisting the movement to overthrow the Czar in Russia and also to carry on an extended propaganda among the workers of this country in order to win recruits for the International Revolutionary cause. The activities of these radicals centered largely about the Russian Socialist Federation, which was a branch of the Socialist Party of America.

An official organ was established, published in the Russian language, called the "Novy Mir," which was edited by Nicholas Bucharin, now one of the foremost leaders of the Soviet regime in Russia. It was with this publication that Leon Trotzky was associated while staying in this country. Prior to the overthrow of the Kerensky government in Russia, the plans for the coming proletarian revolution in that country were fully discussed and perfected by revolutionary committees of the Russian Socialist Federation in the United States.

During his stay in America Leon Trotzky, then known as Leon Braunstein, was an active propagandist, delivering numerous

* See Addendum, Part I.

lectures before radical audiences throughout New York City and elsewhere. He appears to have been particularly welcome to the German Socialist groups at the Labor Temple in 84th Street and Second Avenue, New York City, and in the Harlem River Casino, 127th Street and Second Avenue. He spoke in both the German and the Russian languages.

On February 2, 1917, in the course of a speech delivered at Beethoven Hall, 210 East 5th Street, New York City, he said:

> "You do not want any militarism or any government which is not of any help to the working class, but which is always prepared ready to fire on the working class, and is the enemy of the working class. It is now time that you do away with it once and forever."

On the evening of March 26, 1917, Leon Trotzky delivered his last speech in this country, prior to his departure for Russia, at the Harlem River Casino, New York City. The audience consisted of about 800 German and Russian Socialists. Speaking in Russian, after having delivered an address in German, Trotzky said:

> "Those who are going back to Russia are going to push the revolution ahead, and those that remain in the United States should work hand in hand in the revolutionary movement in order to bring about a revolution in the United States."

The admonition here given was fully in accord with the principles of revolutionary Socialism. On the eve of his departure to overthrow the democratic regime of Kerensky, Trotzky urged his comrades to continue their efforts to undermine the institutions of this country, so that a proletarian dictatorship might be erected on these shores. The object thus expressed more than three years ago has never been lost sight of by the leaders of the Russian revolution, and the subsequent conduct of its agents and sympathizers in this country has made perfectly clear their purpose to carry out the injunction thus given.

On March 27, 1917, Trotzky, accompanied by his wife, sailed on a Norwegian liner for Russia.

On the following evening at 534 East 5th Street, New York City, a meeting was held at which a committee was appointed to pass upon the character of Russian revolutionaries and anarchists, who sought to return to Russia to help the revolution. At this time members of the Russian Socialist Federation, and those identified with the Union of Russian Workers and other anarchistic groups, worked in co-operation. At a meeting of the committee above referred to on the 30th of March, one Schnabel is reported to have said:

> "I want to tell you comrades if you know anything about any of our comrades, or that they would do any harm to our movement, don't hesitate to tell us what you know about him. Don't wait until some of these dirty sneaks are sent to Russia to work in our movement and then tell us what you know."

The propaganda carried on by the Russian Socialist Federation met with a ready response from the other Socialist organizations throughout the country. Leon Trotzky was permitted to proceed to Russia, and the events leading up to the November revolution in which he participated have been previously described in this report.

During the early days of the war the machinery for investigation and information of Federal, State and local governments was not thoroughly perfected, and the activities of revolutionary Socialists and of propagandists were not closely followed, attention being centered upon the movements of German agents. For this reason the work of spreading revolutionary propaganda was carried on without attracting much public notice.

Conflicting and contradictory reports from Russia indicated that all was not well with the provisional government. The fall of Kerensky came as an unpleasant surprise to the general public, although those informed of the events transpiring in Russia knew that the weak and vacillating policy which he had adopted of necessity led to such a catastrophe.

The cause of the proletarian revolution was immediately espoused by Socialist and anarchist elements in this country. Their propaganda was aided by a number of newspaper correspondents and writers returning from Russia. Among these the most active were John Reed, Louise Bryant, his wife, and Albert Rhys Williams. John Reed returned to this country to assume the post of Consul-General of the Soviet regime. His activities were somewhat interfered with by the seizure of all his official documents by the Federal authorities; but he immediately began a campaign in various liberal newspapers, and toured the country making speeches in which he pictured the Russian Soviets as a new social order destined to destroy the "effete" democracies of the western countries. Albert Rhys Williams, during his stay in Russia as a newspaper man, had also become enthusiastic over the revolution, and had joined the International Revolutionary Propaganda Bureau set up by the Soviet regime in Petrograd. He returned to the United States as an avowed propagandist for that regime, writing numerous pamphlets and making many speeches favoring the recognition of the Soviet regime by the United States, painting its great superiority over the principles of government in vogue in this country.

The work of these two propagandists was extremely well received in liberal circules, and added greatly to the number of sympathizers for the Russian revolutionary cause.

At the same time the opinion of the American public was still further clouded by public utterances of certain members of the American Red Cross Commission, as well as some returning members of the Y. M. C. A. These all spoke in the highest terms of the character and ability of Leon Trotzky and Nicolai Lenin, and also of the efficiency of the regime which they had set up. The utterances and writings of these persons were immediately seized upon by revolutionary groups in this country and widely distributed in all languages to the working classes for the purpose of proving that the Soviet regime was in fact a new and higher order of society.

The extremely wide publicity given to all these favorable statements respecting Soviet Russia has made it difficult to counteract the first impression created, and has enabled agitators to carry on revolutionary propaganda with impunity. The Russian revolution had occurred at a moment critical to the allied cause. The collapse of the Eastern front foreshadowed disaster in Flanders and along the banks of the Somme. It was extremely natural, therefore, that the American public was eager to receive information respecting the new regime set up in Russia, in order to determine whether or not it would continue the armed struggle against Imperial Germany. The opportunity thus given to revolutionary Socialists and those "intellectuals" who had espoused their cause to disseminate "information" about Soviet Russia was unlimited.

The opportunity for propaganda was further enlarged by the proletarian revolution which took place in Finland on the 27th of January, 1918. The government which called itself the Provisional Government of the People's Republic of Finland, although of extremely short life, established the first official, though unrecognized, mission in the United States. According to the testimony of Santeri Nuorteva, (who for a number of years had been a leading figure in the Finnish Socialist Federation, having a controlling interest in the "Raivaaja," official organ of that group, published at Fitchburg, Mass.), he received on February 19, 1918, a cablegram from Y. Sirola, asking him to act in the United States as representative of the newly formed Finnish government. (Pages 1535 *et seq.*, stenographic minutes, Committee Hearings.) Mr. Nuorteva accepted the appointment; and although he received no specific instructions, organized the Finnish Information Bureau, with offices located at 299 Broadway, New York City.

It should be stated that the so-called People's Republic of Finland was a proletarian regime based upon the same principles as the Soviet regime of Russia.

An attempt was made to finance Nuorteva's Bureau by his European comrades, through the sending of drafts by messenger outside of the due course of the mails. Whether any money actually reached Mr. Nuorteva the Committee was not able to ascertain. When examined, Mr. Nuorteva stated that none had reached him. One of the messengers, carrying money for the Finnish Information Bureau, was Carl Sandberg, a radical poet. On his arrival in this country he was searched, and the drafts found among his effects for the Finnish Information Bureau were confiscated by the Federal authorities.

This situation reduced Mr. Nuorteva to the necessity of undertaking an active speaking campaign in order to raise money to support his bureau which issued a bulletin to a selected list of educators, members of the United States Congress and other persons of standing. Although Mr. Nuorteva posed before the American people as being solely interested in placing the truth respecting the Finnish revolution before the public, in reality he had constantly in mind the promotion of International revolutionary propaganda.

This is illustrated by many of the letters which came into the possession of this Committee through execution of the search warrant upon the Russian Soviet Bureau on June 12, 1919. The correspondence with one Charles Samolar, of Cleveland, may be taken as typical. We, therefore, reproduce these letters in full:

"MARCH 7, 1919.

"SANTERI NUORTEVA:

"DEAR COMRADE:—We understand the Scheidemann local here has arranged a meeting for you in Cleveland for March 28th. In the name of the Left Wing, we want you to cancel meeting and we will arrange meeting for you.

"The E. S. S. P. Com. is the Soviet of ten Bolshevik organizations in Cleveland, and since the local is doing their damnedest to sabotage our John Reed meeting, we want to sabotage them as far as you are concerned. They have asked him to cancel same, explaining that we are anarchists, etc. You understand their dirty game. We are demanding Reed to stick to his agreement and if he don't stick with us we will of course have our own speaker.

"The integrity of the Reds is concerned in this matter, for if they succeed in getting Reed away from us, they will have won a victory. We must balk them, and not only that, we must take you away from them.

"They got Fraina here for three meetings and he was sabotaged by those who ran the meeting. They"ll do the same to you. You must therefore cancel their meeting.

"(Signed) E. S. S. P. COM.

"CHAS. SAMOLAR, *Sec'y.*

"Special request for concurrence in above from:

"N. SHAFFER, S. No. 3, Y. P. S. L.
"KITCHIN, President, International Workers Council.
"BILL DEMSON, Twelfth Ward Branch.
"BERNARD TAMARKIN, Proletarian University.
"PAUL POSCHENKO, Russian Branch.
"TONY TRUPPO, I. W. W.
"KARATH, Lettish Branch.
"CASPAR, Lithuanian Y. P. S. L.

"P. S.—Address your answer to Chas. Samolar, 2200 E. 97th, Cleveland, O. Yours in haste."

"MARCH 12, 1919.

"MR. CHARLES SAMOLAR, 2200 *East 97th Street, Cleveland, Ohio:*

"DEAR COMRADE SAMOLAR: — I have your letter of March 7th in which you say that you want me to cancel the meeting which Local Cleveland has arranged for me on March 24th. You state as a reason for this strange request that you want to 'sabotage the Scheidemann Local' because they have been sabotaging some of your meetings. Now, dear comrade, the arrangement for the meeting has been agreed upon by me and Comrade Ruthenberg. I have known Comrade Ruthenberg for years and I know he is a radical Socialist who certainly cannot have anything in common with 'Scheidemann's people.'

"As to the alleged sabotage perpetrated against you and as to your desire to retaliate by sabotage on your part, I do not think it is fair to ask me to be a party to your house quarrels, which I know nothing about and I think it is very unfair on your part to make such squabbles a hindrance to Socialist propaganda work.

"I am interested in presenting the case of the Russian Soviets and in nothing else. I must therefore decline to heed your request. If you would on some other date which we could agree on, arrange a meeting for the same purpose for which the meeting of March 24th is arranged, I shall be glad to speak there and I suggest that we should agree on some date when I come to Cleveland.

"Fraternally yours."

It is evident from this correspondence that serious difficulties had arisen in Socialist circles in Cleveland, and Mr. Nuorteva's attitude on such questions is plainly shown where he says: "I think it very unfair on your part to make such squabbles a hindrance to Socialist propaganda work."

With the fall of the revolutionary regime in Finland, Mr. Nuorteva began to turn his attention to propaganda for the Russian Soviet regime. According to his testimony, after consultation with Mr. Gregory Weinstein, at that time editor of the "Novy Mir," the official organ of the Russian Socialist Federation, he determined to open a Russian Information Bureau, to be operated in conjunction with his Finnish Bureau.

In his testimony before the Committee (p. 1538) Mr. Nuorteva said: "I gave out typewritten statements throughout the existence of the Bureau, and about February of this year (1919) I think I began to issue a printed bulletin." In answer to the question, what were the sources of his information, Mr. Nuorteva said: "Newspaper reports of Russian newspapers; reports of the activities of the Russian Soviet government, which reached me from time to time; verbal reports of people who had come from Russia; my deductions based on my knowledge of the situation in Russia in January, and news I received from time to time."

His typewritten bulletin, he said, was sent to a selected list of three or four hundred persons, while his printed bulletin was distributed widely throughout the United States. The propaganda thus disseminated has unquestionably had a marked effect, and in large measure made it possible for the Soviet regime to open the Russian Soviet Bureau in New York City in April, 1919. In the meantime all the agencies of radical revolutionary organizations had been engaged in spreading revolutionary doctrines, praising the Soviet regime, and utilizing the policy of the Allied governments and the United States toward Russia as a means for stirring up hatred of government institutions in general.

One of the fruits of this propaganda was to bring together various radical and revolutionary organizations, which had previously been antagonistic to one another, in the common purpose of aiding the Russian revolutionaries and in spreading the spirit of revolt in the United States.

This may best be illustrated by a series of cables which, being intercepted, have come into the hands of the Committee. They show anarchist, Socialists and intellectuals vieing with one another in the expression of solidarity with the Russian regime.

The attitude of the Russian Socialist Federation of this country toward the Russian Bolsheviki is evidenced by a cable which was sent from New York on March 2, 1918, addressed to the Council of People's Commissaires, Smolny Institute, Petrograd, signed by Novy Mir, A. Menshoy, as follows:

> "You have our unqualified faith and support. The whole colony is with you. Are ready to organize Red Guard for Russia. Americans will help."

In a cable addressed on the 28th of February, 1918, to Boris Reinstein. Commissaire of International Propaganda, Russian

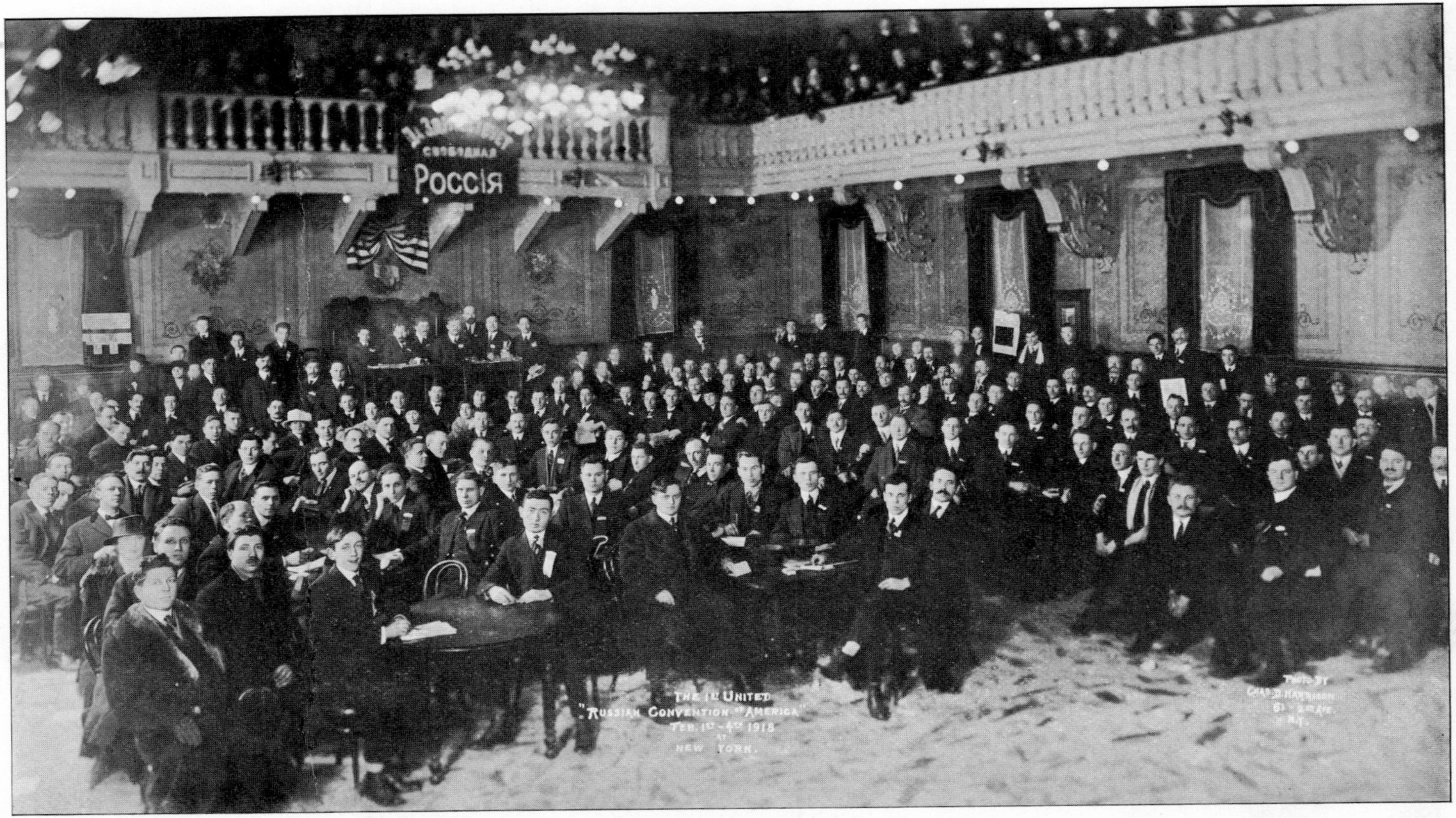

PHOTOGRAPH OF FIRST UNITED "RUSSIAN CONVENTION OF AMERICA," FEB. 1–4, 1918

Foreign Office, Petrograd, and signed by Louise Bryant, we find the following:

"All American revolutionists roused by German advance. Offer their services and their lives to saving of Russian revolution and world freedom. Are organizing revolutionary army mass meetings; tremendous sentiment. Beg Russians to hold out for original peace formula."

A cable addressed to the Council of People's Commissaires, Smolny Institute, on the 2d of March, 1918, signed by Louis Fraina, for Bolshevist Information Bureau, states:

"Bolshevik Information Bureau organized here two months ago to interpret actions of Commissaires and arouse solidarity of American workers with Russian proletariat. Widespread sympathy of American workers with you. Have taken steps to organize Red Guards."

Another interesting cablegram showing the activities of certain groups is one addressed to Lenin and Trotzky, Council of People's Commissaires, Smolny Institute, Petrograd, signed by Rose Baron, for International Social Revolutionary Group, of 319 Second Avenue, New York City, dated the 2d of March, 1918:

"You have our whole-hearted faith and support. Ready to organize and send you international revolutionary army from America."

On the 28th of February, 1918, Louise Bryant addressed to Maria Spiridonova, Chairman, Executive Committee, All-Russian Peasants' Soviets, Smolny Institute, Petrograd, the following cable:

"All-American revolutionists offer their sympathy and their lives to Russian revolutionists in this hour of peril. In your fight against the invaders we are with you to the end. Will come back and fight, and many thousand American Socialists will do same."

An interesting cable was addressed on the second of March to the People's Commissaires at Smolny Institute, Petrograd, signed by Fraina, Rutgers and Mrs. Ravitch, 1562 Madison Avenue, as follows:

"Socialist Propaganda League has unqualified faith in you. Have started recruiting Red Guard for service in

Russia. Great enthusiasm among American workers. Your cause is ours. Cable instructions. Can League help any other way."

At a convention of the United Russian parties held at 175 East Broadway, New York City, on February 1–4, 1918, an Executive Committee was formed, of which Gregory Weinstein was the chairman. On the 2d of March, 1918, Weinstein, acting for the Executive Committee, addressed a cable to Lenin and Trotzky, Council of People's Commissaires, Petrograd, as follows:

"First United Russian convention in America held in New York February 1st to 4th send Greetings to Revolutionary Russia as represented by the People's Commissaires. We are heart and soul with you. Are ready to organize Revolutionary Legions for Russia. Reply."

The interest of the Socialist Party of America, particularly the New York Local, is shown by a cable addressed to the Social Democratic Party, Copenhagen, by Algernon Lee, Educational Director of the Rand School of Social Science, and member of the Executive Committee of the State organization, on the 2d day of March, 1918, as follows:

"Socialists of Greater New York ask you to help convey message to working classes of Germany and Austria-Hungary as follows: 'We beg you vigorously to oppose your rulers' efforts to crush Russian revolution. On you at this moment rests responsibility for success or failure of world-wide efforts for people's peace. German invasion of Russia is blow against labor and democracy in all lands.'"*

Bearing in mind that the Russian Soviet regime is founded on the principle enunciated by Marx, "Workers of the World, Unite! you have nothing to lose but your chains and a world to gain," the establishment of the International Revolutionary Propaganda Bureau in Petrograd may be understood. As a part of the work of that Bureau a letter written to the American workingmen from the Russian Socialist Federated Soviet Republic by Nicolai Lenin, dated August 20, 1918, was sent to America for distribution. This letter will be found in full at the close of this chapter. Many thousand copies of the letter have been distributed throughout the United States in various languages

* The attitude of American Anarchists toward Soviet Russia is disclosed by cables printed on pp. 846–7 of this report.

through the agency of the Socialist Publication Society, with which Mr. Gregory Weinstein, editor of "Novy Mir," is connected, as well as by the newly created Communist Party, Communist Labor Party, and through the agency of the Young People's Socialist League. The letter constitutes a frank appeal to the American working people to forsake the conservative leadership of organized labor, and to adopt the principles and tactics followed by the Russian proletariat in their November revolution.

Lenin labors under no misapprehension as to the meaning of the course which he advocates, for he says, after urging the American workingmen to take up the class struggle: "In reality the class struggle in revolutionary times has always inevitably taken on the form of civil war; and civil war is unthinkable without the worst kind of destruction, without terror and limitations of form of democracy in the interests of the war. One must be a sickly sentimentalist not to be able to see, to understand and appreciate this necessity."

Although the general public was unable to form any very definite estimate of the character of the Russian Soviet regime at that time, the true character of the events transpiring in Russia was known to the State Department through the various intelligence services operating on behalf of the United States in that unhappy country.

The results of the information thus gathered were presented by President Wilson in an appeal to neutrals to assist in ending the Russian reign of terror. This appeal was sent through America's diplomatic representatives to all neutral countries on September 21, 1918, and is as follows:

> "This government is in receipt of information from reliable sources revealing that the peaceable Russian citizens of Moscow, Petrograd, and other cities are suffering from an openly avowed campaign of mass terrorism and are subject to wholesale executions. Thousands of persons have been shot without even a form of trial; ill-administered prisons are filled beyond capacity and every night scores of Russian citizens are recklessly put to death; and irresponsible bands are venting their brutal passions in the daily massacre of untold innocents.
>
> "In view of the earnest desire of the people of the United States to befriend the Russian people and lend them all possible assistance in their struggle to reconstruct their nation

> upon principles of democracy and self-government, and acting therefore solely in the interest of the Russian people themselves, this government feels that it cannot be silent or refrain from expressing its horror at this existing state of terrorism. Furthermore, it believes that in order successfully to check the further increase of the indiscriminate slaughter of Russian citizens all civilized nations should register their abhorrence of such barbarism.
>
> "You will inquire, therefore, whether the government to which you are accredited will be disposed to take some immediate action, which is entirely divorced from the atmosphere of belligerency and the conduct of war, to impress upon the perpetrators of these crimes the aversion with which civilization regards their present wanton acts."

The attitude assumed by this government, as well as the Allied governments toward the Soviet regime, and the lack of any well-defined and fearlessly prosecuted policy which at that period would have succeeded in crushing so subversive and dangerous a movement, enabled Lenin, Trotzky and their adherents to consolidate their power and fasten the chains of their military dictatorship upon an unwilling peasantry.

The revolutionary Socialist elements of America were in constant touch with their Russian comrades, and a continual flow of propaganda material was coming into the United States outside of the due course of the mails.

Military expeditions were sent to North Russia and to Siberia to protect the vast shipments of Allied war supplies and merchandise, which protection gave agitators here an opportunity to invoke the doctrine of so-called self-determination of nations. Moreover, their propaganda was reinforced by the incessant cry of pacifist intellectuals who sought to raise the Russian blockade and to withdraw troops from Russian territory.

In January, 1919, the leaders of the Russian Soviet regime were convinced that propaganda had sufficiently confused American public opinion, so as to allow the establishment of a bureau in the United States for the purpose of directing propaganda looking toward the recognition of Soviet Russia by the United States, the re-establishment of commercial intercourse, and also for the purpose of guiding the propaganda for the International Revolution.

In the first week of April, 1918, Ludwig C. A. K. Martens announced himself as the representative in the United States of the Russian Socialist Federated Soviet Republic, and opened an extensive office in the World Tower Building, 110 West 40th Street, New York City.

The opening of this office was greeted with enthusiasm by radical revolutionaries of all types in this country. The following are typical of the greetings which Mr. Martens received at that time:

"THE SOCIALIST PARTY, EIGHTH ASSEMBLY DISTRICT,
"122 Second Avenue,
"NEW YORK, *April* 21, 1919.

"Comrade L. C. A. K. MARTENS, *Official Representative, Russian Socialist Federated Soviet Republic:*

"GREETINGS: — The members of the Eighth Assembly District, Local New York Socialist Party of America, in regular meeting assembled this 3d day of April, 1919, sends greetings to you and pledge our co-operation in establishing the first representative of the Workers' Government of Russia in America. We also pledge ourselves to work unceasingly for the propagation of those principles and policies and tactics that will aid directly in the establishment of a Socialist Federated Soviet Republic in America. Be it further resolved that a copy of this resolution be printed in the New York 'Call.'

"REBECCA BUHAY, *Sec.*"

In reply to this document Mr. Martens wrote as follows:

"MAY 6, 1919.

"Comrade REBECCA BUHAY, *Sec., Eighth Assembly District, Socialist Party,* 122 *Second Avenue, New York:*

"DEAR COMRADE: — I thank you in the name of the Russian Socialist Federated Soviet Republic for the greetings you sent me.

"I trust that your devotion to the cause of the Russian Soviet Republic will serve the Russian proletariat as well as the proletariat of other countries as a support in their struggle for their final emancipation."

Thus Martens shows himself to be in full accord with the hope expressed for world revolution.

Another letter was addressed to Mr. Martens in a like tenor:

"YOUNG PEOPLE'S SOCIALIST LEAGUE,
"1538 Madison Avenue, New York,
"APRIL 2, 1919.

"*Representative of the Russian Federated Socialist Soviet Republic:*

"Comrade L. C. A. K. MARTENS: — We, the membership of Circle 6 of Manhattan, of the Young People's Socialist League, herewith extend our heartiest greetings to you, and through you to our Russian comrades across the sea. The spirit of brotherhood shall never be stamped out of the hearts of the young. We are ready to meet and battle for the future. There shall come a time when these United States of America will send a representative of their Soviet Republic to Russia. Until then, we are yours for a world revolution and brotherhood.

"CIRCLE 6, MANHATTAN,
"DAVID LEVISON, *Organizer.*"

And a third in Russian:

"RUSSIAN BRANCH OF AMERICAN SOCIALIST PARTY,
"PASSAIC, N. J.

"UKR. FED. OF SOCIALIST PARTY, PASSAIC, N. J.

"ODDZ POL. SOC. PAR. ZWYCIESTWO LUDU.,
"W. PASSAIC, N. J.

"*Greetings to the Representative of the Russian Socialist Federated Soviet Republic, from the Russian, Polish and Ukrainian Branches of the American Socialist Parties of the City of Passaic, N. J.:*

"At a special business meeting of the three branches which occurred on March 31st in the branches' club. No. 118 3d

Street, it was resolved to send to you, as the representative of the Russian Republic in the U. S. the following greetings:

"We, the members of the three branches in the presence of persons and members of the branches, warmly greet you, Comrade L. C. A. K. Martens, as the first representative of the Russian Socialist Federated Soviet Republic. We wish you a rapid success in your activities for the benefit of the Russian Republic.

"We hope that your activities will become a strong impress for the benefit of the entire laboring proletariat of the whole world, and that by your activities there will be established a connection between the American proletariat and the Russian revolutionary proletariat Soviet government.

"We also protest and demand the immediate recall from the limits of the Russian Soviet Republic, of the Allied troops, and the opening by the Allies of the frontiers for the free passage of European citizens to their fatherland.

"*Secretary of Russian Branch,* M. DORESEVIN, (?)
"*Secretary, Polish Branch,* JOE KOSTECK,
"*Secretary Ukrainian Branch,* T. BABAK."

(The signature of the Secretary of the Russian Branch is not distinct.)

To all these messages of greetings Martens replied in the same manner. These documents came into the possession of the Committee through the issuance of the search warrant against the premises occupied by Ludwig C. A. K. Martens at 110 West 40th Street, New York City, on the 12th day of June, 1919.

When examined before the Committee, Mr. Martens stated that he had been duly appointed representative in the United States of the Russian Socialist Federated Soviet Republic, and produced as evidence of his authority a document which he translated as follows:

"Be it known that the Russian citizen, Ludwig Christian Alexander Karl Martens, who is living in the United States of America, is appointed as a representative of the People's Commissariat for Foreign Affairs in the United States of America.

"PEOPLE'S COMMISSARY FOR FOREIGN AFFAIRS.
"(Signed) CHICHERIN and
"*Secretary* F. SHENKIN."

(Page 1494, stenographer's minutes, Committee Hearings.)

In this connection it is well to call attention to the fact that Mr. Martens was and is in fact a German subject.

According to his testimony before this Committee he was born in Russia of German parents and was registered as a German subject. While a student at the Technological Institute in St. Petersburg he became affiliated with a revolutionary organization known as the Union for Liberation of Russian Working Class, with which Nicholai Lenin was identified. His activities in connection with this organization led to his arrest in 1896 and his incarceration for a period of three years. After this, being a German subject, he was deported to Germany where he continued his revolutionary activities in favor of the Socialist revolution in Russia, and was closely identified with the Central Revolutionary Committee, corresponding with both Lenin and Trotzky. He later moved to London, where he was active in international revolutionary circles, and at the outbreak of the war he registered as an alien enemy in that country.

In 1916 he was permitted to go to the United States and entered this country as a German subject. While resident in New York he states that he made application to the Provisional Government of Russia for Russian citizenship. He informed the Committee that the only word which he received concerning action taken upon his application was a letter from his sister, stating that he had been granted Russian citizenship. Acting upon this letter he refrained from registering as an enemy alien during the late war as required by Presidential Proclamation.

It appears from the official message designating Mr. Martens as representative of the Soviet government that he is recognized by that regime as a Russian citizen.

When asked the question: "Is there anything to prevent any resident of this country at this time from acquiring Russian citizenship in the same way that you acquired it?" Mr. Martens replied: "Nothing; only that he be an honest man."

> "Q. So that any person living in the United States who is admittedly an honest man can become a citizen of Soviet Russia simply by proving that he is an honest man? A. Yes, sir.
>
> "Q. There is no requirement imposed by the Bolshevist government that a person make that fact known to this country? A. No."

In other words, any person who adheres to the principles of the International Socialist revolution as exemplified by the Russian Soviet regime, while resident in the United States may make application for and become a citizen of Soviet Russia without any public declaration, or publicly renouncing in any way his allegiance to this country. Whether any large number of radical revolutionary Socialists of this country have availed themselves of this privilege extended by the Soviet regime and renounced their allegiance to the United States, without publicly dispensing with the privileges and protection granted by this government to its citizens, the Committee is not able to ascertain.

When questioned with respect to how he received his appointment, Mr. Martens showed great reticence. He finally admitted that a courier who was not known to him had brought it to his office some time in January, 1919.

Acting upon the authority thus granted to him he immediately set about organizing the bureau, and choosing a staff to carry out such instructions as he might receive from the Soviet regime. As might have been expected, his staff was recruited largely from the most violent revolutionary elements to be found in this vicinity.

The members of the departments selected were as follows:

Commercial Department, A. A. Heller.
Legal Department, Morris Hillquit.
The Chancellory, Gregory Weinstein.
Railroad Department, Prof. J. M. Lomonosoff.
Diplomatic Department, Santeri Nuorteva.

In public announcements Mr. Martens stated that the object of opening his Bureau was to re-establish trade relations between the United States and Soviet Russia. This was undoubtedly a very important part of the program he was to carry out, it being obviously necessary for the Russian Soviet regime to obtain many raw materials and manufactured products available only in this country, in order to supply the wants of the Russian people, to re-establish transportation facilities in that country, and to reconstruct industry.

These things being essential to the consolidation of the Soviet regime and the perpetuation of that form of government, it was obvious that Mr. Martens' first duty was to attempt to re-establish such trade relations.

The testimony taken before the Overman Committee of the United States Senate, as well as information coming through other channels succeeded in bringing home to the American people, in a measure, the nature of the regime set up in Soviet Russia. Mr. Martens' first acts, therefore, as representative of his government was to initiate a nation-wide propaganda looking to counteract this information. He immediately established a weekly magazine known as "Soviet Russia," the object of which was to picture the proletarian government in Russia in its most favorable light. All statements made by reliable observers respecting conditions in that unhappy country were characterized as lies, and an attempt was made in its pages to convince the American people that a new and higher order of society had been created by the working class of Russia.

Members of Mr. Martens' staff accepted invitations to speak at numerous radical and revolutionary meetings throughout the country, and Mr. Martens himself, on many occasions, participated in such meetings. His mission received the hearty support of the Socialist Party of America, and later of the Communist Labor Party. Serious difficulties, however, arose between him and the Communist Party which grew out of a desire on the part of the members of the Russian Federation to control the activities of Mr. Martens in this country. This Federation feeling that it had been in a large measure instrumental in making effective the proletarian revolution in Russia, desired to direct Mr. Martens' activities in this country. This, however, did not fall within the scope of the plans of the Russian Minister of Foreign Affairs, it being clear that Mr. Martens could carry on his work much more effectively in this country if he was not directly affiliated with and subject to the direction of any particular faction of the revolutionary movement. So much was made clear by documents presented to and identified by Mr. Martens in his examination before the sub-committee of the Foreign Relations Committee of the United States Senate, of which Senator George H. Moses was chairman.

In his testimony before this Committee Mr. Martens stated positively that he was a member of the Communist Party of Russia, and that he approved of its principles and its objects. The principles and objects of this party were shown, in Chapter XVI of Section I, to be the realization of the world Socialist revolution; the destruction of the democratic governments of the Western Nations, and the establishment of a world Soviet regime.

It is, therefore, necessary to study the activities of Mr. Martens and his Bureau in the light of the purposes for which it was created. His activities in this country have been carried on with great skill and judgment. In order to effect his purposes it was necessary for him to appear to be conducting his propaganda and regulating his conduct in accordance with the laws of this land. The success of his mission depended in large measure upon his discretion.

Bearing in mind that one of the objects of the regime which he represents in this country is the overthrow of the system of government now existing here, every act which he commits in this country, which is beneficial to the Bolshevist regime, whether a direct violation of any existing statute in this country or not, is unquestionably an act of hostility against the government and the people of the United States.

It is true that the articles published in "Soviet Russia" do not constitute a violation of any statute which has been brought to the attention of this Committee. They are designed, however, to create sympathy for the Russian regime, to make the American public believe in the innocence of its motives, to obscure the hostile intent of that regime. This is effected by invoking the principle of self-determination of peoples, by picturing the desperate straits to which the Russian people have been reduced by the blockade, and by holding out a prospect of vast commercial possibilities, in order to stimulate the cupidity of American manufacturers and business men.

The success of the propaganda which Martens has so skillfully employed is shown by the growing sentiment among members of Congress favoring the recognition of Soviet Russia. The commercial Bureau established under the direction of A. A. Heller has circularized all of the important manufacturing and industrial enterprises in this country, offering to purchase vast quantities of supplies and engaging to pay exorbitant commissions, with the result that legislators are bombarded with requests that trade relations be re-established. By these methods legislators who pride themselves upon being independent thinkers have become the unconscious tools of the Russian proletariat. In other words Mr. Martens has appealed to the sympathy of the American people, as well as to their cupidity, in order to bring about a recognition of the Soviet regime, which would mean giving that regime not only the financial and material support of the people of this untry, but the opportunity through such support to consolidate eir control of the Russian people, and thus enable them to prepare for the final struggle for the overthrow of Western Democracy.

The fact that the Russian Soviet regime had appropriated moneys to carry out a propaganda for a world wide revolution was admitted by Mr. Martens before this Committee, as well as before the sub-committee of the Committee of Foreign Relations of the United States Senate. In excusing this action of his government, Mr. Martens stated that it was adopted as a measure of self-defense against the incursion of alleged counter- revolutionists who had gained the support of the Entente Powers.

Part of the propaganda which he has been carrying on is to state in behalf of his government that this propaganda would be discontinued if recognition were granted, the blockade raised and troops withdrawn from Russian territory. The insincerity of this proposition is made manifest by the fact that the leaders of the Russian Soviet regime are actually in control of the Third International, which has set up a Bureau in Moscow for the very purpose of guiding and directing the activities of revolutionary organizations in all countries of the world.

On the first of May, 1919, Mr. Martens issued a statement which was published in the New York " Call," which in a measure shows his relations with the Third International, and his sympathy with its objects. This statement is as follows:

> " By L. C. A. K. Martens, Representative of the Russian Socialist Soviet Republic.
>
> " On this, the great holiday of the International labor movement, I take the occasion to express through your columns the greetings of the Russian workers and their Soviet Republic to the workers all over the world. The Republic of the Workers of Russia finds itself today cut off from the rest of the world by walls of villification and prejudice and by physical isolation established for the purpose of starving the Russian workers into submission to that economic and political slavery which they threw off on November 7, 1919. Yet no barriers can prevent the workers in various parts of the world from understanding each other. The solidarity of the working class has never been illustrated better than by the whole-hearted sympathy and support which

LUDWIG C. A. K. MARTENS

A German subject acting as Russian Soviet Agent in the United States.

Copyright by Clinedinst, Washington, D. C., from Underwood & Underwood, N. Y.

SANTERI NUORTEVA

Secretary to Ludwig C. A. K. Martens, an able propagandist.

everywhere has been evinced towards Soviet Russia. No barriers have been able to prevent them from realizing that what the Russian workers are striving for represents the highest ideals of the liberation of the working class from exploitation. In the dark hours of the past year the Republic of the Workers of Russia was encouraged in its struggle for liberty of labor by the sympathetic understanding evinced towards it by the workers everywhere.

"On this, the holiday of the international movement, we feel that the night is passing and that the bright day is beginning. The attitude of the workers of the world towards the Russian workers' revolution has proved that the spirit of international solidarity of workers is not dead. It also has proved that the International is not dead.

"It is resurrecting in the Third International in new glory. Long live the Third International."

The interest taken by this Third International in the revolutionary movements carried on in the United States is demonstrated by documents seized from a messenger representing the Third International, who was bearing a message from Zinoviev to the comrades in this country.

A portion of one of the important documents thus seized is here given, and the circumstances attending it may be gathered from the record of the sub-committee of the Foreign Relations Committee of the Senate at pages 413 et seq.

I. Address by G. Zinoviev as president of the executive committee of the Communist International to the Central Committees of the American Communist Party and the American Communist Labor Party:

"From reports of comrades who have arrived from America the executive committee of the Communist International has acquainted itself with the open split between the two American parties. This question has been submitted to and considered by the members of the executive committee, together with representatives of the American parties and the other nationalities. This split is a heavy blow to the movement; unprecedented sacrifices must be made by the American proletariat. The question of tactics is the principal source of disagreement, and this split is therefore unjustified."

Here follows an exposition of the different viewpoints of the two American factions. The American Communist Party principally consists of foreign or so-called national federations and the American Communist Labor Party comprises the English-speaking element.

"With the aim of bringing about unification, the executive committee of the communist international proposes an immediate joint convention, whose decision shall be binding on both parties.

"The following matters are pointed out to American comrades:

"1. The communist party should unite to seize power and to establish the dictatorship of the proletariat. A determined struggle should be made to overthrow the power of the bourgeoisie. For this aim all differences are inadmissible."

Here follows the statement that frank discussion is desired between the various more or less radical groups, but that there must be an absoute final submission of the minority to the decision of the majority.

"The complete break with the old Socialist and Socialist Labor Parties is naturally a condition for the creation of the American Communist Party.

"Individual members or entire groups of these can be received by Communists when they come over whole-heartedly. The Communist Party will be for them the best school for Communism.

"The party must take into account the every-day incidents of the class war. The stage of verbal propaganda and agitation has been left behind. The time for decisive battles has arrived. The most important task confronting the American Communists at the present moment is to draw the wide proletarian masses into the path of revolutionary struggle. The party must have (for its goal) the dissolution of the American Federation of Labor and other unions associated with it and must strive to establish the closest connections with the I. W. W., the One Big Union, and the W. I. I. U. The party must support the formation of factory workers' committees in factories, these serving as bases for the every-day struggle and for training the advanced guard of labor in managing industry."

The amalgamation of the foreign-speaking national federations with the English-speaking party is insisted upon. Being better trained theoretically and more closely bound by the Russian revolutionary traditions, the members of the national federations may in the future have a guiding influence. The employment of the referendum should be reduced to a minimum.

"One of the most important tasks for the American communists is the establishment of a large daily political paper, not for theoretical propaganda in training, but for giving information on all public events from the Communist point of view. The executive committee urges American comrades to establish immediately an underground organization for the purpose of revolutionary propaganda among the masses and for carrying on the work in case of violent suppression of the legal party organization. The fewer people who know about it the better.

"G. ZINOVIEV,

"*President of Executive Committee of the Communist International.*"

II. Agreement for the unification of the American Communist and the American Communist Labor Parties:

"1. A committee is to be established in America for the purpose of uniting both parties, each committee to be composed of three members of each party.

"2. This committee is to call a convention.

"3. The convention is to further consolidation under the name United Communist Party of America.

"4. The convention is to be the party's supreme organ.

"5. The convention is to elect a central committee for directing matters in the intervening periods between conventions.

"6. Party conferences are to be called in case of necessity.

"7. Referendums are considered undesirable during the period of disagreement.

"8. A new executive of national federations must be retained particularly for propaganda among the non-English-speaking masses which must be Anglicized as rapidly as possible. The central committee is to further amalgamation.

"9. Dues are to be paid to the local and State committees.

"10. All present propaganda of the national federations is to be subject to the control of the party's central committee.

"11. The suspension of a member is to be possible only through the central committee of the local party units.

"12. There is to be one federation only for each foreign language group."

The foregoing is dated Moscow, January 12, 1920, and bears the statement that it is signed by the delegates of the American International Communist Labor Party and of various Russian federations.

III. Appeal of the executive committee of the Communist International to the I. W. W., signed by G. Zinoviev, and dated Moscow, January, 1920:

"This communication from the Communist International to the I. W. W is made so that the I. W. W. may understand the Communist principles and program."

Here follows an outline of the common aims of the Communist International and the I. W. W., and a description of recent American legislative measures to bolster up capitalism. It is asserted that the American government and the capitalists are attempting to enslave the factory workers, and that the blood and sweat of laborers must be turned into gold to pay the war debts of the ruined capitalists' governments.

"Unless the workers of other countries rise against their own capitalists the Russian revolution can not last.

"The capitalistic state exposes its real functions as merely protecting capital, this being particularly true of the American Constitution."

In discussing the dictatorship of the proletariat, an argument is made for recognition of the necessity of overthrowing the State and of substituting for it an industrial admnistrative body similar to the general executive committee of the I. W. W.

In discussing the workers' state, a description of various institutions of the Russian Soviet Republic and how they function is given in detail.

Here follows a paragraph on the organization of production and distribution, citing a number of Russian workers' organizations.

In discussing democratic centralization Zinoviev says:

"I. W. W. is opposed to centralization only for the common good of the working class."

This paragraph continues by endeavoring to show how industries and private property must be administered by a centralized authority for the common benefit.

In a paragraph on politics, the "yellow" Socialists are reviled and this declaration is made by Zinoviev:

> "We communists do not believe it possible to capture State power by using the political machinery of the capitalist state."

Zinoviev stated that the general strike as advocated by the I. W. W. is insufficient to wrest power from the capitalist state. Armed insurrection must be employed.

In discussing revolutionary parliamentarism, Zinoviev said:

> "Communists elected to Congress or Legislatures have as their function to make propaganda."

Victor Berger, William Haywood, and Vincent St. John, convicted in the Chicago Federal courts in 1918, are all extolled by Zinoviev as useful examples of the political use of government institutions for communistic purposes.

> "The particular business of the I. W. W. is to train workers for the seizure and management of industry. All workers must be members of the revolutionary industrial union of their industry and of the political party advocating Socialism."

Then follows a paragraph on social revolution and future society.

> "The I. W. W. should take the initiative in trying to establish a basis for uniting all unions having a class-conscious revolutionary character, such as the W. I. I. U. the One Big Union, and insurgents from the American Federation of Labor. They should not repel the attempts of American communists to come to an agreement.
>
> "G. ZINOVIEV,
>
> "*President of the Executive Committee of the Communist International.*"

The interesting feature of these documents is the policy therein revealed of attempting to compose differences between revolutionary factions in this country.

This is further illustrated by other correspondence which has passed between the International Bureau of Moscow and certain revolutionary comrades in this country, showing the central bureau keeps in relatively close touch with the revolutionary activities of parties and groups in other countries.

A sharp divergence of opinion which had arisen between various organizations in the Russian colony in this country, manifested itself at the Pan Colonial Congress of Soviets of the United States, held in New York City in the month of January, 1919. This Congress of revolutionary delegates made up largely from the Russian Socialist Federation, Ukranian Socialist Federation and such groups as the Union of Russian Workers, divided upon the questions of tactics to be employed in carrying out the revolutionary activities in this country.

The leaders of the respective factions were the representatives of the "Novy Mir" and the "Robotchi-i-Kristianin" ("Worker and Peasant"). These differences of opinion were apparently looked upon with great concern by the Bureau of the Third International at Moscow.

A letter taken from the person of a courier addressed to this group illustrates the interest taken by the Moscow Bureau in this matter:

> "DEAR BRETHREN.— We write you in the name of the Bureau of the Third, Communistic, International Committee.
>
> "We have heard about your quarrels and misunderstandings, about the second Congress of the Russian colony, which the 'N. M.' boycotted, about differences between the party and Soviets, etc. Conflicting forces have been created in your work the destructiveness of which you cannot imagine or estimate.
>
> "In the name of our common interests the Bureau of the Third International Committee demands the immediate termination of all quarrels and conflicts, the immediate junction of both papers ('N. M.' and 'R. K.') into one and the immediate co-ordination of Soviet and party labor.
>
> "We know that your quarrels do not rest on questions of principle. All consideration of personal ambition and all factional intolerance must be put aside. You have to aim for the co-operation of large masses of immigrant laborers on the Soviet platform (but not in the narrow sense of a

party), to try to influence American public opinion (information work) and to influence the American labor movement (agitation work). These aims are impossible as long as there are quarrels and misunderstandings amongst you wasting your forces, whilst much depends upon your efforts in America.

"The International Bureau insists on the junction of all groups that stand on the Soviet platform. The work of the party must be done in co-operation with the work of the Soviets. Anarchists, former Menshevists (Minimalists) and Social Revolutionaries, Intelligentsia, etc., who express the wish to co-operate with the Soviets must not be rejected. There must be no splits or separations.

"The legation and Brother Martens are under no control of any local organization; the organizations are only asked to work in entire co-operation with the legation, which is responsible only before the All-Russian Central Acting Committee of the Soviets. There can be no question of any control of local organizations over the legation.

"Along with this letter we are sending you some information and propaganda which immediately must be published.

"With fraternal regards.

"A. MENSHOY
"J. A. BEHRSINSH."

In this letter the initials "N. M." stand for 'Novy Mir," and the "R. K." stand for "Rebotchi-i Kristianin."

Perhaps the most significant passage in this letter is the admonition that "Anarchists, former Menshevists (Minimalists) and Social Revolutionaries, Intelligentsia, etc., who express the wish to co-operate with the Soviets must not be rejected. There must be no splits or separations." In other words, it appears to be the purpose and hope of the Bureau of the International to co-ordinate all of the agencies which seek the overthrow of the present government and system of society, so that this object may be obtained.

In January, 1919, Lenin addressed a second letter to the workers of Europe and America, calculated to stir up a revolutionary spirit in the minds of the workers. This letter as well as the first letter were found in considerable quantities in the office of Mr. Martens, when it was entered pursuant to a search warrant on June 12, 1919, by agents of this Committee.

In his testimony before the Committee Mr. Martens denied that he was engaged in the circulation of these documents. They were, however, freely circulated by the Socialist Party, Communist Party and Communist Labor Party, from which organizations his staff was recruited.

In order to have the record complete we append the new letter to the workers of Europe and America at the close of this chapter.

We have mentioned among the activities of Martens his propaganda to promote trade relations with Soviet Russia. In his first announcements he claimed to be ready to expend in the United States at least $200,000,000; and it developed on examination before this Committee that $150,000,000 which he anticipated employing in commercial transactions was the money in the hands of Mr. Bakhamtieff, Russian Ambassador under the Kerensky regime. Mr. Martens based his claim to this money upon a document which he had received from Soviet Russia signed by Chicherin, as follows:

"REPUBLIQUE RUSSE FEDERATIVE DES SOVIETS

COMMISSARIAT DU PEUPLE POUR LES AFFAIRES ETRANGÈRES

LE 25th *Mai* 1919.

(TO1 4–23–65 — No. 534/k MOSCOU)

"*To whom it may concern:*

"The People's Commissariat for Foreign Affairs of the Russian Federated Socialist Soviet Republic declares that citizen Ludwig Martens is authorized to take in charge and administration, in the name of the Russian Federated Socialist Soviet Republic, all movable and real estates of the former Embassy and Consulates and all properties on the territory of the United States of America belonging to the Russian Federated Socialist Soviet Republic. Citizen L. Martens is also entrusted with the right to solicit and answer claims within the limits of the United States in all cases where material interests of the Russian Federated Socialist Soviet Republic are engaged, to prosecute all civil and criminal cases on behalf of the Russian Federated Socialist Soviet Republic in tribunals, courts and other institutions of the United States of America.

"Citizen L. Martens is entrusted to defray all expenses incurred on behalf of the Russian Federated Socialist Soviet

Republic and to receive all moneys claimed by the Russian Federated Socialist Soviet Republic in the United States of America, and issue receipts.

"PEOPLE'S COMMISSARY FOR FOREIGN AFFAIRS

"(Signed) G. CHICHERIN,

[Seal of the People's Commissary.] *Secretary*

"(Signed) J. LEWON.

"I hereby testify that the above is a true copy of the original document.

" New York, Dec. 11, 1919.

" (Signed) S. NUORTEVA,

Secretary of the Russian Soviet Government Bureau."

Martens' demand on Mr. Bakhmatieff for this money was ignored.

The demands of Mr. Martens to gain recognition from the State Department were also futile.

In the meantime his office which occupied two floors of the building in 110 West 40th Street, New York City, was extremely busy in spreading the propaganda which we have already described.

The personnel of the bureau, other than the heads of departments, is as follows:

Kenneth Durant, Miss Dorothy Keen, Mary Modell, Alexander Coleman, Blanche Abushevitz, Nestor Kuntzevich, Lieut. Col. Boris Leonidovitch Tagueeff Roustam Bek, Ella Tuch, Rose Holland, Henrietta Meerowich, Rose Byers, Vladimir Olchovsky, Evans Clark, Nora G. Smitheman, Etta Fox, Wilfred R. Humphries, Arthur Adams, William Malissoff, Leo A. Huebsch, D. H. Dubrowsky, Isaac A. Hourwich, Eva Joffe, Elizabeth Goldstein, Jacob W. Hartmann, Ray Trotsky, Theodore Breslauer, Vasily Ivanoff, David Oldfield, I. Blankstein.

Mr. Martens testified before this Committee that the funds necessary to pay the expenses of his office were received by him from Soviet Russia. He stated that in March, 1919, he received $20,000; in May $10,000, and in July $20,000, making a total, up to the time Mr. Martens appeared before this Committee, of $90,000. He stated further that this money was brought to him in currency by couriers from Europe, and that his custom was to deposit only so much of the funds in bank as was necessary to pay the current expenses of his office; the money he either kept about his person or in "a safe place."

He testified that he was in constant communication with his government by courier, and constantly receiving messages from his government by the same means. He refused to disclose to the Committee the names of his couriers, their routes of travel or the contents of his reports to his government or the instructions received from it.

In the course of his examination he had recourse to the Court to enjoin the Committee from continuing its examination. This was denied, and when pressed by the Committee to divulge information which it required he again refused. The Committee deemed it of extreme importance and relevancy to its investigation that Mr. Martens disclose the papers which he had received from Soviet Russia, as well as copies of the reports which he had made to his government, because it believed that in this way would be disclosed the full purpose of his mission here, as well as full reports of what he had done to forward the interest of the Soviet regime.

It is particularly interesting to note his testimony to the effect that he had destroyed many of the documents which he had received from Russia, through fear that their contents would be distorted by counsel to this Committee.

It further developed that since his examination before the Committee began, he had caused all of his papers to be removed out of the jurisdiction of the State. An application was made by the Committee to punish Martens for contempt; and an attempt was made to elicit much of the same information from Mr. Santeri Nuorteva, secretary of the Soviet Bureau, and head of the Diplomatic Department. Mr. Nuorteva likewise refused to answer the vital questions, and when papers were prepared seeking to punish these witnesses for contempt of the Committee, they both left this jurisdiction and have not since returned.

This action on the part of Mr. Martens and Mr. Nuorteva has made it impossible for this Committee to determine the extent of Mr. Martens' activities in forwarding revolutionary propaganda in this country. His intimate associates, however, have not been idle. Mr. Gregory Weinstein, the chancellor of his Bureau who acts under his immediate direction, has been active in circulating the propaganda of the Communist Labor Party.

At a meeting held at the Central Opera House, under the auspices of the Socialist Party on March 27, 1919, Mr. Gregory Weinstein spoke in the presence of Mr. Martens, making the following statement: "We have come here to tell Comrade Martens that we have come prepared to take over this great country, just as the working class is taking over Russia."

Although Mr. Martens denies, under oath, that he heard Mr. Weinstein make this statement, Weinstein is duly reported in a verbatim copy of his speech to have made that statement. It is also consonant with innumerable published statements in the "Novy Mir," of which Mr. Gregory Weinstein at that time was editor.

In dealing with this subject the Committee has found it necessary to withhold from the report much of the evidence which has come into its hands, for the reason that it may be necessary to employ it in criminal prosecutions. The purpose of this chapter is simply to indicate briefly some of the phases of Russian activity in this country.

APPENDIX

CHAPTER III

Official Documents.

1. A Letter to American Workingmen.—(N. Lenin.)
2. A New Letter to the Workers of Europe and America.—(N. Lenin.)

Document No. 1

A LETTER TO AMERICAN WORKINGMEN

BY N. LENIN

MOSCOW, *August* 20, 1918.

COMRADES.— A Russian Bolshevik who participated in the Revolution of 1905 and for many years afterwards lived in your country has offered to transmit this letter to you. I have grasped this opportunity joyfully for the revolutionary proletariat of America — in so far as it is the enemy of American imperialism — is destined to perform an important task at this time.

The history of modern civilized America opens with one of those really revolutionary wars of liberation of which there have been so few compared with the enormous number of wars of conquest that were caused, lke the present imperialistic war, by squabbles among kings, landholders and capitalists over the division of ill-gotten lands and profits. It was a war of the American people against the English who despoiled America of its resources and held in colonial subjection, just as their "civilized" descendants are draining the lifeblood of hundreds of millions of human beings in India, Egypt and all corners and ends of the world to keep them in subjection.

Since that war 150 years have passed. Bourgeois civilization has borne its most luxuriant fruit. By developing the productive forces of organized human labor, by utilizing machines and all the wonders of technique America has taken the first place among free and civilized nations. But at the same time America, like a few other nations, has become characteristic for the depth of the abyss that divides a handful of brutal millionaires who are stagnating in a mire of luxury, and millions of laboring starving men and women who are always staring want in the face.

Four years of imperialistic slaughter have left their trace. Irrefutably and clearly events have shown to the people that both imperialistic groups, the English as well as the German, have been playing false. The four years of war have shown in their effects the great law of capitalism in all wars; that he who is richest and mightiest profits the most, takes the greatest share of the spoils while he who is weakest is exploited, martyred, oppressed and outraged to the utmost.

In the number of its colonial possessions, English imperialism has always been more powerful than any of the other countries. England has lost not a span of its "acquired" land. On the other hand it has acquired control of all German colonies in Africa, has occupied Mesopotamia and Palestine.

German imperialism was stronger because of the wonderful organization and ruthless discipline of "its" armies, but as far as colonies are concerned, is much weaker than its opponent. It has now lost all of its colonies, but has robbed half of Europe and throttled most of the small countries and weaker peoples. What a high conception of "liberation" on either side! How well they have defended their fatherlands, these "gentlemen" of both groups, the Anglo-French and the German capitalists together with their lackeys, the social patriots.

American plutocrats are wealthier than those of any other country, partly because they are geographically more favorably situated. They have made the greatest profits. They have made all, even the weakest countries, their debtors. They have amassed gigantic fortunes during the war. And every dollar is stained with the blood that was shed by millions of murdered and crippled men, shed in the high, honorable and holy war of freedom.

Had the Anglo-French and American bourgeoisie accepted the Soviet invitation to participate in peace negotiations at Brest-Litovsk, instead of leaving Russia to the mercy of brutal Germany, a just peace without annexations and indemnities, a peace based upon complete equality could have been forced upon Germany, and millions of lives might have been saved. Because they hoped to re-establish the Eastern Front by once more drawing us into the whirlpool of warfare, they refused to attend peace negotiations and gave Germany a free hand to cram its shameful terms down the throat of the Russian people. It lay in the power of the Allied countries to make the Brest-Litovsk negotiations the forerunner of a general peace. It ill becomes them to throw the blame for the Russo-German peace upon our shoulders!

The workers of the whole world, in whatever country they may live, rejoice with us and sympathize with us, applaud us for having burst the iron ring of imperialistic agreements and treaties, for having dreaded no sacrifice, however great, to free ourselves, for having established ourselves as a socialist republic, even so rent asunder and plundered by German imperialist, for having raised the banner of peace, the banner of Socialism over the world. What wonder that we are hated by the capitalist class the world over. But this hatred of imperialism and the sympathy of the class-conscious workers of all countries give us assurance of the righteousness of our cause.

He is no Socialist who cannot understand that one cannot and must not hesitate to bring even that greatest of sacrifice, the sacrifice of territory, that one must be ready to accept even military defeat at the hands of imperialism in the interests of victory over the bourgeoisie, in the interests of a transfer of power to the working-class. For the sake of "their" cause, that is for the conquest of world-power, the imperialists of England and Germany have not hesitated to ruin a whole row of nations, from Belgium and Servia to Palestine and Mesopotamia. Shall we then hesitate to act in the name of the liberation of the workers of the world from the yoke of capitalism, in the name of a general honorable peace; shall we wait until we can find a way that entails no sacrifice; shall we be afraid to begin the fight until an easy victory is assured; shall we place the integrity and safety of this "fatherland" created by the bourgeoisie over the interests of the international socialist revolution?

We have been attacked for coming to terms with German militarism. Is there no difference between a pact entered upon by Socialists and a bourgeoisie (native or foreign) against the working-class, against labor, and an agreement that is made between a working-class that has overthrown its own bourgeoisie and a bourgeoisie of one side against a bourgeoisie of another nationality for the protection of the proletariat? Shall we not exploit the antagonism that exists between the various groups of the bourgeoisie. In reality every European understands this difference, and the American people, as I will presently show, have had a very similar experience in its own history. There are agreements and agreements, fagots et fagots, as the Frenchman says.

When the robber-barons of German imperialism threw their armies into defenseless, demobilized Russia in February, 1918, when Russia had staked its hopes upon the international solidarity of the proletariat before the international revolution had completely ripened, I did not hesitate for a moment to come to certain agreements with French Monarchists. The French captain Sadoul, who sympathized in words with the Bolsheviki while in deeds he was the faithful servant of French imperialism, brought the French officer de Lubersac to me. "I am a Monarchist. My only purpose is the overthrow of Germany," de Lubersac, declared to me. "That is self understood (cela va sans dire), "I replied. But this by no means prevented me from coming to an understanding with de Lubersac concerning certain services that French experts in explosives were ready to render in order to hold up the German advance by the destruction of railroad lines. This is an example of the kind of agreement that every class-conscious worker must be ready to adopt, an agreement in the interest of Socialism. We shook hands with the French Monarchists although we knew that each one of us would rather have seen the other hang. But temporarily our interests were identical. To throw back the rapacious advancing German army we made use of the equally greedy interests of their opponents, thereby serving the interests of the Russian and the international Socialist revolution.

In this way we furthered the cause of the working-class of Russia and of other countries; in this way we strengthened the proletariat and weakened the bourgeoisie of the world by making use of the usual and absolutely legal practice of manœuvreing, shifting and waiting for the moment the rapidly growing proletarian revolution in the more highly developed nations had ripened.

Long ago the American people used these tactics to the advantage of its revolution. When America waged its great war of liberation against the English oppressors, it likewise entered into negotiations with other oppressors, with the French and the Spaniards who at that time owned a considerable portion of what is now the United States. In its desperate struggle for freedom the American people made "agreements" with one group of oppressors against the other for the purpose of weakening all oppressors and strengthening those who were struggling against tyranny. The American people utilized the antagonism that existed between the English and the French, at times even fighting side by side with the armies of one group of oppressors, the French and the Spanish against the others, the English. Thus it vanquished first the English and then freed itself (partly by purchase) from the dangerous proximity of the French and Spanish possessions.

The Great Russian revolutionist Tchernychewski once said: Political activity is not as smooth as the pavement of the Nevski Prospect. He is no revolutionist who would have the revolution of the proletariat only under the "condition" that it proceed smoothly and in an orderly manner, that guarantees against defeat be given beforehand, that the revolution go forward along the broad, free, straight path to victory, that there shall not be here and there the heaviest sacrifices, that we shall not have to lie in wait in besieged fortresses, shall not have to climb up along the narrowest path, the most impassible, winding, dangerous mountain roads. He is no revolutionist, he has not yet freed himself from the pedantry of bourgeois intellectualism, he will fall back, again and again, into the camp of the counter-revolutionary bourgeoisie.

They are little more than imitators of the bourgeoisie, these gentlemen who delight in holding up to us the "chaos" of revolution, the "destruction" of industry, the unemployment, the lack of food. Can there be anything more hypocritical than such accusations from people who greeted and supported the imperialistic war and made common cause with Kerensky when he continued the war? Is not this imperialistic war the cause of all our misfortune? The revolution that was born by the war must necessarily go on through the terrible difficulties and sufferings that war created, through this heritage of destruction and reactionary mass murder. To accuse us of "destruction" of industries and "terror" is hypocrisy or clumsy pedantry, shows an incapability of understanding the most elemental fundamentals of the raging, climatic force of the class struggle, called revolution.

In words our accusers "recognize" this kind of class struggle, in deeds they revert again and again to the middle class Utopia of "class-harmony" and the mutual "interdependence" of classes upon one another. In reality the class struggle in revolutionary times has always inevitably taken on the form of civil war, and civil war is unthinkable without the worst kind of destruction, without terror and limitations of form of democracy in the interests of the war. One must be a sickly sentimentalist not to be able to see, to understand and appreciate this necessity. Only the Tchechov type of the lifeless "Man in the Box" can denounce the Revolution for this reason instead of throwing himself into the fight with the whole vehemence and decision of his soul at a moment when history demands that the highest problems of humanity be solved by struggle and war.

The best representatives of the American proletariat—those representatives who have repeatedly given expression to their full solidarity with us, the Bolsheviki, are the expression of this revolutionary tradition in the life of the American people. This tradition originated in the war of liberation against the English in the eighteenth and the Civil War in the nineteenth century. Industry and commerce in 1870 were in a much worse position than in 1860. But where can you find an American so pendantic so absolutely idiotic who would deny the revolutionary and progressive significance of the American Civil War of 1860–1865?

The representatives of the bourgeoisie understand very well that the overthrow of slavery was well worth the three years of Civil War, the depth of destruction, devastation and terror that were its accompaniment. But these same gentlemen and the reform Socialists who have allowed themselves to be cowed by the bourgeoisie and tremble at the thought of a revolution, cannot, nay, will not, see the necessity and righteousness of a civil war in Russia, though it is facing a far greater task, the work of abolishing capitalist wage slavery and overthrowing the rule of the bourgeoisie.

The American working class will not follow the lead of its bourgeoisie. It will go with us against the bourgeoisie. The whole history of the American people gives me this confidence, this conviction. I recall with pride the words of one of the best loved leaders of the American proletariat, Eugene V. Debs, who said in the "Appeal to Reason," at the end of 1915, when it was still a Socialist paper, in an article entitled "Why Should I Fight?" that he would rather be shot than vote for war credits to support the present criminal and reactionary war, that he knows only one war that is sanctified and justified from the standpoint of the proletariat; the war against the capitalist class, the war for the liberation of mankind from wage slavery. I am not surprised that this fearless man was thrown into prison by the American bourgeoisie. Let them brutalize true internationalists, the real representatives of the revolutionary proletariat. The greater the bitterness and brutality they sow, the nearer is the day of the victorious proletarian revolution.

We are accused of having brought devastation upon Russia. Who is it that makes these accusations? The train-bearers of the bourgeoisie, of that same bourgeoisie that almost completely destroyed the culture of Europe, that has dragged the whole continent back to barbarism, that has brought hunger and destruction to the world. This bourgeoisie now demands that we find a different basis for our Revolution than that of destruction, that we shall not build it upon the ruins of war, with human beings degraded and brutalized by years of warfare. O, how human, how just is this bourgeoisie!

Its servants charge us with the use of terroristic methods. Have the English forgotten their 1649, the French their 1793? Terror was just and justified when it was employed by the bourgoisie for its own purposes against feudal domination. But terror becomes criminal when workingmen and poverty stricken peasants dare to use it against the bourgeoisie. Terror was just and justified when it was used to put one exploiting minority in the place of another. But terror becomes horrible and criminal when it is used to abolish all exploiting minorities, when it is employed in the cause of the actual majority, in the cause of the proletariat and the semi-proletariat, of the working-class and the poor peasantry.

The bourgeoisie of international imperialism has succeeded in slaughtering 10,000,000, in crippling 20,000,000 in its war.

Should our war, the war of the oppressed and the exploited, against oppressors and exploiters cost a half or a whole million victims in all countries, the bourgeoisie would still maintain that the victims of the World War died a righteous death, that those of the civil war were sacrificed for a criminal cause.

But the proletariat, even now, in the midst of the horrors of war, is learning the great truth that all revolutions teach, the truth that has been handed down to us by our best teachers, the founders of modern Socialism. From them we have learned that a successful revolution is inconceivable unless it breaks the resistance of the exploiting class. When the workers and the laboring peasants took hold of the powers of state, it became our duty to quell the resistance of the exploiting class. We are proud that we have done it, that we are doing it. We only regret that we did not do it, at the beginning, with sufficient firmness and decision.

We realize that the mad resistance of the bourgeoisie against the Socialist revolution in all countries is unavoidable. We know, too, that with the development of this revolution, this resistance will grow. But the proletariat will break down this resistance and in the course of its struggle against the bourgeoisie the proletariat will finally become ripe for victory and power.

Let the corrupt bourgeois press trumpet every mistake that is made by our Revolution out into the world. We are not afraid of our mistakes. The beginning of the revolution has not sanctified humanity. It is not to be expected that the working-classes who have been exploited and forcibly held down by the clutches of want, of ignorance and degradation for centuries should conduct its revolution without mistakes. The dead body of bourgeois society cannot simply be put into a coffin and buried. It rots in our midst, poisons the air we breathe, pollutes our lives, clings to the new, the fresh, the living with a thousand threads and tendrils of old customs, of death and decay.

But for every hundred of our mistakes that are heralded into the world by the bourgeoisie and its sycophants, there are 10,000 great deeds of heroism, greater and more heroic because they seem so simple and unpretentious, because they take place in the everyday life of the factory districts or in secluded villages, because they are the deeds of people who are not in the habit of proclaiming their every success to the world, who have no opportunity to do so.

But even if the contrary were true — I know, of course, that this is not so — but even if we had committed 10,000 mistakes to every 100 wise and righteous deeds, yes, even then our revolution would be great and invincible. And it will go down in the history of the world as unconquerable. For the first time in the history of the world not the minority, not alone the rich and the educated, but the real masses, the huge majority of the working-class itself, are building up a new world, are deciding the most difficult questions of social organization from out of their own experience.

Every mistake that is made in this work, in this honestly conscientious co-operation of 10,000,000 plain workingmen and peasants in the re-creation of their entire lives — every such mistake is worth thousands and millions of "faultless" successes of the exploiting minority, in outwitting and taking advantage of the laboring masses. For only through these mistakes can the workers and peasants learn to organize their new existence, to get along without the capitalist class. Only thus will they be able to blaze their way, through thousands of hindrances to victorious Socialism.

Mistakes are being made by our peasants who, at one stroke, in the night from October 25 to October 26 (Russian calendar), 1917, did away with all private ownership of land, and are now struggling, from month to month, under the greatest difficulties, to correct their own mistakes, trying to solve in practice the most difficult problems of organizing a new social state, fighting against profiteers to secure the possession of the land for the worker instead of for the speculator, to carry on agricultural production under a system of communist farming on a large scale.

Mistakes are being made by our workmen in their revolutionary activity, who, in a few short months, have placed practically all of the larger factories and workers under state ownership, and are now learning, from day to day, under the greatest difficulties, to conduct the management of entire industries, to reorganize industries already organized, to overcome the deadly resistance of laziness and middle-class reaction and egotism. Stone upon stone they are building the foundation for a new social community, the self-discipline of labor, the new rule of the labor organizations of the working-class over their members.

Mistakes are being made in their revolutionary activity by the Soviets which were first created in 1905 by the gigantic upheaval of the masses. The Workmen's and Peasants' Soviets are a new type of state, a new highest form of Democracy, a particular form of the dictatorship of the proletariat, a mode of conducting the business of the state without the bourgeoisie and against the bourgeoisie. For the first time democracy is placed at the service of the masses, of the workers, and ceases to be a democracy for the rich, as it is, in the last analysis, in all capitalist, yes, in all democratic, republics. For the first time the masses of the people, in a nation of hundreds of millions, are fulfilling the task of realizing the dictatorship of the proletariat and the semi-proletariat, without which Socialism is not to be thought of.

Let incurable pedants, crammed full of bourgeois democratic and parliamentary prejudices, shake their heads gravely over our Soviets, let them deplore the fact that we have no direct elections. These people have forgotten nothing, have learned nothing in the great upheaval of 1914–1918. The combination of the dictatorship of the proletariat with the new democracy of the proletariat, of civil war with the widest application of the masses to political problems, such a combination cannot be achieved in a day, cannot be forced into the battered forms of formal parliamentary democratism. In the Soviet Republic there arises before us a new world, the world of Socialism. Such a world cannot be materialized as if by magic, complete in every detail, as Minerva sprang from Jupiter's head.

While the old bourgeoisie democratic constitutions, for instance, proclaimed formal equality and the right of free assemblage, the constitution of the Soviet Republic repudiates the hypocrisy of a formal equality of all human beings. When the bourgeoisie republicans overturned feudal thrones, they did not recognize the rules of formal equality of monarchists. Since we here are concerned with the task of overthrowing the bourgeoisie, only fools or traitors will insist on the formal equality of the bourgeoisie. The right of free assemblage is not worth an iota to the workman and to the peasant when all better meeting places are in the hands of the bourgeoisie. Our Soviets have taken over all usable buildings in the cities and towns out of the hands of the rich and have placed them at the disposal of the workmen and peasants for meeting and organization purposes. That is how our right of assemblage looks — for the workers. That is the meaning and content of our Soviet, of our Socialist constitution.

And for this reason we are all firmly convinced that the Soviet Republic, whatever misfortune may still lie in store for it, is unconquerable.

It is unconquerable because every blow that comes from the powers of madly raging imperialism, every new attack, by the international bourgeoisie will bring new, and hitherto unaffected, strata of workingmen and peasants into the fight, will educate them at the cost of the greatest sacrifice, making them hard as steel, awakening a new heroism in the masses.

We know that it may take a long time before help can come from you, comrades, American Workingmen, for the development of the revolution in the different countries proceeds along various paths, with varying rapidity (how could it be otherwise!) We know full well that the outbreak of the European proletarian revolution may take many weeks to come, quickly as it is ripening in these days. We are counting on the inevitability of the international revolution. But that does not mean that we count upon its coming at some definite, nearby date. We have experienced two great revolutions in our own country, that of 1905 and that of 1917, and we know that revolutions cannot come neither at a word of command nor according to prearranged plans. We know that circumstances alone have pushed us, the proletariat of Russia, forward, that we have reached this new stage in the social life of the world not because of our superiority but because of the peculiarly reactionary character of Russia. But until the outbreak of the international revolution, revolutions in individual countries may still meet with a number of serious setbacks and overthrows.

And yet we are certain that we are invincible, for if humanity will not emerge from this imperialistic massacre broken in spirit, it will triumph. Ours was the first country to break the chains of imperialistic warfare. We broke them with a greatest sacrifice, but they are broken. We stand outside of imperialistic duties and considerations, we have raised the banner of the fight for the complete overthrow of imperialism for the world.

We are in a beleaguered fortress, so long as no other international Socialist revolution comes to our assistance with its armies. But these armies exist, they are stronger than ours, they grow, they strive, they become more invincible the longer imperialism with its brutalities continues. Workingmen the world over are breaking with their betrayers, with their Gompers and their Scheidemanns. Inevitably labor is approaching communistic Bolshevistic tactics, is preparing for the proletarian revolution that alone is capable of preserving culture and humanity from destruction.

We are invincible, for invincible is the Proletarian Revolution.

Document No. 2

A NEW LETTER TO THE WORKERS OF EUROPE AND AMERICA

COMRADES.—At the end of my letter the 20th of August, 1918, addressed to the American workers, I wrote that we shall find ourselves in a beleaguered fortress as long as the rest of the armies of the international Socialist revolution do not come to our aid. I added that the workers will have to break with Gompers and Renner. Slowly but surely the workers are approaching communistic or Bolshevistic tactics.

Less than five months have passed since I wrote these words. It can be said that during this time the world revolution of the proletariat has matured with tremendous rapidity, and the workers in various countries have gone over to Communism and Bolshevism.

At the time of my writing the above-mentioned letter, on the 20th of August, 1918, our Bolshevik Party was the only one which determinedly fought the old Second International, which lasted from 1889 to 1914, and which was shamefully bankrupted during the imperialistic war of 1914–18. Our party was the only one which unqualifiedly took the new road, which leads away from Socialism and Social Democracy, contaminated by an alliance with the brigand bourgeoisie, and toward Communism—the road which leads away from petty-bourgeois reformism and opportunism, which had completely permeated and still permeates the official Social Democracy and Socialist parties, and toward real proletarian and revolutionary tactics.

Now, on the 12th of January, 1919, we find a great number of Communist proletarian parties, not only within the confines of the former Empire of the Czar, as in Lettonia, Finland, Poland, but also in Western Europe—in Austria, Hungary, Holland, and finally in Germany. When the German Spartacus League—lead by its world renowned and celebrated leaders, by such real supporters of the cause of the laboring class as Liebknecht, Rosa Luxemburg, Clara Zetkin, and Franz Mehring — finally broke off its co-operation with the Socialist traitors of the Scheidemann and Suedekum stamp, these social chauvinists (Socialists in words, but chauvinists in action), who forever contaminated themselves by their alliance with the imperialistic brigand bourgeoisie of Germany and with Wilhelm II; when the Spartacus League took the name of the Communist Party of Germany, then the foundation was laid for the real proletarian, the real international, the real revolutionary Third International. The Communist International became a reality. Its formation has not yet been formally established, yet, in fact, the Third International is already acting.

Now, no conscious workingman, and no sincere Socialist, can fail to see what shameful treason against Socialism was perpetrated by those who, in line with the Mensheviks and "social revolutionists" of Russia, with the Scheidemanns and Suedekums of Germany, with the Renaudels of France, and the Vanderveldes in Belgium, with the Hendersons and Webbs in England and with Gompers and Co. in America, supported "their" bourgeoisie in the war of 1914–18. This war has completely revealed itself as an imperialistic and reactionary war of brigandage on the part of Germany, as well as on the part of the English, French, Italian, and American capitalists. They now begin to quarrel between themselves about the division of the captured spoils, about the division of Turkey, Russia, of the African and Polynesian colonies, of the Balkans, etc. The hypocrisy of phrases about democracy and the "League of Nations" is being rapidly exposed when we see that the left bank of the Rhine is being taken by the French bourgeoisie, when we see that Turkey and parts of Russia (Siberia, Archangel, Baku, Krasnovodsk, Aschabad, etc.) are being captured by French, British and American capitalists, when we see that the division of the spoils of brigandage makes for increased hostility between Italy and France, between France and England, between England and America, between America and Japan.

Side by side with these cowardly penny-wise mongers who are stuffed with the prejudices of bourgeois democracy, side by side with these "Socialists," who yesterday defended "their" imperialistic governments, and who to-day confine themselves to platonic "protests" against "military" intervention in Russia —

side by side with them we see in the Allied countries an increase in the number of those who have chosen the Communist road, or the road of MacLean, Debs, Loriot, Lazzari, Serrati—the number of those who understand that only the overthrow of the bourgeoisie and the annihilation of the bourgeois parliament, only Soviet rule and proletarian dictatorship can put an end to imperialism and safeguard the victory of Socialism, safeguard a permanent peace.

Then, on the 20th of August, 1918, the social revolution was still confined within the borders of Russia, and the power of the Soviets, i. e., the whole state power, in the hands of the council of the representatives of the workers, soldiers and peasants, seemed to be (and in fact was), a purely Russian institution. Now, on the 12th of January, 1919, we may notice the powerful Soviet movement, not only in parts of the former Czar's Empire, as Lettonia, Poland, and Ukraine, but also in Western European countries; in neutrals: Switzerland, Holland, Norway; (of those that have suffered from war), Austria, Germany. The German revolution, which is particularly important and characteristic, as it takes place in one of the most developed capitalistic countries, at once took the Soviet form. The whole trend of the evolution of the German revolution, and, especially, the struggle of the Sparticides, the sincere and only representatives of the proletariat against the alliance of the Scheidemannist and Suedekumist elements, with the bourgeoisie; all this clearly shows the historic aspect of the conditions in Germany.

It is a question of either Soviet power or bourgeois parliament, under whatever name (as a national or constitutional convention) it may appear.

This is the world-historic formulation of the question. Now it can be said, and it must be said, without any exaggeration: The "Soviet power" is the second world-historic step, or stage, in the development of proletarian dictatorship. The first step was the Paris Commune. Marx's genial analysis of the meaning and importance of this Commune in his book entitled "The Civil War in France" shows that the Commune gave birth to a new type of state, the proletarian state. Every state at this time, even the most democratic republic, is nothing but an apparatus of one class for the purpose of suppressing the other classes. The proletarian state is the apparatus whereby the proletariat suppresses the bourgeoisie. Such suppression is unavoidable because of the savage, desperate and unscrupulous opposition which is evinced by the landowners and capitalists, the whole bourgeoisie and all its supporters, all exploiters, when their downfall begins, when the exploiting of the exploiters begins.

As long as the property of the capitalists and their power is being protected the bourgeois parliament, even the most democratic parliament in the most democratic republic, is an apparatus for the suppression of millions of toilers through small groups of exploiters. Socialists who are fighting for the deliverance of the toilers from exploitation must use the bourgeois parliaments as a tribunal, as one of their bases of propaganda, agitation and organization, as long as our struggle confines itself within the boundaries of the bourgeois social order. Now, when world history has placed on the order of the day the question of the destruction of this whole system, the question of the crushing and suppression of the exploiters and the transition from capitalism to Socialism — to confine ourself now to bourgeois parliamentarism, to bourgeois democracy, to picture it as "democracy" in general, to cloak its bourgeois character, to forget that universal suffrage, as long as capitalist property is being protected, is merely acting for the bourgeois state — means shamefully to betray the proletariat, to go over to its class enemies, the bourgeoisie, to become a traitor and a renegade.

These two currents within world Socialism, of which the Bolshevik press was already tirelessly speaking as early as in 1915, appears before us with particular clarity when illustrated by the bloody struggle and civil war in Germany.

Karl Liebknecht — his name is known by workers in all countries, everywhere, but especially in the Allied countries, for it stands as a symbol for the fidelity of a leader to the interest of the proletariat, and for fidelity to the socialistic revolution; this name is a symbol for the real convinced, devoted, self-sacrificing, pitiless struggle against capitalism; this name is a symbol for the ruthless war against imperialism — not in words, but in action, a struggle ready for sacrifice, even when one's own country is in the grip of the hysteria of imperialistic victories. Together with Liebknecht and the Spartacides stand everything that has remained pure and really revolutionary among the German Socialists, all that is the most conscious within the proletariat, the exploited, in whose heart the spirit of rebellion is rising and giving birth to revolution.

Against Liebknecht stand the satellites of Scheidemann and Suedekum and the whole gang of despicable servants of the Kaiser and bourgeoisie. They are traitors to Socialism, such as Samuel Gompers, Webb, Renaudel and Vandervelde.

Here we have that upper stratum of the working-class which has been bought by the bourgeoisie, and which we, the Bolsheviks, addressing ourselves to the Russian Suedekums, the Mensheviks, used to call "the agents of the bourgeoisie within the labor movement," and which in America is more appropriately designated by an expression that is magnificent in its expressiveness and striking truthfulness, "labor lieutenants of the capitalist class." The newest and most modern form of Socialist treason has found expression in this feature: In all the civilized countries the bourgeoisie, either by colonial exploitation, or by pressing financial profits from formally independent weaker nations, is plundering a population many times as numerous as the population in their own country. Here we have the economic possibility of the "super-profit" for the imperialistic bourgeoisie. And the fact that this bourgeoisie, to some extent, can use this "super-profit" in order to bribe that renown upper stratum of the proletariat and change it into a reformistic, opportunistic, revolution-scared petty bourgeoisie. Between the Spartacides and the Scheidemanns are fluctuating the Kautskians, the soul mates of Koutsky— in the name independent, in action the most dependent in everything and in all connections dependent today upon the bourgeoisie and the Scheidemanns and tomorrow on the Spartacides. Sometimes following the first mentioned, sometimes the other ones. People without ideas, without character, without politics, without honor . . . a living embodiment of Philistine confusion. In words they recognize the social revolution, but in fact they can not grasp it when it begins, instead of which, in their renegade manner, they advocate "democracy" in general, whereas, as a matter of fact, they are advocates of bourgeois democracy.

In all capitalistic countries, any thinking worker can recognize in this treasonable position, which is analogous to conditions of national and historical nature, just these three fundamental tendencies, both among Socialists and syndicalists; for the imperialistic war and the beginning of the world revolution of the proletariat, has revealed with the utmost clearness these idealogical-political tendencies. * * *

The above lines were written before the base and bestial murder of Karl Liebknecht and Rosa Luxemburg was accomplished by the Ebert-Scheidemann government. These beadles and lackeys of the bourgeoisie intrusted the German White Guards, who were defending the sacred possessions of capital, with the task of lynching Rosa Luxemburg and shooting Karl Liebknecht in the back, under the manifestly fraudulent pretext that he had sought to "escape." (Russian Czarism, which choked the revolution of 1905 in blood, frequently found it a useful pretext, in shooting down offenders, to accuse them of having attempted to "escape.") Simultaneously these beadles vested the White Guards with authority, as if they had been guilty of nothing, since their government, of course, stood above all parties. One cannot find words to express all the vile, contemptible devices resorted to by these creatures who pretend to be Socialists. Evidently history has chosen a course which is to compel the "labor lieutenants of the capitalist class" to "run the whole gamut" of low-down, bestial, vile actions. The stupid Kautskyans, in their paper "Die Freiheit," may talk about a "judgment seat" to consist of representatives of "all the Socialist parties" for they continue to call the Scheidemanns, those beadles, and serf-like lackeys "Socialists."

These heroes of Philistine obtuseness and party bourgeois timidity do not even understand that "a court" is an organ of state power; but the struggle and the civil war in Germany are precisely concerned with the question of who is to hold this power, either the bourgeoisie whom the Scheidemanns will "serve" as beadles and instigators of pogroms, or the Kautskyans, the jurists of "pure democracy," or the proletariat, which will overthrow the exploiting capitalists and break down their opposition.

The best men of the proletarian world international, the unforgettable leaders of the proletarian Socialistic revolution, have fallen, but their blood admonishes new and ever new masses of workers to desperate struggle, if not for life then for death. This struggle will lead to victory. In the summer of 1917, we in Russia passed through the "July days," in which the Russian Scheidemanns, Mensheviks, and Social-Revolutionists also were cloaking the victories of the White Guards over the Bolsheviks, by calling them victories of the "state power," when the Cossacks in the city of Petrograd lynched the worker Veinoff for circulating Bolshevik proclamations. We know from experience, how quickly such "victories" of the bourgeoisie and their slaves cured the masses of their illusions as to bourgeois democracy, as to "universal suffrage," and other such things.

Within the bourgeois governing classes of the Entente we can now observe a certain hesitation. One section of these circles recognizes that the process of dissolution of the Entente troops in Russia, where they are aiding the White Guards by advancing the blackest monarchism and feudal landlordism, has already begun, that a continued military intervention and an attempt to influence Russia by force would require an army of occupation a million strong for a long period, the surest way of swiftly transplating the proletarian revolution to the Entente countries. The example of the German Army of Occupation in Ukraine is sufficiently convincing. Another section of the bourgeoisie in the Entente countries clings as firmly as ever to the idea of military intervention in Russia, together with an "economic siege" (Clemenceau) and of crushing the Soviet Republic. The entire press that serves this bourgeoisie, that is, the greater part of the daily papers in England and France which have been purchased by the capitalists, predicts an immediately impending collapse of the Soviet power, depicts the horror of hunger in Russia, and spreads lies about "disorders" and the instability of the Soviet government. The White Guards, the troops of the capitalists, aided by the Entente with officers and war supplies, with money and auxiliary troops, these officers cut off Russia's hungry center and north from the grain districts of Siberia and the Don region. Famine among the workers in Petrograd and Moscow, in Ivanoff-Voznessensk, and other labor centers, is, as a matter of fact, great. Never have the masses of the workers suffered such depths of misery, such pangs of hunger, as those which they are now condemned to by the military intervention of the Entente, an intervention which is partly masked behind a hypocritical assurance that they will not send "their own" troops, while they are continuing to send mercenaries as well as war materials, money, and officers. The masses could not bear such misery, if they did not understand that they are defending the work of Socialism both in Russia and the rest of the world.

The Entente and White Guard forces are holding Archangel, Perm, Rostov-on-the-Don, Baku, Ashabad, but the "Soviet movement" has taken control of Riga and Kharkov. Lettonia and Ukraine are becoming Soviet republics. The workers see that these tremendous sacrifices are not being made in vain, that the

Soviet power is great and spreading, growing and establishing itself all over the world. Each month of severe struggle and tremendous sacrifice strengthens the cause of the Soviet power all over the world and weakens its enemies, the exploiters.

Undeniably, the exploiters still have forces at their disposal with which to murder and lynch the finest leaders of the world revolution of the proletariat, to multiply the sufferings and tribulations of the workers in the occupied or conquered countries and districts. Yet all the exploiters in the world have not enough power to conquer the world revolution of the proletariat which will bring to the human race a liberation from the yoke of capital, from the constant threat of new and unavoidable imperialistic wars in the interest of capitalism.

N. LENIN.

January 21, 1919.

CHAPTER IV

The Left Wing Movement in the Socialist Party of America

Evidence of a marked divergence of opinion in the ranks of the Socialist Party began to be manifest after the declaration of war on Germany by the United States. These differences were greatly aggravated by the success of the Russian proletarian revolution of November, 1917, the foreign language federations being the first to show marked impatience with the policies of the party leaders. The consequence of these events was the development of the so-called Left Wing movement in the Socialist Party, which culminated in the spring and summer of 1919 in an attempt by the hot-headed and less calculating elements to gain control of the party machinery. While no material difference of opinion existed between the so-called Left Wing elements and the party management as to the ultimate object of the Socialist movement and as to the probable necessity of employing other than parliamentary means to set up the co-operative commonwealth in this country, a very distinct difference of opinion arose over the question of immediate tactics. Whereas, the old party managers believed that America was not ripe for the social revolution and that industrial organization had not proceeded sufficiently to give promise of a successful revolution through industrial action, those who headed the so-called Left Wing movement, inspired by the success of the Russian proletariat, believed the time had come when a successful attempt might be made to overthrow our government by the use of the general strike or, if necessary, by force and violence. This extremely radical tendency seems to have been manifested first in the Russian Socialist Federation, which under the leadership of Alexander Stoklitsky, Oscar Tywerowsky, Michael Mislig, and others, kept in intimate touch with Russian affairs. This was the natural consequence of the part some of its members had played in the Bolshevik revolution in Russia.

The official organ of this federation, the "Novy Mir," had since its inception advanced the principles represented by Lenin and Trotzky; its former editor, N. Bucharin, having returned to Russia, assumed a prominent position in the Moscow government. Leon Trotzky, the Bolshevik Minister of War, was on its staff during his stay in this country in 1917, and Ludwig C. A. K. Martens, now unofficially representing in the United States the

Russian Socialist Federated Soviet Republic, was connected with the paper after his arrival here in 1916. Many members of this federation had returned to Russia and taken part in the November revolution, or had gone to Russia after its success to participate in Soviet affairs.

When Santeri Nuorteva accepted the appointment to represent the Finnish Socialist Republic in this country in 1918 and later undertook to represent the interests of the Russian Soviet regime before the appointment of Mr. Martens, it was to the Russian Socialist Federation that he turned for assistance, and was aided by Mr. Gregory Weinstein, at that time editor of the "Novy Mir."

The result of this intimate relationship between this federation of the Socialist Party and the leaders of the Russian proletariat, was to commit the federation to the policies of the Russian Communist Party.

Evidence that some of the leaders in other branches of the party were beginning to call for a more militant program appeared from several of the party publications and various independent Socialist organs of this period, notably the "Revolutionary Age," which was the official organ of Local Boston, Socialist Party; "Der Kampf," the official organ of the Jewish Socialist Federation; and the publications of the Socialist Publication Society, which included the monthly magazine known as the "Class Struggle," as well as many pamphlets and leaflets designed to impress upon their readers that the Bolsheviki were the true representatives of the working-class of the world. The so-called Left Wing movement, as such, however, was crystallized on February 15, 1919, when certain delegates from Local Kings and Queens, New York City, to the Central Committee of Greater New York bolted the meeting and procured a hall in the Rand School of Social Science, 7 East 15th Street. There they elected a Committee of Fourteen to prepare resolutions and manifestos. This committee was authorized to call meetings in the various boroughs to discuss the formation of a Left Wing organization within the Socialist Party.

The committee proceeded to do this, a draft of the manifesto and program appeared, and a convention was called. The following officers were elected:

Executive secretary, Maximilian Cohen; recording secretary, L. L. Wolfe, later succeeded by Fanny Horowitz; treasurer, Rose Pastor Stokes; financial secretary, Rose Spaniar, later succeeded by Milton Goodman.

A City Committee of Fifteen was elected to carry on the work of the organization, as follows:

Benjamin Gitlow, Nicholas I. Hourwich, Fanny Horowitz, Jay Lovestone, James Larkin, Harry Hiltzik, Edward I. Lindgren, Milton Goodman, John Reed, Joseph Brodsky, Dr. Julius Hammer, Jeanette D. Pearl, Karl Brodsky, Mrs. L. Ravitch and Bertram D. Wolfe.

An Executive Committee was selected to carry on actively the work of organizing the Left Wing Section, which consisted of:

Benjamin Gitlow, Nicholas I. Hourwich, George Lehman, James Larkin, L. Himmelfarb, George C. Vaughn, Benjamin Corsor, Edward I. Lindgren and Maximilian Cohen.

At the convention a manifesto and program were adopted.

To illustrate the nature of this document, we need quote only the following provisions:

> "It is the task of a revolutionary Socialist Party to direct the struggles of the proletariat and provide a program for the culminating crisis. Its propaganda must be so directed that when this crisis comes, the workers will be prepared to accept a program of the following character:
>
> > "(a) THE ORGANIZATION OF WORKMEN'S COUNCILS; recognition of, and propaganda for, these mass organizations of the working-class as instruments in the immediate struggle, as the form of expression of the class struggle, and as the instruments for the seizure of the power of the state and the basis of the new proletarian state of the organized producers and the dictatorship of the proletariat.
> >
> > "(b) WORKMEN'S CONTROL OF INDUSTRY, to be exercised by the industrial organizations (industrial unions or Soviets) of the workers and the industrial vote, as against government ownership or state control of industry.
> >
> > "(c) REPUDIATION OF ALL NATIONAL DEBTS — with provisions to safeguard small investors.
> >
> > "(d) EXPROPRIATION OF THE BANKS—a preliminary measure for the complete expropriation of capital.
> >
> > "(e) EXPROPRIATION OF THE RAILWAYS, AND THE LARGE (TRUST) ORGANIZATIONS OF CAPITAL — no compensation to be paid, as 'buying-out' the capitalists would insure a continuance of the exploitation of the

workers; provision, however, to be made during the transition period for the protection of small owners of stock.

"(f) THE SOCIALIZATION OF FOREIGN TRADE.

"These are not the 'immediate demands' comprised in the social reform planks now in the platform of our party; they are not a compromise with the capitalist state, but imply a revolutionary struggle against that state and against capitalism, the conquest of power by the proletariat through revolutionary mass action. They imply the new Soviet state of the organized producers, the dictatorship of the proletariat; they are preliminary revolutionary measures for the expropriation of capital and the introduction of Communist Socialism." (Page 13 of pamphlet entitled "Manifesto and Program of Left Wing Section Socialist Party Local Greater New York.")

The position taken in this manifesto by the supporters of the Left Wing Section, is one completely in accord with that of the Russian Communist Party. It involves a program which, if an attempt were made to put it into effect, would necessarily result in violence and bloodshed. It was the evident hope of the leaders of this movement that they would be able to capture the machinery of the Socialist Party, and this is made clear by the program which was adopted at the convention:

"1. We stand for a uniform declaration of principles in all party platforms both local and national and the abolition of all social reform planks now contained in them.

"2. The party must teach, propagate and agitate exclusively for the overthrow of capitalism, and the establishment of Socialism through a Proletarian Dictatorship.

"3. The Socialist candidates elected to office shall adhere strictly to the above provisions.

"4. Realizing that a political party can not reorganize and reconstruct the industrial organizations of the working class, and that that is the task of the economic organizations themselves, we demand that the party assist this process of reorganization by a propaganda for revolutionary industrial unionism as part of its general activities. We believe it is the mission of the Socialist movement to encourage and assist the proletariat to adopt newer and more effective forms of organization and to stir it into newer and more revolutionary modes of action.

"5. We demand that the official party press be party owned and controlled.

"6. We demand that officially recognized educational institutions be party owned and controlled.

"7. We demand that the party discard its obsolete literature and publish new literature in keeping with the policies and tactics above mentioned.

"8. We demand that the National Executive Committee call an immediate emergency national convention for the purpose of formulating party policies and tactics to meet the present crisis.

"9. We demand that the Socialist Party repudiate the Berne Congress or any other conference engineered by 'moderate Socialists' and social patriots.

"10. We demand that the Socialist Party shall elect delegates to the International Congress proposed by the Communist Party of Russia (Bolsheviki); that our party shall participate only in a new International with which are affiliated the Communist Party of Russia (Bolsheviki), the Communist Labor Party of Germany (Spartacaus), and all other Left Wing parties and groups." (Page 14 of pamphlet entitled "Manifesto and Program of the Left Wing Section Socialist Party Local Greater New York.")

This manifesto and program is appended in full at the close of this chapter.

This document was thereupon published in pamphlet form and distributed widely in the branches of the Socialist Party, sold by the Rand School of Social Science and other radical book stores, and was reprinted in an issue of the "Revolutionary Age" on March 22, 1919. (See letter from Secretary of Local Boston Socialist Party, dated April 1, 1919, to the Left Wing Section Headquarters, signed by Amy Collyer, Assistant Secretary *pro tem,* Exhibit No. 215, page 454 stenographer's minutes, Committee Hearings.) Also in the "Soviet World" of Philadelphia and in "Truth" of Duluth, Minnesota. (Report of Maximilian Cohen. Executive Secretary to Left Wing Section, dated April 19, 1919.)

Headquarters were immediately opened at 43 West 29th Street, New York City, and a vigorous campaign was carried on to enroll members of the Socialist Party in the Left Wing section.

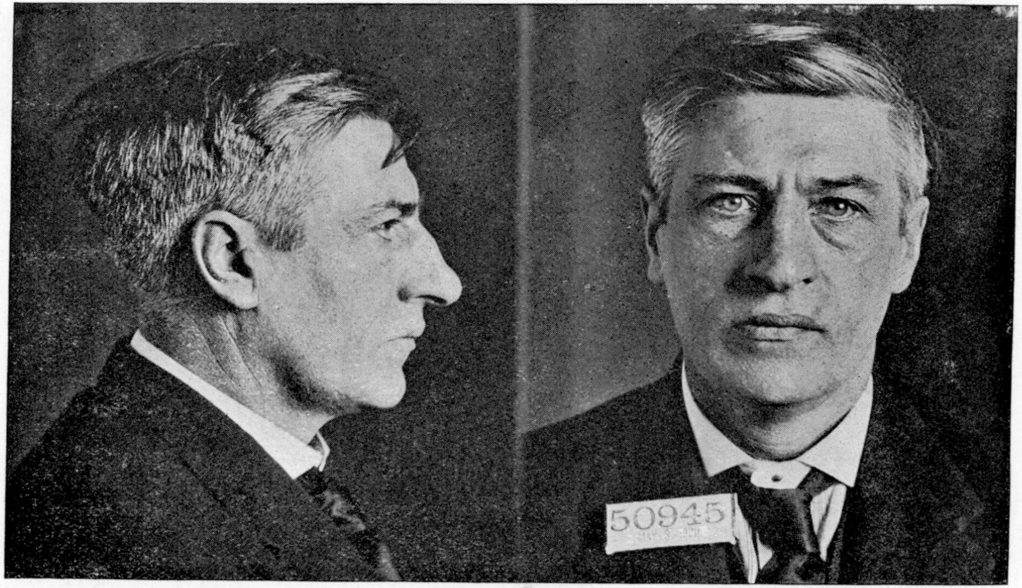

JAMES LARKIN

Member of the Executive Committee of Left Wing Section Socialist Party.

Arrested on charge of Criminal Anarchy by the direction of the Committee, November 8, 1919, tried, convicted and sentenced to State Prison for not less than five years nor more than ten years.

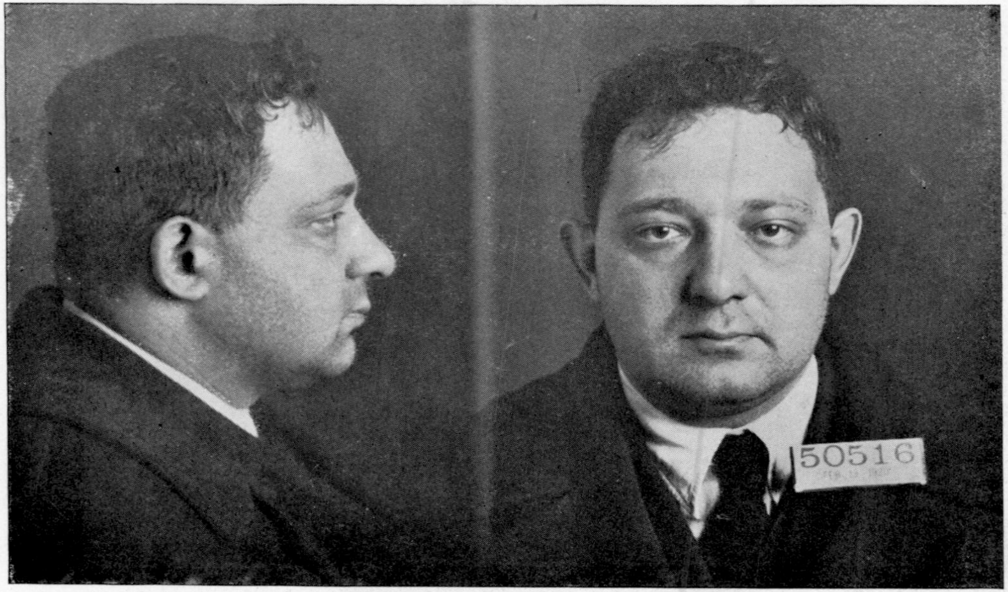

BENJAMIN GITLOW

Business Manager of "The Revolutionary Age," official organ — Left Wing Section of Socialist Party.

Arrested on charge of Criminal Anarchy by direction of the Committee, December 1, 1919, tried, convicted and sentenced to State Prison for not less than five years nor more than ten years.

The radical revolutionary movement thus started appears to have had the full sympathy and support of Ludwig C. A. K. Martens, the Bolshevik representative in this country, as appears from the minute book taken from the headquarters of the Left Wing Section in New York City, which contained the following entry as a part of the minutes of the meeting held on April 20, 1919, at Manhattan Lyceum, 64 East Fourth Street:

> "A message sent to the gathering by Mr. Ludwig C. A. K. Martens, who was unable to attend in person, extending his allegiance and support to the Left Wing movement, was delivered by Dr. Hammer." (Committee's Exhibit 231, Public Hearings.)

In order to insure that the members of the new movement should be in full accord and sympathy with the principles enunciated in its manifesto and program a membership application blank was prepared in the following form:

APPLICATION BLANK

LEFT WING SECTION SOCIALIST PARTY

The undersigned members of the Socialist Party hereby subscribe to the Manifesto, Program and Rules of Organization of the Left Wing Section of the Socialist Party.

Name ....
Street and No. .... County ....
Local .... Branch ....
Age .... Occupation .... Labor Union..........
How long in the party ....
Other Socialist organizations ....
Where .... What period ....

The activity of the leaders of this movement led to the enrollment of a large number of members of the Socialist Party in this organization.

Dr. Maximilian Cohen, executive secretary of the so-called Left Wing Section, reported to the Executive Committee, on April 19, 1919 (referring to the adoption of the Left Wing manifesto and program), as follows:

> "It has been adopted by Local Boston, Philadelphia, Cleveland, Rochester, Buffalo, Essex County, New Jersey, the States of Michigan, Minnesota and Massachusetts, and

many smaller Locals throughout the country, as their platform. In Greater New York we have won some notable victories. Local Queens on April 3d adopted the manifesto and program and joined the Left Wing organization.

"At the next Central Committee meeting they elected Comrades William Ahrens and Fred Scheff as their delegates. Local Bronx after holding three membership meetings finally passed the same resolution as Local Queens and also joined the Left Wing organization."

His report further states that all the Russian, Ukrainian, Lettish, Lithuanian, Esthonian and Hungarian branches as well as the Deutsche Ungarische branch, the Finnish branch, Bronx, Murray Hill German branch, and many Jewish branches, and the Third, Fifth, Eighth and Tenth Assembly districts had endorsed the manifesto and program.

At the time of making this report, the executive secretary states:

"Membership to date is approximately about 4,000, and when all the cards are in from Queens and Bronx and Kings (which is holding a membership meeting in about three weeks when it will go as Bronx and Queens) the total will rise to about 6,000."

On June 21, 1919, the headquarters of the Left Wing Section at 43 West 29th Street was searched pursuant to a search warrant issued by the Chief City Magistrate, William McAdoo, on application of this Committee. At that time, approximately 2,000 signed membership cards were taken.

The propaganda of the Left Wing Section was carried on through the medium of the "Revolutionary Age" in Boston, "Novy Mir" and "Der Kampf," in New York City. Several attempts were made to induce Local Boston to transfer the "Revolutionary Age" to New York City, but on April 1, 1919, the letter of Amy Collier, above referred to, states:

"Local Boston intends to keep the 'Revolutionary Age' in Boston until a National Convention of the Left Wing organization shall be held. Organizations taking part in said convention should agree with the tactics of Bolshevik Russia and the Left Wing manifesto as published in the March 22d issue of the 'Revolutionary Age.'" (See p. 454 of the Stenographer's minutes, Committee Hearings).

In the meantime, an official organ of the Left Wing Section was started in New York under the title "New York Communist," of which John Reed was the editor, Eadmonn MacAlpine, associate editor, and Dr. Maximilian Cohen, business manager. The first issue appeared on April 19, 1919. It states the position taken by the leaders of the Left Wing movement in an editorial on page 2 of that issue, which closes with the following:

> "We take our stand with the Russian Communist Party (Bolsheviki), with the Spartacides of Germany, and the Communists of Hungary and Bavaria, believing that only through the dictatorship of the proletariat can the Socialist order be brought about.
>
> "And in token of our position, we have named our official organ the 'New York Communist.'"

The second issue of this periodical shows the addition of an editorial board, consisting of Nicholas I. Hourwich, Bertram D. Wolfe, Morris Zucker and J. Wilenkin. The last issue of this paper came out on the day of the execution of the search warrant above referred to.

Although the organization of the Left Wing Section began in New York City, it apparently had a wide response from other parts of the country. Local Boston initiated a call for a National Left Wing Conference, which was endorsed by the Committee of Massachusetts, Locals Cleveland, Philadelphia, Essex County, New Jersey, and the City Committee of the Left Wing Section, Local Greater New York. (Report of Dr. Maximilian Cohen of April 19, 1919.)

The National Conference of the Left Wing met pursuant to call in New York City on June 21, 1919. The purpose of this conference was to unify and organize the so-called Left Wing elements in the Socialist Party throughout the country. The first subject under discussion was whether this element should organize immediately as a Communist Party, or whether it should continue the fight to control the National Emergency Convention of the Socialist Party, which had been called for the latter part of August in that year.

The conference, however, decided that the fight for party domination should continue until September, "in order to rally all revolutionary elements for a Communist Party, meanwhile organizing temporarily as the Left Wing Section of the Socialist

Party." (National Left Wing Conference, "Revolutionary Age," issue July 5, 1919, page 4.)

The conference was composed of over ninety delegates from twenty different cities, principally from the large industrial centers, such as New York, Boston, Buffalo, Rochester, Philadelphia, Providence, Pittsburgh, Hartford, Minneapolis, Duluth, St. Paul, Detroit, Kansas City, Mo., Denver, Cleveland and Oakland, Cal.

It was reported to the conference that the Left Wing had taken firm hold in New England and on the Pacific Coast, Northwest and Middle Western States, and in New Mexico.

The temporary chairman of the conference was Louis C. Fraina, editor of the "Revolutionary Age," who, in his opening address, stated as the cause for the Left Wing movement:

> "The Proletarian Revolution in action has modified the old tactical concepts of Socialism; and the inspiration of the Bolshevik conquests, joining with the original minority Socialism in the Socialist Party, has produced the Left Wing."

William Bross Lloyd, of Chicago, was selected as permanent chairman, A. Renner, of Detroit, as vice chairman, and Fanny Horowitz, of New York, as permanent secretary.

The following committees were also chosen:

Manifesto and Program Committee.— Louis C. Fraina, of Boston; Dennis E. Batt, of Detroit; Alexander Stoklitsky, of Chicago; C. E. Ruthenberg, of Cleveland; I. E. Ferguson, of Chicago.

Organization, Finance and Press.— Maximilian Cohen, New York; A. Wagenknecht, Chicago; Nicholas I. Hourwich, New York; Edward I. Lindgren, Brooklyn; Eadmonn MacAlpine, New York.

Labor Committee.— John Reed, New York; Benjamin Gitlow, Bronx, N. Y.; A. Anderson, Boston; Jack Carney, Duluth; Jurgis, Boston.

A National Council of nine members was selected consisting of Louis C. Fraina, of Boston; C. E. Ruthenberg, Cleveland; I. E. Ferguson, Chicago; John Ballam, Boston; James Larkin, New York; Eadmonn MacAlpine, New York; Benjamin Gitlow, New York; Maximilian Cohen, New York, and Bertram D. Wolfe, New York.

At a meeting of the National Council held in New York County on June the 26th, 1919, a new Left Wing manifesto was prepared and adopted, which is printed in full on page 6 of the July 5, 1919, issue of the "Revolutionary Age," and is reproduced at the close of this chapter.

It is an analytical statement of the necessity for the Left Wing or revolutionary movement of the Socialist Party, a criticism of the dominant or moderate Socialism, and a statement of the objects, purposes, methods and tactics to be employed to bring about the destruction of the form of government now existing in the United States and other civilized countries.

In analyzing this manifesto, it will be convenient to state briefly the reasons given for the necessity of the Left Wing movement. These will be found in the first part of the manifesto, from which is quoted the following:

> "The world is in crisis. Capitalism, the prevailing system of society, is in process of disintegration and collapse. Out of its vitals is developing a new social order, the system of Communist Socialism; and the struggle between this new social order and the old is now the fundamental problem of international politics. . . . Imperialism is the final stage of capitalism; and imperialism means sterner reaction, and new wars of conquest—unless the rovlutionary proletariat acts for Socialism. . . . Humanity can be saved from its last excesses only by the Communist revolution. There can now be only the Socialism which unites the proletariat of the whole world in proletarian revolutionary struggle. There can be only the Socialism which unites the proletariat of the whole world in the general struggle against the desperately destructive imperialisms—the imperialisms which array themselves as a single force against the on-sweeping proletarian revolution."

Reference is here unquestionably made to the governments as they now exist in their attitude toward Soviet Russia.

The manifesto then takes up the collapse of the Second International. This Second International, as has been previously pointed out, was an international body organized in 1889, consisting of delegates representing the various elements of the Socialist movement in all countries. It created the International Socialist Bureau at Brussels for the purpose of carrying on the propaganda of the International Socialist revolution. This organization was disrupted by the World War in August, 1914, because the controlling elements of the International supported their respective governments in the war. The manifesto criticizes the action of the so-called dominant Socialists which were the controlling elements of the Second International, in the following terms:

> "The dominant Socialism in accepting and justifying the war, abandoned the class struggle and betrayed Socialism. The class struggle is the heart of Socialism. Without strict conformity to the class struggle, in its revolutionary implications, Socialism becomes either sheer Utopianism, or a method of reaction. . . . The dominant Socialism united with the governments against Socialism and the proletariat, . . . nationalism, social patriotism, and social imperialism determined the policy of the dominant Socialism, and not the proletarian class struggle and Socialism."

Moderate Socialism is further criticized for its recognition of what is called the "bourgeois state," a term which is applied to the Government of the United States as well as to the governments of such countries as Great Britain, France, Italy, and the other civilized nations of the world in the following words:

> "This moderate Socialism initiated the era of 'constructive social reforms.' It accepted the bourgeois state as the basis of its activity and strengthened that state. Its goal became 'constructive reforms' and cabinet portfolios — 'the co-operation of classes,' the policy of openly or tacitly declaring that the coming Socialism was a concern 'of all the classes,' instead of emphasizing the Marxian policy that the construction of the Socialist system is the task of the revolutionary proletariat alone. In accepting Social reformism, 'the co-operation of the classes,' and the bourgeois parliamentary state as the basis of its action, moderate Socialism was prepared to share responsibility with the bourgeoisie in the control of the capitalist state, even to the extent of defending the bourgeoisie against the working class and its revolutionary mass movements. . . . What the parliamentary policy of the dominant moderate Socialism accomplished was to buttress the capitalist state, to promote state capitalism — to strengthen imperialism! . . . When

the economic and political crisis did develop potential revolutionary action in the proletariat, the dominant Socialism immediately assumed an attitude against the revolution. . . . The dominant Socialism united with capitalist governments to prevent a revolution."

Then follows a discussion of the Russian proletarian revolution, and a discussion of the German revolution. The patriotic attitude of the dominant Socialists of Europe is severely criticized thus:

"There is, accordingly, a common policy that characterizes moderate Socialism, and that is its conception of the state. Moderate Socialism affirms that the bourgeois, democratic parliamentary state is the necessary basis for the introduction of Socialism; accordingly, it conceived the task of the revolution, in Germany and Russia, to be the construction of the democratic parliamentary state, after which the process of introducing Socialism by legislative reform measures could be initiated."

Contrasted with the attitude of the moderate Socialist, is the policy of revolutionary Socialism as expressed in the Left Wing movement. The manifesto says:

"Revolutionary Socialism, on the contrary, insists that the democratic parliamentary state can never be the basis for the introduction of Socialism; that it is necessary to destroy the parliamentary state, and construct a new state of the organized producers, which will deprive the bourgeoisie of political power, and function as a revolutionary dictatorship of the proletariat.

"The proletarian revolution in action has conclusively proven that moderate Socialism is incapable of realizing the objectives of Socialism. Revolutionary Socialism alone is capable of mobilizing the proletariat for Socialism, for the conquest of the power of the state, by means of revolutionary mass action and proletarian dictatorship."

In speaking of the conditions in the United States, the manifesto says:

"Imperialism is dominant in the United States. It controls all the factors of social action. Imperialism is uniting all non-proletarian social groups in a brutal state capitalism, for reaction and spoilation. Against this, revolutionary Socialism must mobilize the mass struggle of the industrial proletariat. . . . Revolutionary Socialism adheres to the class struggle, because through the class struggle alone — the mass struggle — can the industrial proletariat secure immediate concessions and finally conquer power by organizing the industrial government of the working class."

The political character of the class struggle referred to is shown by the following statement:

"The class struggle is a political struggle. It is a political struggle in the sense that its objective is political — the overthrow of the political organization upon which capitalistic exploitation depends, and the introduction of a new social system. The direct objective is the conquest by the proletariat of the power of the state.

"Revolutionary Socialism does not propose to 'capture' the bourgeois parliamentary state, but to conquer and destroy it."

The purpose of the authors of this manifesto to bring about the destruction of our government by other than parliamentary means, is indicated by the following quotation:

"*Revolutionary Socialism, accordingly, repudiates the policy of introducing Socialism by means of legislative measures on the basis of the bourgeois state.*

"This state is a bourgeois state, the organ for the coercion of the proletarian by the capitalist: how, then, can it introduce Socialism? As long as the bourgeois parliamentary state prevails, the capitalist class can baffle the will of the proletariat, since all the political power, the army and the police, industry and the press, are in the hands of the capitalists, whose economic power gives them complete domination. The revolutionary proletariat must expropriate all these by the conquest of the power of the state, by annihilating the political power of the bourgeoisie, before it can begin the task of introducing Socialism."

In reading the foregoing, it must be noted that revolutionary Socialism, represented in this instance by the so-called Left Wing movement of the Socialist Party, repudiates the policy of introducing Socialism by means of legislative measures. It aims not to capture the bourgeois parliamentary state, by which is meant the governments of the United States and of the State of New York, but to conquer and destroy both. This is still further emphasized by the following paragraphs:

> "But parliamentarism cannot conquer the power of the state for the proletariat. The conquest of the power of the state is an extra-parliamentary act. It is accomplished, not by the legislative representatives of the proletariat, but by the *mass power of the proletariat in action.* The supreme power of the proletariat inheres in the *political mass strike,* in using the industrial mass power of the proletariat for political objectives.
>
> "Revolutionary Socialism, accordingly, recognizes that the supreme form of proletarian political action *is the political mass strike.* . . . The power of the proletariat lies fundamentally in its control of the industrial process. The mobilization of this control in action *against the bourgeois state and capitalism,* means the end of capitalism, the initial form of the revolutionary mass action that will conquer the power of the state."

The provisions of this manifesto show clearly that the purpose of the adherents to the Left Wing movement was the destruction of the American form of government, the tearing up of the Constitution of the United States, the expropriation of private property. That this destruction of our government and this expropriation of private property cannot be accomplished by means of the ballot and the exercise of legislative powers, but must be accomplished by means of the mass or general strike of the workers in industry. They also aimed to set up a dictatorship of the proletariat only, to the exclusion of all other classes of our society, and believed that this was to be accomplished by revolutionary mass action, which is stated in the manifesto to be an outgrowth of the general political strike.

In defining mass action, the manifesto says:

> "Mass action is the proletarian response to the facts of modern industry, and the forms it imposes upon the proletarian class struggle. Mass action starts as the spontaneous activity of unorganized workers massed in the basic industry; its initial form is the mass strike of the unorganized proletariat. . . . Mass action is industrial in its origin;

> but its development imposes upon it a political character, since the more general and conscious mass action becomes, the more it antagonizes the bourgeois state, becomes political mass action. . . . Mass action concentrates and mobilizes the forces of the proletariat, organized and unorganized; it acts equally *against the bourgeois state and the conservative organizations of the working class. The revolution starts with strikes of protest, developing into mass political strikes and then into revolutionary mass action for the conquest of the power of the state. Mass action becomes political in purpose while extra-parliamentary in form.*"

Here is presented a graphic picture of the method sought to be employed by the adherents to the principles of this manifesto, in seeking the overturn of the government of the United States and this State. As if in fear that the manifesto might be misunderstood, its authors have continued to reiterate the purpose and object of the revolution which they advocate, and the methods which they advise for its achievement. This is illustrated by the following quotation:

> "The final objective of mass action is the conquest of the power of the state, the annihilation of the bourgeois parliamentary state and the introduction of the transition proletarian state, functioning as a revolutionary dictatorship of the proletariat."

The purpose of the dictatorship of the proletariat is thus expressed:

> "The state is an organ of coercion. The bourgeois parliamentary state is the organ of the bourgeoisie for the coercion of the proletariat. The revolutionary proletariat must, accordingly, destroy this state. But the conquest of political power by the proletariat does not immediately end capitalism, or the power of the capitalists, or immediately socialize industry. It is therefore necessary that the proletariat organize its own state — for the coercion and suppression of the bourgeoisie."

The Government of the United States, as well as all other democratic governments, is viewed by the authors of this manifesto as an autocracy.

"In form a democracy, the bourgeois parliamentary state is in fact an autocracy, the dictatorship of capital over the proletariat. . . . The proletarian revolution disrupts bourgeois democracy. It disrupts this democracy in order to end class divisions and class rule, to realize that industrial self-government of the workers which alone can assure peace and liberty to the peoples.

"Proletarian dictatorship is a recognition of the necessity for a revolutionary state to coerce and suppress the bourgeoisie; it is equally a recognition of the fact that, in the Communist reconstruction of society, the proletariat as a class alone counts. . . .

"The old machinery of the state cannot be used by the revolutionary proletariat. It must be destroyed. The proletariat creates a new state, based directly upon the industrially organized producers, upon the industrial unions or soviets, or a combination of both. It is this state alone, functioning as a dictatorship of the proletariat that can realize Socialism."

The tasks of this dictatorship are then enumerated.

Among the preliminary measures advanced as necessary are:

"(a) Workers' control of industry to be exercised by the industrial organizations of the workers, operating by means of the industrial vote.

"(b) Expropriation and nationalization of the banks, as a necessary preliminary measure for the complete expropriation of capital.

"(c) Expropriation and nationalization of the large (trust) organizations of capital. Expropriation proceeds without compensation, as 'buying out' the capitalists is a repudiation of the tasks of the revolution.

"(d) Repudiation of all national debts and the financial obligations of the old system."

This is advocating the repudiation of Liberty Bonds and all other government obligations and is a part of the plan for the expropriation of the so-called bourgeoisie which has been previously referred to.

The closing section of the manifesto has to do with the Communist International, which phrase refers to the International body set up at Moscow in March, 1919, under the leadership of Lenin and Trotzky, and known as the Third International. This organization is contrasted with the attempt to resurrect the Second International at Berne, Switzerland:

> "The Communist International, on the contrary, represents a Socialism in complete accord with the revolutionary character of the class struggle. It unites all the consciously revolutionary forces. It wages war equally against the dominant moderate Socialism and imperialism,— each of which has demonstrated its complete incompetence on the problems that now press down upon the world. . . .
>
> "The Communist International, moreover, issues its call to the subject peoples of the world, crushed under the murderous mastery of imperialism. . . .
>
> "The Communist International, accordingly, offers an organization and a policy that may unify all revolutionary forces of the world for the conquest of power, and for Socialism."

The manifesto closes with this revolutionary appeal:

> "The old order is in decay. Civilization is in collapse. The proletarian revolution and the Communist reconstruction of society — the struggle for these — is now indispensable. This is the message of the Communist International" which "calls the proletariat of the world to the final struggle!"

A careful consideration of the foregoing shows that the authors of this authoritative statement of the objective methods and tactics of the Left Wing movement not only teach and advise the propriety of overthrowing organized government, including the government of the United States and the State of New York by force, violence and unlawful means, but urge immediate action on the part of the working-classes of this country in co-operation with the proletariat of other countries to bring about the world revolution. The means advocated to accomplish the revolution and the setting up of a proletarian dictatorship in this country, is the mass strike. Legislative reforms and the alteration of our Constitution by legal means, are specifically repudiated.

It is apparent that an attempt to put into operation such a program, including the seizure and confiscation of private property without compensation to its owners, would, of necessity, lead to violence, and that such program could not be put into operation without the employment of armed force. The program contemplates the exclusion from participation in the revolutionary government, sought to be set up of all elements of society except the proletariat. No reasonable man will believe that so large an element of American society can be coerced, robbed and crushed without force and violence, and without civil war. Although this manifesto is a labyrinth of phrases, a perfect maze of words, throughout can be clearly discerned the avowed purpose of its authors to advocate the destruction of our government. To change that government not by lawful means, not by the ballot, not by legislative reform, but by a brutal autocratic dictatorship of a comparatively small element of the community, designated the proletariat — in other words, the propertyless class — with the avowed purpose of setting up in this country a duplicate of the government which Lenin and Trotzky, the followers and disciples of Marx, have temporarily reared in Russia. All that has been said with respect to the methods of bringing about Socialism by means of forceful revolution as advocated by the leaders of the Left Wing movement, is further emphasized by an article that appears on page 10 of the "Revolutionary Age" in the issue of July 19, 1919, entitled "The Communist Party," by N. Bucharin. The author of this article, as heretofore stated, was a member of the Russian Socialist Federation in this country, and editor of the "Novy Mir," which later became one of the official organs of the Left Wing movement. This article deals with the dictatorship of the proletariat as understood and applied by the Communist Party of Russia, the sponsors for the Third International above referred to, and with whom the Left Wing elements are allied.

The article opens with this question:

> "By what means is the Communist world order to be established? How are we to attain it? The answer of the Communist Party to these questions is 'through the dictatorship of the proletariat.'
>
> "'Dictatorship' means a power as strong as iron, a power which gives no quarter to its enemies. The 'Dictatorship of the Proletariat' means the government of the working class which abolishes the land owners and capitalists.
>
> "A workers' government can only be produced by a social revolution of the working-class; a revolution which will

destroy the capitalist state and erect on its ruins a new power; the power of the working-class, and the poor peasants who support the workers' government.

"We Communists, therefore, stand for a workers' government until the workers have gained complete control over their adversaries; until they have crushed the entire employing class and knocked out its pride, and until the employing class itself has given up all hopes of ever again coming into power. Of course, it will be said: 'Then you Communists are believers in force?'

"We shall answer: 'Most certainly; but our belief is in revolutionary force. We are convinced that by soft words the working-class will gain nothing from the capitalists. No good will come from reconciliation. Nothing short of a revolution, which will overthrow capitalism and destroy the bourgeoisie can liberate the working-class.'

"*Every revolution means using force against the form of government.* Force was used against the tyrannical landlords and Czar in the Russian revolution of March, 1917, and in the revolution of November, 1917, force was used against the capitalists by the workers, peasants, and soldiery. Such force — the use of force against those who are oppressing millions of workers — is not merely free from evil; it is sacred."

No more clear statement could be made indicating that those participating in the Left Wing movement, advocate, advise and teach the doctrine that organized government should be overthrown by force, violence and unlawful means. All doubt as to the precise meaning of the word "force" as employed in this article is removed by reference to the methods employed in Russia both in bringing about the revolution of March, 1917, and the revolution of November, when the Bolsheviki usurped the power of the state at the point of the bayonet.

It may be urged that many of the phrases used and principles enunciated in the manifesto and program of the Left Wing Section and the article above referred to may be found in the works of Marx, Engels, and other well-known writers on Socialism. Many of these principles have undoubtedly been stated by these authors, but if any of this number were to advocate such principles in the State of New York at the present time, they would unquestionably be subject to the penalties imposed by our statutes.

Evidence of the publication of this manifesto in the "Revolutionary Age" and of the connection therewith of the editors and the members of the National Executive Committee was presented to a Special Grand Jury sitting in and for the County of New York in November, 1919. Indictments were found against all concerned, and at the time of the preparation of this report, one of the defenders, namely, Benjamin Gitlow, had been tried and convicted of the crime of Criminal Anarchy.

The National Left Wing Conference in addition to the adoption of this manifesto, decided that the "Revolutionary Age" of Boston and the "New York Communist" should be combined and published in New York City as the national organ of the Left Wing of the Socialist Party. This was done and the new publication made its appearance on Saturday, July 5, 1919, with Louis C. Fraina and Eadmonn MacAlpine, editors, and Benjamin Gitlow, business manager.

On the third day of the conference, thirty-one delegates, consisting mostly of those from the foreign language federations, decided after a caucus, that they would withhold further activity in the conference because of its refusal to act upon the question of the immediate organization of a Communist Party. These delegates resigned from all the committees, having previously declined nominations to the National Council, and thereupon left the Conference.

The report of the Committee on Labor was duly accepted. It clearly demonstrated the methods advocated by the Left Wing to carry out the program enunciated in its manifesto. The report says in part:

> "The purpose of the Left Wing organization is to create a revolutionary working class movement in America, which, through the action of the working masses themselves, will lead to workers' control of industry and the state, as the only means of expropriating capitalist property and abolishing classes in society. The capitalist state, as has been clearly proven, expresses the existing dictatorship of the capitalist class, a weapon to defend capitalist interests and to extend them at the expense of the workers. Capitalist control of the machinery of politics and publicity makes it impossible for the workers to conquer this state power by use of the ballot; but even if it were possible, the State could not be used by the workers for their own purpose so long

as the factories, mills, mines, land, transportation systems and financial institutions remained in the hands of private capitalist owners.

"With the legislatures, courts, police and armies under control of the capitalists, the workers can only win the state power by extra-parliamentary action which must have its basis in the industrial mass action of the workers.

"*The first act of the workers' dictatorship must be the destruction of the capitalist state and the creation of a new form of Government based on the workers' organizations, whose purpose shall be the permanent destruction of capitalist power by the expropriation of capitalist property. . . . It is the intention of the Left Wing to help prepare the American workers for their historic role, so that when the hour strikes they may take their places in the front ranks of the Social revolution.*

"(1) Revolutionary Industrial Unionism. By the term 'revolutionary industrial unionism' is meant the organization of the workers into unions by industries with a revolutionary aim and purpose; that is to say, those whose purpose is, not merely to defend and strengthen the status of the workers as wage-earners, but to gain control of industry.

"In any mention of revolutionary industrial unionism in this country, there must be recognition of the immense effect upon the American labor movement of the propaganda and example of the Industrial Workers of the World, whose long and valiant struggles and heroic sacrifices in the class-war, have earned the respect and affection of all workers everywhere. We greet the revolutionary industrial proletariat of America in the ranks of the I. W. W. and pledge them our whole-hearted support and co-operation in their struggles against the capitalist class. . . ."

"We suggest that some plan of labor organization be inaugurated along the lines of the Shop Stewards' Committees of Scotland and England or the Factory Shop Committees of Russia. These committees can serve as a spur or check upon the unions. Such committees will necessarily reflect the spirit and the wishes of the rank and file, and will enable the National Left Wing to keep in direct touch with the workers. In this way, the workers can be educated on the job and prepare for the taking over of industry."

The report closes with the following recommendations:

"(1) That a Committee of Seven be elected by the Convention to be known as the Labor Committee.

"(2) That the functions of this committee shall be to carry on revolutionary propaganda among the workers on the job.

"(3) Those workers found to be radical shall be organized into Shop Committees.

"(4) These Shop Committees shall distribute literature, supply information to the Labor Committee, and generally keep in touch with the National Left Wing organization.

"(5) At places where a number of these committees are formed, they shall elect delegates to a local Workers' Council.

"(6) An appropriation shall be made for the purpose of carrying on the work of this committee.

"(7) A general propaganda periodical shall be issued by the National Left Wing Council for the special purpose of reaching the workers at their jobs. And this project shall be referred for further elaboration to the Labor Committee."

It will be noted that in this report and by its adoption, it became the settled purpose of the National Left Wing organization to institute a thoroughly organized agitation among the workers with the view to reorganize them along the lines which had been adopted in Russia, and to create a Workmen's Council which it was hoped might ultimately take the form of Soviets. The plan thus promulgated demonstrated a hostility toward and the determination to destroy the conservative organizations of labor affiliated with the American Federation of Labor. This animosity is apparent in all of the propaganda issued by the Left Wing. An example might be cited in an editorial appearing on page 2 of the "Revolutionary Age," of July 19, 1919, entitled "Union Bureaucracy":

"Wherever militant labor gets in action, it meets the antagonism of the bureaucracy of the old unions. The American labor movement is familiar with the contemptible intrigues of the A. F. of L. bureaucracy against I. W. W. strikes, and particularly during the great Lawrence strike of 1912, when the A. F. of L. officials did all in their power to break the workers' struggle. This tendency also characterized the recent general strike in Seattle.

> "The union bureaucrats are particularly against industrial unionism, since industrial unionism ends craft divisions and craft disputes, which constitute the power of the union bureaucracy. In Canada, the One Big Union — Industrial Unionism — has captured the imagination of the organized workers. The One Big Union directed the great general strike in Canada; but, says an observer, '*The International Brotherhoods have come out against the strikers, shrewdly foreseeing in the One Big Union the destruction of their organization.*' This is a damning indictment of the old unionism."

In July, 1919, the disruption of the Socialist movement of the United States became complete. As has been pointed out in the chapter of this report dealing with the activities of the Socialist Party of America, the principle Foreign Language Federations have been expelled from the Socialist Party, and those Locals which had joined the Left Wing Section and had refused to repudiate it, were also expelled.

The original hope of the leaders of the Left Wing movement to harmonize all of the elements who were in opposition to the Socialist Party leadership, disappeared at the Left Wing Conference in June, when the delegates from the Russian Federation, together with four delegates from the State of Michigan, withdrew from the conference.

In the early part of July, the Michigan Federation issued a call for the organization of the Communist Party at Chicago on September 1st. The convention was called by a "National Organization Committee," consisting of Dennis E. Batt, D. Elbaum, O. C. Johnson, John Keracher, S. Kopnagel, I. Stilson and Alexander Stoklitsky. The Michigan Federation in their call, attacked the National Left Wing for their policy in endeavoring "to capture the old party machinery and the stagnant elements who have been struggling for conference unity and who are only too ready to abandon the ship when it sinks beneath the wave of reaction."

This criticism of the Left Wing movement was violently denounced in Left Wing organs and made the task of reconciling the Left Wing and the Michigan Party difficult. This, however, was in large measure effected at a later date.

To the fair and impartial observer, the element of personal antagonism to the party leaders rather than any fundamental difference of principles seems the occasion for the splits which occurred in the Socialist Party ranks. (See article by Louis C. Fraina in the "Revolutionary Age," July 19, 1919, page 7, entitled "The Left Wing," and an unsigned article in the same issue on page 3, entitled "The Party Fight.")

The attempt to control the National Emergency Convention of the Socialist Party, however, was not abandoned. A large number of the State organizations and Locals which were expelled by the National Executive Committee of the Socialist Party, refused to recognize such expulsion, and prepared to send delegates to the Emergency Convention at Chicago.

Resolutions similar to those adopted by Local Boston were generally adopted. We quote here the statement issued by Local Boston, as given in the "Revolutionary Age" of the issue of July 12, 1919, page 15, as follows:

> "(1) We refuse to recognize the expulsion by the National Executive Committee of the Socialist Party of the State organization of Michigan and Massachusetts, and the suspension of the Hungarian, Lettish, Lithuanian, Polish, South Slavic, Russian and Ukrainian Federations.
>
> "(2) We note that the members of the Executive Committee responsible for this action charged that the Language Federations made plans to vote for a 'slate.' Such procedure has always been recognized within the party as a legitimate method of giving effect to majority opinion in elections. As a matter of fact, James Oneal, one of the objectors, was himself elected on a 'slate,' as State Secretary of Massachusetts, a few years ago.
>
> "(3) Another charge is that five federations issued a statement that they would not assist in the so-called Amnesty Convention called by the National Executive Committee, and even affirmed their opposition to such convention. The purpose of that convention was, in our judgment, to use the Socialist Party as an instrument in securing the release of the bourgeois 'conscientious objectors' and then to abandon the imprisoned victims of the class struggle. Therefore, we declare that the five federations in this matter adhered to the party pledge, while its National Executive Committee violated the third paragraph of that pledge which reads as follows:
>
> > 'I am opposed to all political organizations that support and perpetuate the present capitalist profit system, and I am opposed to any form of trading or

fusing with any such organizations to prolong that system.'

"(4) The members of the outgoing National Executive Committee who voted to hold up the tabulation of votes upon National membership referendums, rendered themselves liable to expulsion from office under Article XIII, section 4, of the party constitution, which reads:

'Any officer who attempts to interfere with the processes of the membership shall be expelled from office.'

"(5) The state organizations of Michigan and Massachusetts were expelled without even the decency of a hearing. Those members of the National Executive Committee who were responsible for this outrage, are now straining every nerve to prevent an appeal against their action to a referendum vote of the party membership. Even in capitalist courts, the accused is given a hearing and a trial, with right of appeal if convicted. The guilty members of the National Executive Committee are seeking to deprive the accused comrades of rights such as are granted to Socialists by a hostile capitalist civilization. Comrades, the Socialist movement of the world is everywhere swinging to the Left. Sweep out of your path the handful of fossilized officials who are trying to stop the swing in America!

"For Local Boston,

"LOUIS E. HENDERSON,
"WILLIAM GOLDBERG,
"LEON GOLOSOV,
"W. T. COLYER,
"Authorized Committee."

The New National Executive Committee met in Chicago on July 26 and 27, 1919, at Bradley Hall. There were present: Louis C. Fraina, Edward I. Lindgren, Fred Harwood, Marguerite Prevey, C. E. Ruthenberg, William Bross Lloyd, L. E. Katterfeld and H. M. Wicks. Other members of the Committee not present were: Denis E. Batt, Nicholas I. Hourwich, John Keracher, Dan Hogan, Mary R. Millis, Pat Nagle, and Kate Greenhalgh.

A committee to tabulate the votes reported that Louis C. Fraina, John Reed, C. E. Ruthenberg and A. Wagenknecht were elected overwhelmingly as International delegates, and Kate Richards O'Hare as International secretary. The new committee made a demand upon the executive secretary of the Socialist

Party, Adolf Germer, to turn over the National headquarters to the New National Executive Committee, and appear at its sessions. This demand was presented in writing to Germer, who is reported to have refused.

At the afternoon session of this National Executive Committee the following motion was adopted:

> "That we declare the office of National Executive Secretary vacant, inasmuch as the present incumbent violates his functions by refusing to tabulate the vote on referendums expressing the will of the membership, and refuses to recognize the regularly elected N. E. C."

Thereupon, A. Wagenknecht was chosen to act as temporary secretary until the National Emergency Convention of August 30th.

A motion was also adopted "That the Massachusetts and Michigan State Organizations be reinstated in the Party, and that the suspension of the Russian, Polish, Lithuanian, South Slavic, Hungarian, Lettish, and Ukrainian Socialist Federations be revoked.

It is reported that this new National Executive Committee decided to assume full control of the Emergency Convention, and resolved:

> "That we recognize the National Council of the Left Wing Section, Socialist Party organized at the National Left Wing Conference, June 21–24, and its official organ, the 'Revolutionary Age,' as an organized expression of the revolutionary sentiments of the party, and that we request their co-operation."

It must be borne in mind that the regular organization of the Socialist Party did not recognize the validity of the elections which resulted in the choice of this Executive Committee, and that they retained control of the party machinery, including the party newspapers and party funds and records. However, the so-called New National Executive Committee proceeded to transact business as though it was in full charge of party affairs, and issued a statement in which it appears by unanimous decision in the session of July 26th and 27th, the Committee decided:

> "(1) To oust National Executive Secretary Germer, who refuses to recognize your N. E. C. as the organ

of the party. (2) To re-instate the expelled State organizations of Michigan and Massachusetts, and the suspended language Federation, restoring to the party with all rights, more than 35,000 comrades. (3) To reorganize the Socialist Party as a Communist Party in harmony with our affiliation with the Communist International. (4) To call upon the members, regardless of the party wrecking old N. E. C. to rally to the support of the class war prisoners. (5) To consider seriously and comprehensively problems of organization shamefully neglected by the old party administrations. (6) To request the co-operation of the National Council of the Left Wing Section, Socialist Party (and its official organ, 'Revolutionary Age,') as an organized expression of the revolutionary sentiments of the party. (7) To assume full control of the Emergency National Convention on August 30th, the old N. E. C. and its executive secretaries leaving no authority to organize or postpone this convention. We will shortly inform you of the place where the convention will meet, together with the roster of delegates. Our temporary executive secretary will call the convention to order."

On the issues of the Emergency Convention, this so-called National Executive Committee adopted the following declaration:

"The movement which culminated in the calling of the Emergency National Convention of August 30th, did not have its origin in a contest over administrative actions of the party Executive Committee; its origin was a demand by large sections of the party membership, for a reformulation of the party tactics; and a restatement of its principles in harmony with the revolutionary Socialist practice of the Bolsheviki of Russia.

"Local after Local, in resolutions and demonstrations urged the National Executive Committee to call a convention, great masses of the membership declared their adherence to the new revolutionary principles, but the National Executive Committee, the representative of moderate Socialism — the Socialism of Scheidemann and Kerensky — acting as self-appointed guardians of the party, refused to accede to the demand of the membership for a convention.

"It was only after the membership itself had taken the matter out of the hands of the National Executive Committee and had endorsed the convention by an overwhelming vote, that the convention was finally called.

"In their effort to maintain their rule of the party the moderate Socialists of the National Executive Committee did not hesitate to disrupt the organization. Members have been expelled and suspended wholesale in order to influence the vote of the referendum election, and to give the old National Executive Committee and moderate Socialism control of the convention and the party. These reactionary and treacherous acts have injected into the present party situation a bitter struggle for control of the party organization and the danger exists that this factional struggle over democracy against autocracy within the organization may overshadow the original purpose of the call for a national convention — to reorganize the Socialist Party of the United States on the basis of the Communist Socialism which is sweeping through the ranks of the proletarian movement of the world and everywhere bringing new inspiration and courage to the workers in their struggle for emancipation. The old National Executive Committee consciously inspired this process by attempting to refer to the convention the controversial questions over administrative actions, which is disruptive.

"Recognizing this danger we call upon the membership to elect representatives to the Emergency National Convention, not merely on the basis of settling questions arisen out of the reactionary administrative action of the old National Executive Committee — the issue is not party democracy as against party autocracy, but revolutionary Socialism against moderate Socialism — but on the basis of reorganizing the party for the achievement of Communist Socialism.

"The action of the membership in this question has already been indicated in the overwhelming and all but unanimous endorsement by referendum vote of affiliation with the Communist International, side by side with the Communist Party (Bolsheviki) of Russia and the Communist Labor Party (Spartacans) of Germany and other Communist parties of Europe. The work of the Emergency National Convention of August 30th, will be to reorganize the Socialist Party on the basis of the Communist Socialist principles and tactics outlined in the declaration of the Communist International. *Out of the Emergency National Convention came the Communist Party of the United States.*

"To carry out this purpose we adopt the following program:

> "I. We reaffirm the call for the Emergency National Convention to be held on August 30th, in Chicago, and call upon all party units to send delegates irrespective of any action which the usurping members of the former National Executive Committee may take.
>
> "II. The convention will be held under the direction of this committee and the executive secretary elected by it will make up the roster of delegates and will call the convention to order.
>
> "III. We call upon all sections of the party expelled or suspended by the reactionary Executive Committee and reinstated by this committee, to send delegates as provided in the rules of party procedure.
>
> "IV. We call upon all party units expelled by state or local organizations to take such actions, in accordance with their local rules, as will insure them representation."

At about the same time an effort was being made to compromise the differences between the Russian Language Federation and the National Council of the Left Wing. These negotiations resulted in the calling of a conference on July 27, 1919, in New York, between the Russian Federation Executive Committee and representatives of the National Council of the Left Wing.

As a result of that Conference, the following resolution was submitted to the National Council:

> "Having discussed the written statements issued by the National Left Wing Council and the telegram of the so-called 'New N. E. C.' of the Socialist Party, reported by the Secretary of the National Left Wing Council, we, the Central Executive Committees of the Lettish, Lithuanian, Esthonian, Ukrainian, Polish and Russian Federations, came to the conclusion that these documents justify once again the position taken by the minority of the Left Wing Conference, and call upon all our members to carry on the work of the creation of the Communist Party. We appeal

to the comrades of the majority group to clarify their desire in forming the Communist Party through participation in the Convention which is being called by the minority of the Left Wing Conference on September 1, 1919. In case of reply in the affirmative, we are prepared to instruct our National Organization Committee to combine with the National Left Wing Council in the common work of calling the convention for the purpose of organizing the Communist Party of America on September 1, 1919, in Chicago.

"*For the Lettish, Lithuanian, Esthonian, Ukrainian, Polish and Russian Central Executive Committees,*

"(Signed) O. TYWEROWSKY,

"*Secretary.*"

This resolution was submitted to the National Council of the Left Wing on July 28, 1919, and the following motions were made and carried:

"(1) The National Left Wing Council stands for a Communist Party on September 1st, and we repeat the call of the Left Wing Conference for a Convention on September 1st to form the Communist Party of America, inviting all revolutionary Socialist groups to join with us.

"(2) We invite the minority group of the Left Wing Conference and the Federations to work with us on the basis of a September 1st Convention to form the Communist Party.

"(3) We associate ourselves with the N. E. C. in relation to the August 30th Emergency Socialist Party Convention only as a preliminary to the September first Communist Party Convention."

At this meeting of the National Council, there appeared a new divergence of opinion, Benjamin Gitlow and James Larkin apparently disagreeing with the majority of the council. This action on the part of the National Council of the Left Wing in reality ended the movement to organize for the control of the Socialist Party of America by the so-called Left Wing elements, and marked the definite beginning of the movement to organize the Communist Party of America, which will be dealt with in the following chapter of this report.

APPENDIX

CHAPTER IV

Official Documents

1. Manifesto of Left Wing Section Socialist Party Local Greater New York.
2. Left Wing Manifesto adopted by National Left Wing Council.

Document No. 1

MANIFESTO

Prior to August, 1914, the nations of the world lived on a volcano. Violent eruptions from time to time gave warning of the cataclysm to come, but the diplomats and statesmen managed to localize the outbreaks, and the masses, slightly aroused, sank back into their accustomed lethargy with doubts and misgivings, and the subterranean fires continued to smoulder.

Many trusted blindly — some in their statesmen, some in the cohesive power of Christianity, their common religion, and some in the growing strength of the international Socialist movement. Had not the German Social-Democracy exchanged dramatic telegrams with the French Socialist Party, each pledging itself not to fight in case their governments declared war on each other! A general strike of workers led by these determined Socialists would quickly bring the governments to their senses!

So the workers reasoned, until the thunder-clap of Sarejevo and Austria's ultimatum to Serbia. Then, suddenly, the storm broke. Mobilization everywhere. Everywhere declarations of war. In three or four days Europe was in arms.

The present structure of society — Capitalism — with its pretensions to democracy on the one hand, and its commercial rivalries, armament rings and standing armies on the other, all based on the exploitation of the working class and the division of the loot, was cast into the furnace of war. Two things only could issue forth: either international capitalist control, through a League of Nations, or Social Revolution and the Dictatorship of the Proletariat. Both of these forces are to-day contending for world-power.

The Social Democracies of Europe, unable or unwilling to meet the crisis, were themselves hurled into the conflagration, to be tempered or consumed by it.

THE COLLAPSE OF THE SECOND INTERNATIONAL

Great demonstrations were held in every European country by Socialists protesting against their governments' declarations of war, and mobilizations for war. And we know that these demonstrations were rendered impotent by the complete surrender of the Socialist parliamentary leaders and the official Socialist press, with their "justifications" of "defensive wars" and the safeguarding of "democracy."

Why the sudden change of front? Why did the Socialist leaders in the parliaments of the belligerents vote the war credits? Why did not Moderate Socialism carry out the policy of the Basle Manifesto, namely: the converting of an imperialistic war into a civil war — into a proletarian revolution? Why did it either openly favor the war or adopt a policy of petty-bourgeois pacifism?

THE DEVELOPMENT OF MODERATE "SOCIALISM"

In the latter part of the nineteenth century, the Social-Democracies of Europe set out to "legislate Capitalism out of office." The class struggle was to be won in the capitalist legislatures. Step by step concessions were to be wrested from the state; the working class and the Socialist parties were to be strengthened by means of "constructive" reform and social legislation; each concession would act as a rung in the ladder of Social Revolution, upon which the workers could climb step by step, until finally, some bright sunny morning, the peoples would awaken to find the Cooperative Commonwealth functioning without disorder, confusion or hitch on the ruins of the capitalist state.

And what happened? When a few legislative seats had been secured, the thunderous denunciations of the Socialist legislators suddenly ceased. No more were the parliaments used as platforms from which the challenge of revolutionary Socialism was flung to all the corners of Europe. Another era had set in, the era of "constructive" social reform legislation. Dominant Moderate Socialism accepted the bourgeois state as the basis of its action and strengthened that state. All power to shape the policies and tactics of the Socialist parties was entrusted to the parliamentary leaders. And these lost sight of Socialism's original purpose; their goal became "constructive reforms" and cabinet portfolios — the "cooperation of classes," the policy of openly or tacitly declaring that the coming of Socialism was a concern "of all the classes," instead of emphasizing the Marxian policy that the construction of the Socialist system is the task of the revolutionary proletariat alone. "Moderate Socialism" accepted the bourgeois state as the leaders, was now ready to share responsibility with the bourgeoisie in the control of the capitalist state, even to the extent of defending the bourgeoisie against the working class — as in the first Briand Ministry in France, when the official party press was opened to a defense of the shooting of striking railway-workers at the order of the Socialist-Bourgeois Coalition Cabinet.

"SAUSAGE SOCIALISM"

This situation was brought about by mixing the democratic cant of the eighteenth century with scientific Socialism. The result was what Rosa Luxemburg called "sausage Socialism." The "Moderates" emphasized petty-bourgeois social reformism in order to attract tradesmen, shop-keepers and members of the professions, and, of course, the latter flocked to the Socialist movement in great numbers, seeking relief from the constant grinding between corporate capital and awakening labor.

The Socialist organizations actively competed for votes, on the basis of social reforms, with the bourgeois-liberal political parties. And so they catered to the ignorance and prejudices of the workers, trading promises of immediate reforms for votes.

Dominant "moderate Socialism" forgot the teachings of the founders of scientific Socialism, forgot its function as a proletarian movement — "the most resolute and advanced section of the working class parties"— and permitted the bourgeois and self-seeking trade union elements to shape its policies and tactics. This was the condition in which the Social-Democracies of Europe found themselves at the outbreak of the war in 1914. Demoralized and confused by the cross-currents within their own parties, vacillating and compromising with the bourgeois state, they fell a prey to social-patriotism and nationalism.

SPARTICIDES AND BOLSHEVIKI

But revolutionary Socialism was not destined to lie inert for long. In Germany, Karl Liebknecht, Franz Mehring, Rosa Luxemburg and Otto Ruhle organized the Spartacus Group. But their voices were drowned in the roar of cannon and the shrieks of the dying and the maimed.

Russia, however, was to be the first battle-ground where "moderate" and revolutionary Socialism should come to grips for the mastery of the state. The breakdown of the corrupt, bureaucratic Czarist regime opened the flood-gates of Revolution.

Three main contending parties attempted to ride into power on the revolutionary tide; the Cadets, the "moderate Socialists" (Mensheviki and Social Revolutionists), and the revolutionary Socialists — the Bolsheviki. The Cadets were first to be swept into power; but they tried to stem the still-rising flood with a few abstract political ideals, and were soon carried away. The soldiers, workers, and peasants could no longer be fooled by phrases. The Mensheviki and Social Revolutionaries succeeded the Cadets. And now came the crucial test: would they, in accord with Marxian teachings, make themselves the ruling class and sweep away the old conditions of production, and thus prepare the way for the Cooperative Commonwealth? Or would they tinker with the old machinery and try to foist it on the masses as something just as good?

They did the latter and proved for all time that "moderate Socialism" cannot be trusted.

"Moderate Socialism" was not prepared to seize the power for the workers during a revolution. "Moderate Socialism" had a rigid formula — "constructive social reform legislation within the capitalist state" and to that formula it clung. It believed that bourgeois democracy could be used as a means of constructing the Socialist system; therefore, it must wait until the people, through a Constituent Assembly, should vote Socialism into existence. And in the meantime, it held that there must be established a Government of Coalition with the enemy, the bourgeoisie. As if, with all the means of controlling public opinion in the hands of the bourgeoisie, a Constituent Assembly could or would ever vote the Socialists into power!

Revolutionary Socialists hold, with the founders of scientific Socialism, that there are two dominant classes in society — the bourgeoisie and the proletariat; that between these two classes a struggle must go on, until the working class, through the seizure of the instruments of production and distribution, the abolition of the capitalist state, and the establishment of the dictatorship of the proletariat, creates a Socialist system. Revolutionary

Socialists do not believe that they can be voted into power. They struggle for the conquest of power by the revolutionary proletariat. Then comes the transition period from Capitalism to Socialism, of which Marx speaks in his "Critique of the Gotha program": when he says: "Between the capitalistic society and the communistic, lies the period of the revolutionary transformation of the one into the other. This corresponds to a political transition period, in which the state cannot be anything else but the dictatorship of the proletariat."

Marx and Engels clearly explain the function of the Socialist movement. It is the "moderate Socialists" through intellectual gymnastics, evasions, misquotations and the tearing of sentences and phrases from their context, who make Marx and Engels sponsors for their perverted version of Socialism.

PROBLEMS OF AMERICAN SOCIALISM

At the present moment, the Socialist Party of America is agitated by several cross-currents, some local in their character, and some a reflex of cleavages within the European Socialist movements. Many see in this internal dissention merely an unimportant difference of opinion, or at most, dissatisfaction with the control of the party, and the desire to replace those who have misused it with better men.

We, however, maintain that there is a fundamental distinction in views concerning party policies and tactics. And we believe that this difference is so vast that from our standpoint a radical change in party policies and tactics is necessary.

This essential task is being shirked by our party leaders and officials generally.

Already there is formidable industrial unrest, a seething ferment of discontent, evidenced by inarticulate rumblings which presage striking occurrences. The transformation of industry from a war to a peace basis has thoroughly disorganized the economic structure. Thousands upon thousands of workers are being thrown out of work. Demobilized sailors and soldiers find themselves a drug upon the labor market, unless they act as scabs and strikebreakers. Skilled mechanics, fighting desperately to maintain their war-wage and their industrial status, are forced to strike. Women, who during the war have been welcomed into industries hitherto closed to them, are struggling to keep their jobs. And to cap the climax, the capitalists, through their Chambers of Commerce and their Merchants and Manufacturers' Associations, have resolved to take advantage of the situation to break down even the inadequate organizations labor has built up through generations of painful struggle.

The temper of the workers and soldiers, after the sacrifices they have made in the war, is such that they will not endure the reactionary labor conditions so openly advocated by the master class. A series of labor struggles is bound to follow — indeed, is beginning now. Shall the Socialist Party continue to feed the workers with social reform legislation at this critical period? Shall it approach the whole question from the standpoint of votes and the election of representatives to the legislatures? Shall it emphasize the consumers' point of view, when Socialist principles teach that the worker is robbed at the point of production? Shall it talk about the Cost of Living and Taxation when it should be explaining how the worker is robbed at his job?

There are many signs of the awakening of labor. Strikes are developing which verge on revolutionary action; the trade unions are organizing a Labor Party, in an effort to conserve what they have won and wrest new concessions from the master class. The organization of the Labor Party is an immature expression of a new spirit in the Labor movement; but a Labor Party is not the instrument for the emancipation of the working class; its policy would be in general what is now the official policy of the Socialist Party — reforming Capitalism on the basis of the bourgeois state. Laborism is as much a danger to the revolutionary proletariat as "moderate" Socialism; neither is an instrument for the conquest of power.

CAPITALIST IMPERIALISM

Imperialism is the final stage of Capitalism, in which the accumulated capital or surplus of a nation is too great to be reinvested in the home market. The increased productivity of the working class, due to improved machinery and efficiency methods, and the mere subsistence wage which permits the worker to buy back only a small portion of what he produces, causes an ever-increasing accumulation of commodities, which in turn become capital and must be invested in further production. When Capitalism has reached the stage in which it imports raw materials from undeveloped countries and exports them again in the shape of manufactured products, it has reached its highest development.

This process is universal. Foreign markets, spheres of influence and protectorates, under the intensive development of capitalist industry and finance in turn become highly developed. They, too, seek for markets. National capitalist control, to save itself from ruin, breaks its national bonds and emerges full-grown as a capitalist League of Nations, with international armies and navies to maintain its supremacy.

The United States no longer holds itself aloof, isolated and provincial. It is reaching out for new markets, new zones of influence, new protectorates.

The capitalist class of America is using organized labor for its imperialistic purposes. We may soon expect the capitalist class, in true Bismarckian fashion, to grant factory laws, old-age pensions, unemployment insurance, sick benefits, and the whole litter of bourgeois reforms, so that the workers may be kept fit to produce the greatest profits at the greatest speed.

DANGERS TO AMERICAN SOCIALISM

There is danger that the Socialist Party of America might make use of these purely bourgeois reforms to attract the workers' votes, by claiming that they are victories for Socialism, and that they have been won by Socialist political action; when, as a matter of fact, the object of these master class measures is to prevent the growing class-consciousness of the workers, and to divert them from their revolutionary aim. By agitating for these reforms, therefore, the Socialist Party would be playing into the hands of the American imperialists.

On the basis of the class struggle, then, the Socialist Party of America must re-organize itself, must prepare to come to grips with the master class during the difficult period of capitalist re-adjustment now going on. This it can do only by teaching the working class the truth about present-day conditions; it must preach revolutionary industrial unionism, and urge all the workers to organize into industrial unions, the only form of labor organization which can cope with the power of great modern aggregations of capital. It must carry on its political campaigns, not merely as a means of electing officials to political office, as in the past, but as a year-round educational campaign to arouse the workers to class-conscious economic and political action, and to keep alive the burning ideal of revolution in the hearts of the people.

POLITICAL ACTION

We assert with Marx that "the class struggle is essentially a political struggle," and we can only accept his own oft-repeated interpretation of that phrase. The class struggle, whether it manifest itself on the industrial field or in the direct struggle for governmental control, is essentially a struggle for the capture and destruction of the capitalist state. This is a political act. In this broader view of the term "political," Marx includes revolutionary industrial action. In other words, the objective of Socialist industrial action is "political," in the sense that it aims to undermine the bourgeois state, which "is nothing less than a machine for the oppression of one class by another and that no less so in a democratic republic than under a monarchy."

Political action is also and more generally used to refer to participation in election campaigns for the immediate purpose of winning legislative seats. In this sense, too, we urge the use of political action as a revolutionary weapon.

But both in the nature and the purpose of this form of political action, revolutionary Socialism and "moderate Socialism" are completely at odds.

Political action, revolutionary and emphasizing the implacable character of the class struggle, is a valuable means of propaganda. It must at all times struggle to arouse the revolutionary mass action of the proletariat—its use is both agitational and obstructive. It must on all issues wage war upon Capitalism and the state. Revolutionary Socialism uses the forum of parliament for agitation; but it does not intend to and cannot use the bourgeois state as a means of introducing Socialism: this bourgeois state must be destroyed by the mass action of the revolutionary proletariat. The proletarian dictatorship in the form of a Soviet state is the immediate objective of the class struggle.

Marx declared that "the working class cannot simply lay hold of the ready-made state machinery and wield it for its own purposes." This machinery must be destroyed. But "moderate Socialism" makes the state the centre of its action.

The attitude towards the state divides the Anarchist (anarcho-syndicalist), the "moderate Socialist" and the revolutionary Socialist. Eager to abolish the state (which is the ultimate purpose of revolutionary Socialism), the Anarchist and Anarcho-Syndicalist fail to realize that a state is necessary in the transition period from Capitalism to Socialism; the "moderate Socialist" proposes to use the bourgeois state with its fraudulent democracy, its illusory theory of "unity of all the classes," its standing army, police and bureaucracy oppressing and baffling the masses; the revolutionary Socialist maintains that the bourgeois state must be completely destroyed, and proposes the organization of a new state — the state of the organized producers — of the Federated Soviets — on the basis of which alone can Socialism be introduced.

Industrial Unionism, the organization of the proletariat in accordance with the integration of industry and for the overthrow of Capitalism, is a necessary phase of revolutionary Socialist agitation. Potentially, industrial unionism constructs the basis and develops the ideology of the industrial state of Socialism; but industrial unionism alone cannot perform the revolutionary act of seizure of the power of the state, since under the conditions of Capitalism it is impossible to organize the whole working class, or an overwhelming majority, into industrial unions.

It is the task of a revolutionary Socialist party to direct the struggles of the proletariat and provide a program for the culminating crisis. Its propaganda must be so directed that when this crisis comes, the workers will be prepared to accept a program of the following character:

(a) *The organization of Workmen's Councils;* recognition of, and propaganda for, these mass organizations of the working class as instruments in the immediate struggle, as the form of expression of the class struggle, and as the instruments for the seizure of the power of the state and the basis of the new proletarian state of the organized producers and the dictatorship of the proletariat.

(b) *Workmen's control of industry,* to be exercised by the industrial organizations (industrial unions or Soviets) of the workers and the industrial vote, as against government ownership or state control of industry.

(c) *Repudiation of all national debts* — with provisions to safeguard small investors.

(d) *Expropriation of the banks* — a preliminary measure for the complete expropriation of capital.

(e) *Expropriation of the railways, and the large (trust) organizations of capital* — no compensation to be paid, as "buying-out" the capitalists would insure a continuance of the exploitation of the workers; provision, however, to be made during the transition period for the protection of small owners of stock.

(f) *The socialization of foreign trade.*

These are not the "immediate demands" comprised in the social reform planks now in the platform of our party; they are not a compromise with the capitalist state, but imply a revolutionary struggle against that state and against capitalism, the conquest of power by the proletariat through revolutionary mass action. They imply the new Soviet state of the organized producers, the dictatorship of the proletariat; they are preliminary revolutionary measures for the expropriation of capital and the introduction of communist Socialism.

PROGRAM

1. We stand for a uniform declaration of principles in all party platforms both local and national and the abolition of all social reform planks now contained in them.

2. The party must teach, propagate and agitate exclusively for the overthrow of Capitalism, and the establishment of Socialism through a Proletarian Dictatorship.

3. The Socialist candidates elected to office shall adhere strictly to the above provisions.

4. Realizing that a political party cannot reorganize and reconstruct the industrial organizations of the working class, and that that is the task of the economic organizations themselves, we demand that the party assist this process of reorganization by a propaganda for revolutionary industrial unionism as part of its general activities. We believe it is the mission of the Socialist movement to encourage and assist the proletariat to adopt newer and more effective forms of organization and to stir it into newer and more revolutionary modes of action.

5. We demand that the official party press be party owned and controlled.

6. We demand that officially recognized educational institutions be party owned and controlled.

7. We demand that the party discard its obsolete literature and publish new literature in keeping with the policies and tactics above-mentioned.

8. We demand that the National Executive Committee call an immediate emergency national convention for the purpose of formulating party policies and tactics to meet the present crisis.

9. We demand that the Socialist Party repudiate the Berne Congress or any other conference engineered by "moderate Socialists" and social patriots.

10. We demand that the Socialist Party shall elect delegates to the International Congress proposed by the Communist Party of

Russia (Bolsheviki); that our party shall participate only in a new International with which are affiliated the Communist Party of Russia (Bolsheviki), the Communist Labor Party of Germany (Spartacus), and all other Left Wing parties and groups.

Document No. 2

THE LEFT WING MANIFESTO

(Issued on Authority of the Conference by the National Council of the Left Wing.)

The world is in crisis. Capitalism, the prevailing system of society, is in process of disintegration and collapse. Out of its vitals is developing a new social order, the system of Communist Socialism; and the struggle between this new social order and the old, is now the fundamental problem of international politics.

The predatory "war for democracy" dominated the world. But now it is the revolutionary proletariat in action that dominates, conquering power in some nations, mobilizing to conquer power in others, and calling upon the proletariat of all nations to prepare for the final struggle against capitalism.

But Socialism itself is in crisis. Events are revolutionizing captalism *and Socialism* — an indication that this is the historic epoch of the proletarian revolution. Imperialism is the final stage of Capitalism; and Imperialism means sterner reaction and new wars of conquest — unless the revolutionary proletariat acts for Socialism. Capitalism cannot reform itself; it cannot be reformed. Humanity can be saved from its last excesses only by the Communist revolution. There can now be only the Socialism which is one in temper and purpose with the proletarian revolutionary struggle. There can be only the Socialism which unites the proletariat of the whole world in the general struggle against the desperately destructive Imperialisms — the Imperialisms which array themselves as a single force against the onsweeping proletarian revolution.

The War and Imperialism

The prevailing conditions, in the world of Capitalism and of Socialism, are a direct product of the war; and the war was itself a direct product of Imperialism.

Industrial development under the profit system of Capitalism is based upon the accumulation of capital, which depends upon the expropriation of values produced by the workers. This accumulation of capital promotes, and is itself promoted by, the concentration of industry. The competitive struggle compels each capitalist to secure the most efficient means of production, or a group of capitalists to combine their capital in order to produce more efficiently. This process of concentration of industry and the accumulation of capital, while a product of competition, ultimately denies and ends competition. The concentration of industry and of capital develops monopoly.

Monopoly expresses itself through dictatorial control exercised by finance-capital over industry; and finance-capital unifies Capitalism for world exploitation. Under Imperialism, the banks, whose control is centralized in a clique of financial magnates, dominate the whole of industry directly, purely upon the basis of investment exploitation, and not for purposes of social production. The concentration of industry implies that, to a large extent, industry within the nation has reached its maturity, is unable to absorb all the surplus-capital that comes from the profits of industry. Capitalism, accordingly, must find means outside the nation for the absorption of this surplus. The older export trade was dominated by the export of consumable goods. American exports, particularly, except for the war period, have been largely of cotton, foodstuffs, and raw materials. Under the conditions of Imperialism it is *capital* which is exported, as by the use of concessions in backward territory to build railroads, or to start native factories, as in India, or to develop oil fields, as in Mexico. This means an export of locomotives, heavy machinery, in short, predominantly a trade in iron goods. This export of capital, together with the struggle to monopolize the world's sources of raw materials and to control undeveloped territory, produces Imperialism.

A fully developed capitalist nation is compelled to accept Imperialism. Each nation seeks markets for the absorption of its surplus capital. Undeveloped territory, possessing sources of raw material, the industrial development of which will require the investment of capital and the purchase of machinery, becomes the objective of capitalistic competition between the imperialistic nations.

Capitalism, in the epoch of Imperalism, comes to rely for its "prosperity" and supremacy upon the exploitation and enslavement of colonial peoples, either in colonies, "spheres of influence," "protectorates," or "mandatories"—savagely oppressing hundreds of millions of subject peoples in order to assure high profit and interest rates for a few million people in the favored nations.

This struggle for undeveloped territory, raw materials, and investment markets, is carried on "peacefully" between groups of international finance-capital by means of "agreements," and between the nations by means of diplomacy; but a crisis comes, the competition becomes irreconcilable, antagonisms cannot be solved peacefully, and the nations resort to war.

The antagonisms between the European nations were antagonisms as to who should control undeveloped territory, sources of raw materials, and the investment markets of the world. The inevitable consequence was war. The issue being world power, other nations, including the United States, were dragged in. The United States, while having no direct territorial interests in the war, was vitally concerned, since the issue was world power; and its Capitalism, having attained a position of financal world power, had a direct imperialistic interest at stake.

The imperialistic character of the war is climaxed by an imperialistic peace—a peace that strikes directly at the peace and liberty of the world, which organizes the great imperialistic powers into a sort of "trust of nations," among whom the world is divided financially and territorially. The League of Nations is simply the screen for this division of the world, an instrument for joint domination of the world by a particular group of Imperialism.

While this division of the world solves, for the moment, the problems of power that produced the war, the solution is temporary, since the Imperialism of one nation can prosper only by limiting the economic opportunity of another nation. New problems of power must necessarily arise, producing new antagonisms, new wars of aggression and conquest—unless the revolutionary proletariat conquers in the struggle for Socialism.

The concentration of industry produces monopoly, and monopoly produces Imperialism. In Imperialism there is implied the *socialization of industry, the material basis of Socialism.* Production moreover, becomes international; and the limits of the nation, of national production, become a fetter upon the forces of production. The development of Capitalism produces world economic problems that break down the old order. The forces of production revolt against the fetters Capitalism imposes upon production. The answer of Capitalism is war; the answer of the proletariat is the Social Revolution and Socialism.

THE COLLAPSE OF THE INTERNATIONAL

In 1912, at the time of the first Balkan War, Europe was on the verge of a general imperalistic war. A Socialist International Congress was convened at Basle to act on the impending crisis. The resolution adopted *stigmatized the coming war as imperialistic and as unjustifiable on any pretext of national interest.* The Basle resolution declared:

1. That the war would create an economic and political crisis; 2. That the workers would look upon participation in the war as a crime, which would arouse "indignation and revulsion" among the masses; 3. That the crisis and the psychological condition of the workers would create a situation that Socialists should use "to rouse the masses and hasten the downfall of capitalism;" 4. That the governments "fear a proletarian revolution" and should remember the Paris Commune and the revolution in Russia in 1905, that is, a civil war.

The Basle resolution indicted the coming war as imperialistic, a war necessarily to be opposed by Socialism, which should use the opportunity of war to wage the revolutionary struggle against Capitalism. The policy of Socialism was comprised in the struggle to transform the imperialistic war into a civil war of the oppressed against the oppressors, and for Socialism.

The war that came in 1914 was the same imperialistic war that might have come in 1912, or at the time of the Agadir crisis. But, upon the declaraton of war, *the dominant Socialism, contrary to the Basle resolution, accepted and justified the war.*

Great demonstrations were held. The governments and war were denounced. But, immediately upon the declaration of war, there was a change of front. The war credits were voted by Socialists in the parliaments. The dominant Socialism favored the war; a small minority adopted a policy of petty bourgeois pacifism, and only the Left Wing groups adhered to the policy of revolutionary Socialism.

It was not alone a problem of preventing the war. The fact that Socialism could not prevent the war, was not a justification for accepting and idealizing the war. Nor was it a problem of immediate revolution. The Basle manifesto simply required opposition to the war and the fight to develop out of its circumstances the revolutionary struggle of the proletariat against the war and capitalism.

The dominant Socialism, in accepting and justifying the war, abandoned the class struggle and betrayed Socialism. The class struggle is the heart of Socialism. Without strict conformty to the class struggle, in its revolutionary implications, Socialism becomes either sheer Utopiaism, or a method of recreation. But the dominant Socialism accepted "civil peace," the "unity of all the classes and parties" in order to wage successfully the imperialistic war. The dominant Socialism united with the governments against Socialism and the proletariat.

The class struggle comes to a climax during war. National struggles are a form of expression of the class struggle, whether they are revolutionary wars for liberation or imperialistic wars for spoilation. It is precisely during a war that material conditions provide the opportunity for waging the class struggle to a conclusion for the conquest of power. The war was a war for world-power — a war of the capitalist class against the working class, since world power means power *over* the proletariat.

But the dominant Socialism accepted the war as a war for democracy — as if democracy under the conditions of imperialism is not directly counter-revolutionary! It justified the war as a war for national independence — as if Imperialism is not necessarily determined upon annihilating the independence of nations!

Nationalism, social patriotism, and social Imperialism determined the policy of the dominant Socialism, and not the proletarian class struggle and Socialism. The coming of Socialism was made dependent upon the predatory war and Imperialism, upon the international proletariat cutting each other's throats in the struggles of the ruling class!

The Second International on the whole merged in the opposed imperialistic ranks. This collapse of the International was not an accident, nor simply an expression of the betrayal by individuals. It was the inevitable consequence of the whole tendency and policy of the dominant Socialism as an organized movement.

MODERATE SOCIALISM

The Socialism which developed as an organized movement after the collapse of the revolutionary First International was moderate, petty bourgeois Socialism. It was a Socialism adapting itself to the conditions of national development, abandoning in practice the militant idea of revolutionizing the old world.

This moderate Socialism initiated the era of "constructive" social reforms. It accepted the bourgeois state as the basis of its activity and *strengthened* that state. Its goal became "constructive reforms" and cabinet portfolios — the "co-operation of classes," the policy of openly or tacitly declaring that the coming of Socialism was the concern "of all the classes," instead of emphasizing the Marxian policy that the construction of the Socialist system is the task of the revolutionary proletariat alone. In accepting social reformism, the "co-operation of classes," and the bourgeois parliamentary state as the basis of its action, moderate Socialism was prepared to share responsibility with the bourgeoisie in the control of the capitalist state, even to the extent of defending the bourgeoisie against the working class and its revolutionary mass movements. The counter-revolutionary tendency of the dominant Socialism finally reveals itself in open war against Socialism during the proletarian revolution, as in Russia, Germany and Austria-Hungary.

The dominant moderate Socialism was initiated by the formation of the Social Democratic Party in Germany. This party united on the basis of the Gotha program, in which fundamental revolutionary Socialism was abandoned. It evaded completely the task of the conquest of power, which Marx, in his *Criticism of the Gotha Program,* characterized as follows: "Between the capitalistic society and the communistic, lies the period of the revolutionary transformation of the one into the other. This corresponds to a political transition period, in which the state cannot be anything else than the revolutionary dictatorship of the proletariat."

Evading the actual problems of the revolutionary struggle, the dominant Socialism of the Second International developed into a peaceful movement of organization, of trades-union struggles, of co-operation with the middle class, of legislation and bourgeois State Capitalism as means of introducing Socialism.

There was a joint movement that affected the thought and practice of Socialism; on the one hand, the organization of the skilled workers into trade unions, which secured certain concessions and became a semi-privileged caste; and, on the other, the decay of the class of small producers, crushed under the iron tread of the concentration of industry and the accumulation of capital. As one moved upward, and the other downward, they met, formed a juncture, and united *to use the state to improve their conditions.* The dominant Socialism expressed this unity, developing a policy of legislative reforms and State Capitalism, making the revolutionary class struggle a parliamentary process.

This development meant, obviously, the abandonment of fundamental Socialism. It meant working on the basis of the bourgeois parliamentary state, instead of the struggle to destroy that state; it meant the "co-operation of classes" for State Capitalism, instead of the uncompromising proletarian struggle for Socialism. Government ownership, the objective of the middle class, was the policy of moderate Socialism. Instead of the revolutionary theory of the necessity of conquering capitalism, the official theory and practice was now that of *modifying* Capitalism, of a gradual peaceful "growing into" Socialism by means of legislative reforms. In the words of Jean Jaures: "we shall carry on our reform work to a complete transformation of the existing order."

But Imperialism exposed the final futility of this policy. Imperialism unites the non-proletarian classes, by means of state capitalism, for international conquest and spoilation. The small capitalists, middle class and the aristocracy of labor, which previously acted against concentrated industry, now compromise and unite with concentrated industry and finance-capital in imperialism. The small capitalists accept the domination of finance-capital, being allowed to participate in the adventures and the fabulous profits of Imperialism, upon which now depends the whole of trade and industry; the middle class invests in monopolistic enterprises, an income class whose income depends upon finance-capital, its members securing "positions of superintendence," its technicians and intellectuals being exported to undeveloped lands in process of development, while the workers of the privileged unions are assured steady employment and comparatively high wages through the profits that come from the savage exploitation of colonial peoples. All these non-proletarian social groups accept Imperialism, their "liberal and progressive" ideas becoming factors in the promotion of Imperialism, manufacturing the democratic idealogy of Imperialism with which to seduce the masses. Imperialism requires the centralized state, capable of uniting all the forces of capital, of unifying the industrial process through state control and regulation, of maintaining "class peace," of mobilizing the whole national power in the struggles of Imperialism. *State capitalism is the form of expression of Imperialism,*— precisely that State Capitalism promoted by moderate, petty bourgeois Socialism. What the parliamentary policy of the dominant moderate Socialism accomplished was to buttress the capitalist state, to promote State Capitalism — to strengthen imperialism!

The dominant Socialism was part and parcel of the national liberal movement,— but this movement, under the compulsion of events, merged in Imperialism. The dominant Socialism accepted capitalistic democracy as the basis for the realization of Socialism, — but this democracy merges in Imperialism. The world war was waged by means of this democracy. The dominant Socialism based itself upon the middle class and the aristocracy of labor — but these have compromised with Imperialism, being bribed by a "share" in the spoils of Imperialism. Upon the declaration of war, accordingly, the dominant moderate Socialism accepted the war and united with the imperialistic state.

Upon the advent of Imperialism, Capitalism emerged into a new epoch — an epoch requiring new and more aggressive proletarian tactics. Tactical differences in the Socialist movement almost immediately came to a head. The concentration of industry, together with the subserviency of parliaments to the imperialistic mandates and the transfer of their vital functions to the executive organ of government, developed the concept of industrial unionism in the United States and the concept of mass action in Europe. The struggle against the dominant moderate Socialism became a struggle against its perversion of parliamentarism, against its conception of the state, against its alliance with non-proletarian social groups, and against its acceptance of State Capitalism. Imperialism made mandatory a reconstruction of the Socialist movement, the formulation of a practice in accord with its revolutionary fundamentals. But the representatives of moderate Socialism refused to broaden their tactics, to adapt themselves to the new conditions. The consequence was a miserable collapse under the test of the war and the proletarian revolution — the betrayal of Socialism and the proletariat.

THE PROLETARIAN REVOLUTION

The dominant Socialism justified its acceptance of the war on the plea that a revolution did not materialize, that the masses abandoned Socialism.

This was conscious subterfuge. When the economic and political crisis *did* develop potential revolutionary action in the proletariat, the dominant Socialism immediately assumed an attitude *against the* revolution. The proletariat was urged *not* to make a revolution. The dominant Socialism united with the capitalist governments to prevent a revolution.

The Russian Revolution was the first act of the proletariat against the war and Imperialism. But while the masses made the Revolution in Russia, the bourgeoisie usurped power and organized the regulation bourgeois-parliamentary republic. This was the first stage of the Revolution. Against this bourgeois republic organized the forces of the proletarian Revolution. Moderate Socialism in Russia, represented by the Mensheviki and the Social-Revolutionists, acted against the proletarian revolution. It united with the Cadets, the party of bourgeois Imperialism, in in a coalition government of bourgeois democracy. It placed its faith in the war "against German militarism," in national ideals, in parliamentary democracy and the "co-operation of classes."

But the proletariat, urging on the poorer peasantry, conquered power. It accomplished a proletarian revolution by means of the Bolshevik policy of "all power to the Soviets, "organizing the new transitional state of proletarian dictatorship. Moderate Socialism, even after its theory, that a proletarian revolution was impossible, had been shattered by life itself, acted against the proletarian revolution and mobilized the counter-revolutionary forces against the Soviet Republic, assisted by the moderate Socialism of Germany and the Allies.

Apologists maintained that the attitude of moderate Socialism in Russia was determined not by a fundamental policy, but by its conception that, Russia not being a fully developed capitalist country, it was premature to make a proletarian revolution and historically impossible to realize Socialism.

This was a typical nationalistic attitude, since the proletarian revolution in Russia could not persist as a national revolution, but was compelled by its very conditions to a struggle for the international revolution of the proletariat, the war having initiated the epoch of the proletarian revolution.

The revolution in Germany decided the controversy. The first revolution was made by the masses, against the protests of the dominant moderate Socialism, represented by the Social-Democratic Party. As in Russia, the first stage of the revolution realized a bourgeois parliamentary republic, with power in the hands of the Social-Democratic Party. Against this bourgeois republic organized a new revolution the proletarian revolution directed by the Spartacan-Communists. And, precisely as in Russia, the *dominant moderate Socialism opposed the proletarian revolution,* opposed all power to the Soviets, accepted parliamentary democracy and repudiated proletarian dictatorship.

The issue in Germany could not be obscured. Germany was a fully developed industrial nation, its economic conditions mature for the introduction of Socialism. In spite of dissimilar economic conditions in Germany and Russia, the dominant moderate Socialism pursued a similar counter-revolutionary policy, and revolutionary Socialism, a common policy, indicating the the international character of revolutionary proletarian tactics.

There is, accordingly, a common policy that characterizes moderate Socialism, and that is *its conception of the state.* Moderate Socialism affirms that the bourgeois, democratic parliamentary state is the necessary basis for the introduction of Socialism; accordingly, it conceived the task of the revolution, in Germany and Russia, to be the construction of the democratic parliamentary state, after which the process of introducing Socialism by legislative reform measures could be initiated. Out of this conception of the state developed the counter-revolutionary policy of moderate Socialism.

Revolutionary Socialism, on the contrary, insists that the democratic parliamentary state can never be the basis for the introduction of Socialism; that it is necessary to destroy the parliamentary state, and construct a new state of the organized producers, which will deprive the bourgeoisie of political power, and function as a revolutionary dictatorship of the proletariat.

The proletarian revolution in action has conclusively proven that moderate Socialism is incapable of realizing the objectives of Socialism. Revolutionary Socialism alone is capable of mobilizing the proletariat for Socialism, for the conquest of the power of the state, by means of revolutionary mass action and proletarian dictatorship.

AMERICAN SOCIALISM

The upsurge of revolutionary Socialism in the American Socialist Party, expressed in the Left Wing, is not a product simply of European conditions. It is, in a fundamental sense, the product of the experience of the American movement — the Left Wing tendency in the Party, having been invigorated by the experience of the proletarian revolutions in Europe.

The dominant moderate Socialism of the International was equally the Socialism of the American Socialist Party.

The policy of moderate Socialism in the Socialist Party comprised its policy in an attack upon the larger capitalists, the trusts, maintaining that all other divisions in society, including the lesser capitalists and the middle class, the *petite bourgeoisie,* are material for the Socialist struggle against capitalism. The moderate Socialism dominant in the Socialist Party asserted, in substance: Socialism is a struggle of *all the people* against the trusts and big capital, making the realization of Socialism depend upon the unity of "the people," of the workers, the small capitalists, the small investors, the professions, in short the official Socialist Party actually depended upon the *petite bourgeoisie* for the realization of Socialism.

The concentration of industry in the United States gradually eliminated the small producers, which initiated the movement for government ownership of industry — and for other reforms proposed to check the power of the plutocracy; and this bourgeois policy was the animating impulse of the practice of the Socialist Party.

This party, moreover, developed into an expression of the unions of the aristocracy of labor — of the A. F. of L. The party refused to engage in the struggle against the reactionary unions, to organize a new labor movement of the militant proletariat.

While the concentration of industry and social developments generally conservatized the skilled workers, it developed the typical proletariat of unskilled labor, massed in the basic industries. This proletariat, expropriated of all property, denied access to the A. F. of L. unions, required a labor movement of its own. This impulse produced the concept of industrial unionism, and the I. W. W. But the dominant moderate Socialism rejected industrial unionism and openly or covertly acted against the I. W. W.

Revolutionary industrial unionism, moreover, was a recognition of the fact that extra-parliamentary action was necessary to accomplish the revolution, that the political state should be destroyed and a new proletarian state of the organized producers constructed in order to realize Socialism. But the Socialist Party not only repudiated the form of industrial unionism, it still more emphatically repudiated its revolutionary political implications, clinging to petty bourgeois parliamentarism and reformism.

United with the aristocracy of labor and the middle class, the dominant Socialism in the Socialist Party necessarily developed all the evils of the dominant Socialism of Europe, and, particularly, abandoning the immediate revolutionary task of reconstructing unionism, on the basis of which alone a militant mass Socialism could emerge.

It stultified working class political action, by limiting political action to elections and participation in legislative reform activity. In every single case where the Socialist Party has elected public officials they have pursued a consistent petty bourgeois policy, abandoning Socialism.

This was the official policy of the party. Its representatives were petty bourgeois, moderate, hesitant, oblivious of the class struggle in its fundamental political and industrial implications. But the compulsion of life itself drew more and more proletarian masses in the party, who required simply the opportunity to initiate a revolutionary proletarian policy.

The war and the proletarian revolution in Russia provided the opportunity. The Socialist Party, under the impulse of its membership, adopted a militant declaration against the war. But the officials of the party sabotaged this declaration. The *official* policy of the party on the war was a policy of petty bourgeois pacifism. The bureaucracy of the party was united with the bourgeois People's Council, which accepted a Wilson Peace and betrayed those who rallied to the Council in opposition to the war.

This policy necessarily developed into a repudiation of the revolutionary Socialist position. When events developed the test of accepting or rejecting the revolutionary implications of the declaration against the war, the party bureaucracy immediately exposed its reactionary policy, by repudiating the policy of the Russian and German Communists, and refusing affiliation with the Communist International of revolutionary Socialism.

PROBLEMS OF AMERICAN SOCIALISM

Imperialism is dominant in the United States, which is now a world power. It is developing a centralized, autocratic federal government, acquiring the financial and military reserves for aggression and wars of conquest. The war has aggrandized American Capitalism, instead of weakening it as in Europe. But world events will play upon and influence conditions in this country — dynamically, the sweep of revolutionary proletarian ideas; materially, the coming construction of world markets upon the resumption of competition. Now all-mighty and supreme, Capitalism in the United States must meet crises in the days to come. These conditions modify our immediate task, but do not alter its general character; this is not the moment of revolution, but it is the moment of revolutionary struggle. American Capitalism is developing a brutal campaign of terrorism against the militant proletariat. American Captalism is utterly incompetent on the problems of reconstruction that press down upon society. Its "reconstruction" program is simply to develop its power for aggression, to aggrandize itself in the markets of the world.

These condtions of Imperialism and of multiplied aggression will necessarily produce proletarian action against Capitalism. Strikes are developing which verge on revolutionary action, and in which the suggestion of proletarian dictatorship is apparent, the striker-workers trying to usurp functions of municipal government, as in Seattle and Winnipeg. The mass struggle of the proletariat is coming into being.

A minor phase of the awakening of labor is the trades unions organizing a Labor Party, in an effort to conserve what they have secured as a privileged caste. A Labor Party is not the instrument for the emancipation of the working class; its policy would in general be what is now the official policy of the Socialist Party — reforming Capitalism on the basis of the bourgeois parliamentary state. Laborism is as much a danger to the revolutionary proletariat as moderate, petty bourgeois Socialism, the two being expressions of an identical tendency and policy. There can be no compromise either with Laborism or the dominant moderate Socialism.

But there is a more vital tendency — the tendency of the workers to initiate mass strikes — strikes which are equally a revolt against the bureaucracy in the unions and against the employers. These strikes will constitute the determining feature of proletarian action in the days to come. Revolutionary Socialism must use these mass industrial revolts to broaden the strike, to make it general and militant; use the strike for political objectives, and, finally, develop the mass political strike against Capitalism and the state.

Revolutionary Socialism must base itself on the mass struggles of the proletariat, engage directly in these struggles while emphasizing the revolutionary purposes of Socialism and the proletarian movement. The mass strikes of the American proletariat provide the material basis out of which to develop the concepts and action of revolutionary Socialism.

Our task is to encourage the militant mass movements in the A. F. of L. to split the old unions, to break the power of unions which are corrupted by Imperialism and betray the militant proletariat. The A. F. of L., in its dominant expression, is united with Imperialism. A bulwark of reaction — it must be exposed and its power for evil broken.

Our task, moreover, is to articulate and organize the mass of the unorganized industrial proletariat, which constitutes the basis for a militant Socialism. The struggle for the revolutionary industrial unionism of the proletariat becomes an indispensable phase of revolutionary Socialism, on the basis of which to broaden and deepen the action of the militant proletariat, developing reserves for the ultimate conquest of power.

Imperialism is dominant in the United States. It controls all the factors of social action. Imperialism is uniting all non-proletarian social groups in a brutal State Capitalism, for reaction and spoliation. Against this, revolutionary Socialism must mobilize the mass struggle of the industrial proletariat.

Moderate Socialism is compromising, vacillating, treacherous, because the social elements it depends upon — the *petite bourgeoisie* and the aristocracy of labor — are not a fundamental factor in society; they vacillate between the bourgeois and the proletariat, their social instability produces political instability; and, moreover, they have been seduced by Imperalism and are now united with Imperialism.

Revolutionary Socialism is resolute, uncompromising, revolutionary, because it builds upon a fundamental social factor, the industrial proletariat, which is an actual producing class, expropriated of all property, in whose consciousness the machine process has developed the concepts of industrial unionism and mass action. Revolutionary Socialism adheres to the class struggle because through the class struggle alone — the mass struggle — can the industrial proletariat secure immediate concessions and finally conquer power by organizing the industrial government of the working class.

POLITICAL ACTION

The class struggle is a political struggle. It is a political struggle in the sense that its objective is political — the overthrow of the political organization upon which capitalistic exploitation depends, and the introduction of a new social system. The direct objective is the conquest by the proletariat of the power of the state.

Revolutionary Socialism does not propose to "capture" the bourgeois parliamentary state, but to conquer and destroy it. Revolutionary Socialism, accordingly, repudiates the policy of introducing Socialism by means of legislative measures on the basis of the bourgeois state. This state is a bourgeois state, the organ for the coercion of the proletarian by the capitalist: how, then, can it introduce Socialism? As long as the bourgeois parliamentary state prevails, the capitalist class can baffle the will of the proletariat, since all the political power, the army and the police, industry and the press, are in the hands of the capitalists, whose economic power gives them complete domination. The revolutionary proletariat must expropriate all these by the conquest of the power of the state, by annihilating the political power of the bourgeoisie, before it can begin the task of introducing Socialism.

Revolutionary Socialism, accordingly, proposes to conquer the power of the state. It proposes to conquer by means of political action — political action in the revolutionary Marxian sense, which does not simply mean parliamentarism, but the *class action* of the proletariat *in any form* having as its objective the conquest of the power of the state.

Parliamentary action is necessary. In the parliament, the revolutionary representatives of the proletariat meet Capitalism on all general issues of the class struggle. The proletariat must fight the capitalist class on all fronts, in the process of developing the final action that will conquer the power of the state and overthrow Capitalism. Parliamentary action which emphasizes the implacable character of the class struggle is an indispensable means of agitation. Its task is to expose through political campaigns and the forum of parliament, the class character of the state and the reactionary purposes of Capitalism, to meet Capitalism on all issues, to rally the proletariat for the struggle against Capitalism.

But parliamentarism cannot conquer the power of the state for the proletariat. The conquest of the power of the state is an extra-parliamentary act. It is accomplished, not by the legislative representatives of the proletariat, but by *the mass power of* the proletariat in action. The supreme power of the proletariat inheres in the *political mass strike,* in using the industrial mass power of the proletariat for political objectives.

Revolutionary Socialism, accordingly, recognizes that the supreme form of proletarian political action is *the political mass strike.* Parliamentarism may become a factor in developing the mass strike; parliamentarism, if it is revolutionary and adheres to the class struggle, performs a necessary service in mobilizing the proletariat against Capitalism.

Moderate Socialism refuses to recognize and accept this supreme form of proletarian political action, limits and stultifies political action into legislative routine and non-Socialist parliamentarism. This is a denial of the mass character of the proletarian struggle, an evasion of the tasks of the Revolution.

The power of the proletariat lies fundamentally in its control of the industrial process. The mobilization of this control in action against the bourgeois state and Capitalism means the end of Capitalism, the initial form of the revolutionary mass action that will conquer the power of the state.

UNIONISM AND MASS ACTION

Revolutionary Socialism and the actual facts of the class struggle make the realization of Socialism depend upon the industrial proletariat. The class struggle of revolutionary Socialism mobilizes the industrial proletariat against Capitalism,—that proletariat which is united and disciplined by the machine process, and which actually controls the basic industry of the nation.

The coming to consciousness of this proletariat produces a revolt against the older unionism, developing the concepts of industrial unionism and mass action.

The older unionism was implicit in the skill of the individual craftsmen, who united in craft unions. These unions organized primarily to protect the skill of the skilled workers, which is in itself a form of property. The trades unions developed into "job trusts," and not into militant organs of the proletarian struggle; until to-day the dominant unions are actual bulwarks of Capitalism, merging in Imperialism and accepting state Capitalism. The trades unions, being organized on craft divisions, did not and could not unite the workers as a class, nor are they actual class organizations.

The concentration of industry, developing the machine process, expropriated large elements of the skilled workers of their skill, but the unions still maintained the older idealogy of property contract and caste. Deprived of actual power, the dominant unionism resorts to dickers with the bourgeois state and an acceptance of imperialistic State Capitalism to maintain its privileges, *as against* the industrial proletariat.

The concentration of industry produced the industrial proletariat of unskilled workers, of the machine proletariat. This proletariat, massed in the basic industry, constitutes the militant basis of the class struggle against Capitalism; and, deprived of skill and craft divisions, it turns naturally to mass unionism, to an industrial unionism in accord with the integrated industry of imperialistic Capitalism.

Under the impact of industrial concentration, the proletariat developed its own dynamic tactics — mass action.

Mass action is the proletarian response to the facts of modern industry, and the forms it imposes upon the proletarian class struggle. Mass action starts as the spontaneous activity of unorganized workers massed in the basic industries; its initial form is the mass strike of the unorganized proletariat. The mass movements of the proletariat developing out of this mass response to the tyranny of concentrated industry antagonized the dominant moderate Socialism, which tried to compress and stultify these militant impulses within the limits of parliamentarism.

In this instinctive mass action there was not simply a response to the facts of industry, but the implicit means for action against the dominant parliamentarism. Mass action is industrial in its origin; but its development imposes upon it a political character, since the more general and conscious mass action becomes the more it antagonizes the bourgeois state, becomes *political* mass action.

Another development of this tendency was Syndicalism. In its mass impulse Syndicalism was a direct protest against the futility of the dominant Socialist parliamentarism. But Syndicalism was either unconscious of the theoretical basis of the new movement, or where there was an articulate theory, it was a derivative of Anarchism, making the proletarian revolution an immediate and direct seizure of industry, instead of the conquest of the power of the state. Anarcho-Syndicalism is a departure from Marxism. The theory of mass action and of industrial unionism, however, are in absolute accord with Marxism — *Revolutionary Socialism in action.*

Industrial unionism recognizes that the proletariat cannot conquer power by means of the bourgeois parliamentary state; it recognizes, moreover, that the proletariat cannot use this state to introduce Socialism, but that it must organize a new "state" — the "state" of the organized producers. Industrial unionism, accordingly, proposes to construct the forms of the government of Communist Socialism — the government of the producers. The revolutionary proletariat cannot adapt the bourgeois organs of government to its own use; it must develop its own organs. The larger, more definite and general the conscious industrial unions, the easier becomes the transition to Socialism, since the revolutionary state of the proletariat must reorganize society on the basis of union control and management of industry. Industrial unionism, accordingly, is a necessary phase of revolutionary Socialist agitation and action.

But industrial unionism alone cannot conquer the power of the state. Potentially, industrial unionism may construct the forms of the new society; but only potentially. Actually the forms of the new society are constructed under the protection of a revolutionary proletarian government; the industrial unions become simply the starting point of the Socialist reconstruction of society. Under the conditions of Capitalism, it is impossible to organize the whole working-class into industrial unions; the concept of organizing the working-class industrially *before* the conquest of power is as Utopian as the moderate Socialist conception of the gradual conquest of the parliamentary state.

The proletarian revolution comes at the moment of crisis in Capitalism, of a collapse of the old order. Under the impulse of the crisis, the proletariat acts for the conquest of power, by means of mass action. Mass action concentrates and mobilizes the forces of the proletariat, organized and unorganized; it acts equally against the bourgeois state and the conservative organizations of the working-class. The revolution starts with strikes of protest, developing into mass political strikes and then into revolutionary mass action for the conquest of the power of the state. Mass action becomes political in purpose while extra-parliamentary in form; it is equally a process of revolution and the revolution itself in operation.

The final objective of mass action is the conquest of the power of the state, the annihilation of the bourgeois parliamentary state and the introduction of the transition proletarian state, functioning as a revolutionary dictatorship of the proletariat.

DICTATORSHIP OF THE PROLETARIAT

The attitude toward the state divides the Anarchist (and Anarcho-syndicalist), the moderate Socialist and the revolutionary Socialist. Eager to abolish the state (which is the ultimate purpose of revolutionary Socialism), the Anarchist (and Anarcho-Syndicalist) fails to realize that the state is necessary in the transition period from Capitalism to Socialism. The moderate Socialist proposes to use the bourgeois state, with its fraudulent democracy, its illusory theory of the "unity of all the classes," its standing army, police and bureaucracy oppressing and baffling the masses. The revolutionary Socialist maintains that the bourgeois parliamentary state must be completely destroyed, and proposes the organization of a new state, the dictatorship of the proletariat.

The state is an organ of coercion. The bourgeois parliamentary state is the organ of the bourgeoisie for the coercion of the proletariat. The revolutionary proletariat must, accordingly, destroy this state. But the conquest of political power by the proletariat does not immediately end Capitalism, or the power of the capitalists, or immediately socialize industry. It is, therefore, necessary that the proletariat organize its own state *for the coercion and suppression of the bourgeoisie.*

Capitalism is bourgeois dictatorship. Parliamentary government is the expression of bourgeois supremacy, the form of authority of the capitalist over the worker. The bourgeois state is organized to coerce the proletariat, to baffle the will of the masses. In form a democracy, the bourgeois parliamentary state is in fact an autocracy, the dictatorship of capital over the proletariat.

Bourgeois democracy promotes this dictatorship of capital, assisted by the pulpit, the army and the police. Bourgeois democracy seeks to reconcile all the classes; realizing, however, simply the reconciliation of the proletariat to the supremacy of Capitalism. Bourgeois democracy is political in character, historically necessary, on the one hand, to break the power of feudalism, and on the other, to maintain the proletariat in subjection. It is precisely this democracy that is now the instrument of Imperialism, since the middle class, the traditional carrier of democracy, accepts and promotes Imperialism.

The proletarian revolution disrupts bourgeois democracy. It disrupts this democracy in order to end class divisions and class rule, to realize that industrial self-government of the workers which alone can assure peace and liberty to the peoples.

Proletarian dictatorship is a recognition of the necessity for a revolutionary state to coerce and suppress the bourgeoisie; it is equally a recognition of the fact that, in the Communist reconstruction of society, the proletariat as a class alone counts. The new society organizes as a communistic federation of producers. The proletariat alone counts in the revolution, and in the reconstruction of society on a Communist basis.

The old machinery of the state cannot be used by the revolutionary proletariat. It must be destroyed. The proletariat creates a new state, based directly upon the industrially organized producers, upon the industrial unions or Soviets, or a combination of both. It is this state alone, functioning as a dictatorship of the proletariat, that can realize Socialism.

The tasks of the dictatorship of the proletariat are:

(a) To completely expropriate the bourgeoisie politically, and crush its powers of resistance.

(b) To expropriate the bourgeoisie economically, and introduce the forms of Communist Socialism.

Breaking the political power of the capitalists is the most important task of the revolutionary dictatorship of the proletariat, since upon this depends the economic and social reconstruction of society.

But this political expropriation proceeds simultaneously with an immediate, if partial, expropriation of the bourgeoisie economically. The scope of these measures being determined by industrial development and the maturity of the proletariat. These measures, at first, include:

(a) Workmen's control of industry, to be exercised by the industrial organizations of the workers, operating by means of the industrial vote.

(b) Expropriation and nationalization of the banks, as a necessary preliminary measure for the complete expropriation of capital.

(c) Expropriation and nationalization of the large (trust) organizations of capital. Expropriation proceeds without compensation, as "buying out" the capitalists is a repudiation of the tasks of the revolution.

(d) Repudiation of all national debts and the financial obligations of the old system.

(e) The nationalization of foreign trade.

(f) Measures for the socialization of agriculture.

These measures centralize the basic means of production in the proletarian state, nationalizing industry; and their partial character ceases as reconstruction proceeds. Socialization of industry becomes actual and complete only after the dictatorship of the proletariat has accomplished its task of suppressing the bourgeoisie.

The state of proletarian dictatorship is political in character, since it represents a ruling class, *the proletariat,* which is now supreme; and it uses coercion against the old bourgeois class. But the task of this dictatorship is to render itself unnecessary; and it becomes unnecessary the moment the full conditions of Communist Socialism materialize. While the dictatorship of the proletariat performs its negative task of crushing the old order, it performs the positive task of constructing the new. Together with the government of the proletarian dictatorship, there is developed a new "government," which is no longer government in the old sense, since it concerns itself with the management of production and not with the government of persons. Out of workers' control of industry, introduced by the proletarian dictatorship, there develops the complete structure of Communist Socialism—industrial self-government of the communistically organized producers. When this structure is completed, which implies the complete expropriation of the bourgeoisie economically and politically, the dictatorship of the proletariat ends, in its place coming the full and free social and individual autonomy of the Communist order.

THE COMMUNIST INTERNATIONAL

The Communist International, issuing directly out of the proletarian revolution in action and in process of development, is the organ of the international revolutionary proletariat; just as the

League of Nations is the organ of the joint aggression and resistance of the dominant Imperialism.

The attempt to resurrect the Second International, at Berne, was a ghastly failure. It rallied the counter-revolutionary forces of Europe, which were actually struggling against the proletarian revolution. In this "International" are united all the elements treasonable to Socialism, and the wavering "center" elements whose policy of miserable compromise is more dangerous than open treason. It represents the old dominant moderate Socialism; it based affiliation on acceptance of "labor" parliamentary action, admitting trades unions accepting "political action." The old International abandoned the earlier conception of Socialism as the politics of the Social Revolution — the politics of the class struggle in its revolutionary implications — admitting directly reactionary implications, admitting directly reactionary organizations of Laborism, such as the British Labor Party.

The Communist International, on the contrary, represents a Socialism in complete accord with the revolutionary character of the class struggle. It unites all the consciously revolutionary forces. It wages war equally against the dominant moderate Socialism and Imperialism, each of which has demonstrated its complete incompetence on the problems that now press down upon the world. The Communist International issues its challenge to the conscious, virile elements of the proletariat, calling them to the final struggle against Capitalism on the basis of the revolutionary epoch of Imperialism. The acceptance of the Communist International means accepting the fundamentals of revolutionary Socialism as decisive in our activity.

The Communist International, moreover, issues its call to the subject peoples of the world, crushed under the murderous mastery of imperialism. The revolt of these colonial and subject peoples is a necessary phase of the world struggle against capitalist Imperialism; their revolt must unite itself with the struggle of the conscious proletariat in the imperialistic nations. The Communist International, accordingly, offers an organization and a policy that may unify all the revolutionary forces of the world for the conquest of power, and for Socialism.

It is not a problem of immediate revolution. It is a problem of the immediate revolutionary struggle. The revolutionary epoch of the final struggle against Capitalism may last for years and tens of years; but the Communist International offers a policy and program immediate and ultimate in scope, that provides for the immediate class struggle against Capitalism, in its revolutionary implications, and for the final act of the conquest of power.

The old order is in decay. Civilization is in collapse. The proletarian revolution and the Communist reconstruction of society — *the struggle for these* — is now indispensable. This is the message of the Communist International to the workers of the world.

The Communist International calls the proletariat of the world to the final struggle!

CHAPTER V

The Communist Party of America *

In the previous chapter dealing with the development of the Left Wing movement in the Socialist Party, mention was made of a divergence of opinion which manifested itself in the First National Conference of the Left Wing, which was held in New York on the 25th day of June, 1919.

At that conference the delegates representing the Russian Socialist Federation and the Michigan delegates, together with some others, numbering thirty-one in all, insisted that the conference should take immediate action looking toward the formation of a Communist Party in the United States. The majority of that conference, as we have already shown, still believed there was a prospect of gaining control of the machinery of the Socialist Party, and was reluctant to abandon the organization at that time. The minority immediately withdrew from the conference, and formed a National Organization Committee to issue a call for a convention with the object of organizing a Communist Party. This move had the full support of the Russian Socialist Federation.

This organization committee, which consisted of Dennis E. Batt, D. Elbaum, O. C. Johnson, John Keracher, S. Kopnagel, I. Stilson, and Alexander Stoklitsky, opened offices at 1221 Blue Island Avenue, Chicago, Ill. The call issued by this committee was printed in the "Novy Mir" in the issue of July 7, 1919, a translation of which is as follows:

"CALL FOR A NATIONAL CONVENTION FOR THE PURPOSE OF ORGANIZING A COMMUNIST PARTY IN AMERICA

"In this, the most momentous period of the world's history, capitalism is tottering to its ruin. The proletariat is straining at the chains which bind it. A revolutionary spirit is spreading throughout the world. The workers are rising to answer the clarion call of the Third International.

"Only one Socialism is possible in this crisis. A Socialism based upon understanding. A Socialism that will express in action the needs of the proletariat. The time has passed for temporizing and hesitating. We must act. The Communist call of the Third International, the echo of the Communist Manifesto of 1848, must be answered.

* See Addendum, Part I.

"The National Executive Committee of the Socialist Party of America has evidenced by its expulsion of nearly half of the membership that they will not hesitate at wrecking the organization in order to maintain control. A deadlock has been precipitated in the ranks of revolutionary Socialism by the wholesale expulsion or suspension of the membership comprising the Socialist Party of Michigan, locals and branches throughout the country, together with seven Language Federations. This has created a condition in our movement that makes it manifestly impossible to longer delay the calling of a convention to organize a new party. Those who realize that the capturing of the Socialist Party as such is but an empty victory will not hesitate to respond to this call and leave the 'Right' and 'Center' to sink together with their 'revolutionary' leaders.

"The majority of the delegates to the Left Wing Conference in New York meekly neglected to sever their connections with the reactionary National Executive Committee. Rendered impotent by the conflicting emotions and lack of understanding present they continued to mark time as Centrists in the wake of the Right. Their policy is one of endeavor to capture the old party machinery and the stagnant elements who have been struggling for a false unity and who are only ready to abandon the ship when it sinks beneath the waves of reaction.

"This condition confronting the minority delegates representing the following organizations — Socialist Party of Michigan; Left Wing State Convention of Minnesota; Locals, Buffalo; Chicago; Union Local, N. J.; Cudahy, Wis.; Rochester, N. Y.; Rockford, Ill.; Kenosha, Wis.; New York; Providence; Nanticoke, Pa.; Milwaukee, Wis.; Boston, Mass.; Polish, Lettish, Russian, Jewish, Lithuanian, Esthonian Federations — at the Left Wing Conference has been met by this call for the organization of a Communist Party in America.

"No other course is possible, therefore, we, the minority delegates at the Left Wing Conference, call a convention to meet in the city of Chicago on September 1, 1919, for the purpose of organizing a Communist Party in America.

"This party will be founded upon the following principles:

"1. The present is the period of the dissolution and collapse of the whole capitalist world system; which will mean the complete collapse of world culture, if capitalism with its unsolvable contradictions is not replaced by Communism.

"2. The problem of the proletariat consists in organizing and training itself for the conquest of the powers of the state. This conquest of power means the replacement of the state machinery of the bourgeoisie with a new proletarian machinery of government.

"3. This new proletarian state must embody the dictatorship of the proletariat, both industrial and agricultural, this dictatorship constituting the instrument for the taking over of property used for exploiting the workers, and for the reorganization of society on a communist basis.

"Not the fraudulent bourgeois democracy — the hypocritical form of the rule of the finance-oligarchy, with its purely formal equality — but proletarian democracy based on the possibility of actual realization of freedom for the working masses; not capitalist bureaucracy, but organs of administrations which have been created by the masses themselves, with the real participation of these masses in the government of the country and in the activity of the communistic structure — this should be the type of the proletarian state. The workers' councils and similar organizations represent its concrete form.

"4. The dictatorship of the proletariat shall carry out the abolition of private property in the means of production and distribution, by transfer to the proletarian state under Socialist administration of the working class; nationalization of the great business enterprises and financial trust.

"5. The present world situation demands the closest relation between the revolutionary proletariat of all countries.

"6. The fundamental means of the struggle for power is the mass action of the proletariat, a gathering together and concentration of all its energies; whereas methods such as the revolutionary use of bourgeois parliamentarism are only of subsidiary significance.

"In those countries in which the historical development has furnished the opportunity, the working class has utilized the regime of political democracy for its organization against capitalism. In all countries where the conditions for a workers' revolution are not yet ripe, the same process will go on.

"But within the process the workers must never lose sight of the true character of bourgeois democracy. If the finance-oligarchy considers it advantageous to veil its deeds of violence behind parliamentary votes, then the capitalist power has at its command in order to gain its ends, all the traditions and attainments of former centuries of upper class rule, demagogism, persecution, slander, bribery, calumny and terror. To demand of the proletariat that it shall be content to yield itself to the artificial rules devised by its mortal enemy, but not observed by the enemy, is to make a mockery of the proletarian struggle for power — a struggle which depends primarily on the development of separate organs of the working-class power.

"7. The old Socialist International has broken into three main groups: (a) Those frankly social patriots who since 1914 have supported their bourgeoisie and transformed these elements of the working class which they control into hangmen of the international revolution.

"(b) The 'Center,' representing the elements which are constantly wavering and incapable of following a definite plan of action, and which are at times positively traitorous; and

"(c) The Communists.

"As regards the social patriots, who everywhere in the critical moment oppose the proletarian revolution with force of arms, a merciless fight is absolutely necessary. As regards the 'Center,' our tactics must be to separate the revolutionary elements by pitilessly criticizing the leaders. Absolute separation from the organization of the 'Center' is necessary.

"It is necessary to rally the groups and proletarian organizations who, though not as yet in the wake of revolutionary trend of the Communist movement, nevertheless have manifested and developed a tendency leading in that direction.

"Socialist criticism has sufficiently stigmatized the bourgeois world order. The task of the International Communist

Party is now to overthrow this order and to erect in its place the structure of the Socialist world order. Under the Communist banner, the emblem under which the first great victories have already been won; in the war against imperialistic barbarity, against the privileged classes, against the bourgeois state and bourgeois property, against all forms of social and national oppression — we call upon the proletarians of all lands to unite!

"PROGRAM OF THE CALL

"1. We favor International alliance of the Socialist movement of the United States only with the Communist groups of other countries, such as the Bolsheviki of Russia, Spartacans of Germany, etc., according to the program of Communism as above outlined.

"2. We are opposed to association with other groups not committed to the revolutionary class struggle, such as labor parties, non-partisan leagues, people's council, municipal ownership leagues and the like.

"3. We maintain that the class struggle is essentially a political struggle, that is, a struggle by the proletariat to conquer the capitalist state, whether its form be monarchistic or democratic-republican, and to destroy and replace it by a governmental structure adapted to the Socialist transformation.

"4. The party shall propagandize class-conscious industrial unionism against the craft form of unionism, and shall carry on party activity in co-operation with industrial disputes that take on a revolutionary character.

"5. We do not disparage voting nor the value of success in electing our candidates to public office — not if these are in direct line with the class struggle. The trouble comes with the illusion that political or industrial immediate achievements are of themselves steps in the revolution, the progressive merging of capitalism into the co-operative commonwealth.

"The basis of our political campaign should be:

"(a) To propagandize the overthrow of capitalism by proletarian conquest of the political power and the establishment of a dictatorship of the proletariat.

"(b) To maintain a political organization as a clearing-house for proletarian thought, a center of political education for the development of revolutionary working-class action.

"(c) To keep in the foreground our consistent appeal for proletarian revolution; and to analyze the counter-proposals and reformist palliatives in their true light of evasion of the issue; recognizing at all times the characteristic developments of the class conflict as applicable to all capitalistic nations.

"(d) To propagandize the party organization as the organ of contact with the revolutionary proletariat of other lands, the basis for international association being the same political understanding and the common plan of action, tending toward increasing unity in detail as the international crisis develops.

"6. Socialist platforms, proceeding on the basis of the class struggle, recognizing that the Socialist movement has come into the historic period of the social revolution, can contain only the demand for the dictatorship of the proletariat.

"(a) The basis of this demand should be thoroughly explained in the economic, political and social analysis of the class struggle, as evolving within the system of capitalism.

"(b) The implications of this demand should be illustrated by the first steps and general modes of social reconstruction dependent upon and involved within the proletarian domination of the political life of the nation.

"(c) A municipal platform of Socialism cannot proceed on a separate basis, but must conform to the general platform, simply relating the attainment of local power to the immediate goal of gaining national power. There are no city problems within the terms of the class struggle, only the one problem of capitalist versus proletarian domination.

"7. We realize that the coming of the social revolution depends on an overwhelming assertion of mass power by the proletariat, taking on political consciousness and the definite direction of revolutionary Socialism. The manifestations of this power and consciousness are not subject to precise precalculation. But the history of the movement of the proletariat toward emancipation since 1900 shows the close connection between the revolutionary proletarian assertion and the political mass strike.

"The mass action conception looks to the general unity of the proletarian forces under revolutionary provocation and stimulus. In the preliminary stages, which alone come within our predetermination and party initiative, the tactics of mass action includes all mass demonstration and mass struggles which sharpen the understanding of the proletariat as to the class conflict and which separate the revolutionary proletariat into a group distinct from all others.

"Mass action, in time of revolutionary crisis, or in the analogous case of large scale industrial conflict, naturally accepts the council form of organization for its expression over a continued period of time.

"8. Applying our declarations of party principal to the organization of the party itself, we realize the need, in correspondence with the highly centralized capitalist power to be combated, of a centralized party organization.

"Organizations indorsing the principles and program outlined as a tentative basis for the organization of a Communist Party are invited to send delegates to the convention in Chicago on September 1, 1919.

"The basis of representation to be one delegate for every organization and one additional for every additional 500 members or major fraction thereof.

"Provided, also, that each Language Federation shall have one fraternal delegate at the convention.

"Provided further, that in states where the states are organized, they shall send delegates as states. In states which are not organized, the locals shall send delegates as such. In locals which are not organized a part of the local may send a delegate.

"NATIONAL ORGANIZATION COMMITTEE.

"DENNIS E. BATT,
"D. ELBAUM,
"O. C. JOHNSON,
"JOHN KERACHER,
"S. KOPNAGEL,
"I. STILSON,
"ALEXANDER STOKLITSKY.

"P. S.—Send communications to the National office of the organization committee: O. C. Johnson, Secretary, 1221 Blue Island Ave., Chicago, Ill."

In commenting editorially upon the circumstances which led up to the issue of this call, the "Novy Mir," in the same issue of July 7, 1919, page 3, says:

"From the Editor.— As we already pointed out, among the delegates to the All-American Conference of the Left Wing that recently took place, a serious disagreement was disclosed on the question of organizing a new Communist Party in America. The minority, numbering thirty-one delegates, i. e., a little more than one-third of all the delegates present at the conference, stood for an immediate break with the official Right Wing of the American Socialist Party in the person of its National Executive Committee, and for the immediate formation of an American Communist Party.

"Encountering an evasive, full of hesitation and half heartedness attitude toward this question from the majority numbering fifty-five delegates, the minority, which consisted in part of representatives of All Russian Socialist Federations excluding the Ukrainian (the representative of Ukrainain Federation joined the 'majority' of the conference, but we have information that in this respect, he did not represent the opinion of his federation) resolved, not leaving officially the conference, not breaking with the Left Wing, the majority of which this 'minority' really was, to take immediately independent measures for the purpose of organizing an American Communist Party.

"With this purpose in view, the 'minority' has decided to appeal to the true revolutionary elements in the ranks of the American Socialist Party to refuse to participate in the Emergency Convention, called by the National Executive Committee for August 30th, but, instead, to participate in the Constituent Convention of the Communist Party, called in Chicago, September 1st.

"Principles of the Third International, and also, with a few modifications, the full program, adopted by the conference of the Left Wing, were embodied in the appeal by the 'minority.'"

During the month of July, 1919, the hope of the so-called Left Wing elements to control the National Emergency Convention of the Socialist Party having apparently weakened, the majority of the National Council of the Left Wing effected a compromise with the National Organization Committee. The result was the issuance of a joint call for a Communist Party Convention to take place on September 1, 1919, in Chicago, Ill., by the National Council of the Left Wing Section, and the National Organization Committee, representing the delegates which had bolted the National Left Wing Conference in June. This joint call was almost identical in terms with the call published in "Novy Mir" on July 7, 1919, and is published in the "Revolutionary Age," issue of Saturday, August 23, 1919, on page 8.

In commenting upon this call the "Revolutionary Age" says:

> "After considerable negotiations seeking to eliminate the differences existing between the Communist elements of the Left Wing, as represented by the so-called Minority and Majority of the Left Wing Conference held in New York, June 21st to 24th, the National Council of the Left Wing Section Socialist Party, realizing the necessity of the organization of the Communist Party of America, in accordance with the decisions of the National Left Wing Conference, realizing also the futility of participating in the proposed Emergency Convention of the Socialist Party, does hereby join with the National Organization Committee in issuing the following call for the organization of the Communist Party:"

As this call was the official call for the Communist Party Convention which took place in Chicago on September 1, 1919, we deem it expedient to reproduce it in full at the close of this chapter, although it is almost identical with that which had previously appeared in "Novy Mir."

On July 19, 1919, the National Organization Committee, above referred to, issued the first number of the "Communist" as the official organ of the Communist Party of America. This paper is published in Chicago. Dennis E. Batt appears as the editor. The names of the organizing committee are given with Dennis E. Batt as secretary of the committee, Alexander Stoklitsky as organizer, and I. Stilson as treasurer. It should be noted that Stilson was the translator-secretary of the Lithuanian branch of the Socialist Party which had been suspended by action of the National Executive Committee of that party. The business manager is given as A. J. McGregor.

Prior to the meeting of the National Convention on September 1, 1919, the organizing committee announced in the August 2d issue of the "Communist" (p. 8) that they were prepared to supply temporary charters, application for membership cards, dues stamps and membership cards to organizations endorsing the call for the organization convention of September 1st.

The committee had printed delegates' credentials and membership cards, and issued instructions for the organization of the Communist locals, and in every way prepared for the coming convention.

Pursuant to call the Communist Party Convention opened in Chicago on September 1, 1919. It is evident from the accounts of the convention that the delegates were animated by a real revolutionary fervor. We quote from the report on the convention by I. E. Ferguson, in the September 27th issue of the "Communist," as follows:

> "There was one moment which revealed the tense enthusiasm of this Convention, a moment never to be forgotten. On Monday, September 1st, near the hour of noon, an orchestra struck the first chord of the Internationale. Instantly there was a thunderous accompaniment of sustained cheering and spontaneous singing. There was no mistaking the martial challenge. It was as if the voices of the millions had come into this colorless hall to impress upon these delegates their deprivations and longings, their strength and readiness for the final conflict. It was a rare signing of the Internationale. So began the Communist Party of America."

The convention was called to order in the name of the National Left Wing Council, and the National Organization Committee, representing the minority group of the Left Wing Conference.

Louis C. Fraina, of New York, was elected temporary Chairman.

In the opening sessions of this convention, a sharp division among the delegates developed. Those representing the Foreign Language Federations, together with the Michigan delegation on the one hand, which constituted a majority, and the delegates under the leadership of the National Left Wing Council on the other, representing the minority. There were, however, on the side of the minority, delegates from South Slavic and Hungarian Federations; and also from the Lithuanian, Polish and Jewsh Federations. The differences between these two groups having been compromised, the work of the convention proceeded, the principal business being the formulation of a constitution and program. A committee to formulate the program was appointed, consisting of Louis C. Fraina, D. Elbaum, Alexander Stoklitsky, Nicholas I. Hourwich, Bittleman, Dennis E. Batt, Maximilian Cohen, Jay Lovestone, and Wicks.

The Constitution Committee consisted of Hiltzig, C. E. Ruthenberg, George Ashkenouzi, I. E. Ferguson, Oscar Tywerowsky, J. G. Stilson, and Forsinger. The constitution which was prepared by this committee, and adopted by the convention, contained several fundamental points of difference from the constitution of the Socialist Party of America.

The provisions relating to party membership are contained in Article III and are as follows:

"III. Membership

"Section 1. Every person who accepts the principles and tactics of the Communist Party and the Communist International and agrees to engage actively in the work of the party shall be eligible to membership. It is the aim of this organization to have in its ranks only those who participate actively in its work.

"Section 2. Applicants for membership shall sign an application card reading as follows:

'The undersigned, after having read the constitution and program of the Communist Party, declares his adherence to the principles and tactics of the party and the Communist International; agrees to submit to the discipline of the party as stated in its constitution and pledges himself to engage actively in its work.'

"Section 3. Every member must join a duly constituted branch of the party. There shall be no members-at-large.

"Section 4. All application cards must be endorsed by two persons who have been members for not less than three months.

"Section 5. Applications for membership shall not be finally acted upon until two months after presentation to the branch, and in the meantime applicant shall pay initiation fee and dues and shall attend meetings and classes. He shall have a voice and no vote. Provided that this rule shall t apply to the charter members of new branches nor to the mbers who make application to newly organized branches ng the first month.

"Section 6. No person who is a member or supporter of any other political organization shall be admitted to membership.

"Section 7. No person who has an entire livelihood from rent, interest or profit shall be eligible to membership in the Communist Party.

"Section 8. No person shall be accepted as a member who enters into the service of the national, state or local governmental bodies otherwise than through the civil service, or by legal compulsion.

"Provided, that the civil employment by the government is of a non-political character.

"Section 9. No members of the Communist Party shall contribute articles or editorials of a political or economic character to publications other than those of the Communist Party or of parties affiliated with the Communist International. (This clause shall not be considered as prohibiting the contribution of articles written from an economic or scientific standpoint to scientific or professional journals. Permission to answer an attack upon the Communist Party in the bourgeois press may be granted by the Central Executive Committee)."

It should be noted that those making application for membership were obliged to state that they had read the constitution and program of the party and to declare their adherence to the principles and tactics of the party, and of the Communist International. This has reference to the Third International of Moscow (Sec. I Chap. XVII), and pledges the candidate to engage actively in the work of the organization.

Section 7 bars from membership in the party all persons who have their entire livelihood from rents, interest or profits.

Section 8 bars all persons from membership who have entered the service of the United States, in the army, navy or other governmental employment.

Section 9 shows that the party intends to exercise complete control over its party membership.

The constitution will be found in full at the close of this chapter.

PHOTOGRAPH OF FIRST CONVENTION, COMMUNIST PARTY OF AMERICA, CHICAGO ILL., SEPT. 1–7, 1919.

1. Al. Renner, Chairman
2. Alexander Stocklitzky
3. Dr. Koppnagle, Chicago
4. Dennis E. Batt, Chicago
10. Nicholas Hourwich, New York
12. Louis C. Fraina, Boston and New York
19. Rose Pastor Stokes, New York
20. Isaac E. Ferguson, Chicago
23. Oscar Tiverowsky, New York
36. Charles Jannsen, Massachusetts
52. O. C. Johnson, Missouri
37. Max Cohen, New York
39. H. A. Rosenthal, Philadelphia
40. A. Forsinger, Philadelphia
43. Jay Lovestone, New York
44. G. Azkenuzi, New York
53. M. Wicks, Chicago
45. H. Hiltzik
46. J. V. Stilson
47. A. Bittleman, New York
49. Mrs. Nicholas Hourwich, New York
51. Carl Ruthenberg

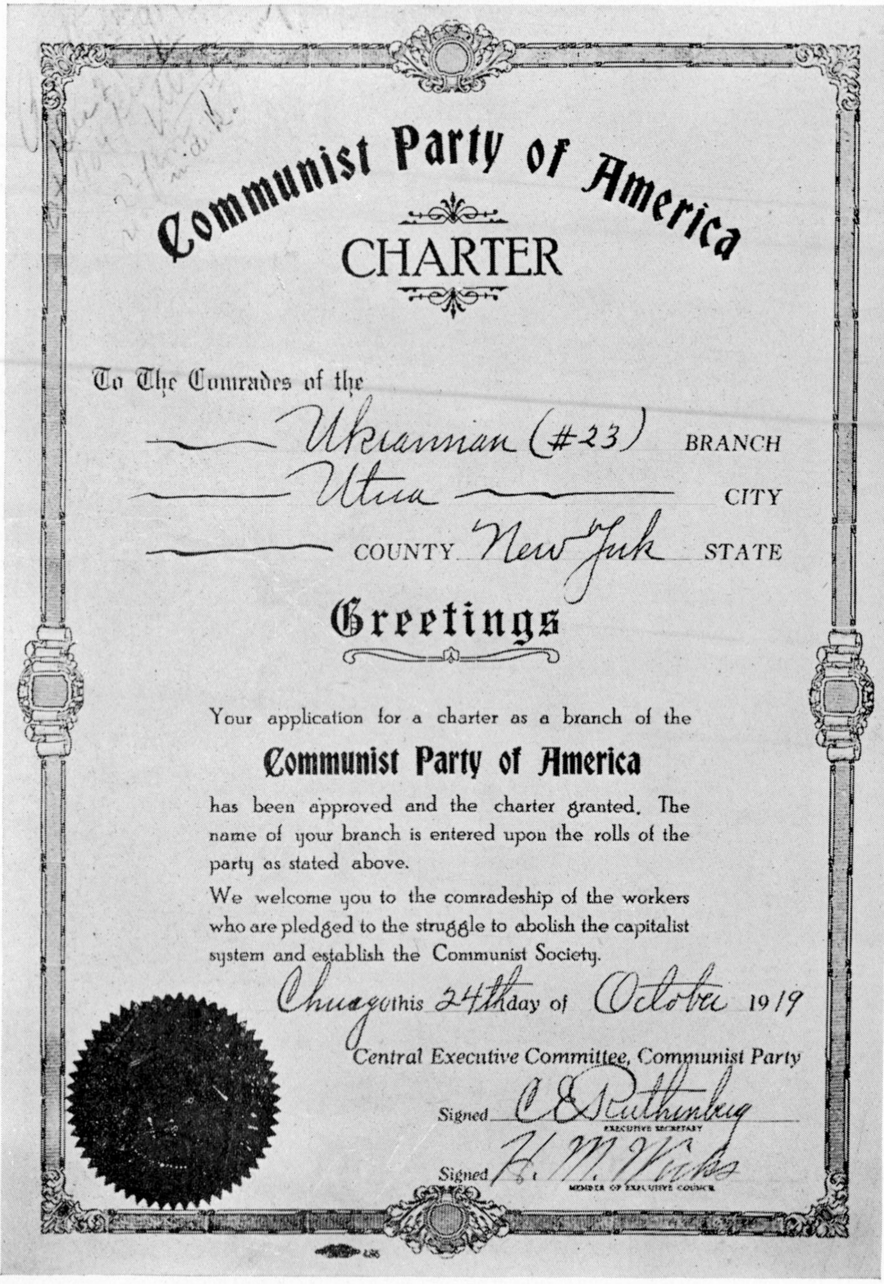

Communist Party of America
CHARTER

To The Comrades of the

Ukrainian (#23) BRANCH

Utica CITY

COUNTY New York STATE

Greetings

Your application for a charter as a branch of the

Communist Party of America

has been approved and the charter granted. The name of your branch is entered upon the rolls of the party as stated above.

We welcome you to the comradeship of the workers who are pledged to the struggle to abolish the capitalist system and establish the Communist Society.

Chicago this 24th day of October 1919

Central Executive Committee, Communist Party

Signed C. E. Ruthenberg
EXECUTIVE SECRETARY

Signed H. M. Wicks
MEMBER OF EXECUTIVE COUNCIL

CHARTER OF COMMUNIST PARTY OF AMERICA.

C. E. RUTHENBERG AND I. E. FERGUSON.

Leaders of the Communist Party of America. Tried and convicted on charge of criminal anarchy upon evidence furnished the District Attorney of New York County by this Committee; now serving sentence in State Prison from 5 to 10 years.

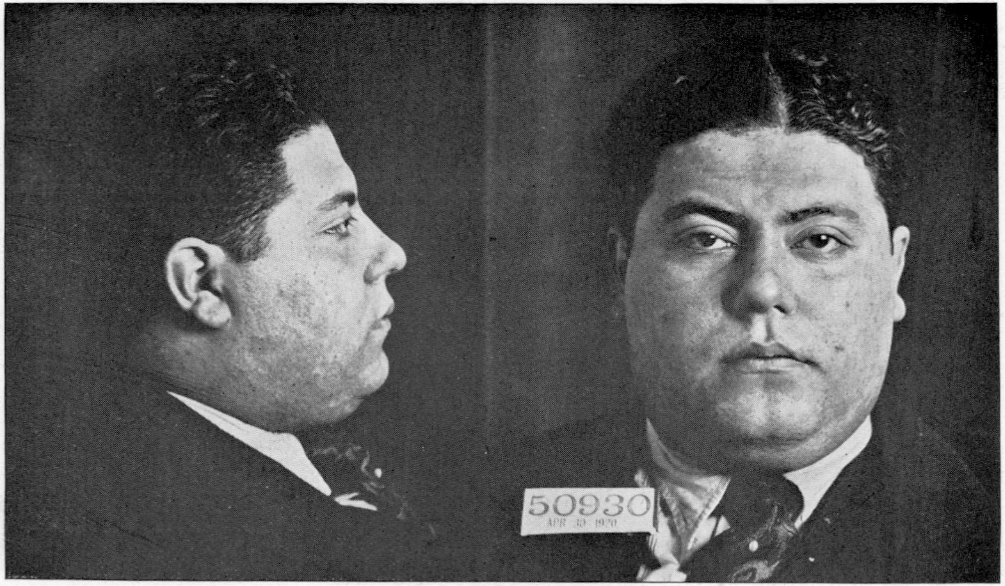

HARRY M. WINITSKY

Executive Secretary, Local New York, Communist Party of America.

Arrested on charge of Criminal Anarchy by direction of the Committee, November 8, 1919, tried, convicted and sentenced to State Penitentiary for not less than five years nor more than ten years.

Two drafts of the manifesto and program were presented to the Program Committee. One by Dennis E. Batt of Detroit, and the other by Louis C. Fraina, of Boston. The latter, after much condensation, was adopted by the committee, Batt and Wicks being in the minority.

The majority report of this committee was adopted by the convention, and the Communist manifesto and program became the statement of the party principles and tactics. The principles and objects of the Communist Party as stated in this manifesto are almost identical with those set forth in the Left Wing Manifesto, which has been previously referred to in this report.

Much of the redundancy of that manifesto was removed. The new manifesto opens with the following statement:

> "The world is on the verge of a new era. Europe is in revolt. The masses of Asia are stirring uneasily. Capitalism is in collapse. The workers of the world are seeing a new life and securing new courage. Out of the night of war is coming a new day. . . .
>
> "The call to action has come. The workers must answer the call.
>
> "The Communist Party of America is the party of the working class. The Communist Party proposes to end Capitalism and organize a workers' industrial republic. . . . The Communist Party insists that the problems of the American worker are identical with the problems of the workers of the world."

The inspiration of Soviet Russia and the international character of the movement which the Communist Party sought to represent is illustrated in the following expression which appears in this document:

> "A giant struggle is convulsing the world. The war is at end, but peace is not here. *The struggle is between the capitalist nations of the world and the international proletariat, inspired by Soviet Russia.*" (*Page 1.*)

The dominant Socialist parties are criticized for their participation in the World War. The collapse of the Second International is characterized as marking "the transition from the older moderate Socialism to the new Socialism of revolutionary practice and promise in the Communist International." (Page 3.)

The parliamentarism of the majority parties of European countries is criticised, and the conservative organizations of labor, as well as the parliamentary Socialists, are stated to have proved their utter incompetence to cope with the new conditions of the class struggle. The existing forms of government are discarded. The parliamentary state is denounced. "Communism rejects this conception of the state. It rejects the idea of class reconciliation and the parliamentary conquest of Capitalism. The Communist Party alone is capable of mobilizing the proletariat for the revolutionary mass struggle to conquer the power of the state. The Communist Party realizes that it is necessary to develop separate organs of working class political power by means of which to crush the resistance of Capitalism and establish the Communist Commonwealth." (Page 6.)

In commenting upon American conditions, the Socialist Party is characterized as "a movement of isolated and indefinite protest." The Socialist Labor Party, on the other hand, is stated to have "developed a purely theoretical activity, of real value" (Page 7) but isolated from the masses. The United States is described as a world power "developing a centralized, autocratic Federal government, acquiring financial and military reserves for aggression and wars of conquest." The recent war is stated to have strengthened American capitalism, instead of weakening it, as in Europe. It is declared to be developing "a brutal campaign of terrorism" which is characterized as "utterly incompetent on the problems of reconstruction that press down upon society."

In commenting on the present situation in the United States, the manifesto says: "While this is not the moment of actual revolution, it is a moment of struggles pregnant with revolution."

It is pointed out: "Strikes are developing, verging on revolutionary action, and in which the suggestion of proletarian dictatorship is apparent. The striker-workers try to usurp functions of industry and government, as in the Seattle and Winnepeg general strikes." (Page 8.)

The formation of a labor party is deprecated, and laborism is considered as great a danger to the proletariat as moderate Socialism.

The opportunity afforded the party in the general labor unrest is stated as follows: "But there is a more vital tendency, the tendency of the workers to start mass strikes, strikes which are equally a revolt against the bureaucracy of the unions and the capitalists. The Communist Party will endeavor to broaden and deepen these strikes, making them general and militant, developing the general political strike."

The purpose of the Communist Party is indicated in the opening paragraph of the program of the party, in which it says: "Its aim is to direct this struggle to the conquest of political power, the overthrow of capitalism and the destruction of the bourgeois state." (Page 14.)

This statement is explained by the following quotation from the manifesto: "Communism does not propose to 'capture' the bourgeois parliamentary state, but to conquer and destroy it. As long as the bourgeois state prevails, the capitalist class can baffle the will of the proletariat."

In other words, the Communist Party does not intend to employ the ballot as a means of bringing about Socialism. This is made especially clear by the following provisions of its party program:

> "(a) The Communist Party shall keep in the foreground its consistent appeal for proletarian revolution, the overthrow of capitalism and the establishment of a dictatorship of the proletariat. . . .
>
> "(b) Participation in parliamentary campaigns which in the general struggle of the proletariat is of secondary importance, *is for the purpose of revolutionary propaganda only.*"

Such participation in elections is intended solely for propaganda purposes, and not with the intention of seeking to utilize the machinery of government to bring about any reforms of benefit to the working-class. This is made clear by the following provision in the party program:

> "Parliamentary representatives of the Communist Party shall not introduce or support reform measures." (Page 15.)

In other words, should members of the Communist Party be elected to legislative positions their sole purpose would be to use such office as a means of revolutionary agitation.

The purpose of the party to overthrow and destroy the existing government of this country being clearly established, the manifesto proceeds to outline the methods by which this objective may be obtained. "The conquest of the power of the state is accomplished by the mass power of the proletariat. Political mass strikes are a vital factor in developing this mass power, preparing the working class for the conquest of capitalism. *The power of the proletariat lies fundamentally in its control of the industrial process.* The mobilizing of this control against capitalism means the initial form of the revolutionary mass action that will conquer the power of the state."

In this brief paragraph the method by which the revolution is to be made effective is clearly revealed. It is pointed out that the workers, if properly organized, may assume actual control of industries. Then by use of the general or mass strike having for its objective the overthrow of government, the workers can shut off the sources of the nation's supply, block the avenues of transportation and by these means prevent the government from mobilizing its resources, thus rendering the authorities impotent to prevent the carrying out of a program of revolution.

Mass action is described as "industrial in its origin, but it acquires political character and it develops fuller forms. . . . Mass action concentrates and mobilizes the forces of the proletariat, organized and unorganized; it acts equally against *the bourgeois state* and the conservative organizations of the working class."

The development of this mass action is described as follows:

> "Strikes of protest develop into general political strikes and then into revolutionary mass action for the conquest of the power of the state."

In order to make perfectly clear that the revolutionary action contemplated by this party is in no sense to be an orderly exercise of the power of the ballot, and that the change of our form of government is sought by means not prescribed by the constitution either of the nation or the state, the manifesto goes on to say: "Mass action becomes political in purpose while extra-parliamentary in form; it is equally a process of revolution and the revolution itself in operation."

The necessity for the revolution is declared to be for the following reasons:

> "The state is an organ of coercion. The bourgeois parliamentary state is the organ of the bourgeoisie for the coercion of the proletariat. Parliamentary government is

the expression of bourgeois supremacy, the form of authority of the capitalist over the worker. Bourgeois democracy promotes the dictatorship of capital, assisted by the press, the pulpit, the army and the police. . . . Therefore it is necessary that the proletariat organize its own state *for the coercion and suppression of the bourgeoisie.* Proletarian dictatorship is a recognition of that fact; it is equally a recognition of the fact that in the Communist reconstruction of society the proletariat alone counts as a class."

This passage of the manifesto indicates clearly that it is the purpose of the Communist Party to seek the establishment of a government patterned after the regime set up in Soviet Russia from which all elements of society, except the propertyless class, shall be excluded from participation in its affairs.

The manifesto closes with the recognition of the Communist International of Moscow:

"The Communist International calls!
"Workers of the World, Unite! (Page 14.)

The Communist Party recognizes that the working class of America is in the main contented; that it does not recognize that it is oppressed by the government and by employers in general. The Party, therefore, conceives it to be its duty to bring "to the workers a consciousness of their oppression, of the impossibility of improving their conditions under capitalism. The Communist Party directs the workers' struggle against capitalism, developing fuller forms and purposes in this struggle, culminating in the mass action of the revolution."

The program also indicates that the party is to intervene in all strikes. "not only to achieve the immediate purposes of the strike, but to develop the revolutionary implications of the mass strike."

The program of the party recognizes that the American Federation of Labor is reactionary "and a bulwark of capitalism," and urges that the "Communist Party must engage actively in the struggle to revolutionize the trade unions."

It is stated that it will be the "major task of the Communist Party to agitate for the construction of a general industrial union organization, embracing the I. W. W., W. I. I. U., independent and secession unions, militant unions of the A. F. of L., and the unorganized workers, on the basis of the revolutionary class struggle."

Workers' councils are to be organized in shops "for the purpose of carrying on the industrial union struggle in the old unions, uniting and mobilizing the militant elements; these councils to be unified in a Central Council wherever possible."

In brief, the Communist manifesto, which was adopted at the Communist Party Convention of September 1, 1919, calls for the destruction of our government, the substitution therefor of a dictatorship of the proletariat, and advocates as a means the use of industrial action involving general strikes and the coercion of government officials to abandon their posts, the seizure of private property, the destruction of the conservative organizations of labor, and the placing of the propertyless class in control. It is obvious that such a program could not be attempted without the use of force and violence, and the rejection of the lawful means of changing our form of government prescribed by our Constitution indicates that the program announced by this party is a flagrant violation of the provisions of the Criminal Anarchy Statute of the State of New York.

The international character of the struggle which the Communist Party has sought to stimulate is clearly shown in the closing paragraphs of the report to the Executive Committee of the Communist International of Moscow, prepared by Louis C. Fraina, as follows:

> "The Communist Party realizes the immensity of its task; it realizes that the final struggle of the Communist proletariat will be waged in the United States, our conquest of power alone assuring the world Soviet Republic. Realizing all this, the Communist Party prepares for the struggle.
>
> "Long live the Communist International! Long live the World Revolution!" (Page 40.)

Before the close of the convention of September 1st the following officers were elected: Louis C. Fraina was chosen International Secretary; C. E. Ruthenberg, of Cleveland, National Secretary. International delegates: C. E. Ruthenberg, Nicholas I. Hourwich, editor of "Novy Mir;" Alexander Stoklitsky, translator-secretary of the Russian Federation; I. E. Ferguson, secretary of the National Left Wing Council and associate editor of the Communist Party publications. The alternates, as International delegates, were D. Elbaum, editor of the Polish Federation daily newspaper in Detroit; Bittleman, editor of the Jewish Federation paper, "Der Kampf;" John Ballam, member of the National Left Wing Council and editor of the "New England Worker," the official organ of the Communist Party in Massachusetts, and Jay Lovestone. Other delegates elected to the executive committees were Schwartz of Boston, of the Lettish Federation; Oscar Tywerowsky, New York Executive Secretary of the Russian Federation; Petras of Chicago, of the Hungarian Federation; Karosses, of the Lithuanian Federation of Philadelphia; and Dr. Maxmilian Cohen, of the National Left Wing Council; Dirba, State Secretary of the Socialist Party of Minnesota, and Wicks of Oregon.

The Executive Council chosen consisted of C. E. Ruthenberg, Louis C. Fraina, I. E. Ferguson, Schwartz, Karosses, Dirba and Wicks.

After the convention the Executive Committee began the immediate work of organizing the party nationally, and preparing and distributing party propaganda. The "Communist," of Chicago, constituted the official organ of the party in English. The following were the Communist publications in other languages:

German: Weekly, "Die Kommunistische Internationale," 1219 Blue Island Ave., Chicago.

Hungarian: Daily, "Elore," 5 E. Third St., New York, N. Y.

Jewish: Weekly, "Der Kampf," 179 East Broadway, New York.

Lettish: Weekly, "Strahdneeks," 49 Dudley St., Roxbury, Mass.

Polish: Daily, "Glos Robotniczy," 1689 Michigan Ave., Detroit, Mich.

Lithuanian: Weekly, "Musu Tiesa," 601 Metropolitan Ave., Brooklyn, N. Y.

——: Weekly, "Zarija," 1219 Blue Island Ave., Chicago, Ill.

Russian: Daily, "Novy Mir," 113 E. Tenth St., New York, N. Y.

Ukrainian: Semi-weekly, "Robitnik," 222 E. Fifth St., New York, N. Y.

South Slavic: Weekly, "Znanje," 2741 W. Twenty-second St., Chicago, Ill.

——: Monthly, "Glas Komunista," 1219 Blue Island Ave., Chicago, Ill.

After the Chicago convention the work of organizing locals and branches proceeded rapidly. The local for Greater New York was organized, with Harry M. Winitsky as Executive Secretary. Its headquarters were moved from the place occupied by the old Left Wing at 43 West Twenty-ninth Street, to 207 East Tenth Street, and a new weekly publication was established as the official organ of the Communist Party, Local Greater New York. This paper was called "Communist World." Maximilian Cohen was elected editor; Bertram D. Wolfe, associate editor, and George Ashkenouzi, business manager. The first issue of this periodical appeared on November 1, 1919.

In an editorial appearing in this issue the purpose of the organization is clearly stated:

> "Our object is the abolition of the wage system and the establishment of the Communist commonwealth through the dictatorship of the proletariat. No mere tinkering with the present capitalist structure; no peaceful growing out of capitalism into Socialism; no parliamentary reforms; no waiting until exhausted capitalism recuperates from the effects of the World War; no aiding of that recuperation under the guise of 'interior reconstruction,' as our Right Wing Socialists would have us do, but the immediate, continuous, bitter, implacable, uncompromising struggle with the master class until Communism is a reality."

The propaganda of this party in New York City opened with a proclamation boycotting the elections, which closes with the following paragraph:

> "Workers, the United States seems to be on the verge of a revolutionary crisis. The workers, through their mass strikes, are challenging the State. The Communist Party's task is to unify these strikes, to develop them into political strikes, aiming at the very power of the capitalist state itself. Out of these mass industrial struggles must issue the means and the inspiration for the conquest of power by the workers. *BOYCOTT THE ELECTIONS!*"

Agitators from the Communist Party began immediately to circulate incendiary leaflets among the longshoremen who were then engaged in a prolonged strike. A typical example of such propaganda is as follows:

"TO THE STRIKING LONGSHOREMEN

"PROCLAMATION ISSUED BY THE COMMUNIST PARTY OF AMERICA, LOCAL GREATER NEW YORK

"*Longshoremen!*

"Sixty-thousand of you are out on strike. You struck against the Bosses and the Government Wage Adjustment Board. You also struck in defiance of the union officials. You are striking against the 'scab unionism' of the A. F. of L. The Wage Adjustment Board refused to grant your demands. Your leaders wanted arbitration. Angered beyond endurance at the Board's award and the treachery of your leaders, you walked out. Your officials are breaking your strike. The prostitute press is trying to break your strike. The bosses with the able assistance of your leaders and the Government are preparing to break your strike. You are determined to stay out.

"Workers! You have repudiated your leaders. You have repudiated your scab form of A. F. of L. unionism. You must form a Transport Workers' Industrial Union. Unite with the striking expressmen, truck-drivers, chauffeurs, freight-handlers, etc., unite with all those who are employed in the transportation industry for One Big Industrial Transport Workers' Union. Already the Shipping Board is advertising that it will protect scabs at seventy-five cents an hour. The Government will send soldiers to take your places. Some are doing this dirty work already. Eighteen thousand more soldiers are on the way. Before the war the bosses hired their strike-breakers from strike-breaking agencies.

"*Now they use the army itself as a strike-breaking agency.*

"Do you see whose Government this is? The Bosses own the State, its army, its police, its press. The Government Wage Adjustment Board represents the State. Did it decide in your favor? The Army is being sent to the piers. To protect you or to scab on you? The Police: Whose heads are they going to crack when you go on the picket line, yours or the scabs? The Press! Whose side are the newspapers taking, yours or the Bosses? Don't you see that the Bosses own and control the whole governmental machinery? Did you ever receive a square deal from the Bosses? How then can you expect to receive a square deal from the Bosses' Government?

"The Government will place squads of soldiers at the piers, with rifles and machine guns to shoot you down. If you hold your ground they will establish martial law; they will break up your meetings; raid your homes, arrest you — just as they are doing to the steel strikers in Gary now. In other words, they will try to crush your spirit, break your solidarity with your fellow-workers and send you back to work like a lot of beaten dogs.

"Will you submit tamely to all this? Forming an industrial union will of itself not solve your problems. It is only a step. Going to the polls on election day will not bring you victory. Don't expect politicians to free you from capitalism and its misery. Depend upon yourselves. The only way is to get rid of the present Bosses' Government and establish a Workers' Government in its place. A Workers' Government like the Soviet Republic of Russia. The present Government is a government of the capitalists, by the capitalists, for the capitalists. You must aim for the establishment of a Workers' Republic of the workers, by the workers, for the workers.

"Look over the whole country today. What do you see? Strikes! Strikes! Nothing but strikes! You are on strike. The steel-workers are on strike. The expressmen are on strike. The machinists are on strike. The shipbuilders are on strike. The lumbermen are on strike. The bricklayers are on strike. The carpenters are on strike. The tailors are on strike. Every industry is tied up with strikes. The coal miners will have a general strike on November 1st. The railroad workers may break out any day against the Government anti-strike law. These workers are all striking for the same reason.

"They can't get along on the wages they get. They must get more, but the Bosses, who made huge fortunes out of the war and the miseries of the poor, refuse to give it to them. The Cost of Living is rising higher and higher. A dollar today is worth less than fifty cents before the war. The whole rotten system is going to pieces. The struggle between the workers and the capitalists is going on all over the world.

"There is only one way out for the workers of America.

> The workers must capture the powers of the State. They must conquer the means by which the capitalist class maintains itself in power. The answer to the Dictatorship of the Capitalists is the Dictatorship of the Workers.
>
> *"All power to the workers!"*

By November 8, 1919, approximately sixty-five branches of the Communist Party had been established in Greater New York. These included English-speaking branches, as well as Russian, Ukranian, Lithuanian, Lettish, Hungarian and Jewish branches. These branches were turned into local district clubs, libraries were collected, reading-rooms established, musical clubs organized, courses of instruction in English for foreigners established, and in so far as their financial means allowed, these were made centers of attraction and amusement for the neighborhoods in which they were located. By these means large numbers of persons who were not familiar with the object and purpose of the organization were enticed to frequent the rooms of the branches. In some of the larger branches refreshments could be had at reasonable prices, and weekly dances were held. All persons who had previously been members of the Left Wing Section of the Socialist Party were admitted to membership in the Communist Party without making the usual application for membership provided for in the constitution (statement made to counsel of this Committee by Harry M. Winitsky, executive secretary).

New applicants for membership in the party were required to sign the following application card:

APPLICATION FOR MEMBERSHIP

COMMUNIST PARTY OF AMERICA

The undersigned, after having read the constitution and program of the Communist Party, declares his adherence to the principles and tactics of the party and the Communist International; agrees to submit to the discipline of the party as stated in its constitution and pledges himself to engage actively in its work.

Name .... Occupation....................

Address .... City.........................

Where employed ....

Endorsed by ....

Applications must be endorsed by two members in good standing.

(REVERSE SIDE)

RECORD

Name of branch..

Name of Local..

Article III, section 5, of Communist Party Constitution provides:

Applications for membership shall not be finally acted upon until two months after presentation to the branch, and in the meantime applicant shall pay initiation fee and dues and shall attend meetings and classes. He shall have a voice and no vote. Provided that this rule shall not apply to the charter members of new branches nor to the members who make application to newly organized branches during the first month.

Application presented to branch ....

Application approved by branch ....

...............................*Sec.*

Address . . . .

Approved by CITY CENTRAL COMMITTEE.

Signed. . . . .*Sec.*

Address . . . .

Those who had been duly endorsed and admitted to membership were given red membership cards.

It will be noted that all those who were accepted for membership had pledged themselves to be active in the work of organization, and to spread its propaganda.

A copy of the instructions from the National office to all Communist branches was seized at the headquarters of Local Buffalo. We reproduce it here in full.

"*Communist Party of America, to all Communist Branches:*

"The distribution and sale of literature is one of the most important functions of every Communist organization. Mass meetings and lectures are valuable, but the solid work of educating the masses and agitation work to build a powerful organization must be done through literature. Meetings can be stopped by White Terror persecution, but the circulation of literature cannot be stopped.

"The work of distribution and selling literature must no longer be left to the few. Every Communist Party member should actively participate in this work. Every branch should organize to give its whole membership a part in the work of spreading information about Communism through the sale and distribution of literature.

"Make the matter of the sale and distribution of literature a special order of business at your next meeting. Place an order for a supply of literature. Do not lock it away in a cupboard. Do not give it to one comrade. When the books come in give a number to each member to take to his shop, to sell among friends and acquaintances. Charge him with the literature and require him to make an accounting at the next meeting. When the books have been sold order a new supply and draw more and more members into the work of selling literature.

"Do the same thing with papers and magazines. The profits on the literature you sell will give you a fund for the purchase of leaflets for free distribution.

"We can thus build a great machine for agitation and propaganda. It will mean a tremendous development of our movement.

"Act at once.

(Signed) C. E. RUTHENBERG,
Executive Secretary."

(See pp. 1619–20 stenographer's minutes, Committee Hearings.)

This was a form letter addressed to all branches of the Communist Party, and from evidence which has come into the hands of the Committee, the advice and instructions therein contained have been faithfully carried out by the party branches. The thorough and systematic methods for the distribution of seditious propaganda are here made plain. It was part of the purpose of the organization, as stated in its program, to bring the workers of America to consciousness of their alleged oppression by disseminating false statement respecting conditions. By stimulating the cupidity of discontented workmen, the party sought to add materially to its membership. A typical example of the leaflets freely distributed in the shops throughout the state is as follows:

"Your Shop. It should be your shop (or your factory, your store, your mill, your mine or your railroad), yours to work in, yours to produce in, yours to manage with the help of your fellow-workers.

"You spend most of your waking hours in the shop. The conditions under which you work and produce determine your life, your happiness.

"If you and your fellow-workers controlled the shop, determined the hours of labor, the working conditions, and apportioned the rewards for the services rendered, you would be able to create the conditions that would bring happiness to you. You would so arrange your work that you would not have your life sapped by long hours and bad working conditions and so that the wealth you produced would be yours, yours to secure the enjoyment of good food, good clothing, a good home and the opportunity for education and healthy recreation.

"There is enough wealth produced to give these things to all who work. But the capitalists own the shops that should be yours. The capitalists make you work long hours under bad working conditions; they take from you as their profit the lion's share of what you produce.

"They will do that as long as they own and control the shop. There is no hope as long as the shop is not yours.

"Workingmen everywhere are learning this. The workingmen of Russia have shown the way. In Russia the shops, as well as all other means of production and distribution, belong to the workers.

"The Russian workers organized their power. They created shop committees in every plant and united these in workers' councils. Thus they built up the means for united action. When the crisis came they were prepared to use their mass power. Before their mass power the government of the capitalists and landowners broke up and disappeared. The workers' councils became the organs of the working-class government. The workers controlled the state power, the police, the army.

"Having taken from the capitalists the governmental power through which the capitalists maintain their control of the shop and the exploitation and oppression of the workers, the workers took control of the shops. The shop committees they elected took over the management. They told the capitalists that their days as autocrats, Czars and Kaisers, of industry were over. They told them there would be no more robbery of the workers through paying them for only a part of what they produced. They told them that the shops now belonged to all the workers and that they, the capitalists, would have to go work for a living.

"And in Russia the workers are building the society that means happiness for all in spite of all the efforts of the capitalists of the world to overthrow their government and strike down their new economic system.

"The workers everywhere are growing more and more dissatisfied with the capitalists' control of the shops in which they work and spend most of their lives. That is the meaning of the great strikes in England and of the great industrial struggles in this country.

"But the workers must organize to secure control of the shops. The first step is to organize a shop committee in the shop in which you work.

"Bring together all the enlightened workers who are ready to participate in the struggle to win control of the shop. Organize them in a Communist Party Shop Branch. This committee will carry on the work of agitation and education among the other workers. It will collect funds and secure papers and pamphlets for distribution in the shop.

"The work of the committee will be to unite all the workers in the shop in a shop organization, machinists, carpenters, shipping clerks, workers of every trade, all must unite in the one workers' organization in their shop.

"Workers! You must build up the organs of working-class power if you are to win your freedom. The shop organization is the basis for the organization of the mass power of the workers.

"Prepare to take control of your shop, of your work, of your lives and happiness.

"Organize and make it your shop."

(See pp. 1636-7-8-9 stenographer's minutes, Committee Hearings.)

Demands which could be made the subject of popular protest and demonstration were used for that purpose. For instance, amnesty for so-called political prisoners, the raising of the Russian blockade and the celebration of the second anniversary of the Bolshevik revolution in Russia. Leaflets and handbills on these subjects were widely distributed throughout the country, and mass meetings were held in all industrial centers under the auspices of the party. These mass meetings were used as recruiting agencies for party membership, and also for the purpose of stirring up a hatred for the government of the United States and the public authorities, and to stimulate class hatred.

The International aspect of the Communist movement is constantly kept before the party in its propaganda literature, and in the correspondent from National headquarters. As an illustration, we here give in full an undated letter addressed to the Secretary of local Buffalo, Communist Party.

> "DEAR COMRADE: Your charter application has been received and charter issued. It has been mailed to you today.
>
> "We extend greetings to the comrades of your branch on their affiliation with the Communist Party of America, which, in co-operation and as a branch of the Communist International, will carry on the struggle for proletarian dictatorship and the establishment of the Communist Society.
>
> "We look forward to your active participation in our work and assure you this office will extend you every assistance in building up your organization.
>
> "Long Life to your Communist Organization!
>
> "Fraternally yours,
>
> (Signed) C. E. RUTHENBERG,
>
> *Executive Secretary.*"

Although this party claimed in its literature and propaganda to be the American representative of the Russian Communist Party, and to be in full and complete accord with the Russian Soviet regime, a coldness developed between Ludwig C. A. K. Martens and the leaders of this organization. This arose out of an attempt on the part of the leaders of the Russian Socialist Federation to control the activity of Martens and the Russian Soviet Bureau in the United States.

This controversy is fully described in Chapter III of this Subsection which deals with the Russian Soviet Bureau and the activities of its agents in this country.

In the foregoing statement of the history of the development of the party, its principles, methods and tactics, we believe that sufficient information has been presented to give the reader a clear conception of the meaning of the movement.

It is the object of this party to destroy the Government of the United States, and to substitute therefor a dictatorship of the proletariat involving the exclusion from participation in government of all classes of society, except the property-less classes. From this follows the expropriation without compensation of private property, all natural resources, instruments of production and means of distribution. This program is sought to be carried out by industrial action, namely, the general strike and the consequent paralyzation of industry and transportation. The practical methods by which this mass action and general strike are to be brought about is, first, the preaching of class hatred and discontent among the workers; the organization of shop committees within conservative organizations of labor for the purpose of destroying such organizations and the American Federation of Labor, and the transformation of trade unions into industrial unions, and ultimately into one big industrial union. This form of labor reorganization is sought because it gives the power to a small executive committee to call a general strike, whereas in the trade union form of organization, the officers and committees of a large number of trade unions must agree upon the necessity of such strike before it can be called. In outlining this program the leaders of the Communist Party have followed scrupulously the plans laid down by the Russian Communist Party, the revolutionary parties of Hungary, the Spartacides of Germany, and other similar groups.

This Committee having come into possession of information relative to the purposes and objects of the Communist Party through correspondence and the publications of that party falling into its hands, felt that in order to check the process of organization, positive and drastic action must be taken. In consequence of this determination, evidence as to the location of the various branches which had been opened by the party in Greater New York, and the nature of the seditious activities being carried on, having been obtained, search warrants were prepared by counsel to the Committee for all these branches, and the same were issued by Chief Magistrate William McAdoo. The hearty co-operation of the Police Department of the City of New York having been obtained, and also that of the New York State police, plans were laid for the service of the search warrant on each of the headquarters simultaneously.

On the evening of November 8, 1919, sixty-five branches in four boroughs of the Greater City were entered simultaneously. Pursuant to the direction of the search warrant all literature and matter of a seditious nature, or evidence of seditious activities, were seized, together with all male persons found in the various branches. These were brought to Police Headquarters in New York City. In all something over a thousand persons were taken into custody. These were examined by counsel for the Committee, and those who admitted being members of the Communist Party, or upon whom was found evidence that they were members, were placed under arrest at the request of the Committee, the remainder being allowed to return to their homes.

In the course of the examination of these persons it was found that not more than 2 per cent. were American citizens, and a large percentage of them had to be interrogated through an interpreter.

Among those taken into custody were Benjamin Gitlow who had formerly been a Socialist Assemblyman from the Borough of the Bronx, New York City, and James Larkin, a noted labor agitator both here and in England; also Jay Lovestone.

On the evening of December 28th the Committee caused to be issued and executed search warrants on all Communist headquarters in the cities of Buffalo, Rochester and Utica.

On Saturday, the third of January, this Committee caused search warrants to be issued against the premises of the "Elore," the Hungarian daily paper, at 5 East Third Street, New York City, at which plant the "Communist World" was also published; "Der Kampf," 179 East Broadway, New York City; and the "Robitnik," the official organ of the Ukranian Federation, 222 East Fifth Street, New York City.

The action thus taken by the Committee at the very inception of the party's organization, has done much to frustrate its plans for developing a strongly organized and closely knit revolutionary body in the United States. Subsequent to the action taken by this Committee the State's attorney in Chicago raided the headquarters of the Communist Party in Chicago, and the Federal Government undertook nation-wide raids which have effectually crippled the organization. Many of its leaders have been indicted, others are fugitives from justice. In New York City the executive secretary, Harry M. Winitsky, has been tried and convicted on the charge of Criminal Anarchy and sentenced to the penitentiary for not less than five nor more than ten years. The leaders of the party, however, have not given up their work.

Various of the party publications are appearing sporadically, published clandestinely in different plants, and it is evident that constant vigilance must be exercised in order to prevent the party from effecting a reorganization and pursuing its destructive plans.

Up to the time when the party fell under the band of the authorities it reported 58,000 dues-paying members, of which 35,000 belonged to the Russian Federation. It is estimated that not more than 16,000 were members of English-speaking branches.

Before closing the description of the activities of this party, it is necessary to refer to the action taken by the Young People's Socialist League in a National Emergency Convention which was held in the city of Rochester on the evening of December 28, 1919. A new constitution was adopted at this convention, which resulted in an affiliation between the Young People's Socialist League and the Communist Party of America. We quote from this instrument as follows:

> "We call on the youth of America to join with us in exerting every effort and making every needed sacrifice toward the realization of these aims.
>
> "ARTICLE I. NAME
>
> "Section 1. This organization shall be known as the Independent Social League of America affiliated with the Third International. . . .
>
> "ARTICLE II. OBJECT
>
> "Section 1. The object of this organization shall be to draw into a compact body all young people interested in the emancipation of the working class. Its foremost and primary function shall be to train them in the principles of International Communism."

(Stenographer's minutes, Committee Hearings, page 1888–1889.)

This organization is of particular interest because it shows the systematic way in which the leaders of the Communist movement seek to influence the minds of young people so as to train them to take part in the revolutionary program which they have adopted.

APPENDIX

CHAPTER V

Official Documents

1. Joint Call for Constituent Assembly.
2. The Communist Party Manifesto.

Document No. 1

JOINT CALL FOR CONSTITUENT ASSEMBLY TO ORGANIZE COMMUNIST PARTY OF AMERICA (Issued by the National Organization Committee and the National Council of the Workers Left Wing Section of the Socialist Party).

In this the most momentous period of the world's history capitalism is tottering to its ruin. The proletariat is straining at the chains which bind it. A revolutionary spirit is spreading throughout the world. The workers are rising to answer the clarion call of the Third International.

Only one Socialism is possible in the crisis. A Socialism based upon understanding. A Socialism that will express in action the needs of the proletariat. The time has passed for temporizing and hesitating. We must act. The Communist call of the Third International, the echo of the Communist Manifesto of 1848, must be answered.

The National Executive Committee of the Socialist Party of America has evidenced by its expulsion of nearly half of the membership that it will not hesitate at wrecking the organization in order to maintain control. A crisis has been precipitated in the ranks of revolutionary Socialism by the wholesale expulsion or suspension of the membership comprising the *Socialist Party of Michigan and Massachusetts, locals and branches throughout the country, together with seven Language Federations.* This has created a condition in our movement that makes it manifestly impossible to longer delay the calling of a convention to organize a new party. Those who realize that the capturing of the Socialist Party as such is but an empty victory will not hesitate to respond to this call and leave the "Right" and "Center" to sink together with their leaders.

No other course is possible; therefore, we, the National Left Wing Council and the National Organization Committee, call a convention to meet in the city of Chicago on September 1, 1919, for the purpose of organizing a Communist Party in America.

This party will be founded upon the following principles:

1. The present is the period of the dissolution and collapse of the whole capitalist world system, which will mean the complete collapse of world culture, if capitalism with its unsolvable contradictions is not replaced by Communism.

2. The problem of the proletariat consists in organizing and training itself for the conquest of the powers of the state. This conquest of power means the replacement of the state machinery of the bourgeoisie with a new proletarian machinery of government.

3. This new proletarian state must embody the dictatorship of the proletariat, both industrial and agricultural, this dictatorship constituting the instrument for the taking over of property used for exploiting the workers, and for the reorganization of society on a Communist basis.

Not the fraudulent bourgeois democracy — the hypocritical form of the rule of the finance-oligarchy, with its purely formal equality — but proletarian democracy based on the possibility of actual realization of freedom for the working masses; not capitalist bureaucracy, but organs of administration which have been created by the masses themselves, with the real participation of these masses in the government of the country and in the activity of the communistic structure — this should be the type of the proletarian state. The workers' councils and similar organizations represent its concrete form.

4. The dictatorship of the proletariat shall carry out the abolition of private property in the means of production and distribution, by transfer to the proletarian state under Socialist administration of the working class; nationalization of the great business enterprises and financial trusts.

5. The present world situation demands the closest relation between the revolutionary proletariat of all countries.

6. The fundamental means of the struggle for power is the mass action of the proletariat, a gathering together and concentration of all its energies; whereas methods such as the revolutionary use of bourgeois parliamentarism are only of subsidiary significance.

In those countries in which the historical development has furnished the opportunity, the working class has utilized the regime of political democracy for its organization against capitalism. In all countries where the conditions for a worker's revolution are not yet ripe, the same process will go on.

But within the process the workers must never lose sight of the true character of bourgeois democracy. If the finance-oligarchy considers it advantageous to veil its deeds of violence behind parliamentary votes, then the capitalist power has at its command, in order to gain its ends, all the traditions and attainments of former centuries of upper class rule, demagogism, persecution, slander, bribery, calumy and terror. To demand of the proletariat that it shall be content to yield itself to the artificial rules devised by its mortal enemy, but not observed by the enemy, is to make a mockery of the proletarian struggle for power — a struggle which depends primarily on the development of separate organs of the working-class power.

7. The old Socialist International has broken into three main groups:

(a) *Those frankly social patriots who since* 1914 *have supported their bourgeoisie and transformed those elements of the working class which they control into hangmen of the international revolution.*

(b) *The "Center," representing elements which are constantly wavering and incapable of following a definite plan of action, and which are at times positively traitorous; and*

(c) *The Communists.*

As regards the social patriots, who everywhere in the critical moment oppose the proletarian revolution with force of arms, a merciless fight is absolutely necessary. As regards the "Center" our tactics must be to separate the revolutionary elements by pitilessly criticizing the leaders. Absolute separation from the organization of the "Center" is necessary.

8. It is necessary to rally the groups and proletarian organizations who, though not as yet in the wake of the revolutionary trend of the Communist movement, nevertheless have manifested and developed a tendency leading in that direction.

Socialist criticism has sufficiently stigmatized the bourgeois world order. The task of the International Communist Party is to carry on propaganda for the abolition of this order and to erect in its place the structure of the Communist world order. Under the Communist banner, the emblem under which the first great victories have already been won; in the war against imperialistic barbarity, against the privileged classes, against the bourgeois state and bourgeois property, against all forms of social and national oppression — we call upon the proletarian of all lands to unite!

PROGRAM OF THE CALL

1. We favor international alliance of the Communist Party of the United States only with the Communist groups of other countries, such as the Bolsheviki of Russia, Spartacans of Germany, etc., according to the program of Communism as above outlined.

2. We are opposed to association with other groups not committed to the revolutionary class struggle, such as Labor parties, Non-Partisan leagues, People's Councils, Municipal Ownership Leagues and the like.

3. *We maintain that the class struggle is essentially a political struggle by the proletariat to conquer the capitalist state, whether its form be monarchistic or democratic-republican, and to destroy and replace it by a governmental structure adapted to the Communist transformation.*

4. The Party shall propagandize class-conscious industrial unionism as against the craft form of unionism, and shall carry on party activity in co-operation with industrial disputes that take on a revolutionary character.

5. *We do not disparage voting nor the value of success in electing our candidates to public office — not if these are in direct line with the class struggle. The trouble comes with the illusion that political or industrial immediate achievements are of themselves steps in the revolution, the progressive merging of capitalism into the co-operative commonwealth.*

The basis of our political campaign should be:

(a) To propagandize the overthrow of capitalism by proletarian conquest of the political power and the establishment of a dictatorship of the proletariat.

(b) To maintain a political organization as a clearing-house for proletarian thought, a center of political education for the development of revolutionary working-class action.

(c) To keep in the foreground our consistent appeal for proletarian revolution; and to analyze the counter-proposals and reformist palliatives in their true light of evasions of the issue; recognizing at all times the characteristic development of the class conflict as applicable to all capitalistic nations.

(d) To propagandize the party organization as the organ of contact with the revolutionary proletariat of other lands, the basis for international association being the same political understanding and the common plan of action, tending toward increasing unity in detail as the international crisis develops.

6. Communist platforms, proceeding on the basis of the class struggle, recognizing that the Socialist movement has come into the historic period of the social revolution, can contain only the demand for the dictatorship of the proletariat.

(a) The basis of this demand should be thoroughly explained in the economic, political and social analysis of the class struggle, as evolving within the system of capitalism.

(b) The implication of this demand should be illustrated by the first steps and general modes of social reconstruction dependent upon and involved within the proletarian domination of the political life of the nation.

(c) A municipal platform of Communism cannot proceed on a separate basis, but must conform to the general platform, simply relating the attainment of local power to the immediate goal of gaining national power. There are no separate city problems within the terms of the class struggle, only the one problem of capitalist versus proletarian domination.

7. We realize that the coming of the social revolution depends on an overwhelming assertion of mass power by the proletariat, taking on political consciousness and the definite direction of revolutionary Socialism. The manifestations of this power and consciousness are not subject to precise precalculation. But the history of the movement of the proletariat toward emancipation since 1900 shows the close connection between the revolutionary proletarian assertion and the political mass strike.

The mass action conception looks to the general unity of the proletarian forces under revolutionary provocation and stimulus. In the preliminary stages, which alone come within our pre-determination and party initiative, the tactic of mass action includes all mass demonstrations and mass struggles which sharpen the understanding of the proletariat as to the class conflict and which separate the revolutionary proletariat into a group distinct from all others.

Mass action, in time of revolutionary crisis, or in the analogous case of large scale industrial conflict, naturally accepts the council form of organization for its expression over a continued period of time.

8. Applying our declarations of party principle to the organization of the party itself, we realize the need, in correspondence with the highly centralized capitalist power to be combated, of a centralized party organization.

Organizations endorsing the principles and program outlined above as a tentative basis for the organization of a Communist Party are invited to send delegates to the convention at Chicago on September 1, 1919.

The basis of representation to be one delegate for every organization and one additional for every additional 500 members or major fraction thereof.

Provided, that states which are organized and endorsing this call shall send delegates as states. In states which are not organized the organized locals accepting this call shall send delegates as locals. In locals which are not organized a part of the local may send delegates.

Provided further, that organizations composed of less than 251 members shall be given fractional votes; and provided that the total vote for each State represented at the convention shall not exceed one, plus one per 500 members or major fraction thereof.

Organizations sending delegates will be assessed $50 for each delegate. This fund will be applied to equalize the railroad fare of all delegates to the convention. Organizations having less than 251 members which are unable to pay all of this amount ($50) are urged* will be created to defray their traveling expenses. Expenses other than railroad fares will be paid by the organizations sending delegates. In the event the delegates are not provided with funds for rooms and meals, effort will be made to assist them.

Do not fail to be represented at this historic convention. All delegates, either directly or through their local secretaries, are requested to communicate with the National secretary immediately following their election. Uniform credential blanks will be furnished.

FOR THE NATIONAL LEFT WING COUNCIL,

I. E. FERGUSON,
Secretary.

FOR THE NATIONAL ORGANIZATION COMMITTEE,

DENNIS E. BATT,
Secretary.

On all matters relating to the Communist Convention, address: 1221 Blue Island avenue, Chicago, Ill.

* So in original.

Document No. 2

THE COMMUNIST PARTY MANIFESTO

The world is on the verge of a new era. Europe is in revolt. The masses of Asia are stirring uneasily. Capitalism is in collapse. The workers of the world are seeing a new life and securing new courage. Out of the night of war is coming a new day.

The spectre of Communism haunts the world of capitalism. Communism, the hope of the workers to end misery and oppression.

The workers of Russia smashed the front of international Capitalism and Imperialism. They broke the chains of the terrible war; and in the midst of agony, starvation and the attacks of the capitalists of the world, they are creating a new social order.

The class war rages fiercely in all nations. Everywhere the workers are in a desperate struggle against their capitalist masters. The call to action has come. The workers must answer the call!

The Communist Party of America is the party of the working class. The Communist Party proposes to end capitalism and organize a workers' industrial republic. The workers must control industry and dispose of the products of industry. The Communist Party is a party realizing the limitations of all existing workers' organizations and proposes to develop the revolutionary movement necessary to free the workers from the oppression of Capitalism. The Communist Party insists that the problems of the American worker are identical with the problems of the workers of the world.

THE WAR AND SOCIALISM

A giant struggle is convulsing the world. The war is at end, but peace is not here. The struggle is between the capitalist nations of the world and the international proletariat, inspired by Soviet Russia. The Imperialisms of the world are desperately arraying themselves against the onsweeping proletarian revolution.

The League of Nations is dividing the world financially and territorially. It is directing the fight against the workers. It is the last effort of Capitalism to save itself.

The reactionary League of Nations is the logical result of this imperialistic war. And the war was the product of Capitalism.

Capitalism oppresses the workers. It deprives them of the

fruit of their labor — the difference between wages and product constituting the profits of the capitalists. As the capitalists compete with each other, while exploiting the workers, new and more efficient means of production develop. This compels the concentration of industry which results in monopoly. Under monopoly there is rapid accumulation of capital, producing a surplus which it is necessary to export for investment. This export of capital, together with the struggle to monopolize the world's sources of raw materials and to control undeveloped territory for purposes of investment, is the basis of Imperialism.

Imperialism produced the war. The war now being at an end, the victorious nations are concerned almost exclusively with these economic, territorial and financial problems. The United States was vitally concerned in the war, the issue being world power; and its capitalism, having secured a position of financial supremacy, had a direct imperialistic interest at stake.

The war made a shamble of civilization. It proved the utter incapacity of capitalism to direct and promote the progress of humanity. Capitalism has broken down.

But the Socialist movement itself broke down under the test of war. The old dominant moderate Socialism accepted and justified the war. It acted against the proletarian revolution and united with the capitalists against the workers. Out of this circumstance developed the forces of revolutionary Socialism now expressed in the Communist International.

Socialism had repeatedly emphasized the menace of war. It had urged the workers to act against the war. The Socialist Congress at Basle in 1912, when Europe was on the verge of a general war, condemned the war as imperialistic and as unjustifiable on any pretext of national interest. It urged using the crisis of war to "rouse the masses and to hasten the downfall of capitalism."

The war that came in 1914 was the same imperialistic war that might have come in 1912. But upon the declaration of war, the dominant opportunistic Socialist parties accepted and justified the war of plunder and mass murder!

This was a direct betrayal of Socialism. It was an abandonment of the class struggle. The class struggle is the very heart of revolutionary Socialism. Unless the Socialist movement wages the class struggle under any and all conditions in its revolutionary implications, it becomes either Utopian or reactionary. But moderate Socialism accepted the war and the "unity of the classes," and united with the capitalist governments against the working class.

The Socialist parties accepted the war as a war for democracy —as if democracy under Imperialism is not directly counter-revolutionary. They justified the war as a war for the independence of nations. Not the proletarian class struggle, but nationalism, social-patriotism and social-imperialism determined the policy of the dominant Socialism. The coming of Socialism was made dependent upon the workers cutting each others' throats in the struggles of their own ruling class!

SOCIALISM AND COMMUNISM

The collapse of the Socialist International during the war marks the transition from the older moderate Socialism to the new Socialism of revolutionary practice and promise in the Communist International.

Moderate Socialism, which perverted the revolutionary Socialism of the First International, placed its faith in "constructive" social reforms. It accepted the bourgeois state as the basis of its activities and then strengthened that state. It developed a policy of "class reconciliation," affirming that the coming of Socialism was a concern of "all the classes" instead of emphasizing the Marxian policy that it was the task of the revolutionary proletariat alone. There was a joint movement that affected the thought and practice of Socialism; on the one hand, the organization of the skilled workers into trade unions, which secured certain concessions and became a semi-privileged caste; and, on the other hand, the decay of the class of small producers, crushed under the iron tread and of industrial concentration. As one moved upward and the other downward, they met and formed a political juncture to use the state to improve their conditions. The dominant Socialism expressed this compromise. It developed a policy of legislative reforms and State Capitalism.

The whole process was simple. The workers were to unite with the middle class and government ownership of industry was to emancipate the working class. Parliamentarism was to revolutionize the old order of slavery and power, of oppression and destruction.

It was simple, but disastrous. The state, as owner of industry, did not free the workers, but imposed a sterner bondage. The capitalist state was made stronger by its industrial functions.

The parliamentary representatives of the workers played at the parliamentary comedy, while Capitalism developed new powers of oppression and destruction.

But Imperialism exposed the final futility of this policy. Imperialism united the non-proletarian classes, by means of State Capitalism, for international conquest and spoliation. The small capitalists, middle class and the aristocracy of labor, which previously acted against concentrated industry, now compromise and unite with concentrated industry and finance-capital in Imperalism. The small capitalist accept the domination of finance-capital, being allowed to participate in the adventures and the fabulous profits of Imperialism, upon which now depends the whole of trade and industry. The middle class invests in monopolistic enterprises; its income now depends upon finance-capital, its members securing "positions of superintendence," its technicians and intellectuals being exported to lands in process of development. The workers of the privileged unions are assured steady employment and comparatively high wages through the profits that come in from the savage exploitation of colonial peoples. All these non-proletarian social groups accept imperialism, their "liberal and progressive" ideas becoming camouflage for Imperialism with which to seduce the masses. Imperialism requires the centralized state, capable of uniting all the forces of capital, of unifying the industrial process through state regulation, of maintaining "class peace," of mobilizing the whole national power for the struggles of imperialism. *State Capitalism is the expression of Imperialism,* precisely that State Capitalism promoted by Moderate Socialism. What the parliamentary policy of Socialism accomplished was to buttress the capitalistic state, to promote State Capitalism to strengthen imperialism.

Moderate Socialism developed while Capitalism was still competitive. Upon the advent of monopoly and Imperialism, Socialism emerged into a new epoch — an epoch requiring new and more aggressive proletarian tactics. Capitalism acquired a terrific power in industry and the state. The concentration of industry, together with the subserviency of parliaments to the imperialistic mandates and the transfer of their vital functions to the executive organ of government, made more clear the impossibility of the parliamentary conquest of power. The older unionism and parliamentary Socialism proved their utter incompetence for the new conditions of struggle. These conditions developed the concept of industrial unionism in the United

States and the concept of mass action in Europe. Imperialism made it necessary to reconstruct the Socialist movement.

But Moderate Socialism itself did not change under the necessity of events. The consequence was a miserable collapse under the test of the war and the proletarian revolution in Russia and Germany.

In the Russian Revolution, the proletariat, urging on the poorer peasantry, conquered the power of the state after the first revolution had established the democratic parliamentary republic. It established a **dictatorship of the proletariat.** This proletarian revolution was accomplished in spite of the opposition of Moderate Socialism, represented by the Mensheviki and the Social Revolutionists. These Moderates argued that since Russia was economically an undeveloped country, it was premature to make a proletarian revolution in Russia and historically impossible to realize Socialism.

Moderate Socialism in Germany also acted against the proletarian revolution. It offered a capitalist parliamentary republic as against proletarian dictatorship.

The issue in Germany could not be obscured. Germany was a fully developed nation industrially, its economic conditions were mature for the introduction of Socialism. But Moderate Socialists rejected the revolutionary task.

There is a common policy that characterizes Moderate Socialism; that is, its conception of the state. Out of the conception that the bourgeois parliamentary state is the basis for the introduction of Socialism developed a directly counter-revolutionary policy.

Communism rejects this conception of the state. It rejects the idea of class reconciliation and the parliamentary conquest of Capitalism. The Communist Party alone is capable of mobilizing the proletariat for the revolutionary mass struggle to conquer the power of the state. The Communist Party realizes that it is necessary to develop separate organs of working-class political power by means of which to crush the resistance of Capitalism and establish the Communist Commonwealth.

AMERICAN SOCIALISM

Socialism in the United States, prior to the appearance of the Socialist Labor Party, was a movement of isolated and indefinite protest. It was the spur of middle-class movements, while itself split by Socialist and Anarchist factions.

The Socialist Labor Party, after casting off the non-Socialist elements, developed as a consistent party of revolutionary Socialism. Particularly, the S. L. P. realized the importance of imparting a Socialist character and consciousness to the unions. The Socialist Labor Party, together with the experience of the Western Federation of Miners and the American Labor Union, developed the theory and practice of Industrial Unionism.

The struggle of the Socialist Labor Party against the old unionism developed a secession from the party of elements who considered protecting the reactionary American Federation of Labor more important than revolutionary Socialism. These, together with bourgeois and agrarian radicals, organized the Socialist Party.

The Socialist Party was a party of Moderate Socialism. Its policy was that of government ownership of industry, not the proletarian conquest of power. It maintained that the middle class and the lesser capitalists are necessary in the Socialist struggle against capitalism. The Socialist Party asserted in substance: Socialism is a struggle of all the people against the trusts, making the realization of Socialism depend upon the "unity of the common people," the workers, the small capitalists and investors, the professions. In short the official policy of the Socialist Party was to attain Socialism by means of capitalist democracy.

The Socialist Party stultified proletarian political action by limiting it to elections and participation in legislative reform activity. The party favored reactionary trade unionism as against revolutionary industrial unionism.

The Socialist Labor Party developed a purely theoretical activity, of real value, but was isolated from the masses. The Socialist Party attained a considerable membership, but largely of a petty bourgeoisie character. The war brought in new industrial proletarian elements but the party still isolated itself from revolutionary theory and practice. The proletarian masses in the Socialist Party required simply the opportunity to develop a revolutionary proletarian policy.

The Socialist Party under the impulse of its proletarian membership adopted a militant declaration against the war. But the officials of the party sabotaged this declaration. The official policy of the party on the war was that of liberal pacifism. The party bureaucracy united with the People's Council which propagandized a Wilson peace. The 1918 party platform accepted the

Wilson "fourteen points" as adopted by the pro-war Interallied Labor and Socialist Conference.

The war and the proletarian revolution in Russia sharpened the antagonism between the party policy and the revolutionary proletarian temper in the party. Revolt broke loose. The Socialist Party was crushed. The Communist Party is the response to this revolt and to the call of the Communist International.

COMMUNIST PARTY PROBLEMS

The United States is now a world power. It is developing a centralized, autocratic federal government, acquiring financial and military reserves for aggression and wars of conquest. Imperialism now consciously dominates the national policy.

The war strengthened American Capitalism, instead of weakening it as in Europe. But the collapse of Capitalism in other countries will play upon and affect events in this country. Feverishly, American capitalism is developing a brutal campaign of terrorism. It is utterly incompetent on the problems of reconstruction that press down upon society. Its "reconstruction" program aims simply to develop power for aggression and plunder in the markets of the world. While this is not the moment of actual revolution, it is a moment of struggles pregnant with revolution.

Strikes are developing verging on revolutionary action, and in which the suggestion of proletarian dictatorship is apparent. The striker-workers try to usurp functions of industry and government, as in the Seattle and Winnipeg general strikes.

A minor phase of proletarian unrest is the trade unions organizing a Labor Party, in an effort to conserve what they have secured as a privileged caste. A Labor Party is not the instrument of aggressive working-class struggle; it can not break the power of the capitalists and the profit system of oppression and misery, since it accepts private property and the "rights of capital." The practice of a Labor Party is in general the practice of the Socialist Party — co-operation with bourgeois "progressives" and reforming Capitalism on the basis of the capitalist parliamentary state. Laborism is as much a danger to the proletarian as moderate petty bourgeois Socialism — the two being expressions of an identical social tendency and policy. There can be no compromise either with Laborism or reactionary Socialism.

But there is a more vital tendency, the tendency of the workers to start mass strikes — strikes which are equally a revolt against the bureaucracy of the unions and the capitalists. The Communist Party will endeavor to broaden and deepen these strikes making them general and militant, developing the general political strike.

The Communist Party accepts as the basis of its action the mass struggles of the proletariat, engaging directly in these struggles and emphasizing their revolutionary implications.

POLITICAL ACTION

The proletarian class struggle is essentially a political struggle. It is a political struggle in the sense that its objective is political, — overthrow of the political organizations upon which capitalist exploitation depends, and the introduction of a proletarian state power. The objective is the conquest by the proletariat of the power of the state.

Communism does not propose to "capture" the bourgeoisie parliamentary state, but to conquer and destroy it. As long as the bourgeoisie state prevails, the capitalist class can baffle the will of the proletariat.

In those countries in which historical development has furnished the opportunity, the working class has utilized the regime of political democracy for its organization against Capitalism. In all countries where the conditions for a workers' revolution are not yet ripe, the same process will go on. The use of parliamentarism, however, is only of secondary importance.

But within this process the workers must never lose sight of the true character of bourgeois democracy. If the finance-oligarchy considers it advantageous to veil its deeds of violence behind parliamentary votes, then the capitalist class has at its command in order to gain its end, all the traditions and attainments of former centuries of working class rule, multiplied by the wonders of capitalist technique — lies, demagogism, persecution, slander, bribery. To the demand of the proletariat that it shall be content to yield itself to the artificial rules devised by its mortal enemy but not observed by the enemy is to make a mockery of the proletarian struggle for power, a struggle which depends primarily on the development of separate organs of working class power.

The parliamentarism of the Communist Party performs a service in mobilizing the proletariat against Capitalism, emphasizing the political character of the class struggle.

The conquest of the power of the state is accomplished by the mass power of the proletariat. Political mass strikes are a vital factor in developing this mass power, preparing the working class for the conquest of Capitalism. The power of the proletariat lies fundamentally in its control of the industrial process. The mobilizing of this control against Capitalism means the initial form of the revolutionary mass action that will conquer the power of the state.

UNIONISM AND MASS ACTION

The older unionism was based on the craft divisions of small industry. The unions consisted primarily of skilled workers, whose skill is itself a form of property. The unions were not organs of the militant class struggle. Today the dominant unionism is actually a bulwark of Capitalism, merging in Imperialism and accepting State Capitalism.

The concentration of industry and the development of the machine process expropriated large numbers of the skilled workers of their skill; but the unions still maintained the ideology of property contract and caste. Deprived of actual power by the ineffectiveness of its localized strikes as against large scale industry, trade unionism resorts to dickers with the bourgeois state and accepts imperialistic State Capitalism to maintain its privileges as against the unskilled industrial proletariat.

The concentration of industry produces the industrial proletariat — the machine workers. This proletariat, massed in the basic industry, constitutes the militant basis of the class struggle. Deprived of skill and craft divisions, the old petty isolated strike is useless to these workers.

These facts of industrial concentration developed the concept of industrial unionism among the organized workers, and mass action among the unorganized.

Mass action is the proletarian response to the facts of modern industry, and the forms it imposes upon the proletarian class struggle. Mass action develops as the spontaneous activity of unorganized workers in the basic industry; its initial form is the mass strike of the unskilled. In these strikes large masses of workers are unified by the impulse of the struggle, developing a new tactic and a new ideology.

Mass action is industrial in its origin, but it acquires political character as it develops fuller forms. Mass action, in the form of general political strikes and demonstrations, unites the energy and forces of the proletariat, brings proletarian mass pressure upon the bourgeois state. The more general and conscious mass action becomes, the more it becomes political mass action. Mass action is responsible to life itself, the form of aggressive proletarian struggle under Imperialism. Out of this struggle develops revolutionary mass action, the means for the proletarian conquest of power.

The conception of mass action has little in common with Syndicalism. In its mass impulse, Syndicalism was a protest against the futility of parliamentarism. But Anarcho-Syndicalism tactically and theoretically is a departure from Marxism. It does not appreciate the necessity of a proletarian state during the transition period from Capitalism to Communism (which implies the disappearance of all forms of the state). Syndicalism makes the proletarian revolution a direct seizure of industry, instead of the conquest of the power of the state.

Industrial Unionism, also, cannot conquer the power of the state. Under the conditions of Capitalism it is impossible to organize the whole working class into industrial unions. It will be necessary to rally the workers, organized and unorganized, by means of revolutionary mass action. Moreover, industrial unionism does not actually construct the forms of the Communist administration of industry, only potentially. After the conquest of power the industrial unions may become the starting point of the Communist reconstruction of society. But the conception that the majority of the working class can be organized into conscious industrial unions and construct under Capitalism the form of the Communist society, is as Utopian as the moderate Socialist conception of the gradual "growing into Socialism."

DICTATORSHIP OF THE PROLETARIAT

The proletarian revolution comes at the moment of crisis in Capitalism, of a collapse of the old order. Under the impulse of the crisis, the proletariat acts for the conquest of power, by means of mass action. Mass action concentrates and mobilizes the forces of the proletariat, organized and unorganized; it acts equally against the bourgeois state and the conservative organizations of the working class. Strikes of protest develop into general political strikes and then into revolutionary mass action for the conquest of the power of the state. Mass action becomes political in purpose while extra-parliamentary in form; it is equally a process of revolution and the revolution itself in operation.

The state is an organ ofcoercion. The bourgeois parliamentary state is the organ of the bourgeoisie for the coercion of the proletariat. Parliamentary government is the expression of bourgeois supremacy, the form of authority of the capitalist over the worker. Bourgeois democracy promotes the dictatorship of capital, assisted by the press, the pulpit, the army and the police. Bourgeois democracy is historically necessary, on the one hand, to break the power of feudalism, and, on the other, to maintain the proletarian in subjection. It is precisely this democracy that is now the instrument of Imperialism, since the middle class, the traditional carrier of democracy, accepts Imperialism. The proletarian revolution disrupts bourgeois democracy. It disrupts this democracy in order to end class divisions and class rule, to realize industrial self-government of the workers. Therefore it is necessary that the proletariat organize its own state *for the coercion and suppression of the bourgeoisie.* Proletarian dictatorship is a recognition of the fact; it is equally a recognition of the fact that in the Communist reconstruction of society the proletariat alone counts as a class.

While the dictatorship of the proletariat performs the negative task of crushing the old order, it performs the positive task of constructing the new. Together with the government of the proletarian dictatorship, there is developed a new "government," which is no longer government in the old sense, since it concerns itself with the management of the production and not with the government of persons. Out of workers' control of industry, introduced by the proletarian dictatorship, there develops the complete structure of Communist Socialism — industrial self-government of the communistically organized producers. When this structure is completed, which implies the complete expropriation of the bourgeoisie, economically and politically, the dictatorship of the proletariat ends, in its place coming the full, free social and individual autonomy of the Communist order.

THE COMMUNIST INTERNATIONAL

The Communist International, issuing directly out of the proletarian revolution in action, is the organ of the international revolutionary proletariat; just as the League of Nations is the organ of the joint aggression and resistance of the dominant Imperialism.

The Communist International represents a Socialism in complete accord with the revolutionary character of the class struggle. It unites all the conscious revolutionary forces. It wages war equally against Imperialism and moderate Socialism — each of which has demonstrated its complete inability to solve the problems that now press down upon the workers. The Communist International issues its call to the conscious proletariat for the final struggle against Capitalism.

It is not a problem of immediate revolution. The revolutionary epoch may last for years, and tens of years. The Communist International offers a program both immediate and ultimate in scope.

The old order is in decay. Civilization is in collapse. The workers must prepare for the proletarian revolution and the Communist reconstruction of society.

The Communist International calls!

Workers of the world, unite!

THE PROGRAM OF THE PARTY

The Communist Party is the conscious expression of the class struggle of the workers against capitalism. Its aim is to direct this struggle to the conquest of political power, the overthrow of capitalism and the destruction of the bourgeois state.

The Communist Party prepares itself for the revolution in the measure that it develops a program of immediate action, expressing the mass struggles of the proletariat. These struggles must be inspired with revolutionary spirit and purposes.

The Communist Party is fundamentally a party of action. It brings to the workers a consciousness of their oppression, of the impossibly of improving their conditions under capitalism. The Communist Party directs the workers' struggle against capitalism, developing fuller forms and purposes in this struggle, culminating in the mass action of the revolution.

I

The Communist Party maintains that the class struggle is essentially a political struggle; that is, a struggle to conquer the power of the state.

(a) The Communist Party shall keep in the foreground its consistent appeal for proletarian revolution, the overthrow of capitalism and the establishment of a dictatorship of the proletariat. As the opposition of the bourgeoisie is broken, as it is expropriated and gradually absorbed in the working groups, the proletarian dictatorship disappears, until finally the state dies and there are no more class distinctions.

(b) Participation in parliamentary campaigns, which in the general struggle of the proletariat is of secondary importance, is for the purpose of revolutionary propaganda only.

(c) Parliamentary representatives of the Communist Party shall not introduce or support reform measures. Parliaments and political democracy shall be utilized to assist in organizing the working class against capitalism and the state. Parliamentary representatives shall consistently expose the oppressive class character of the capitalist state, using the legislative forum to interpret and emphasize the class struggle; they shall make clear how parliamentarism and parliamentary democracy deceive the workers; and they shall analyze capitalist legislative proposals and reforms palliatives as evasions of the issue and as of no fundamental significance to the working class.

(d) Nominations for public office and participation in elections are limited to legislative bodies only, such as municipal councils, state legislatures and the national congress.

(e) The uncompromising character of the class struggle must be maintained under all circumstances. The Communist Party accordingly, in campaigns and elections, and in all its other activities shall not co-operate with groups or parties not committed to the revolutionary class struggle, such as the Socialist Party, Labor Party, Non-Partisan League, People's Council, Municipal Ownership Leagues, etc.

II

The Communist Party shall make the great industrial struggles of the working class its major campaigns, in order to develop an understanding of the strike in relation to the overthrow of capitalism.

(a) The Communist Party shall participate in mass strikes, not only to achieve the immediate purposes of the strike, but to develop the revolutionary implications of the mass strike.

(b) Mass strikes are vital factors in the process out of which develops the workers' understanding and action for the conquest of power.

(c) In mass strikes under conditions of concentrated capitalism there is latent the tendency toward the general mass strike, which takes on a political character and manifests the impulse toward proletarian dictatorship.

In these general mass strikes the Communist Party shall emphasize the necessity of maintaining industry and the taking over of social functions usually discharged by the capitalists and the institutions of capitalism. The strike must cease being isolated and passive; it must become positive, general and aggressive, preparing the workers for the complete assumption of industrial and social control.

(a) Every local and district organization of the Party shall establish contact with the industrial units in its territory, the shops, mills and mines — and direct its agitation accordingly.

(b) Shop Committees shall be organized wherever possible for the purpose of Communist agitation in a particular shop or industry by the workers employed there. These committees shall be united with each other and with the Communist Party, so that the party shall have actual contact with the workers and mobilize them for action against capitalism.

III

The Communist Party must engage actively in the struggle to revolutionize the trade unions. As against the unionism of the American Federation of Labor, the Communist Party propagandizes industrial unionism and industrial union organization, emphasizing their revolutionary implications. Industrial Unionism is not simply a means for the everyday struggle against capitalism; its ultimate purpose is revolutionary, implying the necessity of ending the capitalist parliamentary state. Industrial Unionism is a factor in the final mass action for the conquest of power, as it will constitute the basis for the industrial administration of the Communist Commonwealth.

(a) The Communist Party recognizes that the A. F. of L. is reactionary and a bulwark of capitalism.

(b) Councils of workers shall be organized in the shops as circumstances allow, for the purpose of carrying on the industrial union struggle in the old unions, uniting and mobilizing the militant elements; these councils to be unified in a Central council wherever possible.

(c) It shall be a major task of the Communist Party to agitate for the construction of a general industrial union organization, embracing the I. W. W., W. I. I. U., independent and secession unions, militant unions of the A. F. of L., and the unorganized workers, on the basis of the revolutionary class struggle.

IV

The Communist Party shall encourage movements of the workers in the shops seeking to realize workers' control of industry, while indicating their limitations under capitalism; concretely, any movement analogous to the Shop Stewards of England. These movements (equally directed against the union bureaucracy) should be related to the Communist Party.

V

The unorganized unskilled workers (including the agricultural proletariat) constitute the bulk of the working class. The Communist Party shall directly and systematically agitate among these workers, awakening them to industrial union organization and action.

VI

In close connection with the unskilled workers is the problem of the Negro worker. The Negro problem is a political and economic problem. The racial oppression of the Negro is simply the expression of his economic bondage and oppression, each intensifying the other. Ths complicates the Negro problem, but does not alter its proletarian character. The Communist Party will carry on agitation among the Negro workers to unite them with all class conscious workers.

VII

The United States is developing an aggressive militarism. The Communist Party will wage the struggle against militarism as a phase of the class struggle to hasten the downfall of Capitalism.

VIII

The struggle against Imperialism, necessarily an international struggle, is the basis of proletarian revolutionary action in this epoch.

(a) There must be close unity with the Communist International for common action against the Imperialism.

(b) The Communist Party emphasizes the common character of the struggle of the workers of all nations, making necessary the solidarity of the workers of the world.

THE PARTY CONSTITUTION

I. NAME AND PURPOSE

Section 1. The name of this organization shall be The Communist Party of America. Its purpose shall be the education and organization of the working class for the establishment of the Dictatorship of the Proletariat, the abolition of the capitalist system and the establishment of the Communist Society.

II. EMBLEM

Section 1. The emblem of the party shall be a button with the figure of the earth in the center in white with gold lines and a red flag across the face bearing the inscription, "All Power to the Workers;" around the figure of the earth a red margin shall appear with the words "The Communist Party of America" and "The Communist International" on this margin in white letters.

III. MEMBERSHIP

Section 1. Every person who accepts the principles and tactics of the Communist Party and the Communist International and agrees to engage actively in the work of the party shall be eligible to membership. It is the aim of this organization to have in its ranks only those who participate actively in its work.

Section 2. Applicants for membership shall sign an application card reading as follows:

> "The undersigned, after having read the constitution and program of the Communist Party, declares his adherence to the principles and tactics of the party and the Communist International; agrees to submit to the discipline of the party as stated in its constitution and pledges himself to engage actively in its work."

Section 3. Every member must join a duly constituted branch of the party. There shall be no members-at-large.

Section 4. All application cards must be endorsed by two persons who have been members for not less than three months.

Section 5. Applications for membership shall not be finally acted upon until two months after presentation to the branch, and in the meantime applicant shall pay initiation fee and dues and shall attend meetings and classes. He shall have a voice and no vote. Provided that this rule shall not apply to the charter members of new branches nor to the members who make application to newly organized branches during the first month.

Section 6. No person who is a member or supporter of any other political organization shall be admitted to membership.

Section 7. No person who has an entire livelihood from rent, interest or profit shall be eligible to membership in the Communist Party.

Section 8. No person shall be accepted as a member who enters into the service of the national, state or local governmental bodies otherwise than through the Civil Service or by legal compulsion.

Provided, that the civil employment by the government is of a non-political character.

Section 9. No members of the Communist Party shall contribute articles or editorials of a political or economic character to publications other than those of the Communist Party or of parties affiliated with the Communist International. (This clause shall not be considered as prohibiting the contribution of articles written from an economic or scientific standpoint to scientific or professional journals. Permission to answer an attack upon the Communist Party in the bourgeoisie press may be granted by the Central Executive Committee).

IV. UNITS OF ORGANIZATIONS

Section 1. The basic organization of the Communist Party shall be branches of not less than seven members. (Applicants for a charter shall fill out the form provided by the National Organization.)

Section 2. Two or more branches located in the same city shall form a City Central Committee. City Central Committees may include branches in adjacent territory, subject to supervision of the central management of the party.

Section 3. City Central Committees and all other branches in the same state shall form State Organizations. Provided, that under the control of the Central Executive Committee more than one state may be included in a single District Organization; and provided also that District Organizations may be formed by the Central Executive Committee along the lines of industrial rather than state divisions.

Section 4. Branches of the Communist Party made up of members who speak a foreign language, when there are ten or more of such branches, consisting of a total not less than 750 members, may form a Language Federation. Provided, that this rule shall not apply as to members of those Federations affiliating with the party at the time of its organization or within four months thereafter. No more than one Federation of the same language may exist in the party.

Section 5. All language branches shall join and become part of the Federations of their language, if such a Federation exists.

Section 6. All subsidiary units shall be combined in the Communist Party. Branches of the cities, states, districts and federations shall be units of the Communist Party.

V. ADMINISTRATION

Section 1. The supreme administrative body of the Communist Party shall be the convention of the party.

Section 2. Between the meetings of the conventions the supreme body shall be the Central Executive Committee elected by the convention. The Central Executive Committee shall consist of fifteen members. The convention shall also elect five alternates who shall take their places as members of the Central Executive Committee in case of vacancies in the order of their vote.

Section 3. The Central Executive Committee shall elect from its members a sub-committee of five members, who together with the executive secretary and the Editor of the central organ of the party shall be known as the Executive Council. The members of the Executive Council shall live in the city in which the National Headquarters are located or in adjacent cities. This Executive Council shall carry on the work of the party under the supervision of the Central Executive Committee.

Section 4. The Convention shall elect an Executive Secretary and the Editor of the central organ of the party. All other officials shall be appointed by the Central Executive Committee.

Section 5. The Executive Secretary and Editor shall conduct their work under the direction of the Central Executive Committee.

Section 6. The supreme administrative power of the State, District, Federation or City units shall be vested in the conventions of these respective units. Conventions of the State or District Organization shall be held in May or June each year.

Section 7. Between conventions of the district, state and federations the Central Executive Committee of these organizations shall be the supreme bodies.

Section 8. The Central Executive Committee of these organizations shall in each case be elected by the conventions, which shall also determine the number of members.

Section 9. The City Central Committees shall consist of delegates elected by the branches upon the basis of proportional representation. They shall meet at least once each month. The City Central Committees shall elect their executive committees and Executive Officers.

Section 10. Each Federation shall elect a Translator-Secretary, who shall have an office in the National Headquarters and whose salary shall be paid by the National Organization. Translator-Secretaries are the representatives of their organizations in the National Headquarters, and shall serve as mediums of communicaton. They shall submit monthly to the Executive Secretary and the State and District Organizations a statement showing all the dues stamps sold during the previous month. Translator-Secretaries shall not be eligible to membership in the Central Executive Committee but shall meet with the Committee and the Executive Council and have a voice but no vote.

VI. DUES

Section 1. Each applicant for membership shall pay an initiation fee of fifty cents, which shall be receipted for by an initiation stamp furnished by the National Organization. The fifty cents shall be divided between the branch and City Central Committee. Where there is no City Central Committee its share shall be paid to the State or District Organization.

Section 2. Each member shall pay forty cents per month in dues. Stamps shall be sold to the State or District Organization at fifteen cents; State or District Organizations shall sell stamps to the City Central Committees and branches in cases where there are no City Committees at twenty-five cents; City Central Committees shall sell stamps to branches at thirty cents.

Section 3. Branches of Language Federations shall purchase their dues stamps through their Federations. Translator-Secretaries shall pay ten cents per stamp to the National Organization and shall remit to each State or District Organization ten cents for each stamp sold for each month. Where a City Central Committee exists the State or District Organization shall remit five cents of this amount to the City Central Committee. Members of Language Federation branches pay forty cents per stamp, ten cents going to the branch and ten cents to the federation.

Section 4. Special assessment may be levied by the National Organization, Federations or the Central Executive Committee. No member shall be considered in good standing unless he purchases such special assessment stamps.

Section 5. Husband and wife belonging to the same branch may purchase dual stamps, which shall be sold at the same price as the regular stamps. Special assessments must be paid by both husband and wife.

Section 6. Members unable to pay dues on account of unemployment, strikes, sickness or for similar reasons shall, upon application to their financial secretary, be furnished exempt stamps. Provided that no State or District Organization or Federation shall be allowed exempt stamps in a proportion greater than 5 per cent. of its monthly purchase of regular stamps.

Section 7. Members who are three months in arrears in payment of their dues shall cease to be members of the party in good standing. Members who are six months in arrears shall be stricken from the rolls. No member shall pay dues in advance for a period of more than three months.

VII. Discipline

Section 1. All decisions of the governing bodies of the party shall be binding upon the membership and subordinate units of the organizations.

Section 2. Any member or organization violating the decisions of the party shall be subject to expulsion by the organization which has jurisdiction. Charges against members shall be made before branches, subject to appeal by either side to the City Central Committee or State or District Organization where there is no City Central Committee. Charges against the branches shall be made before the City Central Committee, or where there is no City Central Committee, before the State or District Organization. Decisions of the City Central Committee in the case of branches shall be subject to revision by the State or District Organization. Charges against State or District Organizations shall be made before the Central Executive Committee. When a City Central Committee expels a Federation branch, the branch shall have the right to present its case to the Central Executive Committee of the Federation. If the Central Executive Committee of the Federation decides to that effect it may bring an appeal for reinstatement before the Central Executive

Committee of the party, which shall make final disposition of the matter.

Section 3. Members and branches of the Federation shall be subject to the discipline of the Federation. Branches expelled by the Federation shall have the right to appeal to the City Central Committee, or, when there is no City Central Committee, to the State or District Organization. If the City Central Committee or the State or District Organization does not uphold the expulsion the matter shall be referred to the Central Committee upon documentary evidence, and if the decision of the City Central Committee or State or District Organization is upheld, the branch shall be reinstated as a branch of the Federation.

Section 4. Each unit of the party organization shall restrict its activities to the territory it represents.

Section 5. A member who desires to transfer his membership to another branch shall secure a transfer card from the financial secretary of his branch. No branch shall receive a member from another branch without such a transferral card, and upon presentation of the transfer card the secretary of the branch receiving the same shall make inquiry about the standing of the member to the secretary issuing the card.

Section 6. All party units shall use uniform application cards, dues books and accounting records, which shall be printed by the National Organization.

Section 7. All employees of the party must be party members.

VIII. HEADQUARTERS

Section 1. The National Headquarters of the party shall be located in Chicago. In an emergency District or State Office may be used as the National Headquarters.

IX. QUALIFICATIONS

Section 1. Members of the Central Executive Committee, the Executive Secretary, Editor, International Delegates and International secretary and all candidates for political office must have been members of the party for two years at the time of their election or nomination. Those shall be eligible to election to party offices or nomination to public office on June 1, 1920, who join the Communist Party before January 1, 1920. All who state their intention of joining the Communist Party shall be eligible at this convention.

X. CONVENTIONS

Section 1. National Conventions shall be held annually during the month of June, the specific date and place to be determined by the Central Executive Committee. The Central Executive Committee may call Emergency Conventions, and such conventions may also be called by referendum vote.

Section 2. Representation at the National Convention shall be upon the basis of one delegate for each 500 members or major fraction thereof; provided, that when the number of delegates would exceed a total of 200 the Central Executive Committee shall increase the basis of representation so that the number of delegates shall not exceed that figure.

Section 3. Delegates shall be apportioned to the State or District Organizations on the basis of one delegate for each such organization, and the apportionment of the balance on the basis of the average membership for the six months prior to the issue of the call for the convention. Delegates shall be elected at the Convention of the State or District Organization.

Section 5. Delegates to the National Convention shall be paid their traveling expenses and a per diem of $5.00.

Section 6. The call for the convention and the apportionment of delegates shall be published not later than April 1.

XI. REFERENDUM AND RECALL

Section 1. Referendums on the question of party platform policy or constitution shall be held upon the petition of twenty-five or more branches representing 5 per cent. of the membership; (2) or by initiative of the Central Executive Committee; (3) or by initiative of the National Convention.

Section 2. All officers of the National Organization or those elected to public office shall be subject to recall upon initiative petition of twenty-five or more branches, representing 5 per cent. of the membership. A recall vote of the membership may also be initiated by the Central Executive Committee.

Section 3. Each motion and resolution shall be printed in the official bulletin and remain open for ninety days from the date of first publication, and, if it has not received the requisite number of seconds, it shall be abandoned. The vote on each referendum shall close sixty days after its submission.

Section 4. Referendums shall be submitted without preamble or comment, but the party press shall be open for discussion of the question involved during the time the referendum is pending.

XII. INTERNATIONAL DELEGATE AND SECRETARY

Section 1. Delegates to the International Congress and alternates and an International Secretary and alternate shall be elected by the convention.

SCHEDULE

Any branch of the Socialist Party or Socialist Labor Party which endorses the program and constitution of the Communist Party and applies for a charter before January 1, 1920, shall be accepted as a branch.

The provisions of Article III, section 4, shall not be enforced until after December 1, 1919, except as to the two signatures.

RECOMMENDATION

That this convention authorize the secretary immediately to issue a Special Organization Stamp to sell at fifty cents to create a fund for the organization of the party.

CHAPTER VI

Communist Labor Party *

In the latter part of August, 1919, a divergence of opinion arose in the National Left Wing council over the issuance of a joint call for a convention to organize the Communist Party which has previously been described.

The majority of the delegates of the Left Wing conference held in New York City in June, 1919, had decided that the policy of the Left Wing should be to organize for the purpose of capturing the national emergency convention of the Socialist Party which had been called for the latter part of August in that year.

The delegates to that conference from the Language Federations having withdrawn because of this decision, succeeded later in inducing the majority of the National Council of the Left Wing to abandon its attempt to control that convention, and to issue a joint call for a convention to organize a Communist Party. Certain members of the National Council, as well as a large number of locals and branches which had endorsed the Left Wing movement, still retained the hope of capturing the Socialist Party machinery, or at least, of influencing its decision at the coming convention.

The August 23d issue of the "Revolutionary Age" announced the simultaneous resignations from its staff of John Reed, Eadmonn MacAlpine and Benjamin Gitlow, due to their opposition to the joint call referred to above.

Pursuant to the policy of attempting to participate in the Socialist Party Emergency Convention, certain of the Left Wing delegates presented themselves as delegates to that convention when it convened on August 30, 1919, in Chicago.

Reports of that convention, from various party organs, indicate that the credentials committee of the Socialist Party refused to seat these delegates and they were excluded from the convention.

A description of what transpired there appears in the "Class Struggles" issue of November, 1919, page 389, in an article entitled "Convention Impressions" by William Bross Lloyd. The excluded Left Wing delegates thereupon met in a separate convention.

"The first thing the Left Wing delegates to the Emergency Convention did," says William Bross Lloyd, "was to appoint a

* See Addendum, Part I.

committee of five to meet the Organization Committee of the Communist Party and later a like committee of the Communist Convention for the purpose of seeking unity." These negotiations came to nothing, and the delegates organized themselves into a Communist Labor Party Convention. The Communist Party is criticized for several reasons. First, because it is controlled by the Russian Language Federation with a membership of 35,000 out of a total of 58,000 of that party's membership. Second, because the remaining portion of the Communist Party were members of the expelled State organization of Michigan and the followers of the National Council of the Left Wing which approved of the call of the Communist Convention. Mr. Lloyd, commenting on the situation, says, "These Russian Federations openly regard themselves as the only Simon-pure 'Bolsheviks' in the world — not even excluding Russia. Yet they broke from the Conference on a question not of principle but one of clique control. Yet they united with Michigan, a purely political parliamentarian non-Bolshevik organization, disbelieving in industrial unionism, industrial organization of working class political power and in mass action. All through July the Federations were maligning the Left Wing Council as centrists, as a fetid swamp. Meanwhile, the council was maligning Michigan as parliamentarian and non-Bolsheviks and both Michigan and the Federations as petty political intriguers.

The National Council (Left Wing) was elected under carefully drawn instructions which made it an administrative, ministerial body and in no sense an Executive Committee with power to act on questions of policy. Those instructions were to organize to capture the Socialist Party at the Emergency Convention, and, failing that, afterwards to organize a Communist Party. The Council advertised for money to carry on that work. And in August, the Council publicly renounced the struggle to control the Socialist Party and joined with Michigan and the Federations in calling the Communist Convention. In so doing it violated its instructions and exceeded its authority and if any unexpended funds so secured by advertisement were expended in the Council's new venture, these funds were misapplied." (Pages 392 and 393 of "Class Struggle.")

These are the reasons given for the failure of the promoters of the Communist Labor Party to unite with the Communist Party

Convention. The convention elected A. Wagenknecht executive secretary; and as members of the National Executive Committee, M. Bedacht, of California; Alexander Bilan, Ohio; Jack Carney, Minnesota; L. E. Katterfeld, Kansas; and Edward Lindgren of New York. Alternates, L. K. England, Illinois; Edgar Owens, Illinois. Labor Committee, Charles Baker, Ohio; Benjamin Gitlow, New York; R. E. Richardson, Utah; and Arne Swabeck, Washington. International delegates, John Reed, New York, and A. Wagenknecht, Ohio.

National Headquarters were opened at 3207 Clark Ave., Cleveland, Ohio.

The convention adopted a platform and program for the party. The platform contains the following provision:

> "The Communist Labor Party of the U. S. A. declares itself in full harmony with the revolutionary working class parties of all countries and stands by the principles stated by the Third International formed at Moscow. . . . The Communist Labor Party proposes the organization of the workers as a class, the overthrow of capitalist rule and the conquest of political power by the workers. The workers organized as the ruling class, shall, through their government, make and enforce the laws; they shall own and control land, factories, mills, mines, transportation systems and financial institutions. All power to the workers! . . . To this end we ask the workers to unite with the Communist Labor Party for the conquest of political power to establish a government adapted to the Communist transformation."

The program of the party restates the principles of the Third Moscow International:

> "1. The present is the period of the dissolution and collapse of the whole system of world capitalism. Unless capitalism is replaced by the rule of the working class, world civilization will collapse.
>
> "2. The working class must organize and train itself for the capture of state power. This capture means the establishment of the new working class government machinery, in place of the state machinery of the capitalists.
>
> "3. This new working class government — the Dictatorship of the Proletariat — will reorganize society on the basis of Communism, and accomplish the transition from Capitalism to the Communist Commonwealth. . . .

"4. The Dictatorship of the Proletariat shall transfer private property in the means of production and distribution to the working class government, to be administered by the workers themselves. It shall nationalize the great trusts and financial institutions. It shall abolish capitalist agricultural production.

"5. The present world situation demands that the revolutionary working class movements of all countries shall closely unite.

"6. The most important means of capturing state power for the workers is the action of the masses, proceeding from the place where the workers are gathered together — in the shops and factories. The use of the political machinery of the capitalist state for this purpose is only secondary."

It must here be noted that the objects and methods advocated in this program are identical with those stated by the Communist Party. A slight difference, however, may be noted in the following:

"7. In those countries in which there is a possibility for the workers to use this machinery" (political machinery) "in the class struggle, they have, in the past, made effective use of it as a means of propaganda, and of defense. In all countries where the conditions for a working class revolution are not ripe, the same process must go on."

In other words, the promoters of the Communist Labor Party see greater advantage in using the present political machinery of government for the purpose of propaganda in view of present conditions than do their comrades of the Communist Party.

The party however is distinctly revolutionary. They state:

"1. We favor international alliance of the Communist Labor Party only with the Communist groups of other countries, those which have affiliated with the Communist International.

"2. We are opposed to association with other groups not committed to the revolutionary class struggle.

"3. We maintain that the class struggle is essentially a political struggle, that is, a struggle by the proletariat to conquer the capitalist state, whether its form be monarchial or democratic-republican, and to replace it by a governmental structure adapted to the Communist transformation. . . .

"5. We favor organized Party activity and co-operation with class-conscious industrial unions, in order to unify industrial and political class-conscious propaganda and action. Locals and Branches shall organize shop branches, to conduct the Communist propaganda and organization in the shops, and to encourage the workers to organize in One Big Union.

"6. The Party shall propagandize industrial unionism and industrial union organization, pointing out their revolutionary nature and possibilities.

"7. The Party shall make the great industrial battles its major campaigns, to show the value of the strike as a political weapon."

A special report on labor organization was made to the convention. In it revolutionary industrial unionism is defined as "organization of the workers into unions by industries with a revolutionary aim and purpose; that is to say, a purpose not merely to defend or strengthen the status of the workers as wage earners, but to gain control of industry."

After stating that labor, and labor alone, is industrially responsible, the report makes the following recommendations:

"I. That all Locals shall elect Committees on Labor Organization, composed so far as is possible of members of Labor Unions, whose functions shall be:

"(a) To initiate, or support, the creation of Shop Committees in every industry in their district, the uniting of these Committees in Industrial Councils, District Councils, and the Central Council of all Industries.

"(b) To propagandize and assist in the combining of craft Unions, by industries, in One Big Union.

"(c) To bring together in the centers of Party activity — Locals and Branches — delegates from factories and shops to discuss tactics and policies of conducting the class struggle.

"(d) To propagandize directly among the workers on the job the principles of Communism, and educate them to a realization of their class position.

"(e) To find a common basis for the uniting of all existing economic and political organizations based on the class struggle.

"(f) To mobilize all members who can serve as organizers to fill the demand for men and women who can organize bodies of workers along the lines indicated above.

"(g) To direct the activities of local Party organizations in assisting the workers whole-heartedly in their industrial battles, and making use of these battles as opportunities for educating the workers."

The latter recommendation is of especial significance. It shows the purpose of the leaders of this party to intervene in all strikes; to take advantage of the passions and prejudices which are always engendered by such struggles; to inflame the strikers; to stimulate class hatred; to direct the hatred thus engendered against the government and institutions of this country.

The party platform and program, as well as the special report on labor organization, so clearly state the purpose and objects of this quasi-political party that the Committee deems it expedient to give them in full at the close of this chapter.

As in the case of other revolutionary bodies of this character, persons seeking to become members were required to sign an application card. In the case of the Communist Labor Party the form adopted was very similar to that of the Socialist Party of America. Copy of such card is here given:

APPLICATION FOR MEMBERSHIP

COMMUNIST LABOR PARTY

I, the undersigned, recognizing the class struggle between the capitalist class and the working class, and the necessity of the working class organizing itself politically and industrially for the purpose of establishing Communist Socialism, hereby apply for membership in the Communist Labor Party. I have no relations (as member or supporter) with any other political party. I am opposed to all political organizations that support the present capitalist profit system, and I am opposed to any form of trading or fusing with any such organizations. In all my actions while a member of the Communist Labor Party I agree to be guided by the constitution and platform of that party.

Name ....Occupation ....

(If a member of a labor organization give name and number.)

Street Address .... Ward ....

City .... State .... County ....

Proposed by .... Age ....

Date .... Citizen (yes or no)

Total amount received from applicant, $..........

OFFICIAL RECEIPT

This Certifies that

....

has made application for membership in the Communist Labor Party and has paid the initiation fee of $1.00 and .... months dues at the rate of 50c per month.

For the COMMUNIST LABOR PARTY,

By ....

NOTICE TO APPLICANT.— The sub-division of the Communist Labor Party which will consider your application meets

Place ....

Address ....

Date ....

Successful applicants for membership were given red membership cards for the purpose of identification.

In the matter of propaganda the new party was very active. A number of Socialist newspapers and periodicals as well as new organs began to appear as the official organs of the Communist Labor Party. In New York City a fortnightly entitled "The Voice of Labor" which was first issued on August 15, 1919, as the organ of the Labor Committee of the Left Wing Section of the Socialist Party, edited by John Reed and with Benjamin Gitlow as business manager, became on November 1st an official organ of the Communist Labor Party. From August 30th to October 15th, inclusive, this paper had been published by the Joint Council of Shop Committees, an independent group waiting upon the organization of the Communist Labor Party.

The "Class Struggle" which had previously been an independent Socialist magazine of extremely radical tendency, became an organ of the Communist Labor Party, with a new board of editors consisting of Jack Carney, Ludwig Lore and Gregory Weinstein who had formerly been the editor of "Novy Mir," the official organ of the Russian Socialist Federation, and who is now chancellor of the Russian Soviet Bureau of which Mr. Ludwig C. A. K. Martens is the head.

"The Communist Labor Party News" published in Cleveland, Ohio, was issued as the official organ of the Communist Labor Party

Two very strong papers became the official organs of the Communist Labor Party, one published in Duluth, Minnesota, called the "Truth and then the "Toiler" which had formerly been the "Ohio Socialist."

All of these papers dedicate much space to the official pronouncements of the Soviet Government of Russia, and carry communications from various commissars of the Soviet regime. It should also be noted that the party kept in close touch with the Russian Soviet Bureau through Mr. Gregory Weinstein; and when James Larkin, one of the party's leading organizers was arrested on the charge of criminal anarchy, and later released on $15,000 bail, he was a frequenter of the Soviet Bureau at 110 West 40th Street, New York City. Although a very much smaller group than the Communist Party, its members are active; its propaganda is exceedingly effective, and its ranks are growing despite the difficulties it has gotten into with the federal and local authorities throughout the country.

Since the attacks of the government upon the Communist Labor Party have rendered its work difficult, the official organ of the party has come out in new form under the name of "Communist Labor." Its place of publication and the names of persons connected with the party do not appear.

A new call to action by the National Executive Committee is extremely interesting because it carries with it the spirit which animates the leaders. It also indicates that a May Day demonstration is contemplated by the party.

The Call follows:

"A Call to Action

"Comrades: The echoes of the thunder of the social revolution in Russia, in Europe, are heard by the ruling powers in Capitalist United States.

"They rely with confidence upon their power and hope to prevent the inevitable, like King Kanute tried to sweep back the tide.

"They heard the crash of falling capitalism in Russia.

"But they learned nothing from it.

"They do not acknowledge the elementary forces of the Revolution and believe it man-made.

"Hang the man that talks, that thinks revolution, and Capitalism will be saved. That is their slogan.

"The Capitalist governing powers in the United States import the medicine of force so long employed by Czarism against the revolutionary movement in Russia, import it in spite of the fact that the patient in Russia died while taking it, and apply it here in the hope that the effect will be a different one, that it will save Capitalism here.

"Capitalism in the United States has given the lie to its omnipresent phrases of law and order.

"Its present campaign against the communist movement is a travesty on law, and does violence to the very term of order.

"Like Caesar, the head policeman of capitalism in our country, Mr. Mitchell Palmer, in glory telegraphs over the universe, 'veni, vidi, vici. I have destroyed the revolutionary movement by putting thousands that dared to talk, that dared to think, into prison.'

"But that poor subaltern of American Capitalism, Mitchell Palmer, will soon realize that he is fighting a medusa. Where he succeeds in cutting off one head, two will grow in its place.

"Comrades: The Revolution marches forward in spite of Mitchell Palmer and all that. The spirit of Revolution will march on, until the prison doors burst open and the class-war prisoners march out joining their victorious brothers in a triumphant revolution.

"But that day must find us prepared. The revolutionary power of the workers, when set in motion by the elementary forces of economic evolution, must find a guide in a well-developed communist movement, which consciously and knowingly leads the Revolution along the path to Communism.

"Comrades: We, the National Executive Committee of the Communist Labor Party call upon you to double your efforts for our cause in the same ratio as the efforts of capitalism double to escape its destiny.

"We call upon you to rally under the banners of the Communist Labor Party.

"The raids of head policeman Palmer have shaken the foundation of our organization, but have not disrupted it. We found a new, a more solid foundation upon which we will build with your help. Extensive plans have been made for our future organization and its activities. Your co-operation is needed. We need your support as workers for the cause. We need your financial support.

"Comrades: For many of our rank our cause was worth the sacrifice of their liberty for terms of years.

"WHAT IS IT WORTH TO YOU?

"In order to realize our plans of organization, our plans for the printing and distribution of revolutionary literature we need money. We need not a given sum, but as much as the revolutionary workers of America are able to spare for our, for their cause.

"Comrades: Is the cause of communism, is the cause of Soviet Russia, is the cause of the working-class worth a day's wage to you every three months?

"The workers of Russia give their blood for it. Those unable to bring this supreme sacrifice in Russia, work. Half starving, they work every Saturday, without wages, for their government. They call it Communist Saturday.

"We ask you to work one Saturday in thirteen for your cause. We ask you to pledge one day's wage in every three months for your cause. Make one Saturday in every three months a Communist Saturday.

"Comrades: We need money at once. What can you do? What will you do?

"You cannot, and you will not make your inactivity, your failure to respond, responsible for the failure of our movement.

"Therefore, Comrades, act, and act at once.

"International Labor Day, May 1st, is close at hand.

"May 1st comes upon a Saturday this year.

"**MAKE MAY FIRST YOUR FIRST COMMUNIST SATURDAY.**

"Contribute your first day's wage for the cause on May 1st. Make every revolutionary worker you know contribute a day's wage on May 1st to the cause of Communism.

"The Communist Labor Party will issue an International Labor Day Stamp. This stamp will be issued in books of twenty which will be sold to the members at $5.00 each. Every member will be called upon to purchase a full book of these stamps. Every member will be asked to sell another book of stamps to his fellow workers.

"Comrades: This is your fight. Do your duty.

"Translate your enthusiasm into action so you need not keep on wishing to be in Russia to be in a free country." ("Communist Labor," March 25, 1920, Volume 1, No. 4.)

APPENDIX

CHAPTER VI

Official Documents

1. Platform and Program Communist Labor Party.

Document No. 1

PLATFORM AND PROGRAM COMMUNIST LABOR PARTY

PLATFORM

(1) The Communist Labor Party of the United States of America declares itself in full harmony with the revolutionary working class parties of all countries and stands by the principles stated by the Third International formed at Moscow.

(2) With them it thoroughly appreciates the complete development of capitalism into its present form of Capitalist Imperialism with its dictatorship of the capitalist class and its absolute suppression of the working-class.

(3) With them it also fully realizes the crying need for an immediate change in the social system; it realizes that the time for parleying and compromise has passed; and that now it is only the question whether all power remains in the hands of the capitalist or is taken by the working class.

(4) The Communist Labor Party proposes the organization of the workers as a class, the overthrow of capitalist rule and the conquest of political power by the workers. The workers, organized as the ruling class, shall, through their government make and enforce the laws; they shall own and control land, factories, mills, mines, transportation systems and financial institutions. All power to the workers!

(5) The Communist Labor Party has as its ultimate aim: The abolition of the present system of production, in which the working class is mercilessly exploited, and the creation of an industrial republic wherein the machinery of production shall be socialized so as to guarantee to the workers the full social value of the product of their toil.

(6) To this end we ask the workers to unite with the Communist Labor Party for the conquest of political power to establish a government adapted to the Communist transformation.

PARTY AND LABOR PROGRAM

Part I

The Communist Labor Party of America declares itself in complete accord with the principles of Communism, as laid down in the Manifesto of the Third International formed at Moscow.

In essence, these principles are as follows:

(1) The present is the period of the dissolution and collapse of the whole system of world capitalism. Unless capitalism is replaced by the rule of the working class, world civilization will collapse.

(2) The working-class must organize and train itself for the capture of state power. This capture means the establishment of the new working-class government machinery, in place of the state machinery of the capitalists.

(3) This new working-class government — the Dictatorship of the Proletariat — will reorganize society on the basis of Communism, and accomplish the transition from Capitalism to the Communist Commonwealth.

Communist society is not like the present fraudulent capitalist democracy — which, with all its pretensions to equality, is merely a disguise for the rule of the financial oligarchy — but it is a proletarian democracy, based on the control of industry and the state by the workers, who are thereby free to work out their own destiny. It does not mean capitalist institutions of government, which are controlled by the great financial and industrial interests, but organs of administration created and controlled by the masses themselves; such as, for example, the Soviets of Russia.

(4) The Dictatorship of the Proletariat shall transfer private property in the means of production and distribution to the working class government, to be administered by the workers themselves. It shall nationalize the great trusts and financial institutions. It shall abolish capitalist agricultural production.

(5) The present world situation demands that the revolutionary working class movements of all countries shall closely unite.

(6) The most important means of capturing state power for the workers is the action of the masses, proceeding from the place where the workers are gathered together — in the shops and factories. The use of the political machinery of the capitalist state for this purpose is only secondary.

(7) In those countries in which there is a possibility for the workers to use this machinery in the class struggle, they have, in the past, made effective use of it as a means of propaganda, and of defense. In all countries where the conditions for a working-class revolution are not ripe, the same process must go on.

(8) We must rally all groups and proletarian organizations which have manifested and developed tendencies leading in the direction above indicated, and support and encourage the working class in every phase of its struggle against capitalism.

Part II

(1) The economic conditions in every country determine the form of organization and method of propaganda to be adopted. In order efficiently to organize our movement here, we must clearly understand the political and economic structure of the United States.

(2) Although the United States is called a political democracy there is no opportunity whatever for the working class through the regular political machinery to effectively oppose the will of the capitalist class.

(3) The years of Socialist activity on the political field have brought no increase of power to the workers. Even the million votes piled up by the Socialist Party in 1912, left the Party without any proportionate representation. The Supreme Court, which is the only body in any Government in the world with the power to review legislation passed by the popular representative assembly, would be able to obstruct the will of the working class even if Congress registered it, which it does not. The Constitution, framed by the capitalist class for the benefit of the capitalist class, cannot be amended in the workers' interest, no matter how large a majority may desire it.

(4) Although all the laws and institutions of government are framed and administered by the capitalists in their own interests, the capitalists themselves refuse to be bound by these laws or submit to these institutions whenever they conflict with these interests. The invasion of Russia, the raids into Mexico, the suppression of governments in Central America, and the Carribean, the innumerable wars against working class revolutions now being carried on — all those actions have been undertaken by the Administration without asking the consent even of Congress. The appointment by the President of a Council of National De-

fense, the War Labor Board, and other extra constitutional governing bodies without the consent of Congress, is a direct violation of the fundamental law of republican government. The licensing by the Department of Justice of anti-labor strike-breaking groups of employers — such as the National Security League, the American Defense Society, the Knights of Liberty, the American Protective League — whose express purpose was the crushing of labor organization and all class activities of the workers, and who inaugurated in this country a reign of terror similar to that of the Black Hundreds in Russia — was entirely opposed to the principles of the American government.

(5) Moreover, the War and its aftermath have demonstrated that governing power does not reside in the regularly-elected, or even the appointed officials and legislative bodies. In every State, county and city in the Union, the so-called "police power" is shown to be superior to every law. In Minnesota, Wisconsin and many other states, so-called Public Safety Commissions and similar organizations were constituted by authority of the Governors, made up of representatives of Chambers of Commerce and Employers' Associations, which usurped the powers of Legislatures and municipal administrations.

(6) Not one of the great teachers of scientific Socialism has ever said that it is possible to achieve the Social Revolution by the ballot.

(7) However, we do not ignore the value of voting, or of electing candidates to public office, so long as these are of assistance to the workers in their economic struggle. Political campaigns, and the election of public officials, provide opportunities for showing up capitalist democracy, educating the workers to a realization of their class position, and of demonstrating the necessity for the overthrow of the capitalist system. But it must be clearly emphasized that the chance of winning even advanced reforms of the present capitalist system at the polls is extremely remote; and even if it were possible, these reforms would not weaken the capitalist system.

Part III

(1) In America the capitalist class has never had a feudal aristocracy to combat, but has always been free to concentrate its power against the working class. This has resulted in the

development of the American capitalist class wholly out of proportion to the corresponding development in other countries. By their absolute control of the agencies of publicity and education, the capitalists have gained a control over the political machinery which is impossible to break by resorting to this machinery.

(2) Moreover, in America there is a highly-developed Labor movement. This makes it impossible to accomplish the overthrow of capitalism except through the agency of the organized workers.

Furthermore, there is in America a centralized economic organization of the capitalist class which is a unit in its battle with the working class, and which can be opposed only by a centralized economic organization of the workers.

(3) The economic conditions of society, as Marx foretold, are pushing the workers toward forms of organization which are, by the very nature of things, forced into activity on the industrial field with a political aim—the overthrow of capitalism.

(4) It is our duty as Communists to help this process, to hasten it, by supporting all efforts of the workers to create a centralized revolutionary industrial organization. It is our duty as Communists, who understand the class struggle, to point out to the workers that upon the workers alone depends their own emancipation and that it is impossible to accomplish this through capitalist political machinery, but only by the exercise of their united economic power.

PROGRAM

(1) We favor international alliance of The Communist Labor Party only with the Communist groups of other countries, those which have affiliated with the Communist International.

(2) We are opposed to association with other groups not committed to the revolutionary class struggle.

(3) We maintain that the class struggle is essentially a political struggle, that is, a struggle by the proletariat to conquer the capitalist state, whether its form be monarchial or democratic-republican, and to replace it by a governmental structure adapted to the Communist transformation.

(4) Communist platforms, being based on the class struggle, and recognizing that this is the historical period of the Social Revolution, can contain only one demand: The establishment of the Dictatorship of the Proletariat.

(5) We favor organized party activity and co-operation with class conscious industrial unions, in order to unify industrial and political class conscious propaganda and action. Locals and branches shall organize shop branches, to conduct the Communist propaganda and organization in the shops and to encourage the workers to organize in One Big Union.

(6) The Party shall propagandize industrial unionism and industrial union organization, pointing out their revolutionary nature and possibilities.

(7) The Party shall make the great industrial battles its major campaigns, to show the value of the strike as a political weapon.

(8) The Party shall maintain strict control over all members elected to public office — not only the local organizations, but the National Executive Committee. All public officials who refuse to accept the decisions of the Party shall be immediately expelled.

(9) In order that the Party shall be a centralized organization, capable of united action, no autonomous groups or federations independent of the will of the entire Party shall be permitted.

(10) All party papers and publications endorsed by the Party, and all educational and propaganda institutions endorsed by the Party, shall be owned and controlled by the regular Party organization.

(11) Party platforms, propaganda, dues and methods of organization shall be standardized.

Special Report on Labor Organization

The purpose of the Party is to create a unified revolutionary working-class movement in America.

The European war has speeded up social and industrial evolution to such a degree that capitalism throughout the world can no longer contain within itself the vast forces it has created. The end of the capitalist system is in sight. In Europe it is already tottering and crashing down, and the proletarian revolutions there show that the workers are at the same time becoming conscious of their power. The capitalists themselves admit that the collapse of European capitalism and the rise of the revolutionary working class abroad cannot help but drag American capitalism into the all-embracing ruin.

In this crisis the American working class is facing an alternative. Either the workers will be unprepared, in which case they will be reduced to abject slavery, or they will be sufficiently conscious and sufficiently organized to save society by reconstructing it in accordance with the principles of Communism.

II

(1) By the term "revolutionary industrial unionism" is meant the organization of the workers into unions by industries with a revolutionary aim and purpose; that is to say, a purpose not merely to defend or strengthen the status of the workers as wage earners, but to gain control of industry.

(2) In any mention of revolutionary industrial unionism in this country, there must be recognized the immense effect upon the American labor movement of the propaganda and example of the Industrial Workers of the World, whose long and valiant struggles and heroic sacrifices in the class war have earned the respect and affection of all workers everywhere. We greet the revolutionary industrial proletariat of America, and pledge them our whole-hearted support and co-operation in their struggles against the capitalist class. Elsewhere in the organized Labor movement a new tendency has recently manifested itself as illustrated by the Seattle and Winnipeg strikes, the One Big Union and Shop Committee movements in Canada and the West, and the numerous strikes all over the country of the rank and file, which are proceeding without the authority of the old reactionary Trade Union officials, and even against their orders. This tendency, an impulse of the workers toward unity for common action across the lines of craft divisions, if carried to its logical conclusion would inevitably lead to workers' control of industry.

(3) This revolt of the rank and file must not be allowed to end in the disorganization of the ranks of organized labor. We must help to keep the workers together, and through rank and file control of the Unions, assist the process of uniting all workers in One Big Union.

(4) With this purpose in view, the Communist Labor Party welcomes and supports, in whatever labor organization found, any tendency toward revolutionary industrial unionism. We urge all our members to join industrial unions. Where the job control of the reactionary craft unions compels them to become members of these craft unions, they shall also join an industrial organization, if one exists. In districts where there are no industrial unions, our members shall take steps to organize one.

III

To Labor and Labor alone is industry responsible. Without the power of Labor, industry could not function. The need of the hour is that Labor recognize the necessity of organization and education. This cannot be achieved by attempting to influence the leaders of the Labor movement, as has been clearly shown by the actions of the recent Convention of the American Federation of Labor. It can only be done by getting the workers on the job to come together and discuss the vital problems of industry.

(3) Because of the industrial crisis created by the World War, together with the break down of industry following the cessation of hostilities, and the interruption of the processes of exchange and distribution, there is great dissatisfaction among the workers. But they can find no means of dealing with the situation. Their Unions have refused to take any steps to meet the grave problems of today; and, moreover, they obstruct all efforts of the rank and file to find some way by which the workers can act.

(4) We suggest that some plan of labor organization be inaugurated along the lines of the Shop Steward and Shop Committee movements. These Committees can serve as a spur or check upon the officials of the Unions; they will necessarily reflect the spirit and wishes of the rank and file, and will educate the workers on the job in preparation for the taking over of industry.

RECOMMENDATIONS

We recommend the following measures:

(1) That all Locals shall elect Committees on Labor Organization, composed so far as is possible of members of Labor Unions, whose functions shall be:

(a) To initiate, or support, the creation of Shop Committees in every industry in their district, the uniting of these Committees in Industrial Councils, District Councils, and the Central council of all industries.

(b) To propagandize and assist in the combining of craft unions, by industries, in One Big Union.

(c) To bring together in the centers of Party activity — Locals and Branches — delegates from factories and shops to discuss tactics and policies of conducting the class struggle.

(d) To propagandize directly among the workers on the job the principles of Communism, and educate them to a realization of their class position.

(e) To find a common basis for the uniting of all existing economic and political organizations based on the class struggle.

(f) To mobilize all members who can serve as organizers to fill the demand for men and women who can organize bodies of workers along the lines indicated above.

(g) To direct the activities of local Party organizations in assisting the workers whole-heartedly in their industrial battles, and making use of these battles as opportunities for educating the workers.

(2) That a National Committee on Labor Organization be elected by this Convention, which shall co-operate with the local committees above mentioned. In addition, the National Committee shall be charged with the task of mobilizing national support for strikes of national importance, and shall endeavor to give these a political character.

(a) It shall collect information concerning the revolutionary labor movement from the different sections of the country, and from other countries, and through a Press Service to Labor and Socialist papers, shall spread this information to all parts of the country.

(b) It shall mobilize on a national scale all members who can serve as propagandists and organizers who cannot only teach, but actually help to put into practice, the principles of revolutionary industrial unionism and Communism.

CHAPTER VII

Socialist Labor Party

Prior to 1898 the leading Socialist organization claiming to be a political party was the Socialist Labor Party, which in that year had gained its zenith, polling 82,204 votes throughout the United States. During that year a bitter controversy arose with organized labor, which resulted in a split in the party, the rigid discipline exacted by Daniel De Leon being in large measure responsible for the differences which arose. As pointed out in Chapter I of this subsection, the bulk of Socialist adherents left the party to form the nucleus of what afterward became the Socialist Party of America. Those who remained in the old organization continued to function as the Socialist Labor Party, under the leadership of Daniel De Leon.

The Socialist Labor Party as it exists today is a small group, effective for its propaganda and for its connections with the Workers' International Industrial Union. The aims and purposes of this party differ very little from those of the Socialist Party of America. They both desire the creation of a co-operative commonwealth and favor industrial unionism as opposed to trade unionism of the type of the American Federation of Labor. Though the two parties profess to differ fundamentally, in the final analysis very little difference between them may be discerned.

The party stands for the overthrow of the present system of government, by the use of industrial action to be made effective by organizing the workers in industrial unions and by the carrying on of the class struggle. Its purposes and objects are manifest from a reading of the platform adopted at the national convention on April 30, 1916, which is as follows:

> "We hold that the purpose of government is to secure to every citizen the enjoyment of this right; but taught by experience we hold furthermore that such right is illusory to the majority of the people, to wit, the working class, under the present system of economic inequality that is essentially destructive of their life, their liberty, and their happiness.
>
> "We hold that the true theory of economics is that the means of production must be owned, operated and controlled by the people in common. Man cannot exercise his right

DANIEL DeLEON (Now Deceased)
Leader of Socialist Labor Party — Workers' International Industrial Union

to life, liberty and the pursuit of happiness without the ownership of the land on, and tools with which to work. Deprived of these, his life, his liberty and his fate fall into the hands of that class which owns these essentials for work and production.

"We hold that the existing contradiction between social production and capitalist appropriation — the latter resulting from the private ownership of the natural and social opportunities—divides the people into two classes: the capitalist class and the working class; throws society into the convulsions of the class struggle; and perverts government in the interests of the capitalist class.

"Thus labor is robbed of the wealth it alone produces, is denied the means of self-employment, and, by compulsory idleness in wage slavery, is even deprived of the necessaries of life.

"Against such a system the Socialist Labor Party raises the banner of revolt, and demands the unconditional surrender of the capitalist class.

"In place of such a system the Socialist Labor Party aims to substitute a system of social ownership of the means of production, industrially administered by the working class,—the workers to assume control and direction as well as operation of their industrial affairs.

"This solution of necessity requires the organization of the working class as a class upon revolutionary political and industrial lines.

"We, therefore, call upon the wage workers to organize themselves into a revolutionary political organization under the banner of the Socialist Labor Party; and to organize themselves likewise upon the industrial field into a revolutionary industrial union in keeping with their political aims.

"And we also call upon all other intelligent citizens to place themselves squarely upon the ground of working class interests, and join us in this mighty and noble work of human emancipation, so that we may put summary end to the existing barbarous class conflict by placing the land and all the means of production, transportation, and distribution into the hands of the people, as a collective body, and substituting the Co-operative Commonwealth for the present state of planless production, industrial war and social disorder —

a commonwealth in which every worker shall have the free exercise and full benefit of his faculties, multiplied by all the modern factors of civilization."

The attitude of the party on war is made clear by a letter addressed to the Copenhagen Conference, in which it is stated:

"So long as this theory (of national defense) is adhered to, a repetition of the present mass-murder of Europe's proletariat may occur at any time. Nothing can prevent a capitalist class of one country, through its various agencies, from starting a war with another nation, unless the respective Socialist parties are organizing the working class industrially, *i. e.*, for the immediate overthrow of capitalism."

The cause of the collapse of the Second International is attributed by this party to "Lack of proper economic organization is the mediate, and the superstition of 'nationalism' the immediate cause of the downfall of the International."

An attempt was made, at a conference held in New York City on January 6, 1917, to effect a union between the Socialist Party and the Socialist Labor Party. This, however, came to naught.

The fundamental principles of the Socialist Labor Party were made clear in a statement of minimum demands presented at that conference, as follows:

"(a) As to aim: Abolition of the capitalist system and establishment of collectivism, i. e., Socialism.

"(b) As to political action: Declaration in favor of uncompromising revolutionary political action.

"(c) As to economic action: Declaration in favor of industrial unionism, and a condemnation, generally, of craft unionism.

"(d) As to militarism and war: Declaration to the effect that military establishments are maintained partly for the purpose of crushing working-class rebellion and partly to protect foreign interests of the capitalist class.

"Prohibition (on the part of elected officials) to vote for men or money, for war or militarism, under pain of expulsion, to vote for preparedness either on an increased or the present scale. Also a declaration to the effect that the workers 'have no country to defend but a country and a world to gain from the capitalist class of this country and of the world.'"

The party, according to the report of Arnold Peterson, national secretary of the Socialist Labor Party, appearing at page 366 of the American Labor Year Book for 1917–18, had a membership of 3,185 on December 31, 1916, and had at that time five foreign Language Federations affiliated with it. They were:

The Scandinavian Socialist Labor Federation.
The South Slavonian Socialist Labor Federation.
The Hungarian Socialist Labor Federation.
The Lettish Socialist Labor Federation.
The Jewish Socialist Labor Federation.

According to Arnold Petersen's report, appearing in the American Labor Year Book for 1919–20, the membership of the party has increased up to the present year, and he says that they have "succeeded in putting our message 'across' despite the almost insuperable difficulties which were engendered by the war."

The Socialist Labor Party published a number of papers, among them the following:

The "Volksfreund und Arbeiter Zeitung." This publication, printed in German, was compelled to suspend by reason of its deprivation of second-class mailing privileges.

The "Weekly People," the party's official organ, also deprived of second-class mailing privileges but still continuing to be published.

The "Proletareets," the Lettish organ of the party, which discontinued publication in 1917 by reason of the provisions of the Trading With the Enemy Act.

"A Munkas," the Hungarian organ of the party, which also lost its second-class mailing privileges but which is still continuing to be published.

Arnold Peterson (pages 420 and 421, American Labor Year Book for 1919–20) has this to say about the work and theories of the Socialist Labor Party:

> "The theories of the Socialist Labor Party have received a startling, and in a certain sense, unexpected vindication in Russia. To be sure, Russia economically was not so situated as to present a most favorable soil for the application of the Socialist Labor Party's principles. But so far advanced, generally, is capitalism now, that Russia, under the leadership of Lenin, soon found it necessary to proceed along the lines laid down by the Socialist Labor Party, namely, to discard the political state machinery and to organize the workers and peasants along occupational lines. This process of organization, and the result — the Soviets, corresponds

to the industrial union program long ago formulated by the Socialist Labor Party, with such differences, of course, as naturally result from the differences between the two countries (Russia and the United States of America). Furthermore, the soundness of the principles of the Socialist Labor Party has been recognized by no less an authority than Lenin himself, who, it is said, has been much impressed with Daniel De Leon's writings, which it is further reported, are being translated into the Russian language.

"Thus, while the party as such has not increased much in membership and votes, it can, nevertheless, look back with satisfaction upon the harvest so far reaped, and look forward with confidence to the harvest yet to be reaped, and, if all signs do not fail, a harvest to be reaped in a not too distant future.

"More recently, since the signing of the armistice, the party decided that besides the general broad propaganda always carried on, the time had come to concentrate upon a given field so as to pull in shape, more rapidly, the industrial forces of the working-class. The mining industry was selected and invaded and the propaganda of the S. L. P. carried to the workers in the mines. This move, carefully planned and energetically executed, met with instant success. The State of Illinois, the key position of the United Mine Workers of America, was taken in hand first. There the miners are today in full revolt against both the mine owner and the reactionary labor leader — the latter always a working partner of the former. The miners are now determined to take their organization into their own hands, to place all power with the rank and file and they are taking a decided revolutionary position that aims, ultimately, at the overthrow of capitalism.

"The party membership in the coal fields is now growing and so is the dissemination of the party organs and of party literature."

The aims and purposes of the Socialist Labor Party are summarized in an open letter addressed by the National Executive Committee of that party to Senator Lee S. Overman, Chairman of the Senate Judiciary Committee which investigated Bolshevism about a year ago. The relevant portions of this letter follow:

"The Socialist Labor Party is a revolutionary organization. In this day and age, and above all to an American and an American legislator, it certainly should not be necessary to apologize for, nor even to define, the word revolution. So tremendous is the confusion of ideas, however, that the word is continually coupled with murder, bloodshed, anarchy, arson, and a general reign of terror. We, shall therefore, take no chances of being misunderstood. Technically, and as employed by the Socialist Labor Party, revolution means a fundamental and internal change in government. The particular change which the Socialist Labor Party advocates is a change from the capitalist class-ownership to the social ownership of the means of production, with the management and control lodged with the workers themselves, the power originating from below, in the industries. Hence we hold that under such a system the present Political State with all its trappings and machinery must die out or be abolished, while its place is taken by an industrial government, a government of things instead of men. It is plain that the political ballot would have no further function. The industrial ballot would take its place. The voting would be done on the basis of industry and industrial employment, and, accordingly, could be exercised by workers only. But, Sir, as private ownership in the means of production would naturally cease, there would remain no way of exploitation, no profits, no windfalls, no bonuses, no stock-gambling, and, therefore, in order to live, each and every able-bodied person of proper age would be forced to perform some kind of useful labor. Therefore, as soon as useless folks learned, probably from necessity that 'he who will not work neither shall he eat,' they would hasten to obtain useful employment and become members and voters in the Industrial Commonwealth. . . . The modern wage working-class, that is to say, the intelligent portion of it, in every country and clime, is Socialist or at least 'Socialistic.' The world is on the verge of a social revolution. The Socialist believes, and believes intensely, that your class, Sir, the capitalist class, has fulfilled its mission in human history and that willingly or unwillingly it will have to step aside and give place to the next class on the social ladder. It is for this social change, this revolution, that we Socialists of the Socialist Labor Party agitate. . . .

"Now we come to another phase of the matter. We stated at the outset that the name of the Socialist Labor Party has been closely coupled with the Soviet Republic of Russia, and, of course, you have already perceived that our revolutionary program for the reconstruction of society on industrial, instead of the present political, lines, bears a close resemblance to the constructive program of the Soviet Republic. Perhaps you have already made up your mind that all revolutionary relations of that 'murderous crew' of Russia, the S. L. P., must be 'stamped out' at once. But we claim your indulgence for yet another moment, Sir. We have determined to speak frankly, and we shall hide nothing. If it is real 'American Bolshevism' which you are interested to trace out and to investigate, honored Sir, it is the Socialist Labor Party you will have to investigate first and last. In a public address during January, 1918, Nicolai Lenin paid tribute to Daniel De Leon of the Socialist Labor Party of America, and showed that the governmental construction on the basis of industry, such as outlined by the Socialist Labor Party, fits admirably into the Soviet construction of the state. In an interview with the artist, Robert Minor, reported in the New York "World" of Feb. 4, 1919, Lenin said: 'The American Daniel De Leon first formulated the idea of a Soviet government, which grew up on his idea. Future society will be organized along Soviet lines. There will be Soviet rather than geographical boundaries for nations. Industrial unionism is the basic thing. That is what we are building.'

"The idea of constructive Industrial Unionism, the conception that such a union is the germ of the future Industrial Government, the discovery and amplification of the idea belongs to the American Daniel De Leon, a member and the acknowledged leader of the Socialist Labor Party from the time he became connected with the Labor Movement in the late eighties until his death in 1914. This is S. L. P. ism or, what all our opponents in the Labor Movement have scoffingly designated, 'De Leonism.'

"But, we hear you say, if the Socialist Labor Party are the original 'Bolshevists,' and they appear to be proud of it, what is the use of that Party trying to dodge behind the American Constitution and the Declaration of Independence, of talking about 'civilized methods' and 'orderly procedure?' That 'vicious crew,' the Russian Bolshevists, not only belive in physical force tactics, but they have used and are using them in no uncertain manner. Dear Sir, kindly note that as far as revolutionary tactics are concerned, we have not presumed to lay down any general law. We are not Utopians. We have spoken of American conditions, the only ones we as a Party have to deal with. We have spoken of, and we advocate, what we consider the best and most expedient tactics under American political democracy. As for general revolutionary tactics and methods we have no creed. We are Socialists and revolutionists, and as such we will and must adopt such tactics as will bring about the revolution and insure order in the new social structure in the quickest and most expedient manner. This has ever been the case in history. As to the Russian Bolsheviki we have nothing to do or to say about their tactics; we have no reliable information as to what has actually taken place; and as to whether the Russian revolutionists have adopted the best possible methods under their trying circumstances, or whether they have committed blunder upon blunder which has cost hundreds or thousands of lives, not we, Mr. Senator, but future history alone has the right and power to judge. We are Americans, and Americans, above all people, should be tolerant with those who may be forced, as the American revolutionists were forced, to suffer privation, to starve, and to die, to organize armies and fight their own flesh and blood for the cause they hold dear — a cause which means the happiness of the future. Such moments in history, Sir, are occasions for sackcloth and ashes, not for rash condemnation and harsh judgment."

The attitude of the party towards this country is further illustrated by a statement which appears in the report of the national secretary, Arnold Petersen, published in the American Labor Year Book, 1917–18, at page 364:

"When in 1916, therefore, we at the very outset commenced our campaign on the burning question of the hour — 'preparedness'— basing our arguments on the principle that the workers have no interests in militarism in any form, having no interest in defending a country in which they as yet owned nothing, and whose political institutions had largely outlived their usefulness, we did so in line with our previous pronouncements."

As a typical example of the expression of sympathy which this organization holds for the Russian Soviet regime, we quote from a resolution adopted at the meeting of the National Executive Committee of the party on May 4, 1919, which appears in the May 10, 1919, issue of the "Weekly People:"

"When, on November 7, 1917, the Workers, Soldiers and Poor Peasants of Russia, by a revolutionary act, put an end to the painful attempt on the part of the Russian bourgeoisie to assume the heritage of czarism, and when, as a result of that act, the power in that vast realm passed over to the hitherto disinherited and oppressed, a thrill of delight went through the hearts of the revolutionary workers the world over.

"Here at last, they experienced the first visible triumph of the class struggle, the first fruit of the world war which, unlike all its others, was wholly acceptable and was of corresponding bitterness to the capitalist foe.

". . . And we declare that, with all the power that in us lies, we shall assist them in their struggle by incessant revolutionary propaganda in order to awaken America's proletariat and, by unflagging efforts, to organize that proletariat into a class-conscious, militant body on both the political and the industrial field, bent upon ending capitalist misrule on this side of the Atlantic; and . . . Resolved, that we condemn all military intervention in the territories of these countries and insist upon adherence to a policy of absolute non-interference with the affairs of the people of these countries now engaged in the work of building the only real democracies the world has ever seen; and be it further

"Resolved, That we denounce and condemn the vicious campaign of slander and vituperation carried on by the capitalist plunderbund against Soviet Russia, a campaign conducted with such brazen mendacity and utter disregard of the dictates of common decency — to say nothing of common sense — as to throw into bold relief the strumpet character of capitalist society. We view with disgust the spectacle of a committee of the United States Senate permitting itself to be made the depository of foul tales about the nationalization of Russian women, but we realize that, in its anger and its fright, the capitalist class, when hawking these prurient tales, is only revealing its debauched inner self — repeating history as it were, by imitating a profligate Roman patriciate which habitually charged the early Christians with their own moral decay."

Owing to the dogmatic stand taken by the leaders of this party, it plays no very significant part in the general revolutionary movement in this country.

The national headquarters of this organization are located at 45 Rose street, New York City.

CHAPTER VIII

Investigation into Radical Activities in Upper Part of the State

While a large part of the work of this Committee of necessity concerned itself with conditions existing in the City of New York and vicinity, a fairly comprehensive survey of radical activities existing in the upper part of the state of New York was made. This survey was by no means exhaustive, owing to the limited resources and limited time at the disposal of this Committee.

The upper part of the State, for purposes of convenient reference, was divided into certain zones, and annexed to this chapter are maps of these zones with a reference to the centers of radical activity in each particular zone. The extent of the activity in each place indicated on these various zone maps, of course, varies. In the case of some cities indicated, such as Utica, Rochester and Buffalo, there is considerable well-organized revolutionary radical activity. In the case of other towns and cities indicated on these various zone maps, the revolutionary activities are more or less sporadic, and the sole reason for referring to them on the maps is that there is some activity that requires attention.

As a general rule, the revolutionary radicals sought to gain a foothold in industrial centers, and numerous unjustified strikes may be traced directly to the efforts and the propaganda of Communist and Socialist agitators.

In this chapter we will briefly summarize the results of our investigations in the various sections of the State indicated on the attached zone maps marked, respectively, Zone A, B, C, E, G, and H.

Zone A

Zone A includes the counties of Erie, Niagara, Chautauqua and Wyoming. For purposes of convenience in reference we will include Buffalo, Niagara Falls, Tonawanda, North Tonawanda, and Depew as one group.

Buffalo has been a center of radical activity for some time, and until a wholesale round-up, conducted by agents of this Committee and of the District Attorney of Erie County on the 29th day of December, 1919, practically disrupted their organization, there was a large and growing Communist movement in that city. The headquarters of the Communist Party in Buffalo were situated in the Teck Theatre Building, and the organizer of the party was one George Till. He is an American citizen and has been a revolutionary radical leader for some time. The membership of the party in the late part of 1919 was some 600, and the organization was rapidly increasing in numbers, owing to the agitation carried on by Till and his followers, until his arrest and indictment on the charge of criminal anarchy was brought about by this Committee. Mr. Moore, the District Attorney of Erie County, worked in the closest co-operation with this Committee and caused the indictment of eighteen members of the Communist Party Local on the charge of violating the Criminal Anarchy Statutes of this State.

The literature, books, pamphlets and propaganda found in Buffalo were practically the same as that found in New York City and were, of course, part of the same general scheme of creating industrial unrest, class hatred and revolutionary aims as was found in New York City.

The Committee ascertained that there were in Buffalo the following branches of the Communist Party: The Central branch, which met in the Teck Theatre Building, 760 Main Street, Buffalo; the English-speaking branch, at 7 South Niagara Street, Tonawanda; the Ukrainian East Side branch, which also met at the Teck Theatre Building; the Russian branch, which met in the same place; the Bulgarian branch, which met at 194 Oak Street; the Williamsville branch, which met in the homes of various members on each Sunday of the month; the German branch, whose headquarters were at Sycamore and Smith Streets; and the Polish branch, of Depew, which met at 77 Main Street, Depew.

There were found in this section also other revolutionary organizations, among them a branch of the W. I. I. U., and some forty-five members of the Union of Russian Workers, of whom twenty were arrested by the Department of Justice and held for deportation.

The membership in the various branches of the Communist Party was ascertained to be as follows:

Central branch, 220; Polish branch, 150; Russian branch, 90; Ukrainian and Black Rock, 60; North Tonawanda, 36; Ukrainian East Side, 32; Bulgarian, 22; Williamsville, 16; Lithuanian, 15; German, 10.

Information came to the Committee of the presence of an anarchist group at Niagara Falls. This group was composed exclusively of Spaniards, who are working "under cover" and concerning whom very little information was available. It will be recalled that in February, 1919, a certain number of men were arrested, suspected of plotting against the life of President Wilson, and of that number two were from Niagara Falls and probably belonged to the small group of Spanish anarchists who make their headquarters in that city.

Several branches of the Workers' International Industrial Union, better known as the W. I. I. U., were found in Buffalo. The Polish branch, No. 1, held its meetings at 1036 Broadway, Buffalo, and the English branch met at Harigari Hall, 431 Genesee Street.

The Social Labor Party also had a section there, known as Section Erie County, and meeting at Fleming's Hall, 431 Genesee Street. Practically the whole Socialist organization in Buffalo went Communist, and a conservative appraisal of the number of revolutionary radicals to be found in Buffalo and vicinity would be about 2,000.

At Niagara Falls there was also found a branch of the Union of Russian Workers, but not particularly well organized, and composed of but twelve members.

A circular, entitled "Your Shop," and marked "Propaganda Leaflet No. 3 of the Communist Party of America," was distributed by the tens of thousands in the various industrial plants in and around Buffalo, and was but one of a series of leaflets which preached the doctrine of class hatred and discontent and urged the workers to seize the industries in which they were employed and expropriate them for themselves. A copy of this leaflet appears in full in Chapter V of the subsection dealing with the Communist Party.

It was ascertained by the investigators of this Committee that there were in Zone A thirty-one towns and cities in which were found evidences of revolutionary radical activities. Boris Reinstein, who is one of the members of the International Propaganda Committee of Soviet Russia in Moscow, came from Buffalo and left this country without a passport. The daughter of Boris Reinstein is married to a Dr. Kabanoky of Buffalo, who is very active in revolutionary radical circles in that city.

In the rural communities in Zone A, such as Mayville, Sheridan, Findlay, Findlay Lake, Clymer and Jamestown, in Chautauqua County, and Warsaw and Casteel, in Wyoming County, radical activity is conducted almost exclusively by correspondence. Small schools or classes are conducted in these various communities, and an attempt is made to gain proselytes to the cause of revolutionary radicalism.

The Jamestown strike of the summer of 1919 was conducted by the Workers' International Industrial Union, which is known as a syndicalist organization and is practically conducted on the same lines and on the same principles as the I. W. W. As pointed out in another section of this report, it discards the theory of a fair day's pay for a fair day's work and advocates the seizure of industries by the workers themselves.

The numbers running from 1 to 31 on the map of Zone A indicate the towns in which radical revolutionary activity is extant to some appreciable extent. It must not be thought, however, that the fact of a town's being indicated as a center of radical activity on these maps necessarily means that that activity has assumed any large or dangerous proportions.

ZONE B

Zone B includes the counties of Monroe, Orleans, Genesee, Livingston, Ontario and Wayne. The principal center of activity in Zone B is Rochester. The headquarters of the Communist Party in this city were in Labor Lyceum at 580 St. Paul Street, better known as Dynamite Hall, that being the term commonly used throughout the city in describing this radical headquarters. The organizer of the party in this city was one C. M. O'Brien, who is now under indictment, charged with Criminal Anarchy, and who was arrested by the agents of this Committee, acting in co-operation with the local police and the District Attorney, on the night of December 29, 1919.

A description of Dynamite Hall and the activities there conducted is to be found in another chapter of this report dealing with the general subject of subversive education.

There have been several large strikes in Rochester during the past year, particularly in the Bausch & Lomb Optical Works and in the clothing industry, and there are indications that both of these strikes were fomented by the leaders of radical revolutionary organizations. One Komorowsky, who was a delegate to the Communist Party Convention at Chicago in September, 1919, was one of the leaders of the Bausch & Lomb strike.

The radical revolutionary unions have secured a very firm foothold in the clothing industry at Rochester, and there is but one concern, the Michael Stern Company, which is running a 100 per cent American shop; that is, a shop in which all the employees are American citizens and members of the American Federation of Labor.

There are a number of members of the Union of Russian Workers in Rochester, and records in the possession of the Committee indicate that 150 copies of "Khlieb-y-Volya," the anarchist paper of Peter Bianki, were regularly sent to Rochester.

There are several towns in Zone B in which there was found some evidence of radical activity, these towns being, in addition to Rochester, Mt. Hope, Pittsford, Palmyra, Lyons, Geneva, Batavia and Geneseo, but with the exception of Rochester there is no organized radical activity in any of these places.

ZONE C

Zone C comprises Cattaraugus and Allegany Counties. The principal city in this zone is Olean. There was found an Ukrainian branch of the Communist Party, which went out of existence some six months ago. The towns in this zone in which there was found some evidence of radical activity are Olean, Allegany, Salamanca, Onoville, Little Valley, Gowanda, Franklinville, Angelica, Wellsville, Allentown and Bolivar.

The radical activity in this zone also is practically negligible.

ZONE E

This zone includes the following counties: Oswego, Onondaga, Cayuga, Seneca, and Madison, and evidences of radical activity were found in the following cities and towns: Syracuse, Hamilton, Cazenovia, Manlius, Sherwood, Union Springs, Auburn, Westbury, Fulton, Oswego, Oneida, and Solvay.

In Syracuse there were found Russian, Ukrainian, Polish and Italian branches of the Communist Party. There were found about 150 paid-up members of the Communist Party in Syracuse. The Central branch, which is a Communist Labor Party branch, was composed in large measure of American citizens. No headquarters of the I. W. W. were found, although there was an organizer for the I. W. W. named Phillip Pherry, who was acting as literary agent and soliciting membership for the I. W. W., but apparently with very little success. One J. G. Baldenkoff, residing at 808 South State Street, Syracuse, was acting as the literary agent for the Union of Russian Workers, and in one communication he signed himself as follows: "I remain, in the struggle for the ideals of anarchist Communism."

Most of the activities of the revolutionary radicals in this section are centered around the factories and the industrial plants. In Auburn was found an Ukrainian branch of the Communist Party, very well organized and with a membership of eighty odd, holding its meetings on the third floor of the Auditorium Building on Water Street, in what is known as Woodmen's Hall. John Malyso, of 67½ South Division Street, was the organizer of the Ukrainian branch of the Communist Party in Auburn, and Michael Bazar, address unknown, was the financial secretary.

In Syracuse, a radical newspaper, known as "Hard Times," was published by one M. L. Tourtellot, but this went out of existence several months ago. A letter in possession of the Committee and signed by this man Tourtellot closes with the following words: "Fraternally yours, for Communism." Considerable I. W. W. literature was being circulated in Syracuse by one Phillip Pherry, of 1306 Carbon Street, Syracuse, and a letter in possession of the Committee indicates that he was busily engaged in promulgating the idea of the O. B. U., the One Big Union.

ZONE G

Zone G includes the Counties of Broome, Chenango, and Otsego, and evidences of revolutionary radical activity were found in the following towns: Binghamton, Norwich, Endicott, Oneonta and Morris. The largest city in this zone is Binghamton.

In Binghamton there was a branch of the Communist Party, known as the Lithuanian Communist Party, with a membership of seventy-two. The leader of this branch was one Joseph Klekunas, who lived on Clinton Street, Binghamton. The meetings of this local were held at Lithuanian Hall, 267 Clinton Street. There was also an Ukrainian branch of the Communist Party in Binghamton, comprising some fifteen members, and having as its secretary one Frank Lakoduk, who resided at 7 Judson Avenue. The organizer was one Harajchuk, living on Hazel Street, and another was one Tkachuk, also living on Hazel Street. One of the most active members was Harry Saroka, living on Hazel Street, and John Valchuk, a resident of New York City, who lived in Binghamton for awhile and was a violent agitator.

The Slovak branch of the Socialist Party, comprising some seventy-two members, met in Slovak Hall on Star Avenue, Binghamton. It had as its secretary Joe Horvatt, and the other officers were John Poliachuk, of 192 Murray Street, and Matthew J. Maxian. Maxian organized the cigarmakers' strike in Binghamton in the summer of 1919, and had previously taken a correspondence course at the Rand School of Social Science.

In Endicott there was a Russian branch of the Communist Party, with a membership of 150, with headquarters formerly at 24 Squires Avenue, Endicott, and later at 18 Odell Avenue. The leaders in that organization were Peter Kleskoniv, Wasyl Nosiak, Peter Ilnitsky and W. Pawlosky.

ZONE H

Zone H comprises the following counties: Lewis, Oneida, Herkimer, Hamilton, Fulton and Montgomery. The cities and towns in which evidences of radical revolutionary activities were discovered by the agents of this Committee are Utica, Clinton, Vernon, Rome, Glenfield, Gloversville, Tribes Hill, Amsterdam, Johnstown, St. Johnsville, Dolgeville, Little Falls, Ilion and Frankfort.

There are two branches of the Socialist Party in Utica, the largest city in this zone: the Jewish branch, which meets at its headquarters at 130 Washington Street, and whose organizer is one Max Meyers, and the American branch, the active members of which are John Lattimer and Harvey Brucke. Lattimer is also a member of the I. W. W. The Communist Party has several branches in Utica, the names of which here follow: The Ukrainian branch, which met at 704 Bleeker Street and of which the secretary was Theodore Talley of 406 Millgate Street; Demytno Pastuch, of 1901 Broad Street, was the literature agent, and one Wosyhreczam, whose address was not procurable, acted as financity secretary. Dentryo Choptinay, of 442 Wilkesbarre Street, acted as treasurer. The recording secretary was one Mike Zlepko, who lived in the suburb of Clarkmills.

The Russian branch of the Communist Party in Utica met at 704 Bleeker Street, and one John Korolinok, of 1127 Schuiler Street, was the organizer. One of the most active members was Alex Kruchka.

The Polish branch of the Communist Party met at the same premises, 704 Bleeker Street, and its officers were Joe Gregoros,

411 Mills Street, its organizer, and Joe Skulsky, of Lincoln Avenue, recording secretary.

In the same premises were held the meetings of the Lithuanian branch of the Communist Party. There was an Italian branch of the party, but this group was more or less independent.

At 704 Bleecker street various radical groups meet, of which some 200 are active revolutionary radicals. The investigator of the Committee reported that they were anarchists, syndicalists, cammorists, blackhanders and others.

There is an I. W. W. organization in Utica, which meets in the hall of the Sons of Italy, on Third avenue, and the most active members of which were, at the time of our investigation, Frank Cisirian, Joe Adden, Patsy Urino and one Amandola.

It was customary for the radicals to conduct a sort of open forum at 704 Bleeker street on Saturday nights. The radicals gathered together and discussed various phases of what to them is the most important subject in life, revolutionary radicalism.

To these meetings and these organizations may be traced in a large measure the recent strike in the textile industries in Utica. Testimony given before the Committee by Captain John A. Wright of the Utica Police Force, indicated that in the latter part of August, 1919, a strike was called by the Amalgamated Clothing and Textile Workers of America, composed practically of all foreigners, mostly Poles, Italians, and Syrians. He testified that most of the employees out on strike went out more through fear than through dissatisfaction, threats being made against those who wished to continue their employment, by the strike agitators, who made threats of violent bodily harm and in one instance carried out their threat by setting fire to a building in the night time. Several riots took place, one on Kossuth avenue, near the entrance of the Oneida mill. A number of police officers were injured by being struck by stones.

The strikers compelled merchants in the city to post placards in their windows, reading, "Close in protest to Police Cossacks," and if the merchant refused to put this placard in his window the plate glass was broken by the strikers. Officer John B. Grande of the Utica Police Force testified that one Joseph Gramaldi, a member of the Communist Party in Utica, lead a movement to compel the closing of the stores. As an example of the sort of appeal that was made to the strikers by their leaders, we quote from a speech made by Antonio Carvelli to the Amalagamated

Textile strikers, in a garage on Mary street east of Third avenue, Utica, on October 24, 1919. Carvelli was an organizer of the Amalagamated Clothing and Textile Workers of America:

> "We will open their eyes. They call us anarchists, but as long as we give our wives to the priests and the capitalists we are all right, but when we don't they call us Bolsheviki. We are Bolsheviki. This is the first time that I have spoken between three flags. The Italian flag stands for peace, although they did take it into the war of France. The American flag, the one with the stars in it, the one that Washington and Lincoln fought for, now stands for Wall Street and the fleecers. The best flag of all is the Red flag. I kiss it. It stands for liberty. (Here he held up the Red flag and cried, 'Hurrah for the Bolsheviki.') We are in a critical period, not for you, but for the bosses. For you it is victory. They are insulting the Amalgamated, but every knock is a boost. If we don't win, when we go back the bosses will realize you have no prestige, and if we do go back we will strike in a month or two."

We give here a few excerpts from a speech of another organizer, William H. Derrick, made in Polish Hall, Jay and Nichols streets, on October 3, 1919:

> "If I could get in, I would go back to work, but because I am a Socialist and an agitator they will not employ me. I am a Socialist, and I am not ashamed of it. I am running in the Seventh District of Jersey for the Assembly, and the people respect me and they know that Derrick will fight to wipe out the wrongs. . . . When some one picks your pocket and you holler 'stop thief,' you know who hollers the loudest. It is always the thief. It is the same now with the manufacturers. They are the damndest thieves on the face of the earth. They are not as good as a jack-ass, and they understand less. I wish that they did have the same sense as a jack-ass, even if they did not have the long ears, because even a jack-ass when he gets enough knows enough to stop. . . . They told you that we were Bolsheviki. I wonder if Utica is the only country in the United States that is infested with this Bolshevism. There are at present 2,000 strikes in the United States. Does that look as though you were

alone? . . . When you do win, then I will go to some other place and start another fight. I have lived for forty-seven years, but I guess I am good for thirty more unless some one beats me up. So I guess I will be good for at least 100 more battles. . . . If they kill me there will be ten more speakers and agitators on this platform the next night. Agitators are not born, they are made."

Another speech was made by a man named Ouderkirk, on October 23, 1919, in a garage on Mary street, Utica, at which there were present three or four hundred men and women mill workers. Ouderkirk said:

"The time has come when you should use your brains and your hands to keep the scabs out of the mills. If it is necessary for some to go to the electric chair, the gallows, we will go, but where we leave off there will be many more to carry on our banner. The Amalgamated will open co-operative stores and we will not deal with the profiteers. We will be free from the democratized, Catholicised scab, whether he is an American or just a plain gink. It is you that produced the nice automobile, the fine steam yacht, the Parlor and Pullman cars, and all the wealth for the capitalists, and instead of you using them you get the second-hand bicycle and a dusty, dirty old coach, and have your sons sent to France to fight for these damned profiteers. Go out to the mills and keep the scabs from work. Keep them out anyway. There is no use of disguising it any longer. It is a battle. Go out and fight it."

It was also discovered by the investigators of the Committee that in the premises 704 Bleeker street, Utica, there was an anarchist group known as the Francesco Ferrer Circle. This circle had quite a substantial anarchist library, and among the books that appeared to be particularly popular was one called "L' Emigrazion Sconoscuita". This book dealt with various groups, such as the Black Hand, the Camorra and others, and the preface was written by Luigi Galliani, one of the leading anarchists in the world to-day, who was deported from the United States, in May, 1919. A large mass of revolutionary anarchistic material was found at these premises, 704 Bleeker street, which had been prepared for circulation among the workers in the shops and factories of Utica.

In Rome considerable revolutionary radical activity was noted. In the summer of 1919 there was conducted a very violent strike, and at times this assumed such proportions that companies of the State Constabulary had to be sent into the city to suppress violent riots. This strike was precipitated by I. W. W. agitators and the names of 115 of these men were obtained by the Committee.

A large part of the information obtained as a result of the investigation of this Committee in those portions of the State referred to in the preceding zones cannot be given with any greater detail, by reason of the fact that a large number of indictments under the Criminal Anarchy Statute of this State are pending. These indictments will in the very near future be tried by the prosecuting officers of the counties in which the offenses occurred, and it might defeat the ends of justice if the information obtained were at this time divulged. It is for this reason that this chapter does not give with greater particularity facts that might be of considerable interest in the report.

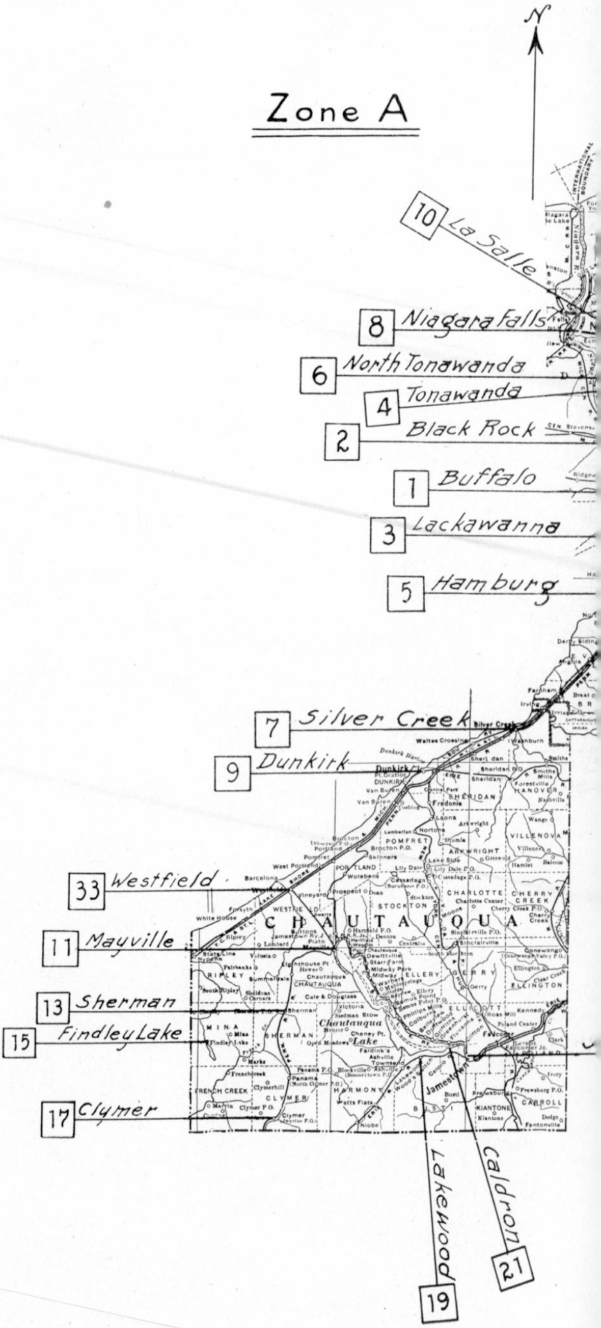
Zone A
N
10 La Salle
8 Niagara Falls
6 North Tonawanda
4 Tonawanda
2 Black Rock
1 Buffalo
3 Lackawanna
5 Hamburg
7 Silver Creek
9 Dunkirk
33 Westfield
11 Mayville
13 Sherman
15 Findley Lake
17 Clymer
19 Lakewood
21 Caldron
CHAUTAUQUA

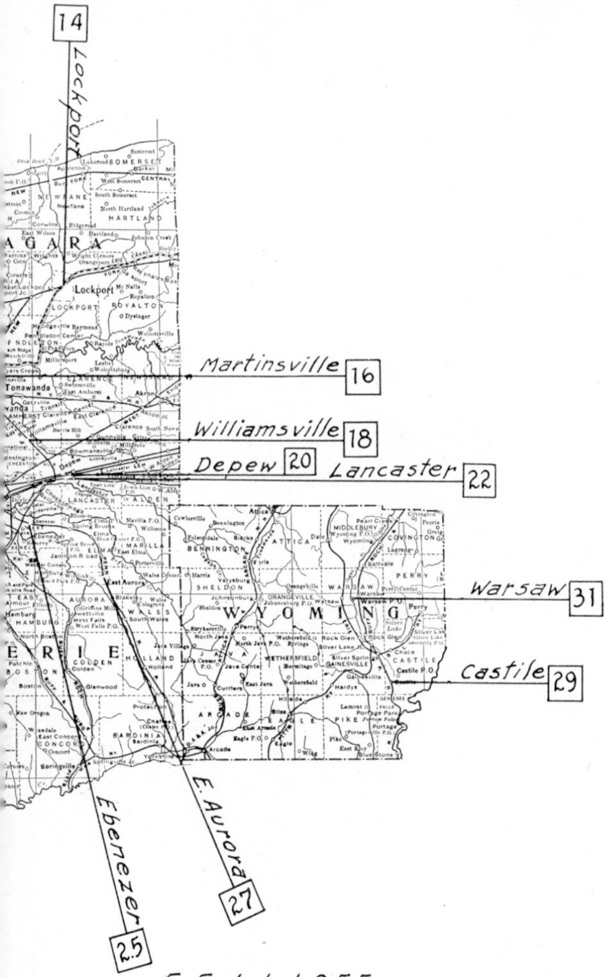

E. Exhibit 355
Dec. 27/19

own 23

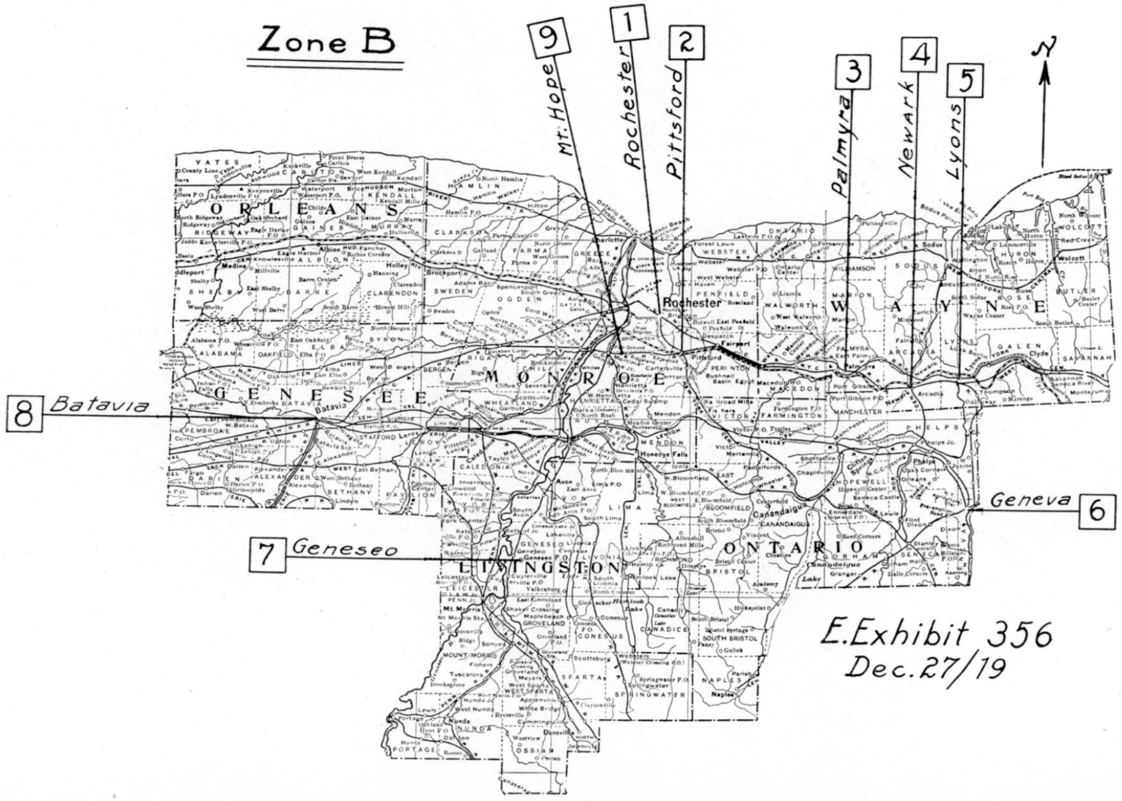
Zone B
N
1 Rochester
2 Pittsford
3 Palmyra
4 Newark
5 Lyons
6 Geneva
7 Geneseo
8 Batavia
9 Mt. Hope
ORLEANS
GENESEE
MONROE
WAYNE
ONTARIO
LIVINGSTON
E.Exhibit 356
Dec. 27/19

Zone C

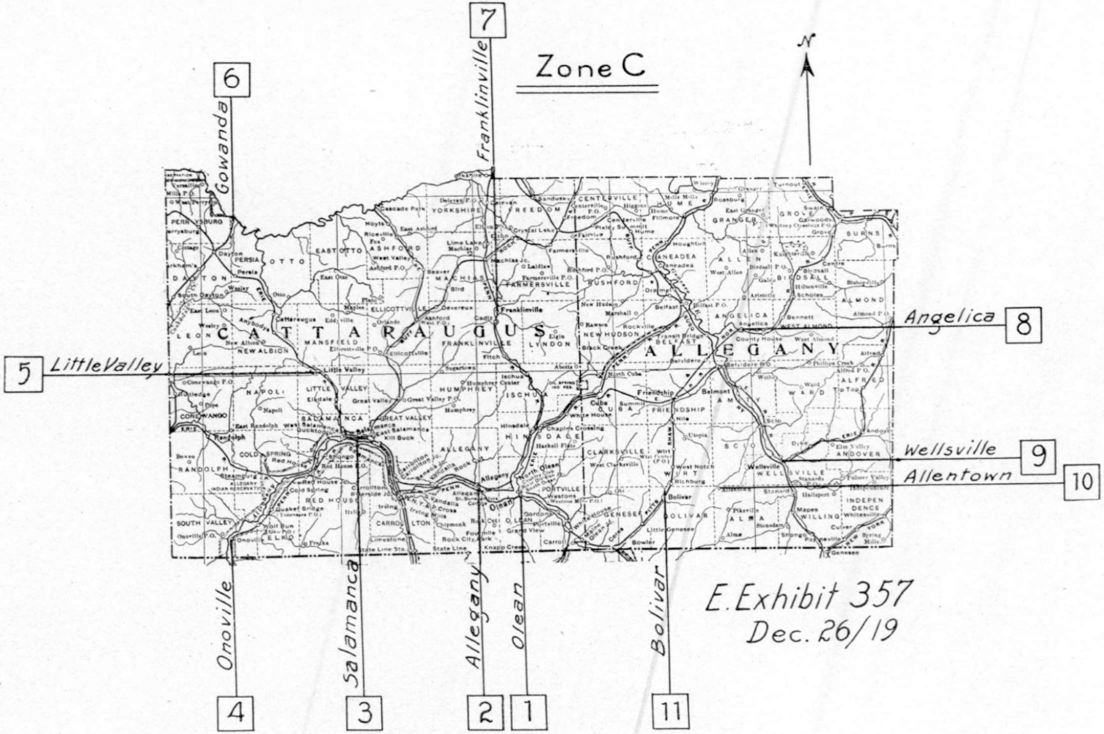

E. Exhibit 357
Dec. 26/19

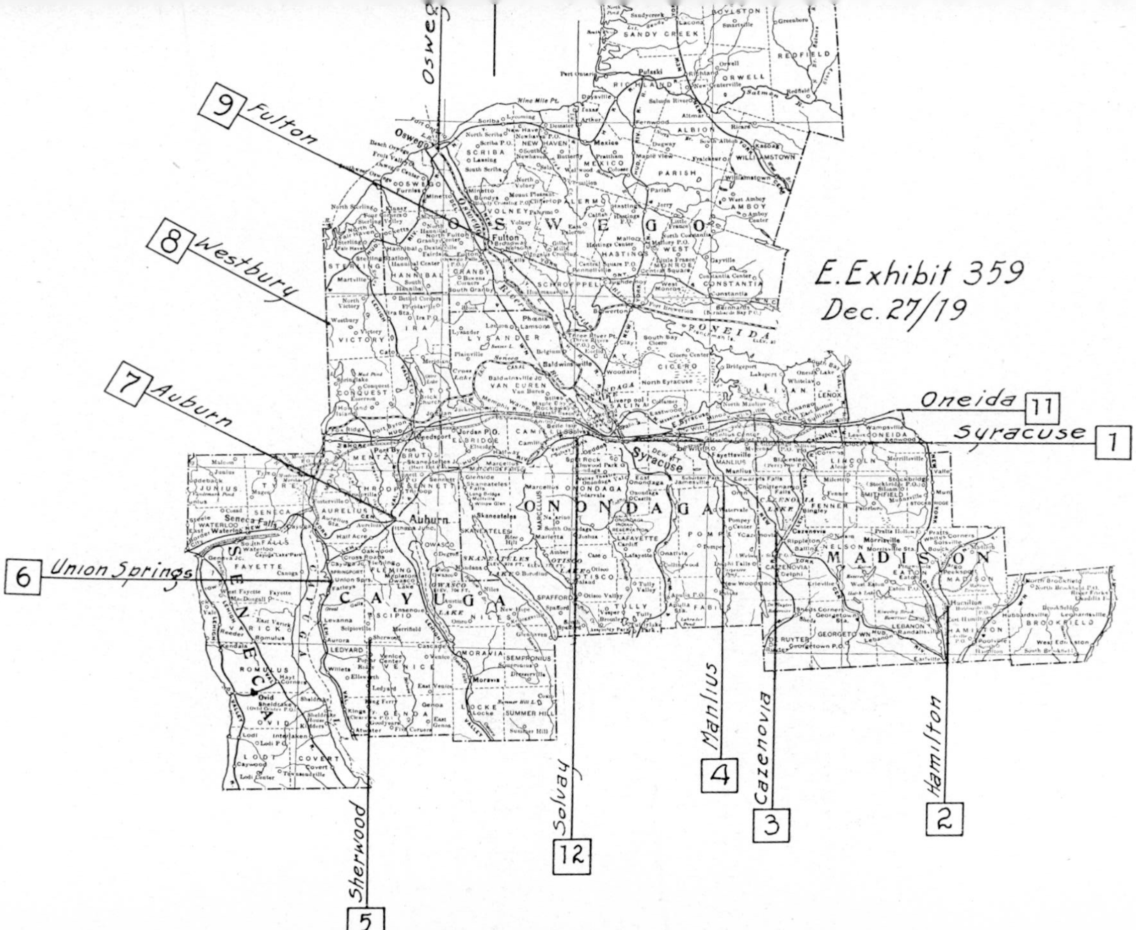
E. Exhibit 359
Dec. 27/19
1 Syracuse
2 Hamilton
3 Cazenovia
4 Manlius
5 Sherwood
6 Union Springs
7 Auburn
8 Westbury
9 Fulton
11 Oneida
12 Solvay
OSWEGO
ONONDAGA
CAYUGA
MADISON
SENECA

Zone G

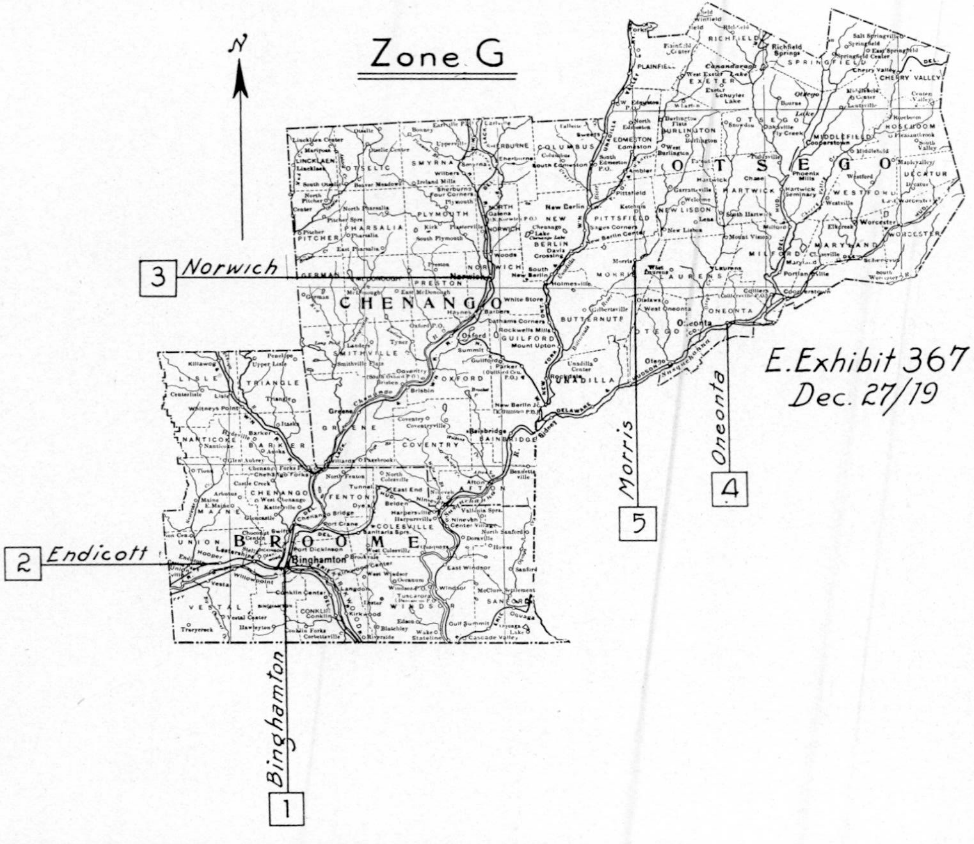

E. Exhibit 367
Dec. 27/19

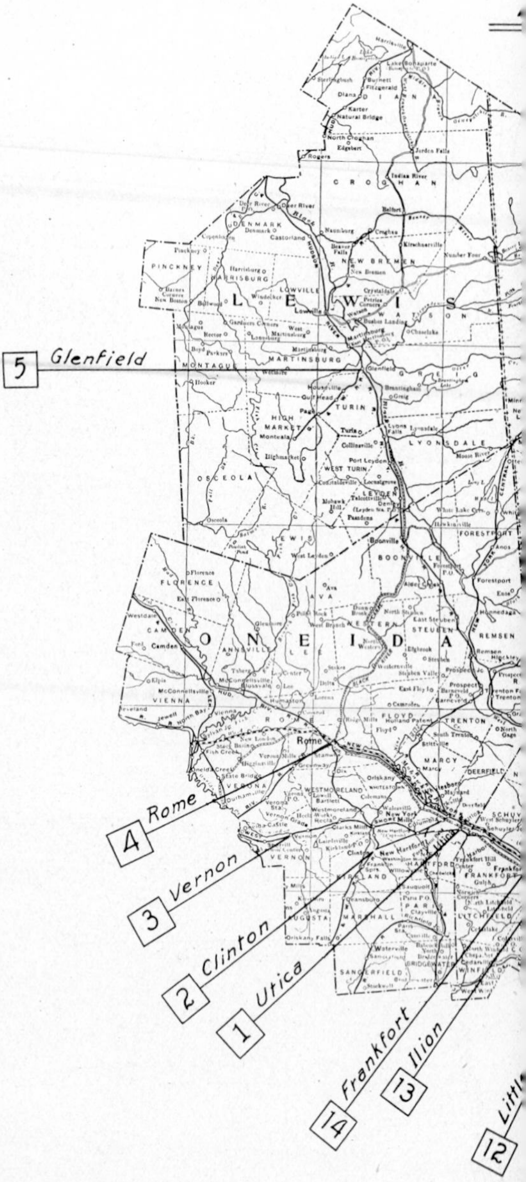

5 Glenfield
4 Rome
3 Vernon
2 Clinton
1 Utica
14 Frankfort
13 Ilion
12
LEWIS
ONEIDA

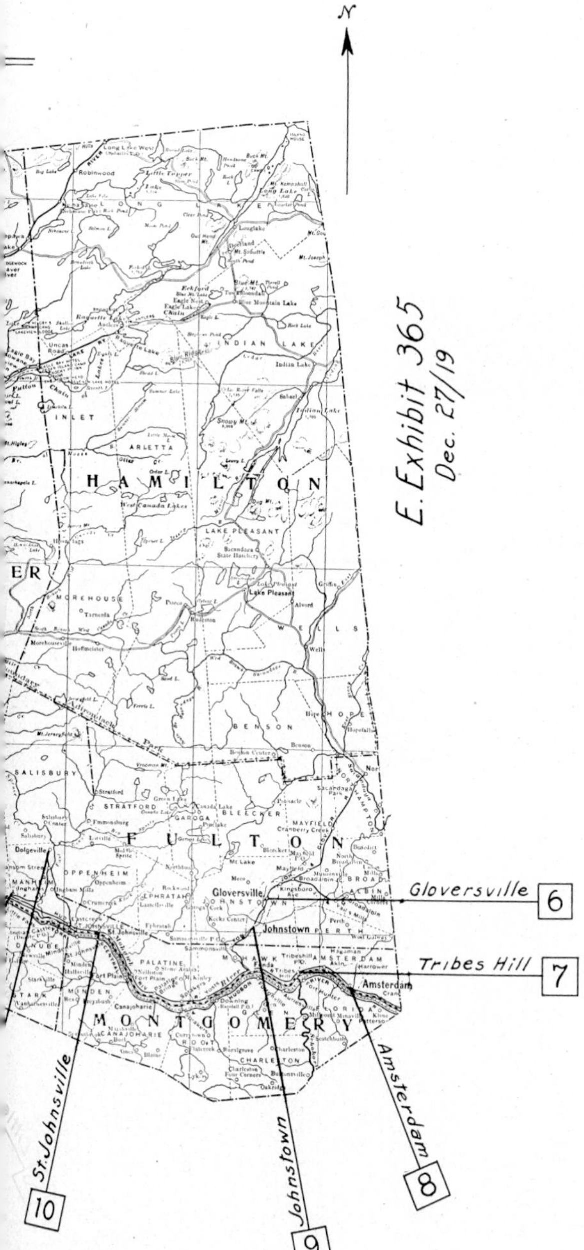

E. Exhibit 365
Dec. 27/19

SUB-SECTION II

ANARCHIST MOVEMENT IN AMERICA

SUB-SECTION II

ANARCHIST MOVEMENT IN AMERICA

CHAPTER I

Historical Sketch and Definition

It is not necessary in this report to trace the history and devel opment of the various theories of social and economic order which may properly be grouped under the term "Anarchism." From the very nature of its philosophy a precise definition is wanting.

Each writer or speaker who advocates it gives expression to his or her own peculiar concept.

Anarchism is defined in the literature issued by Emma Goldman, who for many years was one of the leading anarchists in this country, as "The philosophy of a new social order based on liberty unrestricted by man-made law; the theory that all forms of government rest on violence, and are therefore wrong and harmful as well as unnecessary." (See p 7, stenographer's minutes, Committee Hearings.)

The advocates of theoretical anarchism are not necessarily men of violence, nor men familiar with the use of the torch or bomb, but the picture of a society, free from all restraint, has won to the ranks of the anarchists those irreconcilable and ungoverned spirits who want liberty transformed to license and who seek to indulge their passions and greed without incurring the penalties imposed by organized society. As a result, the term "Anarchism" has come to be applied indiscriminately to all persons who resort to violence and defy the law of the land, even though their acts may have been inspired by other than political motives.

Many writers on theoretical anarchism express a horror of deeds of violence which cannot in themselves bring political or economic results. The anarchism of Bakunin was the expression of an open warfare against the military and autocratic powers of Russia and elsewhere, rather than terrorism of the individual, or attacks upon individuals or civilians without political purpose.

It is interesting to recall that at the time Bakunin evolved his theories, the spirit of revolution was rife throughout Europe, and the aspirations of small and subject nationalities were finding expression in attacks upon the then constituted authorities.

The nihilists of Russia, although claimed by some writers not to be anarchists, may safely be classed with this group, and their tactics were in the nature of demonstrations against the oppression of an autocratic government, and were sanctioned only with apparent reluctance by the leaders of the group.

Theoretical anarchism is the expression of extreme individualism. The anarchist in theory strives after the most complete self-development of the individual which is compatible with the equal claims of his fellow men. He dispenses with the central authority of the State. He rejects universal suffrage on the ground that "It must always turn to the profit of the dominating and exploiting minority against interest of the majority enslaved." (Bakunin).

Government is considered the instrument for the establishment of monopoly; as the invention of the few to protect their vested interests. The anarchist refuses to participate in government; to form a political party or to take any part in the scheme of society which he deems to be a bar to progress. Anarchism is, therefore, the very antithesis of state Socialism.

The philosophy of anarchism is not a spontaneous expression of any one thinker or group of thinkers, but has developed slowly from the earliest time. Socrates and Zeno have both expressed theories analogous of the modern anarchist. Rabelais and Rousseau, and many mediaeval writers, have expressed similar thoughts. It remained for Godwin, however, in his work entitled "Inquiry Concerning Political Justice, and Its Influence on General Virtue and Happiness," published in 1793, to formulate the more modern ideas of anarchism, although in his work he did not employ the word "anarchism" to designate the theories which he so effectually portrayed. He believed it was essential to abolish all laws and the courts for their administration in order to allow real justice development.

During the French Revolution the term "anarchist" first made its appearance, and was applied by Girondists to extremists.

The first memoir of Proudhon, published in 1840, entitled "Qu'Est — ce Que la Propriete'" describes his conception of Mutuellisme, and applies the term "anarchy" to describe the ideal society.

For the purposes of this report it is not necessary to detail the various mutations anarchistic thought has undergone.

In the United States it attained prominence in the latter part of the nineteenth century. Several congresses of anarchists were held, and several newspapers established, notably "The Anarchist" at Boston, "The Arbeiter-Zeitung" of Chicago, and "The Voice of the People" at St. Louis. In 1883 at Pittsburgh, a

Congress of twenty delegates representing anarchists and social revolutionaries issued an address to the workmen of America with the following program:

(1) Destruction of the existing class rule by all means, i. e., energetic, relentless, revolutionary and international action.

(2) Establishment of a free society, based upon co-operative organization of production.

(3) Free exchange of equivalent products by and between productive organizations, without commerce and profit-mongering.

(4) Organization of education on a secular, scientific and equal basis for both sexes.

(5) Equal rights for all, without distinction of sex or race.

(6) Regulation of all public affairs by free contracts between the autonomous — (independent) communes and associations, resting on a federalistic basis.

This, together with the appeal to the workmen to organize, was published in Chicago, in November, 1883, by the local committee, among whom was August Spies, who was later convicted and executed for his participation in the Haymarket affair in the year 1887. (See Enc. Brit. 11th Ed., Vol. I, p. 917.)

It should be noted from the foregoing that anarchism has many points in common with Socialism and syndicalism. Both Marx, the founder of scientific Socialism, and Bakunin, the author of systematic anarchism, desire the final abolition of classes in society; political, economic and social equality for both sexes; that the land and instruments of production and of capital become collective property of the community; that this should be utilized only by the proletariat so long as so-called class distinctions remain in society.

Communist anarchism, therefore, which was the parent of the Social Revolutionary Party in Russia, is closely identified with the Communist Socialism of Germany, and the syndicalism of France. Many anarchists believe that Communism is a necessary step in the attainment of true anarchy which in theory can only be instituted when the mass of society have been schooled to freedom.

It is therefore apparent that anarchism is in theory the extreme Left Wing of the Socialist movement. In fact, for a time, the anarchists were admitted to the International Workingmen's Association, but were expelled in the year 1872 owing to differences which arose between Marx and Bakunin. The importance of the anarchist movement, however, was not great in the past, nor does it now play any important part in the revolutionary or seditious movement in this country. Its practical influence upon the affairs of government is limited, being confined principally to political assassinations, such as the murder of King Humbert of Italy in 1900, and President McKinley at Buffalo in 1901, and as more recently illustrated, by the bomb outrages of May 1st and June 2d, last year.

In the United States the activities of the anarchists played no significant part in the development of the radical movement until the outbreak of the war. Their numbers were not great and were confined largely to the foreign elements of the working-class, notably the Italians, Spanish and Russians.

The ideas of Proudhon, especially as regards mutual banking, have had a considerable following in the United States. The principal followers of his doctrine were Stephen P. Andrew, William Green and Lysander Spooner. A prominent position among the anarchists of the country was acquired by Benjamin R. Tucker of Boston, who started in 1881 a periodical called "Liberty", which advocated Proudhon's ideas in modified form. The anarchism of this American group, however, found little sympathy among the working-class, its devotees being limited to small numbers of so-called intellectuals. Such workingmen in our country as believe in anarchism were anarchist Communists, who rarely knew anything about the theoretical anarchism of the older groups. It is with this type of anarchy that this Committee has to deal.

Sporadic demonstrations have occurred, notably in the nineteenth century, through the agitation of Johann Most, a German anarchist, who came to America after his imprisonment in England, and established "The Freiheit," an anarchist periodical, in New York City.

The agitation of this period culminated in the Haymarket riots, when August Spies, et al., were tried and executed for murder.

CHAPTER II

Anarchist Communism*

The anarchism with which the American public is most familiar may be classified as anarchist Communism, which is defined in the March 15, 1919, issue of "Freedom" as follows:

> "*Anarchist Communism.*— Voluntary economic co-operation of all towards the needs of each. A social arrangement based on the principle: To each according to his needs; from each according to his ability."

Most prominent among the leaders of this movement in America, so far as prolific propaganda is concerned, were Emma Goldman and Alexander Berkman, who were recently deported to Russia on the steamship "Buford." Their official organs were "Mother Earth" and "The Blast," respectively. The anarchists under the leadership of Goldman and Berkman, took an active part in the pacifist movement during the war, and immediately prior thereto, distributing a large amount of anti-draft and anti-military literature, and organizing the No Conscription League, with offices at 20 East 125th street, New York City.

It is impossible to give any coherent or comprehensive statement of this movement in the United States, because it is carried on by isolated groups, clustering about individual leaders, in large measure carrying on their work clandestinely.

During the war many anonymous leaflets were distributed, signed "Anarchist," "Underground Press," etc.

On June 15, 1917, Emma Goldman and Alexander Berkman were arrested in the office of the No Conscription League, in the presence of several of their assistants, namely, M. Eleanor Fitzgerald, Carl Newlander, Walter Merchants and W. P. Bales. They were subsequently indicted for violation of the Espionage Act and later convicted.

With the imprisonment of the leaders of this movement the anarchists organized the League for Amnesty of Political Prisoners, with offices at 857 Broadway, New York City. The purpose of the league is stated in its literature, and is:

(1) To educate the public to the fundamental distinction between political offenses and common crimes.

---

* See Addendum, Part I.

(2) To work for the recognition in the United States of the status of political offenders.

(3) To crystalize public sentiment regarding political prisoners through various activities.

(4) To obtain the immediate release of all political offenders.

The secretary of the league at the time of its organization was M. Eleanor Fitzgerald. The finance committee consisted of Jessie Ashley, now deceased, and Leonard D. Abbott. The legal advisory board consisted of Isaac A. Hourwich, the head of the statistical department of the Russian Soviet Bureau under Ludwig C. A. K. Martens, Jessie Ashley, Theodore Schroeder, Harry Weinberger (counsel for Alexander Berkman and Emma Goldman), and Bolton Hall. The general committee consisted of Leonard D. Abbott, Lillian Brown-Olf, Dr. Frederick A. Blossom, Lucy Robins, Helen Keller, Elizabeth Freeman, Prince Hopkins, Margaret Sanger, Rose Baron, Robert Minor, Anna M. Sloan, Stella Comyn, Lincoln Steffens, Alexander Cohen, Roger N. Baldwin, and Rose Strunsky.

From the brief statement of the principles of anarchism which have been given here it will be seen that, although differing in many fundamental respects from Socialism and syndicalism, particularly with regard to the ultimate objective, there are sufficient points in common to make the followers of this group willing and able to co-operate with these other groups in the advancement of the radical movement. Of the many organizations of anarchist Communists one of the most interesting is the Ferrer Association, which is located at the Ferrer Colony, Stelton, N. J.

It was created as a memorial to the Spanish anarchist, Francesco Ferrer. It has branches in many parts of the country. Its chairman is Leonard B. Abbott. The New York branch has carried on a series of lectures at Pythian Hall, 1941 Madison avenue, New York City.

In executing search warrants on the headquarters of the Communist Party in the City of Utica at 704 Bleeker street, it was found that a branch of the association had its headquarters there. One of the trustees of the association and colony at Stelton, N. J., is Harry Kelly. He is also editor of a magazine known as "Freedom," published by the Freedom publishing group at New Brunswick, N. J., the associate editor being Leonard D. Abbott; the business manager, J. Isaacson. This paper was formerly published at 133 East 15th street, New York City, at the same place where the Union of Russian Workers, another anarchist organization, which will be described later, had its headquarters.

The Freedom group is closely identified with the Ferrer Colony.

In the June issue, on page 1, we find the following interesting comments which bear upon the attitude of the anarchists toward the other groups representative of the revolutionary movements in this country, or their sympathizers. It says: "It may well be asked, 'Why another paper?' when the broadly libertarian and revolutionary movement is so ably represented by Socialist publications like 'Revolutionary Age,' 'Liberator,' 'Rebel Worker,' 'Workers World,' and many others, and the advanced liberal movement by 'The Dial,' 'Nation,' 'The World Tomorrow,' and to a lesser degree, 'The New Republic,' and 'Survey.' These publications are doing excellent work in their several ways, and with much of that work we find ourselves in hearty agreement. They are, however, either liberal in the best sense of the word, Bolshevik, or Socialist, and we are none of these, even if we look with a kindly eye on all of them. We are Anarchists, because we see in the State an enemy of liberty and human progress; and we are Communists, because we conceive Communism, as the most rational and just economic theory yet proposed. . . . As anarchists we seek the abolition of the State or organized government, and would substitute for it a society founded upon the principles of voluntary association and free Communism. The Left Wing Socialists now advocate the same thing. So our differences are merely in the tactics pursued."

The method of attack upon the government is to all intents and purposes the same as that commonly agreed upon by the various groups of radicals which have come under the observation and investigation of this Committee:

> "Industrial unionism, with the shop as the unit of control, backed by a revolutionary proletariat, is the method of attack we advocate. We are not particular if these shop committees are called Shop Stewards, Soviets or Syndicates; the all-important thing is that industry be controlled at the point of production by the workers in groups that shall be self-governing, for without this, emancipation from wage slavery is impossible."

As a further illustration of the attitude of this association, we quote from a cablegram intercepted on March 2, 1918, addressed to Leon Trotzky, Smolny Institute, Petrograd, from Leonard

Abbott, for Ferrer Association: "Ferrer Association is with you to the death. Are forming Red Guards to help you defend the Revolution."

Another cablegram addressed to Lenin and Trotzky, Council of People's Commissars, Smolny Institute, Petrograd, from Rose Baron, one of the members of the general committee of the League for Amnesty of Political Prisoners above referred to, but in this instance representing the International social revolutionary group of 319 Second avenue, New York City, sent on the same date as above, is as follows: "You have our wholehearted faith and support. Ready to organize and send you international revolutionary army from America."

On the same date another cable was sent to William Shatoff, Smolny Institute, Petrograd, by M. Eleanor Fitzgerald, "Mother Earth group with our lives and our last cent are with you in your fight."

The relations of Lincoln Steffens to this group make it proper to refer to the following cablegram, which was sent on the fourth of March to Lenin and Trotzky, Smolny Institute, Petrograd, signed by Louise Bryant and Lincoln Steffens: "Important you designate unofficial representative here who can survey situation, weigh facts and cable conclusions you might accept and act upon. Will undertake secure means of communication between such man and yourself."

It is interesting to recall at this point that Mr. Lincoln Steffens accompanied Mr. Bullitt on his official mission to Russia.

A cablegram was also sent to William Shatoff, Revolutionary Committee, Smolny Institute, Petrograd, by Leonard Abbott, for Ferrer Association, on February 28, 1918, which read as follows: "Ferrer Association is with you to the death. Will send recruits for the Red Guard."

It is this group which carries on a school for children at Stelton, N. J., under the management of William Thurston Brown, a Yale graduate, and formerly a Unitarian minister. The purpose of the school was made clear by Leonard Abbott in his testimony at the trial of Emma Goldman and Alexander Berkman, above referred to. In answer to the question put by the court, Mr. Abbott said: "Q. Are the Ferrer children taught to disobey the laws of the country? A. It teaches them to criticize all laws and prepare themselves for a free society. Q. When you speak of criticizing laws, do you include the laws of this Government? A. Yes, sir."

The nature of the philosophy taught at this school may be gathered from the statement of the principles of anarchy taken from an essay, entitled "Anarchism," by Emma Goldman, published by Mother Earth Publishing Association, 226 Lafayette street, New York City, in 1917, where we find on page 58 the following: "Anarchism is the only philosophy which brings to man the consciousness of himself; which maintains that God, the State, and Society are non-existent, that their promises are null and void, since they can be fulfilled only through man's subordination."

On page 59 is found: "Religion, the dominion of the human mind; Property, the dominion of human needs; and Government, the dominion of human conduct, represent the stronghold of man's enslavement and all the horrors it entails."

Of patriotism we find the following on page 134: "Indeed, conceit, arrogance and egotism are the essentials of patriotism."

On page 138 we find: "The awful waste that patriotism necessitates ought to be sufficient to cure the man of even average intelligence from this disease."

In her essay on "Marriage and Love," Emma Goldman says, at page 242, "Love, the strongest and deepest element in all life, the harbinger of hope, of joy, of ecstasy; love, the defier of all laws, of all conventions; love, the freest, the most powerful moulder of human destiny; how can such an all-compelling force be synonymous with that poor little state and church-begotten weed, marriage?"

That the advocates of this doctrine are strongly and violently revolutionary is apparent from the words of Emma Goldman in the same essay, on page 72, where we find, "Direct action, having proven effective along economic lines, is equally potent in the environment of the individual . . . Direct action against the authority in the shop, direct action against the authority of the law, direct action against the invasive, meddlesome authority of our moral code, is the logical, consistent method of Anarchism. Will it not lead to a revolution? Indeed it will. No real social change has ever come about without a revolution. People are either not familiar with their history, or they have not yet learned that revolution is but thought carried into action."

To give a still clearer conception of the doctrines which are promulgated, we quote from the periodical "Freedom" for the April-May issue, in which an editorial appears on page 4, containing the following: "They invent Governments, Senates and Assemblies, in order to bulldoze us into the idea that we 'govern ourselves;' but we must not forget that these institutions are only the economic expression of the ruling class which enslave, murder and imprison us. These institutions must not be bargained with — they must be abolished."

In commenting upon the bill which was recently introduced in the Legislature of the State of Michigan, making it a felony to advocate or teach crime, sabotage, violence, etc., this same editorial says: "Workers, read it again! Digest it! Do you realize what this means to you? This is war! Are you ready for war? The guns of Capitalism are strong! What are you doing to strengthen yours? The time has come when we should quit quibbling. Socialism is on wings, ready to take flight when the time for action appears. So it remains for you to formulate energetic and effective Anarchist groups and make the Revolution."

It is hardly necessary to characterize the teaching of such documents to children as utterly subversive of moral character and good citizenship. That such an institution has been permitted to exist and to carry on courses of instruction in this state, as well as in neighboring states, shows how little cognizance has been taken of the radical movements in this country.

The school has been in existence for nine years, and is supported by contributions made by various Ferrer groups throughout the country.

There are numerous other groups, particularly among Italian, Russian and Spanish, who find expression for their ideals in "propaganda by deed," or direct action.

Luigi Galliani, a noted anarchist, living, prior to his deportation, at Lynn, Mass., was the leader of a group of Italian anarchists active throughout the eastern states. He was the publisher of the Italian paper called "The Cronaca Sovversiva," published at Lynn, Mass., with a post-office box, No. 678. This was an extremely radical and revolutionary sheet, advocating the overthrow of our government by use of force and violence. As a result of the publication of this paper, and various meetings he conducted in and about Boston, Mass., he was deported by the Federal Government in June, 1919, and the publication of "The Cronaca Sovversiva" was suspended. Thereafter, his printing presses were taken apart and secretly shipped to Providence, R. I. One of the associates of Galliani was a man named Schiviano, who was also deported. He is reputed to have been the publisher of the clandestine sheet known as "Il Dritto," which also advocated the overthrow of our government by force and violence. The publication of this paper was discovered by an agent of this Committee, it having previously escaped the notice of the authorities. It was first published in September, 1918, with Schiviano and one Vito Mariani as its editors. In the issue of March 8, 1919, of "Il Dritto," although published in the Italian language, is found the following appeal in English:

"To the working people of America: The war is over. Your exploiters have quickly placed their profits in safety. You, the working slaves, will soon find yourselves on the streets, facing a hard winter, looking for work. For it is your only means to supply yourselves with the necessities of life. Because you lack the courage to use their methods!

"You have tolerated all the moral and physical slaveries during this war.

"When you dare open your mouths in protest, you are quickly railroaded to jail. What were your profits out of this war? You lost all the little liberty you had, and you gave your sons, brothers and fathers away to be shot down like dogs, and left to rot in the field of France!

"For what?

"For the glory of the American Flag!

"So that your masters may have bigger markets to sell their merchandises and exploit other people like you.

"The workers of Russia, Germany, Austria and other countries have risen and have overthrown their rulers.

"Not by ballots, but by arming themselves as it is your only means. You alone no not budge. Are you afraid to follow their example? Are you afraid to take by force what rightly belongs to you?

"Will you be meek and slavish? Will you wallow under the iron heel of your masters?

"Or will you *tear* your way by the revolution to a better and happier life? *Which will you choose?*

"(Signed) A GROUP OF WORKINGMEN."

"We have risen at the will of the sword with a smile on the face. It is time to consign to hell every kind of tyrant and every form of exploitation of man over man.

"To hell with every race of warriors of brutalized patriots in the art of butchering and of causing butchery beyond the sea.

"To the devil with all who have made war and who are working now to conclude peace.

"The peace of atrocious sorrow and of horrible misery.

"GLORIES IN REVOLUTION

"Down with peace and long live revolution.

"To hell with all the countries who offer to the workingmen whom they condemn to hunger and deportation.

"Long live the restless Satan of Bolshevism, fomentor of revolts and of destruction everywhere beyond the sea.

"To hell with everybody, from Woodrow Wilson to the last citizen of this inquisitional and deporting republic. They will send us beyond the Atlantic with contempt and scorn as undesirables. We want to be near to the conflagaration.

"We the internationalists of every country, know no peace. We wish war to the death without truce or quarter.

"Long live the blood revolution.

"With sword and fire against every enemy of the world."

Although the English of this quotation is not perfect, the spirit which animated its author is quite apparent.

After the deportation of Galliani and Schiviano, their friends and believers took up their work and continued it with extreme caution.

Mariani, who had been associated with them, came to New York and changed his name to Mario Viogeria, and became active in anarchistic circles in New York City. Other associates of Galliani are known to this Committee, but pending the continuation of the investigations it is deemed unwise to go into their activities here.

The deportation warrant for Galliani was issued in May, 1919, and on June 2, 1919, certain bombs were sent to various officials in the United States, each of whom, in one way or another, had been instrumental in bringing to justice certain members of the Galliani group.

On February 27, 1920, Vito Mariani, was arrested at the instance of an agent of this Committee and charged with criminal anarchy for the publication of a newspaper, entitled "Il Refrattario," an anarchist sheet published in Italian, and advong the overthrow of this Government by force and violence. ore his arraignment in the Magistrates' Court, Mariani stated was the sole owner, publisher and editor of "Il Refrattario," and that the business address of the paper was 311 East 106th street, New York City; that only one issue had been published; that in the month of November, 1919, he admitted 2,000 copies were printed, and that he had mailed 1,500 copies to various people in Boston, Lynn, Chicago and other cities; that he had received from Schiviano the list of subscribers of the "Cronaca Sovversiva," and that he had sent "Il Refrettario" to the same people. He also stated that he was the sole publisher with Schiviano of "Il Dritto."

To give a general idea of the nature of the propaganda carried on by "Il Refrettario," we give the following quotation:

> "It is on this account, that anarchy which follows only its own laws, will break the power of the priests and smash the crowns of the powerful; it is on this account that the anarchist, an enemy of all phantoms, must open a way for himself, by using bombs and revolvers (Brownings), as Bonnot did from the red automobile. . . .
>
> "It is the belief amongst many of us, and I have had the same opinion in the past, that the anarchistic regime will be installed immediately after the revolution.
>
> "Therefore, it is imperative for us, to conduct an incessant propaganda, in order to destroy all the prejudices which may prolong the coming of a revolution, and to win over the forces, and to make them realize that only through force will the bourgeoisie society be destroyed. . . .
>
> "Economic organization cannot solve any of the present day problems. It cannot but provoke a useless dispersion of the forces and always render the masses less revolutionary. The temporary benefits which can be obtained from strikes, are but illusory, because the high cost of living will always in proportion automatically keep above the salary received.
>
> "Therefore these benefits are useless. The disease lies in the trunk which must be destroyed. Take away these false notions from the people and teach them the necessity of violence. . . .
>
> "Perhaps the writer may be mistaken but he is convinced that an anarchist, who sincerely believes in revolution and is willing to start one, he could do so in America, as well as in Italy or in China.

EMMA GOLDMAN
Deported on S.S. *Buford*.

PETER BIANKI

Chief Organizer of Union of Russian Workers. Arrested by direction of the Committee and indicted for Criminal Anarchy in New York County. Deported S.S. *Buford*.

"This is the background of the gray picture, who stands out from the Penumbra? The individual Anarchist. Anarchist, I say, because according to my opinion an Anarchist is one who refuses to obey none other but his own laws. . . . It is on this account that the anarchist remains isolated and is not understood. It is on this account that he is classed as a splendid egoist and a powerful enemy. It is on this account that he must open a passageway for himself by using bombs or Brownings (revolvers) as Bonnot did from the red automobile. It is the atrocious struggle without quarters. I expect nothing from the revolution. This is an affair for the multitudes. . . .

"I, an Anarchist, am not avoiding the tragedy.

"SMELL OF POWDER

"In spite of H. M., the Emperor, Woodrow Wilson and of the Wall Street sharks, five hundred thousand coal miners have left the subterranean caves. It is a gigantic strike, rendered still greater if we take into consideration that the steel workers' strike is going on for several weeks.

"The coal miners, who have often given words of their combativeness, not with words in Colorado, and precisely in Ludlow, ask for six hours work a day for five days with sixty per cent. increase.

"The Democratic Government of Uncle Sam with Czar W. Wilson at its head, issued a decree forbidding the eighty-four leaders of the United Miners Workers of America to communicate in any way with the strikers and to stop the distribution of weekly benefits they are entitled to during the strike. To such an end $15,000,000 have been requested by the United States Supreme Court. The Draconian order completely isolates the organizers of the strike who can not help the miners neither morally nor financially.

"War measures have been proclaimed in all mining districts.

"MINERS! STRIKERS IN GENERAL! REMEMBER!

"In this Republic of sharks and 'pimps' nothing can be obtained without violence!

"Tooth for tooth and FORWARD!"

Mariani has been held by the city magistrate under $15,000 bail for action by the Grand Jury.

It may be noted in passing that this paper was first found by an agent of this Committee, and turned over to the Department of Justice.

At the time of the arrest of Mariani, several other clandestine anarchist sheets were found, they being "Inconoclasta," "Il Nuova Vassillo," "Aurora," "Il Libertiore," "Il Proletariat," "Volonta."

An interesting illustration of the character of the propaganda circulated during the war by anonymous anarchist groups is the following:

"REFUSE TO KILL OR BE KILLED

"You are against murder and bloodshed, you have no special grievance against the working class of Germany. All you ask for is to get along peacefully, express yourself, make a living, and take care of your family. You don't want war and you didn't ask the president or any one else to declare war.

"But you will ask: What can I do if I am drafted and ordered to fight? Well; what would happen if you did obey the president and fought for your country? You would probably be killed and lose what little you have, and your family would suffer. Now, if you don't become a professional murderer (a soldier); and refuse to obey the president, nothing worse can happen to you, can it? Oh, but you will say, 'I would have a chance to live.' Well, those ten million men who were killed in Europe, and those twenty million who were injured, didn't have much of a chance, did they? And those who lived didn't get much joy out of life. It isn't a very happy feeling to realize that you have deliberately killed hundreds of inoffensive fellows just like yourself, and who never did you any harm, and who didn't want to fight any more than you do. You may think that you could avoid killing anyone. Nearly everybody who puts on a uniform thinks that, but when once you put on a soldier's clothes and get into the crowd of trained murderers, you are lost and you will do just as you are ordered. No man is brave or strong or lucky enough to escape killing when once he has the uniform on. Now this is the truth, and the history of a hundred million men in arms proves it. Don't try to bluff yourself or anyone else. You must realize that if you join the army you will do just as you are told to do, and if you have any courage or humanity to assert, the time to do it is before you get into the uniform.

"You may agree with all of this, but still you ask, 'What can I do?' We don't believe in telling people what to do. You have a mind and a conscience and you believe in brotherhood and real democracy. If you think murder is wrong, REFUSE TO JOIN THE ARMY or any military body. Then if the government wants to kill you or put you in jail, you will have done your part, and have been faithful to your conscience and humanity, and the world will be the better for your courage and determination.

"No matter what the government or the other fellow does, let's you and I be faithful to mankind and REFUSE TO GO TO WAR.

(Form No. 50950–M — Underground Press.)

"ANARCHISTS"

For the circulation of such propaganda, Jacob Abrams and six associates were arrested, tried and convicted under the Espionage Act, and the judgment of conviction affirmed by the United States Supreme Court.

A group of anarchists, styling themselves, "The American Anarchist Federated Commune Soviets," conduct a systematic campaign, publishing numerous handbills and a bulletin known as "Anarchist Soviet Bulletin." It is particularly interesting because of the sympathy shown for the Russian Soviet regime in these documents, more particularly so because in Soviet Russia the anarchist group themselves have been declared to be counter-revolutionary.

The July issue of the "Anarchist Soviet Bulletin" was found in large quantities at the New York Public Library, where it had been left so that it might be picked up and read by passersby.

A typical article in this issue is entitled, "Time for Action," which we quote as follows:

"TIME FOR ACTION

"This important question must be answered and answered quickly by you the workers of America! The Allies and the United States have not only thrown off their masks and shown you their treachery and hypocrisy by giving out their shameful peace to Germany, together with the now-shown-up-in-mud-besmeared hypocritical snake Woodrow Wilson, they have done something which is EVEN MORE TREACHEROUS AND SHAMEFUL than the German peace treaty; That is; They have openly come out and recognized the Russian Czar's successor Czar Kolchak, they have given him openly (until now it was done secretly) all the guns, ammunition, money, spies and murderers needed in order to enthrone the old czardom and crush THE WORKERS COMMUNE SOVIETS OF RUSSIA.

"They are going to continue the blockade against the Russian people and by this starvation war, through which the allies have already murdered hundreds of thousands of men, women and children, thus trying to force THE WORKERS COMMUNE SOVIETS to submit to the old czardom!

"This the allies are doing, not against the People that was 'OUR' enemy but a people that were fighting with the allies and sacrificed more lives than any other allied country! Do you WORKERS know the reason why the allies are doing it? Because the SUCCESS OF THE WORKERS COMMUNE SOVIETS MEANS THE BEGINNING OF THE DOWNFALL OF CAPITALISM ALL OVER THE WORLD!

"It means that no workers of any other country will continue to live in economic slavery, while the Workers of Russia are free from it. That this is true we can see that since the Russian Revolution started the Workers of Hungary followed next in taking over all industries through their WORKERS COMMUNE SOVIETS. In Germany the workers Soviets are getting stronger. Every day workers Soviets are making uprisings in Spain, Italy, Austria, England and nearly every other country in the world.

"Over in Canada the general strike is only a forerunner to the final battle that is soon to take place there; which will surely result in a victory for THE WORKERS SOVIETS OF CANADA.

"So, if capitalism through the allied government has taken upon itself to crush the WORKERS SOVIETS OF RUSSIA and bring back the rule of czardom, then it only shows that it is their final stand, in order to maintain their dying system, for they have taken up a war not only AGAINST THE WORKERS OF RUSSIA BUT AGAINST THE WORKERS OF THE WHOLE WORLD!

"For this reason we the ANARCHISTS ask you THE WORKERS OF AMERICA; What are you going to do about it? What is your answer to this challenge of capitalism?

"Mass meetings, with addresses by 'prominent liberals' are of no avail to prevent this greatest of all crimes ever committed against a people. Revolutions of protest and paper petitions will be powerless to block the shameful plan of the Allied capitalistic governments.

"What is needed, is not appeals to capitalism and its political tools to save that which it is to their interest to destroy. The only way to stop this hideous, heart-breaking, murderous crime against our fellow workers in Russia is for us to TAKE MATTERS INTO OUR OWN HANDS AND ACT QUICKLY!

"We must follow the example of the 'Triple Alliance' of England — the railway workers, miners and transport workers — DECLARE A GENERAL STRIKE AT ONCE and not resume work until the brutal blockade of Russia is raised, the allies' troops are withdrawn and the sending of money and supplies to the Czarist Kolchak is stopped.

"We must act quickly! In our shops, mines, mills, and factories, in our unions, forums and societies, wherever the workers gather, this matter must be taken up. Let a ringing message echo around the world that the workers of America have called a General Strike, not only to block the attempt to revive the old czardom, but also to organize WORKERS COMMUNIST SOVIETS in every center in America and begin to — take over every industry in the country.

"Let our message to the workers Soviets of Russia be 'KEEP UP YOUR COURAGEOUS BATTLE FOR FREEDOM! THE WORKING CLASS OF THE ENTIRE WORLD WILL SOON BE FIGHTING ON THE BARRICADES OF THE SOCIAL REVOLUTION AGAINST CAPITALISM ITS AGENTS AND UP-

HOLDERS, THE GOVERNMENT, THE CHURCH AND THE PRESS.

"WE THE WORKERS OF THE WORLD, HAVE COMMITTED A GREAT CRIME AGAINST YOU RUSSIAN WORKERS, BY REMAINING SILENT AND SUBMISSIVE, BUT NOW WE WILL SUBMIT AND KEEP SILENT NO LONGER! WE WILL BEGIN TO ACT NOT ONLY TO SAFEGUARD YOUR FREEDOM BUT ALSO TO FREE OURSELVES!"

"Workers of America! Unite into Workers Soviets everywhere, get ready to respond to the call of the GENERAL STRIKE THROUGHOUT THE COUNTRY for that great day will mark the beginning of the social revolution. The Workers Soviets of Russia shall never be destroyed!

"Their destruction means our continuation in slavery!

"Their victory means our liberation and the liberation of the workers of the World!

"Therefore we call upon the WORKERS OF ALL COUNTRIES AND UPON THE WORKERS OF AMERICA TO ACT!!

"AND ACT AT ONCE!!"

One of the typical handbills is as follows:

"REFUSE to LOAD AMMUNITION!

To You — Transport and Marine Workers:

"At last the news leaked out from Washington that the United States government of capitalism is secretly, without the knowledge of the American Workers, preparing within the next few days to smuggle on the Vladimir ship now at Brooklyn 28,000 rifles and 3,000,000 rounds of ammunition, besides the ordinary cargo of 'farm implements.'

"It also leaked out that 80,000 more rifles with millions of rounds of ammunition, are being shipped from various depots to San Francisco, to be transported to the allies 'favorite' — the czars follower — Kolchak.

"It also becomes quite clear now that all the arms ordered by the old czar, will be shipped to the new czar — Kolchak, whose barbarity surpasses even the Spanish inquisition — a HUMAN BEAST that could bungle together overloaded cars, with men, women and children and keep this TRAIN OF DEATH RUNNING FOR WEEKS TILL EVERYONE IN THESE CARS DIED, ROTTING ONE ON TOP OF ANOTHER!

"This beast Kolchak who FORCES members of the Russian workers communes TO DIG THEIR OWN GRAVES, and whom the Allies and the double-faced 'innocent,' cold-blooded-liar-murder-hypocrite Woodrow Wilson, have decided by the order of capitalism to furnish him, with all the money and ammunition needed, until he will succeed in destroying the Workers Commune Soviets of Russia.

"THE STEVEDORS OF ITALY, FRANCE AND ENGLAND HAVE PREVENTED THE SHIPMENT OF ANY AMMUNITION FOR MURDERING RUSSIAN WORKERS, BY SIMPLY REFUSING TO HANDLE ANY GUNS OR AMMUNITION INTENDED FOR SUCH PURPOSES!

"French, Italian, English, Canadian and American soldiers are being withdrawn from Russia, because THEY HAVE REFUSED TO MURDER RUSSIAN WORKERS, FOR NO OTHER REASON, THAN, OF COLLECTING WAR DEBTS FOR CAPITALISM, which, is willing to KILL EVERY WORKER—BUT NOT ONE CAPITALIST in order to accomplish this 'holy' mission.

"What will your answer and action be, *Transport and Marine Workers* of America?

"*Are you going to help handling guns and ammunition,* for to *murder our brother workers of Russia,* or, are you going to *stand up like the workers of all countries and refuse to do it?*

"When you, the TRANSPORT AND MARINE WORKERS are asked to handle or load any murder implements to be used against workers, then, either REFUSE TO DO IT, or DUMP ALL THE GUNS AND AMMUNITION INTO THE RIVERS!

"Let the message echo throughout the entire world, that; the American Workers REFUSE TO LEND ANY HELP WHATSOEVER IN CRUSHING THE ASPIRATIONS OF THE COURAGEOUS STRUGGLING WORKING CLASS OF ANY EUROPEAN COUNTRY AGAINST

> THEIR ENSLAVERS—CAPITALISM SUPPORTED BY ITS GOVERNMENTS!
>
> "TRANSPORT and MARINE WORKERS of America! YOUR ACTION OF SOLIDARITY towards our brother workers, will mean that American capitalism will NOT BE ABLE TO SEND ANY MURDER IMPLEMENTS for to be used in CRUSHING THE STRUGGLING WORKERS OF EUROPE.
>
> "AMERICAN ANARCHIST FEDERATED COMMUNE SOVIETS."

In conclusion, the interesting feature of this movement is the similarity of its methods and tactics with those of the Socialist Party, Communist groups and I. W. W.:

(1) It stands for the international solidarity of the working class. This is well-illustrated by the quotations from the propaganda which we have given, and also by the words of Emma Goldman during her trial: "Tell all friends that we will not waver, that we will not compromise, and that if the worst comes we shall go to prison in the proud consciousness that we have remained faithful to the spirit of internationalism and to the solidarity of all the people of the world." (See "Mother Earth," Vol. 12, No. 5, page 129, July, 1917.)

(2) It advocates industrial unionism as the best instrument for affecting the social revolution.

(3) It advocates direct action, meaning thereby the general strike and sabotage.

(4) It sympathizes with and supports Soviet Russia.

(5) It advocates amnesty for so-called political prisoners.

(6) It advocates the raising of the Russian Blockade.

CHAPTER III

Anarcho-Syndicalism

As distinguished from the isolated groups which advocate doctrines of theoretical anarchism, and the doctrine of the anarchist Communist to which we have referred, there are other groups of anarchists which may be classified as anarcho-syndicalists. These groups are at one with the other anarchists in the principles sought to be attained, but differ in the methods advocated, in that they believe that success in attaining their objective can only come through co-ordinated organization, working exclusively in industrial unions. These principles differentiate them in large measure from the Syndicalist group, which is described in the subsection dealing with industrial unionism.

The principal representative of this group in this country is the Union of Russian Workers, which had its headquarters at 133 East 15th street, New York City, in what was known as the Russian People's House, although this organization might be classed with almost equal propriety with the anarchist Communists.

This union was organized in 1914 as a split from the more conservative organizations of the Russian laborers. By the spring of 1919 its membership had increased to about 7,000; and when its headquarters were searched under search warrants issued at the request of this Committee, the record showed that it had slightly over 9,000 members scattered throughout the entire United States in seventy locals. Seventeen locals had been organized in Canada, the largest locals in this country being located in Detroit, Chicago, Baltimore, Philadelphia and New York City.

The New York Local had a dues-paying membership of 237.

Two membership cards were issued to each of the members, one known as the blue card, with simply the name of the member and the local of which he was a member, and with the reverse having blanks reserved for membership dues, stamps, and what was known as a red card, which contained the following statement:

> "Amicable agreement of the Unions of Russian Workers of the United States and Canada, who have united in the Federation.

Purposes of the Federation

"1. The Unification of the organizations of Russian Workers in the United States and Canada for the joint struggle with capital and authority.

"2. The support of the liberative movement in Russia.

"3. The support of the revolutionary departures of the American workers.

"4. Moral and material support of the organ of the Federation, and

"5. The creation of organizations where there are none and the support of the old existing organizations."

In the early spring the headquarters of this organization had been raided by the Bomb Squad of the New York Police Force, and at that time membership cards were found which contained a statement of the organization's principles, including the overthrow of the government by force and violence. It was evident that subsequent to that raid the organization had issued the membership cards from which these violent provisions were eliminated.

The official organ of this organization was known as "Khlieb-y-Volya" (meaning Bread and Freedom), and was characterized by the extreme violence of its articles. The books and the papers which came into the hands of the Committee indicated that this paper had a circulation of 4,547. The union also published a large number of books, pamphlets, leaflets and handbills to spread their propaganda among Russian laborers. All of their publications were in the Russian language.

The secretary of the organization at this period was Naum Stepanuk, but the moving spirit and actual leader was Peter Bianki, a Russian of Italian parentage.

The college of editors which supervised the publication of "Khlieb-y-Volya," and the preparation and dissemination of the propaganda literature, included Marcus Orodowsky, Peter Bianki, Peter Kravchuk, Hyman Percus and several others.

As an illustration of the propaganda issued by this group we give here a translation made from the May 8, 1919, issue of "Khlieb-y-Volya" on page 4, entitled "The Law of Truth," which deals with the trial of Cottin, who had attempted to assassinate Clemenceau.

"One more of the bold and loyal sons of the oppressed masses has gone to jail for an ideal as old as time is old,

PHOTOGRAPH OF MEMBERS OF LOCAL NEW YORK, UNION OF RUSSIAN WORKERS, 133 EAST 15TH STREET, NEW YORK CITY.

as noble as human nature is noble; for the ideal of protest against the arbitrary law which put him, the defendant of the eternal laws of truth, in jail for ten years.

"The hearts of the sincere and the bold will think with gratitude of him who fulfilled his holy duty. Among them there are hearts no less sincere, although not agreeing in part with his teachings.

"Emile Cottin, realizes this, while behind the grating, in the damp, foul, health-draining, stone bag. He does not need sympathy. He is freer than those who remained 'at liberty.' He is calmer than they. He did all that one man could do.

"While meditating, you are astounded by the inability of people to understand the lesson, which truth has taught them since the beginning of time.

"For what is Cottin sitting in jail? Because he dared to bring to life the word preached by him.

"But neither court nor jail will compel Cottin to alter his opinion, alter his action, or alter even a particle his convictions. These thoughts and convictions are more close to the truth than the laws of the judges who tried Cottin, and tomorrow they will throw off, sweep away, the judges and the hypocritical arbitrary laws of people.

"At least it is not by law that the judges will stop the spread of the idea of Cottin, more likely the judicial law will bring the hour of the 'end' nearer. And this law, the law of condemning and punishing people who have violated the laws arbitrarily created by people for personal purposes, this law will now be put to its utmost use, for the hour of revolution approaches: They who have ruled and rule people have lost their heads under the fear of the approaching end.

"A man condemned for a bold and brave protest against war and dissension in human society cannot but become dear to millions of honest hearts.

"According to the laws of truth this savagry and arbitrariness and law of people interpreted only by wilful book-learned men, law of personal gain, could sentence Cottin to such a punishment!

"The law of truth, the law of nature, crying to man about lawlessness, and the necessity of full freedom of the person and society of mankind — this law is violated.

"The law is violated, and the realization of its violation penetrates into the minds of the broad masses, oppressed by covetous people, who create by their brute strength their own laws!

"The law of nature will no longer be violated without retaliation. The law of arbitrariness will have to give way to the law of nature — human society without laws.

"We are living through days of much promise, days of destruction of everything old, days bringing nearer the liberation of mankind from the arbitrariness of people's laws.

"We believe in that great day.

"We await its arrival."

One of the pamphlets published by this organization, written by one Novymirsky, contains a chapter entitled "Our Tactics," which illustrates clearly the nature and purpose of the organization, a translation of which is as follows:

"What should be our means of fight?

"The tactics of the working class can as little as its ideal — the overthrowing of capital and state — be devised, composed, introduced from the outside. No! It must be discovered in the bosom of contemporary society. It is necessary to study carefully, where those elements are, the development of which destroys the contemporary society and creates a new one. After having discovered these elements we must with our tactics consciously hasten their development.

"As the contemporary professional labor organizations — the embryo of the future free organizations, thus the natural weapon of the working class, the strike, is the seed of our tactics.

"We saw that the proletariat, together with the development of capitalism, is more and more widening and deepening its fight: partial strikes lose their meaning, even mass strikes become general.

"What must we do — the vanguard of the proletariat? We must consciously hasten the elementary course of battle of the working class; we must turn the small strikes into general, and turn the latter into an armed revolt of the laboring masses against capital and the state.

"During this revolt we must, at the first convenient chance, begin the immediate seizure of all means of production and all products of consumption and make the working class in fact the master of the public wealth. Simultaneously, we mercilessly destroy all remnants of state authority and class rules, destroy the jails and police stations, after having liberated those imprisoned, destroy all judicial acts regarding private property, all field fences and boundary lines, burn the certificate of debt — in short, we must take care to wipe off the face of the earth everything that reminds of the right to private property, to blow up the barracks, the gendarme and police administrations, to shoot to death the most eminent military and police chiefs, must be an important concern of the revolted working people."

It was upon the evidence of the publication of this and similar documents, gathered by this Committee, that the Extraordinary Grand Jury of New York County brought in indictments against Peter Bianki, Naum Stepanuk and Peter Kravchuk.

The case was never brought to trial, owing to the fact that these offenders were turned over to the Federal authorities and were deported on the S. S. "Buford."

All lists of names and other data obtained by the Committee have been turned over to the District Attorney of New York County and to the Federal authorities.

Closely identified with the Union of Russian Workers and occupying the same premises is the Soviet of Workmen's Deputies of the United States and Canada, which publishes an anarchistic paper in Russian, entitled "Rabochey-i-Krestyanin," the editorial staff of which consisted of Ivan Okountzoff, M. Korneev and Zioubovich. The treasurer of this organization is Mr. Juschnob.

The nature of the propaganda issued by this and other Russian papers will be described in the subsection of the report which deals with propaganda.

DECENTRALIST MOVEMENT OF THE I. W. W.

Among the documents and papers seized by agents of this Committee in the execution of a search warrant against the headquarters of the I. W. W. at 27 East 4th street, on June 21, 1919, were several issues of a magazine published in the Finnish language, entitled "Luokkataistelu." This purorpted to be the organ of the Finnish branch of the I. W. W., and was advertised in the "One Big Union" monthly, the official organ of the I. W. W., as an independent I. W. W. paper.

Attention was focused upon this publication through an article which appeared in the March, 1919, issue, entitled "The Activity of the Rioting Masses," the significant portion of which is as follows:

> "And thus a rioting mob is the one and only possible means for organizing a fight in the everyday as well as in these last open and decisive blood-battles between the capitalists and the working classes. The above mentioned are illustrations of the pure morals of the working classes. To hell with the teachings of peaceful revolution. The bloody seizure of power by the working classes is the only possible way. Because as long as our enemies are able to raise even one sword a bloodless fight is a day dream."

The publication did not bear the name of any editor or publisher, and the address printed on the paper was a Finnish boarding house at 58 East 123d street, at which address could be found no one connected with the paper.

The Committee thereupon, in co-operation with the Attorney-General of this State, began an investigation to ascertain what persons were behind the publication. This resulted in locating the printer, and finally in the discovery of the editors, Carl Paivio and Gust Alonen. Gust Alonen was located in New York City, and was immediately arrested. From correspondence seized upon the premises, the address of Carl Paivio in Detroit was found, and a member of the Bomb Squad of the New York City Police was sent to that city to effect his arrest. From the correspondence found in the rooms of Carl Paivio and that found in the possession of Gust Alonen, the history of the decentrist or anarchistic movement within the I. W. W. was found.

Three other men joined with Alonen and Paivio in the editing of "Luokkataistelu," namely, Elmer Wirta, Matti Sari and John Helberg. These men represented a group of Finnish members of the I. W. W., who claimed to represent a decentralistic group within that organization. They were anarchists adhering to syndicalist principles but did not believe in any kind of centralized power, centralized organization or centralized government.

One of their principal assertions was that all rules are old even while they are being made. There should be no rules whatsoever.

The individual should govern everything according to his will and pleasure. Members of this group retained their membership cards of the I. W. W., but the character of the group is well expressed in a letter written by one Hans Johnson of 4404 Clinton avenue, Ohio, on July 21, 1919, to Gust Alonen, 864 Caldwell avenue, Bronx, New York City, of which the following is a correct translation:

> "It is my opinion that we should start to publish the 'Class Struggle' as a real anarchistic publication from now on. Why should we care, because we are as a matter of fact anarchists. We cannot get away from it even into hell. We will always be able to fix the K. P. in a discussion if it comes to that. Let us publish in the 'Class Struggle' that it is the only Finnish anarchistic publication in the world, and we start there to wipe out the principles of all the violent and all the Finnish K. P."

The initials "K. P." refers to the Finnish equivalent of the pseudonym of a group of men who published the Finnish I. W. W. paper, "Tia Vaupautin" (Road to Freedom).

While the Luokkataistelu group was thoroughly anarchistic, it was apparent that they desired to carry on their propaganda under the cover of the I. W. W., and as exponents of the doctrine of decentralism.

In a letter written by Carl Paivio from 58 High street West, Detroit, which is not dated, we find statements of which the following is a correct translation:

> "Hans wrote me that he had written you to announce to 'Luokkataistelu,' or 'Class Struggle,' publicly to be an anarchistic publication. I want to mention only that much, that such special announcement should not be made until the discussion about it is submitted to the backers. Always in such things we should find out the opinion of the men upon whom the distribution of 'Luokkataistelu' depends, because here it is much harder to distribute any publication than in New York. Thus, it is much better to be here under the cover of decentralism. The contents in spite of that can be as anarchistic as they please."

The propaganda of this group was carried on throughout the United States in large measure by itinerant workers going from place to place and selling copies of the "Luokkataistelu," leaflets, and booklets; organizing small groups of workmen and in general stirring up discontent.

This is illustrated by a letter written by Carl Paivio on July 28th, to Gust Alonen in New York City, a translation of an excerpt from this letter being as follows:

> "And Ben is going to make a trip in the fall, in the mining villages of Utah and Wyoming, and he is going to sell on that trip the 'K. H.' (meaning 'From Trench to the Grave,' a new book to be published by William Risto). The 'V. S..' (meaning 'Revolutionary Syndicalism,' a book by the same author), and 'Luokkataistelu.'"

A letter from one Ben Harkonen, written from Salt Lake City, Utah, dated May 16, 1919, to Carl Paivio in New York City, contains the following:

> "I received your letter dated the 11th of this month and trust that you will succeed with the 'Class Struggle,' 'Luokkataistelu,' as well as before, which is a good thing because the longing for 'Luokkataistelu' seems to spread all over the country. I got a letter from my brother in Red Lodge, Montana. He wrote that 'Luokkataistelu' is selling there as before. . . . I received also those ten copies of 'Luokkataistelu.' The union secretary has now four copies. I took them over. When the boys happen to go there he can sell them. . . . I am going to cover all mining camps during the summer. I have also thought that maybe I will be able to go in the fall to the coal districts in Wyoming, Diamondville and Cumberland."

Another letter undated written by Carl Paivio in Detroit to Gust Alonen states that 150 copies of "Luokkataistelu" "may be sent here to be sold when it appears." He also states that "Up to now I have sold here 15 copies of the 'Revolutionary Syndicalism.'"

Further on in the letter he states, "Ben is going to make little trips into the mining states, likewise Miettinen; Risto is going to go to the central states and will have to do the same in the East. I thought you should cover Ohio, Pennsylvania, Massachusetts and Maine, and take along the 'Revolutionary Syndicalism,' 'From Trench to the Grave,' and the 'Class Struggle,' and other small books, if they are in."

The literary agent of this group appears to have been a man by the name of William Risto, author of a book called "Revolutionary Syndicalism" and "From Trench to the Grave."

In an advance advertisement of the "Revolutionary Syndicalism" Mr. Risto himself states: "The 'Revolutionary Syndicalism' is anti-patriotic. 'Revolutionary Syndicalism' is anti-nationality. It is anti-militaristic, and it is anti-parliamentary. It is against the private property," etc.

The backers of this book are the same group as those who financed the "Luokkataistelu."

Those particularly engaged in collecting of money for the printing of this book are Vaino Tikka, Otto Hulitella, Carl Paivio, Olga Savolannin, Gust Alonen, Ida Aho, and Elmer Wirta.

SUB-SECTION III

REVOLUTIONARY INDUSTRIAL UNIONISM

INTRODUCTION

SUB-SECTION III

REVOLUTIONARY INDUSTRIAL UNIONISM

INTRODUCTION

In the preceding chapters dealing with the Socialist and anarchist movements in America a brief outline has been given of the principles and objects of various groups masquerading as political parties which seek the overthrow of the present political system as well as the establishment of a new social order.

The succeeding chapters deal with the fruit of the propaganda carried on by such organizations. Although the political and economic theories taught by the Socialists, Communists and anarchists are the product of intellectuals, they have been carried to the working masses by the constant dissemination of propaganda which has spread a spirit of revolt in the ranks of labor, not only against the present social system and organized government, but also against the conservative and constructive organizations of labor.

The movement thus created in the ranks of labor has been given many titles. In England it is known as syndicalism; in France as revolutionary syndicalism, while in the United States it has come to be known as industrial unionism. The object of the movement is to break up the system of craft or trade unions, and to organize workers into One Big Union having subdivisions along the lines of industry, rather than those of trade. The success of this movement is indicated in the following chapters of this sub-section.

The organizations thus created carry on their propaganda in co-operation with the propaganda of the so-called political organizations above referred to, the purpose of which is to create class consciousness, to stimulate in and among the workers the idea that they alone count in the social order; that only among the toiling masses is found the knowledge and ideals which can reconstruct society.

An intense hatred for all other classes of society is encouraged, and the workers are urged to accentuate what is known as the class struggle. The purpose of this propaganda is to cultivate among workers, first, the desire, and then the will to seize industry, and to overturn, or overthrow, organized government and to set up in its place the so-called co-operative commonwealth. The success of the proletarian revolution in Russia has given a clear definition of the meaning of the co-operative commonwealth which now, in the minds of most of the workers affected by this propaganda, means a Soviet form of government modeled after the Russian Soviet regime.

It is impossible for the Committee here to enter into a detailed discussion of all the independent labor organizations which are formed along industrial lines, or which may be affiliated with the I. W. W. or the W. I. I. U. Those concrete examples which are here given will make clear the trend of the movement, and indicate what measure of success it has attained.

The Committee emphasizes at this point that the real danger to American government, and to the structure of American society and its institutions, rests in the continuous activity of such organizations as are here mentioned. Revolution, if it shall be attempted in this country, will not be the work of armed bands of revolutionaries secretly coming together in conspirative organizations. Such a movement would hold out no promise of success. On the other hand, the propaganda of class hatred stimulating in thousands of workers who are ignorant of our institutions and laws, a contempt for our form of government and its institutions, must inevitably lead to a division in our society fraught with the most serious consequences to the public peace and safety.

It is difficult to give a precise definition of the terms, "Revolutionary Industrial Unionism" or "Syndicalism." They are employed to designate the theories and practices of certain revolutionary labor organizations which have for their purposes the seizure and control of the means of production and distribution, as well as the overthrow of the existing forms of government, and the setting up of working class rule.

These labor organizations should be looked upon as the weapons forged by quasi-political parties for the purpose of making effective the revolution. Such labor organizations are characterized by the advocacy of direct action, meaning thereby the use of the general strike and sabotage, and the repudiation of parliamentary action. It should be noted that at the present time the distinction between syndicalism or revolutionary industrial unionism and revolutionary Socialism are purely theoretical, for the latter now approves all of the tactics which formerly characterized syndicalism alone.

The term "syndicalism" is devised from the French syndicates, or trade unions. It is synonymous with revolutionary industrial unionism, but in its restricted sense it refers particularly to the principles and tactics adopted by the French labor organizations which were united in the *Confederation Generale du Travail.* These theories and practices combine in large measure the doctrines of Bakunin, Marx, and Proudhon. The doctrine involves not only the co-operation between various industrial unions in order to effect immediate demands for wage increase, shorter hours, and better working conditions, but insists that all wealth is produced by the workers and that, therefore, such wealth, both productive and distributive, should be controlled and owned by various labor organizations to the exclusion of the capitalists and the state. The bourgeoisie have no place in this scheme save experts in finance, engineering or technology may be hired by the various unions.

As has been stated the chief weapon employed by syndicalists is propaganda by deed or direct action. This includes the general strike and sabotage. Their doctrine teaches that the employees and their employers have nothing in common; that society is divided into two contending groups, on the one hand the employers described as exploiters, and on the other the employees designated as the exploited. It also teaches that there can be no peace so long as the wage system lasts, that the struggle must go on until the workers have gained control of industry and set up a working class government. In other words, it's basic principle is the teaching of the class struggle. This involves the application of physical force.

In order to carry out the doctrine thus promulgated and make effective the tactics advocated it is necessary to have a highly centralized control of the workers in each industry, so that the general strike may be called by a central committee affecting the workers of various trades engaged in the same industry.

Trade unionism as represented by the American Federation of Labor is organized for the purpose of protecting its members against the capricious action of a small committee.

Before a general strike can be called involving different trades the questions in dispute must be of sufficient importance to convince the officers of the different trades of the necessity of such strike. It is for this reason that the revolutionary agitator finds it necessary to seek to destroy these conservative organizations of labor.

As an illustration of the attitude assumed by such agitators towards the American Federation of Labor we quote from a manifesto issued by the Communist League of New Jersey which was reprinted with complete approval in the "Rebel Worker," the official organ of the I. W. W. in New York City in the spring of 1919:

> "We must reverse the historic attitude of the Socialist Party towards the American Federation of Labor. Since its formation in 1898, the Socialist Party has pursued a policy of friendship and alliance with the A. F. of L. Our members have gone into the craft unions and have struggled to 'bore from within.' After twenty years we may read the result. Our efforts have collapsed in a heartbreaking failure.
>
> "The A. F. of L. has ceased to be a labor union. It has allied itself with the master-class. . . . It has invoked the aid of the capitalist government to exterminate the revolutionary minorities within its unions."

While the quotation just given would seem to indicate that the process of "boring from within" had not been successful, evidence daily accumulates that the radical agitators are fast undermining the American Federation of Labor and similar conservative organizations. The large number of unauthorized strikes illustrated vividly at the time of writing this report by the walkout of railway employees, which threatens to tie up the transport system of this country, are the direct result of the propaganda spread by various subversive organizations to which this report refers.

Owing to the wide field of inquiry covered by this Committee it has been impossible for it to make a thorough investigation into the spread of revolutionary ideas among labor unions in general. This is the most important problem which at the present confronts the American people. The Committee can do little but point the direction in which further inquiry must be made.

The general strike which is the principal expression of industrial action has been successfully employed in foreign countries to gain political objectives by extra-parlimentary means. The general strike was employed in Russia to overthrow the provisional government under Kerensky. The general strike was the instrument employed by President Ebert of the present German regime to tie the hands of the Von Kapp provisional government.

Winnipeg, Manitoba, was the scene of a general strike in the summer of 1919 that lasted for some six weeks. This general strike resulted in the complete paralysis of all utilities and industries in Winnipeg. At the stroke of the clock the telephone and telegraph operators, the firemen, the street cleaners, the scavengers, the drivers of all vehicles, all transportation facilities, both of human beings and of merchandise ceased, and had it not been for a volunteer citizens committee which had the courage to resist the efforts of the participants of the general strike, the conditions in Winnipeg would have been appalling and disastrous. The hands of the city government were tied by the strikers.

It must be borne in mind that the general strike here referred to is used for political objectives, and is used to usurp the function of the ballot. It is not a strike for merely better conditions of labor, shorter hours, or sanitary conditions, or increased pay, and in decrying the use of the general strike for political objectives this Committee must not be understood as taking a stand in opposition to the ordinary strikes of organized labor, nor to the efforts of the American Federation of Labor from time to time to enforce its demands for better conditions. The American Federation of Labor appears as much opposed to the general strike for political objectives as any person or group can be.

The purposes of the general strike and of industrial mass action were very frankly and forcibly stated by Dr. Maximilian Cohen who was one of the prime movers in the formation of the Communist Party in Chicago in September, 1919. Doctor Cohen was examined in the office of Attorney-General Newton in New York City on August 14, 1919, by Frederick R. Rich, special deputy attorney-general, Archibald E. Stevenson, associate counsel for this Committee, and by Samuel A. Berger, deputy attorney-general.

Some of the statements made by Doctor Cohen in the course of his examination are here given and will, we believe, make clear the meaning of the general strike. Doctor Cohen said "the agricultural workers would organize and immediately take over the factory or the dairy just as they would take over an industry or a store or anything else."

Doctor Cohen, being further questioned, replied as follows:

> "Q. Instead of delivering it and selling it, they would deliver it to you people? A. Yes, exactly, to the strike committee, as they did in Seattle, and recently in Belfast.

The strikers had enough organizing ability to see that the people did get that minimum amount necessary.

" Q. You mean to assume the government to the exclusion of the elected representatives? A. We are not interested at all in what Congress would do. . . .

" If capitalism is, as we believe it is, on the verge of a breakdown in all countries, which brings with it a greater and greater discontent and a growing class consciousness among the unskilled workers, who are in the vast majority, and they will organize and listen to our propaganda, the time must necessarily come when a state of chaos is at hand. The workers and Soviets on one hand, and the constituent assemblies on the other hand, both wrestling for power. That will be the situation. Whether or not it will be orderly depends on you people, because we want to assume these organizations.

" Q. But if there is any resistance?

" A. Well, you will show the resistance, we will not; you will fight to retain power and the workers will fight to wrest it away from you. On the one hand the Workers' Council, on the other hand the Constituent Assemblies.

" What you are trying to get from me is an admission that force will be necessary.

" Q. No, no; if you have any other way to do it, we would like to know your idea.

" A. The question of force does not rest with us. We base our philosophy on life itself — mass action. Our Socialist brethren berate us for our loose way of talking, but we say mass action is dependent on life itself. We cannot make a narrow definition of it, because it involves all of life itself.

" Q. Laying all the cards right on the table, let us get at this a little. My understanding is that the Communist Party is purely and simply a propaganda organization?

" A. Right.

" Q. For the express purpose of encouraging and stimulating in the workers' minds the idea that they must organize, industrially, economically, politically —

" A. In the Communist Party.

" Q. Not necessarily.

" A. Necessarily.

"Q. Well, in co-operation with it. For instance, the W. I. I. U. is pretty close to the Socialist Labor Party, isn't it?

"A. No, it is an industrial organization—

"Q. Isn't that about the relation there would be between the industrial organization and the Communist Party?

"A. No, because if a revolutionary crisis were to come, you would find the Communist Party would stand aloof as a party, but individually their representatives were in the Soviets even at the time the Mensheviki were in control. Now, then, the workers' councils will be the revolutionary organizations. They will be composed of all the workers' organizations, skilled or unskilled, that will have organized and sent representatives to the Soviets, and the Soviets will be the actual revolutionary organizations, not the Bolsheviks or the Communist Party. If that is what you mean, you are right.

"Q. What do you mean by social revolution?

"A. Social revolution means the overthrow of the existing system.

"Q. In what way?

"A. It is immaterial, but it is not by the methods of the present ruling class, that is plain.

"Q. What other way?

"A. By organizing the revolutionary workers, making them class conscious. It is like the depositors in a bank: So long as there is a feeling that the bank is stable, they will deposit their money, but as soon as a doubt gets in their minds, there is a mass movement, a panic seems to enter them all at once, and they will rush pell mell to draw out the money.

"Q. Their own money?

"A. I just want to develop my idea: The workers will be in the same position as the depositors in the bank, to the present government. They will feel that they have lost all faith in it — through our propaganda, I admit, and though the gradual breakdown of the existing system — wages will not rise to meet it and they will feel they are always on the ragged edge. When that condition prevails and we can instil into their minds doubt and distrust and lack of faith in the present capitalistic methods, even in the Plumb plan, to meet the tremendous reforms necessary.

The reforms granted in Germany under Bismarck, they did not do any good. We have to show them that all social reformers are worthless to them and that the one thing they must do is to organize in the Communist Party. When that stage has reached its development, and the breakdown of industry comes, the revolutionary organizations will probably spring into existence and will attempt to take over the control of the government from your capitalist class—

"Q. How?

"A. Well, let us see, in Russia they made a raid on the—of course, they abolished all the constituent assemblies—but they raided the offices of the powers that be, and installed themselves, and immediately organized Red Guards to protect themselves in their newly found power.

"Q. And you would approve of that method?

"A. Unquestionably.

"Q. That would mean, of course, force.

"A. Well, suppose the capitalist class did not desire to come to us, would use force against us—

"Q. Of course you don't expect they would desire to go to you?

"A. Then the onus is on your side, not on ours. We merely protect ourselves. We all know enough to know that no ruling class will give up power without a fight. But we must have the initiative. All submerged classes must assume the initiative if they are to get what they want.

"Q. Therefore the onus of the result rest with you?

"A. Of course, if we establish a dictatorship of the proletariat we will accept whatever onus is involved?

"Q. Whether the result is successful or not?

"A. You see, of course, it is a peculiar situation: We are being tried in the capitalist court, and there can be no justice, because we tell you frankly what we aim for is the overthrow of your government.

"Q. And you expect to take all the institutions and all of the property of the capitalists?

"A. Communize it, nationalize it, immediately.

"Q. Well, you mean take it away from the present owners and do what you please with it?

"A. Yes.

"Q. You don't expect a man is going to give up property and money without resistance, therefore you are going to supply the means of taking it from him, and you have the initiative in bringing about the means, therefore it cannot be done except by force.

"A. It can be done without force, but if force is used, we blame you people because you are prepared to use force. Now we are going to win over the army and navy —

"Q. How would you try to win it over?

"A. Through propaganda. How do you think any revolutionary organization ever won anybody over, except through propaganda?

"Q. Then you will try to win over the army and navy, the members of which have sworn to uphold the government, and to resist the efforts of anyone who seeks to overthrow the government, and you will try to get them in such a frame of mind as to be untrue to that oath, and not do that which they are sworn to do, to wit, to uphold law and order?

"A. To tell you frankly, we don't care a fig for your oaths. We don't hold them as meaning anything to us, because necessarily if we did we would have to stop and go out of business.

"Q. You are not under oath now, but if you were put under oath, would that mean anything to you? As a gentleman, you would tell the truth. You have been very frank and I would take your word as well without an oath as with an oath.

"A. My oath would mean nothing at all to me.

"Q. It would mean nothing to you?

"A. Nothing at all.

"Q. May I ask, is that anything personal with you, that is the general principle?

"A. No, that is the principle of all revolutionary organizations.

"Q. I certainly want to say that I want to express my personal respect for your frankness.

"A. I must be frank or be untrue to my principles. They are universal so far as those who hold these beliefs are concerned. If I were to get on the stand and say that I don't believe in a class war and in overthrowing the capitalist government, I would be lying. I know if I come before your capitalistic court I must be convicted. I cannot help myself.

"Q. Are these the same ideas that actuate and are followed by the men who publish this Revolutionary Age?

"A. Well, you must make allowance for human equation, but barring that, that is the principle that actuates every member of the Left Wing and every convert that comes into the Left Wing. Ever since the inception of the Socialist movement — if it were not for its hesitancy — they have preached the overthrow of the capitalist system.

"Q. That is rather an indefinite term.

"A. We will say the capitalist class. I mean the system that bases its mode of production on profits, rent, interest and capital.

"Q. Do you mean by that our present form of government as now constituted?

"A. Exactly.

"Q. That is a capitalistic government?

"A. Yes.

"Q. And you understand that the United States government is a capitalistic government?

"A. Yes.

"Q. And when you say that you want to abolish the capitalist government, you mean the United States government?

"A. I mean the United States government in so far as the term applies to this country. If we are carrying on revolutionary propaganda in this country, we mean the overthrow of the United States government; and in France, it would mean the overthrow of the French government, that is it exactly.

"Q. And when the words 'Capitalist system' appear in any of your Communist publications, you mean the United States government?

"A. In so far as it functions for the capitalist class, and it does today function for the capitalist class.

"Q. Doesn't it function for the laboring class?

"A. No.

"Q. Are not they giving the protection of our government in housing, in their lives, or their property? If some one attempts to rob them, does not the government do everything in its power to apprehend the malefactor?"

We have here from the lips of one of the leading advocates of industrial mass action a clear exhibition of how that mass action is to be used, and what its purposes are. It is this sort of propaganda, and the advocacy of principles such as those enunciated by Doctor Cohen that constitute a far more grave menace to the institutions of their country than that presented by bomb-throwing anarchists. The latter can be much more easily apprehended, and his work, at best, is sporadic. But, the activities of the intellectual of the type of Doctor Cohen are so widely diffused and so broadly prevalent that they constitute a very perplexing problem.

The rise and development of this movement in Europe is touched upon in section one of this report. Attention here will be confined to the development of those labor organizations in this country which in the main represent the principles of syndicalism or revolutionary industrial unionism. The principal organizations of this character in the United States are the Industrial Workers of the World, and the Workers International Industrial Union.

In the succeeding chapters typical examples will be given of independent industrial unions organized on the same principles.

The questions here presented deserve the earnest consideration of all persons who hold in esteem the institutions of the United States.

CHAPTER I

The Industrial Workers of the World *

Prior to the organization of the Industrial Workers of the World there was evidence of a growing radical tendency in certain labor unions. The Knights of Labor had fallen under Socialist control which resulted in their dissolution. The Western Federation of Miners, under the leadership of Wm. D. Haywood and Vincent St. John, manifested a violent disregard for law and order which forecast, in a measure, the tactics which were later made the basis for the organization of the Industrial Workers of the World. It was not, however, until the fall of 1904 that the I. W. W. movement really began. Its originators were Isaac Cowan, American representative of the Amalgamated Society of Engineers of Great Britain, Clarence Smith, general secretary-treasurer of the American Labor Union, Thomas J. Hagerty, editor of the "Voice of Labor," the then official organ of the American Labor Union, George Estes, president of the United Brotherhood of Railway Employees, an organization with which Eugene V. Debs was associated, W. L. Hall, general secretary-treasurer of the same organization, and William E. Trautmann, editor of the "Brauer Zeitung," the official organ of the United Brewery Workers of America.

It was at a meeting of these men in the fall of 1904 that the plans for a secret conference in January were laid. As a result of this meeting a conference was held in Chicago, Ill., on January 2, 1905, at which an industrial manifesto was adopted.

The work of circulating this instrument was handled by an executive committee chosen at this conference by the American Labor Union and Western Federation of Miners.

This document is of great historical interest and is therefore reprinted in full at the close of this chapter. It constitutes an attack upon the trade union system, and designates the wage system as slavery. It outlines a plan for the organization of a great industrial union embracing all industries having an international aspect. "It must be founded on the class struggle and its general administration must be conducted in harmony with the recognition of the irrepressible conflict between the capitalist class and the working class."

---

* See Addendum, Part I

The signers of this manifesto were:

A. G. Swing, A. M. Simons, W. Shurtleff, Frank M. McCabe, John M. O'Neil, John Guild, Daniel McDonald, Eugene V. Debs, Thomas J. De Young, Thos. J. Hagerty, Geo. Estes, Wm. D. Haywood, Mother Jones, Ernest Untermann, W. L. Hall, Chas. H. Moyer, Clarence Smith, William Ernest Trautmann, Fred D. Henion, W. J. Bradley, Charles O. Sherman, M. E. White, William J. Pinkerton, Frank Kraffs, J. E. Fitzgerald, Frank Bohn, Jos. Schmidt.

The presence of these persons at this conference and their co-operation in the forming of this industrial organization is of extreme interest because they represent various quasi-political organizations which were apparently antagonistic to one another, namely, the Socialist Party, the Socialist Labor Party and the anarchists.

It should be pointed out that the American Federation of Labor had no part in or in any way countenanced the new movement. In fact, the whole spirit of the conference as crystallized in this manifesto constitutes an attack upon the trade union organizations as they existed in the American Federation of Labor, and pointed the way for a reorganization of labor unions along revolutionary industrial lines, so that they could be used to stimulate so-called class consciousness among the workers, and as effective instruments of attack in the class struggle.

The manifesto called upon all workers who agreed with the principles therein set forth to meet at a convention in Chicago on the 27th day of June, 1905, for the purpose of forming an economic organization of the working class along the lines indicated.

The constitutional convention met, as planned, in Chicago on the 27th day of June, 1905, with 203 delegates representing forty-three different labor organizations of extraordinarily varied character. The difficulties of this first convention was greatly enhanced by the fact that the delegates represented various extreme types of radical thought, and according to Vincent St. John, one of the historians of the I. W. W., included parliamentary Socialists, Impossibilists, Opportunists, Marxists, Reformists, Anarchists, Industrial Unionists and Labor Union Fakers. The divergence of opinion in these various groups of radical thinkers was, however, finally compromised, and the purposes and objects

AT THE PARTING OF THE WAYS
A cartoon appearing in the May, 1919, *One Big Union* which speaks for itself.

A CLOSE CALL

A cartoon appearing in the September, 1919, *One Big Union* which speaks for itself.

of the new organization were stated in the preamble to the first constitution, as follows:

> "The working class and the employing class have nothing in common. There can be no peace so long as hunger and want are found among millions of working people and the few, who make up the employing class, have all the good things of life.
>
> "Between these two classes a struggle must go on until all the toilers come together on the political, as well as on the industrial field, and take and hold that which they produce by their labor through an economic organization of the working class, without affiliation with any political party.
>
> "The rapid gathering of wealth and the centering of the management of industries into fewer and fewer hands make the trade unions unable to cope with the ever-growing power of the employing class, because the trade unions foster a state of things which allows one set of workers to be pitted against another set of workers in the same industry, thereby helping defeat one another in wage wars. The trade unions aid the employing class to mislead the workers into the belief that the working class have interests in common with their employers.
>
> "These sad conditions can be changed and the interests of the working class upheld only by an organization formed in such a way that all its members in any one industry, or in all industries, if necessary, cease work whenever a strike or lockout is on in any department thereof, thus making an injury to one an injury to all." (See pp. 18, 19, 20, stenographer's minutes, Committee Hearings.)

It must be noted that in this original preamble recognition was given to the fact that the toilers must come together on the political as well as on the industrial field.

The factions of the new organization who repudiated the use of parliamentary means to effect their revolutionary purpose, however, gained control of the organization at the Fourth Annual Convention in 1908, at which time the preamble of the constitution was amended to read as follows:

> "The working class and the employing class have nothing in common. There can be no peace as long as hunger and want are found among millions of the working people and

the few, who make up the employing class, have all the good things of life.

"Between these two classes a struggle must go on until the workers of the world organize as a class, take possession of the earth and the machinery of production, and abolish the wage system.

"We find that the centering of the management of industries into fewer and fewer hands makes the trade unions unable to cope with the ever-growing power of the employing class.

"The trade unions foster a state of affairs which allows one set of workers to be pitted against another set of workers in the same industry, thereby helping to defeat one another in wage wars. Moreover, the trade unions aid the employing class to mislead the workers into the belief that the working class have interests in common with their employers.

"These conditions can be changed and the interest of the working class upheld only by an organization formed in such a way that all its members in any one industry, or in all industries, if necessary, cease work whenever a strike or lockout is on in any department thereof, thus making an injury to one an injury to all.

"Instead of the conservative motto, 'A fair day's wage for a fair day's work,' we must inscribe on our banner the revolutionary watchword, 'Abolition of the wage system.'

"It is the historic mission of the working class to do away with capitalism. The army of production must be organized, not only for the every day struggle with capitalists, but also to carry on production when capitalism shall have been overthrown. By organizing industrially, we are forming the structure of the new society within the shell of the old." (See pp. 20, 21 and 22, stenographer's minutes, Committee Hearings.)

In this preamble all reference to action on the political field is stricken out. This action on the part of the convention resulted in a split in the organization. The elements believing that parliamentary action was of use in the class struggle, led by Daniel De Leon, organized the Detroit I. W. W., which later changed its name to the Workmen's International Industrial Union. This organization will be described in a later chapter.

The Industrial Workers of the World are organized into twelve unions, the General Recruiting Union and several small locals in different industries which have not yet been organized in industrial unions.

These unions are as follows:

1. Agricultural Workers' Industrial Union No. 400, Headquarters, Chicago, Illinois.
2. Construction Workers' Industrial Union No. 573, Headquarters, Chicago, Illinois.
3. Hotel, Restaurant and Domestic Workers' Union.
4. Marine Transport Workers' Union, Nos. 100 and No. 700.
5. Lumber Workers' Industrial Union No. 500, Headquarters, Portland, Oregon.
6. The Metal and Machinery Workers' Industrial Union No. 300, Headquarters, Chicago, Illinois.
7. Metal Mine Workers' Industrial Union No. 800, Headquarters, Butte, Mont.
8. Printers' and Publishers' Industrial Union No. 1200, recently organized in New York City.
9. Railroad Workers' Industrial Union No. 600, Headquarters at Chicago.
10. Shipbuilders' Union, Headquarters formerly at Seattle.
11. Textile Workers' Industrial Union No. 1000, Headquarters, Paterson, New Jersey.

The frankest statement of the tactics and methods employed by the I. W. W. is to be found in the pamphlet of Vincent St. John, from which the above quotations are taken, and from which we quote the following:

> "As a revolutionary organization the Industrial Workers of the World aims to use any and all tactics that will get the results sought with the least expenditure of time and energy. The tactics used are determined solely by the power of the organization to make good in their use. The question of 'right' and 'wrong' does not concern us.
>
> "No terms made with an employer are final. All peace so long as the wage system lasts is but an armed truce. At any favorable opportunity the struggle for more control of industry is renewed. . . . No part of the organization is allowed to enter into time contracts with the employers. Where strikes are used, it aims to paralyze all branches of the industry involved, when employers can least afford a

cessation of work — during the busy season and when there are rush orders to be filled. . . . Failing to force concessions from the employers by the strike, work is resumed and 'sabotage' is used to force the employers to concede the demands of the workers. The great progress made in machine production results in an ever-increasing army of unemployed. To counteract this, the I. W. W. aims to establish the shorter working day, and to slow up the working pace, thus compelling the employment of more and more workers. . . . Interference by the government is resented by open violation of government orders, going to jail en masse, causing expense to the taxpayers, which is but another name for the employing class.

"In short, the I. W. W. advocates the use of 'militant direct action' tactics to the full extent of our power to make good."

It will be noted that the employment of sabotage is here frankly advocated. This term, which though comparatively new, has become quite familiar, is somewhat hard to define.

In attempting to define the word at the convention of the Socialist Party of America held in Indianapolis in May, 1912, Delegate Slaydon said as follows:

"Sabotage as it prevails today means interfering with the machinery of production without going on strike. It means to strike but stay on the payroll. It means that instead of leaving the machine the workers will stay at the machine and turn out poor work, slow down their work and in every other way that may be practicable interfere with the profits of the boss, and interfere to such extent that the boss will have to come around and ask, 'what is wrong; what can I do to satisfy you people?'"

Sabotage is described rather than defined by Robert Hunter in his book entitled "Violence and the Labor Movement" (published by Macmillan Company, New York, 1919 — on page 236), as follows:

"If a strike is lost, and the workmen return only to break the machines, spoil the products, and generally disorganize a factory, they are Saboteurs. The idea of Sabotage is that any dissatisfied workman shall undertake to break the machine in order to render the conduct of industry unprofitable, if not actually impossible. It may range all the way from machine obstruction or destruction to dynamiting, train-wrecking, and arson." (See pp. 15, 16, stenographer's minutes, Committee Hearings.)

A careful study of the present preamble of the I. W. W., and the statement of the tactics made by Vincent St. John, which we have quoted, as well as a study of official newspapers of the organization and other literature, shows that it is the purpose of the organization to teach its members that they owe no obligation whatsoever to employers in return for the wages which they receive; that it is their duty to their cause to break any solemn agreement they have entered into if to do so will result in any temporary advantage; to seek the highest possible wages, and to do the least possible work in return therefor; to spoil the products upon which they are engaged and in every way to render unprofitable the carrying on of industry.

It teaches the workers that they have no moral obligations either to their country or to those they serve.

The object sought is not the immediate improvement of the workers' conditions, but to create a condition in industry which would make it impossible for employers to carry on business so that industries may be seized and operated by the workers, and a new government set up in place of the governments of the United States and of the State of New York.

This is well brought out in a booklet entitled "The Revolutionary I. W. W." by Grover H. Perry, published by the I. W. W. Publishing Bureau, 1001 West Madison street, Chicago, Illinois:

"ORGANIZING A NEW SOCIAL SYSTEM

"The I. W. W. is fast approaching the stage where it can accomplish its mission. This mission is revolutionary in character.

"The preamble of the I. W. W. Constitution says in part: 'By organizing industrially we are forming the structure of the new society within the shell of the old.' That is the crux of the I. W. W. position. We are not satisfied with a fair day's wage for a fair day's work. Such a thing is impossible. Labor produces all wealth. Labor is therefore entitled to all wealth. We are going to do away with capitalism by taking possession of the land and the machinery of production. We don't intend to buy them, either. The capitalist class took them because it had the power to control the muscle and brain of the working class in industry. Organized, we, the working class, will have the power. With that power we will take back that which has been stolen from us. We will demand more and more wages from our employers. We will demand and enforce shorter and shorter hours. As we gain these demands we are diminishing the profits of the bosses. We are taking away his power. We are gaining that power for ourselves. All the time we become more disciplined. We become self-confident. We realize that without our labor power no wealth can be produced. We fold our arms. The mills close. Industry is at a standstill. We then make our proposition to our former masters. It is this: We, the workers, have labored long enough to support idlers. From now on, he who does not toil, neither shall he eat. We tear down to build up. . . . The Industrial Workers of the World are laying the foundation of a new government. This government will have for its legislative halls the mills, the workshops and factories. Its legislators will be the men in the mills, the workshops and factories. Its legislative enactments will be those pertaining to the welfare of the workers.

"These things are to be. No force can stop them. Armies will be of no avail. Capitalist governments may issue their mandates in vain. The power of the workers — industrially organized — is the only power on earth worth considering, once they realize that power. Classes will disappear, and in their place will be only useful members of society — the workers." (Pages 10, 11 and 12.)

The purpose to overthrow the government is also frankly stated in an article entitled "The Ku-Klux-Klan Government," in the August, 1919, number of the "One Big Union Monthly," in which we find:

"That government, we frankly confess, we intend to overthrow and that is going to be accomplished by organizing the productive and distributive forces of the world along industrial lines so that the people themselves can take over production and distribution."

The purpose of the organization to expropriate private property without compensation is well stated by John T. Doran in his trial of the United States against William D. Haywood et al., in Chicago, in the summer of 1918, as follows:

> "We I. W. W.'s say: 'Listen. What is the good of buying railroads? We don't want to buy railroads. We don't want to buy brickyards nor the mills nor the factories. We don't have to indulge in a co-operative plan or a co-operative program. This is what we mean to do, organize the slaves in the brickyards, and then we own the brickyards; organize the slaves on the railroads and then we own the railroads. Organize the slaves everywhere, and all these things are ours. But to buy them and attempt to compete with the capitalistic masses, it is nonsense. We are not there."

The foregoing is from page 36 of a pamphlet published by the I. W. W. Publishing Bureau, entitled "Evidence and Cross Examination of J. T. (Red) Doran."

In order to strengthen the organization, gather recruits and stimulate in the rank and file a revolutionary spirit a thoroughly organized propaganda has been instituted. Many newspapers and magazines are published in industrial centers, thousands of pamphlets and leaflets are distributed, amplifying and expounding the principles which have been here shown and calling upon the workers of America to organize in industrial unions under the leadership of the I. W. W. Agitators are sent into various districts and, in many cases, under assumed names, join well-established and conservative organizations of labor in order to carry out the process which has come to be known as "boring from within."

The purpose of these agitators is to create discontent, dissatisfaction in such labor unions and, if possible, bring about strikes. In cases of strikes the I. W. W. agitators enter the territory with their propaganda and seek to detach the strikers from their conservative leadership, so that a basis may be found to convert the legitimate labor organization into a revolutionary industrial union.

An examination of the propaganda discloses that the continuous effort on the part of the organization is to stimulate the most violent hatred of employers in general and also to create a spirit of contempt for the government and institutions of this country. The success of the Russian proletariat in bringing about the

November revolution in Russia has been used as a text showing that when properly organized the laboring masses are capable, have the power to overthrow existing forms of government and institute a government of their own.

The despotic character of that government is not disclosed to the workers, its limitations of democracy are hidden and a glowing picture is painted which inevitably appeals to a worker, particularly if his passions are stirred as in the case of almost any strike.

In order to capitalize the value of the stimulus of the Russian revolution, the I. W. W. claims to be the sole representative in the United States of those principles and tactics which had proved so successful in Russia.

In an article appearing in the March issue, 1919, of the "One Big Union Monthly," John Gabriel Saltis contributes an article on the Bolsheviki in America, in which he says:

> "The I. W. W. contains the identical potentialities of the Soviet. . . . The capitalist class realize full well the political significance of the I. W. W. . . . The real clash of power in this country is between the I. W. W. and the A. F. of L. . . . The I. W. W. is the American soviet."

It is particularly noticeable that the leaders of this movement recognize the necessity of organizing the workers in essential industrials and, in particular, in the transportation lines. They realize that they can gain their objective only in case of causing a strike of sufficient magnitude to paralyze transportation and distribution so that the government will be seriously hampered, if not prevented from mobilizing its resources to combat the industrial action.

On June 21, 1919, at the instance of this Committee, a search warrant was issued against the headquarters of the I. W. W., then located at 27 East 4th street, in the Borough of Manhattan, City of New York. Among the documents seized at that time was an interesting series of correspondence, which indicates that a plan was then being worked upon by the I. W. W. to organize its forces throughout the entire world in one big union, so as to control the international transportation facilities. A call for an international conference, to take place in Chicago on April 28, 1919, was issued from the Chicago headquarters on February 27, 1919, by the Conference Committee, consisting of James

Scott, J. J. McMurphy, W. I. Fisher, John Burke, John Korpi, Tom Doyle, Pete Stone and John Sandgren, secretary. (Exhibit 245 of the Committee Record at page 634.) This document follows:

"CHICAGO. ILL., *February* 27, 1919.

"FELLOW-WORKERS OF THE MARINE TRANSPORT INDUSTRY.— The undersigned Conference Committee is elected by the Industrial Union of Marine Transport Workers, of the Industrial Workers of the World, and as we speak in behalf of tens of thousands of marine transport workers, in this and in other countries, we request your respectful attention for the following proposition:

"Already before the great world war the promptings were constantly pouring in on our main office, asking our organization to take the initiative in calling a conference that might lead to a world union of our industry, a union built on such modern principles that it could count on the support of the most advanced elements of marine transport workers.

"The war temporarily ended all efforts in that direction. But no sooner was the war over, before the same persistent demands began crowding upon us again. Men of all nations are now clamoring for us to take the initiative in such a move for a modern World Union of Marine Transport Workers.

"In taking this step and sending out this call, we do so in connection with the calling of a general conference of our own delegates from the North American continent, proposing to take advantage of this conference and make it an international conference, as far as the short time intervening will allow.

"We hereby issue a formal call to all organizations of marine transport workers in the United States, Canada, and Mexico, and all other countries which this call reaches to send instructed delegates to a conference to take place in Chicago, Ill., U. S. A., on April 28, 1919, with the object of elaborating plans for such a world union of marine transport workers.

"In view of the concerted attack of our masters upon our ranks, it is to be hoped that every organization, local, district or national, that possibly has a chance to send a delegate will do so, in order that our deliberations and decisions may rest on the broadest possible basis.

"The attendance of as many foreign delegates as possible is desirable, in order that we may work out a plan for a world-wide organization. We have positive proof that such an organization and such co-operation is demanded all over the earth. It is only a matter of finding the best forms for this co-operation, and the longed-for World Union of Marine Transport Workers will become a living reality, instead of a sailors' Utopian dream.

"The place in Chicago where the conference will meet will be decided on later, and will be made known to all concerned. In the meantime we suggest that you immediately enter into correspondence with the Conference Committee, and beg to remain,

"Yours for world-wide solidarity,

"THE CONFERENCE COMMITTEE,
Per JOHN SANDGREN, *Sec'y.*

"Address all communications to the secretary, 1001 West Madison street, Chicago, Ill., U. S. A."

Delegates were appointed to represent the Marine Transport Workers of the I. W. W. in carrying out the organization's work in foreign countries, the appointment of one of whom is illustrated by Committee's Exhibit 246, appearing on page 638 of the Committee Record, as follows:

June 10, 1919.

"*To Whom It May Concern:*

"The bearer, Fellow-worker Gustave Johnson, has been duly authorized to represent the Marine Transport Workers of the Industrial Workers of the World for the purpose of presenting to the workers of all countries the proposed Marine Transport Workers' Federation.

"Any courtesy that you may show him will be greatly appreciated.

"Yours for international solidarity,

"MARINE TRANSPORT WORKERS' INDUSTRIAL UNION,

....

"*Acting Sec-Treas.*"

Progress made in the organization is well illustrated by Committee's Exhibit 247, page 639, which is as follows:

"FELLOW-WORKERS.— The Marine Transport Workers' Organizations of the I. W. W. have combined under the name of the Marine Transport Workers' Industrial Union No. 8, of the I. W. W., and are planning an intensive campaign of organization amongst the workers of all nationalities and especially so amongst the Finnish speaking workers of the marine industry.

"We are also forming a revolutionary international Marine Transport Workers' Organization and already have an understanding with the workers of Argentine, Uruguay, Chile, Mexico, Cuba, Spain, Ireland and Holland and are in touch with many other countries.

"But on account of the heavy re-organization expenses we are not financially able to properly carry out our plans for organization amongst the Finnish workers, or to properly meet the opposition of the conservative elements and reactionary factions that are fighting the proposed International. We would therefore like the co-operation of all the Finnish speaking workers and members of the I. W. W. for the purpose of putting our Finnish literature amongst the Finnish seafaring men and longshoremen and other Marine Workers in North and South America.

"Remember, fellow-workers, that the transportation is the keystone of the present industrial system and that, when transportation stops industry stops. The opportunity is ours. All that is required is a little co-operation. If we will work together an International Marine Transport Workers' Organization is an assured fact.

"All money donated by the Finnish workers will be used to educate and organize the Finnish speaking transport workers and to finance the international organization.

"Thanking you in advance for your kind co-operation and trusting that you will be united with us to push this good work, I am,

"Yours for international solidarity,

(Signed) "JAMES SCOTT,

"*Acting Secretary-Treasurer,*

"MARINE TRANSPORT WORKERS' INDUSTRIAL UNION NO. 8 OF THE I. W. W."

A letter showing the point of view of those engaged in this work appears as Committee's Exhibit No. 248, page 641, as follows:

"ERIE, PA., *June* 11, 1919.

"FELLOW-WORKERS:— To let you know that I have left the big city I drop these few lines. As I arrived here on the tenth I cannot tell you much of the slave market here, the boys say that there is not any activities here for the O. B. U.

"The Finns here are mostly 'invertebrate' type, waiting for the bloodless revolution.

"I do not know whether I will stay or not, as it depends on the price, the bourgeoisie of this little town are going to pay for my skin. Anyway I drop you a line in case if I will go to elsewhere.

"Take a notice when the Finns succeed in getting me out of the organization.

"Yours for revolutionary I. W. W.

"Address: J. Helberg, 315 Plum St., Erie, Pa."

Efforts on the part of the Marine Transport Workers of the I. W. W. to co-ordinate their activities with foreign workers in the same industry is illustrated by the following correspondence with William O'Brien, Liberty Hall, Dublin, Ireland:

"FELLOW-WORKERS: — Through Fellow-worker Jim Hayes we have learnt that the Irish Marine Transport Workers' General Union has a program which closely resembles the program of the I. W. W., i. e., industrial organization of the workers for the double purpose of fighting the everyday battles and finally to take over the industry.

"Fellow-worker Hayes also says that he thinks you would be willing to enter into communication with us in regard to a closer affiliation and co-operation. As you will see from the enclosed circular we have proposed to have a general conference in Chicago on April 28th with such ends in view. If you are not able to have a representative with us we should still be glad to hear from you at an early date.

"A proposition is frequently being made that we try to establish a transfer system with other countries, by which it would be possible to collect dues wherever the holder of this is, so that an American marine transport worker of the

Patrick Quinlan, Carlo Tresca, Miss Elizabeth Gurley Flynn, A. Lessig, William D. Haywood

JUSTICE PLEADS WITH THE PRISON GUARD.

A cartoon appearing in the November, 1919, *One Big Union* which speaks for itself.

I. W. W. could pay his regular dues in Ireland, or Spain, as the case may be, while we would accept the dues of an Irish or Spanish fellow-worker in the same manner.

"It is also proposed that any member of organizations in such co-operation shall have the right to have his grievances taken up by the organizations thus affiliated.

"Ultimately, we would, of course, aim at organizing all the Marine Transport Workers of the World as one body, this in our opinion being the only way in which we could take over the responsibility for marine transportation when capitalism goes bankrupt and tumbles over, as it is bound to do in the near future.

"By writing this letter we merely wish to get in touch with your organization, so that we could get an exchange of view in regard to the possibilities of the proposed World Union of Marine Transport Workers.

"Yours for the ONE BIG UNION."

(See pp. 663, 664 stenographer's minutes, Committee Hearings.)

A letter addressed under date of June 12, 1919, to the Irish Transport and General Workers' Union is also interesting:

"FELLOW-WORKERS:— Some time ago several of the Marine Transport Workers' Organizations of the I. W. W. sent communications to you in regards to affiliation with the International Transport Workers' Organization that we were proposing. To date we have received no official answer. Although one of our members, Jim Hayes, stated that when he was in Ireland you had written to us.

"The marine transport workers of Argentine, Uruguay, Chile, Mexico, Cuba and all the marine organizations affiliated with the I. W. W. in North and South America have accepted the international organization as outlined by us. The marine workers in Barcelona and Rotterdam, Holland, have it under consideration at present. A dozen other organizations that we are in touch with are expected to favorably consider the plan.

"This briefly is as follows: That we organize an International Marine Transport Workers' Federation. That all organizations in this federation recognize the membership books of each other and shall be authorized to collect dues from members of affiliated bodies when such members are working in localities that fall under their jurisdiction. All dues so paid shall be accepted by the organization of which the member who paid same belongs. In case of strikes nobody affiliated with the federation shall unload, handle or help transport any commodities that have been loaded by strike-breakers when same arrives at their ports. The federation shall endeavor to bring about an international wage scale and better the conditions of labor.

"All this is directly in line with James Connelly's efforts to organize the workers in One Big Union. And we trust that your organization will co-operate with us to bring about Connelly's dream of a One Big Union of the Workers of the World.

"With best wishes, I am,

"Yours for International Solidarity.

Acting Secretary-Treasurer,

"MARINE TRANSPORT WORKER'S INDUSTRIAL UNION."

(See pp. 665-66 stenographer's minutes, Committee Hearings.)

Previous to this date correspondence had been entered into with the Irish Workers, as is illustrated by the following letter.

"FELLOW-WORKERS: GREETINGS:—We of the local branch Marine Transport Workers' Industrial Union No. 100, I. W. W., Port of New York, are in receipt of information from one of our fellow-workers, who recently visited Ireland. While there he was much inspired by the enthusiasm and solidarity displayed by your members in their fight against the exploiting class in your fair country. This fellow-worker assures us that your aims and objects are the same as ours, namely, organizing the One Big Union of all workers the world over for working class control.

"Believing that the time is now ripe for the taking over of industry by and for the workers, we cordially invite your co-operation towards the end of welding the transport workers of the world in one big powerful union. By courier we are sending you literature which outlines the program of the I. W. W. Should this meet with the favor of your membership we look forward to further correspondence relating to this matter. May we hope for an early and favorable reply?

"We remain yours for industrial freedom,

"ORGANIZATION COMMITTEE FOR THE PORT OF NEW YORK,
"JOHN MURRY,
"F. GONZALES,
"FRANK HART,

"NEW YORK BRANCH, I. W. W., MARINE TRANSPORT WORKERS, INDUSTRIAL UNION No. 100, NEW YORK, N. Y. *March,* 21, 1919."

(See pp. 667–68 stenographer's minutes, Committee Hearings.)

It is evident also that attempts were made to bring about co-operation between the I. W. W. and the Nederlandsche Federatie van Transport–Arbeider, as is illustrated by a confidential letter on the letterhead of that organization, dated April 9, 1919, and addressed to the Marine Transport Workers' Industrial Union No. 1000 of the I. W. W. 27 East 4th street, New York:

"DEAR COMRADES.—We acknowledge receipt of your letter forwarded to us by Comrade F. J. Leamans and handed at our office today by a sailor of the Dutch S. S. 'De Leve Provinciens.' As for your invitation to attend an international conference of syndicalist transport workers which will be held at some place on the European continent in May, we shall put your proposal before our executive committee. In the meantime we shall be pleased to meet one of your delegates to discuss the matter with him, in order to get the necessary informations.

"Awaiting the favor of an early reply, we remain with fraternal greetings, "Yours truly,

"NED: FEDERATIE VAN TRANSPORTARBEIDERS,
"S. VANDEN BERG, *Secretary.*"

(See p. 672 stenographer's minutes, Committee Hearings.)

Another letter on the letterhead of the same organization, dated May 15, 1919, is as follows:

"MARINE TRANSPORT WORKERS INDUSTRIAL UNION, No. 100 OF THE I. W. W.,
27 East 4th Street, New York

"DEAR COMRADE:.—On the 29th and 30th of April last a conference of transport workers was held at Amsterdam with a view of re-establishing the International Transport Workers' Federation. Delegates from Great Britain, Belgium, Germany and Holland were present and a resolution was carried as to the reconstruction of the International. A provisional central committee was appointed to convene a full conference in September and draft new rules which correspond to the actual (present) international social and political conditions.

"Our federation is represented in the provisional bureau so that we as syndicalists have a voice in the preparatory arrangements. We are in touch with the British Transport Workers' Federation that is supporting us to break down the policy of the Germans and their Dutch satellites.

"In order to strengthen the revolutionary element in the new I. T. F., we beg to suggest you to affiliate. Application should be made to Mr. Oudegeest, Nederlandsch Verband Van Vakvereenigingen, Reguliersgracht 80 at Amsterdam.

"Trusting you will agree with our proposition, we remain,

Yours fraternally,

"NED: FEDERATIE VAN TRANSPORTARBEIDERS,
S. VANDEN BERG, *Secretary.*"

(See pp. 670–71, stenographer's minutes, Committee Hearings.)

The reply to this last communication, dated June 5, 1919, is as follows:

"FELLOW-WORKERS.— Enclosed you will find reply to your communication of May 15th and also a letter addressed to Mr. Oudegeest, Amsterdam which kindly deliver for us.

"Kindly get in touch with the other syndicalist organization and let us know the general sentiment in your union for a revolutionary International.

"With many thanks for your kind co-operation, I am,

"Fraternally yours,
"*Acting Secretary-Treasurer,*
M. T. W. I. U. No. 8."

(See p. 669, stenographer's minutes, Committee Hearings.)

The enclosure with this letter is as follows:

"FELLOW-WORKERS.—Your communication of May 15th received and proposal for our affiliation with the proposed I. T. F. noted and carefully considered. In reply we would state that we have also issued a call for the establishment of a new International to be composed only of syndicalist and revolutionary organizations of the marine transport workers. Cuba, Mexico and those of the U. S. A., that are affiliated with us, have agreed to form this new revolutionary International. The marine workers of Barcelona, Spain, and the Irish transport workers are also considering the matter.

"It appears to us that it would be best for the revolutionary marine transport workers and the syndicalist organizations to try and form their own International, as from past experience it has been found almost impossible to combine the conservative and radical workers under one head. Conditions in the marine transport industry are such that only a clear-cut program and an organization that is so organized that it can meet international capital on a real international basis will be able to survive the coming critical period in the international labor movement.

"Kindly consider our proposition and refer it to the comrades of other countries with whom you may be in touch so that we can get together for the purpose of organizing a real International instead of one in name only. An International that will meet international capital with an international organization and whose motto will be:

"'An injury to one is an injury to all.'

"Trusting to hear favorably from you and the other comrades, we remain,

"Yours for the One Big Union of the Marine Transport Workers,

"*Acting Secretary-Treasurer,*
"M. T. W. I. U. of the I. W. W."

(See pp. 673–74 stenographer's minutes, Committee Hearing.)

This series of correspondence also includes letters from the marine transport workers of Spain by Martorell, president, from Sociedad da Resistencia Obrieros de Puerto del La Capital Seccion. This letter from Buenos Aires is extremely interesting and is, therefore, reproduced here in full:

"FELLOW-WORKER: GREETINGS.— In reply to your letter would like to say, as secretary of this organization, that your communication brings us a new spirit of solidarity to bring to the end the exploitation of what the toilers are victims, forming an International across the whole world, with the hopes that the dreams of yesterday are going to be a real feast in the very near future.

"Your communication was just delivered at the same very time that our union was holding a meeting. Having read it to the members present, your delegate has noted the enthusiasm amongst them to hear the good news from miles away distance. Also we gave the opportunity to your delegate to express the feelings of our comrades on the other side giving to us in detail the strength of your organization and giving to us an idea of the persecution that your organization has been victim. Your delegate's visit is the beginning of our great effort and ideas to see the workers of the entire world organize to abolish once forever the slavery and the capitalist system, building so the great bulwark of the workers solidarity.

"Immediately two delegates were eleccted to bring your position to the different bodies and other various organizations of our industry. Also a proposition was carried to print 1,000 copies of the same communication to be distributed in order to put up for discussion and vote in pro or against.

"We really believe and can assure to you that everyone will be in favor of your proposition, as it will be the only way of defeating our great enemies the vampires of capitalism.

"Herewith you will find two copies of your letter and you can be assured that our organization will like to keep in touch with you through your delegates system in order to put you on the real track of what is going on in this country.

"Hoping that you will not exhaust your efforts to reach to an understanding in the very near future, with best wishes, I remain yours for the proletarian cause. (Copy)

"(Seal)

"FOR THE ORGANIZATION COMMITTEE,

"G. MALVIDO, *Secretary*."

(See pp. 679–80, stenographer's minutes, Committee Hearings.)

Similar correspondence was received from Federacion Obriera del Marine Uruguay.

These letters indicate in a measure the methods by which the Marine Transport Workers of the I. W. W. attempt to organize throughout the world, and they disclose fully the purpose for which the co-operation is sought.

The propaganda conducted by the Industrial Workers of the World will be discussed in the succeeding chapters of this report dealing with the general subject of propaganda.

MANIFESTO CALLING CONVENTION TO ORGANIZE INDUSTRIAL WORKERS OF WORLD

Social relations and groupings only reflect mechanical and industrial conditions. The *great facts* of present industry are the displacement of human skill by machines and the increase of capitalist power through concentration in the possession of the tools with which wealth is produced and distributed.

Because of these facts trade division among laborers and competition among capitalists are alike disappearing. Class divisions grow ever more fixed and class antagonisms more sharp. Trade lines have been swallowed up in a common servitude of all workers to the machines which they tend. New machines, ever replacing less productive ones, wipe out whole trades and plunge new bodies of workers into the evergrowing army of tradeless, hopeless unemployed. As human beings and human skill are displaced by mechanical progress, the capitalists need use the workers only during that brief period when muscles and nerves respond most intensely. The moment the laborer no longer yields the maximum of profits, he is thrown upon the scrap pile, to starve alongside the discarded machine. A *dead line* has been drawn, and an age limit established, to cross which, in this world of monopolized opportunities, means condemnation to industrial death.

The worker, wholly separated from the land and the tools, with his skill of craftsmanship rendered useless, is sunk in the uniform mass of wage slaves. He sees his power of resistance broken by craft divisions, perpetuated from outgrown industrial stages. His wages constantly grow less as his hours grow longer and monopolized prices grow higher. Shifted hither and thither by the demands of profit-takers, the laborer's home no longer exists. In this hopeless condition he is forced to accept whatever humiliating conditions his master may impose. He is subjected to a physical and intellectual examination more searching than was the chattel slave when sold from the auction block. Laborers are no longer classified by differences in trade skill, but the employer assigns them according to the machines to which they are attached. These divisions, far from representing differences in skill or interests among the laborers, are imposed by the employers that workers may be pitted against one another and spurred to greater exertion in the shop, and that all resistance to capitalist tyranny may be weakened by artificial distinctions.

While encouraging these outgrown divisions among the workers the capitalists carefully adjust themselves to the new conditions. They wipe out all differences among themselves and present a united front in their war upon labor. Through employers' associations, they seek to crush, with brutal force, by the injunctions of the judiciary, and the use of military power, all efforts at resistance. Or when the other policy seems more profitable, they conceal their daggers beneath the Civic Federation and hoodwink and betray those whom they would rule and exploit. Both methods depend for success upon the blindness and internal dissensions of the working class. The employers' line of battle and methods of warfare correspond to the solidarity of the mechanical and industrial concentration, while laborers still form their fighting organizations on lines of long-gone trade divisions. The battles of the past emphasize this lesson. The *textile* workers of Lowell, Philadelphia, and Fall River; the *butchers* of Chicago, weakened by the disintegrating effects of trade divisions; the *machinists* on the Santa Fe, unsupported by their fellow-workers subject to the same masters; the long-struggling *miners* of Colorado, hampered by a lack of unity and solidarity upon the industrial battlefield, all bear witness to the helplessness and impotency of labor as at present organized.

This worn out and corrupt system offers no promise of improvement and adaptation. There is no silver lining to the clouds of darkness and despair settling down upon the world of labor.

This system offers only a perpetual struggle for slight relief within wage slavery. It is blind to the possibility of establishing an industrial democracy, wherein there shall be no wage slavery, but where the workers will own the tools which they operate, and the product of which they alone will enjoy.

It shatters the ranks of the workers into fragments, rendering them helpless and impotent on the industrial battlefield.

Separation of craft from craft renders industrial and financial solidarity impossible.

Union men scab upon union men; hatred of worker for worker is engendered, and the workers are delivered helpless and disintegrated into the hands of the capitalists.

Craft jealousy leads to the attempt to create trade monopolies.

Prohibitive initiation fees are established that force men to become scabs against their will. Men whom manliness or circumstances have driven from one trade are thereby fined when they seek to transfer membership to the union of a new craft.

Craft divisions foster political ignorance among the workers, thus dividing their class at the ballot box, as well as in the shop, mine and factory.

Craft unions may be and have been used to assist employers in the establishment of monopolies and the raising of prices. One set of workers are thus used to make harder the conditions of life of another body of laborers.

Craft divisions hinder the growth of class consciousness of the workers, foster the idea of harmony of interests between employing exploiter and employed slave. They permit the association of the misleaders of the workers with the capitalists in the Civic Federations, where plans are made for the perpetuation of capitalism, and the permanent enslavement of the workers through the wage system.

Previous efforts for the betterment of the working class have proven abortive because limited in scope and disconnected in action.

Universal economic evils afflicting the working class can be eradicated only by a universal working-class movement. Such a movement of the working class is impossible while separate craft and wage agreements are made favoring the employer against other crafts in the same industry, and while energies are wasted in fruitless jurisdiction struggles which serve only to further the personal aggrandizement of union officials.

A movement to fulfill these conditions must consist of one great industrial union embracing all industries — providing for craft autonomy locally, industrial autonomy internationally, and working-class unity generally.

It must be founded on the class struggle, and its general administration must be conducted in harmony with the recognition of the irrepressible conflict between the capitalist class and the working class.

It should be established as the economic organization of the working class, without affiliation with any political party.

All power should rest in a collective membership.

Local, national and general administration, including union labels, buttons, badges, transfer cards, initiation fees, and per capita tax should be uniform throughout.

All members must hold membership in the local, national or international union covering the industry in which they are employed, but transfers of membership between unions, local, national, or international, should be universal.

Workingmen bringing union cards from industrial unions in foreign countries should be freely admitted into the organization.

The general administration should issue a publication representing the entire union and its principles which should reach all members in every industry at regular intervals.

A *central defense fund,* to which all members contribute equally, should be established and maintained.

All workers, therefore, who agree with the principles herein set forth, will meet in convention at Chicago the 27th day of June, 1905, for the purpose of forming an economic organization of the working class along the lines marked out in this manifesto.

Representation in the convention shall be based upon the number of workers whom the delegate represents. No delegate, however, shall be given representation in the convention on the numerical basis of an organization unless he has credentials — bearing the seal of his union, local, national or international, and the signatures of the officers thereof — authorizing him to install his union as a working part of the proposed economic organization in the industrial department in which it logically belongs in the general plan of the organization. Lacking this authority, the delegate shall represent himself as an individual.

Adopted at Chicago, January 2, 3 and 4, 1905.

A. G. SWING,	JOHN GUILD,
A. M. SIMONS,	DANIEL MCDONALD,
W. SHURTLEFF,	EUGENE V. DEBS,
FRANK M. MCCABE,	THOS. J. DE YOUNG,
JOHN M. O'NEIL,	THOS. J. HAGERTY,
GEO. ESTES,	FRED. D. HENION,
WM. D. HAYWOOD,	W. J. BRADLEY,
MOTHER JONES,	CHAS. O. SHERMAN,
ERNEST UNTERMANN,	M. E. WHITE,
W. L. HALL,	WILLIAM J. PINKERTON,
CHAS. H. MOYER,	FRANK KRAFFS,
CLARENCE SMITH,	J. E. FITZGERALD,
WILLIAM ERNEST TRAUTMANN,	FRANK BOHN.
JOS. SCHMIDT,	

(Pages 46, 47, 48, 49, "The Launching of the Industrial Workers of the World," by Paul Brissenden, published by the University of California, November 25, 1913.)

CHAPTER II

Workers' International Industrial Union

A comparatively small but aggressive group of industrial unionists are represented in the Workers' International Industrial Union, familiarly known as the W. I. I. U. This organization is an offshoot of the I. W. W. The schism occurred at the annual convention of the I. W. W. in 1908, when the elements which wholly repudiated political action gained control of that organization. The leader of the seceding group was Daniel Le Leon, who, for more than twenty years, was editor of "The Weekly People," and one of the principal figures of the Socialist Labor Party. This group was first known as the Detroit I. W. W., but in 1915 the name was changed to the Workers' International Industrial Union.

This group claims to retain the original Socialist principles which were incorporated in the preamble of the first constitution of the I. W. W. It works in close harmony with the Socialist Labor Party whose leaders are active in its ranks. The similarity between the present preamble of the constitution of the Workers' International Industrial Union and the original preamble of the I. W. W. will be apparent from its reading.

It is as follows:

> "The working class and the employing class have nothing in common. There can be no peace so long as hunger and want are found among millions of working people, and the few who make up the employing class have all the good things of life.
>
> "Between these two classes a struggle must go on until the toilers come together on the political field under the banner of a distinct revolutionary political party governed by the workers' class interests, and on the industrial field under the banner of one great Industrial nion to take and hold all means of production and distribution, and to run them for the benefit of all wealth producers.
>
> "The rapid gathering of wealth and the centering of the management of industries into fewer and fewer hands make the trades union unable to cope with the ever-growing power of the employing class, because the trades unions foster a state of things which allows one set of workers to be pitted

against another set of workers in the same industry, thereby helping defeat one another in wage wars. The trades unions aid the employing class to mislead the workers into the belief that the working class have interests in common with their employers.

"These sad conditions must be changed, the interests of the working class upheld and while the capitalist rule still prevails, all possible relief for the workers must be secured. That can only be done by an organization aiming steadily at the complete overthrow of the capitalist wage system, and formed in such a way that all its members in any one industry or in all industries, if necessary, cease work whenever a strike or lockout is on in any department thereof, thus making an injury to one an injury to all." (See pp. 54, 55, stenographer's minutes, Committee Hearings.)

It will be noticed from the foregoing that the W. I. I. U., while aiming at the destruction of the rights of private property, is distinguishable from the I. W. W. by its willingness to employ parliamentary methods as a means of propaganda until such time as direct action offers a prospect of success. The purpose of this organization is to facilitate the use of the general strike as a weapon of offense.

The success of this organization has been largely among metal and machinery workers. A typical example of the propaganda distributed to workmen is as follows:

"ONE GREAT UNION

"THE WAGE WORKERS' MEANS OF EDUCATION AND DEFENSE, A LEVER FOR SOCIAL PROGRESS

"A PLACE FOR EVERY WORKER, EVERY WORKER IN HIS PLACE

(Leaflet No. 4)

"If men should cease to aid each other, mankind would perish.

"Mutual help is one of the necessary conditions of existence. The working class labor together to produce the things required to sustain life. Producing plentifully, the workers have to live stingily; creating by their labor — skill, ingenuity and sacrifice — the wealth of the world, they are *restrained by conditions* from possessing all that they produce.

"The working class and the employing class have nothing in common. There can be no peace so long as hunger and want are found among millions of working people, and the few who make up the employing class have all the good things of life.

"Between these two classes a struggle must go on until the toilers come together on the *political field* under the banner of a *distinct revolutionary political party*, governed by the workers' class interests, and on the *industrial field* under the banner of *one great industrial union*, to take and to hold all means of production and distribution, and to run them for the benefit of all wealth-producers.

"The rapid gathering of wealth, and the centering of the management of industries into fewer and fewer hands, make the trade unions unable to cope with the ever-growing power of the employing class, because the trades unions foster a state of things which allows one set of workers to be pitted against another set of workers in the same industry, thereby helping to defeat one another in wage wars. The trades unions aid the employing class to mislead the workers into the belief that the working class have interests in common with their employers.

"The time has now come when the workers must organize on lines of industry instead of lines of crafts.

"*Loose federation or grouping up of existing trade unions will not do.*

"Industrial solidarity must be aimed at, along with local autonomy.

"No one industrial union or branch shall act arbitrarily, independently or to the disadvantage of other local union groups in the same industry, union branches to recognize and be operated and directed by one central authority in an industry, and that industry to recognize the general, central authority of the general administration.

"In case the members of any subordinate organization of the *one great union* are involved in a strike, regularly ordered by the organization or general executive board, or involved in a lockout, the general executive board must have full power to call out any other union or unions if necessary.

"*Real wages are being reduced, owing to the lessened purchasing power of money, your standard of living is being daily lowered by the fact that your wages are not keeping pace with soaring prices.*

"These sad conditions must be changed, the interests of the working class upheld, and while the capitalist rule still prevails, all possible relief for the workers must be secured. That can only be done by an organization aiming steadily at the complete overthrow of the capitalist wage system, and formed in such a way that all its members in any one industry, or in all industries, if necessary, cease work whenever a strike or lockout is on in any department thereof, thus making an injury to one an injury to all.

"A labor organization, truly to represent the working class, must have two things in view:

"1. It must combine the wage workers in such a way that it can successfully fight the battles and protect the interests of the workers in their struggle for less hours, more wages and better conditions generally.

"2. It must offer a final solution of the labor problem — an emancipation from strikes, lockouts, injunctions, jailing of strikers, officers and organizers, and the scabbery of the workers against one another.

"*Study the plan of the Workers' International Industrial Union,* and learn to know how, while giving recognition to control of shop branch affairs, perfect industrial unionism is provided for, and the strength of all organized workers directed to a common center, from which any weak point can be strengthened and protected. *An injury to one is an injury to all.*

"Know also, that the growth of the Workers' International Industrial Union will build up within itself the structure of an industrial democracy — a Workers' Industrial Republic of Labor — which must finally burst the shell of capitalistic government and be the agency by which the workers will operate the industries and appropriate the products to themselves.

"How is the Industrial Union organized?

"INITIAL TEMPORARY STEPS

"1. *Individual members at large.* Any wage worker in a place where no local union has been organized, joins by application to general headquarters.

"Initiation fee, $2, to include six months' subscription to I. U. News, and monthly dues, 50 cents.

"2. *Local Recruiting Unions.* Organizing of wage workers employed in different industries, until such time as the respective industry has been organized in the locality. Application for charter is sent to general headquarters, etc. Charter and outfit in books cost $20. Initiation fee and local dues are decided by the local, in accordance with the constitution. Its purpose is to agitate for organizing the workers in their respective industries.

"ORGANIZING INDUSTRIES

"1. A local industrial union, or a branch thereof is organized by ten or more wage workers employed in the same industry applying for a charter from the general administration of the W. I. I. U. The financial obligations are the same as those of a recruiting local.

"2. National industrial union for each industry is organized when enough local industrial unions have been formed, as provided by the constitution.

"3. Departments of industries are organized, of national industrial unions of kindred industries, according to the rules governing these administrations. Such departments elect each a member of the general executive board of the W. I. I. U. Till such departments of industries are organized, the G. E. B. members (7) are elected at large.

"General administration of the W. I. I. U.

"The members of the general executive board.

"The general secretary-treasurer.

"The general organizer.

"The editor of the official organ.

"A literature committee of three members.

"*Supplemental Organization.* Industrial Councils are organized in each locality or district, of local unions organized therein, to insure action and counsel on all matters affecting all locals, and to communicate direct with the general administration of the Workers' International Industrial Union.

"The following diagram will help to illustrate the structural formation of the One GreatUnion:

"Join the W. I. I. U today.

"ONE GREAT UNION

"Structure of W. I. I. U.

"LOCAL INDUSTRIAL UNION

"Unite all the actual wage workers in a given industry in a given locality, subdivided into branches as the particular requirements of said industry may call for

"Branch 1 Branch 2 Branch 3

"NATIONAL INDUSTRIAL UNION

"Unites all local industrial unions of the same industry in a country or continent.

"DISTRICT INDUSTRIAL UNION

"For the purpose of establishing in a given district solidarity of action, a council is organized, composed of delegates of local unions of at least five or more, located in that district. Councils are chartered from the General Administration of the W. I. I. U.

"DEPARTMENTS OF INDUSTRIES

"Are organized of National Industrial Unions of kindred industries, in accordance with the provisions governing such body.

"INTERNATIONAL BUREAU OF THE W. I. I. U.

"American administration.
"Australian administration.
"British administration.

"General Organization

"*American Administration*

"The General Executive Board elected by departments, and referendum of membership. The general secretary-treasurer, the general organizer, editor of official paper and literature committee, elected by the regular convention of the Workers' International Industrial Union composed of delegates from all subdivisions of the organization.

"Membership at Large

"Wage workers in a locality where no local is organized.

"LOCAL RECRUITING UNIONS

"Organized by wage workers employed in different industries where no Industrial Local Union has yet been organized.

"The International Bureau is not fully constituted, the American Administration is serving in a temporary manner at present.

"The subdivisions — industrial and national industrial unions — shall have complete autonomy in their respective internal affairs, within the limits of the general constitution and the control of the G. E. B. in matters concerning the general welfare. All members and divisions of the organization are integral parts of the *One Great Union.*

"Universal transfer from one union to another, and admittance of all wage workers to membership, without regard to race, creed or color, makes possible that solidarity so much needed for direct improvement of working conditions and social progress generally.

"Every wage worker should be a member of the W. I. I. U.

"Join today.

"Join the Industrial Union of your class.

"THE WORKERS' INTERNATIONAL INDUSTRIAL UNION.

"(Issued by the American Administration Headquarters; address, P. O. Box 651, Detroit, Mich., U. S. A. Write for further information, samples of literature and papers. Distributed locally by the Workers' International Industrial Union. This leaflet, $3.50 a thousand; 35 cents a hundred.)"

(Label.)

The organization is international in character and revolutionary in aim. It is in complete accord with the Russian Communist Party, as is illustrated by the following quotations from an article entitled "The Russian Revolutionary and Social Industrial Unionism," by S. F. Friedun, which appears on page 12 of the "First of May" magazine for May 1, 1919:

"The feat of the Russian workers has compelled universal attention and heartfelt applause from the class-conscious workers everywhere. The Socialist Industrial Unionist, always on the alert to learn from a defeat of the working class and to be guided by its successes, has eagerly watched the passing of events in Russia. Unfortunately, a sea and continent lie between us and our Russian fellow-workers; yet the reliable information received and the impartial reports of those who have no interest in adulterating the truth, convery a clear idea of what has transpired and is transpiring. The Russian revolution has proved a thundering endorsement of the principles of Socialist Industrial Unionism. The Russian workers, first in the throes of Revolution, and now in working out a stable Socialist structure of government, have been compelled by the force of events to adopt the underlying truths of Socialist Industrial Unionism. They are making realities of our theories. It is my purpose to point out, from the facts on hand, wherein the principles of the W. I. I. U. are confirmed by the actual events in Russia." (Pages 58, 59, stenographer's minutes, Committee Hearings.)

Their approval of the Third International which was launched at Moscow under the leadership of the Russian Communist Party is shown by an article in the same issue of the same magazine, entitled "Revolutionary Socialism and the Third International," appearing on page 3:

"To quote Lenin: 'America is a great country, great in technical achievements. Marvelous developments are possible there. The American Daniel De Leon first formulated the idea of a Soviet government, which grew up in Russia on his idea. Future society will be organized along Soviet lines. There will be Soviet rather than geographical boundaries for nations. Industrial Unionism is the basic state. That is what we are building.'

. . . .

"The Second International is dead! Long live the Third International of Revolutionary Socialism! Long live the International Solidarity of the Workers, reared and cemented by Socialist Industrial Unionism!

"Workers of the World, Unite! You have nothing to lose but your chains; you have a world to gain!

"Fellow-workers: Vote and strike as a class, by joining as a mass the union of your class — the W. I. I. U." (Pages 60, 61, stenographer's minutes, Committee Hearings.)

The organization has branches or affiliated organizations in other countries, namely, the British administration, with headquarters at 47 Oswald street, Glascow, Scotland; general secretary, Thomas L. Smith. Its official organ is "Industrial Unionist." The Australian administration headquarters is at Hatte's Arcade, King street, Newton, Sydney, New South Wales, and its official organ is "The One Big Union Herald."

Metal and machinery locals of the W. I. I. U. in and about New York are as follows:

Local 228, Branch 1, meets every first and third Friday, 8 P. M., at 411 East 83d street, New York.

Local 217, meets every first and third Tuesday, 8 P. M., at Parkway Assembly, 51st street and Fourth avenue, Brooklyn, N. Y.

Local 221, branches 1 and 2, meet first and third Friday, at 7:30 P. M., at 62 Cannon street, Bridgeport, Conn.

Auto Workers Industrial Union, Local 556, branch 1, meets at 411 East 83d street, New York, every second and fourth Thursday.

Recruiting Local 100, branch 1, meets at 411 East 83d street, New York, every second and fourth Tuesday.

You are invited to the meetings of the above locals. Lectures and discussion at every meeting.

The propaganda carried on by this organization will be treated in that section of this report which deals with propaganda in general.

CHAPTER III

International Federation of Workers in the Hotel, Restaurant, Club and Catering Industries

A typical example of industrial unionism is also found in an organization known as the International Federation of Workers in the Hotel, Restaurant, Club and Catering Industry. This is an organization of employees in the industry indicated by its name which has come together in an attempt to form "One Big Union" based upon the same principles as the I. W. W. It is the result of the agitation in this field, of members of the I. W. W., and although a separate organization, is very closely identified with that movement.

In January, 1917, members of this organization opened their headquarters at 158 West 46th street, Borough of Manhattan, City of New York.

In 1918 the membership had reached approximately 7,000.

At the present time, however, the membership has reached approximately 20,000. (See March 15, 1920, issue of the "Hotel Worker.")

At the convention held in New York City on July 8 to 13, 1918, a new preamble was adopted to the federation's constitution, which is as follows:

> "The Workers of the Hotel, Restaurant, Club and Catering Industry have organized this federation with the intention to give an opportunity to all workers employed in the industry to improve their conditions according to the necessities and conditions of life.
>
> "Taking into consideration the facts of past experience that it is impossible to accomplish anything worth while by following the old system of craft or trade unionism, we have come to the conclusion that in order to cope with the present situation successfully, the workers must organize and combine industrially on the economic field on the principle of the class struggle. In advocating these principles we recognize the necessity for the workers to fight continuously to shorten the work day, to increase the pay according to the conditions obtaining where they live, and to co-operate with all other workers who struggle for the abolishment of the wage system, for the complete emancipation of labor. We, therefore, unite under the following constitution."

It should be noted that this preamble is identical in principle with that of the I. W. W.; that the basis of its operation is the *class struggle* and that it clearly contemplates the seizure of the industry by the workers, and the abolition of the wage system.

An examination of the minutes of the convention above referred to shows that on July 12th, on motion of one Bergen, seconded by one Reichhardt, it was resolved:

> "That our present and future officers shall see that our membership will be instructed in the class struggle that is leading all to a great crisis which will occur in the near future. Therefore, it is necessary for all workers to be prepared to show their solidarity in the final overthrow of capitalism."

The propaganda contemplated by this resolution was carried on, and during the summer of 1918 such agitators as Carla Tresca and Arturo Giovannitti were among the lecturers at club meetings.

Lectures are still being given, and the character of the subjects discussed before the organization is illustrated by a notice appearing in the March 1, 1920, issue of the "Hotel Worker" the official organ of the organization, as follows:

> "We are holding weekly lectures every Thursday at 3 P. M.
>
> "Thursday, March 4, to be announced later.
>
> "Thursday, March 11, 'The Life and Activities of Eugene Victor Debs,' by D. C. Gitz.
>
> "Thursday, March 18, 'The One Big Union in Canada,' by Ben Legere."

The organization occupied until recently the entire premises at 158 West 46th street, and in addition to the executive offices of various branches of the organizations, club rooms were provided, entertainments given, refreshments served, and clubs organized. Everything was done to make the place attractive from a social point of view, so as to bring in new members and retain their interest in the organization.

These headquarters were raided by agents of the Bureau of Investigation of the United States Department of Justice in the summer of 1918. A large number of cooks and waiters who were coming into the premises to attend a meeting at that time were examined, and a number were found to carry I. W. W. cards on their person, in addition to the cards of the International Federation. It also developed that the then organizer, Caesar Lesino, was a member of the I. W. W., and in close correspondence with William D. Hayward of that association. Large quantities of the "Almanacco Sovversivo," meaning the "Almanac of the Revolution," published by Libraria Sociologica, of 278 Straight street, Paterson, N. J., were found upon the premises. This is an anarchistic document of extremely incendiary character. There were also found upon the premises a number of seditious books, and propaganda articles. Among them were copies of "Mentanas' Faccio a Faccio Col Nemino" ("Face to Face with the Enemy"), a revolutionary and anarchistic story designed to instruct the reader in the manufacture of explosive bombs. There were also a large number of posters containing the phrase in conspicuous type, "We, the New York waiters, will stand on the principles of the Bolsheviki."

The propaganda of the organization is carried on through a fortnightly newspaper known as the "Hotel Worker," formerly edited by Vincenzo Vacirca, but now edited by Jack Williams. This paper prints articles in English, French, Italian, Greek, German and Russian.

The character and purpose of the organization is clearly revealed by a study of this periodical. In the issue for Monday, December 15, 1919, in an editorial on page 4, entitled "Our Basic Principles," we find the following:

> "Do you know what our basic principles are? Do you know the tendency in the modern labor movement? Are you aware that labor is sick and tired with the mismanagement of industry, education and everything else that should interest you as an intelligent being?
>
> "Labor has had enough of rulership and wage slavery, it proposes a new system of society. It realizes that the class struggle is coming to a head, and that labor after thousands of years of struggle must come into its own."

At a combined business meeting of the kitchen and dining-room workers at the newly organized branch, New York, a resolution was adopted indicating the purpose of the organization, in which we find the following:

> "To function with the world-wide working class in the world-wide movement to establish by class conscious, edu-

cated, well disciplined, industrial effort, a social era wherein the wealth of the world shall belong to the world's producers." (See Issue of Saturday, October 15, 1919.)

The following notice appearing in the same issue of this paper is indicative of the systematic method by which propaganda of this character is carried on:

"LABOR ORGANIZATIONS, FRIENDS OF LABOR AND MEMBERS!

"TAKE NOTICE

"Education, enlightenment and class-consciousness are the mightiest weapon of the working class in their struggle for emancipation.

"We are about to inaugurate a campaign of education through lectures, debates and a Library for our members.

"We need books. Books on economics, history, organization, sociology, fiction; in short, Books on all topics and in all languages, preferably English, Italian and French.

"Will you help this important undertaking? Remember, knowledge in the possession of the working class is the deadliest foe of Capital.

"All Books are welcome and will be received with thanks by Secretary Lyons of the International Catering Workers Club at headquarters, 158 West 46th street."

The strong sympathy of members of this organization for the Russian Soviet regime and the principles for which it stands is illustrated by numerous quotations from Lenin and other writers on the Soviet which appear in its pages.

A typical example is found on page 8 of the March 1, 1920, issue, as follows:

"THE SOVIET ONLY OPPRESSES THE OPPRESSORS

"It is the Soviet, or proletarian democracy, which has first brought about a democracy for the masses, for those who toil, for the workers and small peasants. There has never yet been in the history of the world such exercise of State power by the majority of the population as under the Soviets. This power suppresses the 'liberty' of the exploiters and their aiders and abettors. It deprives them of the 'liberty' to exploit.

LENIN."

It is further illustrated by an article appearing in the January 15, 1920, issue, on page 8, entitled "All Power to the Worker," in which appears the following:

> "We are living in a time when old values and beliefs are constantly undergoing great changes. We realize that it is difficult for a considerable number of people to cast off their old party ideas — and take the new issues as they arise."

The article then refers to the Russian revolution and ends with the following statement:

> "Labor in all countries is preparing for the time when it too will be called upon to take over industry and operate it on a new radical basis. Radical labor resounds to the inspiring call of the Moscow Soviet; 'All Power to the Workers.'
>
> "We greet you, free revolutionary Russia! Long live the Soviets! All power to the workers!"

It is interesting to see the influences which are playing upon this organization. Articles are contributed to the official organ by Frederick A. Blossom, a member of the Freedom group of anarchists; also by L. S. Chumley, who, for a considerable period, was editor of "The Rebel Worker," the official organ in New York City of the I. W. W., which has recently changed its name to "The Fellow-worker."

In an article appearing in the November 15, 1919, issue of the "Hotel Worker," at page 3, is found the explanation for the advocacy of industrial unionism as follows:

"INDUSTRIAL UNIONISM — THE WORKERS' ONLY HOPE

> "Industrial Unionism is the only form of organization that has any chance against the highly organized business world of today.
>
> "By clinging blindly to the old system of organization by trades and crafts, the workers put a millstone around their necks and give the employers tremendous advantage in industrial disputes.
>
> "Under industrial unionism, all the Workers in one industry form One Big Union of that industry.

"Instead of being split up into a lot of separate unions, with divided and often conflicting interests, they strengthen and unite their forces in one mighty and irresistible combination."

The detailed method of organization by which agitation is carried on is illustrated by the program of the shop committee system, which is outlined in the December 15, 1919, issue and the January 1, 1920, issue of this paper. We think this document of sufficient interest to introduce it here in full, as follows:

"THE SHOP COMMITTEE SYSTEM

"The general membership of the International Federation of Workers in the Hotel, Restaurant, Lunchroom, Club and Catering Industry, realize the importance and value of the Shop Committee System as adopted and ratified by the Federation.

"Therefore, we wish to issue to the membership these general rules to guide all workers in each shop as to their duties and responsibilities, so as to make no member responsible to another, but to make each member responsible to all other members, by working hand in hand. With this point in view, we will enable the Federation as a whole to function properly 'An organization without system is like a steamship without a propeller.'

"DUTIES OF JOB ORGANIZERS

"Members of any Branch or its subsections may be appointed as Job Organizers, by its Executive Board through recommendation of the Organization Committee of said Branch or its subsections.

"All Job Organizers should be intelligent and active, their identity shall be private.

"It is the duty of Job Organizers to work in unorganized places, to be in a better position to organize all workers employed there, on general working conditions.

"Job Organizers shall be reimbursed whenever found necessary.

"All Job Organizers may be called to delegate meetings from time to time for reports.

"After the necessary quota of workers have been organized, the workers of said shop shall elect their representative from each department; one of whom shall be the Shop Delegate.

"All Job Organizers shall notify the Employment Bureau whenever a vacancy occurs, or a change in any department. This should be done immediately.

"FORMATION OF SHOP COMMITTEES

"In all establishments where there are less than three departments (such as K. D. and D. R. D. only), the workers shall elect enough representatives at large to bring the total number of representatives up to three, one of which shall act as the Shop Delegate and one shall act as Shop Secretary.

"They shall elect from each department one representative and two assistant representatives; one from each watch and from the total amount of department representatives, one shall act as Shop Delegate, who shall represent all the workers of that shop and at the delegate meetings and shall have the power of one vote. One of the shop representatives at least shall act as Shop Secretary.

"Elections of Shop Delegates shall be held every three months by the workers of each shop at Branch Headquarters. Secret ballots shall be used.

"All Shop meetings shall be held at Branch Headquarters.

"DUTIES OF SHOP WORKERS

"No shop worker shall discuss internal union affairs or be permitted to give information of union activities to any person.

"Workers in each department of any establishment shall not permit themselves to work with non-union workers.

"All members of this Federation shall turn in to the Branch Secretary their membership books of the A. F. of L.

"Any worker found acting in a disorderly manner on the job at meetings or attempting to disrupt the harmony amongst the fellow-workers in the shop or refusing to attend meetings after being notified by mail or through the delegate, shall be dealt with according to the findings of the Shop Committee.

"Whenever a worker has any grievance with the employer or head of the department, the worker shall immediately report to the assistant representative or representatives of the department who shall in turn report same to the Shop Delegate to be taken up with the parties concerned (trivial cases should be avoided, serious cases shall be attended to by the proper officials of the Federation and Shop officials).

"All workers shall assist the Shop Committee in seeing that all employees are engaged in or from the employment bureau and not otherwise.

"Workers in each shop shall be supplied with working cards for job control.

"All steady stations shall be abolished in organized houses.

"Any worker known to pay or buy a position or bribe another for a position, shall be tried on written charges before the Grievance Committee.

"Any worker who is employed in this industry and at the same time carrying on another business (such as Candy, Stationery and Cigar Stores, Boarding Houses, etc.) after being investigated shall be requested to leave the industry and ask for a withdrawal card.

"Any worker starting work, who may have a receipt of a book and found to be over three months in arrears, shall be taken off the job immediately.

"Any Shop Delegate allowing a non-union worker to be engaged at the door and this non-union worker showing a willingness to join the Federation, the non-union worker may do so, but will have to come to headquarters, make out an application and be placed on the unemployed list, which shall be used in rotation.

"Any Delegate who permits this aforementionel rule to be broken, shall be fined heavily or taken from the job after being tried and convicted by the Grievance Committee.

"Any worker who fails to secure satisfactory action through the Shop Committee, shall have the right to appeal to the Executive Board of the Branch and if their decision is not satisfactory, may again appeal to the Executive Board of the federation.

"Members of any shop who should happen to become head of a department or departments that has more than five workers employed, shall immediately apply for a withdrawal card.

"There shall be no permanent chairman on Shop Committee.

"All Recording Secretaries shall be held responsible for the minutes. Secretary, or any proper official after each meeting shall give the minutes to the Shop Secretary.

"Any organized establishment having a shop committee which refuses to function as such, action shall be taken against the shop as a whole by the Branch.

"Shop meetings shall be called by the Shop Delegate or by a petition of one-third of the workers in any establishment, or Organizers.

"Workers in all organized establishments shall help the Organization Committee whenever called upon to assist in organizing any places that are to be organized.

"Gambling shall not be permitted on the job or in any shop meeting or in any office of the headquarters.

"Organizers shall attend shop meetings in an advisory capacity only.

"Members of the Executive Board and Organization Committee shall be empowered to attend shop meetings, to assist and guard against hasty actions being taken that may involve the whole organization.

"Any member of the shop when acting as chairman at a meeting of any description, shall always use sound judgment and seek to advise the workers rather than dictate to them.

"Any organized establishment wishing to hold parties, balls, picnics, etc., may do so after obtaining the consent of the branch.

"No Captain or House Secretary is eligible as Shop Delegate (according to the Constitution).

"All casual workers (such as those who work extra and those who are unemployed, regardless in what department they may work in this industry) shall elect from themselves a Casual Workers' Committee, with a representative, secretary and delegate. This Committee shall hold its meetings and carry on its work on lines similar to a Shop Committee.

"Any worker when on strike found having any communication, personal or otherwise, with the employer or head of any department, in the struck shop, or going to work without the written consent of the Strike Committee or Committee on Organization, shall be brought before the Grievance Committee.

"Any worker found guilty of breaking any of the aforementioned rules which are found necessary to maintain discipline and system, for the general welfare of this Federation, shall be fined by the Shop Committee or Grievance Committee, all fines derived from this source shall be turned over to the Strike Fund.

(Jan. 1, 1920)

"DUTIES OF DEPARTMENT REPRESENTATIVES AND ASSISTANTS

"It is the purpose of this system to advise and request the workers in each shop to see that at all times the most intelligent workers are elected to represent them on their Shop Committee and other official positions in their union.

"An assistant representative from each watch in all departments shall be elected, the assistant shall see that every worker on the watch is a member, should any worker not be a member of the union, the assistant shall report the non-union worker to his representative for action to be taken. It shall be the duty of the assistant to examine all membership books, receive dues, keep the addresses of all workers on the watch — turn same over to the department representative, who shall in turn give books, dues and address list to the Shop Secretary and receive receipt for same. This shall be done monthly.

"Any grievance that may arise, shall in all cases be reported to the Shop Delegate immediately or by whoever is agreed upon to take his place in his absence.

"The department representative and assistants shall see that these general rules shall at all times be carried out in their department and shall be held responsible to the workers of the shop and the Branch for any infringement in the aforementioned rules.

"The department representatives and assistants shall attend all Shop Committee Meetings which shall be held by each house or combined with other Shop Committees at headquarters, they shall have a voice and vote, give their reports, discuss grievances in general and report back to their fellow-workers whatever has been decided upon.

"The representatives of each department, Shop Secretary and Shop Delegate shall constitute the executive of each shop.

"GENERAL MEETINGS

"General meetings of the Branch and its sub-sections shall be held once a month, with additional meetings as the Branch may desire.

"All meetings of the Branch shall be called by the Labor Secretary.

"Shop meetings shall be held at least once a month. Each shop shall arrange the regular date for their meetings. Emergency meetings may be arranged through the Labor Secretary.

"Shop Committees shall meet at least once in two weeks. Combined Shop Committee meetings shall be held as the occasion may require.

"Combined Executive Board and Delegate meetings shall be held from time to time.

"SHOP MEETINGS

"A roll call shall be taken at Shop meetings, Shop committee meetings and Shop Delegate meetings, which shall be recorded in the minutes, those absent intentionally may be fined by the shop workers as provided for in the duties of shop members.

"All workers at their meetings shall elect a chairman and a Recording Secretary. The Recording Secretary shall see that a clear record of all that is transacted is recorded in the minutes. All minutes shall be typwritten and posted in the minute book of that shop. Also, copies of demands shall be kept for future reference. It is important that these rules are insisted upon. The Recording Secretary shall see that all minutes and reports are turned over to the Labor Secretary for filing. The minutes of each meeting should be signed by the Chairman, and the Secretary should sign the minutes and date same after each meeting.

"SHOP COMMITTEE MEETINGS

"All Shop Committee meetings shall be attended by the delegate, Shop Secretary and department representatives, along with the assistants, elect their Chairman and Recording Secretary and transact their business as provided for in the rules for Shop meetings.

"Whenever there are combined Shop meetings held, copies of the minutes shall be posted in the respective minute books of the shops attending said meetings. No secret meetings shall be permitted, except in cases of strikes.

"After a Shop Committee meeting, those present shall return to their shops and notify the workers. This should be done in the most effective manner.

"SHOP DELEGATE MEETINGS

"The Shop Delegate meetings shall have a roll call taken, and record any delegate being absent intentionally and not having a representative to act as substitute, shall be fined in accordance with the aforementioned rules.

"The delegates shall elect their Chairman and Recording Secretary and carry on their business as provided for in Shop Committee meetings and Shop Delegate meetings. The delegates shall use the Branch minute book for their records of minutes and reports, and copies of minutes shall be posted in minute books of shops represented at Delegate meetings.

"Note: Executive Board Committees be made up by group representation.

"GROUP REPRESENTATION

"The workers employed in the various departments of Hotels, Restaurants, Clubs, Lunchrooms and other branches of the Catering Industry, shall have group representation on the Executive Board of this Federation. This shall be done after the shop committee system has been drawn up in detail and presented to the membership in printed form; the Shop Committees installed and each shop working this system in a uniform manner. Then we shall install Group Representation. Representatives from the following groups shall be elected to the Executive Board to represent all workers of that department in the City of said Branch and sub-sections.

"GROUP A

"Shall be composed of all Chef Deporties, Pastry Cooks, Bakers, Confisiers, Glasiers, all Commis, Leguminers, Firemen, Casseroliners, Oystermen.

"GROUP B

"Captains, Assistant Head waitresses, Waiters, Commis, Bussboys.

"*GROUP C*

"Chambermaids, Scrubwomen, Parlormaids, Assistant Housekeepers, Housemaids, Housemen, Valets, Ladies' Maids.

"*GROUP D*

"Bellboys, Captains, Elevatormen, Starters, Coatroom men, Messengers.

"*GROUP E*

"Porters, Baggagemen, Doormen, Chauffeurs.

"*GROUP F*

"All Casual workers.

"*GROUP G*

"Storeroom workers.

"*GROUP H*

"Laundry workers, Seamstresses.

"*GROUP I*

"Dishwashers, Glasswashers, Silver cleaners, Pantry workers, Useful men.

"*GROUP J*

"Salesmen, Soda Fountain workers, Bartenders, Lunch-counter workers.

"*GROUP K*

"Barbers, Manicurists, Hairdressers, Shoe Cleaners.

"*GROUP L*

"Watchmen, Timekeepers, Yardmen.

"*GROUP M*

"Engineers, Electricians, Firemen, Oilers, Icemen, Helpers.

"*GROUP N*

"Plasterers, Painters, Plumbers, Steamfitters, Carpenters, Cabinetmakers, Upholsterers, Decorators, Tailors, Silversmiths, Helpers.

"GROUP O

"Musicians, Performers.

"GROUP P

"Cashiers, Checkers, Clerks, Telephone workers.

"According to the number of organized workers in any of the above groups they shall be entitled to proportionate representation."

On January 1, 1920, the organization moved its headquarters to its new building, 133 West 51st street. The New York branch also took up its headquarters in the new building where a free employment bureau was placed in charge of John Chastony. The secretary's office is also there. The restaurant and lunch-room workers' branch, secretary, J. Salomka, has offices at 28 St. Mark's place, New York City, and also a free employment bureau. Other branches are Brooklyn, N. Y., secretary, S. Fret, 327 Livingston street; Philadelphia, Secretary, H. Chernow, 218 North 13th street; Atlantic City, N. J., 108 So. Arkansas avenue, Bridgeport, Conn., secretary, D. H. Howell, 382 Wood avenue; New Haven, Conn., 153 Crown street; Washington, D. C., 1008 Pennsylvania avenue, N. W.; Newark, N. J., 49 Bank street. The officers of the organization for the present year are:

General secretary-treasurer, John Assel.

General organizer, Rudolf Sheerbarth.

Executive Board of the Federation.— New York branch — F. Lalli, S. Ferrari, S. Cutter, M. Obermeyer, J. Bergen, C. Spagnoli, J. Perrachio, C. Coner, J. Serret, A. Dominico, J. Mackrell, S. Kromberg, H. Hahn, S. Lovie, F. Lasser, C. Tempesta, S. Guanzini, J. Gramola, A. Suchant, J. Fecci.

Philadelphia.— A. Bollenghi, A. Baltera, V. Raviola.

Lunchroom Workers.— J. Feingold, J. Brilensky, J. Haley

Brooklyn.— S. Popper, A. Reiss, E. Gassman.

Branch Philadelphia.— Secretary-treasurer, H. Chernow.

Executive Board.— P. Dallas, F. Roffino, B. Briganti, F. Holtz, P. Bleeker, P. Totti, L. Giliote, J. Malatesta, C. Maegel, J. Winn, J. Probst, A. Rolleri, C. Berndort, J. Scanzarolli, A. Cairoli, W. Uram.

Branch Brooklyn.— Secretary-treasurer, J. Drimmer.

Executive Board.— A. Demos, J. Antonion, A. Holmes, S. Frey, F. Shultz, J. Anderson, S. Weiss, A. Mueller.

Lunchroom Workers' Section.— Secretary-Treasurer, H. Koenig.

Executive Board.— Bodak, Slobodjin, Jery, Pytlar, Greenberg, Wheeler, Budny, Koch, Salomkai.

From all of the foregoing it is quite apparent that this Federation of Hotel Workers is in all respects a revolutionary organization based upon the One Big Union principle, having for its objective the establishment of a new social order, and the seizure of industry.

It is also evident that its propaganda is calculated to stimulate the so-called "class struggle," and to point out the "Principle that the worker has only one enemy, that is, the boss." (See p. 3, October 5, 1919, issue of the "Hotel Worker.")

CHAPTER IV

Journeymen Bakers' and Confectioners' International Union of America

The growing tendency to transform trade unions into revolutionary industrial unions which is being affected by diligent and continuous propaganda of Socialists, Communists, I. W. W. and other allied groups, is well illustrated by the record of a conference of Journeymen Bakers' and Confectioners' International Union of America which took place on October 25, 26, 1919, in the Labor Temple, in New York City.

On the second day of the conference the record states:

> "At two o'clock Comrade Dieners called the meeting to order again. The credentials of the I. W. W. delegation were read. The conference decided to admit the committee and to allow it to take the floor for ten minutes.
>
> "George Speed explained, as the speaker of the I. W. W. delegation, the objects of the industrial union which are recognized by the whole working class movement. There was no debate concerning this point.
>
> "Then a vote was taken on the resolution and the motion of Local Union No. 164, which was the most far-reaching proposals on point 5. (This point dealt with 'Our Attitude on the Question of the Industrial Union.') They were carried, in the following form:
>
>> "Be it decided that the Journeymen Bakers' and Confectioners' International Union, as an independent organization, resolves to accept the principle of industrial organization but that it, at the present juncture, shall not join any existing industrial union. For the time being, the efforts of the union shall, on the main, be devoted to the organization of the bakery workers; as soon as this work is completed, the organization of an industrial union shall be started." (Page 4 of the official organ of the union known as the "Free Voice.")

This was the first convention of this organization.

There was a proposal to get in touch with the International Federation of Workers in the Hotel, Restaurant, Lunch Room and Catering Industry with a view to determining the advisability of merging with that federation in the organization of One Big Union for all workers in the food industry organized on an industrial basis. A committee consisting of August Burckhardt, secretary of the organization, Gus Ritter and Herman Gund, was appointed on behalf of the central committee.

The report of this committee is printed in the February, 1920, issue of the "Free Voice." This committee had a conference with the Hotel Workers' Federation and summarizes the report as follows:

> "If a big union shall be formed it can be done only by the amalgamation of the two organizations at present existing, the Federation of Hotel Workers, and the journeymen bakers, which are closely related and are pretty similar also in their management and their kind of leadership.
>
> "It must be mentioned that this amalgamation once it becomes a fact will of necessity exert a great moral pressure on those separate unions which are still undecided — but which are considering the question. These unions feel that here is the only solution of the problem, but, as explained in the foregoing, there is still indecision in their ranks on account of certain antiquated notions."

This report shows that progress is being made towards the organization of One Big Union along I. W. W. lines to control all the workers in the food industry in this State, as well as in a greater part of the country.

The attitude of this organization toward other elements of the radical movement is further illustrated by certain resolutions which were adopted at the first annual convention above referred to. They were proposed by the general secretary, August Burckhardt, and unanimously carried. The first of these resolutions reads as follows:

> "In consideration that the New Yorker 'Volkszeitung,' the only workingmen's paper of the Germon tongue, always and fearlessly stands for the interest of the progressive working class in all its fights.
>
> "Be it resolved, that we indorse the editorial attitude of this newspaper to the full extent, and that we recommend to our German speaking members to regard the New Yorker 'Volkszeitung' as their official organ, and to work for its circulation among all workers of the German tongue."

The text of the second resolution is as follows:

> "In consideration that our best friends and advisors are being martyrized by the capitalistic system, in the present period of worst reaction, and have been thrown into jail for long terms.
>
> "Be it resolved that the Journeymen Bakers' and Confectioners' International Union of America, assembled in its first convention, does everything in its power in order to open the gates of the jail to those comrades, men and women, and particularly to Comrade Eugene V. Debs."

The membership of this organization on December 31, 1919, is reported in their official report as 4,621. A large portion of the membership is apparently German, the official paper being published both in German and in English.

CHAPTER V

Brotherhood of Metal Workers' Industrial Union

In 1909, a split occurred in the International Association of Machinists and the disaffected group organized the Brotherhood of Metal Workers which has since been organized into an industrial union, having for its motto " The One Big Union for All Workers in the Metal Industry."

The organization publishes a monthly paper entitled the " Metal Worker," edited by F. G. Biedenkapp, general secretary and treasurer of the organization; the associate editors are Stephen Bircher and Morris Sorkin. The organization's present headquarters are in the Rand School Building, 7 East 15th street, New York City.

In the November 1919 issue of this paper there appears an article which states:

> " The long delayed plan for the amalgamation of all Independent Unions within the Metal Industry is now being completed and will soon be submitted to the rank and file of the different unions represented in the conference now taking place.
>
> " Those present at the various meetings held represented either officially or unofficially the following organizations:
>
> " Brotherhood of Chandelier, Brass and Metal Workers' Union.
>
> " Brotherhood of Metal Workers.
>
> " Dental Mechanics' Union.
>
> " Engineer and Firemen's Public Service Organization.
>
> " Inside Iron Workers' Union.
>
> " International Association of Machinists.
>
> " International Tinsmiths' and Metal Workers' Union.
>
> " Metal and Machine Workers' Industrial Union.
>
> " Metal Spinners' Union of New York and Vicinity.
>
> " United Auto, Aircraft and Vehicle Workers.
>
> " With a number of changes made in the Tentative Plan submitted by the Committee it appears as if the delegates were very well satisfied with their work up to date and they expect to complete it at the next meeting, which is to take place on Saturday, November 8th, at 2:30 P. M., in Room 409, 7 East 15th street, New York City."

The character and objective of the organization appears in the same issue of the paper, in an article entitled "Americanism," from which we quote the following:

> "The workers, not only of America, but of all countries, are determined to get the full value of the price they paid and will yet pay. There can be no peace until the workers not only control, but also own, the means of life, liberty, and happiness. To accomplish this, it necessitates the ownership of all industries by a government of workers, for the workers, which can and will be accomplished by the One Big Union.
>
> "No issue can be of interest to the worker unless that issue stands for the Brotherhood of Mankind, founded upon the principle of 'Do unto others as you would have them do to you.' A worker is a worker everywhere, regardless of where he or she first saw the light of day.
>
> "*This only can mean Americanism as the workers would understand it. In that sense let us have and hail Americanism.*"

The nature of the propaganda carried on in this union is made clear in an article in the March 1920 issue of the "Metal Worker" by F. G. Biedenkapp, from which we quote the following:

> "And yet, in the face of this overwhelming horror (the comprehension of which drives men insane), the governments of the various countries, including the United States, continue to support a system of capitalism which is solely and directly responsible for the war and all of its accompanying evils.
>
> "In the support of such a system the United States today is imprisoning and deporting men and women who are opposed to a continuation of capitalism, and who voice their sentiments regarding same. There is no clause in the Constitution of the United States which gives the government the right to interfere with the freedom of the press, speech and assemblage of its citizens, be they I. W. W., Communists, Socialists, or any other —ists; if it is a crime to impose a system as vile as the most poisonous reptile, then we are criminalizing the finest instincts of the human race."

As a further illustration of the character of propaganda used to fan the flames of discontent among the workers of this organization, we quote an article appearing on page 2 of the January, 1920, issue of the "Metal Worker" as follows:

"THE BANKRUPTCY AND DOWNFALL OF CAPITALISM

"By F. G. B.

"Great events forecast their shadows.

"The downfall of capitalism is no longer a question of doubt, but an assured fact.

"Historians of the next generations will record the years from 1914 up to their time as the great period of the World's War and Revolutions, which forced the power of control and dictatorship out of the hands of Capital and into the hands of Labor.

"They will speak of that period as the bloodiest time in the history of mankind. Their writings will speak of the present generation as the most destructive and legalized criminal since the time of man-made laws. Philosophers and analysists, fifty years hence, will give conclusive proof to the world that what today is going under the name of I. W. W.'ism, Communism, Anarchism and Radicalism in general, is but the unavoidable result of a mismanaged and exploited world of workers, under a system of capitalism and militarism.

"They will show by the exposures of secret understanding and written agreements, that the capitalist class of all countries, the bankers, brokers, industrial magnates, and big business men had an understanding with the elected officials of their respective governments to scheme and frame up riots, mob lynchings, charges of attempt to overthrow the government by violence, arson and murder.

"They will show that the most dastardly, cowardly and inhuman acts of bestiality were committed by the hired gunmen, private detectives and other degenerated imbeciles of Capitalism, under the false cry of Patriotism and Americanism.

"They will show that the very persons responsible for these outrages never cared anything about America and its people, but merely sought to provide and maintain their hold upon the natural wealth and resources of the country for their own selfish purposes.

"They will show that the very men and women who are being ruthlessly thrown into foul prisons for years without ever having a trial, and when finally brought to trial, never given half a chance to defend themselves, and then sentenced to terms of imprisonment from two to thirty years, that these men and women were not guilty of the charges brought against them. They will show that the men and women being deported today as alien enemies and dangerous radicals were in reality such who advocated Americanism as our forefathers fought for 150 years ago — under the slogan 'No taxation without representation.'

"They will show that the outrageous raids of the day, carried on by the Lusk Committee and the Department of Justice, with the loud approval of Capital, against political and industrial organizations of a progressive and radical nature, were nothing else than acts of violence against a suffering people and a gross violation of the Constitution of the United States.

"They will show that the great daily, weekly and monthly publications were owned body and soul by the money masters of the day, and used as propaganda mediums to mould the minds of the great mass of people to the acceptance of exploitation.

"They will show by producing now buried evidence that gold was paid to capitalist-hired journalists to write and print malicious, false and dastardly statements about workers who went out on strike for a better living; deliberately falsifying the true meaning of the names of such organizations as were opposed to Capitalism, whether politically or industrially.

"They will show that gold was paid by the henchmen of capitalists to anyone who was willing to debase himself in the interest of profits, even to the extent of committing murder upon the working class to keep the workers down.

"They will show that the courts of today were owned and controlled by Capital, which instructed the issuing of injunctions, forbidding workers to go on strike under penalty of being sent to jail.

"They will show by evidence already before us in the form of the demand by the bankrupt countries of Europe upon the governments of the United States, Japan, and others, of the unimaginable sum of $35,000,000,000, on the mere promise to pay it back if they live long enough, that the whole system of Capitalism was already in its last stages of consumption, and undergoing its death struggle, and that no power of mankind, no matter how brutal and atrocious, could have saved it.

"And, finally, they will prove by figures and facts how Capitalism lived upon the sweat and brow of Labor. How Labor produced everything and got nothing, while Capitalism, which produced nothing, got everything, and that this was possible only because of the ignorance of the great mass of workers, who did not realize that life was a gift of nature and could exist only upon the labor power of the workers and not upon the glint of stored-up gold.

"The annals of history will record the death struggle of Capitalism now going on as its last struggle for Life."

The methods by which the organization advocates the attainment of its objective are clearly illustrated in an article entitled "Industrialism" in the December number of the "Metal Worker" on page 4, as follows:

"The Ballot Box may be, and is, no doubt a means to more liberty and privileges so far as social conditions are concerned, but as to *Industrial Democracy* — that can be achieved only on the *industrial* field through *industrial* action carried on by the organized workers of an *industrial* union — by use of the *General Strike*.

"*Industrial Unionism* means combined strength of the workers within the industry (not trade) in which they are engaged, brought about by having all workers of an industry belong to the same industrial union with but one constitution to guide them, and that constitution should be based clearly and uncompromisingly upon the *Class Struggle*.

"*Industrial Unionism* means that when, for instance, a strike occurs in a plant where, say, a dozen different trades are employed, such as pattern makers, moulders, machinists, brass workers, polishers, electricians, and helpers of all kinds, including time clerks, shipping clerks, porters, etc., proper industrial action would demand that all of these workers, while having their own locals, should belong to one and the same *industrial* union, with but one constitution to guide them. In this case it should be the *Brotherhood of Metal Workers' Industrial Union,* because metal is the basic material used in a plant employing the mechanics above named.

"*Industrial Unionism* as represented in the Brotherhood of Metal Workers means that the workers themselves would decide as to what to do—strike or not strike—and *not* the officials. The members who make up the organization and pay the piper are the ones to say what kind of a settlement *shall* or *shall not* be made.

"*Industrial Unionism* means that it would not be possible for one set of craftsmen to scab on the others, since they would *all* be concerned in the calling of a strike. It would not be a case, for instance, of machinists going out on strike while the polishers and buffers remain at work as they do now, or vice versa.

"*Industrial Unionism* means that everybody that works in the plant or plants for one and the same boss, would fight against that boss at *one* and the *same* time, all together—*one for all and all for one.*

"So, friend reader, if you know of anyone that thinks he can lick the bosses any other way, tell him he still has a whole lot to learn. Tell him to forget the old *craft* line and organize *industrially.*"

The relations between this organization and the I. W. W. were indicated by a statement in the "Metal Worker" on page 4 of the issue of February, 1920, as follows:

"In an interview today Mr. Biedenkapp told a representative of the 'Times' that his organization was not a dual organization, nor was it affiliated with the I. W. W., although he wished it to be understood that his organization was not antagonistic to the I. W. W."

This organization has already established international communications and has become affiliated with the International Metal Workers' Federation, and the question is now before the union whether it shall send delegates to the next International Congress to be held in April of this year at Berne, Switzerland.

The call for this Congress is in part as follows:

"According to the resolutions of the Seventh International Metal Workers' Congress at Berlin, 1913, the next Congress was to take place in 1916 at Vienna. The war rendered that impossible. Time and place could no more be considered. Even today the place fixed upon at the time is out of the question, no less than any other town in the former belligerent countries. And since my manifesto of January last has practically remained without response, the next Congress cannot be held this year, for according to paragraph 13 of our Federal Statutes, six months must elapse between the invitation to and the holding of the Congress. The invitation must be made by the secretary after consultation with the Central Committee.

"In accordance with these rules, I am again addressing myself to the members of the Central Committee, with the urgent request immediately to consider the following proposals:

"(1) To hold the Eighth International Metal Workers' Congress in April, 1920, in a neutral country."

This notice has apparently been acted upon and the proposed Congress is to be held in April of this year at Berne, Switzerland.

Throughout the propaganda of this organization continuous attacks are made against the American Federation of Labor and all other conservative organizations of workmen.

It is apparent that the leaders of this organization work are in complete harmony with all other radical groups for the purpose of spreading the so-called class consciousness and to stimulate the spirit of revolution in the workers of the particular industry in which they operate.

The following are local lodges in and about Greater New York:

New York Lodge, No. 1 — Meets every Friday, 8 P. M., 227 East 84th Street, New York City.

Winthrop Lodge, No. 3 — Meets every first, third, fifth Friday, 8 P. M., Labor Lyceum, 949 Willoughby Avenue, Brooklyn.

Progressive Lodge, No. 4 — Meets every Monday, 8 P. M., Labor Temple, 243 East 84th Street, New York City.

Bushwick Lodge, No. 5 — Meets every Tuesday, 8 P. M., Labor Lyceum, 949 Willoughby Avenue, Brooklyn.

Harrison Lodge, No. 10 — Meets every second and fourth Wednesday, 8 P. M., Labor Lyceum, 15 Ann Street, Harrison, N. J.

Metropolitan Lodge, No. 11 — Meets every second and fourth Friday, 8 P. M., 169 Garrison Avenue, Maspeth, L. I.

Newark Lodge, No. 14 — Meets every Friday, 8 P. M., Labor Lyceum, 704 South 14th Street, Newark, N. J.

Hudson Lodge, No. 16 — Meets every second and fourth Tuesday, 8 P. M., Engle's Cafe, 105 Bowers Street, Jersey City, N. J.

Elizabeth Lodge, No. 19 — Meets every Thursday, 8 P. M., 652 Fulton Street, Elizabeth, N J.

Plumbers Supply Workers' Lodge, No. 30 — Meets every Tuesday at 69 St. Marks Place, New York City.

Outside Erectors Lodge, No. 31 — Meets every fourth Thursday of the month, at 200 Blum Street, Union Hill, New Jersey.

Plumbers and Fitters Lodge, No. 32 — Meets every Thursday at 94 Clinton Street, New York City.

CHAPTER VI

Amalgamated Clothing Workers of America *

The radical and socialistic tendencies which developed in the locals of the United Garment Workers of America, an organization affiliated with the American Federation of Labor, resulted in the exclusion of a number of Socialist delegates at the convention of that organization held in Nashville, Tenn., in October, 1914.

The excluded delegates constituted themselves a separate convention, elected a general executive board and Sidney Hillman general secretary. The action thus taken was ratified by principal locals of the union in Chicago, Rochester, Baltimore and New York, all of which had fallen under control of the Socialist Party of America.

The new organization continued to use the name United Garment Workers of America, and made application to the convention of the American Federation of Labor held in Philadelphia in that year for recognition. This was denied.

A special convention was called by the new organization which took place in New York on December 26 to 28, 1914, at which time the name Amalgamated Clothing Workers of America was adopted. The change was rendered necessary by reason of the legal action taken by officers of the United Garment Workers of America, which still remained affiliated with the American Federation of Labor.

The character of this organization is shown by the preamble of its Constitution, which is as follows:

> "The economic organization of labor has been called into existence by the capitalist system of production under which the division between the ruling class and the ruled class is based upon the ownership of the means of production. The class owning those means is the one that is ruling; the class that possesses nothing but its labor power, which is always on the market as a commodity, is the one that is being ruled.
>
> "A constant and unceasing struggle is being waged between these two classes.
>
> "In this struggle the economic organization of labor, the union, is a natural weapon of offense and defense in the hands of the working class.

---

* See Addendum, Part I.

"But in order to be efficient and effectively serve its purpose the union must in its structure correspond to the prevailing system of the organization of industry.

"Modern industrial methods are very rapidly wiping out the old craft demarcations and the resultant conditions dictate the organization of labor along industrial lines.

"The history of the class struggle in this country for the past two decades amply testifies to the ineffectiveness of the form, methods and spirit of craft unionism. It also shows how dearly the working class has paid for its failure to keep apace with industrial development.

"The working class must accept the principles of industrial unionism or it is doomed to impotence.

"The same forces that are making for industrial unionism are likewise making for a close inter-industrial alliance of the working class.

"This inevitable process will ultimately lead to a universal working class organization, united along the entire line of the class struggle, economically and politically, instead of being split up and divided against itself, as it unfortunately is at present, under the antiquated teachings and methods.

"For the consummation of this great end the education of the working class is most essential. This must therefore be a very important part of the mission of the labor movement.

"Every oppressed class in history achieved its emancipation only upon its attaining economic supremacy. The same law operates also in the struggle between capital and labor.

"The industrial and inter-industrial organization built upon the solid rock of clear knowledge and class consciousness will put the organized working class in actual control of the system of production, and the working class will then be ready to take possession of it." (Vol. I, No. 1, March 9, 1917, "The Advance," the official organ of the Amalgamated Clothing Workers of America.)

Like all of the other subversive organizations its tactics are those of the class struggle. Its ultimate object is to take possession of the industry. Its principles and methods are almost identical with those of the Workingmen's International Industrial

Union. It constitutes a typical example of revolutionary industrial unionism, being founded on the One Big Union idea.

The general attitude of the organization and its leaders, toward the government of this country, may be gathered from scanning the pages of its official organ, in English, the "Advance," in the earlier issues at the time the Government of the United States declared war on the Imperial German Government.

In Volume I, No. 5, of the "Advance," being the April, 1917, issue, there appears a proclamation with the following headlines:

> "Workers are urged to protest on May Day against all wars."

The text of the proclamation is as follows:

> "Members of Amalgamated Clothing Workers of America are urged by general office to prepare for demonstrations May 1, against slaughter of toilers in quarrels of masters—will pledge loyalty to international labor movement.
>
> "The general office of the Amalgamated Clothing Workers of America has issued a call to all members to participate in the celebration of International Labor Day on May 1st as part of the great protest of all workers against war. In a letter to all district councils, joint boards and local unions the General Secretary says:
>
> "GREETING:
>
> "The First of May is again at hand. If there ever was urgent necessity for the working class to celebrate this universal holiday, it is now.
>
> "The European War, began two and a half years ago, is still raging. Oceans of blood are flooding the civilized world. Labor of centuries is being destroyed. A continent laid waste. The roar of cannon is the only voice that is now heard throughout Europe and in a good part of Asia.
>
> "At the time of this writing the catastrophe is also threatening our country. By the time this is read to the members we might be one of the powers engaged in the terrific slaughter.
>
> "And just at this time freedom has scored her greatest triumph in the successful Russian revolution. Czardom lies buried in its own filth. Democracy and freedom are now enthroned in the great Russian Empire.

The triumph of democracy in Russia has found an echo in the hearts of the German people and the foundation is shaking under the throne of despotism in Prussia.

"Never before was there such an historic occasion for the working class to raise its voice in protest against oppression of all forms, against the crime of war in particular and in the proclamation of universal proletarian solidarity.

"Last year, and the year before last, we called upon our members to give full expression to the spirit of May Day because on the European continent the workers could not speak and we had to speak for them. We did our duty to keep alive labor's voice and raise a mighty protest against the war carried on in another hemisphere.

"Today we have the additional duty of protesting against war by our own country, against saddling the yoke of militarism upon the working class at home.

"It is to make this protest as effective as the situation calls for, and it is likewise for the purpose of giving full expression to our joy over the birth of freedom in Russia, that the May Day celebration of this year must be such as to send a message of warning to our murder-loving masters and a message of hope and encouragement to our fellow-workers.

"You are, therefore, called upon to immediately make all preparations for the coming May Day Celebration." (Pages 1031–33, stenographer's minutes, Committee Hearings.)

The comment made in the issue of April 6, 1917, of the "Advance" on President Wilson's war message is also a clear indication of the attitude of the organization:

"President Wilson is a master of the English language and there can be no doubt that he exercised all the care called for by the occasion in framing his message. We humbly submit, however, that if the word 'American' be substituted for 'German' and the word 'capitalism' for 'dynastics' the German people may with full propriety address that statement to the American people.

"Capitalism wants war and war there will be, regardless of the will of the people. The people were not consulted here as they were not consulted in any other country."

An editorial appearing in the issue of March 9, 1917, of the "Advance," closes with the following paragraph, which discloses the character and object of the organization quite clearly:

> "We have unfurled the crimson banner of the Amalgamated Clothing Workers of America for the tens of thousands of workers to rally around it. It is bearing a message of hope and salvation for the workers. Our banner will never be furled before we reach the goal — the emancipation of the working class."

And again in an article in the March 16, 1917, issue entitled "High Cost of Living," page 4, appears the following illuminating paragraphs:

> "The labor union that accepts capitalism as a finality can hold out no hope for the workers in the face of the above condition.
>
> "Only the labor organization that recognizes the class struggle as a means for the abolition of the misrule of capitalism, holds out hope for the working class. While it organizes the working class for its emancipation it affords them all the relief conditions may permit from the evil of the high cost of living, as well as from all other evils inherent in capitalism." (Pages 1029–33, stenographer's minutes, Committee Hearings.)

This organization is in reality an industrial arm of the Socialist Party of America, working for the objects of that party, carrying out in every detail the program announced by that party in the war proclamation and program adopted at the St. Louis Convention in April, 1917, and seizing upon the critical conditions created in this country by the war as a moment opportune for increasing the so-called class struggle. It has gained control of the clothing industry in the State of New York, and in many other of the industrial centers.

In the city of Rochester every clothing manufacturer was compelled, under threat of strike, to sign up agreements with this organization and all have done so with the exception of Michael Sterns & Company.

In New York City they practically control the labor market in this industry.

In his testimony before this Committee James P. Holland, president of the State Federation of Labor, in answer to the question: "Has it ever come to your attention what the principles of the Amalgamated Clothing Workers are with reference to government and the control of industry?" Mr. Holland said, "A. They do not believe in the government. They preach it today even behind closed doors, and some of them even have preached it outside of the doors. There is not a place where one of the speakers goes that he does not ridicule the form of government of the United States. Only a few weeks ago one of their speakers was in Buffalo, and at McKinley square spoke — I think his name was Walden, I would not be positive of his name — when he ridiculed the government and the method of doing business. . . . ." (Page 694, stenographer's minutes, Committee Hearings.)

The means employed by the Amalgamated Clothing Workers of America to gain control of industry is perhaps best illustrated by their participation in the textile strikes of Lawrence, Mass., and Utica, N. Y. Although the latter strike was technically the strike of the textile workers, the textile workers union was, at that time, a new organization ill-equipped to carry on such a strike. The direction of the strike, therefore, devolved in large measure upon the experienced leaders of the Amalgamated Clothing Workers. For some time an attempt had been made to organize the textile industries of Utica into locals of the Amalgamated Textile Workers' Organization.

A strike was called in the latter part of August. A description of the methods employed by the strike organizers to effect their purpose was given to this Committee by Captain John R. Wright, of the Utica police. Captain Wright testified that organizers of the Amalgamated Clothing Workers of America, and the newly created Amalgamated Textile Workers had been working in Utica some time prior to the strike, holding secret meetings, and that the principal agent sent there for that purpose was one Paul Blanchard. The working men and women who joined the new union were largely Poles, Italians and some Syrians. Meetings were held in different parts of the city, and in West and East Utica. The strike was called on the 28th of August. In describing what followed Captain Wright said:

"They paraded around in mass form. There would be as many as two or three or four hundred in their picket lines. They would go in front of the mill and they would picket back and forth on the sidewalk single file. During the time that the people were going to work they would picket; when they would come back at noon or night time, and intimidate the people as they went by where we could not keep close watch on them."

In answer to the question whether there was any threatened violence, Captain Wright said threats were made to the workmen who still worked at the mills "that they would burn up their houses and kill them, or kill some member of their family if they continued to work. The intimidation was in the night time mostly. They would go out in groups from house to house and intimidate the workers in that manner by threatening them with bodily harm, or burning their buildings, or something of that kind. . . . We found by questioning different people that they were out on strike more through fear than through dissatisfaction. There were a great many, especially among the women, who were entirely satisfied with their wages, because they were getting from $20 to $30 a week, and as high as $35. . . . In one place, in East Utica, they carried out their threats by setting fire to a building in the night time. We were never able to get the ones that did that." (See stenographer's minutes, Committee Hearings.)

Several riots occurred after which the merchants along Bleecker street, for a mile and a half, were compelled to close their shops through intimidation, and to post in their windows a placard stating, "*Closed in protest to police cossacks.*" In reference to this matter Captain Wright said, "They went to the merchants along Bleecker street and Tilden avenue, probably a mile and a half, a body of twenty to fifty men, and invited them to close their places, and place one of these placards in their window. If they refused to do it, they would smash their windows in. The Police Department, with our limited number of men, were all located at the mills, so that I could not possibly take them up into Bleecker street to stop this thing."

The nature of the propaganda which fired the hatred of the workmen not only against their employers, but also the government, may be gathered from reading the speeches made by the agitators who represented this union. A typical example of the speeches made is one by an agitator named Ouderkirk, from which we quote the following:

"The time has come when you should use your brains and your hands to keep the scabs out of the mills. If it is necessary for some to go to the electric chair, the gallows, we will go, but where we leave off there will be many more to carry on our banner. The Amalgamated will open co-operative stores and we will not deal with the profiteers. We will be free from Democraticized, Catholicized scab, whether he is an American or just a plain gink. It is you that produce the nice automobile, the fine steam yacht, the Parlor and Pullman cars and all the wealth for the capitalists and instead of you using them you get the second-hand bicycle, a dusty, dirty old coach and have your sons sent to France to fight for these damn profiteers. Go out to the mills and keep the scabs from work. Keep them out any way. There is no use of disguising it any longer. It is a battle, go out and fight it. They tell you that they will not deal with the outside agitators or with the Amalgamated, but they will deal with John D. Strain, that $5,000 per year agitator, to keep you in poverty. They are all organized. The Chamber of Commerce; the Employers' Association is nothing more than a union of the bosses and a criminal union at that. It is up to the workers of this city to break up this criminal union. They are digging graves for themselves and we will see that they are ducked into them. They try to do all in their power to crush and disorganize you but we can stand and overpower the whole damned bunch." (See stenographer's minutes, pp. 1765–6, Committee Hearings.)

In another speech he said: "Strike and strike hard, and we will receive better wages and better conditions, and when the time comes that they tell us they cannot afford to pay us, then we will say, 'All right, we'll take it over and run it ourselves,' and if this is Bolshevism, I say, as Patrick Henry did, 'Make the best of it.'"

This strike was carried on by the combined Amalgamated Clothing and Textile Workers, who publish a paper entitled, "The Clarion," in which Paul D. Blanchard is named as editor, with offices at 670 Bleecker street, Utica, N. Y.

The propaganda of this organization reaches its members through the publication of the following periodicals: "The

Advance," the official English organ, which is published at 31 Union square, New York City, and which circulates largely in New York State; the "Fortschritt," a weekly printed in Yiddish; the "Industrial Democracy," in Polish, and "Industrial Democracy," in Bohemian; "Rabochy Golos," in Russian, and "Il Lavoro," in Italian.

For the circulation and character of the propaganda carried on in these periodicals see the section of this report dealing with newspapers.

CHAPTER VII

The Amalgamated Textile Workers of America *

An industrial union under the domination of the Socialist Party, and having a revolutionary objective is the Amalgamated Textile Workers of America. This organization is an outgrowth of the Lawrence, Mass., strike in 1919, which was promoted and assisted by the Amalgamated Clothing Workers of America. The relationship, therefore, between the organization which we now describe and that of the Amalgamated Clothing Workers of America is extremely close. The new organization took shape at a meeting held at Labor Temple, 14th street and Second avenue, New York City, on April 12, 1919, by a group of textile workers representing textile employees of Lawrence, Paterson, Passaic, Hudson County, N. J., and the New York Knit Goods Workers.

In explaining the success of the new organization A. J. Muste, general secretary of the Amalgamated Textile Workers, says:

> "They were being advised and encouraged by the great Amalgamated Clothing Workers of America." (March 27, 1920, issue "The New Textile Worker.")

The object of the organization is revealed in the article from which we have just quoted. Mr. Muste says:

> "And let us remember that the most fitting way to celebrate our anniversary is to dedicate ourselves anew to the glorious task of building One Big Union for the textile workers of America; a class conscious, honest, democratic, responsible and fighting organization; the Amalgamated Textile Workers of America. Everywhere a new day is dawning for the workers. We must do our share."

The statement of principles contained in the preamble of the constitution adopted by this organization is practically identical with those of the Amalgamated Clothing Workers of America. It shows that the organization is based upon the class struggle; that it repudiates the conservative organizations of trade unions, and that the purpose of the organization is to bring about the seizure of the industry by the workers. It is in full harmony and accord with the principles advocated by the Socialist Party of America, as well as the more radical groups.

---

* See Addendum, Part I.

The preamble of the constitution is as follows:

"The economic organization of Labor has been called into existence by the capitalist system of production, under which the division between the ruling class and the ruled class is based upon the ownership of the means of production. The class owning those means is the one that is ruling; the class that possess nothing but its labor power, which is always on the market as a commodity, is the one that is being ruled.

"A constant and unceasing struggle is being waged between these two classes.

"In this struggle, the economic organization of Labor, the union, is a natural weapon of offense and defense in the hands of the working class.

"But in order to be efficient, and effectively serve its purpose, the union must in its structure correspond to the prevailing system of the organization of industry.

"Modern industrial methods are very rapidly wiping out the old craft demarcations, and the resultant conditions dictate the organization of Labor along industrial lines.

"The history of the Class Struggle in this country for the past two decades amply testifies to the ineffectiveness of the form, methods and spirit of craft unionism. It also shows how dearly the working class has paid for its failure to keep apace with industrial development.

"The working class must accept the principles of Industrial Unionism or it is doomed to impotence.

"The same forces that have been making for Industrial Unionism are likewise making for a close inter-industrial alliance of the working class.

"This inevitable process will ultimately lead to a universal working class organization, united along the entire line of the class struggle, economically and politically, instead of being split up and divided against itself, as it unfortunately is at present, under the antiquated teachings and methods.

"For the consummation of this great end the education of the working class is most essential. This must, therefore, be a very important part of the mission of the Labor Movement.

"Every oppressed class in history achieved its emancipation only upon its attaining economic supremacy. The same law operates also in the struggle between Capital and Labor.

"The industrial and inter-industrial organization built upon the solid rock of clear knowledge and class consciousness will put the organized working class in actual control of the system of production, and the working class will then be ready to take possession of it."

The headquarters of the organization is at 113 East 26th street, New York City. Its official organ is "The New Textile Worker," a weekly of which A. J. Muste, secretary of the organization, is editor; associate editor, Russell Palmer; general treasurer, Matthew Pluhar.

The nature of the intellectual stimulus received by members of this organization is made clear by naming the speakers chosen for the mass meeting of New York Locals scheduled to be held on April 12, 1920, at Cooper Union, to celebrate the first anniversary of the Union's organization. They are Sidney Hillman, president of the Amalgamated Clothing Workers of America; Abraham Shiplacoff, Socialist Alderman of New York City; Arturo Giovannitti, an extreme radical with marked anarchistic tendencies; Scott Nearing of the Rand School of Social Science; Elizabeth Gurley Flynn, of the Workers' Defense Union; and Henry Jaeger, also of the Rand School of Social Science. Each of these speakers is thoroughly committed to the proposition of revolutionary action on the part of workers in order to overthrow the government as now constituted and substitute therefor the co-operative commonwealth.

The general tactics employed by this organization in dealing with industrial disputes have been described in the preceding chapter dealing with the strike in Utica of August and September, 1919.

The progress of organizing the union is illustrated by the number of locals which have taken headquarters.

These are as follows:

Allentown, Pa.— Room 11, Stiles Building, Hamilton street.

Chicago, Ill.— Local One (Knit Goods), Local Two (Textile Trimming Workers), 1145 Blue Island avenue.

Local Hudson County — 347 West street, W. Hoboken, N. J.

Local Lawrence, Mass.— 175 Essex street.

New York, N. Y.— Greater New York Knit Goods Workers, 802 Broadway, Brooklyn.

Textile Trimming Workers, 233 East 14th street, New York City.

Silk Workers — 1152 Second avenue.

Local Passaic, N. J.— 52 Second street.

Local Paterson, N. J.— 90 Market street.

Philadelphia, Pa. Local One — (Cloth Workers) — 188 Diamond street.

Local Two (Knit Goods) — 1202 Race street.

Local Providence, R. I.— 1753 Westminster street.

Local Utica, N. Y.— 670 Bleecker street.

The following leaflet used in the campaign to recruit membership in this union illustrates the methods employed to approach prospective members, and in it can be observed the principles and policies for which the union stands:

"TEXTILE WORKERS

"The Amalgamated Textile Workers of America is the Union that is lining up all the textile workers of America, and there are a million of them, in one big organization.

"It was organized April 12–13, 1919, in New York City, Lawrence, Paterson, Hudson County, N. J., Passaic and New York textile workers taking part in the first convention.

"WE STAND FOR:

"1. Democratic Control.— The rank and file rule in the A. T. W. of A., not officials. All officers are elected, all laws passed, by referendum vote. Final decisions in strike action rest, after consultation with the National office, with the Local membership.

"2. Industrial Organization.— All the workers in the shop in one union, and not divided up into the old fashioned craft unions that cannot accomplish anything in these days of production on a large scale.

"3. The freeing of the workers from exploitation and autocracy. We believe the workers are entitled to get *all* they earn. We believe that it is un-American that in industry bosses should be czars and kaisers, and the workers have practically nothing to say about his job.

"4. Organization and education of the workers, by the workers, as the means to freedom.

"OF THE TEXTILE WORKERS
"BY THE TEXTILE WORKERS, and
"FOR THE TEXTILE WORKERS.

"The purpose of this organization is to bring the American principle of democracy into the textile mills.

"This organization holds that it is necessary for a free people to have a voice and vote as to how the places in which they spend the greatest part of their lives — the mills — are to be run.

"This organization is of the textile workers, the tens of thousands of workers who have been repeatedly betrayed and misled by self-seeking union officials. Those workers who, to the great satisfaction of the textile manufacturers, have been divided and sub-divided into weak craft organizations by labor mis-leaders. The thousands of workers, American born and foreign, who produce millions of dollars worth of textiles, and who get a mere pittance in return for their labor. This organization, the Amalgamated Textile Workers of America, is of these tens of thousands of textile workers now banded together in One Big Union.

"It is run by the textile workers. Its national officers are elected by referendum. The delegates to its conventions are elected by referendum. The general executive board is elected by referendum. Every law passed at the national convention must be voted by the membership through the referendum.

"No national official can order the members of any local union to strike unless the members of that local union so decide by majority vote. No national official can order them back to work, nor sign a contract for any local union, nor make a settlement for any local union. The rank and file decides and disposes of its affairs, and with them alone rests final decision in settling disputes with their employers.

"It is run by the textile workers, and no assessments can be levied unless so voted by a majority of these workers.

"That the A. T. W. of A. is for the textile workers; to better their conditions; to increase their wages, shorten the hours of labor and secure more freedom in the shops, is no more a promise.

"In the short time of its existence, because the membership has the initiative, because they are imbued with the spirit of class consciousness and solidarity, because they have the whole-hearted support of enthusiastic and conscientious officers, many things have already been accomplished for the textile workers.

"Greater things will be accomplished by a greater amalgamated, and the textile worker who lines up with this organization at once, brings nearer the day of greater health and happiness to himself and his family; brings nearer the day of freedom and democracy for the workers in the textile industry.

"WHAT WE HAVE ACCOMPLISHED IN EIGHT MONTHS

"Organized tens of thousands of workers.

"Locals in Greater New York (seven), Utica, Fulton, Hudson County, N. J., Passaic, Paterson, Trenton, Bayonne, Englewood, Phillipsburg, Philadelphia (three), Easton, Allentown, Reading, Rockville, Norwalk, Stafford Springs, Mystic, Providence, Burrillville, New Bedford, Taunton, Plymouth, Chelsea, Lawrence, Maynard, Clinton, Waltham, Fitchburg, Nashua.

"*Carried the great Lawrence strike to successful conclusion. Result, forty-eight hour week in cotton and woolen industry in North.*

"*Forty-four hour week established in silk industry in Hudson County, N. J., Paterson and New York City. After short and well-fought strikes.*

"*Forty-six hour week, minimum wage, twenty per cent. increase, union recognition for thousands of knit goods workers in New York.*

"*Forty-four hour week, minimum wage, large increases for Chicago knit goods workers.*

"*Forty-four hour week and wage incrases for the dyers of New York, Paterson and Allentown, some of the worst exploited workers in the whole country.*

"Twenty to twenty-five per cent. increases in Rockville. Conn.

"Twenty-five per cent. increases in Utica, N. Y., after seventeen weeks' strike. Because of this heroic fight of the

Utica Workers, there was *a general twelve and a half per cent. increase in the textile industry in December,* 1919.

"Wage increases and improved conditions in Philadelphia, Fulton, Burrillville, New Bedford, Chelsea, Passaic, Bayonne, Englewood and other places.

"*Don't you want more wages?*

"*Don't you want shorter hours?*

"*Don't you want better shop conditions?*

"*Don't you want better food, clothing, housing and a better life for your wife and children?*

"Others are getting these things. Why not you?

"*Wake up!*

"Textile workers, ours is the biggest industry in the country. But we are the lowest paid of all workers.

"*All we need to do is to get together. Then only can we improve our conditions. Now is our chance! The union to carry America's textile workers to victory is here!* Join the A. T. W. of A. at once. In order to reach all the workers in the industry, we have organizers who speak all languages.

"*The Local in your town is at*...................

"Look it up, and become a member. If there is no Local in your town, write to the National office, A. T. W. of A., 113 East 26th street, New York, N. Y. They will send all necessary information about the organization.

"*Do it now!*"

"Membership Application

Name ....

Address ....

Where employed ....

Kind of work ....

Send this application to.......................
or to the National office."

CHAPTER VIII

The International Ladies' Garment Workers Union*

The International Ladies' Garmen Workers Union is organized along industrial lines and shows marked radical tendencies. The preamble of the constitution illustrates that it is founded upon the principles of the class struggle; that it adopts the One Big Union idea and seeks to bring about the overthrow of the present system of society. We give the preamble here in full:

"PREAMBLE

"Whereas, The history of the world and of the labor movement has shown that progress is best accomplished by organization, and

"Whereas, Industry has become organized and concentrated to such an extent that the individual worker is powerless against the oppression of the profit-seeking employer:

"Therefore, We, the Workers engaged in the production of ladies' garments, have

"Resolved, That the only way to secure our rights as producers and to bring about a system of society wherein the workers shall receive the full value of their product, is to *organize industrially* into a class conscious labor union politically represented on the various legislative bodies by representatives of a political party whose aim is the abolition of the capitalist system so that we may be able to defend our common interests, and we have

"Further resolved, That to accomplish this purpose, the workers in this industry should be organized locally into local unions and that these local unions should be effectively bound together so as to mutually strengthen each other."

"With this object in view we have established the International Ladies Garment Workers Union through which we hope to organize all workers engaged in every branch of the ladies' garment-making industry, and through which we shall co-operate with organizations of workers in other industries, either by affiliation with the American Federation of Labor or otherwise."

It is closely affiliated with the Socialist Party of America, and stands for the principles and tactics advocated by the party. Its

* See Addendum, Part I.

official organ "Justice" is published weekly. It is discreet in its news and editorial column, and few inflammatory articles are found. However, reference is constantly made to conditions in Soviet Russia, and always with approval.

It is affiliated with the Workers' Defense Union of which Elizabeth Gurley Flynn is the leader, and with which F. G. Biedenkapp of the Metal Workers' Union is secretary. The headquarters are located at 31 Union square, New York City. The president is Benjamin Schlesinger, and secretary-treasurer is E. Baroff. The editor of its official organ "Justice" is S. Wyonopsky, and the business manager is E. Lieberman.

This Union recognizes the need of educating its members in Economics, Sociology and other cultural subjects so that they may be prepared to conduct and manage the industry if their program of seizure is carried out.

In a report signed by Fania M. Cohn, Vice-President of the International Ladies' Garment Workers' Union, printed in the American Labor Year Book for the year 1920, page 204, we find the statement:

> "The International Ladies' Garment Workers' Union began its educational work in 1914 in conjunction with the Rand School of Social Science. About 150 members of the Union were sent to the school to receive instruction in Labor Problems, the History of the Trade Union Movement in the United States and abroad, Economics, Sociology and other cultural subjects."

In order to reach the large membership of the organization, permission was obtained from the Board of Education of New York City to use public school buildings for educational centers and extensive courses of training are now carried on. Much of the work is excellent but throughout there is a manifest purpose of getting before the membership of the organization the principles of government and of industrial reorganization which are the basis of Socialist psychology.

CHAPTER IX

The International Fur Workers' Union of the United States and Canada

The workers in the fur trade have come together in an independent union having much in common with the other industrial unions that have been described in this report, and which is thoroughly under the influence of the Socialist Party of America.

Their organization is called the International Fur Workers' Union of the United States and Canada. Its jurisdiction extends to the following branches of the fur trade:

Fur cutters.
Fur squarers.
Fur operators.
Fur nailers.
Fur finishers and liners.
Fur ironers and examiners.
Fur beaters and cleaners.
Fur pointers.
Fur glove makers.
Fur cap makers.
Fur band makers.
Fur persian makers.
Fur skull makers.
Fur rug makers.
Fur muff bed makers.
Fur head and tail makers.
Fur trimmings and fur pieces.
Fur garments of all descriptions.
Fur hand dressers.
Fur hand shavers.
Fur machine shavers.
Fur machine fleshers.
Fur floor workers.
Fur dyers.
Fur hand and machine pickers and shearers.
Fur scrapers.
Fur combers.
Fur dyeing of all descriptions.
Hatters' fur workers.

Sheepskin workers.
Sheepskin tanners.
Sheepskin dyers.

Although the principles of the organization set out in the preamable are not as outspoken as many of the unions that have been described, it will be seen that the class struggle is the basis for their organization. The preamble of the constitution which is in force in 1920 is as follows:

"PREAMBLE

"Whereas, A struggle is going on in all the nations of the civilized world between the oppressors and the oppressed of all countries, a struggle between the capitalist and the laborer, which grows in intensity from year to year, and will work disastrous results to the toiling millions if they are not combined for mutual protection and benefit.

"Experience has demonstrated that the inroads made into our craft have been due to lack of unity and confidence in each other, and recognizing that unity, guided by intelligence, is a source of strength that can withstand all attacks, and that by intelligent organization we acquire the discipline that enables us to act together, concentrate our strength and direct our efforts to the desired end.

"Therefore, for the purpose of promoting unity of sentiment and action among those employed at the fur craft in the United States and Canada, and joining them closely together for mutual protection, we shall endeavor to further our interests and promote the following:

"To thoroughly organize and elevate the fur craft.

"To establish a perfect apprenticeship system.

"To establish uniform wages for same class of work, regardless of sex.

"To reduce the hours of labor to eight hours per day.

"To substitute arbitration for strikes whenever possible to do so.

"To seek the abolition of sweat-shop and child labor.

"To promote the use of the union label as the sole guarantee of union made furs.

"To support the union label of all other bona fide trade unions, and assist all trade unions to the full extent of our power."

The official news of the organization is carried in a monthly paper entitled "The Fur Workers," published in Long Island City, New York. This paper indicated the tendency of the organization.

Soviet Russia is continually praised in this organ, and the advantages of the regime set up in that country over the form of society existing in America is persistently pointed out.

A page devoted to "Echoes of the Labor Movement" has to do solely with information respecting the Amalgamated Clothing Workers of America, amnesty for political prisoners, nomination of Debs for President, activities of the united labor education committee, referring particularly to "Classes for trade union officials, a course in labor economics, with Dr. Scott Nearing as instructor, meets every Thursday from 1:30 to 2:30 P. M. in the office of the Neckwear Makers' Union, 7 East 15th street."

Another indication of the character of the organization may be gathered from the fact that Dr. Judah L. Magnes is chairman of the conference committee of the fur industry.

In the March, 1920, issue of the "Fur Workers" an article entitled "Americanism: true and false," by Dr. Magnes, we find the following:

> "Soviet Russia stands as a beacon on the hilltops, cheering on the agonizing peoples with a light in the darkness, with new hopes and philosophies, with wondrous longings. . . .
>
> "During the war Americans were welcomed 'most everywhere,' because the plain peoples of Europe had in mind the old America, the America of freedom, of liberty, of independence, the America that had always given shelter to political refugees and to the tens of thousands of families that had come here seeking work and education and happiness. But now, when the peoples of Europe are freeing themselves of their tyrannous masters and of the old systems that wore them down, what a disillusionment in the answer that comes to them across the seas from America! Deportations of political prisoners, the torture of conscientious objectors in dark, damp prisons, suppression of political parties, the invasion of private homes without warrant, the clubbing of innocent men and women, the prostitution of newspapers and other publications, the breaking up of economic organizations, and all the while the land flows with milk and honey and our population is bidden to rest easy

under the official declaration that America has had her revolution and has achieved finality in political, economic and spiritual ideas. . . .

"Let us use intelligence and help to organize the great forces of labor, and let us throw in our lot with the lot of free and liberty-loving men everywhere. Let us uphold the ideal of internationalism in the name of the old America that was free and is now dead, and in the name of that new America which is now in the process of being born!"

The general office of this union is at 9 Jackson avenue, Long Island City, New York.

The names of the officers are as follows:

Morris Kaufman, New York City, general president.

Andrew Wenneis, Brooklyn, general secretary-treasurer.

Harris J. Algus, New York City, first vice-president.

Hyman Sorkin, New York City, second vice-president.

H. F. Somins, New York City, third vice-president.

Lucchi Pietro, Brooklyn, fourth vice-president.

O. Shachtman, Chicago, fifth vice-president.

Albert Roy, Montreal, sixth vice-president.

Charles Gmeiner, St. Paul, seventh vice-president.

Benjamin Lederman, Boston, eighth vice-president.

Max Zarchin, New York City, ninth vice-president.

The officers of the various joint boards affiliated with this organization are as follows:

Joint Board Furriers' Union, New York, 109 East 29th street, New York City.

Joint Board Fur Cap and Trimming Makers' Union, 133 Second avenue, New York City.

Joint Board of Fur Dressing Industry, 949 Willoughby avenue, Brooklyn.

Joint Board Fur Workers of Newark, 161 Belmont avenue, Newark, N. J.

Joint Board Fur Workers of Twin Cities, 206 Dakota Building, St. Paul, Minn.

Joint Board Fur Workers of Montreal, 182 St. Catherine street, E. Montreal, Canada.

Names and addresses of secretaries of local unions:

Local 1, Chas. Fendler, 114 Nagle avenue, New York City.

Local 2, Gustav Schubert, 949 Willoughby avenue, Brooklyn, N. Y.

Local 3, Philip Silberstein, 949 Willoughby avenue, Brooklyn, N. Y.

Local 4, John Gorsky, 192 Nassau avenue, Brooklyn.

Local 5, Sam Malamud, 111 East 7th street, New York City.

Local 10, M. Spivack, 614 East 140th street, New York City.

Local 15, I. Hoffinger, 1652 Washington avenue, Bronx.

Local 20, A. L. Merkin, 133 Second avenue, New York City.

Local 25, Morris Katz, 161 Belmont avenue, Newark, N. J.

Local 30, Benj. Lederman, 694 Washington street, Boston, Mass.

Local 31, Mrs. W. A. Boyd, 3747 Cook avenue, St. Louis, Mo.

Local 35, Frank A. Currie, 152 Bay street, Toronto, Ont., Can.

Local 40, Frank A. Currie, 152 Bay street, Toronto, Ont., Can.

Local 45, O. Shachtman, 26 W. Quincy street, Chicago, Ill.

Local 50, Josef Tichy, 219 N. Gilmore street, Baltimore, Md.

Local 51, A. L. Merkin, 133 Second avenue, New York City.

Local 52, Charles Gmeiner, 206 Dakota Building, St. Paul, Minn.

Local 53, David Granoff, 2533 S. Galloway street, Philadelphia, Pa.

Local 54, Rubin Feilschuss, 161 Belmont avenue, Newark, N. J.

Local 55, Max Geller, 173 Amboy street, Brooklyn, N. Y.

Local 56, Robert Schwartz, 7315 Perry avenue, Chicago, Ill.

Local 57, Charles Gmeiner, 206 Dakota Building, St. Paul, Minn.

Local 58, Lucchi Pietro, 949 Willoughby avenue, Brooklyn.

Local 59, John Gorsky, 192 Nassau avenue, Brooklyn, N. Y.

Local 60, A. L. Merkin, 133 Second avenue, New York City.

Local 61, Charles Rizzo, 64 Ellery street, Brooklyn, N. Y.

Local 62, Frank Cappola, 47 Mt. Prospect avenue, Newark, N. J.

Local 63, A. L. Merkin, 133 Second avenue, New York City.

Local 65, Frank A. Currie, 152 Bay street, Toronto, Ont., Can.

Local 66, Albert Roy, 182 St. Catherine street, East Montreal, Quebec, Can.

Local 67, Albert Roy, 182 St. Catherine street, East Montreal, Quebec, Can.

Local 68, Albert Roy, 182 St. Catherine street, East Montreal, Quebec, Canada.

Local 69, Robert Behling, 2123 N. Dupont avenue, Minneapolis, Minn.

Local 72, Harry Smith, 617 Lamont street, N. W., Washington, D. C.

Local 73, Emil Eisenberg, 915 Rosemore avenue, Pittsburg, Pa. P. O. South Hills Branch.

Local 75, Jack Boobar, 1329 Pacific avenue, Atlantic City, N. J.

Local 76, Harry Siegel, 34 Russel street, Hartford, Conn.

Local 77, Julius Schleider, 438 Newton avenue, Shorewood, Wis.

Local 79, Robert E. Barth, 361–29th street, San Francisco, Cal.

Local 80, Clara C. Bock, 59 Lexington avenue, Detroit, Mich.

Local 81, A. Rogat, 2500 Verde street, Los Angeles, Cal.

Local 79, Helen F. Earth, 3711 20th street, San Francisco, Cal.

SUB-SECTION IV

SPREAD OF SOCIALISM IN EDUCATED CIRCLES THROUGH PACIFIST, RELIGIOUS, COLLEGIATE SOCIETIES, ETC.

SUB-SECTION IV

SPREAD OF SOCIALISM IN EDUCATED CIRCLES THROUGH PACIFIST, RELIGIOUS, COLLEGIATE SOCIETIES, ETC.

INTRODUCTION

It is the purpose of the Committee in the succeeding chapters of this section to show the use made by members of the Socialist Party of America and other extreme radicals and revolutionaries of pacifist sentiment among people of education and culture in the United States as a vehicle for the promotion of revolutionary Socialist propaganda. The facts here related are important because they show that these Socialists, playing upon the pacifist sentiment in a large body of sincere persons, were able to organize their energies and to capitalize their prestige for the spread of their doctrines.

The group here treated is of particular significance because it is recruited largely from among educators, authors, newspaper writers and the clergy, thus giving entree to the public prints, influencing opinion, and invading public office during the war, also attempting to influence the foreign policy of this country toward Soviet Russia.

In dealing with the subject, the Committee has used only original documents which have come into its possession through subpoena of the files of the National Civil Liberties Bureau and other organizations. The Committee does not seek to question the motives of any person or question the patriotism of the persons named, but in all instances allows the documents to speak for themselves.

These chapters may, in large measure, tend to explain the sympathetic attitude toward Soviet Russia and to the radical and revolutionary groups in this country which is maintained by numerous periodicals and newspapers, as will more fully be shown in the section of this report dealing with propaganda.

CHAPTER I

Emergency Peace Federation — October, 1914, to March, 1915

In reading the following report it will be well to recall a statement made during the war by Eduard David, Socialist member of the German Reichstag, in discussing "a good peace" for Germany: "Our tactics," said Dr. David, "would be to promote peace currents in enemy countries." (N. Y. Times, June 16, 1917.)

As we go on we shall see that in the United States not only has Socialism been used to spread "peace currents," but the pacifist movement has been exploited to inject Socialist and internationalist ideas among the educated classes. The two organizers who from 1914 on were most successful in the employment of this propaganda were Mme. Rosika Schwimmer, of Budapest, Hungary, representative of the International Suffrage Alliance (but in reality German agent), and Louis P. Lochner, a Socialist of German descent and sympathies, who for several years had been Secretary of the International Federation of Students.

Mme. Schwimmer appears to have been the first to engage in a peace movement favorable to Germany. In October, 1914, she spoke before the Woman's Peace Party of Minneapolis and fired her audience into passing a Tentative Program for Constructive Peace, calling for a Conference of Neutrals with the object of bringing peace to warring Europe. This Neutral Conference note, from 1914 on, continued to be sounded more and more insistently in the Pacifist-Socialist movement.

When her work was done in Minneapolis Mme. Schwimmer went to Chicago. There, in co-operation with Louis Lochner and Jane Addams, was held "A preliminary meeting early in November, which arranged for a citizen's mass meeting at the Garrick Theatre on December 5th. The speakers were Mme. Rosika Schwimmer, of Hungary, and Mrs. Pethick-Lawrence, of England. The large and enthusiastic audience present unanimously endorsed the project for a movement for constructive peace, and many individual signatures were received from persons anxious to co-operate." [1] Out of this grew a "meeting of delegates of various peace, labor, civic, religious, social and other organizations, on December 19th," six of the twenty-one represented being Socialist and others, as, for example, the Single Tax Club and the Woman's

[1] Minutes Emergency Peace Committee Meeting, Dec. 19, 1914.

Trade Union League, being sympathetic to Socialism. "The meeting was called to order by Miss Jane Addams, chairman pro-tem. The minutes of the previous meeting were read by the secretary. The committee, consisting of Messrs. Mez, Kennedy and Lochner, was appointed to submit a digest of the various proposals for the settlement of the World War and therefrom construct a minimum program."[1] Dr. John Mez is described as "of Munich, Germany, president of the International Federation of Students, 'Corda Fratres,'" and Mr. John Kennedy as "secretary of the National Socialist Party." The outcome of this second meeting was the forming of the Chicago Emergency Peace Federation, with a "tentative program for constructive peace" as its formal purpose.[1]

When we come to examine this program we find it, first of all, to be "in line on the whole with those of other international organizations," among them, the National Executive Committee of the Socialist Party, the South German Socialist Democrats, the Anti-War Council of Holland, the Internationl Peace Bureau, and the Union for Democratic Control of England. And when we analyze the specific planks of the platform we find — in the arguments for "neutralization of the seas, and international action to remove *economic causes* of the war," as well as in those "against the export of munitions, any balance of power league or any war indemnities"[1] — the same formulae which characterized German Socialist propaganda in this country. (From Tentative Program for a Constructive Peace.[2]

After the Emergency Peace Federation was committed to these policies, Lochner, as its executive secretary, at once set January 17, 1915, as the date for another mass meeting; and about the same time he and Miss Addams began to lay plans for a national conference of pacifists for February 27th and 28th, this date being chosen to meet the convenience of the National Executive Committee of the Socialist Party. This is illustrated by a letter from Carl D. Thompson of the Socialist Party, dated January 4, 1915, to "Miss Addams and Mr. Lochner":

> "DEAR FRIENDS.— Just a word as to the reason that I would like very much to have the Peace Conference on February 28th, if possible.
>
> "The National Executive Committee of the Socialist Party has a meeting here in Chicago on March 6th. Some

[1] Emergency Peace Federation Bulletin, 1914–15.
[2] Frau Schwimmer is reported as co-author of this program.

WOMAN'S PEACE PARTY

MASSACHUSETTS BRANCH

NATIONAL CHAIRMAN
JANE ADDAMS

TEMPORARY HEADQUARTERS
12 OTIS PLACE
BOSTON, MASS.

STATE OFFICERS

CHAIRMAN
MRS. J. MALCOLM FORBES

VICE-CHAIRMEN
MRS. FANNIE FERN ANDREWS
MRS. LOUIS D. BRANDEIS
MISS HESTER CUNNINGHAM
MRS. NORWOOD P. HALLOWELL
MRS. HENRY COOLIDGE MULLIGAN
MISS KATHARINE MCDOWELL RICE
MRS. QUINCY A. SHAW
MRS. ROBERT GOULD SHAW
MRS. WILLIAM B. THURBER
MRS. JAMES H. VAN SICKLE

EXECUTIVE SECRETARY
MRS. ELIZABETH GLENDOWER EVANS

TREASURER
MRS. J. PENNINGTON GARDINER

CHAIRMAN ON PUBLICATIONS
MRS. EDWIN D. MEAD

CHAIRMAN COMMITTEE ON MEETINGS
MISS ROSE STANDISH NICHOLS

March 22d, 1915.

Mr. Louis Lockler, Sec'y.,
116 So. Michigan Ave.,
Chicago, Ill.

My dear Mr. Lockler:--

Mr. Edward G. Smith, the one pacifist in Great Britain who from the very first moment of the war kept up his pacifistic attitude and who wrote that excellent little pamphlet of which I gave you a copy, "Letter of an Ex-pacifist," wrote me lately a letter, copy of which I am enclosing here.

I beg you to make up a parcel of every kind of printed matter that you have used for the Chicago Federation of Peace Forces, the programme of the February conference and the adopted platform and rules. Will you also have a parcel of the Women's Peace Party printed matter made up and will you please send the whole thing straightway to Mr. Smith.

I would advise you to keep on with him. It is very worth while. He is a fine worker and a fine speaker. He is Secretary of the Arbitration League, but had the same experience you had with your Chicago Peace Committee in the beginning. They suppressed his activities and hampered all his efforts. The Meads and the other Pacifists who used to go to London know Mr. Smith very well personally.

I take this opportunity also to say Good Bye to you, as I leave on the 7th of April. I go to Christiana, Stockholm and Copenhagen before I proceed to The Hague and will try to see statesmen and pacifists of these countries. I know that I have shocked the professional pacifists of this country very much and that they will be very glad to know that they have got rid of me and that they will have a quieter time. Nevertheless, I am very glad to have seen that it is not the people nor the nation which lacks enthusiasm, but the leaders are to be blamed for everything that is blameable. It was a great comfort to have found in you such a fine-spirited, active pacifist and I am sure you will keep things alive and going.

May I suggest to you to send a circular to all the Women's Peace Parties and to tell them that a part of their work is to get the men organized into the National Peace Federation. I see that the men are most eager to join any organization that is ready for action. They are only unwilling to join Peace

FACSIMILE OF ORIGINAL LETTER — ROSIKA SCHWIMMER TO LOUIS P. LOCHNER

Mr. Louis Lockler -2-

Societies where they are treated like children who have to sit still and look at the professionals who teach. People, like children, want activity. But I don't need to teach and preach to you. You know these things yourself. I have wonderful meetings on and on.

May I beg you to keep me informed and to send me every kind of printed matter that you may publish in the future to my temporary address Care Mrs. Wulffton-Pathe, 35 van Stolkweg, Hague, Netherlands. It depends upon the decisions of The Hague Conference whether I go home to Hungary or whether I will have to work in another part of Europe. As the correspondence with other countries is at any rate better to go through Holland, this Dutch address may remain until I notify otherwise.

I wonder whether you could let me have those photographs which were sent for the use of your conference and of which I could make now good use, and I wonder whether I can do something for you in Europe. Be sure to let me know. My address until the 7th of April is Hotel McAlpin, New York.

With very best regards for Mrs. Lockler and a kiss to the dear little Peace baby, I am, with greatest consideration for all your work and with a warm handshake,

Yours sincerely,

Rosika Schwimmer

Please send W.P.P. printed matter for distribution to Rev. Harold Marshall Melrose Forum
Melrose, Mass.

Mr Charles Laird
Pres. of Forum
Brockton, Mass.

Mr Coleman
Ford Hall
Boston, Mass.

of the members will be here before that. So I think that if we can arrange to have the conference on the 28th of February we could get several of these to attend."

To this Lochner replied on January 6th:

"MY DEAR FRIEND THOMPSON.—I saw Miss Addams this morning and we talked over your letter of January 4th. Miss Addams asks me to say as far as she is concerned, she will only be too glad to have the national meeting take place on February 28th."

So much settled, Lochner concentrated his efforts for the moment in making the January 17th meeting successful.

On January 4th he wrote to a prominent New Yorker, urging assistance for the Emergency Peace Federation from the Carnegie Endowment in the form "of a subvention of $2,500. . . . "Would it not be feasible for the Association for International Conciliation to publish our Tentative Program with commentary for the widest possible distribution?"[1] The result of the correspondence which followed was an agreement that the Carnegie Endowment should pay a certain sum and traveling expenses to each speaker assigned to Emergency Peace Federation meetings, among them Dr. Mez, Mme. Schwimmer and Morris Hilquit.[2]

During this time Lochner was also busy corresponding with many other persons. He arranged with Carl Thompson to distribute the Program among Socialists;[3] thanked M. A. Stolar, of the Vegetarian Society for giving "peace publicity in Russian and Yiddish newspapers;"[4] urged Anthony Czarnecki to "interest the Arch-bishop in pushing the program,"[5] and begged Ethelwyn Mills, of the Women's Socialist League, "if you will just pass the word along on every occasion, I am sure that we can get a big turnout. We are counting on you Socialists to make the demonstration a memorable one."[6]

About this time Lochner was also engaged in an important correspondence with Dr. John Mez, "the young German, president of the International Federation of Students," who was then at one of its American branches, the Cornell Cosmopolitan Club. The

[1] Lochner to Nicholas Murray Butler, Jan. 4, 1915.
[2] Henry S. Haskell to Lochner, Feb. 5, 1915. Also Lochner to Haskell, Feb. 8, 1915.
[3] Lochner to Thompson, Jan. 4, 1915.
[4] Lochner to Stolar, Jan. 7, 1915.
[5] Lochner to Zaruecki, Jan. 5, 1915.
[6] Lochner to Miss Mills, Jan. 11, 1915.

correspondence between the two men, partly in German (early in January, 1915) showed clearly that Mez was Lochner's adviser, that they were intimate friends, equally sympathetic to Germany and in spreading "constructive peace ideas" in this country. In illustration of this we will quote from the translation of Mez's German letter to Lochner, under date of January 8, 1915:

> "DEAR LOCHNER.— Please wire a word on Saturday to Cornell Cosmopolitan Club for its Tenth Anniversary. . . . I expect in the near future the annual report of the Chicago Peace Society. . . . The German Peace Society ought to be founded now. Please ask permission to call on Mrs. Consul Singer, room 1608, La Salle Hotel, in order to discuss a meeting of organization."[1]

Lochner, though he took pains to deny his German sympathies to outsiders, showed every intention of following these directions to the letter,[2] all the while making ready for the January 17, 1915, mass meeting. When this came off it is curious to note, according to the Emergency Peace Federation Bulletin, that the meeting "without a dissenting voice, voted in favor of a nation-wide conference at Chicago on February 27th and 28th" — curious, because we know that on January 4, 1915, Lochner, Miss Addams, and Carl Thompson, of the National Socialist Party, had already definitely settled upon these exact dates for the February conference. Aside from the publicity story of the January 17th meeting we have a glowing account of it (along with other Peace meetings), in Lochner's report, under the heading of "Central West Department," Jan. 18, 1915. We quote from the report:

> "It will be to the everlasting credit of the Peace Committee of the Political Equality League that it brought to Chicago one of Europe's most eloquent women, Mme. Schwimmer, of Budapest, Hungary, Secretary of the International Suffrage Alliance. No matter where Mme. Schwimmer appeared, whether before the Association of Commerce or an auditorium of university students or a church, or a woman's organization, or a meeting of journalists, she stirred the hearts of everyone with her fervent appeal to America to stop the war by sending envoys to Europe. . . .
>
> "Almost coincident with Mme. Schwimmer came a noted

[1] John Mez to Lochner (in German), Jan. 8, 1915.
[2] Lochner to Mez, Jan. 11, 1915.

Englishwoman, Mrs. Pethick-Lawrence of London, England. For several weeks she was a guest of Miss Addams and came before many organizations with her 'Woman's Movement for Constructive Peace.'"

After mentioning Dr. Mez and two other "aggressive pacifist" speakers, Pastor Furnajeff of Bulgaria, and Dr. George Nasmyth of Boston, who both made fervent peace appeals, the report ends with the following statement:

"Through the efforts of Dr. Mez and Mme. Schwimmer it also appears likely that a German-American branch of the Chicago society will be organized in the near future."

Towards the end of January, 1915, Lochner began to receive some adverse criticisms of his peculiar peace policies from Arthur Call, of the American Peace Society:

"It's all right to stir up the animals and to advocate throwing all 'conventionality to the winds' and start out upon 'aggressive lines,' so long as you are not obliged to define 'conventionality' and 'aggressive lines.' I could say with equal sincerity, and I believe truth, that the one thing is needed just now is to remember 'conventionality' and avoid 'aggressive lines,' if I were permitted to define my terms."[1]

Lochner's defense — much clever verbiage covering adroit explanations and hedging — is a masterpiece of its hind.[2]

Another characteristic Lochner letter of this period was to Edwin H. Mead, of the World Peace Foundation of Boston who, unlike Mr. Call, was rather more sympathetic to the Emergency Peace Federation viewpoint. Here Lochner at once takes off the "peace" mask in confiding to Mead his ambition to draw into the Emergency Peace Federation "the rank and file of the people," other than pacifists, and his conviction that "the only hope of the Federation lies in keeping the organized peace societies in the background. . . . To give you an illustration: the packed theatre last Sunday at the Powers Theatre, at which the enclosed splendid resolutions were adopted without dissenting voice, and at which the constructive program for peace was carefully dis-

[1] Arthur Call to Lochner, Jan. 15, 1915.
[2] Lochner to Call, Jan. 18, 1915.

cussed, two-thirds of the audience, I believe, was made up of laboring men, traveling salesmen, who happened to be in Chicago for Sunday, and the like. In other words, our annual meeting of the Peace Society the day before had taken care of the regular converts, while the popular meeting on Sunday interested a great many new organizations."[1]

Perhaps, however, nowhere was the real scheme put as simply as in the postscript of a letter from Lochner to Jane Addams of August 19, 1917.[2]

"Who would have thought in February, 1915," writes Lochner to Miss Addams, "when you called the Emergency Peace Federation Conference that your dream for a federation of all liberal and peace forces would be so completely realized!"

That Miss Addams was further active in organizing the February conference is evidenced by a letter to her from Zevin, of the Jewish "Daily News," under date of February 14, 1915, promising for her peace sentiments, "full publicity in both our English and Yiddish departments."

The main preparatory work for the conference, however, fell to Lochner. His letter of invitation, for instance, to the secretaries of Socialist parties and labor unions was carefully differentiated from those to peace, religious and similar orders[3] — the name of Morris Hillquit usually being dangled before "the rank and file," while that of Jane Addams served as stock attraction for the pacifists. When it came to bringing into line a hybrid organization, such as the Chicago Ethical Culture Society, Lochner had his friend, Dr. Mez, on hand. They both spoke before this body on February 18, 1915, and both praised a certain peace plan "suggesterd by Miss Wales."[4] This plan, as will be seen later, was incorporated into the Conference platform.

As February 27th drew near and Lochner corresponded with more and more pacifists all over the country, he selected with unerring precision those on whose radical sympathies he could count. Thus he wrote, Jan. 25, 1915, to Miss Frances L. Dusenberry, of Chicago, the owner of a radical bookshop, enclosing copies of the tentative program:

> "At the suggestion of Mr. W. A. Stolar, I take the liberty of sending you 100 copies of the tentative program. . . .

[1] Lochner to Edwin Mead, Jan. 23, 1915.
[2] Lochner to Miss Addams, from Minneapolis.
[3] Form letters of invitation signed Lochner.
[4] Lochner to Arnold B. Hall, Madison, Wis., Feb. 19, 1915.

If you can pass these on to interested persons and if you can interest people in other cities, I hope you will do so."

About the same time Lochner wrote to Dean Keppel, commending Dr. Mez "as the best trained pacifist" speaker permanently for the Carnegie Endowment.

A Lochner letter dated Feb. 1, 1915, to J. Stitt Wilson, of Berkeley, Cal., sets forth:

> "There is every hope that we shall have a splendid Congress" (February 27th and 28th). "Now, we are definitely counting upon your being here at that time. In fact, the date of the Congress was set with reference to the meeting of the National Central Committee of the Socialist Party. Comrade Thompson told us that you would be here the week following and that he could practically guarantee your taking part in our meeting. Be sure not to fail us. You were the prime mover in this project and should be one of the principal speakers."

Other letters from Lochner at this period were:

To C. E. Parsons, of Grand Blanc, Mich., in reference to the question of delegates to the Conference, he advises: "If there are bodies that are not outspoken in support of our platform, but none the less interested and will become more so by hearing the discussions of the congress, by all means invite them to take part."

To Mrs. Fannie Fern Andrews, of the American School Peace League, Boston: "I hope by all means that you can arrange to be with us on February 27th and 28th. . . . We shall need your counsel and advice, for while the populace is applauding the speakers there must be some trained pacifists behind the scenes to see to it that the proper program is constructed and the proper resolutions passed."

To Stolar, the Socialist vegetarian, thanking him for the Russian translation of the Conference program, which had been published in "Novy Mir."

We quote from a letter of Lochner to Rabbi Hirsch, of Chicago, of Feb. 18, 1915: "There was another matter about which I wanted to talk to you. Our friend, Mr. Edwin D. Mead, whose sympathetic attitude toward the German point of view is of course well known to you, writes me that he will arrive here on Wednesday next and will be with us throughout the convention."

As to the major meetings of the conference we have no complete record; but through Lochner's correspondence early in March we learn a number of things concerning it:

That though Stitt Wilson could not be present, Hamilton Holt, Dr. Mez, Mme. Schwimmer, Dr. Mead and Mr. Hillquit all spoke and were paid by the Carnegie Endowment;[1] that Mr. Holt delivered a speech decrying all preparedness as "mob hysteria" and urging "that the United States lead the world in disarmament;"[2] that Mrs. Lucia Ames Mead, another Conference speaker and a very ardent internationalist, asked to have copies of the platform sent to "the foreign members of the Berne Bureau;"[3] that Dr. Emil Hirsch acted as chairman at one of the Conference sessions;[4] that the Emergency Peace Federation transformed itself into the National Peace Federation;[5] and finally, that, an International Plan for Continuous Meditation without Armistice, called the Wisconsin Plan for short, was incorporated into the regular platform.[6]

This plan, which was the one written by Miss Julia Wales of the University of Wisconsin, and praised by Lochner, Mez, Dr. David Starr Jordan and Dr. George Nasmyth, was briefly the old Neutral Conference idea expanded into a nebulous program for a premature and negotiated peace, as usual obliquely favorable both to Germany and internationalism.

As we read these and other formal peace documents of the period, the similarity of certain points with the program of the Russian Workmen's and Soldiers' Council of 1917 is somewhat apparent. In the case of the Wisconsin Plan it is interesting to note that its author, Miss Wales, though probably well meaning, was a strategist of no mean order, for in a letter to Jane Addams of November 14, 1915, Miss Wales, in referring to a manuscript copy of the Wisconsin Plan, wrote as follows: "What I wanted to do was to discuss it generally under the title of the 'Principle of Continuous Mediation,' and mention the present war only incidentally. People get hold of the idea more easily if they think of the plan only as a new device for the future, and then they make the application themselves without first getting on the defensive."

Another document on file, bearing a striking resemblance to later pronouncements, is called "A Plan for a Rehabilitation

---

[1] Lochner to Henry S. Haskell of Carnegie Endowment, March 6, 1915.
[2] Hamilton Holt to Lochner, March 15, 1915, enclosing résumé of address.
[3] Mrs. Mead to Lochner, March 11, 1915.
[4] Lochner to Dr. Hirsch, March 2, 1915.
[5] Lochner to Mme. Schwimmer, March 24, 1915.
[6] Lochner to David Starr Jordan, March 2, 1915.

Fund Contributed by Neutral Countries as a Substitute for War Indemnities."

Still another resolution passed at the February Conference provided for "a delegation of five to wait upon President Wilson in an endeavor to secure action" (for the Wisconsin Plan, of course). The President, however, never received this committee, even though Miss Addams was its leader.[1]

After these Conference records, one of the most important documents on file, is a letter from the National office of the Socialist Party, March 4, 1915, enclosing a bill from the "American Socialist," "for the display ad. which we ran of the Peace Conference."

Another letter to Lochner, dated March, 1915, is from Dr. Frederick Lynch, of The Church Peace Union urging. . . . "Let me know when you need more money."

Following these developments there is nothing of significance to record until March 24, 1915, when Mme. Schwimmer writes from Washington, D. C., announcing her sailing on April 7, 1915, "for Christiania, Stockholm and Copenhagen before I proceed to the Hague; and will try to see the statesmen and pacifists of those countries . . . It depends upon the decisions of the Hague Conference whether I go home to Hungary or whether I will have to work in another part of Europe." Mme. Schwimmer further requests that all peace and Emergency Peace Federation literature be sent to Mr. Edward G. Smith of London, "who has kept up his pacifistic attitude during the war. . . . The Meads and other pacifists who used to go to London know Mr. Smith very well personally. . . . May I suggest to you to send a circular to all of the Women's Peace Parties and to tell them that a part of their work is to get their men organized into the National Peace Federation? I see that the men are most eager to join any organization that is ready for action. They are only unwilling to join peace societies when they are treated like children who have to sit still and look at the professionals who teach . . . May I beg you to keep me informed and to send me every kind of printed matter that you may publish in the future to my temporary address, care of Mrs. Wulffen-Palthe, 35 van Stolweg, Hague, Netherlands? As the correspondence with other countries is at any rate better to go through Holland, this Dutch address may remain until I notify otherwise." As a postscript, Mme. Schwimmer adds: "Please send National Peace Federa-

[1] John Alyward to Lochner, March 10, 1915.

tion printed matter for distribution to the Rev. Harold Marshall, Melrose Forum, Melrose, Mass.; Mr. Charles Laird, Brockton, Mass.; and Mr. John Codman, Ford Hall, Boston, Mass.

Lochner, who replied to Mme. Schwimmer at once (March 24, 1915), was only too eager to follow her advice. He announced that Miss Addams was urging a Congress of Women at the Hague "to be followed immediately by one of men and women of the neutral powers. . . . I have just returned from a trip through Kentucky and you will be amused to hear that I had first to bring people to see that peace is desirable. They are very backward in their views there. . . . You may be sure that I gave them 'red hot stuff.' . . . Finally, may I not take this means of introducing to you a Miss Angelica Post, 218 West Springfield street, Boston, whom I have never met personally, but who, I take it from her letters has stood almost alone in Boston in urging upon her German fellow citizens that they abandon their jingoistic attitude and see whether something cannot be done to stop the war."

These letters are the last words to be heard in this country from either Mme. Schwimmer or Lochner for some months. We must therefore, leave the Emergency Peace Federation for the time being — with its fortunes to be taken overseas by Mme. Schwimmer. With her, or about the same time, forty-two other pacifist or radical American women, including Emily Greene Balch, Alice Hamilton, Leonora O'Reilly, Fannie Fern Andrews, Florence Holbrook, as well as Mrs. Pethick-Lawrence of England, sailed for Rotterdam, in order to attend the meeting of the International Congress of Women at the Hague on May 1, 1915. (From "Women at the Hague.") As will be seen, Lochner a little later followed with Jane Addams herself, as delegate to the Congress.

The next time we hear of The Emergency Peace Federation in this country is in Chicago, September, 1915, under its new name of the National Peace Federation.

CHAPTER II

National Peace Federation — September, 1915, to December 4, 1915

That Frau Schwimmer and her group were followed by Lochmer and Miss Addams in April, 1915, is evidenced by a picture post card of the S. S. *Rotterdam* (sent to an official of the National Peace Federation in Chicago) dated April 13 and signed "Jane Addams, Sophonisba Breckenridge and Louis P. Lochner."[1]

Concerning the activities of the group after reaching the Hague, we note from a memorandum of one of the National Peace Federation officials of the period:

> "During the summer of 1915, when Miss Jane Addams, Miss Sophonisba Breckenridge and Mr. Lochner (acting as special secretary to Miss Addams) went to the Hague, they organized with the assistance of different European delegates (including Mme. Schwimmer) the International Committee of Women for Permanent Peace. The British delegate Miss Chrystal McMillan, delegate from a Suffrage Alliance of England, is the present Recording Secretary of the International Suffrage Alliance. Miss Addams, Mr. Lochner and other members of Congress also went to Germany, giving lectures there."

Further evidence that these "Pacifists" were establishing European Headquarters for American Peace Socialists in 1915 may be found in the following notations on the letter-head of the Woman's Peace Party of New York City: "National Woman's Peace Party, Jane Addams, Chairman, Washington, D. C., Jan. 10, 1915; Woman's Peace Party of New York City, Mrs. Amos Pinchot, Chairman, Feb. 19, 1915; International Committee of Women for Permanent Peace, The Hague, Apr. 28, 1915."

We have indeed Lochner's written word for it that Miss Addams spent some of her time abroad "in interviewing the leading statesmen of the warring countries." (Form letter Sept. 16, 1915.)[2] Certain it is that by September Frau Schwimmer, Miss Addams and Lochner were all back in this country, co-operating presently with Miss McMillan (who seems to have been closely associated with Mme. Schwimmer's enterprises), in sending out under the auspices of the National Peace Federation

[1] See illustration.

[2] See Addendum Part I. The Woman's International Congress.

"The Manifesto issued by the envoys of the International Congress of Women." (Letter Oct. 17, 1915, from Albert H. Hall, Minneapolis, to Lochner.) There was also evolved a resolution in favor of a Mediatory Commission of Neutrals, generally called the Jane Addams Resolution. This, according to a form letter of Lochner, ". . . came out of a series of meetings, held by small but influential groups in New York and Chicago after the return of Miss Addams from the capitals of Europe. It attempts to secure action along the lines which Miss Addams (and others who have had an opportunity to study the European situation at first hand) as a result of her interviews with leading statesmen in the warring countries believes practicable" . . . (Form letter, Sept. 16, 1915.)

Concretely the Resolution urged ". . . the appointment of an International Commission, drawn from the neutral nations of Europe as well as the United States, which shall explore the issue involved in the present struggle and on the basis of its findings submit propositions to the belligerent nations, in the hope that such effort will not only clear the ground for final peace negotiations, but also influence such terms of settlement as will make for constructive and lasting peace." (From Jane Addams Resolution adopted by Henry Booth House, Chicago, Sept. 19, 1915.)

In connection with the Manifesto we quote from a letter to Miss Addams from Mr. Kellogg of "The Survey," dated October 8, 1915: ". . . I sent copies of the manifesto to Mr. Lochner. Miss McMillan and Mme. Schwimmer have copies and you have given one to Mrs. Mead. I fancy all four of them are to be at the San Francisco peace meeting, and it occurs to me that they might get together in some signal use of the manifesto on the 15th, and that word from you might get them to join in any plan rather than go their own ways. It could of course be read from the platform on that date. Mrs. Mead sent us ten days ago her address in San Francisco which we are running in an early issue as enclosed . . . Is there any way in which on or about the 15th something could be gotten out, some interview perhaps which would use this manifesto as a text and put the thing straight up to the White House? Why would it not be possible for Mrs. Mead, Mme. Schwimmer, Mr. Lochner and Miss McMillan to arrange for such a resolution at San Francisco?"

Though we have no acknowledgment of this letter from Miss Addams, we have one from Lochner to Kellogg, dated October 29, 1915, as follows: ". . . Enclosed is our next stunt." "Under another cover I am sending you additional copies."

No doubt Kellogg's suggestion of the manifesto being "used as a text and put the thing straight up to the White House" was the germ of the idea to organize meetings all over the country with the object of sending thousands of peace messages to President Wilson on November 8, 1915, all clamoring for a peace dictated by the inevitable Conference of Neutrals. Dr. George Nasmyth, for instance, wired Lochner on Nov. 1, 1915: "Send ten more sets, Nov. 8, Neutral Conference material," to which request Lochner complied on Nov. 2d, adding: "I am relying on Miss Balch and you to swing Massachusetts for us . . ."

Miss Chrystal McMillan's part in the program of the "Mediatory Commission of Neutrals" may be indicated by quoting from two letters, the first to her from Lochner of October 29, 1915. ". . . Under separate cover I am sending you a bunch of the material that we are getting out for a nation-wide demonstration. The very next day after you left we plunged into this job, *and I hope it was done to your satisfaction."* The second letter from Miss McMillan herself to Frau Schwimmer is dated Washington, D. C., Nov. 2, 1915, and reports some very ambitious efforts on her part in behalf of The Case of Continuous Meditation. . . . "Villard gave me an introduction to Lansing, Secretary Lane and Polk. . . . Kirchwey, though his time is much engaged with Sing Sing prison, is getting together some people likely to have influence on the President to bring pressure on him." . . . On the whole, Miss McMillan (who was one of the delegates to the 1920 Peace Conference at Berne this summer) could not report any definite success for her endeavors. She closes by hoping that Frau Schwimmer "will have a good meeting at Detroit and success with Ford."

During the series of these peace meetings in Detroit early in November, 1915, begun under the auspices of the Envoys of the International Congress of Women, one Rebecca Shelly telegraphed Lochner Nov. 3d as follows:

> "Parsons wants meeting under auspices of your Federation. I have agreed to it on Mme. Schwimmer's advice. . . . Angell to come but now ill. Have telegraphed Kirchwey and LaFollette. . . . Wire possible speakers. Send any literature wish distributed."

Lochner's answer reads:

"Charlotte Perkins Gilman can be had through us for fifty dollars and expenses. Mrs. Philip Snowden for hundred dollars net. Carl Thompson for fifty. Probably Dr. Mez would come from Washington."

The Parsons mentioned by Miss Shelly was the Rev. C. E. Parsons, an official of the National Peace Federation in Detroit, who wrote to Lochner on Nov. 6, 1915:

". . . A splendid impression has been made in Detroit by the mass meeting. . . . An impression that the meeting was a beginning of a series under the auspices of the Woman's International Congress was for some time prevailing, despite my constant endeavor to change it . . ." (referring apparently to Frau Schwimmer and Miss Shelly's decision to continue meetings under National Peace Federation auspices).

Lochner, in answering Parsons, said:

". . . I am rather sorry you are so emphasizing the fact that you worked hard to avoid the impression that the meeting was under the auspices of the Woman's International Congress. . . . The thing that I am just now interested in is that we immediately get a good bunch of money . . ."

Though Miss Shelly, Frau Schwimmer and Parsons (a member of the Flint, Michigan, Board of Commerce) were all excellent organizers, yet there had undoubtedly been difficulty in raising a sufficient "bunch of money" for Lochner's purposes. On October 26, 1915, when Frau Schwimmer had telegraphed to Dr. Kirchwey at Columbia College:

"Secretary Lochner of National Peace Federation prepared all material for organization of nation-wide meetings to be held November 8, to impress Wilson for Neutral Conference. Everything ready but lack one thousand dollars may spoil whole splendid work. Can you get this sum pledged through your friends immediately . . ."

and a similar appeal to Mrs. Joseph Fels at Philadelphia,— we know that Dr. Kirchwey at least was unable to meet her wishes. This is set down in a long letter to Kirchwey from Lochner, dated Nov. 2, 1915, from which we quote:

"Here in Chicago we hope to have about 50 simultaneous meetings rather than one big one. We want to get the White House bombarded with messages . . . We can probably use the entire machinery that we have set in motion several times now, and that we are hiding under the all-inclusive name of the National Peace Federation for getting up a tremendous protest against increased armaments."

He ends by offering to submit to Kirchwey "the underlying scheme for a National Peace Federation."

Now that we know the National Peace Federation, with its affiliated peace and civic societies, was merely an instrument of the International Congress of Women; that its envoys, Jane Addams, Mme. Schwimmer and Miss McMillan, were using the forces of the Peace Federation of this country in order to bring about a bombardment of the White House on November 8th, and that the hidden object of this peace drive was to create a protest against increased armament — the air is somewhat cleared and we can proceed to follow further developments of the campaign.

While Miss Shelly, Mme. Schwimmer et al., were busy in the field, Lochner at National Peace Federation headquarters in Chicago had naturally not been idle. As early as September 16, 1915, Lochner was forwarding the Jane Addams Resolution with his request for endorsements[1] to his followers. On October 26th he sent a telegram to Hamilton Holt, President of the Federation, which had the flavor of Mme. Schwimmer's own fund-raising messages: "Plans complete for simultaneous meetings throughout the country November 8th to practically force President's hand for Neutral Conference. Need thousand dollars at once from New York. Can you raise it by tomorrow? If not what is earliest possible date?" We have no answer on record from Mr. Holt.

On October 29th Lochner again sent out many letters working toward the November 8th demonstration. His letters to peace, civic, Socialist, fraternal, labor, business men's, religious and other societies, exhibit as usual in each case skillful differentiation.[2]

[1] From letter to Joseph J. Russell, Charleston, Mo., Sept. 16, 1915.
[2] Bulletin letters of October 29, 1915.

About this time several affiliated organizations of the National Peace Federation began to give valuable co-operation in the November 8th drive, among the Woman's Peace Party, through Crystal Eastman;[1] the World Peace Foundation, through Edwin C. Mead; [2] the Federal Council of Churches, through Rev. Martin Hardin;[3] and certain peace groups in Boston, through Dr. George Nasmyth. [4] Apparently things seemed to be going so well that a cablegram was drafted (in Mme. Schwimmer's handwriting) for Lochner to send to the Women's Peace Committee at Amsterdam. It reads as follows:

> "National Peace Federation organizing thousands of meetings throughout America for November eighth urging Wilson's co-operation to form Neutral Conference. Give publicity.— LOCHNER."

We have also on file the draft of a telegram, in Lochner's handwriting, to Mr. John Gavit, of the New York "Evening Post," which reads:

> "Can you see that Reuter and Wolff International News Service are informed that National Peace Federation, in response to urgent requests, is organizing nation-wide demonstration November 8th, urging Wilson to form Neutral Conference. Meetings to be held throughout the country. Hamilton Holt is president of Federation and Jane Addams vice-president.— L. P. LOCHNER, *Secretary.*

Though these messages throw further light on the European sources of the Lochner-Schwimmer workings in this country, if we are to follow closely the actual details of those plans, we must read Lochner's letter of November 4, 1915, to Frank P. Williams of the Buffalo Peace Society, who thought he could secure the co-operation of his local Congressman. In his letter to Williams, Lochner brings out a number of points:

> "We want to see the White House simply bombarded with messages. . . . Dr. Jordan will see the President four days later, and after consultation with Jordan last night— this confidential—I find that he thinks that will have a decided influence in making the President listen to his proposal. . . .

---

[1] November 1, 1915.
[2] Mead to Lochner, 1915.
[3] Lochner to Rabbi Hirsch, Nov. 2, 1915.
[4] Telegram from Nasmyth to Lochner, Nov. 1, 1915.

"I am sending you a bundle of manifolds and resolutions.

"As for the names of governors, senators, etc., I enclose a list herewith.

"When you speak to Congressman ——, it may be well to emphasize to him that what we are after is not primarily that the United States call the conference, but rather that it co-operate with the European neutrals, who, we understand, at least Sweden and Holland, are ready to act if they have assurances from us that we will act with them."

As for the aftermath of the campaign, we must rely principally upon the letters of the "departmental secretary," who, when Lochner accompanied by Dr. Jordan on his visit to President Wilson, attended to the correspondence of the National Peace Federation. This Secretary, then, writing "in behalf of Mr. Lochner and Miss Addams," took care to thank the co-operating friends of the Federation and to keep in touch with others, notably Mr. Kellogg of the "Survey" and Miss Julia Wales, author of the "Wisconsin Plan." To Miss Wales was sent, on November 12, 1915, the following suggestive letter, referring to the Jordan-Lochner conference with the President:

"I have just received the following telegram from Mr. Lochner:

'"Appointment decidedly worth while. Smith (Wilson) more mellow than David ever saw him and more inclined to listen. Had forty minutes with him and feel sure that he would not approve affirmative action from another country. I tried hard to make him absolutely commit himself but he refused to do that.'"

After this there is only to record in this connection a letter against preparedness from Jane Addams to Walter Fisher — "at Mr. Lochner's request" — and to refer again to the letter of November 3d from Chrystal McMillan, in Washington, to Mme. Schwimmer, in which she hoped that Mme. Schwimmer would have "good success with Ford in Detroit."

This brings us to the "Ford Peace Party," which, after much advertising and gathering of forces — once more under the generalship of Mme. Schwimmer and Lochner — set sail on December 4, 1915, with a strange collection of pacifists, radicals and newspaper men on board, "to get the boys out of the trenches before Christmas."

CHAPTER III

The Ford Peace Party

In the present records, the only reference to the organization of the Ford Peace Party is Miss McMillan's wish of November 3, 1915, that Mme. Schwimmer would have good success with Ford. Nevertheless, we know from newspaper files of the period (New York "Times" Dec. 5, 1915) that Mme. Schwimmer organized the party, that Lochner acted as general secretary, and that the strange admixture of pacifists, radicals, philanthropists, press representatives, adventurers and professional organizers, sailed for Stockholm on the Oscar II — the Peace Ship — December 4, 1915.

Besides Mr. Ford, who paid all expenses of the expedition,[1] there were on board, or connected with the undertaking in some way, persons of a certain importance not mentioned on the passenger lists. Among these were Rebecca Shelly, Lella Faye Secor and several officials of the Ford Motor Company.

Among the passengers actually listed (New York "Times," Dec. 5, 1915) we find the names of some thirty odd men and women afterward active in furthering "peace," pro-German or internationalist movements, many of whom are active revolutionaries today. Some of these propagandists merely gave prestige to the movement by lending their names; while others actually organized affiliated societies, which worked in turn against preparedness, our joining the Allies, conscription and the Espionage Act.

List of Persons of the Ford Peace Party Afterwards Active in Radical Movements

The Rev. Charles F. Aked, San Francisco.—"People tell me that Aked was so pro-German, even before he went on the expedition, that people used to get up and leave his church during his sermons." (Mrs. Ada Morse Clark to Lochner, August, 1917.)

William C. Bullitt, Philadelphia.— Famous for his attacks on the Peace Treaty, President Wilson, Lloyd George, and so forth. Well known radical.

Edwin Ralph Cheney.— Co-operated with the Emergency Peace Federation, 1917.

---

[1] From R. S. Neely of Ford Motor Co. to Lochner, May 22, 1917; Lochner to Neely, May 25, 1917; "The Case of Miss Balch," Jan. 26, 1917; and Lochner to Miss Kellog, May 12, 1917.

Mrs. Ada Morse Clark, Palo Alto, Cal.— Offered to organize for People's Council, etc., 1917.

Miss Grace de Graff, Portland, Ore.— Organizer for Emergency Peace Federation, 1917.

Mrs. Joseph Fels, Philadelphia. — Active in single tax movement.

B. W. Huebsch, New York.— Wrote Miss Shelly, July, 1916: "My Ford lecture devoted mainly to the idea of a Neutral Conference Committee came off successfully." Huebsch is now a publisher of radical books, and editor of "The Freeman."

Ellis O. Jones, Forest Hills, N. Y.— Co-operated in 1917 by sending a list of names to the Emergency Peace Federation; started a little "revolution" in December, 1918, in Central Park.

Christian Sorensen, Nebraska.— Organizer for Emergency Peace Federation, May, 1917.

Mrs. G. B. Latus, Pittsburgh.— Co-operated in 1917 with Emergency Peace Federation.

Mrs. J. Reece Lewis, Lansdowne, Pa.—A delegate to First Conference of Democracy and Terms of Peace, May 30, 1917.

Lola Maverick Lloyd (since divorced from Wm. Bross Lloyd of Chicago).— Co-operated and organized for Emergency Peace Federation, 1915; again in 1917. Also active in Conference and People's Council.

Lewis Maverick, San Antonio, Tex., brother of Lola Maverick Lloyd. Co-operated with Emergency Peace Federation, 1917, and also First Conference for Democracy and Terms of Peace.

Alice Park, Palo Alto, Cal.— Of the National Women's Suffrage Party. Organized for Emergency Peace Federation, 1917. I. W. W. sympathizer.[1]

Senator Helen Ring Robinson, Denver, Col.— Speaker for and sympathizer with Emergency Peace Federation, 1917.

Mrs. May Wright Sewall.— Co-operated with Emergency Peace Federation, 1917.

Mrs. William I. Thomas, Chicago.— Co-operated with People's Council, 1917.

Carl D. Thompson.— Official of National Socialist Party; and co-operated with Emergency Peace Federation, 1917.

Miss Julia Grace Wales, Wisconsin.— Co-operated with Emergency Peace Federation, 1917, and Author of "Wisconsin Plan."

---

[1]Alice Park to Roger Baldwin (Legal Defense, Vol. 1, p. 395); Alice Park to Roger Baldwin (Legal Defense, Vol. 1, p. 425): "Of all the pacifist workers in the U. S. since April, 1917, you have the most useful and most successful job."

Miss Nora Smitheman.—On staff of Soviet Bureau, New York City, 1919.

F. O. Van Galder, Rock Island, Ill.—Wrote to Miss Shelly, August 1, 1916: "Immediately upon my return I gave many talks before churches, clubs and societies on the Peace Expedition and have been on the stump fighting the attempt to commercialize our patriotism."

Mme. Malberg.—Finnish Socialist who recruited soldiers in Finland for German army in 1916. (Statement of member of Ford Party, 1920.)

G. F. Milton, Chattanooga, Tenn.—Wrote to Lochner May 8, 1917: "I appreciate your asking me to join the call of the meeting for May 30th, as your statement of principles meets my hearty approval. I fear, however, this is a little premature. I believe if you will wait a few weeks and allow events in Europe, especially in Russia, to develop, you will have some tangible European movement to which you can connect up with the ones in this country. . . . I am enclosing several editorial clippings which will indicate that I am working already along your own line." (Milton was president of the "Chattanooga News" in 1917.)

Thos. Seltzer.—Publisher of radical books.

Frederick H. Holt of Detroit.—(Letter from Lochner to Holt, August 27, 1917.)

As has already been noted, though the Ford Peace trip was generally ridiculed as the irresponsible venture of nebulous dreamers, Lochner and Mme. Schwimmer had in the undertaking a perfectly practical object. This was to effect a powerful international "Conference of Neutrals," to which the Ford pilgrims were to be delegates, and the foreign delegates of the Central Organization for a Durable Peace a sort of steering committee. The project, however, may be best set forth by quoting from a letter of Lochner, May 25, 1917, to R. S. Neely, of the Ford Motor Company, Long Island City:

> "As regards the question of a Central Organization at The Hague, I have seen with my own eyes a statement in writing made by Mr. Holt and countersigned by Miss Balch as member of the executive committee of the Neutral Conference, in which are sums, as I remember it, of one thousand kroner, promised for the support of each of the nine or ten study commissions of the Central Organization."

Another document which will no doubt explain the workings of the Ford Peace pilgrims once they reached the other side is "The Case of Miss Balch" — this a memoranda enclosed by Lochner with his letter to Neely:

"When Miss Balch, after due election to the position of alternate delegate to the Neutral Conference (the election made by the members of the Ford Expedition before disbanding at The Hague) was invited to come to Stockholm instead of Miss Jane Addams, whose illness prevented her from coming, the undersigned as general secretary of the conference invited Miss Balch to come to Stockholm; and in the letter, a copy of which the undersigned holds and the original of which is in the hands of Miss Balch, promised her that the payment of the substitute as well as her expenses would be met by Mr. Ford. Contrary to the advice of Mme. Schwimmer, then in supreme charge of the conference, I *did not* offer any honorarium besides (thought the European delegates were paid $500 per month plus expenses) because I felt that Miss Balch herself would not consent to such an arrangement. . . . Also when she left Stockholm early in July, 1916, she was given the definite task of organizing the August demonstrations in this country. During this time she was to have an expense allowance for her living expenses in New York, Washington, Detroit, . . ."

"(Expense account follows).

"In the opinion of the undersigned Mr. Ford should not only repay this sum but also compensate Miss Balch for the loss of interest.

"Respectfully submitted,

"(Signed) LOUIS P. LOCHNER."

In still another letter, this time from Lochner to Neely, the following additional information is set forth:

"I understand that either Mr. Holt (referring to Mr. Frederick Holt of Detroit), or yourself made that arrangement with the Central Organization at The Hague,, whereby they were to receive something like two thousand dollars. . . ."

Precisely why and how Mr. Ford became disillusioned — or perhaps illuminated — as to all the underlying motives of the expedition, we may never know, since we have only Lochner's vague explanation, "because Mr. Ford and I differed over the question of the wisdom of his continuing his work in Europe. I felt now that the war was imminent it was more necessary than ever to have an unofficial commission sitting in Europe, while he was of the opinion that with America's severance of diplomatic relations with Germany the whole game was up and all effort of that sort was worthless."

Nevertheless, it is on record that Lochner considered a great deal had been gained for the "cause" through the Ford Party.

In summing up, then, the results of the Ford peace Party, as far as we know, the venture did accomplish certain definite things: The "Conference of Neutral Internationalists and Pacifists" entirely financed by Mr. Ford was held in Stockholm from about March to July, 1917; Miss Balch was appointed to organize an American Neutral Conference Committee in New York on her return; the Central Organization for a Durable Peace was enriched by at least $2,000; and finally a definite break occurred between Lochner and Ford.

Miss McMillan, as has been noted, is still an officer of the International Suffrage Alliance; and Mme. Schwimmer has had the distinction of being the first Bolshevik Ambassador from Hungary to Switzerland in 1919, her career being cut short by the fall of Bela Kun. Since we did not hear of her again in America after 1915 (except through her disciples), perhaps then the Ford Peace Party may have served a useful purpose not generally understood.

During the spring of 1916, though we have no record of any peace activities in the United States, we find in Lochner's files of March of that year a full list of a Precinct Committeemen of the Non-Partisan League. Whether or not, therefore, he was actually engaged in organizing for the league during this period, it is apparent that there must have been some connection between the Non-Partisan League and the peace forces of this country.

Our first record of peace activities directly at work again in the United States after the Ford Expedition was June 9, 1916, when Jane Addams wired Dr. Frederick Lynch, "Accept place on Committee with pleasure." Following this, in July, 1916, Rebecca Shelly (apparently co-operating with Miss Balch under orders from the Stockholm Conference) began formally to organize the American Neutral Conference Committee in New York City.

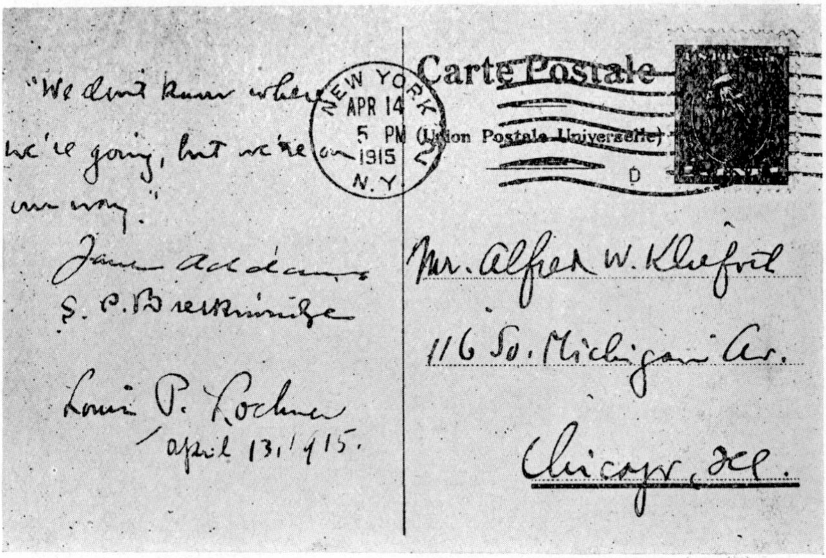

FACSIMILE OF POSTAL OF S. S. NOODAM, HOLLAND-AMERICAN LINE, APRIL 14, 1915.

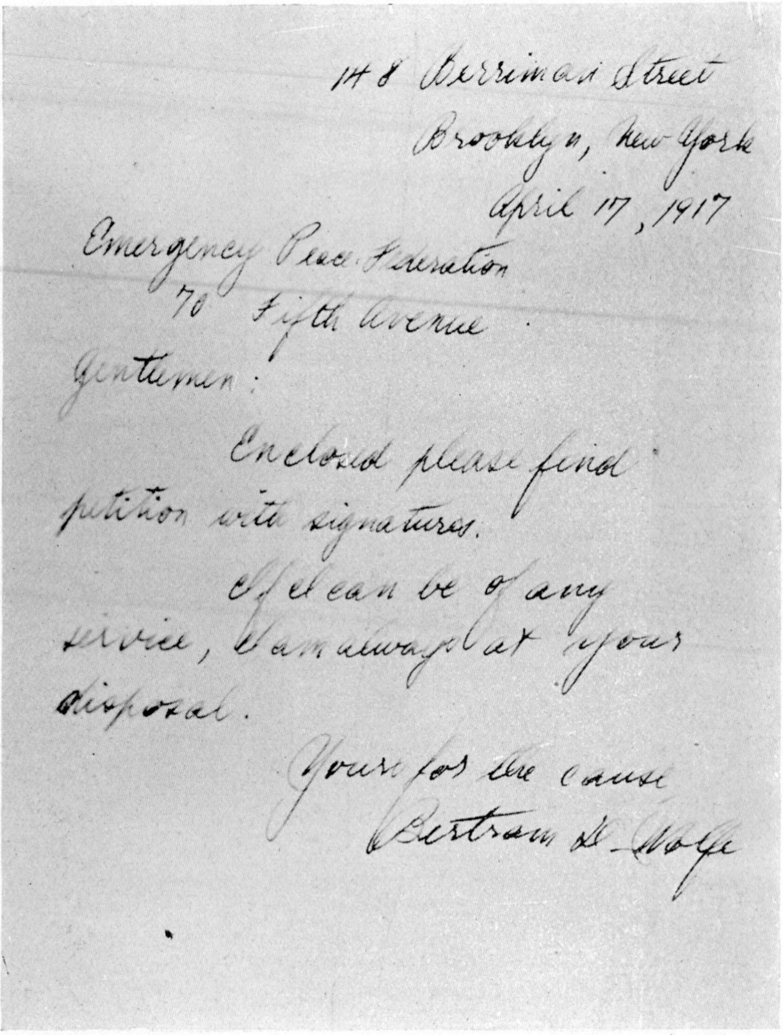

148 Berriman Street
Brooklyn, New York
April 17, 1917

Emergency Peace Federation
70 Fifth Avenue

Gentlemen:

Enclosed please find petition with signatures.

If I can be of any service, I am always at your disposal.

Yours for the cause
Bertram D. Wolfe

Winnetka — March 19 '17

Please return

Dear Lochner,

You will be surprised to hear that I saw your nice wife yesterday in Milwaukee. I went up on an errand concerning an exhibition of Chas Haag's sculpture but also largely to see Victor Berger, and Mrs. Lochner was good enough to meet me and spend an interesting hour with me. What a sick feeling we have to know the terrible weakness of Henry Ford!

Facsimile of Original Letter — Lola M. Lloyd to Louis P. Lochner

Its the mean spirited Mrs. Ford who makes all the dirty work possible against Ford's peace activities, but finally its his <u>own</u> <u>fault</u>.

Well I'm writing now to ask you to send Berger all your available material I would have carried in the letter to Wilson you sent me but I had already sent it to Fred. A. Moore — Both of these men should be on your list. Berger is very straight on peace, he is one of the best in the Socialist ranks & he will push the party his way in their emergency conference in St. Louis April 6 or so. But especially he promised to print anything new I could send him — He had used the Trevelyan letter but had not seen those statements of Buxton & Ponsonby — Send him the whole collection —

Have you anything from foreign pacifists since the break with Germany? Wilfrid Wilson Gibson the English poet told me he hoped & believed the U.S. could never be forced into the war, but he can't speak on this point in public because he promised his government to keep still over here before he got his passport.

Berger said the Russian revolution meant first increased activity of the army but soon a break-up in military discipline that would mean an early peace.

How the rail chiefs used the strike & the settlement both to increase the war scare!

When - if ever - we get a La Follette meeting here Berger wants one in Chicago. I wish he would wire directly to La Follette & I will write him to do so, but meanwhile use this request if you can. He even urged that Milwaukee was a better place for a big meeting than Chicago since they have a newspaper & its La F's

native State: Berger's home address is: Victor L. Berger
980 First St.
Milwaukee

Mr. Moore's you probably have but it's: Fred. A. Moore
2024 Washington Blvd.

Good luck to your efforts to get a Commission of inquiry started with Jordan Chairman! The aim is a joint Commission of Germans & Americans in some possible neutral spot, isn't it?

Norris's challenge to the Nebraska legislature to let his constituents speak their mind is a fine step! I wish everybody's constituents had a chance at a plain issue like that!

Cordially yours, Lola M. Lloyd

The Methodist Federation for Social Service

FRANCIS J. McCONNELL, President
Bishop, Denver, Colorado

HERBERT WELCH, Vice-President
President Ohio Wesleyan University, Delaware, Ohio

HARRY F. WARD, Secretary

Office of the Secretary, 72 Mt. Vernon Street, Boston, Massachusetts

May 2, 1917

Miss Lella Faye Secor,
Emergency Peace Committee,
#70 Fifth Ave.
New York City.

My dear Miss Secor:-

I shall be very glad to accept your invitation to act upon the Council of the Emergency Peace Federation.

Sincerely yours,

Harry F. Ward

Oregon - Illinois August 12 '17.

Dear Lochner,

Mary O'Reilly called on Miss Addams and found her enthusiastic about the growth of the People's Council. She would like to go to Minneapolis and speak and even if she can't stay six days she would like to be a delegate.

I was delighted to hear this and of course something can be arranged at

FACSIMILE OF ORIGINAL LETTER — LOLA M. LLOYD TO LOUIS P. LOCHNER

once — Mrs. Thomas & Mrs. Karsten are delegates but the Chicago Branch of the Woman's Party has no delegate yet. Wish Miss Addams would swing the National Committee of the W.P.P. into line for us! But if she can't she may be willing to represent the Chicago Branch (which is a great deal more radical than its officers and can surely be persuaded to affiliate at its next meeting). I was

thinking of asking for
that job myself but if
Miss Addams can get right
into the thick of things, I'd
give up my chances
cheerfully.

Miss O'Reilly said that if
three delegates could go from
the Chicago People's Council
she'd try to get Lovett
and Wentworth sent —
I might go in as a third
there — if all went well.

She has to teach school
the first of September

but she rather hopes to get her pension cinched by serving a few weeks of this term & then resigning to go on with peace work. I find her work very good & her spirit fine. She isn't a hide-bound socialist & she's had all kinds of experience. I hope she'll keep the job here. It depends on our executive Committee.

I'd like to see you all in Minneapolis but if I can't

go for either family reasons or because I can't get anything to elect me a delegate, I will know that things are at last going so well that they don't need pushing! Isn't it great!

La Follette's action Saturday opens up the congressional discussion — & Henderson's doings in England must give Northcliff apoplexy!

Gompers' rival organization is the best sign of our growing influence with labor.

This is all the news I gathered Saturday when I went up to

town. None of it may be of any use to you, but then it might!

Don't kill yourself –

Cordially yours,

Lola M. Lloyd

Would Karl von Wiegand speak for us on peace movements in Germany? He's in N.Y.

30.

THE CHURCH PEACE UNION

(FOUNDED BY ANDREW CARNEGIE)

70 FIFTH AVENUE

NEW YORK

OFFICE OF
REV. FREDERICK LYNCH, D.D.
SECRETARY

May 10, 1917.

My dear Mr. Lochner:

Members of my Board of Trustees have expressed the feeling that it would be wiser for me not to have my name identified with any of the peace organizations at this time except those with which I am at this time connected in an executive capacity. As I do not wish to disrupt organizations like the World Alliance of Churches and The Church Peace Union, which have a high potency of good in them, and thus lose what radical sentiment still exists in these boards, I think it wise to comply with this request. I cannot, therefore, sign my name to the Call for the First American Conference on Democracy and Terms of Peace.

Yours sincerely,

Frederick Lynch,

Secretary. H.G.N.

Mr. Louis P. Lochner, Organizing Secretary,
First American Conference for Democracy and Terms of Peace,
70 Fifth Ave.,
N.Y. City.

17

Organizing Committee
EMILY G. BALCH
JAMES J. BAGLEY
JOSEPH D. CANNON
HARRY L. W. DANA
WALTER FULLER
MORRIS HILLQUIT
JUDAH L. MAGNES
REBECCA SHELLY
NORMAN L. THOMAS

Treasurer
ALFRED J. BOULTON

Executive Staff
LOUIS P. LOCHNER
ELISABETH FREEMAN
ROY BRAZZLE
S. ADA FLATMAN

First American Conference for Democracy and Terms of Peace

Headquarters: ROOM 61, HOLLAND HOUSE

May 30 and 31, 1917, New York City

CHANGE OF ADDRESS
230-
057

Not sent to Mrs. Charles J. Rhoads because she had written me that she could not help this year E. G. Balch

May twenty-third
1917

My dear Mrs. Roades:

We are confident of your hearty sympathy with the purpose of the First American Conference for Democracy and Terms of Peace. We therefore appeal to you for help in the most difficult side of its organization. We come to you for money.

You know of course that friends of peace throughout the country are discouraged - many are hopeless. The successful outcome of the proposed conference is therefore of utmost importance for both present and future.

You know, and we all know, that the peace sentiment is there - but it is not organized. The individual is not heard; grouped and organized these individuals will exert a powerful influence upon our own community, upon Congress and upon President Wilson. To coordinate and organize the democratic and peace loving forces of the country is the primary aim of the conference.

Once the friends of peace are organized they will undoubtedly rally in support of the conference program. But we must look to a few men and women to launch the movement. The enclosed budget asks for $5379.50. Of this a little over $1000 has already been contributed. The finance committee has carefully gone over its list of possible supporters and has taken the liberty of asking individuals for specific sums.

May we depend upon for a contribution of 200 - dollars? This is not the ordinary sort of contribution; it is rather an investment in a big enterprize which is sure to bring returns. Please let us count on you,

Faithfully yours,

Fannie Garrison Villard
P.P.E.

Joseph D. Cannon

Morris Hillquit

Emily G. Balch

Leonora O'Reilly

CHAPTER IV

American Neutral Conference Committee — July, 1916 to February 3, 1917

When it came to the actual organizing of an American Neutral Conference Committee, Miss Balch seems to have turned the work bodily over to Miss Shelly, who showed herself as in 1915 once more to be a worthy emissary of the Stockholm headquarters. By July 15th, 1916, when her first appeal was issued for a committee of 100 representative Americans, she already had a letter-head registering the following officers of an American Neutral Conference Committee:

Chairman.— Hamilton Holt.

Vice-chairman.— Jane Addams, Prof. Irving Fisher, Dr. John Harvey Kellogg and Dr. George Kirchwey.

Executive Committee.— Bertha Kuntz Baker, B. W. Heubsch, Paul U. Kellogg, Dr. Frederick Lynch, Lella Faye Secor, Dr. James J. Walsh and Rabbi Stephen S. Wise.

In other words, Miss Shelly followed the example of Frau Schwimmer and Lochner in securing names for her enterprise likely to inspire confidence in the general public for peace projects.

In her campaign there were three separate appeals sent out to representative Americans under the date of July 15, 20 and 26, 1916, respectively, all urging the formation of a Committee of 100. The first of the bulletins began:

> "The American Neutral Conference Committee was organized to bring before the public the idea of a Conference of Neutral Nations irrespective of peace platforms, preparedness and the terms of the war settlement.
>
> "The warring nations assert that their purpose is to make future wars impossible. Guarantees to that end can best be secured by a Neutral Conference. This idea is widely accepted in the neutral countries of Europe, as is attested by the strength of their Neutral Conference Committees, and the enthusiasm of the May 18th demonstrations called to urge governmental action in that direction.
>
> "Carl Lindhagen, Mayor of Stockholm,[1] has a Neutral Conference bill pending in the Riksdag; it passed the Lower

[1] Lindhagen was a Socialist, afterwards cooperating with the Russian Bolshevists. (Statement of member of Ford Party.)

House unanimously. Similar bills are pending in the Parliaments of Switzerland and Norway. What about the United States? . . ."

Always in summing up, Miss Shelly brought out the points that Europe was waiting for America to lead in making future wars impossible; and that the aim of her committee was to crystallize and direct public opinion in any effort President Wilson might make to stop the war through a conference of neutrals.

In composing these letters Miss Shelly showed a versatility and an ingenuity which perhaps deserved more success than she actually achieved at the moment. For though there were certain notables, such as Jane Addams, Luther Burbank, Gov. Capper of Kansas, Rear Admiral Chadwick, Philander Claxton, Dr. Frank Crane, Oswald Villard, Judge Ben Lindsey, Mrs. Joseph Fels, Prof. Jacques Loeb, Mrs. Percy Pennybacker, Thomas Mott Osborne, Senator Helen Ring Robinson, John Hays Hammond, Leo T. Rowe and Frank Walsh. who accepted service on the committee, and others like Senator La Follette, Raymond Robins and Dudley Field Malone, who declined with deep regret, yet these totalled only about thirty-five altogether. There were also some decidedly unregretful and clear-thinking declinations from equally important persons approached, refusing to interfere with the policies of the United States Government. Among these names were Joseph H. Choate, Charles J. Bonaparte, Winston Churchill, Harry Pratt Judson, A. Lawrence Lowell, George B. McClellan, Gifford Pinchot, Ex-Gov. Fielder of New Jersey, Emerson McMillin, Lyman Abbott, Chas. Van Hise, Charles F. Thwing, Thomas Burke of Seattle, Frances Lynd Stetson, George W. Wickersham, Samuel Gompers, and John Mitchell.

Until the end of December, 1916, Miss Balch and Miss Shelly's committee seems to have been largely a paper organization. There is only one November letter on record from Miss Shelly's office — this to Louis Lande, of 290 Broadway, New York City, thanking him for his "co-operation and the generous list of names." That there was, however, co-operation with other anti-war agencies during November, 1916, is evidenced by a document in the conference files called "The Near-at-Hand World League to Prevent Aggression," by George H. Sibley, issued November 14, 1916, under the auspices of the League for World Peace, and sent originally to Jacob H. Schiff. Briefly, the article pointed out that Germany was ready to agree to the Allies' peace terms and give up Belgium if England would relinquish control of the seas; that the United States, on the strength of a provision of the Naval Appropriation Bill, should call a conference of the great governments in the interests of peace; that Mr. Taft's League to Enforce Peace was "reactionary"; and that the United States must lead the world in disarmament.

After this peace manifestation there was apparently a further lull in the American Neutral Conference Committee activities until December 23, 1916, when another form letter signed by Rebecca Shelly was issued.

According to the letterhead Miss Balch was now vice-chairman of the executive committee, to which the names of John Haynes Holmes, Governor Arthur Capper, and John Hays Hammond had been added. The letter itself, which was more intimate and flurried into one than preceding ones, announced that: "The war and peace situation calls for immediate action. Will you not write or telegraph to your congressmen and senators, asking them to support some such resolution as was introduced a few days ago? The enclosed letter to President Wilson was received by our committee under most interesting circumstances. Mr. Bertrand Russell had written this letter to President Wilson on December 4th. About that time he saw in the London "Times" that the American Neutral Conference Committee had given publicity to Mr. Trevelyan's letter, and he determined to send it to us. The identity of the messenger cannot be revealed for obvious reasons."

Concerning the letter mentioned by Miss Shelly, we quote from a letter to the Conference Committee from J. C. Skemp, of the Brotherhood of Painters and Decorators, January 3, 1917:

> "I should be pleased to use in the January 'Painter and Decorator' the Bertrand Russell letter. Assuring the Committee of my heartiest sympathy and co-operation in its work, I am,"

On January 13, 1917, Miss Shelly sent out a petition for peace, with notices of a meeting in its interests of the American Neutral Conferences Committee, for January 17th:

> "We are circulating a petition to which hundreds of thousands of names have already been signed. Within the next few weeks we want thousands of New Yorkers to add their names in order to assure President Wilson that he has the support of the people in any effort he may make towards

peace. Organized churches, civic bodies and so forth are co-operating with us. Will you help us get the petition before all the people in your district. . . ."

"Next Wednesday morning, January 17th, at ten o'clock we will meet in the University Settlement, 184 Eldridge street, to talk over plans for this vital work."

The next document on file is a Conference Committee form letter issued on January 26, 1917, and signed by its new chairman, George Foster Peabody. This displays an impressive list of some 100 names as a general committee, and announces a peace mass meeting on February 2d, with William Jennings Bryan as speaker and Dr. George Kirchwey as presiding officer. A special invitation to the meeting under date of January 30, 1917, declares that:

". . . The occasion will be neutral and non-partisan. . . . But those who attend will be united by one common belief: That the war should be ended by negotiation rather than by a peace dictated to a crushed opponent or a peace due to exhaustion."

This letter was signed by Frederic C. Howe and Anna M. Sloan.

When February 2d arrived Mr. George Foster Peabody, as chairman, presided over a crowded mass meeting; and to judge by the applause following Mr. Bryan's most anti-British and pro-German allusions, the audience must have been made up largely of German sympathizers. His address covered the following points:

Insinuations against the veracity of American newspapers, against munition makers and other alleged "interests" back of the newspapers, and against England for interning German merchantmen; a plea that blame for the war should rest equally on all belligerents; for a peace without victory; for freedom of the seas; for a referendum on a possible declaration of war; a statement that Germany (presumably) never intended to injure the United States; that we should firmly refuse in any case to fight anybody until the present European War was over; and finally, that there would be great honor in refusing eternally to go to war, in order that we, the United States of America, might play the disinterested part of a great neutral.[1]

[1] Transcript of Stenographer's Minutes of Meeting Feb. 2, 1917. Marked passages.

In spite of Mr. Bryan's eloquence, negotiations with Germany, as we know, were officially discontinued on February 3, 1917, the very next day after he made this speech. On the same day the officers of the American Neutral Conference Committee, together with some "well known radicals," got together hurriedly in order to reorganize into a second Emergency Peace Federation, — this time with the definite object of keeping America out of the war. The history of this rejuvenated federation may be followed in detail under the heading "Emergency Peace Federation of 1917."

CHAPTER V

Emergency Peace Federation, New York City — February to May, 1917

Our best record of the transformation of the American Neutral Conference Committee in New York, on February 3, 1917, into a rejuvenated Emergency Peace Federation, may be found in a letter from Rebecca Shelly, dated May 16, 1917, to J. Barnard Walton, of Swarthmore College and the Religious Society of Friends, who had previously described this organization as "all siding with the more radical wing." [1]

> "The Emergency Peace Federation," wrote Miss Shelly, as field secretary, "had its beginning on February 3, 1917, the date Count Von Bernstorff was handed his passports. On that day we formed a little 'keep out of war committee,' which held a mass meeting at Carnegie Hall on February 5th. On February 7th the Emergency Peace Federation was more formally organized with the object 'to keep America from war and its attendant consequences.' In the three strenuous months of our existence we have built up a strong national organization and raised over $76,000, most of which has been spent in advertising."

As the above excerpt takes us forward three months, we must return to February 8, 1917, when the American Neutral Conference Committee sent out a bulletin announcing its transformation into the Emergency Peace Federation.

Under the same date the Peace Federation issued a letter which begins as follows: "If the American people do not want to go to war, they must let Congress know how they feel about it. There is no silence on the part of those clamoring for military aggression."

In examining the officers of this Emergency Peace Federation — Mrs. Henry Villard, chairman; Emily Greene Balch, Louis Lochner, Ella Flagg Young, and Phillip S. Florence, vice-chairmen; Dr. Frederick Lynch, treasurer, Lella Faye Secor, secretary; and Rebecca Shelly, field secretary — we find "Internationalist" interests represented by Lochner, Miss Shelly, Miss

[1] J. Barnard Walter to Miss Shelly, March 15, 1917.

Secor and Miss Balch, four ex-members of the Ford Peace Neutral Conference at Stockholm. Clearly Lochner, who, according to a later statement,[1] had spent a year in Europe after the Ford party disbanded, had come back at the first sign of serious trouble between Germany and the United States, to steer "emergency" peace ventures once more.

Simultaneously with the central office in New York, an Emergency Peace Federation Committee was formed in Washington, D. C., according to a bulletin letter sent out to members of the Woman's Peace Party by Miss Secor, February 9, 1917, "On the initiative of Miss Balch and Dr. Kirchwey." This "legislative branch" of the federation, which represented the American Union against Militarism, the American Peace Party, and the Women's Peace Party, at once proceeded to co-operate with New York headquarters in arranging with them for a great peace demonstration to be held in Washington on February 12, 1917.[2]

In Chicago, though, no new peace federation was formally organized at this time, the Woman's Peace Party of Chicago, representing the International Committee of Women for Permanent Peace, led by such women as Jane Addams, Mrs. Carrie Chapman Catt, Anna Garlin Spencer, and Mrs. Louis F. Post, became very active along the old Emergency Peace Federation lines. On February 7, 1917, Miss Addams, as chairman, sent out a bulletin letter which proved, among other things, that she, as well as the Ford veterans in New York, was still faithful both to the International and German comrades. The bulletin covered the following points:

(a) A telegram sent by Miss Addams on February 3, 1917, to President Wilson, urging an alliance with neutral nations in an endeavor to avoid war.

(b) (1) Cablegram from several peace organizations to Dr. Anita Augspurg, secretary of the national committee in Germany: "Many American women join with the members of our international committee in sending messages of good will to our German sisters and share our hopes that war may yet be averted."

(2) A cablegram to Dr. Aletta Jacobs, of the International Committee of Women for Permanent Peace at Amsterdam: "Members of our international committee have sent greetings to German women and are making utmost efforts to allay war spirit."

[1] Lochner's statement, May 30, 1917, p. 29, First Amer. Conference for Democracy and Terms of Peace.

[2] Form letter of Woman's Peace Party, Feb. 9, 1917.

(c) A petition to President Wilson to avert war through an official neutral conference and a referendum vote: This to be signed by as many members of the Woman's Peace Party as possible.

(d) The creation of a clearing house for peace activities under the auspices of the Woman's Peace Party of New York.

(e) Urging members of the Woman's Peace Party to co-operate with the American Union against Militarism in telegraphing the President, senators and congressmen endorsing "Mr. Bryan's statement to the American people."[1]

Following the Addams bulletin letter a somewhat similar one was issued on February 9, 1917, jointly by the secretaries of the Chicago Woman's Peace Party and the New York Emergency Peace Federation, urging attendance of members at the proposed peace demonstration in Washington on February 12, 1917. Though the heavy work leading up to this pilgrimage fell on the shoulders of Miss Secor, at Emergency Peace Federation headquarters in New York, she was aided by two influential local women in Mrs. Henry Villard and Mrs. J. Sargent Cram, both of whom were delegates to the meeting. Further, as Mrs. Villard was honorary chairman, not only of the Emergency Peace Federation, but of the Woman's Peace Party of New York as well, with such women as Crystal Eastman, Mrs. Amos Pinchot, Mrs. James Warbasse, Madeline Doty, Mary Austin, Mrs. Frederic Howe, Carrie Chapman Catt, Mrs. Florence Kelley, Mary Shaw, Lillian Wald, Anna Strunsky Walling, Margaret Lane, Agnes Brown Leach, Mrs. Jacques Loeb, Tracy Mygatt, and Nellie M. Smith on her staff, she was able to give Miss Secor substantial aid in many directions.

About the same time Miss Secor was receiving some expert advice in organizing pacifists from W. E. Williams, at the time publicity manager of the Commonwealth Construction Corporation of New York City. Among other things he advised:

(1) A committee of American Federation of Labor people, to persuade unions in all parts of the country to endorse the peace program; Miss Secor personally to influence the farmers' organizations to the same end.

(2) Each local representative of the Emergency Peace Federation to form a committee representing union labor, Socialism and

[1] Letter of Woman's Peace Party of N. Y. City.

other radical groups, peace parties, farmers' organizations and religious societies opposed to war.

(3) Emphasis to be laid on the fact that since the platform of the federation was "merely tentative" delegates would not necessarily be required to endorse it.[1] Thus it will be seen that the old method of federating radicals with pacifists was again followed, even to reassuring those who were alarmed by the socialistic platform with its "tentative program manoeuvre." That the radical delegates themselves understood this strategy perfectly is clear from a letter from W. J. Wright, representing the Socialist Party of Allegheny County, Pennsylvania, at the Washington demonstration:

> "Dear Comrade," wrote Mr. Wright, May 7, 1917, to Miss Secor, ". . . So let us get together — 'the Emergency Peace Federation' to be its name, but let us merge it into the American Union against Militarism, Socialist Party and all societies who oppose Prussianizing the United States for the purpose of crushing militarism in Germany. Formulate some plan that we may all co-operate."

Among other early advisers of Miss Secor in the field about this period were Rear Admiral Chadwick, (Telegram, Feb. 10, 1917), Benjamin Marsh, of Washington, D. C., (Telegram, Feb. 8, 1917), Robert Bringler, of the State Socialist Party of Pennsylvania, (Telegram, Feb. 10, 1917), and C. H. Sorensen of Lincoln, Nebraska (another Ford veteran), all of whom sent encouraging and helpful telegrams to her, Sorensen being especially so in his message:

> Feb. 8, 1917.
>
> "I am bringing with me president of organization representing 40,000 farmers . . ."

On February 7, 1917, a mass meeting was held at Cooper Union, at which Mrs. Warbasse, Norman Thomas, Lochner, and Dr. Henry Neumann, all spoke. Whether or not this meeting actually recruited pilgrims for the February 12th celebration, when Lincoln's birthday of 1917 arrived, there were 250 delegates, headed by Mrs. Villard and Mrs. Cram, who appeared at the White House with a view "of urging that no action be taken which would plunge this country into war."

[1] W. E. Williams to Miss Secor, from 18 E. 41st, N. Y. City.

And if at the crucial moment the ladies had to content themselves with pouring out their pacifism to Mr. Tumulty, nothing in the formal history of the occasion is allowed to hint of any chagrin on their part.[1]

The expense, of course, of 250 delegates to and from Washington, particularly since they chartered two special trains, one at $6,000,[2] were heavy; but no doubt the delegates felt themselves justified.

As Miss Shelly has said, a great part of the money collected went into peace publicity from time to time. This seems to have been accomplished entirely through the firm of Joseph Ellner & Co., Ltd., which received altogether nearly $50,000 from the Emergency Peace Federation for advertising.[3]

After the Washington demonstration was over the Emergency Peace Federation officials began to receive some valuable contributions in their anti-war drive from pacifists in many parts of the country. For instance, B. F. Koopman, a "pacifist" of Davenport, Iowa, offered to spread propaganda in this fashion: "As a 'traveling man,'" wrote Mr. Koopman, Feb. 13, 1917, "covering Eastern Iowa and Western Illinois, it seems to me I might do some good in the distribution of 'peace literature,' petitions, etc."

To this letter Miss Shelly wired an appreciative answer Feb. 17, 1917, which said, in part:

> "Imperative that members of Congress hear immediately from constituents opposing war. You can best help by organizing Emergency Peace Committees in all localities you touch. No need elaborate organization. Simply see that active group pledges itself to stimulate sending letters and telegrams Congress daily. As soon as group is formed wire name of chairman to this office. Urge friends and traveling acquaintances to wire and write to Congress immediately opposing war."

Later, Miss Teresa McMahon, of the University of Washington, at Seattle agreed to do what she could for the "legislative committee" of the Emergency Peace Federation, in the way of bring-

[1] Typewritten account of Feb. 12, 1917 demonstration.

[2] Check for $6,000 to Penn. R. R. from Emergency Peace Federation, March 31, 1917.

[3] Exhibit Series of checks to Ellner & Co.

ing pressure on Congress; and giving the names of Dr. Anna Louise Strong and Mrs. Thomas Crahan as Seattle women who would make better propagandists than herself.[1] Mrs. Jessie Hardy Mackaye, of the Congressional Union for Woman Suffrage in Washington, used her office to send out peace letters and telegrams. On February 13, 1917, she reported sending "the following night letter to radicals:"[2]

> "Will you co-operate with legislative committee Emergency Peace Federation at Washington by organizing peace committee in your Congressional District? Wire your Senators, Congressman and President. Arrange mass meetings, pass resolutions. Immediate action imperative. Please wire me name and address chairman your committee.
>
> "(Signed) JESSIE HARDY MACKAYE,
>
> "*Acting Secretary.*"

About the same time, Mrs. A. D. Warbasse, of Brooklyn, wrote to report cheerfully:[3]

> "I have paid the bill for advertising in the 'Post' this morning, and am very glad that the investment has brought such splendid returns. . . ."[3]

Mrs. Lola Maverick Lloyd, of Chicago, (since divorced from Wm. Bross Lloyd the Communist), one of the faithful pacifists of 1915, and special friend of Frau Schwimmer, suggested calling a conference of English, Germans and well-known Americans . . "just as the American Union against Militarism called the Americans and Mexicans to El Paso. . . . Could the Allies safely prevent?[4] . . ."

Mr. Prince Hopkins, of Boyland, California, formed a branch of the Emergency Peace Federation at Santa Barbara, Cal.;[5] Dr. Jacques Loeb, of the Rockefeller Institute, submitted his article on "Biology and the War," to be used as campaign literature by the federation;[6] and some faithful comrade sent to headquarters a copy of a Socialist-pacifist message, from Arthur LeSueur, of the Non-Partisan League, to Dante Barton.[7]

[1] Letter to Jessie Mackaye, Feb. 14, 1917.
[2] Memorandum, Feb. 13, 1917 (typed).
[3] A. D. Warbasse to Miss Secor, Feb. 22, 1917.
[4] Lola M. Lloyd to Miss Secor, in post-script.
[5] Letter from Dr. M. M. Yates to E. P. F. Apr. 17, 1917.
[6] Dr. Loeb to Conference Committee, Feb. 9, 1917.
[7] Le Sueur to Barton on Government confiscation, etc., Feb. 29, 1917.

Occasionally, it is true, the Emergency Peace Federation officials came into possession of a vigorous anti-peace letter, whose writer not only saw through the pro-German and defeatist schemes, but said so. For instance, Congressman Walter M. Chandler received from H. L. Chase, one of his constituents, a most discerning letter on the activities of the Emergency Peace Federation, Feb. 19, 1917, which ended as follows:

> "I cannot believe that you will give a moment's consideration to the pro-German propaganda of the so-called Emergency Peace Federation, but I feel that you should hear from those who condemn it as traitorous and dangerous, not alone to the United States, but to world civilization."

The Emergency Peace Federation officials presently organized another anti-war pilgrimage to Washington for February 22, 1917, this time in the form of a student delegation.[1] While arrangements to this end were being made, Miss Secor attempting to secure a list of all pacifist students through the International Polity Clubs, she received some interesting letters from Miss Shelly, who was "legislating" in Washington. These, besides touching on the difficulties of lobbying, went on to say, in part:

> (1) "The most important thing for me to report is my work with the farmers. Mrs. Cram and I had a gratifying hearing before the legislative gathering of the Farmers' Co-operative Union, and feel that we made a distinct impression. . . ."
>
> (2) "I talked with Mr. MacSparran, of the National Grange today, and am still hoping that he will sign the telegrams to the state grange masters urging them to bring delegates. . . ."
>
> (3) "I am sending you the Lynn Haynes list as far as we have completed it, also the names of others to whom we have written. As I said before our hands will be more than full taking this poll of Congress for the next few days."
>
> (4) "We have almost finished the complete cataloging of the Members of Congress, and I can give you a typewritten copy of names, state and district, together with our individual tab on them, whether militarist, pacifist, uncertain or co-operative. . . ."
>
> (5) "Some people felt that we were putting in an undue amount of time on this poll because, as some one expressed

[1] Typed account of Feb. 22, 1917, peace demonstration.

it, every Congressman will vote for the side that scares him the most. It is up to us at all events to see that a sufficient number of our telegrams and letters come into Congress and tell the representative members in unmistakable terms what their constituents expect of them. . . ."

(6) "Let us send out, as you have already taken steps to do, a strong letter to every person whose name we have been able to secure by hook or crook. . . . If within the next few days we could spend five to ten thousand dollars sending out your inimitable letters with definite instructions on the congressional situation, I would feel at least 50 per cent easier about the 'crucial moment' when our forces must be ready. So much for the letter campaign."

(7) "Would it be possible to utilize the many splendid volunteer workers in a great series of about fifty street meetings? The automobiles from which the speakers would address the crowds should be commandeered and the speakers organized immediately with the understanding that the meetings would be pulled off when most needed. . . ."

(8) "Another point about which we did not have time to speak yesterday is that of sending out the ten organizers and arranging a nation-wide series of mass meetings. In connection with the latter a kind of speakers' bureau should be organized. Perhaps you could give to Freda Kirchwey and a few other good workers the particular task of organizing such a bureau."

(9) "Now about the student delegation: I am having serious trouble in getting actual university students here. Mr. Meade has been negotiating with Mr. Rappaport, who felt he could not guarantee more than ten students. We are to have a meeting tomorrow, and hope to realize some local publicity on it. . . ." [1]

That the student delegation, eighty-three strong, representing forty-one colleges (including the Rand School) did travel safely to Washington on February 22, 1917, at much less cost than the Villard-Cram expedition, we know from the expense account and a congratulatory letter from Lochner in Milwaukee to Miss Secor on "having gotten away with the stunt." (Feb. 19, 1917.) But whether the students pierced with their pacifism into the White House, even as far as Mr. Tumulty, we do not know.

[1] From Miss Shelly's letters to Miss Secor, Feb. 17, 20, 23 & 26.

About this time and later the Emergency Peace Federation was receiving lists of over 200 labor union locals, together with valuable information concerning them, through the co-operation of A. W. Ricker, of Pearson's Magazine, which was apparently engaged in spreading Socialism through the labor unions.[1] There are on file a number of letters from the secretaries of central bodies in different parts of the country to Mr. Ricker, all submitting their lists and agreeing to advertise the magazine at meetings. A characteristic letter of this series was from Otto E. Musselman, recording secretary of the Scranton Central Labor Union, which reads as follows:

"*February* 16, 1917.

"PEARSON'S MAGAZINE, MR. A. W. RICKER, *Business Manager:*

"DEAR SIR: — Replying to yours of the 14th, I am enclosing a list of the local unions of labor affiliated with the Scranton General Labor Union, together with those of the United Mine Workers' Local that are affiliated. The majority of the miners' locals are not affiliated. Therefore I do not have the address of the secretaries. These, I think, you can get by writing to John M. Mack, secretary District No. 1, Miller Building, Scranton, Pa. However, you need not mention the fact that I directed you to address him, as I have no right to give out this list, without first taking up the matter with the executive board of the Central Labor Union, and knowing the personnel of the board I took the matter upon myself to furnish this list without their consent."

A second letter worth quoting from is from Hugh Watson of Tony, Ill., March 24, 1917 who, after offering to co-operate with Mr. Ricker, went on to say:

". . . I have read Pearson's for several years, long before it became a socialist periodical, and have been agreeably surprised by its ardent stand for Socialism, and it has done better than I expected with your writers, and they are the very best in the country. Of course it is true that I buy them out of the newsstand, but when I go for mine I often times persuade some one else to buy a copy. . ."

Another publication in thorough sympathy with the Emergency Peace Federation and its policies was the "Medical World,"

[1] Typed list of Unions sent to Ricker by Musselman.

published by Dr. C. F. Taylor, of Philadelphia. "It reaches some 20,000 physicians in all parts of the world," according to a letter from Dr. Taylor to the Emergency Peace officials.[1]

Soon after the Washington Birthday demonstration, Lochner, who seemed to have been in the West, comparatively inactive for some weeks,[2] arrived at the Emergency Peace Federation office in Washington, to cooperate with the "legislative committee" there.[3] Here he lost no time in geting to work, and on March 2d, 1917, he was telegraphing New York headquarters as follows:

> "Kirchwey leaving for New York tonight. Will get in touch with our friends on arrival. He, therefore, prefers to give his views in person."

Following up the telegram, on March 2, Lochner wrote to his fellow-workers in New York, reporting:

> ". . . As I have just wired you Dean Kirchwey is leaving for New York tonight. He shares the general pessimism of Bryan and our friends on the hill, who all of them feel that while they are fighting to the last ditch they are on the losing side. Even in La Follette's office — the Senator was too much on the vigil on the floor to come out — the same pessimism is shared. He will put up a stiff fight but sees little hope ahead."

On March 3d, apparently more cheerful, Lochner wired the Woman's Peace Party of Chicago as follows, with true Lochner tactics:

> "Get flood of telegrams off today from prominent men to Senator Sherman opposing armed neutrality. Send us preferably non-German and not avowed pacifists. Miss Addams and Mrs. Thomas join in this request."

On March 4th both Lochner and Miss Balch wired Dr. David Starr Jordan, in California, asking his advice on German-American or "international" mediation in the interests of peace; and on March 5th Dr. Jordan sent two answering telegrams discouraging both plans for the moment as "desirable but impracticable." Nevertheless, the idea bore fruit, for on March 17, 1917, Dr.

[1] Dr. Taylor to Mrs. Fannie Garrison Villard, March 27, 1917. Dr. Taylor to Miss Balch, Apr. 25, 1917.

[2] Lochner to Miss Secor, Feb. 19, 1917.

[3] Telegram from Miss Balch to Lochner, Feb. 24, 1917.

Jordan and Mrs. Villard issued a joint Emergency Peace appeal, saying, in part:

> ". . . It is for you to demand that Congress and the President stand by the slogan on which they were elected and continue to keep us out of war. . . . Help save America from the shame of a cowardly and useless war.[1] . . ."

After this appeal there was an actual meeting of the long desired "Unofficial Commission in New York City." This developed into a series of conferences at the Holland House, lasting from March 17 to March 24, 1917:

> ". . . to devise ways and means of solving international problems without resort to arms."

The findings of the commission disclose that Lochner came over to the meetings from Washington, Joseph D. Cannon from Colorado, Arthur LeSueur from the Non-Partisan League of North Dakota (and has his expenses paid),[2] as well as certain other distinguished pro-Germans, radicals and Socialists from various localities.

The commission, besides recommending everybody to bring anti-war pressure on the administration, urged under the headings of "A Joint High Commission of Inquiry and Conciliation," "An Open Letter to the President," "Conference of Neutrals," and "Consequences of Entering the War," that still another peace demonstration be effected in Washington, this time on April 2, 1917.[3]

Besides the formal findings of the commission, we read in the minutes of one meeting a long and impassioned anti-war speech by Lochner. This exonerated Germany from any special blame for the war and from all intent to injure the United States with the gentle submarine,—finding pathetic excuses for the Germans and insisting that they were really very fond of Americans. He touched upon the outrage of England controlling the seas, on the horrors of war, on the nobility of pacifists in general (and congressional ones in particular) and the fundamental baseness of so-called patriotism, ending with a fervent plea for "true patriots" to bring pressure on the President. ". . . Write him,

[1] From letter, beginning "Dear Friend of Peace."
[2] Check of $100 to LeSueur and his receipt.
[3] Findings of Unofficial Commission (typed) March 19-24, 1917.

wire him from every hamlet, from every fireside, 'America refuses to go to war.'"[1]

While these meetings of the unofficial commission were going on, followers of the Emergency Peace Federation all over the country were faithfully bombarding members of the administration with letters, telegrams and even original literature.

From San Francisco, on March 25, 1917, Daniel O'Connell submitted to the Federation (through Dr. Jordan) a series of specious but ingenious leaflets called "The Truth" (respectively), about Russia, England, France, Italy, Germany and the War, which will perhaps be found to represent about the most subtle defeatist propaganda on record, and which may explain in part the confused thinking of many an American today. From Chicago, Mrs. Lloyd wrote Lochner March 19, 1917, another characteristic letter about Victor Berger (whom she greatly admired) as "being able to push the Socialist Party his way," and as having said that "the Russian revolution meant first increased activity in the army, *but soon a break up in military discipline.*" Then she added, "Good luck to you. . . . The aim is a joint commission of Germans and Americans in a neutral country, is it not?"[2]

Other valuable Emergency Peace Federation allies in the field about this time were S. A. Stockwell, of Minneapolis, who on March 28, 1917, held a big peace meeting in St. Paul with a view to sending delegates to Washington;[3] and Ellis O. Jones, of Forest Hills, New York, who (though on March 28, 1917, merely submitted a list of promising pacifists to Miss Secor) started a little revolution in Central Park in December, 1918.

Other persons who co-operated in more or less degree are Bertram D. Wolfe,[4] of Brooklyn, N. Y., one of the organizers of the Communist Party, April 17, 1917; John P. Trowbridge, of Pittsfield, Mass.; Mrs. G. Frederick Washburn, of Brookline, Mass., Feb. 28, 1917; Mrs. Lydia Avery Coonley Ward, of Illinois, March 30, 1917; Rudolph Spreckels, of San Francisco, April 5, 1917; H. C. Hull, of Swarthmore, Pa., April 2, 1917; Jessie Hardy Mackaye, at the time of the charge of the National Defence League, at Washington, D. C.; Mr. I. Wolf, of Philadelphia, Pa.;

---

[1] Speech attached to findings and ,signed "Louis P. Lochner, former Secretary Neutral Conference for Continuous Mediation, founded by Henry Ford."

[2] See illustration.

[3] Stockwell to Miss Secor, March 20, 1917.

[4] See illustration.

Winter Russell, of New York City; George Fred Williams, of Boston, March 28, 1917; Rev. John Nevin Sayre, of Suffern, N. Y., March 30, 1917; Benjamin A. Javitz, New York City, and J. D. Schmidlapp, of Cincinnati, March 26, 1917.

Perhaps, however, the most far-reaching co-operation in anti-war propaganda received about this time by the Federation was the Congress of Forums, Inc., of New York City. "The forum is not an experiment," wrote Mr. de Jarnette, its secretary, to Lochner, in March, 1917, "since Cooper Union for twenty years has been a weekly demonstration; but the organization of a Congress of Forums to spread a movement for the promotion of democracy throughout the nation is something new."[1]

As war drew near and Congress was about to convene, there was a feverish speeding up of pacifist aggressiveness everywhere. Lochner arranged for another mass meeting in New York, importuning Senator La Follette to speak there, but the Senator, though always sympathetic to Emergency Peace Federation policies, usually declined to speak under its auspices.

On March 21, 1917, he wrote Miss Secor as follows:

> ". . . It would be personally gratifying to speak with the friends of peace in the east, but if I could go out it would be to so organize the public opinion of that part of the country where it is right so as to make it express itself in the votes of congressmen and senators and where it might have some effect here in Washington, where a declaration of war is to be voted upon in ten days . . ."

A little later, March 24, 1917, Miss Katherine Leckie, of New York City (Frau Schwimmer's manager of 1915), wrote to Miss Shelly:

> "Do you think there is any way in which I may receive the news of what is going out from your various organizations about peace? A great many people come into my office. Also I belong to the Gamut, the Pen and Brush, the Women's City Club, all of which are strongly militaristic organizations. You asked me the other night at the Woman's Peace party where I stood on war. I stand just exactly where I stood before this war started, and I have never failed to lift my voice for peace . . ."

About the same time, Mr. Sorenson, of Nebraska, and Miss DeGraff, of Oregon (both Ford veterans), wired that they were

[1] Letter to Lochner, March 6, 1917.

sending delegates to Washington and working up anti-war enthusiasm in their respective states; the German Publishing Company of Brookline, Oregon, asked the Emergency Peace Federation to "let us run your full page advertisement in our German-American daily for $40. Guarantee over 11,000 circulation — every reader friendly and co-operative;"[1] there was an important meeting of war veterans on March 29, 1917, where "a prominent pacifist will be allowed twenty minutes for a speech;" the secretary of the Williamsburg, New York, Anti-High Cost of Living Conference, "representing 30 labor and social societies," offered to lend the Emergency Peace Federation aid "in any kind of propaganda and agitation necessary;"[2] Jenkin Lloyd Jones wired encouraging words about influencing President Wilson toward peace; Mrs. Lloyd, of Chicago, again wrote one of her frank letters of advice to Lochner, counselling him this time on the ground that he had been severely criticized in Chicago: "Don't make everybody merge under your banner. Let them have a little leeway when it comes to the scratch. This does not apply to the convention or lobby that is to work later on, but get every element you can into the parade and kick 'em all out afterwards. I can promise some Socialists and some trade union women." (March 29, 1917.)

Other co-operating forces with the Emergency Peace Federation were as follows: Louis J. Kantor, who wired from Washington to Jesse Kramer, Young Men's Anti-Militarism League, in New York, April 3, 1917:

> "War crisis acute but hopeful. Rush all telegrams possible to congressmen demanding support Mason bill providing Commission on Peace Terms before instead after war. . . . Protest sending American conscript army to Europe."

James W. Donahy, President of the Collegiate Anti-Militarism League, at Columbia College, telegraphed the Emergency Peace Federation, April 4, 1917, for "$1,000, immediately to cover fifty universities with live issues of war."

Arthur K. Pope, of Berkeley, California, wired, March 27, 1917:

> "Preparing telegram to President to be signed by seventy-five members of faculty. Other telegrams have gone forward. Am arranging symposium in newspaper. . . ."

[1] March 30, 1917.
[2] March 31, 1917.

Miss Lillian Wald, of the American Union against Militarism, and of the Henry Street Settlement, put on "Black 'ell", a strong anti-war play, on April 2, 1917, in the heart of the New York ghetto, which ran even after war was declared.[1]

The New York Vegetarian Society telegraphed its "Uncompromising stand against war" to Washington;[2] and finally all manner of fish, fowl and good red herring pacifists, singly and in groups, hiding now as in 1915, "under the all inclusive term of Emergency Peace Federation,". once more bombarded Congress with anti-war messages.[3]

There is on file an answering telegram to Miss Secor from Secretary Redfield, dated March 21, 1917, as follows:

> "Replying to your telegram I believe your organization and doctrine *to be directly promotive of attacks on American citizens and property.* To accept your policy would, in my judgment, mean more ruthless slaughter. *You are among these who are doing more than anyone else to bring about war.*
>
> WILLIAM C. REDFIELD,
> *Secretary of Commerce.*

There are a number of other replies less stinging from congressmen and senators, as well as a few sympathetic and noncommittal ones.

After April 6th, however, when, in spite of all efforts of these "Emergent" pacifists, war with Germany was nevertheless declared, the answers of congressmen to the peace bombardment, with the conspicuous exception of the fifty who voted for peace, were generally war-like.

The Emergency pacifists, however, far from standing behind the President, immediately gathered themselves together to devise other "unofficial peace measures" to circumvent him. Perhaps the new members of the Emergency Peace Federation Executive Board — Joseph D. Cannon, a Socialist leader; Mrs. J. Sargent Cram, H. W. L. Dana, Mrs. Elsie Borg Goldsmith, Robert W. Hale, Professor Harry Overstreet, Tracy Mygatt, Dr. Henry Neumann, and Frances M. Witherspoon[4] — gave fresh impetus to the *old-guard pacifists,* or perhaps it was the extraordinary zeal and organizing ability of certain comrades in the field, as for instance,

[1] Fly leaf of Black'ell, with date, etc., of performance.
[2] Telegram from A. R. Gold, April 13, 1917.
[3] Important Request form and night letter forms.
[4] Letter-head, Emergency Peace Federation, dated April 7, 1917.

Professor Frederick W. Keasbey, of the University of Texas,[1] which spurred the Emergency Peace Federation officers on. At all events, on April 6, 1917, the very day that war was declared, Miss Secor, who had secured the names of the fifty congressmen and six senators who just had voted against war, sent each one the following day letter:

"On behalf of the Emergency Peace Federation I extend sincere thanks for your patriotic stand in opposing war. May I request that you communicate at once with Representative Kitchin, to whom I have written a letter suggesting co-operation between ourselves and pacifists in Congress."

Attached to the copy of the telegram was a newspaper clipping entitled:

ANTI-WAR VOTES

"The members of the House who voted against the resolution were:

"Democrats, sixteen — Almon, Alabama; Burnett, Alabama; Church, California; Connelly, Kansas; Decker, Missouri; Dill, Washington; Dominick, South Dakota; Hensley, Missouri; Hilliard, Colorado; Igoe, Missouri; Keating, Colorado; Kitchin, North Carolina; McLemore, Texas; Shackleford, Missouri; Sherwood, Ohio; Van Dyke, Minnesota.

"Republicans, thirty-two — Bacon, Michigan; Britten, Illinois; Browne, Wisconsin; Cary, Wisconsin; Cooper, Wisconsin; Davidson, Wisconsin; Davis, Minnesota; Dillon, South Dakota; Esch, Wisconsin; Frear, Wisconsin; Fuller, Illinois; Haugen, Iowa; Hayes, California; Hull, Iowa; Johnson, South Dakota; King, Illinois; Kinkaid, Nebraska; Knutson, Minnesota; La Follette, Wisconsin, Little, Kansas; Lundeen, Minnesota; Mason, Illinois; Nelson, Wisconsin; Rankin, Montana; Reavis, Nebraska; Rodenberg, Illinois; Sloan, Nebraska; Stafford, Wisconsin; Voigt, Wisconsin; Wheeler, Illinois; Woods, Iowa.

"Prohibitionist, one — Randall, California.

"Socialist, one — London, New York.

"Six members were announced as paired — Hill and Webb, Fields and Meeker, and Lee and Powers.

[1] Keasbey to Miss Secor, April 6, 1917.

"Speaker Clark did not vote. Representative Capstick of New Jersey and Helgesen of Minnesota were absent owing to illness. Representative Bleakley of Pennsylvania has resigned. With the two vacancies in the House due to death this completes the roster."

Approximately at the same time of the day letter, Miss Secor rushed a telegram to Representative Claude Kitchin, as follows:

"Will you summon immediately caucus of all senators and representatives who voted for peace to discuss the following plan suggested by Emergency Peace Federation: Let Congress communicate directly with Reichstag asking that German commission be appointed responsible only to Reichstag to confer with commission appointed by Congress, in hope that President's declared purpose may be accomplished without shedding American blood. Ample precedent for appealing directly to people over head of irresponsible government. If you and associates will lead such fight we will publish appeal throughout nation and strengthen your hand in every possible way. Rev. Irwin Tucker, emissary from federation, arrives Washington this afternoon,"[1] (April 7, 1917.)

A little later, April 7, 1917, Miss Shelly, who was also forehanded, had ready a perfectly fresh and timely bulletin letter thanking all of her dear friends for their previous support of emergent pacifism, and easily asking for further funds — this, of course, in order to bring about peace negotiations on the part of a "Joint High Commission from the German Reichstag in our own Congress."

Though the Emergency Peace Federation invoked for the fulfilment of this plan a certain German intermediary named Ritter,[2] the Joint High Commission plan ended finally in smoke because the peace forces, seeing the Espionage bill on the horizon, found it imperative to concentrate all of their strength in its defeat.[3] Accordingly on April 9, 1917, Lochner, Miss Balch and Miss Elizabeth Freeman, representing the "legislative committee" of the Federation in Washington, sent headquarters the following telegram:

"First hearing on spy bill, 2:30 today. Have able speakers ready to go down tonight."

[1] Typed copy of telegram signed Lella Faye Secor.
[2] To Lochner from Miss Secor, April 5, 1917.
[3] Lochner to Miss Secor, April 9, 1917.

On the same date Lochner wrote a long illuminating letter to Miss Secor from which we quote:

"The big feature of to-day has been the hearing on the Espionage bill. That bill would have been railroaded through I firmly believe, except for the efforts of our little group here. . . . What is more, the committee will conduct another public hearing on Thursday, beginning at 10 o'clock in the morning. Now the word that we would unanimously urge most solemnly upon you people in New York is this: send a group of the very ablest people down here for Thursday — men like Gilbert Roe, Amos Pinchot, etc. . . . Let the representatives of labor come here to protest against the bill in its present form. . . .

"The reason why we feel so strongly about this whole thing is that if that bill passes we fear that we might as well shut up our shop. And another thing! Do not have all the people you send represent the federation but rather a great variety of interests. John Haynes Holmes and Norman Thomas ought to be two good persons to testify. . . This spy bill matter so engrossed us today and was so all important that the other matters of the Congress — Reichstag communications, had to take second place. . . .

"Another thing, the statement in the papers about the telegram you sent out was as you see given out by 'one of the fifty,'" (evidently referring to the fifty congressmen who voted for peace) "who is afraid lest he be indentified with us. . . Now Miss Freeman and I after feeling out various members of Congress are of the opinion that these men simply will not enter into closer relations with us; and that your suggestion that Kitchin and the others hold a caucus at which our federation can be represented by a delegation, far from eliciting applause is calculated to make them shy of us."

It was about this time that two bulletins were sent out from the *Central Organization for a Durable Peace* at The Hague, addressed to the members of the "International Committee of Research No. VII," the same committee it may be remembered that Mr. Ford endowed when he was abroad. Both bulletins were signed B. De Jong Van Beek en Donk and read as follows:

No. 1. "I herewith beg to hand you copy of the answer to the questionnaire of your committee which we received from Professor Charles Gide and Mr. H. J. Lange," and "No 2. "I herewith beg to hand you copy of the answers to the questionnaire of your committee which we received from Mr. Hamilton Holt. At the same time I have the pleasure of informing you that Mr. Antonio Huneess, professor and former minister of San Diego, has become a member of your committee."

We know that Lochner was a member of this committee of research, through his acknowledgement of the bulletins under date of May 12, 1917, when he wrote to Mr. de Jong in part:

> "As you will see from the enclosed we are now engaged in trying to unify the constructive forces of this country. We of course meet with the usual difficulties that democrats have in wartime."

That there was then in Washington the American branch of an international organization called the Inter-Parliamentary Union (composed of government officers of certain countries who are supposed to work "unofficially" for peace against the very policies of each government in question) may be verified by reading fragments of Lochner's letter to Miss Shelly of April 16th:

> "I discussed the inter-parliamentary scheme with Slayden of Texas, who is now chairman of the American group of the Inter-Parliamentary Union. But he was very skeptical about the plan, and said that after the war they would do great things, but not now. . . .
>
> "May I suggest that you send us the replies, or copies thereof, of the fifty congressmen and six senators whom Miss Secor invited to confer with Mr. Kitchin. . . . It might be that Mayor Lindhagen might be induced to extend an invitation to the German and American members of the Inter-Parliamentary Union to come to Stockholm."[1]

Apparently Mr. Slayden relented enough to introduce Mr. Lochner to the chairman of the American group of the Inter-Parliamentary Union, for under date of April 17, 1917, we have "Record of a conversation with Dr. North of the Carnegie Foundation," which reads in part:

> "I was directed to see Dr. North by Congressman Slayden. I had asked Mr. Slayden for a list of the American members in the union and was referred to Dr. North, who though not a parliamentarian himself, is acting as secretary of the group."

[1] It should be remembered that Lindhagen was the Socialist Mayor of Stockholm.

After a rather unsatisfactory talk (from Lochner's point of view) on the subject of the Espionage bill, the co-operation of the Carnegie Endowment with the Emergency Peace forces, and a heated difference of opinion on the subject of the Conscription bill, the subject changed.

"If I remember correctly I then asked why the American group of the Inter-Parliamentary Union had not seen fit to reply favorably to the repeated requests from the European neutral group, especially Switzerland and Scandinavia, to get together in joint session during the war. Dr. North said that Dr. Lange, the secretary-general, had written him reams of stuff about it and that he was a charming fellow and all that, but that the American group had remained in close touch with the State Department and had been advised by it not to meddle with the international situation. I said that was one of the great criticisms that I made of the American democracy, that everybody seemed to leave everything to the President and State Department.

"Dr. North then tried to explain to me that in a way the American members of the Inter-Parliamentary Union were responsible to the government and that it would look very bad if they took up one line of action and the State Department another. I told him that if that was true of the United States it was certainly just as much true of the European members, and that they had not seen any reason against their acting in the fact that they were members of the government. I stated that the chairman of the Swiss group, for instance, was not only, as a member of the Upper House of the Swiss Parliament, a member of the government, but that he was a member of the Neutral Board of the Swiss Parliament, yet he was one of the prime movers in trying to get the neutrals together.

"To which Dr. North exclaimed tartly, 'Well, what has been done in Switzerland cannot be done here.'

"I replied, 'That is probably true because they have more democracy and we less,' at which the honorable gentleman again lost his temper.

"He concluded the chapter on the Inter-Parliamentary Union by saying, 'We were given reasons by the State Department that seemed to us conclusive, and I think present events have justified our action.'

"I said to Dr. North that my experience abroad had convinced me that the great masses of the people in the neutral countries there were exacting a tremendous pressure upon their governments and upon their parliamentarians to do something in view of the world situation, and that it was in response to this demand that the European members of the Inter-Parliamentary Union were urging their American colleagues to come together with them.

"Thereupon Dr. North said that in this country there had been very powerful and official pressure brought upon the government, and that it had led to exceedingly foolish things. 'Poor old Ford, for example.'

"To this I replied, 'Possibly you did not know what happened in Europe after Mr. Ford's party got over there. Mr. Ford's efforts stand forth as the one constructive thing for peace that was done in Europe during the entire war.'"

Another suggestive reference to the inter-parliamentary idea is in a letter from Miss Shelly, April 11, 1917, to Mr. R. G. Wagner, who seems to have contributed $6,000 altogether to the Emergency Peace Federation:

"Be sure that your contribution has not been wasted," she writes, "for the strong anti-war feeling which our advertising campaign produces will be within the next few weeks focused on our Inter-Parliamentary Peace plan which is now being worked out in detail by our Congressional representatives in conference with the Congressional leaders in Washington."

Still another reference to this matter is contained in Miss Shelly's letter dated April 14, 1917, to Dr. J. Wolf, 161 West 85th street, New York City, also thanking him for a check:

". . . I told you in a previous letter that we are working on an Inter-Parliamentary Peace Commission plan, which will be published in full as soon as completed. We want to submit the plan to every possible authority so as to be sure of our grounds before attempting to arouse a demand for political action. In the meantime we are trying to build up a strong catalogue system recording the names of all who have the courage to stand firm against the encroachments of militarism and its demand for war to the finish."

Though there is no further mention of The Central Organization in this report, there is to be found a little later a most significant reference by Lochner to the Inter-Parliamentary Union.

As we have seen, after war was declared in April, 1917, the inter-parliamentarians, pacifists, "neutrals," "internationalists," socialists, and Germans alike were unable to interfere seriously with the war policies of the United States Government. They did, however, largely through the Emergency Peace Federation, manage to harass administration officials in various ways. In turn they exerted all possible pressure against the Chamberlain, War College, Press Censorship, Espionage and Selective Draft bills, as well as against any loans to the Entente or working agreements with the Allies.[1] Further, about this time co-operation from the pacifist, religious or quasi-religious societies, began to aid in the defeatist plans of the Federation. Notable among these was the Fellowship of Reconciliation, which under the guidance of Norman Thomas on April 13, 1917, developed a plan to "Experiment with social, industrial and international problems."

The program though pretentious is of course vague, unless indeed one examines carefully each committee where, together with a group of unknown persons, two or three names of well-known radicals are always bracketed. In the first group the names Miss Jessie Hughan, Walter Rauschenbusch and Dr. Harry F. Ward appear; in the second, Miss Balch, Dr. John Haynes Holmes, and O. G. Villard; in the third, Jane Addams, L. Hollingsworth Wood and the Reverend Jonathan Day.

It is also suggestive to note that one large committee of the Fellowship of Reconciliation was "devoted to the carrying on of the propaganda of the society in foreign countries."[2]

In the way of "Emergency Strategy" at this point we find a number of instances: Mr. Owen Lovejoy on April 27, 1917, declined to serve on the Emergency Peace Federation Board, only because he was already pledged to the American Union against Militarism. "I think it adds immensely to our strength to have the lists quite distinct so that it will not appear that the same group of people is simply playing another role, because we are not able to get enough people to take all the parts."

Again when a purely ornamental pledge of $250 was made to the Emergency Peace Federation by Mr. Ralph Pearson of

[1] Form letter sent Representative W. P. Borland, April 11, 1917, in form of questionnaire.

[2] Document: Committees appointed by Fellowship of Reconciliation Committee, April 13, 1917.

New York City, Miss Secor wrote to him "not to worry about being held to it."[1]

Presently there was another sharp change in the policy of those pseudo-pacifists. On April 30, 1917, Miss Shelly wrote to Lochner asking him and Miss Freeman to come to a meeting of the Emergency Peace Federation Committee at Hotel Astor in New York on May 2. This turned out to be virtually a co-ordinating and federating of the various anti-war, pro-German and Socialist leagues then existing in the United States, "as an informal Conference on War Problems, according to a letter, May 3, 1917, from Miss Shelly to Miss Trevett of Portland, Oregon:

> "About forty people were present last night," continued Miss Shelly, "including Morris Hillquit, a great Socialist leader, Prof. Emily Greene Balch, of international standing, Rabbi Judah L. Magnes, a Jewish leader, John Haynes Holmes, one of the outstanding ministers of the country, Edward J. Cassidy, President of the Big Six Typographical Union, (the largest in New York), Miss Lillian Wald, of Henry Street Settlement, Mr. Linville of the School Teachers' Union, George Foster Peabody and about 35 other prominent labor, socialist, church and social reform leaders."

The Emergency Peace Federation bulletin of May 3, 1917, however, does not lay undue emphasis upon this significant federating of anti-war societies, merely stating, "We were beaten, but we were right. We did not succeed in stemming the destructive tide, but we stirred a tremendous sentiment against it." It then goes on to set forth conspicuously as the future praiseworthy object of the Federation "to defend American ideals of liberty and democracy in wartime and to work for an early and enduring peace."

Reasonable as this sounds, here we have the first definite warning of the significant part which so-called free speech and civil liberties were to play in the defeatist plans of the socialistic-pacifists from this time on, invoking and perverting the meaning of one section of the Constitution precisely in order to undermine the strength of the Constitution itself. The rest of the May 3d bulletin sets forth the "Immediate Program" of the federation, as follows:

[1] April 19, 1917.

"No. 1. The free speech clause.

"No. 2. To oppose the enactment of measures for compulsory military service.

"No. 3. To assert the right of the people to know and discuss the aims, scope and method of our participation in the war and their right at any time to advocate terms of peace.

"No. 4. To oppose the adoption of any treaty, alliance or policy which would prevent the United States from making an independent decision as to when and on what terms it shall make peace.

"No. 5. To urge our government to seize every opportunity for bringing about peace negotiations and establishing an international organization as a guarantee against future wars."

This "Program," which bears resemblance to Lochner's 1915 program, was one of the first fruits of the meeting of May 2, 1917, to which Lochner had been summoned, and where representatives of the Emergency Peace Federation, the American Union against Militarism, the Socialist movement, the Labor Party, the Woman's Peace Party,[1] etc., merged under the suprising title of "The First American Conference for Democracy and Terms of Peace."

At a subsequent meeting of May 4th, to which also came individual radicals of all varieties, an amicable arrangement was reached whereby the officers of the American Union against Militarism and the Emergency Peace Federation were to co-operate jointly in the interest of the First American Conference for Democracy and Terms of Peace, set to meet formally at the Holland House in New York on May 30 and 31, 1917.

Since the chairman of the American Union against Militarism at that time was Miss Lillian Wald, supported by a staff including Amos Pinchot, L. Hollingsworth Wood, Crystal Eastman, Roger Baldwin and Charles T. Hallinan, it would seem that our "emergency group" had found strong allies. And promptly on May 3, 1917, Roger Baldwin, Associate Director of the American Union against Militarism (who has since served a year in jail for violating the Draft Law, and who was described as an "intellectual anarchist" by Norman Thomas), wrote a long letter to Miss Balch, giving expert advice as to how similar conferences for "democracy

[1] Lochner to Miss Wald, May 9, 1917, 1st and 2nd drafts.

and terms of peace" should be organized in Chicago, San Francisco and elsewhere. His main points were as follows:

"No. 1. That every effort should be made to get the labor, socialist and farmer group to back these conference meetings, "because they will carry most weight with the country *and in dealing with similar groups abroad.*"

"No. 2. "That the pacifist organizations ought to stand in the background." (Old Emergency Peace Federation strategy, of course.)

"No. 3. More emphasis to be placed on the international aspects of these conferences. . . . 'It may be well even to think of sending delegates from our own people's conferences to similar conferences to be held in other countries, *particularly Germany and Austria.*' Emphasis should be placed upon the co-operation of the peoples — not the governments — on a program of internationalism."

Surely in this last point of Baldwin we have the old German-Socialist-Internationalist pacifism of the Lochner-Schwimmer 1915 period, coming out into the open, under wartime conditions in 1917, as international revolutionary Socialism.

Though Lochner and his Emergency Peace Federation associates were in perfect accord with these policies of Baldwin, apparently the arrangements for Lochner to be in supreme charge of the Conference, seems not to have been satisfactory to certain officers of the American Union against Militarism,— notably Miss Wald, the chairman, undoubtedly the leader of the group. So that presently the executives of the American Union against Militarism, who had expected themselves to be in command, withdrew their names from the First American Conference.[1]

The history of the misunderstandings and difficulties which led to the withdrawal is rather complicated, but in Lochner's long letter of explanation to Miss Wald[2] he says in effect that both Dr. Judah Magnes and Mr. Hillquit, who were apparently directing the organization of the Conference, objected to the American Union against Militarism being its steering committee.

The American Union thereupon concentrated its efforts upon defending the rights of conscientious objectors; and presently developed branch offices both in Washington and in New York under the name of the Civil Liberties Bureau. Though this

[1] Lochner to Mrs. Wm. Thomas, May 12, 1917, 2nd draft.

[2] Lochner to Miss Wald, May, 1917, Draft 1.

bureau under Baldwin continued to co-operate in an advisory way with the First American Conference, for the most part it created and developed entirely new machinery for hampering the military strength of the country, during the war and afterward.

After following therefore the manoeuvres of Lochner's Conference forces to their logical conclusion, we shall return to observe those of the Baldwin American Union against Militarism group which seceded from the conference in May, 1917.

CHAPTER VI

First American Conference for Democracy and Terms of Peace, May 1 to 30, 1917

PART I

CO-OPERATION OF EMERGENCY PEACE FEDERATION

Certain definite phases of the withdrawal of the American Union against Militarism officers from the Conference appeared in Lochner's letter of explanation early in May, 1917, to Miss Lillian Wald. Lochner wrote, pointing out as delicately as possible, that the American Union against Militarism was expected to be merely a co-ordinating unit of the Conference on equal terms with the Emergency Peace Federation. In doing this, however, he threw the responsibility of the decision upon the shoulders of Dr. Magnes.[1]

Nevertheless Rabbi Magnes, on May 11, 1917, telegraphed Lochner from Kansas City, as follows:

> "Strongly urge making every possible concession to American Union even to extent of modifying platform and nature of conference. Task before us so long and arduous, would be unfortunate if at beginning complete understanding lacking. Call meeting of committee. Thresh matters out. Come to an agreement."

There is no record of the exact outcome of the matter, but though the names and the officers of the American Union Against Militarism never appeared formally on the Conference lists, the Union as an organization did nevertheless act informally as one of the co-ordinating forces in a somewhat less degree than the Emergency Peace Federation. There is indeed memoranda on co-operation between the anti-militaristic organizations, dated May 18, 1917, to the following effect:

> "(1) Organizations actively in the field working nationally are:
>
> "American Union against Militarism.
>
> "Emergency Peace Federation.

[1] Lochner to Miss Wald, May 9, 1917.

"Woman's Peace Party.
"Socialist Party.
"Occasionally other national peace organizations (Church Peace Union and the American Peace Society).
"(2) Co-operation in New York:

"(1) Weekly conference of the National executives of the American Union against Militarism, Emergency Peace Federation, and other bodies represented by national officers.

"(2) Exchange of minutes, bulletins, plans, copies of circular letters, etc., between the executives of all these organizations. Each should keep a full file of the publications and minutes of the other.

"(3) A joint registration bureau of the names of co-operating local organizations and individuals throughout the United States should be established in New York under a committee representing the agencies which maintain it, in charge of a clerk appointed by this committee.

"(3) Co-operation in Washington:

"(1) During session of Congress through a weekly conference of legislative agents.

"(2) Through congressional campaigns planned in advance, distributing the work among the organizations.

"(4) General co-operation:

"(1) A written agreement as to the division of organizing work throughout the country.

"(2) A joint program agreed upon by the organizations showing what matters each will handle and in exactly what way."

The Emergency Peace Federation, of course, having been largely responsible for the very birth of the First American Conference for Democracy and Terms of Peace, strained every nerve, in the combined efforts of the Misses Shelly and Secor in its behalf.

In other words, while Lochner was federating the various forces of the radical and pacifist leagues under the banner (and letterhead) of the Conference itself, these ladies were stirring up old followers, inspiring new ones and generally feeding fuel to the central fires in the name of the Emergency Peace Federation.

Before, therefore, going on to Lochner's own organizing activities for the Conference, we will consider a little those of his principal aides. At the same time it might be well to mention the fact once more that there were many high-minded and genuine pacifists in the movement, some not understanding it in the least, and others becoming gradually converted, or hypnotized into believing that a revolution leading to Socialism would make a paradise of the world.

Naturally, the several women on the staff of the Emergency Peace Federation knew well enough that they were helping Lochner to develop for the Conference a thoroughly practical platform. Miss Secor's letters to New York pacifists may have been a little vague as to method but those of Miss Shelly to the Emergency Peace Federation organizers in the field, enclosing the "Call to Action"[1] of the Conference, were altogether specific. Between the first and the third weeks of May, 1917, Miss Shelly wrote to the following persons:

1. To Mrs. Lola Maverick Lloyd, of Chicago, (May 5, 1917):

> . . . "I wish very much that you could stir them and other Chicago pacifists up to some action after May 18th. . . . The issue now is specific terms of peace. Your devoted soul will leap to hear that there is a powerful movement on foot to bring together all democratic forces in America to discuss and push for this very thing. . . . The Organization Committee meets tonight. This conference will be somewhat parallel to your Chicago Emergency Conference in 1915, except if I read the signs correctly, it will be more all-inclusive. . . . I am sending you twenty-five copies of our latest pamphlet 'In Time of War Prepare for Peace,' which I wish you would distribute judiciously."

2. To the Reverend E. R. Wagner, of Huntingdon, Pa., (May 8, 1917):

> . . . "The first chapter of our existence was chiefly one of emergency action and protest. The second must be one of careful planning, thorough organization and constructive action. . . . Any plans we make are effective only as we can induce friends of peace all over the country to co-operate with us. Will you help to organize an Emergency Peace Federation in Huntingdon."

3. To Mr. Joseph Schonfield, (May 21, 1917), Minneapolis,

[1] **"Call to Action" as issued by Conference Organizers, May 7, 1917.**

Minn., and Prof. A. O. Lovejoy, (May 9, 1917), of Johns-Hopkins University, Baltimore, Md., the regular form letter beginning:

"The Emergency Peace Federation had its beginning on February 3d, the day Count von Bernstorff was handed his passports."

4. To Senator LaFollette and Representative William Mason, both in Washington, D. C., (May 16, 1917):

"This is to introduce to you Mrs. J. Sargent Cram of New York City, who has been one of the mainstays of the Emergency Peace Federation, *and who is now especially devoting herself to the problem of the conscientious objectors. Her home is the rallying point for a great number of young men who are unalterably opposed to war, and who are looking to her for guidance as to what course to pursue when once the Conscription Act has been passed. . . .*" (Italics ours.)

5. Mr. Elmer Willis Serl, River Falls, Wis.:

. . . "It is hoped by the leaders that every peace organization in the country, every Socialist and Labor Local, and all other radical groups, will push this program and demand peace negotiations based on the principles therein enunciated." (May 8, 1917).

6. Mr. Albert Steinhauser, New Ulm, Minn.:

. . . "While individual co-operation through correspondence is essential as furnishing the basis for more solid organization, group organization and group action is inevitably the method by which we will effect our purpose." . . . (May 9, 1917).

7. Dr. C. F. Taylor, of the "Medical World," Philadelphia:[1]

. . . "The first American Conference on Democracy and Terms of Peace will be held on May 30th. It will formulate a program of principles, and the plan of action on which all supporters of peace and democracy may unite. This program will *undoubtedly be in thorough accord with that of the Russian Council of Workmen and Soldiers.*[2] *We* want the people of America to join hands with the people of Russia in a respectable demand that the government cease to

[1] Dated May 19, 1917.
[2] Italics ours.

juggle alternately with words and millions of human lives, and state concretely what they are fighting for."

8. Rev. Arthur L. Weatherly (a Ford Pilgrim), of Lincoln, Neb., (May 9, 1917):

> . . . "To be frank, the Emergency Peace Federation is a much more radical organization, and will step in the vanguard of the fight more actively and uncompromisingly, than the American Union against Militarism. This is not disparaging the latter . . . Finally, please tell me just what organizations or societies in Lincoln we can depend upon for radical peace action."

9. To Arthur LeSueur, Non-Partisan League, North Dakota:

> . . . "If, however, the people of America do not bring pressure on the government to back up demoracy in Russia and Germany, the war may continue as long as the war party wishes it." (May 11, 1917.)

A very interesting piece of co-operation with Miss Shelly from the field about this time was on the part of J. Barnard Walton of the Religious Society of Friends (and of Swarthmore College), who wrote to her in answer to a letter on May 24, 1917:

> "Dr. Hull forwarded to me your letter to him with the name of your members in Swarthmore, and I have also received your letter of the 16th . . . We have already two active organizations, the local group which at least is absolutely in agreement with the platform of the Emergency Peace Federation. They are the Fellowship of Reconciliation and the Woman's Peace Party. They contain the persons named on your list and several others. I would therefore suggest that you put on your list exactly as if they were secretaries of local groups of the Emergency Peace Federation:—Mrs. Elizabeth W. Collins, Swarthmore, Pa., for the Fellowship of Reconciliation, and Emilie W. Pollard, Swathmore, Pa., for the Woman's Peace Party." . . .

Not only Mr. Walton, but virtually all persons addressed by Conference officials were sympathetic to her peace overtures. Among those eager to co-operate were Dr. John Lovejoy Elliot, of the New York Ethical Culture Society[1]; Dr. John Herman

[1] Dr. Elliot to Miss Secor, April 28, 1917.

Randall of Mt. Morris Baptist Church[1]; Prof. Harry F. Ward, of the Methodist Federation for Social Service, now the Union Theological Seminary[2]; Prof. Harry Overstreet, of the College of the City of New York[3]; Dr. Harvey Dee Brown, of the Church of the Messiah (May 9, 1917); Dr. Richard W. Hogue, of the Prisoners' Aid Association of Maryland (April 28, 1917); Norman Thomas, George Foster Peabody,[4] and J. Levin of the Jewish Socialist Labor Party of America.

Occasionally, however, Miss Shelly, as well as Miss Secor and even Miss Balch, encountered some penetrating criticism, as for instance from Judge Robert F. Walker, of Jefferson City, Mo., or from an honest though clear-headed pacifist named G. Ulbricht, who wrote on May 14th, 1917:

> . . . "Though I am heartily in favor of any efforts that can be made to bring about peace, I am opposed to the trend of your federation towards Socialism and Single Tax". . . .

Other points worth noting in the files of the Emergency Peace Federation of this period are as follows:

A list of the Open Forum Speakers' Bureau of Boston for 1917–18, which upon close examination today discloses many of the speakers as radicals and Socialists.

A telegram from Louis Kantor, to the Emergency Peace Federation: "Send accurate information as to number of members affiliated with the following societies: Citizens' Emergency, Bronx; Anti-Conscription Collegiate; Anti-Militarists; Young Men's Anti-Conscription; East Side Conscription; Third and Tenth Districts Anti-Conscription; Harlem Union against Conscription; Leagues World Patriots; American Union against Militarism. Prominent Senator wants to use them in his speech."

A letter from Miss Warneson, Kansas City, Mo. (May 23, 1917):

> "Your getting a note from Dr. How" (James Eads How, the hobo millionaire Socialist) "reassured me somewhat as to his fate. I was afraid that he might be shut up with the German prisoners in Halifax as were Trotzky and the other Russians who attempted to return to their native land after the revolution.

---

[1] Dr. Randall to Miss Secor, May 1, 1917.
[2] Dr. Ward to Miss Secor, May 2, 1917.
[3] Lochner thanking Overstreet for signing "The Call," May 15, 1917.
[4] Peabody to Miss Balch, May 17, 1917.

"I sometimes wonder that the Russian radicals in Kansas don't beat it back to freedom now there is such a thing on earth, but they seem to want to do their bit to give this country a taste of it" . . .

There are further minutes of two Emergency Peace Federation meetings on file for May 9 and May 25, 1917, respectively, at one of which Mr. Villard was made chairman; also a bulletin of the Fellowship of Reconciliation announcing "Mr. Villard and John Haynes Holmes speakers at the next religious conference;" and finally an Emergency Peace Federation Bulletin May 25, 1917, announcing that the Federation officials had joined the forces of the First Conference for Democracy and Terms of Peace.

Since from this date on we hear nothing further from the Emergency Peace Federation as such, we must take it for granted that it was swallowed whole on May 30, 1917, at the first meeting of the Conference.

PART II

FIRST AMERICAN CONFERENCE FOR DEMOCRACY AND TERMS OF PEACE

To return to Lochner and his own organizing activities leading up to the May 30–31 Conference of 1917, a telegram from him to Morris Hillquit and Miss Balch on May 12, 1917, will show that they were even higher authorities in the matter of Conference policies than Rabbi Magnes. The telegram reads:

> "Magnes after consultation with Jane Addams and on receipt of letter from me wires 'Strongly urge making every possible concession to American Union, even to extent of modifying platform and nature of conference. Task before all so long and arduous, would be unfortunate if at beginning complete understanding lacking. Call meeting of committee. Thresh matters out. Come to an agreement. What do you advise? Literature ready for mailing today. Shall I go ahead or wait?"

Though there is no answer on record from either Hillquit or Miss Balch, it is evident that they advised Lochner to "go ahead," for the platform of the Conference was not in the least modified, and the only name of the American Union Against Militarism Executive Board signed to the "Call" was that of Norman Thomas.

The "Tentative Program" issued on May 7, 1917, though a Socialistic document to the discerning eye, (as was evidenced by a notation on one copy reading, "Not my ideal of a democracy," and signed by Mrs. T. H. Tillinghast, New Bedford, Mass.) with its protestation of love for America, insistence on the "tentative platform" statement and the reiterated misuse of the words "democracy" and "democratic," the program was likely enough to mislead the average pacifist. Further, even as late as May 23, 1917, when an appeal for funds went out under the names of Mrs. Villard, Miss Balch, Leonora O'Reilly, Joseph D. Cannon and Morris Hillquit, the letter reading: "To co-ordinate and organize the democratic and peace loving forces of the country is the primary aim of the conference,"—how were the sincere peace loving ones to know that by "democratic" the committee really meant Socialistic?

Of course the names of the signers to the invitation to the Conference, which today, with few exceptions, stand for Socialism, are now generally recognized as such. In May, 1917, however, a goodly proportion of the men and women whose names were signed —

Emily G. Balch, Joseph D. Cannon, Morris Hillquit, Rabbi Magnes, J. H. Maurer, Victor L. Berger, A. J. Boulton, James J. Bagley, Rose Schneidermann, John C. Kennedy, Edward J. Cassidy, Joseph Schlossberg, E. Baroff, Henry Bereche, Roy Brazzle, Mary Kenney O'Sullivan, Arthur LeSueur, Algernon Lee, James Oneal, Harry Laidler, Julius Gerber, Julian Pierce, Job Harriman, Winter Russell, Harry Weinberger, Rt. Rev. Paul Jones, Jenkin Lloyd Jones, Rev. Richard W. Hogue, Rev. Sidney Strong, Rev. H. L. Canfield, L. Hollingsworth Wood, David Starr Jordan, Prof. Simon N. Patten, Scott Nearing, William I. Hull, Harry W. L. Dana, Lindley Miller Keasbey, Prof. Harry A. Overstreet, Rev. Irwin St. John Tucker, Brent Dow Allinson, Grace De Graff, James McKeen Cattell, Randolph Bourne, May Wright Sewall, Daniel Kiefer, Amy Mali Hicks, Frank Stephens, Mrs. Glendower Evans, Helena S. Dudley, Lenora Warneson, Mrs. Lola Maverick Lloyd, Mrs. Elsie Borg Goldsmith, Margaret Lane, Edward Berwick, John Reed, Edward T. Hartman, L. C. Beckwith, Miss Crystal M. Eastman, Anna F. Davies, and Henry R. Linville —

termed themselves merely "liberals," and had a large following of perfectly well intentioned Americans. These, as cannot be mentioned too often, went ahead joyously, working against the interests of the country without ever suspecting as much. That Lochner and his associates were well aware of the importance of having these "liberals" and their following of Americans in high standing connected with his Conference, may be illustrated in several ways.

For instance, the Rev. S. G. von Bosse, a German from Wilmington, Del., in answering an appeal for the National German-American alliance to co-operate in the organization of the Conference, wrote on May 8, 1917, disapproving of German-Americans taking any part in peace propaganda during war-time: "Any such efforts," he adds, "must come from men who cannot be identified with any German affiliations." Another illustration of Lochner's difficulties about this time was the determined and outspoken opposition of Samuel Gompers to the Conference officials as "conscious or unconscious agents of the Kaiser in America." After this statement of Gompers was published in the Washington

"Herald," early in May, 1917, Miss Balch wrote to Lochner, asking among other things:

> "Cannot some strong labor man get after Gompers explaining to him that he 'misunderstood the conference?'"

Evidently no labor man was found strong enough to persuade Gompers, for on May 11, 1917, Lochner wired Miss Balch:

> "Baldwin and I urge strongly that you or Hallinan see Grant Hamilton and Morrison of A. F. of L. personally to solicit signatures to 'Call.' Also suggest you get Jackson H. Ralston to sign."

There are other instances to prove that Baldwin and other officers of the American Union Against Militarism, who had not allowed Lochner the use of their names in the "Call," did nevertheless help him unofficially in organizing the Conference. Aside from the regular organized aid of the American Union Against Militarism, the Emergency Peace Federation, etc., Lochner commanded some valuable co-operation from individual Socialists. Significant among these was C. W. Barzel of Portland, Ore., who, in organizing "Peace" societies for Lochner, thoroughly understood the un-pacific nature of the undertaking. He reported his endeavors as follows (May 19, 1917):

> "No. 1 appealed to was a minister of very socialistic tendencies and well up to date for the ministry. His conclusion was that it might be the right thing to do but gave no assurance that he would take an active part therein. My second appeal was to a druggist who is known to be very far advanced in economic and social lines. He seemed to favor it" (a Peace Conference) "but gave no pledge as to the part he would take. My third was a foreman in a grocery business known to be anti-war. He seemed not to grasp the necessity of immediate action. My fourth was another druggist known to be only partially informed. He seemed to think the move was to play into the hands of Germany and gave no evidence of favorable interest. A fifth was a real estate dealer who hesitated to talk, etc. My sixth was another merchant interested but not informed. . . . If my prospectus is of interest, you may send me literature and I will distribute it, as may be accepted by my friends and neighbors."

Still other examples of strategy of one kind or another which helped build up or disguise the true nature of the First American Conference for Democracy and Peace were as follows:

1. A telegram dated May 7, 1917, from Judge Lindsey to Lochner: "Am in sympathy with your purposes, but for reasons that I will write you more at length it is better at this time that my name should not be signed to 'Call.'"

2. A letter from Lochner to Miss Balch[1] quoting Rabbi Magnes as advising the Conference to go more or less easy on conscription and other "anti" issues, putting stress instead upon "constructive measures looking toward a re-establishment of international relations."

3. A long letter from Lochner to Mrs. Robert La Follette, in an endeavor to make the Senator appear publicly at the conference, and a similar letter from Miss Secor to young Robert La Follette, son of the Senator.[2]

4. A letter from Miss Lenora Warneson, who organized a conference in Kansas City, Mo., under the name of the "Kansas City Federation for Democratic Control." "We chose that title as less alarming to the easily terrorized than our former name, 'American Union Against Militarism.'" (May 7, 1917.)

5. A letter from the secretary of Rev. Frederick Lynch of the Church Peace Union (May 25, 1919) (who had previously been compelled by his board to resign as treasurer of the Emergency Peace Federation) enclosing check nevertheless, signed by Dr. Lynch, and asking that the date of his letter of resignation be accordingly brought forward. A letter from Dr. Lynch himself to Lochner on his staying in the Church Peace Union, "in order not to lose what radical sentiment there still exists in these boards."

6. A letter from Alice Cassidy of 530 West 123d street, New York City, of May 16, 1917, offering to do propaganda work for Lochner. We quote from the letter: "I have been quietly arousing a peace sentiment since the beginning of the war two and a half years ago, and previous to that I was active in almost all the big strikes, as I was at that time connected with the Woman's Trade Union League. You may telephone Miss Mary E. Dreier, and she will tell you that my work was always effective."

---

[1] May 18, 1917.
[2] May 10, 1917.

In a second letter, dated May 22, 1917, Miss Cassidy writes: "I am enclosing a list of colored organizations which meet uptown. . . . I presume you will have to communicate with them in case you intend sending speakers to address them."

7. A letter of adverse criticism (May 25, 1917) from Richard H. Rice, of Lynn, Mass.: "I consider that participation in this conference is an act of treason and that the propaganda which you apparently are intending to launch is probably inspired by German influence and financed by German capital;" and Lochner's propitiatory, protesting answer, a specimen of his juggling with the truth with which he usually tried to disarm his critics.

8. A letter to Lochner from George Nasmyth, May 21, 1917, introducing Rev. Linley Gordon, "who has been doing a splendid piece of work speaking and organizing against conscription in Australia." And a second Nasmyth letter, May 25, 1917, advising Miss Balch against including "opposition to compulsory military training during the war as a permanent policy" in the Conference program,—this however purely for strategic reasons.

9. A letter from Henry R. Linville of the Teachers' Union, objecting among other things to Morris Hillquit being sent to Russia as a representative of the Conference Committee: "I have never been able," Mr. Linville goes on, "to detect anything American in sympathy in the psychology of Hillquit. . . . I have had some difficulty in assuring myself that the American Conference contained the elements that would be able to make an effective appeal to American Democracy any more successfully than would the Socialist Party . . . The party of which I am a member . . ."

10. Correspondence with J. Harris Crook of the League for Democratic Control of Boston, who promised May 19, 1917, to send three delegates to the Conference (besides himself) and offering some moderation of the program, also on tactical grounds.

11. A letter from John Jay Cisco, Jr., of Greenwich, Conn., May 18, 1917, who wished to co-operate with Lochner in organizing a "No-conscription Fellowship of the World" (Mr. Cisco's chief claim to distinction — aside from his pride in being a conscientious objector — seems to have been a sort of left handed acquaintanceship, twice removed, with Bertrand Russell, the English Pacifist).

12. A letter from Harry Lashkowitz of Fargo, N. D., May 11,

1917, to Morris Hillquit, expressing a wish to bring about "a consolidation of the people of this state to help secure peace with . . . no indemnities nor forcible annexations, no foreign alliances; international organization after the war, opposition to conscription and statement of terms by our government."

13. A note of introduction to labor unions of New York City and vicinity from Lochner, May 19, 1917, reading as follows: "This is certify that Mr. James J. Bagley and Mr. Walter F. Rockstroh have been duly appointed to represent the Conference before labor unions, with a view to enlisting the co-operation of the labor movement and securing delegates for the Conference."

14. A letter from the Massachusetts Council of the Friends of Irish Freedom, expressing sympathy with the aims of the Conference. (May 5, 1917.)

15. A letter from Miss Balch to her Conference associates giving the news that the Federal Council of Churches would have the subject of conscientious objectors "strongly presented;"[1] and quoting the following telegram from Mrs. Lloyd in Chicago: "Radical group including Addams decided Saturday to hold auditorium protest meeting Sunday, May 27. Can you get anyone in Congress to promise to speak. . . . Try La Follette again, if unsuccessful try Thomas Cooper, Keating, Gronna, Anthony, Rankin. . . ."

16. A letter from Miss Mabel H. Williamson, of Teachers' College, May 8, 1917, asking for "fifty of our resolutions; I speak for the branch here of the Fellowship of Reconciliation."

17. A letter from C. S. Longacre of the Religious Library Association of Washington, D. C., suggesting that he would submit "a list of our ministers" to Lochner, if called for. (May 10, 1917.)

18. A letter from Rev. Edw. Blakeman, of the University Methodist Episcopal Church of Madison, Wis., to Lochner, congratulating him upon his "tenacity and inguenuity. . . . (April 10, 1917.) Men who can over three or four years promote these manoeuvres under the conditions prevailing should be able to outdo Milton in Paradise Lost. . . ."

19. A letter from Robert W. Dunn, of the Yale "Courant" (May 21, 1917), promising to distribute Lochner's invitations to the Conference among the Yale pacifists. "Our organizations

[1] May 14, 1917.

are distinctly collegiate. Yet I shall use my personal influence to have the Socialist Party, perhaps some of the labor bodies, Woman's Peace Party, etc., in the city send representatives."

20. Another letter from Cisco, giving Bertrand Russell's address. (May 26, 1917.) He then adds: "Will you try to secure the co-operation of the Emergency Peace Federation, the American Union against Militarism and most important, the innumerable locals of the Socialist Party in rounding up the helter-skelter anti-conscription organizations under one great purposeful head?"

21. Suggestions of Scott Nearing for the Conference, in some detail.[1] He urges as a working program the joining of forces of the Woman's Peace Party, the American Legal Defense League, the American Union against Militarism, the Emergency Peace Federation, the labor unions, American Association for Labor Legislation, the Socialist Party and the Socialist Labor Party — all with a view to having "every agency in the United States that stands for democracy working together in this common cause." As a final word Mr. Nearing adds: "The League will work towards the establishment of industrial democracy in the United States after the war."

22. A letter from Louis Kopelin, owner and editor of the "Appeal to Reason," to Morris Hillquit, May 31, 1917, offering his publication for sale to the Peace Conference, "which I understand is the central body of all the peace associations and the Socialist Party."

23. From Paul U. Kellogg to Miss Balch, May 10, 1917, regretting that the Conference dates conflict with that Conference on Foreign Relations, the results of your work, Mr. Villard's and mine . . ."

In these, as well as many other sources of co-operation, Lochner, Miss Freeman and Miss Balch, aided by Hillquit and Magnes proceeded with the building up of the "Peace" Conference, which as it came nearer and nearer became less and less peaceful and more and more openly socialistic. In spite of all criticism, friendly and unfriendly, in spite of the fact that the Holland House, the place originally set for the Conference meeting, put the radicals out, Lochner and his fellow campaigners continued the building up of their anti-war, anti-conscription, anti-

[1] Suggestions of Scott Nearing, Toledo, O., May 26, 1917.

allies, in a word, anti-democratic (in the true sense) Federation. And, finally, the conference of May 30 and 31, 1917, was called at Madison Square Garden.[1]

Anyone who wishes to learn the entire happenings of these two days will do well to read every word of the first session of the "First American Conference of Democracy and Terms of Peace" in pamphlet form. But for the benefit of those who prefer short cuts, a digest of the pamphlet will follow.

---

[1] Title page of Report of Conference.

PART III

PUBLISHED REPORT OF FIRST AMERICAN CONFERENCE FOR DEMOCRACY AND TERMS OF PEACE

Before considering the published report of the First American Conference of Democracy and Terms of Peace, held in New York City May 30 and 31, 1917, it may be well to recall that at that time the United States had been at war with Germany for two months; and in an endeavor to make up for some of its unpreparedness had passed the Conscription bill. Patriotic citizens, therefore, realizing that if Germany were allowed to defeat the Allies, this country must inevitably be the next target, willingly accepted any burdens that insured a successful prosecution of the war. There were of course hundreds of thousands of aliens and citizens of German sympathies among us; the newspapers were reporting acts of destruction by them; the air was full of rumors of draft riots; very disquieting news kept coming from the ranks of the Allies in France; and finally, through the Russian revolution of March, 1917, there loomed the added danger of the Russians making a separate peace and joining forces with the enemy. Surely this was a time for every staunch American, every lover of democracy in its true sense to stand by and fight the enemies of all democracy.

The Conference group, however, guided by Lochner and other persons of similar opinions, subtly twisting and perverting the meaning of honest words, chose this time to present a thoroughly socialistic, pro-German and undemocratic program under the name of "Democracy."

In the very foreword of this peculiarly un-American document, in the very act of shrieking aloud its Americanism, we find this sinister juggling of words and motives. After a diatribe against militarism justifying the organization of the Conference, representing the combined Socialist, pacifist and anti-military leagues of the country, we are told that these are "a mighty force demanding that American democracy, American ideals, American peace be preserved inviolate."[1] The foreword then continues:

> "Such an organization was rendered doubly necessary by the revolution in Russia . . . They (the American people) wanted to make known to this free Russian people that the

[1] Page 3, Report of First American Conference for Democracy and Terms of Peace.

feelings of those who dwell in America were not truly expressed by the war-like and undemocratic action of the official government that was elected to represent them. They wanted to show that they stand solid behind the Russian democracy and are ready to work with *them until the autocracy of the entire world is overthrown.*"[1]

In plain words, the Socialists and their pacifist allies of this country, thoroughly in sympathy with the Socialist program of Russia, were preparing to join them in an effort to overthrow the so-called autocracies (our own Government included, as we shall presently see) of the world.

That this program of international Socialism is sounded over and over again in the proceedings of the Conference — and along with it more or less open sympathy with Germany — we are about to illustrate step by step. Before doing so, however, it is only fair to give further explanation of some words generally in use by radicals. In the radical dictionary then, the word "autocracy" refers as often as not to a genuine democracy, such as our own; the words "democracy", "democratic" and "democrats" are used to connote Socialism, Socialistic and Socialists; and the very word "Americanism" has been prostituted to mean things as wholly un-American as, let us say, the Socialist Party.

In the report of the Conference itself we read:

1. Under the heading of "Peace": "The Conference favors an early democratic peace, to be secured through negotiation in harmony with the principles outlined by the President of the United States and by revolutionary Russia, and substantially by the progressive and democratic forces of France, England, Italy, Germany, Austria, etc., namely: (a) No forcible annexations of territory; (b) no punitive indemnities; (c) free development of all nationalities."

The committee of delegates in charge of these "peace" resolutions were Morris Hillquit, Jenkin Lloyd Jones, Emily Greene Balch, Wm. I. Hull, Randolph Bourne, Anne Withington, Alfred J. Boulton, Leonora O'Reilly, Algeron Lee and Prof. Lindley M. Keasbey.[2]

2. Under "American Liberties" the Conference protested (among other things) "against conscription, compulsory military training;" and demanded "democratic control of our foreign

[1] Page 3 of Conference report. (Italics our own).
[2] Pages 7 and 8 of Report.

policy." The committee in charge of "American Liberties" read as follows:

Richard W. Hogue, chairman; Lola Maverick Lloyd, Winnetka, Ill.; J. Barnard Walton, Swarthmore, Pa.; Prof. H. W. L. Dana, New York City, now of Boston; Harry Weinberger, New York City; Rev. Norman Thomas, New York City; Victor Berger, Milwaukee; Donald Stephens, Delaware; Alex. L. Trachtenberg, New York City.[1]

3. Under "Industrial Standards" we find: . . . "The American people, joining hands with the new democracy of Russia, must lay the basis for permanent world peace by establishing industrial democracy." In charge of this overseas joining of hands project, were Scott Nearing, Toledo, Ohio, chairman; James Bagley, New York City; Edward J. Cassidy, New York City; Henri Bereche, New York City; Owen R. Lovejoy, New York City; Mrs. Florence Kelley, New York City; E. Baroff, New York City; Miss Amy Hicks, New York City.[2]

Under "Permanent Organization and Future Activities" we have in Point 3: . . . "To create at once a committee on international co-operation representing all the democratic forces in the United States field, to work in co-operation with the democratic forces of other countries both during and after the war," and further; "that the committee arrange for a similar conference on democracy and terms of peace in Illinois immediately and in California as soon as practicable thereafter." The committee appointed to look after these matters was James Maurer, Harrisburg, Pa., chairman; Frank Stephens, Arden, Del.; Mary Ware Dennett, New York City; Crystal Eastman, Croton-on-Hudson, N. Y.; Job Harriman, Los Angeles, Cal.; Rebecca Shelly, New York City; Daniel Roy Freeman, Grand Rapids, Mich.; Willard C. Wheeler, Boston, Mass.; Rose Schneidermann, New York City; Arthur Fisher; Adolf Germer, Chicago; Max Pine, New York City; Max Eastman; Edward Hartman, Boston, Mass.; Harold Rotzel, Worcester, Mass.; Fola La Follette, New York City; Harry W. Laidler, New York City; Louis P. Lochner, Chicago, Ill.; Joseph Schlossberg, New York City; Daniel Kiefer, Cincinnati, Ohio; Charles W. Ervin, New York City; Elizabeth Freeman, New York City; Margaret Lane, New York City.[3]

---

[1] Page 8 of Conference report.
[2] Page 9 of Conference report.
[3] Page 10 of Conference report.

Other persons who gave valuable assistance were Frank Stephens, Arden, Del.; Lewis A. Maverick, San Antonio, Tex.; Marian B. Cothren, Brooklyn, N. Y.; Darwin J. Meserole, Brooklyn; Jacob Panken, New York City; Ludwig Lore, New York City, and Job Harriman.[1]

The speeches delivered at the first session of the Conference on May 30, 1917, are extremely illuminating. The chairman, Rabbi Magnes, said in his opening appeal that their purpose was "to rededicate ourselves to the cause of democracy and international brotherhood." Later he makes the veiled threat: "America must understand that the Russian armies will have the spirit to continue the war on one condition — that their own idealistic war aims be made the war aims of their Allies." A little later Rabbi Magnes puts this in another way: "We want them (the Russians) to know that the American democracy does not intend to lag behind the Russian in the development of political and economic internationalism, and in all the constructive arts of peace."[2]

Following Dr. Magnes, Mr. Algernon Lee, of the Rand School, spoke on "Forces Making for Democracy and Peace in Europe," confining himself to the workings of the International Socialist Bureau and the Socialist parties in the various countries of Europe. In so doing he brought out that the Socialist movement in Europe was largely that of organized labor and that in many countries "numerous and influential non-Socialist elements are earnestly working in the same direction so far as concerns the effort for a general, democratic and lasting peace," especially mentioning the co-operation of the Union of Democratic Control of Great Britain and pacifists on the order of Bertrand Russell. Mr. Lee went on to tell in detail of the activities of the Societies abroad during the war to submit their peace platform beginning with the familiar "no punitive indemnities," including a demand for the "democratization of governments"— taking care, however, not to draw attention to the fact that our own government was to be no exception to the rule. He referred with pride that the Socialists of Great Britain in the summer of 1916 were responsible for "the Union for Democratic Control and similar organizations, getting more than a hundred thousand signers within a few weeks to a so-called 'Stop the War Petition.'"[3]

---

[1] Page 5 of Conference report.
[2] Pages 11 to 17.
[3] Pages 18, 20, and 24 of Conference report.

After Mr. Lee had finished his own address he read one by Morris Hillquit which had to do with international Socialist Conferences during the war and a coming one to be held in Stockholm to which Mr. Hillquit had been denied passports. We find a peculiar significance in his statement:

> "As far as the Socialist Party of the United States is concerned it called such a conference as early as September 24, 1914, and renewed the suggestion on several subsequent occasions. As a result of these movements some conferences of neutrals and some separate conferences of the Socialists in the Allied countries and in the central powers were held."[1]

For it proves beyond doubt that the many conferences of neutrals recorded in this report (those on paper as well as those which actually came together) were directed by the Socialist Party.

Mr. Hillquit also reported on "Efforts during the war to bring a general International Conference of Socialists for the purpose of working out a peace program acceptable to all parties to the conflict and particularly to the Socialists of all countries." Here at last we had plain speaking; for Mr. Hillquit not only refrained from using the "democratic" camouflage for socialistic doctrines, but he stated bluntly that the "peace program" devised by the Socialists would be particularly acceptable to Socialists all over the world.

Mr. Alexander Trachtenberg, the next speaker, took as his subject merely a variant of the preceding ones in "The Russian Situation." After announcing that the revolution in Russia was effected by the workers and soldiers rather than by the liberals, he emphasized the fact "that the entire Russian Socialist democracy now in control of the affairs of Russia is completely international. The whole Russian working class is imbued with internationalism. It has been taught so from the very beginning." Mr. Trachtenberg wound up his address with the rather illogical remark: "As a fugitive myself — one who has found a haven here in America as a political refugee — I wish to invite to free Russia all those working for peace who find themselves uncomfortable here."[2]

---

[1] Page 25 of Conference report.
[2] Pages 28 and 29, Report of Conference, May 30, 1917.

At this, Rabbi Magnes again took the floor (in order to make clear Mr. Trachtenberg's meaning) with the following statement:

> "I cannot resist taking some of our valuable time by saying I understand that a society has actually been projected in Russia — somewhat copying the name of a society that has done very good work here for a number of years before the Russian revolution. Some of us have been connected with it — the American Friends of Russian Freedom. I understand that they have projected a society in Russia known as the Russian Friends of American Freedom."[1]

Those who remember Emma Goldman's parting reference to this Russian enterprise to "free" America, may now note further that the Russian Friends of American Freedom was functioning as long ago as 1917.

The speaker following Dr. Magnes was Mr. Louis Lochner who, though he probably compiled and wrote the report itself, now contented himself with a short talk on "The Scandinavian Countries." Though short, the speech was altogether illuminating, dealing as it did with the question of the Inter-Parliamentary Union. After pointing out that in Scandinavia "people are very democratic — possibly even more so than in America," Lochner proceeded to give a concise definition of this inter-parliamentary group — government officials in Scandinavian and other countries pledged to work against the policies of their respective governments in the cause of internationalism. To quote verbatim from Lochner:

> "This Inter-Parliamentary Union is made up of members of Parliament of all countries who believe in the cause of arbitration, international organization, etc. During the war the groups of the Inter-Parliamentary Union of the three Scandinavian countries, as well as of Switzerland and Holland, have made it their special business to try from time to time to bring pressure to bear upon their governments to renew their peace efforts, but from every side came the answer, 'We cannot do anything as long as the American group does not answer.'" He ended by urging fervently upon the conference "to send forth from the American movement" (for democracy and peace) "a delegation that will stay in touch with Europe at some spot in Scandinavia where

[1] Page 29, Report of Conference, May 30, 1917.

there is real democracy, where they can breathe the free air and be in touch constantly with those many international currents with which they can come in contact there, so that we on this side of the water may be better informed than we are now as to the progress that democracy is making in Europe."[1]

At the afternoon session of May 31st we find Mrs. Florence Kelley, chairman,[2] and Morris Hillquit, the first speaker. His subject was "Terms of Peace." This time Mr. Hillquit after proving to his own satisfaction that true patriotism should cry out for peace in time of war; that the war was "essentially a war for international trade and markets;" and that "the self-interest of every great nation will be in the direction of establishing an international organization between the nations"—goes on to asseverate that this league would be entirely different from the proposed League to Enforce Peace. Complete disarmament by all governments (even as the old army of Russia was demobilized) was the only thing to satisfy the Socialists.

Hillquit after bringing one specious argument after another in favor of disarmament, said: "I maintain that even if the governments, or rather the peoples of the various governments, repudiate the tremendous war debts *as they should* (italics our own), even then I say there will be no resources left in the various nations to maintain standing armies."[3]

Another speaker to present the subject of International Relations was Prof. Wm. I. Hull of Swarthmore College, under the title of "Entangling Alliances."

This address, under the cloak of international ideals and international conciliation, was an attack not only upon the national ambitions of the Allies but upon any national ambitions or ideals whatever. Specifically, Prof. Hull urged that an International Commission be appointed, in order to avoid possible atrocities, to follow in the wake of all advancing armies.[4]

The next dissertation: "The Democratization of Diplomacy," was delivered by Prof. Lindley M. Keasbey of the Uinversity of Texas, who, to begin with, deplored the fact that "the democratization of diplomacy will not come until we have democratized our state." Though he had no definite plan of international

[1] Pages 30 and 31, Report of Conference, May 30, 1917.
[2] Page 32, Report of Conference, May 30, 1917.
[3] Pages 33, 34 and 35, Report of Conference, May 30, 1917.
[4] Pages 38 to 41, Report of Conference, May 30, 1917.

co-operation to urge and apparently forgot to revert to the democratization of Diplomacy altogether, the professor, in his belief that "labor must be organized, capital socialized and the land liberated" was certainly in line with the pet theories of the International Socialists.[1]

Victor Berger, the next speaker, with "The War and High Finance" as his subject began facetiously as follows:

> "This war to me, ladies and gentlemen, is the Morganatic marriage, an illegal marriage between Lombard Street, London, and Wall Street, New York. The issues are illegitimate war babies down in Wall Street, and every time you mention peace one of these babies is ready to die . . . and we will stay in this war until our American people follow in the footsteps of the Rusian people and establish a social democracy."[2]

Miss Emily Balch, who discussed "Terms of Peace" after announcing that "the internationalism which we must build up is the internationalism of effective co-operation between friendly nations," proceeded to dilate upon how cruel it would be to levy a huge indemnity on Germany, even as in 1870 Germany mistakenly levied a huge indemnity upon France. (P. 44.)

The third session, on the evening of the first day, opened with Mr. James Maurer, of the Pennsylvania State Federation of Labor, who spoke briefly on "Labor Legislation and the War."[3]

Scott Nearing who followed said: "The American people, joining hands with the new democracy of Russia, must lay the basis for permanent world peace by establishing industrial democracy." A little later Mr. Nearing added: "We know how to exploit and they (the working people) know how to produce. We exploit them of a part of their product and then we tell ourselves that we are the intelligent, enlightened, beneficial party of the community."[4]

Mrs. Florence Kelley then spoke on the subject of "Labor Standards in War Time" in a destructive rather than a constructive way, attacking in the first place virtually all of the legislators in Albany. In turn she held up to scorn John

---

[1] Pages 41 and 42, Report of Conference, May 30, 1917.
[2] Pages 43 and 44, Report of Conference, May 30, 1917.
[3] Pages 45 to 47, Report of Conference, May 30, 1917.
[4] Pages 47 to 50, Report of Conference, May 30, 1917.

Mitchell, James Lynch, Elon R. Brown, Governor Whitman, Mayor Mitchel and finally Commissioner John H. Finley.[1]

Following Mrs. Kelly, there came Owen R. Lovejoy, on "Child Labor and the War;" Miss Elizabeth Freeman on "Finances of the Conference;" Stephen Bircher, of the Brotherhood of Metal Workers, on "Labor in War Time;" Edward J. Cassidy, of the Central Federated Union, on "Labor and Peace;" and Abraham Shiplacoff, on "Labor Laws in War." Each gave a short talk (more or less alike), each agitating against some war measure, each claiming to be altogether patriotic in the "new democratic sense."[2]

With the advent of the next speaker, Miss Leonora O'Reilly of the National Woman's Trade Union League, whose subject was "Safeguarding Labor in War Time," the beauty and nobility of "true democracy" was once more strongly emphasized. "One thing is certain," said Miss O'Reilly, "not only the labor movement, not only the trade unionists, not only these Socialists, not only these agitators, but the whole people together will begin to sense how fundamental are the teachings of that much abused labor movement which teaches that every child that is born be taught that labor creates all wealth and that all wealth belongs to those who create it." (P. 60.)

Mary Ware Dennett closed the third session of the first day with an address on "Taxation of Wealth During War Time," in which she called "for a land value tax that would force them to use the land they are holding out of use" during war time and forever afterward. (P. 62.)

On the morning of May 31, 1917, Rabbi Magnes, after announcing the presence of Department of Justice agents, for the purpose of reporting any anti-draft utterances on the part of speakers, declared the inflexible purpose of the Conference to keep within the law.[3] Following this, he introduced five speakers, all of whom attacked conscription in terms altogether subversive, yet so carefully within the letter of the law that no arrests seem to have followed.

As examples of what these advocates of "democracy" allowed themselves to insinuate against the draft during war time, we quote a fragment from the address of each speaker in turn:

---

[1] Pages 50 to 53, Report of First Amer. Conference, 1917.
[2] Pages 53 to 59, Report of First Amer. Conference, 1917.
[3] Page 64, Report of First Amer. Conference, 1917.

Mr. Daniel Kiefer, on "Conscription and Democracy," said in part:

"The conscription act is both immoral and unconstitutional. . . . We are not at war because we are attacked but because certain persons with authority wish to have us at war, regardless of necessity and regardless of the popular wishes. . . . We have been told that it is a war for democracy. Well, any people that are determined to have democracy can have it without war. When Russia definitely decided to send the Czar packing she did not have to wait for a victory over Germany to do so. She simply sent him away. We can get democracy in the United States too whenever we get as ready for it as Russia is." (Pp. 64and 65.)

Rev. Richard W. Hogue of the Prisoners' Association of Maryland and of the Open Forum, Baltimore, Md., said:

"We are at war with our government in the announced motive and purpose of the country's call to arms. We are sincere and conscientious objectors to the adoption of the method set before us not only because of history's evidence of its futility, but because of its injury to liberty, its damage to democracy and its substitution of autocratic compulsion for their inalienable freedom of conscience which is the very foundation of the republic." (P. 66.)

Mr. Gilbert Roe, President Free Speech League of America, after protesting his patriotism, said:

"Do not be bluffed on this subject of free speech. Remember that the first amendment of the Constitution stands. I would say it with greater emphasis if I were a member of the forces of the present Administration; for I want to say that if any administration in this country wants to seek trouble it will find it along the line of denying the constitutional rights of free speech and free press."[1]

Rev. Norman Thomas, of the Fellowship of Reconciliation, after protesting both his love of America and of the Church, said:

"To substitute the Prussian ideal" (conscription) "for the American ideal in a war to make the world safe for democracy is a cause for anguish on the part of those who

[1] Page 70, Report of First Amer. Conference, 1917.

love America. What is there then that we can do for this thing? I have already said that we can educate the public looking to the repeal of conscription." (P. 74.)

Mr. Harry Weinberger of the American Defense League:

"I don't believe we should wait till the end of the war to demand and take our liberties in this country. I don't believe any country has the right to force into the army or to compel any individual to do any work against his conscience. . . . The tyrannies of majorities are as bad as the tyrannies of kings. Are you going to wait for peace to maintain your rights or are you going to maintain them here and now?" (P. 75.)

So much for the patriotic, democratic, pacifistic gentlemen who invoked the First Amendment of the Constitution in order to undetermine the Constitution itself — and to save their own skins in the doing!

At the afternoon session of the May 31st Conference, after Fola La Follette had read the report of the Committee on Permanent Organization and Future Activity (p. 77), Rebecca Shelly took the floor with "Suggestions for a People's Council of America."

The most original statements put forth by her were as follows:

"Congress as now constituted does not represent the will of the American people. . . . We propose therefore that this Conference commit itself to the immedate organization of a People's Council, modeled after the Council of Workmen's and Soldiers' Delegates which is the sovereign power in Russia today. . . . The majority of delegates should come from the progressive trade union locals, the single taxers, the vigorous Socialist locals, the Granges, the Farmers' Co-operative Union and other agricultural organizations. . . . The first session of the People's Council might begin . . . with the immediate object 'To consider ways and means of re-establishing representative government in America and to work for an early and lasting peace' . . . The Council should also act as a medium through which the democratic leaders and groups in Europe could speak to the people of America."[1]

[1] Pages 77 and 78, Report of First Amer. Conference, 1917.

At the evening and last session of the Conference Dr. Magnes spoke briefly again, mainly to introduce the other speakers and to announce that the outcome of the Conference was to be the organization of a People's Council. Mr. Maurer followed with an anti-war speech. Mr. Hillquit again spoke against war from another angle; the Rev. Jenkin Lloyd Jones added his voice to the protest, including an appeal for a peace without victory; and Seymour Stedman ended up the symposium by dwelling once more upon the rights of free speech and striking his final note with the favorite refrain of the Conference:

> "Let us make one thing emphatic, that as liberty rises in Russia it shall not perish here."[1]

If it should be necessary to prove further our assertion that the First American Conference for Democracy and Terms of Peace presented during the second month of our war with Germany a thoroughly socialistic, pro-German and defeatist program, all the proof in the world may be found by following the manoeuvres of the Conference officials under its brand-new name of the People's Council of America. The next chapter of this report deals with the events leading up to the Convention of the People's Council, called to convene in Minneapolis from September 1 to September 6, 1917.

[1] Pages 79 to 81, First Amer. Conference for Democracy and Terms of Peace.

CHAPTER VII

People's Council of America, June, 1917, to April, 1920

As will be recalled, in June 1917 the People's Council of America, "modeled after the Council of Workmen's and Soldiers' Council, the sovereign power of Russia today,"[1] was the outgrowth of the First American Conference of Democracy and Terms of Peace. Similarly the Conference was a reorganization of the 1917 Emergency Peace Federation, and the 1917 Emergency Peace Federation an outgrowth of the American Neutral Conference Committee, which in turn was a development of the Ford Peace Party, this a result of the original Lochner-Schwimmer Emergency Peace manoeuvres of 1914. By 1917, the old peace strategy having worn rather thin, and the revolution in Russia having made the sham Pacifists very bold, Lochner and his followers came more and more into the open with their revolutionary Socialism, scantily disguised as peace measures.

When we examine the names of the organizing committee of the People's Council, we find the following:

James J. Bagley, former president of the Central Labor Union, Brooklyn, N. Y.; Emily Greene Balch, College Professor, Economist, author; Joseph D. Cannon, organizer, International Mine, Mill and Smelter Workers' Union, N. Y.; H. W. L. Dana, professor, Columbia University; Eugene V. Debs, former Socialist nominee for President, Terre Haute, Ind.; Mary Ware Dennett, former head of the Woman's Bureau of the Democratic National Commission, New York; Crystal Eastman, Executive Secretary of the American Union Against Militarism; Max Eastman, editor "Masses," New York; Edmund C. Evans, architect, member Single Tax Society, Philadelphia, Pa.; P. Geliebter, Recording Secretary, Workmen's Circle, New York; Edward T. Hartman, secretary, Civic League, Boston, Mass.; Amy Mali Hicks, artist and author, New York; Morris Hillquit, international secretary of Socialist Party and its nominee for Mayor of New York City; Richard Hogue, minister, Baltimore, Md.; Bishop Paul Jones, Episcopal Bishop of Utah, Salt Lake City; Linley M. Keasby, author, economist, former professor of Institutional History, University of Austin, Tex.; Daniel Kiefer, Chairman, Fels Fund Commission, Cincinnati, Ohio; Charles Kruse, president Inter-

[1] Page 77, First Amer. Conference for Democracy and Terms of Peace.

national Welfare Brotherhood, St. Louis, Mo.; Algernon Lee, member of executive committee, Socialist Party of the State of New York, Educational Director, Rand School of Social Science; Duncan McDonald, General Organizer of Co-operative League of America, Springfield, Ill.; Rabbi Judah L. Magnes, religious leader, New York; James H. Maurer, member Pennsylvania State Legislature, President, Pennsylvania State Federation of Labor; Rev. Howard Mellish; Pat Nagle, editor, "Tenant Farmer," Kingfisher, Okla.; Scott Nearing, college professor, economist, Toledo, Ohio; James Oneal; Jacob Panken; Elsie Clews Parsons; Max Pine, Secretary, United Hebrew Trades, New York; A. W. Ricker, publisher "Pearson's Magazine," New York; Winter Russell, lawyer, counsel Bureau of Legal First Aid, New York; Benjamin Schlesinger, president of International Ladies' Garment Workers Union, New York City; Joseph Schlossberg; Rose Schneidermann; Western Starr, farmer and single taxer, Westover, Md.; Frank Stephens, founder Single Tax Colony, Arden, Del.; Sidney Strong, minister, author, Seattle, Wash.; Mrs. William I. Thomas, Secretary Woman's Peace Party of America, Chicago, Ill.; Irwin St. John Tucker, College President, editor, Christian Socialist, Chicago, Ill.; John D. Works, former United States Senator, Los Angeles, Cal.; Lella Faye Secor, organizing secretary, People's Council; Rebecca Shelly, financial secretary, People's Council; Elizabeth Freeman, Legislative; William E. Williams, publicity director, People's Council; Louis Lochner, executive secretary, People's Council and David Starr Jordan, Treasurer. Here we discover (with the exception of the American Union Against Militarism group, conducting their own anti-war agitation under the cloak of the Civil Liberties Bureau) most of the old guard "emergency" pacifists, together with some noteworthy additions from Socialist and other radical sources.

Besides his strong central committee, Lochner had an invaluable "legislative committee" in the person of his Treasurer, Dr. David Starr Jordan, who at the time was making Washington, D. C., his headquarters. Under date of June 10, 1917, this gentleman, who had already done so much in the cause of "peace" and "internationalism," reported to Lochner as follows:[1]

> "My course in 'university extension for statesmen' goes on nicely. Friday night under the lead of Huddleston, I had numerous members of the House. Monday I have a

[1] See illustration of original Jordan letters.

Seminar of Senators under Vardaman. . . . I have never been received with such deference before. . . . But it is also clear that I must not stay around so as to be regarded as a lobbyist. Thus far all this has been received as a personal favor and the men asked me to visit them. Kitchin has asked that for Monday, and there are numerous others of the same sort. So I think it best to go home in a few days. I am advising:

"1. Not to adjourn at all before December.

"2. If adjourned, not to grant a single blanket authorization to the Administration.

"3. It is the duty and privilege of Congress, not the President, to declare war, to state purpose of war, to make known terms of peace.

"4. To oppose every Prussian authorization.

"Next week (or this) bills will be offered:

"a. Restating meaning of treason under the Constitution.

"b. Reminding that constitutional guarantees were intended to be valid in war time. They were established for that purpose.

"c. Repealing the Conscription Act which is apparently unconstitutional.

"d. Repealing (for the future) the non-tax feature of bonds.

"I doubt if it is wise for me to do any mass-meeting speaking just now. It might, through false reports interfere with my relations with Congress. . . . I can play here best, a lone hand, but I do not forget other matters. . . .

"Among Congressmen involved in my 'Courses of Instruction' are Senators La Follette, Norris, Johnson, Borah, Vardaman, Gronna, Smoot, Curtis and New. Representatives *Kitchen, *Huddleston, *Crosser, *Hilliard, *Dill, *Gordon, Little, *Rankin, Randall, Dillon, *Cooper (Wis.), Cooper (W. Va.), Bowers, Crampton, Mondell, *Frear, Woods (Iowa), *Lundeen, *La Follette (an excellent man), *Sisson, *Slayden, Ragsdale, *Mason, London. . . . I hope that Miss Freeman can be here before I leave. But her work is different from mine." (The meaning of the starring of names is unexplained.)

These excerpts speak for themselves as to Dr. Jordan's co-operation with Lochner and other revolutionaries during war times. On another page Dr. Jordan continues:

"I have just analyzed the President's unfortunate letter to Russia. It is weak and verbose, not hitting any of the points vital to these people. Why not say (for the United States):

"We have entered the war in the spirit of altruism asking no reward, acting through sympathy with British efforts to redeem Belgium and France. When this is achieved and the seas made the world's safe open highway, we shall hope to lay down our arms. . . . We shall approve of no forced annexations, no forced indemnities and of no exploitation of fruits of victory. We know no guarantees save those involved in the good will of free peoples. We appeal to all nations to grant, through autonomy and federation, relief to repressed nationalities; believing that in conciliation and co-operation, not in unlimited national sovereignty, the future of civilization can be conserved."

Under the date of June 12, 1917, Dr. Jordan again writes Lochner as follows:

"Slayden agrees with me that a strong impression, without staying about the lobbies, is to use such force as I have to best advantage.

"This morning I used a syllabus which I send: Twenty were present at my University Extension in the Immigration Committee Room to-day."

There follows a list of the twenty, as well as twenty-two additional names of representatives and senators. Dr. Jordan closes with: "My bill is enclosed. Make returns to me at Carmel-by-the-Sea."

There is further this interesting postscript, at the top of the first page of the letter: "Keep the People's Council in touch with Miss Rankin."

When we consider that Mr. Slayden was prominent in the

American branch of the Inter-Parliamentary Union[1] (the international group of government officials pledged to co-operate in opposing the war policies of each respective government) and that certain members of Jordan's university extension course have since shown an apologetic attitude toward Socialism, it will be seen that Dr. Jordan's co-operation with Lochner was in part effective. As an illustration of this statement, we quote part of a telegram from Senator Gronna published in the first bulletin issued by the People's Council on August 7, 1917:

> "The people know that Congress cannot make laws 'abridging the freedom of speech or of the press; or the right of the people peaceably to assemble, and to petition the government for a redress of grievances.'"

Early in June, 1917, Mr. Lochner wrote to a number of California citizens and congressmen, in regard to a People's Council Conference set for San Francisco early in July: "to be analogous as far as our American conditions permit, to the Council of Workingmen and Soldiers of Russia and to a similar body just created in England."

In Miss Shelly's revised plan for a People's Council which Lochner was working out, the same note of Russian Socialism was sounded and the following measures planned, along near-Soviet lines:

> "The People's Council would be made up of delegates duly elected by any organization which has a thousand bona-fide members and subscribers to the fundamental aims of the People's Council, real democracy at home, and an early peace based on the terms already announced by the Russian government. . . . The majority of delegates would come from the forward looking trade union locals, the vigorous Socialist branches, the single taxers, the Granges, Farmers' Co-operative Unions and other farmers' organizations. The Council should represent ideas, territorial sections and voting power. Most of all it should represent the productive working classes which, if welded together, will make their voices effective in the councils of the Nation. . . . The first session of the People's Council might well begin in the Middle West on July 4. . . . then to meet in the large cities of different sections of the country; and thereby draw

[1] See Chapter IV of this Section, Lochner's report of his conversation with Dr. North.

to itself the strength to be gained by actual contact with all possible phases of American industrial and social life. The Council should ultimately sit in Washington. . . . with the immediate object of considering ways and means of re-establishing representative government in America. . . . Other acts of the Council might deal with the repeal of the conscription laws, the defense of our fundamental American liberties. . . . the recent disclosures about our hospital ships, the death of two nurses by defective shell, and the crooked labor trials. . . . At the outset the basis of representation of the Council might be one delegate for every thousand constituents, aiming at a council of five hundred delegates. . . . The Council should act as a medium through which the democratic leaders and groups of Europe would find publicity in America. . . . If our government persists in refusing passports to the delegates of the Stockholm Conference, the People's Council might invite representatives from the Stockholm Conference to lay its findings before the American people through the medium of the Council."

This program boiled down amounts to: a drawing together of all the radical forces of workingmen, suggesting mass action; a plan of Soviet representation and a discrediting of that now in force; a scheme to agitate for discontent and disloyal measures; and finally for an international co-operation with the Socialist forces of Europe.[1]

Another suggestive instance of co-operation of certain radical and Socialist Committee members operating with Lochner is indicated by the following telegram to him, dated June 9, 1917:

"Have Hillquit meet Walsh at Cosmos Club, Washington, D. C. Arrange with him by wire. You sign telegram. Cannot determine date until I arrive Seattle. Le Sueur out of city.

"(Signed) JOB HARRIMEN."

Though the tactics here are obvious, they do not surpass those of still another crafty ally of Lochner in organizing the People's

[1] Basis of Discussion of a Tentative Plan for a People's Council, marked "Shelly," and having at close a written addition in Miss Shelly's handwriting.

Telephone 1937 Chelsea

Hudson Guild
436-438 WEST 27th STREET
NEW YORK

May 23, 1917.

Dear Mr. Lochner:-

I am sorry that your letter of May 18th did not reach me before. I am expecting to attend the meeting of the American Conference for Democracy and Terms of Peace but it would not be wise for me at present to sign the call even if this letter should get to you in time. I am anxious however to co-operate with you and your organization for permanent work in the future.

Yours sincerely,

John L Elliott

Mr. Louis P. Lochner,
Room 61, Holland House,
New York

FRONT OF CARD AND REVERSE SIDE

This card was freely circulated in American colleges during the war by the American Union Against Militarism.

"WHY! What has made our hero a Bolshevist?"

"Oh, chiefly the Students' Army Training Corps."

College Membership

To the American Union Against Militarism

Westory Building, Washington, D. C.

Gentlemen: What I know about Compulsory Military Training is plenty,—enroll me as a member!

____

____

*Here's my contribution*____________

1919

150

My dear Mr Baldwin:

Can't get off—

Now if you have important facts that would help Judge Anderson (Don't use his name to any one) send them (few as possible a so arranged at least that he can get at their significance easily) at once to

Judge Geo. A. Anderson Cosmos Club

Wash. D.C.

You can count on him

152

to do all that can be done in ways of which we spoke. I shall send you some more questions from him to me— in a day or two

G.—

J.G.B.

Facsimile of Original Letter — John Graham Brooks to Roger N. Baldwin, Relating to Judge Anderson's Willingness to Assist in Quashing I. W. W. Indictments at Chicago.

Council, Roger Baldwin of the American Union Against Militarism and the Civil Liberties Bureau. Baldwin had already advised both Lochner and Miss Balch early in May as to the details of organizing the Council along national lines; and he now wrote another masterly letter of advice.

"It seems to me important that we should have every point carefully thought out," wrote Baldwin, "in order that this movement may take the greatest possible hold upon public opinion throughout the United States." (May 9, 1917.)

In another letter to Lochner (Aug. 21, 1917), referring mainly to the proposed Convention of the People's Council in September, 1917, Baldwin wrote as follows:[1]

> "1. Do steer away from making it look like a Socialist enterprise. Too many people have already gotten the idea that it is nine-tenths a Socialist movement. You can of course avoid this by bringing to the front people like Senator Works, Miss Addams and others who are known as substantial Democrats.
>
> "2. Do get into the movement just as strong as possible the leaders in the labor circles, particularly the substantial men, not the radical Socialists, both of whom ought to be recognized. But the substantial men will begin to start the big Irish Democratic Labor movement our way, and that is important. Also bring to the front the farmers, not confining it to the new agrarian movement in the northwest.
>
> "3. I think it would be an error to get the public thinking that we are launching a political party in Minneapolis. To be sure we are launching a political movement, but that is quite another matter from a political point. It is a mistake already to have tied up with the name of Mr. La Follette fine as he is. If we begin to mix personalities with principles we will find at these early stages we are going to get into a lot of trouble. Our main job is to keep peace terms and a larger democracy for the United States in the foreground of public discussion.
>
> "4. We want also to look like patriots in everything we do. We want to get a lot of good flags, talk a good deal about the Constitution and what our forefathers wanted to make of this country, and to show that we are the folks that really stand for the spirit of our institutions."

---

[1] **See illustration of Baldwin's letter of August 21, 1917, to Lochner.**

Lochner in answering agreed to all four points, even to: "I agree with you that we should keep proclaiming our loyalty and patriotism. I will see to it that we have flags and similar paraphernalia." (Aug. 24, 1917.)

All this while, Lochner's official family, to which had been added an assistant in the person of James Waldo Fawcett (afterward a member of the Left Wing Socialist Party and editor of a radical magazine called "The Modernist)" had not been idle. By the middle of July, 1917, due to good team work with certain comrades in the field and by judicious use of the "American Conference camouflage" as an entering wedge,[1] Lochner and his associates succeeded in organizing a number of locals of the People's Council in many parts of the country, all of which were pledged to work for the proposed September Central Convention in Minneapolis.

Records of these local People's Councils formed during the summer of 1917, are as follows:

California — Los Angeles.— New councils have been formed in Pasadena, Santa Ana, Anaheim, Orange, Long Beach, Santa Monica, South Pasadena, Santa Barbara, San Diego and Pomona.

Colorado — Denver.

Georgia — Macon.

Idaho — Nampa.

Iowa — Postville.

Massachusetts — Boston.— A local branch which is rapidly gaining new members has been organized here under the leadership of Mr. Robert L. Wolfe, assistant in the department of economics at Harvard.

Michigan — Detroit.

Minnesota — St. Paul.— The St. Paul Lodge No. 112 of the International Association of Machinists has voted to participate in the Minneapolis Conference.

Missouri — Kansas City.

Nebraska — Haskins.

New Jersey — Camden.— A council has been started here and branches are under way at Vineland, Montclair, Bridgeton, Millville and several other New Jersey towns. Paterson.— Paterson Workers' Conference, representing twelve organizations, has voted to affiliate with the People's Council and has elected two delegates to the Minneapolis Convention.

---

[1] Press Matter, People's Council, July 20, 1917, giving account of Third American Conference for Democracy and Terms of Peace in Los Angeles.

New York — Syracuse.— The Cigar Makers' Local No. 6 of this city has indorsed the principles of the People's Council. Buffalo.

Ohio — Youngstown, Canton.

Pennsylvania — Pittsburgh.—A strong council is at work in this city, with headquarters at 415 Fourth avenue, opposite the United States Postoffice and Federal Building.

Utah — Salt Lake City.— Under the leadership of Rev. Paul Jones, Bishop of Utah, a strong council has been formed in this state, with headquarters in this city.

Vermont — West Woodstock.

Wisconsin — Milwaukee.— The local council has held three largely attended meetings, printed 50,000 copies of a leaflet and is gaining the affiliation of all progressive bodies.

Job Harriman of Los Angeles reports that the farmers of the Middle West are deeply interested in the movement and will be strongly represented at the Assembly in Minneapolis.

Max Eastman, editor of "The Masses," is speaking for the People's Council at mass meetings in the Middle West. He reports that the movement is growing among labor unions and working people beyond the most enthusiastic hopes.

James H. Maurer, president of the Pennsylvania State Federation of Labor, has addressed twenty-five mass meetings for the People's Council in various centers throughout the West. Many of these meetings were attended by members of trade unions only. Mr. Maurer says that the sentiment of organized labor is for peace and that feeling against the action of officials of the American Federation of Labor is growing resentful. (People's Council Bulletin, August 27, 1917.)

Besides these smaller centers, we have records of two more important People's Councils in Chicago and Philadelphia. In Chicago the frankly radical and pro-German Mrs. Lloyd had a great deal of trouble in persuading both Senator La Follette and Jane Addams to ally themselves openly with the Socialists connected with the People's Council there. By way of illustration of this we quote from several of Mrs. Lloyd's letters to Lochner.

> "Saturday our Conference made Irvin St. John, secretary for lack of a willing non-Socialist; and Miss Addams hesitated about the chairmanship. Today she refused it because of an unfortunate leak in the papers — a premature announcement of the meeting under Socialist auspices. She said by

telephone and not very clearly, she hoped the Socialists would now take up the meeting and push it as a Socialist affair and co-operate with your Conference fully. I knew Miss Breckenridge and Mrs. Karsten were on that track a week ago. The Socialists know better than to run this affair that way, and besides the auditorium wouldn't rent to us most likely. To-morrow if Magnes can't win over Miss Addams. . . I shall strongly urge a combination committee minus Miss Addams. . . . She herself recommended Norman Thomas before you did, and I hope he can come on and give us full details of the New York Conference. If we could have for speakers Norman Thomas, Gronna, a home Socialist, a young man (probably Arthur Fisher), and Miss Addams, I'd die happy." (May 13, 1917.)

When it came to other matters Mrs. Lloyd was equally frank, writing to Lochner and Miss Secor at different times during 1917:

> "Why can't we wire freely to Germany? . . . I'm hoping and praying for the success of the Russian Socialists. . . . I wired La Follette again about our auditorium meeting. He replied that the legislative situation would prevent. Do you really think he would injure anything there by absenting himself over Saturday and Sunday. . . . Can you do anything about it?" (May 5, 1917.)

In Lochner's answers among several things worth quoting are:

> "The leak in the newspapers was indeed unfortunate, though Socialism just now is getting to be mighty respectable. . . . As you have probably already surmised the ultimate aim of our organization will be to get America out of the war that we were unable to keep her out of." (May 16, 1917.)

As for Jane Addams, though she, like La Follette, was always sympathetic to Lochner's plans during the early period of the peace movement, from 1917 on, she was extremely loth to allow her name to appear on his Conference Committee and People's Council lists. It will be remembered that when Lochner began his peace agitation in 1914, Jane Addams helped him, not only with her sympathy publicly expressed, but with the prestige of her name on his letter heads. By 1917, however, when his socialistic program was more boldly announced,

Miss Addams persistently refused anything but private co-operation. Some of her concessions at this stage were as follows: "As your plans" (for the Conference) "develop, do keep us informed, and it is possible that out of this meeting a similar organization might be formed.[1] . . . I am feeling queer to be going to the conference of foreign relations of the United States, financed it is rumored by the Carnegie people, when you and my other friends will be having a conference on the 30th."

Another time, in response to Miss Balch's urgent wire, Miss Addams telegraphed. "Am not as well as usual and not able to preside, but hope to attend conference. Would advise Mr. Tucker as the best man for suggested work." (May 25, 1917.)

Later in the summer, (August 22, 1917), Miss Secor wired in reference to the People's Council Convention to Lochner, "Jane Addams in letter to Balch accepts place on program." But as there is not the slightest mention of the name of Jane Addams in the record of the September Convention, she must have withdrawn at the psychological moment.

There was, nevertheless, an American Conference for Democracy and Terms of Peace organized in Chicago and delegates appointed to the Convention of the People's Council from Chicago, without the public support of Miss Addams.[2] Also in Philadelphia on July 20, 1917, where the Conference met boldly under the auspices of the Workmen's Branch of the People's Council in the first place, Norman Thomas spoke in high praise of conscientious objectors, and Jacob Panken, after a subtle attack on Mr. Gompers and the American Federation of Labor, said:

> "They (the people) must realize that this war has no appeal to the American Workers, nor are there any principles or interests of the American people vitally involved. . . . It is held out to us that we are to make these sacrifices for democracy and civilization. If it is the democracy and civilization that is sought to be saddled upon us by the government, it were better that democracy and civilization perish entirely." (Bulletin of Philadelphia People's Council.)

---

[1] Jane Addams to Lochner, May 7, 1917.

[2] From Mrs. Lloyd to Lochner, Aug. 12, 1917; from Mrs. Thomas to Lochner, Aug. 25 and Aug. 26, 1917.

Approximately at the same time the People's Council issued a bulletin announcing the dispatch of an open letter to all members of Congress, the gist of which is given as:

> "'We appeal to you, our representatives, immediately to set aside adequate time for a frank and free debate on a resolution accepting the Russian formula as a basis for immediate, general peace, and we urge upon you the advisability of calling into conference in Washington, without delay, representatives to the elected assemblies of all the Allied powers for the purpose of formulating a concrete statement of terms, upon which a just and permanent peace can be arranged.
>
> "The letter was written immediately following the speech of Senator Borah in which he urged that the nation deserves to know 'more definitely and more specifically the terms and conditions upon which we were fighting and the terms and conditions upon which we would cease to fight.'
>
> "The letter also called attention to a recent similar utterance upon the part of Senator Lewis and one of Mr. Asquith in the English House of Commons, in which he said 'it cannot be stated too clearly that this is a matter for the people rather than for the governments.'
>
> "This is but one of the activities of the organization committee of the Council. In conjunction with the Legal First Aid Bureau and the Civil Liberties Bureau, 70 Fifth avenue, New York City, it is providing legal defense for conscientious objectors. It is also urging throught its branches agitation for the repeal of conscription act.
>
> "In conjunction with the Workmen's Council, which is the labor wing of the People's Council movement, the organizing committee arranged a great mass meeting of protest against the suppression of the labor and radical press by denial of the use of the mails." (Press matter, People's Council, August, 1917.)

It was towards the central convention set for September 2–6, 1917, that Lochner and his colleagues both at New York headquarters and in the field now devoted their energies. Miss Freeman for instance was particularly active, traveling from Seattle, August 13th, to Everett, Wash., August 17th, then to Deer Lodge, Mont., August 22d, and finally to Butte, Mont., on August 27th, agitating constantly for the People's Council. We quote passages from her voluminous letters to Lochner:

From Seattle, August 13, 1917, in reference to the San Francisco meeting of the People's Council she wrote:

> "The man Thompson you see on the program is a member of the I. W. W. and made a wonderful speech."

From Everett, Wash., describing the Seattle meeting where Kate Sadler "a splendid live soul but very radical" was arrested:

> ". . . I leaped on the table and started to speak — most of the crowd remaining. I told the purposes of the People's Council and something about the Russian democracy. . . . Then Colonel Wood of Portland came and I closed. Just then eight policemen came up . . . and declared they would arrest me. A great shout of indignation went up but they seemed very determined. . . . I jumped from the table and a policeman caught hold of my arm. . . . People surged in between us, the hand suddenly loosened and I slipped into the crowd easily and back to the hall, in time to do my usual job of asking for the collection. . . . The I. W. W. situation here is one to be reckoned with. They are very powerful here, and our meetings were rather swamped owing to the lumber strike. . . . The screws are getting tighter. 'These are great times for democracy.' . . . By the way get in touch with Lincoln Steffens. . . ."

From Deer Lodge, Mont., August 22, 1917, to Miss Alice Park of the Woman's Suffrage Party:

> "The situation here is vastly different from the Seattle vicinity. One has to soft-pedal very much. . . . The splendid boys who formed the committee had worked very hard and were very anxious. They feared the least radical remark would upset the apple cart. I made my speech in the form of questions; and so got by with many statements. . . . I am leaving here tonight. . . . Will see you in Minneapolis."

From Butte, to Lochner, August 27, 1917:

> "I haven't done anything to speak of here. The situation is most delicate. Mary O'Neill will handle it. . . . She is very deep in it all here and so is Miss Rankin who, by the way is at her home in Missoula, Mont. Mary is her

first lieutenant in this State, and very wise and careful. . . ."

"Great Falls are planning to go out on a sympathetic strike, and it means careful handling."

In view of these letters it can perhaps be said without any exaggeration that Miss Freeman did her bit in the way of spreading radicalism through People's Council propaganda, in this country during the war.

Among the agents organizing in the field during the summer of 1917 for the People's Council were Irwin St. John Tucker who co-operated with Mrs. Lloyd in Chicago,[1] Grace Scribner, of Boston;[2] S. A. Stockwell, of Minneapolis;[3] M. A. Brantland, of Ada, Minn.; Thos. Vollom, Erskine, Minn.; Olof M. Grover, Mentor, Minn.;[5] and C. A. Ryan of the World Peace Association, Northfield, Minn.,[4] were also active. One of Lochner's aides who did particularly effective work was James Maurer. He wrote in August 20, 1917, submitting his expense account to the People's Council:

"On my tour I spoke at the following places:

Chicago	3 meetings	
Los Angeles	3 meetings	
Frisco	2 meetings	
Oakland	1 meeting	
Portland	1 meeting	
Everett	1 meeting	
Seattle	2 meetings	
Spokane	1 meeting	
Pocatello	1 meeting	
Salt Lake City	2 meetings	(Union men only)
Denver	1 meeting	
Trinidad	1 meeting	
Kansas City	2 meetings	
St. Louis	3 meetings	(1 to Union men only)
Granite City	1 meeting	

All told twenty-five meetings. All excepting two were very well attended. Meeting at Seattle was broken up by soldiers, after I had spoken just one hour. The meeting at Pocatello

[1] Telegram, Tucker to Lochner, Aug. 21, 1917.
[2] June 19, 1917.
[3] Aug. 4, 1917.
[4] C. A. Ryan, soliciting funds for People's Council, Aug. 17, 1917.
[5] Aug. 15 and 25, 1917.

was broken up by police and plain clothes rough necks, after I had spoken about twenty minutes. . . . All told, I feel that my efforts left good results at each place visited.

"People's Council of New York, agree to pay my expenses from Chicago to the Coast and return to Chicago.

Chicago	3 days
At Los Angeles	3 days
At Everett	1 day
Salt Lake City	1 day
Return to Chicago	3 days

All other meetings were paid for by Socialists and others, who arranged them. That is, wages and hotel was paid."

"I feel that my tour has done much good among Socialists, Union men and others." (August 21, 1917.)

Other valuable Lochner allies of this period who wrote interesting letters were:

1. Mr. Erich C. Stern, of Milwaukee, from whom we quote: "Your telegram received today and so Mr. Haessler and I called upon Mr. Gustav Trostel (brother of Albert Trostel). He said that La Follette's secretary, Mr. Hanna, was in town last week and had collected a considerable sum of money to be used for peace purposes — and had received a considerable amount from the Trostels. Mr. Trostel therefore thought we ought to appeal to others as well as him and his brother. He gave us his own check for $100 for the local treasury and turned over to us $508 from another source for the national treasury. Mr. Haessler took this check and promised to forward the money to you at once. . . . I must confess to being disappointed that you are meeting with so much difficulty in raising the initial $50,000. It seems to me that even $1 membership fees should have made out a very large sum in the aggregate if your membership is as numerous as I had supposed. . . . Do you know what La Follette does with the money he collects?"[1] Lochner in answering Stern[2] said: "I think La Follette is using the money he collects for two purposes — first, to ascertain the name of one peace man in each precinct of the Union; second, to enable him to circularize his splendid articles such as, 'The right of the citizen to criticise the government in war times.'"

[1] Aug. 15, 1917.
[2] Aug. 23, 1917.

2. From Mrs. Harriet Thomas of the Woman's Peace Party at Chicago (section for the United States of the International Committee of Women for Permanent Peace), who showed what manner of pacifist she was by the following: "At Dixon, Ill., night before last, a People's Council was formed with a signed-up membership of more than a thousand, mostly farmers. They elected their delegate and alternate to Minneapolis and are enthusiastic over the movement. Let the good work go on."[1] Lochner's answer[2] in which he advised Senator Works for permanent chairman of the People's Council is also illuminating: "At first there was talk of having Rabbi Magnes, but finally the suggestion prevailed of having Senator Works preside for the simple reason that we felt that the authorities would be less liable to stop a man just recently from the Senate. . . . His conception of our meeting is that of a movement that will go beyond the war. . . ."

3. From Chapin Hoskins, of the Book House, Chicago, to Lochner (August 28, 1917):

> "So it has been suggested to me that inasmuch as the Book House is one of the few book stores that make a specialty of the sort of books that People's Council members want to and ought to read, it would be a great gain for the cause as well as for me if I carried on an advertising campaign in your bulletin. Some of the directors were very anxious to have me repeat the stunt I pulled off at the Chicago meeting, of having a table of books on display, but I did not think it feasible at a distance from Chicago. Let me say, though, that the eagerness with which people at the Conference examined and bought sensible war literature shows that we really did a service.
>
> "If you see things in the same light as my Chicago friends — and of course I shall not urge the matter on you, for nothing is further from my wishes than to make money through my connection with the movement — an arrangement will have to be made somewhat as follows: I will give my full services to Mr. Fuller for the week and receive proper compensation; I will be permitted to buy adequate advertising space in the bulletin at a reasonable rate; the net result must be that the cost of my trip to Minneapolis will not exceed the value of the advertising to me.

[1] Aug. 25, 1917.
[2] Lochner to Mrs. Thomas, Aug. 28, 1917.

"This is rather a peculiar proposition, isn't it? But the fact is, I suppose, that most propositions are as intricate at bottom, but the proposers are less frank about their motives."

4. From J. Muhlon Barnes of Chicago,[1] in reference to People's Council propaganda literature: "I am mailing out a mimeographed letter, dated today, to only 400 unions eliminating those farthest removed from Minneapolis. . . . I think I should spend next week there working among the unions."

5. From Fawcett (writing from the New York office of the People's Council of which he was in charge when Lochner transferred his headquarters, the second week in August, 1917, to Minneapolis):

"It seems that there is a possibility that Alexander Berkman will be elected to the Assembly by one of the local groups. Also, Miss Secor suggests that Emma Goldman may be present in the same capacity. Mr. Panken is annoyed at this prospect and Mr. Hillquit has been asked to think the matter over, which probably means that the two in question will be asked not to permit their names to be offered as delegates. You know Mr. Hillquit is Berkman's attorney.

"Mr. Panken fears are based on the ground that publicity will be concentrated on the presence of anarchists at the convention and that the best purposes of the Council will be lost sight of and injured.

"I suppose if the matter is in Mr. Hillquit's hands it will be taken care of correctly. You had better advise me however as to what I might do in case of emergency. I could appeal to Berkman personally if it seemed necessary."

6. A telegram from Congressman Wm. A. Mason dated August 20, 1917, in reply to Lochner's urgent request for him to speak at the September Convention: "Expect to be in Washington then fighting same cause. . . ."

Some of the official matter turned out by the People's Council office during the first weeks of August, 1917, was as follows:

A financial statement from June 1 to August 18, 1917, showing contributions amounting to $29,918.75 and an expenditure of $23,910.44; a bulletin form letter announcing "A mouthpiece for the People's Council" in the form of a weekly bulletin; a second form letter requesting People's Council members who "voted on

[1] Barnes to Lochner, Aug. 22, 1917.

the referendum in favor of the Hardwick bill" which bill provides that no person drafted into the military service of the United States be sent, except voluntarily, outside the territorial limits of the country.[1] "This is to adopt resolutions and send a copy to Senator Chamberlain." "This is a real chance to save our boys from slaughter at the front."

Lochner, in Minneapolis, almost from the moment of his arrival found himself in the midst of perplexities. One of these came from the outside so to speak, and from an old Ford friend — Mrs. Ada Morse Clark, of Palo Alto, Cal., an ardent pacifist thoroughly trained in regarding all capitalists as devils but not as yet prepared to consider the I. W. W. angels. We quote from Mrs. Clark's letter (August 19, 1917):

> "Another thing . . . I want to say is that I am told that at the meeting of the People's Council here in San Francisco, one of the speakers was an I. W. W. Is that true? If so, it is the greatest possible calamity, for that wild I. W. W. will queer any movement whatever. I cannot believe it is true that one of that group would be allowed to speak, and would be very glad if you would at once send me a denial of that rumor. Of course I know better than to believe newspaper reports about the People's Council, but I have my information from other sources in this case. . . .
>
> "In the paper this morning I read an interview from Hale. He mentioned his trip to Holland while you were in the States — the old scoundrel. When I remember what he told me about having Gerard in his room every night for two weeks before the latter sailed for America to see President Wilson, it makes me wonder if Gerard is 'hand-in-glove' with a man like Hale, or if the whole yarn was untrue. What is your private opinion of Gerard? At present there is a serial running through the Hearst papers, written by Gerard, but somehow it does not ring true to me. I don't feel any confidence in it whatever, though I could not say why. . . .
>
> "People tell me that Aked was so Pro-German even before he went on the expedition, that people used to get up and leave the church during his sermons!"

[1] Aug. 17, 1917.

Lochner in his answer, though forced to admit that I. W. W.'s were in good standing with the People's Council, explained: "It is not our business to ask whether a man is an I. W. W. or a high churchman. The fact that he is willing to stand for the splendid program that we have worked out and is willing to sign up is enough. . . . As a matter of fact you will find that the I. W. W. have been badly misrepresented. There are extreme elements among them as there are in every movement."

This difficulty, however, was as nothing to the local situation in Minneapolis which may be best pictured by quoting from Lochner's first report to the organizing committee of the People's Council, sent soon after his arrival (August 19, 1917):

> "Two days of work in Minneapolis have brought the following results:
>
> "First, the press of the city is totally hostile to us. There is a most deliberate turning and twisting of every thing that is said and done by either Mr. Stockwell, in charge of local arrangements, or myself.
>
> "Second, the business men of the city are being intimidated in hope of their refusing to let us have a meeting place. We had secured the Mozart Hall, but our check was returned the following day and we were told we were undesirable. Practically my whole time has been consumed in looking up halls, only to find them denied us. If everything else fails, we may secure the building of the Finnish societies, with good committee rooms and a good auditorium seating 500. My only misgiving is that this hall will, I fear, be far too small.
>
> "Third, the mayor of the city is entirely in sympathy with us and will give the address of welcome. The chief of police, too, is heart and soul for us. He is a Socialist.
>
> . . . .
>
> "Eighth, I rather anticipate that there may be hundreds if not thousands of people coming from neighboring territory who will want to attend in an individual capacity. We may be forced to run two 'shows'—one the convention of delegates, doing serious business from day to day, the other a talk-fest for the edification of the masses that will have come in good faith thinking this to be a free-for-all, and whom we cannot afford to send away without giving them inspirational dope to take home with them."

As a specimen of the sort of local criticism which the People's Council have received during August, 1917, the following will serve:

> "*People's Council of America, i. e., Agents of the Kaiser:*
>
> "Your request for rooms received and though I need *very much* to rent my rooms, I would no more think of renting them to you than to any other enemy of my country — an outspoken enemy being far less dangerous than the wolves masquerading in sheep's clothing.
>
> "Yours in need but not in such need as to harbor traitors.
>
> "MRS. J. H. BURNS."

In spite of all hostile opposition, however, and all of his tremendous handicaps in finding accommodations for his People's Council Convention, Lochner kept driving on. He did, it is true, permit himself to write to Fawcett: "As for Berkman and and Goldman, I do hope they will not be elected. Here the people are awfully stirred up about the I. W. W. . . . but if in addition we have those two splendid fighters for liberty with us that may be too big a burden to carry. . . . Personally, I have only the highest regard for the two."[1] And he wrote uneasily to A. L. Sugarman of St. Paul to "-send me a copy of the letter which the Secretary of War wrote to the national executive of the Socialist Party, stating that interference with meetings on the part of soldiers would not be tolerated."[2] Taken all in all Mr. Lochner showed a surprising un-pacifistic battle spirit in his determined fight to hold his convention against all comers. Perhaps a letter from Morris Hillquit dated August 15, 1917, clearly Lochner's superior officer, may explain this persistence:

> "The main thing after all will be the organization and the work of the council after the Minneapolis meeting. If you will succeed in your work of organizing the convention upon a solid basis, a few mistakes here will not matter much,
>
> "As to your proper designation, I believe it will be best for everybody concerned that you forget about it, at least for the time being. However, we shall have ample opportunity to discuss the entire situation when we meet in Minneapolis."

---

[1] Aug. 17, 1917.
[2] Aug. 24, 1917.

That Lochner was a most careful organizer is illustrated by two letters: The first to Wm. Kruse, secretary of the Young People's Socialist League,[1] which reads in part:

"It is going to be a big job to have all details arranged for the convention, and your help in lining up some of the young Socialist League fellows will be invaluable.

"I should like to make you responsible for the collections. As our plans are now arranged, we anticipate that in addition to the working body of delegates there will be frequent open air mass meetings in the grove near our tent. Now, people who will be coming to these mass meetings will be the farmers for miles around. My friends tell me that the Minnesota farmer is mighty well off and that he is so stirred up about the war that he is quite willing to dig into his pockets, so there is your golden opportunity to extract many dollars from our visitors. Please let me know as soon as possible when you are coming. With kindest regards."

The second letter, to Dr. Williams Bayard Hale,[2] reads:

"I don't think you can afford to stay from our big show here at Minneapolis. I thought I knew something about the peace sentiment in this country, but have had to come here to see with my own eyes before I believed the intensity of it. . . One evidence of the tremendous possibilities of our movement is to be found in the fact that as a counter-attraction Mr. Gerard is to speak here tomorrow night, and that on the fifth of September, Samuel Gompers, Charles Edward Russell, John Spargo and others are to come here to offset our work.

"As we shall concern ourselves very much with the question of peace terms there is an added reason why we wish you here to acquaint us with Germany's point of view. So I think you had better make your plans to be here and see this big event staged. As all big halls have been denied us we have leased thirty-five acres of ground and are going to pitch a huge tent besides several smaller tents for committee work."

All this while the publicity committee of the People's Council had been working actively, having produced and widely distributed two strong bulletins.

---

[1] Aug. 24, 1917.
[2] Aug. 23, 1917.

The first, dated August 7th, after protesting the patriotism of the People's Council, made the following statements, first under the heading of "Peace":

"*Our program demands:*

"Concrete statements of America's war aims.

"Early general peace based on *no forcible annexations, no punitive indemnities, and free development for all nationalities.*

"International organization for world peace.

"Repeal of conscription laws.

"Democratic foreign policy.

"Referendum on question of war and peace.

"Freedom of speech, and of the press, right of assembly and right to petition the government.

"Safeguarding of labor standards.

"Taxation of wealth to pay for the war.

"Reduction of the high cost of living."

A second section of this bulletin contains the strange appeal: "Be a true American citizen and an Internationalist and join this great new world movement of democracy."

The inner section is a verbatim copy of the bulletin of the Petrograd Council of Workers' and Soldiers' Deputies, issued March 5, 1917, and printed both in Russian and English, with the explanatory statement:

> "The original copy of this bulletin was smuggled over to this country. . . ."

After an appeal for contributions, the proclamation follows "To the People of the Whole World," which declares in part:

> "Long live liberty! Long live the international solidarity of the proletariat and its struggle for final victory!
>
> "Our cause has not been fully won; the shades of the old regime have not yet vanished and many enemies are gathering their forces against the Russian revolution. Nevertheless our victories are enormous. The peoples of Russia will express their will through the Constituent Assembly, which is to be called in the near future on the basis of universal, equal, direct and secret suffrage. It is certain that a democratic republic will be established in Russia. . . .
>
> "Workers of all countries! In extending to you our

fraternal hand over mountains of corpses of our brothers, across rivers of innocent blood and tears, over smoldering ruins of cities and villages, over destroyed treasures of civilization, we beseech you to re-establish and strengthen international unity. Therein lies the security for our future victories and the complete emancipation of humanity.

"Proletarians of all countries, unite!" (Signed) The Petrograd Council of Workers' and Soldiers' Deputies.

After this extremely revolutionary appeal to the proletarians of the world to unite against all other classes, it cannot surprise us that the so-called Constituent Assembly of the People's Council was never allowed to meet in Minneapolis.

To return to the People's Council of America bulletin of August 7, 1917, we have in Lochner's running footnotes further proof of the altogether socialistic co-operation of these pacifistic People's councillors, as well as a forecast of the Bolshevist revolution of November, 1917.

"Speaking in obedience to the will of the Russian people, made known through the Councils of Workers, Soldiers and Peasants, the Russian government has said, 'We are for immediate, general peace, based on no forcible annexations — no punitive indemnities and free development for all nationalities.'

"The governments of the Allies and our own government as well have met this common-sense and intelligible declaration with silence, denials or reservations, and as a direct and certain consequence, the Russian people are withholding full military co-operation in the war. *This is the true interpretation of the present situation in Russia.* . . . The democracy of America must quickly send back an answer to the Russian people. If the Congress of the United States will not speak for the people, the people must speak for themselves — and this should be our message: 'Your war aims are ours. We are with you against the imperialists who would continue this war for their own ends.' The movement represented by the People's Council of America is plain, genuine democracy and those who oppose it are reactionary and un-American. Again we urge all American citizens to join the People's Council and to stand with the people of all nations in demanding immediate, general peace based on the terms first formulated, not by statesmen and diplomatists, but by the common people—*no forcible annexations, no punitive indemnities and free development of all nationalities.*"

The second bulletin, dated August 27, 1917, containing no hint of the determined opposition of Minneapolis people to having the People's Council meet there, began with the query: "Who are the anti-Americans?" The answer, as might be expected, was Messrs. Gompers, Russell and Spargo. In other words, the very men who were straining every nerve to keep the laboring men of the United States loyal during the war.

Another heading was: "And yet we have no quarrel with the German people" (this referring to the refusal of our State Department to forward a cablegram of the People's Council to the German Reichstag).

These two bulletins no doubt had their share in adding to the hostile attitude of the loyal people of Minneapolis and the State of Minnesota itself. Since, however, (as has been mentioned) Van Lear, Mayor of Minneapolis and his Chief of Police, both were Socialists, Lochner apparently felt secure in his plan for holding the convention. The following day letter to the New York "Call" will illustrate:

> "Attention Weitzenkorn! Avoid sensation account local conditions. Stick close to spirit of this. The abolition of secret diplomacy as a prolific cause of war, referenda on questions of peace and war, proposals to render President's cabinet responsible to Congress and the people as in England, the right of representatives of the people in Congress to pass upon any proposed peace settlement, just as treaties are ratified, Russian peace formula, Pope's peace proposal and Stockholm peace proposals, peace resolutions now pending in Congress, repeal of conscription acts, proposals to send only volunteers abroad, will be among the subjects discussed at the national assembly of the People's Council at Minneapolis. . . .
>
> "Committees of experts will lay before the information bearing on this subject, also upon disarmament, international organization for peace as proposed by the League to Enforce Peace, as well as those by the International Socialist Bureau. The proposed Stockholm conference for which some of our delegates were refused passports will be discussed. . . ."

Notwithstanding (or perhaps because of) these elaborate plans, Lochner and his comrades in Minneapolis were literally driven from pillar to post in seeking a meeting place for their convention; and on August 27, 1917, public opinion rose to such a pitch that Governor Burnquist of Minnesota issued a proclamation forbidding the People's Council Convention to be held anywhere in the State of Minnesota on the ground that the sheriff has "advised me that said convention and meeting if held, in his opinion, would result in bloodshed, rioting and loss of life; and whereas, said convention and meeting can, in my opinion, under the circumstances, have no other effect than that of aiding and abetting the enemies of this country."

Following this proclamation Lochner still persisted according to the following telegram from Mayor Van Lear both to the New York "Call" and the New York "Tribune":

> "Lochner, executive secretary, wired Burnquist's proclamation to President Wilson with protest against that document. Also announced that no attempt would be made to hold meeting in Minnesota. Arrangements being made for meeting in another city but no announcement tonight."

Evidently, however, the governor's proclamation was effective; for on August 29, 1917, one of the Lochner conference officials, D. Shier, sent out the following day letter to the "Forward," the Yiddish newspaper at 175 East Broadway, New York City:

> "Governor Burnquist barred People's Council from Minnesota acting on instructions from Sheriff Langum that if the convention was held it would result in bloodshed, rioting and loss of life. Invitations from two different states for the People's Council to meet there. Governor Phillip of Wisconsin agreed to permit meeting in Milwaukee. Following telegram was received from Governor Frazier of North Dakota: 'The People's Council of America for Democracy and Peace will be guaranteed their constitutional rights in North Dakota — we are loyal and patriotic and believe in freedom of speech for all people. (Signed, Lynn J. Frazier.)'
>
> "Attorney General Langer of North Dakota wires he is going to pick a town for us — he is on the job now."

Both Fargo, N. D., and Hudson, Wis., were presently suggested as the meeting place for the convention, but both were found impracticable. Finally, all delegates, speakers, publicity people, special trains, etc., had to be notified that the People's Council's Congress would have to be held in Chicago.[1]

Here on September 2, 1917, the forces gathered, held several mild meetings,[2] issued a mild bulletin, and were finally dispersed by order of the Governor of the State of Illinois.

From this time on, the People's Council, though working effectively enough in its many centers throughout the country, did so more or less quietly. Naturally there was no publicity given to Lochner's cablegram of March 3, 1918, to the People's Commissaires at Petrograd.[3] This, which was signed also by Scott Nearing and James Maurer, read as follows:

> "People's Council of America for democratic peace representing 300 radical groups in forty-two states, has consistently stood for Russian formula of no annexations, no indemnities and self determination. We urge you to make no other terms."

There remains only to record a mass meeting of the People's Council at Madison Square Garden, New York, May 25, 1919, called "Justice to Russia," which protested against the blockade and intervention generally. The speakers were Magnes, Lincoln A. Colcord, Frederic C. Howe and Amos Pinchot. Louis Lochner presided.[4]

Lochner, who was a lecturer at the Rand School in 1919, today is in charge of People's Print at 138 W. 13th street, New York City, which is the department of publications of the People's Freedom Union, virtually a clearing house for ultra-radical leaflets and pamphlets. The People's Print is under the same roof with the American Civil Liberties Union.[5].

---

[1] Copy of telegram sent to list of delegates, Aug. 30, 1917.
[2] Convention number, People's Council Bulletin, Sept., 1917.
[3] Photostat of intercepted cablegram.
[4] Document, "Justice to Russia," May 25, 1917.
[5] See Addendum, Part I, for later information.

CHAPTER VIII

Development of American League to Limit Armaments, December 18, 1914, Into The American Civil Liberties Union, January, 1920.*

In order properly to understand the attitude taken by the American Civil Liberties Union in March, 1920, we must go back to December 18, 1914, when, almost on the same day that the Emergency Federation of Peace forces in Chicago began their campaign, the American League to Limit Armaments was organized in New York City. With the outbreak of the war in 1914, the majority of the American public was in sympathy with the Entente, this feeling increasing with each new violation of international law by the German army of occupation in Belgium, and the action of the German navy on the high seas. German propagandists saw that public opinion in the United States was slowly driven toward the point which would require the Administration to enter the conflict on the side of the Entente.

To compel American neutrality and to still the growing demand for military preparation by the United States, it became necessary for German propagandists to stimulate pacifist sentiment in this country. In order to prevent the entry of the United States into the war and to create a sentiment looking toward intervention by this country (thus bringing about a peace favorable to Germany), existing German and certain other societies were employed. Also new organizations were created for the purpose of holding mass meetings, distributing pacifist literature, using their influence with Congress to prevent the enactment of laws enlarging our military establishment, as well as disturbing the harmony existing between the United States and Great Britain.

The activities of these German propagandists is now a matter of history, having been thoroughly inquired into by the Judiciary Committee of the United States Senate. The effect of this propaganda was to encourage American citizens of pacifist tendencies to organize and to co-operate in order to achieve the same purpose. In the preceding chapters, the history of the pacifist movement has been traced; and it is the purpose of this chapter to trace the history of the anti-military movement, begin-

---

* See Addendum, Part I.

ning with the organization of the American League to Limit Armaments, which had its offices at 43 Cedar street, New York City.

This association was created for the following purposes:

> "The American League to Limit Armaments is organized to combat militarism and the spread of the militaristic spirit in the United States. It will use its influence to promote a sane national policy for the preservation of international law and order, with the least reliance upon force, and to secure the efficient use of moneys appropriated for that purpose. Any person in sympathy with these purposes will be eligible to membership without payment of dues." (Taken from the letterhead of this organization.)

At a meeting of the organizers of this league, held on December 18, 1914, at the Railroad Club, 30 Church street, New York City, it was resolved:

> "That the true policy of this country is not to increase its land and sea forces but to retain for productive and humanizing outlay the vast sums demanded for armaments, and to wait steadfastly for the day when we may offer our disinterested aid in helping the nations of Europe, crippled by excesses of militarism, to free themselves and the world from the waste and terror of built-up instruments of destruction." (Minutes of proceedings of that meeting.)

Among the active organizers of this league will be found the names of many who were at the same time active in the movement directed by Louis Lochner in Chicago, under the name of the Emergency Peace Federation. Among them are: Jane Addams, Rev. John Haynes Holmes, David Starr Jordan, Dr. Jacques Loeb, Dr. George W. Nasmyth, George Foster Peabody, Oswald Garrison Villard, Morris Hillquit, Hamilton Holt, Elsie Clews Parsons, Lillian D. Wald, Stephen S. Wise, and L. Hollingsworth Wood, secretary.[1]

These persons, with others in high standing, were able to enlist the support of a large number of thoroughly patriotic citizens, who withdrew from the movement as soon as they became acquainted with the intentions of its leaders,

[1] From Minutes of First Meeting of League to Limit Armaments, Dec. 18, 1914.

and also as they began to see more clearly the nature of the international problems confronting the United States.

In the early part of 1915, the members of the executive committee of this league felt that its scope was not wide enough and, therefore, the anti-preparedness committee was formed, which later became the American Union against Militarism, with headquarters at 70 Fifth avenue, New York City. As time went on, the activity of German propagandists became less and less conspicuous, whereas the American Union against Militarism became increasingly more active. It is not intended to intimate here that those who participated in this movement were all German propagandists, or received any compensation or other benefits from German forces. It is necessary, however, to point out that their activities carried out to the letter the plans which had previously been outlined by German propagandists, though unquestionably many were not aware of this fact.

The work of the American Union against Militarism, beyond seeking to prevent legislation looking toward the increase of the military establishment of the United States, and seeking to bring about intervention in the European conflict, does not assume real significance, so far as the report of this Committee is concerned, until America had actually entered the conflict.

The passage of the draft act, after our entry into the war, caused the American Union Against Militarism to increase its activity. It immediately undertook to assist all persons desiring to avoid the draft, and to protect all persons from so-called "infringement of civil liberties," opening branch offices under the name of the Civil Liberties Bureau, both in Washington and New York, for this purpose.

The avowed intention of these branch offices was to protect all persons (and especially conscientious objectors) from so-called infringement of civil liberties, but throughout the history of the Civil Liberties Bureau, the effect was certainly to suggest to men to become "conscientious objectors."

The American Union against Militarism then, with the specific free speech issue taken care of by its branch offices, devoted itself largely to working out an elaborate organization plan for an anti-conscription campaign, both local and national.

Under date of April 9, 1917, we find a memorandum for the executive committee of the American Union against Militarism, in part as follows:

"ANTI-CONSCRIPTION CAMPAIGN

"1. Publicity.

"(a) One good dodger for wholesale distribution throughout the country.

"(b) Newspaper copy with statements by the Union on specific issues. List all newspapers opposed to conscription.

"(c) Bulletins to members and all locals at regular intervals.

"2. Organizing pressure on Congress.

"(a) Get all existing organizations to act.

"(b) Get our locals and members into action.

"(c) Meetings in critical Congressional districts.

"(d) A test referendum vote conducted, if possible, through newspapers.

"(e) Card index all members of Congress and circularize them from every source possible.

"(f) Line up the strongest possible opponents of conscription in both the Senate and House.

"(g) Send out speakers on a midwestern tour to the cities reached by the Security League.

"(h) Send out speaker into the South to counteract the Taft tour.

"(i) Get the Pacific Coast representatives to organize a tour west of the Rockies.

"(j) Campaign committee to serve with representatives of other organizations opposed to conscription; agreeing upon a platform at once in conference at New York and Washington."

"NATIONAL ORGANIZATION

"1. Use of existing organizations and groups for:

"(a) Getting individuals to co-operate.

"(b) Organized action.

"(c) Holding meetings for discussion and agitation.

"Under these get in touch throughout the country with the Socialist locals, intercollegiate Socialist society locals, radical groups, open forums and the like. Labor unions, women's organizations, church organizations, settlements, social workers' clubs, college clubs, racial groups, *especially Jewish and colored,* nationalistic societies, other peace organizations, farmers' organizations. (Italics ours.)

"2. Organize local units in the larger cities to bring together interested individuals and all local groups as a branch of the American Union.

"3. Furnish them a model constitution and by-laws, with full directions for getting to work.

"4. Furnish duplicate registration card so that a copy must be sent to the American Union central office to be filed.

"5. Send an organizer around to the larger cities in the Middle West and get an organizer on the Pacific Coast.

"6. Get one live wire in each State to stimulate organizing in the larger cities of each State.

"7. Send out one general call for organizing to every large city and then take up the work systematically based upon the returns.

"8. Call mass meetings at particular crises throughout the country on the same day."

"Program

"1. Immediate anti-conscription campaign.

"2. Co-operation in the defense of free speech and free assemblage during the war and the rights of conscientious objectors.

"3. Organize groups throughout the country to discuss the terms of peace after the war, and to form a medium of contact with similar groups in other countries after the war.

"4. Note that the printed program of the American Union calls for a number of activities, all of which are impracticable of agitation during the war, namely:

"Honesty and efficiency in the army and navy.

"Government manufacture of munitions.

"Solution of the Oriental problem.

"Conference of the twenty-one American republics, and certain declarations of national policy."[1]

---

[1] Memorandum of Executive Committee Meeting, April 9, 1917.

Another document of interest in this connection, under date of May 18, 1917, entitled, " Memorandum on co-operation between the anti-militarist organizations " follows:

" 1. Organizations actively in the field working nationally are:

" American Union against Militarism.

" Emergency Peace Federation.

" Woman's Peace Party.

" Socialist Party.

" Occasionally other national peace organizations (Church Peace Union and the American Peace Society).

" 2. Co-operation in New York:

"(1) Weekly conference of the national executives of the American Union against Militarism, Emergency Peace Federation, and other bodies represented by national offices.

" (2) Exchange of minutes, bulletins, plans, copies of circular letters, etc., between the executives of all these organizations. Each should keep a full file of the publications and minutes of the other.

"(3) A joint registration bureau of the names of co-operating local organizations and individuals throughout the United States, should be established in New York under a committee representing the agencies which maintain it, in charge of a clerk appointed by this Committee.

" 3. Co-operation in Washington:

"(1) During session of Congress through a weekly conference of legislative agents.

"(2) Through Congressional campaigns planned in advance, distributing the work among the organizations.

" 4. General co-operation:

"(1) A written agreement as to the division of organizing work throughout the country.

"(2) A joint program agreed upon by the organizations showing what matters each will handle and in exactly what way."

Since both the conscription and espionage bills were soon passed by Congress it was not very long before the American

Union against Militarism virtually withdrew, leaving the field in the hands of its branch offices.

It will be remembered that the American Union against Militarism in the spring of 1917 had organized these branch offices under the name of the Civil Liberties Bureau, both in New York and Washington. For the purposes of this record, therefore, we shall proceed with the history of the Civil Liberties Bureau, except for certain instances when the American Union against Militarism may again emerge for a moment.

A full list of the officers and executive committees of the Civil Liberties Bureau was as follows:

Lillian D. Wald, chairman.
Amos Pinchot, vice-chairman.
L. Hollingsworth Wood, treasurer.
Crystal Eastman, executive secretary.
Charles T. Hallinan, editorial director.

EXECUTIVE COMMITTEE

Roger N. Baldwin, director of Civil Liberties Bureau.

Jane Addams, A. A. Berle, Frank Bohn, William F. Cochran, John Lovejoy Elliott, John Haynes Holmes, Paul U. Kellogg, Alice Lewisohn, Frederick Lynch, James H. Maurer, Scott Nearing, Oswald Garrison Villard, Emily Greene Balch, Herbert S. Bigelow (of Cincinnati), Sophonisba P. Breckenridge, Max Eastman, Zona Gale, David Starr Jordan, Agnes Brown Leach, Owen R. Lovejoy, John A. McSparran, Henry R. Mussey, Norman M. Thomas, James P. Warbasse and Stephen S. Wise.

As the Civil Liberties Bureau had for its ostensible object "the maintenance in war times of the rights of free speech, free press, peaceful assembly, liberty of conscience and freedom from unlawful search and seizure," [1] it naturally became very popular with the drove of slackers, pro-Germans, Socialists, etc., who grasped at any chance to pose as conscientious objectors. Moreover, the Civil Liberties Bureau gradually became known as a sort of clearing house for conscientious objectors; and in October, 1917, it enlarged both its offices and scope under the name of National Civil Liberties Bureau.

The American Union, however, merely retired, so to speak, for the time being, according to a bulletin issued on November

[1] From the letter-head of the organization.

1, 1917, announcing the establishment of the National Civil Liberties Bureau as a distinct organization with a directing committee and an executive staff of its own. "Thus the American Union is now free to undertake a far-reaching program toward the practical achievement of international federation and disarmament after the war." It is interesting to note that enclosed with this bulletin was "a reprint of the detailed peace terms recently proposed by the Russian Council of Workmen's and Soldiers' Delegates." [1]

Under the same date, November 1, 1917, the National Civil Liberties Bureau issued a bulletin from which we quote:

> "On the matter of the conscientious objector, we are in constant touch with the War Department, which is showing a liberal and sympathetic attitude. Secretary Baker is personally interested, having spent a day recently with a group of objectors at Camp Meade. . . . All the men who claim conscientious objection are treated on the same basis, whether members of religious sects or not. Most have accepted non-combatant service. Although we cannot get accurate figures as to the total number . . . there seem to be altogether considerably less than one thousand conscientious objectors in the sixteen cantonments.
>
> "A bulletin containing all the facts up to date on this matter is being sent out at this itme to the 3,500 conscientious objectors and others interested in the problem registered with us. . . ." [2]

Though, as has been noted, the ostensible object of this bureau was to protect free speech and civil liberties during war times, an exhaustive examination of its files shows that aside from assisting a very small number of bona fide conscientious objectors, some of the real objects of the bureau were:

1. Encouraging naturally timid boys and discontents to register as conscientious objectors.

2. To assist any radical movement calculated to obstruct the prosecution of the war, as evidenced by the bureau's activities in collecting funds for the I. W. W. and "Masses" defense.

3. In issuing propaganda literature through publications in high standing, in order to influence public sympathy toward the I. W. W., conscientious objectors and radical organizations.

[1] Bulletin of A. U. A. M., Nov. 1, 1917.
[2] From Nat'l Civil Liberties Bureau Bulletin, Nov. 1, 1917.

4. To discourage in every possible way any conscientious objector (applying to it for information) from doing his military duty in the war; and pointing out to mothers and friends the means employed by others to escape military service.

5. To furnish attorneys for conscientious objectors and persons prosecuted for violation of the Espionage Act, as well as for other anti-war activities.

6. " Boring from within " in churches, religious organizations, women's clubs, American Federation of Labor, etc., in order to spread radical ideas and propaganda sympathetic to conscientious objectors.

7. Working towards an after-the-war radical program, usually referred to as a " democratic program of constructive peace."

In illustration of the co-operation of the Emergency Peace Federation forces with the National Civil Liberties Bureau in the mobilizing of conscientious objectors, we quote from a letter of one of the officials of the Emergency Peace Federation, May 16, 1917, to Senator LaFollette:

> " My Dear Mr. LaFollette: This is to introduce to you Mrs. J. Sargent Cram, of New York City, who has been one of the mainstays of the Emergency Peace Federation, and who is now especially devoting herself to the problem of the conscientious objectors. *Her home is a rallying point for a great number of young men who are unalterably opposed to war and who are looking to her for guidance as to what course to pursue when once a conscription act has been passed."* (Italics ours.)

Other illustrations of the National Civil Liberties Bureau methods of mobilizing conscientious objectors are as follows:

(a) To Roger Baldwin from C. C. Cheshire, conscientious objector at Camp Lewis, who objected to fighting Germans:

> "Have you a correspondent in this camp who I could see? I have several friends that feel the same as I do. I would (try) to organize them as you asked in your literature, but do not know how to start, . . ." (C. O. Camps, Vol. 6, p. 38.)

(b) On page 39 of the same volume, Baldwin answered cordially, giving the name of Clyde Crobaugh as his " camp correspondent."

(c) From Chapin Hoskins, an organizer for the American Union against Militarism, reporting the arrest of anti-draft Socialist agitators to Baldwin:

> ". . . they (Socialists) asked today for three hundred membership blanks of the Union against Militarism. . . . Our letter has been sent to the national mailing list of chapters of the Young People's Socialist Party League; 27th Ward has given us 1000 names. . . . We sent a man to Hammond, Ind., who returned with 100 conscientious objectors names." (Legal Defense, III, p. 2.)

(d) Leo Mittelheimer, secretary Erie County Local, Socialist Party of Pennsylvania, wrote to John Bartram Kelly, of the National Civil Liberties Bureau:

> "I'm in position to state that the People's Council of Erie, Pa., is organizing all conscientious objectors in this locality." (C. O. Camps, Vol. 5, p. 197.)

(e) On page 198 of the same volume, Kelly answered:

> "I think the organization of conscientious objectors is the greatest work that can be done at this time."

As examples of the methods employed by the National Civil Liberties Bureau, among the men within the camps, we note from the correspondence of

(a) Ernest R. Reichmann, supposed conscientious objector at Camp Meade, April 30, 1918, that he was both a German sympathizer and a Socialist (I. W. W., Vol. II, p. 215.)

(b) Jacob Rose, supposed "vegetarian" and conscientious objector at Camp Meade, wrote to Baldwin:

> "By the way, I shall state officially that I am an tuberculosis case." (C. O. Camps, Vol. VII, p. 354.)

A little later on F. E. Evans, of the Friends' Service Committee reported Rose most unpopular with other conscientious objectors and unreasonable. Further, that the other objectors at Camp Meade reported that they were "treated white" and had no ground for complaint. Baldwin, nevertheless, continued urging relief for Rose, bringing all sorts of pressure on Secretary Baker and other officials. In the end Rose was court martialed and sentenced to ten years.

(c) From Baldwin to Brent Allinson, former president of the International Polity Clubs, afterwards tried and convicted:

> "I don't think there is much use playing a role of objector in camp under the present regulations." (C. O. Camps, Vol. IV, p. 19.)

(d) From Harold Story, Bellflower, Cal. (a "Quaker conscientious objector"), to the American Union against Militarism, July, 1917, offering to organize a branch in the west:

> "I am convinced that there is a considerable amount of anti-conscription and anti-war sentiment in this district that could be crystallized into tangible protest in co-operation with similar movements in other parts of the country. *The Quakers here are inactive, but their reputation might be capitalized to effect, if they would grant their support, which I think could be secured.*" (Italics ours.) (C. O. Camps, Vol. V, p. 144.)

Considerable correspondence passed to and from Frederick Keppel, of the War Department, to Roger Baldwin and Norman Thomas of the Civil Liberties Bureau, indicating the efforts of that organization to influence the War Department with respect to its treatment of conscientious objectors. A letter from Baldwin to Manley Hudson contains the following:

> "Lippman and Frankfurter are of course out of that particular job now, (war office) and I have to depend entirely upon Keppel." (C. O. Camps, Vol. IV, p. 13.)

As examples of other activity for and concerning conscientious objectors, we find the following:

(a) Baldwin, writing to Mrs. Cooper, of the Liberty Defense Union, Chicago:

> "Isn't it possible for some one of the objectors there (at camp) who has taken non-combatant service, and whom you know, to get out word about the other men? I can get that from practically all the other places by that method." (C. O. Camps, Vol. IV, p. 114.)

(b) Baldwin to the father of a conscientious objector:

> "I shall see the Board of Inquiry in a few days which handles the conscientious objector cases. I will take up your son's case with them." (C. O. Camps, Vol. III, p. 36.)

The moving spirit of the organizing activities of the National Civil Liberties Bureau was its Director Roger N. Baldwin; and there can be no better example of his type of mind than to quote again from his advisory letter of August, 1917, to Louis Lochner, in reference to organizing the People's Council Convention:

"Do steer away from making it look like a Socialist enterprise. Too many people have already gotten the idea that it is nine-tenths a Socialist movement. You can, of course, avoid this by bringing to the front people like Senator Works, Miss Addams, and others, who are known as substantial Democrats. . . . I think it would be an error to get the public thinking that we are launching a political party in Minneapolis. To be sure, we are launching a political movement, but that is quite a different matter from a political point. . . .

"*We want also to look patriots in everything we do. We want to get a good lot of flags, talk a good deal about the Constitution and what our forefathers wanted to make of this country, and to show that we are really the folks that really stand for the spirit of our institutions.*" (Italics ours.)

The advice to have plenty of flags and to seem patriotic in everything was particularly characteristic of Baldwin, to the naked eye a charming, well-bred liberal, of good American stock and traditions, in reality a radical to the very bone, with a strong leaning towards the I. W. W. According to the sworn testimony of Norman Thomas, Baldwin was a philosophical anarchist. His point of view is also illustrated by the statement to the Court at the time he was sentenced for a violation of the Selective Service Act, as follows:

"Though, at the moment, I am of a tiny minority, I feel myself just one protest in a great revolt surging up from among the people — the struggle of the masses against the rule of the world by the few — profoundly intensified by the war. It is a struggle against the political state itself, against exploitation, militarism, imperialism, authority in all forms. It is a struggle to break in full force only after the war. Russia already stands in the vanguard, beset by her enemies in the camps of both belligerents — the central empires break asunder from within, the labor movement gathers revolutionary forces in Britain — and in our own country the Non-Partisan League, radical labor and the Socialist

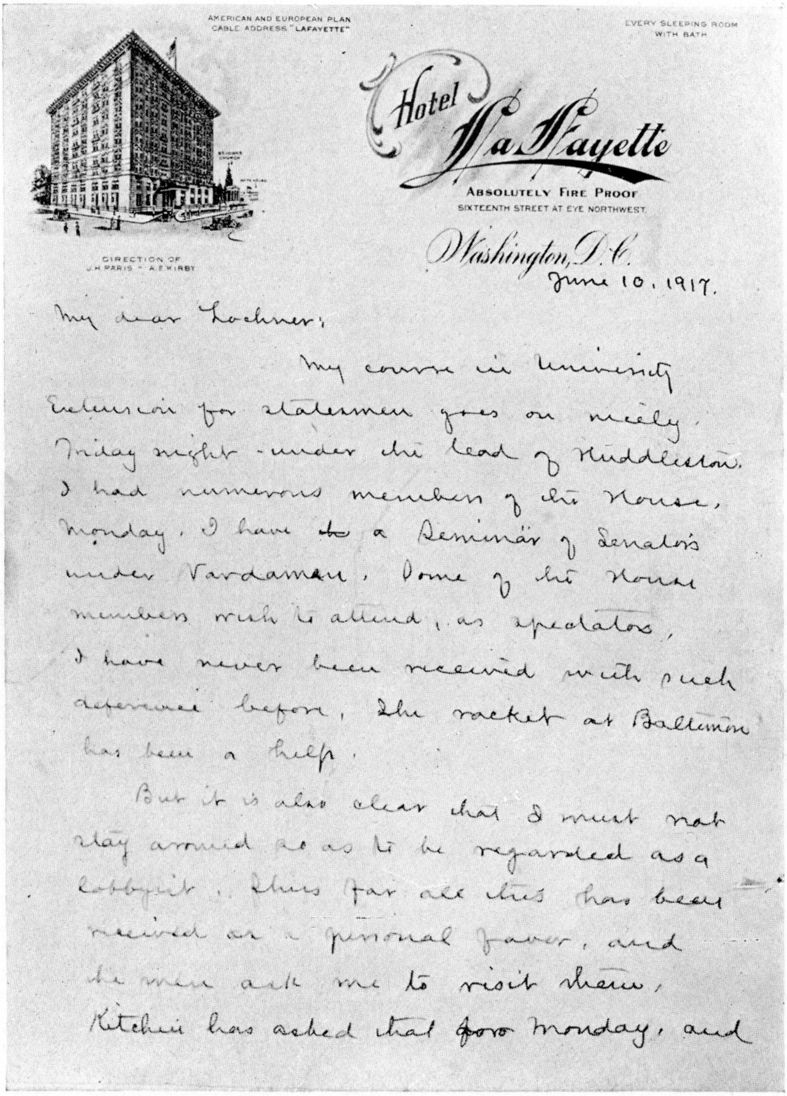
AMERICAN AND EUROPEAN PLAN
CABLE ADDRESS "LAFAYETTE"

EVERY SLEEPING ROOM WITH BATH

Hotel LaFayette

ABSOLUTELY FIRE PROOF
SIXTEENTH STREET AT EYE NORTHWEST

DIRECTION OF
J.H. PARIS — A.E. KIRBY

Washington, D.C.
June 10, 1917.

My dear Lochner:

My course in University Extension for statesmen goes on nicely. Friday night - under the lead of Huddleston I had numerous members of the House. Monday I have ~~to~~ a Seminär of Senators under Vardaman. Some of the House members wish to attend, as spectators. I have never been received with such deference before. The racket at Baltimore has been a help.

But it is also clear that I must not stay around so as to be regarded as a lobbyist. Thus far all this has been received as a personal favor, and the men ask me to visit them. Kitchin has asked that ~~for~~ Monday, and

FACSIMILE OF ORIGINAL LETTER — DAVID STARR JORDAN TO LOUIS P. LOCHNER

AMERICAN AND EUROPEAN PLAN
CABLE ADDRESS "LAFAYETTE"

EVERY SLEEPING ROOM
WITH BATH

DIRECTION OF
J. H. PARIS – A. E. KIRBY

Hotel LaFayette

ABSOLUTELY FIRE PROOF
SIXTEENTH STREET AT EYE NORTHWEST.

Washington, D.C.

there are numerous others of the same sort. So I think it best to go home in a few days.

I am advising:

1. Not to adjourn at all before December.
2. If adjourned, not to grant a single blanket authorization to the Administration
3. It is the Duty and privilege of Congress, not the President, to declare war, to state purpose of war, to ~~[illegible]~~ make known terms of peace.
4. To oppose every Prussian authorization.

Next week (or this) bills will be offered:

Restating the meaning of Treason under the Constitution.

Reminding that Constitutional Guarantees were intended to be valid in war time. They

AMERICAN AND EUROPEAN PLAN
CABLE ADDRESS "LAFAYETTE"

EVERY SLEEPING ROOM
WITH BATH

6c

DIRECTION OF
J. H. PARIS - A. E. KIRBY

Hotel LaFayette
ABSOLUTELY FIRE PROOF
SIXTEENTH STREET AT EYE NORTHWEST.
Washington, D.C.

were established for that purpose.

Repealing the Conscription Act, which is apparently unconstitutional.

Repealing (for the future) the non-tax feature of bonds.

I have promised to speak to the N.E.A. at Portland about July 10. I doubt if it is wise for me to do any mass-meeting speaking just now. It might – through false reports, interfere with my relations with Congress.

There is profound dissatisfaction here. About half the democrats have lost their patronage. Some are sorry – others take a different view.

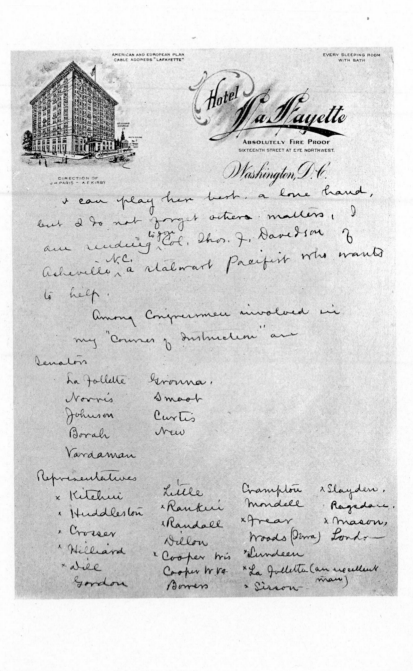

AMERICAN AND EUROPEAN PLAN
CABLE ADDRESS "LAFAYETTE"

EVERY SLEEPING ROOM
WITH BATH

DIRECTION OF
J.H. PARIS — A.E. KIRBY

Hotel LaFayette

ABSOLUTELY FIRE PROOF
SIXTEENTH STREET AT EYE NORTHWEST.

Washington, D.C.

& can play her best, a lone hand, but I do not forget others matters. I am sending to you Col. Thos. J. Davidson of Asheville, N.C. a stalwart Pacifist who wants to help.

Among Congressmen involved in my "Courses of Instruction" are

Senators

La Follette	Gronna.
Norris	Smoot
Johnson	Curtis
Borah	New
Vardaman	

Representatives

x Kitchin	Little	Crampton	x Slayden,
x Huddleston	x Rankin	Mondell	Ragsdale.
x Crosser	x Randall	x Frear	x Mason,
x Hilliard	Dillon	Woods (Iowa)	London—
x Dill	x Cooper Wis	x Lundeen	
Gordon	Cooper W Va	x La Follette (an excellent man)	
	Bowers	x Sisson—	

AMERICAN AND EUROPEAN PLAN
CABLE ADDRESS "LAFAYETTE"

EVERY SLEEPING ROOM WITH BATH

[illegible]ayette

ABSOLUTELY FIRE PROOF
SIXTEENTH STREET AT EYE NORTHWEST

Washington, D.C.

DIRECTION OF
J.H. PARIS – A.E. KIRBY

I have just analyzed the President's unfortunate letter to Russia. It is weak and verbose, not hitting any of the points vital to these people, why not say –

We have entered the war in the spirit of altruism, asking no reward, acting through sympathy with British efforts to redeem Belgium and France. When this is achieved and the seas made the ~~safe~~ World's safe open highway we shall hope to lay down our arms, returning to our normal status of Peace. We shall approve of no forced annexations, of no forced indemnities and of no exploitation of fruits of victory. We know no guarantees save those involved in the good will of free peoples. We appeal to all nations, to grant, through autonomy and federations, relief to repressed nationalities; believing that in conciliation and cooperation, not in unlimited national sovereignty, the future of Civilization can be conserved. Special problems should be solved in peace by peoples concerned, with the [illegible] and counsel of an International League of Peace

AMERICAN AND EUROPEAN PLAN
CABLE ADDRESS "LAFAYETTE"

EVERY SLEEPING ROOM WITH BATH

62.

Hotel LaFayette

ABSOLUTELY FIRE PROOF

SIXTEENTH STREET AT EYE NORTHWEST.

Washington, D.C.

DIRECTION OF
J.H. PARIS – A.E. KIRBY

I do not think it best to stay in or to go to Chicago, much as I should like to have your driving power. I can be most effective in my fashion, and I shall have done all that it is best to attempt just now.

I hope that Miss Freeman can be here before I leave. But her work is different from mine.

I have written Miss Shelly doubting if I ought to be "treasurer", not having any of the "treasure" to handle, being too far away to draw checks and the like. I think that point well taken.

Sincerely yours,

J.

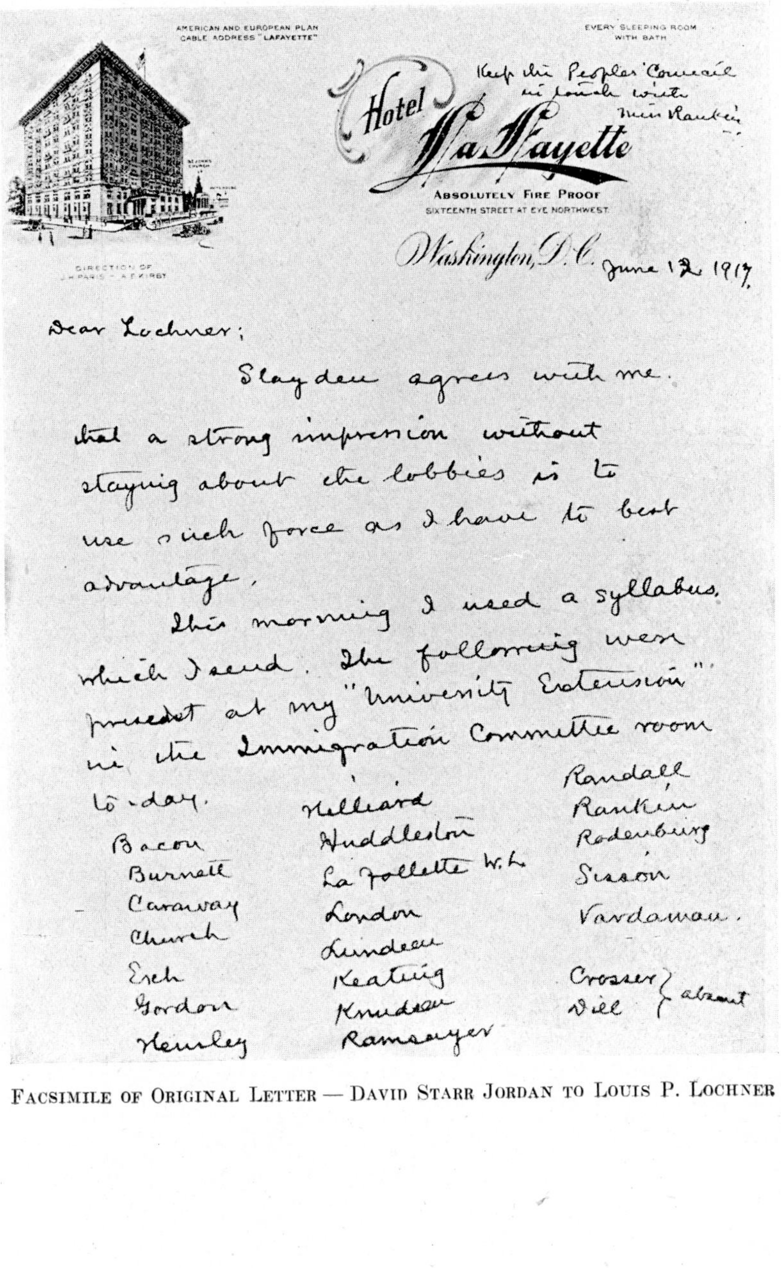

AMERICAN AND EUROPEAN PLAN
CABLE ADDRESS "LAFAYETTE"

EVERY SLEEPING ROOM WITH BATH

Hotel LaFayette
ABSOLUTELY FIRE PROOF
SIXTEENTH STREET AT EYE NORTHWEST

DIRECTION OF
J.H. PARIS — L.A. KIRBY

Keep the Peoples' Council in touch with Miss Rankin

Washington, D.C. June 12 1917

Dear Lochner;

Slayden agrees with me that a strong impression without staying about the lobbies is to use such force as I have to best advantage.

This morning I used a syllabus which I send. The following were present at my "University Extension" in the Immigration Committee room to-day.

Bacon
Burnett
Caraway
Church
Esch
Gordon
Hensley

Hilliard
Huddleston
La Follette W. L.
London
Lundeen
Keating
Knudsen
Ramsayer

Randall
Rankin
Rodenburg
Sisson
Vardaman.

Crosser } absent
Dill }

FACSIMILE OF ORIGINAL LETTER — DAVID STARR JORDAN TO LOUIS P. LOCHNER

DIRECTION OF
J. H. PARIS — A. E. KIRBY

AMERICAN AND EUROPEAN PLAN
CABLE ADDRESS "LAFAYETTE"

EVERY SLEEPING ROOM
WITH BATH

Hotel LaFayette

ABSOLUTELY FIRE PROOF
SIXTEENTH STREET AT EYE NORTHWEST

Washington, D.C.

To these add

Crosser, Hill, Kitchin, Webb, Little

Hawley, Cooper W Va, Osborne, Frear, Bowers

Slayden, Hayden, Cooper Wis, Nolan.

of private interviews.

Senators

La Follette, Borah, Stone

Gronna, Norris, New

Smoot, Curtis.

The only point as to the Treasurer is the actual work. You must be Asst. Treasurer, with authority to sign checks. or to sign David Starr Jordan, per Louis P. Lochner

My bill is enclosed, Make returns to me at Carmel-by-the-Sea, California go home to Stanford about July 1.

Sincerely yours
David Starr Jordan

Party hold the germs of a new social order. Their protest is my protest." (Quoted from a leaflet issued by friends of Roger Baldwin, November, 1918.)

After the conviction of Roger Baldwin above referred to, the National Civil Liberties Bureau continued its activities; and on November 18, 1918, its officers were as follows:

L. Hollingsworth Wood, chairman; Norman M. Thomas, vice-chairman; Helen Phelps Stokes, treasurer; Albert de Silver, director; William G. Simpson, associate director; Walter Nelles, counsel.

The directing committee was John S. Codman, John Lovejoy Elliott, Walter W. Haviland, Agnes Brown Leach, Crystal Eastman, Edmund C. Evans, John Haynes Holmes, Judah L. Magnes, and John Nevin Sayre.

An examination of the various accounts for the formation of the bureau from October, 1917, to August 31, 1918, showed a turnover of $17,000. Of this amount, about $10,000 was received from the following subscribers:

Eliza Cope, William P. Bancroft, Sarah J. Eddy, Mrs. J. Sargent Cram, A. G. Scattergood, Harold A. Hatch, Mary McMurtrie, Alexander Fleischer, Edith Borg, Albert de Silver, Agnes Brown Leach, Helen Phelps Stokes, John Nevin Sayre, James H. Post and Mrs. Maurice Lowenstein.

One of the principal activities of the National Civil Liberties Bureau, as will be disclosed in this chapter, was to create sympathy for the Industrial Workers of the World, commonly known as the I. W. W. In order to be acquainted with the precise character of the I. W. W., Part I, Sec. 2, Sub-sec. 3, Chapter I of this report, should be read. There will be found a statement of the purposes, objects, methods and tactics of the I. W. W. as defined by its own membership.

Perhaps the one organization which was most active in assisting the defense committees of the I. W. W., both in the matter of raising funds and securing bail for William D. Haywood and in carrying on a widespread publicity campaign to create sympathy for the I. W. W., was the National Civil Liberties Bureau.

In a letter of Baldwin to Justin Ebert, 233 Richmond street, Brooklyn, dated November 8, 1917, he speaks of proposed pamphlets against "the silly and outrageous indictments against the I. W. W." In preparing the proposed pamphlet on the I. W. W.

(which was issued as a bulletin of the National Civil Liberties Bureau) he discussed its contents first on November 13, 1917, with the secretary of the I. W. W., C. E. Payne, of 19 South La Salle street, Chicago, receiving Payne's approval on November 17, 1917.

A further examination of the National Civil Liberties Bureau's files indicates that a movement was set on foot about this time to exert influence upon officials to quash the indictment in the I. W. W. cases; and on December 26, 1917, Mr. Frank P. Walsh, at that time co-chairman with ex-President William H. Taft, of the War Labor Board, addressed a letter to the National Civil Liberties Bureau, introducing J. A. Law, and L. S. Chumley, both of the Defense Council of the I. W. W. Thereafter Mr. Chumley took up his offices with the National Civil Liberties Bureau, working with them in the plans for raising funds for the I. W. W. defense, and in putting out propaganda literature justifying the position of the I. W. W.[1] Chumley is now the organizer of the I. W. W. in New York, and editor of the "Rebel Worker."

Presently a conference was proposed to take place in Washington on January 10, 1918, for the purpose of taking certain action in regard to the I. W. W. trial. On January 7th, Mr. George Creel, chairman of the Committee on Public Information, addressed a letter to the National Civil Liberties Bureau, in regard to the I. W. W., as follows:

> "Please omit my name from any lists that you send out, and be at particular pains not to give the impression that I am a part of your organization or connected with it in any way. I will see Mr. Walsh when he comes."[2]

Mr. Baldwin's reply to Mr. Creel, on January 8, 1918, states that he appreciates Mr. Creel's position and says Mr. Walsh wants Creel at the meeting, "in the interests of a harmonious handling of a matter of such great public merit."

On January 11th, Roger Baldwin sent to Clarence Darrow at 140 North Dearborn street, Chicago, a copy of the report of the I. W. W. meeting in Washington on January 9, 1918. Further copies of this report were sent to Gilbert E. Roe, George P. West,

[1] I. W. W., Vol. I, Page 1991.
[2] I. W. W., Vol. I, Pages 2006 and 2007.

Charles Merz, Jack Law, Laurence Todd, Ned Cochran, Basil Manly.[1] The report says in effect:

> No action taken in the absence of Messrs. Walsh and Darrow. (Clearly Walsh and Darrow were unable to be present.)

In reference to the sending of material for the I. W. W. pamphlet under separate cover, L. S. Chumley wrote about the same date in part to Baldwin: that Frank P. Walsh would do the same, and asked for suggestions how to raise the $25,000 bail for Haywood.[2]

In answer to this telegram Mr. Baldwin on the 22d of January wired:

> "Wiring Carlton Parker about having Haywood's bail reduced.[3]

There are a number of other examples to illustrate that the relation between the National Civil Liberties Bureau and the I. W. W. was intimate. For instance, the mailing list of the bureau was put at the disposal of William D. Haywood, who, in a letter of May 28, 1918, said that he had engaged Harrison George to write letters to be sent to the National Civil Liberties Bureau mailing list. Assistance was also given by the bureau in gathering material to help the I. W. W. trial.

Again on June 18, 1918, Mr. Baldwin wrote to Prof. Irving Fisher, at 460 Prospect street, Chicago, asking him to give him information on material for "social extravagance," this to be used by the defense in the I. W. W. trial. It is also on record that Professor Fisher gave the required information.

Other co-operation between the National Civil Liberties Bureau in regard to the I. W. W. trial itself was as follows:

(1) A letter from George F. Vandeveer, on June 22, 1918, referring to Scott Nearing's "Social Extravagance," which he enclosed for Baldwin's benefit. Much further correspondence between Baldwin and Vandeveer about various books on social extravagance. (Emphasis to be placed upon this phase of capitalism for the I. W. W. trial.)

(2) A letter from Baldwin, June 25, 1918, to Charles W. Ervin, present editor of the New York "Call," and later candi-

[1] I. W. W., Vol. I, 2004 and 2005.
[2] I. W. W., Vol. III, Page 137.
[3] I. W. W., Vol. III, Page 138.

date for governor on the Socialist ticket in this State. In this letter Baldwin confirmed the arrangement to pay the "Call" $400 for reporting the I. W. W. trial, it being understood that David Karsner, Chicago representative of the "Call," would write an article once a week about the trial for the National Civil Liberties Bureau.

(3) Vincent St. John, convicted as one of the I. W. W. defendants, on July 9, 1918, writing from Chicago, acknowledged receipt from the National Civil Liberties Bureau of $1,167, and on July 13th of an additional $1,021, which payment seems to have been made for publicity, etc., concerning the I. W. W. trial.

(4) A letter from the I. W. W. defense committee to Baldwin:

> "Vanderveer advises us of your offer to handle all I. W. W. cases where the right to agitate and organize is concerned."

(5) Paul Hanna, publicity agent for the I. W. W., outlined to Baldwin a "side door plan" to make the public sympathetic to the I. W. W. "The front door to fair publicity on the I. W. W. trial is shut and closed. But the side door stands wide open."[1]

It was this idea of creating sympathy on the part of the public for the I. W. W. that was perhaps, after all, the most important contribution that the National Civil Liberties Bureau gave to "The Cause," for just at the psychological moment there was issued a pamphlet called "The Truth About the I. W. W.," published by the National Civil Liberties Bureau. On the first page of this pamphlet the following quotations from the reports of the President's Mediation Committee was printed:

> "The I. W. W. has exercised its strongest hold in those industries and communities where employers have most resisted the trade movement and where some form of protest against unjust treatment was inevitable."

The object of the pamphlet, as stated in the introductory paragraph, was:

> "To furnish interested citizens with a fair statement about the I. W. W. by unprejudiced observers. This is necessary in view of the flood of unfounded and partisan 'information' constantly given to the public."

[1] I. W. W., Vol. III, Pages 18 to 21.

The most important contributor to the pamphlet was Mr. John Graham Brooks, of Cambridge, Mass., whose high standing as a writer among the scholars and intellectuals of the country naturally went far toward commanding some strong, if sentimental, sympathy for the I. W. W. All the while Brooks was co-operating with both Baldwin and Judge George Anderson (in Washington, D. C.), in preparing I. W. W. pamphlets. It must be admitted that he went to no end of trouble in preparing the pamphlet, traveling to New York several times in order to consult with Baldwin and his other collaborators.[1]

Among these was Prof. Carlton Parker, of the University of Washington, a young professor who, though a radical, had been given a position by the government as a special agent of the War Department in dealing with the I. W. W. of the Northwest.

Prof. Parker, who had previously published an equivocal article in the "Atlantic Monthly" on the I. W. W., was considered more or less of an authority on the subject. It is, therefore, interesting to note that during the time he was serving the government as a mediator, he was collaborating in the writing of the pamphlet in question, urging sympathy for the I. W. W. As a matter of fact, this idea seems to have occurred to Prof. Parker himself (as it happened just before he died in 1918), for there are on file several urgent telegrams and letters from him to Baldwin, insisting that his name be not signed to that portion of the pamphlet which he (Parker) composed. (I. W. W., Vol. II, pp. 183–214.)

Perhaps the most striking of these messages from Parker to Baldwin is as follows, dated January 17, 1918:

> "Developments here make it highly inadvisable to use my name in pamphlet. You can naturally use any of material I have sent on. I. W. W. are striking and rioting in the camps in which I have obtained for them all their demands, and this is compromising my position as Government Mediator and makes it impossible to join officially in pamphlet publicity. Extremely sorry." (I. W. W., Vol. II, p. 203.)

[1] I. W. W., Vol. II, Pages 150–183.

Baldwin, who apparently received other urgent telegrams from Parker in the meantime wrote him on March 12, 1918:

> ". . . . You may be dead sure we won't refer to you as special agent of the War Department. . . . (I. W. W., Vol. II, p. 212.)

Among other contributors or men helpful in the publication of the I. W. W. W pamphlet were: Robert W. Bruere; Harold Callender, of Detroit, Mich., special investigator for Frank P. Walsh into the labor situation during the war in industries where the I. W. W. were strong; John A. Fitch, industrial editor of "The Survey;" Prof. Thorstein Veblen, of the School of Social Research in New York, and George P. West, of New York City.[1]

Each of these men was an apologist for the I. W. W., and the whole pamphlet was an attempt to represent favorably the position of the I. W. W. and to throw great blame upon employers.

John Graham Brooks even went so far as to suggest to Baldwin how he might co-operate with "the Stokers' I. W. W., and other more recent organizations for propaganda purposes."[2]

Another characteristic co-operative effort on the part of the National Civil Liberties Bureau in coloring or confusing public opinion concerning the I. W. W. was the placing of an advertisement in the "New Republic," June 22, 1918, of which the following is a copy:[3]

> "Never mind what you think about the I. W. W. they are at least entitled to a fair trial and an open minded public hearing. That is a primary American right.
>
> "One hundred and ten of their leaders are now before the Federal Court at Chicago, charged with conspiring to obstruct the war, but the trial involves essentially the activities of the I. W. W. as a labor organization.
>
> "The I. W. W. are entitled to the best legal defense they can make. They must bring scores of witnesses long distances. The trial will probably last months.
>
> "The Department of Justice, the court and the jury can be relied upon to deal effectually with any criminal acts that may be disclosed. It is for American liberals to make it financially possible for the defense to present fully the industrial evils underlying the I. W. W. revolt against intolerable conditions of labor.
>
> "Such a labor trial is, of necessity, enormously expen-

---

[1] I. W. W., Vol. II.

[2] I. W. W., Vol. II, Page 225.

[3] Copied from official report.

sive. It will cost over $100,000. Of this about $50,000 has already been raised from the membership alone. But it is impossible to raise the entire fund from the members. The whole sum needed cannot be secured without the liberal financial support of those Americans who believe in the right of a fair trial, even for the I. W. W.

"The undersigned, therefore, appeal to all liberals for financial help. Checks should be made out to Albert De Silver, treasurer, 2 West 13th street, New York City.

"ROBERT W. BRUERE, "JOHN DEWEY,
"JOHN A. FITCH, "PERCY STICKNEY GRANT,
"CARLTON J. H. HAYES, "INEZ HAYNES IRWIN,
"HELEN KELLER, "JAMES HARVEY ROBINSON,
"THORSTEIN VEBLEN, "GEORGE P. WEST."
"WALTER E. WEYL,

In this connection it is interesting to note the endeavors of the League for Democratic Control of Boston (one of the co-operating organizations of the National Civil Liberties Bureau) to raise money for the I. W. W. defense. A letter from Harold L. Rotzel, organizing secretary (who once signed himself "Yours for Bolshevik democracy"),[1] on July 29, 1918, reads:

"MY DEAR BALDWIN: . . . Our appeal for the I. W. W. among the supposedly liberal members of the Twentieth Century Club, to whom we had sent the pamphlet. The I. W. W." fell flat. . . . I made bold to use them as an illustration in a sermon in a Quaker church yesterday. . . . I think that a regular murderer would have a higher standing in the eyes of most people than an I. W. W. But of such is the Kingdom of War."[2]

It is worth noting further that the National Civil Liberties Bureau, under its new name of the American Civil Liberties Bureau, today is as active as ever working up sympathy for revolutionaries, influencing public opinion, and generally spreading subversive propaganda.

One of the most subtle of the weapons used by these radicals is the discrediting of any conservative force intent on exposing them. For instance, one of the leaflets published lately by the National Civil Liberties Bureau, entitled "Memorandum Regard-

[1] I. W. W., Vol. 3, Page 199.
[2] C. O. General, Vol 3, Page 71.

ing the Persecution of the Radical Labor Movement in the United States," tries to discredit the Department of Justice for its raids from September 5, 1917, on. As a result, there has been a tremendous amount of sentimental indignation created against these raids, which have, in effect, protected the very people complaining against them.

Another instance on the part of the National Civil Liberties Bureau forces and their more openly radical allies, the I. W. W., etc., to undermine the American Federation of Labor, may be illustrated by Baldwin's letter to Mr. John Haynes Holmes, in May, 1917, concerning the proposed Conference for Democracy and Terms of Peace:

> "I am hoping that the conference will at least serve the useful purpose of a new radical attack on the hidebound leadership of the American Federation of Labor."

Still another method of Baldwin and his friends may be set forth by the following excerpt from Baldwin's letter to Wm. Hard, June 13, 1918:

> "We wonder whether you would not be willing to let us send you exclusive material from time to time, with the understanding that you would be willing to look it over, with the idea of using such of it as appeals to you. We are particularly anxious to see that the case is constantly and vigorously stated by pro-war liberals and radicals whose motive is above question." . . .

Hard, who was supposed to be a "pro-war liberal," answered June 21, 1918:

> ". . . I think I see my way perfectly clear now to writing something about free speech in general and about the Post Office dep't in particular." . . . (General, Vol. II, pp. 175 and 176.)

Again, in writing to George Vandeveer, Baldwin suggests that unorganized labor could work against the American Federation of Labor "with a view to staging a revolution."

Other instances of this "boring-from-within" policy of Baldwin will be found in:

(1) Letters from Baldwin in regard to influencing and spreading propaganda in churches. (C. O. General, Vol. IV, pp. 2147, 2148.)

(2) Arthur W. Calhoun, of Clark University, offers to organize a branch of the National Civil Liberties Bureau in Worcester with "Ministers, Friends, radicals and Socialists co-operating." (C. O. States, Vol. III, p. 780) and on page 781 Mr. Calhoun gets specific directions from Baldwin as to how to go about this organization process.

The National Civil Liberties Bureau, though leaving no stone unturned to hamper the military strength of the United States Government during the war, was at the same time forehanded enough to look toward an after-the-war program, which should be altogether along the same lines. In this connection it should be remembered that when the American Union against Militarism withdrew from the active field of propaganda, this was only in order to conserve its forces for an after-the-war drive against military protection.

One of the chief members of the American Union, Miss Lillian Wald, followed this line of thought when, in October, 1917, she resigned from the executive board, not only of the American Union, but also of the National Civil Liberties Bureau. In writing to Baldwin, explaining her resignation, she ended by saying, "I am not at all out of the movement, even though I am not on the committee."[1]

Baldwin, in answering this letter, said, in part:

> "It is a comfort to know that we can call on you with such assurance of response in any emergency."

Again, when Baldwin sent Chumley, Collector for the I. W. W., with the suggestion that Miss Wald introduce him "to Miss Lewisohn, Col. Thompson and Mrs. Willard Straight," Miss Wald replied:

> ". . . I believe it would be a great deal better for you to introduce him to the people you mention. If I have the opportunity I will be glad to say the encouraging word." (I. W. W., Vol. II, p. 96.)

Other instances suggesting after-the-war plans of both the American Union against Militarism and the National Civil Liberties Bureau are as follows:

(1) From Laurence Todd, Baldwin's "inside information" newspaper man in Washington, to Baldwin in 1917:

> "A million employees on the railroad are going to stand together to get democratic consideration of their demands,

[1] C. O. General, Vol. 4, Pages 2255 and 2256.

and they in turn are going to give the postal employees and other big groups their help in securing the same treatment. We are on the way to a big liberalization of industrial relations."[1]

(2) Baldwin, August 20, 1918, addressing F. S. Fash, a conscientious objector, at Fort Worth:

"It is men like you . . . who will be the centers of influence in the reconstruction of democracy which is bound to follow the war." (Legal Defense, Vol. VIII, p. 101.)

(3) Baldwin, in General, Vol. III, page 3:

"Villard is saving himself for a program of agitation for disarmament and against universal military service after the war."

(4) Baldwin, in writing to Kenneth Darling, a "conscientious objector" (in regard to court martial sentences of conscientious objectors), that he judges from what he hears from the War Department "that the men will all be freed as soon as the war is over."

At this point it may be interesting to note some of the general tactics, aside from that with conscientious objectors, employed by Baldwin in accomplishing his ends:

(1) Baldwin to Sugarman, of Detroit:

"We have found it best to use plain envelopes . . . without any indication of our identity." (Legal Defense, Vol. IV, p. 1405.)

(2) John Haynes Holmes, writing to Baldwin, May 6, 1918:

"There is nothing in the past that has pleased me more or more deeply stirred my admiration than the fine co-operation which you established between our bureau and the two Departments of War and Justice." (General, Vol. II, p. 114.)

(3) From Laurence Todd to Baldwin:

"I'm informed on good authority in G. C's bureau, that the Colonel House influence is now being thrown in favor of democratic liberties. . . . People's Council will henceforth be free to do as it pleases. Labor revolt is brewing. . .

[1] General, Vol. 1, Page 133.

Socialists and radicals are to be welcome in respectable official circles." (General, Vol. I, p. 144.)

(4) Baldwin to Harold Evans, Philadelphia (April 13, 1918):

"While the administration is full of liberals, they unfortunately are not in the two departments which enforce this war legislation, namely, the Post Office Department and Department of Justice." (General, Vol. I, p. 59.)

(5) Wire from Baldwin to Liberty Defense League, soliciting letters of complaint from drafted conscientious objectors to Secretary Baker at once:

"Administration plan depends on number and kind of such letters received before Tuesday." (C. O. General, Vol. III, p. 122.)

(6) Baldwin to Herbert Bigelow, in regard to proposed protest meeting, November, 1917:

"We will endeavor to get all of the pro-war men who still stand for constitutional rights, and if we can't get many of them we will put up the least objectionable among the radicals and the so-called pacifists. Men, for instance, like Amos Pinchot, John Haynes Holmes, Mr. Villard . . . and, very likely, Jane Addams." (Legal Defense, Vol. IV, p. 1165.)

(7) A letter from Mrs. Agnes Brown Leach to Baldwin, in praise of Baldwin and mentioning $500 given by her to People's Council, November 6, 1917:

"The radical who is going to help the people's cause most is not the unconventional freak, . . . but . . . engaging gentleman, like yourself, who will bring things to pass." (General, Vol. II, p. 66.)

(8) From Laurence Todd to B. W. Nelles, (May 14, 1918):

"Its strategy. . . . (The Non-Partisan League) is first to get the legislative and administrative power, and then quietly remove the autocrats and inciters of mob violence from the places of influence they have held." . . . (General, Vol. I, p. 180.)

(9) Mr. Charles Zueblin, declining to serve on a committee, to Baldwin, January 8, 1918:

"I think lobbying in Washington much more valuable." (than mass meetings.) Round up congressmen and senators, as suffragists and prohibitionists. . . . I believe in unrestricted free speech, but nationalization of railways and mines is more important." (Conferences, p. 103.)

(10) Baldwin writes to advise Kenneth Darling, conscientious objector and a radical Socialist, to apply for work in the Department of Justice, as German translator. He advises Darling to write to Mr. Keppel. (Darling never achieved this end. (C. O. Camps, Vol. VI, p. 269.)

(11) From Alice Park, suffragist, on staff of "Votes for Women," to Baldwin, congratulating him on his I. W. W. pamphlets and protesting against the activities of the home defense leagues of California against seditious activities. (Legal Defense, Vol. I, p. 395.)

General, Vol. I, page 88 — Baldwin writes to Rabbi Judah Magnes:

"We need you, your point of view and your connections in building up an increasingly effective movement."

General, Vol. I, page 115 — Baldwin to James Warbasse:

". . . We are trying to preserve the fundamental rights of agitation, so that those who oppose war or who advocate peace may have a chance to talk more freely. . . ." (November 10, 1917.)

General, Vol. I, page 32 — from Baldwin to George Nasmyth:

". . . This work is only half with objectors, half directly with freedom of expression as regards labor and radical movements." (August, 1918.)

From "Novy Mir," the Russian Socialist newspaper, to Baldwin, March 12, 1918:

"Your address was given us by Comrade Charles Ervin, secretary of the newly organized American Liberty Union, having for its purpose the protection of free speech in this country and giving aid to those caught in the net." (Legal Defense, Vol. VI, p. 138; on p. 139, Baldwin answers in a co-operative spirit.)

In Legal Defense, Vol. VII, page 60, Baldwin explains regretfully why he could not oppose Liberty Bond drives, etc.:

"Our main job is to help keep people's mouths open and their printing presses free. Our business is to see that all those who want to get any ideas across are protected in their rights."

It remains, in recording this history of the pacifist-Socialist movement in this country, to bring the National Civil Liberties Bureau up to date under its lately acquired name of the American Civil Liberties Union and to follow the achievements of some of the chief organizers of the movement to the present day.

A late bulletin (March, 1920) of the American Civil Liberties Union, representing the American Freedom Foundation, 1541 Unity Building, Chicago, Ill.; the Labor Defense League, 230 Russ Building, San Francisco, Cal.; the League for Democratic Control, 2 Park Square, Boston, Mass.; the Workers' Defense Building, San Francisco, Cal., and the Workers' Defense Union, 7 East 15th street, New York City, discloses as its officers:

Harry F. Ward, chairman; Duncan McDonald, Illinois, and Jeanette Rankin, of Montana, as vice-chairmen; Helen Phelps Stokes, treasurer; Albert de Silver and Roger N. Baldwin, directors; Walter Nelles, counsel; Lucille B. Lowenstein, field secretary; and Louis F. Budenz, publicity director.

National Committee:

Jane Addams, Chicago, Ill.
Herbert S. Bigelow, Cincinnati, Ohio.
Sophonisba P. Breckenridge, Chicago, Ill.
Robert M. Buck, Chicago, Ill.
John S. Codman, Boston, Mass.
Lincoln Colcord, Washington, D. C.
James H. Dillard.
Crystal Eastman, New York City.
John Lovejoy Elliott, New York City.
Edmund C. Evans, Philadelphia, Pa.
Edward W. Evans, Philadelphia, Pa.
William M. Fincke, Katonah, N. Y.
John A. Fitch, New York City.
Elizabeth Gurley Flynn, New York City.
Felix Frankfurter, Harvard.
William Z. Foster.
Paul J. Furnas, New York City.
Zona Gale, Portage, Wis.
A. B. Gilbert, St. Paul, Minn.
Arthur Garfield Hays, New York City.
Morris Hillquit, New York City.

John Haynes Holmes, New York City.
Frederic C. Howe, Washington, D. C.
James Weldon Johnson, New York City.
Helen Keller, Forest Hills, L. I.
Harold J. Laski, Cambridge, Mass.
Agnes Brown Leach, New York City.
Arthur Le Sueur, St. Paul, Minn.
Henry R. Linville, New York City.
Robert Morss Lovett, Chicago, Ill.
Allen McCurdy, New York City.
Grenville S. MacFarland, Boston, Mass.
Oscar Maddaus, Manhasset, L. I.
Judah L. Magnes, New York City.
James H. Maurer, Reading, Pa.
A. J. Muste, New York City.
George W. Nasmyth, New York City.
Scott Nearing, New York City.
Julia O'Connor, Boston, Mass.
William H. Pickens, Baltimore, Md.
William Marion Reedy, St. Louis, Mo.
John Nevin Sayre, Katonah, N. Y.
Rose Schneidemann, New York City.
Vida D. Scudder, Wellesley, Mass.
Norman M. Thomas, New York City.
Oswald Garrison Villard, New York City.
L. Hollingsworth Wood, New York City.
George P. West, Oakland, Cal.[1]

These names will nearly all be familiar to any one who has read the preceding chapters of this section; and the association here of women like Jane Addams and Helen Keller with extreme radicals like Elizabeth Gurley Flynn and leaders of the Socialist movement in America will explain, in large measure, the Socialist tendencies which manifest themselves in many so-called liberal papers and in some collegiate settlement and religious circles.

The National Civil Liberties Bureau has lately issued some fifteen pamphlets, among which are "Your Amish Mennonite," by William Hard, reprinted from the "New Republic," which is described in a foreword as "The following striking story of the conscientious objector in America;" "Why Freedom Matters," by Norman Angell; and "Amnesty for Political Prisoners," by Judah L. Magnes.

[1] See Addenda for later corrections and additions. (July, 1920.)

Under its new title, the American Civil Liberties Union has, as far as our knowledge goes, issued four pamphlets:

(1) "General Amnesty," by Dr. Frank Crane, of the New York "Globe," ending: "I am in favor of a general amnesty for all political prisoners."

(2) "The Old America and the New," by Judah L. Magnes, ending, "Let us uphold the ideals of internationalism in the name of the old America that was free and is now dead, and in the name of the New America which is now being born."

(3) "Do We Need More Sedition Laws?"

(4) "The Issues in the Centralia Murder Trial," an attempted defense of the Centralia I. W. W. murderers of American soldiers.

The Bureau has also issued the reprint copy of an article from the January 31, 1920, issue of the "New Republic," called "The Force and Violence Joker.[1]

This includes more or less open attacks on Attorney-General Palmer, Mr. Lansing, the House Immigration Committee, the New York "Times," Senator Fall, this Committee, etc. It also quotes the dissenting opinions in the Abrams case, of Justices Holmes and Brandeis, and ends by making light of the danger of revolution in America.

This belittling of the very real danger to the institutions of this country, as well as the attempted discrediting of any investigating group (or individual), has become thoroughly characteristic of our "Parlor-Bolshevik" or "Intelligensia."

Concerning the present status of some of these:

As we have seen, Roger Baldwin, though he spent a year in prison for his "conscientious objector beliefs," is now again one of the directors of the American Civil Liberties Union.

Many of the original organizers of the American Union against Militarism are at present on the list of officers or members of committees of the American Civil Liberties Union.

During the period which has been described, there were a large number of organizations co-operating with those described in the preceding chapter (in many cases having interlocking directorates), starting in the beginning with anti-militarism as their objective, but in nearly all cases winding up in the closest possible contact with extreme radicals and revolutionaries. The Committee feels that anyone who has followed closely the progress of

---

[1] See Addenda for July 1920 publications.

the movement described in this and preceding chapters will recognize the influences which have been at play on public opinion and the efforts which have been exerted to stimulate the radical movement among persons of means and education.

(NOTE: The quotations from letters to and from the National Civil Liberties Bureau and allied organizations in this chapter, containing citations to various volumes, refer to the volumes of bound correspondence subpoenaed from the National Civil Liberties Bureau by this Committee, from which this data is gathered.)

CHAPTER IX

People's Freedom Union*

In addition to the particular organizations which have been enumerated in the preceding chapters of this section, there also were a large number of similar organizations with interlocking directorates, both in New York City and scattered throughout the United States. The notable feature of the entire movement which is here treated is the striking activity of many of those participating in it. If the committees representing these numerous organizations be scanned, it will be found that in almost every one the leading spirits are the same. So great is the activity of a number of these agitators that one is inclined to believe that the different organizations serve simply as so many aliases under which this same movement is carried on.

One of the latest organizations to appear, which has begun to spread its propaganda broadcast, is the People's Freedom Union, successor to the People's Council, with offices at 138 West 13th street, New York City. It will be noted that this is the same premises occupied by the People's Print, the American Civil Liberties Union, and a number of other questionable organizations. The purpose and object of this union is well stated in a mimeographed statement issued from its headquarters. The Committee feels that it is of sufficient interest to reproduce here in full, as follows:

"THE PEOPLES' FREEDOM UNION

"WHAT IT IS AND WHY IT IS

"A New Alignment Necessary In America

"Never has there been so urgent a need as comes with the end of the Great War for just-minded men and women to unite their efforts on behalf of a saner world order. The forces of reaction are more active today than ever. They now work internationally. But a consolidation of strength and a new orientation of the forces working for peace and freedom has become indispensable. In the first place, it is imperative that the forward-looking forces in this country, whose morale has become weakened by discouragement and whose energies dissipated, be reco-ordinated. During the war a number of groups sprang up, devoted to such

---

* See Addendum, Part I.

objects as the securing of amnesty for political prisoners, defending and regaining civil rights and liberties abrogated under the hysteria of war, and promoting international understanding and friendship even while the conflict raged. In the beginning each tried to appeal to a different group for support, moral and financial. Gradually, however, each found itself assuming other functions than that originally conceived to be its central purpose. To each phase of this general program went a fraction of the energy of the group, with the result that no single function was carried out in such manner as to achieve relative success. In the same way, each group appealed in the end approximately to the same clientele of progressive citizens for financial and moral support.

"*With Europe*

"Equally important with the revitalizing of the American movement is the resumption of intercourse between ourselves and the liberal forces of the various countries, made possible by the lifting, to a degree at least, of international censorship. Each foreign mail brings us tidings of European groups ready to take up the task of world building in their own country, and eager for news of what is transpiring in America.

"THE PROPORTIONS OF THE PROBLEM

"An intelligent public opinion on world affairs must be stimulated. A first pre-requisite to a saner world order is an enlightened public opinion on international affairs. But do people know what is going on in other lands? Do the majority of our fellow citizens in America, for example, know the facts about Russia or about Hungary, or Ireland, or India, or Egypt, or China, and a dozen other scenes of strife?

"When the Egyptian people rose this year and demanded that Great Britain keep her promise to withdraw her sovereignty, Lloyd George reaffirmed the British 'protectorate,' and President Wilson pledged America to recognize it. Were our people consulted?

"When delegates from Korea wished to leave for Paris to present to the Peace Conference their country's claim to independence from Japan, they were denied passports by our State Department. How many of our people had a voice in these decisions?

"Thus, instance after instance might be mentioned of transactions of the utmost importance, in which the American people have had neither part nor knowledge. At this moment policies are being shaped which may call our young men to kill and be killed in Mexico, in Europe, Asia and Africa.

"Everywhere the stage is being set for the next war. Shall that next war be allowed to break? The time to stop it is now, by throwing the light of pitiless publicity upon the machinations of secret diplomacy.

"IMPERIALISM AND MILITARISM MUST BE CRUSHED

"Imperialism is not dead, even though the kaiser and other emperors have gone. Any people which rules other people without their consent, whether directly (as in India) or indirectly (through 'protectorates,' 'spheres of influence' and the like, as in Persia), is imperialistic.

"Imperialism has been sharpened by the war. The British Empire has been increased a million square miles; France gets Syria; Japan practically gets Shantung; Italy is prepared to fight Jugo-Slavia over Adriatic territory, and Greece over Smyrna, in Asia Minor.

"In our own country, American imperialists want us to keep the Philippines and continue the policies which have extended American dominion over Porto Rico, Panama, Haiti, Santo Domingo, Nicaragua and Honduras. The annexation of Mexico and Costa Rica may be next. A clash may come with Japan or some other former ally over financial interests in China.

"Shall the liberal and radical forces of the world bestir themselves only when the next war has burst? They must come together and get ready now before the passions of war again sweep them aside.

"MILITARISM IS RAMPANT THROUGHOUT THE WORLD

"The war which was to have ended all war leaves the nations more militaristic than ever.

"In our own country Secretary Daniels complains to Congress that its appropriation of $15,000,000 for navy aviation is too small in view of Great Britain's appropriation of ten times that amount for the same purpose. Congress is practically committed to a large army and the principle of conscription, the only question now being whether the standing army is to consist of 570,000 men or only 300,000.

"In Europe the same fever is raging. Though Germany has been beaten to the dust, France and Great Britain are less inclined than ever to reduce their armaments. In Japan the politicians are pointing to the military preparations of the Western Powers as a reason for speeding up the martial activities of their own empire.

"OUR CIVIL LIBERTIES MUST BE REDEEMED AND THE VICTIMS OF COERCION FREED

"Democracy without the unrestricted right to discuss public policies is the shabbiest of pretenses. Painful and abundant illustrations exist of the dangers to real democracy at the present hour.

"Legal meetings have been forbidden or broken up; newspapers suppressed and spokesmen for uncongenial opinions deported or imprisoned. For voicing in words a protest against the war, Eugene V. Debs received a jail sentence three times as heavy as that inflicted by an Austrian court upon the men whose protest took the form of assassinating an Austrian premier.

"Even after the signing of the armistice, men have been sent to jail for violating the Espionage Act, a law ostensibly framed to prevent the giving of aid to Germany, but in practice used to jail radical protestants against social injustice. There is no disposition evident to repeal this measure. On the contrary, the Attorney-General of the United States, Congress and the various State legislatures are preparing even more drastic laws to choke off the radical tendencies which they fear to allow men and women to discuss openly and democratically.

"Meantime, reactionary forces further the candidacies of incompetent politicians, on the sole strength of their war records. They silence constructive criticism and defeat needed changes in our social structure by dishonestly identifying the plea for those changes with the 'agitation' of 'foreigners.'"

"THE PEOPLE'S FREEDOM UNION

"WHAT THE PEOPLE'S FREEDOM UNION IS

"The People's Freedom Union, then, is a federation to which several New York groups have committed themselves to the end of a more effective handling than any could attain in its separate strength of the above program. It is the One Big Union idea applied to the peace-and-freedom movement.

"HOW IT WILL WORK

"The Peoples' Freedom Union will proceed on the principle of specialization on concrete tasks not already covered by their organizations, each task to be assigned to a committee or group especially qualified to direct the campaign for its accomplishment. It hopes gradually to absorb other groups, and to give them the added strength that comes from union and from the generous infusion of new blood. It will strive constantly to reach out to those millions of fellow citizens who, profiting by the lessons of the Great War, are ready now to join in the effort to build a new and better world. It stands ready, as specific issues necessitate the formation of special and temporary groups, to welcome these as a part of the federation and to extend to them facilities for economizing on clerical help and other overhead expenses.

"HOW IT IS ADMINISTERED

"The affairs of the Peoples' Freedom Union are administered by an executive committee, by the officers and departmental directors, and by special committees in charge of specific phases of the work. In its headquarters at 138 West 13th street are located the following administrative departments: Organizations, publicity, publications, speakers and finances.

"The department of organization aims to stimulate in other centers the co-ordination of existing forces now being accomplished in New York as well as to promote committees to specialize on activities not already provided for.

"The publicity department transmits all official pronouncements of the union to the press, plans systematic campaigns for popularizing the principles of the union through the daily and weekly press, and keeps the daily, weekly, and monthly publications of this and other countries informed of the activities of the union.

"The department of publications, under the imprint of the 'People's Print,' issues weekly leaflets on some important current topic for free distribution in large quantities. It publishes from time to time pamphlets on vital questions of the day; it issues the special publications authorized by the various sub-committees. At an early date this department will establish a monthly journal which will chronicle the work of the Peoples' Freedom Union and of similar groups, which will comment fearlessly upon existing international injustices, and which will serve as an exponent of the American movement for peace and freedom to similar movements in other countries.

"The speakers' bureau arranges tours for men and women of national and international note who have a message bearing upon the objects for which the union stands. For terms, available speakers and their topics, application should be made to the executive secretary.

"The Financial department, under a financial secretary, is in charge of the raising and collection of the funds necessary for carrying on the work of the union. Contributions may be made either for the general purposes of the union or for some specific object."

The curious combination of so-called liberals, educators, writers, anarchists and revolutionary socialists which bend their energies toward controlling public opinion through the medium of this association, is revealed by the following list of officers of the union and the members of the committee, which is known as the Free Political Prisoners Committee:

John Lovejoy Elliott, chairman; Arthur S. Leeds, treasurer; Frances M. Witherspoon, executive secretary.

Committee members: Tracy D. Mygatt, secretary; Pauline Cahn, Evans Clark, Joe Coffin, Stella Daljord, Lottie Fishbein, Anne Peck Fite, M. E. Fitzgerald, Elizabeth G. Flynn, Paul Furnas, Lewis Gannett, Gratia Goller, Ruth Gordon, Alfred Hayes, Helen Holman, Wilfred Humphries, Virginia Hyde, Harry W. Laidler, Gertrude U. Light, Winthrop D. Lane, Florence Lattimore, Alice E. Mauran, Therese Mayer, Donald McGraw, Leland Olds, Ida Rauh, Florence Rauh, Merrill Rogers, Jessica Smith,

Evan Thomas, Norman Thomas, Pauline H. Turkel, Albert Rhys Williams, Jacob Wortsman, Jules Wortsman.

It will be recalled that it was this organization that sponsored a rather melodramatic demonstration on Christmas Day, parading on Fifth avenue, in New York city, in single file, with touching banners, for the purpose of arousing sympathy for so-called political prisoners. A number of similar examples might be given, but the Committee feels that anyone who has read this section will realize why so many of the papers and periodicals which believe themselves to represent the so-called liberal point of view have been led astray with respect to the great forces at play on the public opinion of the American people. The persons who have participated in this movement, not necessarily thoroughly familiar with the objects and the purposes which actuate it, are sowing the seeds of disorder and doing their part to imperil the structure of American institutions.

CHAPTER X

Academic and Scholastic Socialist Activities

It is not easy to know how deeply Socialism has penetrated the majority of our colleges and universities, how much of the teachings of economics and sociology is purely scientific, and how much has a tinge of propaganda.

As early as 1909, in an address to college alumni, a former Secretary of the Treasury, also a banker, said:

> "I am alarmed at the trend towards Socialism in this country today. If there is any power in this country to stem it, it ought to be the trained minds of college men. Four out of five commencement day orations are purely Socialistic. I have met many of the teachers of sociology in our schools and universities. With few exceptions these teachers are Socialists, though they hesitate to admit it and most of them will deny it. Unconsciously there is a great deal of Socialism being taught in these days from the pulpit. The Chautauqua is also full of it. I do not recall a Chautauqua popular speaker who is not talking and teaching Socialist doctrine. The trend of the newspapers is towards Socialism, and, I repeat, the trend is dangerous to this country."

The work from which this quotation is taken is "Christianizing the Social Order," by Walter Rauschenbusch, then professor of history in Rochester Theological Seminary. The author was an eminent and popular writer and lecturer before seminaries and universities. His books have a wide circulation and influence.

His attitude towards Socialism can be easily understood by two or three quotations (p. 404):

> "The Socialists found the Church against them and thought God was against them, too. They have had to do God's work without the sense of God's presence to hearten them. . . . Whatever the sins of individual Socialists, and whatever the shortcomings of Socialist organizations, they are tools in the hands of the Almighty. . . . Whatever tares grow in the field of Socialism, the field was plowed and sown by the Lord and He will reap it. Socialism is one of the chief powers of the coming age. . . . God had to raise up Socialism because the organized Church was too blind, or too slow, to realize God's ends."

He advises the weekly reading of the "Survey," and says that if a man reads the Bible and the "Survey," he ought to find salvation.

It is a commentary on the increasing prevalence of revolutionary Socialist ideas among university men, that in 1917 and 1918 there did not exist in the United States a single purely literary weekly review that was not of this character. The "Nation" and the "New Republic" were its exponents. So was the "Dial." The situation called for immediate remedy. A group of patriotic university men planned a new weekly, the "Review," to present to the public and patriotic view of every current issue and event. In connection with this question it is interesting to publish a letter written by a professor of sociology at the Ohio State University, Arthur W. Calhoun, written July 29, 1919, to an instructor in sociology at the University of Minnesota, named Zeuch, who since then has gone as instructor in sociology to Cornell University, and who also lectures at the Rand School. The letter reads:

> Dear Zeuch.— I think I accept all you say about the condition of the proletariat and the impossibility of the immediate revolution. But I am less interested in the verbiage of the Left Wing than in the idea of keeping ultimates everlastingly in the center of attention to the exclusion of mere muttering reforms. One of the things that will hasten the revolution is to spread the notion that it *can* come soon. If the Left Wing adopt impossibilist methods of campaign, I shall stand aloof, but if they push for confiscation, equality of economic status, and the speedy elimination of class privilege, and keep their heads, I shall go with them rather than the yellows. If Gras is doing what he says and I am doing what he says, he is right in saying that he is doing the better job. I wonder, however, how many of his students draw the "necessary" conclusions: and I wonder whether I do all my students' thinking for them.
>
> "Ellery is feeling at Columbus and also at Illinois. I had a letter from Hayes about him.
>
> "I have accepted the professorship of sociology at De Pauw University. The job pays $2,200 this year with assurance of $2,400 if I stay the second year. The president has been here three times and had long interviews with me. Besides we have written a lot. I told him I belonged to the radical Socialists. I expounded my general principles

on all important points. He knows also of the circumstances of my leaving Clark and Kentucky. He says he is in substantial agreement with most of what I have said and that he sees no reason why I cannot get along at De Pauw. He says he feels confident it will be a permanency. Ross had some hand in the game. President Grose interviewed him at Madison last week and Ross wrote encouraging me to take the place. I did not make any great effort. Grose knows that I did not care much one way or the other. He took the initiative almost from the start and I sat back and waited. I am afraid Greencastle is too small to do much with the Co-Op. Population 4,000, 30 miles north of Bloomington, 800 students, mostly in college, a few in school of music, a few graduate students. Hudson is professor of Ec. (economics) there.

"Beals was here last week. He is pushing the "Nation." Says the circulation has quadrupled since they became Bolshevists.

"As ever,

"(Signed) A. W. C."

There are many things in this letter that make it more than the expression of one man's opinions. In the first place, the president of De Pauw University at Greencastle, Indiana, offers the professorship of sociology to a man whom he knows to be a radical Socialist, a teacher of revolutionary Socialism and a member of the Left Wing. The Gras who is mentioned in the letter is Professor N. S. B. Gras of the University of Minnesota, who evidently is teaching revolutionary Socialism as well, if not better than Calhoun, and leaving his students to draw the "necessary" conclusions. Professor Ellery evidently belongs to the same group, as he is "feeling" at Columbus and Illinois universities; and E. C. Hayes also is professor of sociology at Illinois University. Another member of the group is Professor E. A. Ross, a professor of sociology at the University of Wisconsin and advisory editor of the American Journal of Sociology. The Beals who is mentioned as pushing the "Nation," was previously a university professor and an open Bolshevist. One of the side activities of Professor Calhoun, which explains his reference to the "Co-Ops." in his letter, is his position with the Tri-State Cooperative Society of Pittsburgh, which promotes the production and distribution of Red propaganda. It would seem as if there was a pretty wide circle of revolutionary Socialist professors in western faculties. How deeply rooted the teaching is in the minds of the phalanxes of students who pass year after year under the instruction of these men, would be impossible to calculate, but it goes even further back in certain sections into the school system. In a certain state library the following books were selected to send around to country schools:

"Socialism and Modern Science," by Ferri (leader of one of the Socialist groups in Italy).

"Evolution of Property," by LaFargue. (A revolutionary Socialist propagandist.)

"Love and Marriage," by Ellen Key.

"Love and Ethics," by Ellen Key. (Ellen Key is an outspoken advocate of free love and of the dissolution of marriage.)

"The Bolsheviki and World Peace," by Leon Trotzky.

"The Profits of Religion," by Upton Sinclair. (A violent literary Socialist.)

"Anarchism and Socialism," by Harris.

"Anarchism and Free Love," by Harris. (Harris is a professional Bolshevist.)

See for the above the "Iowa Magazine," February 5, 1920.

Prof. Calhoun has finally found his proper place among the teachers of the Rand School.

Quite a number of the university men have given their adhesion to the Rand School: such as Prof. Wm. I. Hull of Swarthmore, who speaks from the same platform as Trachtenberg, Algernon Lee and Hillquit.

In a recent address (Feb. 21, 1920) by W. A. Atterbury, vice-president of the Penn. R. R., to the alumni of the University of Pennsylvania, Mr. Atterbury deplored the prevalence of the diffusion of Socialist ideas of a revolutionary character at our universities, and their invasion of the select ranks of the American Economic Association and the American Sociological Society.

There are two dangerous centers of Revolutionary Socialist teaching of a university type in ecclesiastical institutions. One is the Union Theological Seminary of New York, where Christian Ethics are taught by Dr. Harry F. Ward; the other is St. Stephens College at Annandale, N. Y., where the president is the Rev. Iddings-Bell, and the professor of economics the Socialist, Dr. Edwards. The latter especially will be spoken of here more fully than in the following chapter.

Dr. Ward is the author of "The New Social Order," in which he shows a decided sympathy for Socialist social forms and is friendly to Bolshevism in Russia. He also wrote "The Labor Movement," which contained addresses delivered before the Boston School of Theology, when he was professor of social science at that institution. He expressed in it approval of the I. W. W. It is reported in a recent issue of the National Civic Federation Review that he gave his endorsement to the new gospel of Bolshevism which he considers a spiritual movement replacing the outworn Christianity of the Russian Orthodox Church. He characterized the cognate I. W. W. "philosophy" as the most ideal and practical Christian philosophy since the days of Jesus Christ, and as expressing the ideas of Christ much more closely than any church of the present day.

The activities of Dr. Ward, as shown in other parts of this report, are entirely consistent with this point of view. He is chairman of the American Civil Liberties Union, which champions the I. W. W., and presided over the I. W. W. meeting of Feb. 9, 1920, held at the Rand School, to raise money for the defense of the I. W. W. murderers of the four members of the American Legion at Centralia. He has also been prominent in numerous pacifist and radical societies such as the "Fellowship of Reconciliation," the "Emergency Peace Conference" and "People's Council," the "Liberty Defense Union."

The pro-Bolshevik articles which Dr. Ward contributed to "The Social Service Bulletin" of the Methodist Federation for Social Service were considered particularly objectionable because the Bulletin was circulated not only by the Methodist Church but by the Congregational, Northern Baptist and other organizations. They called attention to Dr. Ward's textbooks circulated by the Graded Sunday School Syndicate. Dr. Ward is also connected with the Y. M. C. A., the Y. W. C. A. and the Inter-Church World Movement.

The Philadelphia Annual Conference of the Methodist Church protested against the pro-Bolshevism of Dr. Ward being circulated in the name of the denomination. Such specialists in Bolshevism as Lieutenant Klieforth and Wm. English Walling have characterized Dr. Ward's statements as downright falsehoods or distorted facts, and as a kind of Bolshevism far worse than the Bolshevism of Russia.

The same attempt to swing existing educational institutions to the support of the atheism and materialism of the I. W. W. and Bolshevism, is shown in the movement in the Episcopal Church of which the nominal leader is the Rev. Bernard Iddings Bell. He is at the head of St. Stephen's College at Annandale, where so many young ministers of the Episcopal Church receive university education. The head of the department of economics is the Rev. Lyford P. Edwards, an able expositor of Socialism and member of the Socialist Party. He gives courses at the College on the I. W. W., on Syndicalism, Socialism and Bolshevism. As a Socialist who was selected to represent this party in the Episcopal Church at last year's Convention in England, he teaches these movements to the young Episcopalians sympathetically.

What the President, Dr. Bell himself, thinks, can be judged from his book, "Right and Wrong after the War." He here bases the whole history and character of civilization on what he calls the two great "Urges," the Hunger Urge and the Sex Urge, which we have in common with the animal kingdom. He accepts, in other words, the lowest form of the Karl Marx materialistic conception of history, in which there is absolutely no place for a God in the evolution of the universe. Logically this is inescapable atheism. As a corollary he states two fundamental articles of faith: (1) that private property should be absolutely abolished, and (2) that interest on invested property, rents, savings, etc., is robbery. He also condemns, as the Bolsheviki do, the present institution of the family, which he regards as a purely sexual relation, except insofar as it subserves the raising of the young.

In a sermon delivered on May 23, 1920, in the Cathedral of St. John the Divine, Dr. Bell announced his sympathy with the revolutionary element of labor which demands the abolishing of the wage system and the communistic assumption of control. He states that the New Social Order is here and must be accepted. He says, "The world has already determined that the change shall be, and the real question is now whether it shall be by orderly, decent, law-abiding methods or brought about by blood and iron — by working-class revolution or by common sense." He favors, as a matter of course, internationalism as against national patriotism.

The campaign to weed out from the ranks of our school teachers any disloyal element, calls attention to certain extraordinary expressions of opinion by members of the New York Local of the

American Federation of Teachers, which is affiliated with the American Federation of Labor. Its organ is the "American Teacher," which in its May-June issue of 1918, page 105, in connection with running an exchange advertisement of the "Liberator," which is a self-confessed organ of Bolshevism, I. W. W.ism and revolutionary Communism by violence, takes occasion to praise the "Liberator," to state that its editors "now support the Government," and to condemn, implicitly, any attack on them. On another page (108) the revolutionary industrial theory is expressed that the children in the schools must be taught to demand industrial democracy and this is defined as a condition in which "it is by the people who do the work that the hours of labor, the conditions of employment and the definition of property is to be made. It is by them the captains of industry are to be chosen, and chosen to be the servants, not masters."

Is this the doctrine we wish taught to our children?

The attitude of the New York Board of Education toward radical teaching in the schools is well expressed by Dr. John L. Tildsley, associate superintendent of schools of New York, as quoted in the American Labor Year Book, 1919–20, page 89, from a statement made by him April 26, 1919:

> "No person who adheres to the Marxian program, the program of the Left Wing of the Socialist Party in this country, should be allowed to become a teacher in the public school system, and if discovered to be a teacher, should be compelled to sever his connection with the school system, for it is impossible for such a person to carry out the purpose of the public schools as set forth by Commissioner Finegan, that the public school of any country should be the expression of the country's ideals, the purpose of its institutions, and the philosophy of its life and government."

A typical example of such teaching was the case of Benjamin Glassberg, New York high school teacher, who was discharged by the Board of Education on May 29, 1919, after being charged with supporting Bolshevism. That the accusation was accurate was shown by a subsequent open connection with the Rand School as a teacher of revolutionary Socialist doctrines.

Other prominent cases are those of Sadie Ginsberg, probationary teacher in the New York public schools; of three teachers in the DeWitt Clinton High School; of Miss Alice Wood, of the Washington, D. C., high school; of B. H. Mattingly, of the

Poughkeepsie schools, and of Mary McDowell, of the Brooklyn public schools, who were dismissed in 1918 and 1919.

On the whole, it may be safely said that our public school system is comparatively free from the taint of revolutionary teaching.

The American Labor Year Books of 1916 and of 1919–1920 give accounts of the invasion of Academic Freedom, as it calls it, through the dismissal or disciplining of a number of professors and instructors on account of their socialistic teachings or sentiments. Among these is Arthur W. Calhoun, whose letter was published above, who was dismissed in 1915 from Maryville College, Tennessee, from the professorship of economics, the probable cause being economic radicalism. The case of Prof. Scott Nearing is treated in detail, including his dismissal from the University of Pennsylvania, and then from the University of Toledo in 1915–16. Other cases mentioned are the dismissal of W. C. Fisher, professor of economics at Wesleyan; of A. E. Morse, professor of economics at Marietta College; of G. B. L. Arner, instructor in economics at Dartmouth, and so forth. Dr. H. W. L. Dana was dismissed from the faculty of Columbia University in October, 1917, on account of his pacifist activities. This was followed by the withdrawal from Columbia faculty of Professors Charles A. Beard and Henry R. Mussey, both of whom became active in radical teachings, especially in connection with the new School for Social Research.

It was in 1905 that there was organized in New York the Inter-Collegiate Socialist Society, "for the purpose of promoting an intelligent interest in Socialism among college men and women, graduates and under-graduates." It was in charge of a group selected to represent the largest possible number of universities and colleges in different parts of the country, all alumni taking an active interest in Socialism, and who could promote it among the students and faculties. It developed shortly into open advocacy of, instead of merely interest in, Socialism. Chapters were established in a large number of colleges and universities, cities and towns. It founded a quarterly which became a monthly magazine, called the "Socialist Review." It arranges to send lecturers on tours to various institutions, where it also organizes conferences, discussions and conventions. It also publishes pamphlets and books, and directs in a systematic way, the Socialist propaganda among students and graduates, collaborating with the socialistically inclined members of the faculties. The secretary of the society, Mr. Harry W. Laidler, has recently published "Socialism in Thought and Action," which is an able review of the tenets and history of Socialism, well adapted for text-book use in colleges and universities. It is a work of propaganda.

In the American Labor Year Book for 1916 (p. 157) a list of alumni chapters is given as existing in Buffalo, Central California, Chicago, Cleveland, Detroit, Los Angeles, New York, Portland, Schenectady, Seattle, St. Louis, Springfield, Washington and Wilkesbarre.

It also lists under-graduate chapters in the following institutions: Albion; Amherst; Bernard; Bates; Beloit; Berkeley Divinity; Brown, Cal.; Carnegie Institute of Technology; Chicago; Cincinnati; City College, N. Y.; Clark; Colorado; Columbia; Cornell; Dartmouth; East Tennessee Normal; Emory and Henry; George Washington; Grinnell; Hamline; Harvard; Howard; Illinois; Indiana; Iowa; Iowa State; John Marshall Law; Johns-Hopkins; Kansas Agricultural; LaCrosse Normal; Los Angeles Osteopathic; Nast Technology; Miami; Michigan; Middle Tennessee Normal; Minnesota; Nevada; New York; New York Dental; New York Law; North Carolina; North Dakota; Oberlin; Ohio State; Ohio Wesleyan; Pennsylvania; Pittsburgh; Princeton; Radcliffe; Randolph; Macon; Richmond; Rutgers; Simmons; Simpson; South Carolina; Springfield; Syracuse; Temple; Trinity; Union Theological; Utah; Valparaiso; Vassar; Virginia; Washington, Wash.; Washington-Jefferson; Washington and Lee; Wisconsin; Yale.

The Year Book states that "in 1915–1916 John Spargo, Rose Pastor Stokes and Harry W. Laidler spoke in 120 colleges before over 30,000 students and 12,000 others. They addressed some eighty economic and other classes and spoke before over a score of entire college bodies."

A so-called Bureau of Industrial Research, established at West 23d street, New York City, describes itself as being "organized to promote sound human relationships in industry." In addition to the courses in employment administration, the bureau offers expert industrial counsel and technical assistance to employers and trade union executives. Its research department maintains a library of current information covering the field of industrial relations, from which it is prepared to supply documentary and statistical data at moderate cost to individuals, corporations, labor organizations and the press.

Co-operating Attorneys

[illegible]

CIVIL LIBERTIES BUREAU

of the

American Union Against Militarism

For the maintenance in war time of the rights of free press, free speech, peaceful assembly, liberty of conscience, and freedom from unlawful search and seizure.

Directing Committee

L. Hollingsworth Wood, *Chairman*
Roger N. Baldwin, *Director*
Norman M. Thomas
Agnes Brown Leach
Amos Pinchot
John Haynes Holmes
John Lovejoy Elliott

Munsey Bldg.
Washington, D. C.

70 Fifth Avenue
New York

New York, August 21, 1917

Mr. Louis P. Lochner,
Hotel Majestic,
Minneapolis, Minn.

Dear Mr. Lochner:

I hoped before you left that we might have the conference we talked over in regard to the Minneapolis program. I don't know that my views are worth anything to you, but my services are entirely at your disposal, together with these two thoughts that I have on what I regard as the most important, political, social and economic movement in the country.

In the first place, let me say I am planning to leave St. Louis in time to be in Minneapolis the day before the Council Meeting opens. I may be able to get in Thursday afternoon. Please figure out just what job you can put me to, and if you can send me in advance the sketch of your plan for the programme and for the organization work, I would appreciate it. Please address me at 911 Locust St. St. Louis, Mo. where I shall be from next Saturday until Wednesday.

The points I want to make about the meeting

are briefly as follows:

1st. Do steer away from making it look like a Socialist enterprise. Too many people have already gotten the idea that it is nine-tenths a Socialist movement. You can of course avoid this by bringing to the front people like Senator Works, Miss Addams and others who are known as substantial Democrats.

2nd. Do get into the movement just as strong as possible the leaders in the Labor circles particularly the substantial men, not the radical socialist, both of whom of course ought to be recognized. But the substantial men will begin to start the big Irish Democratic Labor movement our way, and that is important. Also bring to the front the farmers, not confining it to the new agrarian movement in the north-west.

3rd. I think it would be an error to get the public thinking that we are launching a political party in Minneapolis. Tobe sure we are launching a political movement, but that is quite a different matter from a political point. It is a mistake already to have us tied up with the name of Mr. LaFollette, fine as he is. If we begin to mix personalities with principles, we will find that at these early stages of the movement we are going to get into a lot of trouble. Our main job is to keep peace terms, and a larger democracy for the U. S. in the foreground of public discussion.

4th. We want to also look like patriots in everything we do. We want to get a lot of good flags, talk a good deal about the constitution, and what our forefathers wanted to make of this country, and to show that we are the folks that really stand for the spirit of our institution.

5th. The plan of organization ought to be most carefully thought out, and I think you would do best by having it mimeographed or printed, so that the delegates can take the proposed tentative plan in sending it. It ought not to be shoved on us in a committee report at a meeting. It is too comprehensive and too big a thing to handle that way. A definite four page scheme of organization and statement of purposes will do more to crystallize sentiment in the right direction than a whole lot of things.

Call on me for anything in the world you think I can do, and if by any chance you need me two days ahead of time, say so.

With best of good wishes, I am,

Sincerely yours,

RNB.RB

Roger N Baldwin.

HENRY STREET SETTLEMENT
NEW YORK

2255

MAIN HOUSE
265 HENRY STREET

October 12, 1917.

Dear Mr. Baldwin:-

I think that I ought to have the facts about the Tribune in order to properly answer the letter that I read to you over the telephone. If you can give me concrete evidence of the things that are considered unfair, I will be very glad to present them. At present the correspondence seems to be related to certain phrases that the Tribune used which the American Union thought inaccurate and which they defend by producing letters and so forth.

Thank you very much for your very cordial note of the 11th. The reason that I resigned from the American Union was so clearly expressed in the various letters that I presented to the Committee, that I thought that you were fully aware of every incident that led up to the final decision. I did not resign at all because of my other responsibilities, for I consider that everybody who cares about it should use their energies and influence against dangers to the American democracy, it was because of the difficulties of administration of the American Union as it had developed. I do not know whether to be glad or sorry that the Union followed my judgment so many months after our discussions.

I hope that you are coming to the Settlement a good deal during the winter, and I am not at all out of the movement even though I am not on the Committee.

Sincerely and cordially yours,

Lillian D. Wald

Mr. Roger Baldwin,
70 Fifth Avenue,
New York City.

1991

Frank P. Walsh
Kansas City, Mo.

December 26, 1917.

Mr. Roger N. Baldwin,
National Civil Liberties Bureau,
70 Fifth Avenue,
New York City.

Dear Mr. Baldwin:

This will introduce Mr. J. A. Law and Mr. L. S. Chumley, who are members of the Defense Council of the Industrial Workers of the World.

They are endeavoring to make a defense of their associates, as you know, under very difficult circumstances. I have outlined a little rough plan for a conference which might be gotten together, and I showed them your letter to me of December 11th, which gave them an idea of the good work you were trying to do for them. My advice to them was to get in close touch with you and I was sure you could help them.

I have been expecting to be in New York every few days for the past month. It now looks as though I will be there between the first and the 8th. I will, of course, call upon you.

Sincerely,

Frank P. Walsh

Its director is Robert W. Bruere; its treasurer, Herbert Crowley, of the "New Republic." Its other members are Ordway Tead, Henry C. Metcalf, P. Sargent Florence, Leonard Outhwaite, Carl G. Karsten, Mary D. Blankenhorn.

It also has special lecturers: John A. Fitch and Irwin H. Schell.

This organization co-operates with the "New School for Social Research," which has been established by men who belong to the ranks of near-Bolshevik Intelligentsia, some of them being too radical in their views to remain on the faculty of Columbia University.

CHAPTER XI

Socialism and the Churches

All church organizations have entered since the war into a period of tremendous activity, with a view to meeting, from the point of view of Christianity, the difficulties and problems of the present. The churches have realized that a rebirth of religious beliefs and of moral conscience is absolutely necessary among the masses if present civilization is to endure. In large numbers the masses during the present generation have been drifting away from religion. In order to insure that the churches shall take the part that really belongs to them, two currents have been set in motion; one, based upon the historical principles that lie at the foundation of Christianity, and, the other, experimenting with new more or less radical principles as the basis for a renewal of society.

While the Committee presents in this chapter a number of data which illustrate dangerous revolutionary tendencies, it wishes emphatically to state that such tendencies are embodied in a comparatively small number of members of the clergy of the different denominations. By far the larger bulk of all religious teachers are working in an old-fashioned crusade against the inroads of materialism and revolutionary thought. The new activity and enthusiasm was embodied, in the Protestant sphere, in the Inter-Church World-Wide Movement, which was started during the latter part of 1919. It aimed not only to raise over $300,000,000 for spreading the right kind of Christianity among the people, but it aimed at increasing church membership and unity of Christian faith and endeavor to an extent hitherto unknown in this generation. It is true that radical elements attained prominence in certain spheres of this work, but it remains to be seen how influential they will be when their real aims are known.

Not long ago a pastoral letter was issued by the leaders of the Catholic Church in America, which expresses on behalf of the Catholic Church their attitude and their hopes. This pastoral letter was prepared by a committee belonging to the American Hierarchy, including Cardinals Gibbons and O'Connell and the Rector of the Catholic University at Washington, Thomas J. Shaham, and more than one hundred bishops of the Church. It is issued to the 20,000,000 Catholics in the United States and is the first pastoral letter issued by the general organization of the

Catholic Church since one sent out thirty-five years ago in 1884, to the then 7,000,000 Catholics of the United States.

As the Catholic Bulletin of Cleveland expresses it:

> "Materialism and its formidable sons, anarchy, Bolshevism and unrest, have thrown down the gauge of battle. We must catch it up and wage the good fight for God and for country."

The pastoral letter says:

> "It is an error to assert that the issues involved are purely economic. They are, at bottom, moral and religious.
>
> "It is necessary (it states), to insist that the rights of the community shall prevail; that law and order shall be preserved; and that the public shall not be made to suffer while the contention goes on from one state to another."

The letter agrees that there are wrongs that must be righted, fundamental wrongs. It says:

> "This is not a time for makeshifts. . . . Rightly or wrongly, the movements which are shaking the foundations of order come out of men's souls. They embody a demand for right. They may be stopped for a time or diverted; but, if, in keeping with American principles, order is to rest on the willingness of the people and their free co-operation, their souls must be right. They must be trained to think rightly and to do as they think. . . . What we have chiefly to fear is educated intelligence devoid of moral principles. . . . The right of labor to a living wage, with decent maintenance for the present and provision for the future, is generally recognized. The right of capital to a fair day's work for a fair day's pay, is equally plain. To secure the practical recognition and exercise of both rights, good will, no less than adherence to justice is required. Animosity and mistrust should first be cleared away. When this is done, when the parties meet in a friendly rather than militant spirit, it will be possible to effect a reconciliation."

A considerable portion of the men who are doing yeoman's service in country-wide speaking and writing against the revolutionary movement, are laymen of the Catholic Church. It is an interesting and significant fact that the work that all Christian leaders are doing in this campaign is bringing all the branches of Christian believers closer together and breaking down as comparatively unimportant the denominational walls of separation.

The Committee has given elsewhere, especially in the educational section, a conspectus of the work done by the different branches of the Protestant Church in connection with education of the aliens, and other constructive work to stamp out all forms of radicalism, materialism and anarchy.

What is of the greatest importance for churchmen to understand, in order that they may not be led astray by specious arguments of so-called Christian Socialists and so-called liberals and self-styled partisan of free speech, is that Socialism as a system as well as anarchism and all its ramifications from high-brow Bolshevism to the Russian Anarchist Association, are all the declared enemies of religion and of all recognized moral standards and restraints.

Unless this movement is killed and unless the constructive movement of church leaders leads to a revival of religious belief, the necessary foundations for a permanent social reconstruction will be wanting.

The object of the present chapter is to clarify the situation from this point of view and to point out the danger to church leaders who are carried away by false, specious idealism masquerading as progress.

Nothing has attracted public attention more strongly than the attitude of the different churches and religious organizations either semi-officially, through their various agencies, or unofficially through individual action. This attitude relates to both the revolutionary and the labor questions. Before reporting on this question it would be well to state the attitude toward religion of the Soviet system and of Socialism in general. As elsewhere stated, the system of Karl Marx is a pure materialism which abolishes religion of any sort. Of this there can be no question. Marx was an avowed atheist. The Marxian philosophy being the recognized basis of the Soviet government of Russia, of every Communist, every Socialist and every Social Democratic Party, it follows that the whole revolutionary movement is atheistic, is anti-religious. One of the common rallying cries of the Soviet army is, 'We have abolished God.'"

The official attitude of Bolshevism as an atheistic theory seeking to destroy all religion, all belief in a God, is clearly expressed in an article by N. Bucharin, entitled "Church and School in the

Soviet Republic," published in the "Class Struggle" for May, 1919. This Bucharin is recognized all over the world as the official literary mouthpiece and program maker of Lenin, as the leader in the Soviet educational system. What he says, therefore, is authoritative.

"One of the instruments for the obscuring of the consciousness of the people is the belief in God and the devil, in good and evil spirits, angels, saints, etc., in short, religion. The masses of the people have become accustomed to believe in these things, and yet, if we approach these beliefs sensibly, and come to understand where religion comes from, and why religion receives such warm support from the bourgeois gentlemen, we shall clearly understand that the function of religion at present is to act as a poison with which the minds of the people have been and continue to be corrupted. And then we shall also understand why the Communist Party is so resolutely opposed to religion.

"Present day science has pointed out that the most primitive form of religion was the worship of the souls of dead chieftains, and that this worship began at the moment that, in ancient human society, the elders of the tribe, old men more wealthy, experienced and wise than the rest of the tribe, already had secured power over the remaining members. At the very outset of human history, when men still were in the semi-ape stage, they were equal. The elders did not put in their appearance until later, and then began the subjugation of the other members. Then also the latter began to worship the former, and this worship of the souls of the dead rich is the foundation of religion; these 'saints,' these little gods, were later transformed into a single threatening deity, who punishes and rewards, judges and regulates. . . . The world also has its master, a great powerful, threatening creature, on whom all depends, and who will severely punish all disobedience. Now, this master over all the world is God. . . .

"God, so to speak, is a really rich, powerful master, a slaveholder, one who 'rules the heavens,' a judge — in a word, a precise counterfeit and copy of the earthly power of the elder, later of the prince. . . .

"In short, the belief in God is an expression of the vile conditions on earth, is the belief in slavery, which is present, as it were, not only on earth, but in the whole universe besides. It is of course clear that there is no truth in these things. And it is also clear that these fairy tales are a hindrance in the path of human progress. Humanity will not advance until it has become accustomed to seek for a phenomenon as its natural explanation.

"But when, instead of explanations, faith is put in God or in the saints, or in the devils and wood-sprites, there is no likelihood that any useful purpose will be attained . . really, religious people are not fit for any kind of fighting. Religion, therefore, not only causes the people to remain in a state of barbarism, but fits them also for the condition of slavery. The religious man is more readily inclined to accept everything without a murmur (since everything, of course, comes from God), and to submit to the powers that be, and to suffer in patience ('for everything will be required a hundredfold up yonder'). It is therefore not surprising that the powers in control under capitalism should consider religion an extremely useful instrument for the deceiving of the people. . . .

"From the above the program of the Communists with regard to Church and State is clear. We must fight the Church, not with force, but with conviction. The Church must be separated from the State. This means, the priests may continue to exist, but let them be supported by those who wish to purchase their poison, or who may have some other interest in their continued existence. Another poison of this type is opium. Those who have smoked it behold all sorts of lovely visions, are at once transported to paradise. But the use of opium later results in a complete undermining of the health, and the user gradually becomes a complete idiot. It is the same with religion. . . . The priests are now in the camp of the 'oppressed bourgeoisie.' They are working below ground and above against the working class. But the times are bad, and the great masses of the workers no longer fall for the bait as they used to. That is the great educative accomplishment of the revolution. It liberates from economic slavery. But it also liberates from spiritual slavery."

One of the sources of Bucharin's atheistic argumentation is the writings of the famous prophet of anarchism, Michael

Bakunin, in whose essay "God and the State" we find sentences that are almost repeated by Bucharin. For example:

> "All religions, with their gods, their demi-gods, and their prophets, their Messiahs, and their Saints, were created by the more credulous of men who have not attained the full development and full possession of their faculties. . . . If God is, man is a slave; now, man can and must be free; then, God does not exist. . . . Is it necessary to point out to what extent and in what manner religions debase and corrupt the people? They destroy their reason, the principal instrument of human emancipation, and reduce them to imbecility, the essential condition of their slavery."

The American Socialist Party has acknowledged in its meetings that it is atheistic: that about 99 per cent of its members are actual atheists. A work recently issued by J. J. Mereto, entitled "The Socialist Conspiracy against Religion" shows clearly both the Amercan and the international character of Socialist atheism. Morris Hillquit is quoted in the official proceedings of the National Convention of the Socialist Party of 1908 as saying that 99 per cent. of the Socialists were agnostics. At that time the "International Socialist Review" said, "Religion spells death to Socialism, just as Socialism to religion . . . the thinking Socialists are all free-thinkers." Bob Minor, who came near to a military trial for spreading Bolshevism in our army, writes in the "Liberator" that he is glad he does not believe in God. The German Socialist "New Yorker Volkszeitung" says: "Socialism is logical only when it denies the existence of God."

The plank regarding religion in the Socialist Party platform of 1908 states: "The Socialist movement is primarily an economic and political movement. It is not concerned with the institutions of marriage and religion." The plank as it was first proposed read "that religion be treated as a private matter — a question of individual conscience." Now, this clause is cited by many persons as proof that Socialism does not antagonize religion. But the whole discussion at the convention before its adoption in its final form shows that its aim and purpose was distinctly for nothing else than to fool the public and to help Socialist propaganda. This was made clear in the speeches of the Socialist

Delegates Lewis and Unterman. Arthur M. Lewis of Illinois opposed having any statement about religion inserted.

"I know," he said, "that the Socialist position . . . in the question of religion does not make a good campaign subject . . . . therefore I am willing that we should be silent about it. But if we must speak, I suppose that we shall go before this country with the truth and not with a lie. . . . I do not propose to state in this platform the truth about religion from the point of view of the Socialist philosophy as it is stated in almost every book of standard Socialist literature; but if we do not do that, let us at least have the good grace to be silent about it, and not make hypocrites of ourselves."

However, Unterman, the delegate from Idaho, had the majority behind him in inducing the Convention to insert the plank that made of them, as Comrade Lewis says, both "liars" and "hypocrites." Unterman begins by declaring himself a thorough materialist and athiest, but insists that for propaganda purposes it would be foolish to let Socialism be known to the public as an atheistic system. "Would you expect," he says: "to go out among the people of this country, people of different churches, of many different religious factions, and tell them that they must become athiests before they can become Socialists? That would be nonsense. We must first get these men convinced of the rationality of our economic and political program." Another prominent delegate who favored inserting the plank was Victor Berger of Milwaukee, who speaks of himself as being well-known to be a pronounced agnostic.

After the plank had been dropped in 1912, Socialists were freer in their conventions in denouncing religion. In the account of the State of Michigan Socialist Convention at Grand Rapids of February 24, 1919, John R. Ball reports in the "Communist" of Chicago: "A Socialist who understands the materialistic conception of history cannot have faith in superstition of any kind. In other words, a religious or Christian Socialist is a contradiction of terms and the statement that religion is a private matter (allusion to the 1908 plank) is a lie."

There would seem, then, to be no possible excuse for members, much less for teachers of any church organizations, to help or adhere to, Socialism as it is at present officially constituted, unless such members or teachers have already lost their belief in God. Certain ex-clergymen and certain clergymen have done so frankly: others are deceiving themselves or the public or both. Geo. D. Herron left the ministry and wrote in 1901: "When the gods are dead to rise no more, man will begin to live." Irwin St. John Tucker of Chicago, convicted under the Espionage Act, is equally frank. So is Wm. T. Brown, once pastor of Plymouth Church, Rochester. Such Unitarian ministers as J. M. Evans and A. L. Weatherly can abjure God without leaving their ministry. John Haynes Holmes changed the name of his so-called church from "Church of the Messiah" to "Community Church" as an outward mark of his change of heart from Christianity to Communism. An insidious anti-religious campaign is being carried on by these men and their colleagues in such reviews as "The World Tomorrow" (New York) and "Unity" (Chicago).

What, now, is the point of view of the church leaders of supposedly liberal views who without leaving their churches are giving support to the revolutionary Socialist movement? Their influence is of tremendous importance as they are, to borrow an economic term, "boring from within." Certain of these leaders, like Percy Stickney Grant, whose forum has been until recently the sporting-ground of parlor Bolsheviki, are, consciously or unconsciously playing into the hands of revolutionary propaganda.

It is interesting to see the situation in the Protestant Episcopal Church, especially as it is viewed by the official exponent of Socialist activities or the Rand School's American Labor Year Book (Vol. II, pp. 358–60). This report is signed by Rev. A. L. Byron-Curtiss, secretary, and is headed, "The Christian Socialists."

"THE CHRISTIAN SOCIALISTS"

"The Christian Socialist movement in the United States in the late seventies and during the eighties was sporadic in character but was led by very sincere and earnest men. Dissatisfied with the existing social order, having a keen discernment of the evolution of society and a penetrating vision of the future, they groped persistently for bearings from which to direct their shafts of denunciation and warning. They were fearsome of the word Socialism but were none the less vehement in their attacks upon the existing order and demands for a more Christian state of society. The Transcendentalists and others experimented with colonies, all of which had religion as a basis. During the last decade of the nineteenth century the word Socialism began to be used by them and the Socialist program presented as a theory or plan, and considerable cohesion or unanimity appeared among the devotees. Among the leaders may be mentioned Rev. W. D. P. Bliss and Professors George D. Herron and R. T. Ely.

"Probably the Episcopal Church was the only one within which there arose a society bearing any semblance to a working class movement. This society was made up of a few parsons and pious women, and was called the Church Association for the Advancement of the Interests of Labor, C. A. I. L. for short, and still exists. During its early career, under the inspiration of Rev. Father Huntington, an Anglican monk of the Order of the Holy Cross, and of other single taxers, it was quite radical, but of late years it has been rather colorless in its activities. To a few very radical Episcopalians is also to be credited the importation of a distinctively Socialist organization from the mother Church of England, the Christian Social Union, which sprang from the Christian Socialist movement of Kingsley and Maurice, both priests of the Church of England. A branch of the union was formed in 1893 with Right Rev. F. D. Huntington of the diocese of Central New York as president. The union gave considerable promise and much was hoped of it by Bishop Huntington who was at heart a thorough Socialist; but, aside from issuing a few brochures, nothing came of it. Its ultimate affiliation with the Association for the Advancement of the Interests of Labor marked its quick decline.

"The distinct advance of Socialist sentiment and movement among the church people of America was coincident with the spread of Socialism beyond the groups of the foreign born. At the national convention of the Socialist Party in Chicago in 1902 there were among the regular delegates a number of clergy and lay officials of different churches. Since that date two Christian Socialist organizations have been formed and are now very active, with the avowed purpose of extending the principles of Socialism among church people of America.

"The first and largest of these is the Christian Socialist Fellowship, an interdenominational organization with offices in Chicago. It was organized in Louisville, Kentucky, in June, 1906. From the beginning its general secretary has been Rev. Edward Ellis Car, Ph.D. It publishes a weekly and monthly paper called 'The Christian Socialist,' with offices in Chicago. It has over fifty branches and a large proportion of its members are allied with the Socialist movement and party. It holds annual and frequent district conferences. Through its general offices and local centers, Socialist sermons and lectures have been delivered in thousands of churches. Millions of copies of the official paper of the Fellowship have been circulated to preachers, teachers and social workers. Churches, Y. M. C. A.'s and colleges are opened to the message of Socialism as put forth by the Fellowship.

"In 1911 the Church Socialist League in America was organized by a few clergy and lay people of the Episcopal Church. For some years there had been a strong and very pronounced Socialist league in England. The organization of an American Church Socialist League was fortunate, as the pulpits of the Episcopal Church are not generally open to clergy of different denominations. As the influence of the Episcopal Church is greater throughout the country than in proportion to its members, so is it with the league. Its influence within the Episcopal Church is not at all measured by its numerical strength. In spite of the conservatism of the Episcopal Church and of its members, yet that Church has officially adopted radical and even revolutionary resolutions, and the influence of the Church Socialist League is discernible as giving color to them. A considerable share of the clergy are tinctured with Socialism. With but 6,000 clergy, several hundred are avowed Socialists and nearly one hundred are members of the Socialist Party. The league is able to present the parallel demands of militant Socialism to this communion as no other society can. Rev. A. L. Byron-Curtiss is the national secretary, and the official organ is a quarterly, 'The Social Preparation,' the official address of both being Utica, N. Y. Officers and executive committee embrace the following well known names:

"President: Rt. Rev. Paul Jones, D. D.; Vice Presidents: Rev. William A. Guerry, D. D., Rt. Rev. Benjamin Brewster, D. D., Rev. Eliot White; Executive Committee: Rev.

G. Israel Browne, Rev. William H. Tomlins, Very Rev. Bernard I. Bell, Rev. A. L. Byron-Curtiss, William F. Cochran, M. H. Reeves, E. M. Parker, Vida D. Scudder, Charlotte E. Lee, Ellen Gates Starr.

"A. L. B.-C."

That this report of the Rev. Byron-Curtiss is not an exaggerated statement has been shown by the three triennial reports of the Joint Commission on Social Service of the Protestant Episcopal Church, presented to the general conventions of the Church at the close of 1913, 1916 and 1919. The last of these reports has suggested an inquiry by Mr. Ralph M. Easley in the "National Civic Federation Review," in which attention is called to the revolutionary Socialist utterances of Rev. J. H. Melish, secretary; Rev. F. M. Crouch, field secretary; Rev. B. Iddings-Bell, member of the commission, as well as president of St. Stephens College, who were also leaders in the Church Socialist League. The official organ of the League, the "Social Preparation," asserts:

"We are not reformers trying to patch up an outworn garment, but revolutionists."

This is not an isolated statement. The Rev. Mr. Crouch, at a conference in October, 1919, of the Inter-Church movement, advocated the overthrow of our present social system, when he said:

"The system of industrialism which we still largely know, working out the exploitation of fellowmen by fellowmen, cannot endure in the face of justice."

In the first report of the Social Service Commission in 1913, the Rev. Franklin S. Spaulding, in an address on "Christianity and Democracy" (p. 12), declared himself as opposed to private property and opposed to nationalism. He said:

"I believe that all value is created by the application of labor to land."

He takes as his great authority Prof. Scott Nearing.

He accepts Karl Marx as his prophet.

In an address by the Rev. J. H. Melish (p. 68), "The Church's Relation to Workingmen's Organizations," is an apology for the "wobblies:"

"Syndicalism, as every investigation has shown, finds a field only in our industrial centers where immigrants are herded, etc."

In a third paper, "The Ethics of the Wage System," Helen S. Dudley (p. 74) pleads for the abolishment of the wage system.

These Socialist tendencies are emphasized in more systematic and propagandist form in the second report of 1916 under the headings (p. 8): "The Study of Social and Industrial Conditions," and (p. 16) "The Encouragement of Sympathetic Relations between Capital and Labor."

In discussing the attitude of union labor in the open and closed shop question, the liberty of the open shop is ridiculed and the claim of the unions to the closed shop is supported, denying the right of the employer to employ non-union labor (p. 23).

> "The plea of the employer that denial of the right of freedom and contract is un-American, as the new case of the now notorious recent issue in Colorado is either specious or due to an entire misconception of the real situation."

In its discussion of Socialism and syndicalism the statement is made that syndicalism "would not have developed in this country had organized capital on the one hand and organized labor on the other been disposed to give the 'man farthest down' a fair chance. It is precisely because the lowest grade of labor — the least skilled and least literate voters, recruited as they are now largely from our newer Americans — have been exploited by manufacturers and comparatively neglected by trade unions that syndicalism has developed. . . . Now, it is obvious that these three (union labor, Socialism, syndicalism) relate to divers movements, represent legitimate aspirations and hopes of the various groups from which they are respectively recruited. . . . To take advantage of their lack of present co-operation and unity is unworthy either of the self-respecting employer or the Church of which he is a member."

The so-called welfare work initiated by many employers of labor is described as but "a means of giving with one hand while continuing to take with the other."

Other schemes, such as bonuses, profit-sharing, scientific management, are also discredited. It is concluded that: "Despite, therefore, the attempts of capital to meet demands of labor, while still retaining their essential control of industry, labor today is perhaps even more bitter than formerly toward the employing class. This the Church must frankly recognize. Some members of the commission there are, indeed, who feel that the most effective method of discharging this part of the responsibility laid upon them by the general convention is to encourage the gradual assumption by government — Federal, State, local — of the whole system of production and distribution of life's necessities, or, as an alternative, democratization of our industrial order; though it is true that there are members who favor less radical measures. The challenge, however, of industrial democracy cannot be evaded. What the workers of today want is not only a living wage, reasonable hours, and decent conditions of toil, but some effective participation in the management and control of the enterprise in which they are engaged. In the modern 'co-operative movement' they have made a beginning in this direction. To allege, as is so commonly done, that labor as we know it today lacks present or potential capacity to handle its own affairs, and that there must be always a more favored class at the top in direction of industrial enterprises is to fly in the face of history."

The commission recommends in closing its report that the Church should help along the coming of the fundamental change in the economic structure which is involved in the term "Industrial Democracy."

The commission states that is will embark on a wide campaign of social propaganda, not only through meetings and the work of the field secretaries throughout the country, but through the publication of numerous pamphlets. One of its purposes was to train a large number of men for intelligent social service with a clear viewpoint.

The third triennial report of the Social Service Commission, submitted in October, 1919, to the Convention of the Episcopal Church at Detroit, attempts to give a scientific survey of the entire social and industrial field with a characterization of all the different groups and theories now current, and the criticism and evaluation of every one. The report states that there has been recently a significant change in the temper of American labor which has caught much of the aggressiveness of the British workers who, on the other hand, had given new and signal proof of their determination to secure hearing by launching a general railroad strike which may ultimately involve the other members of the English triple industrial alliance — miners and dockers.

Labor throughout the world, indeed, is clamoring for its own, and can scarcely be balked with impunity. If the Church would help it must be by counselling, not repression, but sympathetic consideration of the workers' needs.

The report, again, discussing the various plans that are being carried out on the basis of a continuation of the present system, largely based on the various demands of and arrangements with trade unionism, includes such rather radical movements as those of the shop stewards and the shop committees, the district and national councils and conferences, including the British Whitley plan. But it concludes (p. 59) that, to the radical group of workers, "the whole plan just considered looks like another concordat between mutually hostile parties: those who have a sense of humor would liken it to a mutual agreement between slaves and slaveholders, which would, at the same time, not abrogate the institutions."

The report then studies the revolutionary program of Socialism, Communism, syndicalism, industrial unionism, Guild Socialism, the co-operative movement, etc. It shows considerably more sympathy with all these revolutionary movements than it had shown with the previously discussed revisionist movements. It supports Marxism, saying of Marx that the modern leader "is compelled to recognize that the central position for which he stood is not only tenable but is really impregnable" (page 65), namely:

> "the principles of pristine Socialism evolved by the central fact, since Marx's time increasingly apparent to many, that there is and must be under present conditions exploitation of the workers by those who are in a position to profit by their labor."

In speaking of syndicalism in the United States it states that in the United States it has been "in large measure deliberately or unconsciously misconstrued by the great body of American public. . . . There is in the syndicalist movement, if we can for the moment leave out of consideration its violent tactics, a possibility of social and even ultimately of religious value which neither the church nor the state can afford to ignore or condemn until it has given the movement a fair hearing."

Some doubt is cast on the genuineness of the opposition of many American citizens and christians, "professedly" good citizens to syndicalism and Bolshevism which they "profess" to abhor.

The commission enjoins the Church from opposing syndicalism and I. W. W.'ism and quotes the words of Gamaliel: "Refrain from these men and let them alone; for if this council or this work be of men, it will come to naught, but if it be of God, ye cannot overthrow it; lest happily ye be found even to fight against God."

In other words, it places the I. W. W.'s under God's protection, adding that its theories have some affiliation with "aspects of Christian faith." In this connection it excuses the syndicalist strikes in Lawrence, Mass., and Paterson, N. J.; but the radical movement which enlists the committee's greatest sympathy is the Guild Socialism.

> "Viewed from within as a constructive industrial program, Guild Socialism offers much ground for hope."

The theory of Guild Socialism involves ownership by the State, operation by the workers, the State being entirely subject to the industrial workers' supreme organization. In other words, there would be no political State at all. As a part of this taking over of the State, the co-operative organization would take charge of the distribution of the production engineered by the guilds. The summary of conclusions (p. 104) is this:

> "Either, therefore, the theory and practice of state-craft must be so revised as to attend to the well-being of all citizens — not of one favored class — or it must make way for more constructive methods of association, through groups, unions, syndicates, which shall enable workers in whatever country to register their convictions and their will. The modern state, as it has been justly remarked, is no more sacrosant than any other secular institution. It must stand or fall on the basis of its achievement for the common good."

It acknowledges that "the workers' contention is largely right." The Church must fight "against an economic and industrial system which drives human beings to the limit as semi-mechanical tools, and robs them of their birthright of due leisure."

Toward the close the report (p. 162) states the amusing theory that the Christian Church from the beginning until the reformation took a consistent stand against private property. It says that while the practice of the communistic theory and philosophy may have been abandoned, "the theory itself remained a determining factor in the Church's attitude until well toward the close of the Middle Ages. . . . Practically until the modern era in the world, the primitive Christian believed that God had made all things for the common property and the common enjoyment of all men, iterated and reiterated in the most uncompromising and drastic terms by the representative Fathers of the Greek and Latin Churches was the background against which the entire structure of the Church Canon Law and ethics as related to Socialist and economic duty was developed. Private property, by contrast, was recognized as a concession to the infirmity of human nature."

Canon Law is depicted as fighting uselessly for the recognition of Communism!

One of the few clergymen who have declared themselves frankly to be Bolshevist is Bishop William M. Brown, a retired Episcopal clergyman, now at Galion, Ohio, a friend of radical Socialists and Communists, who has been active for many years.

A more influential clerical leader is the Rev. Harry F. Ward, professor in Union Theological Seminary, New York, and also high in the councils of the Methodist Episcopal church. He is a leader in the intellectual field of the radical movement. His friendly attitude toward Bolshevism, expressed in a text-book published by the Methodist Church, caused quite a public scandal, especially after it had been approved by an examining board of his church. His position has been fully described in the preceding chapter.

Advocates and sympathizers of extreme radical opinion have crept into places of influence in such quasi-religious bodies as the Y. M. C. A. Dr. Hecker, a prominent Methodist minister, has been placed in an authoritative relation to the Russian population of this country as Director of the Russian Investigation Bureau of the International Y. M. C. A. He is a German Russian who has not lived in Russia since boyhood but who has become a propagandist of Bolshevism.*

---

* The radical views of Dr. Hecker being questioned, he made a statement of them at a Conference Meeting of the Methodist Episcopal Church in New York, on June 7, 1920. At that meeting he showed himself to be in general sympathy and accord with the Russian Soviet Regime, as well as with American Communism and other revolutionary groups. He is attempting to publish a book on Religion in Revolutionary Russia, in which he clothes Communism in Russia with a quasi-religious character, thus disregarding the fact that the Communists of Russia deny the existence of God. At this meeting a Methodist clergyman present is reported to have stated publicly that if Dr. Hecker believed what he said, he laid himself open to serious charges.

The most recent proof of the invasion of the churches by subversive influences is the Report on the Steel Strike by a committee appointed by the

There have been two collective protests by groups of clergymen that placed them in the field of Socialist and pacifist sympathizers.

On July 6, 1919, five clergymen issued a protest against the repression exercised against the Reds, against arrests and deportations, and against the application of the Espionage Act. The clergymen signing this document were Rev. Arthur C. McGiffert, president of Union Theological Seminary; Rev. Howard C. Robbins, dean of the Cathedral of St. John the Divine; Rev. Charles R. Brown, dean of the Yale School of Religion; Rev. Henry S. Coffin, of the Madison Avenue Presbyterian Church; Rev. William A. Smith, editor of "The Churchman."

A more extreme attitude was taken by a meeting of Episcopal clergymen belonging to the Church Socialist League held on June 29, 1919, at the Rand School. This group issued a manifesto calling for a "complete revolution of our present economic and social disorder." It affirmed that the church "must repudiate its affiliation and support of the capitalist system of production, with its unholy emphasis on profits, privileges and exploitations."

The signers of this document belonging to the clergy were:

Rev. John Paul Jones, former Bishop of Utah; Rev. Joseph P. Morris, Rev. Charles H. Collett, Rev. James L. Smiley, Rev. William B. Spofford, Rev. James G. Mythen, Rev. Alfred Pridis, Rev. Irwin St. John Tucker, Rev. A. L. Byron-Curtiss, Rev. Horace Fort, Rev. Robert Johnson, Rev. Richard M. Doubs, Rev. Alfred Farr, Rev. George J. Miller, Rev. John M. Horton.

Among these men, particular attention should be called to St. John Tucker, whose radicalism is well known, and A. L. Byron-Curtiss, who is secretary of the Socialist League of the Episcopal Church, and is elsewhere mentioned.

Two of the above clergymen, Smiley and Spofford, sent on behalf of this same conference a message to President Wilson, which expresses its absolute sympathy with the Soviet government

---

Interchurch World Movement. Not satisfied with the investigation of the Steel Strike by the Senate's Committee (Kenyon), this new organization of the churches employed certain specialists to make a detailed inquiry, involving the cross-examination of hundreds of workmen. It is not generally known that the direction of this inquiry was not in the hands of unbiased investigators. The principal "experts" are David J. Saposs and George Soule, whose radical viewpoints may be gathered from their association with Mr. Evans Clark, acting under the direction of Ludwig C. A. K. Martens, head of the Soviet Bureau in the United States; their connection also with the Rand School of Social Science, and certain revolutionary Labor organizations further emphasizes their unfitness to carry on an unbiased investigation.

of Russia. It asks him to cease intervention in Russia and asks him to act against "any attempt of the Allies to strangle European democracy in its cradle." In other words, it characterizes the Soviet government as the one budding system of democracy in Europe.

A certain group in the Catholic Church with leanings toward Socialism, under the leadership of the Rev. Dr. Ryan, professor at the Catholic University of Washington, issued in January, 1918, a pamphlet called "Social Reconstruction; a General Review of the Problems, and a Survey of Remedies." It was issued by the Committee on Special War Activities of the National Catholic Council in Washington, and was signed by four bishops: Peter J. Muldoon, Bishop of Rockford; Joseph Schrembs, Bishop of Toledo; Patrick J. Hayes, Bishop of Tagaste, William T. Russell, Bishop of Charleston.

It begins by a disapproval of the famous social reconstruction program of the British Labor Party because this program, it considers, would lead ultimately to complete Socialism. It considers the program of the American Federation of Labor not to give sufficient expression to the weaker sections of the working class, and calls attention to its failure to even imply that the workers should become owners as well as users of the instruments of production. It examines other plans, such as that of the National Chamber of Commerce, and especially the proposals of the interdenominational conference of social service unions, comprising ten religious bodies of Great Britain.

The committee itself outlines in a rather general way its own proposed solution. Among other things, it favors the co-operative societies owned and managed by the consumers. It favors a large participation of labor in industrial management. Where the socialistic tendency of the committee shows itself most clearly is in what is said under the heading of "Co-operation and Copartnership." This statement is of sufficient importance to be quoted:

> "Nevertheless, the full possibilities of increased production will not be realized so long as the majority of the workers remain mere wage earners. The majority must somehow become owners, or at least in part, of the instruments of production. They can be enabled to reach this stage gradually through co-operative productive societies and copartnership arrangements. In the former, the workers own and manage

the industries themselves; in the latter, they own a substantial part of the corporate stock and exercise a reasonable share in the management. However slow the attainment of these ends, they will have to be reached before we can have a thoroughly efficient system of production, or an industrial and social order that will be secure from the danger of revolution. It is to be noted that this particular modification of the existing order, however far-reaching and involving to a great extent the abolition of the wage system, would not mean the abolition of private ownership. The instruments of production will still be owned by individuals, not by the State."